LIFE-SPAN DEVELOPMENT

Fourth Edition

LIFE-SPAN DEVELOPMENT

John W. Santrock
University of Texas at Dallas

 Wm. C. Brown Publishers

Book Team

Editor *Michael Lange*
Developmental Editor *Sheralee Connors*
Production Editor *Gloria G. Schiesl*
Art Editor *Carla Marie Heathcote*
Photo Editor *Carrie Burger*
Permissions Editor *Karen L. Storlie*
Visuals Processor *Joseph P. O'Connell*

 Wm. C. Brown Publishers

President *G. Franklin Lewis*
Vice President, Publisher *Thomas E. Doran*
Vice President, Operations and Production *Beverly Kolz*
National Sales Manager *Virginia S. Moffat*
Group Sales Manager *John Finn*
Executive Editor *Edgar J. Laube*
Director of Marketing *Kathy Law Laube*
Marketing Manager *Carla J. Aspelmeier*
Managing Editor, Production *Colleen A. Yonda*
Manager of Visuals and Design *Faye M. Schilling*
Production Editorial Manager *Julie A. Kennedy*
Production Editorial Manager *Ann Fuerste*
Publishing Services Manager *Karen J. Slaght*

WCB Group

President and Chief Executive Officer *Mark C. Falb*
Chairman of the Board *Wm. C. Brown*

Cover photo: Monet, *Train in the Countryside,* c. 1872, detail. Musée d'orsay Paris. (Giraudon/Art Resource, New York)

Interior and cover design by Heidi J. Baughman

The credits section for this book begins on page C-1 and is considered an extension of the copyright page.

Library of Congress Catalog Card Number: 91–73295

ISBN 0–697–11894–0 (cloth)
    0–697–10517–2 (paper)

Printed in the United States of America by Wm. C. Brown Publishers, 2460 Kerper Boulevard, Dubuque, IA 52001

10 9 8 7 6 5 4 3 2

To my parents, Ruth and John Santrock

BRIEF CONTENTS

CONTENTS

Contents

S·E·C·T·I·O·N

X

DEATH AND DYING

CHAPTER 21
Death and Dying 632

PERSPECTIVES ON LIFE-SPAN DEVELOPMENT

CULTURAL WORLDS OF DEVELOPMENT

PREFACE

Life-Span Development is about life's rhythm and meaning and about weaving together a portrait of who we were, are, and will be. This text is about you and it is about me; it is about the life of every human being. It tells the story of human development from conception to death—from the point in time when life as we know it begins until the point in time when it ends. The complex and exciting story of how we develop and how we become who we are is written and presented in a manner that is both informative *and* enjoyable.

You will see yourself as an infant, as a child, and as an adolescent, and you will be asked to reflect on how those years have influenced who you are today. And what about your adult years? Isn't what has happened, or will happen, to you as an adult also important? You will see yourself as a young adult, as a middle-aged adult, and as an adult in old age, and you will be asked to imagine how your experiences today will influence your development throughout the remainder of your life. You might think about how marriage, the birth of a child, divorce, the time when children leave home, a new career, and the death of a spouse change our lives in ways that require adaptation.

Balance, Integration, and Rhythm

Understanding the meaning of life's human cycle involves balance and integration. Different strands of human development—biological, cognitive, and social processes—are interwoven to make up an integrated human being. *Life-Span Development* is similarly composed of interwoven elements, and provides a balanced approach to the study of human development. It involves science and research, writing, motivation, learning, and teaching. Each of these elements contributes to more insightful understanding of life-span development. But as is true in understanding the human life cycle, so is the whole of *Life-Span Development* equal to more than the sum of its parts. Woven together, these elements combine to tell the odyssey of life's human cycle.

Science and Research

Beginning with the first edition and continuing with this, the fourth edition, *Life-Span Development* is above all else an extremely up-to-date presentation of research in the three primary domains of human development: biological processes, cognitive processes, and social processes. Research on biological, cognitive, and social processes continues to represent the core of *Life-Span Development*. This core includes both classic and leading edge research. Approximately 45 percent of the references in the fourth edition of *Life-Span Development* are new. More than 500 new references come from 1990, 1991, and *in press* sources, with more than 200 from 1991 and *in press* sources. Life-span development's research is expanding on many frontiers, and in each chapter, I have attempted to capture the excitement of these new discoveries as well as the classic studies that are the foundation of the discipline.

Writing

With the entire life span to cover, it is important that this book be written in a clear, efficient manner. In the third edition, I rewrote virtually every paragraph and section—adding, subtracting, integrating, and simplifying. Because this strategy was so well received, I have applied it to this edition as well. You may wonder why I have spent so much time rewriting the book when most authors with successful books make only cosmetic changes in the third and fourth editions. Considering the continued expansion of research on many frontiers of life-span development, this strategy has the important benefits of eliminating ideas and references that have become dated, retaining the theories, concepts, and research that are the core of the discipline, adding the newly developed theoretical and research ideas that have appeared, and integrating these changes so that the presentation of the material is clear, efficient, and easy to read. I have also continued to examine alternative ways of presenting ideas and have asked college students to give me feedback on which strategies are the most effective. For example, every key term is now defined in the text where it is first presented, a strategy that gives students a clear, precise understanding of key concepts. The reviewers of the manuscript for this fourth edition have consistently commented on the significant improvements in the writing and presentation of the material.

Motivation

In writing *Life-Span Development*, fourth edition, I wanted to convey the excitement of research—the rich moments of learning about the fetus's developmental changes, the infant's fathoming the permanence of the world, the young child's imaginative play, the adolescent's search for an identity, the young adult's motivation for intimacy, the middle-aged adult's coping with bodily changes, and the older adult's perceived control over the world. I wanted to communicate the discoveries in life-span development with enthusiasm, energy, and a constant awareness of their relevance to readers. When a concept is introduced, lively examples and applications of the concept are provided. Each chapter opens with a high-interest look at a topic related to the content of the chapter. **Perspective on Life-Span Development** inserts appear in every chapter—a brief glimpse through any chapter reveals their special appeal to students.

Learning

Life-Span Development incorporates an effective and challenging learning system. It is designed to enhance student comprehension and encourage critical thinking. My intent is to challenge students with the latest knowledge in the field of life-span development. I want them to think, to analyze, and to understand this information. Topics are explored in sufficient depth to challenge students, and the complex nature of life-span development is presented in such a way as to encourage critical thinking skills. Three or four **critical thinking questions** appear in the margins of each chapter.

Not only did I want to encourage thinking skills, but I also wanted to use textbook pedagogy to help students learn. Thus, the text is built around a carefully designed pedagogical framework. Critical to

this framework are the **concept tables** that appear two or three times in every chapter. They are designed to activate students' memory and comprehension of major topics or key concepts that have been discussed to that point. They help students to understand complex concepts and ideas and how they are interrelated. Concept tables provide a cognitive framework of the most important information in each section.

A very important aspect of *Life-Span Development's* learning system is the way the **key terms** are now presented. The key terms appear in **bold-faced type** in the text with their definitions following immediately in *italics*. This provides students with a clear understanding of important concepts in life-span development. The key terms are also listed with page references at the end of each chapter and are defined in a page-referenced **glossary** at the end of the book.

The presentation of figures and tables has been dramatically improved in the fourth edition of *Life-Span Development*. Every chapter has a number of visual figures and tables that include both a description of important content information and photographs to illustrate the content. In many instances, the visual figures and tables represent summaries or reviews of important concepts. For example, in chapter 2, a visual figure summarizes Erikson's stages of development; in chapter 6, a visual figure summarizes the key features of Piaget's sensorimotor stage; in chapter 9, a visual table highlights the different types of play; in chapter 13, a visual figure summarizes the new look in parent-adolescent relationships; in chapter 17, a visual figure portrays Levinson's stages of adult development; and in chapter 20, a visual figure presents the social construction-reconstruction view of aging. The combination of summary descriptions and carefully selected photographs in the form of visual figures and tables presented periodically

during a chapter enhances students' retention and makes the book a more attractive learning tool.

An **Outline** of major topics and subtopics at the beginning of each chapter shows the overall hierarchical organization of the material. At the end of the chapter, a detailed **summary** in outline form provides a helpful review. An annotated list of **suggested readings** also appears at the end of every chapter. These features should help students learn and, more important, understand the field of life-span development.

Teaching

My final goal has been to write a *teachable* text. I hope that the combination of solid, up-to-date research, presented in a readable, interesting writing style with an effective student-oriented learning system will produce a text that is as enjoyable to teach from as it is to study.

The publisher and the ancillary team have worked together to produce an outstanding integrated teaching package to accompany *Life-Span Development*. The authors of the ancillaries are all experienced teachers of the life-span course. The ancillaries have been designed to make it as easy as possible to customize the entire package to meet the unique needs of professors and their students.

Highlights of Changes in the Fourth Edition of Life-Span Development

Although the fourth edition of *Life-Span Development* is organized basically the same as the third edition, a number of changes have been made in the book's format and style. In addition to the extensive research updating and rewriting, the fourth edition of *Life-Span Development* has a new chapter on aging and increased emphasis on many topics, including ethnicity and culture, gender and women's development, prenatal development and infancy, and health, stress, and coping.

New Chapter on Aging

Research on older adults and the aging process has mushroomed in recent years. To accommodate this research effort and the increased attention given to aging in our culture, Section IX, "Late Adulthood," now has three chapters rather than two. Physical and cognitive development in late adulthood, which were combined in the same chapter in the third edition, have been given separate chapter status in this fourth edition.

Ethnicity and Culture

Special attention has been given to the role of ethnicity and culture in understanding life-span development. This increased coverage reflects the growing interest in ethnic-minority and cross-cultural research. A special new feature in the fourth edition of *Life-Span Development* is the **Cultural Worlds of Development** inserts in every chapter. A look through any chapter of the book reveals their special appeal. Reviewers of the fourth edition of the book consistently commented about the importance of the new material on ethnic and cultural issues, underscoring that *Life-Span Development* has far more discussion of ethnicity and culture than other life-span texts.

Gender and Women's Development

An equally important change in the fourth edition is the increased coverage of gender and women's development. Throughout the discussion of different periods in the life span, an effort has been made to expand the presentation of ideas about gender issues and to consider the nature of how girls and women develop. This coverage includes expanded presentation of Carol Gilligan's views, as well as those of Nancy Chodorow and Jean Baker Miller.

Prenatal Development and Infancy

Research has not only expanded enormously at the end of the life span, but also at the beginning of the life span. Issues that have been given increased attention include: cocaine babies, pre-term infants, prenatal care around the world, stimulation of preterm infants, and quality child care.

Health, Stress, and Coping

An extensive amount of new material on health practices, exercise, nutrition, and coping with stress has been added. The importance of these topics is addressed throughout the human life span.

Increased Coverage of Other Topics

In addition to the increased coverage of topics already mentioned, the following areas have been given more attention: AIDS, sexuality, rape, attachment, Bronfenbrenner's ecological theory, cohort effects, information processing, developmentally appropriate practice in preschools, Damon's conception of empathy and altruism, the new look in parent-adolescent relationships, career development, generativity, wisdom, and a developmental perspective on death.

Supplementary Materials

Wm. C. Brown Publishers has gathered a group of talented individuals with many years of experience in teaching life-span development to create supplementary materials that will assist instructors and students who use this text. The supplements are designed to make it as easy as possible to customize the entire package for the unique needs of professors and their students.

Instructor's Course Planner The key to this teaching package was created by Lori Temple of the University of Nevada, Las Vegas. This flexible planner provides a variety of useful tools to enhance your teaching efforts, reduce your workload, and increase your enjoyment. For each chapter of the text, the Planner provides an outline, overview, learning objectives and key terms. These items are also contained in the Student Study Guide. The Planner also contains lecture suggestions, classroom activities, discussion questions, integrative essay questions, a film list, and a transparency guide. The Instructor's Course Planner is conveniently housed within an attractive 11″ × 13″ × 9″ carrying case. This case is designed to accommodate the complete ancillary package by containing each chapter's material within a separate hanging file, allowing you to keep all your class materials organized at your fingertips.

The **Test Item File** was constructed by Lori Temple, at University of Nevada, Las Vegas and the team of Allen Keniston, Jerry Harper, and Robert Tomlinson, all of the University of Wisconsin–Eau Claire. This comprehensive test bank includes over 2000 new multiple choice test questions that are keyed to the text and learning objectives. Each item is designated as factual, conceptual, or applied.

The **Student Study Guide** was also created by Lori Temple. For each chapter of the text, the student is provided with an outline, an overview, learning objectives, key terms, a guided review, study questions (with answers provided for self-testing), and an integration and application question. The study guide begins with a section on "Developing Good Study Habits" to help students study more effectively and efficiently.

The **WCB Developmental Psychology Transparency/Slide Set** consists of 100 newly developed acetate transparencies or slides. These full color illustrations include graphics from various outside sources. These transparencies, created by Lynne Blesz Vestal, were expressly designed to provide comprehensive coverage of all major topic areas generally covered in life-span development. A comprehensive annotated guide provides a brief description for each transparency and helpful suggestions for use in the classroom.

WCB Customized Reader allows instructors to select over 80 different journal or magazine articles from a menu provided by a WCB sales representative. These readings can be custom printed and bound into an attractive 8½ × 11 book, giving instructors an opportunity to tailor-make their own student reader.

WCB TestPak, a computerized testing service, provides instructors with either a mail-in/call-in testing program or the complete test item file on diskette for use with the Apple® and IBM® PC computers. WCB TestPak requires no programming experience.

A large selection of **Videotapes,** including *Seasons of Life,* is also available to instructors based upon the number of textbooks ordered from Wm. C. Brown Publishers by your bookstore.

Acknowledgments

This book was produced by many minds and hands. William C. Brown Publishers has provided excellent support for the book. Michael Lange, Acquisitions Editor, is a wonderful editor, whose friendship and guidance I cherish. Carla Aspelmeier, Developmental Editor, showed a special enthusiasm for this book and should feel a sense of pride in competently guiding it through the revision process. The production team deserves special thanks for their excellent work: Gloria Schiesl, production editor; Heidi Baughman, designer; Karen Storlie, permissions editor; Carrie Burger, photo editor; Carla Heathcote, art editor; and Joe O'Connell, visual processor. Thanks also go to Lori Temple, who prepared an excellent Student Study Guide and a very useful Instructor's Course Planner, and to Lori Temple, Allen Keniston, Jerry Harper, and Robert Tomlinson, who prepared the Test Item File.

The fourth edition of this book benefited enormously from a carefully selected board of reviewers who provided in-depth reviews of chapters dealing with their area of expertise and/or a page-by-page analysis of the entire manuscript. For their generous help and countless good ideas, I would like to thank:

Furman, Duwayne
Western Illinois University

Green, Michael
University of North Carolina

Hulbert, Kathleen Day
University of Lowell

Kalichman, Seth
Loyola University

Macht, Jean Hill
Montgomery County Community College

Macias, Salvador
University of South Carolina–Sumter

Muzi, Malinda
Community College of Philadelphia

Nelson, Gordon K.
Pennsylvania State University

Offenbach, Stuart
Purdue University

Osborne, Sandra
Montana State University

Pierce, Richard
Pennsylvania State University–Altoona

Temple, Lori L.
University of Nevada, Las Vegas

I also remain indebted to the following individuals who reviewed previous editions and whose helpful guidance has been carried forward into the current edition of this text:

Alegre, Joanne M.
Yavajai College

Benedict, Helen E.
Baylor University

Blackburn, James A.
University of Wisconsin–Madison

Blevin-Knabe, Belinda
University of Arkansas–Little Rock

Bowers, Donald
Comm Coll of Philadelphia

Cannon, Joan B.
University of Lowell

Feldman, Shirley
Stanford University

Flickinger, Linda E.
St. Clair Community College

Goldstein, David
Temple University

Gram, Peter C.
Pensacola Junior College

Hoyer, Stephen
Pittsburgh State University

Kirkendall, Karen
Sangaman State University

Miller-Schwartz, Teri M.
Milwaukee Area Technical College

Murphy, Martin D.
University of Akron

Siaw, Susan Nakayama
California St Polytechnical Univ

Simmons, Vicki
University of Victoria

Snodgrass, Jon
California State University–LA

Stanley, Donald
North Dallas County College

Whetstone, B. D.
Birmingham Southern College

White, Sarah
Reynolds Community College

Wickelgren, Lyn W.
Metropolitan State College

Williams, Ann M.
Luzerne County Comm College

The quality of this text is greatly due to the ideas and insights of many other colleagues. I would like to thank the following individuals for sharing their thoughts and beneficial suggestions for improving *Life-Span Development:*

Adams, Berkeley
Jamestown Community College

Busky, Jack
Harrisburg Area Community College

Carter, Jeri
Glendale Community College

Castranovo, Vincent
Community College of Philadelphia

Chappeleau, Ginny
Muskingum Area Technical College

Christenberry, M. A.
Augusta College

Crown, Cynthia
Zavier University

Davis, Diane
Bowie State University

DeSantio, Doreen
West Chester University

De Villiers, Jill
Smith College

Ewy, Richard
Penn State University

Ferrara, Roberta
University of Kentucky

Gat, John
Humboldt State University

Gelman, Marvin
Montgomery County College

Glare, Rebecca J.
Weber State College

Goodell, Judy
National University

Heavilin, Robert
Greater Hartford Community College

Holt, Sharon
Allegany Community College

Janek, Erwin
Henderson State University

Jasper-Jacobsen, James
Indiana University–Purdue

Joyce, Ursula
St. Thomas Aquinas College

Kane, Barbara
Indiana State University

Keeney, James L.
Middle Georgia College

Kinarthy, Elinor
Rio Hondo College

Klingner, A.
Northwest Community College

Krump, Jane
North Dakota State College of Science

Lavoie, Joe
University of Nebraska

Macrae, Karen
University of South Carolina

McGinnis, Robert C.
Ancilla College

McKinney, Clara
Barstow College

Newton, Michael
Sam Houston State University

Norrie, Beatrice
Mount Royal College

O'Neil, Jean
Boston College

Pipes, David
Caldwell Community College

Rainey, Bob
Florida Community College

Ratner, H.
Wayne State University

Riley, Russell
Lord Fairfax Community College

Romeno, Clarence
Riverside Community College

Roodin, Paul
SUNY–Oswego

Russac, Ron
University of North Florida

Scheibe, Cynthia
Ithica College

Schell, Robert
SUNY–Oswego

Sharkey, Owen
University of Prince Edward Island

Stanley, Donald
North Harris Community College

Thomas, Barbara
National University

Turcott, James
Kalamazoo Valley Community College

Turhan, Stephen
Winston Salem State University

Williams, Myron D.
Great Lakes Bible College

A final note of thanks goes to my wife Mary Jo for her continued support of my work and for the companionship she has provided.

LIFE-SPAN DEVELOPMENT

S·E·C·T·I·O·N
I

THE LIFE-SPAN DEVELOPMENTAL PERSPECTIVE

All the world's a stage,
And all the men and women merely players;
They have their exits and their entrances,
And one man in his time plays many parts . . .

William Shakespeare

CHAPTER 1

History, Issues, and Methods

*W*hy study life-span development? Perhaps you are or will be a parent or teacher. Responsibility for children is or will be a part of your everyday life. The more you learn about them, the better you can deal with them. Perhaps you hope to gain some insight into your own history—as an infant, a child, an adolescent, or a young adult. Perhaps you want to know more about what your life will be like as you grow through the adult years—as a middle-aged adult, as an adult in old age, for example. Or, perhaps you just stumbled onto this course thinking that it sounded intriguing and that the topic of the human life cycle would raise some provocative and intriguing issues about our lives as we grow and develop. Whatever your reasons, you will discover that the study of life-span development *is* provocative, *is* intriguing, and *is* filled with information about who we are, how we have come to be this way, and where our future will take us.

This book tells the story of human development from conception to death—from the point in time when life begins until the point in time when it ends, at least life as we know it. You will see yourself as an infant, as a child, and as an adolescent, and be stimulated to think about how those years influenced the kind of individual you are today. And you will see yourself as a young adult, a middle-aged adult, and as an adult in old age, and be stimulated to think about how your experiences today will influence your development through the remainder of your adult years.

In this chapter, you will be introduced to some contemporary concerns in life-span development and to a historical perspective on child, adolescent, and life-span development. You will learn what development is, what issues are raised by a life-span perspective on development, and what methods are used to study life-span development.

Life-Span Development—Today and Yesterday

Everywhere an individual turns in contemporary society, the development and well-being of children and adults capture public attention, the interest of scientists, and the concern of policymakers. Through history, though, interest in the development of children and adults has varied.

Some Contemporary Concerns

Consider some of the topics you read about in newspapers and magazines everyday: genetic research, child abuse, homosexuality, mental retardation, parenting, intelligence, career changes, divorce, the increasing ethnic minority population, gender issues, retirement, and aging. What the experts are discovering in each of these areas has direct and significant consequences for understanding children and adults and our decisions as a society about how they should be treated. Let's think about five of these areas in more detail: genetics, child abuse, ethnic issues, gender, and the aging population.

Genetics researchers are discovering new techniques to diagnose potential problems both before and after conception. They are learning to predict genetic disturbances in development, various forms of deformities and retardation, and the child's sex. Some remarkable breakthroughs have also occurred in the ability to fertilize a human egg outside of its natural mother. All of these techniques and capabilities have profound consequences on genetic counseling for parents, arguments about when life really begins, debates about the legal right of women to have abortions, and ethical dilemmas about tampering in the laboratory with the genetic makeup of unborn children.

Another contemporary social issue whose widespread occurrence has just become understood in the last decade is child abuse (Schneider-Rosen &

The changing tapestry of the American culture involves the dramatic increase in ethnic minority individuals. An important agenda for the life-span perspective is to become more sensitive to ethnic issues and the role of ethnicity in development.

• *Critical Thinking* •

Genetic research, child abuse, homosexuality, mental retardation, parenting, intelligence, career changes, divorce, the increasing ethnic minority population, retirement, and aging are some contemporary concerns in life-span development. What other contemporary concerns related to life-span development can you generate?

Cicchetti, 1991). Although there are no sure data on how many cases of abuse occur each year, we do know something about the profile of the individuals who abuse children, the emotional consequences of the children being abused, and short-term remedies for the abused and abusers. Medical professionals and social service practitioners have formed child abuse teams throughout the country to spot cases of abuse in their early stages and to offer help to the victims. Some progress is being made, but the hurdles are difficult to overcome. Chief among these is the complex historical and legal tradition in our country that places families in the driver's seat in any conflict over a child's welfare.

The tapestry of American culture has changed dramatically in recent years. Nowhere is the change more noticeable than in the increasing ethnic diversity of America's citizens. In 1989, ethnic minority groups—Blacks, Hispanics, Native Americans (American Indians), and Asians, for example—made up 20 percent of all children and adolescents under the age of 17. By the year 2000, projections indicate that one-third of all school-aged children will fall into this category. This changing demographic tapestry promises not only the richness diversity produces but also difficult challenges in extending the American dream to individuals of all ethnic groups. Historically, ethnic minorities have found themselves at the bottom of the economic and social order. They have been disproportionately represented among the poor and the inadequately educated. Half of all Black children and one-third of all Hispanic children live in poverty. School dropout rates for minority youth reach the alarming rate of 60 percent in some urban areas. These population trends and our nation's inability to prepare ethnic minority individuals for full participation in American life have produced an imperative for the social institutions that serve ethnic minorities (Allen & Santrock, in press; Gibbs & Huang, 1989; Gordon, 1991; Jones, 1990; Marín & Marín, 1991; Ramirez, 1989; Spencer & Dornbusch, 1990; Sue, 1990). Schools, colleges, social services, health and mental health agencies, juvenile probation services, and other programs need to become more sensitive to ethnic issues and provide improved services to ethnic minority and low-income individuals.

(a)   (b)

Figure 1.1 *Artists' renditions of children as miniature adults. (a) Maria Teresa de Borbon by Francisco Goya; (b) Don Manuel Osorio de Zuniga by Francisco Goya. These artistic impressions show how children were viewed as miniature adults earlier in history. However, artists' renditions of children as miniature adults may have been too stereotypical.*

The changing tapestry of American culture also encompasses gender roles (Bronstein & Quina, 1988; Doyle & Paludi, 1991). A special concern is that historically females have grown up in a male-dominated society and that much of psychology portrays human development with a "male dominant theme" (DeFour & Paludi, in press; Unger, 1990). Feminist scholars are developing new perspectives that focus on girls' life experiences and development. These perspectives include an emphasis on girls and women as authorities on their own experiences, or as Harvard psychologist Carol Gilligan (1990, 1991; Gilligan, Brown, & Rogers, 1990) advocates, listening to females' voices. The perspectives also include an emphasis on females' competence in relationships, emotional development, and development of the self. Throughout the book you will find discussions of the increasing interest in gender issues.

Another major change in our culture is the increasing age of our population. Individuals are living longer and, in addition, are breaking the close link to their families. Because of this, the elderly no longer maintain as strong a socializing role in the child's development as they once did. Who is to care for the elderly who do not live with or close to their own children and grandchildren? What kinds of social services are needed for the elderly, and how can they be implemented? Should we reconsider the age of retirement for workers because of their increased longevity? Are there alternative work patterns in late adulthood that need to be explored? We address these and many other questions in our study of life-span development.

The Historical Perspective

Interest in children has a long and rich history. Interest in adolescents is more recent, and in adults has only seriously begun to develop in the latter half of the twentieth century (Havighurst, 1973).

Child Development

Childhood has become such a distinct period that it is hard to imagine it was not always thought of in that way. However, in medieval times, laws generally did not distinguish between childhood and adult offenses. And, after analyzing samples of art along with available publications, historian Philippe Aries (1962) concluded that European societies did not accord any special status to children prior to 1600. In the paintings, children were often dressed in smaller versions of adultlike clothing (see figure 1.1).

We reach backward to our parents and forward to our children, and through their children to a future we will never see, but about which we need to care.

~ *Carl Jung*

Were children actually treated as miniature adults with no special status in medieval Europe? Aries' interpretation has been criticized. He primarily sampled aristocratic, idealized subjects, which led to the overdrawn conclusion that children were treated as miniature adults and not accorded any special status (Borstelmann, 1983). In medieval times, children did often work and their emotional bond with parents may not have been as strong as it is for many children today. However, in medieval times, childhood was probably recognized as a distinct phase of life more than Aries believed. Also, we know that in ancient Egypt, Greece, and Rome, rich conceptions of children's development were held.

Through history, philosophers have speculated at length about the nature of children and how they should be reared. Three such philosophical views are: original sin, *tabula rasa,* and innate goodness. In the perspective of **original sin,** *especially advocated during the Middle Ages, children were perceived as basically bad, being born into the world as evil beings.* The goal of childrearing was salvation, which was believed to remove sin from the child's life. Toward the end of the seventeenth century, the **tabula rasa** *view was proposed by English philosopher John Locke. He argued that children are not innately bad, but instead they are like a "blank tablet,"* a tabula rasa *as he called it.* Locke believed that childhood experiences are important in determining adult characteristics. He advised parents to spend time with their children and help them become contributing members of society. In the eighteenth century, the **innate goodness** *view was presented by Swiss-born French philosopher Jean Jacques Rousseau, who stressed that children are inherently good.* Rousseau said that because children are basically good, they should be permitted to grow naturally with little parental monitoring or constraint.

During the past century and a half, interest in the nature of children and ways to improve their well-being have continued to be important concerns of our society. We now conceive of childhood as a highly eventful and unique period of life that lays an important foundation for the adult years and is highly differentiated from them. In most approaches to childhood, distinct periods are identified in which special skills are mastered and new life tasks are confronted. Childhood is no longer seen as an inconvenient "waiting" period during which adults must suffer the incompetencies of the young. We now value childhood as a special time of growth and change, and we invest great resources in caring for and educating our children. We protect them from the excesses of adult work through strict child labor laws; we treat their crimes against society under a special system of juvenile justice; and we have government provisions for helping them when ordinary family support systems fail or when families seriously interfere with the child's well-being (Cohen & Naimark, 1991; Hart, 1991; Melton, 1991).

Adolescence

Twentieth century poet essayist Roger Allen once remarked, "In case you are worried about what's going to become of the younger generation, it's going to grow up and start worrying about the younger generation." Virtually every society has worried about its younger generation, but it was not until the beginning of the twentieth century that the scientific study of adolescence appeared. In 1904, American psychologist G. Stanley Hall wrote the first scientific book on the nature of adolescence. The **storm and stress view** *is G. Stanley Hall's concept that adolescence is a turbulent time charged with conflict and mood swings.* Thoughts, feelings, and actions oscillate between conceit and humility, good and temptation, and happiness and sadness. The adolescent may be nasty to a peer one moment and kind the next moment. At one time the adolescent may want to be alone but seconds later seek companionship.

As we move toward the close of the twentieth century, experts on adolescence are trying to dispel the myth that adolescents are abnormal and deviant (Hill, 1983; Feldman & Elliott, 1990; William T. Grant Foundation Report, 1988). Too often all adolescents are stereotyped and described in sweeping generalizations based on a small group of highly visible adolescents. A recent investigation by Daniel Offer and his colleagues (1988) documented that the vast majority of adolescents are competent human beings who are not experiencing deep emotional turmoil. The self-images of adolescents were sampled from around the world—from the United States, Australia, Bangladesh, Hungary, Israel, Japan, Taiwan, Turkey, and West Germany. A positive self-image characterized three of every four adolescents studied. The adolescents were moving toward adulthood with a healthy integration of their identity, being happy most of the time, enjoying life, valuing work and school, having positive feelings about their family and friends, expressing confidence in their sexual selves, and believing they have the ability to cope with life's stresses—not exactly a storm and stress portrayal of adolescence.

While adolescence has a biological base, sociohistorical conditions contributed to the emergence of the concept of adolescence. American society may have "inflicted" the status of adolescence on its youth through child-saving legislation (Elder, Caspi, & Burton, 1988; Lapsley, Enright, & Serlin, 1985). By developing laws for youth only, the adult power structure placed young people in a submissive position that restricted their options, encouraged dependency, and made their move into the world of adult work more manageable. From 1890 to 1920, virtually every state developed laws that excluded youth from work and required them to attend school. In this time frame, a 600 percent increase in the number of high school graduates occurred! (Tyack, 1976). And by 1950, the developmental period we refer to as adolescence had come of age. Not only did it possess physical and social identity, but it possessed legal identity as well. By this time, every state had developed special laws for youth between the ages of 16 and 21.

Life-Span Development

The *traditional* approach to development emphasizes extreme change from birth to adolescence, little or no change in adulthood, and decline in old age. By contrast, the *life-span approach* emphasizes that developmental change occurs during adulthood as well as during childhood (Baltes, 1987; Baltes, Featherman, & Lerner, 1990; Cummings, Greene, & Karraker, 1991; Hetherington & Baltes, 1989). Figure 1.2 reveals how the traditional view of development contrasts with the life-span perspective. In the traditional view, notice the powerful role allotted to infancy and early childhood and the absence of change in early and middle adulthood.

The first interest in the adult part of the life cycle was toward the end of the cycle—in aging (Riegel, 1977). Improvements in sanitation, nutrition, and medical knowledge led to dramatic increases in life expectancy. In table 1.1, the average life expectancy of individuals from prehistoric to contemporary times is shown. Until the twentieth century most individuals did not live to be 50 years of age. In 1900, only 1 American in 25 was over 65; today, 9 in 25 live to be this old. By the middle of the next century, 1 American in 4 will be 65 years of age or older. Figure 1.3a shows the number (in millions) of Americans over 65 in 1900, 1940, and 1980, and the projected numbers for the year 2040. Not only will we experience a substantial increase in the number of people over 65, but the same trend will occur for individuals over the age of 85 (see figure 1.3b).

In youth, we clothe ourselves with rainbows, and go as brave as the zodiac.

~ *Ralph Waldo Emerson,*
The Conduct of Life, 1860

• *Critical Thinking* •

In what ways are today's adolescents the same as or different from the adolescents of ten years ago? twenty years ago?

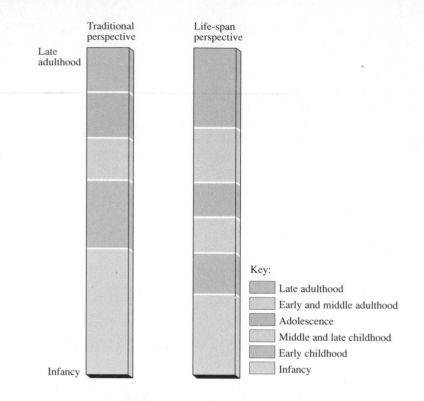

Figure 1.2 Two contrasting perspectives on developmental change. In the traditional perspective, dramatic change occurs in infancy and early childhood, while little or no change takes place in adult development. In the life-span perspective, developmental change takes place throughout the human life cycle.

Table 1.1: Human Life Expectancy at Birth from Prehistoric to Contemporary Times

Time Period	Average Life Expectancy (in years)
Prehistoric Times	18
Ancient Greece	20
Middle Ages, England	33
1620, Massachusetts Bay Colony	35
19th Century, England	41
1900, USA	47
1915, USA	54
1954, USA	70
1983, USA	75

Source: Data from Monroe Lerner, "When, Why, and Where People Die" in E. S. Shneidman (ed.), *Death: Current Perspectives,* 2d ed., pp. 89–91, 1980.

Consequently, we have developed an interest in old age, and also in the psychological changes between adolescence and old age. For too long we believed that development was something that only happened to children. To be sure, growth and development are dramatic in the first two decades of life, but a great deal of change goes on in the next five or six decades of life, too. In the words of American developmental psychologists Robert Sears and Shirley Feldman (1973):

But the next five or six decades are every bit as important, not only to those adults who are passing through them but to their children, who

The Life-Span Developmental Perspective

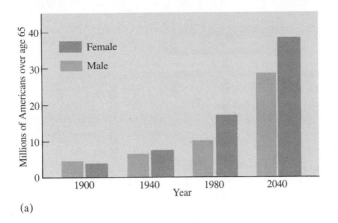

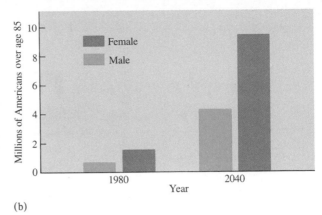

(a)

(b)

*Figure 1.3   The aging of America.
(a) Millions of Americans over age
65 from 1900 to the present and
projected to the year 2040.
(b) Millions of Americans over age
85 in 1980 and projected in the year
2040.*

*must live with and understand parents and grandparents. The changes
in body, personality, and abilities through these later decades is great.
There are severe developmental tasks imposed by marriage and parenthood, by the waxing and waning of physical prowess and of some intellectual capacities, by the children's flight from the nest, by the achievement
of an occupational plateau, and by the facing of retirement and the prospect of final extinction. Parents have always been fascinated by their children's development, but it is high time adults began to look objectively
at themselves, to examine the systematic changes in their own physical,
mental, and emotional qualities, as they pass through the life cycle, and
to get acquainted with the limitations and assets they share with so many
others of their age (pp. v–vi).*

Our society's increasing interest in older adults is reflected by a law en-
acted by Congress in 1986, which states that employers can no longer require
workers to retire when they reach age 70—with certain exceptions, such as
police officers and pilots (Riley, 1989). This act does not end discrimination,
but it does increase the freedom of choice of many older adults and sends a
strong message that the work contributions of older adults are valued. This
act may signify a reversal of the century-long decline in labor force participation of workers over the age of 65.

As the elderly population continues to grow into the twenty-first century,
life-span developmentalists are concerned that an increasing number of older
adults will be without either spouse or children, who have traditionally been
major sources of support for older adults (House, 1989; Featherman, 1989).
In recent decades, American adults were less likely to be married, more likely
to be childless, and more likely to be living alone than earlier in the twentieth
century. As these individuals become older, their need for social relationships,
networks, and supports appears to be increasing at the same time the supply
is dwindling. (More about the role of social supports for older adults appears
in chapter 20.)

The Life-Span Perspective

In this book we take a life-span perspective on understanding development.
What does it mean to adopt a life-span perspective? According to life-span
development expert Paul Baltes (1987), the **life-span perspective** *involves seven
basic contentions: Development is life-long, multidimensional, multidirectional, plastic, historically embedded, multidisciplinary, and contextual.* We
consider each of these characteristics of the life-span perspective in turn.

*Paul Baltes has developed a number
of important ideas about the life-
span perspective and conducted
many research studies documenting
the nature of developmental changes
in adulthood. His most recent
research interests have focused on
the developmental aspects of wisdom
in adulthood.*

Figure 1.4 *Characteristics of the life-span perspective.*

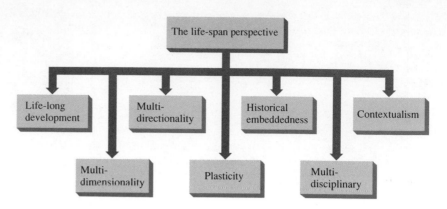

The Life-Span Perspective's Characteristics

Development is *life-long.* No age period dominates development. Researchers increasingly study the experiences and psychological orientations of adults at different points in their development. Development includes both gains and losses, which interact in dynamic ways throughout the life cycle (Baltes, 1989; Lerner, 1990).

Development is *multidimensional.* Development consists of biological, cognitive, and social dimensions. Even within a dimension such as intelligence, there are many components, such as abstract intelligence, nonverbal intelligence, social intelligence, and so on.

Development is *multidirectional.* Some dimensions, or components of a dimension may increase in growth, while others decrease. For example, older adults may become wiser by being able to call on experience as a guide to intellectual decision making, but perform more poorly on tasks that require speed in processing information.

Development is *plastic.* Depending on the individual's life conditions, development may take many paths. A key developmental agenda is the search for plasticity and its constraints. For example, researchers have demonstrated that the reasoning abilities of older adults can be improved through training (Kliegl, Smith, & Baltes, 1990; Smith & Baltes, 1991; Willis, 1990).

Development is *embedded in history,* being influenced by historical conditions. The experiences of 40-year-olds who lived through the Depression were very different from the experiences of 40-year-olds who lived in the optimistic aftermath of World War II. The career orientation of many 30-year-old females in the 1990s is very different from the career orientation of most 30-year-old females in the 1950s.

Development is *studied by a number of disciplines.* Psychologists, sociologists, anthropologists, neuroscientists, and medical researchers all study human development and share a concern for unlocking the mysteries of development through the life span.

Development is *contextual.* The individual continually responds to and acts on contexts, which include one's biological makeup, one's physical environment, and one's social, historical, and cultural contexts. In the contextual view, individuals are thought of as changing beings in a changing world. A summary of the characteristics of the life-span perspective is presented in figure 1.4.

The life-span perspective has been beneficial to the health and well-being of individuals, families, and communities. Many different careers now include positions that involve an application of knowledge about life-span development. For example, a knowledge of life-span development is relevant to genetic counselors and family planning specialists, health specialists and nurses, directors of day-care centers and preschool teachers, crisis intervention counselors, juvenile probation officers, social workers and therapists, and gerontologists (those who study or work with older adults).

Contextualism: Age-Graded, History-Graded, and Nonnormative Influences

One characteristic of the life-span perspective—contextualism—merits further attention. In the contextual view, development can be understood as the outcome of the interaction among three systems: (1) normative age-graded influences, (2) normative history-graded influences, and (3) nonnormative life-events (Baltes, 1987).

Normative age-graded influences *are biological and environmental influences that are similar for individuals in a particular age group.* These influences include biological processes such as puberty and menopause, and they include sociocultural, environmental processes such as entry into formal education (usually at about age 6 in most cultures) and retirement (usually occurring in the fifties and sixties).

Normative history-graded influences *are biological and environmental influences that are associated with history. These influences are common to people of a particular generation.* Normative history-graded influences include economic changes (the Depression of the 1930s), war (World War II in the 1940s), the changing roles of women, the computer revolution, and political upheaval and change (such as the decrease in hard-line communism in the late 1980s and early 1990s).

Nonnormative life events *are unusual occurrences that have a major impact on an individual's life. The occurrence, patterning, and sequence of these events are not applicable to many individuals.* These events do not follow a general and predictable course. Such events may include the death of a parent when a child is young, pregnancy in early adolescence, a disaster (such as a fire that destroys a home), or an accident (such as a serious car wreck). Nonnormative life events can also include positive occurrences such as winning a lottery or being offered a unique career opportunity with special privileges. An important aspect of understanding the role of nonnormative life events is how individuals adapt to them.

The Nature of Development

Each of us develops in ways that are like all other individuals, like some other individuals, and like no other individuals. Most of the time, our attention is directed to an individual's uniqueness. But psychologists who study life-span development are drawn to our shared as well as our unique characteristics. As humans, each of us has traveled some common paths. Each of us—Leonardo Da Vinci, Joan of Arc, George Washington, Martin Luther King, Jr., and you—walked at about 1 year, talked at about 2 years, engaged in fantasy play as a young child, and became more independent as a youth. Each of us, if we live long enough, will experience hearing problems, and the death of family and friends.

Just what do psychologists mean when they speak of an individual's development? **Development** *is the pattern of movement or change that begins at conception and continues through the life cycle.* Most development involves

Each of you, individually, walkest with the tread of a fox, but collectively ye are geese.

~ *Solon, Ancient Greece*

growth, although it also includes decay (as in death and dying). The pattern of movement is complex because it is the product of several processes—biological, cognitive, and social.

Biological, Cognitive, and Social Processes

Biological processes *involve changes in the individual's physical nature.* Genes inherited from parents, the development of the brain, height and weight gains, motor skills, the hormonal changes of puberty, and cardiovascular decline all reflect the role of biological processes in development.

Cognitive processes *involve changes in the individual's thought, intelligence, and language.* Watching a colorful mobile swinging above the crib, putting together a two-word sentence, memorizing a poem, imagining what it would be like to be a movie star, and solving a crossword puzzle, all reflect the role of cognitive processes in development.

Social processes *involve changes in the individual's relationships with other people, changes in emotions, and changes in personality.* An infant's smile in response to her mother's touch, a young boy's aggressive attack on a playmate, a girl's development of assertiveness, an adolescent's joy at the senior prom, and the affection of an elderly couple, all reflect the role of the social processes in development.

Remember as you read about biological, cognitive, and social processes that they are intricately interwoven. You will read about how social processes shape cognitive processes, how cognitive processes promote or restrict social processes, and how biological processes influence cognitive processes, for example. Although it is helpful to study the different processes involved in children's development in separate sections of the book, keep in mind that you are studying the development of an integrated individual with one interdependent mind and one body (see figure 1.5).

Periods of Development

For the purposes of organization and understanding, we commonly describe development in terms of periods. The most widely used classification of developmental periods involves the following sequence: prenatal period, infancy, early childhood, middle and late childhood, adolescence, early adulthood, middle adulthood, and late adulthood. Approximate age ranges are listed for the periods to provide a general idea of when a period first begins and when it ends.

The **prenatal period** *is the time from conception to birth.* It is a time of tremendous growth—from a single cell to an organism complete with brain and behavioral capabilities, produced in approximately a nine-month period.

Infancy *is the developmental period extending from birth to 18 or 24 months.* Infancy is a time of extreme dependence upon adults. Many psychological activities are just beginning—language, symbolic thought, sensorimotor coordination, and social learning, for example.

Early childhood *is the developmental period extending from the end of infancy to about 5 or 6 years; this period is sometimes called the preschool years.* During this time, young children learn to become more self-sufficient and to care for themselves, develop school readiness skills (following instructions, identifying letters), and spend many hours in play with peers. First grade typically marks the end of early childhood.

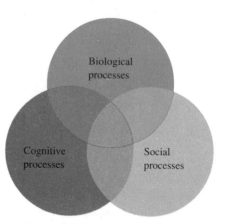

Figure 1.5 Biological, cognitive, and social processes in life-span development. Changes in development are the result of biological, cognitive, and social processes. These processes are interwoven in the development of the individual through the human life cycle.

Middle and late childhood *is the developmental period extending from about 6 to 11 years of age, approximately corresponding to the elementary school years; this period is sometimes called the elementary school years.* The fundamental skills of reading, writing, and arithmetic are mastered. Formal exposure to the larger world and its culture takes place. Achievement becomes a more central theme of the child's world, and self-control increases.

Adolescence *is the developmental period of transition from childhood to early adulthood, entered at approximately 10 to 12 years of age and ending at 18 to 22 years of age.* Adolescence begins with rapid physical changes—dramatic gains in height and weight, changes in body contour, and the development of sexual characteristics such as enlargement of the breasts, development of pubic and facial hair, and deepening of the voice. At this point in development, the pursuit of independence and an identity are prominent; thought is more logical, abstract, and idealistic; and more and more time is spent outside of the family.

Early adulthood *is the developmental period beginning in the late teens or early twenties and lasting through the thirties.* It is a time of establishing personal and economic independence, a time of career development, and for many, a time of selecting a mate, learning to live with someone in an intimate way, starting a family, and rearing children.

Middle adulthood *is the developmental period beginning at approximately 35 to 45 years of age and extending to the sixties.* It is a time of expanding personal and social involvement and responsibility; of assisting the next generation in becoming competent, mature individuals; and of reaching and maintaining satisfaction in one's career.

Late adulthood *is the developmental period beginning in the sixties or seventies and lasting until death.* It is a time of adjustment to decreasing strength and health, life review, retirement, and adjustment to new social roles.

The periods of the human life cycle are shown in figure 1.6 along with the processes of development—biological, cognitive, and social. The interplay of biological, cognitive, and social processes produces the periods of the human life cycle.

In our description of the periods of the life cycle, we placed approximate age bands on the periods. However, one expert on life-span development, Bernice Neugarten (1980, 1988; Neugarten & Neugarten, 1989) believes we are rapidly becoming an age-irrelevant society. She says we are already familiar with the 28-year-old mayor, the 35-year-old grandmother, the 65-year-old father of a preschooler, the 55-year-old widow who starts a business, and the 70-year-old student. Neugarten says that she has had difficulty clustering adults into age brackets that are characterized by particular issues. She stresses that choices and dilemmas do not spring forth at ten-year intervals, and decisions are not made and then left behind as if they were merely beads on a chain. Neugarten argues that most adulthood themes appear and reappear throughout life's human cycle. The issues of intimacy and freedom can haunt couples throughout their relationship. Feeling the pressure of time, reformulating goals, and coping with success and failure are not the exclusive property of adults of a particular age. As an indication that age itself may be becoming a less important marker, developmentalists have found that older adults are just as satisfied with their lives as younger adults. To learn more about feelings of happiness and life satisfaction at different points in the life cycle, turn to Perspective on Life-Span Development 1.1.

One's children's children's children. Look back to us as we look to you; we are related by our imaginations. If we are able to touch, it is because we have imagined each other's existence, our dreams running back and forth along a cable from age to age.

~ *Roger Rosenblatt, 1986*

Some life-span theorists believe that age is rapidly becoming a poor predictor of adult development. For example, Bernice Neugarten says we are already familiar with the 28-year-old mayor, the 35-year-old grandmother, the 65-year-old father of a preschooler, the 55-year-old widow who starts a business, and the 70-year-old student.

Figure 1.6 Processes and periods of life-span development. The unfolding of the life-cycle's periods of development is influenced by the interplay of biological, cognitive, and social processes.

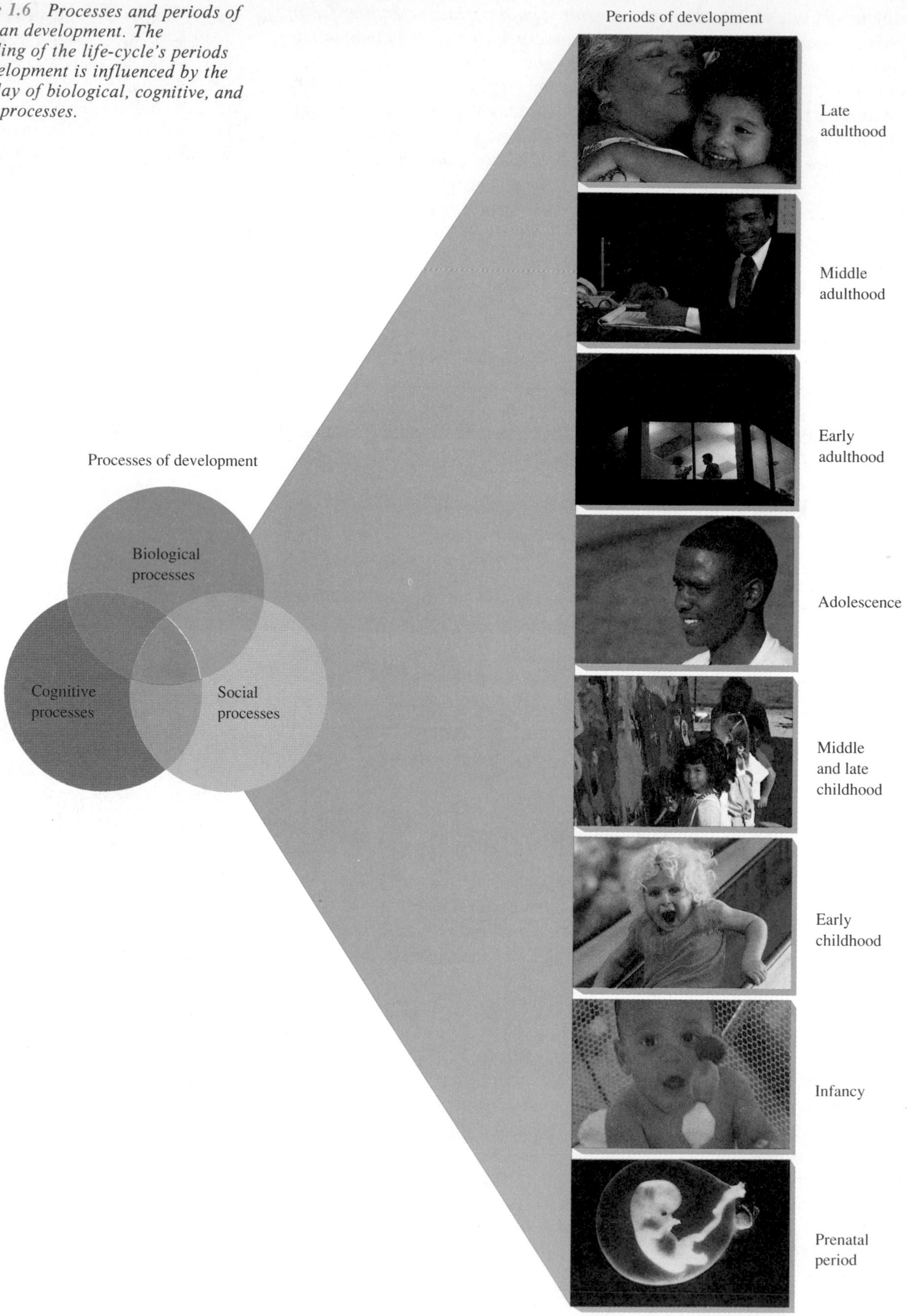

Periods of development

Late adulthood

Middle adulthood

Early adulthood

Adolescence

Middle and late childhood

Early childhood

Infancy

Prenatal period

Processes of development

Biological processes

Cognitive processes

Social processes

WHAT IS THE BEST AGE TO BE?

*E*ach of us is curious about what the best years of our life were or will be. That is, how do people feel about their phase of the life course? Which age group do you feel is probably the happiest? Is it carefree, independent youth? Optimistic, energetic young adults? Successful, experienced middle-aged adults? Or fulfilled, retired older adults? A common belief is that the adolescent years and the older adult years are the unhappiest years of life. After all, aren't the adolescent years filled with stress, identity confusion, insecurity, mood swings, and peer pressure? And aren't the late adulthood years a time of reduced income, less energy, a deteriorating body, decreasing cognitive skills, death of friends and family, and thoughts of one's own impending death? As we discuss adolescence and late adulthood later in the text, you will discover that people have many misconceptions and stereotypes about adolescents and older adults.

When individuals report how happy they are and how satisfied they are with their lives, no particular age group reports that they are happier or more satisfied than any other age group (Stock & others, 1983). In one report of life-satisfaction in eight Western

What is the best age to be? When individuals report how happy they are and how satisfied they are with their lives, no particular age group reports that they are happier or more satisfied than any other age group.

European countries, there was no difference in the percentage who reported an overall satisfaction with life at different ages: 78 percent of 15 to 24-year-olds, 78 percent of 35 to 44-year-olds, and 78 percent of those 65 years and older (Ingelhart & Rabier, 1986). Similarly, slightly less than 20 percent of each of the age groups reported that they were "very happy."

Why might older people report just as much happiness and life satisfaction as younger people? Every period of the life cycle has its stresses, its pluses and minuses, its hills and valleys. While adolescents must cope with developing an identity, feelings of insecurity, mood swings, and peer pressure, the majority of adolescents develop positive perceptions of themselves, feelings of competence about their skills, positive relationships with friends and family, and an optimistic view of their future. And while older adults face a life of reduced income, less energy, decreasing physical skills, and concerns about death, they are also less pressured to achieve and succeed, have more time for leisurely pursuits, and have accumulated many years of experience that help them adapt to their lives with a wisdom they may not have had in their younger years. Since growing older is a certain outcome of living, we can derive considerable pleasure from knowing that we are likely to be just as happy as older adults as when we were younger (Myers, 1989).

Developmental Issues

A number of issues generate spirited debate among developmentalists. The extent to which development is influenced by maturation and experience (nature and nurture), is characterized by continuity and discontinuity, and involves stability and change are among the most intensely discussed issues. We consider each of these issues in turn.

Maturation and Experience (Nature and Nurture)

Not only can we think of development as produced by the interplay of biological, cognitive, and social processes, but also by the interplay of maturation and experience. **Maturation** *is the orderly sequence of changes dictated by* *the genetic blueprint we each have.* Just as a sunflower grows in an orderly way—unless flattened by an unfriendly environment—so does the human grow in an orderly way, according to the maturational view. The range of environments can be vast, but the maturational approach argues that the genetic blueprint produces communalities in our growth and development. We walk before we talk, speak one word before two words, grow rapidly in infancy and less so in early childhood, experience a rush of sexual hormones in puberty after a lull in childhood, reach the peak of our physical strength in late adolescence and early adulthood and then decline, and so on. The maturationists acknowledge that extreme environments—those that are psychologically barren or hostile—can depress development, but they believe basic growth tendencies are genetically wired into the human.

By contrast, other psychologists emphasize the importance of experiences in life-span development. Experiences run the gamut from the individual's biological environment—nutrition, medical care, drugs, and physical accidents—to the social environment—family, peers, schools, community, media, and culture.

The debate about whether development is primarily influenced by maturation or by experience has been a part of psychology since its beginning. This debate is often referred to as the **nature-nurture controversy.** *Nature refers to an organism's biological inheritance, nurture to environmental experiences. The "nature" proponents claim biological inheritance is the most important influence on development and the "nurture" proponents claim that environmental experiences are the most important.*

Ideas about the nature of development have been like a pendulum, swinging between nature and nurture. In the 1980s we witnessed a surge of interest in the biological underpinnings of development, probably because the pendulum had swung too far toward thinking that development was exclusively due to environmental experiences (Hinde & Gorebel, 1989). As we enter the 1990s, a heightened interest in sociocultural influences on development is emerging, probably because the pendulum in the 1980s had swung so strongly toward the biological side (Brislin, 1990; Bruner, 1989, 1991; Ceci, 1991; Jones, 1990; Rogoff, 1989; Spencer, 1991; Sue, 1990). As we indicated earlier in the chapter, an important dimension of life-span development is the changing cultural tapestry of America, which is especially apparent in the increasing ethnic diversity of America's citizens. More about the changing cultural worlds of life-span development appears in Cultural Worlds of Development 1.1.

Continuity and Discontinuity

Think about your development for a moment. Did you gradually become the person you are, like the slow, cumulative growth of a seedling into a giant oak? Or did you experience sudden, distinct changes in your growth, like the way a caterpillar changes into a butterfly (see figure 1.7)? For the most part, developmentalists who emphasize experience have described development as a gradual, continuous process; those who emphasize maturation have described development as a series of distinct stages (Bornstein & Krasnegor, 1989).

Some developmentalists emphasize **continuity of development,** *the view that development involves gradual, cumulative change from conception to death.* A child's first word, while seemingly an abrupt, discontinuous event, is actually the result of weeks and months of growth and practice. Puberty, while also seemingly an abrupt, discontinuous occurrence, is actually a gradual process occurring over several years.

Figure 1.7 Continuity and discontinuity in development. Is development more like a seedling gradually growing into a giant oak or a caterpillar suddenly becoming a butterfly?

The Life-Span Developmental Perspective

THE HETEROGENEITY OF ETHNIC AND CULTURAL GROUPS

*A*n especially important idea in considering the nature of cultural and ethnic groups is that not only is there ethnic diversity within a culture—our American culture includes Anglo Americans, Black Americans, Hispanic Americans, Native Americans, Asian Americans, Italian Americans, Polish Americans, and so on—but there is diversity within each ethnic group. No cultural characteristic is common to all or nearly all Black Americans, or to all or nearly all Hispanic Americans, and absent in Anglo Americans, unless it is the experience of being Black or of being Hispanic and the beliefs that develop from that experience (Havighurst, 1987).

Black Americans make up the largest easily visible ethnic minority group in the United States. Black Americans are distributed through the social class structure, although they constitute a larger proportion of low-income individuals than the majority Anglo American group (Bell-Scott, 1989; Belle, 1990; Gibbs, 1989; McLoyd, in press). The majority of Black youth stay in school, do not take drugs, do not get married prematurely, and grow up to lead productive lives in spite of social and economic disadvantages. Hispanic Americans also are a diverse group of individuals. All Hispanic Americans are not Catholic. Many are, but some are not. All Hispanic Americans do not have a Mexican heritage. Many do, but many others have cultural ties with South American countries, with Puerto Rico or other Caribbean countries, or with Spain (Pacheco & Valdez, 1989; Ramirez, 1989).

Native Americans are also an extremely diverse and complex ethnic group (Trimble, 1989, in press). There are more than 450 identifiable tribal

To help buffer the stress in their lives, many ethnic minority groups have developed their own social structures, which include Mexican American kin systems, the African American church, Chinese American family associations, and Native American tribal associations.

units. So are Asian Americans, with more than 30 distinct groups listed under this designation (Sue, 1990).

America has embraced new ingredients from many cultures. The cultures often mix their beliefs and identities. Some of the culture of origin is retained, some of it is lost, and some of it is mixed with the American culture. As ethnic minority groups continue to expand at a rapidly increasing rate, one of life-span development's most important agendas is to give increased attention to the role of culture and ethnicity in understanding development.

Recognizing the importance of better understanding ethnic minorities, the Gerontological Association of America recently established a task force on minority issues (Anderson,

1989). Both the demographic and health status data for older minorities suggest they are in a disadvantaged position relative to Whites. However, it is important to note that not all ethnic minority individuals live in poverty—for example, Asian Americans show a poverty rate similar to that of Anglo Americans (Jackson, 1989). And in the face of covert or overt attempts at segregation, ethnic minority groups have developed their own communities and social structures—which include Black churches, Vietnamese mutual assistance associations, Chinese American family associations, and Mexican American kin systems. At the same time they are learning to negotiate with the dominant White culture in America (Gibbs & Huang, 1989).

Other developmentalists emphasize **discontinuity of development,** *the view that development involves distinct stages in the life span.* Each of us is described as passing through a sequence of stages in which change is qualitatively rather than quantitatively different. As the oak moves from seedling to giant oak, it becomes *more* oak—its development is continuous. As the caterpillar changes to a butterfly, it is not just more caterpillar, it is a *different kind* of organism—its development is discontinuous. For example, at some point a child moves from not being able to think abstractly about the world to being able to. This is a qualitative, discontinuous change in development, not a quantitative, continuous change.

Stability and Change

Another important developmental topic is the **stability-change issue,** *which addresses whether development is best described by stability or by change. The stability-change issue involves the degree to which we become older renditions of our early experience or whether we develop into someone different than we were at an earlier point in development.* Will the shy child who hides behind the sofa when visitors arrive be a wallflower at college dances, or will the child become a sociable, talkative individual? Will the fun-loving, carefree adolescent have difficulty holding down a nine-to-five job as an adult or become a straitlaced, serious conformist?

One of the reasons adult development was so late in being studied was the predominant belief for many years that nothing much changes in adulthood. The major changes were believed to take place in childhood, especially during the first five years of life. Today, most developmentalists believe that some change is possible throughout the human life cycle, although they disagree, sometimes vehemently, about just how much change can take place, and how much stability there is. The important issue of stability and change in development will reappear on many occasions in our journey through the human life cycle.

The issue of stability and change raises the question of which is the more dominant and desired characteristic of human development: stability or change? Some life-span developmentalists, such as Klaus Riegel (1975), have argued that change, not stability, is the key to understanding development. Riegel's view is called the **dialectical model,** *which states that each individual is continually changing because of various forces that push and pull development forward. In the dialectical model, each person is viewed as acting on and reacting to social and historical conditions.* Consider the push and pull between independence and dependence. In the first year of life, the infant is dependent on parents for support and sustenance. In the second year of life, as development proceeds, the infant becomes more independent, seeking to engage in more autonomous adventures. But as toddlers encounter fears and stressors, their independent efforts become moderated as they sense their need to maintain some dependence on their parents. Thus the push and pull between independence and dependence continues throughout life, waxing and waning, as we, others, and sociohistorical conditions develop and change. As individuals enter adolescence, they push for independence from their parents, who struggle to pull them toward dependence. While all adolescents push for independence, sociohistorical conditions influence the intensity of the push. The adolescent rebelliousness of the late 1960s and the 1970s can be partly understood as a reaction to their parents' conservative values, which were likely an outgrowth of the difficult times of the Depression and World War II. In subsequent years, the so-called generation gap between parents and adolescents decreased as both parents and adolescents, as well as sociohistorical conditions, changed. In the dialectical model, such change also characterizes the push and pull that we experience in the development of masculinity-femininity, competitiveness-cooperation, introversion-extraversion, and so on.

Evaluating the Developmental Issues

As we further consider these three salient developmental issues—nature and nurture, continuity and discontinuity, and stability and change—it is important to point out that most life-span developmentalists recognize that extreme positions on these issues are unwise. Development is not all nature or nurture, not all continuity or discontinuity, and not all stability or change. Both nature and nurture, continuity and discontinuity, stability and change characterize our development through the human life cycle. For example, in considering the nature-nurture issue, the key to development is the *interaction* of nature and nurture rather than either factor alone (Plomin, 1989, 1991; Scarr, 1991). For example, the individual's cognitive development is the result of heredity-environment interaction, not heredity or environment alone. (Much more about the role of heredity-environment interaction appears in chapter 3.)

Although most developmentalists do not take extreme positions on these three important issues, there is, nonetheless, spirited debate about how strongly development is influenced by each of these factors. Are girls less likely to do well in math because of their "feminine" nature, or because of society's masculine bias? How extensively can the elderly be trained to reason more effectively? How much, if at all, does our memory decline in old age? Can techniques be used to prevent or reduce the decline? If children experienced a world of poverty, neglect by parents, and poor schooling, can enriched experiences in adolescence remove the "deficits" they encountered earlier in their development? The answers given by developmentalists to such questions depend on their stance regarding the issues of nature and nurture, continuity and discontinuity, and stability and change. The answers to these questions also influence public policy decisions about children, adolescents, and adults, and influence how we each live our lives as we go through the human life cycle.

At this point we have discussed a number of ideas about the contemporary and historical perspectives on life-span development, the life-span perspective, and the nature of development. A summary of these ideas is presented in concept table 1.1. The life-span perspective is more than just a perspective. It is a developmental *science* with goals of studying life changes, improving conditions of life through intervention efforts, and promoting the health and well-being of individuals. What do we mean when we say the life-span perspective is a *science?*

The Science Base of Life-Span Development

Some individuals have difficulty thinking of life-span development as a science in the same way physics, chemistry, and biology are sciences. Can a discipline that studies how babies develop, parents nurture children, adolescents' thoughts change, adults form intimate relationships, and aging adults engage in self-control, be equated with disciplines that investigate the molecular structure of a compound and how gravity works? Science is not defined by *what* it investigates but by *how* it investigates. Whether you are studying photosynthesis, butterflies, Saturn's moons, or human development, it is the way you study that makes the approach scientific or not.

Concept Table 1.1: History and Issues in Life-Span Development

Concept	Processes/Related Ideas	Characteristics/Description
Life-Span Development— Today and Yesterday	Contemporary Concerns	Today, the well-being of children and adults is a prominent concern in our culture—four such concerns are genetic research, child abuse, ethnic diversity, and aging.
	The Historical Perspective	Interest in children has a long and rich history. In the Renaissance, philosophical views were prominent, including original sin, *tabula rasa,* and innate goodness. The scientific study of adolescence was promoted by G. Stanley Hall in the early 1900s. His storm and stress view contrasts with the belief that sociohistorical conditions produced the concept of adolescence. The traditional approach emphasizes extensive change in childhood but stability in adulthood; the life-span perspective emphasizes that change is possible throughout the life span.
The Life-Span Perspective	Characteristics	The life-span perspective involves seven basic contentions: Development is life-long, multidimensional, multidirectional, plastic, historically embedded, contextual, and multidisciplinary.
	Contextualism	In the contextual view, development can be understood as the outcome of the interaction of normative age-graded influences, normative history-graded influences, and nonnormative life events.
The Nature of Development	What Is Development?	Development is the pattern of movement or change that occurs throughout the life span.
	Biological, Cognitive, and Social Processes	Development is influenced by an interplay of biological, cognitive, and social processes.
	Periods of Development	The life cycle is commonly divided into the following periods of development: prenatal, infancy, early childhood, middle and late childhood, adolescence, early adulthood, middle adulthood, and late adulthood. Some experts on life-span development, such as Neugarten, however, believe too much emphasis is placed on age. She believes we are moving toward a society in which age is not a good predictor of development in adulthood.
Developmental Issues	Maturation and Experience (Nature and Nurture)	The debate about whether development is primarily influenced by maturation or experience is another version of the nature-nurture controversy.
	Continuity and Discontinuity	Developmentalists describe development as continuous (gradual, cumulative change) or as discontinuous (abrupt, sequence of stages).
	Stability and Change	Is development best described as stable or changing? The stability-change issue focuses on the degree to which we become older renditions of our early experience or develop into someone different than we were earlier in development. The dialectical model emphasizes change.
	Evaluating the Developmental Issues	Most developmentalists recognize that extreme positions on the nature-nurture, continuity-discontinuity, and stability-change issues are unwise. Despite this consensus, spirited debate still characterizes these issues.

Theory and the Scientific Method

According to nineteenth century French mathematician Henri Poincaré, "Science is built of facts the way a house is built of bricks, but an accumulation of facts is no more science than a pile of bricks a house." Science *does* depend upon the raw material of facts or data, but as Poincaré indicated, science is more than just facts. As you will soon learn, psychology's theories are more than just facts; they are the mortar that tie the facts together.

A **theory** *is a coherent set of ideas that helps to explain data and to make predictions.* A theory has **hypotheses,** *assumptions that can be tested to determine their accuracy.* For example, a theory about depression among the elderly would explain our observations of depressed elderly individuals and predict why elderly people get depressed. We might predict that elderly individuals get depressed because they fail to focus on their strengths but instead dwell excessively on their shortcomings. This prediction would help to direct our observations by telling us to look for overexaggerations of weaknesses and underestimations of strengths and skills.

The **scientific method** *is an approach that can be used to discover accurate information about behavior and development, which includes the following steps: identify and analyze the problem, collect data, draw conclusions, and revise theories.*

For example, you decide that you want to help elderly individuals overcome their depression. You *identified a problem,* which does not seem to be a difficult task. But as part of this first step, you need to go beyond a general description of the problem by isolating, analyzing, narrowing, and focusing on what you hope to investigate. What specific strategies do you want to use to reduce depression among the elderly? What aspect of depression do you want to study—its biological characteristics, cognitive characteristics, or behavioral characteristics? One group of psychologists believe the cognitive and behavioral aspects of depression can be improved through a course on coping with depression (Lewinsohn & others, 1984; Zeiss & Lewinsohn, 1986). One of the course's components involves teaching elderly individuals to control their negative thoughts. In this first step of the scientific method, the researchers identified and analyzed a problem.

The next step in the scientific method involves *collecting information (data).* Psychologists observe behavior and draw inferences about thoughts and emotions. For example, in the investigation of depression among the elderly, you might observe how effectively individuals who complete the course on coping with depression monitor their moods and engage in an active lifestyle.

Once psychologists collect data, they use *statistical (mathematical) procedures* to understand the meaning of quantitative data. Psychologists then *draw conclusions.* In the investigation of the elderly's depression, statistics help the researchers determine whether their observations are due to chance. After psychologists analyze data, they compare their findings with what others have discovered about the same issue or problem.

The final step in the scientific method is *revising theory.* Psychologists have developed a number of theories about why people become depressed and how they can cope with depression. Data such as those collected in our hypothetical study force us to study existing theories of depression to determine if they are accurate. Over the years, some theories of life-span development have been discarded and others revised. Theories are so important in the study of life-span development that an entire chapter has been set aside for their discussion (see chapter 2).

• *Critical Thinking* •

Theories help us to make predictions about how we develop and how we behave. Do you believe that we can predict an individual's behavior and development? Explain your answer.

Truth is arrived at by the painstaking process of eliminating the untrue.

~ *Arthur Conan Doyle,*
Sherlock Holmes

Collecting Information about Life-Span Development

Systematic observations can be conducted in a variety of ways. For example, we can watch behavior in the laboratory or in a more natural setting such as a home or a street corner. We can question people using interviews and surveys, develop and administer standardized tests, conduct case studies, or carry out physiological research or research with animals. To help you understand how psychologists use these methods, we will apply each method to the study of aggression.

Observation

Sherlock Holmes chided Watson, "You see but you do not observe." We look at things all the time, but casually watching a mother and her infant is not scientific observation. Unless you are a trained observer and practice your skills regularly, you may not know what to look for, you may not remember what you saw, and you may not communicate your observations effectively.

For observations to be effective, we have to know what we are looking for, who we are observing, when and where we will observe, how the observations will be made, and in what form they will be recorded. That is, our observations have to be made in some *systematic* way. Consider aggression. Do we want to study verbal or physical aggression, or both? Do we want to study children or adults, or both? Do we want to evaluate them in a university laboratory, at work, at play, or at all of these locations? A common way to record our observations is to write them down, using shorthand or symbols; however, tape recorders, video cameras, special coding sheets, and one-way mirrors are used increasingly to make observations more efficient and more objective.

When we observe, frequently it is necessary to *control* certain factors that determine behavior but are not the focus of our inquiry. For this reason, much psychological research is conducted in a **laboratory,** *a controlled setting from which many of the complex factors of the "real world" are removed.* For example, Albert Bandura (1965) brought children into a laboratory and had them observe an adult repeatedly hit a plastic, inflated Bobo doll about three feet tall. Bandura wondered to what extent the children would copy the adult's behavior. After the children saw the adult attack the Bobo doll, they also hit the inflated toy aggressively. By conducting his experiment in a laboratory with adults the children did not know as models, Bandura had complete control over when the child witnessed aggression, how much aggression the child saw, and what form the aggression took. Bandura could not have had as much control in his experiment if other factors—such as parents, siblings, friends, television, and a familiar room—had been present.

Laboratory research, however, does have some drawbacks. First, it is almost impossible to conduct without the participants' knowing they are being studied. Second, the laboratory setting may be *unnatural* and therefore cause unnatural behavior from the participants. Subjects usually show less aggressive behavior in a laboratory than in a more familiar natural setting, such as a park or at home. They also show less aggression when they are unaware they are being observed than when they are aware that an observer is studying them. Third, some aspects of life-span development are difficult if not impossible to examine in a laboratory. Certain types of stress are difficult (and unethical) to study in the laboratory, such as recreating the circumstances that stimulate marital conflict.

Although laboratory research is a valuable tool for developmentalists, naturalistic observation provides insight we sometimes cannot achieve in the

The Life-Span Developmental Perspective

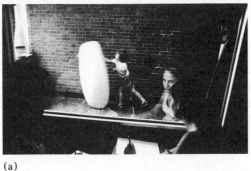

(a)   (b)

Figure 1.8   *Observation of children's aggression in laboratory and in naturalistic conditions. (a) In this situation, the child's aggressive behavior is being observed through a one-way mirror. This allows the observer to exercise control over the observation of aggression. (b) In this situation, the child's aggressive behavior is being observed in a naturalistic situation. This allows the observer to obtain information about the everyday occurrence of behavior.*

laboratory. In **naturalistic observation,** *the scientist observes behavior in real-world settings and makes no effort to manipulate or control the situation.* Developmentalists conduct naturalistic observations at day-care centers, hospitals, schools, parks, homes, malls, dances, and other places where people live and frequent. In contrast to Bandura's observations of aggression in a laboratory, developmentalists observe the aggression of children in nursery schools, of adolescents on street corners, and of marital partners at home (Bronfenbrenner, 1989; Patterson, Capaldi, & Bank, 1991). Figure 1.8 shows a comparison of aggression in the laboratory and in a naturalistic situation.

Interviews and Questionnaires

Sometimes the best and quickest way to get information from people is to ask them for it. Psychologists use interviews and questionnaires to find out about an individual's experiences and attitudes. Most interviews occur face-to-face, although they can take place over the telephone.

Interviews range from highly unstructured to highly structured. Examples of unstructured interview questions are: How aggressive do you see yourself? and How aggressive is your child? Examples of structured interview questions are: In the last week how often did you yell at your spouse? and How often in the last year was your child involved in fights at school? Structure is imposed by the questions themselves, or the interviewer can categorize answers by asking the respondent to choose from several options. For example, in the question about your level of aggressiveness, you might be asked to choose from "highly aggressive," "moderately aggressive," "moderately unaggressive," and "highly unaggressive." In the question about how often you yelled at your spouse in the last week, you might be asked to choose "0," "1–2," "3–5," "6–10," or "more than 10 times."

An experienced interviewer knows how to put respondents at ease and encourage them to open up. A competent interviewer is sensitive to the way the person responds to questions and often probes for more information. A person may respond with fuzzy statements to questions about the nature of marital conflict, for example, "Well, I don't know whether we have a lot of conflict or not." The skilled interviewer pushes for more specific, concrete answers, possibly asking, "If you had it to do over, would you get married?" or "Tell me the worst things you and your husband said to each other in the last

"Would you say you are, 'extremely happy,' 'happy,' 'average' or 'bored stiff'?"

week?" Using these interviewing strategies forces researchers to be involved with, rather than detached from, their subjects, which yields a better understanding of development.

Interviews are not without drawbacks. When interviewed, some individuals simply do not tell the truth. Other individuals respond with socially desirable answers, in which they tell the interviewer what they think is most socially acceptable or desirable rather than what they truly think or feel. When asked about her marital conflict, Jane may not want to disclose that arguments have been painfully tense during the last month. Sam, her husband, may not want to divulge his extramarital affair when asked about his sexual relationships. Skilled interviewing techniques and questions to help eliminate such defenses are critical in obtaining accurate information.

Psychologists also use questionnaires or surveys to gather information. A **questionnaire** *is similar to a highly structured interview except that respondents read the questions and mark their answer on paper rather than respond verbally to the interviewer.* One major advantage of surveys and questionnaires is that they can be given to a large number of people easily. Good surveys have concrete, specific, and unambiguous questions, and allow assessment of the authenticity of the replies.

Case Studies

A **case study** *is an in-depth look at one individual; it is used mainly by clinical psychologists when the unique aspects of an individual's life cannot be duplicated, either for practical or ethical reasons.* A case study provides information about an individual's fears, hopes, fantasies, traumatic experiences, upbringing, family relationships, health, or anything that helps the psychologist understand the person's mind and behavior.

Traumatic experiences have produced some truly fascinating case studies in psychology. Consider the following. A 26-year-old male school teacher met a woman with whom he fell intensely in love. But several months after their love affair began, he became depressed, drank heavily, and talked about suicide. The suicidal ideas progressed to images of murder and suicide. His actions became bizarre. On one occasion he punctured the tires of her car. On another he stood on the roadside where she frequently passed in her car, extending his hand in his pocket so she would think he was holding a gun. His relationship with the woman vascillated between love and hate. Only eight months after meeting her, the teacher shot her while he was a passenger in the car she was driving. Soon after the act, he ran to a telephone booth to call his priest. The girlfriend died (Revitch & Schlesinger, 1978).

This case reveals how depressive moods and bizarre thinking can precede violent acts, such as murder. Other vivid case studies appear throughout this text, among them a modern-day wild child named Genie, who lived in near isolation during her childhood.

While case histories provide dramatic, in-depth portrayals of people's lives, we need to exercise caution when generalizing about this information. The subject of a case study is unique, with a genetic makeup and experiences no one else shares. In addition, case studies involve judgments of unknown reliability, in that no check is usually made to see if other psychologists agree with the observations.

Standardized Tests

Standardized tests *require people to answer a series of written or oral questions. They have two distinct features. First, psychologists usually total an individual's score to yield a single score, or a set of scores, that reflects something about the individual. Second, psychologists compare the individual's* *score to the scores of a large group of similar people to determine how the individual responded* relative *to others.* Scores are often described in percentiles. For example, if you scored in the 92nd percentile on the SAT, this measure tells you how much higher or lower you scored than the large group of individuals who previously took the test. Among the most widely used standardized tests in psychology are the Stanford-Binet intelligence test and the Minnesota Multiphasic Personality Inventory (MMPI).

To continue our look at how psychologists use different methods to evaluate aggression, consider the MMPI, which includes a scale to assess an individual's delinquency and antisocial tendencies. The items on this scale ask you to respond whether or not you are rebellious, impulsive, and have trouble with authority figures. The 26-year-old teacher who murdered his girlfriend would have scored high on a number of the MMPI scales, including one designed to measure how strange and bizarre are our thoughts and ideas.

The main advantage of standardized tests is that they provide information about *individual differences* among people. But information obtained from standardized tests does not always predict behavior in nontest situations. Standardized tests are based on the belief that an individual's behavior is consistent and stable. Although personality and intelligence, two of the primary targets of standardized tests, have some stability, they *can* vary, depending on the situation in which a person is evaluated. A person may perform poorly on a standardized test of intelligence but when observed in a less anxious context, such as at home, may display a much higher level of intelligence. This criticism is especially relevant for members of minority groups, some of whom have been inappropriately classified as mentally retarded on the basis of their scores on standardized intelligence tests. For example, one Black child from a low-income family scored in the mentally retarded range on a standardized intelligence test, yet he was bright enough to plan an elaborate escape from the institution where he lived. And, cross-cultural psychologists also caution that while many psychological tests may work reasonably well in Western cultures, they may not always be appropriate in cultures where they were not developed (Lonner, 1990).

Physiological Research and Research with Animals
Two additional methods that psychologists use to gather data about life-span development are physiological research and research with animals. Increased research into the biological basis of life-span development has produced remarkable insights. For example, electrical stimulation of certain areas of the brain has turned docile, mild-mannered individuals into hostile, vicious attackers; and higher concentrations of some hormones have been associated with delinquent behavior in male adolescents (King, 1961; Nottelmann & others, 1990; Susman & Dorn, 1991).

Much physiological research cannot be carried out with humans, so psychologists use animals. With animals, we can control genetic background, diet, experiences during infancy, and countless other factors. In human studies, these factors have to be treated as random variation, or "noise," and they may interfere with accurate results. With animals, we can investigate the effects of treatments (brain implants, for example) that would be unethical to attempt with humans. Moreover, it is possible to track the entire life cycle of some animals over a relatively short period of time. Laboratory mice, for example, have a life span of approximately one year.

With regard to aggression, castration has turned ferocious bulls into docile oxen by acting on the male hormone system. After a number of breedings of aggressive mice, researchers have created mice who are absolutely ferocious, attacking virtually anything in sight (Lagerspetz, 1979). Do these findings with animals apply to humans? Hormones and genes do influence human aggression, but this influence is less than in animals. Because humans differ from animals in many ways, one disadvantage of research with animals is that the results may not apply to humans.

Strategies for Setting up Research Studies

How can we determine if responding nurturantly to an infant's cries increases attachment to the caregiver? How can we determine if listening to rock music lowers an adolescent's grades? How can we determine if an active life-style in old age increases longevity? When designing research to answer such questions, a developmentalist must decide whether to use a correlational strategy or an experimental strategy.

Correlational Strategy

In the **correlational strategy,** *the goal is to describe the strength of the relation between two or more events or characteristics. This is a useful strategy because the more strongly events are correlated (related, or associated), the more we can predict one from the other.* For example, consider one of our major national health problems in adulthood, high blood pressure. If we find that high blood pressure is strongly associated with the inability to manage stress, then we can use the inability to manage stress to predict high blood pressure.

The next step, taken all too often, is to conclude from such evidence that one event *causes* the other. Following this line of reasoning, we would erroneously conclude that the inability to manage stress causes high blood pressure. Why is this reasoning *wrong?* Why doesn't a strong correlation between two events mean that one event causes the other? A strong correlation could mean that the inability to manage stress causes high blood pressure, but it could *also* mean that high blood pressure causes an inability to manage stress. A third possibility also exists: Although strongly correlated, the inability to manage stress and high blood pressure do not cause each other at all. How could this be? Possibly a third factor underlies their association, such as a genetic tendency, poor nutrition, or lack of exercise (see figure 1.9). Throughout this text, you will read about studies based on a correlational strategy. Keep in mind that it is easy to think that because two events or characteristics are correlated, one causes the other; as we have just seen, this is not always the case.

Experimental Strategy

While the correlational strategy only allows us to say that two events are related, the **experimental strategy** *allows us to precisely determine behavior's causes. The psychologist accomplishes this task by performing an experiment, a carefully regulated setting in which one or more of the factors believed to influence the behavior being studied is manipulated and all others are held constant.* If the behavior under study changes when a factor is manipulated, we say that the manipulated factor causes the behavior to change. Experiments are used to establish cause and effect between events, something correlational studies cannot do. *Cause* is the event being manipulated and *effect* is the behavior that changes because of the manipulation. Remember that in testing correlation, nothing is manipulated; in an experiment, the researcher actively changes an event to see the effect on behavior.

The following example illustrates the nature of an experiment. The problem to be studied is whether aerobic exercise during pregnancy affects

Observed correlation

Possible explanations for this correlation

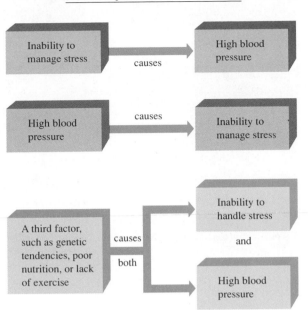

As the inability to manage stress increases, blood pressure increases

Inability to manage stress → causes → High blood pressure

High blood pressure → causes → Inability to manage stress

A third factor, such as genetic tendencies, poor nutrition, or lack of exercise → causes both → Inability to handle stress and High blood pressure

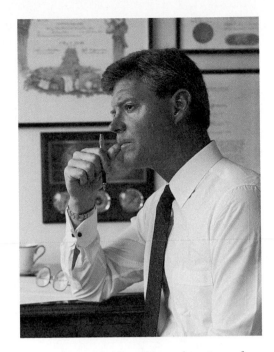

Figure 1.9   Possible explanations of correlational data. An observed correlation between two events cannot be used to conclude that one event causes a second event. Other possibilities are that the second event caused the first event, or that a third, unknown event caused the correlation between the first two events.

the development of the infant. We need to have one group of pregnant women engage in aerobic exercise and the other not engage in aerobic exercise. We randomly assign our subjects to these two groups. **Random assignment** *occurs when researchers assign subjects by chance to experimental and control conditions, thus reducing the likelihood that the results of the experiment will be due to some preexisting differences in the two groups.* For example, random assignment greatly reduces the probability of the two groups differing on such factors as age, social class, prior aerobic exercise, intelligence, health problems, alertness, and so on.

The **independent variable** *is the manipulated, influential, experimental factor in the experiment. The label* independent *is used because this variable can be changed independently of other factors.* In the aerobic exercise experiment, the amount of aerobic exercise was the independent variable. The experimenter manipulated the amount of the aerobic exercise by having the pregnant women engage in aerobic exercise four times a week under the direction of a trained instructor.

The **dependent variable** *is the factor that is measured in an experiment; it may change because of the manipulation of the independent variable. The label* dependent *is used because this variable depends on what happens to the subjects in the experiment.* In the aerobic exercise experiment, the dependent variable was represented by two measures—breathing and sleeping patterns of the infants. The subjects' responses on these measures depended on the influence of the independent variable (whether or not pregnant women engaged in aerobic exercise). An illustration of the nature of the experimental strategy, applied to the aerobic exercise study, is presented in figure 1.10. In our experiment, we tested the two sets of offspring during the first week of life. We found that the experimental group infants had more regular breathing and sleeping patterns than their control group counterparts. We conclude that aerobic exercise by pregnant women promotes more regular breathing and sleeping patterns in newborn infants.

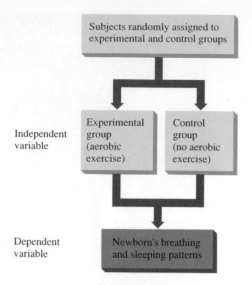

Independent variable

Experimental group (aerobic exercise)

Control group (no aerobic exercise)

Dependent variable

Newborn's breathing and sleeping patterns

Figure 1.10 Principles of the experimental strategy applied to a study of the effects of aerobic exercise by pregnant women on the breathing and sleeping patterns of their newborn infants.

Remember that the correlational study of the relation between stress and blood pressure gave us little indication of whether stress influences blood pressure, or vice versa. A third factor may have caused the correlation. A research study that determined if stress management reduces high blood pressure will help you to understand further the experimental strategy (Irvine & others, 1986). Thirty-two males and females with high blood pressure were randomly assigned to either a group who were trained in relaxation and stress management (experimental group) or a group who received no training (control group). The independent variable consisted of ten weekly one-hour sessions that included educational information about the nature of stress and how to manage it, as well as extensive training in learning to relax and control stress in everyday life. The blood pressure of both groups was assessed before the training program and three months after it was completed. Nurses who were unaware of which group the subjects had been in measured blood pressure at the three-month follow-up. The results indicated that the relaxation and stress management program (the independent variable) was effective in reducing high blood pressure.

It might seem as if we should always choose an experimental strategy over a correlational strategy, because the experimental strategy gives us a better sense of the influence of one variable on another. Are there instances when a correlational strategy might be preferred? Three such instances are (1) when the focus of the investigation is so new that we have little knowledge of which variables to manipulate (as when AIDS first appeared), (2) when it is physically impossible to manipulate the variables (such as factors involved in suicide), and (3) when it is unethical to manipulate the variables (for example, in determining the association between illness and exposure to dangerous chemicals).

Time Span of Inquiry

A special concern of developmentalists is the time span of a research investigation. Studies that focus on the relation of age to some other variable are common in life-span development. We have several options: We can study different individuals of different ages and compare them; we can study the same individuals as they age over time; or we can use some combination of these two approaches. We consider each of these in turn.

The Life-Span Developmental Perspective

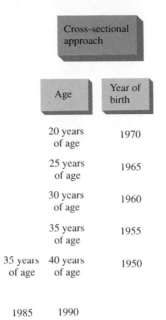

Figure 1.11 Comparison of cross-sectional and longitudinal approaches. In the cross-sectional approach different individuals born at different points in time are assessed all at one time (in our example, in 1990). In the longitudinal approach, the same individuals are assessed at different points in time over a period of years (in our example, 1970, 1975, 1980, 1985, and 1990).

Cross-Sectional Approach

The **cross-sectional approach** *is a research strategy in which individuals of different ages are compared at one time.* A typical cross-sectional study might include a group of 5-year-olds, 8-year-olds, and 11-year-olds; another might include a group of 15-year-olds, 25-year-olds, and 45-year-olds. The different groups can be compared with respect to a variety of dependent variables: IQ, memory, peer relations, attachment to parents, hormonal changes, and so on. All of this can be accomplished in a short time. In some studies data are collected in a single day. Even large-scale cross-sectional studies with hundreds of subjects do not usually take longer than several months to complete the data collection.

The main advantage of the cross-sectional study is that the researcher does not have to wait for the individuals to grow up or become older. Despite its time efficiency, the cross-sectional approach has its drawbacks. It gives no information about how individuals change or about the stability of their characteristics. The increases and decreases of development—the hills and valleys of growth and development—can become obscured in the cross-sectional approach. For example, in a cross-sectional approach to perceptions of life satisfaction, average increases and decreases might be revealed. But the study would not show how the life satisfaction of individual adults waxed and waned over the years. It also would not tell us whether adults who had positive or negative perceptions of life satisfaction as young adults maintained their relative degree of life satisfaction as middle-aged or older adults. While cross-sectional studies cannot answer such questions, longitudinal studies can.

The **longitudinal approach** *is a research strategy in which the same individuals are studied over a period of time, usually several years or more.* For example, if a study of life satisfaction were conducted longitudinally, the same adults might be assessed periodically over a 70-year time span—at the ages of 20, 35, 45, 65, and 90, for example. The cross-sectional and longitudinal research designs are compared in figure 1.11.

As an example of a longitudinal study, Jacqueline Lerner and her colleagues (1988) studied 75 White, middle-class children from early in their infancy through the adolescent years. They wanted to know if negative emotional and behavioral characteristics (such as aggression, anxiety, undercompliance, and depressive mood) in the infancy and childhood years were related

BY BILL HOEST

"That's my dad when he was 10 . . . He was in some sort of cult."

to adjustment in the adolescent years. They found that early negative emotional states in the years 1 through 6 were strongly related to adolescent adjustment problems with parents and peers. This pattern was specific to the type of emotional difficulty—aggression predicting poor family adjustment, and anxiety predicting peer adjustment problems.

Although longitudinal studies provide a wealth of information about such important issues as stability and change in development and the importance of early experience for later development, they are not without their problems. They are expensive and time-consuming. The longer the study lasts, the more subjects drop out—they move, get sick, lose interest, and so forth. Subjects can bias the outcome of a study because those who remain may be dissimilar to those who drop out. Those individuals who remain in longitudinal study over a number of years may be more compulsive and conformity oriented, for example. Or they might have more stable lives.

Sequential Approach

Sometimes developmentalists also combine the cross-sectional and longitudinal approaches to learn about life-span development (Schaie, 1973, 1989, 1991). The **sequential approach** *is the term used to describe the combined cross-sectional, longitudinal design. In most instances, this approach starts with a cross-sectional study that includes individuals of different ages. A number of months or years after the initial assessment, the same individuals are tested again—this is the longitudinal aspect of the design. At this later time, a new group of subjects is assessed at each age level.* The new groups at each level are added at the later time to control for changes that might have taken place in the original group of subjects—some may have dropped out of the study, or retesting might have improved their performance, for example. The sequential approach is complex, expensive, and time-consuming, but it does provide information that is impossible to obtain from cross-sectional or longitudinal approaches alone. The sequential approach has been especially helpful in examining cohort effects in life-span development, which we discuss next.

Cohort Effects

Cohort effects *are due to a subject's time of birth or generation but not to actual age.* For example, cohorts can differ in years of education, childrearing practices, health, attitudes toward sex, religious values, and economic status (see figure 1.12). Cohort effects are important because they can powerfully

• *Critical Thinking* •

You are faced with the task of designing an investigation of intergenerational relations. What problem do you want to study? What measure(s) would you use? What strategy would you follow— experimental or correlational? What would be the time span of your inquiry?

The Life-Span Developmental Perspective

(a)

Figure 1.12 Cohort effects. Cohort effects are due to a subject's time of birth or generation but not actually to age. Think for a moment about how growing up in (a) the Roaring Twenties, (b) the Great Depression, (c) the 1940s, (d) the 1950s, (e) the late 1960s, and (f) the early 1990s might influence the nature of an individual's development through the life span.

(b)

(c)

(d)

(e)

(f)

33

affect the dependent measures in a study ostensibly concerned with age. Researchers have shown that cohort effects are especially important to investigate in the assessment of adult intelligence (Willis, 1990; Willis & Schaie, 1986). Individuals born at different points in time—such as 1920, 1940, and 1960—have had varying opportunities for education, while individuals born in earlier years have had less access.

Now that we have considered the main ways that developmentalists conduct research, it is also important to consider whether research on life-span development is value free, how life-span development research can become less sexist, and what ethical issues must be considered in developmental research.

Reducing Sexist Research

Traditional science is presented as being value free and thus a more valid way of studying mental processes and behavior. However, there is a growing consensus that science in general, and psychology in particular, are not value free (Doyle & Paludi, 1991). A special concern is that the vast majority of psychological research has been male oriented and male dominated. Some researchers believe male-dominated sciences such as psychology need to be challenged to examine the world in a new way, one that incorporates girls' and women's perspectives and respects their ethnicity, sexual orientation, age, and socioeconomic status (Denmark & others, 1988; McHugh, Koeske, & Frieze, 1986; Quina, 1986). For example, Florence Denmark and her colleagues (1988) provided the following three recommendations as guidelines for nonsexist research:

1. Research methods:
   - Problem: The selection of research participants is based on stereotypic assumptions and does not allow for generalizations to other groups.
   - Example: On the basis of stereotypes about who should be responsible for contraception, only females are studied.
   - Correction: Both sexes should be studied before conclusions are drawn about the factors that determine contraceptive use.
2. Data analysis:
   - Problem: Gender differences are inaccurately magnified.
   - Example: While only 24 percent of the females were found to . . . fully 28 percent of the males were. . . .
   - Correction: The results should include extensive descriptions of the data so that inappropriate presentation of differences are not exaggerated.
3. Conclusions:
   - Problem: The title or abstract (a summary) of an article makes no reference to the limitations of the study participants and implies a broader scope of the study than is warranted.
   - Example: A study purporting to be about "perceptions of the disabled" uses only blind, White subjects. . . .
   - Correction: Use more precise titles and clearly describe the sample and its selection criteria in the abstract or summary.

Ethics in Research on Life-Span Development

When Anne and Pete, two 19-year-old college students, agreed to participate in an investigation of dating couples, they did not consider that the questionnaire they filled out would get them to think about issues that might lead to conflict in their relationship and possibly end it. One year after this investigation, nine of ten participants said that they had discussed their answers with their dating partner (Rubin & Mitchell, 1976). In most instances, the discussions helped to strengthen the relationships, but in some instances, the participants used the questionnaire as a springboard to discuss problems or concerns previously hidden. One participant said, "The study definitely played a role in ending my relationship with Larry." In this circumstance, the couple had different views about how long they expected to be together. She anticipated that the relationship would end much sooner than Larry thought. Discussion of their answers to the questions brought the long-term prospects of the relationship out in the open, and eventually Larry found someone who was more interested in marrying him.

At first glance, you would not think that a questionnaire on dating relationships would have any substantial impact on the participants' behavior. But psychologists increasingly recognize that considerable caution must be taken to ensure the well-being of subjects in a study of life-span development. Today colleges and universities have review boards that evaluate the ethical nature of research conducted at their institutions. Proposed research plans must pass the scrutiny of an ethics research committee before the research can be initiated. In addition, the American Psychological Association (APA) has developed guidelines for its members' ethics.

The code of ethics adopted by APA instructs researchers to protect their subjects from mental and physical harm. The best interests of the subjects need to be kept foremost in the researcher's mind. All subjects must give their informed consent to participate in the research study, which requires that subjects know what their participation will involve and any risks that might develop. For example, research subjects who date one another should be told beforehand that a questionnaire might stimulate thought about issues they might not anticipate. The subjects should also be informed that in some instances a discussion of the issues raised can improve their dating relationships, while in other cases, it can worsen the relationship and even terminate it. After informed consent is given, the subject reserves the right to withdraw from the study at any time while it is being conducted.

Special ethical concerns govern the conduct of research with children. First, if children are to be studied, informed consent from parents or legal guardians must be obtained. Parents have the right to a complete and accurate description of what will be done with their children and may refuse to let them participate. Second, children have rights, too. The psychologist is obliged to explain precisely what the child will experience. The child may refuse to participate, even after parental permission has been given. If so, the researcher must not test the child. Also, if a child becomes upset during the research study, it is the psychologist's obligation to calm the child. Failing to do so, the activity must be discontinued. Third, the psychologist must always weigh the potential for harming children against the prospects of contributing some clear benefits to them. If there is the chance of harm—as when drugs are used, social deception takes place, or the child is treated aversively (that is, punished

Concept Table 1.2: The Science Base of Life-Span Development

Concept	Processes/Related Ideas	Characteristics/Description
Theory and the Scientific Method	Theory	General beliefs that help us explain what we observe and make predictions. A good theory has hypotheses, which are assumptions that can be tested.
	Scientific Method	A series of procedures (identifying and analyzing a problem, collecting data, drawing conclusions, and revising theory) to obtain accurate information.
Ways of Collecting Information—Measures	Observation	A key ingredient in life-span development research that includes laboratory and naturalistic observation.
	Interviews and Questionnaires	Used to assess perceptions and attitudes. Social desirability and lying are problems with their use.
	Case Studies	Provides an in-depth look at an individual. Caution in generalizing is warranted.
	Standardized Tests	Designed to assess an individual's characteristics relative to those of a large group of similar individuals.
	Physiological Research and Research with Animals	Focus is on the biological dimensions of the organism. While greater control over conditions can be achieved with animals, generalization to humans may be problematic.
Strategies for Setting Up Research Studies	Correlational Strategy	Describes how strongly two or more events or characteristics are related. It does not allow causal statements.
	Experimental Strategy	Involves manipulation of influential factors, the independent variables, and measurement of their effect on the dependent variables. Subjects are randomly assigned to experimental and control groups in many studies. The experimental strategy can reveal the causes of behavior and how one event influences another.
Time Span of Inquiry	Cross-Sectional Approach	Individuals of different ages are compared at one time.
	Longitudinal Approach	The same individuals are studied over a period of time, usually several years or more.
	Sequential Approach	A combined cross-sectional, longitudinal approach that highlights the importance of cohort effects in life-span development.
Cohort Effects	Their Nature	Effects due to a subject's time of birth or generation but not actually to age. The study of cohort effects underscores the importance of considering the historical dimensions of life-span development.
Reducing Sexist Research	Its Nature	A special concern is that the vast majority of research in psychology has been male oriented and male dominated. Some researchers believe that developmentalists need to be challenged to examine development in a new way, one that incorporates girls' and women's perspectives. Recommendations have been made for conducting nonsexist research.
Ethics in Research on Life-Span Development	Their Nature	Researchers must ensure the well-being of subjects in life-span development research. The risk of mental and physical harm must be reduced, and informed consent should be obtained. Special ethical considerations are involved when children are research subjects.

or reprimanded)—the psychologist must convince a group of peers that the benefits of the experience clearly outweigh any chance of harm. Fourth, since children are in a vulnerable position and lack power and control when facing an adult, the psychologist should always strive to make the professional encounter a positive and supportive experience.

At this point we have discussed a number of ideas about the science base of life-span development. A summary of these ideas is presented in concept table 1.2. In this chapter we discovered that, as a science, the life-span perspective stresses the importance of theories and methods in understanding development. In the next chapter we turn our attention exclusively to theories of life-span development.

Summary

I. Life-Span Development—Today and Yesterday

Today, the well-being of children and adults is an important concern in our culture. Four such concerns are genetic research, child abuse, ethnic diversity, and aging. The history of interest in children is long and rich. In the Renaissance, philosophical views were prominent, including original sin, *tabula rasa,* and innate goodness. The scientific study of adolescence was promoted by G. Stanley Hall in the early 1900s. His storm and stress view contrasts with the belief that sociohistorical conditions contributed to the concept of adolescence. The traditional approach emphasizes extensive change in childhood but stability in adulthood; the life-span perspective emphasizes that change is possible throughout the life span.

II. The Life-Span Perspective

The life-span perspective involves seven basic contentions: Development is life-long, multidimensional, multidirectional, plastic, historically embedded, multidisciplinary, and contextual. In the life-span perspective's contextual view, development can be understood as the outcome of the interaction of three systems: normative age-graded influences, normative history-graded influences, and nonnormative life events.

III. The Nature of Development

Development is the pattern of movement or change that occurs throughout the life span. Development is influenced by an interplay of biological, cognitive, and social processes. The life cycle is commonly divided into the following periods of development: prenatal, infancy, early childhood, middle and late childhood, adolescence, early adulthood, middle adulthood, and late adulthood. Some experts on life-span development, such as Neugarten, however, believe too much emphasis is placed on age. She believes we are moving toward a society in which age is not a good predictor of development in adulthood.

IV. Developmental Issues

Three important developmental issues are to what extent is development (1) influenced by maturation and experience (or nature and nurture), (2) characterized by continuity and discontinuity, and (3) distinguished by stability and change? The debate of whether development is primarily due to maturation or to environment is another version of the nature-nurture controversy. Some developmentalists describe development as continuous (gradual, cumulative change), others as discontinuous (abrupt, sequence of stages). The stability-change issue focuses on the degree to which we become older renditions of our early experience or develop into someone different than we were earlier in development. The dialectical model emphasizes change. Most developmentalists recognize that extreme positions on these issues are unwise. Despite this consensus, spirited debate characterizes the issues.

V. Theory and the Scientific Method

Theories are general beliefs that help us to explain what we observe and make predictions. A good theory has hypotheses, which are assumptions that can be tested. A series of procedures (identifying and analyzing a problem, collecting data, drawing conclusions, and revising theory) called the scientific method are followed to obtain accurate information about life-span development.

VI. Ways of Collecting Information—Measures

Observation is a key ingredient in life-span development research that includes laboratory and naturalistic observation. Interviews and questionnaires are used to assess perceptions and attitudes. Social desirability and lying are problems with their use. Case studies provide an in-depth look at an individual. Caution in generalizing is warranted. Standardized tests are designed to assess an individual's characteristics relative to those of a large group of similar individuals. Physiological research and research with animals focus on the biological dimensions of the organism. While greater control over conditions can be achieved with animals, generalization to humans may be problematic.

VII. Strategies for Setting Up Research Studies

The correlational strategy describes how strongly two or more events or characteristics are related. It does not allow causal statements. The experimental strategy involves the manipulation of influential factors—the independent variables—and the measurement of their effect on the dependent variables. Subjects are randomly assigned to experimental and control groups in many studies. The experimental strategy can reveal the causes of behavior and tell us how one event influenced another.

VIII. **Time Span of Inquiry**

In the cross-sectional approach, individuals of different ages are compared all at one time. In the longitudinal approach, the same individuals are studied over a period of time, usually several years or more. In the sequential approach, a combination of the cross-sectional and longitudinal approaches are used. The sequential approach highlights cohort effects.

IX. **Cohort Effects**

Cohort effects are those due to a subject's time of birth or generation but not actually to age. The study of cohort effects underscores the importance of considering the historical dimensions of development.

X. **Reducing Sexist Bias**

A special concern is that the vast majority of psychological research has been male oriented and male dominated. Some researchers believe that developmentalists need to be challenged to examine development in a new way, one that incorporates girls' and women's perspectives. Recommendations have been made for conducting nonsexist research.

XI. **Ethics in Research on Life-Span Development**

Researchers must ensure the well-being of subjects in life-span development research. The risk of mental and physical harm must be reduced, and informed consent should be sought. Special ethical considerations are involved when research with children is conducted.

Key Terms

Suggested Readings

Baltes, P. B. (1987). Theoretical propositions of life-span developmental psychology: On the dynamics between growth and decline. *Developmental Psychology. 23,* 611–626.
In this article, leading life-span development conceptualizer Paul Baltes describes the basic dimensions of the life-span perspective. Special attention is given to how these dimensions influence intelligence.

Borstelmann, L. J. (1983). Children before psychology: Ideas about children from antiquity to the late 1800s. In P. H. Mussen (Ed.), *Handbook of Child Psychology* (4th ed., Vol. 1.) New York: Wiley.
A comprehensive treatment of the historical conception of children from ancient times until the eighteenth century.

Brim, O. G., & Kagan, J. (Eds.) (1980). *Constancy and change in human development.* Cambridge, MA: Harvard University Press.
A number of developmental experts contributed articles to this book, which focuses on how stable or changeable our lives are as we go through the life span.

Child Development, Developmental Psychology, Journal of Gerontology.
These are three of the leading journals in the field of life-span development. Go to your library and leaf through the issues of the last several years to get a feel for the research interests of developmentalists.

Hall, G. S. (1904). *Adolescence* (Vol. 1). Englewood Cliffs, NJ: Prentice-Hall.
This is an intriguing look into the mind of the father of the scientific study of adolescent development. Be sure to read about his views of sexuality in the early twentieth century.

McClusky, K. A., & Reese, H. W. (Eds.) (1985). *Life-span developmental psychology: Historical and cohort effects.* New York: Academic Press.
This book gives insight into how historical events and year of birth influence life-span development.

CHAPTER 2

Theories

S igmund Freud and Carl Rogers, whose theories we discuss in this chapter, are giants in the field of psychological theorizing. The lives of theorists and their experiences have a major impact on the content of their theories. As with each of us, the search for understanding human behavior begins by examining our own.

Sigmund Freud's theory emphasizes the sexual basis of development. What were Freud's sexual interests like as he was growing up? History shows that Freud repressed most of his sexual desires while busily pursuing intellectual matters. In all of the writings about Freud's life, only one incident during his youth reveals something about his sexual desires:

> The story relates to his first love experience at the age of 16 when—for the first time in his life—he revisited his birthplace. He stayed there with the Fluss family . . . with their daughter, Gisela, a year or two younger than himself, a companion of his early childhood, he fell in love with her on the spot. He was too shy to communicate his feelings or even to address a single word to her, and she went away to her school after a few days. The disconsolate youth had to content himself with the fantasy of how pleasant life would have been had his parents not left that happy spot where he could have grown up a stout country lad, like the girl's brothers, and married the maiden. So it was all his father's fault (Jones, 1953, pp. 25–26).

Carl Rogers' theory stresses the importance of developing positive conceptions of ourselves and sensitivity to others' feelings. What was Rogers' youth like? He had virtually no social life outside his family, although he does not remember that this bothered him (Rogers, 1967). At the age of 12, his family moved to a farm; apparently his mother wanted to shield her children from the evils of city life. Even though he was saddled with extensive chores at home, such as milking the cows every morning at 5:00 A.M., Rogers managed to make straight A's in school. He had little time for friendship and dating, and never had what could be called a real date in high school. Once Carl had to take a girl to a class dinner as a matter of custom. He vividly remembers the anxiety of having to ask her to the dinner. She agreed to go, but Rogers said he does not know what he would have done if she had turned him down.

These experiences of Freud and Rogers are examples of how theorists' own experiences and behavior influence their thinking. Perhaps Freud's own sexual repression in adolescence contributed to his theory that behavior has a sexual basis. And perhaps Rogers' anxieties about social contact as a youth fostered his theoretical emphasis on warmth in social relationships.

Freud's and Rogers' theories are but two of many theories you will read about in this chapter. The diversity of theories make understanding life-span development a challenging undertaking. Just when you think one theory has the correct explanation of life-span development, another theory crops up and makes you rethink your earlier conclusion. To keep from getting frustrated, remember that life-span development is a complex, multifaceted topic and no single theory has been able to account for all aspects of it. Each theory has contributed an important piece to the life-span development puzzle. While the theories sometimes disagree about certain aspects of life-span development, much of their information is complementary rather than contradictory. Together they let us see the total landscape of life-span development in all its richness.

There is nothing quite so practical as a good theory.

Kurt Lewin,
Psychologist, 1890–1947

• Critical Thinking •

What personal experiences in your own life might influence the kind of developmental theory you would construct?

Sigmund Freud, the founder of psychoanalytic theory.

Psychoanalytic Theories

For psychoanalytic theorists, life-span development is primarily unconscious (that is, beyond awareness) and is heavily colored by emotion. Psychoanalytic theorists believe that behavior is merely a surface characteristic and that to truly understand someone's development, we have to analyze the symbolic meanings of behavior and the deep inner workings of the mind. Psychoanalytic theorists also stress that early experiences with parents extensively shape our development. These characteristics are highlighted in the main psychoanalytic theory, that of Sigmund Freud.

Freud's Theory

Loved and hated, respected and despised, for some the master, for others misdirected, Sigmund Freud—whether right or wrong in his views—has been one of the most influential thinkers of the twentieth century. Freud was a medical doctor who specialized in neurology. He developed his ideas about psychoanalytic theory from his work with patients with mental problems. He was born in 1856 in Austria and died in London at the age of 83. Most of his years were spent in Vienna, though he left the city near the end of his career because of the Nazis' anti-Semitism.

The Structure of Personality

Freud (1917) believed that personality had three structures: the id, the ego, and the superego. One way to understand the three structures is to consider them as three rulers of a country (Singer, 1984). The id is king or queen, the ego is prime minister, and the superego is high priest. The id is an absolute monarch, owed complete obedience; it is spoiled, willful, and self-centered. The id wants what it wants right now, not later. The ego as prime minister has the job of getting things done right; it is tuned into reality and is responsive to society's demands. The superego as high priest is concerned with right and wrong; the id may be greedy and needs to be told that nobler purposes should be pursued.

The **id** *is the Freudian structure of personality that consists of instincts, which are the individual's reservoir of psychic energy.* In Freud's view, the id is unconscious; it has no contact with reality. The id works according to the pleasure principle. The **pleasure principle** *is the Freudian concept that the id always seeks pleasure and avoids pain.*

It would be a dangerous and scary world if our personalities were all id. As young children develop, they learn they cannot slug several children in the face. Sometimes they are not even allowed to slug one. They also learn they have to use the toilet instead of their diaper. As children experience the demands and constraints of reality, a new structure of personality is formed, the **ego**—*the Freudian structure of personality that deals with the demands of reality. The ego is called the executive branch of personality because it makes rational decisions.* The ego abides by the **reality principle**—*the Freudian concept by which the ego tries to bring the individual pleasure within the boundaries of reality.* Few of us are cold-blooded killers or wild wheeler-dealers; we take into account obstacles to our satisfaction that exist in our world. We recognize that our sexual and aggressive impulses cannot go unrestrained. The ego helps us test reality—to see how far we can go without getting into trouble and hurting ourselves.

They cannot scare me with their empty spaces
Between stars—on stars where no human race is.
I have it in me so much nearer home
To scare myself with my own desert places.

~ *Robert Frost*

If it were possible to talk to the unborn, one could never explain to them how it feels to be alive, for life is washed in the speechless real.

~ *Jacques Barzun,*
The House of Intellect, *1959*

The Life-Span Developmental Perspective

While the id is completely unconscious, the ego is partly conscious. It houses our higher mental functions—reasoning, problem solving, and decision making, for example. For this reason, the ego is referred to as the executive branch of the personality; like an executive in a company, it makes the rational decisions that help the company succeed.

The id and ego have no morality. They do not consider whether something is right or wrong. The **superego** *is the Freudian structure of personality that is the moral branch of personality. The superego takes into account whether something is right or wrong.* Think of the superego as what we often refer to as our "conscience." Like the id, the superego does not consider reality; it doesn't deal with what is realistic, only with whether the id's sexual and aggressive impulses can be satisfied in moral terms. You are probably beginning to sense that both the id and the superego make life rough for the ego. Your ego might say, "I'll only have sex occasionally and I'll be sure to take the proper precautions because I don't want the intrusion of a child in the development of my career." But your id is saying, "I want to be satisfied; sex is pleasurable." And your superego is at work too, "I feel guilty about having sex."

Remember that Freud considered personality to be like an iceberg; most of personality exists below our level of awareness, just as the massive part of the iceberg is beneath the surface of the water. Figure 2.1 illustrates this analogy and how extensive the unconscious part of our mind is, in Freud's view.

Defense Mechanisms

How does the ego resolve the conflict between its demands for reality, the wishes of the id, and the constraints of the superego? Through **defense mechanisms,** *the psychoanalytic term for unconscious methods, the ego distorts reality, thereby protecting it from anxiety.* In Freud's view, the conflicting demands of the personality structures produce anxiety. For example, when the ego blocks the pleasurable pursuits of the id, inner anxiety is felt. This diffuse, distressed state develops when the ego senses that the id is going to cause some harm to the individual. The anxiety alerts the ego to resolve the conflict by means of defense mechanisms.

Repression *is the most powerful and pervasive defense mechanism, according to Freud; it works to push unacceptable id impulses out of awareness and back into the unconscious mind.* Repression is the foundation from which all other defense mechanisms work; the goal of every defense mechanism is to repress or push threatening impulses out of awareness. Freud said that our early childhood experiences, many of which he believed were sexually laden, are too threatening and stressful for us to deal with consciously. We reduce the anxiety of this conflict through the defense mechanism of repression.

Among the other defense mechanisms we use to protect the ego and reduce anxiety are rationalization, displacement, sublimation, projection, reaction formation, and regression. **Rationalization** *is the psychoanalytic defense mechanism that occurs when the real motive for an individual's behavior is not accepted by the ego and is replaced by a cover motive.* For example, you are studying hard for an exam tomorrow. You are really getting into the material when a friend calls and says he is having a party in an hour. He tells you that a certain person you find attractive will be there. You know that if you don't stay in your room and study you will do poorly on tomorrow's exam.

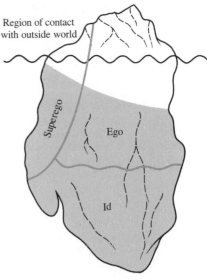

Figure 2.1 *Conscious and unconscious processes: the iceberg analogy. This rather odd-looking diagram illustrates Freud's belief that most of the important personality processes occur below the level of conscious awareness. In examining people's conscious thoughts and their behaviors, we can see some reflections of the ego and the superego. But, whereas the ego and superego are partly conscious and partly unconscious, the primitive id is the unconscious, totally submerged part of the "iceberg."*

But you tell yourself, "I did well on the first test in this class and I have been studying hard all semester; it's time for some fun." So you go to the party. The real motive is going to the party, having fun, and seeing the attractive person. But then you might think: if that is the reason, then I should stay home and study. Your ego now steps in and fixes the motive to look better. Your ego says that you have worked hard all semester and you need to unwind, and that you will probably do better on the exam if you relax a little—a rationale that is more acceptable than just going to have fun and meet the desirable other person.

Displacement *is the psychoanalytic defense mechanism that occurs when the individual shifts unacceptable feelings from one object to another, more acceptable object.* For example, a woman is harrassed by her boss. She gets angry but she knows she can't take the anger out on the boss because she might get fired. When she gets home that evening, she yells at her husband, thus transferring her feelings toward her boss to her husband.

Sublimation *is the psychoanalytic defense mechanism that occurs when a socially useful course of action replaces a distasteful one.* Sublimation is actually a type of displacement. For example, an individual with strong sexual urges may turn them into socially approved behavior by becoming an artist who paints nudes.

Projection *is the psychoanalytic defense mechanism that occurs when we attribute our own shortcomings, problems, and faults to others.* For example, a man who has a strong desire to have an extramarital affair keeps accusing his wife of flirting with other men. The manipulative businesswoman who takes advantage of everyone to push herself up the corporate ladder tells her associate, "Everybody around here is so manipulative; they never consider my feelings." When we can't face our own unwanted feelings, we project them onto others and see others as having the trait.

Reaction formation *is the psychoanalytic defense mechanism that occurs when we express an unacceptable impulse by transforming it into its opposite.* For example, an individual who is attracted to the brutality of war becomes a peace activist. Or a person who fears his sexual urges becomes a religious zealot.

Regression *is the psychoanalytic defense mechanism that occurs when we behave in a way that characterizes a previous developmental level.* When anxiety becomes too great for us, we revert to an early behavior that gave us pleasure. For example, a woman may run home to her mother every time she and her husband have a big argument.

Two final points about defense mechanisms need to be underscored. First, they are unconscious; we are not aware we are calling on them to protect our ego and reduce anxiety. Second, when used in moderation or on a temporary basis, defense mechanisms are not necessarily unhealthy. For example, such defense mechanisms as denial—protecting oneself from unpleasant aspects of reality by refusing to acknowledge them—can help an individual cope with impending death. For the most part, though, we should not let defense mechanisms dominate our behavior and prevent us from facing the demands of reality.

The Development of Personality
As Freud listened to, probed, and analyzed his patients, he became convinced that their problems were the result of experiences early in life. Freud believed that we go through five stages of psychosexual development, and that at each stage of development we experience pleasure in one part of the body more than

The Life-Span Developmental Perspective

THE FAR SIDE By GARY LARSON

"So, Mr. Fenton . . . Let's begin with
your mother."

others. **Erogenous zones** *refer to Freud's concept that at each stage of development one part of the body has especially strong pleasure-giving qualities.*

Freud thought that our adult personality was determined by the way conflicts between these early sources of pleasure—the mouth, the anus, and then the genitals—and the demands of reality were resolved. When these conflicts are not resolved, the individual may become fixated at a particular stage of development. **Fixation** *is the psychoanalytic defense mechanism that occurs when the individual remains locked into an earlier developmental stage because needs are under- or over-gratified.* For example, a parent may wean a child too early, be too strict in toilet training the child, punish the child for masturbation, or smother the child with warmth. We will return to the idea of fixation and how it may show up in an adult's personality, but first we need to learn more about the early stages of personality development.

The **oral stage** *is the first Freudian stage of development, occurring during the first 18 months of life, in which the infant's pleasure centers around the mouth.* Chewing, sucking, and biting are chief sources of pleasure. These actions reduce tension in the infant.

The **anal stage** *is the second Freudian stage of development, occurring between 1½ and 3 years of age, in which the child's greatest pleasure involves the anus or the eliminative functions associated with it.* In Freud's view, the exercise of anal muscles reduces tension.

The **phallic stage** *is the third Freudian stage of development occurring between the ages of 3 and 6; its name comes from the Latin word phallus, which means penis. During the phallic stage, pleasure focuses on the genitals as the child discovers that self-manipulation is enjoyable.*

In Freud's view, the phallic stage has a special importance in personality development because it is during this period that the Oedipus complex appears. This name comes from Greek mythology, in which Oedipus, the son of the King of Thebes, unwittingly killed his father and married his mother. The **Oedipus complex** *is the Freudian concept in which the young child develops an intense desire to replace the parent of the same sex and enjoy the affections of the opposite-sexed parent.* Freud's concept of the Oedipus complex

GENDER-BASED CRITICISMS OF FREUD'S THEORY

*T*he Oedipus complex was one of Freud's most influential concepts pertaining to the importance of early psychosexual relationships for later personality development. Freud's theory was developed during the Victorian era of the late nineteenth century when the male was dominant and the female was passive, and when sexual interests, especially the female's, were repressed. According to Freud, the sequence of events in the phallic stage for the girl begins when she realizes that she has no penis. According to Freud, she recognizes that the penis is superior to her own anatomy, and thus develops *penis envy*. Since her desire for having a penis can never be satisfied directly, Freud said that the young girl develops a wish to become impregnated by her father. Holding her mother responsible for her lack of a penis, she renounces her love for her mother and becomes intensely attached to her father, thus forming her own version of the Oedipus complex, sometimes referred to as the Electra complex. Thus the sequence of events becomes reversed: for the boy, the Oedipal complex produces castration anxiety; whereas for the girl, penis envy—the parallel to castration anxiety—occurs first and leads to the formation of the Oedipus complex (Hyde, 1985).

Many psychologists believe Freud overemphasized behavior's biological determinants and did not give adequate attention to sociocultural influences and learning. In particular, his view on the differences between males

Bwaitalu village carvers in the Trobriand islands of New Guinea with children. In the Trobriand islands, the authoritarian figure in the young boy's life is the maternal uncle, not the father. The young boys in this culture fear the maternal uncle, not the father. Thus, it is not sexual relations in a family that create conflict and fear for a child, a damaging finding for Freud's Oedipus complex theory.

has been criticized by some female psychoanalysts and feminist writers. To learn more about the cultural and gender-based criticisms of Freud's theory, turn to Perspective on Life-Span Development 2.1.

How is the Oedipus complex resolved? At about 5 to 6 years of age, children recognize that their same-sex parent might punish them for their incestuous wishes. To reduce this conflict, the child identifies with the same-sex

Karen Horney developed the first feminist-based criticism of Freud's theory. Horney's model emphasizes women's positive qualities and self-evaluation.

Nancy Chodorow has developed an important contemporary feminist revision of psychoanalytic theory that emphasizes the meaningfulness of emotions for women.

and females, including their personality development, has a strong biological flavor, relying mainly on anatomical differences. That is, because they have a penis, boys are likely to develop a dominant, powerful personality, girls a submissive, weak personality. In basing his view of male/female differences in personality development on anatomical differences, Freud ignored the enormous impact of culture and experience in determining the personalities of the male and the female.

More than half a century ago, English anthropologist Bronislaw Malinowski (1927) observed the behavior of the Trobriand islanders of the Western Pacific. He found that the Oedipus complex is not universal but depends on cultural variations in families. The family pattern of the Trobriand islanders is different than found in many cultures. In the Trobriand islands, the biological father is not the head of the household, a role reserved for the mother's brother, who acts as a disciplinarian. Thus, the Trobriand islanders tease apart the roles played by the same person in Freud's Vienna and in many other cultures. In Freud's view, this different family constellation should make no difference: the Oedipal complex should still emerge, in which the father is the young boy's hated rival for the mother's love. However, Malinowski found no indication of conflict between fathers and sons in the Trobriand islanders, though he did observe some negative feelings directed by the boy toward the maternal uncle. Thus, the young boy feared the man who was the authoritarian figure in his life, which in the Trobriand island culture was the maternal uncle, not the father. In sum, Malinowski's study documented that it was not the sexual relations within the family that created conflict and fear for a child, a damaging finding for Freud's Oedipal complex theory.

The first feminist-based criticism of Freud's theory was proposed by psychoanalytic theorist Karen Horney (1967). She developed a model of women with positive feminine qualities and self-evaluation. Her critique of Freud's theory included reference to a male-dominant society and culture. Rectification of the male bias in psychoanalytic theory continues today. For example, Nancy Chodorow (1978, 1989) emphasizes that many more women than men define themselves in terms of their relationships and connections to others. Her feminist revision of psychoanalytic theory also emphasizes the meaningfulness of emotions for women, as well as the belief that many men use the defense mechanism of denial in self-other connections.

parent, striving to be like him or her. If the conflict is not resolved, though, the individual may become fixated at the phallic stage. Table 2.1 reveals some possible links between adult personality characteristics and fixation, sublimation, and reaction formation involving the phallic stage, as well as the oral and anal stage.

Table 2.1: Possible Links Between Adult Personality Characteristics and Fixation at Oral, Anal, and Phallic Stages

Stage	Adult Extensions	Sublimations	Reaction Formations
Oral	Smoking, eating, kissing, oral hygiene, drinking, chewing gum	Seeking knowledge, humor, wit, sarcasm, being a food or wine expert	Speech purist, food faddist, prohibitionist, dislike of milk
Anal	Notable interest in one's bowel movements, love of bathroom humor, extreme messiness	Interest in painting or sculpture, being overly giving, great interest in statistics	Extreme disgust with feces, fear of dirt, prudishness, irritability
Phallic	Heavy reliance on masturbation, flirtatiousness, expressions of virility	Interest in poetry, interest in acting, striving for success	Puritanical attitude toward sex, excessive modesty

From *Introduction to Personality* by E. Jerry Phares. Copyright © 1984 by Scott, Foresman and Company. Reprinted by permission of HarperCollins Publishers.

The **latency stage** *is the fourth Freudian stage of development, which occurs between approximately 6 years of age and puberty; the child represses all interest in sexuality and develops social and intellectual skills.* This activity channel's much of the child's energy into emotionally safe areas and aids the child in forgetting the highly stressful conflicts of the phallic stage.

The **genital stage** *is the fifth and final Freudian stage of development, occurring from puberty on. The genital stage is a time of sexual reawakening; the source of sexual pleasure now becomes someone outside of the family.* Freud believed that unresolved conflicts with parents reemerged during adolescence. When resolved, the individual was capable of developing a mature love relationship and functioning independently as an adult. Figure 2.2 summarizes Freud's psychosexual stages.

Erikson's Theory

Erik Erikson (1902–   ) spent his childhood and adolescence in Europe. After working as a young adult under Freud's direction, Erikson came to the United States in 1933. He became a U.S. citizen and taught at Harvard University.

Erikson recognized Freud's contributions but he believed Freud misjudged some important dimensions of human development. For one, Erikson (1950, 1968) says we develop in *psychosocial stages,* in contrast to Freud's psychosexual stages. For another, Erikson emphasized developmental change

Oral stage

Anal stage

Phallic stage

Latency stage

Genital stage

Figure 2.2 Freudian psychosexual stages. Freud said we go through five stages of psychosexual development. In the oral stage, pleasure centers around the mouth. In the anal stage, pleasure focuses on the anus: the nature of toilet training is important here. In the phallic stage, pleasure involves the genitals: the opposite-sex parent becomes a love object here. In the latency stage, the child represses sexual urges: same-sex friendship is prominent. In the genital stage, sexual reawakening takes place: the source of pleasure now becomes someone outside of the family.

Erik Erikson developed a theory that consists of eight psychosocial stages of human development.

Know thyself, for once we know ourselves, we may learn how to care for ourselves, otherwise we never shall.

~ *Socrates*

throughout the human life cycle, whereas Freud argued that our basic personality is shaped in the first five years of our life. The **epigenetic principle** *is Erikson's term for the process that guides development through the life cycle. The epigenetic principle states that anything that grows has a blueprint, each having a special time of ascendency, until all of the parts have arisen to form a functioning whole.* In Erikson's theory, eight stages of development unfold as we go through the life cycle. Each stage consists of a unique developmental task that confronts the individual with a crisis that must be faced. For Erikson, this crisis is not a catastrophe, but a turning point of increased vulnerability and enhanced potential. The more the individual resolves the crises successfully, the healthier development will be.

Trust versus mistrust *is Erikson's first psychosocial stage, which is experienced in the first year of life. A sense of trust requires a feeling of physical comfort and a minimal amount of fear and apprehension about the future.* Trust in infancy sets the stage for a lifelong expectation that the world will be a good and pleasant place to live.

Autonomy versus shame and doubt *is Erikson's second stage of development, occurring in late infancy and toddlerhood (1 to 3 years). After gaining trust in one's caregiver(s), infants and toddlers begin to discover that their behavior is their own.* They start to assert their sense of independence, or autonomy. They realize their will. If infants and toddlers are restrained too much or punished too harshly, they are likely to develop a sense of shame and doubt.

Initiative versus guilt *is Erikson's third stage of development, occurring during the preschool years. As preschool children encounter a widening social world, they are challenged more than they were as infants. Active, purposeful behavior is needed to cope with these challenges.* Children are asked to assume responsibility for their body, their behavior, their toys, and their pets. Developing a sense of reponsibility increases initiative. Uncomfortable guilt feelings may arise, though, if the child is irresponsible and is made to feel too anxious. Erikson has a positive outlook on this stage. He believes most guilt is quickly compensated for by a sense of accomplishment.

Industry versus inferiority *is Erikson's fourth developmental stage, occurring approximately during the elementary school years. Children's initiative brings them in contact with a wealth of new experiences. As they move into middle and late childhood, they direct their energy toward mastering knowledge and intellectual skills.* At no other time is the child more enthusiastic about learning than at the end of early childhood's period of expansive imagination. The danger during the elementary school years is a sense of inferiority—of feeling incompetent and unproductive. Erikson believes teachers have a special responsibility for children's development of industry. They should "mildly but firmly coerce children into the adventure of finding out that one can learn to accomplish things which one would never have thought of by oneself" (Erikson, 1968, p. 127).

Identity versus identity confusion *is Erikson's fifth developmental stage, experienced by individuals during the adolescent years. At this time, individuals are faced with finding out who they are, what they are all about, and where they are going in life.* Adolescents are confronted with many new roles and adult statuses—vocational and romantic, for example. Parents need to allow adolescents to explore many different roles and different paths within a particular role. If the adolescent explores these roles in a healthy manner and arrives at a positive path to follow, then a positive identity will be achieved. If an identity is pushed on the adolescent by parents, if the adolescent does not adequately explore many roles, and if a positive future path is not defined, then identity confusion reigns.

Intimacy versus isolation *is Erikson's sixth developmental stage, experienced by individuals during the early adulthood years. At this time, individuals face the developmental task of forming intimate relationships with others.* Erikson described intimacy as finding yet losing oneself in another. If the young adult forms healthy friendships and an intimate close relationship with another individual, intimacy will be achieved; if not, isolation will result.

Generativity versus stagnation *is Erikson's seventh developmental stage, experienced by individuals during middle adulthood. A chief concern is to assist the younger generation in developing and leading useful lives; this is what Erikson meant by generativity.* The feeling of having done nothing to help the next generation is stagnation.

Integrity versus despair *is Erikson's eighth and final developmental stage, experienced by individuals during late adulthood when they review their life and evaluate it as having been either primarily positive or primarily negative.* Through many different routes the older person may have developed a positive outlook in most or all of the previous stages of development. If so, the retrospective glances will reveal a picture of a life well spent, and the person will feel a sense of satisfaction; integrity will be achieved. If the older adult resolved many of the earlier stages negatively, the retrospective glances will likely yield doubt or gloom; this is the despair Erikson talks about.

Erikson does not believe the proper solution to a stage crisis is always completely positive in nature. Some exposure or commitment to the negative end of the person's bipolar conflict is sometimes inevitable—you cannot trust all people under all circumstances and survive, for example. Nonetheless, in the healthy solution to a stage crisis, the positive resolution dominates. A summary of Erikson's stages is presented in figure 2.3.

Evaluating the Psychoanalytic Theories

While psychoanalytic theories have become heterogeneous, nonetheless, they share some core principles. Our development is determined not only by current experiences but also by those from early in our life. The principles that early experiences are important determinants of personality and that we can better understand personality by examining it developmentally have withstood the test of time. The belief that environmental experiences are mentally transformed and represented in the mind likewise continues to receive considerable attention. Psychoanalytic theorists forced psychologists to recognize that the mind is not all consciousness; the mind has an unconscious portion that influences behavior. Psychoanalytic theorists' emphasis on the importance of conflict and anxiety requires us to consider the dark side of our existence, not just its bright side. Adjustment is not always easy, and the individual's inner world often conflicts with the outer demands of reality.

However, the main concepts of psychoanalytic theories have been difficult to test. Inference and interpretation are required to determine whether psychoanalytic ideas are accurate. Researchers have not successfully investigated such key concepts are repression in the laboratory. Much of the data used to support psychoanalytic theories come from patients' reconstruction of the past, often the distant past, and are of doubtful accuracy. Other data come from clinicians' subjective evaluations of clients; in such cases, it is easy for clinicians to see what they expect because of the theory they hold. Some psychologists object that Freud overemphasized sexuality and the unconscious mind. The psychoanalytic theories also provide a model of the individual that is too negative and pessimistic. We are not born into the world with only a bundle of sexual and aggressive impulses; our compliance with the external demands of reality does not always conflict with our biological needs.

> You come to a place in your life when what you've been is going to form what you will be. If you've wasted what you have in you, it's too late to do much about it. If you've invested yourself in life, you're pretty certain to get a return. If you are inwardly a serious person, in the middle years it will pay off.
>
> ~ *Lillian Hellman*

Figure 2.3 *Erikson's eight stages of the human life cycle.*

Erikson's stages	Developmental period	Characteristics
Trust versus mistrust	Infancy (first year)	A sense of trust requires a feeling of physical comfort and a minimal amount of fear about the future. The infant's basic needs are met by responsive, sensitive caregivers.
Autonomy versus shame and doubt	Late infancy toddlerhood (1 to 3 years)	After gaining trust in caregivers, infants start to discover that they have a will of their own. They assert their sense of autonomy or independence. They realize their will. If infants are restrained too much or punishment is too harsh, they are likely to develop a sense of shame and doubt.
Initiative versus guilt	Early childhood (preschool years, ages 3 to 5)	As preschool children encounter a widening social world, they are challenged more and need to develop more purposeful behavior to cope with these challenges. Children are now asked to assume more responsibility. Imaginative play develops. Uncomfortable guilt feelings may arise, though, if the child is irresponsible and is made to feel too anxious.
Industry versus inferiority	Middle and late childhood (elementary school years, 6 to puberty)	At no other time is the child more enthusiastic than at the end of early childhood's expansive imagination. As children move into the elementary school years, they direct their energy toward mastering knowledge and intellectual skills. The danger at this stage involves feeling incompetent and unproductive.

Cognitive Theories

Exploring the human mind has been regarded with a kind of mystical awe throughout most of human history. Now, ten thousand years after the dawn of civilization, a new understanding of the mind is flourishing. Mind is a complex term but it is primarily our cognitive activity: perception, attention, memory, language, reasoning, thinking, and the like. Whereas psychoanalytic

Erikson's stages	Developmental period	Characteristics
Identity versus identity confusion	Adolescence (10 to 20 years)	Individuals are faced with finding out who they are, what they are all about, and where they are going in life. An important dimension is the exploration of alternative solutions to roles. Career exploration is important.
Intimacy versus isolation	Early adulthood (20s, 30s)	Individuals face the developmental task of forming intimate relationships with others. Erikson described intimacy as finding oneself yet losing oneself in another person.
Generativity versus stagnation	Middle adulthood (40s, 50s)	A chief concern is to assist the younger generation in developing and leading useful lives.
Integrity versus despair	Late adulthood (60s -)	Individuals look back and evaluate what they have done with their lives. The retrospective glances can either be positive (integrity) or negative (despair).

theories emphasize unconscious thoughts, cognitive theories emphasize conscious thoughts. The developing individual is perceived as rational and logical, capable of using the mind to effectively interact with and control the environment. The cognitive theory that has dominated the study of development is that of Swiss psychologist Jean Piaget. A second important cognitive approach is information processing.

Jean Piaget, famous Swiss developmental psychologist, changed forever the way we think about the development of the child's mind. For Piaget, the child's mental development is a continuous creation of increasingly complex forms.

• Critical Thinking •

What experiences in your own life provide examples of Piaget's concepts of assimilation and accommodation?

Piaget's Theory

Jean Piaget was born in 1896 in Switzerland. Piaget was a child genius. At the age of 10, he wrote an article about a rare albino sparrow, which was published in the *Journal of the Natural History of Neuchatel.* The article was so brilliant that the curators of the Geneva Museum of Natural History, who had no idea the article had been written by a 10-year-old, offered young Piaget the job of museum curator. The museum heads quickly rescinded their offer when they realized Piaget was only a child. Piaget continued to live in Switzerland as an adult and became one of the most influential forces in child development in the twentieth century. In a eulogy to Piaget following his death at the age of 84 in 1980, it was said that we owe him the present field of cognitive development. What was the theory of this giant in developmental psychology like?

Piaget's theory will be covered in greater detail later in this book when we discuss cognitive development in infancy, early childhood, middle and late childhood, and adolescence. Here we briefly present the main ideas of his theory. Piaget stressed that individuals actively construct their own cognitive world; information is not just poured into their mind from the environment. Two processes underlie the individual's construction of the world: organization and adaptation. To make sense of our world, we organize our experiences. For example, we separate important ideas from less important ideas. We connect one idea to another. But we not only organize our observations and experiences, we also *adapt* our thinking to include new ideas because additional information furthers understanding. Piaget (1954) believed that we adapt in two ways: assimilation and accommodation.

Assimilation *occurs when individuals incorporate new information into their existing knowledge.* **Accommodation** *occurs when individuals adjust to new information.* Consider a circumstance in which a 5-year-old girl is given a hammer and nails to hang a picture on the wall. She has never used a hammer, but from observation and vicarious experience she realizes that a hammer is an object to be held, that it is swung by the handle to hit the nail, and that it is usually swung a number of times. Recognizing each of these things, she fits her behavior into information she already has (assimilation). However, the hammer is heavy, so she holds it near the top. She swings too hard and the nail bends, so she adjusts the pressure of her strikes. These adjustments reveal her ability to alter her conception of the world slightly (accommodation).

Piaget thought that assimilation and accommodation operate even in the very young infant's life. Newborns reflexively suck everything that touches their lips (assimilation), but after several months of experience, they construct their understanding of the world differently. Some objects, such as fingers and the mother's breast, can be sucked, and others, such as fuzzy blankets, should not be sucked (accommodation).

Piaget also believed that we go through four stages in understanding the world. Each of the stages is age-related and consists of distinct ways of thinking. Remember, it is the *different* way of understanding the world that makes one stage more advanced than another; knowing *more* information does not make the child's thinking more advanced in the Piagetian view. This is what Piaget meant when he said the child's cognition is *qualitatively* different in one stage compared to another. What are Piaget's four stages of cognitive development like?

The **sensorimotor stage,** *which lasts from birth to about 2 years of age, is the first Piagetian stage. In this stage, infants construct an understanding of the world by coordinating sensory experiences (such as seeing and hearing)* *with physical, motoric actions—hence the term sensorimotor.* At the beginning of this stage, newborns have little more than reflexive patterns with which to work. At the end of the stage, 2-year-olds have complex sensorimotor patterns and are beginning to operate with primitive symbols.

The **preoperational stage,** *which lasts from approximately 2 to 7 years of age, is the second Piagetian stage. In this stage, children begin to represent the world with words, images, and drawings.* Symbolic thought goes beyond simple connections of sensory information and physical action. Although preschool children can symbolically represent the world, according to Piaget, they still lack the ability to perform *operations,* the Piagetian term describing mental operations that allow the child to do mentally what was done physically before. For example, preschool children cannot mentally reverse the liquid from one beaker to another and understand that the volume is the same even though the beakers are different in height and width. The inability to perform operations is the reason Piaget described this stage as *pre*operational.

The **concrete operational stage,** *which lasts from approximately 7 to 11 years of age, is the third Piagetian stage. In this stage, children can perform operations. Logical reasoning replaces intuitive thought as long as the principles can be applied to specific or concrete examples.* For instance, concrete operational thinkers cannot imagine the steps necessary to complete an algebraic equation, which is too abstract for thinking at this stage of development.

The **formal operational stage,** *which appears between the ages of 11 and 15, is the fourth and final Piagetian stage. In this stage, individuals move beyond the world of actual, concrete experiences and think in abtract and more logical terms.* As part of thinking more abstractly, adolescents develop images of ideal circumstances. They may think about what an ideal parent is like and compare their parents with this ideal standard. They begin to entertain possibilities for the future and are fascinated with what they can be. In solving problems, formal operational thinkers are more systematic, developing hypotheses about why something is happening the way it is, and then they may test these hypotheses in a deductive fashion.

Piaget's stages are summarized in figure 2.4. A comparison of Piaget's stages with Freud's and Erikson's stages is presented in figure 2.5. Notice that only Erikson describes changes in the adulthood years. And remember that Piaget's theory stresses conscious thought while Freud's and Erikson's theories stress unconscious thought.

The Information Processing Approach

The **information processing approach** *is concerned with how individuals process information about their world—how information enters our minds, how it is stored and transformed, and how it is retrieved to perform such complex activities as problem solving and reasoning.* A simple model of cognition is shown in figure 2.6. Cognition begins when information from the world is detected through sensory and perceptual processes. Then information is stored, transformed, and retrieved through the processes of memory. Notice in our model that information can flow back and forth between memory and perceptual processes. For example, we are good at remembering the faces we see, yet our memory of an individual's face may be different from how the individual actually looks. Keep in mind that our information processing model is a simple one, designed to illustrate the main cognitive processes and their interrelations. We could have drawn other arrows—between memory and language, between thinking and perception, and between language and perception,

Man is a reed, the weakest in nature; but he is a thinking reed.

~ *Pascal, 1670*

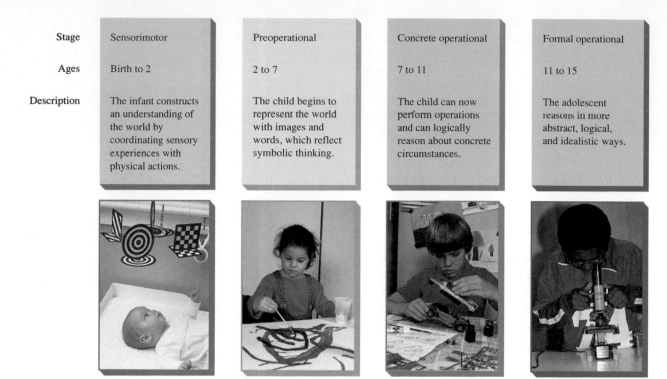

Stage	Sensorimotor	Preoperational	Concrete operational	Formal operational
Ages	Birth to 2	2 to 7	7 to 11	11 to 15
Description	The infant constructs an understanding of the world by coordinating sensory experiences with physical actions.	The child begins to represent the world with images and words, which reflect symbolic thinking.	The child can now perform operations and can logically reason about concrete circumstances.	The adolescent reasons in more abstract, logical, and idealistic ways.

Figure 2.4 Piaget's stages of cognitive development.

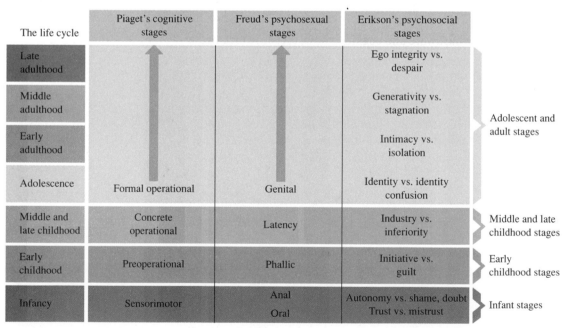

The life cycle	Piaget's cognitive stages	Freud's psychosexual stages	Erikson's psychosocial stages	
Late adulthood			Ego integrity vs. despair	
Middle adulthood			Generativity vs. stagnation	Adolescent and adult stages
Early adulthood			Intimacy vs. isolation	
Adolescence	Formal operational	Genital	Identity vs. identity confusion	
Middle and late childhood	Concrete operational	Latency	Industry vs. inferiority	Middle and late childhood stages
Early childhood	Preoperational	Phallic	Initiative vs. guilt	Early childhood stages
Infancy	Sensorimotor	Anal / Oral	Autonomy vs. shame, doubt / Trust vs. mistrust	Infant stages

Figure 2.5 Comparison of Piaget's, Freud's, and Erikson's stage theories.

for example. Also, it is important to know that the boxes in the figure do not represent sharp, distinct stages in processing information. There is continuity and flow between the cognitive processes as well as overlap.

By the 1940s, the first successful computer suggested that machines could perform logical operations. This indicated that some mental operations might be modeled by computers, and possibly computers could tell us something about how cognition works. Cognitive psychologists often use the computer to help explain the relation between cognition and the brain. The physical brain is

The Life-Span Developmental Perspective

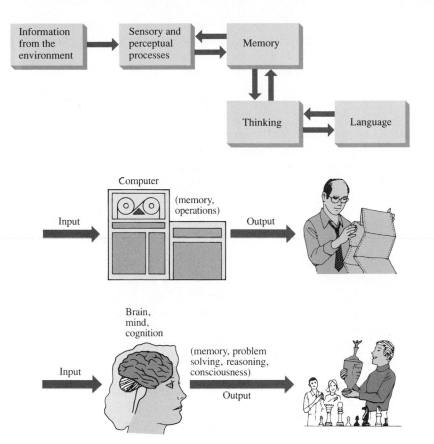

Figure 2.6 A model of information processing. In this simplified model of how individuals process information, sensory and perceptual processes, memory, thinking, and language are described as important cognitive processes. Notice the flow of information back and forth between these cognitive processes.

Figure 2.7 Computers and cognition: an analogy. The computer revolution has influenced the way cognitive psychologists view cognition. Cognitive psychologists have often used the computer to help explain the relation between cognition and the brain. The physical brain is described as the computer's hardware, cognition as its software.

described as the computer's hardware and cognition as its software (see figure 2.7). The ability to process information has highlighted psychology's cognitive revolution since the 1950s.

The information processing approach raises important questions about changes in cognition across the life span (Kuhn, 1991; Smith & Baltes, 1991). One of these questions is: Does processing speed increase as children grow older and decrease as adults grow older? Speed of processing is an important aspect of the information processing approach. Many cognitive tasks are performed under real time pressure. For example, at school we have a limited amount of time to add and subtract and take tests; at work we have deadlines for completing a project. A good deal of evidence suggests that processing speed is slower in younger children than older children, and slower in elderly adults than in young adults. But the causes of these differences have not been determined. Although some might be biological in origin, they might reflect differences in knowledge about or practice on a task (Santrock & Bartlett, 1986).

Evaluating the Cognitive Theories

Both Piaget's cognitive-developmental theory and the information processing approach contribute in important ways to our knowledge about life-span development. Today, researchers enthusiastically evaluate the accuracy of Piaget's theory with the result that some of his ideas remain unscathed while others are requiring extensive modification. The information processing approach has opened up many avenues of research, offering detailed descriptions of cognitive processes and sophisticated methods for studying cognition. The cognitive theories provide an optimistic view of human development, ascribing to children and adults the ability and motivation to know their world and to cope with it in constructive ways.

• Critical Thinking •

What can a computer do that a human mind cannot do? What can a human mind do that a computer cannot?

Like all theories, the cognitive theories have their weaknesses. There is skepticism about the pureness of Piaget's stages and his concepts are somewhat loosely defined. The information processing approach has not yet produced an overall perspective on development. Both the Piagetian and information processing approaches may have underestimated the importance of the unconscious mind and environmental experiences, especially those involving families, in determining behavior.

So far we have discussed two main theories of life-span development—psychoanalytic and cognitive. A summary of the main ideas in these two theories is presented in concept table 2.1. The psychoanalytic and cognitive-developmental theories are stage theories, each highlighting the ascendence of certain characteristics at particular points in development. The remaining theories we will discuss do not specify stages in life-span development.

Behavioral and Social Learning Theories

Tom is engaged to marry Ann. Both have warm, friendly personalities and they enjoy being with each other. Psychoanalytic theorists would say that their warm, friendly personalities are derived from long-standing relationships with their parents. They would also argue that the reason for their attraction is unconscious; they are unaware of how their biological heritage and early life experiences have been carried forward to influence their adult personality.

Behaviorists and social learning theorists would observe Tom and Ann and see something quite different. They would examine their experiences, especially their most recent ones, to understand the reason for their attraction. Tom would be described as rewarding Ann's behavior, and vice versa, for example. No reference would be made to unconscious thoughts, the Oedipus complex, defense mechanisms, and so on.

Behaviorists believe we should examine only what can be directly observed and measured. At approximately the same time Freud was interpreting his patients' unconscious minds through their early childhood experiences, behaviorists such as Ivan Pavlov and John B. Watson were conducting detailed observations of behavior under controlled laboratory conditions. Out of the behavioral tradition grew the belief that development is observable behavior, learned through experiences with the environment. The two versions of the behavioral approach that are prominent today are the behavioral view of B. F. Skinner (1904–1990) and social learning theory.

Skinner's Behaviorism

During World War II, B. F. Skinner constructed a rather strange project—a pigeon-guided missile. A pigeon in the warhead of the missile operated the flaps on the missile and guided it home by pecking at an image of a target. How could this possibly work? When the missile was in flight, the pigeon pecked the moving image on the screen. This produced corrective signals to keep the missile on its course. The pigeons did their job well in trial runs, but top Navy officials just could not accept pigeons piloting their missiles during a war. Skinner, however, congratulated himself on the degree of control he was able to exercise over the pigeons.

Following the pigeon experiment, Skinner (1948) wrote *Walden Two*, a novel in which he presented his ideas about building a scientifically managed society. Skinner envisioned a utopian society that could be engineered through behavioral control. Skinner viewed existing societies as poorly managed because individuals believe in myths such as free will. He pointed out that humans

B. F. Skinner, the prominent American behaviorist.

The Life-Span Developmental Perspective

Concept Table 2.1: The Psychoanalytic and Cognitive Theories

Concept	Processes/Related Ideas	Characteristics/Description
Psychoanalytic Theories	Freud's Theory	Freud said that our personality has three structures—id, ego, and superego—that conflict with each other. Most of our thoughts are unconscious in Freud's view and the id is completely unconscious. The conflicting demands of personality structures produce anxiety; defense mechanisms, especially repression, protect the ego and reduce anxiety. Freud was convinced that problems develop because of childhood experiences. He said we go through five psychosexual stages—oral, anal, phallic, latency, and genital. During the phallic stage, the Oedipus complex is a main source of conflict.
	Erikson's Theory	Erikson developed a theory that emphasizes eight psychosocial stages of development: trust vs. mistrust, anatomy vs. shame and doubt, initiative vs. guilt, industry vs. inferiority, identity vs. identity confusion, intimacy vs. isolation, generativity vs. stagnation, and integrity vs. despair.
	Evaluating the Psychoanalytic Theories	Strengths are an emphasis on the past, the developmental course of personality, mental representation of environment, unconscious mind, and emphasis on conflict. Weaknesses are difficulty in testing main concepts, lack of an empirical data base and overreliance on past reports, too much emphasis on sexuality and the unconscious mind, and a negative view of human nature.
Cognitive Theories	Piaget's Theory	Piaget's theory is responsible for the field of cognitive development. He believes we are motivated to understand our world and use the processes of organization and adaptation (assimilation, accommodation) to do so. Piaget says we go through four cognitive stages; sensorimotor, preoperational, concrete operational, and formal operational.
	Information Processing Approach	This approach is concerned with how we process information about our world. It includes how information gets into our mind, how it is stored and transformed, and how it is retrieved to think and solve problems. The development of the computer promoted this approach; the mind as an information processing system was compared to how a computer processes information. The information processing approach raises questions about life-span development, among them the rise and decline of speed of processing information.
	Evaluating the Cognitive Theories	Both the Piagetian and information processing approaches have made important contributions to life-span development. They have provided a positive, rational portrayal of humans as they develop, although they may have underestimated the importance of unconscious thought and environmental experiences. The purity of Piaget's stages have been questioned and the information processing approach has not yet produced an overall perspective on development.

are no more free than pigeons; denying that our behavior is controlled by environmental forces is to ignore science and reality, he argued. In the long run, Skinner said we would be much happier when we recognized such truths, especially his concept that we could live a prosperous life under the control of positive reinforcement.

Behaviorism *emphasizes the scientific study of observable behavioral responses and their environmental determinants.* In Skinner's behaviorism, the mind, conscious or unconscious, was not needed to explain behavior and development. For him, development was the individual's behavior. For example, observations of Sam reveal that his behavior is shy, achievement oriented, and caring. Why is Sam's behavior this way? For Skinner, rewards and punishments in Sam's environment have shaped him into a shy, achievement-oriented, and caring individual. Through interactions with family members, friends, teachers, and others, Sam has *learned* to behave in this fashion. Because behaviorists believe that development is learned and often changes according to environmental experiences, it follows that rearranging experiences can change the individual's development. For the behaviorist, shy behavior can be changed into outgoing behavior; aggressive behavior can be shaped into docile behavior; lethargic, boring behavior can be turned into enthusiastic, interesting behavior.

Skinner describes how behavior is controlled in the following way. The individual *operates* on the environment to produce a change that will lead to a reward (Skinner, 1938). Skinner chose the term *operants* to describe the responses that are actively emitted because of the consequences for the individual. The consequences—rewards and punishments—are *contingent,* or depend on the individual's behavior. For example, an operant might be pressing a lever on a machine that delivers a candy bar; the delivery of the candy bar is contingent on pressing the lever. In sum, **operant conditioning** *is a form of learning in which the consequences of behavior lead to changes in the probability of that behavior's occurrence.*

More needs to be said about reinforcement and punishment. **Reinforcement** *(or reward) is a consequence that increases the probability of a behavior occurring.* By contrast, **punishment** *is a consequence that decreases the probability of a behavior occurring.* For example, if someone smiles at you and the two of you continue talking for some time, the smile has reinforced your talking. However, if someone you meet frowns at you and you quickly leave the situation, the frown has punished your talking with the individual.

Social Learning Theory

Some psychologists believe the behaviorists are basically right when they say development is learned and is strongly influenced by environmental experiences. But they believe Skinner went too far in declaring that cognition is unimportant in understanding development. **Social learning theory** *is the view of psychologists who emphasize behavior, environment,* and *cognition as the key factors in development.*

The social learning theorists say we are not like mindless robots, responding mechanically to others in our environment. And we are not like weathervanes, behaving like a Communist in the presence of a Communist, or like a John Bircher in the presence of a John Bircher. Rather, we think, reason, imagine, plan, expect, interpret, believe, value, and compare. When others try to control us, our values and beliefs allow us to restrict their control.

American psychologists Albert Bandura (1977, 1986, 1989) and Walter Mischel (1973, 1984) are the main architects of social learning theory's contemporary version, which was labeled *cognitive social learning theory* by Mischel (1973). Bandura believes we learn by observing what others do. Through observational learning (also called modeling or imitation), we cognitively represent the behavior of others and then possibly adopt this behavior ourselves. For example, a young boy may observe his father's aggressive outbursts and hostile interchanges with people; when observed with his peers, the young boy's style of interaction is highly aggressive, showing the same characteristics as

• *Critical Thinking* •

Think about your life during the last 24 hours. How did rewards and punishments influence the way you behaved during this time frame?

The Life-Span Developmental Perspective

(a)   (b)

(a) Albert Bandura and (b) Walter Mischel crafted social learning theory's contemporary version, labeled cognitive social learning theory by Mischel.

his father's behavior. Or, a young female executive adopts the dominant and sarcastic style of her boss. When observed interacting with one of her subordinates, the young woman says, "I need this work immediately if not sooner; you are so far behind you think you are ahead!" Social learning theorists believe we acquire a wide range of such behaviors, thoughts, and feelings through observing others' behavior; these observations form an important part of our development.

Social learning theorists also differ from Skinner's behavioral view by emphasizing that we can regulate and control our own behavior. For example, another young female executive who observed her boss behave in a dominant and sarcastic manner toward employees found the behavior distasteful and went out of her way to encourage and support her subordinates. Imagine that someone tries to persuade you to join a particular social club on campus and makes you an enticing offer. You reflect about the offer, consider your interests and beliefs, and make the decision not to join. Your *cognition* (your thoughts) leads you to control your behavior and resist environmental influence in this instance.

Bandura's (1986, 1989, 1991) most recent model of learning and development involves behavior, the person, and the environment. As shown in figure 2.8, behavior, cognitive and other personal factors, and environmental influences operate interactively. Behavior can influence cognition and vice versa, the person's cognitive activities can influence the environment, environmental influences can change the person's thought processes, and so on.

Let's consider how Bandura's model might work in the case of a college student's achievement behavior. As the student diligently studies and gets good grades, her behavior produces positive thoughts about her abilities. As part of her effort to make good grades, she plans and develops a number of strategies to make her studying more efficient. In these ways, her behavior has influenced her thought and her thought has influenced her behavior. At the beginning of the semester, her college made a special effort to involve students in a study skills program. She decided to join. Her success, along with that of other students who attended the program, has led the college to expand the program next semester. In these ways, environment influenced behavior, and behavior changed the environment. And the college administrators' expectations that the study skills program would work made it possible in the first place. The program's success has spurred expectations that this type of program could work in other colleges. In these ways, cognition changed the environment, and the environment changed cognition. Expectations are an important variable in Bandura's model.

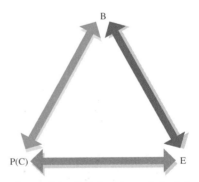

Figure 2.8 Bandura's model of the reciprocal influence of behavior, personal and cognitive factors, and environment. P(C) stands for personal and cognitive factors, B for behavior, and E for environment. The arrows reflect how relations between these factors are reciprocal rather than unidirectional. Examples of personal factors include intelligence, skills, and self-control.

Like the behavioral approach of Skinner, the social learning approach emphasizes the importance of empirical research in studying development. This research focuses on the processes that explain development—the social and cognitive factors that influence what we are like as people.

Evaluating the Behavioral and Social Learning Theories

The behavorial and social learning theories emphasize that environmental experiences determine development. These approaches have fostered a scientific climate for understanding development that highlights the observation of behavior. Social learning theory emphasizes both environmental influences and cognitive processes in explaining development; this view also suggests individuals have the ability to control their environment.

The criticisms of the behavioral and social learning theories are sometimes directed at the behavioral view alone and at other times at both approaches. The behavioral view has been criticized for ignoring the importance of cognition in development and placing too much importance on environmental experiences. Both approaches have been described as being too concerned with change and situational influences on development, not paying adequate tribute to the enduring qualities of development. Both views are said to ignore the biological determinants of development. Both are labeled as reductionistic, which means they look at only one or two components of development rather than at how all of the pieces fit together. And critics have charged that the behavioral and social learning theories are too mechanical. By being overly concerned with several minute pieces of development, the most exciting and rich dimensions of development are missed, say the detractors. This latter criticism—that the creative, spontaneous, and human characteristics of development are missing from the behavorial and social learning theories—has been made on numerous occasions by adherents of the humanistic approach, which we consider next.

Phenomenological and Humanistic Theories

Remember our example of the engaged couple, Tom and Ann, who were described as having warm, friendly personalities. Phenomenological and humanistic psychologists would describe their warm, friendly personalities as reflecting their inner self; they would emphasize that a key to understanding their attraction is their positive perception of each other. Tom and Ann are not viewed as controlling each other's behavior; rather they have determined their own course of action and each freely chosen to marry. No recourse to biological instincts or unconscious thoughts as determinants of their attraction occurs in the phenomenological and humanistic theories.

The **phenomenological approach** *stresses the importance of our perceptions of ourselves and our world in understanding personality; for each individual, reality is what is perceived.* The **humanistic approach** *is the most widely known phenomenological approach to personality. It stresses the person's capacity for personal growth, freedom to choose one's own destiny, and positive qualities.* Humanistic psychologists believe each of us has the ability to cope with stress, control our lives, and achieve what we desire. Each of us has the ability to break through and understand ourselves and our world; we can burst the cocoon and become a butterfly, say the humanists.

You probably sense that the phenomenological and humanistic perspectives provide stark contrasts to the psychoanalytic perspective, which is based on conflict and little faith in the ability of individuals to understand their own personality, and to the behavorial perspective, which emphasizes that rewards and punishments from others determine the individual's personality. Carl Rogers and Abraham Maslow were two of the leading architects of the humanistic perspective.

Carl Rogers' Approach

Like Freud, Rogers (1902–1987) began his inquiry about human nature by studying troubled personalities. Rogers (1961) explored the human potential for change. In the knotted, anxious, and defensive verbal stream of his clients, Rogers examined the conditioned, controlling world that kept them from having positive self-concepts and reaching their full potential as human beings.

Our Conditioned, Controlling World

Rogers believed that most individuals have considerable difficulty accepting their own true feelings, which are innately positive. As we grow up, significant others condition us to move away from these positive feelings. Our parents, siblings, teachers, and peers place constraints and contingencies on our behavior; too often we hear, "Don't do that," "You didn't do that right," "How could you be so stupid?" and "You didn't try hard enough." When we don't do something right, we often get punished. And parents may even threaten to take away their love. **Conditional positive regard** *is Rogers' concept that love and praise are often not given unless an individual conforms to parental or social standards.* The result is lower self-esteem.

These constraints and negative feedback continue during our adult lives. As a result, our relationships either carry the dark cloud of conflict, or we conform to what others want. As we struggle to live up to society's standards, we distort and devalue our true self. We may even completely lose our sense of self by mirroring what we think others want.

The Self

Through the individual's experiences with the world a self emerges—this is the "I" or "me" of our existence. Rogers did not believe that all aspects of the self are conscious, but he did believe that they are all accessible to consciousness. The self is a whole, consisting of one's self-perceptions (how attractive I am, how well I get along with others, how good an athlete I am) and the values we attach to these perceptions (good-bad, worthy-unworthy, for example). **Self-concept** *is a central theme in Rogers' and other humanists' views; self-concept refers to individuals' overall perception of their abilities, behavior, and personality.* In Rogers' view, a person who has a positive self-concept is likely to think, feel, and act positively; and a person who has a negative self-concept is likely to think, feel, and act negatively.

In discussing self-concept, Rogers distinguished between the real self, that is, the self as it really is as a result of our experiences, and the ideal self, which is the self we would like to be (figure 2.9 shows a portrait that reflects the ideal self and real self). The greater the discrepancy between the real self and the ideal self, the more maladjusted we will be, said Rogers. To improve our adjustment, we can develop more positive perceptions of our real self, not worry so much about what others want, and increase our positive experiences in the world.

Unconditional Positive Regard, Empathy, and Genuineness

How can others help the individual develop a more positive self-concept? Rogers stressed three factors in this regard: unconditional positive regard, empathy, and genuineness. Rogers said that we need to be accepted by others, regardless

Carl Rogers, one of the architects of the humanistic approach.

Figure 2.9 Picasso's portrait reflecting Rogers' ideal and real selves. Half naked, half clothed, Picasso's 1932 portrayal of a Girl Before a Mirror *reflects the twin images of Carl Rogers' ideal and real selves.*

(Oil on canvas, 64 × 51¼ in. Collection, The Museum of Modern Art. New York. Gift of Mrs. Simon Guggenheim.)

of what we do or say. **Unconditional positive regard** *is Rogers' concept of accepting, valuing, and being positive toward another person regardless of that person's behavior.* Rogers recognized that when a person's behavior is below acceptable standards, inappropriate, or even obnoxious, the person needs the respect, comfort, and love of others. Rogers strongly believed that unconditional positive regard elevates the person's self-worth. However, Rogers (1974) distinguished between unconditional positive regard directed at the individual as a person of worth and dignity and as directed at the individual's behavior. Thus, a Rogerian counselor might say, "I don't like your behavior, but I accept you, value you, and like you as a person."

Rogers also said we can help individuals develop a more positive self-concept if we are *empathic* and *genuine.* Being empathic means being a sensitive listener and understanding another's true feelings. Being genuine means being open with our feelings and dropping our pretenses and facades. For Rogers, unconditional positive regard, empathy, and genuineness are the three key ingredients of human relations. We can use these techniques to get other people to feel good about themselves, and the techniques also help us to get along better with others.

The Fully Functioning Person

Rogers (1980) stressed the importance of becoming a fully functioning person. What are fully functioning persons like? They are open to experience, are not very defensive, are aware of and sensitive to the self and the external world, and for the most part have harmonious relationships with others. A discrepancy between our real self and our ideal self may occur, others may try to control us, and our world may have too little unconditional positive regard; but Rogers believed that we are highly resilient and capable of becoming a fully functioning person. He believed that our good side could not be kept down.

This self-actualizing tendency of ours is reflected in Rogers' comparison of a person with a plant he once observed on the coastline of northern California. Rogers was looking out at the waves beating furiously against the jagged rocks, shooting mountains of spray into the air. Rogers noticed a tiny palmlike seaweed on the rocks, no more than two or three feet high, taking the pounding of the breakers. The plant was fragile and top-heavy; it seemed clear that the waves would crush the tiny specimen. A wave would crunch the plant, bending its slender trunk almost flat and whipping its leaves in a torrent of spray. Yet the moment the wave passed, the plant became erect, tough, and resilient once again. It was incredible that the plant could take this incessant pounding hour after hour, week after week, possibly even year after year, all the time nourishing itself, maintaining its position, and growing. In this tiny palmlike seaweed Rogers saw the tenacity of life, the forward thrust of life, and the ability of a living thing to push into a hostile environment and not only hold its own, but adapt, develop, and become itself. So it is with each of us, in Rogers' view (Rogers, 1963).

Abraham Maslow's Approach

Abraham Maslow (1908–1970) was one of the most powerful forces behind the humanistic movement in psychology. He called the humanistic approach the "third force" in psychology, that is, an important alternative to the psychoanalytic and behavioral forces. Maslow pointed out that psychoanalytic

We carry with us the wonders we seek without us.

~ *Sir Thomas Browne, 1642*

The Life-Span Developmental Perspective

theories place too much emphasis on disturbed individuals and their conflicts, and that behaviorists ignore the person altogether.

The **hierarchy of needs** *is Maslow's concept that certain basic needs (physiological, safety, love and belongingness, and self-esteem) have to be satisfied before we can satisfy the highest need of self-actualization.* **Self-actualization** *is Maslow's term for the highest human need, defined as the motivation to develop one's full potential as a human being.* Maslow (1954, 1971) charted the human potential of creative, talented, and healthy people. Figure 2.10 shows Maslow's hierarchy of human needs.

Abraham Maslow

Maslow believed that needs come in two forms: deficiency needs and metaneeds (also called growth or self-actualized needs). According to Maslow, **deficiency needs**—*physiological (food) and psychological (affection, security, self-esteem)—are needs that individuals try to make up for if they are not fulfilled.* **Metaneeds,** *or growth needs, refer to Maslow's concept of higher, self-actualization needs; they include truth, goodness, beauty, wholeness, aliveness, uniqueness, perfection, justice, richness, and playfulness.* The metaneeds cannot be satisfied until all the lower needs are met. However, the metaneeds are not hierarchically arranged in Maslow's model. For example, although we must satisfy our need for belongingness before our need for self-esteem, we do not have to satisfy our need for goodness before our need for aliveness. When our metaneeds are not fulfilled, we may become maladjusted, said Maslow. For example, unfulfilled metaneeds may cause individuals to become alienated, weak, or cynical.

Maslow developed psychological profiles of famous people and concluded that such individuals as Eleanor Roosevelt, Albert Einstein, Abraham Lincoln, Walt Whitman, William James, and Ludwig van Beethoven were self-actualized.

Evaluating the Phenomenological and Humanistic Approaches

The phenomenological and humanistic approaches sensitized psychologists to the importance of phenomenological experience; our perceptions of ourselves and the world are key determinants of our personality. The emphasis on conscious experience has likewise had a significant influence on how we view personality. The humanistic psychologists reminded us that we need to consider the whole person and the individual's positive nature. The contributions of these approaches are apparent in the area of human relations: many individuals believe the humanistic approach has helped them to understand themselves and others better. And the approaches have facilitated our ability to effectively communicate with others.

A weakness of the humanistic approach is that it is hard to test scientifically. Self-actualization, for example, is not clearly defined. Psychologists are not certain how to study this concept empirically. Some humanists even scorn the experimental approach, preferring clinical interpretation as a data base. Verification of humanistic concepts has come mainly from clinical experiences rather than from controlled experimental studies. Some critics also believe humanistic psychologists are too optimistic about human nature, overestimating the freedom and rationality of humans. And some critics say the humanists encourage self-love and narcissism.

We have seen that the behavioral and social learning approaches, and the phenomenological and humanistic approaches, take different paths to understand development. A summary of the main ideas in these approaches is presented in concept table 2.2.

Figure 2.10   Maslow's hierarchy of motives. Abraham Maslow developed the hierarchy of human motives to show how we have to satisfy certain basic needs before we can satisfy higher needs. In the diagram, lower level needs are shown toward the base of the pyramid, higher level needs toward the peak. The lowest needs (those that have to be satisfied first) are physiological—hunger, thirst, and sleep, for example. The next needs that have to be satisfied are safety needs, which ensure our survival— protection from crime and war, for example. Then, we have to satisfy love and belongingness needs—the security, affection, and attention of others, for example. Almost at the top of Maslow's hierarchy are self-esteem needs—the need to feel good about ourselves as we learn skills, pursue a profession, and deal with people, for example. And finally, at the top of the pyramid and the highest of Maslow's needs, are self-actualization needs—reaching our full potential as human beings. Included among self-actualization needs are a motivation for truth, goodness, beauty, wholeness, and justice.

Self-actualization

Self-esteem

Love and belongingness

Safety

Physiological

Concept Table 2.2: The Behavioral and Social Learning Approaches and the Phenomenological and Humanistic Approaches

Concept	Processes/Related Ideas	Characteristics/Description
The Behavioral and Social Learning Approaches	Skinner's Behaviorism	Behaviorism emphasizes that cognition is unimportant in understanding behavior. Development is observed behavior, which is influenced by rewards and punishments in the environment. Behavior varies according to the situation.
	Social Learning Theory	The environment is an important determinant of behavior, but so are cognitive processes. We have the capability of controlling our own behavior through thoughts, beliefs, and values. Bandura's emphasis on observational learning highlights cognitive aspects of social learning theory.
	Evaluating the Behavioral and Social Learning Approaches	Strengths of both approaches include emphases on environmental determinants and a scientific climate for investigating behavior, as well as an emphasis on cognitive processes and self-control in the social learning approach. The behavioral view has been criticized for taking the person out of development, and for ignoring cognition. These approaches have not given adequate attention to enduring individual differences, to biological factors, and to development as a whole.
The Phenomenological and Humanistic Approaches	Their Nature	The phenomenological approach emphasizes our perceptions of ourselves and our world; it underscores the belief that reality is what is perceived. The humanistic approach is the most widely known phenomenological perspective.
	Carl Rogers' Approach	Each of us is a victim of conditional positive regard. The result is that our real self is not valued. The self is the core of development; it includes both the real and the ideal self. Rogers said we can help others develop a more positive self-concept in three ways: unconditional positive regard, empathy, and genuineness. Rogers also stressed that each of us has the innate, inner capacity to become a fully functioning person.
	Abraham Maslow's Approach	Maslow called the humanistic movement the "third force" in psychology. Each of us has a self-actualizing capacity. Maslow distinguishes between deficiency needs and self-actualization needs, or metaneeds.
	Evaluating the Phenomenological and Humanistic Approaches	They sensitized us to the importance of subjective experience, consciousness, self-conception, the whole person, and our innate, positive nature. Weaknesses focus on the absence of an empirical orientation, a tendency to be too optimistic, and an inclination to encourage self-love.

Figure 2.11 Ethologist Konrad Lorenz and imprinted graylag geese. Lorenz, a pioneering student of animal behavior, is followed through the water by three imprinted graylag geese.

The tide of evolution carries everything before it, thoughts no less than bodies, and persons no less than nations.

~ *George Santayana,*
Little Essays, *1920*

Ethological Theories

Sensitivity to different kinds of experience varies over the individual's life cycle. The presence or absence of certain experiences at particular times in the life span influences the individual well beyond the time that they first occur. Ethologists believe that most psychologists underestimate the importance of these special time frames in early development and the biological influences on development.

Lorenz's Classical Ethological Theory

Ethology emerged as an important view because of the work of European zoologists, especially Konrad Lorenz. **Ethology** *stresses that behavior is strongly influenced by biology, is tied to evolution, and is characterized by critical or sensitive periods.*

Working mostly with graylag geese, Lorenz (1965) studied a behavior pattern that was considered to be programmed within the genes of the animals. A newly hatched gosling seemed to be born with the instinct for following its mother. Observations showed that the gosling was capable of such behavior as soon as it was hatched from the egg. Lorenz proved that it was incorrect to assume that such behavior was programmed in the animal.

In a remarkable set of experiments, Lorenz separated the eggs laid by one female goose into two groups. One group he returned to the female goose to be hatched by her; the other group was hatched in an incubator. The goslings in the first group performed as predicted; they followed their mother as soon as they were hatched. But those in the second group, who saw Lorenz when they were first hatched, followed him everywhere, just as though he were their mother. Lorenz marked the goslings and then placed both groups under a box. Mother goose and "mother" Lorenz stood aside as the box lifted. Each group of goslings went directly to its "mother" (see figure 2.11). Lorenz called this process **imprinting**—*the ethological concept of rapid, innate learning within a limited critical period of time that involves attachment to the first moving object seen.*

The ethological view of Lorenz and the European zoologists forced American developmental psychologists to recognize the importance of the biological basis of behavior. But the research and theorizing of ethology still lacked some ingredients that would elevate it to the ranks of the other theories already discussed in this chapter. In particular, little or nothing was included in the classical ethological view about the nature of social relationships across the human life cycle, something that any major theory of development must explain. And the concept of **critical period**—*a fixed time period very early in development during which certain behaviors optimally emerge*—was overdrawn. Classical ethological theory had been weak in stimulating studies with humans. Recent expansion of the ethological view has improved its status as a viable developmental perspective.

Hinde's Neo-Ethological Theory

British ethologist Robert Hinde (1983, 1989) developed a view that goes beyond classical ethological theory. **Neo-ethological theory** *is Hinde's view that emphasizes sensitive rather than critical periods of development, social development and relationships, and application of ethological theory to human development.* Insight into Hinde's neo-ethological theory appears in the following discussion of selected issues of interest to ethologists.

Robert Hinde, British ethologist, developed the neo-ethological theory of development. Hinde is a professor of psychology at Cambridge University in England.

Like behaviorists, ethologists are careful observers of behavior. Unlike behaviorists, ethologists believe that laboratories are not good settings for observing behavior; rather, they observe behavior in its natural surroundings. Behavior should be meticulously observed in homes, playgrounds, neighborhoods, schools, hospitals, and so on.

Ethologists also point out that children's development is studied by adults, who see the end point of development as mature adulthood. However, ethologists believe that the behavior of infants or children should not always be considered in terms of its importance for mature adulthood. Rather, a behavior may only be adaptive at an early stage of development. For example, caterpillars are excellent leaf eaters, but they do not pretend to be butterflies. Ethologists believe the word development too often diverts attention from viewing each stage of development in its own right.

Ethologists emphasize sensitive periods. Hinde distinguishes between critical and sensitive periods. Classical ethologists, such as Lorenz, argued for the importance of critical periods in development. A **sensitive period** *is the ethological concept that describes a more flexible band of time for behavior to emerge than does the concept of a critical period.* Sensitive periods occur within months or years rather than weeks or days. For children, sensitive periods for language, vision, and attachment have been proposed (Bornstein, 1987; Bowlby, 1989).

Some ethologists are also becoming interested in social relationships and personality. Hinde argues that certain properties of relationships, such as synchrony and competitiveness, do not describe individuals in isolation. Relationships have properties that emerge from the frequency and patterning of interactions over time. For example, if the mother-infant relationship is studied at one point in development, researchers may not be able to describe it as rejecting, controlling, or permissive. But detailed observations over a period of time may make such categorization possible.

Evaluating the Ethological Theories

Ethological theory emphasizes the biological and evolutionary basis of behavior, giving biology an appropriate, prominent role in development. Ethologists use careful observations in naturalistic surroundings to obtain information about development. And ethologists believe development involves sensitive periods.

However, like other theories we have discussed, ethology has its weaknesses. The critical period concept is too rigid for human development, and at times, even the emphasis on sensitive periods seems to be too rigid. The emphasis still slants more toward biological-evolutionary explanations of development than toward a biological-environmental mix. Another criticism of ethological theory is the virtual absence of attention to cognitive processes and development. The theory has been slow in generating research about human development. And the theory is better at explaining behavior retrospectively than prospectively. That is, ethology is better at explaining what caused a child's behavior after it happens than predicting its occurrence in the future.

Ecological Theory

At approximately the same time Robert Hinde was developing his biologically based neo-ethological theory, Cornell University developmental psychologist Urie Bronfenbrenner (1979, 1986, 1989) was proposing a sociocultural view of development. **Ecological theory** *is Bronfenbrenner's sociocultural view of development, which consists of five environmental systems, ranging from the fine-grained inputs of direct interactions with social agents to the broad-based inputs of culture. The five systems in Bronfenbrenner's ecological theory are: microsystem, mesosystem, exosystem, macrosystem, and chronosystem,* each of which we consider in turn. Bronfenbrenner's ecological model is shown in figure 2.12.

Environmental Systems

The **microsystem** *in Bronfenbrenner's ecological theory is the setting in which the individual lives. These contexts include the person's family, peers, school, and neighborhood. It is in the microsystem that the most direct interactions with social agents take place—with parents, peers, and teachers, for example.* The individual is not viewed as a passive recipient of experiences in these settings, but as someone who helps to construct the settings. Bronfenbrenner points out that most research on sociocultural influences has focused on microsystems.

The **mesosystem** *in Bronfenbrenner's ecological theory involves relations between microsystems or connections between contexts. Examples are the relation of family experiences to school experiences, school experiences to church experiences, and family experiences to peer experiences.* For example, children whose parents have rejected them may have difficulty developing positive relations with teachers. Developmentalists increasingly believe it is important to observe behavior in multiple settings—such as family, peer, and school contexts—to obtain a more complete picture of the individual's development.

The **exosystem** *in Bronfenbrenner's ecological theory is involved when experiences in another social setting—in which the individual does not have an active role—influence what the individual experiences in an immediate context.* For example, work experiences may affect a woman's relationship with her husband and their child. The mother may receive a promotion that requires more travel, which might increase marital conflict and change patterns of parent-child interaction. Another example of an exosystem is the city government, which is responsible for the quality of parks, recreation centers, and library facilities for children and adolescents. And yet another example is the federal government through its role in the quality of medical care and support systems for the elderly.

Urie Bronfenbrenner developed ecological theory, a sociocultural approach that emphasizes five environmental systems.

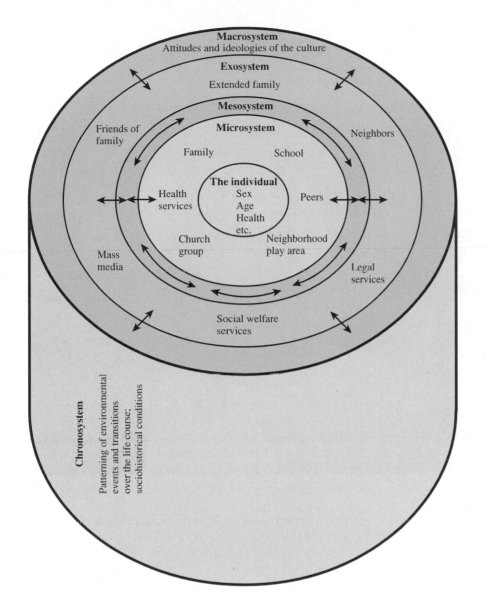

Figure 2.12 Bronfenbrenner's ecological theory of development. Bronfenbrenner's ecological theory consists of five environmental systems: microsystem, mesosystem, exosystem, macrosystem, and chronosystem.

The **macrosystem** *in Bronfenbrenner's ecological theory involves the culture in which individuals live.* **Culture** *refers to the behavior patterns, beliefs, and all other products of a particular group of people that are passed on from generation to generation.* A cultural group can be as large and complex as the United States or it can be as small as an African hunter-gatherer group. Whatever its size, the group's culture influences the identity, learning, and social behavior of its members (Whiting, 1989). For example, the United States is a very achievement-oriented culture with a strong work ethic, but recent comparisons of American and Japanese children revealed that Japanese children were better at math, spent more time working on math in school, and spent much more time doing math homework than American children (Corser, Stevenson, & Lee, 1989). Cross-cultural studies, the comparison of one culture with one or more other cultures, provide information about the generality of life-span development. More information about the role of culture in personality and development is presented in Cultural Worlds of Development 2.1.

Cultural standards for dating and marriage often vary considerably. For example, in Xinjiang, China, courtship involves a horseback chase. A woman mounts a horse and her suitor must chase her, kiss her, and evade her riding crop—all on the gallop. In 1981, a new marriage law took effect in China. The law sets a minimum age for marriage at 22 years for males and 20 years for females. Late marriage and late childbirth are China's critical efforts to control population growth.

Another important dimension of culture is **ethnicity** *(the word ethnic comes from the Greek word for "nation"), which is based on cultural heritage, nationality characteristics, religion, and language.* Every human being is a member of one or more ethnic groups. As we discussed in chapter 1, nowhere are sociocultural changes in American life more profound than the rapidly increasing ethnic diversity of its citizens (Miller, 1989). An important theme of this textbook is to provide a wide-ranging portrait of cultural and ethnic diversity in life-span development.

The **chronosystem** *in Bronfenbrenner's ecological theory involves the patterning of environmental events and transitions over the life course and sociohistorical circumstances.* For example, in one investigation, family processes researcher Mavis Hetherington and her colleagues (Hetherington, 1989; Hetherington, Cox, & Cox, 1982) found that the disruptive effects of divorce peaked one year after the divorce with the effects being more negative for sons than for daughters. By two years after the divorce, family interaction was less chaotic and more stable. In another example of the chronosystem, life-span developmentalist Glenn Elder and his colleagues (Elder & Caspi, in press; Elder, Caspi, & Downey, 1986) found that the presence of an irritable father or an irritable child increases the probability that unemployment will have long-range negative consequences for life-span development. Also critical was the presence of marital conflict, which often arose, or became exacerbated, following the father's loss of a job.

The Life-Span Developmental Perspective

CULTURE AND PERSONALITY—
INDIVIDUALISTIC AND COLLECTIVISTIC ORIENTATIONS

*B*ecause the concept of personality or self, like other concepts, is socially constructed, it is likely to involve at least some cross-cultural variation (Kagitcibasi & Berry, 1989). Many of the assumptions about personality have been developed in Western cultures, cultures that emphasize the individual or self. Self-oriented terms dominate thinking about personality in Western cultures like the United States—self-concept, self-awareness, self-actualization, self-efficacy, self-reinforcement, self-criticism, self-serving, selfishness, self-doubt, and so on (Lonner, 1988).

Many non-Western cultures—including Communist countries such as Russia, and Eastern countries such as Japan, China, and India—are collectivistic rather than individualistic (Hui & Villareal, 1989; Kagitcibasi, 1988; Triandis, 1985). *Individualistic* refers to an individual or self-orientation that involves separating the self from others. *Collectivistic* refers to a group orientation that involves relating the self to others. In one investigation of 40 nations, an individualistic versus a collectivistic orientation was a basic dimension of national culture (Hofstede, 1980).

Critics of the individualistic, self-orientation of Western personality conceptions point out that human beings have always lived in groups, communities, and societies, mutually needing one another. However, the individualistic orientation of many Western cultures, especially the United States, may undermine our species' basic need for relatedness (Kagitcibasi, 1988). Some social scientists believe that many of our problems, such

In Japan, school children wear the same clothes, reflecting the collective orientation of the Japanese culture.

as anxiety, depression, and shyness, would not be as intense if the American cultural emphasis on the self and independence were not so strong (Munroe & Munroe, 1975). The pendulum may have swung too far in the individualistic direction in Western cultures. We underscore the belief that to develop a healthy, optimal personality, all people in all cultures need to develop a positive sense of self *and* a positive connectedness with others.

A cherished attribute for American children is the development of autonomy or independence, which is believed to be a prerequisite for an ideal personality. Many American parents train their children to be independent or self-sufficient at an early age. However, in many non-Western cultures, parents and other adults train children to be more other- or group-oriented. These non-Western cultures include Russia, China, Japan, and Israel. In North America, many Mexican parents also train their children to be more

other- and group-oriented than American parents do (Holtzmann, 1982).

In Russia, from the earliest years in school, the peer group is enlisted to help adult authorities teach and enforce the culture's social values (Bronfenbrenner, 1970). Evaluation of the individual's behavior is primarily in terms of how well it matches the collective's goals and aims. To encourage group identification and pride, interclass and interschool competitions are frequently held. In the school, the social unit may be the rows of pupils in a classroom, later it may be the "cell" of the Communist Youth Organization.

In Japan, beginning in kindergarten, children wear the same uniform, including caps, which are of different colors to indicate their respective classrooms. They have identical sets of equipment kept in identical drawers and shelves. This is not intended to turn the young Japanese children into robots, as some Americans have pondered, but to impress upon them that other people just like them have needs and rights that are equally important (Hendry, 1986). In sum, our American culture needs to emphasize a stronger sense of connectedness as well a positive development of self.

The individualistic-collectivistic dichotomy has not gone uncriticized. Describing entire nations of people as having a basic personality obscures the extensive diversity and individual variation that characterizes a nation's people. Also, certain values serve both individual and collective interests, such as wisdom, mature love, and a broad-minded orientation (Schwartz, 1990).

Evaluating Ecological Theory

Bronfenbrenner's ecological model is one of the few comprehensive frameworks for understanding the environment's role in development. The model includes both micro (molecular) and macro (molar) aspects of environmental, sociocultural influences on development. Bronfenbrenner's most recent addition to the model—the chronosystem—takes into account development over time and sociohistorical influences on development.

The main weaknesses of the ecological model are its failure to adequately account for the influence of both biological and cognitive processes.

An Eclectic Theoretical Orientation

No single indomitable theory is capable of explaining the rich complexity of life-span development. Each of the theories described in this chapter has made important contributions to our understanding of life-span development, but none provides a complete description and explanation. Psychoanalytic theory best explains the unconscious mind. Erikson's theory best describes the changes that occur in adult development. Piaget's theory is the most complete description of children's cognitive development. The behavioral, social learning, and ecological theories have been the most adept at examining the environmental determinants of development. The phenomenological and humanistic theories have given us the most insight about self-conception. And the ethological theories have made us aware of biology's role and the influence of sensitive periods in development. It is important to recognize that, while theories are helpful guides in understanding life-span development, relying on a single theory to explain life-span development probably is a mistake.

An attempt was made in this chapter to present six theoretical perspectives objectively. The same eclectic orientation will be maintained throughout the book. In this way, you can view the study of life-span development as it actually exists—with different theorists making different assumptions about development, stressing different empirical problems, and using different strategies to discover information about life-span development.

These theoretical perspectives, along with the research issues and methods described in chapter 1, provide a sense of life-span development's scientific nature. Table 2.2 compares the main theoretical perspectives in terms of how they view some of the issues we have discussed thus far. By studying table 2.2, you should be able to integrate some of the most important ideas about issues and methods described in chapter 1 with the main theories described in this chapter.

In thinking about theories of life-span development be sure to keep in mind the life-span perspective discussed in chapter 1. Recall that the life-span perspective has been a late-developing view and many of the theories presented in this chapter were already in place when the life-span perspective was formulated. As a perspective, the life-span view coordinates a number of theoretical principles about the nature of development. Although these principles of the life-span perspective are not new, the strength of the beliefs and the coordination of principles represent a novel, unique approach to development (Baltes, 1987).

Remember that from a life-span perspective, development is seen as life-long, multidirectional, multidimensional, plastic, historically embedded, contextual, and multidisciplinary. By considering the ideas of various developmental theorists discussed in this chapter along with the chracteristics of the life-span perspective, we can get a sense of the theoretical concepts that are

The Life-Span Developmental Perspective

Table 2.2: Theoretical Comparisons and Issues and Methods in Life-Span Development

Issues and Methods	Theories					
	Psychoanalytic	*Cognitive*	*Behavioral and Social Learning*	*Phenomenological and Humanistic*	*Ethological*	*Ecological*
Continuity and Discontinuity, Stability and Change	Discontinuity between stages, but continuity between early experiences and later development; later changes in development emphasized in Erikson's theory.	Discontinuity between stages, but continuity between early experiences and later development in Piaget's theory; this has not been an important issue to information processing psychologists.	Continuity (no stages). Experience at all points of development is important.	Continuity (no stages). Experience at all points in development is important, especially immediate experience.	Discontinuity but no stages are given; critical or sensitive periods are emphasized.	Little attention is given to continuity-discontinuity issue; change emphasized more than stability.
Biological and Environmental Factors	Freud stressed biological determination interacting with early experiences in the family; Erikson provides a more balanced biological-cultural interaction perspective.	Piaget emphasizes interaction and adaptation. Environment provides the setting for cognitive structures to develop. Information processing perspective has not addressed this issue extensively, but hardware-software metaphor emphasizes biological-environmental interaction.	Environment is viewed as the cause of behavior in both the behavioral and social learning views.	Environmental influences are emphasized, especially warmth and nurturance.	Strong biological view.	Strong environmental view.
Importance of Cognition	Cognition is emphasized, but in the form of unconscious thought.	Cognition is the primary determinant of behavior.	Cognition is strongly deemphasized in the behavioral approach but plays an important mediating role in the social learning approach.	Cognition is important, especially in the form of self-perception.	Cognition is not emphasized.	Cognition is not emphasized.
Research Methods	Clinical interviews, unstructured personality tests, and psychohistorical analyses of lives.	Interviews and observations.	Observation, especially laboratory observation.	The scientific approach is deemphasized; self-report measures and interviews are used.	Observation in natural settings.	Emphasizes use of varied methods; especially stresses importance of collecting data in different social contexts.

Concept Table 2.3: Ethological Theories, Ecological Theory, and an Eclectic Theoretical Orientation

Concept	Processes/Related Ideas	Characteristics/Description
The Ethological Theories	Lorenz's Classical Ethological Theory	The biological and evolutionary basis of development needs to be emphasized. Critical periods, at which time a characteristic has an optimal time of emergence, occur in development.
	Hinde's Neo-ethological Theory	Neo-ethological theory emphasizes sensitive rather than critical periods; it also places a premium on naturalistic observation and biological/evolutionary ties but also focuses on social relationships and personality.
	Evaluating the Ethological Theories	Strengths include an emphasis on the biological and evolutionary basis of behavior, naturalistic observation, and sensitive periods. Weaknesses include the rigidity of the critical period concept, an overemphasis on biology and evolution, a failure to generate studies of human development, and the inability to predict behavior prospectively.
Ecological Theory	Bronfenbrenner's Model	In Bronfenbrenner's ecological theory, five environmental systems are described: microsystem, mesosystem, exosystem, macrosystem, and chronosystem.
	Evaluation	Bronfenbrenner's theory provides one of the few comprehensive models of environmental influences on development. Both macro and micro aspects of environmental influence are included. Criticisms focus on the lack of emphasis on biological and cognitive processes.
An Eclectic Theoretical Orientation	Its Nature	No single theory can explain the rich, awesome complexity of life-span development. Each of the theories has made a different contribution, and it probably is a wise strategy to adopt an eclectic theoretical perspective as we attempt to understand life-span development. As a perspective, the life-span view coordinates a number of theoretical principles about the nature of development. By considering the ideas of the life-span perspective along with the developmental theories discussed in this chapter, we can get a sense of the theoretical concepts that are important in understanding life-span development.

important in understanding life-span development. You may want to review these characteristics of the life-span perspective at this time (see chapter 1) as you think about an eclectic approach to life-span development.

At this point we have discussed a number of ideas about ethological theories, ecological theory, and an eclectic theoretical orientation. A summary of these ideas is presented in concept table 2.3. This chapter concludes our discussion of Section I: "The Life-Span Developmental Perspective." In Section II: "Beginnings," we begin our journey through the human life cycle, starting with chapter 3, "Biological Beginnings."

The Life-Span Developmental Perspective

Summary

I. Freud's Theory

Freud said that our personality has three structures—id, ego, and superego—which conflict with each other. Most of our thoughts are unconscious in Freud's view, and the id is completely unconscious. The conflicting demands of personality structures produce anxiety; defense mechanisms, especially repression, protect the ego and reduce anxiety. Freud was convinced that problems develop because of childhood experiences. He said we go through five psychosexual stages—oral, anal, phallic, latency, and genital. During the phallic stage, the Oedipus complex is a main source of conflict.

II. Erikson's Theory and Evaluation of the Psychoanalytic Theories

Erikson developed a theory that emphasizes eight psychosocial stages of development: trust vs. mistrust, autonomy vs. shame and doubt, initiative vs. guilt, industry vs. inferiority, identity vs. identity confusion, intimacy vs. isolation, generativity vs. stagnation, and integrity vs. despair. Strengths of the psychoanalytic theories are an emphasis on the past, the developmental course of personality, mental representation of the environment, unconscious mind, and emphasis on conflict. Weaknesses are the difficulty in testing main concepts, lack of an empirical data base and over-reliance on past reports, too much emphasis on sexuality and the unconscious mind, and a negative view of human nature.

III. Piaget's Theory

Piaget's theory is responsible for the field of cognitive development. He believed we are motivated to understand our world and use the processes of organization and adaptation (assimilation and accommodation) to do so. Piaget said that we go through four cognitive stages: sensorimotor, preoperational, concrete operational, and formal operational.

IV. Information Processing Approach and Evaluation of the Cognitive Theories

The information processing approach is concerned with how we process information about our world. It includes how information gets into the mind, how it is stored and transformed, and how it is retrieved to think and solve problems. The development of the computer promoted this approach; the mind as an information processing system was compared to the way a computer processes information. The information processing approach raises questions about life-span development, among them the rise and decline of speed of processing information. Both the Piagetian and information processing approaches have made important contributions to life-span development. They have provided a positive, rational portrayal of humans as they develop, although they may have underestimated the importance of unconscious thought and environmental experiences. The purity of Piaget's stages has been questioned, and the information processing approach has not yet prodocued an overall perspective on development.

V. Behavioral and Social Learning Theories

Skinner's behaviorism emphasizes that cognition is unimportant in development; development is observed behavior, which is influenced by the rewards and punishments in the environment. In social learning theory, the environment is an important determinant of development, but so are cognitive processes. We have the ability to control our own behavior through thoughts, beliefs, and values. Bandura's emphasis on observational learning and his model of the reciprocal influences of behavior, person (cognition), and environment exemplify social learning theory. The contemporary version of social learning theory is called cognitive social learning theory.

VI. Evaluating the Behavioral and Social Learning Theories

The strengths of both theories include emphasis on environmental determinants and a scientific climate for investigating development, as well as a focus on cognitive processes and self-control in social learning theory. The behavioral view has been criticized for taking the person out of development and for ignoring cognition. These approaches have not adequately considered biological factors and development as a whole.

VII. Phenomenological and Humanistic Theories

The phenomenological approach emphasizes our perceptions of ourselves and our world and centers on the belief that reality is what is perceived. The humanistic approach is the most widely known phenomenological approach. In Rogers' theory, each of us is a victim of conditional positive regard. The result is that our real self is not valued. The self is the core of development; it includes the real self and the ideal self. Rogers advocates unconditional positive regard to enhance our self-concept. Each of us has the innate, inner capacity to become a fully functioning person. Maslow called the humanistic approach the third force in psychology. He also proposed that we have a hierarchy of motives, with lower needs requiring satisfaction before higher needs; self-actualization is the highest need. These approaches have sensitized developmentalists to the importance of subjective experience, consciousness, self-conception, the whole person, and our innate, positive nature. Their weaknesses focus on the absence of a scientific orientation, a tendency to be too optimistic, and an inclination to encourage self-love.

VIII. Ethological Theories

Ethological theories emphasize the biological and evolutionary basis of development. In Lorenz's classical ethological theory, critical periods—optimal time periods for the emergence of a characteristic—are emphasized. In Hinde's neo-ethological theory, sensitive periods rather than critical periods are stressed, along with naturalistic observation, social relationships, and personality. Strengths include the emphasis on biological and evolutionary bases of behavior, naturalistic observation, and sensitive periods. Weaknesses include the rigidity of critical periods, an overemphasis on biology and evolution, a failure to generate studies of human development, and the inability to predict behavior prospectively.

IX. Ecological Theory

In Bronfenbrenner's ecological theory, five environmental systems are described: microsystem, mesosystem, exosystem, macrosystem, and chronosystem. Bronfenbrenner's theory provides one of the few comprehensive models of environmental influences on development. Both macro and micro aspects of environmental influence are included. Criticisms focus on the lack of attention to biological and cognitive processes.

X. An Eclectic Theoretical Orientation

No single theory can explain the rich, awesome complexity of life-span development. Each of the theories has made a different contribution, and it is probably wise to adopt an eclectic theoretical perspective as we attempt to understand life-span development. As a perspective, the life-span view coordinates a number of theoretical principles about the nature of development. By considering the ideas of the life-span perspective along with the developmental theories discussed in this chapter, we can get a sense of the theoretical concepts that are important in understanding life-span development.

Key Terms

id 42
pleasure principle 42
ego 42
reality principle 42
superego 43
defense mechanisms 43
repression 43
rationalization 43
displacement 44
sublimation 44
projection 44
reaction formation 44
regression 44
erogenous zones 45
fixation 45
oral stage 45
anal stage 45
phallic stage 45
Oedipus complex 45
latency stage 48
genital stage 48

epigenetic principle 50
trust versus mistrust 50
autonomy versus shame and doubt 50
initiative versus guilt 50
industry versus inferiority 50
identity versus identity confusion 50
intimacy versus isolation 51
generativity versus stagnation 51
integrity versus despair 51
assimilation 54
accommodation 54
sensorimotor stage 54
preoperational stage 55
concrete operational stage 55
formal operational stage 55
information processing approach 55
behaviorism 60
operant conditioning 60
reinforcement 60
punishment 60
social learning theory 60
phenomenological approach 62

humanistic approach 62
conditional positive regard 63
self-concept 63
unconditional positive regard 64
hierarchy of needs 65
self-actualization 65
deficiency needs 65
metaneeds 65
ethology 68
imprinting 68
critical period 69
neo-ethological theory 69
sensitive period 69
ecological theory 70
microsystem 70
mesosystem 70
exosystem 70
macrosystem 71
culture 71
ethnicity 72
chronosystem 72

The Life-Span Developmental Perspective

Suggested Readings

Bandura, A. (1986). *Social foundations of thought and action.* Englewood Cliffs, NJ: Prentice-Hall.
This book presents Bandura's cognitive social learning view of development, including an emphasis on reciprocal connections between behavior, environment, and the individual.

Bronfenbrenner, U. (1986). Ecology of the family as a context for human development: Research perspectives. *Developmental Psychology, 22,* 723–742.
In this article, Bronfenbrenner adds the chronosystem to his other four environmental systems. Includes discussion of a number of research studies involving various environmental systems.

Cowan, P. (1978). *Piaget with feeling.* New York: Holt, Rinehart, & Winston.
Provides a well-written overview of Piaget's theory and draws implications for understanding children's emotional development.

Erikson, E. H. (1968). *Identity: Youth and crisis.* New York: W. W. Norton. *Must reading for anyone interested in developmental psychology. Erikson outlines his eight stages of the life cycle and talks extensively about identity.*

Hinde, R. (1983). Ethology and child development. In P. H. Mussen (Ed.), *Handbook of child psychology* (4th ed. Vol. 2). New York: Wiley. *Hinde's views are strongly influencing thinking about child development. Here he outlines the questions ethologists ask and the issues they research.*

Miller, P. H. (1989). *Theories of developmental psychology* (2nd ed.). New York: W. H. Freeman. *An excellent presentation and evaluation of a number of the developmental theories discussed in this chapter.*

Shostrum, E. (1967). *Man, the manipulator.* New York: Bantam Books. *Shostrum presents an intriguing humanistic perspective on development, including many helpful ideas about adjustment and self-evaluation.*

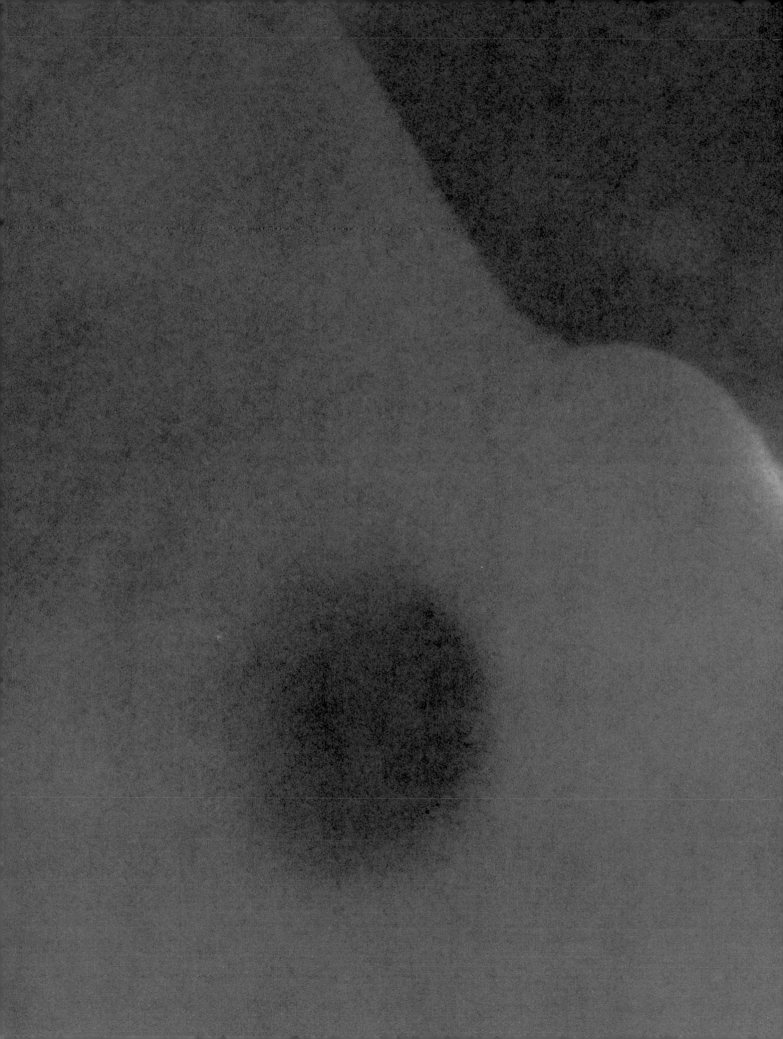

S·E·C·T·I·O·N

II

BEGINNINGS

*W*hat endless questions vex the
thought, of whence and whither,
when and how.

Sir Richard Burton, Kasidah

CHAPTER 3

Biological Beginnings

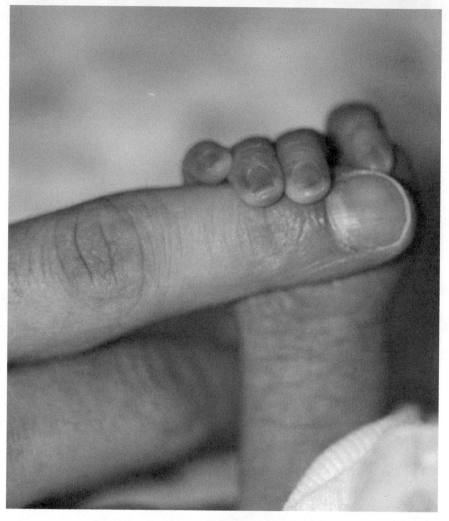

*J*im Springer and Jim Lewis are identical twins. They were separated at 4 weeks of age and did not see each other again until they were 39 years old. Both worked as part-time deputy sheriffs, vacationed in Florida, drove Chevrolets, had dogs named Toy, and married and divorced women named Betty. One twin named his son James Allan, and the other named his son James Alan. Both liked math but not spelling, enjoyed carpentry and mechanical drawing, chewed their fingernails down to the nubs, had almost identical drinking and smoking habits, had hemorrhoids, put on ten pounds at about the same point in development, first suffered headaches at the age of 18, and had similar sleep patterns.

But Jim and Jim had some differences. One wore his hair over his forehead, the other slicked it back and had sideburns. One expressed himself best orally, the other was more proficient in writing. But for the most part, their profiles were remarkably similar.

Another pair, Daphne and Barbara, were called the "giggle sisters" because they were always making each other laugh. A thorough search of their adoptive families' histories revealed no gigglers. And the identical sisters handled stress by ignoring it, avoided conflict and controversy whenever possible, and showed no interest in politics.

Two other female identical twin sisters were separated at 6 weeks and reunited in their fifties. Both had nightmares, which they describe in hauntingly similar ways: Both dreamed of doorknobs and fishhooks in their mouths as they smothered to death! The nightmares began during early adolescence and had stopped in the last 10 to 12 years. Both women were bed wetters until about 12 or 13 years of age, and they reported educational and marital histories that were remarkably similar.

These sets of twins are part of the Minnesota Study of Twins Reared Apart, directed by Thomas Bouchard and his colleagues. They bring identical twins (identical genetically because they come from the same egg) and fraternal twins (dissimilar genetically because they come from two eggs) from all over the world to Minneapolis to investigate their lives. The twins are given a number of personality tests, and detailed medical histories are obtained, including information about diet, smoking, exercise habits, chest X-rays, heart stress tests, and EEGs (brain-wave tests). The twins are interviewed and asked more than 15,000 questions about their family and childhood environment, personal interests, vocational orientation, values, and aesthetic judgments. They are also given ability and intelligence tests (Bouchard & others, 1981; Bouchard & others, 1990; McGue & Bouchard, 1989).

Critics of the Minnesota identical twins study point out that some of the separated twins were together several months before their adoption, that some of the twins had been reunited before their testing (in some cases, a number of years earlier), that adoption agencies often place twins in similar homes, and that even strangers who spend several hours together and start comparing their lives are likely to come up with some coincidental similarities (Adler, 1991). Still, even in the face of such criticism, the Minnesota study of identical twins indicates how scientists have recently shown an increased interest in the genetic basis of human development, and that we need further research on genetic and environmental factors.

The examples of Jim and Jim, the giggle sisters, and the identical twins who had the same nightmares stimulate us to think about our genetic heritage and the biological foundations of our existence. Organisms are not like billiard balls, moved by simple, external forces to predictable positions on life's pool table. Environmental experiences and biological foundations work together to make us who we are. Our coverage of life's biological beginnings focuses on evolution, genetics, heredity's influence on development, and the interaction of heredity and environment.

Biological Beginnings

Jim Springer (a), and Jim Lewis (b). These identical twins were separated at the age of 4 weeks and didn't see each other again until they were 39 years old. As adults they showed remarkably similar behavior patterns.

(a)   (b)

The Evolutionary Perspective

In evolutionary time, humans are relative newcomers to Earth, yet we have established ourselves as the most successful and dominant species. If we consider evolutionary time in terms of a calendar year, humans arrived here late in December (Sagan, 1977). As our earliest ancestors left the forest to feed on the savannahs, and finally to form hunting societies on the open plains, their minds and behaviors changed. How did this evolution come about?

Natural selection *is the evolutionary process that favors individuals of a species that are best adapted to survive and reproduce.* To understand natural selection, let's return to the middle of the nineteenth century, when Charles Darwin was traveling around the world observing many different species of animals in their natural surroundings. Darwin (1859), who published his observations and thoughts in *On the Origin of Species,* observed that most organisms reproduced at rates that would cause enormous increases in the population of most species, yet populations remained nearly constant. He reasoned that an intense, constant struggle for food, water, and resources must occur among the many young born in each generation, because many of the young do not survive. Those that do survive pass their genes on to the next generation. Darwin believed that those who do survive to reproduce are probably superior in a number of ways to those who do not. In other words, the survivors are better adapted to their world than the nonsurvivors. Over the course of many generations, organisms with the characteristics needed for survival would comprise a larger percentage of the population. Over many, many generations, this could produce a gradual modification of the whole population. If environmental conditions change, however, other characteristics might develop, moving the process in a different direction.

Over a million species have been classified, from bacteria to blue whales, with many varieties of beetles in between. The work of natural selection produced the disappearing acts of moths and the quills of porcupines. And the effects of evolution produced the technological advances, intelligence, and longer parental care of human beings (see figure 3.1).

Generally, evolution proceeds at a very slow pace. The lines that led to the emergence of human beings and the great apes diverged about 14 million

What seest thou else in the dark backward and abysm of time.

~ *William Shakespeare,*
The Tempest

I am a brother to dragons, and a companion to owls.

~ *Job 30:29*

Beginnings

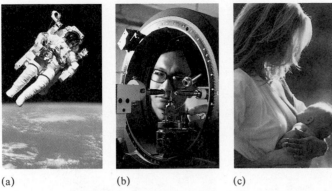

(a)   (b)   (c)

Figure 3.1   The better an animal is adapted, the more successful it becomes. Humans, more than any other mammal, adapt to and control most types of environments. (a) Technological advances give greater freedom of movement and independence; (b) greater intelligence leads to the use of complex objects that enhance life: and (c) longer parental care allows humans to learn more complex behavior patterns, which contribute to adaptation.

years ago! Modern humans, *Homo sapiens,* came into existence only about 50,000 years ago. And the beginning of civilization as we know it began about 10,000 years ago. No sweeping evolutionary changes in humans occurred since then—for example, our brain is not ten times as big, we do not have a third eye in the back of our heads, and we haven't learned to fly.

While no dramatic evolutionary changes have occurred since *Homo sapiens* appeared on the fossil record 50,000 years ago, there have been sweeping cultural changes. Biological evolution shaped human beings into a culture-making species.

Heredity

Every species must have a mechanism for transmitting characteristics from one generation to the next. This mechanism is explained by the principle of genetics. Each of us carries a genetic code that we inherited from our parents. This code is located within every cell in our bodies. Our genetic codes are alike in one important way—they all contain the human genetic code. Because of the human genetic code, a fertilized human egg cannot grow into an egret, eagle, or elephant.

What Are Genes?

Each of us began life as a single cell weighing about one twenty-millionth of an ounce! This tiny piece of matter housed our entire genetic code—the information about who we would become. These instructions orchestrated growth from that single cell to a person made of trillions of cells, each containing a perfect replica of the original genetic code.

The nucleus of each human cell contains 46 **chromosomes,** *which are threadlike structures that come in 23 pairs, one member of each pair coming from each parent. Chromosomes contain the remarkable genetic substance deoxyribonucleic acid, or DNA.* **DNA** *is a complex molecule that contains genetic information.* DNA's "double helix" shape looks like a spiral staircase (see figure 3.2). **Genes,** *the units of hereditary information, are short segments of the DNA "staircase." Genes act as a blueprint for cells to reproduce themselves and manufacture the proteins that maintain life.* Chromosomes, DNA, and genes can be mysterious. To help you turn mystery into understanding, see figure 3.3.

There are one hundred and ninety-three living species of monkeys and apes. One-hundred and ninety-two of them are covered with hair. The exception is the naked ape self-named, homo-sapiens.

~ *Desmond Morris,*
The Naked Ape, *1967*

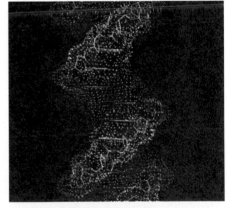

Figure 3.2   The remarkable substance known as DNA. Notice that the DNA molecule is shaped like a spiral staircase. Genes are short segments of the DNA molecule. The horizontal bars that look like the rungs of a ladder play a key role in locating the identity of a gene.

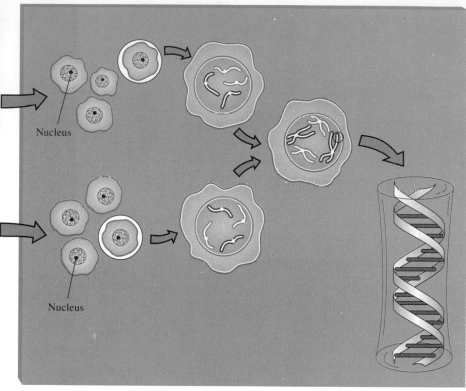

Figure 3.3 *Facts about chromosomes, DNA, and genes. The body contains billions of cells that are organized into tissue and organs. Each cell contains a central structure, the nucleus, which controls reproduction. Chromosomes reside in the nucleus of each cell. The male's sperm and the female's egg are specialized reproductive cells that contain chromosomes. At conception the offspring receives matching chromosomes from the mother's egg and the father's sperm. The chromosomes contain DNA, a chemical substance. Genes are short segments of the DNA molecule. They are the units of hereditary information that act as a blueprint for cells to reproduce themselves and manufacture the proteins that sustain life. The rungs in the DNA ladder are an important location of genes.*

The turtle lives 'twixt plated
decks
Which practically conceal its sex.
I think it clever of the turtle
In such a fix to be so fertile.

~ *Ogden Nash,*
Many Long Years Ago, 1945

Gametes *are human reproduction cells, which are created in the testes of males and the ovaries of females.* **Meiosis** *is the process of cell division in which each pair of chromosomes in the cell separates, with one member of each pair going into each gamete, or daughter cell.* Thus, each human gamete has 23 unpaired chromosomes. **Reproduction** *takes place when a female gamete (ovum) is fertilized by a male gamete (sperm)* (see figure 3.4). A **zygote** *is a single cell formed through fertilization.* In the zygote, two sets of unpaired chromosomes combine to form one set of paired chromosomes—one member of each pair from the mother and the other member from the father. In this manner, each parent contributes 50 percent of the offspring's heredity.

Reproduction

The ovum is about 90,000 times as large as a sperm. Thousands of sperm must combine to break down the ovum's membrane barrier to allow even a single sperm to penetrate the membrane barrier. Ordinarily, females have two X chromosomes and males have one X and one Y chromosome. Because the Y chromosome is smaller and lighter than the X chromosome, Y-bearing sperm can be separated from X-bearing sperm in a centrifuge. This raises the possibility that the offspring's sex can be controlled. Not only are the Y-bearing sperm lighter, but they are more likely than the X-bearing sperm to coat the ovum. This results in the conception of 120 to 150 males for every 100 females. But males are more likely to die (spontaneously abort) at every stage of prenatal development, so only about 106 are born for every 100 females.

Reproduction's fascinating moments have been made even more intriguing in recent years. **In vitro fertilization** *is conception outside the body.* Consider the following situation. The year is 1978. One of the most dazzling occurrences of the 1970s is about to unfold. Mrs. Brown is infertile, but her physician informs her of a new procedure that could enable her to have a baby. The procedure involves removing the mother's ovum surgically, fertilizing it in a laboratory medium with live sperm cells obtained from the father or another male donor (see figure 3.5), storing the fertilized egg in a laboratory solution that substitutes for the uterine environment, and finally implanting the egg in the mother's uterus. For Mrs. Brown, the procedure was successful, and nine months later her daughter Louise was born.

Since the first in vitro fertilization in the 1970s, variations of the procedure have brought hope to childless couples. A woman's egg can be fertilized with the husband's sperm, or the husband and wife may contribute their sperm and egg with the resulting embryo carried by a third party, who essentially is donating her womb. Researchers have not found any developmental deficiencies in children born through in vitro fertilization.

Approximately 10 to 15 percent of couples in the United States are estimated to experience infertility, which is defined as the inability to conceive a child after twelve months of regular intercourse without contraception. The cause of infertility may rest with the woman or the man. The woman may not be ovulating, she may be producing abnormal ova, her fallopian tubes may be blocked, or she may have a disease that prevents implantation of the ova. The man may produce too few sperm, the sperm may lack motility (the ability to move adequately), or he may have a blocked passageway. In one recent investigation, long-term use of cocaine by men was related to low sperm count, low motility, and a high number of abnormally formed sperm (Bracken & others, 1990). Cocaine-related infertility appears to be reversible if users stop taking the drug for at least one year. In some cases of infertility, surgery may correct the problem, in others hormonal-based drugs may improve the probability of having a child. However, in some instances, fertility drugs have caused superovulation, producing as many as three or more babies at a time.

While surgery and fertility drugs can solve the infertility problem in some cases, another choice is to adopt a child. At the time of the adoption, most adoptive parents receive little information about the child's family history, and

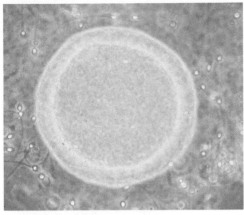

Figure 3.4 *Ovum and sperm. An ovum ready for release has been extracted and put into a nutritive solution together with a drop of specially treated seminal fluid. The sperm are eagerly striving toward the ovum. Notice the difference in size between the ovum and the sperm.*

Figure 3.5 *In vitro fertilization. In vitro fertilization is conception outside of the womb. Here sperm meets egg in a laboratory dish.*

in turn, the child's biological parents are given little information about the adoptive parents. While this policy has been followed by most adoption agencies as being in the child's best interests, it is currently being challenged by a number of activist groups who argue that the sealing of records at the time of adoption violates the basic rights of persons to know about themselves. Researchers have found that adopted children are often more at risk for psychological and school-related problems than nonadopted children (Brodzinky & others, 1984), although some adopted children adapt well to their circumstances (Marquis & Detweiler, 1985). Adolescence is a time when some adopted children show difficulties, when as part of their search for identity, they feel a void and incompleteness because they do not know their biological family's history.

A question that virtually every adoptive parent wants answered is, "Should I tell my adopted child that he or she is adopted? If so, when?" Most psychologists believe that adopted children should be told that they are adopted, because they will eventually find out anyway. Many children begin to ask where they came from when they are approximately 4 to 6 years of age. This is a natural time to begin to respond in simple ways to children about their adopted status. Clinical psychologists report that one problem that sometimes surfaces is the desire of adoptive parents to make life too perfect for the adoptive child and to present perfect images of themselves to the child. The result too often is that adopted children feel that they cannot release any angry feelings and openly discuss problems in this climate of perfection (Warshak, 1991).

Abnormalities in Genes and Chromosomes

Geneticists and psychologists have identified a range of problems caused by some major gene or chromosome defect. **Phenylketonuria (PKU)** *is a genetic disorder in which the individual cannot properly metabolize protein. Phenylketonuria is now easily detected, but if left untreated, mental retardation and hyperactivity result.* When detected, the disorder is treated by diet to keep a poisonous substance from entering the nervous system. Phenylketonuria involves a recessive gene and occurs about once in every 10,000 to 20,000

Beginnings

live births. Phenylketonuria accounts for about 1 percent of institutionalized mentally retarded individuals and it occurs primarily in Whites.

Down syndrome, *the most common genetically transmitted form of mental retardation, is caused by the presence of an extra (47th) chromosome.* An individual with Down syndrome has a round face, a flattened skull, an extra fold of skin over the eyelids, a protruding tongue, short limbs, and retardation of motor and mental abilities. It is not known why the extra chromosome is present, but the health of the male sperm or female ovum may be involved. Women between the ages of 18 and 38 are less likely to give birth to a Down syndrome child than are younger or older women. Down syndrome appears approximately once in every 700 live births. Black children are rarely born with Down syndrome.

Sickle-cell anemia, *which occurs most often in Blacks, is a genetic disorder affecting the red blood cells.* A red blood cell is usually shaped like a disk, but in sickle-cell anemia, a change in a recessive gene modifies its shape to a hook-shaped "sickle." These cells die quickly, causing anemia and early death of the individual because of their failure to carry oxygen to the body's cells. About 1 in 400 Black babies is affected. One in 10 Black Americans is a carrier, as in 1 in 20 Latin Americans (Whaley & Wong, 1989).

Other disorders are associated with sex-chromosome abnormalities. Remember that normal males have an X chromosome and a Y chromosome, and normal females have two X chromosomes. **Klinefelter syndrome** *is a genetic disorder in which males have an extra X chromosome, making them XXY instead of XY.* Males with this disorder have undeveloped testes, and they usually have enlarged breasts and become tall. Klinefelter syndrome occurs approximately once in every 3,000 live male births.

Turner syndrome *is a genetic disorder in which females are missing an X chromosome, making them XO instead of XX.* These women are short in stature and have a webbed neck. They may be mentally retarded and sexually underdeveloped. Turner syndrome occurs approximately once in every 3,000 live female births.

The **XYY syndrome** *is a genetic disorder in which the male has an extra Y chromosome. Early interest in this syndrome involved the belief that the Y chromosome found in males contributed to male aggression and violence.* It was then reasoned that if a male had an extra Y chromosome he would likely be extremely aggressive and possibly develop a violent personality. However, researchers subsequently found that XYY males were no more likely to commit crimes than XY males (Witkin & others, 1976).

Each year in the United States, approximately 100,000 to 150,000 infants are born with a genetic disorder or malformation. These infants comprise about 3 to 5 percent of the 3 million births and account for at least 20 percent of infant deaths. Prospective parents increasingly are turning to genetic counseling for assistance, wanting to know their risk of having a child born with a genetic defect or malformation. To learn more about genetic counseling, turn to Perspective on Life-Span Development 3.1.

Some Genetic Principles

Genetic determination is a complex affair, and much is unknown about the way genes work. But a number of genetic principles have been discovered, among them dominant-recessive genes, sex-linked genes, polygenically inherited characteristics, reaction range, and canalization.

According to the **dominant-recessive genes principle,** *if one gene of the pair is dominant and one is recessive (goes back or recedes), the dominant gene exerts its effect, overriding the potential influence of the other, recessive*

• Critical Thinking •

Imagine that you want to start a family. Probe your family background. What questions would you want to ask a genetic counselor?

GENETIC COUNSELING

◆

*B*ob and Mary Sims have been married for several years. They would like to start a family, but they are frightened. The newspapers and popular magazines are full of stories about infants who are born prematurely and don't survive, infants with debilitating physical defects, and babies found to have congenital mental retardation. The Simses feel that to have such a child would create a social, economic, and psychological strain on them and on society.

Accordingly, the Simses turn to a genetic counselor for help. Genetic counselors are usually physicians or biologists who are well versed in the field of medical genetics. They are familiar with the kinds of problems that can be inherited, the odds for encountering them, and helpful measures for offsetting some of their effects. The Simses tell their counselor that there has been a history of mental retardation in Bob's family. Bob's younger sister was born with Down syndrome, a form of mental retardation. Mary's older brother has hemophilia, a condition in which bleeding is difficult to

When prospective parents visit a genetic counselor, they are asked about the incidence of genetic disorders in their family history. In this situation, the genetic counselor has drawn a chart to visually display how close or far away in genetic relatedness a disorder has appeared.

stop. They wonder what the chances are that a child of theirs might also be retarded or have hemophilia and what measures they can take to reduce their chances of having a mentally or physically defective child.

The counselor probes more deeply, because she understands that these facts in isolation do not give her a complete picture of the possibilities. She

learns that no other relatives in Bob's family are retarded and that Bob's mother was in her late forties when his younger sister was born. She concludes that the retardation was due to the age of Bob's mother and not to some general tendency for members of his family to inherit retardation. It is well known that women over 40 have a much higher probability of giving birth to retarded children than younger women have. Apparently, in women over 40, the ova (egg cells) are not as healthy as in women under 40.

In Mary's case the counselor determines that there is a small but clear possibility that Mary may be a carrier of hemophilia and may transmit that condition to a son. Otherwise, the counselor can find no evidence from the family history to indicate genetic problems.

The decision is then up to the Simses. In this case, the genetic problem will probably not occur, so the choice is fairly easy. But what should parents do if they face the strong probability of having a child with a major birth defect? Ultimately, the decision

gene. *A recessive gene exerts its influence only if the two genes of a pair are both recessive.* If you inherit a recessive gene for a trait from both of your parents, you will show the trait. If you inherit a recessive gene from only one parent, you may never know you carry the gene. Brown eyes, farsightedness, and dimples rule over blue eyes, nearsightedness, and freckles in the world of dominant-recessive genes. Can two brown-eyed parents have a blue-eyed child? Yes, they can. In each parent, the gene pair that governs eye color includes a dominant gene for brown eyes, and a recessive gene for blue eyes. Since dominant genes override recessive genes, the parents have brown eyes. But both may be carriers of blueness and pass on their recessive genes for blue eyes. With no dominant gene to override them, the recessive genes can make the child's eyes blue.

For thousands of years, people wondered what determined the sex of the child. Aristotle believed the father's arousal during intercourse determined the offspring's sex. The more excited the father was, the more likely it would

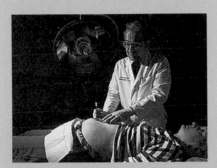

Amniocentesis being performed on a pregnant woman.

potential. The earlier it is performed, the more useful it is in deciding whether a pregnancy should be terminated.

Ultrasound sonography *is a prenatal medical procedure in which high-frequency sound waves are directed into the pregnant woman's abdomen.* The echo from the sounds is transformed into a visual representation of the fetus's inner structures. This technique has been able to detect such disorders as microencephaly, a form of mental retardation involving an abnormally small brain. Ultrasound sonography is often used in conjunction with amniocentesis to determine the precise location of the fetus in the mother's abdomen.

As scientists have searched for more accurate, safe assessments of high-risk prenatal conditions, they have developed a new test. The **chorionic villus test** *is a prenatal medical procedure in which a small sample of the placenta is removed at some point between the 8th and 11th weeks of pregnancy.* Diagnosis takes approximately 10 days.

A 6-month-old infant posing with its ultrasound sonography record taken at four months into prenatal development.

depends on the couple's ethical and religious beliefs.

The decision is even more acute once pregnancy has begun. **Amniocentesis** *is a prenatal medical procedure in which a sample of amniotic fluid is withdrawn by a syringe and tested to discover if the fetus is suffering from any chromosomal or metabolic disorders. Amniocentesis is performed between the 12th and 16th weeks of pregnancy.* The later amniocentesis is performed, the better the diagnostic

The chorionic villus test allows a decision about abortion to be made near the end of the first trimester of pregnancy, a point when abortion is safer and less traumatic than after amniocentesis in the second trimester. These techniques provide valuable information about the presence of birth defects, but they also raise issues pertaining to whether an abortion should be obtained if birth defects are present.

be for a son to be born, he reasoned. Of course he was wrong, but it was not until the 1920s that researchers confirmed the existence of human sex chromosomes, 2 of the 46 chromosomes human beings normally carry. Ordinarily, females have 2 X chromosomes, and men have an X and a Y. (Figure 3.6 shows the chromosome makeup of a male and a female.)

Genetic transmission is usually more complex than the simple examples we have examined thus far. **Polygenic inheritance** *is a genetic principle describing the interaction of many genes to produce a particular characteristic.* Few psychological characteristics are the result of single pairs. Most are determined by the interaction of many different genes. There are as many as 50,000 or more genes, so you can imagine that possible combinations of these are staggering in number. Traits produced by this mixing of genes are said to be polygenically determined.

No one possesses all the characteristics that our genetic structure makes possible. **Genotype** *is the person's genetic heritage, the actual genetic material.* However, not all of this genetic material is apparent in our observed and

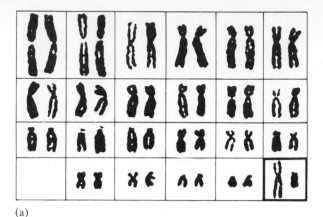

(a)

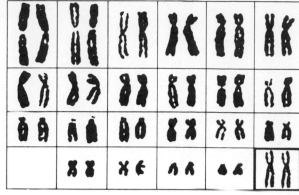

(b)

Figure 3.6   The genetic difference between males and females. Set (a) shows the chromosome structure of a male, and set (b) shows the chromosome structure of a female. The 23rd pair appears in the bottom right box of each set. Notice that the Y chromosome of the male is smaller than that of the female. To obtain this kind of chromosomal picture, a cell is removed from the person's body, usually from the inside of the mouth. The chromosomes are magnified extensively and then photographed.

That which comes of a cat will catch mice.

~ *English Proverb*

measurable characteristics. **Phenotype** *is the way an individual's genotype is expressed in observed and measurable characteristics.* Phenotypes include physical traits—such as height, weight, eye color, and skin pigmentation, and psychological characteristics—such as intelligence, creativity, personality, and social tendencies.

For each genotype, a range of phenotypes can be expressed. Imagine that we could identify all the genes that would make a person introverted or extraverted. Would measured introversion-extraversion be predictable from knowledge of the specific genes? The answer is no, because even if our genetic model was adequate, introversion-extraversion is a characteristic shaped by experience throughout life. For example, parents may push an introverted child into social situations and encourage the child to become more gregarious.

To understand how introverted a person is, think about a series of genetic codes that predispose the child to develop in a particular way, and imagine environments that are responsive or unresponsive to this development. For example, the genotype of some persons may predispose them to be introverted in an environment that promotes a turning inward of personality, yet in an environment that encourages social interaction and outgoingness, these individuals may become more extraverted. However, it would be unlikely for the individual with this introverted genotype to become a strong extravert. The term **reaction range** *is used to describe the range of phenotypes for each genotype, suggesting the importance of an environment's restrictiveness or enrichment* (figure 3.7).

Sandra Scarr (1984) explains reaction range this way: Each of us has a range of potential. For example, an individual with "medium-tall" genes for height who grows up in a poor environment may be shorter than average. But in an excellent nutritional environment, the individual may grow up taller than average. However, no matter how well fed the person is, someone with "short" genes will never be taller than average. Scarr believes that characteristics such as intelligence and introversion work the same way. That is, there is a range within which the environment can modify intelligence, but intelligence is not completely malleable. Reaction range gives us an estimate of how modifiable intelligence is.

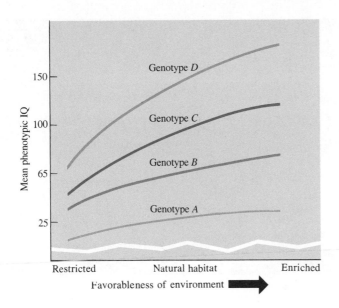

Figure 3.7 Some possible reaction ranges for the development of intelligence under poor to good environmental conditions. Although each genotype responds favorably to improved environments, some are more responsive to environmental deprivation and enrichment than are others.

Genotypes, in addition to producing many phenotypes, may show the opposite track for some characteristics—those that are somewhat immune to extensive changes in the environment. These characteristics seem to stay on a particular developmental course regardless of the environmental assaults on them (Waddington, 1957). **Canalization** *is the term chosen to describe the narrow path or developmental course that certain characteristics take. Apparently, preservative forces help to protect or buffer a person from environmental extremes.* For example, American developmental psychologist Jerome Kagan (1984) points to his research on Guatemalan infants who had experienced extreme malnutrition as infants, yet showed normal social and cognitive development later in childhood. And some abused children do not grow up to be abusers themselves.

However, it is important to recognize that while the genetic influence of canalization exerts its power by keeping organisms on a particular developmental path, genes alone do not directly determine human behavior (Cairns, 1991; Gottlieb, 1991a, b; Lerner, 1991). Gilbert Gottlieb (1991b) points out that genes are an integral part of the organism, but that their activity (genetic expression) can be affected by the organism's environment. For example, hormones that circulate in the blood make their way into the cell, where they influence the cell's activity. The flow of hormones themselves can be affected by environmental events such as light, day length, nutrition, and behavior.

Methods Used by Behavior Geneticists

Behavior genetics *is concerned with the degree and nature of behavior's hereditary basis.* Behavior geneticists assume that behaviors are jointly determined by the interaction of heredity and environment. To study heredity's influence on behavior, behavior geneticists often use either the twin study or the adoption study.

In the **twin study,** *the behaviors of identical and fraternal twins are compared.* **Identical twins** *(called monozygotic twins) develop from a single fertilized egg that splits into two genetically identical replicas, each of which becomes a person.* **Fraternal twins** *(called dizygotic twins) develop from separate eggs, making them genetically less similar than identical twins.* Although fraternal twins share the same womb, they are no more alike genetically than ordinary brothers and sisters, and they may be of different sexes. By comparing groups of identical and fraternal twins, behavior geneticists capitalize

This pair of identical twins developed from a single fertilized egg that split into two genetically identical replicas. In the twin study, identical twins are compared with fraternal twins, who develop from separate eggs, making them genetically less similar than identical twins.

on the basic knowledge that identical twins are more similar genetically than are fraternal twins. In one recent twin study, 7,000 pairs of Finnish identical and fraternal twins were compared on the personality traits of extraversion (outgoingness) and neuroticism (psychological instability) (Rose & others, 1988). On both of these personality traits, identical twins were much more similar than fraternal twins, suggesting the role of heredity in both traits. However, several issues crop up in the interpretation of results from twin studies. Adults may stress the similarities of identical twins more than those of fraternal twins. And identical twins may perceive themselves as a "set" and play together more than do fraternal twins. If so, observed similarities in identical twins could be environmentally influenced.

In the **adoption study,** *investigators seek to discover whether the behavior and psychological characteristics of adopted children are more like their adoptive parents, who contributed a home environment, or their biological parents, who contributed their heredity.* In one investigation, the educational levels attained by biological parents were better predictors of adopted children's IQ scores than the IQs of the children's adopted parents (Scarr & Weinberg, 1983). Because of the genetic relation between the adopted children and their biological parents, the implication is that heredity influenced the children's IQ scores.

So far, our coverage of the biological beginnings of the life cycle have taken us through some important aspects of heredity. A summary of these ideas is presented in concept table 3.1. Now let's turn our attention to some aspects of development influenced by heredity.

Heredity's Influence on Development

What aspects of development are influenced by genetic factors? They all are. However, behavior geneticists are interested in more precise estimates of the variation in a characteristic accounted for by genetic factors. Intelligence and temperament are among the most widely investigated aspects of heredity's influence on development.

Intelligence

Arthur Jensen (1969) sparked a lively and at times hostile debate when he presented his thesis that intelligence is primarily inherited. Jensen believes that environment and culture play only a minimal role in intelligence. Jensen

Concept Table 3.1: The Evolutionary Perspective and Genetics

Concept	Processes/Related Ideas	Characteristics/Description
The Evolutionary Perspective	Its Nature	Natural selection is the evolutionary process that favors individuals within a species best adapted to survive and reproduce. This concept was developed by Darwin. Evolution generally proceeds at a slow pace. Biological evolution shaped human beings into a culture-making species.
Genes, Chromosomes, and Reproduction	Genes and Chromosomes	The nucleus of each human cell contains 46 chromosomes, which are composed of DNA. Genes are short segments of DNA and act as a blueprint for cells to reproduce and manufacture proteins that maintain life.
	Reproduction	Genes are transmitted from parents to offspring by gametes, or sex cells. Gametes are formed by the splitting of cells, a process called meiosis. Reproduction takes place when a female gamete (ovum) is fertilized by a male gamete (sperm) to create a single-celled ovum. In vitro fertilization has helped to solve some infertility problems. Approximately 10 to 15 percent of couples in the United States experience infertility problems, some of which can be corrected through surgery or fertility drugs. Another choice for infertile couples is adoption.
Abnormalities in Genes and Chromosomes	The Range of Problems	A range of problems are caused by some major gene or chromosome defect, among them the PKU syndrome, Down syndrome, sickle-cell anemia, Klinefelter syndrome, Turner syndrome, and the XYY syndrome.
	Genetic Counseling and Tests	Genetic counseling has increased in popularity as couples desire information about their risk of having a defective child. Amniocentesis, ultrasonic sonography, and the chorionic villus test are used to determine the presence of defects after pregnancy has begun.
Genetic Principles	Their Nature	Genetic transmission is complex, but some principles have been worked out, among them dominant-recessive genes, sex-linked genes, polygenic inheritance, genotype-phenotype distinction, reaction range, and canalization.
	Methods Used by Behavior Geneticists	Behavior genetics is the field concerned with the degree and nature of behavior's hereditary basis. Among the most important methods used by behavior geneticists are the twin study and the adoption study.

examined several studies of intelligence, many of which involved comparisons of identical and fraternal twins. Remember that identical twins have identical genetic endowments, so their IQs should be similar. Fraternal twins and ordinary siblings are less similar genetically, so their IQs should be less similar. Jensen found support for his argument in these studies. Studies with identical twins produced an average correlation of .82; studies with ordinary siblings produced an average correlation of .50. Note the difference of .32. To show that genetic factors are more important than environmental factors, Jensen compared identical twins reared together with those reared apart; the correlation for those reared together was .89 and for those reared apart it was .78

(a difference of .11). Jensen argued that if environmental influences were more important than genetic influences, then siblings reared apart, who experienced different environments, should have IQs much farther apart.

Many scholars have criticized Jensen's work. One criticism concerns the definition of intelligence itself. Jensen believes that IQ as measured by standardized intelligence tests is a good indicator of intelligence. Critics argue that IQ tests tap only a narrow range of intelligence. Everyday problem solving, work, and social adaptability, say the critics, are important aspects of intelligence not measured by the traditional intelligence tests used in Jensen's sources. A second criticism is that most investigations of heredity and environment do not include environments that differ radically. Thus, it is not surprising that many genetic studies show environment to be a fairly weak influence on intelligence.

Jensen places the importance of heredity's influence on intelligence at about 80 percent (Jensen, 1969). Thomas Bouchard and his colleagues (1990) also believe heredity has a strong influence on intelligence, placing its influence at about 70 percent. Intelligence is influenced by heredity, but most developmentalists do not put the figure nearly as high as Jensen and Bouchard do. Other experts estimate heredity's influence on intelligence in the 50 percent range (Plomin, 1989; Plomin, DeFries, & McClearn, 1990).

Temperament

Temperament *refers to an individual's behavioral style and characteristic way of responding.* Developmentalists are especially interested in the temperament of infants. Some infants are extremely active, moving their arms, legs, and mouths incessantly. Others are tranquil. Some children explore their environment eagerly for great lengths of time. Others do not. Some infants respond warmly to people. Others fuss and fret. All of these behavioral styles represent a person's temperament (Goldsmith & others, 1991).

A widely debated issue in temperament research is just what the key dimensions of temperament are. Alexander Chess and Stella Thomas (Chess & Thomas, 1977; Thomas & Chess, 1987, 1991) believe there are three basic types or clusters of temperament: easy, difficult, and slow-to-warm-up.

1. The **easy child** *is generally in a positive mood, quickly establishes regular routines in infancy, and adapts easily to new experiences.*
2. The **difficult child** *tends to react negatively and cry frequently, engages in irregular daily routines, and is slow to accept new experiences.*
3. The **slow-to-warm-up child** *has a low activity level, is somewhat negative, shows low adaptability, and displays a low intensity of mood.*

Different dimensions go into making up these three basic clusters of temperament. The three basic clusters and their dimensions are shown in table 3.1. In their longitudinal investigation, Chess and Thomas found that 40 percent of the children they studied could be classified as "easy," 10 percent as "difficult," and 15 percent as "slow-to-warm-up." Researchers have found that these three basic clusters of temperament are moderately stable across the childhood years.

Other researchers suggest that temperament is comprised of different basic components. Personality psychologist Arnold Buss and behavior geneticist Robert Plomin (1984, 1987) believe that the temperament of infants falls into three basic categories: emotionality, sociability, and activity level.

Beginnings

Table 3.1: Chess and Thomas's Dimensions and the Basic Clusters of Temperament

Temperament Dimension	Description	Temperament Cluster		
		Easy Child	*Difficult Child*	*Slow-to-Warm-Up Child*
Rhythmicity	Regularity of eating, sleeping, toileting	Regular	Irregular	
Activity level	Degree of energy movement		High	Low
Approach-withdrawal	Ease of approaching new people and situations	Positive	Negative	Negative
Adaptability	Ease of tolerating change in routine plans	Positive	Negative	Negative
Sensory threshold	Amount of stimulation required for responding			
Predominant quality of mood	Degree of positive or negative affect	Positive	Negative	
Intensity of mood expression	Degree of affect when pleased, displeased, happy, sad	Low to moderate	High	Low
Distractibility/attention span/persistence	Ease of being distracted			

This table shows which of the dimensions were critical in spotting a basic cluster of temperament and what the level of responsiveness was for a critical feature. A blank space indicates that the dimension was not strongly related to a basic cluster of temperament.

1. **Emotionality** *is the tendency to be distressed.* It reflects the arousal of the person's sympathetic nervous system. Distress develops during infancy into two separate emotional responses: fear and anger. Fearful infants try to escape something that is unpleasant; angry ones protest it. Buss and Plomin argue that children are labeled "easy" or "difficult" on the basis of their emotionality.

2. **Sociability** *is the tendency to prefer the company of others to being alone.* It matches up with a tendency to respond warmly to others.

3. **Activity level** *involves tempo and vigor of movement.* Some children walk fast, are attracted to high-energy games, and jump or bounce around a lot; others are more placid.

A number of scholars, including Chess and Thomas, conceive of temperament as a stable characteristic of newborns that becomes shaped and modified by the child's later experiences (Thomas & Chess, 1987; Goldsmith,

IMPERTURBABILITY IN EUROPEAN AMERICAN, CHINESE AMERICAN, AND NAVAHO INDIAN NEWBORNS

*D*o newborns from different cultures have different biological predispositions of temperament? In one investigation, 24 Chinese American and 24 European American 2-day-old babies were observed (Freedman & Freedman, 1969). The Chinese American infants had a less rapid buildup to an excited state of arousal, showed less facial and body reddening, and showed fewer state changes. When placed in the prone position, the Chinese Americans tended to remain inactive, face flat against the bed. By contrast, the European Americans were

Shown here is a Chinese American mother and her young infant. Researchers have found that Chinese American newborns are calmer than European American and Navaho Indian newborns.

more likely to lift their head or turn their face to one side. The Chinese American babies were easier to control when crying and were able to stop by themselves without being consoled. The researchers suggested that these behaviors reflect the temperament of "imperturbability," which affects the way adults care for the infants. Further comparison of this temperament indicated that newborn Navaho Indians were more perturbable than newborn Chinese Americans (Freedman, 1971).

1988). This raises the question of heredity's role in temperament. Twin and adoption studies have been conducted to answer this question (Plomin, 1989; Matheny, Dolan, & Wilson, 1976). The researchers found a heritability index in the range of .50 to .60, suggesting a moderate influence of heredity on temperament. However, the strength of the association usually declines as infants become older (Goldsmith & Gottesman, 1981). This finding supports the belief that temperament becomes more malleable with experience. Alternatively, it may be that as the child becomes older, behavioral indicators of temperament may be more difficult to spot. To read about likely biologically based ethnic differences in temperament, turn to Cultural Worlds of Development 3.1.

The consistency of temperament depends in part on the "match" or "fit" between the child's nature and that of the parents (Nitz & Lerner, 1991; Plomin & Thompson, 1987; Rothbart, 1988). Imagine a high-strung parent with a child who is difficult and sometimes slow to respond to the parent's affection. The parent may begin to feel angry or rejected. A parent who does not need much face-to-face social interaction will find it easy to manage a similarly introverted baby, but he may not be able to provide an extraverted baby with sufficient stimulation. Parents influence infants, but infants also influence parents. Parents may withdraw from difficult children, or they may become critical and punish them; these responses may make the difficult child even more difficult. A more easygoing parent may have a calming effect on a difficult child or may continue to show affection even when the child withdraws or is hostile, eventually encouraging more competent behavior.

In sum, heredity does seem to influence temperament. But the degree of influence depends on parents' responsiveness to the child and other environmental experiences of the child.

• Critical Thinking •

Consider your own temperament. Does it fit into one of the clusters described by Chess and Thomas? How stable has your temperament been in the course of your development? What factors contributed to this stability or lack of stability?

Heredity-Environment Interaction and Development

Both genes and environment are necessary for an organism to even exist. Heredity and environment operate—or cooperate—together to produce an individual's intelligence, temperament, height, weight, ability to pitch a baseball, career interests, and so on. Without genes, there is no organism; without environment, there is no organism (Scarr & Weinberg, 1980). If an attractive, popular, and intelligent girl is elected as president of the student body, would we conclude that her success is due to environment or to heredity? Of course, it is due to both. Because the environment's influence depends on genetically endowed characteristics, we say that the two factors *interact* (Plomin, 1991; Scarr, 1989, 1991; Scarr & Weinberg, 1980; Wahlsten, 1991; Weinberg, 1989).

But as we have seen, developmental psychologists probe further to determine more precisely the influence heredity and environment have on development. What do we know about heredity-environment interaction? According to Sandra Scarr and Kenneth Kidd (1983), we know that hundreds of disorders appear because of miscodings in DNA. We know that abnormalities in chromosomal number adversely influence the development of physical, intellectual, and behavioral features. We know that genotype and phenotype do not map onto each other in a one-to-one fashion. We know that it is very difficult to distinguish between genetic and cultural transmission. There is usually a familial concentration of a particular disorder, but familial patterns are considerably different from what would be precisely predicted from simple modes of inheritance. We know that when we consider the normal range of variation, the stronger the genetic resemblance, then the stronger the behavioral resemblance will be. This holds more strongly for intelligence than for personality or interests. The influence of genes on intelligence is present early in children's development and continues through the late adulthood years. And we also know that being raised in the same family accounts for some portion of intellectual differences among individuals, but common rearing accounts for little of the variation in personality or interests. One reason for this discrepancy may be that families place similar pressures on their children for intellectual development but they do not necessarily direct their children toward similar personalities or interests. That is, most parents would like their children to have above-average intellect, but there is much less agreement about whether or not a child should be highly extraverted.

What do we need to know about the role of heredity-environment interaction in development? Scarr and Kidd (1983) commented that we need to know the pathways by which genetic abnormalities influence development. The

Concept Table 3.2: Heredity's Influence on Development and Heredity-Environment Interaction

Concept	Processes/Related Ideas	Characteristics/Description
Heredity's Influence on Development	Its Scope	All aspects of development are influenced by heredity.
	Intelligence	Jensen's argument that intelligence is primarily due to heredity sparked a lively, and at times bitter, debate. Intelligence is influenced by heredity, but not as strongly as Jensen envisioned.
	Temperament	Temperament refers to behavioral style; temperament has been studied extensively. Chess and Thomas developed three temperament clusters: "easy," "difficult," and "slow-to-warm-up." Temperament is influenced strongly by biological factors in early infancy but becomes more malleable with experience. An important consideration is the fit of the infant's temperament with the parents' temperament.
Heredity-Environment Interaction and Development	Its Nature	Without genes, there is no organism; without environment, there is no organism. Because the environment's influence depends on genetically endowed characteristics, we say that the two factors interact.

• Critical Thinking •

Beyond the fact that heredity and environment always interact to produce development, first argue for heredity's dominance in this interaction, and, second, argue for environment's dominance.

PKU success story is but one such example. Scientists discovered the genetic linkage of the disorder and subsequently how the environment could be changed to reduce the damage to development. We need to know more about genetic-environment interaction in the normal range of development. For example, what accounts for the difference in one person's IQ of 95 and another person's IQ of 125? The answer requires a polygenic perspective and information about cultural and genetic influences.

We also need to know about heredity's influence across the entire life cycle. For instance, puberty is not an environmentally produced accident (Bancroft & Reinisch, 1990; Rowe & Rodgers, 1989); neither is menopause. While puberty and menopause can be influenced by such environmental factors as nutrition, weight, drugs, and health, the basic evolutionary and genetic program is wired into the species. It cannot be eliminated, nor should it be ignored. This evolutionary and genetic perspective gives biology its appropriate role in our quest to better understand human development through the life cycle.

A summary of the main ideas in our discussion of heredity's influence on development and heredity-environment interaction is presented in concept table 3.2. In the next chapter we will continue our discussion of biological beginnings, turning to information about prenatal development and birth.

Summary

I. The Evolutionary Perspective

Natural selection is the evolutionary process that favors individuals within a species best adapted to survive and reproduce. This concept was developed by Darwin. Evolution generally proceeds at a slow pace. Biological evolution shaped human beings into a culture-making species.

II. Chromosomes, DNA, and Genes

The nucleus of each human cell contains 46 chromosomes, which are composed of DNA. Genes are short segments of DNA and act as a blueprint for cells to reproduce and manufacture protein, which maintains life.

III. Reproduction

Genes are transmitted from parents to offspring by gametes, or sex cells. Gametes are formed by the splitting of cells, a process called meiosis. Reproduction takes place when a female gamete (ovum) is fertilized by a male gamete (sperm) to create a single-celled zygote. In vitro fertilization has helped solve some infertility problems. Approximately 10 to 15 percent of couples in the United States experience fertility problems, some which can be corrected through surgery or fertility drugs. Another choice for infertile couples is adoption.

IV. **Abnormalities in Genes and Chromosomes**

A range of problems are caused by some major gene or chromosome defects, among them the PKU syndrome, Down syndrome, sickle-cell anemia. Klinefelter syndrome, Turner syndrome, and the XYY syndrome. Genetic counseling has increased in popularity, as couples desire information about their risk of having a defective child. Amniocentesis and the chorionic villus test are used to determine the presence of defects after pregnancy has begun.

V. **Some Genetic Principles**

Genetic transmission is complex, but some principles have been worked out, among them dominant-recessive genes, polygenic inheritance, genotype-phenotype distinction, reaction range, and canalization.

VI. **Methods Used by Behavior Geneticists**

Behavior genetics is the field concerned with the degree and nature of behavior's heredity basis. Among the most important methods used by behavior geneticists are the twin study and the adoption study. The concept of heritability is used in many of the twin and adoption studies. The heritability index is not without flaws.

VII. **Heredity's Influence on Development**

All aspects of development are influenced by heredity. Jensen's argument that intelligence is influenced primarily by heredity sparked a lively, and at times bitter, debate. Intelligence is influenced by heredity, but not as strongly as Jensen envisioned. Temperament refers to behavioral style; temperament has been studied extensively in infancy. Chess and Thomas developed three temperament clusters: "easy," "difficult," and "slow-to-warm-up." Temperament is strongly influenced by biological factors in early infancy but becomes more malleable with experience. An important consideration is the fit of the infant's temperament with the parents' temperament.

VIII. **Heredity-Environment Interaction and Development**

Without genes, there is no organism; without environment, there is no organism. Because the environment's influence depends on genetically endowed characteristics, we say that the two factors interact.

Key Terms

natural selection 84
chromosomes 85
DNA 85
genes 85
gametes 86
meiosis 86
reproduction 86
zygote 86
in vitro fertilization 86
phenylketonuria (PKU) 88
Down syndrome 89
sickle-cell anemia 89

Klinefelter syndrome 89
Turner syndrome 89
XYY syndrome 89
dominant-recessive genes principle 89
amniocentesis 91
ultrasound sonography 91
chorionic villus test 91
polygenic inheritance 91
genotype 91
phenotype 92
reaction range 92
canalization 92

behavior genetics 93
twin study 93
identical twins 93
fraternal twins 93
adoption study 94
temperament 96
easy child 96
difficult child 96
slow-to-warm-up child 96
emotionality 97
sociability 97
activity level 97

Suggested Readings

Chess, S., & Thomas, A. (1986). *Temperament in clinical practice.* New York: Guilford.
Details of Chess and Thomas's classical longitudinal study of temperament are provided, and applications to clinical problems are described.

Gould, S. (1983). *Hen's teeth and horse's toes: Reflections on natural history.* New York: W. W. Norton. *This book is a collection of fascinating articles by a biologist interested in evolution. The essays originally were published in the magazine* Natural History.

Lewontin, R. C., Rose, S., & Kamin, L. J. (1984). *Not in our genes.* New York: Pantheon.
Argues for an environmental view of development and provides many reasons why heredity's role is overestimated.

Plomin, R., DeFries, J. C., & McClearn, G. E. (1990). *Behavioral genetics: A primer* (2nd ed). New York: W. H. Freeman.
A good introduction to research on genes and behavior by leading behavior geneticists.

Watson, J. D. (1968). *The double helix.* New York: New American Library.
A personalized account of the research leading up to one of the most provocative discoveries of the twentieth century—the DNA molecule. Reading like a mystery novel, it illustrates the exciting discovery process in science.

CHAPTER 4

Prenatal Development and Birth

*T*eresa Block's second pregnancy was difficult. Her amniotic sac ruptured, she contracted an infection that sent her temperature skyrocketing, and she had an exhausting breech delivery. Her son Robert weighed just under 2 pounds at birth. Teresa said she had never imagined a baby looking so tiny. The first time she saw Robert, he was lying on his back attached to a respirator, and wires were connected all over his body. Robert stayed at the hospital until two weeks before his originally projected birth date, at which time he weighed 4 pounds, 8 ounces. Teresa and her husband lived in a small town sixty miles from the hospital; they commuted each day to spend time with Robert, and brought their other child along with them whenever it was practical.

A decade later, Robert is still at the bottom of the weight chart, but he is about average in height and the only physical residue of his early birth difficulties is a "lazy eye." He is 20/20 in his good eye but 20/200 in the other. He is doing special exercises for the bad eye, and his doctor thinks he is not far from the day he can go without glasses. Robert is on the soccer team and the swim team (Fincher, 1982).

Considering his circumstances, Robert had a relatively uncomplicated stay at the hospital. Not all children born so frail survive, and those who do sometimes show the consequences many years in the future.

At one time, you were an organism floating in a sea of fluid within your mother's womb. From the moment you were conceived until the moment you were born, some astonishing developments occurred. This chapter chronicles the truly remarkable developments from conception to birth and the nature of the birth process itself.

Prenatal Development

Imagine how you came to be. From the thousands of eggs and millions of sperm, one egg and one sperm united to produce you. Had the union of sperm and egg come a day or even an hour earlier or later, you might have been very different—maybe even of the opposite sex.

The Course of Prenatal Development

Remember from chapter 3 that conception occurs when a single sperm cell from the male unites with the ovum (egg) in the female's fallopian tube in a process called fertilization. Remember also that the fertilized egg is called a zygote. By the time the zygote ends its three- to four-day journey through the fallopian tubes and reaches the uterus, it has divided into approximately 12 to 16 cells.

The **germinal period** *is the period of prenatal development that takes place in the first 2 weeks after conception. It includes the creation of the zygote, continued cell division, and attachment of the zygote to the uterine wall.* By approximately one week after conception, the zygote is composed of 100 to 150 cells. Differentiation of cells has already commenced as inner and outer layers are formed. The **blastocyst** *is the inner layer of cells that develops during the germinal period. These cells later develop into the embryo.* The **trophoblast** *is the outer layer of cells that develop during the germinal period. They later provide nutrition and support for the embryo.* **Implantation** *is the attachment of the zygote to the uterine wall, which takes place about 10 days after conception.*

The **embryonic period** *is the period of prenatal development that occurs from 2 to 8 weeks after conception. During the embryonic period, the rate of cell differentiation intensifies, support systems for the cells form, and organs appear.* As the zygote attaches to the uterine wall, its cells form two layers.

DENNIS THE MENACE

"My Mom says I come from Heaven. My Dad says he can't
remember an' Mr. Wilson is POSITIVE I came from Mars!"

It is at this time that the mass of cells changes names from *zygote* to *embryo*. The **endoderm** *is the inner layer of cells, which will develop into the digestive and respiratory systems.* The outer layer of cells is divided into two parts. The **ectoderm,** *the outermost layer, will become the nervous system, sensory receptors (ear, nose, and eyes, for example), and skin parts (hair and nails, for example).* The **mesoderm,** *the middle layer, will become the circulatory system, bones, muscle, excretory system, and reproductive system.* Every body part eventually develops from these three layers. The endoderm primarily produces internal body parts, the mesoderm primarily produces parts that surround the internal areas, and the ectoderm primarily produces surface parts.

As the embryo's three layers are formed, life-support systems for the embryo mature and develop rapidly. These life-support systems include the placenta, the umbilical cord, and the amnion. The **placenta** *is a life-support system consisting of a disk-shaped group of tissues in which small blood vessels from the mother and the offspring intertwine but do not join.* The **umbilical cord** *is a life-support system that contains two arteries and one vein and connects the baby to the placenta.* Very small molecules—oxygen, water, salt, food from the mother's blood, and carbon dioxide and digestive wastes from the embryo's blood—pass back and forth between the mother and infant. Large molecules—including red blood cells and harmful substances such as most bacteria, maternal wastes, and hormones—cannot pass through the placental wall. The mechanisms that govern transfer of substances across the placental barrier are complex and still not entirely understood (Rosenblith and Sims-Knight, 1985). The **amnion,** *a sort of bag or envelope containing a clear fluid in which the developing embryo floats, is another important life-support system of the embryo. It provides an environment that is temperature and humidity controlled as well as shock proof.*

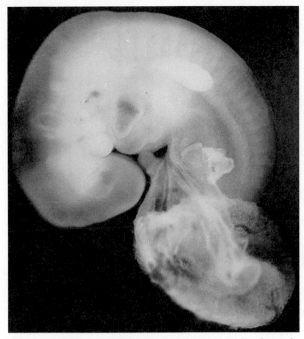

Figure 4.1 *Embryo at 4 weeks. At about 4 weeks the embryo is about .2 inches in length. The head, eyes, and ears begin to show. The head and neck are half the body length; the shoulders will be located where the whitish arm buds are attached.*

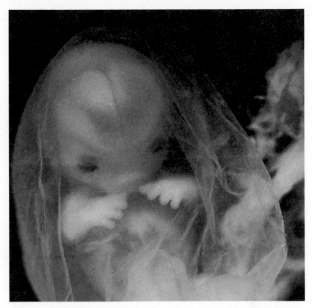

Figure 4.2 *Embryo at 8 weeks. At 8 weeks, 4 centimeters (1.6 inches), the developing organism is no longer an embryo, but a fetus. Everything that will be found in the fully developed human being has now been formed. The fetal stage is a period of growth and perfection of detail. The heart has been beating for a month, and the muscles have just begun their first exercises. Two menstrual periods have now been skipped. At about this time the mother-to-be goes to a doctor or clinic for prenatal care.*

Before most women even know they are pregnant, some important embryonic developments take place. In the third week, the neural tube that eventually becomes the spinal cord forms. At about 21 days, eyes begin to appear, and by 24 days, the cells for the heart begin to differentiate. During the fourth week, the urogenital system first appears, and arm and leg buds emerge. Four chambers of the heart take shape, and blood vessels surface (see figure 4.1). From the fifth to the eighth week, arms and legs differentiate further; at this time, the face starts to form but is still not very recognizable. The intestinal tract develops and the facial structures fuse. At 8 weeks, the developing organism weighs about 1/30 of an ounce and is just over 1 inch long.

Organogenesis *is the process of organ formation that takes place during the first two months of prenatal development.* When organs are being formed, they are especially vulnerable to environmental changes. Later in the chapter, we will describe the environmental hazards that are harmful during organogenesis.

The **fetal period** *is the prenatal period of development that begins 2 months after conception and lasts for 7 months on the average.* Growth and development continue their dramatic course during this time (see figure 4.2). Three months after conception, the fetus is about 3 inches long and weighs about 1 ounce. It has become active, moving its arms and legs, opening and closing its mouth, and moving its head. The face, forehead, eyelids, nose, and chin are distinguishable, as are the upper arms, lower arms, hands, and lower limbs. The genitals can be identified as male or female. By the end of the fourth month, the fetus has grown to 6 inches in length and weighs 4 to 7

If I could have watched you grow
As a magical mother might,
If I could have seen through my
magical transparent belly,
There would have been such
ripening within . . .

~ *Anne Sexton,* Little Girl,
My String Bean, My Lovely Woman

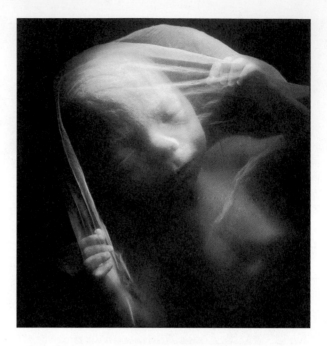

Figure 4.3 The fetus at 4 months. At this point the fetus has grown to approximately 6 inches in length and weighs 4 to 7 ounces. Arm and leg movements can be felt by the mother for the first time.

So the riders of the darkness pass on their circuits: the luminous island of the self trembles and waits, waits for us all, my friends, where the sea's big brush recolors the dying lives, and the unborn smiles.

~ *Lawrence Durrell*

ounces. At this time, a growth spurt occurs in the body's lower parts. Prenatal reflexes are stronger; arm and leg movements can be felt for the first time by the mother (see figure 4.3).

By the end of the fifth month, the fetus is about 12 inches long and weighs close to a pound. Structures of the skin have formed—toenails and fingernails, for example. The fetus is more active, showing a preference for a particular position in the womb. By the end of the sixth month, the fetus is about 14 inches long and has already gained another pound. The eyes and eyelids are completely formed. A fine layer of hair covers the head. A grasping reflex is present and irregular breathing occurs. By the end of the seventh month, the fetus is about 16 inches long and has gained another pound, now weighing about 3 pounds. During the eighth and ninth months, the fetus grows longer and gains substantial weight—about 4 pounds. At birth, the average American baby weighs 7 pounds and is 20 inches long. In these last two months, fatty tissues develop and the functioning of various organ systems—heart and kidneys, for example—is stepped up.

Miscarriage and Abortion

A miscarriage, or spontaneous abortion, happens when pregnancy ends before the developing organism is mature enough to survive outside the womb. This happens when the embryo separates from the uterine wall and is expelled by the uterus. Estimates indicate that about 15 to 20 percent of all pregnancies end in a spontaneous abortion, most in the first two to three months. Many spontaneous abortions occur without the mother's knowledge, and many involve an embryo or fetus that was not developing normally.

Early in history, it was believed that a woman could be frightened into a miscarriage by loud thunder or a jolt in a carriage. Today we recognize that this occurrence is highly unlikely; the developing organism is well protected. Abnormalities of the reproductive tract and viral or bacterial infections are more likely causes of spontaneous abortions. In some cases, severe traumas may be at fault.

Deliberate termination of pregnancy is a complex issue, medically, psychologically, and socially. Carrying the baby to term may affect the woman's health; the woman's pregnancy may have resulted from rape or incest; the woman may not be married; or perhaps she is poor and wants to continue her education. Abortion is again legal in the United States; in 1973, the Supreme Court ruled that any woman could obtain an abortion during the first six months of pregnancy. This decision continues to generate ethical objections from the antiabortion forces. The Supreme Court has also ruled that abortion in the first trimester is solely the decision of the mother and her doctor. Cases have also added that the father, and the parents of minor girls, do not have any say during this time frame. In the second trimester, states can legislate the time and method of abortion for protection of the mother's health. In the third trimester, the fetus's right to live is the primary concern.

What are the psychological effects of having an abortion? In 1989, a research review panel appointed by the American Psychological Association examined more than 100 investigations of the psychological effects of abortion. The panel's conclusions follow. Unwanted pregnancies are stressful for most women. However, it is common for women to report feelings of relief as well as feelings of guilt after an abortion. These feelings are usually mild and tend to diminish rapidly over time without adversely affecting the woman's ability to function. Abortion is more stressful for women who have a history of serious emotional problems and who are not given support by family or friends. According to the American Psychological Association report, only a small percentage of women fall into these high-risk categories. If an abortion is performed, the woman should not only be given competent medical care but her psychological needs should also be addressed.

• *Critical Thinking* •

What are the arguments for and against abortion? Where do you stand on this sensitive ethical issue? Why?

Teratology and Hazards to Prenatal Development

Some expectant mothers carefully tiptoe about in the belief that everything they do and feel has a direct effect on their unborn child. Others behave casually, assuming that their experiences have little effect on the unborn child. The truth lies somewhere in between these two extremes. Although living in a protected, comfortable environment, the fetus is not totally immune to the larger environment surrounding the mother. The environment can affect the child in many well-documented ways. Thousands of babies born deformed or mentally retarded every year are the result of events that the mother experienced as recently as one or two months before conception.

Teratology

A **teratogen,** *which comes from the Greek word tera meaning "monster," is any agent that causes a birth defect. The field of study that investigates the causes of birth defects is called teratology.* So many teratogens exist, that practically every fetus is exposed to at least some of them. For this reason, it is difficult to determine which teratogen causes which birth defect. In addition, it may take a long time for the effects of a teratogen to show up; only about half are present at birth.

Despite the many unknowns about teratogens, scientists have discovered the identity of some of these hazards to prenatal development and the particular point of fetal development at which they do their greatest damage. As figure 4.4 shows, sensitivity to teratogens occurs about 3 weeks after conception. The probability of a structural defect is greatest early in the embryonic period, because this is when organs are being formed. After organogenesis is complete, teratogens are less likely to cause anatomical defects. Exposure later during the fetal period is more likely to stunt growth or to create problems in the way organs function. The preciseness of organogenesis is evident when teratologists point out that vulnerability of the brain is greatest at 15 to 25 days after conception, the eye at 24 to 40 days, the heart at 20 to 40 days, and the legs at 24 to 36 days.

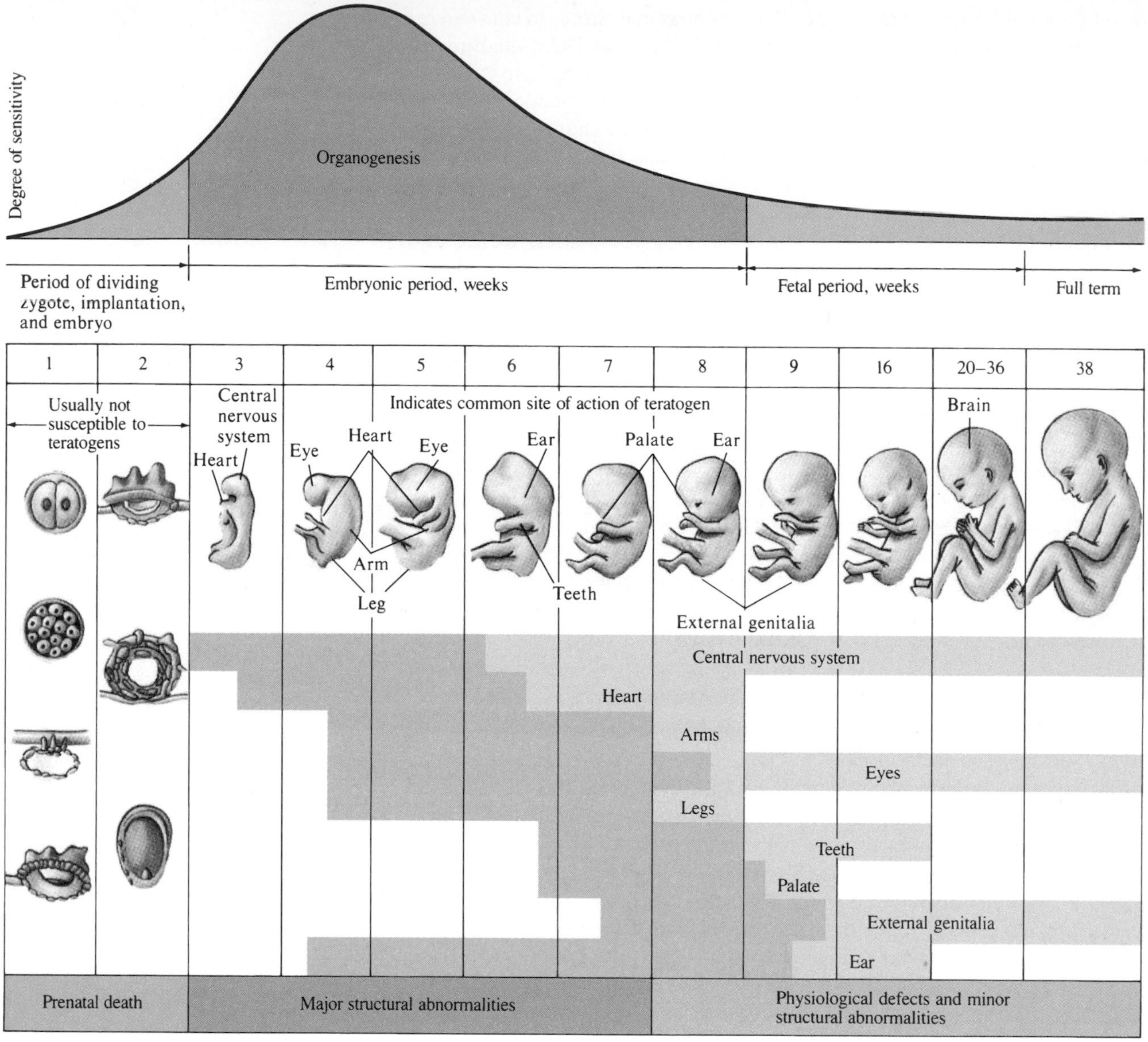

Degree of sensitivity
Organogenesis
Period of dividing zygote, implantation, and embryo
Embryonic period, weeks
Fetal period, weeks
Full term
1
2
3
4
5
6
7
8
9
16
20–36
38
Usually not susceptible to teratogens
Central nervous system
Heart
Indicates common site of action of teratogen
Eye
Heart
Eye
Ear
Palate
Ear
Brain
Arm
Leg
Teeth
External genitalia
Central nervous system
Heart
Arms
Eyes
Legs
Teeth
Palate
External genitalia
Ear
Prenatal death
Major structural abnormalities
Physiological defects and minor structural abnormalities

Figure 4.4 Teratogens and the timing of their effects on prenatal development. The danger of structural defects caused by teratogens is greatest early in embryonic development. This is the period of organogenesis, and it lasts for several months. Damage caused by teratogens during this period is represented by the dark-colored bars. Later assaults by teratogens typically occur during the fetal period and, instead of structural damage, are more likely to stunt growth or cause problems of organ function.

In the following sections, we explore how certain environmental agents influence prenatal development. That is, we examine how maternal diseases and conditions, drugs, and environmental hazards affect the fetus.

Maternal Diseases and Conditions

Maternal diseases or infections can produce defects by crossing the placental barrier, or they can cause damage during the birth.

Rubella (German measles) and syphilis (a sexually transmitted disease) are two maternal diseases that can damage prenatal development. A rubella outbreak in 1964–1965 resulted in 30,000 prenatal and neonatal (newborn) deaths, and more than 20,000 infants were born with malformations, including mental retardation, blindness, deafness, and heart problems. The greatest damage occurs when mothers contract rubella during the third and fourth weeks of pregnancy, although infection during the second month is also damaging. Elaborate efforts ensure that rubella will never again have the same disastrous effects as it did in the mid-1960s. A vaccine that prevents German measles is routinely administered to children, and mothers who plan to have children should have a blood test before they become pregnant to determine if they are immune to the disease.

Syphilis is more damaging later in prenatal development—four months or more after conception. Rather than affecting organogenesis as rubella does, syphilis damages organs after they are already formed. Damage includes eye lesions, which can cause blindness, and skin lesions. When syphilis is present at birth, other problems involving the central nervous system and gastrointestinal tract can develop. Most states require a pregnant woman to be given a blood test to detect the presence of syphilis.

Another infection that has received widespread attention recently is genital herpes. Increased numbers of newborns contract this virus when they are delivered through the birth canal of a mother with genital herpes. About one-third of babies delivered through an infected birth canal die and another one-fourth become brain damaged. If a pregnant woman detects an active case of genital herpes close to her delivery date, a cesarean section can be performed to keep the virus from infecting the newborn (Byer, Shainberg, & Jones, 1991).

AIDS can also be transmitted by the mother to the offspring (Peterson & others, 1991; Seibert & Olson, 1989). The first infant case of AIDS appeared in this country in 1979. By the end of 1991, 3,000 cumulative cases of AIDS in infants were documented. In the majority of cases, the mother's infection is linked to her own or her sexual partner's use of intravenous drugs. Most children develop symptoms in the first year of life, including bacterial infections, neurological impairment, and delayed development. Treatment of AIDS is still in the trial stages. Early recognition and treatment of the symptoms may prolong life (Novick, 1989; Task Force on Pediatric AIDS, 1989), but no cure is forthcoming and the prognosis is always death.

The Mother's Age

When the mother's age is considered in terms of possible harmful effects on the fetus and infant, two time periods are of special interest: adolescence and beyond the age of 30. Approximately one of every five births is to an adolescent; in some urban areas, the figure reaches as high as one in every two births. Infants born to adolescents are often premature. The mortality rate of infants born to adolescent mothers is double that of infants born to mothers in their twenties. While such figures probably reflect the mother's immature reproductive system, they may also involve poor nutrition, lack of prenatal care, and low socioeconomic status. Prenatal care decreases the probability that a child born to an adolescent girl will have physical problems. However, adolescents are the least likely of all age groups to obtain prenatal assistance from clinics, pediatricians, and health services (Osofsky, 1990; Timberlake and others, 1987).

Women are increasingly seeking to establish their careers before beginning a family, delaying childbearing until their thirties. Down syndrome, a form of mental retardation, is related to the mother's age. A baby with Down syndrome is rarely born to a mother under the age of 30, but the risk increases after the mother reaches 30. By age 40, the probability is slightly over 1 in 100, and by age 50 it is almost 1 in 10. The risk also increases before age 18.

Women also have more difficulty becoming pregnant after the age of 30 (Toth, 1991). In one investigation, the clients of a French fertility clinic all had husbands who were sterile (Schwartz & Mayaux, 1982). To increase their chances of having a child, they were artificially inseminated once a month for one year. Each woman had twelve chances to become pregnant. Seventy-five percent of the women in their twenties became pregnant, 62 percent of women 31 to 35 years old became pregnant, and only 54 percent of those women over 35 years old became pregnant.

We still have much to learn about the role of the mother's age in pregnancy and childbirth. As women become more active, exercise regularly, and are careful about their nutrition, their reproductive systems may remain healthier at older ages than was thought possible in the past. Indeed, as we will see next, the mother's nutrition influences prenatal development.

Nutrition

The developing fetus depends completely on the mother for its nutrition, which comes from the mother's blood. Nutritional state is not determined by any specific aspect of diet; among the important factors are the total number of calories and the appropriate levels of protein, vitamins, and minerals. The mother's nutrition even influences her ability to reproduce. In extreme instances of malnutrition, women stop menstruating, thus precluding conception. And children born to malnourished mothers are more likely to be malformed.

One investigation of Iowa mothers documents the important role of nutrition in prenatal development and birth (Jeans, Smith, & Stearns, 1955). The diets of 400 pregnant women were studied and the status of the newborns was assessed. The mothers with the poorest diets were more likely to have offspring who weighed the least, had the least vitality, were born prematurely, or who died. In one investigation, diet supplements given to malnourished mothers during pregnancy improved the performance of offspring during the first three years of life (Werner, 1979).

Emotional State and Stress

Tales abound about the way the mother's emotional state affects the fetus. For centuries it was thought that frightening experiences—a severe thunderstorm or a family member's death—would leave birthmarks on the child or affect the child in more serious ways. Today we believe that the mother's stress can be transmitted to the fetus, but we have gone beyond thinking that these happenings are somehow magically produced. We now know that, when a pregnant woman experiences intense fears, anxieties, and other emotions, physiological changes occur—heart rate, respiration, and glandular secretions among them. For example, the production of adrenaline in response to fear restricts blood flow to the uterine area and may deprive the fetus of adequate oxygen.

The mother's emotional state during pregnancy can influence the birth process, too. An emotionally distraught mother might have irregular contractions and a more difficult labor. This may cause irregularities in the baby's oxygen supply, or it may lead to irregularities after birth. Babies born after extended labor may adjust more slowly to their world and be more irritable. One investigation revealed a connection between the mother's anxiety during pregnancy and the newborn's condition (Ottinger & Simmons, 1964). In this study, mothers answered a questionnaire about their anxiety every three months during pregnancy. When the babies were born, the babies' weights, activity levels, and crying were assessed. The babies of the more anxious mothers cried more before feedings and were more active than the babies born to the less anxious mothers.

Nothing vivifies, and nothing kills, like the emotions.

~ Joseph Roux,
Meditations of a Parish Priest, 1886

Beginnings

Drugs

How do drugs affect prenatal development? Some pregnant women take drugs, smoke tobacco, and drink alcohol without thinking about the possible effects on the fetus. Occasionally, a rash of deformed babies are born, bringing to light the damage drugs can have on the developing fetus. This happened in 1961, when many pregnant women took a popular tranquilizer called thalidomide to reduce their morning sickness. In adults, the effects of thalidomide are mild; in embryos, they are devastating. Not all infants were affected in the same way. If the mother took thalidomide on day 26 (probably before she knew she was pregnant), an arm might not grow. If she took a drug two days later, the arm might not grow past the elbow. The thalidomide tragedy shocked the medical community and parents into the stark realization that the mother does not have to be a chronic drug user for the fetus to be harmed. Taking the wrong drug at the wrong time is enough to physically handicap the offspring for life.

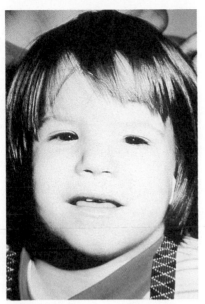

Figure 4.5   Fetal alcohol syndrome. This child has fetal alcohol syndrome. Notice the wide set eyes, flat bones, and thin upper lip. This child is also mentally retarded.

Heavy drinking by pregnant women can also be devastating to an offspring (Coles, Platzman, & Smith, 1991). **Fetal alcohol syndrome (FAS)** *is a cluster of abnormalities that appear in the offspring of mothers who drink heavily during pregnancy. The abnormalities include facial deformities, as well as defective limbs and heart. Most of these children are below average in intelligence and some are mentally retarded.* Figure 4.5 shows a child with fetal alcohol syndrome. While no serious malformations such as those produced by FAS are found in infants born to mothers who are moderate drinkers, in one investigation infants whose mothers drank moderately during pregnancy (for example, one to two drinks a day) were less attentive and alert, with the effects present at 4 years of age (Streissguth & others, 1984).

Cigarette smoking by pregnant women can also adversely influence prenatal development, birth, and postnatal development (Chasnoff, 1991; Fried & O'Connell, 1991; Streissguth & others, 1991). Fetal and neonatal deaths are higher among smoking mothers; also prevalent are higher preterm births and lower birth weights. In one recent investigation, prenatal exposure to cigarette smoking was related to poorer language and cognitive development at 4 years of age (Fried & Watkinson, 1990). In another study, mothers who smoked during pregnancy had infants who were awake more on a consistent basis—a finding one might expect, because the active ingredient in cigarettes is the stimulant nicotine (Landesman-Dwyer & Sackett, 1983). Respiratory problems and sudden infant death syndrome (also known as crib death) are more common among the offspring of mothers who smoked during pregnancy. Intervention programs designed to get pregnant women to stop smoking are successful in reducing some of the negative effects of cigarette smoking on offspring, being especially effective in raising their birth weights (Sexton & Hebel, 1984; Vorhees & Mollnow, 1987).

Marijuana use by pregnant women also has detrimental effects on the developing child (Day, 1991). Marijuana use by pregnant mothers is associated with increased tremors and startles among newborns (Fried, Watkinson, & Dillon, 1987), and poorer verbal and memory development at 4 years of age (Fried & Watkinson, 1990).

It is well documented that infants whose mothers are addicted to heroin show several behavioral difficulties (Hans, 1989; Hutchings & Fifer, 1986). The young infants of these mothers are addicted and show withdrawal symptoms characteristic of opiate abstinence, such as tremors, irritability, abnormal crying, disturbed sleep, and impaired motor control. Behavioral problems are still often present at the first birthday, and attention deficits may appear later in the child's development.

• *Critical Thinking* •

How can we reduce the number of offspring born to drug dependent mothers? If you had $100 million to spend to help remedy this problem, what would you do?

Table 4.1: Drug Use during Pregnancy

Drug	Effects on Fetus and Offspring	Safe Use of the Drug
Alcohol	Small amounts increase risk of spontaneous abortion. Moderate amounts (one to two drinks a day) are associated with poor attention in infancy. Heavy drinking can lead to fetal alcohol syndrome. Some experts believe even low to moderate amounts, especially in the first three months of pregnancy, increase the risk of FAS.	Should be avoided.
Nicotine	Heavy smoking is associated with low birth-weight babies, which means the baby may have more health problems. Smoking may be especially harmful in the second half of pregnancy.	Should be avoided.
Tranquilizers	Taken during the first three months of pregnancy, may cause cleft palate or other congenital malformations.	Avoid if you might become pregnant and during early pregnancy. Use only under doctor's supervision.
Barbiturates	Mothers who have taken large doses may have babies who are addicted. Babies may have tremors, restlessness, and irritability.	Use only under doctor's supervision.
Amphetamines	May cause birth defects.	Use only under doctor's supervision.
Cocaine	Possible drug dependency and withdrawal symptoms at birth, as well as physical and mental problems, especially if used in the first three months of pregnancy. Higher risk of hypertension and heart problems. Possible developmental retardation and possible learning difficulties.	Should be avoided.
Marijuana	May cause a variety of birth defects. Associated with low birth weight and height.	Should be avoided.

Source: Modified from the National Institute on Drug Abuse.

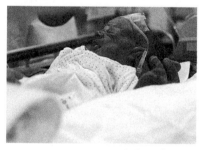

Figure 4.6 A cocaine baby. Shown here is a baby addicted to cocaine, who became addicted because its mother was a cocaine addict. Researchers have found that the offspring of women who took cocaine during pregnancy often have hypertension and heart damage. Many of these infants face a childhood full of medical problems.

With the increased use of cocaine in the United States, there is growing concern about the effects of cocaine on the embryos, fetuses, and infants of pregnant cocaine users (see figure 4.6). To learn more about the efforts of researchers to study the effects of cocaine use by pregnant mothers, turn to Perspective on Life-Span Development 4.1. A summary of the effects of various drugs on the fetus and offspring, and the safe use of these drugs, is presented in table 4.1.

Environmental Hazards

Radiation, chemicals, and other hazards in our modern industrial world can endanger the fetus. Radiation can cause a gene mutation, an abrupt but permanent change in genetic material. For example, chromosomal abnormalities are higher among the offspring of fathers exposed to high levels of radiation in their occupations (Schrag & Dixon, 1985). Radiation from X rays can also affect the developing embryo and fetus, with the most dangerous time being the first several weeks after conception, when a woman does not yet know she is pregnant. It is important for a woman and her physician to weigh the risk of an X ray when an actual or potential pregnancy is involved.

Environmental pollutants and toxic wastes are also sources of danger to the unborn child. Researchers have found defects in animals exposed to high doses of wastes and pesticides. Among the pollutants and wastes believed to

COCAINE BABIES

◆

Cocaine use during pregnancy has recently attracted considerable attention because of concerns about possible harm to the developing embryo and fetus. Surprisingly little is known about the potential adverse health outcomes associated with cocaine abuse during pregnancy, although a number of research studies are beginning to be conducted (Beckwith & Howard, 1991; Behnke & Eyler, 1991; Dixon, 1991; Lester, 1991). The most consistent finding is that infants born to cocaine abusers have reduced birth weight and length (Chasnoff & others, 1989). Increased frequencies of congenital abnormalities in the offspring of cocaine users during pregnancy have been noted, but other factors in the drug addict's life-style, such as malnutrition and other substance abuse, may be responsible for the congenital abnormalities (Eyler, Behnke, & Stewart, 1990; Little & others, 1989; Stewart, 1990). For example, cocaine users are more likely to smoke cigarettes and/or marijuana, drink alcohol, and take amphetamines than non-cocaine users (Little & others, 1989). Teasing apart these potential influences from the effects of cocaine use itself has not been adequately accomplished. Obtaining valid information about the frequency and type of drug use by mothers is also complicated because many mothers fear prosecution or loss of custody because of their drug use.

In one recent investigation of the offspring of cocaine users during pregnancy, 172 mothers who used cocaine prenatally and their offspring were compared with 155 mothers who had not used cocaine prenatally and their offspring (Eyler, Behnke, & Stewart, 1990). Cocaine users were more likely to have more children, be slightly older, enter the prenatal-care system later, and use more alcohol and tobacco. Also, in the cocaine-exposed group, there was a younger gestational age, lower birthweight, more instances of preterm labor, greater need for resuscitation, and a larger number of infants who remained hospitalized.

In another investigation, 75 cocaine-using women who enrolled in a comprehensive perinatal-care program were divided into two groups: those who used cocaine only during the first trimester of pregnancy (23 mothers and their offspring) and those who used cocaine throughout pregnancy (52 mothers and their offspring) (Chasnoff & others, 1989). The outcomes of these pregnancies were compared with the outcomes of a group of pregnant mothers with no history or evidence of substance abuse (40 mothers and their offspring). Both groups of cocaine-exposed infants had significantly impaired orientation, motor, and state regulation behaviors on the Brazelton Neonatal Behavior Assessment Scale. The mothers who used cocaine throughout their pregnancy were more likely to have a preterm delivery and low-birthweight infants than the other two groups of mothers.

Each year 375,000 babies are born to women who use drugs during pregnancy. In recent years, an increasing number of these infants have been cocaine babies. Although some of the babies born to mothers who have taken drugs during pregnancy will suffer little or no long-term effects, many of the drug-affected infants require extra attention. One intervention effort aimed at helping drug abusing mothers and their young children is Operation PAR (Parental Awareness and Responsibility), which serves 28,000 people a year in Florida. Operation PAR includes a day-care center, one of which is located in St. Petersburg and serves 31 2- to 6-year-old children. Much of what goes on in the day care is indistinguishable from any good day-care center. For example, the staff-child ratio is low, teachers are warm and friendly to the children, and there is an abundance of attractive and interesting toys and play areas. What is different are the anti-drug cartoons that start early in the children's attendance at the day-care center. Also, the parents whose children are in the day-care center must seek drug treatment and attend parenting-skill groups.

be dangerous to the developing fetus are carbon monoxide, lead, and mercury. Some children have been exposed to lead because their mothers live in houses where lead-based paint flakes off the walls or they live near a busy highway where there are heavy automobile emissions from leaded gasoline. Researchers believe that early exposure to lead affects children's mental development. For example, in one investigation, 2-year-old infants who prenatally had high levels of lead in their umbilical-cord blood performed poorly on a test of mental development (Bellinger & others, 1987).

Researchers have also found that the manufacturing chemicals known as PCBs are harmful to prenatal development. In one investigation, the extent to which pregnant women ate PCB-polluted fish from Lake Michigan was examined, and subsequently their newborns were observed (Jacobson & others,

Concept Table 4.1: Prenatal Development

Concept	Processes/Related Ideas	Characteristics/Description
The Course of Prenatal Development	Germinal Period	This period begins at conception and lasts about 10 to 14 days. The fertilized egg is called a zygote. The period ends when the zygote attaches to the uterine wall.
	Embryonic Period	This period lasts from about 2 weeks to 8 weeks after conception. The embryo differentiates into three layers, life-support systems develop, and organ systems form (organogenesis).
	Fetal Period	This period lasts from about 2 months after conception until 9 months or when the infant is born. Growth and development continue their dramatic course and organ systems mature to the point where life can be sustained outside the womb.
Miscarriage and Abortion	Its Nature and Ethical Issues	A miscarriage, or spontaneous abortion, happens when pregnancy ends before the developing organism is mature enough to survive outside the womb. Estimates indicate that about 15 to 20 percent of all pregnancies end this way, many without the mother's knowledge. Induced abortion is a complex issue medically, psychologically, and socially. An unwanted pregnancy is stressful for the woman regardless of how it is resolved.
Teratology and Hazards to Prenatal Development	Teratology	Teratology is the field that investigates the causes of congenital (birth) defects. Any agent that causes birth defects is called a teratogen.
	Maternal Diseases and Conditions	Maternal diseases and infections can cause damage by crossing the placental barrier, or they can be destructive during the birth process. Among the maternal diseases and conditions believed to be involved in possible birth defects are rubella, syphilis, genital herpes, AIDS, the mother's age, nutrition, and emotional state and stress.
	Drugs	Thalidomide was a tranquilizer given to pregnant mothers to reduce their morning sickness. In the early 1960s, thousands of babies were malformed as a consequence of their mother taking this drug. Alcohol, nicotine, heroin, and cocaine are other drugs that can adversely affect prenatal and infant development.
	Environmental Hazards	Among the environmental hazards that can endanger the fetus are radiation in occupations and X rays, environmental pollutants, and toxic wastes.

1984). Women who had eaten greater quantities of PCB-polluted fish were more likely to have newborns who were smaller preterm infants and who reacted slower to stimuli.

A recent environmental hazard concern involves women who spend long hours in front of a video display terminal (Becker, 1990). The fear is that the low levels of electromagnetic radiation from the video display terminal will adversely affect the offspring of pregnant women. As yet, there is little research about this potential hazard.

At this point we have discussed a number of ideas about prenatal development. A summary of these ideas is presented in concept table 4.1. Next, we turn to the study of the birth process.

The Birth Process

Delivery can be as difficult for the baby as for the mother, lasting anywhere from 4 to 24 hours. When the newborn emerges, it is covered with a thick, greasy, white material called vernix, which eases movement through the birth canal. The newborn's head is not the most attractive in the world; it may be swollen at the top because of pressure against the pelvic outlet during the last hours of labor. The baby's face may be puffy and bluish; the ears may be pressed against the head in a bizarre position—matted forward on the cheeks, for example. The nose may be flattened and skewed to one side by the squeeze through the pelvis. The baby may be bowlegged, and the feet may be pigeon-toed from being up beside the head for so long in the mother's womb; they can be flexed and put in a normal position at birth. How stunning it must be to be thrust suddenly into a new, bright, airy world so totally different from the dark, moist warmth of the womb. Despite the drama of human birth, newborns who have had a comfortable stay in the womb and are born when due are well equipped by nature to withstand the birth process. There are many intriguing questions about the birth process: What kinds of childbirth strategies are currently being used? What are the stages of birth, and what delivery complications can arise? What are preterm infants like? How can we measure the newborn's health and social responsiveness? How crucial is bonding? We will consider each of these in turn.

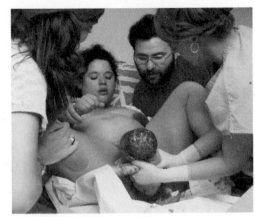

Birth is a time of dramatic transition for the fetus. The baby is on a threshold between two worlds.

Childbirth Strategies

Controversy swirls over how childbirth should proceed. Some critics argue that the standard delivery practices of most hospitals and physicians need to be overhauled. Others suggest that the entire family—especially the father—should be more involved in childbirth. And others argue that procedures that ensure mother-infant bonding should be followed.

In the standard childbirth procedure that was practiced for many years, the expectant mother was taken to a hospital, and was prepared for labor by having her pubic hair shaved and by having an enema. She was then placed in a labor room which was often filled with other pregnant women, some of whom were screaming. When she was ready to deliver, she was taken to the delivery room, which looked like an operating room. She was laid on the table with her legs in the air, and the physician, along with an anesthetist and a nurse, delivered the baby.

What could be wrong with this procedure? Critics list three things: (1) Important individuals related to the mother are excluded from the birth process. (2) The mother is separated from her infant in the first minutes and hours after birth. (3) Giving birth is treated like a disease, and a woman is thought of as a sick patient (Rosenblith & Sims-Knight, 1985). As we will see next, some alternative procedures differ radically from this standard procedure.

The **Leboyer method,** *developed by French obstetrician Frederick Leboyer, is intended to make the birth process less stressful for infants. Leboyer's procedure is referred to as "birth without violence."* Leboyer describes standard childbirth as torture (Leboyer, 1975). He vehemently objects to holding newborns upside down and slapping or spanking them, putting silver nitrite into their eyes, separating them immediately from their mothers, and scaring them with the bright lights and harsh noises of the delivery room. Leboyer also criticizes the traditional habit of cutting the umbilical cord as soon as the infant is born, a situation that forces the infant to immediately inhale oxygen to breathe. Leboyer believes that the umbilical cord should be left intact for several minutes to allow the newborn a chance to adjust to a

> There was a star danced, and under that I was born.
>
> ~ *William Shakespeare*

> We must respect this instant of birth, this fragile moment. The baby is between two worlds, on a threshold, hesitating . . .
>
> ~ *Frederick Leboyer,*
> Birth Without Violence

As the Lamaze method became more popular, it became common for fathers to assist in the birth process. This photograph shows a father participating in Lamaze training.

world of breathing air. In the Leboyer method, the baby is placed on the mother's stomach immediately after birth so the mother can caress the infant. Then the infant is placed in a bath of warm water to relax.

While most hospitals do not use the soft lights and warm baths suggested by Leboyer, they sometimes do place the newborn on the mother's stomach immediately after birth, believing that it will stimulate bonding between the mother and the infant.

Another well-known birth procedure that deviates markedly from the standard practice is the **Lamaze method,** *a form of prepared or natural childbirth developed by Fernand Lamaze, a pioneering French obstetrician. It has become widely accepted in the medical profession and involves helping the pregnant mother to cope with the discomfort of childbirth in an active way to avoid or reduce medication.* Lamaze training for parents is available on a widespread basis in the United States and usually consists of six weekly classes. In these classes, the pregnant woman learns about the birth process and is trained in breathing and relaxation exercises. As the Lamaze method grew in popularity, it became more common for the father to participate in the exercises and to assist in the birth process.

Medical doctors provide most maternity care in the United States. However, in many countries of the world, midwives are the primary caregiver for pregnant and laboring women. In the United States, midwives are not as well established, although all states have provisions for their practice. The emphasis of the midwife's training is that birth is a normal physiological event. Midwives support and promote the woman's physical and emotional well-being. Midwives do not care for women who have complications of pregnancy. In the United States, certified nurse-midwives are the most numerous. They generally work in close cooperation with physicians in hospitals, homes, or birthing centers.

Most births in the United States take place in a hospital. In recent years, hospitals have offered more comfortable, homelike rooms for birth. Many hospitals now have birthing rooms, where the mother can labor, give birth, and spend time with her newborn afterward. And birthing centers also have emerged as an alternative setting to hospitals if the pregnant woman is healthy and no complications are foreseen. Birthing centers provide a sense of community and learning, with social gatherings and classes often being held there.

Labor is a biological process that is virtually the same in all cultures. The *experience* of birth, though, varies extensively from one culture to another. In several cultures, giving birth is thought of as a natural process that requires no special assistance. This orientation toward birth characterizes the hunting and gathering society of the !Kung who live in Africa's Kalahari desert.

Most cultures have at least one or two attendants to help in delivering the baby. The Ngoni women of East Africa view themselves as childbirth experts. They completely exclude men from the birth sequence and keep their pregnancy a secret from the men as long as possible. When the mother-in-law discovers that her daughter-in-law's labor has started, she and other female relatives move into the woman's hut, make the husband leave, and oversee the baby's birth. The women even remove all of the husband's belongings from the hut, including his tools and clothes. Men are not permitted to return to the hut until after the baby's birth (Read, 1968).

Stages of Birth and Delivery Complications

The birth process occurs in three stages, the longest of which is the first stage. For a woman having her first child, the first stage lasts an average of 12 to 24 hours. During this stage, uterine contractions which occur 15 to 20 minutes apart at the beginning and last up to a minute, stretch and open the woman's cervix. As the first stage progresses, the contractions come closer together, appearing every 2 to 5 minutes, and their intensity increases. By the end of the first birth stage, contractions dilate the cervix to an opening of about 4 inches so that the baby can move from the uterus to the birth canal.

The second birth stage begins when the baby's head starts to move through the cervix and the birth canal. It terminates when the baby completely emerges from the mother's body. This stage lasts for approximately 1½ hours. With each contraction, the mother bears down to push the baby out of her body. By the time the baby's head is out of the mother's body, the contractions come almost every minute and last for about a minute.

Afterbirth *is the third birth stage, during which the placenta, umbilical cord, and other membranes are detached and expelled.* This final stage is the shortest of the three birth stages, lasting only minutes.

Complications can accompany the baby's delivery. **Precipitate** *is a delivery that takes place too rapidly. In precipitate delivery, the baby takes less than 10 minutes to be squeezed through the birth canal.* This deviation in delivery can disturb the infant's normal blood flow, and the pressure on the infant's head can cause hemorrhaging. **Anoxia,** *the insufficient availability of oxygen to the infant,* can develop if the delivery takes too long. Anoxia can cause brain damage.

The **breech position** *is the baby's position in the uterus that causes the buttocks to be the first part to emerge from the vagina.* In some breech positions, one or both feet emerge first. Normally, the crown of the baby's head comes through the vagina first. But in 1 of every 25 babies born the head does not come through first, as when the baby is in the breech position. Breech babies have difficulties because their heads are still in the uterus when the rest of their bodies are out, which can cause respiratory problems. Some breech babies cannot be passed through the cervix and must be delivered by cesarean section.

A **cesarean section** *is the surgical removal of the baby from the uterus through the abdomen.* A cesarean section is usually performed when the baby is in a breech position or lying crosswise in the uterus, when the baby's head is too large to pass through the mother's pelvis, when the baby develops complications, or when the mother is bleeding vaginally. The benefits and risks of cesarean section delivery continue to be debated. Cesarean section deliveries

> Birth is not one act
> It is a process.
> ~ *Erich Fromm*

are safer for the mother and child in various circumstances, but a higher infection rate, a longer hospital stay, greater expense, and the stress that accompanies any surgery characterize cesarean section deliveries. Some critics believe too many American babies are delivered by cesarean section. In fact, more cesarean sections are performed in the United States than in any other industrialized nation. From 1979 to 1987 alone, the number of cesarean sections increased almost 50 percent in the United States to an annual rate of 24 percent (Marieskind, 1989). However, growing use of vaginal birth after a previous cesarean, greater public awareness, and peer pressure in the medical community are beginning to slow the rate of increase (Enkin, 1989; Marieskind, 1989).

Use of Drugs during Childbirth

Drugs can be used to relieve pain and anxiety and to speed up delivery during the birth process. The widest use of drugs during delivery is to relieve the expectant mother's pain or anxiety. A wide variety of tranquilizers, sedatives, and analgesics are used for this purpose. Researchers are interested in the effects of these drugs because they can cross the placental barrier and because their use is so widespread. One survey of hospitals found that only 5 percent of deliveries involved no anesthesia (Brackbill, 1979).

Oxytocin, *a hormone that simulates and regulates the rhythmicity of uterine contractions has been widely used as a drug to speed up delivery. Controversy surrounds the use of this drug.* Some physicians argue that it can save the mother's life or keep the infant from being damaged. They also stress that using the drug allows the mother to be well rested and prepared for the birth process. Critics argue that babies born to mothers who have taken oxytocin are more likely to have jaundice, that induced labor requires more pain-killing drugs, and that greater medical care is required after the birth, resulting in the separation of the infant and the mother.

What conclusions can be reached based on research about the influence of drugs during delivery? Four conclusions follow (Rosenblith & Sims-Knight, 1985):

1. Research studies are few in number, and those that have been completed often have methodological problems. However, not all drugs have similar effects. Some drugs—tranquilizers, sedatives, and analgesics, for example—do not seem to have long-term effects. Other drugs—oxytocin, for example—are suspected of having long-term effects.
2. The degree to which a drug influences the infant is usually small. Birth weight and social class, for instance, are more powerful predictors of infant difficulties than drugs.
3. A specific drug may affect some infants but not others. In some cases, the drug may have a beneficial effect, while in others, it may have a harmful effect.
4. The overall amount of medication may be an important factor in understanding the effects drugs have on delivery.

Preterm Infants and Age-Weight Considerations

An infant is full-term when it has grown in the womb for the full 38 to 42 weeks between conception and delivery. A **preterm infant** *(also called a premature infant) is one who is born prior to 38 weeks after conception.* **Low-birthweight infants** *are infants born after a regular gestation period (the length of time between conception and birth) of 38 to 42 weeks, but who weigh less than 5½ pounds.* Both preterm and low-birthweight infants are considered high-risk infants (Crisafi & Driscoll, 1991; Dedrick & others, 1991; Holmes, Reich, & Gyurke, 1989; Hunt & Cooper, 1989).

In one recent study, an intervention program was implemented to improve the developmental outcomes of low-birthweight infants (Achenbach & others, 1990). The program was designed to enhance the mother's adjustment to the care of a low-birthweight infant by (a) enabling the mother to appreciate her baby's specific behavioral and temperamental characteristics; (b) sensitizing her to the baby's cues, especially those that signal stimulus overload, distress, and readiness for interaction; and (c) teaching her to respond appropriately to those cues to facilitate mutually satisfying interactions. The intervention involved seven hospital sessions and four home sessions in which a nurse helped mothers adapt to their low-birthweight babies. At age 7, the low-birthweight babies whose mothers had participated in the intervention program scored higher than a control group of low-birthweight babies on information processing measures. The researchers commented that the intervention prevented cognitive lags among low-birthweight children and that long-term follow-ups are needed to overcome major biological and environmental risks.

A short gestation period does not necessarily harm the infant. It is distinguished from retarded prenatal growth, in which the fetus has been damaged in some way (Kopp, 1983, 1987). The neurological development of the short-gestation infant continues after birth on approximately the same timetable as if the infant were still in the womb. For example, consider an infant born after a gestation period of 30 weeks. At 38 weeks, approximately two months after birth, this infant shows the same level of brain development as a 38-week fetus who is yet to be born.

Some infants are born early and have a precariously low birth weight (Friedman & Caron, 1991; Thompson & Oehler, 1991). "Kilogram kids" weigh less than 2.3 pounds (which is 1 kilogram, or 1,000 grams) and are very premature. The task of saving such a baby is not easy. At the Stanford University Medical Center in Palo Alto, California, 98 percent of the preterm babies survive; however, 32 percent of those between 750 and 1,000 grams do not, and 76 percent of those below 750 grams do not. Approximately 250,000 preterm babies are born in the United States each year and 15,000 to 20,000 of these weigh less than 1,000 grams.

Preterm infants have a different profile than full-term infants. For instance, infant researcher Tiffany Field (1979) found that 4-month-old preterm infants vocalized less, fussed more, and avoided eye contact more than their full-term counterparts. Other researchers have found differences in the information-processing skills of preterm and full-term infants. In one investigation, Susan Rose and her colleagues (1988) found that 7-month-old high-risk preterm infants were less visually attentive to novelty and showed deficits in visual recognition memory when compared with full-term infants.

Some Conclusions about Preterm Infants

What conclusions can we draw from the results of research about preterm infants? Four such conclusions seem appropriate (Kopp, 1983, 1987; Kopp & Kaler, 1989):

1. As intensive-care technology has improved, there have been fewer serious consequences of preterm births. For instance, from 1961 to 1965, the manner of feeding preterm infants changed and intravenous fluid therapy came into use. From 1966 to 1968, better control of hypoxemia (oxygen

Some infants are born very early and have a precariously low birth weight. Shown here is a "kilogram kid," weighing less than 2.3 pounds. In neonatal care units, such as the one shown here, banks of flashing lights, linking numbers, and beeping alarms stand guard over the extremely premature infant. Vital signs such as brain waves, heartbeat, and respiratory rate are constantly monitored.

deficiency) resulted. In 1971, artificial ventilation was introduced. In the mid-1970s, neonatal support systems became less intrusive and damaging to the infant.

2. Infants born with an identifiable problem are likely to have a poorer developmental future than infants born without a recognizable problem (Cohen & others, 1989). For instance, extremely sick or extremely tiny babies are less likely to survive than are healthy or normal-weight babies.

3. Social class differences are associated with the preterm infant's development. The higher the socioeconomic status, the more favorable is the developmental outcome for a newborn. Social class differences are tied to many other differences. For example, quality of environment, cigarette and alcohol consumption, IQ, and knowledge of competent parenting strategies are associated with social class; less positive characteristics are associated with lower-class families.

4. We do not have solid evidence that preterm infants, as a rule, have difficulty later in school. Nor is there substantial evidence that these preterm children perform poorly on IQ and information-processing tests. Such claims to the contrary were made just one or two decades ago.

Despite the advances made in prenatal care and technology in the United States, the availability of quality medical and educational services still needs much improvement. In some countries, especially in Scandinavia and western Europe, more consistent, higher quality prenatal care is provided than in the United States. To read further about the nature of prenatal care in different countries, turn to Cultural Worlds of Development 4.1.

Stimulation of Preterm Infants

Just three decades ago the preterm infant was perceived as being too fragile for stimulation and the recommendation was to handle the infant as little as possible. The climate of opinion changed when the adverse effects of maternal deprivation became known and was interpreted to include a lack of stimulation. A number of research studies followed that indicated a "more is better" approach in the stimulation of the preterm infant. However, today experts on infant development argue that the care of the preterm infant is far too complex to be described only in terms of the amount of stimulation (Field, 1990; Korner, 1990; Lester & Tronick, 1990a).

Experts on the stimulation of preterm infants recently held a roundtable discussion and offered the following recommendations (Lester & Tronick, 1990b):

1. Preterm infants' responses to stimulation vary with their conceptual age, illness, and individual makeup. The immature brain of the preterm infant may be more vulnerable to excessive, inappropriate, or mistimed stimulation. The very immature infant should probably be protected from stimulation that could destabilize its homeostatic condition.

PRENATAL CARE IN THE UNITED STATES AND AROUND THE WORLD

As advanced as the United States has become economically and technologically, it still has more low-birth-weight infants than a number of countries (Grant, 1986, 1991). As indicated in table 4.A, only 4 percent of the infants born in Sweden, Finland, the Netherlands, and Norway, and only 5 percent of those born in New Zealand, Australia, France, and Japan are of low birth weight. In the United States, 7 percent of the infants born are of low birth weight. Also as indicated in table 4.A, in some developing countries such as Bangladesh, where poverty is rampant and the health and nutrition of mothers is poor, the percentage of low-birth-weight infants reaches as high as one-half of all infants.

In the United States, there are also discrepancies in the nature of prenatal development and birth between Black infants and White infants (Edelman, 1987): Black infants:
are twice as likely to
- be born prematurely
- have low birth weight
- have mothers who received late or no prenatal care

are three times as likely to
- have their mothers die in childbirth

are five times as likely to
- be born to unmarried teenage mothers.

In many countries with a lower percentage of low-birth-weight infants than the United States, either free or very low-cost prenatal and postnatal care is available to mothers. This care includes paid maternity leave from work that ranges from 9 to 40 weeks (Miller, 1987). In Norway and the Netherlands, prenatal care is coordinated with a general practitioner, an obstetrician, and a midwife. Twelve prenatal visits are made to these professionals.

Pregnant women in the United States do not receive the uniform prenatal care that women in many Scandanavian and western European countries receive. The United States does not have a national policy of health care that ensures high-quality assistance for pregnant women. The cost of birth is approximately $4000 in the United States (more than $5,000 for a cesarean birth), and more than 25 percent of American women of prime childbearing age do not have insurance that will pay for hospital costs. More than one-fifth of White mothers and one-third of Black mothers do not receive prenatal care in the first trimester of their pregnancy. Five percent of White mothers and 10 percent of Black mothers receive no prenatal care at all (Wegman, 1986). Many infant development experts believe the United States needs more comprehensive medical and educational services to improve the quality of prenatal care and reduce the percentage of low-birth-weight infants.

Table 4.A	*Percentage of Low-Birthweight Infants in Selected Countries*
Country	Percentage of Low-Birthweight Infants
Bangladesh	50%
India	30%
Guatemala	18%
Iran	14%
Mexico	12%
U.S.S.R.	9%
U.S., Great Britain, Israel, Egypt	7%
Canada, China	6%
New Zealand, Australia, France, Japan	5%
Sweden, Finland, the Netherlands, Norway	4%

Source: Data from J. Grant, *State of the World's Children,* 1986.

MASSAGING AND EXERCISING PREEMIES

In one investigation, 40 preterm infants who had just been released from the intensive-care unit and placed in a transitional nursery were studied (Field, Scafidi, & Schanberg, 1987). Twenty of the preterm babies were given special stimulation with massage and exercise techniques for three 15-minute periods at the beginning of three consecutive hours every morning for ten weekdays. For example, the infant was placed on its stomach and gently stroked. The massage began with the head and neck and moved downward to the feet. It also moved from the shoulders down to the hands. The infant was then rolled over. Each arm and leg was flexed and extended, then both legs together were flexed and extended. Next, the massage was repeated.

The massaged and exercised preterm babies gained 47 percent more weight than their preterm counterparts who were not massaged and exercised, even though both groups had the same number of feedings per day and averaged the same intake of formula. The massaged infants were more active, more alert, and performed

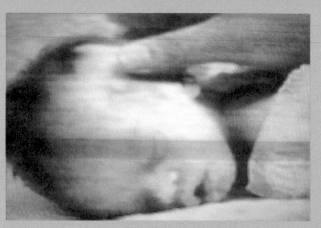

This preterm baby is being massaged as part of Tiffany Field's research investigation of the effects of massaging and exercising on infant development. The massaged and exercised infants were more active, more alert, and performed better on developmental tests than their preterm counterparts who were not massaged.

better on developmental tests. Also, their hospital stay was about six days shorter than the nonmassaged, nonexercised group. This saved about $3,000 per preterm infant.

The increased activity of the massaged, exercised infants would seem to work against weight gain. However, similar findings have been found with animals. The increased activity may increase gastrointestinal and metabolic efficiency.

The massaged, exercised infants also were more socially interactive than the other infants. This may happen because massage stimulates intimacy between the infant and social figures in its world (Field, 1991).

2. As the healthy preterm infant becomes less fragile and approaches term, the issue of what is appropriate stimulation should be considered. Infant behavioral cues can be used to determine appropriate interventions for the individual infant. Signs of stress or avoidance behaviors indicate that the stimulation should be terminated. Positive behaviors indicate that stimulation is appropriate. To read about the stimulation strategies of massage and exercise with preterm infants, turn to Perspective on Life-Span Development 4.2.

3. Intervention with the preterm infant should be organized in the form of an individualized developmental plan. This plan should be constructed as a psychosocial intervention to include the parents and other immediate family members and to acknowledge the socioeconomic, cultural, and home environment factors that will determine the social context in which the infant will be reared. The developmental plan should include assessing the infant's behavior, working with

Table 4.2: The Apgar Scale

Health Sign	Score		
	0	1	2
Heart rate	Absent	Slow—fewer than 100 beats per minute	Fast—100-140 beats per minute
Respiratory effort	No breathing for more than 1 minute	Irregular and slow	Good breathing with normal crying
Muscle tone	Limp and flaccid	Weak and inactive, but some flexion of extremities	Strong, active motion
Body color	Blue and pale	Body pink but extremities blue	Entire body pink
Reflex irritability	No response	Grimace	Coughing, sneezing, and crying

From Virginia A. Apgar, "A Proposal for a New Method of Evaluation of a Newborn Infant" in *Anesthesia and Analgesia*, 32:260–267. Copyright © 1975 International Anesthesia Research Society. Reprinted by permission.

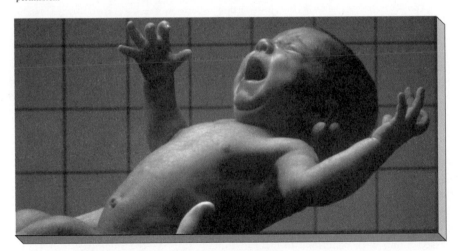

parents to help them understand the infant's medical and behavioral status, and helping the parents to deal with their own feelings (Lester & others, 1990).

Measures of Neonatal Health and Responsiveness

The **Apgar scale** *is a widely used method to assess the health of the newborn 1 and 5 minutes after birth. The Apgar scale is used to evaluate heart rate, respiratory effort, muscle tone, body color, and reflex irritability.* The obstetrician or nurse gives the newborn a reading of 0, 1, or 2 for each of these five signs (see table 4.2). A high total score of 7 to 10 indicates the newborn's

Table 4.3: The 26 Categories on the Brazelton Neonatal Behavioral Assessment Scale (NBAS)

1. Response decrement to repeated visual stimuli
2. Response decrement to rattle
3. Response decrement to bell
4. Response decrement to pinprick
5. Orienting response to inanimate visual stimuli
6. Orienting response to inanimate auditory stimuli
7. Orienting response to animate visual stimuli—examiner's face
8. Orienting response to animate auditory stimuli—examiner's voice
9. Orienting responses to animate visual and auditory stimuli
10. Quality and duration of alert periods
11. General muscle tone—in resting and in response to being handled, passive, and active
12. Motor activity
13. Traction responses as the infant is pulled to sit
14. Cuddliness—responses to being cuddled by examiner
15. Defensive movements—reactions to a cloth over the infant's face
16. Consolability with intervention by examiner
17. Peak of excitement and capacity to control self
18. Rapidity of buildup to crying state
19. Irritability during the examination
20. General assessment of kind and degree of activity
21. Tremulousness
22. Amount of startling
23. Lability of skin color—measuring autonomic lability
24. Lability of states during entire examination
25. Self-quieting activity—attempts to console self and control state
26. Hand-to-mouth activity

condition is good, a score of 5 indicates there may be developmental difficulties, and a score of 3 or below signals an emergency and indicates that survival may be in doubt.

While the Apgar is used immediately after birth to identify high-risk infants who need resuscitation, another scale is being increasingly used in addition to the Apgar. The **Brazelton Neonatal Behavioral Assessment Scale** *is given several days after birth to assess the newborn's neurological development, reflexes, and reactions to people* (Brazelton, 1973, 1984, 1990; Brazelton, Nugent, & Lester, 1987). The Brazelton scale is usually given on the third day of life and then repeated several days later. Twenty reflexes are assessed along with reactions to circumstances, such as the neonate's reaction to a rattle. The examiner rates the newborn on each of 26 different items (see table 4.3). As an indication of how detailed the ratings are, consider item 14 in table 4.3: "cuddliness." As shown in table 4.4, nine categories are involved in assessing this item, with infant behavior scored on a continuum that ranges from the infant being very resistant to being held to the infant being extremely

Table 4.4: The Assessment of Cuddliness on the Brazelton Neonatal Behavioral Assessment Scale

Score	Infant Behavior
1	The infant resists being held and continually pushes away, thrashes, and stiffens.
2	The infant resists being held most of the time.
3	The infant does not resist but does not participate either, acting like a rag doll.
4	The infant eventually molds into the examiner's arms after considerable nestling and cuddling efforts by the examiner.
5	The infant usually molds and relaxes when initially held, nestling into the examiner's neck or crook of the elbow. The infant leans forward when held on the examiner's shoulder.
6	The infant always molds at the beginning, as described above.
7	The infant always molds initially with nestling and turns toward body and leans forward.
8	The infant molds and relaxes, nestles and turns head, leans forward on the shoulder, fits feet into cavity of other arm, and all of the body participates.
9	All of the above take place, and in addition, the infant grasps the examiner and clings.

From *In the Beginning: Development in the First Two Years,* by J. E. Rosenblith and J. E. Sims-Knight. Copyright © 1985 by Wadsworth, Inc., division of Brooks/ Cole Publishing Company, Pacific Grove, CA.

cuddly and clinging. The Brazelton scale is not only used as a sensitive index of neurological integrity in the week after birth, but it is also used widely as a measure in many research studies on infant development. In recent versions of scoring the Brazelton scale, Brazelton and his colleagues (1987) categorize the 26 items into four different categories—physiological, motoric, state, and interaction. They also classify the baby in global terms such as "worrisome," "normal," or "superior," based on these categories.

A very low Brazelton score can indicate brain damage. But if the infant merely seems sluggish in responding to social circumstances, parents are encouraged to give the infant attention and to undergo **Brazelton training,** *which involves using the Brazelton scale to show parents how their newborn responds to people* (Brazelton, 1987, 1989). As part of the training, parents are shown how the neonate can respond positively to people and how such responses can be stimulated. Brazelton training has improved the social interaction of high-risk infants and the social skills of healthy, responsive infants (Widmayer & Field, 1980; Worobey & Belsky, 1982).

Bonding

Bonding *is the establishment of close contact, especially physical contact, between the parent and the newborn in the period shortly after birth. Some physicians believe this period is a critical time for the formation of an important emotional attachment that will provide a foundation for optimal development in years to come.* Special interest in bonding came about when it was recognized that the circumstances surrounding delivery often separate the mother and her infant, preventing or making difficult the development of a bond between the mother and infant. Giving the mother drugs to make her

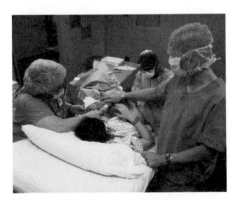

This mother is bonding with her infant moments after the baby was born. How critical is bonding for the development of social competence later in childhood?

Concept Table 4.2: The Birth Process

Concept	Processes/Related Ideas	Characteristics/Description
Childbirth Strategies	Their Nature	A controversy currently exists over how childbirth should proceed. Standard childbirth has been criticized, and the Leboyer and Lamaze methods have been developed as alternatives. Medical doctors deliver most babies in the United States, but midwives sometimes are used. Most babies in the United States are delivered in hospitals, but birthing centers also may be used.
Stages of Birth and Complications	Stages	Three stages of birth have been defined. The first lasts about 12 to 24 hours for a woman having her first child. The cervix dilates to about 4 inches. The second stage begins when the baby's head moves through the cervix and ends with the baby's complete emergence. The third stage is afterbirth.
	Complications	A baby can move through the birth canal too rapidly or too slowly. A delivery that is too fast is called precipitate; when delivery is too slow, anoxia may result. A cesarean section is the surgical removal of the baby from the uterus.
Use of Drugs during Childbirth	Drugs Used to Relieve Pain and Anxiety and to Speed Up Delivery	A wide variety of tranquilizers, sedatives, and analgesics are used to relieve the expectant mother's pain and anxiety, while oxytocin is used to speed up delivery. It is hard to come up with general statements about drug effects, but it is known that birth weight and social class are more powerful predictors of problems than drugs. A specific drug can have mixed effects and the overall amount of medication needs to be considered.

delivery less painful may contribute to the failure of a mother and her infant to bond. The drugs may make the mother drowsy and thus interfere with her ability to respond to and stimulate the newborn. And preterm infants are isolated from their mothers to an even greater degree than full-term infants.

Is there evidence that such close contact between the mother and the newborn is absolutely critical for optimal development later in life? While some research supports the bonding hypothesis (Klaus & Kennell, 1976), a growing body of research challenges the significance of the first few days of life as a critical period (Bakeman & Brown, 1980; Rode & others, 1981). Indeed, the extreme form of the bonding hypothesis—that the newborn must have close contact with the mother in the first few days of life to develop optimally—simply is not true.

Concept	Processes/Related Ideas	Characteristics/Description
Preterm Infants and Age-Weight Considerations	Types	Preterm infants are those born after a briefer-than-regular time period in the womb. Infants who are born after a regular gestation period of 38 to 42 weeks but who weigh less than 5½ pounds are called low-birth-weight infants.
	Conclusions	As intensive-care technology has improved, preterm babies have benefited considerably. Infants born with an identifiable problem have a poorer developmental future than those born without a recognizable problem. Social class differences are associated with the preterm infant's development. There is no solid evidence that preterm infants perform more poorly than full-term infants when they are assessed years later in school.
	Stimulation	Care of the preterm infant is much too complex to be described only in terms of the amount of stimulation. Preterm infants' responses vary according to their conceptual age, illness, and individual makeup. Infant behavioral cues can be used to indicate the appropriate stimulation. Intervention should be organized in the form of an individualized developmental plan.
Measures of Neonatal Health and Responsiveness	Types	For many years the Apgar scale has been used to assess the newborn's health. A more recently developed test—the Brazelton Neonatal Behavioral Assessment Scale—is used for long-term neurological assessment. It assesses not only the newborn's neurological integrity but also social responsiveness. If the newborn is sluggish, Brazelton training is recommended.
Bonding	Its Nature	There is evidence that bonding—establishment of a close mother-infant bond in the first hours or days after birth—is not critical for optimal development, although for some mother-infant pairs it may stimulate interaction after they leave the hospital.

Nonetheless, the weakness of the maternal-infant bonding research should not be used as an excuse to keep motivated mothers from interacting with their infants in the postpartum period, because such contact brings pleasure to many mothers. In some mother-infant pairs—preterm infants, adolescent mothers, or mothers from disadvantaged circumstances—the practice of bonding may set in motion a climate for improved mother-infant interaction after the mother and infant leave the hospital (Maccoby & Martin, 1983).

We have discussed many dimensions of the birth process. To help you remember the main points of this discussion, turn to concept table 4.2. This concludes our discussion of biological beginnings. In the next section, we will turn our attention to the nature of infant development.

Summary

I. The Course of Prenatal Development

Prenatal development is divided into three periods. The germinal period lasts from conception to about 10 to 14 days. The fertilized egg is called a zygote. This period ends when the zygote attaches to the uterine wall. The embryonic period lasts from 2 weeks to 8 weeks after conception. The embryo differentiates into three layers; life-support systems develop; and organ systems form (organogenesis). The fetal period lasts from 2 months after conception until 9 months or when the infant is born. Growth and development continue their dramatic course, and organ systems mature to the point that life can be sustained outside the womb.

II. Miscarriage and Abortion

A miscarriage, or spontaneous abortion, happens when pregnancy ends before the developing organism is mature enough to survive outside the womb. Estimates indicate that about 15 to 20 percent of all pregnancies end this way, many without the mother's knowledge. Induced abortion is a complex issue medically, psychologically, and socially. An unwanted pregnancy is stressful for the woman regardless of how it is resolved.

III. Teratology and the Hazards to Prenatal Development

Teratology is the field that investigates the causes of congenital (birth) defects. Any agent that causes birth defects is called a teratogen. Maternal diseases and infections can cause damage by crossing the placental barrier, or they can be destructive during the birth process itself. Among the maternal diseases and conditions believed to be involved in possible birth defects are rubella, syphilis, genital herpes, AIDS, the mother's age, nutrition, and emotional state and stress. Thalidomide was a tranquilizer given to pregnant mothers to reduce their morning sickness. In the early 1960s, thousands of babies were malformed as a consequence of their mother taking this drug. Alcohol, nicotine, heroin, and cocaine are other drugs that can adversely affect prenatal and infant development. Among the environmental hazards that can endanger the fetus are radiation in occupations and X rays, environmental pollutants, and toxic wastes.

IV. Childbirth Strategies

A controversy exists over how childbirth should proceed. Standard childbirth has been criticized, and the Leboyer and Lamaze methods have been developed as alternatives. Medical doctors deliver most babies in the United States, but midwives are sometimes used. Most babies in the United States are born in hospitals, but birthing centers have provided an alternative in many areas.

V. Stages of Birth and Complications

Three stages of birth have been defined. The first lasts about 12 to 24 hours for a woman having her first child. The cervix dilates to about 4 inches. The second stage begins when the baby's head moves through the cervix and ends with the baby's complete emergence. The third stage is afterbirth. A baby can move through the birth canal too quickly or too slowly. A delivery that is too fast is called precipitate; when delivery is too slow, anoxia may result. A cesarean section is the surgical removal of the baby from the uterus.

VI. Use of Drugs during Childbirth

A wide variety of tranquilizers, sedatives, and analgesics are used to relieve the expectant mother's pain and anxiety, while oxytocin is used to speed up delivery. It is hard to make any general statements about drug effects, but it is known that birth weight and social class are more powerful predictors of problems than are drugs. A specific drug can have mixed effects, and the overall amount of medication needs to be considered.

VII. Preterm Infants and Age-Weight Considerations

Preterm infants are those born after a briefer-than-regular time period in the womb. Infants who are born after a regular gestation period of 38 to 42 weeks but who weigh less than 5½ pounds are called low-birthweight infants. As intensive-care technology has improved, preterm babies have benefited considerably. Infants born with an identifiable problem have a poorer developmental future than those born without a recognizable problem. Social class differences are associated with the preterm infant's development. There is no solid evidence that preterm infants perform more poorly than full-term infants when they are assessed years later in school. Care of the preterm infant is much too complex to be described only in terms of the amount of stimulation. Preterm infants' responses vary according to their conceptual age, illness, and individual makeup. Infant behavioral cues can be used to indicate the appropriate stimulation. Intervention should be organized in the form of an individualized developmental plan.

VIII. Measures of Neonatal Health and Responsiveness

For many years the Apgar Scale has been used to assess the newborn's health. A more recently developed test—the Brazelton Neonatal Behavioral Assessment Scale—is used for long-term neurological assessment. It assesses not only the newborn's neurological integrity but also social responsiveness. If the newborn is sluggish, Brazelton training is recommended.

IX. Bonding

There is evidence that bonding—establishment of a close mother-infant bond in the first hours or days after birth—is not critical for optimal development, although for some mother-infant pairs it may stimulate interaction after they leave the hospital.

Key Terms

germinal period 103
blastocyst 103
trophoblast 103
implantation 103
embryonic period 103
endoderm 104
ectoderm 104
mesoderm 104
placenta 104
umbilical cord 104

amnion 104
organogenesis 105
fetal period 105
teratogen 107
fetal alcohol syndrome (FAS) 111
Leboyer method 115
Lamaze method 116
afterbirth 117
precipitate 117
anoxia 117

breech position 117
cesarean section 117
oxytocin 118
preterm infants 118
low-birthweight infants 118
Apgar scale 123
Brazelton Neonatal Behavioral
Assessment Scale 124
Brazelton training 125
bonding 125

Suggested Readings

Brazelton, T. B., & Lester, B. M. (1982). *New approaches to developmental screenings of infants.* New York: Elsevier.
A group of experts on infant development relate new developments in the assessment of newborns.

Falkner, F., & Macy, C. (1980). *Pregnancy and birth.* New York: Harper & Row.
An easy-to-read description of experiences during pregnancy and the nature of childbearing.

Lester, B. M., & Tronick, E. Z. (1990). (Eds.). *Stimulation and the preterm infant: The limits of plasticity.* Philadelphia: W. B. Saunders.
This book is based on a roundtable discussion by a number of experts in the field of prenatal development and birth. The result is a provocative set of chapters that addresses important issues in intervention with preterm infants.

Nilsson, L. (1966). *A child is born.* New York: Delacourt.
Contains an abundance of breathtaking photographs that take you inside the mother's womb to see the developmental unfolding of the zygote, embryo, and fetus.

S·E·C·T·I·O·N
III

INFANCY

In the end, the power behind development is life.

Erik Erikson,
Harvard Educational Review, 1981

CHAPTER 5

Physical Development in Infancy

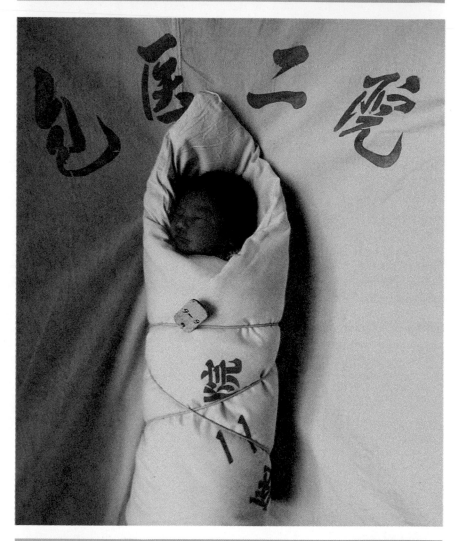

*T*he creature has poor motor coordination and can move itself only with great difficulty. Its general behavior appears to be disorganized, and although it cries when uncomfortable, it uses few other vocalizations. In fact, it sleeps most of the time, about 16 to 17 hours a day. You are curious about this creature and want to know more about what it can do. You ask yourself, "I wonder if it can see? How can I find out?"

You obviously have a communication problem with the creature. You must devise a way that will allow the creature to "tell" you that it can see. While examining the creature one day, you make an interesting discovery. When you move a large object toward it, it moves its head backward, as if to avoid a collision with the object. The creature's head movement suggests that it has at least some vision.

In case you haven't already guessed, the creature you have been reading about is the human infant, and the role you played is that of a developmentalist interested in devising techniques to learn about the infant's visual perception. After years of work, scientists have developed research tools and methods sophisticated enough to examine the subtle abilities of infants and to interpret their complex actions. Videotape equipment makes it possible to investigate elusive behaviors, and high-speed computers make it possible to perform complex data analysis in minutes instead of months and years. Other sophisticated equipment is used to closely monitor respiration, heart rate, body movement, visual fixation, and sucking behavior, which provide clues to what is going on inside the infant.

Among the first things developmentalists were able to demonstrate was that infants have highly developed perceptual motor systems. Until recently, even nurses in maternity hospitals often believed that newborns were blind at birth, and they told this to mothers. Most parents were also told that their newborns could not taste, smell, or feel pain. As you will discover later in this chapter, we now know that newborns can see (albeit fuzzily), they can taste, they can smell, and they can feel pain. Before we turn to the fascinating world of the infant's perception, we will discuss a number of ideas about physical development.

• Critical Thinking •

Other than moving a large object toward a newborn's head to see if the newborn responds to it, can you think of other techniques that could be used to determine whether a newborn can see or not?

Physical Growth and Development

How do infants respond to their world? What are an infant's states like? What is the nature of the infant's nutritional world? We will consider each of these questions in turn.

Reflexes

The newborn is not an empty-headed organism. Among other things, it has some basic reflexes that are genetically carried survival mechanisms. For example, the newborn has no fear of water; it will naturally hold its breath and contract its throat to keep water out.

Reflexes govern the newborn's movements, which are automatic and beyond the newborn's control. They are built-in reactions to certain stimuli. They provide young infants with adaptive responses to their environment before they have had the opportunity to learn. The **sucking reflex** *occurs when newborns automatically suck an object placed in their mouth. The sucking reflex enables newborns to get nourishment before they have associated a nipple with food.* The sucking reflex is an example of a reflex that is present at birth but later disappears. The **rooting reflex** *occurs when the infant's cheek is stroked or the side of the mouth is touched. In response, the infant turns its head toward the side that was touched in an apparent effort to find something to suck.* The sucking and rooting reflexes disappear when the infant is about

3 to 4 months old. They are replaced by the infant's voluntary eating. The sucking and rooting reflexes have survival value for newborn mammals, who must find the mother's breast to obtain nourishment.

The **Moro reflex** *is a neonatal startle response that occurs in response to a sudden, intense noise or movement. When startled, the newborn arches its back, throws its head back, and flings out its arms and legs. Then, the newborn rapidly closes its arms and legs to the center of the body.* The Moro reflex is a vestige from our primate ancestry and it too has survival value. This reflex, which is normal in all newborns, also tends to disappear at 3 to 4 months of age. Steady pressure on any part of the infant's body calms the infant after it has been startled. Holding the infant's arm flexed at the shoulder will quiet the infant.

Some reflexes present in the newborn—coughing, blinking, and yawning, for example—persist throughout life. They are as important for the adult as they are for the infant. Other reflexes, though, disappear several months following birth as the infant's brain functions mature, and voluntary control over many behaviors develops. The movements of some reflexes eventually become incorporated into more complex, voluntary actions. One important example is the **grasping reflex,** *which occurs when something touches the infant's palms. The infant responds by grasping tightly.* By the end of the third month, the grasping reflex diminishes and the infant shows a more voluntary grasp, which is often produced by visual stimuli. For example, when an infant sees a mobile whirling above its crib, it may reach out and try to grasp it. As its motor development becomes smoother, the infant will grasp objects, carefully manipulate them, and explore their qualities.

An overview of the main reflexes we have discussed, along with others, is given in table 5.1. Let's look now at three important reflexes in greater detail—sucking, crying, and smiling.

Sucking

Sucking is the infant's route to nourishment. The sucking capabilities of newborns vary considerably. Some newborns are efficient at forceful sucking and obtaining milk, others are not so adept and get tired before they are full. Most newborns take several weeks to establish a sucking style that is coordinated with the way the mother is holding the infant, the way milk is coming out of the bottle or breast, and the infant's sucking speed and temperament.

An investigation by pediatrician T. Berry Brazelton (1956) involved observations of infants for more than a year to determine the incidence of their sucking when they were nursing and how their sucking changed as they grew older. More than 85 percent of the infants engaged in considerable sucking behavior unrelated to feeding. They sucked their fingers, their fists, and pacifiers. By the age of 1 year, most had stopped the sucking behavior.

Parents should not worry when infants suck their thumbs, fist, or even a pacifier. Many parents, though, do begin to worry when thumb sucking persists into the preschool and elementary school years. As many as 40 percent of children continue to suck their thumbs after they have started school (Kessen, Haith, & Salapatek, 1970). Most developmentalists do not attach a great deal of significance to this behavior and are not aware of parenting strategies that might contribute to it. Individual differences in children's biological makeup may be involved to some degree in the late continuation of sucking behavior.

Nonnutritive sucking, *sucking behavior unrelated to the infant's feeding,* is used as a measure in a large number of research studies with young infants because young infants quit sucking when they attend to something, such as to a picture or to vocalization. Nonnutritive sucking, then, is one of the ingenious ways developmentalists study the young infant's attention and learning.

Infancy

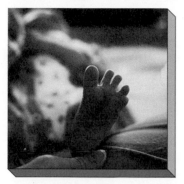

Babinski reflex

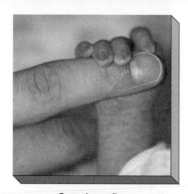

Grasping reflex

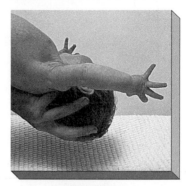

Moro reflex

Reflex	Stimulation	Infant's Response	Developmental Pattern
Blinking	Flash of light, puff of air	Closes both eyes	Permanent
Babinski	Sole of foot stroked	Fans out toes, twists foot in	Disappears 9 months to 1 year
Grasping	Palms touched	Grasps tightly	Weakens after 3 months, disappears after 1 year
Moro (startle)	Sudden stimulation, such as hearing a loud noise or being dropped	Startles, arches back, throws head back, flings out arms and legs and then rapidly closes them to center of body	Disappears 3 to 4 months
Rooting	Cheek stroked or side of mouth touched	Turns head, opens mouth, begins sucking	Disappears 3 to 4 months
Stepping	Infant held above surface and feet lowered to touch surface	Moves feet as if to walk	Disappears 3 to 4 months
Sucking	Object touching mouth	Sucks automatically	Disappears 3 to 4 months
Swimming	Infant put face down in water	Makes coordinated swimming movements	Disappears 6 to 7 months
Tonic neck	Infant placed on back	Forms fists with both hands and usually turns head to the right (sometimes called the "fencer's pose" because the infant looks like it is assuming a fencer's position)	Disappears 2 months

Rooting reflex

Stepping reflex

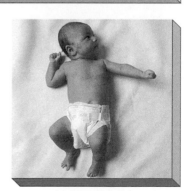

Tonic neck reflex

Crying and Smiling

Crying and smiling are emotional behaviors that are important in the infant's communication with the world. Crying is the infant's first emotional or affective behavior. Newborns spend 6 to 7 percent of their day crying, although some infants cry more, and others less (Gotowiec & Ames, 1989). An infant's earliest cries are reflexive reactions to discomfort. The cries may signify information about the infant's biological state, and possibly indicate distress. They are highly differentiated and have different patterns of frequency, intensity, and pause (Gustafson & Green, 1989).

Most adults can determine whether the infant's cries signify anger or pain (Barr, Desilets, & Rotman, 1991; St. James-Roberts, Bowyer, & Hurry, 1991). In one investigation, even when the crying segments were brief, adults could distinguish between aversive, arousing cries (more distressful) and those indicating hunger (less distressful). Even shortly after birth, infant's cries communicate information (Gustafson, 1989; Lester & Boukydis, 1991; Zeskind & Marshall, 1988).

Should a crying infant be given attention and be soothed, or does this spoil the infant? Many years ago, behaviorist John Watson (1928) argued that parents spend too much time responding to the infant's crying and as a consequence reward the crying and increase its incidence. By contrast, recent arguments by ethologists and attachment theorists such as Mary Ainsworth (1979) stress that it is difficult to respond too much to an infant's crying. Ainsworth views caregivers' responsiveness to infant crying as contributing to the formation of a secure attachment between the infant and the caregiver. One investigation found that mothers who responded quickly to their infant's crying at 3 months of age had infants who cried less later in the first year of life (Bell & Ainsworth, 1972). Other research by behaviorists suggests that a quick, soothing response by a caregiver to crying increases the infant's subsequent crying (Gewirtz, 1977). Controversy, then, still surrounds the issue of when and how caregivers should respond to infant crying.

It is not uncommon for 9- to 12-month-old infants to wake up in the middle of the night and start crying. Sometimes the crying results from illness or other physically based distress, and if so, caregivers should respond to the crying (Ferber, 1989). Most of the time, though, middle-of-the-night crying occurs because the infant is alone, usually in a dark or dimly lit room, is not very sleepy, and does not have much to do. At this point, infants use the one tool that eliminated their boredom in the past—crying. Middle-of-the-night crying is usually motivated by the infant's desire to have the company of others rather than to be alone, awake, and bored. This can become a serious inconvenience to many parents. Some couples spend long hours awake in the wee hours trying to cope with a wide-awake baby. White (1988) described one such encounter. A dentist in Georgia called him long-distance. Mildly embarrassed, the dentist said that he and his wife were taking a minimum of two automobile rides after midnight and before 6 A.M. each night in an attempt to lull their baby to sleep. Like others in the same situation, they could not believe they had gotten themselves into this predicament. They finally went to a pediatrician who checked the baby's health, which was fine. He told the parents the baby was not crying at night because it was hurt or in pain. The pediatrician told them simply to let the baby cry it out at this age. This wasn't easy for the parents to do, but ignoring their 10-month-old's crying in the middle of the night quickly led to much quieter nights for the parents and the infant.

Smiling is another important communicative behavior of the infant. Two kinds of smiling can be distinguished in infants—one reflexive, the other social. A **reflexive smile** *does not occur in response to external stimuli. Reflexive smiling occurs during the first month after birth, usually during irregular patterns of sleep. Reflexive smiling does not occur when the infant is in an alert state.* A **social smile** *occurs in response to an external stimulus, which early in development typically is in response to a face.* Social smiling usually does not occur until 2 to 3 months of age (Emde, Gaensbauer, & Harmon, 1976), although some researchers believe that infants grin in response to voices as early as 3 weeks of age (Sroufe & Waters, 1976). The power of the infant's smiles were appropriately summed up by British attachment theorist John Bowlby (1969), "Can we doubt that the more and better infants smile, the better they are loved and cared for? It is fortunate for their survival that babies are so designed by Nature that they beguile and enslave mothers." More information about Bowlby's ideas on attachment appears in chapter 7, as well as further discussion of the infant's emotional world.

He who binds himself to joy
Does the winged life destroy;
But he who kisses the joy as it
Flies lives in eternity's sun rise.

~ *William Blake*

States

To chart and understand the infant's development, developmentalists have constructed different classification schemes of the infant's states (Berg & Berg, 1987; Brown, 1964; Colombo, Moss, & Horowitz, 1989). One classification scheme (Brown, 1964) describes seven infant states:

1. *Deep sleep.* The infant lies motionless with eyes closed, has regular breathing, makes no vocalization, and does not respond to outside stimulation.
2. *Regular sleep.* The infant moves very little, breathing might be raspy or involve wheezing, and respirations may be normal or move from normal to irregular.
3. *Disturbed sleep.* There is a variable amount of movement, the infant's eyelids are closed but might flutter, breathing is irregular, and there may be some squawks, sobs, and sighs.
4. *Drowsy.* The infant's eyes are open or partly open and appear glassy, there is little movement (although startles and free movement may occur), vocalizations are more regular than in disturbed sleep, and some transitional sounds may be made.
5. *Alert activity.* This is the state most often viewed by parents as being awake. The infant's eyes are open and bright, a variety of free movements are shown, fretting may occur, skin may redden, and there may be irregular breathing when the infant feels tension.
6. *Alert and focused.* This kind of attention is often seen in older children but is unusual in the neonate. The child's eyes are open and bright. Some motor activity may occur, but it is integrated around a specific activity. This state may occur when focusing on some sound or visual stimulus.
7. *Inflexibly focused.* In this state, the infant is awake but does not react to external stimuli; two examples are sucking and wild crying. During wild crying the infant may thrash about, but the eyes are closed as screams pour out.

. . . He cooperates
With a universe of large and
noisy feeling states
Without troubling to place
Them anywhere special, for, to his
eyes, funnyface.
Or elephant as yet
Mean nothing. His distinction
between me and us
Is a matter of taste; his seasons
are dry and wet;
He thinks as his mouth does.

~ *W. H. Auden,* Mundus et Infans

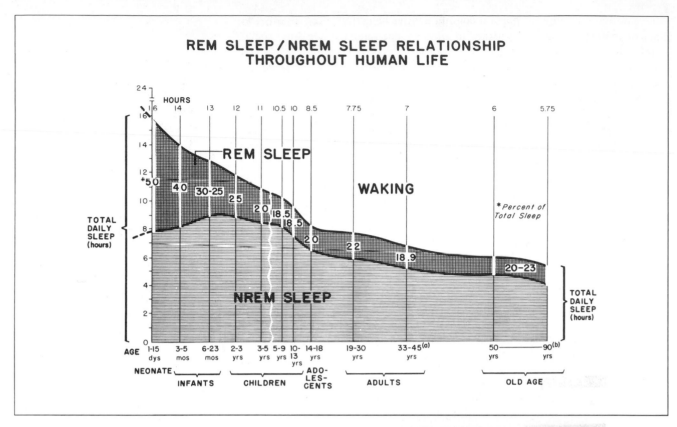

REM SLEEP/NREM SLEEP RELATIONSHIP
THROUGHOUT HUMAN LIFE

Figure 5.1   This graph shows changes (with age) in total amounts of daily sleep, daily REM sleep, and in the percentage of REM sleep. Note the sharp diminution of REM sleep in the early years. REM sleep falls from 8 hours at birth to less than 1 hour in old age. The amount of NREM sleep throughout life remains more constant, falling from 8 to 5 hours. In contrast to the steep decline of REM sleep, the quantity of NREM sleep is undiminished for many years. Although total daily REM sleep falls steadily during life, the percentage rises slightly in adolescence and early adulthood. This rise does not reflect an increase in amount; it is due to the fact that REM sleep does not diminish as quickly as total sleep. Data for the 33- to 45- and 50- to 90-year groups are taken from Kales and others (1967), Feinberg and others (1967) and Kahn & Fisher (1969), respectively (revised by Roffwarg and others since publication in Science, 152: 604–619, 1966).

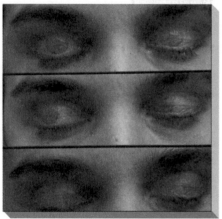

Shown above is rapid eye movement that gives REM sleep its name. In children and adults, dreams are most likely to occur in REM sleep. The function of REM sleep in infancy is debated.

Using classification schemes such as the one just described, researchers have identified many different aspects of the infant's development. One such aspect is the sleeping-waking cycle. Each night, something lures us from our work, our play, and our loved ones; the sandman's spell claims more of our time than any other pursuit. When we were infants, sleep consumed even more of our time than it does now. Newborns sleep for 16 to 17 hours a day, although some sleep more, and others less. The range is from a low of about 10 hours to a high of about 21 hours (Parmalee, Wenner, & Schulz, 1964). The longest period of sleep is not always between 11 P.M. and 7 A.M. While total sleep remains somewhat consistent for young infants, the patterns of sleep during the day do not always follow a rhythmic pattern. An infant might change from sleeping several long bouts of 7 or 8 hours to three or four shorter sessions only several hours in duration. By about 1 month of age, most infants have begun to sleep longer at night, and by about 4 months of age, they usually have moved closer to adultlike sleep patterns, spending their longest span of sleep at night and their longest span of waking during the day (Coons & Guilleminault, 1984).

Infant researchers are intrigued by different forms of infant sleep. They are especially interested in **REM (rapid eye movement) sleep,** *a recurring sleep stage during which vivid dreams commonly occur among children and adults* (Carskadon & Dement, 1989; McCarley, 1989). Most adults spend about one-fifth of their night in REM sleep, and REM sleep usually appears about one hour after non-REM sleep. However, about one-half of an infant's sleep is REM sleep, and infants often begin their sleep cycle with REM sleep rather than non-REM sleep. The extensive amount of REM sleep in infancy is shown in figure 5.1. By the time infants reach 3 months of age, the percentage of time spent in REM sleep falls to about 40 percent and no longer does REM sleep begin the sleep cycle. The large amount of REM sleep may provide young infants with added self-stimulation, which they may require less of as their time awake increases. REM sleep may also promote the brain's development.

Physical Growth and Motor Development

Physically, newborns are limited. They are tiny; from head to heels, they are only about 20 inches long and weigh 7 pounds. They are bound by where they are put, and they are at the mercy of their bodily needs. Their heart beats twice as fast as an adult's—120 beats a minute—and they breathe twice as fast—about 33 times a minute. Within a 24-hour period, they urinate as many as 18 times and move their bowels from 4 to 7 times. On the average, they are alert and comfortable for only about 30 minutes in a 4-hour period.

The infant's pattern of physical development in the first two years of life is exciting. At birth, the neonate has a gigantic head (relative to the rest of the body) that flops around in uncontrollable fashion; she possesses reflexes that are dominated by evolutionary movements. In the span of twelve months, the infant becomes capable of sitting anywhere, standing, stooping, climbing, and usually walking. During the second year, growth decelerates, but rapid increases in such activities as running and climbing take place.

Among the important changes in growth are those involving the cephalocaudal and proximodistal sequences, gross and fine motor skills, and the brain. We examine each of these in turn.

Sleep that knits up the ravelled sleeve of care . . .
Balm of hurt minds, nature's second course,
Chief nourisher in life's feast.

~ *William Shakespeare,*
Macbeth, *1605*

Growth is the only evidence of life.

~ *John Henry,*
Cardinal Newman Apologia
pro Vita Sua, *1864*

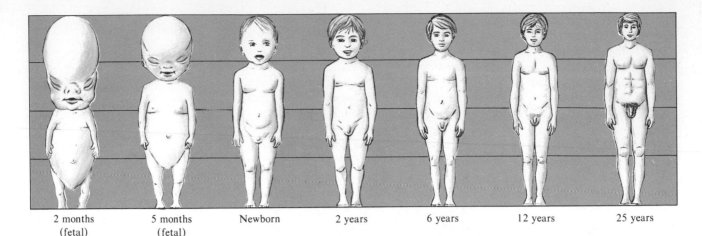

| 2 months (fetal) | 5 months (fetal) | Newborn | 2 years | 6 years | 12 years | 25 years |

Figure 5.2 Changes in body form and proportion during prenatal and postnatal growth.

Cephalocaudal and Proximodistal Sequences

The **cephalocaudal pattern** *means that the greatest growth always occurs at the top—the head—with physical growth in size, weight, and feature differentiation gradually working its way down from top to bottom (for example, neck, shoulders, middle trunk, and so on).* This same pattern occurs in the head area because the top parts of the head—the eyes and brain—grow faster than the lower parts—such as the jaw. As illustrated in figure 5.2 an extraordinary proportion of the total body is occupied by the head during prenatal development and early infancy.

The **proximodistal pattern** *means that growth starts at the center of the body and moves toward the extremities. An example of this is the early maturation of muscular control of the trunk and arms as compared with the hands and fingers.*

Gross and Fine Motor Skills

In addition to cephalocaudal and proximodistal growth patterns, we also can describe growth in terms of **gross motor skills**—*those involving large muscle activities such as moving one's arms and walking,* and **fine motor skills**—*those involving more finely tuned movements like finger dexterity.*

At birth, the infant has no appreciable coordination of the chest or arms. By about 4 months of age, however, two striking accomplishments occur in turn. The first is the infant's ability to hold the chest up when lying in a face-down position (at about 2 months). The other is the ability to reach for objects placed within the infant's direct line of vision, without making any consistent contact with the objects (because the two hands don't work together and the coordination of vision and grasping is not yet possible). A little later, at about 3 to 4 months, there is further progress in motor control. By 5 months, the infant can sit up with some support and grasp objects. By 6 months, the infant can roll over when lying in a prone position.

At birth, the newborn is capable of supporting some weight with the legs. This is proven by formal tests of muscular strength. These tests use a specially constructed apparatus to measure the infant's leg resistance as the foot is pulled away by a calibrated spring device. This ability is also evidenced by the infant's partial support of its own weight when held upright by an adult. If the infant is given enough support by the adult, some forward movement is seen because of a built-in stepping reflex, which disappears in a few months. Each leg is lifted, moved forward, and placed down, as if the infant were taking a series of steps. However, the sequence lasts for only two to three steps, and,

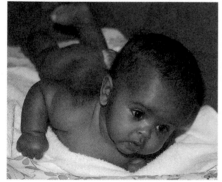

At about 4 months of age, infants develop the ability to hold their chest up when in a face-down position.

1 month Chin up	2 months Chest up	3 months Reach and miss	4 months Sit with support
5 months Sit on lap and grasp objects	6 months Sit unaided	7 months Crawl	8 months Pull to stand
9 months Climb up 6 inches	10 months Cruise (walk while holding onto some- thing, like a chair)	11 months Walk unaided	12 months Climb down 14 inches

Figure 5.3   The development of posture and locomotion in infants. The month shown is the average for American infants. The actual month at which such milestones occur varies as much as four months.

A traditional practice among many Hopi and Navaho Indians is to wrap babies in cloth and strap them to a cradleboard until they are about 6 months old. Infants in the Hopi and Navaho cultures learn to walk at about the same age as babies from cultures that do not constrain them in this way. Even though there are often substantial differences in the opportunity infants have to practice their motor movements across cultures, infants in virtually every culture walk at about the same age.

of course, the infant does not have sufficient balance or strength to execute the movement independently.

By about 6 months of age, infants can sit unaided. By about 7 months, they can pull to sit unaided, and crawl or scoot. By about 8 months, they can pull to a stand. By about 11 months they can walk unaided. By about 13 months, they can ride four-wheel wagons. And by about 26 months, they can ride a tricycle (White, 1988). The average age of infant motor accomplishments in the first year of life are shown in figure 5.3. The actual month at which the milestones occur varies as much as 2 to 4 months, especially among older infants. What remains fairly uniform, however, is the sequence of accomplishments. An important implication of these infant motor accomplishments is the increasing degree of independence they bring. Infants can explore their environment more extensively and initiate social interaction with caregivers and peers.

Not content with their infants reaching the motor development milestones at an average rate, many American parents want to accelerate their infants' physical skills. Is this a wise practice? To learn more about this intriguing question, turn to Perspective on Life-Span Development 5.1.

A baby is an angel whose wings decrease as his legs increase.

~ *French Proverb*

Physical Development in Infancy

BABIES DON'T NEED EXERCISE CLASSES

Six-month-old Andrew doesn't walk yet, but his mother wants him to develop his physical skills optimally. Three times a week she takes him to a recreation center where he participates with other infants in swimming and gymnastics classes. With the increased interest of today's adults in aerobic exercise and fitness, some parents have tried to give their infants a head start on becoming physically fit and physically talented. However, in 1988 the American Academy of Pediatricians issued a statement that recommends against structured exercise classes for babies. Pediatricians are now seeing more bone fractures and dislocations and more muscle strains in babies than in the past. They point out that when an adult is stretching and moving an infant's limbs, it is easy to go beyond the infant's physical limits without knowing it.

The physical fitness classes for infants range from passive fare—with adults putting infants through the paces—to programs called "aerobic" because they demand crawling, tumbling, and ball skills. However, exercise for infants is not aerobic. They cannot adequately stretch their bodies to achieve aerobic benefits. Even

Shown here are mothers and their babies in a swimming class. Pediatricians and child psychologists recommend that exercise classes, and even swimming classes, for infants are not needed, possibly having more negative than positive outcomes.

swimming classes before early childhood have a down side. Children cannot cognitively learn to swim until they are 3 or 4 years of age. It is not uncommon to observe 4-year-olds who have had swim classes since infancy suddenly become terrified of the water because for the first time they understand that they could drown.

For optimal physical development, babies simply need touch, face-to-face contact, and brightly colored toys to manipulate. If infants are not couch potatoes from being babysat extensively by a television set, their normal play will provide them with all the fitness training they need.

The Brain

As the infant walks, talks, runs, shakes a rattle, smiles, and frowns, changes in the brain are occurring. Consider that the infant began life as a single cell and that in 9 months was born with a brain and nervous system containing approximately 100 billion nerve cells. At birth, the infant probably had all of the nerve cells—called neurons—it would have in its entire life. But at birth and in early infancy, the connectedness of all of these neurons was impoverished. As shown in figure 5.4, as the infant moves from birth to 2 years of age, the interconnections of neurons increase dramatically as the dendrites (the receiving part) of the neuron branch out.

Undoubtedly, neurotransmitters change throughout the prenatal period and during the infant years, too. Neurotransmitters are the tiny chemical substances that carry information across gaps from one neuron to the next. Little is known about neurotransmitter changes in infancy, although changes in one important neurotransmitter—dopamine—has been documented in monkeys

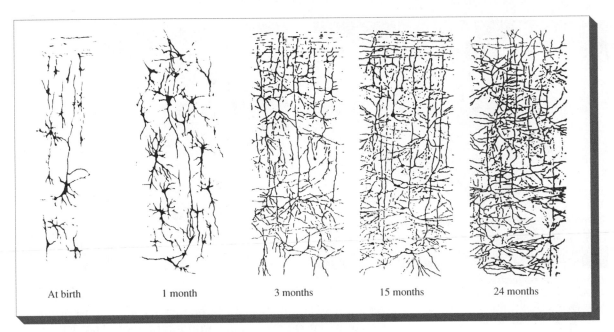

At birth　　　1 month　　　3 months　　　15 months　　　24 months

Figure 5.4　The development of dendritic spreading. Note the increase in connectedness between neurons over the course of the first two years of life.

(Goldman-Rakie & others, 1983). The concentration of dopamine in the prefrontal lobe—the area of the brain involved in higher cognitive functions such as problem solving—peaks at 5 months of age, declines until about 18 to 24 months, and then increases again at 2 to 3 years of age. These changes in dopamine concentration may reflect a switch from growth and nutritional functions to neurotransmitter function for this substance. Such speculation only begins to scratch the surface of the important role neurotransmitter substances might play in the brain's early development.

Nutrition

Four-month-old Robert lives in Bloomington, Indiana, with his middle-class parents. He is well nourished and healthy. By contrast, 4-month-old Nikita lives in Ethiopia. Nikita and his parents live in impoverished conditions. Nikita

Physical Development in Infancy

Which is best: breast-feeding or bottle-feeding? In the United States, the majority of experts favor breast-feeding, but the issue of breast-versus bottle-feeding continues to be hotly debated.

is so poorly nourished that he has become emaciated and lies near death. Our coverage of infant nutrition begins with information about nutritional needs and eating behavior, then turns to malnutrition.

Nutritional Needs and Eating Behavior

The importance of adequate energy and nutrient intake consumed in a loving and supportive environment during the infant years cannot be overstated (Pipes, 1988). From birth to 1 year of age, human infants triple their weight and increase their length by 50 percent. Individual differences of infants in nutrient reserves, body composition, growth rates, and activity patterns make defining actual nutrient needs difficult. However, because parents need guidelines, nutritionists recommend that infants consume approximately 50 calories per day for each pound they weigh—more than twice an adult's requirement per pound.

Human milk, or an alternative formula if needed, is the baby's source of nutrients and energy for the first 4 to 6 months. For years, developmentalists and nutritionists have debated whether breast-feeding has substantial benefits over bottle-feeding. The growing consensus is that breast-feeding is better for the baby's health (Lozoff,1989; Walton & Vallelunga, 1989; White, 1990; Worthington-Roberts, 1988). Breast-feeding provides milk that is clean and digestible, and helps to immunize the newborn from disease. Breast-fed babies gain weight more rapidly than do bottle-fed babies. However, only about one-half of mothers nurse newborns, and even fewer continue to nurse their infants after several months. Mothers who work outside the home find it difficult, if not impossible, to breast-feed their young infant for many months. Even though breast-feeding provides more ideal nutrition for the infant, some researchers argue that there is no long-term evidence of physiological or psychological harm to American infants when they are bottle-fed (Caldwell, 1964; Ferguson, Harwood, & Shannon, 1987; Forsyth, Leventhal, & McCarthy, 1985). Despite the claims by these researchers that no long-term negative consequences of bottle-feeding have been documented in American children, the American Academy of Pediatrics, the majority of physicians and nurses, as well as two leading publications for parents—the *Infant Care* manual and *Parents* magazine—endorse breast-feeding as having physiological and psychological benefits (Young, 1990).

There is a consensus among experts that breast-feeding is the preferred practice, especially in developing countries where inadequate nutrition and poverty are common. In 1991, the Institute of Medicine, part of the National Academy of Sciences, issued a report that women should be encouraged to breast-feed their infants exclusively for the first 4 to 6 months of life. According to the report, the benefits of breast-feeding are: protection against some gastrointestinal infections and food allergies for infants, and possible reduction of osteoporosis and breast cancer for mothers. Nonetheless, while the majority of experts recommend breast-feeding, the issue of breast- versus bottle-feeding continues to be hotly debated. Many parents, especially working mothers, are now following a sequence of breast-feeding in the first several months and bottle-feeding thereafter. This strategy allows the mother's natural milk to provide nutritional benefits to the infant early in development and permits mothers to return to work after several months.

Some years ago, controversy also surrounded the issue of whether a baby should be fed on demand or on a regular schedule. The famous behaviorist John Watson (1928) argued that scheduled feeding was superior because it increased the child's orderliness. An example of a recommended schedule for newborns was 4 ounces of formula every six hours. In recent years, demand feeding—in which the timing and amount of feeding are determined by the infant—has become more popular.

The maturation of oral and fine motor skills indicate appropriate ages for the introduction of semisolid and solid foods. Current recommendations are to introduce semisolid foods at 4 to 6 months of age and finger foods when infants reach out, grasp, and bring items to their mouth. When munching and rotary chewing begin, providing soft-cooked foods is appropriate. Infants can begin to drink from a cup with help between 9 and 12 months of age.

There has been speculation that formula-feeding and the early introduction of semisolid foods might contribute to excessive intakes of energy and the development of infant obesity. It has also been speculated that obese infants often become obese adults. However, neither breast- nor bottle-feeding, nor the age of introduction of semisolid foods, are causes of obesity. Obesity in infancy has not been a very good predictor of obesity in adulthood (Stunkard, 1989).

During the 1980s, we became extremely nutrition conscious. Does the same type of nutrition that makes us healthy adults also make young infants healthy? For the answer to this question, turn to Perspective on Life-Span Development 5.2.

Malnutrition in Infancy

Marasmus *is a wasting away of body tissues in the infant's first year of life, which is caused by severe protein-calorie deficiency.* The infant becomes grossly underweight and the muscles atrophy. The main cause of marasmus is early weaning from breast milk to inadequate nutrients such as found in formulas prepared from unsuitable and unsanitary cow's milk. Something that looks like milk but is not may also be used, usually a form of tapioca or rice. In many of the world's developing countries, mothers used to breast-feed their infants for at least two years. To become more modern, they stopped breast-feeding their infants much earlier and replaced it with bottle-feeding. Comparisons of breast-fed and bottle-fed infants in countries such as Afghanistan, Haiti, Ghana, and Chile document that the rate of infant deaths is much greater among bottle-fed than breast-fed infants, with bottle-fed infants sometimes dying at a rate five times higher than breast-fed infants (Grant, 1991).

WHAT'S GOOD FOOD FOR AN ADULT CAN BE BAD FOOD FOR A BABY

*S*ome yuppie parents may not know the recipe for a healthy baby: whole milk and an occasional cookie, along with fruits, vegetables, and other foods. Some affluent, well-educated parents almost starve their babies by feeding them the lowfat, low-calorie diet they eat themselves. Diets designed for adult weight loss and prevention of heart disease may actually retard growth and development in babies. Fat is very important for babies. Nature's food—the mother's breast milk—is not low in fat or calories. No child under the age of 2 should be consuming skim milk.

In one investigation, seven cases were documented in which babies 7 to 22 months of age were unwittingly undernourished by their health-conscious parents (Lifshitz & others, 1987). In some instances, the parents had been fat themselves and were determined that their child was not going to be. The well-meaning parents substituted vegetables, skim milk, and other lowfat foods for what they called junk food. However, for infants, broccoli is not always a good substitute for a cookie. For growing infants, high-calorie, high-energy foods are part of a balanced diet.

What hazards might the current trends in diet foods and health preoccupation on the part of parents have when it comes to choosing foods for their infants?

Even if not fatal, severe and lengthy malnutrition is detrimental to physical, cognitive, and social development (Super, Herrera, & Mora, 1990). And in some cases even moderate malnutrition can cause subtle difficulties in development. Recently, researchers have shown that nutritional supplements early in development can improve the cognitive development of malnourished children (Engle, 1991; Gorman & Politt, 1991; Super, Herrera, & Mora, 1991). Much of our discussion of malnutrition has focused on developing countries, but in some areas of the United States hunger is also a problem. To read about children living hungry in America, turn to Cultural Worlds of Development 5.1.

At this point we have discussed a number of ideas about physical development in infancy, including information about reflexes, states, physical growth and motor development, and nutrition. A summary of these ideas is presented in concept table 5.1. Now we turn our attention to the world of infant perception.

CHILDREN LIVING HUNGRY IN AMERICA

*H*arlingen, Texas, is a city of approximately 40,000 near the Rio Grande. It is heavily populated by Chicanos. At Su Clinica ("Your Clinic"), which serves many Chicano residents, poverty and unemployment are evident in the waiting list of 800 families needing the low-cost care provided by the clinic. Many of the Chicanos working in Texas agriculture receive no health-care benefits. Few make even the minimum wage. Farm workers usually get less than $1.50 an hour for working long days in the pesticide-infected fields. The infant mortality rate for the region is listed as good, but this figure is wrong. Many of the deaths are not counted. A baby dies and it is buried. People outside the family seldom know. Many infants and young children here experience growth problems because they do not get enough to eat. This is not unique to Harlingen, Texas; many other locations in the United States have their share of impoverished families who have difficulty making ends meet and

Mexican American children playing in Harlingen, Texas. Many Mexican American children living in Texas and other states do not get adequate nutrition and live in poverty conditions.

putting food on the table. Hunger and poverty are seen in children of poor Mississippi tenant farmers, of laid-off coal miners in West Virginia, of neglected parents in the ghettos of New York and Chicago. In many instances, these children are the victims of silent undernutrition, less dramatic than in Africa or Bangladesh, but no less real (Brown & Pizer, 1987).

Sensory and Perceptual Development

At the beginning of this chapter, you read about how the newborn comes into the world equipped with sensory capacities. But what are sensation and perception anyway? Can a newborn see, and if so, what can it perceive? And what about the other senses—seeing, smelling, hearing, tasting, and touching? What are they like in the newborn? These are among the intriguing questions we now explore.

What Are Sensation and Perception?

How do newborns know that their mother's skin is soft rather than rough? How do 5-year-olds know what color their hair is? How do 8-year-olds know that summer is warmer than winter? How do 10-year-olds know that a firecracker is louder than a cat's meow? How does a 40-year-old know its time to get bifocals? Infants, children, and adults "know" these things because of their senses. All information comes to the infant through the senses. Without

> Systematic reasoning is something we could not, as a species of individuals, do without. But neither, if we are to remain sane, can we do without direct perception . . . of the inner and outer world into which we have been born.
>
> ~ *Aldous Huxley*

Concept Table 5.1: Physical Growth and Development in Infancy

Concept	Processes/Related Ideas	Characteristics/Description
Reflexes	Their Nature	The newborn is no longer viewed as a passive, empty-headed organism. Newborns are limited physically, though, and reflexes—automatic movements—govern the newborn's behavior.
	Sucking	For infants, sucking is an important means of obtaining nutrition, as well as a pleasurable, soothing activity. Nonnutritive sucking is of interest to researchers because it provides a means of evaluating attention.
	Crying and Smiling	Crying and smiling are effective behaviors that are important in the infant's communication with the world.
States	Classification	Researchers have put together different classification systems; one classification involves seven infant state categories, including deep sleep, drowsy, alert and focused, and inflexibly focused.
	The Sleeping-Waking Cycle	Newborns usually sleep 16 to 17 hours a day. By 4 months, they approach adultlike sleeping patterns. REM sleep, during which children and adults are most likely to dream, occurs much more in early infancy than in childhood and adulthood. The high percentage of REM sleep—about half of neonatal sleep—may be a self-stimulatory device, or it may promote brain development.
Physical Growth and Motor Development	Cephalocaudal and Proximodistal Sequences	The cephalocaudal pattern is growth from the top down; the proximodistal pattern is growth from the center out.
	Gross Motor and Fine Motor Skills	Gross motor skills involve large muscle activity, as in walking. Fine motor skills involve more fine-grained activities such as manual dexterity. Both gross and fine motor skills undergo extensive change in the first two years of development.
	The Brain	There is a great deal of brain growth in infancy as well as in prenatal development. Dendritic spreading is dramatic in the first two years. Some important changes in neurotransmitters probably also take place, although these changes are just beginning to be charted.
Nutrition	Nutritional Needs and Eating Behavior	Infants need to consume approximately 50 calories per day for each pound they weigh. Human milk, or an alternative formula, is the baby's source of nutrients for the first six months. The growing consensus is that breast-feeding is superior to bottle-feeding, but the increase in working mothers has meant fewer breast-fed babies. Parents are increasingly using a demand feeding schedule. The maturation of oral and fine motor skills indicate appropriate ages for introducing semisolid and solid foods. Obesity in infancy has not been a good predictor of obesity in adulthood. Infants should not be placed on lowfat, low-calorie diets.
	Malnutrition in Infancy	Severe infant malnutrition is still prevalent in many parts of the world. Severe protein-calorie deficiency can cause marasmus, a wasting away of body tissues. It is mainly caused by early weaning from breast milk to unsuitable substitutes. Even if not fatal, severe and lengthy malnutrition is detrimental to physical, cognitive, and social development.

vision, hearing, touch, taste, smell, and other senses, our brain would be isolated from the world; we would live in dark silence, a tasteless, colorless, feelingless void.

Sensation *occurs when information contacts sensory receptors—the eyes, ears, tongue, nostrils, and skin.* The sensation of hearing occurs when waves of pulsating air are collected by the outer ear and transmitted through the bones of the inner ear to the auditory nerve. The sensation of vision occurs as rays of light contact the two eyes and become focused on the retina. **Perception** *is the interpretation of what is sensed.* The information about physical events that contact the ears may be interpreted as musical sounds, for example. The physical energy transmitted to the retina may be interpreted as a particular color, pattern, or shape.

Visual Perception

How do we see? Anyone who has ever taken pictures while on vacation appreciates the miracle of perception. The camera is no match for it. Consider a favorite scenic spot that you visited and photographed some time in the past. Compare your memory of this spot to your snapshot. Although your memory may be faulty, there is little doubt that the richness of your perceptual experience was not captured in the picture. The sense of depth that you felt at this spot probably was not conveyed by the snapshot. Neither was the subtlety of the colors you perceived nor the intricacies of textures and shapes. Human vision is complex, and its development is complex, too.

Psychologist William James (1890/1950) called the newborn's perceptual world a blooming, buzzing confusion. Was James right? A century later we can safely say that he was wrong. To sum up the research on infant perception with one simple statement: Infants' perception of visual information is *much* more advanced than previously thought (Bower, 1989, 1991).

Our tour of visual perception begins with the pioneering work of Robert Fantz (1963). Fantz placed infants in a "looking chamber," which had two visual displays on the ceiling of the chamber above the infant's head. An experimenter viewed the infant's eyes by looking through a peephole. If the infant was fixating on one of the displays, the experimenter could see the display's reflection in the infant's eyes. This allowed the experimenter to determine how long the infant looked at each display. By looking at figure 5.5, you can see Fantz's "looking chamber" and the results of his experiment. In Fantz's experiment, infants preferred to look at patterns rather than color or brightness. For example, they preferred to look at a face, a piece of printed matter, or a bull's eye longer than at red, yellow, or white discs. And in another experiment, Fantz found that younger infants—only 2 days old—looked longer at patterned stimuli, such as faces and concentric circles, than at red, white, or yellow discs. Based on these results, pattern perception likely has an innate basis, or at least is acquired after only minimal environmental experience. The newborn's visual world is not the blooming, buzzing confusion William James imagined.

Just how well can infants see? The newborn's vision is estimated to be 20/200 to 20/600 on the well-known Snellen chart that you are tested with when you have your eyes examined (Haith, 1991). This is about ten to thirty times lower than normal adult vision (20/20). But by 6 months of age, vision is 20/100 or better (Banks & Salapatek, 1983).

The human face is perhaps the most important visual pattern for the newborn to perceive. The infant masters a sequence of steps in progressing toward full perceptual appreciation of the face (Gibson, 1969). At about 3½

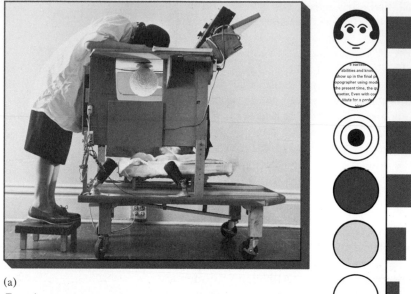

(a)

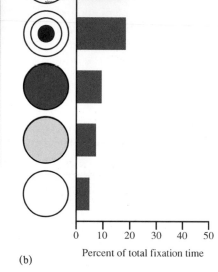

(b)

Percent of total fixation time

0 10 20 30 40 50

Figure 5.5 Fantz's experiment on infants' visual perception. Shown above (a) is the "looking chamber" used by Fantz to study infants' perception of stimuli. As shown in the graph (b), 2- to 3-month-old infants preferred to look at some stimuli more than others. In Fantz's experiment, infants preferred to look at patterns rather than color or brightness. For example, they looked longer at a face, a piece of printed matter, or a bull's eye than at red, yellow, or white discs.

weeks, the infant is fascinated with the eyes, perhaps because the infant notices simple perceptual features such as dots, angles, and circles. At 1 to 2 months of age, the infant notices and perceives contour. At 2 months and older, the infant begins to differentiate facial features: the eyes are distinguished from other parts of the face, the mouth is noticed, and movements of the mouth draw attention to it. By 5 months of age, the infant has detected other facial features—its plasticity, its solid, three-dimensional surface, the oval shape of the head, the orientation of the eyes, and the mouth. Beyond 6 months of age, the infant distinguishes familiar faces from unfamiliar faces—mother from stranger, masks from real faces, and so on.

How early can infants perceive depth? To investigate this question, infant perception researchers Eleanor Gibson and Richard Walk (1960) conducted a classic experiment. They constructed a miniature cliff with a drop-off covered by glass. The motivation for this experiment happened when Gibson was eating a picnic lunch on the edge of the Grand Canyon. She wondered whether an infant looking over the canyon's rim would perceive the dangerous drop-off and back up. In their laboratory, Gibson and Walk placed infants on the edge of a visual cliff and had their mothers coax them to crawl out onto the glass (see figure 5.6). Most infants would not crawl out on the glass, choosing instead to remain on the shallow side, indicating that they could perceive depth. Because the 6- to 14-month-old infants had extensive visual experience, this research did not answer the question of whether depth perception is innate.

Exactly how early in life does depth perception develop? Since younger infants do not crawl, this question is difficult to answer. Research with 2- to 4-month-old infants shows differences in heart rate when the infants are placed directly on the deep side of the visual cliff instead of on the shallow side of the cliff (Campos, Langer, & Krowitz, 1970). However, an alternative interpretation is that young infants respond to differences in some visual characteristic of the deep and shallow cliffs, with no actual knowledge of depth.

Following are appropriate activities for adults to engage in that involve the visual stimulation of infants at various points during the first year (Whaley & Wong, 1989):

Birth to 1 month:
- Look at infant within close range.
- Hang bright, shiny object within eight to ten inches of infant's face and in midline.

2 to 3 months:
- Provide bright objects.
- Make room bright with pictures or mirrors on wall.
- Take infant to different rooms while doing chores.
- Place infant in infant seat for vertical view of environment.

4 to 6 months:
- Place infant so that she/he can look in mirror.
- Give brightly colored toys to infant to grasp (toys that are small enough to grasp).

6 to 9 months:
- Give infant large toys with bright colors, movable parts, and noise-makers.
- Place infant in front of mirror; infant enjoys patting mirror, making sounds at image.
- Infant enjoys peekaboo, especially hiding his/her face in towel.
- Make funny faces to encourage imitation.
- Give infant paper to tear and crumble.
- Give infant ball of yarn or string to pull apart.

9 to 12 months:
- Show infant large pictures in books.
- Take infant to places where there are animals, many people, and different objects (for example, a shopping center).
- Play ball by rolling ball to infant, demonstrating how to "throw" it back.
- Demonstrate building a two-block tower.

Figure 5.6 *Examining the depth perception of infants on the visual cliff. The apparatus consists of a board laid across a sheet of heavy glass, with a patterned material directly beneath the glass on one side and several feet below it on the other. Placed on the center board, the child crawls to his mother across the "shallow" side. Called from the "deep" side, he pats the glass, but despite this tactual evidence that the "cliff" is in fact a solid surface, he refuses to cross over to the mother.*

We have discussed a good deal of research on visual perception in infancy. What can we conclude about the infant's visual perception? Many fundamental aspects of vision are in working order by birth, and many aspects of visual perception are present early in the infant's first year of life (Granrud, 1989). Objects are seen as bounded, unitary, solid, and separate from the background, possibly from birth, but certainly by 3 to 4 months of age (Mandler, 1990). With further development there is still a great deal to learn about objects, but the world must appear both stable and orderly even to very young infants. Perception is not complete by 1 or 2 years of age. Many aspects of perception continue to grow more efficient and accurate during the childhood years (Bornstein, 1988).

Hearing
Immediately after birth, infants can hear, although their sensory thresholds are somewhat higher than those of adults (Trehub & others, 1991). That is, a stimulus must be louder to be heard by a newborn than by an adult. Not only can a newborn hear, but the possibility has been raised that the fetus can hear as it nestles within its mother's womb. To learn more about this possi-

THE FETUS AND *THE CAT IN THE HAT*

◆

*T*he fetus can hear sounds in the last few months of pregnancy: the mother's voice, music, loud sounds from television, the roar of an airplane, and so on. Given that the fetus can hear sounds, two psychologists wanted to find out if listening to Dr. Seuss's classic story *The Cat in the Hat,* while still in the mother's womb, would produce a preference for hearing the story after birth (DeCasper & Spence, 1986). Sixteen pregnant women read *The Cat in the Hat* or a story with a different rhyme and pace, *The King, the Mice and the Cheese,* to their fetuses twice a day over the last six weeks of their pregnancies. When the babies were born, they were given a choice of listening to each of two stories by varying their sucking rate (slow rate, for example) resulted in their hearing a recording of one story. Sucking at another rate (faster rate, for example) resulted in their hearing a recording of the other story. The newborns preferred listening to *The Cat in the Hat,* which they had heard frequently as a fetus.

(a)

(b)

(a) Pregnant mothers read The Cat in the Hat *to their fetuses during the last few months of pregnancy. (b) When the babies were born, they preferred listening to a recording of their mothers reading* The Cat in the Hat, *as evidenced by their sucking on a nipple that produced this recording.*

Two important conclusions can be drawn from this investigation. First, it reveals how ingenious scientists have become at assessing the development not only of infants but of fetuses as well, in this case discovering a way to "interview" newborn babies who cannot yet talk. Second, it reveals the remarkable ability of the brain to learn even before the infant is born.

bility, turn to Perspective on Life-Span Development 5.3. Also, in one recent study, infants were much more proficient at localizing sounds at 28 weeks than at 8 weeks (Morrongiello, Fenwick, & Chance, 1990).

Smell

Newborn infants can differentiate odors. For example, by the expressions on their faces they indicate that they like the way vanilla and strawberry smell, but do not like the way rotten eggs and fish smell (Steiner, 1979). In one investigation, young infants who were breast-fed showed a clear preference for smelling their mother's breast pad when they were 6 days old (MacFarlane, 1975) (see figure 5.7). However, when they were 2 days old, they did not show this preference (compared to a clean breast pad), indicating they require several days of experience to recognize this odor.

Taste

Sensitivity to taste may be present before birth. When saccharin was added to the amniotic fluid of a near-term fetus, increased swallowing was observed (Windle, 1940). Sensitivity to sweetness is clearly present in the newborn. When sucks on a nipple are rewarded with a sweetened solution, the amount

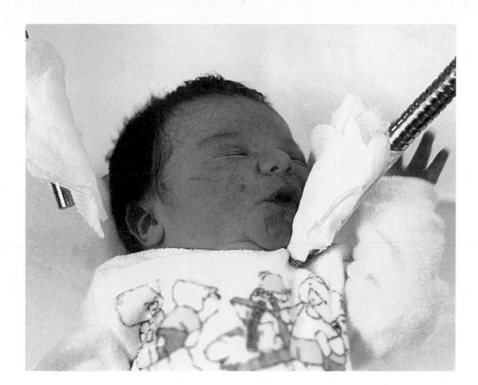

Figure 5.7 Newborns' preference for the smell of their mother's breast pad. In the experiment by MacFarlane (1975), 6-day-old infants preferred to smell their mother's breast pad over a clean one that had never been used, but 2-day-old infants did not show this preference, indicating that this odor preference requires several days of experience to develop.

of sucking increases (Lipsitt & others, 1976). In another investigation, newborns showed a smilelike expression after being stimulated with a sweetened solution but pursed their lips after being stimulated with a sour solution (Steiner, 1979).

Touch

Just as newborns respond to taste, they also respond to touch. A touch to the cheek produces a turning of the head, while a touch to the lips produces sucking movements. An important ability that develops in infancy is connecting information about vision with information about touch. One-year-olds clearly can do this and it appears that 6-month-olds can too (Acredolo & Hake, 1982). Whether still younger infants can coordinate vision and touch is yet to be determined. And in one recent study, 1- to 3-day old infants cried much less when they were given sucrose through a pacifier (Smith, Fillion, & Blass, 1990).

Following are appropriate activities for adults to engage in that involve the infant's sense of touch (Whaley & Wong, 1989):

Birth to 1 month:
• Hold, caress, and cuddle the infant.
• Keep the infant warm.
• The infant may like to be swaddled.

2 to 3 months:
• Caress the infant while bathing and at diaper change.
• Comb the infant's hair with a soft brush.

4 to 6 months:
• Give the infant soft squeeze toys of various textures.
• Allow the infant to splash in bath.
• Place the infant nude on a soft furry rug and move extremities.

6 to 9 months:
- Let the infant play with various textures of fabric.
- Let the infant feel foods of different sizes and textures.
- Let the infant "catch" running water.
- Give the infant a wad of sticky tape to manipulate.

9 to 12 months:
- Give the infant finger foods of different textures.
- Let the infant mess and squash food.
- Let the infant feel cold objects (ice cube) or warm objects, and tell the infant what temperature each is.
- Let the infant feel a breeze blowing (such as from a fan).

Pain

If and when you have a son and need to consider whether he should be circumcised, the issue of an infant's pain perception probably will become important to you. Circumcision is usually performed on young boys about the third day after birth. Will your young son experience pain if he is circumcised when he is 3 days old? Increased crying and fussing occur during the circumcision procedure, suggesting that 3-day-old infants experience pain (Gunnar, Malone, & Fisch, 1987; Porter, Porges, & Marshall, 1988).

In the investigation by Megan Gunnar and her colleagues (1987), the healthy newborn's ability to cope with stress was evaluated. The newborn infant males cried intensely during the circumcision, indicating that it was stressful. The researchers pointed out that it is rather remarkable that the newborn infant does not suffer serious consequences from the surgery. Rather, the circumcised infant displays amazing resiliency and ability to cope. Within several minutes after the surgery, the infant can nurse and interact in a normal manner with his mother. And, if allowed, the newly circumcised newborn drifts into a deep sleep that seems to serve as a coping mechanism. In this experiment, the time spent in deep sleep was greater in the 60 to 240 minutes after the circumcision than before it.

For many years, doctors have performed operations on newborns without anesthesia. The accepted medical practice was followed because of the dangers of anesthesia and the supposition that newborns do not feel pain. Recently, as researchers have convincingly demonstrated that newborns can feel pain, the longstanding practice of operating on newborns without anesthesia is being challenged.

Intermodal Perception

Are young infants so competent that they can relate and integrate information in several sensory modalities? **Intermodal perception** *is the ability to relate and integrate information about two or more sensory modalities, such as vision and hearing.* An increasing number of developmentalists believe the young infant experiences related visual and auditory worlds (Bahrick, 1988; Gibson & Spelke, 1983; Rose & Ruff, 1987). Keep in mind, though, that intermodal perception in young infants remains a controversial concept. For example, in one investigation of 6-month-old infants, the auditory sense dominated the visual sense, restricting intermodal perception (Lewkowicz, 1988).

The claim that the young infant can relate information to another has important conceptual ties. The **direct perception view** *states that infants are born with intermodal perception abilities that enable them to display intermodal perception early in infancy. In this view, infants only have to attend to the appropriate information; they do not have to build up an internal representation of the information through months of experience.* In contrast,

Concept Table 5.2: Perceptual Development in Infancy

Concept	Processes/Related Ideas	Characteristics/Description
What Are Sensation and Perception?	Sensation	Sensation occurs when information contacts sensory receptors—eyes, ears, tongue, nostrils, and skin.
	Perception	Perception is interpretation of what is sensed.
Visual Perception	The Newborn's Visual World	William James said it is a blooming, buzzing confusion; he was wrong. The newborn's perception is more advanced than we previously thought.
	Visual Preferences	Fantz's research—by showing how infants prefer striped to solid patches—demonstrated that newborns can see.
	Quality of Vision	The newborn is about 20/600 on the Snellen chart; by 6 months the infant's vision improves to at least 20/100.
	The Human Face	The human face is an important visual pattern for the newborn. The infant gradually masters a sequence of steps in perceiving the human face.
	Depth Perception	A classic study by Gibson and Walk (1960) demonstrated through the use of the visual cliff that 6-month-old infants can perceive depth.
Other Senses	Hearing	The fetus can hear several weeks before birth; immediately after birth newborns can hear, although their sensory threshold is higher than that of adults.
	Smell, Taste, Touch, and Pain	Each of these senses is present in the newborn. Research on circumcision shows that 3-day-old males experience pain and have the ability to adapt to stress.
Intermodal Perception	Its Nature	Considerable interest focuses on the infant's ability to relate information across perceptual modalities; the coordination and integration of perceptual information across two modalities—such as the visual and the auditory senses—is called intermodal perception. A number of researchers believe young infants have intermodal perception. The direct perception and constructivist views are two important views of perception that make different predictions about intermodal perception.

the **constructivist view** *advocated by Piaget states that the main perceptual abilities—visual, auditory, and tactile, for example—are completely uncoordinated at birth, and that young infants do not have intermodal perception. According to Piaget, only through months of sensorimotor interactions with the world is intermodal perception possible. For Piaget, infant perception involves a representation of the world that builds up as the infant constructs an image of experiences.*

Although the intermodal perception and direct perception/constructivist arguments have not completely been settled, we now know today that young infants know a lot more than we used to think they did. They see more and hear more than we used to think was possible (Bower, 1989, 1991). In our tour of the infant's perceptual world, we have discussed a number of senses—vision, hearing, smell, taste, touch, and pain. Main ideas related to these aspects of infants' perceptual development are summarized in concept table 5.2. In the next chapter, we will continue our discussion of infant development, turning to the nature of infants' cognitive development.

• *Critical Thinking* •

Increasingly, developmentalists have become surprised by the early competencies of newborns and young infants. Are we going too far in believing that newborns and young infants are competent in dealing with their world or are they really as sophisticated as the new wave of research seems to suggest?

Summary

1. **Reflexes**

   The newborn is no longer viewed as a passive, empty-headed organism. Physically, newborns are limited, however, and reflexes (automatic movements) govern the newborn's behavior. Sucking is an important means of obtaining nutrition, as well as a pleasurable, soothing activity, for infants. Nonnutritive sucking is of interest to researchers because it provides a means of evaluating attention. Crying and smiling are affective behaviors that are important in the infant's communication with the world.

II. **States**

   Researchers have put together different classification systems; one classification involves seven infant state categories, including deep sleep, drowsy, alert and focused, and inflexibly focused. Newborns usually sleep 16 to 17 hours a day. By 4 months, they approach adultlike sleeping patterns. REM sleep, during which children and adults are most likely to dream, occurs much more often in early infancy than in childhood or adulthood. The high percentage of REM sleep—about half of neonatal sleep—may be a self-stimulatory device, or it may promote brain development.

III. **Physical Growth and Development in Infancy**

   The cephalocaudal pattern is growth from the top down; the proximodistal pattern is growth from the center out. Gross motor skills involve large muscle activity as in walking; fine motor skills involve more fine-grained activities, such as manual dexterity. Both gross and fine motor skills undergo extensive change in the first two years of a child's development. During the first year, rhythmic motor behavior—involving rapid, repetitious movement of the limbs, torso, and head—is common; this type of movement seems to represent an important adaptive transition in development. A great deal of brain growth occurs in infancy as well as in prenatal development. Dendritic spreading is dramatic in the first two years of life. Some important changes in neurotransmitters probably also occur, although these changes are just beginning to be charted.

IV. **Nutritional Needs and Eating Behavior**

   Infants need to consume about 50 calories per day for each pound they weigh. Human milk, or alternative formula, is the baby's source of nutrients for the first six months. The growing consensus is that breast-feeding is superior to bottle-feeding, but the increase in working mothers has meant fewer breast-fed babies. Parents are increasingly using a demand feeding schedule. The maturation of oral and fine motor skills indicate appropriate ages for introducing semisolid and solid foods. Obesity in infancy has not been a good predictor of obesity in adulthood. Infants should not be placed on lowfat, low-calorie diets.

V. **Malnutrition in Infancy**

   Severe infant malnutrition is still prevalent in many parts of the world. Severe protein-calorie deficiency can cause marasmus, a wasting away of body tissues. It is caused mainly by early weaning from breast milk to unsuitable formulas. Even if not fatal, severe and lengthy malnutrition is detrimental to physical, cognitive, and social development.

VI. **Sensation and Perception**

   Sensation is when information contacts sensory receptors—eyes, ears, tongue, nostrils, and skin. Perception is the interpretation of what is sensed.

VII. **Visual Perception**

   William James said that the newborn's world is like a blooming, buzzing confusion. He was wrong. The newborn's perception is more advanced than previously thought. Fantz's research—by showing that infants prefer stripes to solids—demonstrated that newborns can see. The human face is an important visual pattern for the newborn. The infant gradually masters a sequence of steps in perceiving the human face. A classic study by Gibson and Walk demonstrated through the use of the visual cliff that 6-month-old infants can perceive depth.

VIII. **Other Senses**

   The fetus can hear several weeks before birth; immediately after birth newborns can hear, although their sensory threshold is higher than that of adults. Smell, taste, touch, and pain are present in the newborn. Research on circumcision shows that 3-day-old males experience pain and have the ability to cope with stress.

IX. **Bimodal Perception**

   Considerable interest focuses on the infant's ability to relate information across perceptual modalities; the coordination and integration of perceptual information across two modalities—such as the visual and auditory senses—is called bimodal perception. A number of researchers believe young infants have intermodal perception. The direct perception and constructivist views are two important views of perception that make different predictions about intermodal perception.

Key Terms

sucking reflex   133
rooting reflex   133
Moro reflex   134
grasping reflex   134
nonnutritive sucking   134
reflexive smile   137

social smile   137
REM (rapid eye movement) sleep   139
cephalocaudal pattern   140
proximodistal pattern   140
gross motor skills   140
fine motor skills   140

marasmus   145
sensation   149
perception   149
intermodal perception   154
direct perception view   154
constructivist view   155

Suggested Readings

Banks, M. S., & Salapatek, P. (1983). Infant visual perception. In P. E. Mussen (Ed.), *Handbook of child psychology* (4th ed., Vol. 2). New York: Wiley.
This authoritative version of research on infant perception covers in great detail the topics discussed in this chapter.

Caplan, F. (1981). *The first twelve months of life.* New York: Bantam.
An easy-to-read, well-written account of each of the first 12 months of life. Includes extensive information about motor milestones.

Lamb, M. E., & Bornstein, M. C. (1987). *Development in infancy.* New York: Random House.
This portrayal of the infant by two leading researchers includes individual chapters on perceptual development as well as the ecology of the infant's development.

Mandler, J. M. (1990). A new perspective on cognitive development. *American Scientist, 78,* 236–243.
Cognitive psychologist Jean Mandler describes the revolution that has taken place in infant cognitive development in recent years, which challenges some of Piaget's cherished views.

Osofsky, J. D. (1987). *Handbook of infant development* (2nd ed.). New York: Wiley.
Leading experts in the field of infant development have contributed chapters on a far ranging set of topics about infants.

Williams, S. R., & Worthington-Roberts, B. S. (1988). *Nutrition throughout the life cycle.* St. Louis: Times Mirror/Mosby.
An up-to-date, authoritative examination of nutrition in development with separate chapters on breast-feeding and nutrition in infancy.

CHAPTER 6

Cognitive Development in Infancy

M atthew is 1 year old. He has already seen over 1,000 flash cards with pictures of shells, flowers, insects, flags, countries, and words on them. His mother, Billie, has made almost 10,000 of the 11-inch-square cards for Matthew and his 4-year-old brother, Mark. Billie has religiously followed the regimen recommended by Glenn Doman, the director of the Philadelphia Institute for the Achievement of Human Potential and the author of *How to Teach Your Baby to Read*. Using his methods, learned in a course called "How to Multiply Your Baby's Intelligence," Billie is teaching Matthew Japanese and even a little math. Mark is learning geography, natural science, engineering, and fine arts, as well.

Parents using the card approach print one word on each card using a bright red felt-tipped pen. The parent repeatedly shows the card to the infant while saying the word aloud. The first word is usually *mommy,* then comes *daddy,* the baby's name, parts of the body, and all the things the infant can touch. The infant is lavishly praised when he recognizes the word. The idea is to imprint the large red words in the infant's memory, so that in time, he accumulates an impressive vocabulary and begins to read. The parent continues to feed the infant with all manner of information in small, assimilable bits, just as Billie Rash has done with her two boys.

Using this method, the child should be reading by 2 years of age, and by 4 or 5 should have begun mastering some math and be able to play the violin, not to mention the vast knowledge of the world he should be able to display because of a monumental vocabulary. Maybe the SAT or ACT test you labored through on your way to college might have been conquered at the age of 6 if your parents had only been enrolled in "How to Multiply Your Baby's Intelligence" course and made 10,000 flash cards for you.

Is this the best way for an infant to learn? A number of developmentalists believe Doman's "better baby institute" is a money-making scheme and is not based on sound scientific evidence. They believe that we should not be trying to accelerate the infant's learning so dramatically. Rather than have information poured into infants' minds, infants should be permitted more time to spontaneously explore the environment and construct their knowledge. Jean Piaget called "What should we do to foster cognitive development?" the American question, because it was asked of him so often when he lectured to American audiences. Developmentalists worry that children exposed to Doman's methods will burn out on learning. What is probably more important is providing a rich and emotionally supportive atmosphere for learning.

There was a child who went forth every day And the first object he looked upon, that object he became. And that object became part of him for the day, or a certain part of the day, or for many years, or stretching cycles of years.

Walt Whitman

Here infants and toddlers are being taught in the manner recommended by Glenn Doman, which emphasizes acceleration of learning to read by intensely exposing children to flash cards with many different words on them. Most developmental psychologists believe something is fundamentally wrong with Doman's approach. They believe that rather than pouring information into children's minds in the way Doman advises, children should be permitted to spontaneously explore their environment and to construct their knowledge in an independent manner.

Cognitive Development in Infancy

The excitement and enthusiasm surrounding the infant's cognition has been fueled by an interest in what an infant knows at birth and soon after, by continued fascination about innate and learned factors in the infant's cognitive development, and by controversies over whether infants construct their knowledge (as Piaget believed) or whether they know their world more directly. Primary topics include Piaget's theory of infant development; the nature of attention, memory, and imitation; measurement of infants' intelligence; and where the infant's language comes from and how it develops. We will examine each of these topics in turn.

Piaget's Theory of Infant Development

The poet Noah Perry once asked, "Who knows the thoughts of a child?" Piaget knew as much as anyone. Through careful, inquisitive interviews and observations of his own three children—Laurent, Lucienne, and Jacqueline—Piaget changed the way we think about children's conception of the world. Remember that we studied an overview of Piaget's theory in chapter 2. It may be helpful for you to review the basic features of his theory at this time.

Piaget believed that the child passes through a series of stages of thought from infancy to adolescence. Passage through the stages results from biological pressures to *adapt* to the environment (assimilation and accommodation) and to organize structures of thinking. The stages of thought are *qualitatively* different from one another; the way children reason at one stage is very different from the way they reason at another stage. This contrasts with the quantitative assessments of intelligence made through the use of standardized intelligence tests, where the focus is on what the child knows, or how many questions the child can answer correctly (Ginsburg & Opper, 1988). According to Piaget, the mind's development is divided into four such qualitatively different stages: sensorimotor, preoperational, concrete operational, and formal operational. Here our concern is with the stage that characterizes infant thought—the sensorimotor stage.

The Stage of Sensorimotor Development

Piaget's sensorimotor stage lasts from birth to about 2 years of age, corresponding to the period of infancy. During this time, mental development is characterized by considerable progression in the infant's ability to organize and coordinate sensations with physical movements and actions—hence, the name *sensorimotor* (Piaget, 1952).

At the beginning of the sensorimotor stage, the infant has little more than reflexive patterns with which to work. By the end of the stage, the 2-year-old has complex sensorimotor patterns and is beginning to operate with a primitive system of symbols. Unlike other stages, the sensorimotor stage is subdivided into six substages, which describe qualitative changes in sensorimotor organization. The term **scheme** *(or schema) refers to the basic unit for an organized pattern of sensorimotor functioning.*

Piaget was a masterful observer of his three children. The following observation of his son, Laurent, provides an excellent example of the infant's emerging coordination of visual and motor schemes, and eloquently portrays how infants learn about their hands.

At 2 months, Laurent by chance discovers his right index finger and looks at it briefly. Several days later, he briefly inspects his open right hand, perceived by chance. About a week later, he follows its spontaneous movement for a moment, then he holds his two fists in the air and looks at the left one. Then he slowly brings it toward his face and rubs his nose with it, then his

We are born capable of learning.
~ *Jean Jacque Rousseau*

eye. A moment later the left hand again approaches his face. He looks at it and touches his nose. He does that again and laughs five or six times while moving the left hand to his face. He seems to laugh before the hand moves, but looking has no influence on its movement. He laughs beforehand but begins to smile again on seeing the hand. Then he rubs his nose. At a given moment, he turns his head to the left, but looking has no effect on the direction. The next day, the same reaction occurs. And, then another day later, he looks at his right hand, then at his clasped hands. Finally, on the day after that, Piaget says that Laurent's looking acts on the orientation of his hands, which tend to remain in the visual field (Piaget, 1936).

With a given substage, there may be different schemes—sucking, rooting, and blinking in Substage 1, for example. In Substage 1, the schemes are basically reflexive in nature. From substage to substage, the schemes change in organization. This change is at the heart of Piaget's description of the stages. The six substages of sensorimotor development are (1) simple reflexes; (2) first habits and primary circular reactions; (3) secondary circular reactions; (4) coordination of secondary circular reactions; (5) tertiary circular reactions, novelty, and curiosity; and (6) internalization of schemes.

Simple reflexes *is Piaget's first sensorimotor substage, which corresponds to the first month after birth. In this substage, the basic means of coordinating sensation and action is through reflexive behaviors, such as rooting and sucking, which the infant has at birth.* In Substage 1, the infant exercises these reflexes. More importantly, the infant develops an ability to produce behaviors that resemble reflexes in the absence of obvious reflexive stimuli. The newborn may suck when a bottle or nipple is only nearby, for example. When the baby was just born, the bottle or nipple would have produced the sucking pattern only when placed directly in the newborn's mouth or touched to the lips. Reflexlike actions in the absence of a triggering stimulus is evidence that the infant is initiating action and is actively structuring experiences in the first month of life.

First habits and primary circular reactions *is Piaget's second sensorimotor substage, which develops between 1 and 4 months of age. In this substage, the infant learns to coordinate sensation and types of schemes or structures—that is, habits and primary circular reactions.* A *habit* is a scheme based upon a simple reflex, such as sucking, that has become completely divorced from its eliciting stimulus. For example, an infant in Substage 1 might suck when orally stimulated by a bottle or when visually shown the bottle, but an infant in Substage 2 might exercise the sucking scheme even when no bottle is present.

A **primary circular reaction** *is a scheme based upon the infant's attempt to reproduce an interesting or pleasurable event that initially occurred by chance.* In a popular Piagetian example, a child accidently sucks his fingers when they are placed near his mouth; later, he searches for his fingers to suck them again, but the fingers do not cooperate in the search because the infant cannot coordinate visual and manual actions. Habits and circular reactions are stereotyped in that the infant repeats them the same way each time. The infant's own body remains the center of attention; there is no outward pull by environmental events.

Secondary circular reactions *is Piaget's third sensorimotor substage, which develops between 4 and 8 months of age. In this substage, the infant becomes more object-oriented or focused on the world, moving beyond preoccupation with the self in sensorimotor interactions.* The chance shaking of a rattle, for example, may fascinate the infant, and the infant will repeat this action for the sake of experiencing fascination. The infant imitates some simple actions of others, such as the baby talk or burbling of adults, and some physical gestures. However, these imitations are limited to actions the infant is already able to produce. Although directed toward objects in the world, the infant's schemes lack an intentional, goal-directed quality.

Coordination of secondary circular reactions *is Piaget's fourth sensorimotor substage, which develops between 8 and 12 months of age. In this substage, several significant changes take place involving the coordination of schemes and intentionality.* Infants readily combine and recombine previously learned schemes in a *coordinated* way. They may look at an object and grasp it simultaneously, or visually inspect a toy, such as a rattle, and finger it simultaneously in obvious tactile exploration. Actions are even more outwardly directed than before. Related to this coordination is the second achievement—the presence of *intentionality,* the separation of means and goals in accomplishing simple feats. For example, infants might manipulate a stick (the means) to bring a desired toy within reach (the goal). They may knock over one block to reach and play with another one.

Tertiary circular reactions, novelty, and curiosity *is Piaget's fifth sensorimotor substage, which develops between 12 and 18 months of age. In this substage, infants become intrigued by the variety of properties that objects possess and by the multiplicity of things they can make happen to objects.* A block can be made to fall, spin, hit another object, slide across the ground, and so on. Tertiary circular reactions are schemes in which the infant purposely explores new possibilities with objects, continually changing what is done to them and exploring the results. Piaget says that this stage marks the developmental starting point for human curiosity and interest in novelty. Previous circular reactions have been devoted exclusively to reproducing former events, with the exception of imitation of novel acts, which occurs as early as Substage 4. The tertiary circular act is the first to be concerned with novelty.

Internalization of schemes *is Piaget's sixth and final sensorimotor substage, which develops between 18 and 24 months of age. In this substage the infant's mental functioning shifts from a purely sensorimotor plane to a symbolic plane, and the infant develops the ability to use primitive symbols.* For Piaget, a *symbol* is an internalized sensory image or word that represents an event. Primitive symbols permit the infant to think about concrete events without directly acting them out or perceiving them. Moreover, symbols allow the infant to manipulate and transform the represented events in simple ways. In a favorite Piagetian example, Piaget's young daughter saw a matchbox being opened and closed; sometime later, she mimicked the event by opening and closing her mouth. This was an obvious expression of her image of the event. In another example, a child opened a door slowly to avoid disturbing a piece of paper lying on the floor on the other side. Clearly, the child had an image of the unseen paper and what would happen to it if the door opened quickly. However, developmentalists have debated whether 2-year-olds really have such representations of action sequences at their command (Corrigan, 1981). A summary of Piaget's sensorimotor substages is shown in figure 6.1.

To read further about Piaget's six substages of infant cognitive development, turn to Perspective on Life-Span Development 6.1, where you will find suggestions for a day-care curriculum based on Piaget's substages.

Object Permanence

Object permanence *is the Piagetian term for one of an infant's most important accomplishments: understanding that objects and events continue to exist even when they cannot directly be seen, heard, or touched.* Imagine what thought would be like if you could not distinguish between yourself and your world. Your thought would be chaotic, disorganized, and unpredictable. This

(a)   (b)   (c)

(d)   (e)   (f)

*Figure 6.1   Piaget's six sensorimotor substages. (a) In substage 1, the infant
practices the reflexive behavior of sucking. (b) In substage 2, the infant will
practice the sucking reflex when no bottle is present. (c) In substage 3, the infant
becomes more object oriented. (d) In substage 4, the infant begins to coordinate
action. (e) In substage 5, the infant becomes intrigued by an object's variety of
properties. (f) In substage 6, the infant's functioning shifts to a symbolic plane.*

*Figure 6.2   Object permanence.
Piaget thought that object
permanence was one of infancy's
landmark cognitive accomplishments. For this 5-month-old infant
boy, "out of sight" is literally out of
mind. The infant looks at the toy
monkey (left), but when his view of
the toy is blocked (right), he does
not search for it. Eventually he will
search for the hidden toy monkey,
reflecting the presence of object
permanence.*

is what the mental life of a newborn is like, according to Piaget. There is no
self-world differentiation and no sense of object permanence (Piaget, 1952).
By the end of the sensorimotor period, however, both are present.

The principal way that object permanence is studied is by watching an
infant's reaction when an interesting object or event disappears (see figure
6.2). If infants show no reaction, it is assumed they believe the object no longer

SUGGESTIONS FOR A DAY-CARE CURRICULUM BASED ON PIAGET'S SUBSTAGES OF INFANT COGNITIVE DEVELOPMENT

As more infants spend much of their day in day-care centers, it is important for the caregivers to interact in effective ways with the infants and for the day-care center to develop a curriculum that is appropriate for infant cognitive development. Following is a developmentally appropriate curriculum for infant cognitive development that was proposed by educator/developmentalist LaVisa Wilson (1990).

Piagetian Stage	Materials	Examples of Caregiver Strategies
Stage 1: Simple Reflexes (birth to 1 month)	Visually attractive crib, walls next to crib, and objects; occasional music, singing, talking, chimes	Provide nonrestrictive clothes and uncluttered crib to allow freedom of movement; provide environment that commands attention during the infant's periods of alertness
Stage 2: First Habits and Primary Circular Reactions (1 month to 4 months)	Face and voice, musical toys, musical mobile, rattle; objects infant can grasp and which are safe to go in the infant's mouth; objects the infant can grasp and lift	Provide change in infant's environment; carry infant around, hold infant, place infant in crib; observe, discuss, record changes in the infant; turn on musical toys and place where the infant can see them; place objects in the infant's hands or within the infants reach; provide clothes that allow freedom of movement; provide time and space for repetition of behaviors
Stage 3: Secondary Circular Reactions (4 to 8 months)	Objects that attract attention, such as contrasting colors, changes in sounds, variety of textures, designs; toys; balls	Watch movements the infant repeats, as when an infant waves an arm and hits the crib gym, and then repeats this action; provide materials that facilitate such repetitions (new items on the crib gym, for example); place blocks, dolls, ball, and other toys near the infant so they can be reached; initiate action, wait for the infant to imitate it, then repeat the action (smile, open mouth, for example)

exists. By contrast, if infants are surprised at the disappearance and search for the object, it is assumed they believe it continues to exist. According to Piaget, object permanence develops in a series of substages that correspond to the six substages of sensorimotor development. In table 6.1, how the six substages of object permanence reflect Piaget's substages of sensorimotor development is shown.

At this point we have discussed a number of characteristics of Piaget's stage of sensorimotor thought. To help you remember the main characteristics of sensorimotor thought, turn to figure 6.3.

Piagetian Stage	Materials	Examples of Caregiver Strategies
Stage 4: Coordination of Secondary Circular Reactions (8 to 12 months)	Toys, visually attractive objects	Place objects near the infant; play "hide the doll under the blanket"; place the block behind you; verbalize caregiver's own actions, such as "I put the ball behind me"; introduce new copy games; allow time and space for the infant to play
Stage 5: Tertiary Circular Reactions, Novelty, and Curiosity (12 to 18 months)	Blanket, paper, toys, dolls, spoon, interesting objects; water toys, water basin; narrow-neck milk carton and different sizes and shapes of objects	Play game of "hide the object" with infant—hide the object while the infant watches, let infant watch you move the object to a different place under the blanket, and ask, "Where is it?" "Can you find it?"; observe and allow infant to find the object, praise infant for good watching and thinking; allow infant to play with water and toys to discover different actions of water and of the objects in the water; provide time and materials that stimulate infant to think and try out new ideas; ask questions but do not tell answers or show infant; encourage infant to pretend—to drink from a pretend bottle like baby Gwen, to march like Pearl, to pick up toys; allow infant to repeat own play and develop own preferences
Stage 6: Internalization of Schemes (18 to 24 months)	Developmentally appropriate toys, interesting objects	Allow toddler time to figure out solutions, to think and search for objects; observe toddler's representations and identify the ideas that seem important to the toddler; allow the toddler to act out conflict in play with toys and materials; observe toddler's play and identify consistent themes; provide clothes and materials that help the toddler pretend to be someone else

Although Piaget's stage sequence is the best summary of what might happen as the infant fathoms the permanence of things in the world, some contradictory findings have emerged. Piaget's stages broadly describe the interesting changes reasonably well, but the infant's life is not so neatly packaged into distinct stages as Piaget believed. Some of Piaget's explanations for the causes of change are debated.

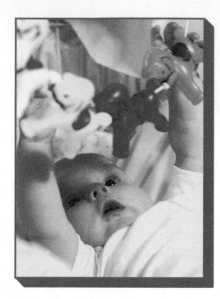

Ability to organize and coordinate sensations with physical movements	Is nonsymbolic through most of its duration	Consists of six substages of cognitive development	Object permanence develops

Figure 6.3 *The main characteristics of sensorimotor thought.*

Table 6.1: The Six Substages of Object Permanence

Sensorimotor Stage	Behavior
Substage 1	There is no apparent object permanence. When a spot of light moves across the visual field, the infant follows it but quickly ignores its disappearance.
Substage 2	A primitive form of object permanence develops. Given the same experience, the infant looks briefly at the spot where the light disappeared, with an expression of passive expectancy.
Substage 3	The infant's sense of object permanence undergoes further development. With the newfound ability to coordinate simple schemes, the infant shows clear patterns of searching for a missing object, with sustained visual and manual examination of the spot where the object apparently disappeared.
Substage 4	The infant actively searches for a missing object in the spot where it disappeared, with new actions to achieve the goal of searching effectively. For example, if an attractive toy has been hidden behind a screen, the child may look at the screen and try to push it away with a hand. If the screen is too heavy to move or is permanently fixed, the child readily substitutes a secondary scheme—for example, crawling around it or kicking it. These new actions signal that the infant's belief in the continued existence of the missing object is strengthening.
Substage 5	The infant now is able to track an object that disappears and reappears in several locations in rapid succession. For example, a toy may be hidden under different boxes in succession in front of the infant, who succeeds in finding it. The infant is apparently able to hold an image of the missing object in mind longer than before.
Substage 6	The infant can search for a missing object that disappeared and reappeared in several locations in succession, as before. In addition, the infant searches in the appropriate place even when the object has been hidden from view as it is being moved. This activity indicates that the infant is able to "imagine" the missing object and to follow the image from one location to the next.

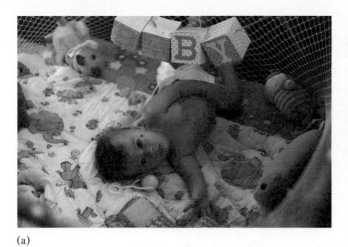

(a)

(b)

Habituation is a common occurrence in the infant's perceptual world. In (a) the infant is attending to the blocks hanging overhead. In (b), the infant has become bored with the blocks and looks away from them. Habituation is like getting bored with a stimulus.

Information Processing

How do information processing psychologists describe infant development? First, we consider the nature of this approach and compare it with Piaget's perspective, and second, we examine several processes—habituation/dishabituation and memory—thought to be important in the way the infant processes information. Third, the fascinating possibility that the newborn can imitate an adult facial expression is discussed.

The Information Processing Perspective and Infant Development

Unlike Piaget, information processing psychologists do not describe infancy as a stage or a series of substages. Rather, information processing psychologists emphasize the importance of such cognitive processes as attention, memory, and thinking in the way the infant processes information about the world.

Piaget believed that the infant's ability to construct sensorimotor schemas, establish a coherent world of objects and events suitable to form the content of ideas, imitate, and form images that can stand for things is completed in the second half of the second year. However, many information processing psychologists believe the young infant is more competent than Piaget believed, with attentional, symbolic, imitative, and conceptual capabilities present earlier in infant development than Piaget envisioned (Mandler, 1990, 1991). In this sense, the information processing psychologists share the view with the direct perception psychologists (discussed in chapter 5) that the young infant is very competent.

Habituation and Dishabituation

If a stimulus—a sight or sound—is presented to infants several times in a row, they usually pay less attention to it each time, suggesting they are bored with it. This is the process of **habituation**—*repeated presentation of the same stimulus that causes reduced attention to the stimulus* (Kaplan, Fox, & Huckeby, 1991; Tamis-LeMonda & Bornstein, 1989). **Dishabituation** *is an infant's renewed interest in a stimulus.* Among the measures infant researchers use to study whether habituation is occurring are sucking behavior (sucking behavior

Man is the only animal that can be bored.

~ *Eric Fromm,*
The Sane Society, *1955*

stops when the young infant attends to a novel object), heart and respiration rates, and the length of time the infant looks at an object. Newborn infants can habituate to repetitive stimulation in virtually every stimulus modality—vision, audition, touch, and so on (Rovee-Collier, 1987). However, habituation becomes more acute over the first three months of life. The extensive assessment of habituation in recent years has resulted in its use as a measure of an infant's maturity and well-being. Infants who have brain damage or have suffered birth traumas such as lack of oxygen do not habituate well and may later have developmental and learning problems.

A knowledge of habituation and dishabituation can benefit parent-infant interaction. Infants respond to changes in stimulation. If stimulation is repeated often, the infant's response will decrease to the point that the infant no longer responds to the parent. In parent-infant interaction, it is important for parents to do novel things and to repeat them often until the infant stops responding. Wise parents sense when the infant shows an interest and that many repetitions of the stimulus may be necessary for the infant to process the information. Parent stop or change behaviors when infants redirect their attention (Rosenblith & Sims-Knight, 1985).

Memory

Memory *is a central feature of cognitive development, pertaining to all situations in which an individual retains information over time.* Sometimes information is retained for only a few seconds, and at others for a lifetime. Memory is involved when we remember a telephone number and dial it, when we remember the name of our best friend from elementary school, when an infant remembers who her mother is, and when an older adult remembers to keep a doctor's appointment.

Infant researcher Carolyn Rovee-Collier and her colleagues (Rovee-Collier, 1987; Borovsky, Hill, & Rovee-Collier, 1987) hung a mobile over an infant's crib and attached a ribbon to one of the baby's limbs (figure 6.4). Six-week-old infants quickly discovered which arm or leg would move the mobile. Two weeks later, the infants were placed in the same situation. They *remembered* which arm or leg to move, even though they were not attached to the mobile. These early signs of memory are the basis of the kinds of learning from experience that continue throughout our lifetime. Ongoing investigation of such abilities underscores just how surprisingly competent young infants are.

Is the infant's memory of the mobile conscious? As children and adults, our memory often involves conscious feelings, such as "I have seen that before," as well as additional retrieval abilities, such as "Where have I seen that before—was it at the zoo?" However, these conscious feelings are probably not present in the memory of young infants, who do not have the ability to consciously recall or reflect about objects when they are not present (Flavell, 1985).

Just when do infants acquire the ability to consciously remember the past? In one investigation, parents kept diaries of their 5- to 11-month-olds' memories (Ashmead & Perlmutter, 1979). An entry in one of the diaries describes the behavior of a 9-month-old girl who was looking for ribbons that had been removed from the drawer where they had been kept. She first looked in the "old" drawer. Failing to find the ribbons, she searched other drawers until she found them. The next day, the young girl went directly to the "new" drawer to find the ribbons. More formal experiments support the existence of such memory in infants over 6 months of age (Fox, Kagan, & Weiskopf, 1979). For example, when an object is shown to an infant and then subsequently removed, a 7-month-old infant will search for it, but a younger infant will not.

Life is all memory, except for the one present moment that goes by you so quick you hardly catch it going.

~ *Tennessee Williams,*
The Milk Train Doesn't Stop
Here Anymore, *1963*

Infancy

Figure 6.4 Studying infant memory. Shown here is the technique used in Rovee-Collier's investigation of infant memory. The mobile is connected to the infant's ankle by the ribbon and moves in direct proportion to the frequency and vigor of the infant's kicks.

The memory of infants in the first six months of life is not like what we, as adults, commonly think of as memory; it is not conscious memory for specific past episodes but rather learning of adaptive skills.

Why does conscious memory develop later than other learning and memory skills? Possibly conscious memory must await the maturation of certain brain structures, such as the hippocampus (Diamond, 1989). Possibly conscious memory depends on the development of cognitive structures, as Piaget's theory suggests.

Despite evidence of conscious memory in the first year of life, such recall is believed to be minimal until the child is about 3 years of age (Nelson, 1991). Try to recall a specific episode in the first three years of your life, such as the birth of a sibling. Can you remember anything at all about the first three years of your life? **Infantile amnesia** *is the lack of memory for anything that happened prior to 3 years of age.* In one investigation (Sheingold & Tenney, 1982), college students who had at least one younger sibling were interviewed and asked such questions as, "Who told you that your mother was leaving to go to the hospital to have a baby?" "What time of day did she go to the hospital?" "Did you visit your mother in the hospital?" Recall for the college students is shown in figure 6.5. Recall was virtually zero unless their siblings were three or more years younger, supporting the concept of infantile amnesia.

Imitation

In the last chapter, we described how infants display a variety of their own emotions. But can they also imitate someone else's emotional expressions? If an adult smiles, will the baby follow with a smile? If an adult protrudes her lower lip, wrinkles her forehead, and frowns, will the baby show a saddened look? If an adult opens his mouth, widens his eyes, and raises his eyebrows, will the baby follow suit? Could infants only 1 day old do these things?

• *Critical Thinking* •

Can you think of ways to measure infantile amnesia other than asking individuals if they remember a sibling being born?

We are, in truth, more than half what we are by imitation.

~ *Lord Chesterfield,*
Letters To His Son, *1750*

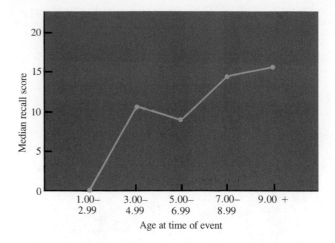

Figure 6.5 Infantile amnesia. As shown in the graph, when college students were asked if they could remember the birth of their young sibling, recall was virtually zero unless their siblings were three or more years younger, supporting the concept of infantile amnesia.

Tiffany Field and her colleagues (1982) explored these questions with newborns only 36 hours after their birth. The model held the newborn's head upright with the model's and the newborn's faces separated by 10 inches. The newborn's facial expressions were recorded by an observer who stood behind the model. The observer could not see which facial expressions the model was showing. The model expressed one of three emotions: happiness, sadness, or surprise. As shown in figure 6.6, infants were most likely to imitate the model's display of surprise by widely opening their mouths. When the infants observed a happy mood, they frequently widened their lips. When the model expressed sadness, the infants followed with lips that reflected pouting. Other research supports the belief that young infants can imitate an adult's emotional expressions.

Infant development researcher Andrew Meltzoff (1988, 1990; Meltzoff & Kuhl, 1989) has conducted numerous studies of the imitative abilities of infants. He believes infants' imitative abilities are biologically based because infants can imitate a facial expression within the first few days after birth before they have had the opportunity to observe social agents in their environment engage in tongue protrusion and other behaviors. He also believes the infant's imitative abilities are not like the ethologist's concept of a hard-wired, reflexive innate releasing mechanism, but rather involve flexibility, adaptability, and intermodal perception. In Meltzoff's observations of infants in the first 72 hours of life, the infants gradually displayed a full imitative response of an adult's facial expression, such as tongue protrusion or a wide-opening of the mouth. Initially, the young infant may only get its tongue to the edge of its lips, but after a number of attempts and observations of the adult behavior, the infant displays a more full-blown response.

Meltzoff has also studied **deferred imitation,** *which is imitation that occurs after a time delay of hours or days.* In one recent investigation, Meltzoff (1988) demonstrated that 9-month-old infants could imitate actions they had seen performed 24 hours earlier. Each action consisted of an unusual gesture—for example, pushing a recessed button in a box (which produced a beeping sound). Piaget did not believe deferred imitation occurs until about 18 months of age; Meltzoff's research suggests it occurs much earlier in infant development.

In sum, rather than assuming that infants' conceptual functioning—involving such important cognitive processes as memory and deferred imitation—can occur only as an outcome of a lengthy sensorimotor stage,

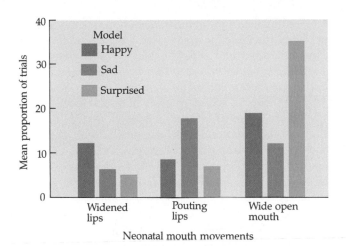

Figure 6.6 *Imitation of adults' emotional facial expressions by 36-hour-old newborns. The graph shows the mean proportion of trials during which newborn mouth movements followed a model's facial expression. Mouth movements included widened lips (happy), pouting lips (sad), and wide open mouth (surprised).*

Shown here is infant development researcher Andrew Meltzoff displaying tongue protrusion and getting an infant to imitate his behavior. Researchers have demonstrated that young infants can imitate an adult's behavior far earlier than traditionally believed.

information processing psychologists believe infants are either born with these capabilities or they acquire them much earlier in infancy than Piaget believed. As we see next, a third perspective on infant cognition also differs from Piaget's approach.

Individual Differences in Intelligence

So far we have stressed general statements about how the cognitive development of infants progresses, emphasizing what is typical of the largest number of infants or the average infant. But the results obtained for most infants do not apply to all infants. Individual differences in infant cognitive development have been studied primarily through the use of developmental scales or infant intelligence tests (Columbo & Fagan, 1991; Green, 1991; Horowitz, 1991).

It is advantageous to know whether an infant is advancing at a slow, normal, or advanced pace of development. In chapter 4, we discussed the Brazelton Neonatal Behavioral Assessment Scale, which is widely used to evaluate newborns. Developmentalists also want to know how development proceeds during the course of infancy as well. If an infant advances at an especially slow rate, then some form of enrichment may be necessary. If an infant develops at an advanced pace, parents may be advised to provide toys that stimulate cognitive growth in slightly older infants.

The infant testing movement grew out of the tradition of IQ testing with older children. However, the measures that assess infants are necessarily less verbal than IQ tests that assess the intelligence of older children. The infant developmental scales contain far more items related to perceptual motor development. They also include measures of social interaction.

The most important early contributor to the developmental testing of infants was Arnold Gesell (1934). He developed a measure that was used as a clinical tool to help sort out potentially normal babies from abnormal ones. This was especially useful to adoption agencies who had large numbers of babies awaiting placement. Gesell's examination was used widely for many years and is still frequently used by pediatricians in their assessment of normal and abnormal infants. The version of the Gesell test now used has four categories of behavior: motor, language, adaptive, and personal-social. The **developmental quotient (DQ)** *is an overall developmental score that combines subscores in motor, language, adaptive, and personal-social domains in the Gesell assessment of infants.* However, overall scores on tests like the Gesell do not correlate highly with IQ scores obtained later in childhood. This is not surprising because the nature of the items on the developmental scales are considerably less verbal than the items on intelligence tests given to older children.

The **Bayley Scales of Infant Development,** *developed by Nancy Bayley (1969), are widely used in the assessment of infant development. The current version has three components: a mental scale, a motor scale, and an infant behavior profile.* Unlike Gesell, whose scales were clinically motivated, Bayley wanted to develop scales that could document infant behavior and predict later development. The early version of the Bayley scales covered only the first year of development; in the 1950s, the scales were extended to assess older infants.

Because our discussion centers on the infant's cognitive development, our primary interest is on Bayley's mental scale, which includes assessment of the following:

- auditory and visual attention to stimuli
- manipulation, such as combining objects or shaking a rattle
- examiner interaction, such as babbling and imitation
- relation with toys, such as banging spoons together
- memory involved in object permanence, such as when the infant finds a hidden toy
- goal-directed behavior that involves persistence, such as putting pegs in a board
- ability to follow directions and knowledge of objects' names, such as understanding the concept of "one"

How well should a 6-month-old perform on the Bayley mental scale? The 6-month-old infant should be able to vocalize pleasure and displeasure, persistently search for objects that are just out of immediate reach, and approach a mirror that is placed in front of the infant by the examiner. How well should a 12-month-old perform? By 12 months of age, the infant should be able to inhibit behavior when commanded to do so, imitate words the examiner says (such as "Mama"), and respond to simple requests (such as "Take a drink").

• *Critical Thinking* •

Is an older infant's intelligence just quantitatively different than a younger infant's intelligence or is it qualitatively different? What would Piaget have said about this question?

Infant tests of intelligence have been valuable in assessing the effects of malnutrition, drugs, maternal deprivation, and environmental stimulation on the development of infants. They have met with mixed results in predicting later intelligence. Global developmental quotient or IQ scores for infants have not been good predictors of childhood intelligence. However, specific aspects of infant intelligence are related to specific aspects of childhood intelligence. For example, in one recent investigation, infant language abilities as assessed by the Bayley test predicted language, reading, and spelling ability at 6 to 8 years of age (Siegel, 1989). Infant perceptual motor skills predicted visual-spatial, arithmetic, and fine-motor skills at 6 to 8 years of age. These results indicate that an item analysis of infant scales like Bayley's can provide information about the development of specific intellectual functions.

The explosion of interest in infant development has produced many new measures, especially tasks that evaluate the way infants process information (Fagan & Khevel, 1989; Rose, 1989). Evidence is accumulating that measures of habituation and dishabituation predict intelligence in childhood (Bornstein, 1989; Sigman & others, 1989; Slater & others, 1989). Quicker decays or less

The Mental Scale of the Bayley test includes assessment of the infant's auditory and visual attention to objects.

cumulative attention in the habituation situation and greater amounts of attention in the dishabituation situation reflect more efficient information processing. Both types of attention—decrement and recovery—when measured in the first six months of infancy, are related to higher IQ scores on standardized intelligence tests given at various times between infancy and adolescence. In sum, more precise assessment of the infant's cognition with information-processing tasks involving attention have led to the conclusion that continuity between infant and childhood intelligence is greater than was previously believed (Bornstein & Krasnegor, 1989).

It is important, however, not to go too far and think that the connections between early infant cognitive development and later childhood cognitive development are so strong that no discontinuity takes place. Rather than asking whether cognitive development is continuous *or* discontinuous, perhaps we should be examining the ways cognitive development is both continuous *and* discontinuous (Pomerleau, 1989; Sternberg & Okagaki, 1989). Some important changes in cognitive development take place after infancy, changes that underscore the discontinuity of cognitive development. We will describe these changes in cognitive development in subsequent chapters that focus on later periods of development.

Thus far, we have described several important ideas about the infant's cognitive development. To help you remember the main points of this discussion, turn to concept table 6.1. Next, we will study another key dimension of the infant's development—language.

Concept Table 6.1: Infant Cognitive Development

Concept	Processes/Related Ideas	Characteristics/Description
Piaget's Theory of Infant Development	Sensorimotor Stage	This stage lasts from birth to about 2 years of age; involves progression in the infant's ability to organize and coordinate sensations with physical movements. The sensorimotor stage has six substages: simple reflexes; first habits and primary circular reactions; secondary circular reactions; coordination of secondary circular reactions; tertiary circular reactions, novelty, and curiosity; and internalization of schemes.
	Object Permanence	Object permanence refers to the development of the ability to understand that objects and events continue to exist even though the infant no longer is in contact with them. Piaget believed that this ability develops over the course of the six substages.
Information Processing	The Information Processing Perspective and Infant Development	Unlike Piaget, information processing psychologists do not describe infancy as a stage or series of substages of sensorimotor development. Rather, they emphasize the importance of cognitive processes such as attention, memory, and thinking. The information processing psychologists believe the young infant is more competent than Piaget envisioned, with attentional, symbolic, imitative, and conceptual abilities occurring much earlier in development than Piaget thought.
	Habituation and Dishabituation	Habituation is the repeated presentation of the same stimulus causes reduced attention to the stimulus. If a different stimulus is presented and the infant pays attention to it, dishabituation is occurring. Newborn infants can habituate, but habituation becomes more acute over the first three months of infancy.
	Memory	Memory is the retention of information over time. In the first six months, infants learn adaptive skills, but conscious memory does not develop until later in the first year. Infantile amnesia is our inability to remember anything that happened in the first three years of our life.
	Imitation	Infants can imitate the facial expressions of others in the first few days of life. Meltzoff demonstrated that deferred imitation occurs at about 9 months of age, much earlier than Piaget believed.
Individual Differences in Intelligence	History	Developmental scales for infants grew out of the tradition of IQ testing with older children. These scales are less verbal than IQ tests. Gesell was an early developer of an infant test. His scale is still widely used by pediatricians; it provides a developmental quotient (DQ).
	Bayley Scales	The developmental scales most widely used today, developed by Nancy Bayley, consist of a motor scale, a mental scale, and an infant behavior profile.
	Conclusions about Infant Tests and Continuity in Mental Development	Global infant intelligence measures are not good predictors of childhood intelligence. However, specific aspects of infant intelligence, such as information-processing tasks involving attention, have been better predictors of childhood intelligence, especially in a specific area. There is both continuity and discontinuity between infant cognitive development and cognitive development later in childhood.

Language Development

In 1799, a nude boy was observed running through the woods in France. The boy was captured when he was approximately 11 years old. It was believed he had lived in the wild for at least six years. He was called the Wild Boy of Aveyron (Lane, 1976). When the boy was found he made no effort to communicate. Even after a number of years he never learned to communicate effectively. The Wild Boy of Aveyron raises an important issue in language, namely, what are the biological, environmental, and cultural contributions to language? Later in the chapter we will describe a modern-day wild child named Genie, who will shed some light on this issue. Indeed, the contributions of biology, environment, and culture figure prominently into our discussion of language.

What Is Language?

Every human culture has language. Human languages number in the thousands, differing so much on the surface that many of us despair at learning more than even one. Yet all human languages have some common characteristics. **Language** *is a system of symbols used to communicate with others. In humans, language is characterized by infinite generativity and rule systems.* **Infinite generativity** *is an individual's ability to generate an infinite number of meaningful sentences using a finite set of words and rules, which makes language a highly creative enterprise.* Language's rule systems include phonology, morphology, syntax, semantics, and pragmatics, each of which we now discuss in turn.

Language is made up of basic sounds or *phonemes*. In the English language there are approximately 36 phonemes. **Phonology** *is the study of a language's sound system.* Phonological rules ensure that certain sound sequences occur (for example, *sp, ba,* or *ar*) and others do not (for example, *zx* or *qp*). A good example of a phoneme in the English language is /k/, the sound represented by the letter *k* in the word *ski* and the letter *c* in the word *cat.* While the /k/ sound is slightly different in these two words, the variation is not distinguished and the /k/ sound is described as a single phoneme. In some languages, such as Arabic, this kind of variation represents separate phonemes.

Morphology *refers to the rules for combining morphemes; a morpheme is the smallest string of sounds that gives meaning to what we say and hear.* Every word in the English language is made up of one or more morphemes. Some words consist of a single morpheme (for example, *help*), while others are made up of more than one morpheme (for example, *helper,* has two morphemes, *help + er,* with the morpheme *er* meaning "one who": in this case "one who helps"). However, as shown in the previous example, not all morphemes are words (for example, *pre-, -tion,* and *-ing*). Just as the rules that govern phonemes ensure that certain sound sequences occur, the rules that govern morphemes ensure that certain strings of sounds occur in particular sequences. For example, we would not reorder *helper* to *erhelp.*

Syntax *involves the way words are combined to form acceptable phrases and sentences.* Because you and I share the same syntactic understanding of sentence structure, if I say to you, "Bob slugged Tom" and "Bob was slugged by Tom," you know who did the slugging and who was slugged in each case. You also understand that, "You didn't stay, did you?" is grammatically correct but that "You didn't stay, didn't you?" is unacceptable and ambiguous.

> The adjective is the banana peel of the parts of speech.
>
> ~ *Clifton Fadiman,*
> Reader's Digest, *1956*

"If you don't mind my asking, how much does a sentence diagrammer pull down a year?"

Reprinted with the permission of Bob Thaves.

A concept closely related to syntax is **grammar,** *the formal description of syntactical rules.* In elementary school and high school, most of us learned rules about sentence structure. Linguists devise rules of grammar that are similar to those you learned in school but are much more complex and powerful. Many contemporary linguists distinguish between the "surface" and "deep" structure of a sentence. **Surface structure** *is the actual order of words in a sentence;* **deep structure** *is the syntactic relation of the words in a sentence.* By applying syntactic rules in different ways, one sentence (the surface structure) can have two very different deep structures. For example, consider this sentence: "Mrs. Smith found drunk on her lawn." Was Mrs. Smith drunk or did she find a drunk on the lawn? Either interpretation fits the sentence, depending on the deep structure applied.

Semantics *refers to the meaning of words and sentences.* Every word has a set of semantic features. Girl and woman, for example, share the same semantic features as the words female and human but differ in regard to age. Words have semantic restrictions on how they can be used in sentences. The sentence "The bicycle talked the boy into buying a candy bar" is syntactically correct but is semantically incorrect. The sentence violates our semantic knowledge—bicycles do not talk.

A final set of language rules involves **pragmatics**—*the ability to engage in appropriate conversation.* Certain pragmatic rules ensure that a particular sentence will be uttered in one context and not in another. For example, you know that it is appropriate to say "Your new haircut certainly looks good" to someone who just had his or her hair styled, but that it is inappropriate to say "That new hairstyle makes you look awful." Through pragmatics we learn to convey intended meaning with words, phrases, and sentences. Pragmatics helps us to communicate more smoothly with others (Anderson, 1989; Pan, Rollins, & Snow, 1991).

Do we learn this ability to generate rule systems for language and then use them to create an almost infinite number of words, or is it the product of biology and evolution?

Biological Influences

How strongly is language influenced by biological evolution? Do animals have language? Is there a critical period for language? We consider each of these questions in turn.

Biological Evolution

A number of experts stress the biological foundations of language (Chomsky, 1957; Maratsos, 1983; Miller, 1981; Studdert-Kennedy, 1991). They believe it is undeniable that biological evolution shaped humans into linguistic creatures. In terms of biological evolution, the brain, nervous system, and vocal system changed over hundreds of thousands of years. Prior to *Homo sapiens,* the physical equipment to produce language was not present. *Homo sapiens* went beyond the groans and shrieks of their predecessors with the development of abstract speech. Estimates vary as to how long ago humans acquired language—from about 20,000 to 70,000 years ago. In evolutionary time, then, language is a very recent acquisition.

Biological Prewiring

Linguist Noam Chomsky (1957) believes humans are biologically prewired to learn language at a certain time and in a certain way. He also said that children are born into the world with a **language acquisition device (LAD),** *a biological prewiring that enables the child to detect certain language categories, such as phonology, syntax, and semantics.* LAD is an innate grammatical ability that underlies all human languages.

Do Animals Have Language?

The role of language in human evolution has stimulated psychologists to think about the possibility that animals have language. No one doubts that animals of many different species have wondrous and ingenious communication systems and that their communication is adaptive in signaling danger, food, and sex. Indeed, some of these communication systems are complex. For example, the females of one firefly species have learned to imitate the flashing signal of another species to lure the aliens into their territory. Then she eats them. But is this language in the human sense? And what about animals higher on the evolutionary scale, such as apes? Is ape language similar to human language? Can we teach language to them? Consider the efforts to teach language to a chimp named Washoe, who was adopted when she was about 10 months old (Gardner & Gardner, 1971). Since apes do not have the physical equipment to speak, the trainers tried to teach Washoe the American Sign Language, which is the sign language of the deaf. Daily routine events, such as meals and washing, household chores, play with toys, and car rides to interesting places provided many opportunities for the use of sign language. In two years, Washoe learned 38 different signs and by the age of 5 she had a vocabulary of 133 signs. Washoe learned how to put signs together in combinations, such as "you drink" and "you me tickle" (see figure 6.7). Most of her sign combinations resembled those of her human companions, but Washoe also combined signs in novel ways: She called her refrigerator the "open food drink" and her toilet chair the "dirty good," even though her companions referred to these as the "cold box" and the "potty chair," respectively. The Gardners have replicated the Washoe study with four additional chimpanzees, Moja, Pili, Tatu, and Dar (Gardner, Gardner, and Van Cantfort, 1989) and a number of other efforts to teach language to chimps have had similar results.

Figure 6.7 Washoe using American Sign "sweet" for lollipop. Washoe learned 133 signs by the age of 5, and also how to put signs together in combinations, such as "you me tickle."

The debate about language in chimpanzees focuses on two key issues. First, can apes understand the meaning of symbols, that is, can they comprehend that one thing stands for another? Second, can apes learn syntax, that is, can they learn systems of rules that give human language its creative productivity? The first of these issues seems to have been recently settled. Sue Savage-Rumbaugh and Duane Rumbaugh have studied two chimps named Sherman and Austin, discovering strong evidence that their subjects understand symbols (see figure 6.8). For example, if Sherman or Austin is sitting in a room, and a symbol for an object is displayed on a screen, they will go into another room, find the object, and bring it back. If the object is not there, they will come back empty-handed (Cowley, 1988). Austin can play a game in which one chimp points to a symbol for food (M&Ms), and the other chimp selects the food from a tray, then they both eat it. These observations are clear evidence that chimps can understand symbols (Rumbaugh & others, 1991; Savage-Rumbaugh, 1991).

Figure 6.8 Sue Savage Rumbaugh and Duane Rumbaugh are shown with their chimpanzee, Austin. A keyboard is reflected in the glass and Austin is using a joystick to select words at the Rumbaugh's laboratory at Georgia State University.

There is still no strong evidence that chimps can learn syntax. However, other animals possibly can. Ron Schusterman has worked with a sea lion named Rocky, teaching him to follow commands such as "ball fetch" and "disc ball fetch." The first command means that Rocky should take a disc to a ball in his tank. The second command means that Rocky should take the ball to the disc. Although Rocky and other sea lions make some errors in decoding these complex commands, they perform much better than chance, indicating they have learned rules linking the ordering of symbols to abstract meaning. Such rules are either syntax or something close to it.

We conclude that animals can communicate with each other and can be trained to manipulate languagelike symbols. Whether animals such as chimpanzees and sea lions can learn language with all the characteristics of human language is doubtful.

Cognitive Development in Infancy

GENIE, MODERN-DAY WILD CHILD

*G*enie was found in 1970 in California. At the time, she was 13 years old and had been reared by a partially blind mother and a violent father. She was discovered because her mother applied for assistance at a public welfare office. At the time, Genie could not speak and could not stand erect. She had lived in almost total isolation during her childhood years. Naked and restrained by a harness that her father had fashioned, she was left to sit on her potty seat day after day. She could only move her hands and feet and had virtually nothing to do every day of her life. At night, she was placed in a kind of straight jacket and caged in a crib with wire mesh sides and an overhead cover. She was fed, although sparingly. When she made a noise, her father beat her. He never spoke to her with words but growled and made barking sounds toward her.

Genie underwent extensive rehabilitation and training over a number of

Artist's drawing of the modern day wild child Genie after she was found.

Illustration by Roger Burkhart.

years (Curtiss, 1977). During her therapy, Genie learned to walk with a jerky motion and was toilet trained. She learned to recognize many words and to speak. At first she spoke in one-word utterances and eventually began to string together two-word utterances. She began to create some two-word sequences on her own, such as "big teeth," "little marble," and "two hand." Later she was able to put together three words—"small two cup," for example.

But unlike normal children, Genie never learned how to ask questions and she never understood grammar. Even four years later, after she began to put words together, her speech sounded like a garbled telegram. Genie never understood the differences between pronouns and between passive and active verbs. She continues as an adult to speak in short, mangled sentences, such as "father hit leg," "big wood," and "Genie hurt."

Is There a Critical Period for Language Learning?

If you have listened to Henry Kissinger, former secretary of state, speak you have some evidence for the belief that there exists a critical period for learning language. If individuals over 12 years of age emigrate to a new country and then start to learn its language, they will probably speak the language with a foreign accent the rest of their lives. Such was the case with Kissinger. But if an individual emigrates as a young child, the accent goes away as the new language is learned (Asher & Garcia, 1969).

Similarly, speaking like a native New Yorker is less related to how long you have lived in the city than to the age at which you moved there. Speaking with a New York "dialect" is more likely if you moved there before the age of 12. Apparently, puberty marks the close of a critical period for acquiring the phonological rules of different languages and dialects.

The experiences of a modern-day wild child named Genie raises further interest in the idea of whether a critical time period for acquiring language exists. To learn more about Genie, turn to Perspective on Life-Span Development 6.2.

Such findings confirm the belief that language must be triggered to be learned and that the optimal time for that triggering is during the early years of childhood. Clearly, biology's role in language is powerful, but even the most heavily inherited aspects of human development require an environment for their expression.

"Letter from Lonso . . . and he sounds pretty lonely."

Behavioral and Environmental Influences

Behaviorists view language as just another behavior, like sitting, walking, or running. They argue that language represents chains of responses (Skinner, 1957) or imitation (Bandura, 1977). But many of the sentences we produce are novel; we have not heard them or spoken them before. For example, a child hears the sentence, "The plate fell on the floor," and then says, "My mirror fell on the blanket," after the child drops the mirror on the blanket. The behavioral mechanisms of reinforcement and imitation cannot completely explain this.

While spending long hours observing parents and their young children, child language researcher Roger Brown (1973) searched for evidence that parents reinforce their children for speaking in grammatical ways. He found that parents sometimes smile and praise their children for sentences they liked, but that they also reinforced sentences that were ungrammatical. Brown concluded that no evidence exists to document that reinforcement is responsible for language's rule systems.

Another criticism of the behavioral view is that it fails to explain the extensive orderliness of language. The behavioral view predicts that vast individual differences should appear in children's speech development because of each child's unique learning history. But as we have seen, a compelling fact about language is its structure and everpresent rule systems. All infants coo before they babble. All toddlers produce one-word utterances before two-word utterances, and all state sentences in the active form before they state them in the passive form.

However, we do not learn language in a social vacuum. Most children are bathed in language from a very early age. We need this early exposure to language to acquire competent language skills (Furrow & Moore, 1991; Hoff, Ginsberg, 1991; Lock, 1991; Schegloff, 1989; Snow, 1989a). The Wild Boy of Aveyron did not learn to communicate effectively after being reared in social isolation for years. Genie's language was rudimentary even after a number of

MOTHER-CHILD INTERACTION IN AN INNER-CITY HOUSING PROJECT

*S*ome young children are brought up in the blighted urban areas of high-rise housing projects. Many of them are the children of single mothers. The small apartments and public housing rules discourage extended families. High-rise buildings frequently eliminate the possibility of free play outside by young children.

Young mothers isolated in these small apartments with their young children are often separated from family members by the expense and trouble of cross-town public transportation. The mothers watch television, talk on the phone, or perform household and caregiving chores. Playmates

for their children are scarce. So are toys. The mother's girlfriends, the older children of neighbors, and visits to the grocery store, the welfare office, and the laundromat may represent the only breaks in daily apartment routines. So may the usually traumatic visits to the health clinic.

One mother agreed to let researcher Shirley Heath (in press) tape-record her interactions with her children over a two-year period and to write notes about her activities with them. Within 500 hours of tape and more than 1,000 lines of notes, the mother living in a high-rise urban housing project initiated talk with one

of her three preschool children on only eighteen occasions (other than giving them a brief directive or asking a quick question). Few of the mother's conversations involved either planning or executing actions with or for her children.

Heath (1989) points out that the lack of family and community supports is widespread in urban housing projects, especially among Black Americans. The deteriorating, impoverished conditions of these inner-city areas severely impede the ability of young children to develop the cognitive and social skills they need to function competently.

years of extensive training. And as discussed in Cultural Worlds of Development 6.1, infants and young children who live in low-income inner-city areas may also experience an impoverished language world.

What are some of the ways the environment contributes to language development? Imitation is one important candidate. Children who are slow in developing their language ability can be helped if parents use carefully selected lists of words and grammatical constructions in their speech to the child (Snow, 1989b; Stine & Bohannon, 1984; Whitehurst & Valdez-Menchaca, 1988). Recent evidence also suggests that parents provide more corrective feedback for children's ungrammatical utterances than Brown originally thought (Bohannon & Stanowicz, 1988; Penner, 1987). Nonetheless, a number of language experts believe that imitation and reinforcement facilitate language but are not absolutely necessary for its acquisition (de Villiers & de Villiers, 1978).

One intriguing role of the environment in the young child's acquisition of language is called **motherese,** *the way mothers and other adults often talk to babies in a higher-than-normal frequency, greater-than-normal pitch, and simple words and sentences.* It is hard to talk in motherese when not in the presence of a baby. But as soon as you start talking to a baby you immediately shift into motherese. Much of this is automatic and something most parents are not aware they are doing. Motherese has the important functions of capturing the infant's attention and maintaining communication (Snow, 1989b). When parents are asked why they use baby talk, they point out that it is designed to teach their baby to talk. Older peers also talk baby talk to infants, but observations of siblings indicate that the affectional features are dropped when sibling rivalry is sensed (Dunn & Kendrick, 1982).

Other than motherese, are there other strategies adults use to enhance the child's acquisition of language? Four candidates are recasting, echoing, expanding, and labeling. **Recasting** *is phrasing the same or a similar meaning of a sentence in a different way, perhaps turning it into a question.* For example, if the child says, "The dog was barking," the adult can respond by asking, "When was the dog barking?" The effects of recasting fit with suggestions that "following in order to lead" helps a child to learn language. That is, letting a child initially indicate an interest and then proceeding to elaborate that interest—commenting, demonstrating, and explaining—may enhance communication and help language acquisition. In contrast, an overly active, directive approach to communicating with the child may be harmful (Rice, 1989).

Echoing *is repeating what the child says to you, especially if it is an incomplete phrase or sentence.* **Expanding** *is restating what the child has said in a linguistically sophisticated form.* **Labeling** *is identifying the names of objects.* Young children are forever being asked to identify the names of objects. Roger Brown (1986) identified this as the great word game and claimed that much of the early vocabulary acquired by children is motivated by this adult pressure to identify the words associated with objects.

Some of the ways parents influence their children's language development is through the use of recasting, echoing, expanding, and labeling.

How Language Develops

In describing language, we have touched on language development many times. You just read about motherese that parents use with their infants. Earlier we discussed the Wild Boy of Aveyron, Genie, and Washoe.

When does an infant utter her first word? The event usually occurs at about 10 to 13 months of age, although some infants take longer. Many parents view the onset of language development as coincident with this first word, but some significant accomplishments are attained earlier. Before babies say words, they babble, emitting such vocalizations as "goo-goo" and "ga-ga." Babbling starts at about 3 to 6 months of age; the start is determined by biological maturation, not reinforcement or the ability to hear (Locke & others, 1991). Even deaf babies babble for a time (Lenneberg, Rebelsky, & Nichols, 1965). Babbling exercises the baby's vocal apparatus and facilitates the development of articulation skills that are useful in later speech (Clark & Clark, 1977). But the purpose of a baby's earliest communication is to attract attention from parents and others in the environment. Infants engage the attention of others by making or breaking eye contact, by vocalizing sounds, or by performing manual actions such as pointing. All of these behaviors involve pragmatics.

A child's first words include those that name important people (dada), familiar animals (kittie), vehicles (car), toys (ball), food (milk), body parts (eye), clothes (hat), household items (clock), or greeting terms (bye). These were the first words of babies fifty years ago and they are the first words of babies today (Clark, 1983). At times it is hard to tell what these one-word utterances mean. One possibility is that they stand for an entire sentence in the infant's mind. Because of limited cognitive or linguistic skills, possibly only one word comes out instead of the whole sentence. The **holophrase hypothesis** *is the concept that a single word is used to imply a complete sentence; it is characteristic of an infant's first words.*

By the time children are 18 to 24 months of age, they usually utter two-word statements. During this two-word stage, they quickly grasp the importance of expressing concepts and the role that language plays in communicating with others. To convey meaning with two-word utterances, the child

Children pick up words as pigeons peas.

~ *John Ray,*
English Proverbs, *1670*

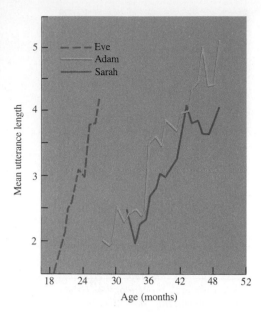

Figure 6.9 An examination of MLU in three children. Shown here is the average length of utterances generated by three children who range in age from 1½ to just over 4 years.

relies heavily on gesture, tone, and context. The wealth of meaning children can communicate with a two-word utterance includes (Slobin, 1972):

Identification: See doggie.
Location: Book there.
Repetition: More milk.
Nonexistence: Allgone thing.
Negation: Not wolf.
Possession: My candy.
Attribution: Big car.
Agent-action: Mama walk.
Action-direct-object: Hit you.
Action-indirect-object: Give papa.
Action-instrument: Cut knife.
Question: Where ball?

One of the most striking aspects of this list is that it is used by children all over the world. The examples are taken from utterances in English, German, Russian, Finnish, Turkish, Samoan, and Luo, but the entire list could be made up from examples from a 2-year-old's speech in any language.

Telegraphic speech *is the use of short and precise words to communicate; it is characteristic of young children's two-word utterances.* When we send telegrams to individuals we try to be short and precise, excluding any unnecessary words. As indicated in the examples of telegraphic speech from children from around the world, articles, auxiliary verbs, and other connectives are usually omitted. Of course telegraphic speech is not limited to two-word utterances. "Mommy give ice cream," or "Mommy give Tommy ice cream," are also examples of telegraphic speech.

One- and two-word utterances classify children's language development in terms of number of utterances. In expanding this concept, Roger Brown (1973) proposed that **mean length of utterance (MLU),** *an index of language development based on the number of words per sentence a child produces in a sample of about 50 to 100 sentences, is a good index of language maturity.* Brown identified five stages based on MLU:

Stage	**MLU**
1	$1+$ to 2.0
2	2.5
3	3.0
4	3.5
5	4.0

The first stage begins when the child generates sentences consisting of more than one word, such as examples of two-word utterances we gave. The $1+$ designation suggests that the average number of words in each utterance is greater than one but not yet two, because some of the child's utterances are still holophrases. This stage continues until the child averages two words per utterance. Subsequent stages are marked by increments of 0.5 in mean length of utterance.

Brown's stages are important for several reasons. First, children who vary in chronological age as much as one-half to three-fourths of a year still have similar speech patterns. Second, children with similar mean lengths of utterance to have similar rule systems that characterize their language. In some ways, then, MLU is a better indicator of language development than chronological age. Figure 6.9 shows the individual variation in chronological age that characterizes children's MLU.

Infancy

Concept Table 6.2: Language Development

Concept	Processes/Related Ideas	Characteristics/Description
What Is Language?	Its Nature	Language involves a system of symbols we use to communicate with each other. The system is characterized by infinite generativity and rule systems. The rule systems include phonology, morphology, syntax, semantics, and pragmatics.
Biological Influences	Biological Evolution	The fact that biological evolution shaped humans into linguistic creatures is undeniable.
	Biological Prewiring	Chomsky argues that humans are biologically prewired to learn language and have a language acquisition device.
	Do Animals Have Language?	Animals clearly can communicate and chimpanzees and sea lions can be taught to use symbols. Whether animals have all of the properties of human language is debated.
	Is There a Critical Period for Learning Language?	The experiences of Genie and other children suggest the early years of childhood are a critical time for learning language. If exposure to language does not occur before puberty, lifelong deficits in grammar occur.
Behavioral and Environmental Influences	The Behavioral View	Language is just another behavior. Behaviorists believe language is learned primarily through reinforcement and imitation, although they probably play a facilitative rather than a necessary role.
	Environmental Influences	Most children are bathed in language early in their development. Among the ways adults teach language to infants are motherese, recasting, echoing, expanding, and labeling.
How Language Develops	Its Nature	Vocalization begins with babbling at about 3 to 6 months of age. A baby's earliest communication skills are pragmatic. One-word utterances occur at about 10 to 13 months; the holophrase hypothesis has been applied to this. By 18 to 24 months, most infants use two-word utterances. Language at this point is referred to as telegraphic. Brown developed the idea of mean length of utterance (MLU). Five stages of MLU have been identified, providing a valuable indicator of language maturity.

As we have just seen, language unfolds in a sequence. At every point in development, the child's linguistic interaction with parents and others obeys certain principles (Conti-Ramsden & Snow, 1991; Maratsos, 1991). Not only is this development strongly influenced by the child's biological wiring, but the language environment the child is bathed in from an early age is far more intricate than was imagined in the past (von Tetzchner & Siegel, 1989). The main ideas we have discussed about language development are summarized in concept table 6.2. In the next chapter, we will continue our discussion of infant development, turning to information about the infant's social worlds.

• *Critical Thinking* •

In our discussion of language, we have emphasized the role of biological and environmental factors. How might cognitive factors be involved in language development?

Summary

1. **Piaget's Theory of Infant Development**

   The stage of sensorimotor development lasts from birth to about 2 years of age. It involves progression in the infant's ability to organize and coordinate sensations with physical movements. The sensorimotor stage has six substages: simple reflexes; first habits and primary circular reactions; secondary circular reactions; coordination of secondary circular reactions tertiary circular reactions, novelty, and curiosity; and internalization of schemes. Object permanence is an important accomplishment in infant cognitive development; it refers to the development of the ability to understand that objects and events continue to exist even though the infant is no longer in contact with them. Piaget believed that this ability developed over the course of the six substages.

II. **Information Processing**

   Unlike Piaget, information processing psychologists do not describe infancy as a stage or series of substages of sensorimotor development. Rather, they emphasize the importance of cognitive processes such as attention, memory, and thinking. The information processing psychologists believe the young infant is more competent than Piaget envisioned, with attentional, symbolic, imitative, and conceptual abilities occurring much earlier than he thought. Habituation occurs when the repeated presentation of the same stimulus causes reduced attention to the stimulus. If a different stimulus is presented and the infant pays attention to it, dishabituation is occurring. Newborn infants can habituate, but habituation becomes more acute over the first three months of infancy. Memory is the retention of information over time. In the first six months, infants can learn adaptive skills, but conscious memory does not develop until later in the first year. Infantile amnesia is the inability to remember anything that happened in the first three years of life. Infants can imitate the facial expressions of others in the first few days of life. Meltzoff demonstrated that deferred imitation occurs at about 9 months of age, much earlier than Piaget believed.

III. **Individual Differences in Intelligence**

   Developmental scales for infants grew out of the tradition of IQ testing with older children. These scales are less verbal than IQ tests. Gesell was an early pioneer in the development of infant scales. His scale is still widely used by pediatricians; it provides a developmental quotient (DQ). The Bayley Scales are the most widely used today. They consist of a motor scale, a mental scale, and an infant behavior profile. Global infant intelligence measures do not predict childhood intelligence. However, specific aspects of infant intelligence, such as information processing tasks involving attention, are better predictors of childhood intelligence, especially in a specific area. There is both continuity and discontinuity between infant cognitive development and cognitive development later in childhood.

IV. **What Is Language?**

   Language involves a system of symbols we use to communicate with each other. The system is characterized by infinite generativity and rule systems. The rule systems include phonology, morphology, syntax, semantics, and pragmatics.

V. **Biological Influences on Language**

   The fact that biological evolution shaped humans into linguistic creatures is undeniable. Chomsky argues that humans are biologically prewired to learn language and have a language acquisition device. Animals can clearly communicate and chimpanzees and sea lions can be taught to use symbols. Whether animals have all of the properties of human language is debated. The experiences of Genie and other children suggest that the early years of childhood are a critical time for learning language. If exposure does not occur before puberty, life-long deficits in grammar occur.

VI. **Behavioral and Environmental Influences on Language**

   In the behavioral view, language is just another behavior. Behaviorists believe that language is learned primarily through reinforcement and imitation, although they probably play a facilitative rather than a necessary role. Most children are bathed in language early in their development. Among the ways adults teach language to infants are motherese, recasting, echoing, expanding, and labeling.

VII. **How Language Develops**

   Vocalization begins with babbling at about 3 to 6 months of age. A baby's earliest communication skills are pragmatic. One-word utterances occur at about 10 to 13 months; the holophrase hypothesis has been applied to this. By 18 to 24 months, most infants use two-word utterances. Language at this point is referred to as telegraphic. Brown developed the idea of mean length of utterance (MLU). Five stages of MLU have been identified, providing a valuable indicator of language maturity.

Key Terms

scheme 160
simple reflexes 161
first habits and primary circular reactions 161
primary circular reaction 161
secondary circular reactions 161
coordination of secondary circular reactions 162
tertiary circular reactions, novelty, and curiosity 162
internalization of schemes 162
object permanence 162
habituation 167

dishabituation 167
memory 168
infantile amnesia 169
deferred imitation 170
developmental quotient (DQ) 172
Bayley Scales of Infant Development 172
language 175
infinite generativity 175
phonology 175
morphology 175
syntax 175
grammar 176
surface structure 176

deep structure 176
semantics 176
pragmatics 176
language acquisition device (LAD) 176
motherese 180
recasting 181
echoing 181
expanding 181
labeling 181
holophrase hypothesis 181
telegraphic speech 182
mean length of utterance (MLU) 182

Suggested Readings

Bruner, J. (1983). *Child talk*. New York: W. W. Norton.
A fascinating view of the child's language development by one of the leading cognitive theorists.

Curtiss, S. (1977). *Genie*. New York: Academic Press.
Susan Curtiss tells the remarkable story of Genie, a modern-day wild child and her ordeal of trying to acquire language.

Ginsburg, H., & Opper, S. (1989). *Piaget's theory of intellectual development* (2nd ed.). Englewood Cliffs, NJ: Prentice-Hall.

One of the best explanations and descriptions of Piaget's theory of infant development.

Maratsos, M. (1983). A leading child language researcher discusses current issues in the study of the acquisition of grammar. In P. H. Mussen (Ed.), *Handbook of child psychology* (4th ed., Vol. 2). New York: Wiley.
A thorough, informative review of what we know about language development.

Rovee-Collier, C. (1987). Learning and memory in infancy. In J. D. Osofsky (Ed.), *Handbook of infant development*. New York: Wiley.

One of the leading researchers on infant memory describes how infants learn and remember; special attention is given to habituation.

Wilson, L. C. (1990). *Infants and toddlers: Curriculum and teaching*. Albany, NY: Delmar.
This excellent book is intended for individuals who provide care for infants and toddlers; it includes information to help caregivers select and use curriculum appropriately individualized for each infant and toddler in their care.

CHAPTER 7

Social Development in Infancy

*T*he newborns of some species function independently in the world; other species are not so independent. At birth, the opossum is still considered fetal and is capable of finding its way around only in its mother's pouch, where it attaches itself to her nipple and continues to develop. This protective environment is similar to the uterus. By contrast, the wildebeest must run with the herd moments after birth, behavior that is far more adult than the opossum's, although the wildebeest does have to obtain food through suckling. The maturation of the human infant lies somewhere between these two extremes; much learning and development must take place before the infant can sustain itself (Maccoby, 1980) (see figure 7.1).

Because it cannot sustain itself, the human infant requires extensive care. What kind of care is needed and how does the infant begin the road to social maturity? Much of the interest in infant care focuses on attachment, although the infant's development of emotions, trust, sense of self, and independence are important as well. Before we tackle these important dimensions of the infant's social development, let's consider some basic ideas about family processes.

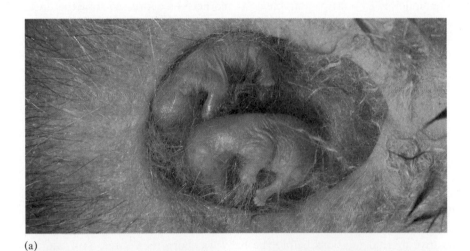

(a)

(b)

(c)

Figure 7.1 Variations in the dependency of newborns in different species. (a) The newborn opossum is fetal, capable of finding its way around only in its mother's pouch, where it attaches itself to her nipple and continues to develop. (b) By contrast, the wildebeest runs with the herd moments after birth. (c) The human newborn's maturation lies somewhere in between that of the opossum and that of the wildebeest.

Family Processes

Most of us began our lives in families and spent thousands of hours during our childhood interacting with our parents. Some of you are already parents; others of you may become parents. What is the transition to parenthood like? What is the nature of family processes?

Transition to Parenthood

When people become parents through pregnancy, adoption, or stepparenting, they face disequilibrium and must adapt. Parents want to develop a strong attachment with their infant, but they still want to maintain strong attachments to their spouse and friends, and possibly continue their careers. Parents ask themselves how this new being will change their lives. A baby places new restrictions on partners; no longer will they be able to rush out to a movie on a moment's notice, and money may not be readily available for vacations and other luxuries. Dual-career parents ask, "Will it harm the baby to place her in day care? Will we be able to find responsible babysitters?"

The excitement and joy that accompany the birth of a healthy baby are often followed by "postpartum blues" in mothers—a depressed state that lasts as long as nine months into the infant's first year (Fleming & others, 1988; Osofsky, 1989). The early months of the baby's physical demands may bring not only the joy of intimacy but also the sorrow of exhaustion. Pregnancy and childbirth are demanding physical events that require recovery time for the mother.

Many fathers are not sensitive to these extreme demands placed on the mother. Busy trying to make enough money to pay the bills, fathers may not be at home much of the time. A father's ability to sense and adapt to the stress placed on his wife during the first year of the infant's life has important implications for the success of the marriage and the family.

Becoming a father is both wonderful *and* stressful. In a longitudinal investigation of couples from late pregnancy until three-and-one-half years after the baby was born, Carolyn and Phillip Cowan (Cowan, 1988, 1991; Cowan & Cowan, 1989; Cowan & others, 1991) found that the couples enjoyed more positive marital relations before the baby was born than after. Still, almost one-third showed an increase in marital satisfaction. Some couples said that the baby had both brought them closer together *and* moved them farther apart. They commented that being parents enhanced their sense of themselves and gave them a new, more stable identity as a couple. Babies opened men up to a concern with intimate relationships, and the demands of juggling work and family roles stimulated women to manage family tasks more efficiently and pay attention to their personal growth.

At some point during the early years of the child's life, parents do face the difficult task of juggling their roles as parents and as self-actualizing adults. Until recently in our culture, nurturing our children and having a career were thought to be incompatible. Fortunately, we have come to recognize that the balance between caring and achieving, nurturing and working—although difficult to manage—can be accomplished.

Reciprocal Socialization

For many years, socialization between parents and children was viewed as a one-way process: Children were considered to be the products of their parents' socialization techniques. Today, however, we view parent-child interaction as reciprocal. **Reciprocal socialization** *is the view that socialization is bidirectional; children socialize parents just as parents socialize children.* For example, the interaction of mothers and their infants is symbolized as a dance

We never know the love of our parents until we have become parents.

~ *Henry Ward Beecher, 1887*

Infancy

The interaction of mothers and their infants is symbolized as a dance or a dialogue in which the successive actions of the partners are closely coordinated. This coordinated dance or dialogue can assume the form of synchrony, as shown here in the interaction of a synchronous mother-infant pair.

or a dialogue in which successive actions of the partners are closely coordinated. This coordinated dance or dialogue can assume the form of mutual synchrony (each person's behavior depends on the partner's previous behavior), or it can be reciprocal in a more precise sense; the actions of the partners can be matched, as when one partner imitates the other or when there is mutual smiling (Cohn & Tronick, 1988).

When reciprocal socialization has been investigated in infancy, mutual gaze or eye contact has been found to play an important role in early social interaction (Fogel, Toda, & Kawai, 1988). In one investigation, the mother and infant engaged in a variety of behaviors while they looked at each other; by contrast, when they looked away from each other, the rate of such behaviors dropped considerably (Stern & others, 1977). In sum, the behaviors of mothers and infants involve substantial interconnection, mutual regulation, and synchronization.

Scaffolding *is a term used to describe an important caregiver's role in early parent-child interaction. Through their attention and choice of behaviors, caregivers provide a framework around which they and their infants interact. One function scaffolding serves is to introduce infants to social rules, especially turn-taking* (Bruner, 1989; Lyon, 1991). For example, in the game peek-a-boo, mothers initially cover their babies, then remove the covering, and finally register "surprise" at the reappearance. As infants become more skilled at peek-a-boo, the infants do the covering and uncovering. Infant researcher Tiffany Field (1987) observed that in addition to peek-a-boo, pat-a-cake, and so-big are other caregiver-infant games that involve scaffolding and its turn-taking sequences (see figure 7.2). In one recent investigation, infants who had more extensive scaffolding experiences with their parents, especially in the form of turn-taking, were more likely to engage in turn-taking as they interacted with their peers (Vandell & Wilson, 1988).

The Family as a System

As a social system, the family can be thought of as a constellation of subsystems defined in terms of generation, gender, and role. Divisions of labor among family members define particular subunits, and attachments define others. Each family member is a participant in several subsystems—some dyadic (involving two people), some polyadic (involving more than two people). The father

(a)

(b)

(c)

Figure 7.2 Caregiver-infant games that involve scaffolding. (a) Pat-a-cake, (b) peek-a-boo, and (c) so-big are excellent games for parents to play with their infants. Through such games, children learn social rules, especially turn taking.

and child represent one dyadic subsystem, the mother and father another; the mother-father-child represent one polyadic subsystem, the mother and two siblings another (Belsky, Rovine, & Fish, 1989).

An organizational scheme that highlights the reciprocal influences of family members and family subsystems is shown in figure 7.3 (Belsky, 1981). As the arrows in the figure show, marital relations, parenting, and infant behavior can have both direct and indirect effects on each other. An example of a direct effect is the influence of the parents' behavior on the child; an example of an indirect effect is how the relationship between the spouses mediates the way a parent acts toward the child. For example, marital conflict might reduce the efficiency of parenting, in which case marital conflict would be an indirect effect on the child's behavior. In the family system, the infant's most important experiences involve the process of attachment.

Attachment

A small curly-haired girl named Danielle, age 11 months, begins to whimper. After a few seconds, she begins to wail. The psychologist observing Danielle is conducting a research study on the nature of attachment between infants and their mothers. Subsequently, the mother reenters the room, and Danielle's crying ceases. Quickly, Danielle crawls over to where her mother is seated and reaches out to be held. This scenario is one of the main ways that psychologists study the nature of attachment during infancy.

What Is Attachment?

In everyday language, attachment refers to a relationship between two individuals who feel strongly about each other and do a number of things to continue the relationship. Many pairs of people are attached: relatives, lovers, a teacher and a student. In the language of developmental psychology, though, attachment is often restricted to a relationship between particular social figures and a particular phenomenon that is thought to reflect unique characteristics of the relationship. In this case, the developmental period is infancy, the social figures are the infant and one or more adult caregivers, and the phenomenon is a bond (Bowlby, 1969, 1989). To summarize, **attachment** *is a close emotional bond between the infant and the caregiver.*

There is no shortage of theories about infant attachment. Freud believed that the infant becomes attached to the person or object that provides oral satisfaction; for most infants, this is the mother, since she is most likely to feed the infant.

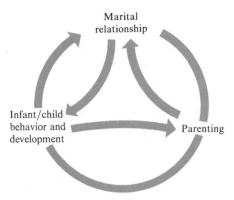

Figure 7.3 *The family as a system of interacting individuals: direct and indirect effects. Jay Belsky developed this model to describe the way that family interaction patterns can have both direct and indirect effects. For example, the parent's behavior can have a direct effect on the infant's or child's behavior, or the marital relationship can have indirect effects on the infant's or child's development by influencing parenting behavior.*

But is feeding as important as Freud thought? A classic study by Harry Harlow and Robert Zimmerman (1959) suggests that the answer is no. These researchers evaluated whether feeding or contact comfort was more important to infant attachment. Infant monkeys were removed from their mothers at birth and reared for six months by surrogate (substitute) "mothers." As shown in figure 7.4, one of the mothers was made of wire, the other of cloth. Half of the infant monkeys were fed by the wire mother, half by the cloth mother. The amount of time the infant monkeys spent with either the wire or the cloth mother was periodically computed. Regardless of whether they were fed by the wire or the cloth mother, the infant monkeys spent far more time with the cloth mother. This study clearly demonstrates that feeding is not the crucial element in the attachment process and that contact comfort is important.

Most toddlers develop a strong attachment to a favorite soft toy or a particular blanket. Toddlers may carry the toy or blanket with them everywhere they go, just as Linus does in the "Peanuts" cartoon strip, or they may run for the toy or blanket only in moments of crisis, such as after an argument or a fall. By the time they have outgrown the security object, all that may be left is a small fragment of the blanket, or an animal that is hardly recognizable, having had a couple of new faces and all its seams resown half a dozen times. If parents try to replace the security object with something newer, the toddler will resist. There is nothing abnormal about a toddler carrying around a security blanket. Children know that the blanket or teddy bear is not the mother, and yet they react affectively to these objects and derive comfort from them as if they were the mother. Eventually they abandon the security object as they grow up and become more sure of themselves.

Might familiarity breed attachment? The famous study by Konrad Lorenz (1965) suggests that the answer is yes. Remember from our description of this study in chapter 2 that newborn goslings became attached to "father" Lorenz rather than to their mother because he was the first moving object they saw. The time period during which familiarity is important for goslings is the first 36 hours after birth; for human beings, it is more on the order of the first year of life.

Figure 7.4 *Harlow's classic "contact comfort" study. Regardless of whether they were fed by the wire mother or by the cloth mother, the infant monkeys overwhelmingly preferred to be in contact with the cloth mother, demonstrating the importance of contact comfort in attachment.*

Soft toys or a particular blanket are common attachment objects of toddlers. Most toddlers eventually abandon the security object as they grow up and become more sure of themselves.

I am what I hope and give.

~ *Erik Erikson*

A child forsaken, waking suddenly,
Whose gaze affeard on all things round doth rove,
And seeth only that it cannot see
The meeting eyes of love.

~ *George Eliot*

Erik Erikson (1968) believes that the first year of life is the key time frame for the development of attachment. Recall his proposal (also discussed in chapter 2) that the first year of life represents the stage of trust versus mistrust. A sense of trust requires a feeling of physical comfort and a minimal amount of fear and apprehension about the future. Trust in infancy sets the stage for a lifelong expectation that the world will be a good and pleasant place to be. Erikson also believes that responsive, sensitive parenting contributes to the infant's sense of trust.

The ethological perspective of British psychiatrist John Bowlby (1969, 1989) also stresses the importance of attachment in the first year of life and the responsiveness of the caregiver. Bowlby believes that the infant and the mother instinctively form an attachment. He argues that the newborn is biologically equipped to elicit the mother's attachment behavior. The baby cries, clings, coos, and smiles. Later the infant crawls, walks, and follows the mother. The infant's goal is to keep the mother nearby. Research on attachment supports Bowlby's view that at about 6 to 7 months of age, attachment of the infant to the caregiver intensifies (Sroufe, 1985).

Individual Differences

Although attachment to a caregiver intensifies midway through the first year, isn't it likely that some babies have a more positive attachment experience than others? Mary Ainsworth (1979) thinks so and says that in **secure attachment** *infants use the caregiver, usually the mother, as a secure base from which to explore the environment. Ainsworth believes secure attachment in the first year of life provides an important foundation for psychological development later in life.* Sensitivity of the caregiver to the infant's signals increases secure attachment. The securely attached infant moves freely away from the mother but processes her location through periodic glances. The securely attached infant responds positively to being picked up by others, and when put back down, moves away freely to play. An insecurely attached infant, by contrast, avoids the mother or is ambivalent toward her. The insecurely attached infant fears strangers and is upset by minor, everyday separations.

Ainsworth believes that the insecurely attached infant can be classified as either anxious-avoidant or anxious-resistant, making three main attachment categories: secure (type B), anxious-avoidant (type A), and anxious-resistant (type C). **Type B babies** *use the caregiver as a secure base from which to explore the environment.* **Type A babies** *exhibit insecurity by avoiding the mother (for example, ignoring her, averting her gaze, and failing to seek proximity).* **Type C babies** *exhibit insecurity by resisting the mother (for example, clinging to her but at the same time fighting against the closeness, perhaps by kicking and pushing away).*

Why are some infants securely attached and others insecurely attached? Following Bowlby's lead, Ainsworth believes that attachment security depends on how sensitive and responsive the caregiver is to the infant's signals. For example, infants who are securely attached are more likely to have mothers who are more sensitive, accepting, and expressive of affection toward them than those who are insecurely attached (Baruch, 1991; Pederson & others, 1989; Waters, 1991).

If early attachment to the caregiver is important, it should relate to the child's social behavior later in development. Research by Alan Sroufe (1985, in press) documents this connection. In one investigation, infants who were securely attached to their mothers early in infancy were less frustrated and happier at 2 years of age than their insecurely attached counterparts (Matas,

Infancy

Arend, & Sroufe, 1978). And, in another longitudinal investigation, securely attached infants were more socially competent and had better grades in the third grade (Egeland, 1989).

Attachment, Temperament, and the Wider Social World

Not all developmentalists believe that a secure attachment in infancy is the only path to competence in life. Indeed, some developmentalists believe that too much emphasis is placed on the importance of the attachment bond in infancy. Jerome Kagan (1987, 1989), for example, believes that the infant is highly resilient and adaptive; he argues that the infant is evolutionarily equipped to stay on a positive developmental course even in the face of wide variations in parenting. Kagan and others stress that genetic and temperament characteristics play more important roles in the child's social competence than the attachment theorists like Bowlby, Ainsworth, and Sroufe are willing to acknowledge (Fish, 1989; Fox & others, 1989). For example, an infant may have inherited a low tolerance for stress; this, rather than an insecure attachment bond, may be responsible for an inability to get along with peers.

Another criticism of the attachment theory is that it ignores the diversity of social agents and social contexts that exist in the infant's world. Experiences with both the mother and the father, changing gender roles, day care, the mother's employment, peer experiences, socioeconomic status, and cultural values are not considered adequately in the attachment concept (Lamb & others, 1984; Takahashi, 1990; Thompson, 1991). In all of these perspectives, the importance of social relationships with parents is recognized; their differences lie in the criticalness of the attachment bond. Keep in mind that a great deal of controversy currently surrounds the concept of secure attachment. Some experts argue for its primacy in influencing the child's competent development (Main, 1990), and others argue that it is given too much weight.

Thus far we have discussed a number of important ideas about family and attachment processes. These ideas are summarized in concept table 7.1. Now we turn our attention to other caregivers and settings in the infant's development, first evaluating the father's role, and second, day care.

Concept Table 7.1: Family Processes and Attachment		
Concept	**Processes/Related Ideas**	**Characteristics/Description**
Family Processes	Transition to Parenthood	The transition to parenthood produces a disequilibrium, requiring considerable adaptation. Becoming a parent is both wonderful *and* stressful.
	Reciprocal Socialization	Children socialize their parents just as parents socialize their children. Scaffolding, synchronization, and mutual regulation are important dimensions of reciprocal socialization.
	The Family as a System	The family is a system of individuals interacting with different subsystems, some dyadic, others polyadic. Belsky's model describes direct and indirect effects.
Attachment	What Is Attachment?	Attachment is a relationship between two people in which each person feels strongly about the other and does a number of things to ensure the relationship's continuation. In infancy, attachment refers to the bond between the caregiver and the infant. Feeding is not the critical element in attachment, although contact comfort, familiarity, and trust are important. Bowlby's ethological theory stresses that the caregiver and infant instinctively trigger attachment. Attachment to the caregiver intensifies at about 6 to 7 months.
	Individual Differences	Ainsworth believes that individual differences in attachment can be classified into secure, avoidant, and resistant categories. Ainsworth believes that securely attached babies have sensitive and responsive caregivers. In some investigations, secure attachment is related to social competence later in childhood.
	Attachment, Temperament, and the Wider Social World	Some developmentalists believe that too much emphasis is placed on the role of attachment; they believe that genetics and temperament, on the one hand, and the diversity of social agents and contexts, on the other, deserve more credit.

In the 1970s, the current image of the father as an active, nurturant, caregiving parent emerged.

The Father's Role

A father gently cuddles his infant son, softly stroking his forehead. Another father dresses his infant daughter as he readies her for her daily trip to a day-care center. How common are these circumstances in the life of fathers and their infants? Has the father's role changed dramatically?

The father's role has undergone major changes (Bronstein, 1988; Lamb, 1986, 1987; Pleck, 1984). During the colonial period in American history, fathers were mainly responsible for moral teaching; they provided more guidance and values, especially through religion. With the Industrial Revolution, the father's role changed; now he had the responsibility as the breadwinner, a role that continued through the Great Depression. By the end of World War II, another role for fathers emerged, that of a gender role model. While being a breadwinner and moral guardian continued to be important father roles, attention shifted to his role as a male, especially for sons. Then, in the 1970s, the current interest in the father as an active, nurturant, caregiving parent emerged. Rather than being responsible only for the discipline and control of older children and with providing the family's economic base, the father is now evaluated in terms of his active, nurturant involvement with his children, even infants.

Are fathers more actively involved with their children than they were ten to twenty years ago? Few data document changes in the father's involvement from one point in history to another. However, in one investigation, the father's involvement in 1975 and 1981 was compared (Juster, 1985). In 1981, fathers spent about one-fourth more time in direct interaction with the child than in 1975. Mothers increased their direct interaction about 7 percent over this time period, but fathers—while increasing their direct interaction—still were far below mothers in this regard. In this study, the father's involvement was about one-third that of the mother, both in 1975 and in 1981. If the mother is employed, does the father increase his involvement with his children? Only slightly. In sum, the father's active involvement with the child has increased somewhat, although this involvement does not approach the mother's, even when she is employed. Although fathers are spending more time with their infants and children, the evidence so far indicates that increased time does not necessarily mean quality time. In one investigation, there was no relation between the amount of time fathers spent with their 5-year-old children and the quality of fathering (Grossman, Pollack, & Golding, 1988).

Can fathers care for their infants as competently as mothers can? Observations of fathers and their infants suggest that fathers have the ability to act sensitively and responsively with their infants (Parke & Sawin, 1980). Probably the strongest evidence of the adaptability of male caregiving abilities is derived from information about male primates who are notoriously low in their interest in offspring but are forced to live with infants whose female caregivers are absent. Under these circumstances, the adult male competently rears the infants (Parke & Suomi, 1981). But remember, while fathers can be active, nurturant, involved caregivers with their infants, most of the time they choose not to follow this pattern.

Do fathers behave differently toward infants than mothers do? While maternal interactions usually center around child-care activities—feeding, changing diapers, bathing—paternal interactions are more likely to include play. Fathers engage in more rough-and-tumble-play, bouncing infants, throwing them up in the air, tickling them, and so on (Lamb, 1986). Mothers do play with infants, but their play is less physical and arousing than that of fathers.

In stressful circumstances, do infants prefer their mother or father? In one investigation, twenty 12-month-olds were observed interacting with their parents (Lamb, 1977). With both parents present, infants preferred neither their mother nor their father. The same was true when the infant was alone with the mother or the father. But the entrance of a stranger, combined with boredom and fatigue, produced a shift in the infant's social behavior toward the mother. In stressful circumstances, then, infants show a stronger attachment to the mother.

Might the nature of parent-infant interaction be different in families that adopt nontraditional gender roles? This question was investigated by Michael Lamb and his colleagues (1982). They studied Swedish families in which the fathers were the primary caregivers of their firstborn, 8-month-old infants. The mothers were working full time. In all observations, the mothers were more likely to discipline, hold, soothe, kiss, and talk to the infants than the fathers. These mothers and fathers dealt with their infants differently, along the lines of American fathers and mothers following traditional gender roles.

All men know their children mean more than life.

~ *Euripides, 426* B.C.

• *Critical Thinking* •

The father's role has changed considerably in the twentieth century. What do you think the father's role in the child's development will be like in the twenty-first century?

The father's role in China has been slow to change, but it is changing. Traditionally, the father has been expected to be strict, and the mother kind. The father is characterized as a stern disciplinarian; the child is expected to fear the father. The notion of the strict father has ancient roots. The Chinese character for father (fu) evolved from a primitive character representing the hand holding a cane, which symbolizes authority. However, the twentieth century has witnessed a decline in the father's authority. Younger fathers are more inclined to allow children to express their opinions and be more independent. Influenced to some degree by the increased employment of mothers, Chinese fathers are becoming more involved in caring for their children. In some instances, intergenerational tension has developed between fathers and sons, as younger generations behave in less traditional ways (Ho, 1987).

CHILD-CARE POLICIES AROUND THE WORLD

*S*heila Kamerman (1989) recently surveyed the nature of child-care policies around the world with special attention given to European countries. Maternity and paternity policies for working parents include paid, job-protected leaves, which are sometimes supplemented by additional unpaid, job-protected leaves. Child-care policy packages also often include full health insurance. An effective child-care policy is designed to get an infant off to a competent start in life and to protect maternal health while maintaining income. More than a hundred countries around the world have such child-care policies, including all of Europe, Canada, Israel, and many developing countries (Kamerman & Kahn, 1988). Infants are assured of at least 2 to 3 months of maternal/paternal care, and in most European countries 5 to 6 months.

The maternity policy as now implemented in several countries involves a paid maternity leave that begins 2 to 6 weeks prior to expected childbirth and lasts from 8 to 20 or even 24 weeks after birth. This traditional maternal policy stems from an effort to protect the health of pregnant working women, new mothers, and their infants. Only since the 1960s has the maternity policy's link with employment become strong. A second child-care policy emphasizes the importance of parenting and recognizes the potential of fathers as well as mothers to care for their infants. In Sweden a parent insurance benefit provides protection to the new mother before birth and for 6 to 12 weeks after birth but then allows the father to participate in the post-childbirth leave. Approximately one-fourth of Swedish fathers take at least part of the post-childbirth leave, in addition to the two weeks of paid leave all fathers are entitled to at the time of childbirth. In a typical pattern in Sweden, the working mother might take off 3 months, after which she and her husband might share child care between them, each working half-time for 6 months. In addition, Swedish parents have the option of taking an unpaid but fully-protected job leave until their child is 18 months old and to work a 6-hour day (without a reduction in pay) from the end of the parental leave until their child is 8 years old. In table 7.A, paid maternity/paternity leave provisions in various Western countries are shown.

In sum, almost all the industrialized countries other than the United States have recognized the importance of developing maternity/paternity policies that allow working parents some time off after childbirth to physically recover, to adapt to parenting, and to improve the well-being of the infant. These policies are designed to let parents take maternity/paternity leave without losing employment or income.

Having fathers assume the primary caregiving role did not substantially alter the way they interacted with the infant. This may be because of biological reasons or because of deeply ingrained socialization patterns in cultures.

In Sweden, mothers or fathers are given paid maternity or paternity leave for up to nine months. Sweden and many other European countries have well-developed child-care policies. To learn about these policies, turn to Cultural Worlds of Development 7.1. In Sweden, day care for infants under 1 year of age is usually not a major concern because one parent is on paid leave for child care. As we see next, because the United States does not have a policy of paid leave for child care, day care in the United States has become a major national concern.

Table 7.A *Paid Maternity/Paternity Leave Provisions in Various Western Countries*

Country	Date	Duration of Paid Leave	Available to Fathers (Y = Yes)	Supplementary Unpaid or Paid Parental Leave
Benefit Level at 100% Earnings[a]				
Norway	1984	4 months	Y	Y
Austria	1987	16 weeks		10 more months, at lower level[b]
F.R. Germany	1987	14 weeks[c]	Y	1 year at flat rate[d]
Portugal	1984	3 months		Y
Netherlands	1984	12 weeks[c]		
Benefit Level at 90% of Earnings				
Sweden	1987	9 months plus 3 months at flat rate	Y	up to 18 months; 6-hour workday, up to 8 years
Denmark	1987	24 weeks	Y	Y
France	1987	16 weeks[c]		up to 2 years
United Kingdom	1987	6 weeks + 12 weeks at flat rate		Y maternity leave
Benefit Level at 80% of Earnings				
Finland	1987	11 months	Y	Y
Italy	1984	5 months[e]		Y
Belgium	1984	14 weeks		
Ireland	1982	14 weeks		
Benefit Level at 75% of Earnings				
Spain	1982	14 weeks		
Israel	1984	12 weeks		
Canada	1984	17 weeks, 15 paid		
Benefit Level at 50% of Earnings				
Greece	1982	12 weeks		

From S. B. Kamerman, "Child Care, Women, Work, and the Family: An International Overview of Child Care Services and Related Policies" in J. S. Lande, S. Scarr, and N. Gunzenhauser (eds.), *Caring for Children: Challenge to America.* Copyright © 1989 Lawrence Erlbaum Associates, Inc., Hillsdale, NJ. Reprinted by permission.
[a]Up to maximum covered under Social Security.
[b]Plus 2 years for low-income single mothers if they cannot find child care.
[c]6 weeks must be taken before expected birth; in other countries this time is voluntary.
[d]Last 6 months available only on an income-tested basis.
[e]100% paid for first 4 weeks; 2 months' leave before birth mandated.

Day Care

Each weekday at 8:00 A.M., Ellen Smith takes her 1-year-old daughter to the day-care center at Brookhaven College in Dallas. Then Mrs. Smith goes off to work and returns in the afternoon to take Tanya home. Now, after three years at the center, Mrs. Smith reports that her daughter is adventuresome and interacts confidently with peers and adults. Mrs. Smith believes that day care has been a wonderful way to raise Tanya.

In Los Angeles, however, day care has been a series of horror stories for Barbara Jones. After two years of unpleasant experiences with sitters, day-care centers, and day-care homes, Mrs. Jones quit her job as a successful real estate agent to stay home and take care of her 2½-year-old daughter, Gretchen.

"I didn't want to sacrifice my baby for my job," said Mrs. Jones, who was unable to find good substitute care in day-care homes. When she put Gretchen into a day-care center, she said that she felt her daughter was being treated like a piece of merchandise—dropped off and picked up.

Many parents worry whether day care will adversely affect their children. They fear that day care will reduce the infant's emotional attachment to them, retard the infant's cognitive development, fail to teach the child how to control anger, and allow the child to be unduly influenced by peers. How extensive is day care? Are the worries of these parents justified?

During the 1990s, far more young children are in day care than at any other time in history; about 2 million children currently receive formal, licensed day care, and more than 5 million children attend kindergarten. Also, uncounted millions of children are cared for by unlicensed babysitters. Day care clearly has become a basic need of the American family (Caldwell, 1991; Phillips, 1989).

The type of day care that young children receive varies extensively. Many day-care centers house large groups of children and have elaborate facilities. Some are commercial operations, others are nonprofit centers run by churches, civic groups, and employers. Child care is frequently provided in private homes, at times by child-care professionals, at others by mothers who want to earn extra money (Lombardi, 1991).

The quality of care children experience in day care varies extensively. Some caregivers have no training, others extensive training; some day-care centers have a low caregiver-child ratio, others have a high caregiver-child ratio. Some experts have recently argued that the quality of day care most children receive in the United States is poor. Infant researcher Jay Belsky (1989) not only believes that the quality of day care children experience is generally poor, but he also believes this translates into negative developmental outcomes for children. Belsky concludes that extensive day-care experience during the first twelve months of life—as typically experienced in the United States—is associated with insecure attachment as well as increased aggression, noncompliance, and possibly social withdrawal during the preschool and early elementary school years.

A recent study supports Belsky's beliefs (Vandell & Corasaniti, 1988). Extensive day care in the first year of life was associated with long-term negative outcomes. In contrast to children who began full-time day care later, children who began full-time day care (defined as more than 30 hours per week) as infants were rated by parents and teachers as being less compliant and as having poorer peer relations. In the first grade, they received lower grades and had poor work habits by comparison.

Belsky's conclusions about day care are controversial. Other respected researchers have arrived at a different conclusion; their review of the day-care research suggests no ill effects of day care (Clarke-Stewart, 1989; Scarr, 1984, 1991; Scarr, Lande & McCartney, 1989).

What can we conclude? Does day care have adverse effects on children's development? Trying to combine the results into an overall conclusion about day-care effects is a problem because of the different types of day care children experience and the different measures used to assess the outcome. Belsky's analysis does suggest that parents should be very careful about the quality of day care they select for their infants, especially those 1 year of age or less. Even Belsky agrees, though, that day care itself is not the culprit; rather it is the quality of day care that is problematic in this country. Belsky acknowledges that no evidence exists to show that children in high-quality day care are at risk in any way (Belsky, 1984; Doll, 1988).

What constitutes a high-quality day-care program for infants? The

WHAT IS QUALITY CARE?

◆

*W*hat constitutes quality child care? The following recommendations were made by the National Association for the Education of Young Children (1986). They are based on a consensus arrived at by experts in early childhood education and child development. It is especially important for parents to meet the adults who will care for their child. They are responsible for every aspect of the program's operation.

The young children shown here are at a day-care center while their parents are at work. Day care has become a basic need of the American family. What are some variations in the type of day care children can experience?

1. The adult caregivers
   - The adults should enjoy and understand how infants and young children grow.
   - There should be enough adults to work with a group and to care for the individual needs of children. More specifically, there should be no more than four infants for each adult caregiver, no more than eight 2- to 3-year-old children for each caregiver, and no more than ten 4- to 5-year-old children for each adult caregiver.
   - They observe and record each child's progress and development.
2. The program activities and equipment
   - The environment fosters the growth and development of young children working and playing together.
   - A good center provides appropriate and sufficient equipment and play materials and makes them readily available.

   - Infants and children are helped to increase their language skills and to expand their understanding of the world.
3. Relation of staff to families and the community
   - A good program considers and supports the needs of the entire family. Parents should be welcome to observe, discuss policies, make suggestions, and work in the activities of the center.
   - The staff in a good center is aware of and contribute to community resources. The staff should share information about community recreational and learning opportunities with families.

4. The facility and the program should be designed to meet the varied demands of infants and young children, their families, and the staff.
   - The health of children, staff, and parents is protected and promoted. The staff should be alert to the health of each child.
   - The facility should be safe for children and adults.
   - The environment should be spacious to accommodate a variety of activities and equipment. More specifically, there should be a minimum of 35 square feet of usable playroom floor space indoors per child and 75 square feet of play space outdoors per child.

demonstration program developed by Jerome Kagan and his colleagues (1978) at Harvard University is exemplary. The day-care center included a pediatrician, a nonteaching director, and an infant-teacher ratio of 3 to 1. Teachers' aides assisted at the center. The teachers and aides were trained to smile frequently, to talk with the infants, and to provide them with a safe environment that included many stimulating toys. No adverse effects of day care were observed in this project. More information about what to look for in a quality

We have all the knowledge necessary to provide absolutely first-rate child care in the United States. What is missing is the commitment and the will.

~ *Edward Zigler, 1987*

Blossoms are scattered by the wind
And the wind cares nothing, but
The blossoms of the heart
No wind can touch.

~ *Youshida Kenko,*
The Harvest of Leisure, 1330

day-care center is presented in Perspective on Life-Span Development 7.1. Using such criteria, one researcher discovered that children who entered low-quality child care as infants were least likely to be socially competent in early childhood (less compliant, less self-controlled, less task-oriented, more hostile, and having more problems in peer interaction) (Howes, 1988).

Edward Zigler (1987, 1991) recently proposed a solution to the day-care needs of families. Zigler says that we should not think of school as an institution, but rather as a building, one that is owned by tax-paying parents who need day care for their children. Part of the school building would be for teaching and part would be for child care and supervision. This system could provide parents with competent developmental child-care services. Zigler believes it should be available to every child over the age of 3. He does not think children should start formal schooling at age 3; they would be in the schools only for day care. At the age of 5, children would start kindergarten, but only for half days. If the child has a parent at home, the child would spend the remainder of the day at home. If the parents are working, the child would spend the second half of the day in the day-care part of the school. For children aged 6 to 12, after-school and vacation care would be available to those who need it.

Zigler does not believe that teachers should provide day care; they are trained as educators and are too expensive. What we need, he says, is a child development associate, someone who is trained to work with children, someone we can afford to pay. This is a large vision, one that involves a structural change in society and a new face for our school system. As Zigler remembers, between the fall of 1964 and the summer of 1965, we managed to put 560,000 children into Head Start programs, an educational program for impoverished children. He believes we can do the same thing with day care (Trotter, 1987). Despite the efforts of Zigler and others, the child-care bills currently being introduced in Congress do not adequately address the quality of child care and the low pay of child-care workers (DeAngelis, 1990).

Emotional and Personality Development

The sociocultural world, family processes, attachment, the father's role, and day care are all important ingredients of the infant's social being. But there is more to understanding the nature of the infant; emotions, trust, independence, and development of a sense of self also play key roles in understanding the infant's social development.

Emotional Development

If you cannot name an emotion, you cannot experience it. That was the dominant view of infant emotion for much of this century. But now a different picture has emerged, one that recognizes the infant's repertoire of emotions. Just as we found in chapters 5 and 6, that vision, hearing, and the ability to remember and learn are more highly developed in infancy than was originally believed, we now know that interest, distress, and disgust are present early in infancy and can be communicated to parents. Much earlier than the arrival of language, infants add other emotions like joy, anger, surprise, shyness, and fear to their capabilities.

What are the functions of emotions in infancy? Emotions are adaptive and promote survival, serve as a form of communication, and provide regulation (Barrett & Campos, 1987; Bretherton & others, 1986; Izard and Malatesta, 1987; Lewis, 1989). For example, various fears—such as fear of the dark and fear of sudden changes in the environment—are adaptive because there are clear links between such events and possible danger. Infants use emotions to inform others about their feelings and needs. Infants who smile are probably telling others that they are feeling pleasant, and infants who cry are probably communicating that something is unpleasant. Infants also use emotions to increase or decrease the distance between themselves and others. The infant who smiles may be encouraging someone to come closer; the infant who displays anger may be suggesting that an intruder should go away. And emotions influence the information the infant selects from the perceptual world and the behaviors the infant displays (Izard, 1991).

How can we find out if the infant is displaying emotion? Carroll Izard (1982) developed a system for decoding the emotional expressions on infants' faces. Izard wanted to discover which emotions were inborn and which emerged later, and under which conditions they were displayed. The conditions included being given an ice cube, having tape put on the backs of their hands, being handed a favorite toy and then having it taken away, being separated from and reunited with their mothers, being approached by a stranger, having their heads gently restrained, having a ticking clock held next to their ears, having a balloon pop in front of their faces, and being given camphor to sniff and lemon rind and orange juice to taste.

Maximally Discriminative Facial Movement Coding System (MAX) *is Izard's system of coding infants' facial expressions related to emotion.* Using MAX, the coder watches slow-motion and stop-action videotapes of the infant's facial reactions to stimuli, such as the circumstances we described earlier. For example, anger is indicated when the brows are sharply lowered and drawn together, the eyes are narrowed or squinted, and the mouth is open in an angular, square shape. The key elements of emotional facial codes are shown in figure 7.5 and the developmental timetable of their emergence in infancy is shown in table 7.1.

Personality Development

The individual characteristics of the infant that are often thought of as central to personality development are trust, the self, and independence.

Trust

According to Erik Erikson (1968), the first year of life is characterized by the stage of development, trust versus mistrust. Following a life of regularity, warmth, and protection in the mother's womb, the infant faces a world that is less secure. Erikson believes that infants learn trust when they are cared for in a consistent, warm manner. If the infant is not well fed and kept warm on a consistent basis, a sense of mistrust is likely to develop.

We briefly described Erikson's ideas about the role of trust in attachment earlier. His thoughts have much in common with Mary Ainsworth's concept of secure attachment. The infant who has a sense of trust is likely to be securely attached and have confidence to explore new circumstances; the infant who has a sense of mistrust is likely to be insecurely attached and to not have such confidence and positive expectations.

Trust versus mistrust is not resolved once and for all in the first year of life; it arises again at each successive stage of development. There is both hope and danger in this. Children who enter school with a sense of mistrust may trust a particular teacher who has taken the time to make herself trustworthy. With this second chance children overcome their early mistrust. By contrast, children who leave infancy with a sense of trust can still have their sense of mistrust activated at a later stage, perhaps if their parents are separated or divorced under conflicting circumstances. An example is instructive (Elkind, 1970). A 4-year-old boy was being seen by a clinical psychologist at a court clinic because his adoptive parents, who had had him for six months, now

Joy
Mouth forms smile, cheeks lifted, twinkle in eyes

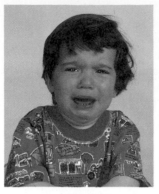

Anger
Brows drawn together and downward, eyes fixed, mouth squarish

Interest
Brows raised or knit, mouth softly rounded, lips pursed

Disgust
Nose wrinkled, upper lip raised, tongue pushed outward

Surprise
Brows raised, eyes widened, mouth rounded in oval shape

Distress
Eyes tightly closed, mouth, as in anger, squared and angular

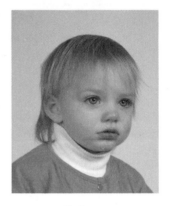

Sadness
Brows' inner corners raised, drawn out and down

Fear
Brows level, drawn in and up, eyelids lifted, mouth retracted

Figure 7.5 Facial expressions of emotion and their characteristics.

• *Critical Thinking* •

In addition to the description of the 4-year-old boy from an adopted family, can you think of other examples in which trust during infancy is an important aspect of development? Try to come up with at least two other specific cases.

wanted to give him back to the agency. They said he was cold and unloving, stole things, and could not be trusted. He was indeed a cold and apathetic boy, but with good reason. About a year after his illegitimate birth, he was taken away from his mother, who had a drinking problem, and was shuttled back and forth among several foster homes. At first he tried to relate to people in the foster homes, but the relationships never had an opportunity to develop because he was moved so frequently. In the end, he gave up trying to reach out to others because the inevitable separations hurt too much. Like the burned child who dreads the flame, this emotionally burned child shunned the pain of close relationships. He had trusted his mother, but now he trusted no one. Only years of devoted care and patience could now undo the damage to this child's sense of trust.

The Developing Sense of Self and Independence

Individuals carry with them a sense of who they are and what makes them different from everyone else. They cling to this identity and begin to feel secure in the knowledge that this identity is becoming more stable. Real or imagined, this sense of self is a strong motivating force in life. When does the individual begin to sense a separate existence from others?

Table 7.1: The Development Course of Infant Emotions

Emotional Expression	Approximate Time of Emergence
Interest *Neonatal smile (a sort of half smile that appears spontaneously for no apparent reason) *Startled response *Distress Disgust	Present at birth
Social smile	4 to 6 weeks
Anger Surprise Sadness	3 to 4 months
Fear Shame/Shyness	5 to 7 months 6 to 8 months
Contempt Guilt	Second year of life

*The neonatal smile, the startled response, and distress in response to pain are precursors of the social smile and the emotions of surprise and sadness, which appear later. No evidence suggests that they are related to inner feelings when they are observed in the first few weeks of life.

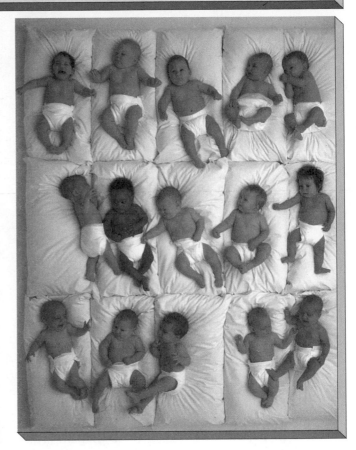

Children begin to develop a sense of self by learning to distinguish themselves from others. To determine whether infants can recognize themselves, psychologists have used mirrors. In the animal kingdom, only the great apes learn to recognize their reflection in the mirror, but human infants accomplish this feat by about 18 months of age. How does the mirror technique work? The mother puts a dot of rouge on her infant's nose. The observer watches to see how often the infant touches his nose. Next, the infant is placed in front of a mirror and observers detect whether nose touching increases (Lewis & Feinman, 1991; Lewis & others, 1989). In two independent investigations in the second half of the second year of life, infants recognized their own image and coordinated the image they saw with the actions of touching their own body (Amsterdam, 1968; Lewis & Brooks-Gunn, 1979) (see figure 7.6).

Not only does the infant develop a sense of self in the second year of life, but independence becomes a more central theme in the infant's life as well. The theories of Margaret Mahler and Erik Erikson have important implications for both self-development and independence. Mahler (1979) believes that the child goes through a separation and then an individuation process. Separation involves the infant's movement away from the mother and individuation involves the development of self.

Social Development in Infancy 203

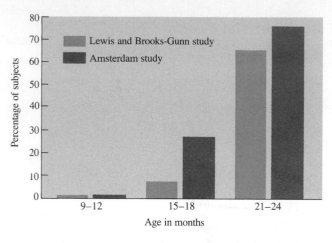

Figure 7.6   The development of self-recognition in infancy. The graph gives the findings of two studies in which infants of different ages showed recognition of rouge by touching, wiping, or verbally referring to it. Notice that self-recognition did not occur extensively until the second half of the second year of life.

Mother-child interaction can interfere with the development of individuation. For example, Anna's mother was often emotionally unavailable. Never certain of her mother's availability, Anna was preoccupied with it; she found it difficult to explore her surroundings. After a brief spurt of practicing, she would return to her mother and try to interact with her in an intense way. Sometimes she would spill cookies on the floor, always with an eye to gaining her mother's attention. Anna's mother was absorbed with her own interests. During the preschool years, Anna threw temper tantrums and clinged to her teacher. Then the clinging would turn to hitting and yelling. In Mahler's view, Anna wanted only one thing to happen: She wanted her mother to return through the door. As can be seen in Anna's case, an unsatisfactory mother-infant relationship led to problems in her development of independence.

Erikson (1968), like Mahler, believes that independence is an important issue in the second year of life. Erikson describes the second stage of development as autonomy versus shame and doubt. Autonomy builds on the infant's developing mental and motor abilities. At this point in development, infants cannot only walk but they can also climb, open and close, drop, push and pull, hold and let go. Infants feel pride in these new accomplishments and want to do everything themselves, whether it is flushing a toilet, pulling the wrapping off a package, or deciding what to eat. It is important for parents to recognize the motivation of toddlers to do what they are capable of doing at their own pace. Then they can learn to control their muscles and their impulses themselves. But when caregivers are impatient and do for toddlers what they are capable of doing themselves, shame and doubt develop. Every parent has rushed a child from time to time. It is only when parents consistently overprotect toddlers or criticize accidents (wetting, soiling, spilling, or breaking, for example) that children develop an excessive sense of shame and doubt about their ability to control themselves and their world.

Erikson also believes that the autonomy versus shame and doubt stage has important implications for the development of independence and identity during adolescence. The development of autonomy during the toddler years gives adolescents the courage to be independent individuals who can choose and guide their own future.

Too much autonomy, though, can be as harmful as too little. A 7-year-old boy who had a heart condition learned quickly how afraid his parents were of any signs of his having cardiac problems. It was not long before he ruled the household. The family could not go shopping or for a drive if the boy did not approve. On the rare occasions his parents defied him, he would get angry, and his purple face and gagging would frighten them into submission. This boy actually was scared of his power and eager to relinquish it. When the parents and the boy realized this, and recognized that a little shame and doubt were a healthy opponent of an inflated sense of autonomy, the family began to function much more smoothly (Elkind, 1970).

Consider also Robert, age 22 months, who has just come home from watching his 5-year-old brother, William, take a swimming lesson. Their mother has gone in the kitchen to get dinner ready when she hears a scream. She hurries into the living room and sees Robert's teeth sunk into William's leg. The next day, Robert is playing with a new game and he can't get it right. He hurls it across the room and just misses his mother. That night his mother tells him it is time for bed. Robert's response: "No." Sometimes the world of 2-year-olds becomes very frustrating. Much of their frustration stems from their inability to control the adult world. Things are too big to manage, to push around, or to make happen. Toddlers want to be in the driver's seat of every car and to push every cart by themselves. Two-year-olds want to play the dominant role in almost every situation. When things don't go their way, toddlers can become openly defiant even though they were placid as babies earlier in life. Called the "terrible twos" by Arnold Gesell, this developmental time frame can try the patience of the most even-tempered parents. Nonetheless, calm, steady affection and firm patience can help to disperse most of toddlerhood's tensions. Fortunately, the defiance is only temporary in most children's development.

Adapting Caregiving to the Developmental Status of the Infant and Toddler, and the Goals of Caregiving

In our discussion of infant social development, the themes of attachment, independence, emotional development, and the development of self have been predominant. We have examined developmental changes in attachment and seen that the push for independence is stronger in the second than in the first year of life. We have seen that different emotions emerge at different points in infancy, and we have seen that the second year is an important point in the emergence of a sense of self. Let's now examine some of these social developmental changes in infancy and see the importance of adapting caregiving to the developmental changes.

Adapting Caregiving to the Developmental Status of the Infant and Toddler

What are some of the ways caregivers can effectively interact with infants and toddlers of different ages to promote their social and emotional development? The following recommendations are based on LaVisa Wilson's (1990) development of a curriculum for people who care for infants and toddlers.

Birth to 4 Months
Caregivers can use several strategies to enhance the young infant's social development. The caregiver should respond quickly to the infant's needs and can initiate social interaction by looking at, holding, stroking, talking with, playing with, carrying, and rocking the infant. Caregivers must become emotionally

involved with the infant. Caregivers need to frequently look at and touch the infant, which contributes to the development of an emotional relationship. Caregivers arrange time and select materials that help infants to learn about themselves. For example, mirrors fascinate infants. Dots on bare feet and hands extend infants' interest in their bodies. Caregivers arrange for infants to interact with other people and with playthings.

4 to 8 Months

Infants are now developing a focused attachment to a primary caregiver; the primary caregiver's presence, consistent care, and emotional involvement with the infant support the development of an attachment. If the infant is in day care, a specific caregiver should be assigned to the infant; one caregiver can be a significant other for several infants. The caregiver should share the infant's pleasure and calm, as well as soothe, stroke, and sing to the infant during the infant's frustrating periods.

Infants now express a wider range of emotions in more elaborate ways. Pleasure, happiness, fear, and frustration are shown through a variety of sounds, such as gurgles, coos, wails, and cries, along with physical movements, such as rapid kicking, arm waving, rocking, and smiling. Many infants show a fear of strangers, or what has been called stranger anxiety. Stranger anxiety often emerges between 5 and 7 months of age. Therefore, strangers should be introduced carefully, and the stranger should not hover close to the infant. Give the infant time to become adjusted to the stranger from a distance.

8 to 12 Months

Social interaction with others is often increasing. Infants' increased mobility in this age period allow them to socially interact with and move away from other people. Caregivers should talk and play with the infant, and allow the infant access to other adults and infants. Infants often continue to fear strangers at this age, so strangers should not be forced on infants immediately. A number of turn-taking games should be initiated with the infant, such as pat-a-cake. Infants are egocentric and want their own pleasure, usually not considering others' needs. Caregivers can begin to verbalize limits and help the infant choose other activities and materials. Infants at this age are very possessive of the caregiver, thus it is important for the caregiver to verbally assure the infant that she or he will come back to talk and play with the infant again.

External controls like a verbal "no" or a firm look may be needed to help infants limit or change their behavior at this age. Restrictive words should be followed by an explanation. For example, if an infant throws food on the floor, the caregiver can say, "No. You need the carrots up here on your plate. Can you put a carrot in your mouth?" Sometimes infants will stop their own negative behaviors, and if so, caregivers should praise the infant for their self-restriction. When infants at this age show anger or frustration, caregivers can determine and remove the causes of the anger or frustration if possible. Use calm talking, and sometimes hold and soothe the infant. Help the infant start a new activity. Tantrums may need to be ignored so they will not be reinforced and will eventually decrease in frequency and intensity.

12 to 18 Months

Toddlers push for independence, but at the same time they are very dependent on their caregivers, needing help for many tasks. Toddlers need emotional support, which affirms their importance as individuals who make some choices and accomplish some tasks all by themselves. Toddlers' negativism may be expressed by "No!" or in tantrums. Their pursuit of independence may lead them to sometimes do the opposite of what the caregiver does.

As toddlers seek independence, allow them to attempt activities by themselves. Don't take over if toddlers can be successful alone. When toddlers express negativism, provide workable alternatives, such as "Do you want to walk or run to the table?" Toddlers also increasingly behave differently toward different people, adjusting their interactions with them. They may be eager and excited with a caregiver and quiet and shy with an adult stranger. Caregivers need to recognize these different responses and accept the toddler's choices. Don't force the toddler to interact with everyone.

18 to 24 Months

The development of self is especially important during this time period, as toddlers begin to use words that identify them as separate people—"I," "mine," "me," and "you," for example. Caregivers can verbally respond to the toddler's use of pronouns referring to the self, reinforcing the distinction the toddler makes between self and others. Toddlers at this age continue to expand their social relationships. Caregivers should encourage children to interact with others and provide support when they do.

Toddlers' behavior often moves to extremes, from lovable to demanding and stubborn. Caregivers need to allow the toddler to express swings in behavior. Show acceptance of the toddler as a person. Help toddlers work on their demands and stubbornness by suggesting alternatives in behavior. And, even though toddlers sometimes reject their caregivers, caregivers should continue to express to toddlers how much they love them and continue to show them a great deal of affection.

Caregivers—whether parents or day-care personnel—play extremely important roles in infants' and toddlers' development. Of special concern are the personal characteristics of competent caregivers. To read about these personal characteristics, turn to Perspective on Life-Span Development 7.2.

Goals of Caregiving

Over the course of the last three chapters, we have chronicled the extensive development—physical, cognitive, and social—that takes place during infancy. On many pages, we have described ways that caregivers can interact with infants in a developmentally appropriate manner. Are there some overarching goals that caregivers should have in being responsible for the development of infants? Infant researcher and parent educator Burton White (1990) believes that caregivers should pursue three basic general goals:

- Giving the infant a sense of being loved and cared for
- Helping the infant to develop specific skills
- Encouraging the infant's interest in the outside world

Giving the Infant a Sense of Being Loved and Cared For

In the first two years of life, all infants and toddlers have a strong need to establish an attachment to one or more older humans. In the process of developing this attachment they begin their long road to being socialized and socializing others. As we have seen, Erikson (1968) believes the central goal of the first year of life is the development of a sense of trust rather than mistrust on the part of the infant. White and I believe this term is an appropriate one. The frequency and degree of discomfort and distress babies feel depends in large part on the kind of treatment they experience. There is no way to prevent a fair amount of unhappiness from such factors as hunger, indigestion, teething, and a cold diaper. However, such unhappiness can be prolonged and allowed to escalate if the avoidable discomfort and distress are not responded to promptly.

PERSONAL CHARACTERISTICS OF COMPETENT CAREGIVERS

◆

*S*ome caregivers are more competent than others. What makes a competent caregiver? That question was recently addressed by child-care expert LaVisa Wilson (1990). She believes the following personal characteristics define a competent caregiver:

- *Competent caregivers are physically healthy.* Good health is necessary to provide the high level of energy required for competent caregiving. In day care, good health is required to resist the variety of illnesses to which caregivers are exposed.
- *Competent caregivers are mentally healthy.* In daily interactions with infants, caregivers need to provide physical closeness and nurturance for an extended period of time, to give emotionally more than they often receive, and to be patient longer than they would like. Emotionally stable caregivers who have learned how to cope

with a variety of emotional demands in their daily experiences are often able to encourage mental health in others.
- *Competent caregivers have a positive self-image.* Feelings of self-confidence and positive self-worth show that caregivers believe in themselves. Caregivers who have positive self-images are people who infants and toddlers want to approach rather than avoid.
- *Competent caregivers are flexible.* Competent caregivers do not get upset if they have to change the daily schedule, daily plans, or responsibilities.
- *Competent caregivers are patient.* Infants and toddlers are very demanding and require considerable attention and monitoring, which can stretch the caregiver's patience. However, competent caregivers

show patience as they respond to the infants' and toddlers' needs.
- *Competent caregivers are positive models for infants.* Caregivers' behaviors are observed and imitated by infants and toddlers. Competent caregivers monitor their own behavior, knowing it is a model for infants and toddlers.
- *Competent caregivers are open to learning.* Competent caregivers seek to develop additional skills and are open to new insights, understanding, and skills.
- *Competent caregivers enjoy caregiving.* Competent caregivers gain considerable enjoyment and satisfaction in providing effective, high-quality care for infants and toddlers. Competent caregivers reflect these positive feelings as they interact with infants and toddlers.

Caregivers who respond to infants with loving care and attention make strong contributions to the development of infants' competence. As White indicates, no requirement of good caregiving is more natural or more rewarding than tending to the baby in a loving and attentive way.

Helping the Infant to Develop Specific Skills
Over the course of the first two years of life, infants develop from a creature who cannot think, use language, socialize with a human being, run, walk, or even deliberately move around to a socialized individual who has accumulated a number of specific skills. Good childrearing in the first two years of an infant's life includes knowing what the normal pattern of emerging skills is and facilitating their emergence and development. Most of these skills evolve unaided under average rearing circumstances, but good parenting ensures the optimal development of these skills. Throughout the three chapters on infant development, we have gone to great lengths to specify what the normal development of physical, cognitive, and social skills are during the infant years and how caregivers can interact with infants in developmentally appropriate ways to enhance these skills. Facilitating the development of the infant's specific skills is tied to White's third general goal of caregiving competence.

Encouraging the Infant's Interest in the Outside World
Whether an infant first learns to reach for objects at 3 months or at 5 months is probably of less consequence than seeing that the babies are regularly involved in activities that interest them. Instead of trying to push infants to develop skills beyond their current level and become a "superbaby," it is important for parents to interact with the infant in ways that keep the infant interested, cheerful, and alert. After the first several months, infants should be actively enjoying themselves at least some of the time.

Problems and Disturbances

Problems and disturbances in infancy can arise for a number of reasons. All development—normal and abnormal—is influenced by the interaction of heredity and environment. In a comprehensive study of children at risk, a variety of biological, social, and developmental characteristics were identified as predictors of problems and disturbances at age 18. They included moderate to severe perinatal (at or near birth) stress and birth defects, low socioeconomic status at 2 to 10 years of age, level of maternal education below 8 years, low family stability between 2 and 8 years, very low or very high infant responsiveness at 1 year, a Cattell score below 80 at age 2 (the Cattell is one of the early measures of infant intelligence), and the need for long-term mental health services or placement in a learning-disability class at age 10. When four or more of these factors were present, the stage was set for serious coping problems in the second decade of life (Werner & Smith, 1982). Among the problems in infancy that deserve special consideration are child abuse and autism.

Child Abuse

Unfortunately, parental hostility toward children in some families escalates to the point where one or both parents abuse the child. Child abuse is an increasing problem in the United States. Estimates of its incidence vary, but some authorities say that as many as 500,000 children are physically abused every year. Laws in many states now require doctors and teachers to report suspected cases of child abuse. Yet, many cases go unreported, especially those of battered infants (Ammerman & Hersen, 1990).

Child maltreatment is such a disturbing circumstance that many people have difficulty understanding or sympathizing with parents who abuse or neglect their children (Crittenden, 1988; Crittenden & Partridge, 1991). Our response is often outrage and anger directed at the parent. This outrage focuses our attention on parents as bad, sick, monstrous, sadistic individuals who cause their children to suffer. Experts on child abuse believe that this view is too simple and deflects attention away from the social context of the abuse and the parents' coping skills. It is especially important to recognize that child abuse is a diverse condition, that it is usually mild to moderate in severity, and that it is only partially caused by individual personality characteristics of parents (Cicchetti & others, 1991; Emery, 1989; Haugard & Emery, in press).

The Multifaceted Nature of Child Maltreatment
While the public and many professionals use the term *child abuse* to refer to both abuse and neglect, developmentalists are increasingly using the term *child maltreatment.* This term reduces the emotional impact of the term *abuse* and acknowledges that maltreatment includes several different conditions. Among the different types of maltreatment are physical and sexual abuse; fostering delinquency; lack of supervision; medical, educational, and nutritional neglect; and drug or alcohol abuse (Garbarino, 1989). Approximately 20 percent of

the reported cases involve abuse alone, 46 percent neglect alone, 23 percent both abuse and neglect, and 11 percent sexual abuse (American Association for Protecting Children, 1986). Abused children are more likely to be angry or wary than neglected children, who tend to be passive (Lynch & Roberts, 1982).

Severity of Abuse

The concern about child abuse began with the identification of the "battered child syndrome" and has retained the characteristic of severe, brutal injury for several reasons. First, the media tend to underscore the most bizarre and vicious incidents. Second, much of the funding for child-abuse prevention, identification, and treatment depends on the public's perception of the horror of child abuse and the medical professions' lobby for funds to investigate and treat abused children and their parents. The emphasis is often on the worst cases. These horrific cases do exist, and are indeed terrible, but they make up only a small minority of abused children. Less than 1 percent of abused children die, and another 11 percent suffer life-threatening, disabling injuries (American Association for Protecting Children, 1986). By contrast, almost 90 percent suffer temporary physical injuries. These milder injuries, though, are likely to be repeatedly experienced in the context of daily hostile family exchanges. Similarly, neglected children, who suffer no physical injuries, often experience extensive, long-term psychological harm.

In China, where physical punishment is rarely used to discipline children, the incidence of child abuse is reported to be very low.

The Cultural Context of Maltreatment

The extensive violence of the American culture is reflected in the occurrence of violence in the family. A regular diet of violence appears on television screens, and parents often resort to power assertion as a disciplinary technique. In China, where physical punishment is rarely used to discipline children, the incidence of child abuse is reported to be very low. In the United States, many abusing parents report that they do not have sufficient resources or help from others. This may be a realistic evaluation of the situation experienced by many low-income families, who do not have adequate preventive and supportive services (Rodriguez-Haynes & Crittenden, 1988).

Community support systems are especially important in alleviating stressful family situations and thereby preventing child abuse. An investigation of the support systems in 58 counties in New York State revealed a relation between the incidence of child abuse and the absence of support systems available to the family. Family resources—relatives and friends, for example—and formal community support systems—such as crisis centers and child abuse counseling—were associated with a reduction in child abuse (Garbarino, 1976).

Family Influences

To understand abuse in the family, the interaction of all family members needs to be considered, regardless of who actually performs the violent acts against the child (Cicchetti & others, 1991; Daro, 1988). For example, even though the father may be the one who physically abuses the child, contributions by the mother, the child, and siblings also should be evaluated. Many parents who abuse their children come from families in which physical punishment was used (Simons & others, 1991). These parents view physical punishment as a legitimate way of controlling the child's behavior, and physical punishment may be a part of this sanctioning. Children themselves may unwittingly contribute to child abuse: An unattractive child receives more physical punishment than an attractive child, and a child from an unwanted pregnancy may be especially vulnerable to abuse (Harter, Alexander, & Neimeyer, 1988).

SHATTERED INNOCENCE—THE SEXUAL ABUSE OF CHILDREN

◆

*H*eadlines about day-care center scandals and feminist protests against sexist exploitation have increased public awareness of what we now know is a widespread problem: sexual abuse of children. It has been estimated that as many as 40 million American children are sexually abused—about one in six. A 1984 Gallup poll of 2,000 men and women in 210 Canadian communities found that 22 percent of the respondents were sexually abused as children. Clearly, children's sexual abuse is more widespread than was thought in the past. One reason the problem of children's sexual abuse was a dark secret for so long is that people understandably kept this painful experience to themselves.

The sexual abuse of children occurs most often between the ages of 9 and 12, although the abuse of 2- and 3-year-olds is not unusual. The abuser is almost always a man, and typically he is known to the child, often being a relative. In many instances, the abuse is not limited to a single episode. No race, ethnic group, or economic class is immune.

While children do not react uniformly to sexual abuse, certain behaviors and feelings occur with some regularity. The immediate effects include sleeping and eating disturbances, anger, withdrawal, and guilt. The children often appear to be afraid or anxious. Two additional signs occur so often that professionals rely on them as indicators of abuse when they are present together. The first is sexual preoccupation—excessive or public masturbation and an unusually strong interest in sexual organs, play, and nudity. The second sign consists of a host of physical complaints or problems, such as rashes, headaches, and vomiting, all without medical explanation. When it is discovered that these children have been sexually abused, a check of their medical records usually produces years of such mysterious ailments. While there are patterns in the immediate effects of sexual abuse of children, it is far more difficult to connect such abuse with later psychological problems. It is impossible to say that every child who has been abused will develop this or that problem, and we still have not developed a profile of the child abuse victim that everyone can agree upon.

Husband-wife violence and financial problems may result in displaced aggression toward a defenseless child. Displaced aggression is commonly involved in child abuse.

In one recent study, abusive families were characterized by the following: Worried parents who did not enjoy parenting and did not express affection to the child, parents who were isolated from the wider community, and parents who did not encourage the child's development of independence yet at the same time placed high achievement demands on the child (Trickett & others, 1991). A number of research studies have found that this pattern of family relationships had negative consequences for children's development (Maccoby & Martin, 1983). One form of child maltreatment can be devastating to the child—sexual abuse, which we discuss in Perspective on Life-Span Development 7.3.

Infantile Autism

As its name suggests, **infantile autism** *has its onset in infancy. It is a severe developmental disturbance that includes deficiencies in social relationships, abnormalities in communication, and restricted, repetitive, and stereotyped patterns of behavior* (Dawson, 1989; Hertzig & Shapiro, in press; Rutter & Schopler, 1987; Tager-Flusberg, in press). Social deficiencies include a failure to use an eye-to-eye gaze to regulate social interaction, rarely seeking others for comfort or affection, rarely initiating play with others, and having no peer relations involving mutual sharing of interests and emotions. As babies, these children require very little from their parents. They do not demand much attention and they do not reach out (literally or figuratively) for their parents. They rarely smile. When someone tries to hold them, they usually withdraw

Concept Table 7.2: The Father's Role, Day Care, Emotional and Personality Development, Caregiving, and Problems and Disturbances

Concept	Processes/Related Ideas	Characteristics/Description
The Father's Role	Its Nature	Over time, the father's role in the child's development has evolved from moral teacher to breadwinner to gender role model to active, nurturant caregiver.
	Father-Child Interaction and Attachment	Fathers have increased their interaction with their children, but they still lag far behind mothers, even when the mother is employed. Fathers can act sensitively to the infant's signals, but most of the time they do not. The mother's role in the infant's development is primarily caregiving. That of the father involves playful interaction. Infants generally prefer their mothers under stressful circumstances even in nontraditional families, as when the father is the main caregiver.
Day Care	Its Nature	Day care has become a basic need of the American family; more children are in day care today than at any other time in history.
	Quality of Care and Effects on Development	The quality of day care is uneven. Belsky concluded that most day care is inadequate and that extensive day care in the first twelve months of the infant's life has negative developmental outcomes. Other experts disagree with Belsky. Day care remains a controversial topic. Quality day care can be achieved and it seems to have few adverse effects on children.
Emotional and Personality Development	Emotional Development	Emotions in infancy are adaptive and promote survival, serve as a form of communication, and provide regulation. Izard developed the MAX system for coding infant facial expressions of emotion. Using this system, it was found that interest and disgust are present in the newborn, and that a social smile, anger, surprise, sadness, fear, and shame/shyness develop in the first year, while contempt and guilt develop in the second year.
	Trust	Erikson argues that the first year is characterized by the crisis of trust versus mistrust; his ideas about trust have much in common with Ainsworth's secure attachment concept.

by arching their back and pushing away. In their cribs or playpens, they appear oblivious to what is going on around them, often sitting and staring into space for long periods of time.

In addition to these social deficiencies, autistic children also show communication abnormalities that focus on the problems of using language for social communication: poor synchrony and lack of reciprocity in conversation, and stereotyped, repetitive use of language. As many as one of every two autistic children never learns to speak. **Echolalia** *is a speech disorder associated with autism in which children echo what they hear.* For example, if you ask, "How are you, Chuck?" Chuck responds, "How are you, Chuck?" Autistic children also confuse pronouns, inappropriately substituting *you* for *I,* for example.

Stereotyped patterns of behavior by autistic children include compulsive rituals, repetitive motor mannerisms, and distress over changes in small details

Concept	Processes/Related Ideas	Characteristics/Description
	Developing a Sense of Self and Independence	At some point in the second half of the second year of life, the infant develops a sense of self. Independence becomes a central theme in the second year of life. Mahler argues that the infant separates herself from the mother and then develops individuation. Erikson stresses that the second year of life is characterized by the stage of autonomy versus shame and doubt.
Adapting Caregiving to the Developmental Status of the Infant and Toddler and the Goals of Caregiving	Adapting Caregiving to the Developmental Status of the Infant and Toddler	From birth to 4 months of age, caregivers should respond quickly to the infant's needs with love, affection, and care. From 4 to 8 months of age, the caregiver's consistent care and emotional involvement with the infant support the development of a focused attachment. From 8 to 12 months of age, caregivers should continue to talk and play with the infant, and allow the infant access to other adults and infants. During this age period, caregivers need to monitor their infants' attentional bids. From 12 to 18 months of age, toddlers' independence needs to be promoted but their negativism needs to be dealt with firmly in the context of a loving and nurturant atmosphere. From 18 to 24 months of age, caregivers can encourage the toddler's development of self, continue monitoring their negativism, and continue giving them considerable affection.
	Goals of Caregiving	White believes that caregivers should pursue three basic general goals: giving the infant a sense of being loved and cared for, helping the infant to develop specific skills, and encouraging the infant's interest in the outside world.
Problems and Disturbances	Child Abuse	An understanding of child abuse requires information about cultural, familial, and community influences. Sexual abuse of children is now recognized as a more widespread problem than was believed in the past.
	Infantile Autism	Infantile autism is a severe disorder that first appears in infancy. It involves an inability to relate to people, speech problems, and upsets over changes in routine or environment. Autism seems to involve some form of organic brain and genetic dysfunction.

of the environment. Rearrangement of a sequence of events or even furniture in the course of a day may cause autistic children to become extremely upset, suggesting that they are not flexible in adapting to new routines and changes in their daily lives.

What causes autism? Autism seems to involve some form of organic brain dysfunction and may also have a hereditary basis. There has been no satisfactory evidence developed to document that family socialization causes autism (Rutter & Schopler, 1987).

At this point we have discussed several ideas about the father's role, day care, emotional development, and personality development in infancy. A summary of these ideas is presented in concept table 7.2. This chapter concludes our discussion of infant development. In the next section, we will continue our journey through development, moving into the early childhood years.

Summary

I. Family Processes

The transition to parenthood produces a disequilibrium that requires considerable adaptation. It is not unusual for postpartum blues to characterize mothers in the several months after the infant's birth. Infants socialize parents just as parents socialize infants—the process of reciprocal socialization. Parent-infant relationships are mutually regulated by the parent and the infant. In infancy, much of the relationship is driven by the parent, but as the infant gains self-control, the relationship is initiated more on an equal basis. The family is a system of interacting individuals with different subsystems, some dyadic, others polyadic. Belsky's model describes direct and indirect effects.

II. What Is Attachment?

Attachment is a relationship between two people in which each person feels strongly about the other and does a number of things to ensure the continuation of the relationship. In infancy, attachment refers to the bond between the caregiver and the infant. Feeding is not the critical element in attachment; contact comfort, familiarity, and trust are also important. Bowlby's ethological theory stresses that the caregiver and infant instinctively trigger attachment. Attachment to the caregiver intensifies at about 6 to 7 months.

III. Individual Differences in Attachment, Temperament, and the Wider Social World

Ainsworth believes that individual differences in attachment can be classified into secure, avoidant, and resistant categories. Ainsworth believes that securely attached babies have sensitive and responsive caregivers. In some investigations, secure attachment is related to social competence later in childhood. Some developmentalists believe that the role of attachment is emphasized too much; they believe that genetics and temperament on the one hand, and the diversity of social agents and contexts on the other, deserve more credit.

IV. The Father's Role

Over time, the father's role has evolved from moral teacher to breadwinner to gender role model to active, nurturant caregiver. Fathers have increased their interaction with their children, but fathers still lag far behind mothers, even when the mother is employed. Fathers can act sensitively to the infant's signals, but most of the time they do not. The mother's role in the infant's development is primarily caregiving, and that of the father involves playful interaction. Infants generally prefer their mother under stressful circumstances. Even in nontraditional families, as when the father is the primary caregiver, the behaviors of mothers and fathers follow traditional gender lines.

V. Day Care

Day care has become a basic need of the American family. More children are in day care today than at any other time in history. The quality of day care is uneven. Belsky contends that most day care is inadequate and that extensive day care in the first twelve months of the infant's life has negative developmental outcomes. Other experts disagree with Belsky. Day care remains a controversial topic. Quality day care can be achieved and it seems to have little adverse effects on children.

VI. Emotional Development

Emotions in infancy are adaptive and promote survival, serve as a form of communication, and provide regulation. Izard developed the MAX system for coding infant facial expressions of emotion. Using this system, it was found that interest and disgust are present in the newborn, and that a social smile, anger, surprise, sadness, fear, and shame and shyness develop in the first year while contempt and guilt develop in the second year.

VII. Personality Development

Erikson argues that the first year of life is characterized by the crisis of trust versus mistrust; his ideas about trust have much in common with Ainsworth's concept of secure attachment. At some point in the second half of the second year of life, the infant develops a sense of self, and independence becomes a central theme. Mahler argues that the infant separates herself from the mother and then develops individuation. Erikson stresses that the second year of life is characterized by the stage of autonomy versus shame and doubt.

VIII. Adapting Caregiving to the Developmental Status of the Infant and the Toddler

From birth to 4 months of age, caregivers should respond quickly to the infant's needs with love, affection, and care. From 4 to 8 months of age, the caregiver's consistent care and emotional involvement with the infant support the development of a focused attachment. From 8 to 12 months of age, caregivers should continue to talk and play with the infant, and allow the infant access to other adults and infants. During this age period, caregivers need to monitor their infants' attentional bids. From 12 to 18 months of age, toddlers' independence needs to be encouraged, but their negativism needs to be dealt with firmly in the context of a loving and nurturant atmosphere. From 18 to 24 months of age, caregivers can encourage the toddler's development of self, continue monitoring their negativism, and continue giving them considerable affection.

IX. Goals of Caregiving
White believes that caregivers should pursue three basic general goals: giving the infant a sense of being loved and cared for, helping the infant to develop specific skills, and encouraging the infant's interest in the outside world.

X. Problems and Disturbances
Abnormal development, like normal development, is caused by the interaction of heredity and environment. An understanding of child abuse requires an analysis of cultural, familial, and community influences. Sexual abuse of children is now recognized as a more widespread problem than was believed in the past. Infantile autism is a severe disorder that first appears in infancy. It involves an inability to relate to people, speech problems, and upsets over changes in routine or environment. Autism seems to involve some form of organic brain and genetic dysfunction.

Key Terms

reciprocal socialization   188
scaffolding   189
attachment   190
secure attachment   192

type B babies   192
type A babies   192
type C babies   192

Maximally Discriminative Facial Movement Coding System (MAX)   201
infantile autism   211
echolalia   212

Suggested Readings

Crittenden, P. (1988). Family and dyadic patterns of functioning in maltreating families. In K. Browne, C. Davies, & P. Stratton (Eds.), *Early prediction and prevention of child abuse.* New York: Wiley. *An excellent overview of family patterns of child maltreatment.*

Izard, C. E. (1982). *Measuring emotion in infants and children.* New York: Cambridge University Press. *Izard, one of the leading figures in the study of infant emotions, describes in fascinating detail how to assess the emotions of infants and young children.*

Kohn, A. (1987). *No contest: The case against competition.* Boston: Houghton Mifflin. *The dark secrets of children's sexual abuse is told with extensive examples of case studies to illustrate its psychological damage.*

Lamb, M. E. (1987). *The father's role: Cross-cultural perspectives.* Hillsdale, NJ: Erlbaum. *Intriguing descriptions of the father's role in different cultures are provided. Includes information about English, American, Israeli, Italian, Chinese, Swedish, and Aka pygmy fathers.*

Lande, J. S., Scarr, S., & Gunzenhauser, N. (Eds.). (1989). *Caring for children: Challenge to America.* Hillsdale, NJ: Erlbaum. *This up-to-date treatment of child care includes chapters on child care in European countries, child care in Black families, licensing of child-care facilities, and future directions of child care in the United States.*

Sroufe, L. A., & Fleeson, J. (1986). Attachment and the construction of relationships. In W. Hartup and Z. Rubin (Eds.), *Relationships and development.* Hillsdale, NJ: Erlbaum. *Gives insight into the importance of attachment in our development of relationships.*

White, B. L. (1990). *The first three years of life.* New York: Prentice-Hall. *Infant expert Burton White provides an excellent overview of how parents can interact with their infants and toddlers to produce competent, happy individuals.*

S·E·C·T·I·O·N
IV

EARLY CHILDHOOD

*You are troubled at seeing him spend
his early years doing nothing. What! Is it
nothing to be happy? Is it nothing to skip, to
play, to run about all day long? Never in his
life will he be so busy as now.*

Jean-Jacques Rousseau

CHAPTER 8

Physical and Cognitive Development in Early Childhood

A t 2 years of age, Tony is no saint. Tony's growing demand for autonomy keeps his mother busy hour after hour. Only a year earlier, he had learned to walk. Now he is running away from her into neighbor's yards and down the aisles of grocery stores. Trying out his new skills, he is constantly testing his parents and finding out the limits of his behavior.

By about his third birthday, Tony's behavior takes a slightly different turn. His temper tantrums have not entirely disappeared—the "terrible twos" can last into the fourth year—but much of his negative behavior has gone away. Every week produces a palate of new words and new tricks of climbing, skipping, and jumping. Tony is beginning to be able to make his body do what he wants it to do. As he moves through the preschool years, he learns how to draw and how to play different ball games. He is boastful, too, about his newly developed competencies. Tony says, "I'm bigger now, aren't I?" "I'm not a little baby anymore, am I?" Tony is right. He is not a baby anymore. His babyhood is gone.

By 4 years of age, Tony has become even more adventuresome, exploring his world with fascination and abandon. By age 5, Tony is a self-assured child. He has good coordination and he delights at alarming his parents with his hair-raising stunts on any suitable climbing object. Our coverage of early childhood in this chapter focuses on physical and cognitive development.

Physical Development in Early Childhood

Remember from chapter 5 that the infant's growth in the first year is extremely rapid and follows cephalocaudal and proximodistal patterns. At some point around the first birthday, most infants have begun to walk. During the infant's second year, the growth rate begins to slow down, but both gross and fine motor skills progress rapidly. The infant develops a sense of mastery through increased proficiency in walking and running. Improvement in fine motor skills—such as being able to turn the pages of a book one at a time—also contribute to the infant's sense of mastery in the second year. The growth rate continues to slow down in early childhood. Otherwise, we would be a species of giants.

Body Growth and Changes

The average child grows 2½ inches in height and gains between 5 and 7 pounds a year during early childhood. As the preschool child grows older, the percentage of increase in height and weight decreases with each additional year. The average height and weight of children as they age from 3 to 6 is shown in figure 8.1. Girls are only slightly smaller and lighter than boys during these years, a difference that continues until puberty. During the preschool years, both boys and girls slim down as the trunks of their bodies lengthen. Although their heads are still somewhat large for their bodies, by the end of the preschool years, most children have lost their top-heavy look. Body fat also shows a slow, steady decline during the preschool years, so that the chubby baby often looks much leaner by the end of early childhood. Girls have more fatty tissue than boys, and boys have more muscle tissue.

Growth patterns vary individually. Think back to your preschool years. This was probably the first time you noticed that some children were taller than you, some shorter; that some were fatter, some thinner; that some were stronger, some weaker. Much of the variation is due to heredity, but environmental experiences are involved to some extent. A review of the heights and weights of children around the world concluded that the two most important contributors to height differences are ethnic origin and nutrition (Meredith,

Physical growth, ages 3 to 6 (50th percentile)				
	Height (inches)		Weight (pounds)	
Age	Boys	Girls	Boys	Girls
3	38	37¾	32¼	31¾
3½	39¼	39¼	34¼	34
4	40¼	40½	36½	36¼
4½	42	42	38½	38½
5	43¼	43	41½	41
5½	45	44½	45½	44
6	46	46	48	47

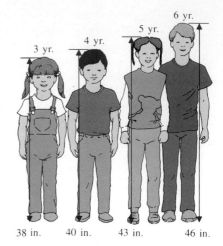

1978). Urban, middle-class, and firstborn children were taller than rural, lower-class, and later-born children. Children whose mothers smoked during pregnancy were ½ inch shorter than children whose mothers did not smoke during pregnancy. In the United States, Black children are taller than White children.

Motor Development

During your preschool years you probably developed the ability to perform all kinds of activities: running as fast as you can, falling down, getting right back up and running just as fast as you can . . . building towers with blocks . . . scribbling, scribbling, and more scribbling . . . cutting paper with scissors.

Gross Motor Skills

The preschool child no longer has to make an effort simply to stay upright and to move around. As children move their legs with more confidence and carry themselves more purposefully, the process of moving around in the environment becomes more automatic (Poest & others, 1990).

At 3 years of age, children are still enjoying simple movements such as hopping, jumping, and running back and forth, just for the sheer delight of performing these activities. They take considerable pride in showing how they can run across a room and jump all of 6 inches. The run-and-jump will win no Olympic gold medals, but for the 3-year-old the activity is a source of considerable pride and accomplishment.

By 4 years of age, children are still enjoying the same kind of activities, but they have become more adventuresome. They scramble over low jungle gyms as they display their athletic prowess. Although they have been able to climb stairs with one foot on each step for some time now, they are just beginning to be able to come down the same way. They often revert to marking time on each step.

By 5 years of age, children are even more adventuresome than they were at 4. As our description of Tony at the beginning of the chapter indicated, it is not unusual for self-assured 5-year-olds to perform hair-raising stunts on practically any climbing object. Five-year-olds run hard and enjoy races with each other and their parents.

You probably have arrived at one important conclusion about preschool children: They are very, very active. Indeed, researchers have found that 3-year-old children have the highest activity level of any age in the entire human life span. They fidget when they watch television. They fidget when they sit

The greatest poem ever known
Is one all poets have outgrown;
The poetry, innate, untold,
Of being only four years old.

~ *Christopher Morley*

Early Childhood

at the dinner table. Even when they sleep, they move around quite a bit. Because of their activity level and the development of large muscles, especially in the arms and legs, preschool children need daily exercise.

Fine Motor Skills

At 3 years of age, children are still learning to place and handle things. Although they have had the ability to pick up the tiniest objects between their thumb and forefinger for some time now, they are still somewhat clumsy at it. Three-year-olds can build surprisingly high block towers, each block being placed with intense concentration but often not in a completely straight line. When 3-year-olds play with a form board or a simple jigsaw puzzle, they are rather rough in placing the pieces. Even when they recognize the hole a piece fits into, they are not very precise in positioning the piece. They often try to force the piece in the hole or pat it vigorously.

At 4 years of age, children's fine motor coordination has improved substantially and become much more precise. Sometimes 4-year-old children have trouble building high towers with blocks because in their desire to place each of the blocks perfectly they may upset those already stacked. By age 5, children's fine motor coordination has improved further. Hand, arm, and body all move together under better command of the eye. Mere towers no longer interest the 5-year-old, who now wants to build a house or a church complete with steeple, though adults may still need to be told what each finished project is meant to be.

How do developmentalists measure motor development? The **Denver Developmental Screening Test** *is a widely used test that measures young children's motor development. It is especially helpful in assessing developmental delay in motor skills and can be used with children from birth through 6 years of age.* The test is individually administered and includes an evaluation of language and social skills, in addition to separate assessments of gross and fine motor skills. Among the gross motor skills that are measured are the child's ability to sit, walk, long jump, pedal a tricycle, throw a ball overhand, catch a bounced ball, hop on one foot, and balance on one foot. Fine motor skills that are measured include the child's ability to stack cubes, reach for objects, and draw a person.

Handedness

For centuries left-handers have suffered unfair discrimination in a world designed for the right-hander. Even the devil himself was portrayed as a left-hander. For many years, teachers forced all children to write with their right hand even if they had a left-handed tendency. Fortunately today, most teachers let children write with the hand they favor.

Some children are still discouraged from using their left hand, even though many left-handed individuals have become very successful. Their ranks include Leonardo da Vinci, Benjamin Franklin, and Pablo Picasso. Each of these famous men was known for his imagination of spatial layouts, which may be stronger in left-handed individuals. Left-handed athletes also are often successful; because there are fewer left-handed athletes, the opposition is not as accustomed to the style and approach of "lefties." Their serve in tennis spins in the opposite direction, their curve ball in baseball swerves the opposite way, and their left foot in soccer is not the one children are used to defending against. Left-handed individuals also do well intellectually. In an analysis of the Scholastic Aptitude Test (SAT) scores of more than 100,000 students, 20 percent of the top scoring group was left-handed, which is twice the rate of left-handedness found in the general population (Bower, 1985). Quite clearly, many

The young child's developing ability to hold a pencil or crayon reveals growth in fine motor coordination. Toddlers tend to grasp the pencil or crayon in the palm of their hand and make rough, crude movements with it. During early childhood, children become more proficient with pencils or crayons, learning to use their fingers and wrist to manipulate the tip rather than the whole pencil or crayon.

Table 8.1: Recommended Energy Intakes for Children
Ages 1 through 10

Age	Weight (kg)	Height (cm)	Energy Needs (calories)	Calorie Range
1–3	13	90	1,300	900 to 1,800
4–6	20	112	1,700	1,300 to 2,300
7–10	28	132	2,400	1,650 to 3,300

Source: Food and Nutrition Board, 1980.

left-handed people are competent in a wide variety of human activities ranging from athletic skills to intellectual accomplishments.

When does hand preference develop? Adults usually notice a child's hand preference during early childhood, but researchers have found handedness tendencies in the infant years. Even newborns have some preference for one side of their body over the other. In one research investigation, 65 percent of infants turned their heads to the right when they were lying on their stomachs in the crib. Fifteen percent preferred to face toward the left. These preferences for the right or left were related to later handedness (Michel, 1981). By about 7 months of age, infants prefer grabbing with one hand or the other, and this is also related to later handedness (Ramsay, 1980). By 2 years of age, about 10 percent of children favor their left hand (Hardyck & Petrinovich, 1977). Many preschool children, though, use both hands, with a clear hand preference not completely distinguished until later in development. Some children use one hand for writing and drawing, and the other hand for throwing a ball. My oldest daughter, Tracy, confuses the issue even further. She writes left-handed and plays tennis left-handed, but she plays golf right-handed. During her early childhood, her handedness was still somewhat in doubt. My youngest daughter, Jennifer, was left-handed from early in infancy. Their left-handed orientation has not handicapped them in their athletic and academic pursuits, although Tracy once asked me if I would buy her a pair of left-handed scissors.

What is the origin of hand preference? Genetic inheritance and environmental experiences have been proposed as causes. In one investigation, a genetic interpretation was favored. The handedness of adopted children was not related to the handedness of their adopted parents but was related to the handedness of their biological parents (Carter-Saltzman, 1980).

Nutrition

Four-year-old Bobby is on a steady diet of double cheeseburgers, french fries, and chocolate milkshakes. Between meals he gobbles up candy bars and marshmallows. He hates green vegetables. Only a preschooler, Bobby has already developed poor nutrition habits. What are a preschool child's energy needs? What is a preschooler's eating behavior like?

Energy Needs

Feeding and eating habits are important aspects of development during early childhood. What children eat affects their skeletal growth, body shape, and susceptibility to disease. Recognizing that nutrition is important for the child's growth and development, the federal government provides money for school lunch programs. An average preschool child requires 1,700 calories per day. Table 8.1 shows the increasing energy needs of children as they move from

Table 8.2: The Fat and Calorie Content of Selected Fast Foods

Food	Calories	% of Calories from Fat
Burger King Whopper, fries, vanilla shake	1,250	43
Big Mac, fries, chocolate shake	1,100	41
McDonald's Quarter-Pounder with cheese	418	52
Pizza Hut 10-inch pizza with sausage, mushrooms, pepperoni, and green pepper	1,035	35
Arby's roast beef sandwich, two potato patties, coleslaw, chocolate shake	1,200	30
Kentucky Fried Chicken dinner (three pieces chicken, mashed potatoes and gravy, coleslaw, roll)	830	50
Arthur Treacher's fish and chips (two pieces breaded and fried fish, french fries, cola drink)	900	42
Typical restaurant "diet plate" (hamburger patty, cottage cheese, etc.)	638	63

Reprinted by permission: Virginia DeMoss, "The Good, the Bad, and the Edible" in *Runner's World,* June 1980.

infancy through the childhood years. Energy requirements for individual children are determined by the **basal metabolism rate (BMR),** *which is the minimum amount of energy a person uses in a resting state.* Energy needs of individual children of the same age, sex, and size vary. Reasons for these differences remain unexplained. Differences in physical activity, basal metabolism, and the efficiency with which children use energy are among the candidates for explanation (Pipes, 1988).

Eating Behavior
A special concern in our culture is the amount of fat we consume. While some health-conscious mothers may be providing too little fat in their children's diets, other parents are raising their children on diets that are too high in fat. Our busy life-styles, in which we often eat on the run and pick up fast-food meals, probably contribute to the increased fat levels in children's diets. Although most fast-food meals are high in protein, especially meat and dairy products, the average American child does not need to be concerned about getting enough protein. What must be of concern is the vast number of young children who are being weaned on fast foods that are high in fat. Eating habits become ingrained very early in life, and unfortunately, it is during the preschool years that many people get their first taste of fast foods. The American Heart Association recommends that the daily limit for calories from fat should be approximately 35 percent. Compare this figure with the figures in table 8.2. Clearly, many fast-food meals contribute to excess fat intake by children.

Being overweight can be a serious problem in early childhood. Consider Ramon, a kindergartner who always begged to stay inside to help during recess. His teacher noticed that Ramon never joined the running games the small superheroes played as they propelled themselves around the playground. Ramon is an overweight 4-year-old boy. Except for extreme cases of obesity, overweight preschool children are usually not encouraged to lose a great deal of weight, but to slow their rate of weight gain so that they will grow into a more normal weight for their height by thinning out as they grow taller. Prevention of obesity in children includes helping children and parents see food as a way to satisfy their hunger and nutritional needs, not as proof of love or as a reward for good behavior. Snack foods should be low in fat, simple sugars, and salt, and high in fiber. Routine physical activity should be a daily occurrence. The child's life should be centered around activities, not meals (Javernik, 1988).

A simple child;
That lightly draws its breath
What should it know of death?

~ *William Wordsworth,*
"We Are Seven," 1878

• *Critical Thinking* •

What responsibility do the wealthier nations of the world have for fostering and financing health and nutrition services for children in developing countries?

The State of Illness and Health in the World's Children

A special concern is the state of children's illness and health in developing countries around the world. One of every three deaths in the world happens to a child under the age of 5 (Grant, 1991). Every week, more than a quarter of a million children die in developing countries in a quiet carnage of infection and undernutrition. The leading cause of childhood death in the world is diarrhea. However, approximately 70 percent of the more than 40 million children killed by diarrhea in 1989 could have been saved if parents had available a low-cost breakthrough known as **oral rehydration therapy (ORT),** *a treatment involving a range of techniques designed to prevent dehydration during episodes of diarrhea by giving the child a large volume of water and other liquids.*

Most child malnutrition, as well as most child deaths, could now be prevented by parental actions that are almost universally affordable and based on knowledge that is already available. Making sure that parents know they can improve their children's health by adequate birth spacing, prenatal care, breast-feeding, immunization, special feeding before and after illness, and regular checking of the child's weight can overcome many causes of malnutrition and poor growth in today's world.

Among the nations with the highest mortality rate under age 5 are Asian nations such as Afghanistan, and African nations such as Ethiopia (Grant, 1991). In 1986, for every 1,000 children born alive in Afghanistan, 325 died before the age of 5; in Ethiopia, the figure was 255 per 1,000. Among the countries with the lowest mortality rate under age 5 in 1986 were Scandinavian countries such as Sweden and Finland, where only 7 of every 1,000 children born died before the age of 5. The United States mortality rate under age 5 was better than that of most countries, but of 131 countries for which figures were available in 1986, 20 countries had better rates than the United States. For every 1,000 children born alive in the United States, 13 died before the age of 5.

Fortunately, in the United States the dangers of many diseases such as measles, rubella (German measles), mumps, whooping cough, diphtheria, and polio are no longer present. The vast majority of children in the United States have been immunized against such major childhood diseases. It is important,

Concept Table 8.1: Physical Development in Early Childhood

Concept	Processes/Related Ideas	Characteristics/Description
Body Growth and Changes	Their Nature	The average child grows 2½ inches in height and gains between 5 and 7 pounds a year during early childhood. Growth patterns vary individually, though.
Motor Development	Gross Motor Skills	Gross motor skills improve dramatically in early childhood. Children become increasingly adventuresome as their gross motor skills improve. Young children's lives are extremely active, more so than at any other period in the human life cycle.
	Fine Motor Skills	Fine motor skills improve substantially during early childhood. The Denver Developmental Screening Test is one widely used measure of gross and fine motor skills.
	Handedness	At one point, all children were taught to be right-handed. In today's world, the strategy is to let children use the hand they favor. Left-handed children are as competent in motor skills and intellect as right-handed children. Both genetic and environmental explanations of handedness have been given.
Nutrition	Energy Needs	Energy needs increase as children go through the childhood years. Energy requirements vary according to basal metabolism, rate of growth, and activity level.
	Eating Behavior	Many parents are raising children on diets that are too high in fat content. Children's diets should include well-balanced proportions of fats, carbohydrates, protein, vitamins, and minerals.
The State of Illness and Health in the World's Children	Extent of Children's Deaths and Their Prevention	One of every three deaths in the world is that of a child under 5. Every week, more than a quarter of a million children die in developing countries. The most frequent cause of children's death is diarrhea. Oral rehydration therapy can be used to prevent death from diarrhea. Most child malnutrition and death could be prevented by parental actions that are affordable and based on knowledge available today.
	Death and Illness in the United States Compared to Other Countries	The United States has a relatively low mortality rate for children compared to other countries, although the Scandinavian countries have the lowest rates. The disorders most likely to be fatal for American children in the preschool years are birth defects, cancer, and heart disease.

though, for parents to recognize that these diseases, while no longer afflicting our nation's children, do require a sequence of vaccinations. Without the vaccinations, children can still get the diseases.

The disorders most likely to be fatal during the preschool years are birth defects, cancer, and heart disease. Death rates from these problems have been reduced in recent years because of improved treatments and health care (Garrison and McQuiston, 1989).

At this point we have discussed a number of ideas about physical development in early childhood. A summary of these ideas is presented in concept table 8.1. Now we turn our attention to cognitive development in early childhood.

"Mrs. Hammond! I'd know you anywhere from little Billy's portrait of you."

Drawing by Frascino; © 1988 The New Yorker Magazine, Inc.

Cognitive Development in Early Childhood

The cognitive world of the preschool child is creative, free, and fanciful. In their art, suns sometimes show up as green, and skies as yellow. Cars float on clouds, pelicans kiss seals, and people look like tadpoles. Preschool children's imagination works overtime and their mental grasp of the world improves. Our coverage of cognitive development in early childhood focuses on Piaget's stage of preoperational thought, information processing, language development, Vygotsky's theory of development, and early childhood education.

Piaget's Stage of Preoperational Thought

Remember from chapter 6 that, during Piaget's sensorimotor stage of development, the infant progresses in the ability to organize and coordinate sensations and perceptions with physical movements and actions. What kinds of changes take place in the preoperational stage?

Since this stage of thought is called preoperational, it would seem that not much of importance occurs until full-fledged operational thought appears. Not so! The preoperational stage stretches from approximately 2 to 7 years of age. It is a time when stable concepts are formed, mental reasoning emerges, egocentrism begins strongly and then weakens, and magical beliefs are constructed. Preoperational thought is anything but a convenient waiting period for concrete operational thought, although the label *preoperational* emphasizes that the child at this stage does not yet think in an operational way. What are operations? **Operations** *are internalized sets of actions that allow the child to do mentally what was done physically before.* Operations are highly organized and conform to certain rules and principles of logic. The operations appear in one form in concrete operational thought and in another form in formal operational thought. Thought in the preoperational stage is flawed and not well organized. Preoperational thought is the beginning of the ability to reconstruct at the level of thought what has been established in behavior. Preoperational thought also involves a transition from primitive to more sophisticated use of symbols. Preoperational thought can be divided into two substages: the symbolic function substage and the intuitive thought substage.

Symbolic Function Substage

The **symbolic function substage** *is the first substage of preoperational thought, occurring roughly between the ages of 2 and 4. In this substage, the young child gains the ability to mentally represent an object that is not present.* The ability to engage in such symbolic thought is called symbolic function, and it vastly expands the child's mental world. Young children use scribbled designs to represent people, houses, cars, clouds, and so on. More on young children's scribbles and art appears in Perspective on Life-Span Development 8.1. Other examples of symbolism in early childhood are the prevalence of pretend play (discussed in chapter 9) and language. In sum, the ability to think symbolically and represent the world mentally predominates in this early substage of preoperational thought. However, although young children make distinct progress during this substage, their thought still has several important limitations, two of which are egocentrism and animism.

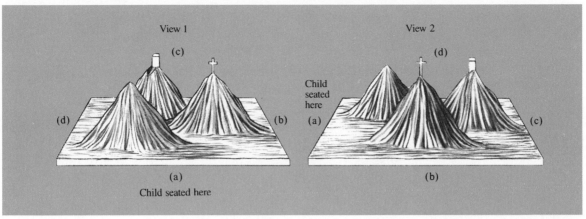

View 1

(c)

(d)

(d)   (b)

(a)

Child seated here

View 2

Child
seated
here

(d)

(a)   (c)

(b)

Figure 8.2   The three mountains task. View 1 shows the child's perspective from where he or she is sitting. View 2 is an example of the photograph the child would be shown mixed in with others from different perspectives. For children to correctly identify this view, they have to take the perspective of a person sitting at spot (b). Invariably, the preschool child who thinks in a preoperational way cannot perform this task. When asked what the perspective or view of the mountains will look like from position (b), children select a photograph taken from location (a), the view they have at the time.

Egocentrism *is a salient feature of preoperational thought. It is the inability to distinguish between one's own perspective and someone else's perspective.* The following telephone conversation between 4-year-old Mary, who is at home, and her father, who is at work, typifies Mary's egocentric thought:

Father: Mary, is Mommy there?
Mary: (Silently nods.)
Father: Mary, may I speak to Mommy?
Mary: (Nods again silently.)

Mary's response is egocentric in that she fails to consider her father's perspective before replying. A nonegocentric thinker would have responded verbally.

Piaget and Barbel Inhelder (1969) initially studied young children's egocentrism by devising the three mountains task (figure 8.2). The child walks around the model of the mountains and becomes familiar with what the mountains look like from different perspectives. The child can see that different objects are on the mountains as well. The child is then seated on one side of the table on which the mountains are placed. The experimenter takes a doll and moves it to different locations around the table, at each location asking the child to select one photo from a series of photos that most accurately reflects the view the doll is seeing. Children in the preoperational stage often pick the photo that shows the view they have rather than the view the doll has. Perspective-taking does not seem to develop uniformly in the preschool child, who frequently shows perspective-taking skills on some tasks but not others (Shantz, 1983).

Animism, *another facet of preoperational thought, is the belief that inanimate objects have "lifelike" qualities and are capable of action.* The young child might show animism by saying, "That tree pushed the leaf off, and it fell down," or "The sidewalk made me mad; it made me fall down." The young child who uses animism fails to distinguish the appropriate occasions for using human and nonhuman perspectives. Some developmentalists, though, believe that animism represents incomplete knowledge and understanding, not a general conception of the world (Dolgin & Behrend, 1984).

False would be a picture which insisted on the brutal egocentrism of the child, and ignored the physical beauty which softens it.

~ *A. A. Milne*

WHERE PELICANS KISS SEALS, CARS FLOAT ON CLOUDS, AND HUMANS ARE TADPOLES

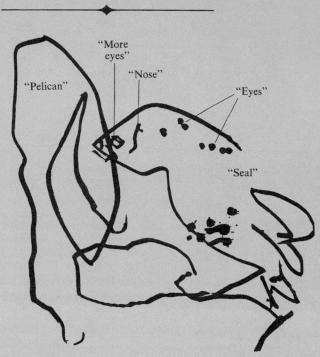

Figure 8.A   *A 3½-year-old's symbolic drawing. Halfway into this drawing, the 3½-year-old artist said it was "a pelican kissing a seal."*

At about 3 years of age and sometimes even 2, children's spontaneous scribbles begin to resemble pictures. One 3½-year-old child looked at the scribble he had just drawn and said it was a pelican kissing a seal (figure 8.A). At about 3 to 4 years of age, children begin to create symbols of humans. Invariably the first symbols look curiously like tadpoles; see the circle and two lines in figure 8.B—the circle represents a head and the two lines are legs.

These observations of children's drawings were made by Denise Wolf, Carol Fucigna, and Howard Gardner at Harvard University. They point out that many people think young children draw a person in this rather odd way because it is the best they can do. Piaget said children intend their drawings to be realistic; they draw what they know rather than what they see. So the tadpole with its strange exemptions of trunk and arms might reflect a child's lack of knowledge of the human body and how its parts fit together. However, children know more about the human body than they are capable of drawing. One 3-year-old child drew a tadpole but described it in complete detail, pointing out where the feet, chin, and neck were. When 3- and 4-year-old children are asked to draw someone

playing ball, they produce symbols of humans that include arms, since the task implicitly requires arms.

Possibly because preschool children are not very concerned about reality, their drawings are fanciful and inventive.

Suns are blue, skies are yellow, trees are purple, and cars float on clouds in the preschool child's symbolic world. The symbolism is simple but strong, not unlike the abstractions found in some contemporary art. In the elementary

Figure 8.B *A 3-year-old's drawing of a person. Many 3-year-olds' drawings of persons look curiously like tadpoles.*

Figure 8.C *Elementary school children's drawings are neater and more realistic than preschool children's, but they also are often less inventive.*

school years, the child's symbols become more realistic, neat, and precise. Suns are yellow, skies are blue, trees are green, and cars are placed on roads (figure 8.C).

A child's ability to symbolically represent the world on paper is related to the development of perceptual motor skills. But once such skills are developed, some artists revert to the style of young children's drawings. As Picasso once commented, "I used to draw like Raphael but it has taken me a whole lifetime to learn to draw like children" (Winner, 1986).

Intuitive Thought Substage

Tommy is 4 years old. Although he is starting to develop his own ideas about the world in which he lives, his ideas are still simple and he is not very good at thinking things out. He has difficulty understanding events he knows are taking place but cannot see. His fantasized thoughts bear little resemblance to reality. He cannot yet answer the question, What if? in any reliable way. For example, he has only a vague idea of what would happen if a car hit him. He also has difficulty negotiating traffic because he cannot do the mental calculations necessary to estimate whether an approaching car will hit him when he crosses the road (Goodman, 1979).

The **intuitive thought substage** *is the second substage of preoperational thought, occurring between approximately 4 and 7 years of age. In this substage, children begin to use primitive reasoning and want to know the answers to all sorts of questions. Piaget called this time period* intuitive *because, on*

Physical and Cognitive Development in Early Childhood

Figure 8.3 Sorting objects. (a) A random array of objects. (b) An ordered array of objects.

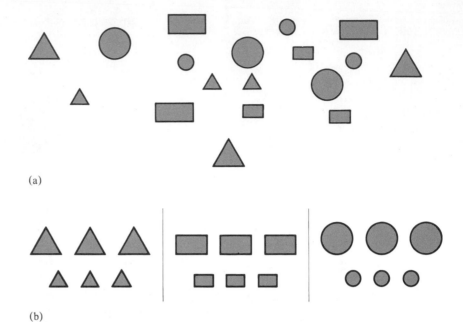

(a)

(b)

Figure 8.4 Piaget's conservation task. The beaker test is a well-known Piagetian test to determine whether a child can think operationally, that is, can mentally reverse actions and show conservation of the substance. (a) Two identical beakers are presented to the child. The experimenter pours the liquid from B into C, which is taller and thinner than A or B. (b) The child is then asked if these beakers (A and C) have the same amount of liquid. The preoperational child says no. When asked to point to the beaker that has more liquid, the preoperational child points to the tall, thin beaker.

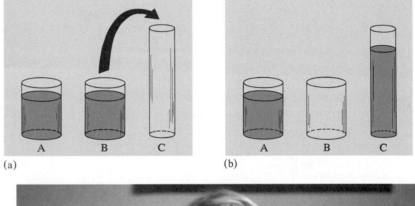

(a)   (b)

the one hand, young children seem so sure about their knowledge and understanding, yet are so unaware of how they know what they know. That is, they say they know something but know it without the use of rational thinking.

An example of young children's reasoning ability is the difficulty they have putting things into correct categories. Faced with a random collection of objects that can be grouped together on the basis of two or more properties, preoperational children are seldom capable of using these properties consistently to sort the objects into appropriate groupings. Look at the collection of objects in figure 8.3a. You would respond to the direction "Put the things together that you believe belong together" by sorting the characteristics of size and shape together. Your sorting might look something like that shown in figure 8.3b. In the social realm, the 4-year-old girl might be given the task of dividing her peers into groups according to whether they are friends and whether they are boys or girls. She would be unlikely to arrive at the following classification: friendly boys, friendly girls, unfriendly boys, unfriendly girls. Another example of classification shortcomings involves the preoperational child's understanding of religious concepts (Elkind, 1976). When asked, "Can you be a Protestant and an American at the same time?" 6- and 7-year-olds usually say no; 9-year-olds are likely to say yes, understanding that objects can be cross-classified simultaneously.

Many of these examples show a characteristic of preoperational thought called **centration**—*the focusing, or centering, of attention on one characteristic to the exclusion of all others.* Centration is most clearly evidenced in young children's lack of **conservation**—*the idea that an amount stays the same regardless of how its containers change.* To adults, it is obvious that a certain amount of liquid stays the same regardless of a container's shape. But this is not obvious at all to young children; instead, they are struck by the height of the liquid in the container. In the conservation task—Piaget's most famous— a child is presented with two identical beakers, each filled to the same level with liquid (figure 8.4). When asked if these beakers have the same amount of liquid, the child usually says yes. Then, the liquid from one beaker is poured into a third beaker, which is taller and thinner than the first two. The child is then asked if the amount of liquid in the tall, thin beaker is equal to that which remains in one of the original beakers. Children who are less than 7 or 8 years old usually say no and justify their answers in terms of the differing height or width of the beakers. Older children usually answer yes and justify their answers appropriately ("If you poured the milk back, the amount would still be the same").

In Piaget's theory, failing the conservation of liquid task is a sign that children are at the preoperational stage of cognitive development, while passing this test is a sign that they are at the concrete operational stage. In Piaget's view, the preoperational child not only fails to show conservation of liquid, but also of number, matter, length, volume, and area (figure 8.5). The child's inability to mentally reverse actions is an important characteristic of preoperational thought. For example, in the conservation of matter shown in figure 8.5, preoperational children almost always say that the longer shape has more clay because they assume that "longer is more." Preoperational children cannot mentally reverse the clay-rolling process to see that the amount of clay is the same in both the shorter ball-shape and the longer stick-shape.

Some developmentalists do not believe Piaget was entirely correct in his estimate of when children's conservation skills emerge. For example, Rochel Gelman (1969; Gelman & Baillargeon, 1983) has shown that by improving the child's attention to relevant aspects of the conservation task, the child is

Figure 8.5 Some dimensions of conservation: number, matter, length, volume, and area.

Type of conservation	Initial presentation	Manipulation	Preoperational child's answer
Number	Two identical rows of objects are shown to the child, who agrees they have the same number.	 One row is lengthened and the child is asked whether one row now has more objects.	Yes, the longer row.
Matter	Two identical balls of clay are shown to the child. The child agrees they are equal.	The experimenter changes the shape of one of the balls and asks the child whether they still contain equal amounts of clay.	No, the longer one has more.
Length	Two sticks are aligned in front of the child. The child agrees that they are the same length.	The experimenter moves one stick to the right, then asks the child if they still are equal in length.	No, the one on the top is longer.
Volume	Two balls are placed in two identical glasses with an equal amount of water. The child sees the balls displace equal amounts of water.	The experimenter changes the shape of one of the balls and asks the child if it still will displace the same amount of water.	No, the longer one on the right displaces more.
Area	Two identical sheets of cardboard have wooden blocks placed on them in identical positions. The child agrees that the same amount of space is left on each piece of cardboard.	The experimenter scatters the blocks on one piece of cardboard and then asks the child if one of the cardboard pieces has more space covered up.	Yes, the one on the right has more space covered up.

more likely to conserve. Gelman has also demonstrated that attentional training on one type of task, such as numbers, improves the preschool child's performance on another type of task, such as mass. Thus, Gelman believes that conservation appears earlier than Piaget thought, and that the process of attention is especially important in explaining conservation.

Yet another characteristic of preoperational children is that they ask a barrage of questions. Children's earliest questions appear around the age of

| More symbolic than sensorimotor thought | Inability to engage in operations; can't mentally reverse actions; lacks conservation skills | Egocentric (inability to distinguish between own perspective and someone else's) | Intuitive rather than logical |

Figure 8.6 Preoperational thought's characteristics.

3, and by the age of 5, they have just about exhausted the adults around them with "Why" questions. The child's questions yield clues about mental development and reflect intellectual curiosity. These questions signal the emergence of the child's interest in reasoning and figuring out why things are the way they are. Samples of the questions children ask during the questioning period of 4 to 6 years of age are (Elkind, 1976):

"What makes you grow up?"
"What makes you stop growing?"
"Why does a lady have to be married to have a baby?"
"Who was the mother when everybody was a baby?"
"Why do leaves fall?"
"Why does the sun shine?"

At this point we have discussed a number of characteristics of preoperational thought. To help you remember these characteristics, turn to figure 8.6.

Earlier we mentioned that Gelman's research demonstrated that children may fail a Piagetian task because of their failure to attend to relevant dimensions of the task—length, shape, density, and so on. Gelman and other developmentalists also believe that many of the tasks used to assess cognitive development may not be sensitive to the child's cognitive abilities. Thus, rather than limitations on cognitive development, the limitations may be due to the tasks used to assess cognitive development. Gelman's research reflects the thinking of information-processing psychologists who place considerable importance on the tasks and procedures involved in assessing children's cognition.

"I still don't have all the answers, but I'm beginning to ask the right questions."

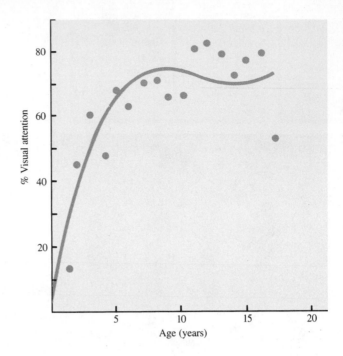

Figure 8.7 Increase in visual attention to TV during the preschool years. Visual attention to television dramatically increased during the preschool years. In this elaborate study, two video cameras and a time lapse recorder were used to observe children's attention to television in their homes.

Information Processing

Not only can we study the stages of cognitive development that young children go through, as Piaget did, but we can also study the different cognitive processes of young children's mental worlds. Two limitations on preschool children's thoughts are attention and memory, important domains involved in the way young children process information. Advances in these two domains are made during early childhood. What are the limitations and advances in attention and memory during the preschool years?

Attention

Remember from chapter 6 that attention was discussed in the context of habituation, which is something like being bored, in that the infant becomes disinterested in a stimulus and no longer attends to it. Habituation can actually be described as a decrement in attention, while dishabituation is the recovery of attention. The importance of these aspects of attention in infancy for the preschool years was underscored by research showing that both decrement and recovery of attention, when measured in the first six months of infancy, were associated with higher intelligence in the preschool years (Bornstein & Sigman, 1986).

While the infant's attention has important implications for cognitive development in the preschool years, significant changes in the child's ability to pay attention take place in the preschool years. The toddler wanders around, shifting attention from one activity to another, generally seeming to spend little time focused on any one object or event. By comparison, the preschool child might be observed watching television for a half-hour. In one investigation, young children's attention to television in the natural setting of the home was videotaped (Anderson & others, 1985). Ninety-nine families that included 460 individuals were observed for 4,672 hours. Visual attention to television dramatically increased during the preschool years (figure 8.7).

One deficit in attention during the preschool years concerns those dimensions that stand out or are *salient* compared to those that are relevant to solving a problem or performing well on a task. For example, a problem might

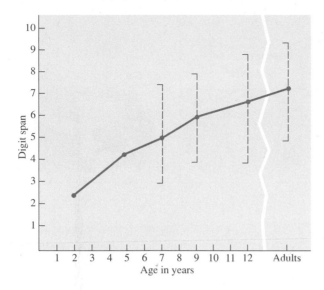

Figure 8.8 Memory span and age. In one investigation, memory span increased from about two digits in 2- to 3-year-old children to about five digits in 7-year-old children (Dempster, 1981). Between 7 and 13 years of age, memory span only increased by 1½ digits. The brackets represent how widely the memory span scores varied at different ages.

have a flashy, attractive clown that presents the directions for solving a problem. Preschool children are influenced strongly by the features of the task that stand out, such as the flashy, attractive clown. After the age of 6 or 7, children attend more efficiently to the dimensions of the task that are relevant, such as the directions for solving a problem. Developmentalists believe this change reflects a shift to cognitive control of attention so that children act less impulsively and reflect more (Paris & Lindauer, 1982).

Memory

Memory is a central process in children's cognitive development; it involves the retention of information over time. Conscious memory comes into play as early as 7 months of age, although children and adults have little or no memory of events experienced before the age of 3. Among the interesting questions about memory in the preschool years are those involving short-term memory.

In **short-term memory,** *individuals retain information for up to 15 to 30 seconds, assuming there is no rehearsal.* Using rehearsal, we can keep information in short-term memory for a much longer period. One method of assessing short-term memory is the memory-span task. If you have taken an IQ test, you were probably exposed to one of these tasks. You simply hear a short list of stimuli—usually digits—presented at a rapid pace (one per second, for example). Then you are asked to repeat the digits. Research with the memory-span task suggests that short-term memory increases during early childhood. For example, in one investigation, memory span increased from about two digits in 2- to 3-year-old children to about five digits in 7-year-old children; yet between 7 and 13 years of age, memory span increased only by 1½ digits (Dempster, 1981) (see figure 8.8). Keep in mind, though, the individual differences in memory span, which is why IQ and various aptitude tests are used.

Why are there differences in memory span because of age? Rehearsal of information is important; older children rehearse the digits more than younger children. Speed and efficiency of processing information are important too, especially the speed with which memory items can be identified. For example, in one investigation, children were tested on their speed at repeating words presented orally (Case, Kurland, & Goldberg, 1982). Speed of repetition was a powerful predictor of memory span. Indeed, when the speed of repetition was controlled, the 6-year-olds' memory spans were equal to those of young adults!

I come into the fields and spacious palaces of my memory, where are treasures of countless images of things in every manner.

~ St. Augustine

• *Critical Thinking* •

How extensively do you think children's memory span can be improved through the use of strategies? Are there limits on how much improvement can be made? Explain your answer.

The speed-of-processing explanation highlights an important point in the information processing perspective. That is, the speed with which a child processes information is an important aspect of the child's cognitive abilities.

Task Analysis

Another major emphasis in the information processing perspective is identifying the components of the task the child is performing (Klahr, 1989). Information processing psychologists are intrigued by the possibility that if tasks are made interesting and simple, children may display greater cognitive maturity than Piaget realized. This strategy was followed to determine if preschool children could reason about a *syllogism*—a type of reasoning problem, consisting of two premises, or statements, assumed to be true, plus a conclusion (Hawkins & others, 1984). To simplify problems, words such as *some* and *all* were made implicit rather than explicit. The problems focused on fantasy creatures alien from practical knowledge. Imagine how wide a child's eyes become when told stories about purple bangas who sneeze at people and merds who laugh don't like mushrooms (see figure 8.9). The following are two syllogisms that were read to children:

Every banga is purple.
Purple animals always sneeze at people.
Do bangas sneeze at people?

Merds laugh when they're happy.
Animals that laugh don't like mushrooms.
Do merds like mushrooms?

By simplifying the problem and making its dimensions more understandable to young children, the researchers demonstrated that preschool children can reason about syllogisms.

Language Development

Young children's understanding sometimes gets way ahead of their speech. One 3-year-old, laughing with delight as an abrupt summer breeze stirred his hair and tickled his skin, commented, "It did winding me!" Adults would be understandably perplexed if a young child ventured, "Anything is not to break, only plates and glasses," when she meant, "Nothing is breaking except plates and glasses." Many of the oddities of young children's language sound like mistakes to adult listeners. But from the children's point of view, they are not mistakes; they represent the way young children perceive and understand their world at that point in their development.

Remember from our discussion of language development in chapter 6 that language consists of rule systems such as those involving morphology, syntax, semantics, and pragmatics. What kinds of changes take place in these rule systems during early childhood?

As children move beyond two-word utterances, there is clear evidence that they know morphology rules. Children begin using the plurals and possessive forms of nouns (e.g., *dogs* and *dog's*), putting appropriate endings on verbs (e.g., *s* when the subject is third-person singular, *-ed* for the past tense, and *-ing* for the present progressive tense), using prepositions (*in* and *on*), articles (e.g., *a* and *the*), and various forms of the verb *to be* (e.g., "I was going to the store"). Some of the best evidence for changes in children's use of morphological rules occur in their overgeneralizations of the rules. Have you ever heard a preschool child say "foots" instead of "feet," or "goed" instead of "went"? If you do not remember having heard such oddities, talk to some parents who have young children, or to the young children themselves. You will hear some interesting errors in the use of morphological rule endings.

In a classic experiment, child language researcher Jean Berko (1958) presented preschool children and first-grade children with cards such as the one shown in figure 8.10. Children were asked to look at the card while the experimenter read the words on the card aloud. Then the children were asked to supply the missing word. This might sound easy, but Berko was interested not just in the children's ability to recall the right word, but also in their ability to say it "correctly" (with the ending that was dictated by morphological rules). "Wugs" would be the correct response for the card in figure 8.10. Although the children's answers were not always accurate, they were much better than chance. Moreover, the children demonstrated their knowledge of morphological rules not only with the plural forms of nouns ("There are two wugs"), but also with possessive forms of nouns and with the third-person singular and past-tense forms of verbs. What makes the study by Berko impressive is that most of the words were fictional; they were created especially for the experiment. Thus, the children could not base their responses on remembering past instances of hearing the words. It seems, instead, that they were forced to rely on *rules*. Their performance suggested that they did so successfully.

Similar evidence that children learn and actively apply rules can be found at the level of syntax. After advancing beyond two-word utterances, children speak word sequences that show a growing mastery of complex rules for how words should be ordered. Consider the case of *wh-* questions: "Where is Daddy going?" and "What is that boy doing?" for example. To ask these questions properly, the child has to know two important differences between *wh-* questions and simple affirmative statements (e.g., "Daddy is going to work" and "That boy is waiting on the school bus"). First, a *wh-* word must be added at the beginning of the sentence. Second, the auxiliary verb must be "inverted"—that is, exchanged with the subject of the sentence. Young children learn quite early where to put the *wh-* word, but they take much longer to learn the auxiliary-inversion rule. Thus, it is common to hear preschool children asking such questions as "Where daddy is going?" and "What that boy is doing?"

As children move into the elementary school years, they become skilled at using syntactical rules to construct lengthy and complex sentences (Singer, 1991). Sentences such as "The man who fixed the house went home" and "I don't want you to use my bike" are impressive demonstrations of how the child can use syntax to combine ideas into a single sentence. How young children achieve the mastery of such complex rules and yet struggle with relatively simple arithmetic rules is a mystery we must still solve.

Figure 8.10 Stimuli in Berko's study of young children's understanding of morphological rules. In Jean Berko's (1958) study, young children were presented cards such as this one with a "wug" on it. Then the children were asked to supply the missing word; in supplying the missing word, they had to say it correctly, too. "Wugs" is the correct response here.

"No, Timmy, not 'I sawed the chair'; it's 'I *saw* the chair' or 'I *have seen* the chair'."

© Glenn Bernhardt.

But whatever the process, the result is wonderful, gradually from naming an object we advance step-by-step until we have traversed the vast difference between our first stammered syllable and the sweep of thought in a line of Shakespeare.

~ *Helen Keller*

Physical and Cognitive Development in Early Childhood

Regarding semantics, as children move beyond the two-word stage, their knowledge of meanings also rapidly advances. The speaking vocabulary of a 6-year-old child ranges from 8,000 to 14,000 words (Carey, 1977). Assuming that word learning began when the child was 12 months old, this translates into a rate of five to eight new word meanings a day between the ages of 1 and 6. After five years of word learning, the 6-year-old child does not slow down. According to some estimates, the average child of this age is moving along at the awe-inspiring rate of 22 words a day (Miller, 1981)! How would you fare if you were given the task of learning 22 new words every day? It is truly miraculous how quickly children learn language (Rice, 1991; Winner & Gardner, 1988).

Although there are many differences between a 2-year-old's language and a 6-year-old's language, none are more important than those pertaining to pragmatics—that is, rules of conversation (Becker, 1991). A 6-year-old is simply a much better conversationalist than a 2-year-old is. What are some of the improvements in pragmatics that are made in the preschool years? At about 3 years of age, children improve in their ability to talk about things that are not physically present; that is, they improve their command of the characteristic of language known as displacement. One way displacement is revealed is in games of pretend. Although a 2-year-old might know the word *table,* he is unlikely to use this word to refer to an imaginary table that he pretends is standing in front of him. But a child over 3 probably has this ability, even if he does not always use it. There are large individual differences in preschoolers' talk about imaginary people and things.

Somewhat later in the preschool years—at about 4 years of age—children develop a remarkable sensitivity to the needs of others in conversation (Gleason, 1988). One way in which they show such sensitivity is their use of the articles *the* and *a* (or *an*). When adults tell a story or describe an event, they generally use *an* (or *a*) when they first refer to an animal or an object, and then use *the* when referring to it later (e.g., "Two boys were walking through the jungle when *a* fierce lion appeared. *The* lion lunged at one boy while the other ran for cover"). Even 3-year-olds follow part of this rule (they consistently use the word *the* when referring to previously mentioned things). However, using the word *a* when something is initially mentioned develops more slowly. Although 5-year-olds follow this rule on some occasions, they fail to follow it on others.

Vygotsky's Theory of Development

Children's cognitive and language development do not develop in a social vacuum. Lev Vygotsky (1896–1934), a Russian psychologist, recognized this important point about children's minds more than half a century ago. Vygotsky's theory is receiving increased attention as we move toward the close of the twentieth century (Belmont, 1989; Glick, 1991; Moll, 1991; Rogoff, in press; Rogoff & Morelli, 1989). Before we turn to Vygotsky's ideas on language and thought, and culture and society, let's examine his important concept called the zone of proximal development.

Zone of Proximal Development
The **zone of proximal development** (**ZPD**) *is Vygotsky's term for tasks too difficult for children to master alone, but that can be mastered with the guidance and assistance of adults or more skilled children.* Thus, the lower limit

Early Childhood

Figure 8.11 Vygotsky's zone of proximal development.

Upper limit — Level of additional responsibility child can accept with assistance of an able instructor

Zone of proximal development (ZPD)

Lower limit — Tasks too difficult for children to master alone; level of problem solving reached on these tasks by child working alone

Vygotsky's zone of proximal development has a lower limit and an upper limit. Tasks in the ZPD are too difficult for the child to perform alone. They require assistance from an adult or a skilled child. As children experience the verbal instruction or demonstration, they organize the information in their existing mental structures so they can eventually perform the skill or task alone.

of the ZPD is the level of problem solving reached by a child working independently. The upper limit is the level of additional responsibility the child can accept with the assistance of an able instructor (see figure 8.11). Vygotsky's emphasis on ZPD underscored his belief in the importance of social influences on cognitive development and the role of instruction in children's development.

The ZPD is conceptualized as a measure of learning potential. IQ is also a measure of learning potential. However, IQ emphasizes that intelligence is a property of the child, while ZPD emphasizes that learning is interpersonal, a dynamic social event that depends on a minimum of two minds, one better informed or more drilled than the other. It is inappropriate to say that the child *has* a ZPD; rather, a child *shares* a ZPD with an instructor.

The practical teaching involved in ZPD begins toward the zone's upper limit, where the child is able to reach the goal only through close collaboration with the instructor. With adequate continuing instruction and practice, the child organizes and masters the behavioral sequences necessary to perform the target skill. As the instruction continues, the performance transfers from the instructor to the child as the teacher gradually reduces the explanations, hints, and demonstrations until the child is able to adequately perform alone. Once the goal is achieved, it may become the foundation for the development of a new ZPD.

Learning by toddlers provides an example of how the ZPD works. The toddler has to be motivated and must be involved in activities that involve the skill at a reasonably high level of difficulty—that is, toward the zone's upper

Physical and Cognitive Development in Early Childhood

end. The teacher must have the know-how to exercise the target skill at any level required by the activity, and must be able to locate and stay in the zone. The teacher and the child have to adapt to each other's requirements. The reciprocal relationship between the toddler and the teacher adjusts dynamically as the division of labor is negotiated and aimed at increasing the weaker partner's share of the goal attainment.

In one research investigation of toddler-mother dyads, the pair was put to work on a number of problems with arrays of various numbers (few versus many objects) and varying complexity (simple counting versus number reproduction) (Saxe, Guberman, & Gearhart, 1987). The mothers were told to treat this as an opportunity to encourage learning and understanding of their children. Based on videotaped interactions of the mothers and their toddlers, the mothers adjusted their task goals to meet their children's abilities. Importantly, the mothers also adjusted the quality of their assistance during the problem-solution period in direct response to the children's successes and failures.

Language and Thought

In Vygotsky's view, the child's mental or cognitive structures are made of relations between mental functions. The relation between language and thought is believed to be especially important in this regard (Langer, 1969; Vygotsky, 1962). Vygotsky said that language and thought initially develop independently of each other but eventually merge.

Two principles govern the merging of thought and language. First, all mental functions have external or social origins. Children must use language and communicate with others before they focus inward to their own mental processes. Second, children must communicate externally and use language for a long period of time before the transition from external to internal speech takes place. This transition period occurs between 3 and 7 years of age and involves talking to oneself. After a while, the self-talk becomes second nature to children and they can act without verbalizing. When this occurs, children have internalized their egocentric speech in the form of inner speech, which becomes the thoughts of the child. Vygotsky believed that children who engage in a large amount of private speech are more socially competent than those who do not use it extensively. He argued that private speech represents an early transition in becoming more socially communicative.

Vygotsky's theory challenges Piaget's ideas on language and thought. Vygotsky argued that language, even in its earliest forms, is socially based, whereas Piaget emphasized young children's egocentric and nonsocially oriented speech. Young children talk to themselves to govern their behavior and to guide themselves (Duncan, 1991). By contrast, Piaget stressed that young children's egocentric speech reflects social and cognitive immaturity.

Culture and Society

Many developmentalists who work in the field of culture and development find themselves comfortable with Vygotsky's theory, which focuses on the sociocultural context of development (Rogoff & Morelli, 1989). Vygotsky's theory offers a portrayal of human development that is inseparable from social and cultural activities. Vygotsky emphasized how the development of higher mental processes such as memory, attention, and reasoning involve learning to use the inventions of society, such as language, mathematical systems, and memory devices. He also emphasized how children are aided in development by the guidance of individuals who are already skilled in these tools. Vygotsky's emphasis on the role of culture and society in cognitive development contrasts with Piaget's description of the solitary little scientist.

Vygotsky stressed both the institutional and the interpersonal levels of social contexts. At the institutional level, cultural history provides organizations and tools useful to cognitive activity through institutions such as schools, inventions such as computers, and literacy. Institutional interaction gives the child broad behavioral and societal norms to guide their lives. The interpersonal level has a more direct influence on the child's mental functioning. According to Vygotsky (1962), skills in mental functioning develop through immediate social interaction. Information about cognitive tools, skills, and interpersonal relations are transmitted through direct interaction with people. Through the organization of these social interactional experiences embedded in a cultural backdrop, children's mental development matures. More information about the role of culture in children's cognitive development appears in Cultural Worlds of Development 8.1, where you will read about cultural similarities and variations in children's thinking apprenticeships.

Early Childhood Education

With increased understanding of how young children develop and learn has come greater emphasis on the education of young children. We explore the following questions about early childhood education: What is child-centered kindergarten? What are developmentally appropriate and inappropriate practices in programs for young children? Does it really matter if children attend preschool before kindergarten? What are the effects of early childhood education? What is the nature of education for disadvantaged young children? We consider each of these questions in turn.

Child-Centered Kindergarten

Kindergarten programs vary a great deal. Some approaches place more emphasis on young children's social development, others on their cognitive development. Some experts on early childhood education believe that the curriculum of too many of today's kindergarten and preschool programs place too much emphasis on achievement and success, putting pressure on young children too early in their development (Bredekamp & Shepard, 1989; Burts & others, in press; Charlesworth, 1989; Elkind, 1987, 1988; Moyer, Egertson, & Isenberg, 1987). Placing such heavy emphasis on success is not what kindergartens were originally intended to do. In the 1840s, Friedrich Froebel's concern for quality education for young children led to the founding of the kindergarten, literally "a garden for children." The founder of the kindergarten understood that, like growing plants, children require careful nurturing. *Unfortunately, too many of today's kindergartens have forgotten the importance of careful nurturing for our nation's young children.*

In the **child-centered kindergarten,** *education involves the whole child and includes concern for the child's physical, cognitive, and social development. Instruction is organized around the child's needs, interests, and learning styles. The process of learning, rather than what is learned, is emphasized.* Each child follows a unique developmental pattern, and young children learn

> Learning is an ornament in prosperity, a refuge in diversity.
>
> ~ *Aristotle*

CULTURAL SIMILARITIES AND VARIATIONS IN THINKING APPRENTICESHIPS

*A*ccording to American developmental psychologist Barbara Rogoff (1990), children's cognitive development is an apprenticeship, which occurs through guided participation in social activity with companions who stretch and support children's understanding of and skill in using the "tools" of the culture. Some of the technologies that are important tools for handling information in a culture are language systems that organize categories of reality and structure ways of approaching situations, literate practices to record information and transform it through written exercises, mathematical systems that handle numerical and spatial problems, and memory strategies that preserve information in memory over time. Some of these technologies have material supports, such as pencils and paper, word-processing programs, alphabets, calculators, abacus and slide rules, notches on sticks, and knots on ropes. These tools provide mechanisms for transmitting information from one generation to the next.

In presenting her ideas on apprenticeship in thinking, Rogoff draws heavily on Vygotsky's theory. Rogoff argues that guided participation is widely used around the world, but with important variations in arrangements for, and communication with, children in different cultures. The most salient differences focus on the goals of development—what lessons are to be learned—and the means available for children either to observe and participate in culturally important activities or to receive instruction outside the context of skilled activity.

The general processes of guided participation appear around the world. Caregivers and children make arrangements for children's activities and

Apprenticeship training is an important aspect of children's cognitive development. Through guided participation, children learn about the skills and tools of the culture. For example, with regard to language, most middle-class American children are given a number of picture books, which their parents read to or with them.

revise children's responsibilities as they gain skill and knowledge. With the guidance of those around them, children participate in cultural activities that socialize them into skilled activities. For example, Mayan mothers in Guatemala help their daughters learn to weave in a process of guided participation (Rogoff, 1990). And in the United States and many other nations, the development of prominent and creative thinkers is promoted by interacting with a knowledgeable person rather than by studying books or by attending classes and exhibits (John-Steiner, 1985).

Skills for the use of cultural tools such as literacy begin to be practiced even before children have contact with the technology itself. American middle-class parents involve their children in extensive conversation long before they

go to kindergarten or elementary school. And they provide their young children with picture books and read stories to them at bedtime as part of their daily routine. Middle-class American parents embed their children in a way of life in which reading and writing are integral parts of communication, recreation, and livelihood (Cazden, 1988; Rogoff, 1990).

By contrast, consider the practices of two communities whose children have trouble reading (Heath, 1983). Parents in an Appalachian mill town taught their children respect for the written word, but did not involve book characters or information in the children's everyday lives. Their children did well in the first several years of learning to read, but the children had difficulty when required to *use* these literate skills to express themselves or interpret text. Children of rural origin in a mill town learned skillful and creative use of language, but were not taught about books or the style of communication and language used in school. These children had difficulty learning to read, which kept them from using their creative skills with language in the school setting. Early childhood in both of these communities did not include school-style reading and writing in the context of daily life, and not surprisingly, the children experienced difficulties with literacy in school.

In sum, Rogoff argues that through guided participation—the participation of children in skilled cultural activities with other people of varying levels of skill and status—children's cognitive development advances. Guided participation may be universal, although communities vary in the goals of socialization and in the means of communication.

best through firsthand experiences with people and materials. Play is extremely important in the child's total development. *Experimenting, exploring, discovering, trying out, restructuring, speaking,* and *listening* are all words that describe excellent kindergarten programs. Such programs are closely attuned to the developmental status of 4- and 5-year-old children. They are based on a state of being, not on a state of becoming (Ballenger, 1983).

*Developmentally Appropriate and Inappropriate Practices
in the Education of Young Children*
It is time for number games in a kindergarten class at the Greenbrook School in South Brunswick, New Jersey. With little prodding from the teacher, twenty-three 5- and 6-year-old children pick up geometric puzzles, playing cards, and counting equipment from the shelves lining the room. At one round table, some young children fit together brightly colored shapes. One girl forms a hexagon out of triangles. Other children gather around her to count up how many parts were needed to make the whole. After about half an hour the children prepare for story time. They put away their counting equipment and sit in a circle around one young girl. She holds up a giant book about a character named Mrs. Wishywashy, who insists on giving the farm animals a bath. The children recite the whimsical lines, clearly enjoying one of their favorite stories. The hallway outside the kindergarten is lined with drawings depicting the children's own interpretations of the book. After the first reading, volunteers act out various parts of the book. There is not one bored face in the room (Kantrowitz & Wingert, 1989).

This is not reading, writing, and arithmetic the way most individuals remember it. A growing number of educators and psychologists believe that preschool and young elementary school children learn best through active, hands-on teaching methods like games and dramatic play. They know that children develop at varying rates and that schools need to allow for these individual differences. They also believe that schools should focus on improving children's social development as well as their cognitive development. Educators refer to this type of schooling as **developmentally appropriate practice,** *which is based upon knowledge of the typical development of children within an age span (age appropriateness) as well as the uniqueness of the child (individual appropriateness). Developmentally appropriate practice contrasts with developmentally inappropriate practice, which ignores the concrete, hands-on approach to learning. Direct teaching largely through abstract, paper-and-pencil activities presented to large groups of young children is believed to be developmentally inappropriate.*

One of the most comprehensive documents addressing the issue of developmentally appropriate practice in early childhood programs is the position statement by the NAEYC (National Association for the Education of Young Children, 1986) (Bredekamp, 1987). This document represents the expertise of many of the foremost experts in the field of early childhood education. By turning to table 8.3, you can examine some of the NAEYC recommendations for developmentally appropriate practice.

A special worry of early childhood educators is that the back-to-basics movement that has recently characterized educational reform is filtering down to kindergarten. Another worry is that many parents want their children to go to school earlier than kindergarten for the purpose of getting a "head start" in achievement.

Table 8.3: Developmentally Appropriate and Inappropriate Practice in Early Childhood Education:

Component	Appropriate Practice	Inappropriate Practice
Curriculum Goals 	Experiences are provided in all developmental areas—physical, cognitive, social, and emotional.	Experiences are narrowly focused on cognitive development without recognition that all areas of the child's development are interrelated.
	Individual differences are expected, accepted, and used to design appropriate activities.	Children are only evaluated against group norms and all are expected to perform the same tasks and achieve the same narrowly defined skills.
	Interactions and activities are designed to develop children's self-esteem and positive feelings toward learning.	Children's worth is measured by how well they conform to rigid expectations and perform on standardized tests.
Teaching Strategies 	Teachers prepare the environment for children to learn through active exploration and interaction with adults, other children, and materials.	Teachers use highly structured, teacher-directed lessons almost exclusively.
	Children select many of their own activities from among a variety the teacher prepares.	The teacher directs all activity, deciding what children will do and when.
	Children are expected to be mentally and physically active.	Children are expected to sit down, be quiet, and listen, or do paper- and-pencil tasks for long periods of time. A major portion of time is spent passively sitting, watching, and listening.
	Children work individually or in small, informal groups most of the time.	Large group, teacher-directed instruction is used most of the time.
	Children are provided with concrete learning activities that include materials relevant to their own life experiences.	Workbooks, ditto sheets, flashcards, and other similarly structured abstract materials dominate the curriculum.
	Teachers move among groups and individuals to facilitate children's involvement with materials by asking questions, offering suggestions, or adding more complex materials or ideas to a situation.	Teachers dominate the environment by talking to the whole group most of the time and telling children what to do.
	Teachers accept that there is often more than one right answer or one right way of doing something. Teachers recognize that children learn from self-directed problem solving and experimentation.	Children are expected to respond correctly with one right answer. Rote memorization and drill are emphasized.
Guidance of Socioemotional Development 	Teachers enhance children's self-control by using positive guidance techniques such as modeling and encouraging expected behavior, redirecting children to a more acceptable activity, and setting clear limits.	Teachers spend considerable time enforcing rules, punishing unacceptable behavior, demeaning children who misbehave, making children sit and be quiet, or refereeing disagreements.
	Children are provided many opportunities to develop social skills such as cooperating, helping, negotiating, and talking with the person involved to solve interpersonal problems.	Children work individually at desks and tables most of the time and listen to the teacher's directions to the total group.

Recommendations by the National Association for the Education of Young Children

Appropriate Practice	Inappropriate Practice	Component
Children are provided many opportunities to see how reading and writing are useful before they are instructed in letter names, sounds, and word identification. Basic skills develop when they are meaningful to children. An abundance of these activities is provided to develop language and literacy: listening to and reading stories and poems, taking field trips, dictating stories, participating in dramatic play; talking informally with other children and adults; and experimenting with writing.	Reading and writing instruction stresses isolated skill development, such as recognizing single letters, reading the alphabet, singing the alphabet song, coloring within predefined lines, or being instructed in correct formation of letters on a printed line.	Language Development and Literacy 
Children develop an understanding of concepts about themselves, others, and the world around them through observation, interacting with people and real objects, and seeking solutions to concrete problems. Learning about math, science, social studies, health, and other content areas is integrated through meaningful activities.	Instruction stresses isolated skill development through memorization. Children's cognitive development is seen as fragmented in content areas such as math or science, and times are set aside for each of these.	Cognitive Development 
Children have daily opportunities to use large muscles, including running, jumping, and balancing. Outdoor activity is planned daily so children can freely express themselves.

Children have daily opportunities to develop small muscle skills through play activities, such as puzzles, painting, cutting, and similar activities. | Opportunity for large muscle activity is limited. Outdoor time is limited because it is viewed as interfering with instructional time, rather than as an integral part of the children's learning environment.

Small motor activity is limited to writing with pencils, coloring predrawn forms, or engaging in similar structured lessons. | Physical Development  |
| Children have daily opportunities for aesthetic expression and appreciation through art and music. A variety of art media is available. | Art and music are given limited attention. Art consists of coloring predrawn forms or following adult-prescribed directions. | Aesthetic Development  |
| Children's natural curiosity and desire to make sense of their world are used to motivate them to become involved in learning. | Children are required to participate in all activities to obtain the teacher's approval, to obtain extrinsic rewards like stickers or privileges, or to avoid punishment. | Motivation  |

Does It Really Matter if Children Attend Preschool before Kindergarten?
According to child developmentalist David Elkind (1987, 1988), parents who are exceptionally competent and dedicated and who have both the time and the energy can provide the basic ingredients of early childhood education in their home. If parents have the competence and resources to provide young children with a variety of learning experiences and exposure to other children and adults (possibly through neighborhood play groups), along with opportunities for extensive play, then home schooling may sufficiently educate young children. However, if parents do not have the commitment, the time, the energy, and the resources to provide young children with an environment that approximates a good early childhood program, then it *does* matter whether a child attends preschool. In this case, the issue is not whether preschool is important, but whether home schooling can closely duplicate what a competent preschool program can offer.

We should always keep in mind the unfortunate idea of early childhood education as an early start to ensure the participants will finish early or on top in an educational race (NAEYC, 1990; Willer & Bredekamp, 1990). Elkind (1988) points out that perhaps the choice of the phrase "head start" for the education of disadvantaged children was a mistake. "Head Start" does not imply a race. Not surprisingly, when middle-class parents heard that low-income children were getting a "head start," they wanted a "head start" for their own young children. In some instances, starting children in formal academic training too early can produce more harm than good. In Denmark, where reading instruction follows a language experience approach and formal instruction is delayed until the age of 7, illiteracy is virtually nonexistent. By contrast, in France, where state-mandated formal instruction in reading begins at age 5, 30 percent of the children have reading problems. Education should not be stressful for young children. Early childhood education should not be solely an academic prep school.

Preschool is rapidly becoming a norm in early childhood education. Twenty-three states already have legislation pending to provide schooling for 4-year-old children, and there are already many private preschool programs. The increase in public preschools underscores the growing belief that early childhood education should be a legitimate component of public education. There are dangers, though. According to child developmentalist David Elkind (1988), early childhood education is often not well understood at higher levels of education. The danger is that public preschool education for 4-year-old children will become little more than a downward extension of traditional elementary education. This is already occurring in preschool programs in which testing, workbooks, and group drill are imposed on 4- and 5-year-old children.

Elkind believes that early childhood education should become a part of public education but on its own terms. Early childhood should have its own curriculum, its own methods of evaluation and classroom management, and its own teacher-training programs. Although there may be some overlap with the curriculum, evaluation, classroom management, and teacher training at the upper levels of schooling, they certainly should not be identical.

Researchers are already beginning to document some of the stress that increased academic pressure can bring to young children (Burts, Charlesworth, & Fleege, 1991; Burts & others, in press; Charlesworth & others, in press). In one recent investigation, Diane Burts and her colleagues (1989) compared the frequencies of stress-related behaviors observed in young children in classrooms with developmentally appropriate and developmentally inappropriate instructional practices. They found that children in the developmentally inappropriate classrooms exhibited more stress-related behaviors than children in the developmentally appropriate classrooms. In another recent investigation, children in a high academically oriented early

EARLY CHILDHOOD EDUCATION IN JAPAN

*I*n the midst of low academic achievement by American children, many Americans are turning to Japan, a country of high academic achievement and economic success, for possible answers. However, the answers provided by Japanese preschools are not the ones Americans expected to find. In most Japanese preschools, surprisingly little emphasis is given to academic instruction. In one recent investigation, 300 Japanese and 210 American preschool teachers, child-development specialists, and parents were asked about various aspects of early childhood education (Tobin, Wu, & Davidson, 1989). Only 2 percent of the Japanese respondents listed "to give children a great start academically" as one of their top three reasons for a society to have preschools. In contrast, over half the American respondents chose this as one of their top three choices. To prepare children for successful careers in first grade and beyond, Japanese schools do not teach reading, writing, and mathematics, but more fundamental preacademic skills like persistence, concentration, and the ability to

In Japan, group experiences and learning how to cooperate are extremely important reasons for the existence of early childhood education.

function as a member of a group. The vast majority of young Japanese children are taught to read at home by their parents.

In the recent comparison of Japanese and American preschool education, 61 percent of the Japanese respondents chose providing children with a group experience as the single most important reason for a society to have preschools (Tobin, Wu, & Davidson, 1989). Ninety-one percent of the Japanese made this one of their top three choices. Americans did not

give group experience as high a priority, although 62 percent of the more individually oriented Americans listed group experience as one of their top three choices. An emphasis on the importance of the group is not only apparent in Japanese early childhood education, but also in elementary school education.

As in America, there is diversity in Japanese early childhood education. Some Japanese kindergartens have specific aims such as early musical training or the practice of Montesorri aims (Hendry, 1986). In large cities some kindergartens are attached to universities where there are also elementary and secondary schools. Some parents believe that if their young children attend the university-based programs, they will increase their chances of eventually being admitted to top-rated schools and universities. The emphasis on intellectual achievement in some Japanese kindergartens has led to the introduction of free play as a specialty in several more progressive programs.

childhood education program were compared with children in a low academically oriented early childhood education program (Hirsch-Pasek & others, 1989). No benefits appeared for children in the high academically oriented early childhood education program, but some possible harmful effects were noted. Higher test anxiety, less creativity, and a less positive attitude toward school characterized the children who attended the high academic program more than the low academic program.

One of the concerns of Americans is that our school children fare poorly when their achievement tests scores in math and science are compared with the test scores of school children from many other industrialized nations, especially such Asian nations as Japan and China (McKnight & others, 1987). Many Americans attribute the differences in achievement scores to a rigid system that sets young children in a lock-step march from cradle to college. In fact, the early years of Japanese schooling are anything but a boot camp. To read further about the nature of early childhood education in Japan, turn to Cultural Worlds of Development 8.2.

The Effects of Early Childhood Education

Because kindergarten and preschool programs are so diverse, it is difficult to make overall conclusions about their effects on children's development. Nonetheless, in one review of early childhood education's influence (Clarke-Stewart & Fein, 1983), it was concluded that children who attend preschool or kindergarten

- interact more with peers, both positively and negatively.
- are less cooperative with and responsive to adults than home-reared children.
- are more socially competent and mature in that they are more confident, extraverted, assertive, self-sufficient, independent, verbally expressive, knowledgeable about the social world, comfortable in social and stressful circumstances, and better adjusted when they go to school (exhibiting more task persistence, leadership, and goal direction, for example).
- are less socially competent in that they are less polite, less compliant to teacher demands, louder, and more aggressive and bossy, especially if the school or family supports such behavior.

In sum, early childhood education generally has a positive effect on children's development, since the behaviors just mentioned—while at times negative—seem to be in the direction of developmental maturity in that they increase as the child ages through the preschool years.

Education for Disadvantaged Children

For many years, children from low-income families did not receive any education before they entered the first grade. In the 1960s, an effort was made to try to break the cycle of poverty and poor education for young children in the United States through compensatory education. **Project Head Start** *is a compensatory education program designed to provide children from low-income families the opportunity to acquire the skills and experiences important for success in school.* Project Head Start began in the summer of 1965, funded by the Economic Opportunity Act, and it continues to serve disadvantaged children today.

Initially, Project Head Start consisted of many different types of preschool programs in different parts of the country. Little effort was made to find out whether some programs worked better than others, but it became apparent that some programs did work better than others. **Project Follow Through** *was implemented in 1967 as an adjunct to Project Head Start. In Project Follow Through, different types of educational programs were devised to determine which programs were the most effective. In the Follow Through programs, the enriched programs were carried through the first few years of elementary school.*

Were some Follow Through programs more effective than others? Many of the different variations were able to produce the desired effects on children. For example, children in academically oriented, direct-instruction approaches did better on achievement tests and were more persistent on tasks than were children in the other approaches. Children in affective education approaches were absent from school less often and showed more independence than children in other approaches. Thus, Project Follow Through was important in demonstrating that variation in early childhood education does have significant effects in a wide range of social and cognitive areas (Stallings, 1975).

The effects of early childhood compensatory education continue to be studied, and recent evaluations support the positive influence on both the cognitive and social worlds of disadvantaged young children (Haskins, 1989;

The preschool children shown here are attending a Head Start program, a national effort to provide children from low-income families the opportunity to experience an enriched environment.

Kagan, 1988; Lee, Brooks-Gunn, & Schnur, 1988). Of special interest are the long-term effects such intervention might produce. Model preschool programs lead to lower rates of placement in special education, dropping out of school, grade retention, delinquency, and use of welfare programs. Such programs might also lead to higher rates of high school graduation and employment. For every dollar invested in high-quality, model preschool programs, taxpayers receive about $1.50 in return by the time the participants reach the age of 20 (Haskins, 1989). The benefits include savings on public school education (such as special-education services), tax payments on additional earnings, reduced welfare payments, and savings in juvenile justice system costs. Predicted benefits over a lifetime are much greater to the taxpayer, a return of $5.73 on every dollar invested.

One long-term investigation of early childhood education was conducted by Irving Lazar, Richard Darlington, and their colleagues (1982). They pooled their resources into what they called a consortium for longitudinal studies, developed to share information about the long-term effects of preschool programs so that better designs and methods could be created. At the time the data from the eleven different early education studies were analyzed together, the children ranged in age from 9 to 19 years. The early education models varied substantially, but all were carefully planned and executed by experts in early childhood education. Outcome measures included indicators of school competence (such as special education and grade retention), abilities (as measured by standardized intelligence and achievement tests), attitudes and values, and impact on the family. The results indicated substantial benefits of competent preschool education with low-income children on all four dimensions investigated. In sum, ample evidence indicates that well-designed and well-implemented early childhood education programs with low-income children are successful (Darlington, 1991; Haskins, 1989; Kagan, 1988).

At this point we have discussed a number of ideas about young children's cognitive development. A summary of these ideas is presented in concept table 8.2. In the next chapter, we will turn our attention to young children's social worlds.

Physical and Cognitive Development in Early Childhood

Concept Table 8.2: Cognitive Development in Early Childhood

Concept	Processes/Related Ideas	Characteristics/Description
Piaget's Stage of Preoperational Thought	Its Nature	This is the beginning of the ability to reconstruct at the level of thought what has been established in behavior, and a transition from primitive to more sophisticated use of symbols. The child does not yet think in an operational way.
	Symbolic Function Substage	This substage occurs roughly between 2 and 4 years of age and is characterized by symbolic thought, egocentrism, and animism.
	Intuitive Thought Substage	This substage stretches from approximately 4 to 7 years of age. It is called intuitive because, on the one hand, children seem so sure about their knowledge, yet on the other hand, they are so unaware of how they know what they know. The preoperational child lacks conservation and asks a barrage of questions.
Information Processing	Attention	The child's attention dramatically improves during early childhood. One deficit in attention in early childhood is that the child attends to the salient rather than the relevant features of a task.
	Memory	Significant improvement in short-term memory occurs during early childhood. For example, memory span increases substantially in early childhood. Increased use of rehearsal and increased speed of processing are related to young children's memory improvement.
	Task Analysis	Information processing advocates believe a task's components should be analyzed. By making tasks more interesting and simple, some aspects of children's cognitive development have been shown to occur earlier than thought possible.
Language Development	Its Nature	Language development in early childhood includes changes in morphology, syntax, semantics, and pragmatics during the early childhood years.
Vygotsky's Theory of Development	Zone of Proximal Development	ZPD is Vygotsky's term for tasks too difficult for children to master alone, but that can be mastered with the guidance and assistance of adults or more skilled children.
	Language and Thought	They develop independently and then merge. The merging occurs between 3 and 7 years of age and involves private speech, that is, talking to oneself.
	Culture and Society	Vygotsky's theory stresses how the child's mind develops in the contexts of the sociocultural world. Cognitive skills develop through social interactions embedded in a cultural backdrop.

Summary

I. Body Growth and Changes

The average child grows 2½ inches in height and gains between 5 and 7 pounds a year during early childhood. Growth patterns vary individually, though.

II. Motor Development

Gross motor skills improve dramatically in early childhood. Children become increasingly adventuresome as their gross motor skills improve. Young children's lives are extremely active, more active than at any other point in the human life cycle. Fine motor skills also improve substantially during early childhood. The Denver Developmental Screening Test is one widely used measure of gross and fine motor skills. At one point, all children were taught to be right-handed. In today's world, the strategy is to let children use the hand they favor. Left-handed children are as competent in motor skills and intellect as right-handed children. Both genetic and environmental explanations of handedness are given.

Concept	Processes/Related Ideas	Characteristics/Description
Early Childhood Education	Child-Centered Kindergarten	Child-centered kindergarten involves the education of the whole child, with emphasis on individual variation, the process of learning, and the importance of play in development.
	Developmentally Appropriate and Inappropriate Practices in the Education of Young Children	Developmentally appropriate practice is based on knowledge of the typical development of children within an age span (age appropriateness), as well as the uniqueness of the child (individual appropriateness). Developmentally appropriate practice contrasts with developmentally inappropriate practice, which ignores the concrete, hands-on approach to learning. Direct teaching largely through abstract, paper-and-pencil activities presented to large groups of young children is believed to be developmentally inappropriate. The National Association for the Education of Young Children has been a strong proponent of developmentally appropriate practice and has developed extensive recommendations for its implementation.
	The Importance of Children Attending Preschool before Kindergarten	Parents can effectively educate their young children just as schools can. However, many parents do not have the commitment, time, energy, and resources needed to provide young children with an environment that approaches a competent early childhood education program. Too often, parents see education as a race, and preschool as a chance to get ahead in the race. However, education is not a race and it should not be stressful for young children. Public preschools are appearing in many states. A concern is that they should not become merely simple versions of elementary school. Early childhood education has some issues that overlap with upper levels of schooling, but in many ways the agenda of early childhood education is different.
	The Influence of Early Childhood Education on Children's Development	This is difficult to evaluate, but the effects overall seem to be positive. However, outcome measures reveal areas in which social competence is more positive, others in which it is less positive.
	Education for Disadvantaged Young Children	Compensatory education has tried to break through the poverty cycle with programs like Head Start and Follow Through. Long-term studies reveal that model preschool programs have positive effects on development.

III. Nutrition

Energy needs increase as children go through the childhood years. Energy requirements vary according to basal metabolism, rate of growth, and activity. Many parents are raising children on diets that are too high in fat. Children's diets should include well-balanced proportions of fats, carbohydrates, protein, vitamins, and minerals.

IV. The State of Illness and Health in the World's Children

One of every three deaths in the world is the death of a child under 5. Every week, more than a quarter of a million children die in developing countries. The most frequent cause of death is diarrhea. Oral rehydration therapy can be used to prevent diarrhea from leading to death. Most child malnutrition and death could be prevented by parental actions that are affordable and based on knowledge available today. The United States has a relatively low rate of child deaths compared to other countries, although the Scandinavian countries have the lowest rates. The disorders most likely to be fatal for American children in the preschool years are birth defects, cancer, and heart disease.

V. Piaget's Stage of Preoperational Thought

Preoperational thought is the beginning of the ability to reconstruct at the level of thought what has been established in behavior, and involves a transition from primitive to more sophisticated use of symbols. The child does not yet think in an operational way. The symbolic function substage occurs roughly between 2 and 4 years of age and is characterized by symbolic thought, egocentrism, and animism. The intuitive thought substage stretches from approximately 4 to 7 years of age. It is called intuitive because, on the one hand, children seem so sure about their knowledge, yet on the other hand, they are so unaware of how they know what they know. The preoperational child lacks conservation and asks a barrage of questions.

VI. Information Processing

The child's attention improves dramatically during early childhood. One deficit in attention in early childhood is that the child attends to the salient rather than the relevant features of the task. Significant improvement in short-term memory occurs during early childhood. For example, memory span increases substantially in early childhood. Increased use of rehearsal and increased speed of processing information are related to the young child's memory improvement. Information processing advocates believe a task's components should be analyzed. By making the tasks more interesting and simple, some aspects of children's cognitive development have been shown to occur earlier than previously thought possible.

VII. Language Development

Changes in language development in early childhood involve morphology, syntax, semantics, and pragmatics.

VIII. Vygotsky's Theory of Development

The zone of proximal development (ZPD) is Vygotsky's term for tasks too difficult for children to master alone, but that can be mastered with the guidance and assistance of adults or more skilled children. According to Vygotsky, language and thought develop independently, then merge. The merging occurs between 3 and 7 years of age and involves private speech, that is, talking to oneself. Vygotsky's theory stresses how the child's mind develops in the contexts of the sociocultural world. Cognitive skills develop through social interaction that are embedded in a cultural backdrop.

IX. Child-Centered Kindergarten, and Developmentally Appropriate and Inappropriate Practices in the Education of Young Children

Child-centered kindergarten involves education of the whole child, with emphasis on individual variation, the process of learning, and the importance of play in development. Developmentally appropriate practice is based upon knowledge of the typical development of children within an age span (age appropriateness) as well as the uniqueness of the child (individual appropriateness). Developmentally appropriate practice contrasts with developmentally inappropriate practice, which ignores the concrete, hands-on approach to learning. Direct teaching largely through abstract, paper-and-pencil activities presented to large groups of young children is believed to be developmentally inappropriate. The National Association for the Education of Young Children (NAEYC) has been a strong proponent of developmentally appropriate practice and has developed extensive recommendations for its implementation.

X. Does It Really Matter If Children Attend Preschool before Kindergarten?

Parents can effectively educate their young children just as schools can. However, many parents do not have the commitment, time, energy, and resources needed to provide young children with an environment that approaches a competent early childhood education program. Too often, parents see education as a race, and preschool as a chance to get ahead in the race. However, education should not be a race and it should not be stressful for young children. Public preschools are appearing in many states. A concern is that they should not become simple versions of traditional elementary schools. Early childhood education has some issues that overlap with upper levels of schooling, but in many ways the agenda of early childhood education is different.

XI. The Influence of Early Childhood Education and Education for Disadvantaged Young Children

The effects of early childhood education on children's development are difficult to evaluate, but overall they seem to be positive. However, while outcome measures reveal areas in which social competence is more positive for children who have experienced early childhood education, other areas reveal less social competence. Compensatory education has tried to break through the poverty cycle with programs like Head Start and Project Follow Through. Long-term studies reveal that model preschool programs have positive effects on disadvantaged children's development.

Key Terms

Denver Developmental
Screening Test 221
basal metabolism rate (BMR) 223
oral rehydration therapy (ORT) 224
operations 226
symbolic function substage 226

egocentrism 227
animism 227
intuitive thought substage 229
centration 231
conservation 231
short-term memory 235
zone of proximal development
(ZPD) 238

child-centered kindergarten 241
developmentally appropriate
practice 243
Project Head Start 248
Project Follow Through 248

Suggested Readings

Clark, J. E., & Humphrey, J. H. (Eds.).
(1985). *Motor development: Current
selected research.* Princeton, NJ:
Princeton Book Company.
*A collection of articles by leading
experts on children's motor
development. Includes detailed
information about the growth of
various motor and athletic skills in
the preschool years.*

Daehler, M. W., & Bukatko, D. (1985).
Cognitive development. New York:
Random House.
*A thorough review of children's
cognitive development is provided.
Topics include the development of
attention, memory, and reasoning.*

Dumtschin, J. U. (1988, March).
Recognize language development and
delay in early childhood. *Young
Children,* pp. 16–24.

Presents an up-to-date overview of
what language delay is, how parents
and preschool teachers can recognize
it, and what can be done about it.

Grant, J. P. (1990). *The state of the
world's children.* New York:
UNICEF and Oxford University
Press.
*Provides an analysis of children's
illness, health, and death in 131
countries around the world. Detailed
charts about death rates and
nutrition. Recommends ways to
reduce the child death rate and
malnutrition.*

Rogoff, B. (1990). *Apprenticeship in
thinking: Cognitive development in
social context.* New York: Oxford
University Press.
*One of the leading scholars in
research on the cultural contexts of*

*cognitive development, Barbara
Rogoff describes the important roles
that social and cultural interaction
play in cognitive development.*

Young Children, published by the
National Association for the
Education of Young Children,
Washington, D.C.
*This journal includes a variety of
articles about young children's
physical, cognitive, and social
development. Special attention is
given to how various aspects of
development can be fostered in our
nation's preschool programs. Look
through the issues of the last five
years to get a feel for the important
concerns in this area.*

CHAPTER 9

Social Development in Early Childhood

*I*magine . . . two 4-year-olds are playing and one says to the other: "You stay here with the baby while I go fishing." Don't you immediately assume that one of the preschool children is a boy and the other is a girl? And don't you also infer that the sex of the child speaking is male? If you made these inferences, you are correct. These two preschool children—Shane and Barbara—were playing at their nursery school. As Shane walked away, Barbara called to him, "I want to go fishing, too." Shane replied, "No. Girls don't go fishing. But I'll take you to a French restaurant when we get back."

Barbara returned to playing with her dolls after Shane left. The director of the nursery school talked to Shane's mother about his behavior. She wanted to know whether Shane was merely mimicking his father's behavior. Shane's mother said that he was not, because the entire family went fishing together. The gender roles children display, then, are not merely replications of parental actions.

Another play scene observed by the nursery school director focused on three boys sitting around a play table in a play kitchen. The boys began issuing orders: "I want a cup of coffee." "Some more jelly for the toast over here." Girls were running back and forth between the stove and the table as they cooked and served breakfast. In one situation, the boys got out of hand, demanding cups of coffee one after another as a 4-year-old, Ann, raced around in a dizzy state. Finally, Ann gained some control over the situation by announcing that the coffee was all gone. It didn't seem to occur to Ann to sit down at the table and demand coffee from the boys.

Gender specific behavior from young children is nothing new, but viewing it as a problem is. Such behavior has become somewhat of an obsession with preschool teachers and directors, and it bothers many parents who are trying to rear their offspring free of sexist bias (Carper, 1978).

Later in the chapter we will further discuss the nature of children's roles and look more closely at their play. We will also focus on young children's peer relations, the role of television, and personality development. But to begin, we continue our emphasis on the importance of families in children's socialization.

> *It is a happy talent to know how to play.*
>
> Emerson,
> Journals, *1834*

Families

In chapter 7, we learned that attachment is an important aspect of family relationships during infancy. Remember that some experts believe attachment to a caregiver during the first several years of life is the key ingredient in the child's social development, increasing the probability the child will be socially competent and well adjusted in the preschool years and beyond. We also learned that other experts believe secure attachment has been overemphasized and that the child's temperament, other social agents and contexts, and the complexity of the child's social world are also important in determining the child's social competence and well-being. Some developmentalists also emphasize that the infant years have been overdramatized as determinants of life-span development, arguing that social experiences in the early childhood years and later deserve more attention than they have sometimes been given.

In this chapter, we will go beyond the attachment process as we explore the different types of parenting styles to which children are exposed, sibling relationships, and how more children are now experiencing socialization in a greater variety of family structures than at any other point in history. Keep in mind as we discuss these aspects of families the importance of viewing the family as a system of interacting individuals who reciprocally socialize and mutually regulate each other.

"Are you going to believe me, your own flesh and blood, or some stranger you married?"

Parenting Styles

Parents want their children to grow into socially mature individuals, and they may feel frustrated in trying to discover the best way to accomplish this. Developmentalists have long searched for the ingredients of parenting that promote competent social development in children. For example, in the 1930s, John Watson argued that parents were too affectionate with their children. In the 1950s, a distinction was made between physical and psychological discipline, with psychological discipline, especially reasoning, emphasized as the best way to rear a child. In the 1970s and beyond, the dimensions of competent parenting have become more precise.

Especially widespread is the view of Diana Baumrind (1971, 1991), who believes parents should be neither punitive nor aloof, but should instead develop rules for their children and be affectionate with them. She emphasizes three types of parenting that are associated with different aspects of the child's social behavior: authoritarian, authoritative, and laissez-faire (permissive). More recently, developmentalists have argued that permissive parenting comes in two different forms: permissive indulgent and permissive indifferent. What are these forms of parenting like?

Authoritarian parenting *is a restrictive, punitive style that exhorts the child to follow the parent's directions and to respect work and effort. The authoritarian parent places firm limits and controls on the child with little verbal exchange allowed. Authoritarian parenting is associated with children's social incompetence.* For example, an authoritarian parent might say, "You do it my way or else. There will be no discussion!" Children of authoritarian parents are often anxious about social comparison, fail to initiate activity, and have poor communication skills.

Authoritative parenting *encourages children to be independent but still places limits and controls on their actions. Extensive verbal give-and-take is allowed and parents are warm and nurturant toward the child. Authoritative parenting is associated with children's social competence.* An authoritative

There's no vocabulary for love within a family, love that's lived in but not looked at, love within the light of which all else is seen, the love within which all other love finds speech. This love is silent.

~ *T. S. Eliot,* The Elder Statesman

Early Childhood

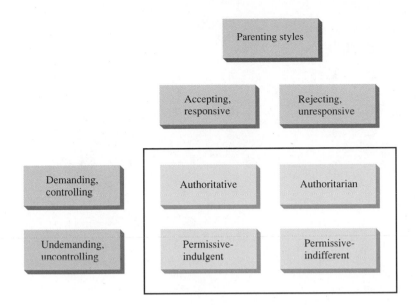

Figure 9.1 Classification of parenting styles. The four types of parenting styles (authoritative, authoritarian, permissive-indulgent, and permissive-indifferent) involve the dimensions of acceptance and responsiveness on the one hand, and demand and control on the other.

parent might put his arm around the child in a comforting way and say, "You know you should not have done that; let's talk about how you can handle the situation better next time." Children whose parents are authoritative are socially competent, self-reliant, and socially responsible.

Permissive parenting comes in two forms: permissive-indifferent and permissive-indulgent (Maccoby & Martin, 1983). **Permissive-indifferent parenting** *is a style in which the parent is very uninvolved in the child's life; it is associated with children's social incompetence, especially a lack of self-control.* This parent cannot answer the question, "It is 10 P.M. Do you know where your child is?" Children have a strong need for their parents to care about them; children whose parents are permissive-indifferent develop the sense that other aspects of the parents' lives are more important than they are. Children whose parents are permissive-indifferent are socially incompetent—they show poor self-control and do not handle independence well.

Permissive-indulgent parenting *is a style of parenting in which parents are highly involved with their children but place few demands or controls on them. Permissive-indulgent parenting is associated with children's social incompetence, especially a lack of self-control.* They let their children do what they want, and the result is the children never learn to control their own behavior and always expect to get their way. Some parents deliberately rear their children in this way because they believe the combination of warm involvement with few restraints will produce a creative, confident child. One boy I knew whose parents deliberately reared him in a permissive-indulgent manner moved his parents out of their bedroom suite and took it over for himself. He is now 18 years old and has not learned to control his behavior; when he can't get something he wants, he still throws temper tantrums. As you might expect, he is not very popular with his peers. Children whose parents are permissive-indulgent rarely learn respect for others and have difficulty controlling their behavior.

The four classifications of parenting just discussed involve combinations of acceptance and responsiveness on the one hand, and demand and control on the other. How these dimensions combine to produce authoritarian, authoritative, permissive indifferent, and permissive indulgent parenting is shown in figure 9.1. Further advice for parents that dovetails with the concept of authoritative parenting is presented in Perspective on Life-Span Development 9.1.

A PRIMER FOR COMPETENT PARENTING

*I*n the 1980s, the Missouri Department of Education hired Michael Meyerhoff and Burton White to design a model parent-education program and help set it up in four school districts across the state: one urban, one suburban, one small town, and one rural town. The families cover a wide range of social and economic backgrounds. The services include get-togethers—at which ten to twenty parents meet with a parent educator at the resource center—and individual home visits by a parent educator. Services begin during the final three months of pregnancy and continue until the child's third birthday, with increasing emphasis on private visits after the child is 6 years old. The average amount of contact with the families is once a month for an hour and a half.

During group and private sessions, parents are given basic information about what kinds of parenting practices are likely to help or hinder their children's progress. Table 9.A shows the dos and don'ts told to parents, advice that makes sense and is likely to promote the child's competence (Meyerhoff & White, 1986; White, 1988).

Parenting practices play an important role in young children's development. What were the characteristics of competent parents found by Meyerhoff and White?

TABLE 9.A	*A Primer in Competent Parenting*

The following recommendations are based on the lessons Michael Meyerhoff and Burton White learned from the parents of competent preschool children.

Things to do:

Provide children with the maximum opportunity for exploration and investigation.

Be available to act as your children's personal consultant as much as possible. You don't have to hover, but be around to provide attention and support as needed.

Respond to your children promptly and favorably as often as you can, providing appropriate enthusiasm and encouragement.

Set limits—do not give in to unreasonable requests or permit unacceptable behavior to continue.

Talk to your children often. Make an effort to understand what they are trying to do and concentrate on what they see as important.

Use words they understand but also add new words and related ideas.

Provide new learning opportunities. Having children accompany you to the supermarket or allowing them to bake cookies with you is more enriching than sitting them down and conducting a flash card session.

Give your children a chance to direct some of your shared activities from time to time.

Try to help your children be as spontaneous emotionally as your own behavior patterns will allow.

Encourage your child's pretend activities, especially those in which they act out adult roles.

Things not to do:

Don't confine your children regularly for long periods of time.

Don't allow them to concentrate their energies on you so much that independent exploration and investigation are excluded.

Don't ignore attention getting to the point where children have to throw a tantrum to gain your interest.

Don't worry that your children won't love you if you say "no" on occasion.

Don't try to win all the arguments, especially during the second half of the second year when most children are passing through a normal period of negativism.

Don't be overprotective.

Don't bore your child if you can avoid it.

Don't worry about when children learn to count or say the alphabet.

Don't worry if they are slow to talk, as long as they seem to understand more and more language as time goes by.

Don't spoil your children, giving them the notion that the world was made just for them.

Source: PSYCHOLOGY TODAY MAGAZINE, September 1986:44. Copyright © 1986 (PT Partners, L. P.).

Adapting Parenting to Developmental Changes in the Child

Parents also need to adapt their behavior toward the child based on the child's developmental maturity. Parents should not treat the 5-year-old the same as the 2-year-old. The 5-year-old and the 2-year-old have different needs and abilities. In the first year, parent-child interaction moves from a heavy focus on routine caretaking—feeding, changing diapers, bathing, and soothing—to later include more noncaretaking activities like play and visual-vocal exchanges. During the child's second and third years, parents often handle disciplinary matters by physical manipulation: They carry the child away from a mischievous activity to the place they want the child to go; they put fragile and dangerous objects out of reach; they sometimes spank. But as the child grows older, parents turn increasingly to reasoning, moral exhortation, and giving or withholding special privileges. As children move toward the elementary school years, parents show them less physical affection.

Cultural, Social Class, and Ethnic Variations in Families

Cultures vary on a number of issues involving families, such as what the father's role in the family should be, the extent support systems are available to families, and how children should be disciplined. Although there are cross-cultural variations in parenting (Whiting & Edwards, 1988), in one study of parenting behavior in 186 cultures around the world, the most common pattern was a warm and controlling style, one that was neither permissive nor restrictive (Rohner & Rohner, 1981). The investigators commented that the majority of cultures have discovered over many centuries a "truth" that has only recently emerged from research in the Western world, namely, that children's healthy social development is most effectively promoted by love and at least some moderate parental control.

Ethnic-minority families differ from White American families in their size, structure, and composition, their reliance on kinship networks, and their levels of income and education (Spencer & Dornbusch, 1990). Large and extended families are more common among ethnic-minority groups than White Americans (Wilson, 1989; Wilson & others, 1991). For example, more than 30 percent of Hispanic American families consist of five or more individuals (Keefe & Padilla, 1987). Black American and Hispanic American children interact more with grandparents, aunts, uncles, cousins, and more distant relatives than do White American Children.

Single parent families are more common among Black Americans and Hispanic Americans than among White Americans (Rogler, Cortes, & Malgady, 1991; Marín & Marín, 1991). In comparison with two-parent households, single parents often have more limited resources of time, money, and energy. This shortage of resources may prompt them to encourage early autonomy among their children and adolescents (Spencer & Dornbusch, 1990). Also, ethnic-minority parents are less well educated and engage in less joint decision making than White American parents. And ethnic-minority children are more likely to come from low-income families than White American children (Committee for Economic Development, 1987; McLoyd, in press). Although impoverished families often raise competent children, poor parents may have a diminished capacity for supportive and involved parenting (McLoyd, in press).

Some aspects of home life can help to protect ethnic-minority children from social patterns of injustice (Spencer & Dornbusch, 1990). The community and family can filter out destructive racist messages, parents can provide alternate frames of reference than those presented by the majority, and

BLACK AND HISPANIC FAMILY ORIENTATIONS

*I*n the 1985 Children's Defense Fund Study, "Black and White Children in America: Key Facts" (Edelman, 1987), Black children were three times as likely as White children to:

- be poor
- live with a parent who was separated from a spouse
- die of child abuse

five times as likely to:

- be dependent on welfare

and twelve times as likely to:

- live with a parent who never married

Nonetheless, it is important to keep in mind that millions of Black American families are not on welfare, have children who stay in school and out of trouble, and find ways to cope with and overcome problems they experience during difficult times. In 1967, Martin Luther King, Jr., reflected on the Black American family and gave the following caution: "As public awareness of the predicament of the Black family increases, there will be danger and opportunity. The opportunity will be to deal fully rather than haphazardly with the problem as a whole, as a social catastrophe brought on by many years of oppression. The danger is that the problems will be attributed to innate Black weaknesses and used to justify further neglect and to rationalize con-

Although Black children are more likely than White children to be poor and live with a parent who has been separated from a spouse, it is important to keep in mind that millions of Black American families are not on welfare, have considerable family support, and find ways to effectively cope with stress.

tinued oppression." In today's world, Dr. King's words still ring true. (McLoyd, in press; Ogbu, 1989; Spencer & Dornbusch, 1990).

The Black cultural tradition of an extended family household—in which one or several grandparents, uncles, aunts, siblings, or cousins, either live together or provide support—has helped many Black parents cope with

adverse social conditions such as economic impoverishment (McAdoo, 1988). The Black extended family can be traced to the African heritage of many Black Americans, where in many cultures a newly married couple does not move away from relatives. Instead, the extended family assists its members with basic family functions. Researchers have found that the extended

parents can also provide competent role models and encouragement (Bowman & Howard, 1985; Jones, 1990). And the extended family system in many ethnic-minority families provides an important buffer to stress. To read further about the extended family system in Black American and Hispanic American families, turn to Cultural Worlds of Development 9.1.

In America and most Western cultures, social class differences in child-rearing have been found. Working class and low-income parents often place a high value on external characteristics such as obedience and neatness, whereas

The Hispanic family reunion of the Limon family in Austin, Texas. Hispanic American children often grow up in families with a network of relatives that runs into scores of individuals.

Black family helps to reduce the stress of poverty and single parenting through emotional support, sharing of income and economic responsibility, and surrogate parenting (McAdoo, 1988). The presence of grandmothers in the households of many Black adolescents and their infants has been an important support system for both the teenage mother and the infant (Stevens, 1984). Active and involved extended family support systems also help a parent or parents from other ethnic-minority groups cope with poverty and its related stress.

A basic value in Mexico is represented by the saying "As long as our family stays together, we are strong." Mexican children are brought up to stay close to their family, often playing with siblings rather than with schoolmates or neighborhood children, as American children usually do. Unlike the father in many American families, the Mexican father is the undisputed authority on all family matters and is usually obeyed without question. The mother is revered as the primary source of affection and care. This emphasis on family attachment leads the Mexican to say, "I will achieve mainly because of my family, and for my family, rather than myself." By contrast, the self-reliant American would say, "I will achieve mainly because of my ability and initiative and for myself rather than for my family." Unlike most Americans, families in Mexico tend to stretch out in a network of relatives that often runs to scores of individuals.

Both cultures—Mexican and American—have undergone considerable change in recent decades. Whether Mexican children will gradually take on the characteristics of American children, or whether American children will shift closer to Mexican children, is difficult to predict. The cultures of both countries will probably move to a new order more in keeping with future demands, retaining some common features of the old while establishing new priorities and values (Holtzmann, 1982).

middle-class families often place a high value on internal characteristics, such as self-control and delay of gratification. Not only are there social class differences in childrearing values but also in parenting behaviors. Middle-class parents are more likely to explain something, use verbal praise, use reasoning to accompany their discipline, and ask their children questions. By contrast, parents in low-income and working-class households are more likely to discipline their children with physical punishment and criticize their children more (Heath, 1983; Kohn, 1977).

More than 80 percent of American children have siblings. Children's sibling relationships include helping, sharing, teaching, fighting, and playing.

• *Critical Thinking* •

Sibling rivalry is a common occurrence in families. What aspects of family life are likely to increase sibling rivalry? What techniques could be used to reduce sibling conflict?

Sibling Relationships and Birth Order

Sandra describes to her mother what happened in a conflict with her sister:

> We had just come home from the ball game. I sat down on the sofa next to the light so I could read. Sally (the sister) said, "Get up. I was sitting there first. I just got up for a second to get a drink." I told her I was not going to get up and that I didn't see her name on the chair. I got mad and started pushing her. Her drink spilled all over her. Then she got really mad; she shoved me against the wall, hitting and clawing at me. I managed to grab a handful of hair.

At this point, Sally comes into the room and begins to tell her side of the story. Sandra interrupts, "Mother, you always take her side." Sound familiar? Any of you who have grown up with siblings probably have a rich memory of aggressive, hostile interchanges; but sibling relationships have many pleasant, caring moments as well. Children's sibling relationships include helping, sharing, teaching, fighting, and playing. Children can act as emotional supports, rivals, and communication partners (Zukow, 1989; Stocker & Dunn, 1991; Vandell, 1987). More than 80 percent of American children have one or more siblings (brothers or sisters). Because there are so many possible sibling combinations, it is difficult to generalize about sibling influences. Among the factors to be considered are the number of siblings, age of siblings, birth order, age spacing, sex of siblings, and whether sibling relationships are different from parent-child relationships.

Is sibling interaction different than parent-child interaction? There is some evidence that it is. Observations indicate that children interact more positively and in more varied ways with their parents than with their siblings (Baskett & Johnson, 1982). Children also follow their parents' dictates more than those of their siblings, and they behave more negatively and punitively with their siblings than with their parents.

In some instances, siblings may be stronger socializing influences on the child than parents are (Cicirelli, 1977). Someone close in age to the child—such as a sibling—may be able to understand the child's problems and be able to communicate more effectively than parents can. In dealing with peers, coping with difficult teachers, and discussing taboo subjects such as sex, siblings may be more influential in the socialization process than parents.

Birth order is a special interest of sibling researchers (McCartney & others, 1991; Musun-Miller, 1991). When differences in birth order are found, they usually are explained by variations in interactions with parents and siblings associated with the unique experiences of being in a particular position in the family. This is especially true in the case of the firstborn child. The oldest child is the only one who does not have to share parental love and affection with other siblings—until another sibling comes along. An infant requires more attention than an older child; this means that the firstborn sibling now gets less attention than before the newborn arrived (Teti & others, 1991). Does this result in conflict between parents and the firstborn? In one research study, mothers became more negative, coercive, restraining, and played less with the firstborn following the birth of a second child (Dunn & Kendrick, 1982). Even though a new infant requires more attention from parents than does an older child, an especially intense relationship is often maintained between parents and firstborns throughout the life cycle. Parents have higher expectations for, put more pressure for achievement and responsibility on, and interfere more with the activities of firstborn than later-born children (Rothbart, 1971).

Birth order is also associated with variations in sibling relationships. The oldest sibling is expected to exercise self-control and show responsibility in interacting with younger siblings. When the oldest sibling is jealous or hostile, parents often protect the younger sibling. The oldest sibling is more dominant, competent, and powerful than the younger siblings; the oldest sibling is also expected to assist and teach younger siblings. Indeed, researchers have shown that older siblings are both more antagonistic—hitting, kicking, and biting—and more nurturant toward their younger siblings than vice versa (Abramovitch & others, 1986). There is also something unique about same-sex sibling relationships. Aggression and dominance occur more in same-sex sibling relationships than in opposite-sex sibling relationships (Minnett, Vandell, & Santrock, 1983).

Given the differences in family dynamics involved in birth order, it is not surprising that firstborns and later-borns have different characteristics. First-born children are more adult oriented, helpful, conforming, anxious, self-controlled, and less aggressive than their siblings. Parental demands and high standards established for firstborns result in these children excelling in academic and professional endeavors. Firstborns are overrepresented in *Who's Who* and Rhodes scholars, for example. However, some of the same pressures placed on firstborns for high achievement may be the reason they also have more guilt, anxiety, difficulty in coping with stressful situations, and higher admission to child guidance clinics.

What is the only child like? The popular conception of the only child is a "spoiled brat" with such undesirable characteristics as dependency, lack of self-control, and self-centered behavior. But researchers present a more positive portrayal of the only child, who often is achievement oriented and displays a desirable personality, especially in comparison to later-borns and children from large families (Falbo & Polit, 1986).

The Changing Family in a Changing Society

Children are growing up in a greater variety of family structures than ever before in history. Many mothers spend the greatest part of their day away from their children, even their infants. More than one of every two mothers with a child under the age of 5 is in the labor force; more than two of every three with a child from 6 to 17 years of age is. And the increasing number of children growing up in single-parent families is staggering. As shown in figure 9.2, a substantial increase in the number of children under the age of 18 who lived in a single-parent family occurred between 1980 and 1988. Also note that a much higher percentage of Black families than White families or Hispanic families are single-parent families. If current trends continue, by the year 2000 one in every four children will also have lived a portion of their lives in a stepparent family. And, as we saw in chapter 7, fathers perform more childrearing duties than in the past.

Working Mothers

Because household operations have become more efficient and family size has decreased in America, it is not certain that children with mothers working outside the home actually receive less attention than children in the past whose mothers were not employed. Outside employment—at least for mothers with school-aged children—may simply be filling time previously taken up by added household burdens and more children. It also cannot be assumed that, if the mother did not go to work, the child would benefit from the time freed by streamlined household operations and smaller families. Mothering does not always have a positive effect on the child. The educated, nonworking mother may overinvest her energies in her children, fostering an excess of worry and discouraging the child's independence. In such situations, the mother may inject more parenting than the child can profitably handle.

Big sisters are the crab grass in the lawn of life.

~ *Charles Schulz,* Peanuts

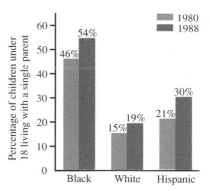

Figure 9.2   Percentage of children under 18 living with one parent in 1980 and 1988. The percentage of children under 18 living with one parent increased from 20 percent in 1980 to 24 percent in 1988. The figures above reveal the breakdown of single parents in Black, White, and Hispanic families. Note the substantially higher percentage of Black and Hispanic single-parent families.

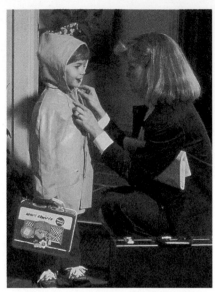

What issues do women face as they combine career and family?

As Lois Hoffman (1979, 1989) comments, maternal employment is a part of modern life. It is not an aberrant aspect of it, but a response to other social changes that meets the needs that cannot be met by the previous family ideal of a full-time mother and homemaker. Not only does it meet the parent's needs, but in many ways, it may be a pattern better suited to socializing children for the adult roles they will occupy. This is especially true for daughters, but it is also true for sons. The broader range of emotions and skills that each parent presents is more consistent with this adult role. Just as his father shares the breadwinning role and the childrearing role with his mother, so the son, too, will be more likely to share these roles. The rigid gender-role stereotyping perpetuated by the divisions of labor in the traditional family is not appropriate for the demands children of either sex will have made on them as adults. The needs of the growing child require the mother to loosen her hold on the child, and this task may be easier for the working woman whose job is an additional source of identity and self-esteem (Lerner & Hess, 1991).

Effects of Divorce on Children

Early studies of the effects of divorce on children followed a father absence tradition, in which children from father-absent and father-present families were compared, and differences in their development were attributed to the absence of the father. But family structure (such as father present, divorced, and widowed) is only one of many factors that influence the child's adjustment. The contemporary approach advocates evaluating the strengths and weaknesses of the child prior to divorce, the nature of events surrounding the divorce, and postdivorce family functioning. Support systems (babysitters, relatives, day care), an ongoing, positive relationship between the custodial parent and the ex-spouse, authoritative parenting, financial stability, and the child's competencies at the time of the divorce are related to the child's adjustment (Block, Block, & Gjerde, 1986; Chase-Landsdale & Hetherington, in press; Hetherington, 1991; Hetherington, Cox, & Cox, 1982; Kelly, 1987; Santrock & Warshak, 1986; Wallerstein & Kelly, 1980).

Developmentalists are especially concerned about single mothers in poverty, more than one-third of whom are in poverty compared to only 10 percent of single fathers (U.S. Bureau of the Census, 1987). Developmentalist Vonnie McLoyd (in press; McLoyd & Wilson, 1990) states that because poor single mothers are more emotionally distressed than affluent mothers, it is not surprising that single mothers in low-income circumstances often show low support, nurturance, and involvement with their children. Among the reasons for the high poverty rate of single mothers are the low pay of women, infrequent awarding of alimony payments, and poorly enforced child support by fathers (Farley, 1990). A concern of most divorced mothers, but especially those in poverty, is the unavailability of low-cost, quality day care for children.

Many separations and divorces are highly emotional affairs that immerse the child in conflict (Parish, 1988; Parish & Osterberg, 1985). Conflict is a critical aspect of family functioning that seems to outweigh the influence of family structure on the child's development. Children in divorced families that are low in conflict function better than children in never-divorced, intact families that are high in conflict, for example (Rutter, 1983; Wallerstein, Corbin, & Lewis, 1988). Although escape from conflict may be a positive benefit for children, in the year immediately following the divorce, the conflict does not decline, but instead increases. At this time, children—especially boys—in divorced families show more adjustment problems than children in homes with both parents present. During the first year after the divorce, the

Early Childhood

child often experiences a poor quality of parenting; parents seem preoccupied with their own needs and adjustment—experiencing anger, depression, confusion, and emotional instability—which inhibits their ability to respond sensitively to the child's needs. During the second year after the divorce, parents are more effective in their childrearing duties, especially with daughters (Hetherington, Cox, & Cox, 1982).

Recent evaluations by Mavis Hetherington and her colleagues (Hetherington, 1989, 1991; Hetherington, Hagan, & Anderson, 1989) of children six years after the divorce of their parents found that living in nonremarried mother-custody homes had long-term negative effects on boys, with negative outcomes appearing consistently from preschool to adolescence. In contrast, most girls from these families recovered from divorce early in their lives. However, although preadolescent girls in divorced families adapted reasonably well, at the onset of adolescence, a subset of these girls—those who were early maturers—engaged in frequent conflict with their mothers, behaved in noncompliant ways, had lower self-esteem, and experienced more problems in heterosexual relations.

The sex of the child and the sex of the custodial parent are important considerations in evaluating the effects of divorce on children. One research study directly compared children living in father-custody and mother-custody families (Santrock & Warshak, 1979, 1986). On a number of measures, including videotaped observations of parent-child interaction, children living with the same-sex parent were more socially competent—happier, more independent, and more mature—and had higher self-esteem than children living with the opposite-sex parent. Other research has supported these findings (Camara & Resnick, 1988; Furstenberg, 1988).

Support systems are especially important for low-income divorced families. The extended family and community services often play a critical role in the functioning of low-income divorced families. These support systems may be crucial for low-income divorced families with infants and young children, because the majority of these parents must work full-time but still may not be able to make ends meet (Wilson, 1989).

The age of the child at the time of the divorce also needs to be considered. Young children's responses to divorce are mediated by their limited cognitive and social competencies, their dependency on their parents, and their restriction to the home or inferior day care (Hetherington, Hagan, & Anderson, 1989). During the interval immediately following divorce, young children less accurately appraise the divorce situation. These young children may blame themselves for the divorce, may fear abandonment by both parents, and may misperceive and be confused by what is happening (Wallerstein, Corbin, & Lewis, 1988).

The cognitive immaturity that creates extensive anxiety for children who are young at the time of their parents' divorce may benefit the children over time. In one study, ten years after the divorce of their parents, adolescents had few memories of their own earlier fears and suffering or of their parents' conflict (Wallerstein, Corbin, & Lewis, 1988). Nonetheless, approximately one-third of these children continued to express anger about not being able to grow up in an intact, never-divorced family. Those who were adolescents at the time of their parents' divorce were more likely to remember the conflict and stress surrounding the divorce some ten years later in their early adult years. They too expressed disappointment at not being able to grow up in an intact family and wondered if their life wouldn't have been better if they had been able to do so.

Concept Table 9.1: Families		
Concept	**Processes/Related Ideas**	**Characteristics/Description**
Parenting Styles	The Four Major Categories	Authoritarian, authoritative, permissive indifferent, and permissive indulgent are four main categories of parenting. Authoritative parenting is associated with children's social competence more than the other styles.
Adapting Parenting to Developmental Changes in the Child	Its Nature	Parents need to adapt their interaction strategies as the child grows older, using less physical manipulation and more reasoning in the process.
Cultural, Social Class, and Ethnic Variations in Families	Cross-Cultural and Social Class Comparisons	Authoritative parenting is the most common childrearing pattern around the world. Working class and low-income parents place a higher value on external characteristics, middle-class parents place a higher value on internal characteristics, and these social classes vary in their childrearing patterns.
	Ethnic Variations	Ethnic-minority families differ from White American families in their size, structure, and composition, their reliance on kinship networks, and their levels of income and education.
Sibling Relationships	Their Nature	More than 80 percent of American children have one or more siblings. Children interact with siblings more negatively and punitively and in less varied ways than with their parents. In some cases, siblings are stronger socializing influences than parents.
	Birth Order	The relationships of firstborn children and their parents are often especially close and demanding, which may account for the stronger achievement orientation and anxiety in firstborn children than later-born children.
The Changing Family	Working Mothers	A mother's working full-time outside the home can have both positive and negative effects on the child; there is no indication that long-term effects are negative overall.
	Divorce	The early father-absent tradition has been supplanted by an emphasis on the complexity of the divorced family, pre- and postdivorce family functioning, and varied responses to divorce. Among the factors that influence the child's adjustment in divorced families are poverty, conflict, time since divorce, sex of the child and sex of the custodial parent.

• *Critical Thinking* •

Imagine you are a judge in a custodial dispute. What are some of the key factors you would consider in awarding custody?

In sum, large numbers of children are growing up in divorced families. Most children initially experience considerable stress when their parents divorce, and they are at risk for developing problem behaviors. However, divorce also can remove children from marriages in which there is a great deal of conflict. Many children emerge from divorce as competent individuals. In recent years, researchers have moved away from the view that single-parent families are atypical or pathological, focusing more on the diversity of children's responses to divorce and the factors that facilitate or disrupt the development and adjustment of children in these family circumstances (Hetherington, 1991; Hetherington, Hagan, & Anderson, 1989; Santrock, 1990a,b).

Thus far, we have discussed a number of ideas about family relationships in early childhood. A summary of these ideas is presented in concept table 9.1. We now turn to the intriguing world of children's peer relations and play.

Peer Relations

Peer relations take up an increasing amount of time during early childhood. Many of children's greatest frustrations and happiest moments come when they are with their peers. **Peers** *are children who are of about the same age or maturity level.* Same-age peer interaction serves a unique role in our culture (Hartup, 1983). Age grading would occur even if schools were not age graded and children were left to choose the composition of their own societies. After all, one can only learn to be a good fighter among age mates: The bigger guys will kill you and the little ones are no challenge. One of the most important functions of the peer group is to provide a source of information and comparison about the world outside the family. From the peer group, children receive feedback about their abilities. Children evaluate what they do in terms of whether it is better than, as good as, or worse than what other children do. It is hard to do this at home, because siblings are usually older or younger.

Are peers necessary for development? When peer monkeys who have been reared together are separated from one another, they become depressed and less advanced socially (Suomi, Harlow, & Domek, 1970). The literature on human development contains a classic example of the importance of peers in social development. Anna Freud studied six children from different families who banded together after their parents were killed in World War II (Freud & Dann, 1951). Intensive peer attachment was observed; the children were a tightly knit group, dependent on one another and aloof with outsiders. Even though deprived of parental care, they became neither delinquent nor psychotic.

Thus, good peer relations may be necessary for normal social development. Social isolation, or the inability to "plug in" to a social network, is linked with many problems and disturbances, ranging from delinquency and problem drinking to depression (Cairns & Cairns, 1989; Kupersmidt & Coie, 1990). In one investigation, poor peer relations in childhood was associated with a tendency to drop out of school and delinquent behavior in adolescence (Roff, Sells, & Golden, 1972). In another investigation, harmonious peer relations in adolescence was related to positive mental health at midlife (Hightower, 1990).

The frequency of peer interaction, both positive and negative, continues to increase throughout early childhood (Hartup, 1983). Although aggressive interaction and rough-and-tumble play increase, the *proportion* of aggressive exchanges to friendly interchanges decreases, especially among middle-class boys. With age, children tend to abandon this immature and inefficient social interaction and acquire more mature methods of relating to peers.

What are some similarities and differences in peer and parent-child relationships? Children touch, smile, frown, and vocalize when they interact with both parents and other children. However, rough-and-tumble play occurs mainly with other children, not with adults. In times of stress, children usually move toward their parents rather than their peers.

The worlds of parent-child and peer relations are distinct, but they are coordinated, too. Some developmentalists believe that secure attachment to parents promotes healthy peer relations (Ainsworth, 1979; Sroufe, in press). However, as we discussed in chapter 7, others believe the route to competency, including positive peer relations, is not always through secure attachment (Kagan, 1987). Nonetheless, the data are consistent with the theory that children's relationships with their parents serve as emotional bases for exploring and enjoying peer relations (Hartup, 1989, Pettit, Dodge, & Brown, 1988).

One investigation revealed how the relationship history of each peer helps to predict the nature of peer interaction (Olweus, 1980). Some boys were highly aggressive and other boys were the recipients of aggression throughout the preschool years. The "bullies" as well as the "whipping boys" had distinctive relationship histories. The bullies' parents treated them with rejection, had an authoritarian orientation, and were permissive toward aggression; the bullies' families were also characterized by discord. By contrast, the whipping boys' parents were anxious and overprotective, taking special care to have their son avoid aggression. The well-adjusted boys were not as involved in aggressive interchanges. Their parents did not sanction aggression; their responsive involvement with their children promoted the development of self-assertion as an adaptive pattern (Olweus, 1989).

Play

An extensive amount of peer interaction during childhood involves play. But while peer interaction can involve play, social play is but one type of play. Just what is play? **Play** *is a pleasurable activity that is engaged in for its own sake.* Our coverage of play includes its functions, Parten's classic study of play, and types of play.

Play's Functions

Play is essential to the young child's health. As today's children move into the twenty-first century and continue to experience pressure in their lives, play becomes even more crucial. Play increases affiliation with peers, releases tension, advances cognitive development, increases exploration, and provides a safe haven in which to engage in potentially dangerous behavior. Play increases the probability that children will converse and interact with each other. During this interaction, children practice the roles they will assume later in life.

For Freud and Erikson, play was an especially useful form of human adjustment, helping the child master anxieties and conflicts. Because tensions are relieved in play, the child can cope with life's problems. Play permits the child to work off excess physical energy and to release pent-up tensions. **Play**

therapy *allows the child to work off frustrations and is a medium through which the therapist can analyze the child's conflicts and ways of coping with them. Children may feel less threatened and be more likely to express their true feelings in the context of play.*

Piaget (1962) saw play as a medium that advances children's cognitive development. At the same time, he said that children's cognitive development *constrains* the way they play. Play permits children to practice their competencies and acquired skills in a relaxed, pleasurable way. Piaget believed that cognitive structures need to be exercised, and play provides the perfect setting for this exercise. For example, children who have just learned to add or multiply begin to play with numbers in different ways as they perfect these operations, laughing as they do so.

Vygotsky (1962), whose developmental theory was discussed in chapter 8, also believed that play is an excellent setting for cognitive development. He was especially interested in the symbolic and make-believe aspects of play, as when a child substitutes a stick for a horse and rides the stick as if it were a horse (Smolucha, 1989). For young children, the imaginary situation is real. Parents should encourage such imaginary play because it advances the child's cognitive development, especially creative thought (Arman-Nolley, 1989).

Daniel Berlyne (1960) described play as exciting and pleasurable in itself because it satisfies the exploratory drive each of us possesses. This drive involves curiosity and a desire for information about something new or unusual. Play is a means whereby children can safely explore and seek out new information—something they might not otherwise do. Play encourages this exploratory behavior by offering children the possibilities of novelty, complexity, uncertainty, surprise, and incongruity.

Parten's Classic Study of Play

Many years ago, Mildred Parten (1932) developed an elaborate classification of children's play. Based on observations of children in free play at nursery school, Parten arrived at these play categories:

1. **Unoccupied play** *occurs when the child is not engaging in play as it is commonly understood and may stand in one spot, look around the room, or perform random movements that do not seem to have a goal.* In most nursery schools, unoccupied play is less frequent than other forms of play.

And that park grew up with me; that small world widened as I learned its secret boundaries, as I discovered new refuges in the woods and jungles: hidden homes and lairs for the multitudes of imagination, for cowboys and Indians, and the tall-terrible half-people who rode on nightmares through my bedroom. But it was not the only world—that world of rockery, gravel path, playbank, bowling green, bandstands, reservoir, dahlia garden, where an ancient keeper named smoky, was the whiskered snake in the grass one must keep off. There was another world where with my friends I used to dawdle on half holidays along the bent and devon-facing seashore, hoping for gold watches or the skull of a sheep or a message in a bottle to be washed up by the tide.

~ *Dylan Thomas*

2. **Solitary play** *occurs when the child plays alone and independently of others*. The child seems engrossed in the activity and does not care much about anything else that is happening. Two- and 3-year-olds engage more frequently in solitary play than older preschoolers do.

3. **Onlooker play** *occurs when the child watches other children play*. The child may talk with other children and ask questions but does not enter into their play behavior. The child's active interest in other children's play distinguishes onlooker play from unoccupied play.

4. **Parallel play** *occurs when the child plays separately from others, but with toys like those the others are using or in a manner that mimics their play*. The older children are, the less frequently they engage in this type of play, although even older preschool children engage in parallel play quite often.

5. **Associative play** *occurs when play involves social interaction with little or no organization*. In this type of play children seem to be more interested in each other than in the tasks they are performing. Borrowing or lending toys and following or leading one another in line are examples of associative play.

6. **Cooperative play** *involves social interaction in a group with a sense of group identity and organized activity*. Children's formal games, competition aimed at winning, and groups formed by the teacher for doing things together are examples of cooperative play. Cooperative play is the prototype for the games of middle childhood. Little cooperative play is seen in the preschool years.

Parten's research on play was conducted more than half a century ago. To determine whether her findings were out of date, Keith Barnes (1971) used Parten's categories of play to observe a group of preschoolers. He found that children in the 1970s did not engage in as much associative and cooperative play as they did in the 1930s. These changes in play probably occurred because children have become more passive as a consequence of heavy television viewing and because toys are more abundant and attractive than they were forty years ago. Today, solitary play may be more natural, and parents may encourage children to play by themselves more than parents did years ago. The developmental changes that were observed by Parten were also observed by Barnes. That is, 3-year-old children engaged in solitary play and parallel play more than 5-year-old children did, and 5-year-old children engaged in associative and cooperative play more than other types of play.

Types of Play

Parten's categories represent one way of thinking about the different types of play. However, today researchers and practitioners who are involved with children's play believe other types of play are important in children's development. Whereas Parten's categories emphasize the role of play in the child's social world, the contemporary perspective on play emphasizes both the cognitive and social aspects of play. Among the most widely studied types of children's play today are: sensorimotor/practice play, pretense/symbolic play, social play, constructive play, and games (Bergin, 1988). We consider each of these types of play in turn.

Sensorimotor/Practice Play

Sensorimotor play *is behavior engaged in by infants to derive pleasure from exercising their existing sensorimotor schemas.* The development of sensorimotor play follows Piaget's description of sensorimotor thought, which we discussed in chapter 8. Infants initially engage in exploratory and playful visual and motor transactions in the second quarter of the first year of life. By 9 months of age, infants begin to select novel objects for exploration and play, especially those that are responsive, such as toys that make noise or bounce. By 12 months of age, infants enjoy making things work and exploring cause and effect. At this point in development, children like toys that perform when they act on them.

In the second year, infants begin to understand the social meaning of objects and their play reflects this awareness. And 2-year-olds may distinguish between exploratory play that is interesting but not humorous and "playful" play, which has incongruous and humorous dimensions (McGhee, 1984). For example, a 2-year-old might "drink" from a shoe or call a dog a "cow." When 2-year-olds find these deliberate incongruities funny, they are beginning to show evidence of symbolic play and the ability to play with ideas.

Practice play *involves the repetition of behavior when new skills are being learned or when physical or mental mastery and coordination of skills is required for games or sports. Sensorimotor play, which often involves practice play, is primarily confined to infancy, while practice play can be engaged in throughout life.* During the preschool years, children often engage in play that involves practicing various skills. Estimates indicate that practice play constitutes about one-third of the preschool child's play activities, but less than one-sixth of the elementary school child's play activities (Rubin, Fein, & Vandenberg, 1983). Practice play contributes to the development of coordinated motor skills needed for later game playing. While practice play declines in the elementary school years, practice play activities such as running, jumping, sliding, twirling, and throwing balls or other objects are frequently observed on the playgrounds at elementary schools. While these activities appear similar to the earlier practice play of the preschool years, practice play in the elementary school years differs from earlier practice play because much of it is ends rather than means related. That is, elementary school children often engage in practice play for the purpose of improving motor skills needed to compete in games or sports.

Pretense/Symbolic Play

Pretense/symbolic play *occurs when the child transforms the physical environment into a symbol* (DeHart & Smith, 1991; Fein, 1986; Howes, Unger & Seidner, 1989; Rogers & Sawyers, 1988). Between 9 and 30 months of age, children increase their use of objects in symbolic play. They learn to transform objects, that is substituting them for other objects and acting toward them as if they were these other objects. For example, a preschool child treats a table as if it is a car and says, "I'm fixing the car," as he grabs a leg of the table.

Many experts on play consider the preschool years the "golden age" of symbolic/pretense play that is dramatic or sociodramatic in nature (Bergin, 1988; Singer & Singer, 1988). This type of make-believe play often appears at about 18 months of age and reaches a peak at 4 to 5 years of age, then gradually declines. In the early elementary school years, children's interests often shift to games.

Catherine Garvey (1977) has spent many years observing young children's play. She indicates that three elements are found in almost all of the pretend play she has observed: props, plot, and roles. Children use objects as *props* in their pretend play. Children can pretend to drink from a real cup or from a seashell. They can even create a make-believe cup from thin air, if nothing else is available. Most pretend play also has a story line, though the *plot* may be quite simple. Pretend play themes often reflect what children see going on in their lives, as when they play family, school, or doctor. Fantasy play can also take its theme from a story children have heard, or a show they have seen. In pretend play, children try out many different *roles*. Some roles, like mother or teacher, are derived from reality. Other roles, like cowgirls or Superman, come from fantasy.

Social Play

Social play *is play that involves social interaction with peers.* Parten's categories, which we described earlier, are oriented toward social play. Social play with peers increases dramatically during the preschool years. In addition to general social play with peers and group pretense or sociodramatic play, another form of social play is rough-and-tumble play. The movement patterns of rough-and-tumble play are often similar to those of hostile behavior (running, chasing, wrestling, jumping, falling, hitting), but in rough-and-tumble play these behaviors are accompanied by signals such as laughter, exaggerated movement, and open rather than closed hands, which indicates this is play (Bateson, 1956).

Constructive Play

Constructive play *combines sensorimotor/practice repetitive activity with symbolic representation of ideas. Constructive play occurs when children engage in self-regulated creation or construction of a product or a problem solution.* Constructive play increases in the preschool years as symbolic play increases and sensorimotor play decreases. In the preschool years, some practice play is replaced by constructive play. For example, instead of moving their fingers around and around in finger paint (practice play), children are more likely to draw the outline of a house or a person in the paint (constructive play). Some researchers have found that constructive play is the most common type of play during the preschool years (Hetherington, Cox, & Cox, 1979; Rubin, Maioni, & Hornung, 1976). Constructive play is also a frequent form of play in the elementary school years, both in and out of the classroom. Constructive play is one of the few playlike activities allowed in work-centered classrooms. For example, having children create a play about a social studies topic involves constructive play. Whether such activities are considered play by children usually depends on whether they get to choose whether to do it (it is play) or whether the teacher imposes it (it is not play), and also whether it is enjoyable (it is play) or not (it is not play) (King, 1982).

Constructive play can also be used in the elementary school years to foster academic skill learning, thinking skills, and problem solving. Many educators plan classroom activities that include humor, encourage playing with ideas, and promote creativity (Bergin, 1988). Educators also often support the performance of plays, the writing of imaginative stories, the expression of artistic abilities, and the playful exploration of computers and other technological equipment. However, distinctions between work and play frequently become blurred in the elementary school classroom.

Games

Games *are activities engaged in for pleasure that include rules and often competition with one or more individuals.* Preschool children may begin to participate in social game play that involves simple rules of reciprocity and turn taking, but games take on a much more salient role in the lives of elementary school children. In one investigation, the highest incidence of game playing

Table 9.1: Types of Play

Sensorimotor/ Practice Play	Pretense/ Symbolic Play	Social Play	Constructive Play	Games
Sensorimotor play is behavior engaged in by infants to derive pleasure from exercising their existing sensorimotor schemas. Sensorimotor play begins in the second quarter of the first year of life. Sensorimotor play is practice play. Practice play involves the repetition of behavior when new skills are being learned or when physical or mental mastery and coordination of skills is required for games or sports. Although sensorimotor play is confined to infancy, practice play continues through life.	Pretense/symbolic play occurs when the child transforms the environment into a symbol. Between 9 and 30 months, children increase their use of objects in symbolic play. Many experts consider the preschool years the "golden years" of symbolic/ pretense play that is dramatic or sociodramatic in nature. This type of play peaks at about 4 to 6 years of age, then gradually declines.	Social play is play that involves social interaction with peers. Parten's categories are oriented toward social rather than cognitive play. Social play with peers increases dramatically in the preschool years. In addition to general social play with peers, a specific form of social play is rough-and-tumble play. Group pretense or sociodramatic play is also social play.	Constructive play combines sensorimotor/practice repetitive activity with symbolic representation of objects and ideas. Constructive play occurs when children engage in self-regulated creation or construction of a product or a problem solution. Constructive play increases in the preschool years as symbolic play increases and sensorimotor play decreases. Constructive play is one of the most frequent types of play in the preschool and elementary school years.	Games are activities engaged in for pleasure that include rules and often competition with other individuals. Preschool children may begin to participate in social game play that involves simple rules of reciprocity and turn taking, but games take on a more salient role in children's lives in the elementary school years.

occurred between 10 and 12 years of age (Eiferman, 1971). After age 12, games decline in popularity, often being replaced by practice play, conversations, and organized sports (Bergin, 1988).

In the elementary years, games feature the meaningfulness of a challenge (Eiferman, 1971). This challenge is present if two or more children have the skills required to play and understand the rules of the game. Among the types of games children engage in are steady or constant games, such as tag, which are played consistently; recurrent or cyclical games, such as marbles or hopscotch, which seem to follow cycles of popularity and decline; sporadic games which are rarely played; and one-time games, such as hula hoop contests, which rise to popularity once and then disappear.

In sum, play is a multidimensional, complex concept. It ranges from an infant's simple exercise of a newfound sensorimotor talent to a preschool child's riding a tricycle to an older child's participation in organized games. An overview of the different forms of play described by contemporary play theorists and researchers is presented in table 9.1.

"Mrs. Horton, could you stop by school today?"

Television

Few developments in society over the past 25 years have had a greater impact on children than television has. Many children spend more time in front of the television set than they do with their parents. Although it is only one mass medium that affects children's behavior, television is the most influential. The persuasion capabilities of television are staggering; the 20,000 hours of television watched by the time the average American adolescent graduates from high school are greater than the number of hours spent in the classroom.

Television's Many Roles

While television can have a negative influence on children's development by taking them away from homework, making them passive learners, teaching them stereotypes, providing them with violent models of aggression, and presenting them with unrealistic views of the world, television can have a positive influence on children's development by presenting motivating educational programs, increasing children's information about the world beyond their immediate environment, and providing models of prosocial behavior (Esty & Fisch, 1991).

Television has been called many things, not all of them good. Depending on one's point of view, it may be a "window on the world," the "one-eyed monster," or the "boob tube." Television has been attacked as one of the reasons that scores on national achievement tests in reading and mathematics are lower now than in the past. Television, it is claimed, attracts children away from books and schoolwork. In one study, children who read printed materials, such as books, watched television less than those who did not read (Huston, Seigle, & Bremer, 1983). Furthermore, critics argue that television trains children to become passive learners: rarely, if ever, does television require active responses from the observer.

Television also is said to deceive; that is, it teaches children that problems are resolved easily and that everything always comes out right in the end.

Early Childhood

For example, TV detectives usually take only 30 to 60 minutes to sort through a complex array of clues to reveal the killer—and they *always* find the killer! Violence is a way of life on many shows. It is all right for police to use violence and to break moral codes in their fight against evildoers. The lasting results of violence are rarely brought home to the viewer. A person who is injured suffers for only a few seconds; in real life, the person might need months or years to recover, or might not recover at all. Yet, one out of every two first-grade children says that the adults on television are like adults in real life (Lyle & Hoffman, 1972).

A special concern is how ethnic minorities are portrayed on television. Ethnic minorities have historically been underrepresented and misrepresented on television. Ethnic-minority characters—whether Black, Asian, Hispanic, or Native American—have traditionally been presented as less dignified and less positive than White characters (Condry, 1989). In one recent investigation, character portrayals of ethnic minorities were examined during heavy children's viewing hours (weekdays 4–6 P.M. and 7–11 P.M.) (Williams & Condry, 1989). The percentage of White characters far exceeded the actual percentage of Whites in the United States; the percentage of Black, Asian, and Hispanic characters fell short of the population statistics. Hispanic characters were especially underrepresented—only 0.6 percent of the characters were Hispanic, while the Hispanic population in the United States is 6.4 percent of the total U.S. population. Minorities tended to hold lower status jobs and were more likely than Whites to be cast as criminals or victims.

There are some positive aspects to television's influence on children. For one, television presents children with a world that is different than the one in which they live. It exposes children to a wider variety of viewpoints and information than they might get from only their parents, teachers, and peers. And some television programs have educational and developmental benefits. One of television's major programming attempts to educate children is *Sesame Street*, which is designed to teach children both cognitive and social skills. The program began in 1969 and is still going strong.

Sesame Street demonstrates that education and entertainment can work well together. Through *Sesame Street*, children experience a world of learning that is both exciting and entertaining. *Sesame Street* also follows the principle that teaching can be accomplished in both direct and indirect ways. Using the direct way, a teacher might tell children exactly what they are going to be taught and then teach them. However, in real life, social skills are often communicated in indirect ways. Rather than merely telling children, "You should cooperate with others," TV can show children so that children can figure out what it means to be cooperative and what the advantages are. More about Sesame Street appears in Cultural Worlds of Development 9.2.

Amount of Television Watching by Children

Just how much television do young children watch? They watch a lot, and they seem to be watching more all the time. In the 1950s, 3-year-old children watched television for less than one hour a day; 5-year-olds watched just over 2 hours a day. But in the 1970s, preschool children watched television for an average of 4 hours a day; elementary schoolchildren watched for as long as 6 hours a day (Friedrich & Stein, 1973). In the 1980s, children averaged 11 to 28 hours of television per week (Huston, Watkins, & Kunkel, 1989), which is more than for any other activity except sleep. Of special concern is the extent

SESAME STREET AROUND THE WORLD

*W*hen *Sesame Street* first appeared in 1969, the creators of the show had no idea that this "street" would lead to locations as distant as Kuwait, Israel, Latin America, and the Philippines. In the twenty years since *Sesame Street* first aired in the United States, the show has been televised in 84 countries. Thirteen foreign language versions of the show have been produced. Following is a sampling of *Sesame Street* productions in various countries:

- **Plaza Sesamo, Latin America** The show is seen in 17 South and Central American countries, as well as in Puerto Rico. The diversity of cultures and lifestyles in Latin America is given special emphasis.
- **Rechov Sumsum, Israel** The set represents a typical Israeli neighborhood, with old houses next to modern apartment buildings. Its puppet characters include Kippy, a full-size pink porcupine who is naive, friendly, and opinionated. Moishe Oofnick is a shaggy grouch. Reflecting the diversity of Israel's population, the cast includes people from different ethnic and religious backgrounds who live in harmony.

Don Pimpón of Spain's "Barrio Sesamo."

- **Sesamstraat, The Netherlands** Children are familiarized with the concept of school and any anxieties they might have about school are dispelled. Some segments encourage children to discuss their fears openly. Other segments show interactions between disabled and nondisabled children. One of the puppets is Pino, a 7-foot-tall blue bird who is eager to learn.

- **Barrio Sesamo, Spain** The bakery is *Barrio Sesamo's* central meeting place. The residents include two full-size puppets. Espinete, a special friend of the children, is a hedgehog who tries to get the cast members to play games whenever possible. Don Pimpón is a shaggy old codger, at times a bit absentminded, who has traveled extensively and entertains with stories of his adventures (Corwin, 1989).

to which children are exposed to violence and aggression on television. Up to 80 percent of the prime-time shows include violent acts, including beatings, shootings, and stabbings. The frequency of violence increases on the Saturday morning cartoon shows which average more than 25 violent acts per hour.

Effects of Television on Children's Aggression and Prosocial Behavior

What are the effects of television violence on children's aggression? Does television merely stimulate a child to go out and buy a Star Wars ray gun, or can it trigger an attack on a playmate? When the child grows up, can television violence increase the likelihood he will violently attack someone?

In one longitudinal investigation, the amount of violence viewed on television at age 8 was significantly related to the seriousness of criminal acts performed as an adult (Huesmann, 1986). In another investigation, long-term exposure to television violence was significantly related to the likelihood of aggression in 1,565 12- to 17-year-old boys (Belson, 1978). Boys who watched the most aggression on television were the most likely to commit a violent crime, swear, be aggressive in sports, threaten violence toward another boy, write slogans on walls, or break windows. These investigations are *correlational* in nature, so we cannot conclude from them that television violence causes children to be more aggressive, only that watching television violence is *associated* with aggressive behavior. In one experiment, children were randomly assigned to one of two groups: one watched television shows taken directly from violent Saturday morning cartoon offerings on eleven different days; the second group watched television cartoon shows with all of the violence removed (Steur, Applefield, & Smith, 1971). The children were then observed during play at their preschool. The preschool children who saw the TV cartoon shows with violence kicked, choked, and pushed their playmates more than preschool children who watched nonviolent TV cartoon shows. Because children were randomly assigned to the two conditions (TV cartoons with violence versus no violence), we can conclude that exposure to TV violence *caused* the increased aggression in children in this investigation.

Although some critics have argued that the effects of television violence do not warrant the conclusion that TV violence causes aggression (Freedman, 1984), many experts argue that TV violence can induce aggressive or antisocial behavior in children (Condry, 1989; Huston, Watkins, & Kunkel, 1989; Liebert & Sprafkin, 1988). Of course, television is not the *only* cause of aggression. There is no *one,* single cause of any social behavior. Aggression, like all other social behaviors, has a number of determinants.

Children need to be taught critical viewing skills to counter the adverse effects of television violence. In one investigation, elementary school children were randomly assigned to either an experimental or a control group (Huesmann & others, 1983). In the experimental group, children assisted in making a film to help children who had been fooled or harmed by television. The children also composed essays that focused on how television is not like real life and why it is bad to imitate TV violence or watch too much television. In the control group, children received no training in critical viewing skills. The children who were trained in critical viewing skills developed more negative attitudes about TV violence and reduced their aggressive behavior.

Television can also teach children that it is better to behave in positive, prosocial ways than in negative, antisocial ways. Aimee Leifer (1973) demonstrated that television is associated with prosocial behavior in young children: she selected a number of episodes from the television show *Sesame Street* that reflected positive social interchanges. She was especially interested in situations that taught children how to use their social skills. For example, in one interchange, two men were fighting over the amount of space available to them; they gradually began to cooperate and to share the space. Children who watched these episodes copied these behaviors, and in later social situations, they applied the prosocial lessons they had learned.

Parents' Role in Children's Television Viewing

How much do parents take an active role in discussing television with their children? For the most part, parents do not discuss the content of television shows with their children (Leifer, Gordon, & Graves, 1974). Parents need to be especially sensitive to young children's viewing habits because the age period of 2½ to 6 is when long-term television-viewing habits begin to be established

(Murphy, Talley, & Huston, 1991). Children from lower socioeconomic status families watch television more than children from higher socioeconomic status families (Huston, Seigle, & Bremer, 1983). And children who live in families involved in high conflict watch more television than children who live in families low in conflict (Price & Feshbach, 1982). In one recent investigation, parents who showed more empathy and were more sensitive to their children had children who preferred less fantasy fare on television (Tangney, in press). In dysfunctional families, children may use the lower developmental level of fantasy-oriented children's programs to escape from the taxing, stressful circumstances of the home environment.

Parents can make television a more positive influence in children's lives. The following guidelines developed by Dorothy and Jerome Singer (1987) can go a long way in reducing television's negative effects and improving its role as a positive influence in children's development.

1. Develop good viewing habits early in the child's life.
2. Encourage planned viewing of specific programs rather than random viewing. Be active with young children between planned programs.
3. Look for children's programs that feature children in the child's age group.
4. Make sure that television is not used as a substitute for participating in other activities.
5. Develop discussion about sensitive television themes with children. Give them the opportunity to ask questions about the programs.
6. Balance reading and television activities. Children can "follow up" interesting television programs by checking out the library book from which some programs are adapted and by pursuing additional stories by the authors of those books.
7. Help children to develop a balanced viewing schedule of education, action, comedy, fine arts, fantasy, sports, and so on.
8. Point out positive examples that show how various ethnic and cultural groups all contribute to making a better society.
9. Point out positive examples of females performing competently both in professions and at home.

So far, we have discussed a number of ideas about peers, play, and television. A summary of these ideas is presented in concept table 9.2. Now we turn our attention to children's personality development in early childhood, beginning with the self.

The Self

We learned in chapter 7, that toward the end of the second year of life, children develop a sense of self. During early childhood, some important developments in the self take place. Among these developments are facing the issue of initiative versus guilt and enhanced self-understanding.

Initiative versus Guilt

According to Erikson (1968), the psychosocial stage that characterizes early childhood is *initiative versus guilt*. By now, children have become convinced that they are a person of their own; during early childhood, they must discover

When I say "I," I mean a thing absolutely unique, not to be confused with any other.

~ *Ugo Betti,*
The Inquiry, *1944*

Early Childhood

Concept Table 9.2: Peers, Play, and Television

Concept	Processes/Related Ideas	Characteristics/Description
Peers	The Nature of Peer Relations	Peers are powerful social agents. The term *peers* refers to children who are of about the same age or maturity level. Peers provide a source of information and comparison about the world outside the family.
	The Development of Peer Relations	The frequency of peer interaction, both positive and negative, increases during the preschool years.
	The Distinct but Coordinated Worlds of Parent-Child and Peer Relations	Peer relations are both like and unlike family relations. Children touch, smile, and vocalize when they interact with parents and peers. However, rough-and-tumble play occurs mainly with peers. In times of stress, children generally seek out their parents. Healthy family relations usually promote healthy peer relations.
Play	Play's Functions	Affiliation with peers, tension release, advances in cognitive development, exploration, and provision of a safe haven in which to engage in potentially dangerous activities, are among the benefits of play.
	Parten's Classic Study of Play	Parten developed the categories of unoccupied, solitary, onlooker, parallel, associative, and cooperative play. Three-year-olds engage in more solitary play and parallel play than 5-year-olds, and 5-year-olds engage in cooperative and associative play more than other types of play.
	Types of Play	The contemporary perspective emphasizes both the cognitive and social aspects of play. Among the most widely studied aspects of children's play today are sensorimotor/practice play, pretense/symbolic play, social play, constructive play, and games.
Television	Its Effects on Children	While television can have a negative influence on children's development by taking them away from homework, making them passive learners, teaching them stereotypes, providing them with violent models of aggression, and presenting them with unrealistic views of the world, television can have a positive influence by presenting motivating educational programs, increasing children's information about the world beyond their immediate environment, and providing models of prosocial behavior. Children watch huge amounts of television, with preschool children watching an average of 4 hours a day. Up to 80 percent of the prime-time shows have violent episodes. Television violence is not the only cause of children's aggression, but most experts conclude that it can induce aggression and antisocial behavior in children. Prosocial behavior on television is associated with increased positive behavior by children. Parents rarely discuss television's contents with their children. Television-viewing habits are often formed in the early childhood years.

what kind of person they will become. They intensely identify with their parents, who most of the time appear to them to be powerful and beautiful, although often unreasonable, disagreeable, and sometimes even dangerous. During early childhood, children use their perceptual, motor, cognitive, and language skills to make things happen. They have a surplus of energy that permits them to forget failures quickly and to approach new areas that seem desirable—even if they seem dangerous—with undiminished zest and some increased sense of direction. On their own *initiative,* then, children at this stage exuberantly move out into a wider social world.

The great governor of initiative is *conscience.* Children now not only feel afraid of being found out, but they also begin to hear the inner voice of self-observation, self-guidance, and self-punishment. Their initiative and enthusiasm may bring them not only rewards, but also punishments. Widespread disappointment at this stage leads to an unleashing of guilt that lowers the child's self-concept.

Whether children leave this stage with a sense of initiative that outweighs their sense of guilt depends in large part on how parents respond to their self-initiated activities. Children who are given freedom and opportunity to initiate motor play such as running, bike riding, sledding, skating, tussling, and wrestling have their sense of initiative supported. Initiative is also supported when parents answer their children's questions and do not deride or inhibit fantasy or play activity. In contrast, if children are made to feel that their motor activity is bad, that their questions are a nuisance, and that their play is silly and stupid, then they often develop a sense of guilt over self-initiated activities that may persist through life's later stages (Elkind, 1970).

Self-Understanding

Self-understanding *is the child's cognitive representation of self, the substance and content of the child's self-conceptions* (Damon & Hart, 1988). For example, a 5-year-old girl understands that she is a girl, has blond hair, likes to ride her bicycle, has a friend, and is a swimmer. An 11-year-old boy understands that he is a student, a boy, a football player, a family member, a video-game lover, and a rock music fan. A child's self-understanding is based on the various roles and membership categories that define who children are (Harter, 1988). Though not the whole of personal identity, self-understanding provides its rational underpinnings (Damon & Hart, 1988).

The rudimentary beginning of self-understanding begins with self recognition, which takes place by approximately 18 months of age. Since children can verbally communicate their ideas, research on self-understanding in childhood is not limited to visual self-recognition, as it was during infancy. Mainly by interviewing children, researchers have probed children's conceptions of many aspects of self-understanding, including mind and body, self in relation to others, and pride and shame in self. In early childhood, children usually conceive of the self in physical terms. Most young children think the self is part of their body, usually their head. Young children usually confuse self, mind, and body (Broughton, 1978). Because the self is a body part, it can be described along many material dimensions, such as size, shape, and color. Young children distinguish themselves from others through many different physical and material attributes. Says 4-year-old Sandra, "I'm different from Jennifer because I have brown hair and she has blond hair." Says 4-year-old Ralph, "I am different from Hank because I am taller, and I am different from my sister because I have a bicycle."

Researchers also believe that the *active dimension* is a central component of the self in early childhood (Keller, Ford, & Meacham, 1978). If we define the category *physical* broadly enough, we can include physical actions as well as body image and material possessions. For example, preschool children often describe themselves in terms of activities like play. In sum, in early childhood, children frequently think of themselves in terms of a physical self or an active self.

Gender

Few aspects of children's social development are more central to their identity and to their social relationships than their sex or gender. What exactly do we mean by gender? What are the biological, cognitive, and social influences on gender? We consider each of these questions in turn.

What Is Gender?

While sex refers to the biological dimension of being male or female, **gender** *refers to the social dimension of being male or female.* Two aspects of gender bear special mention—gender identity and gender role. **Gender identity** *is the sense of being male or female, which most children acquire by the time they are 3 years old.* **Gender role** *is a set of expectations that prescribe how females and males should think, act, and feel.*

Biological Influences

One of Freud's basic assumptions is that human behavior and history are directly related to reproductive processes. From this assumption arises the belief that sexuality is essentially unlearned and instinctual. Erikson (1968) extended this argument, claiming that the psychological differences between males and females stem from anatomical differences. Erikson argued that—because of genital structure—males are more intrusive and aggressive, females more inclusive and passive. Erikson's belief has become known as *"anatomy is destiny."* Critics of the anatomy-is-destiny view believe that Erikson has not given experience adequate importance. They argue that males and females are more free to choose their gender role than Erikson allows. In response to the critics, Erikson has modified his view, saying that females in today's world are transcending their biological heritage and correcting society's overemphasis on male intrusiveness.

Biology's influence on gender roles also involves sex hormones, which we learned about in chapter 3. These are among the most powerful and subtle chemicals in nature. Remember that these hormones are controlled by the brain's master gland, the pituitary. In females, hormones from the pituitary carry messages to the ovaries and produce the hormone estrogen. In males, the pituitary messages travel to the testes where the sex hormone androgen is manufactured.

The secretion of androgen from the testes of the young male fetus (or the absence of androgen in the female) completely controls sexual development in the womb. If enough androgen is produced, as happens with a normal developing boy, male organs and genitals develop. **Hermaphrodites** *are individuals whose genitals become intermediate between male and female because of a hormonal imbalance (as in the developing male with insufficient androgen, or a female exposed to an excess of androgen).* When genetically female infants are born with masculine-looking genitals, surgery is usually performed so that a female genital-female genetic match is achieved. Until they reach puberty, these females often behave in a more aggressive, tomboyish manner than most girls. They also dress and play in ways that are more characteristic of boys than girls (Ehrhardt, 1987; Money, 1987).

Is the behavior of these surgically corrected females due to their prenatal hormones? Or is their behavior due to their social experiences? Experiments with different animal species—rats, monkeys, and many others—reveal that when male hormones are injected into female embryos, the females later display a more masculine appearance and behave in a more masculine way

(Hines, 1982). However, as we move from animals to humans, hormonal control over behavior is usually less dominant. Since the androgenized girls looked more "masculine," others possibly reacted to them more like they were boys. The biological appearance of sex has social consequences for gender.

No one argues about the presence of genetic, biochemical, and anatomical differences between the sexes. Even child developmentalists with a strong environmental orientation acknowledge that boys and girls will be treated differently because of their physical differences and their different roles in reproduction. The importance of biological factors is not at issue. What is at issue is the directness or indirectness of their effects on social behavior (Huston, 1983). For example, if a high androgen level directly influences the central nervous system, which in turn produces a higher activity level, then the effect is more direct. By contrast, if a high level of androgen produces strong muscle development, which in turn causes others to expect the child to be a good athlete and in turn prompts the child to participate in sports, then the biological effect is more indirect.

While virtually everyone thinks that a child's behavior as male or female is due to an interaction of biological and environmental factors, an interactionist position means different things to different people (Hinde, 1989; Maccoby, 1987; Money, 1987). For some it suggests that certain environmental conditions are required to make preprogrammed dispositions appear. For others it suggests that the same environment will have different effects depending on the child's predispositions. For yet others it means that children shape their environments, including their interpersonal environment, as well as vice versa. Processes of influence and counterinfluence unfold over time. Throughout development, males and females actively construct their own version of acceptable masculine and feminine behavior patterns.

Social Influences

In our culture, adults discriminate between the sexes shortly after the infant's birth. The "pink and blue" treatment may be applied to boys and girls before they leave the hospital. Soon afterward, differences in hair styles, clothes, and toys become obvious. Adults and peers reward these differences throughout development. And boys and girls learn gender roles through imitation or observational learning by watching what other people say and do. In recent years, the idea that parents are the critical socializing agents in gender-role development has come under fire (Huston, 1983). Parents are only one of many sources through which the individual learns gender roles. Culture, schools, peers, the media, and other family members are others. Yet it is important to guard against swinging too far in this direction, because—especially in the early years of development—parents are important influences on gender development.

Identification and Social Learning Theories

Two prominent theories address the way children acquire masculine and feminine attitudes and behaviors from their parents. **Identification theory** *stems from Freud's view that the preschool child develops a sexual attraction to the opposite-sex parent, then by approximately 5 or 6 years of age, renounces this attraction because of anxious feelings, and subsequently identifies with the same-sex parent, unconsciously adopting the same-sex parent's characteristics.* However, today many child developmentalists do not believe gender development proceeds on the basis of identification, at least in terms of Freud's emphasis on childhood sexual attraction. Children become gender-typed much earlier than 5 or 6 years of age, and they become masculine or feminine even when the same-sex parent is not present in the family.

Early Childhood

Table 9.2: A Comparison of Identification and Social Learning Views of Gender Development			
Theory	**Processes**	**Outcome**	
Freud's Identification Theory	Sexual attraction to opposite-sex parent at 3 to 5 years of age	Anxiety about sexual attraction and subsequent identification with same-sex parent at 5 to 6 years of age	Gender behavior similar to same-sex parent
Social Learning Theory	Rewards and punishments of gender-appropriate and inappropriate behavior by adults and peers	Observation and imitation of models' masculine and feminine behavior	Gender behavior

The **social learning theory of gender** *emphasizes that children's gender development occurs through observation and imitation of gender behavior, and through the rewards and punishments children experience for gender appropriate and inappropriate behavior.* Unlike identification theory, social learning theory argues that sexual attraction to parents is not involved in gender development. (A comparison of identification and social learning views is presented in table 9.2.) Parents often use rewards and punishments to teach their daughters to be feminine ("Karen, you are being a good girl when you play gently with your doll.") and masculine ("Keith, a boy as big as you is not supposed to cry."). Peers also extensively reward and punish gender behavior. And by observing adults and peers at home, at school, in the neighborhood, and on television, children are widely exposed to a myriad of models who display masculine and feminine behavior. Critics of the social learning view argue that gender development is not as passively acquired as it indicates. Later we will discuss the cognitive views of gender development, which stress that children actively construct their gender world.

Parental Influences

Parents, by action and by example, influence their children's gender development. Both mothers and fathers are psychologically important in children's gender development. Mothers are more consistently given responsibility for nurturance and physical care, fathers are more likely to engage in playful interaction and be given responsibility for ensuring that boys and girls conform to existing cultural norms. And whether or not they have more influence on them, fathers are more involved in socializing their sons than their daughters (Lamb, 1986). Fathers seem to play an especially important part in gender-role development—they are more likely to act differently toward sons and daughters than mothers are, and thus contribute more to distinctions between the genders (Huston, 1983).

Many parents encourage boys and girls to engage in different types of play and activities (Lewis, 1987). Girls are more likely to be given dolls to play with during childhood and, when old enough, are more likely to be assigned baby-sitting duties. Girls are encouraged to be more nurturant and emotional than boys, and fathers are more likely to engage in aggressive play

As reflected in this tug-of-war battle between boys and girls, the playground in elementary school is like going to "gender school." Elementary school children show a clear preference for being with and liking same-sex peers.

with their sons than their daughters. As adolescents increase in age, parents permit boys more freedom than girls, allowing them to be away from home and stay out later without supervision. Parents placing severe restrictions on their adolescent sons has been found to be especially disruptive to the adolescent's development (Baumrind, 1989).

Peer Influences

Parents provide the earliest discrimination of gender roles in development, but before long, peers join the societal process of responding to and modeling masculine and feminine behavior. Children who play in sex-appropriate activities tend to be rewarded for doing so by their peers. Those who play in cross-sexed activities, tend to be criticized by their peers or left to play alone. Children show a clear preference for being with and liking same-sex peers (Maccoby, 1989; Maccoby & Jacklin, in press), and this tendency usually becomes stronger during the middle and late childhood years (Hayden-Thomson, Rubin, & Hymel, 1987). After extensive observations of elementary school playgrounds, two researchers characterized the play settings as "gender school," pointing out that boys teach one another the required masculine behavior and enforce it strictly (Luria & Herzog, 1985). Girls also pass on the female culture and mainly congregate with one another. Individual "tomboy" girls can join boys' activities without losing their status in the girls' groups, but the reverse is not true for boys, reflecting our society's greater sex-typing pressure for boys.

Peer demands for conformity to gender role become especially intense during adolescence. While there is greater social mixing of males and females during early adolescence, in both formal groups and in dating, peer pressure is strong for the adolescent boy to be the very best male possible and for the adolescent girl to be the very best female possible.

School and Teacher Influences

In a recent Gallup poll, 80 percent of the respondents agreed that the federal government should promote educational programs intended to reduce such social problems as poverty and unequal educational opportunities for minorities and females (Gallup & Clark, 1987). Discriminatory treatment involving gender involves all ability groups, but in many cases the stereotypically lower-valued group (by sex, by ethnic group, and so on) is treated similarly to the lower-valued ability group. For example, girls with strong math abilities are frequently given fewer quality instructional interactions from teachers than their male counterparts (Eccles, MacIver, & Lange, 1986). And, minority females are given fewer teacher interactions than other females, who are given fewer than Black males, who are given fewer than White males (Sadker, Sadker, & Klein, 1986).

In one study, researchers were trained in an observation system to collect data in more than a hundred fourth-, sixth-, and eighth-grade classrooms (Sadker & Sadker, 1986). At all three grade levels, male students were involved in more interactions than female students, and male students were given more attention from teachers. Male students were also given more remediation, more criticism, and more praise than female students.

Historically, education in the United States has been male defined rather than gender balanced. In many instances, traditional male activities, especially White male activities, have been the educational norm. Although females mature earlier, are ready for verbal and math training at a younger age, and have control of small-motor skills earlier than males, educational curricula have been constructed mainly to mirror the development of males. Decisions about the grade in which students should read *Huckleberry Finn,* do long division, or begin to write essays are based primarily on male developmental patterns. Some experts believe that this state of educational affairs means that some girls may become bored or give up, with most girls learning simply to hold back, be quiet, and smile (Shakeshaft, 1986).

Three trends in sex equity education research have been identified (Klein, 1988). First, there is a trend toward greater investigation of subtle discrimination and stereotyping. Much of the sex equity research and initial sex equity policies in the 1970s focused on identifying and putting an end to overt discrimination and stereotyping. By 1981, it was noted that while some progress had been made toward equity in areas of overt sex discrimination such as athletics and college admissions, many subtle types of sex discrimination and stereotyping, such as sex bias in classroom interactions, still remained. Sex equity researchers are now calling attention to sex discrimination and stereotyping in less visible problem areas such as home economics, foreign language, visual arts, and sex education (Spencer, 1986).

A second trend in sex equity education research is a shift toward male- and female-valued educational outcome goals. In addition to assisting females in achieving parity with males, researchers and policymakers are focusing more on the development of skills associated with females (Belenky & others, 1986). For example, placing more value on skills such as writing and human relations, areas in which females excel, can change the content covered in many standardized academic achievement tests. This type of change could improve females' achievement test scores, self-esteem, and job prospects.

A third trend in sex equity education research is an increased emphasis on sex equity outcomes. Much of the initial sex equity education research focused on identifying inequities or problems. Once researchers understand how far we are from attaining sex equity goals, they can emphasize the effectiveness of various sex equity solutions in reaching these goals. For example, researchers have found that girls' participation and achievement in mathematics becomes more equal to that of boys through the use of multiple strategies that include anxiety reduction, "hands on" math instructional experiences, career awareness activities, "girl-friendly" classrooms, and role models (Eccles, MacIver, & Lange, 1986; Stage & others, 1985).

Media Influences

As we have described, children encounter masculine and feminine roles in their everyday interactions with parents, peers, and teachers. The messages carried by the media about what is appropriate or inappropriate for males and for females are important influences on gender development as well.

A special concern is the way females are pictured on television. In the 1970s, it became apparent that television was portraying females in less competent ways than males. For example, about 70 percent of the prime-time characters were males, men were more likely to be shown in the work force, women were more likely to be shown as housewives and in romantic roles, men were more likely to appear in higher status jobs and in a greater diversity of occupations, and men were presented as more aggressive and constructive (Sternglanz & Serbin, 1974).

In the 1980s, television networks became more sensitive to how males and females were portrayed on television shows. Consequently, many programs now focus on divorced families, cohabitation, and women in high-status roles. Even with the onset of this type of programming, researchers continue to find that television portrays males as more competent than females (Durkin, 1985). In one investigation, young adolescent girls indicated that television occupations are more extremely stereotyped than real-life occupations (Wroblewski & Huston, 1987).

Gender-role stereotyping also appears in the print media. In magazine advertising, females are shown more often in advertisements for beauty products, cleaning products, and home appliances, while males are shown more often in advertisements for cars, liquor, and travel. As with television programs, females are being portrayed as more competent in advertisements than in the past, but advertisers have not yet given them equal status with males.

So far in our discussion of gender, we have seen that both biological and social factors play important roles in children's gender development. Recently, many child developmentalists have also recognized the important role that cognitive factors play.

Cognitive Influences

What is the cognitive developmental view of gender? What is the gender schema theory of gender development? What role does language play in gender development? We consider each of these questions in turn.

Cognitive Developmental Theory

In the **cognitive developmental theory of gender,** *children's gender-typing occurs after they have developed a concept of gender. Once they consistently conceive of themselves as male or female, children often organize their world on the basis of gender.* Initially developed by psychologist Lawrence Kohlberg (1966), cognitive developmental theory argues that gender development proceeds in the following fashion: I am a girl, I want to do girl things; therefore, the opportunity to do girl things is rewarding. Having acquired the ability to categorize, children strive toward consistency in the use of categories and their actual behavior. Piaget's cognitive developmental theory provided Kohlberg with a basis for his view of children's gender development. As children's cognitive development matures, so does their understanding of gender. While 2-year-olds can apply the labels of "boy" and "girl" correctly to themselves and others, their concept of gender is simple and concrete. Preschool children rely on physical features such as dress and hairstyle to decide who falls in which category. Girls are people with long hair, while boys are people who never wear dresses. Many preschool children believe that people can change their own gender at will by getting a haircut or a new outfit. They do not yet have the cognitive machinery to think of gender as adults do. According to Kohlberg, all the reinforcement in the world won't modify that fact. However, by the concrete operational stage (the third stage in Piaget's theory, entered at about 6 to 7 years of age), children understand gender constancy—that a male is still a male regardless of whether he wears pants or a skirt, or his hair is short or long (Tavris & Wade, 1984). When their concept of gender constancy is clearly established, children are then motivated to become a competent or "proper" boy or girl. Consequently, she or he finds female or male activities rewarding and imitates the behavior of same-sex models.

Gender Schema Theory

A **schema** *is a cognitive structure, a network of associations that organizes and guides an individual's perceptions.* A **gender schema** *organizes the world in terms of female and male.* And **gender schema theory** *argues that children's attention and behavior are guided by an internal motivation to conform to gender-based, sociocultural standards and stereotypes* (Bem, 1981; Levy, 1991; Levy & Carter, 1989; Liben & Signorella, 1987; Martin 1989; Martin & Halverson, 1981, 1987; Martin & Rose, 1991; Murphy & Carter, 1991; Yekel, Bigler, & Liben, 1991). Gender schema theory suggests that gender typing occurs when individuals are ready to encode and organize information along the lines of what is considered appropriate or typical for males and females in a society. Whereas Kohlberg's cognitive developmental theory argues that the attainment of a particular cognitive prerequisite—gender constancy—is necessary for gender-typing, gender schema theory states that a general readiness to respond to and categorize information on the basis of culturally defined gender roles is the key ingredient that fuels children's gender-typing activities. A comparison of the cognitive developmental and gender schema theories of gender development is presented in table 9.3.

While researchers have shown that the appearance of gender constancy in children is related to their level of cognitive development, especially the acquisition of conservation skills (which supports the cognitive developmental theory of gender) (Emmerich & others, 1977; Serbin & Sprafkin, 1986), they have also shown that young children who are pre-gender constant have more gender-role knowledge than the cognitive developmental theory of gender predicts (which supports gender schema theory) (Carter & Levy, 1988; Carter & Taylor, in press). Today, gender schema theorists acknowledge that gender constancy is one important aspect of gender-role development, but stress that other cognitive factors—such as gender schema—are also very important (Levy & Carter, 1989).

As a real-life example of gender schema's influence on adolescents, consider a 17-year-old high school student deciding which hobby to try out from among the many available possibilities. The student could ask about how expensive each possibility is, whether it can be done in cold weather, whether it can be done during the school week, whether it will interfere with studying, and so on. But the adolescent is also likely to look at the hobby through the lens of gender and ask: What sex is the hobby? What sex am I? Do they match? If so, I will consider the hobby further. If not, I will reject it. This student may not be consciously aware of the influence of his or her gender's schema on the decision of which hobby to pursue. Indeed, in many of our everyday encounters we are not consciously aware of how gender schema affects our behavior. In sum, the gender schema approach emphasizes the active cognitive construction of gender but also accepts that societies determine which schema are important and the associations that are involved.

• *Critical Thinking* •

How do cognitive theories of gender differ from the social learning and identification theories of gender discussed earlier?

Social Development in Early Childhood

Table 9.3: A Comparison of Cognitive Developmental and Gender Schema Theories of Gender Development

Theory	Processes		Outcome
Cognitive Developmental Theory	Development of gender consistency, especially around 6 to 7 years of age, when conservation skills develop.	After children develop ability to consistently conceive of themselves as male or female, children often organize their world on the basis of gender, such as selecting same-sex models to imitate.	Gender-typed behavior
Gender Schema Theory	Sociocultural emphasis on gender-based standards and stereotypes.	Children's attention and behavior are guided by an internal motivation to conform to these gender-based standards and stereotypes, allowing children to interpret the world through a network of gender-organized thoughts.	Gender-typed behavior

The Role of Language in Gender Development

Gender is present in the language children use and encounter. The nature of the language children hear most of the time is sexist. That is, the English language contains sex bias, especially through the use of "he" and "man" to refer to everyone (O'Donnel, 1989). For example, in one investigation, mothers and their 1- to 3-year-old children looked at popular children's books, such as "The Three Bears," together (DeLoache, Cassidy, & Carpenter, 1987). The Three Bears were almost always referred to as boys: 95 percent of all characters of indeterminate gender were referred to by mothers as males.

Moral Development

People are hardly neutral about moral development. Many parents worry that their children are growing up without traditional values. Teachers complain that their students are unethical. What is moral development? What is Piaget's view of how children's moral reasoning develops? What is the nature of children's moral behavior? How do children's feelings contribute to their moral development? We consider each of these questions in turn.

What Is Moral Development?

Moral development *concerns rules and conventions about what people should do in their interactions with other people.* In studying these rules, developmentalists examine three different domains. First, how do children *reason* or *think* about rules for ethical conduct? For example, consider cheating. The child can be presented with a story in which someone has a conflict about whether or not to cheat in a particular situation, such as taking a test in school. The child is asked to decide what is appropriate for the character to do and why. The focus is on children's *reasoning* that is used to justify their moral decisions.

Second, how do children actually *behave* in moral circumstances? In our example of cheating, the emphasis is on observing the child's cheating and the environmental circumstances that produced and maintained the cheating. Children might be shown some toys and then be asked to select the one they believe is the most attractive. The experimenter then tells the young child that that particular toy belongs to someone else and is not to be played with. Observations of different conditions under which the child deviates from the prohibition or resists temptation are then conducted.

Third, how does the child *feel* about moral matters? In the example of cheating, does the child feel enough guilt to resist temptation? If children do cheat, do feelings of guilt after the transgression keep them from cheating the next time they face temptation? In the remainder of this section, we will focus on these three facets of moral development: thought, action, and feeling. Then, we will evaluate the positive side of children's moral development: altruism.

Piaget's View of How Children's Moral Reasoning Develops

Interest in how the child thinks about moral issues was stimulated by Piaget (1932), who extensively observed and interviewed children from the ages of 4 to 12. He watched them play marbles, seeking to learn how they used and thought about the game's rules. He also asked children questions about ethical rules—theft, lies, punishment, and justice, for example. Piaget concluded that children think in two distinctly different ways about morality depending on their developmental maturity. **Heteronomous morality** *is the first stage of moral development in Piaget's theory, occurring from approximately 4 to 7 years of age. Justice and rules are conceived of as unchangeable properties of the world, removed from the control of people.* **Autonomous morality** *is the second stage of moral development in Piaget's theory, displayed by older children (about 10 years of age and older). The child becomes aware that rules and laws are created by people and that, in judging an action, one should consider the actor's intentions as well as the consequences.* Children 7 to 10 years of age are in a transition between the two stages, evidencing some features of both.

Let's consider Piaget's two stages of moral development further. The heteronomous thinker judges the rightness or goodness of behavior by considering the consequences of the behavior, not the intentions of the actor. For example, the heteronomous thinker says that breaking twelve cups accidently is worse than breaking one cup intentionally while trying to steal a cookie. For the moral autonomist, the reverse is true. The actor's intentions assume paramount importance. The heteronomous thinker also believes that rules are unchangeable and are handed down by all-powerful authorities. When Piaget suggested that new rules be introduced into the game of marbles, the young children resisted. They insisted that the rules had always been the same and could not be altered. By contrast, older children—who were moral autonomists—accept change and recognize that rules are merely convenient, socially agreed-upon conventions, subject to change by consensus.

The heteronomous thinker also believes in **immanent justice,** *the concept that if a rule is broken, punishment will be meted out immediately.* The young child believes that the violation is connected in some automatic way to the punishment. Thus, young children often look around worriedly after committing a transgression, expecting inevitable punishment. Older children, who are moral autonomists, recognize that punishment is socially mediated and occurs only if a relevant person witnesses the wrongdoing and that, even then, punishment is not inevitable.

Piaget argued that, as children develop, they become more sophisticated in thinking about social matters, especially about the possibilities and conditions of cooperation. Piaget believed that this social understanding comes about through the mutual give-and-take of peer relations. In the peer group, where others have power and status similar to the individual, plans are negotiated and coordinated, and disagreements are reasoned about and eventually settled. Parent-child relations, in which parents have the power and the child does not, are less likely to advance moral reasoning because rules are often handed down in an authoritarian way. Later, in chapter 11, we will discuss another highly influential cognitive view of moral development, that of Lawrence Kohlberg.

Moral Behavior

The study of moral behavior has been influenced by social learning theory. The processes of reinforcement, punishment, and imitation are used to explain children's moral behavior. When children are rewarded for behavior that is consistent with laws and social conventions, they are likely to repeat that behavior. When models who behave morally are provided, children are likely to adopt their actions. And when children are punished for immoral behavior, those behaviors are likely to be reduced or eliminated. However, because punishment may have adverse side effects, it needs to be used judiciously and cautiously.

Another important point needs to be made about the social learning view of moral development: Moral behavior is influenced extensively by the situation. What children do in one situation is often only weakly related to what they do in other situations. A child may cheat in math class, but not in English class; a child may steal a piece of candy when others are not present, and not steal it when they are present; and so on. More than half a century ago, morality's situational nature was observed in a comprehensive study of thousands of children in many different situations—at home, at school, and at church, for example. The totally honest child was virtually nonexistent; so was the child who cheated in all situations (Hartshorne & May, 1928–30).

Social learning theorists also believe that the ability to resist temptation is closely tied to the development of self-control. Children must overcome their impulses for something they want that is prohibited. To accomplish this self-control, they must learn to be patient and to delay gratification. Today, social learning theorists believe that cognitive factors are important in the child's development of self-control. For example, in one investigation, children's cognitive transformations of desired objects helped children to become more patient (Mischel & Patterson, 1976). Preschool children were asked to do a boring task. Close by was an enticing mechanical clown who tried to persuade the children to come play with him. The children who had been trained to say to themselves, "I'm not going to look at Mr. Clown when Mr. Clown says to look at him," controlled their behavior and continued working on the dull task much longer than those who did not instruct themselves.

Moral Feelings

In chapter 2, we extensively discussed Sigmund Freud's psychoanalytic theory, which describes the *superego* as one of the three main structures of personality—the id and ego being the other two. In Freud's classical psychoanalytic theory, the child's superego—the moral branch of personality—develops as the child resolves the Oedipal conflict and identifies with the same-sex parent in the early childhood years. Among the reasons children resolve the Oedipal conflict is the fear of losing their parents' love and of being punished for their unacceptable sexual wishes toward the opposite-sex parent. To reduce anxiety, avoid punishment, and maintain parental affection, children form a superego by identifying with the same-sex parent. Through their identification with the same-sex parent, children internalize the parents' standards of right and wrong that reflect societal prohibitions. And, the child turns inward the hostility that was previously aimed externally at the same-sex parent. This inwardly directed hostility is now felt self-punitively as guilt, which is experienced unconsciously (beyond the child's awareness). In the psychoanalytic account of moral development, self-punitiveness of guilt is responsible for keeping the child from committing transgressions. That is, children conform to societal standards to avoid guilt.

> What is moral is what you feel good after and what is immoral is what you feel bad after.
>
> ~ *Ernest Hemingway,*
> Death in the Afternoon, *1932.*

Positive feelings such as empathy contribute to the child's moral development. **Empathy** *means reacting to another's feelings with an emotional response that is similar to the other's response* (Damon, 1988). Although empathy is experienced as an emotional state, it often has a cognitive component. The cognitive component is the ability to discern another's inner psychological states, or what we have previously called *perspective taking.* Young infants have the capacity for some purely empathic responses, but for effective moral action, children need to learn how to identify a wide range of emotional states in others, and children need to learn to anticipate what kinds of action will improve another person's emotional state.

We have seen that classical psychoanalytic theory emphasizes the power of unconscious guilt in moral development, but that other theorists such as Martin Hoffman and William Damon, emphasize the role of empathy. Today, many child developmentalists believe that both positive feelings, such as empathy, sympathy, admiration, and self-esteem, as well as negative feelings, such as anger, outrage, shame, and guilt contribute to the child's moral development (Damon, 1988). When strongly experienced, these emotions influence children to act in accord with standards of right and wrong. Emotions such as empathy, shame, guilt, and anxiety over other people's violation of standards are present early in development and undergo developmental change throughout childhood and beyond (Damon, 1988). These emotions provide a natural base for the child's acquisition of moral values, both orienting children toward moral events and motivating children to pay close attention to such events. But moral emotions do not operate in a vacuum to build the child's moral awareness, and they are not sufficient in themselves to generate moral

Concept Table 9.3: The Self, Gender, and Moral Development

Concept	Processes/Related Ideas	Characteristics/Description
The Self	Initiative versus Guilt	Erikson believes early childhood is a period when the self involves resolving the conflict between initiative versus guilt.
	Self-Understanding	Self-understanding is the child's cognitive representation of self—the substance and content of the child's self-conceptions. Self-understanding provides the rational underpinnings for identity. While a rudimentary form of self-understanding occurs at about 18 months in the form of self-recognition, in early childhood the physical and active self become a part of self-understanding.
Gender	What Is Gender?	While sex refers to the biological dimension of being male or female, gender refers to the social dimension of being male or female. Gender identity is the sense of being male or female, which most children acquire by 3 years of age. Gender role is the set of expectations that prescribe how females or males should think, act, and feel.
	Biological Influences	Freud's and Erikson's theories promote the idea that anatomy is destiny. Hormones influence gender development, although often not as pervasively as in animals. Hermaphrodites are individuals whose genitals become intermediate male and female because of a hormonal imbalance. Today's child developmentalists are all interactionists when biological and environmental influences on gender are considered. However, interaction means different things to different people.
	Social Influences	Both identification theory and social learning theory, while providing different perspectives on gender development, emphasize the adoption of parents' gender characteristics. Parents, by action and by example, influence gender development. Peers are especially adept at rewarding gender-appropriate behavior. Historically, in the United States, education has been male-defined rather than gender-balanced. Currently, an effort is being made to make schools more gender-balanced. Despite improvements, television still portrays males as more competent than females.

responsivity. They do not give the "substance" of moral regulation—the actual rules, values, and standards of behavior that children need to understand and act on. Moral emotions are inextricably interwoven with the cognitive and social aspects of children's development.

Thus far, we have discussed a number of ideas about the self, gender, and moral development in young children. These ideas are summarized in concept table 9.3. This chapter concludes our discussion of early childhood. In the next section, we will turn our attention to middle and late childhood.

Summary

I. Parenting Styles
Four major categories of parenting styles are authoritarian, authoritative, permissive indifferent, and permissive indulgent. Authoritative parenting is associated with children's social competence more than the other styles. Parents need to adapt their interaction strategies as the child grows older, using less physical manipulation and more reasoning in the process.

II. Cultural, Social Class, and Ethnic Variations in Families
Authoritative parenting is the most common childrearing pattern around the world. Working class and low-income parents place a higher value on external characteristics, middle-class parents place a higher value on internal characteristics, and these social classes vary in their childrearing patterns. Ethnic-minority families differ from

Concept	Processes/Related Ideas	Characteristics/Description
	Cognitive Influences	Both cognitive developmental theory and gender schema theory emphasize the role of cognition in gender development. In cognitive developmental theory, children's gender-typing occurs only after they have a concept of gender. In gender schema theory, children's attention and behavior are guided by an internal motivation to conform to gender-based, sociocultural standards and stereotypes. Gender is present in the language children use and encounter. The nature of language children hear much of the time is sexist.
Moral Development	What Is It?	Moral development concerns rules and regulations about what people should do in their interactions with others. Developmentalists study how children think, behave, and feel about such rules and regulations.
	Piaget's View	Piaget distinguished between the heteronomous morality of younger children and the autonomous morality of older children.
	Moral Behavior	Moral behavior is emphasized by social learning theorists. They believe there is considerable situational variability in moral behavior and that self-control is an important aspect of understanding children's moral behavior.
	Moral Feelings	In psychoanalytic theory, the superego is the moral branch of personality. The superego develops as the child resolves the Oedipal conflict and identifies with the same-sex parent in early childhood. Through identification, children internalize a parent's standards of right and wrong. Children conform to societal standards to avoid guilt. Positive emotions, such as empathy, are important in understanding children's moral development. Empathy means reacting to another's feelings with an emotional response that is similar to the other's response. Empathy often has a cognitive component—perspective taking. Both positive feelings such as empathy, sympathy, admiration, and self-esteem, and negative feelings such as anger, outrage, shame, and guilt contribute to children's moral development. When strongly experienced, these emotions influence children to act in accord with moral standards. Moral emotions do not operate in a vacuum: they are interwoven with the cognitive and social aspects of moral development.

White American families in their size, structure, and composition, their reliance on kinship networks, and their levels of income and education.

III. Sibling Relationships

More than 80 percent of American children have one or more siblings. Children interact with siblings more negatively and punitively, and in less varied ways than with their parents. In some cases, siblings are stronger socializing influences than parents. The relationship of the firstborn child to parents is often especially close and demanding, which may account for the greater achievement and anxiety found in firstborn children than later-born children.

IV. The Changing Family

A mother's working full-time outside the home can have positive or negative effects on the child; there is no indication of long-term negative effects overall. A special concern is the high rate of poverty in single-mother families. Family conflict often outweighs family structure in its impact on the child; conflict is greatest in the first year after the divorce. A continuing, ongoing positive relationship with the ex-spouse is important for the child's adjustment. Support systems are significant in the child's adaptation to divorce. Boys fare better in father-custody families, girls in mother-custody families.

V. Peers

Peers are powerful social agents. The term *peers* refers to children who are of about the same age or maturity level. Peers provide a source of information and comparison about the world outside the family. The frequency of peer interaction, both positive and negative, increases during the preschool years. Peer relations are both similar to and different from family relations.

VI. Play

The functions of play include affiliation with peers, tension release, advances in cognitive development, exploration, and provision of a safe haven in which to engage in potentially dangerous activities. Parten developed the categories of unoccupied, solitary, onlooker, parallel, associative, and cooperative play. The contemporary perspective emphasizes both the cognitive and social aspects of play. Among the most widely studied types of children's play today are sensorimotor play, practice play, pretense/symbolic play, social play, constructive play, and games.

VII. Television

While television can have a negative influence on children's development by taking them away from homework, making them passive learners, teaching them stereotypes, providing them with violent models of aggression, and presenting them with unrealistic views of the world, television can have a positive influence by presenting motivating educational programs, increasing children's information about the world beyond their immediate environment, and providing models of prosocial behavior. Children watch huge amounts of television, with preschool children watching an average of 4 hours a day. Up to 80 percent of the prime-time shows have violent episodes. Television violence is not the only cause of children's aggression, but most experts conclude that it can induce aggression and antisocial behavior in children. Prosocial behavior on television is associated with increased positive behavior by children. Parents rarely discuss television's contents with their children. Television-viewing habits are often formed in the early childhood years.

VIII. The Self

Erikson believes early childhood is a period when the self involves resolving the conflict between initiative and guilt. Self-understanding is the child's cognitive representation of self, the substance and content of the child's self-conceptions.

Self-understanding provides the rational underpinnings for identity. While a rudimentary form of self-understanding occurs at about 18 months in the form of self-recognition, in early childhood the physical and active self becomes a part of self-understanding.

IX. Gender

While sex refers to the biological dimension of being male or female, gender refers to the social dimension. Gender identity is the sense of being male or female, which most children acquire by 3 years of age. Gender role is the set of expectations that prescribe how females or males should think, act, and feel. Freud's and Erikson's theories promote the idea that anatomy is destiny. Hormones influence gender development, although often not as pervasively as in animals. Hermaphrodites are individuals whose genitals become intermediate between male and female because of a hormonal imbalance. Today's developmentalists are all interactionists when biological and environmental influences on gender are considered, although interaction means different things to different people. Identification and social learning theory, while providing different perspectives, both emphasize children's adoption of parents' gender characteristics. Parents, by action and by example, influence gender development. Peers are especially adept at rewarding gender-appropriate behavior. Although historically, in the United States, education has been male-defined rather than gender-balanced, an effort is currently being made to make schools more gender-balanced. Despite improvements, television still portrays males as more competent than females. Both cognitive developmental and gender schema theories emphasize the role of cognition in gender development. In cognitive developmental

theory, gender-typing occurs only after children have a concept of gender. In gender schema theory, children's attention and behavior are guided by an internal motivation to conform to gender-based sociocultural standards. Gender is present in the language children use and encounter. Much of this language is sexist.

X. Moral Development

Moral development concerns rules and regulations about what people should do in their interactions with others. Developmentalists study how children think, behave, and feel about such rules and regulations. Piaget distinguished between the heteronomous morality of younger children and the autonomous morality of older children. Moral behavior is emphasized by social learning theorists. They believe there is considerable situational variation in moral behavior and that self-control is an important aspect of understanding children's moral behavior. In psychoanalytic theory, the superego is the moral branch of personality. The superego develops as the child resolves the Oedipal conflict and identifies with the same-sex parent in early childhood. Children conform to societal standards to avoid guilt. Positive emotions, such as empathy, are important in understanding children's moral development. Both positive feelings such as empathy, sympathy, admiration, and self-esteem, and negative emotions, such as anger, outrage, shame, and guilt contribute to children's moral development. When strongly experienced, these emotions influence children to act in accord with moral standards. Moral emotions do not operate in a vacuum; they are interwoven with the cognitive and social aspects of moral development.

Key Terms

Suggested Readings

Bergen, D. (Ed.). (1988). *Play as a medium for learning and development*. Portsmouth, NH: Heinemann.
This book includes a number of excellent chapters on many diverse aspects of play by leading experts on play. Includes an entire section of chapters on the use of play as a curricular tool.

Damon, W. (1988). *The moral child*. New York: Free Press.
Damon presents his intelligent views on the nature of children's moral development, including some provocative ideas about moral education.

Hartup, W. W. (1983). The peer system. In P. H. Mussen (Ed.), *Handbook of child psychology* (4th ed., Vol. 4). New York: Wiley.
A detailed look at the development of peer relations by one of the leading experts in the field.

Hetherington, E. M., Hagan, M. S., & Anderson, E. R. (1989). Family transitions: A child's perspective. *American Psychologist, 44*, 303–312.
Hetherington is a leading researcher in the investigation of the effects of divorce on children's development. In this article, she and her colleagues review the recent literature on divorce, giving special attention to transitions in divorced and stepparent families.

Levy, G. D., & Carter, D. B. (1989). Gender schema, gender constancy, and gender-role knowledge: The role of cognitive factors in preschoolers' gender-role stereotype attributions. *Developmental Psychology, 25*, 444–449.
The contemporary perspective of gender schema theory is competently presented.

Liebert, R. M., & Spratkin, J. N. (1988). *The early window: Effects of television on children and youth* (3rd ed.). Elmsford, NY: Pergamon.
An updated account of theory and research that addresses the effects of television on children's development.

S·E·C·T·I·O·N
V

MIDDLE AND LATE
CHILDHOOD

*E*very forward step we take we leave some
phantom of ourselves behind.

John Lancaster Spalding

CHAPTER 10

Physical and Cognitive Development in Middle and Late Childhood

*S*tanding on the balance beam at a sports school in Beijing, China, 6-year-old Zhang Liyin stretches her arms outward as she gets ready to perform a backflip on the beam. She wears an elite bright-red gymnastic suit given to only the best ten girls in her class of 6- to 8-year-olds (figure 10.1). But her face wears a dreadful expression; she can't drum up enough confidence to do the flip. Maybe it is because she has had a rough week; a purple bruise decorates one leg, and a nasty gash disfigures the other. Her coach, a woman in her twenties, makes Zhang jump from the beam and escorts her to the high bar, where she is instructed to hang for three minutes. If Zhang falls, she must pick herself up and try again. But she does not fall, and she is escorted back to the beam, where her coach puts her through another tedious routine.

Zhang attends the sports school in the afternoon. The sports school is a privilege given to only 260,000 of China's 200 million students of elementary to college age. The Communist party has decided that sports is one avenue China can pursue to prove that China has arrived in the modern world. The sports schools designed to produce Olympic champions were the reason for China's success in the 1984 and 1988 Olympics. These schools are the only road to Olympic stardom in China. There are precious few neighborhood playgrounds. And there is only one gymnasium for every 3.5 million people.

Many of the students who attend the sports schools in the afternoon live and study at the schools as well. Only a few attend a normal school and then come to a sports school in the afternoon. Because of her young age, Zhang stays at home during the mornings and goes to the sports school from noon until 6 P.M. A part-timer like Zhang can stay enrolled until she no longer shows potential to move up to the next step. Any child who seems to lack potential is asked to leave.

Zhang was playing in a kindergarten class when a coach from a sports school spotted her. She was selected because of her broad shoulders, narrow hips, straight legs, symmetrical limbs, open-minded attitude, vivaciousness, and outgoing personality. If Zhang continues to show progress, she could be asked to move to full time next year. At age 7, she would then go to school there and live in a dorm six days a week. If she becomes extremely competent at gymnastics, Zhang could be moved to Shishahai, where the elite gymnasts train and compete.

> *C*hildren are remarkable for their intelligence and ardor, for their curiosity, their intolerance of shams, the clarity . . . of their vision.
>
> *Aldous Huxley*

Figure 10.1   The training of future Olympians in the sports schools of China. Six-year-old Zhang Liyin (third from the left) hopes someday to become an Olympic gymnastics champion. Attending the sports school is considered an outstanding privilege; only 260,000 of China's 200 million children are given this opportunity.

Physical and Cognitive Development in Middle and Late Childhood

At Shishahai, the day begins at 6 A.M. with breakfast, followed by four hours of academic classes and study until 11:30 A.M. Then follows lunch and a nap until 2:30, four grueling hours of athletic training, dinner at 7, more studies from 7 to 9, and lights out at 9:30. No TVs are allowed in the school, no in-room phones are permitted, and dating is prohibited. Coca-Cola, VCRs, and Colonel Sanders may have arrived in Beijing, but they won't be found at the Shishahai sports school (Reilly, 1988).

By American standards, Zhang's life sounds rigid and punitive. Although achievement in sports has a lofty status in American society, children are not trained with the intensity now being witnessed in China, Eastern European nations, and the Soviet Union.

Later in this chapter we discuss children's sports, physical fitness, and health. Then we turn to the study of children's cognitive development.

Physical Development in Middle and Late Childhood

How do children's bodies change in middle and late childhood? How much exercise do children get? What kind of disabilities do handicapped children have and how should they be educated? We consider each of these questions in turn.

Body Changes

The period of middle and late childhood involves slow, consistent growth. This is a period of calm before the rapid growth spurt of adolescence. Among the important aspects of body change in this developmental period are those involving the skeletal system, the muscular system, and motor skills.

The Skeletal and Muscular Systems

During the elementary school years, children grow an average of 2 to 3 inches a year until, at the age of 11, the average girl is 4 feet 10 inches tall and the average boy is 4 feet, 9½ inches tall. Children's legs become longer and their trunks slimmer. During the middle and late childhood years, children gain about 5 to 7 pounds a year. The weight increase is due mainly to increases in the size of the skeleton and muscular systems, as well as the size of some body organs. Muscle mass and strength gradually increase as "baby fat" decreases. The loose movements and knock knees of early childhood give way to improved muscle tone. The increase in muscular strength is due to heredity and to exercise. Children double their strength capabilities during these years. Because of their greater number of muscle cells, boys are usually stronger than girls (Whaley & Wong, 1989).

Motor Skills

During middle and late childhood, children's motor development becomes smoother and more coordinated than it was in early childhood. For example, only one child in a thousand can hit a tennis ball over the net at the age of 3, yet by the age of 10 or 11, most children can learn to play the sport. Running, climbing, skipping rope, swimming, bicycle riding, and skating are just a few of the many physical skills elementary schoolchildren can master. And when mastered, these physical skills are a source of great pleasure and accomplishment for children. In gross motor skills involving large muscle activity, boys usually outperform girls rather handily.

As children move through the elementary school years, they gain greater control over their bodies and can sit and attend for longer periods of time. However, elementary schoolchildren are far from having physical maturity, and they need to be active. Elementary schoolchildren become more fatigued by long periods of sitting than by running, jumping, or bicycling. Physical action is essential for these children to refine their developing skills, such as batting a ball, skipping rope, or balancing on a beam. An important principle of practice for elementary schoolchildren, therefore, is that they should be engaged in *active,* rather than passive, activities (Katz & Chard, 1989).

Increased myelinization—an insulation of nerves that helps the nerve impulse to travel faster—of the central nervous system is reflected in the improvement of fine motor skills during middle and late childhood. Children's hands are used more adroitly as tools. Six-year-olds can hammer, paste, tie shoes, and fasten clothes. By 7 years of age, children's hands become steadier. At this age, children prefer a pencil to a crayon for printing, and reversal of letters is less common. Printing becomes smaller. Between 8 and 10 years of age, the hands can be used independently with more ease and precision. Fine motor coordination develops to the point where children can write rather than print words. Letter size becomes smaller and more even. By 10 to 12 years of age, children begin to show manipulative skills similar to the abilities of adults. The complex, intricate, and rapid movements needed to produce fine-quality crafts or playing a difficult piece on a musical instrument can be mastered. One final point: Girls usually outperform boys in fine motor skills.

Exercise

Many of our patterns of health and illness are longstanding. Our experiences as children contribute to our health practices as adults. Did your parents seek medical help at your first sniffle, or did they wait until your temperature reached 104 degrees? Did they feed you heavy doses of red meat and sugar or a more rounded diet with vegetables and fruit? Did they get you involved in sports or exercise programs, or did you lie around watching television all the time?

Are children getting enough exercise? The 1985 School Fitness Survey tested 18,857 children aged 6 to 17 on nine fitness tasks. Compared to a similar survey in 1975, virtually no improvement was made on the tasks. For example, 40 percent of the boys 6 to 12 years of age could do no more than one pull-up, and a full 25 percent could not do any! Fifty percent of the girls aged 6 to 17 and 30 percent of the boys aged 6 to 12 could not run a mile in less than 10 minutes. In the 50-yard dash, the adolescent girls in 1975 were faster than the adolescent girls in 1985.

Some experts suggest that television is at least partially to blame for the poor physical condition of our nation's children. In one investigation, children who watched little television were significantly more physically fit than their heavy-television-viewing counterparts (Tucker, 1987). The more children watch television, the more they are likely to be overweight. No one is quite sure whether this is because children spend their leisure time in front of the television set instead of chasing each other around the neighborhood or whether they tend to eat a lot of junk food they see advertised on television.

Some of the blame also falls on the nation's schools, many of which fail to provide physical education classes on a daily basis. In the 1985 School Fitness Survey, 37 percent of the children in the first through the fourth grades take gym classes only once or twice a week. The investigation also revealed that parents are poor role models when it comes to physical fitness. Less than 30 percent of the parents of children in grades 1 through 4 exercised three days a week. Roughly half said they never get any vigorous exercise. In another study, observations of children's behavior in physical education classes at four different elementary schools revealed how little vigorous exercise is done in these classes (Parcel & others, 1987). Children moved through space only 50 percent of the time they were in the class, and they moved continuously an average of only 2.2 minutes. In summary, not only do children's school

Little league baseball, basketball, soccer, tennis, dance —as children's motor development becomes smoother and more coordinated, they are able to master these activities more competently in middle and late childhood than in early childhood.

◆

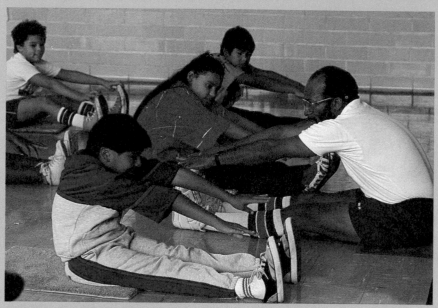

A gymnastics class for third and fourth grades at the Govalle School in Austin, Texas. One of the most important components of heart disease prevention programs is a regular, vigorous exercise workout.

One large-scale investigation, the Bogalusa Heart Study, involves an on-going evaluation of 8,000 boys and girls in Bogalusa, Louisiana (Berensen, 1989; Downey & others, 1987). Observations reveal that the precursors of heart disease begin at a young age with many children possessing one or more clinical risk factors—hypertension or obesity, for example. Based on the Bogalusa Heart Study, a cardiovascular health intervention model for children has been developed. The model is called Heart Smart.

The school is the focus of the Heart Smart intervention. Since 95 percent of children and adolescents aged 5 to 18 are in school, schools are an efficient context in which to educate individuals about health. Special attention is given to teachers, who serve as role models. Teachers who value the role of health in life and who engage in health-enhancing behavior present

weeks not include adequate physical education classes, but the majority of children do not exercise vigorously even when they are in physical education classes. Furthermore, most children's parents are poor role models for vigorous physical exercise.

Does it make a difference if we push children to exercise more vigorously in elementary school? One recent investigation says yes (Tuckman & Hinkle, 1988). One hundred fifty-four elementary schoolchildren were randomly assigned to either three 30-minute running programs per week or to regular attendance in physical education classes. Although the results sometimes varied according to sex, for the most part, the cardiovascular health as well as the creativity of children in the running program were enhanced. For example, the boys in this program had less body fat and the girls had more creative involvement in their classrooms. Information about another school program in which exercise plays an important role is described in Perspective on Life-Span Development 10.1.

The family, in addition to the school, plays an important role in the child's exercise program. A wise strategy is for the family to take up activities involving vigorous physical exercise that parents and children can enjoy together. Running, swimming, cycling, and hiking are especially recommended.

• *Critical Thinking* •

Imagine that you are the physical education coordinator for the elementary schools in a large city. Describe the ideal program you would want to implement to improve children's physical fitness.

children and adolescents with positive models for health. Teacher in-service education is conducted by an interdisciplinary team of specialists including physicians, psychologists, nutritionists, physical educators, and exercise physiologists. The school's staff is introduced to heart health education, the nature of cardiovascular disease, and risk factors for heart disease. Coping behavior, exercise behavior, and eating behavior are discussed with the staff. And a Heart Smart curricula is explained. For example, the Heart Smart curricula for grade 5 includes the content areas of cardiovascular health (such as risk factors associated with heart disease), behavior skills (for example, self-assessment and monitoring), eating behavior (for example, the effects of food on health), and exercise behavior (for example, the effects of exercise on the heart).

The physical education component of Heart Smart involves two to four class periods each week to incorporate a "Superkids-Superfit" exercise program. The physical education instructor teaches skills required by the school system plus aerobic activities aimed at cardiovascular conditioning—including jogging, race walking, interval workouts, rope skipping, circuit training, aerobic dance, and games. Classes begin and end with five minutes of walking and stretching.

The school lunch program serves as an intervention site where sodium, fat, and sugar levels are decreased. Children and adolescents are given reasons why they should eat healthy foods such as a tuna sandwich and why they should not eat unhealthy foods such as a hot dog with chili. The school lunch program includes a salad bar where children and adolescents can serve

themselves. The amount and type of snack foods sold on the school premises is monitored.

High-risk children—those with elevated blood pressure, cholesterol, and weight—are identified as part of Heart Smart. A multidisciplinary team of physicians, nutritionists, nurses, and behavioral counselors work with the high-risk boys and girls and their parents through group-oriented activities and individual-based family counseling. High-risk boys and girls and their parents receive diet, exercise, and relaxation prescriptions in an intensive twelve-session program, followed by long-term monthly evaluations.

Extensive assessment is a part of this ongoing program. Short-term and long-term changes in children's knowledge about cardiovascular disease and changes in their behavior are being assessed.

In encouraging children to exercise more, parents should not push them beyond their physical limits or expose them to competitive pressures that take the fun out of sports and exercise. For example, long-distance running may be too strenuous for young children and could result in bone injuries. Recently, there has been an increase in the number of children competing in strenuous athletic events such as marathons and triathalons. Doctors are beginning to see some injuries in children that they previously saw only in adults. Some injuries, such as stress fractures and tendonitis, stem from the overuse of young, still-growing bodies (Risser, 1989). If left to their own devices, how many 8-year-old children would want to prepare for a marathon? It is recommended that parents downplay cutthroat striving and encourage healthy sports that children can enjoy (Puffer, 1987).

Handicapped Children

The elementary school years are a time when handicapped children become more sensitive about their differentness and how it is perceived by others. One 6-year-old girl came home from school and asked, "Am I disabled or handicapped?" Another articulate 6-year-old girl described in detail how her premature birth was the cause of her cerebral palsy: "I was a teensy-weensy baby.

They put me in an incubator and I almost died." Later, when asked about being teased by her classmates because she could not walk, she replied, "I hate their guts, but if I said anything the teacher would get mad at me." A 7-year-old handicapped boy commented about how he had successfully completed a rocket-making course during the summer; he was the youngest and the most knowledgeable child in the class: "For the first time, some kids really liked me" (Howard, 1982). Life is not always fair, especially for handicapped children. As evidenced by the comments of the handicapped children just mentioned, adjusting to the world of peers and school is often painful and difficult. Our coverage of handicapped children focuses on the scope and education of handicapped children, learning disabilities, and attention-deficit hyperactivity disorder.

Scope and Education of Handicapped Children

An estimated 10 to 15 percent of the United States population of children between the ages of 5 and 18 are handicapped in some way (table 10.1). The estimates range from 0.1 percent who are visually impaired to the 3 to 4 percent who have speech handicaps. Estimates vary because of problems in classification and testing. Experts sometimes differ in how they define the various categories of handicapped children. And different tests may be used by different school systems or psychologists to assess whether a child is handicapped.

Public Law 94–142 *is the federal government's mandate to all states to provide a free, appropriate education for all children. This law, also called the Education for All Handicapped Children Act, was passed by Congress in 1975. A key provision of the bill was the development of an individualized education program for each identified handicapped child.*

Mainstreaming *occurs when handicapped children attend regular school classes with nonhandicapped children. In this way handicapped children enter the "mainstream" of education in the school and are not separated from nonhandicapped students.* However, even under PL 94–142, which emphasizes mainstreaming, certain types of handicapped children, such as those with hearing impairments, usually spend part of each day in separate classes taught by specially trained teachers. The results of mainstreaming have met with mixed results. In some schools, teachers assign children to environments that are not the best contexts for learning (Brady & others, 1988). Some people believe that mainstreaming means there will be a number of profoundly retarded, drugged children sitting in classrooms in dazed, unresponsive states. Others believe that including handicapped children in regular classrooms will detract from the quality of education given to nonhandicapped children. The picture is not as bleak as some of these criticisms suggest. Virtually all profoundly retarded children are institutionalized and will never be schooled in public classrooms. Only the mildly retarded are mainstreamed. Mainstreaming makes children and teachers more aware of the special needs of handicapped people.

In practice, mainstreaming has not been the simple solution its architects hoped for. Many handicapped children require extensive and expensive services to help them become effective learners in the regular classroom. As school systems have become increasingly strapped financially, many services for handicapped children have been cut back. Some teachers, already burdened with heavy course loads and time demands, have felt overwhelmed by the added requirement of developing special teaching arrangements for handicapped children. And the social interaction of handicapped and nonhandicapped children has not always gone smoothly in mainstreamed classrooms (Gallagher, Trohanis, & Clifford, 1989).

Table 10.1: Estimates of the Percentage and Number of Handicapped Children in the United States

Handicap	Percentage of Population	Number of Children Ages 5 to 18*
Visual impairment (includes blindness)	0.1	55,000
Hearing impairment (includes deafness)	0.5–0.7	275,000–385,000
Speech handicap	3.0–4.0	1,650,000–2,200,000
Orthopedic and health impairments	0.5	275,000
Emotional disturbance	2.0–3.0	1,100,000–1,650,000
Mental retardation (both educable and trainable)	2.0–3.0	1,100,000–1,650,000
Learning disabilities	2.0–3.0	1,100,000–1,650,000
Multiple handicaps	0.5–0.7	275,000–385,000
Total	10.6–15.0	5,830,000–8,250,000

*Number of children based on 1985 population estimates.

Table reprinted by permission of Merrill, an imprint of Macmillan Publishing Company, from *The Exceptional Student in the Regular Classroom,* Third Edition, by Bill R. Gearheart and Mel W. Weishahn. Copyright © 1984.

The hope that mainstreaming would be a positive solution for all handicapped children needs to be balanced with the reality of each individual handicapped child's life and that particular child's special needs. The specially tailored education program should meet with the acceptance of the child's parents, counselors, educational authorities, and, when feasible, the children themselves (Hallahan & others, 1988; Kusche, 1991).

Is there a disadvantage to referring to these children as handicapped or disabled? Children who are labeled as handicapped or disabled may feel permanently stigmatized and rejected, and they may be denied opportunities for full development. Children labeled as handicapped or disabled may be assigned to inferior educational programs or placed in institutions without the legal protection given to "normal" individuals. Paradoxically, however, if handicapped or disabled children are not labeled, they may not be able to take advantage of the special programs designed to help them (Hobbs, 1975; Horne, 1988).

• Critical Thinking •

Is mainstreaming the best way for handicapped children to be educated? What needs and concerns of handicapped and nonhandicapped children should be considered?

Public Law 94–142 mandates free, appropriate education for all children. A key provision of the bill was the development of an individualized education program for each identified handicap child. Among the important issues involved in the education of handicapped children are mainstreaming and labeling.

There are no quick fixes for the education of handicapped children. While progress has been made in recent years to provide supportive instruction for handicapped children, increasing effort needs to be devoted to developing the skills of handicapped children (Hynd & Obrzut, 1986). Handicapped children have a strong will to survive, to grow, and to learn. They deserve our very best educational efforts (Wood, 1988).

Learning Disabilities

Paula doesn't like kindergarten and can't seem to remember the names of her teacher or classmates. Bobby's third-grade teacher complains that his spelling is awful and that he is always reversing letters. Ten-year-old Tim hates to read. He says it is too hard for him and the words just don't make any sense to him. Each of these children is learning disabled. Children with **learning disabilities** *(1) are of normal intelligence or above, (2) have difficulties in several academic areas but usually do not show deficits in others, and (3) are not suffering from some other conditions or disorders that could explain their learning problems* (Reid, 1988). The breadth of definitions of learning disabilities has generated controversy about just what learning disabilities are (Chalfant, 1989; Siegel & Ryan 1989; Silver, 1989).

Within the global concept of learning disabilities fall problems in listening, thinking, memory, reading, writing, spelling, and math. Attention deficits involving an inability to sit still, pay attention, and concentrate are also classified under learning disabilities. Estimates of the number of learning-disabled children in the United States are as broad as the definition, ranging from 1 to 30 percent (Lerner, 1988). The U.S. Department of Education puts the number of identified learning-disabled children between the ages of 3 and 21 at approximately 2 million.

Improving the lives of learning-disabled children will come from (1) recognizing the complex, multifaceted nature of learning disablities (biological, cognitive, and social aspects of learning disabilities need to be considered) and (2) becoming more precise in our analysis of the learning environments in which learning-disabled children participate (Lerner, 1989). The following discussion of one subtype of learning disability, attention-deficit hyperactivity disorder, exemplifies consideration of this complexity and preciseness.

Middle and Late Childhood

Attention-Deficit Hyperactivity Disorder

Matthew failed the first grade. His handwriting was messy. He did not know the alphabet and never attended very well to the lessons the teacher taught. Matthew is almost always in motion. He can't sit still for more than a few minutes at a time. His mother describes him as very fidgety. Matthew has **attention-deficit hyperactivity disorder,** *the technical term for what is commonly called hyperactivity. This disorder is characterized by a short attention span, distractibility, and high levels of physical activity* (Barkeley, in press; Silver, 1987). In short, these children do not pay attention and have difficulty concentrating on what they are doing (Loge & Schatz, 1991; Pierce, 1991). Estimates of the number of children with attention-deficit hyperactivity disorder vary from less than 1 percent to 5 percent. While young children or even infants show characteristics of this disorder, the vast majority of hyperactive children are identified in the first three grades of elementary school when teachers recognize that they have great difficulty paying attention, sitting still, and concentrating on their schoolwork.

What makes Jimmy so impulsive, Sandy so distractible, and Harvey so excitable? Possible causes include heredity, prenatal damage, diet, family dynamics, and the physical environment. As we saw in chapter 3, the influence of heredity on temperament is increasingly considered, with activity level being one aspect of temperament that differentiates one child from another very early in development. Approximately four times as many boys as girls are hyperactive. This sex difference may be due to differences in the brains of boys and girls determined by genes on the Y chromosome. The prenatal hazards we discussed in chapter 4 may also produce hyperactive behavior. Excessive drinking by women during pregnancy is associated with poor attention and concentration by their offspring at 4 years of age, for example (Streissguth & others, 1984). With regard to diet, severe vitamin deficiencies can lead to attentional problems. Vitamin B deficiences are of special concern. Caffeine and sugar may also contribute to attentional problems.

The social and physical environments in which children live also contribute to attentional problems (Henker & Whalen, 1989). Children with attention-deficit hyperactivity disorder are more likely to come from families who frequently move and who are more concerned with controlling the child's behavior than with warmly supporting the child's academic work (Lambert & Hartsough, 1984). Hyperactive children are more likely to misbehave when they are in exciting but unstructured circumstances (such as a typical birthday party) or in circumstances with many behavioral demands (such as a typical school classroom). Lead poisoning can also produce attention problems and hyperactive behavior.

Children with attention-deficit hyperactivity disorder may continue to have problems in adolescence, although by that time the attentional problem is usually less severe. By adulthood, approximately one-third to one-half continue to be troubled by their attentional difficulties (Weiss & Hechtman, 1986).

A wide range of psychotherapies and drug therapy have been used to improve the lives of hyperactive children. For unknown reasons, some drugs that stimulate the brains and behaviors of adults have a quieting effect on the brains and behaviors of children. The drugs most widely prescribed for hyperactive children are amphetamines, especially Ritalin. Amphetamines work effectively for some hyperactive children, but not all (Batshaw & Perret, 1986; Buhrmester & MacDonald, 1991; MacDonald & others, 1991). As many as 20 percent of hyperactive children treated with Ritalin do not respond to it.

Concept Table 10.1: Physical Development in Middle and Late Childhood

Concept	Processes/Related Ideas	Characteristics/Description
Body Changes	The Skeletal and Muscular Systems	During the elementary school years, children grow an average of 2 to 3 inches a year. Muscle mass and strength gradually increase. Legs lengthen and trunks slim down as "baby fat" decreases. Growth is slow and consistent.
	Motor Skills	During the middle and late childhood years, children's motor development becomes smoother and more coordinated. Children gain greater control over their bodies and can sit and attend for longer frames of time. However, their lives should be activity oriented and very active. Increased myelinization of the central nervous system is reflected in improved fine motor skills. Improved fine motor development is reflected in children's handwriting skills over the course of middle and late childhood. Boys are usually better at gross motor skills, girls at fine motor skills.
Exercise	Its Nature	Every indication suggests that our nation's children are not getting enough exercise. Television viewing, parents who are poor role models, and the lack of adequate physical education classes in schools may be to blame.
Handicapped Children	Scope and Education of Handicapped Children	Approximately 10 to 15 percent of children in the United States are estimated to be handicapped in some way. Public Law 94–142 ordered free, appropriate education for every handicapped child. The law emphasizes an individually tailored education program for every child and provision of a least restrictive environment, which has led to extensive mainstreaming of handicapped children into the regular classroom. Mainstreaming has been a controversial topic. Another issue is the labeling of handicapped children and its benefits and drawbacks.
	Learning Disabilities	Children with a learning disability have normal or above-normal intelligence, have difficulties in some areas but not others, and do not suffer from some other disorder that could explain their learning problems. Learning disabilities are complex and multifaceted and require precise analysis.
	Attention-Deficit Hyperactivity Disorder	This is the technical term for what is commonly called hyperactivity. This disorder is characterized by a short attention span, distractibility, and high levels of physical activity. Possible causes include heredity, prenatal damage, diet, family dynamics, and physical environment. Amphetamines have been used with some success in treatment, but they do not work with all hyperactive children.

Even when Ritalin works, it is also important to consider the social worlds of the hyperactive child. The teacher is especially important in this social world, helping to monitor the child's academic and social behavior to determine whether the drug works and whether the prescribed dosage is correct.

At this point we have discussed a number of ideas about physical development in middle and late childhood. A summary of these ideas is presented in concept table 10.1. Now we turn our attention to children's cognitive development.

Cognitive Development in Middle and Late Childhood

Our coverage of children's cognitive development focuses on Piaget's theory and concrete operational thought, information processing, children and computers, intelligence, language, and achievement, each of which we discuss in turn.

Piaget's Theory and Concrete Operational Thought

According to Piaget (1967), the preschool child's thought is preoperational. Preoperational thought involves the formation of stable concepts, the emergence of mental reasoning, the prominence of egocentrism, and the construction of magical belief systems. Thought during the preschool years is still flawed and not well organized. Piaget believed that concrete operational thought does not appear until about the age of 7, but as we learned in chapter 8, Piaget may have underestimated some of the cognitive skills of preschool children. For example, by carefully and cleverly designing experiments on understanding the concept of number, Rochel Gelman (1972) demonstrated that some preschool children show conservation, a concrete operational skill. In chapter 8, we explored concrete operational thought by describing the preschool child's flaws in thinking about such concrete operational skills as conservation and classification; here we will cover the characteristics of concrete operational thought again, this time emphasizing the competencies of elementary schoolchildren. Applications of Piaget's ideas to children's education and an evaluation of Piaget's theory are also considered.

Concrete Operational Thought

Remember that, according to Piaget, concrete operational thought is made up of operations—mental actions that allow the child to do mentally what was done physically before. Concrete operations are also mental actions that are reversible. In the well-known test of reversibility of thought involving conservation of matter, the child is presented with two identical balls of clay. The experimenter rolls one ball into a long, thin shape; the other remains in its original ball shape. The child is then asked if there is more clay in the ball or in the long, thin piece of clay. By the time children reach the age of 7 or 8, most answer that the amount of clay is the same. To answer this problem correctly, children have to imagine that the clay ball is rolled out into a long, thin strip and then returned to its original round shape. This type of imagination involves a reversible mental action. Thus, a concrete operation is a reversible mental action on real, concrete objects. Concrete operations allow the child to coordinate several characteristics rather than focus on a single property of an object. In the clay example, the preoperational child is likely to focus on height *or* width. The concrete operational child coordinates information about both dimensions.

Many of the concrete operations identified by Piaget focus on the way children reason about the properties of objects. One important skill that characterizes the concrete operational child is the ability to classify or divide things into different sets or subsets and to consider their interrelationships. An example of the concrete operational child's classification skills involves a family tree of four generations (see figure 10.2) (Furth & Wachs, 1975). This family tree suggests that the grandfather (A) has three children (B, C, & D), each of whom has two children (E through J), and that one of these children (J) has three children (K, L, & M). A child who comprehends the classification system can move up and down a level (vertically), across a level (horizontally), and up and down and across (obliquely) within the system. The concrete operational child understands that person J can at the same time be father,

The thirst to know and understand. . . these are the goods in life's rich hand.

~ *Sir William Watson, 1905*

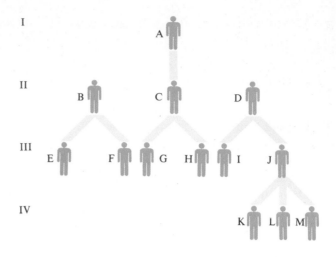

Figure 10.2   An example of a classification problem to demonstrate concrete operational thought. In this family tree of four generations, the preoperational child has trouble classifying the members of the four generations. The concrete operational child can classify the members vertically, horizontally, and obliquely (up and down and across).

Piaget is shown sitting on a bench observing children. Piaget was a genius at observing children. By carefully observing and interviewing children, he constructed a comprehensive theory of children's cognitive development.

brother, and grandson, for example. A summary of concrete operational thought's characteristics is shown in figure 10.3.

Piaget and Education

Piaget was not an educator and never pretended to be. But he did provide a sound conceptual framework from which to view educational problems. What are some of the principles in Piaget's theory of cognitive development that can be applied to children's education? David Elkind (1976) described three. First, the foremost issue in education is *communication*. In Piaget's theory, the child's mind is not a blank slate; to the contrary, the child has a host of ideas about the physical and natural world, but these ideas differ from those of adults. We must learn to comprehend what children are saying and to respond in the same mode of discourse that children use. Second, the child is always unlearning and relearning in addition to acquiring knowledge. Children come to school with their own ideas about space, time, causality, quantity, and number. Third, the child is by nature a knowing creature, motivated to acquire knowledge. The best way to nurture this motivation for knowledge is to allow the child to spontaneously interact with the environment; education needs to ensure that it does not dull the child's eagerness to know by providing an overly rigid curricula that disrupts the child's own rhythm and pace of learning.

Piagetian Contributions and Criticisms

Piaget was a genius at observing children, and his insights are often surprisingly easy to verify. Piaget showed us some important things to look for in development, including the shift from preoperational to concrete operational thought. He also showed us how we must make experiences fit our cognitive framework, yet simultaneously adapt our cognitive orientation to experience. Piaget also revealed how cognitive change is likely to occur if the situation is structured to allow gradual movement to the next higher level.

But Piaget's view has not gone unquestioned. Four sorts of findings question the Piagetian approach to cognitive development (Beilin, 1989; Bjorklund, 1989; Case, 1991; Gelman, 1991; Mandler, 1983; Pascual-Leone & Johnson, 1991; Small, 1990; Spelke, 1991; Sugarman, 1990). First, Piaget conceived of stages as unitary structures of thought, so his theory assumes that there is a synchrony in development. That is, various aspects of a stage should emerge at about the same time. However, several concrete operational concepts do not appear in synchrony. For example, children do not learn to conserve at the same time they learn to cross-classify. Second, small changes in the procedures involved in a Piagetian task sometimes have significant effects on a child's cognition. Third, in some cases, children who are at one cognitive

| Can use operations, mentally reversing action; shows conservation skills | Logical reasoning replaces intuitive reasoning, but only in concrete circumstances | Not abstract (can't imagine steps in algebraic equation, for example) | Classification skills — can divide things into sets and subsets and reason about their inter-relations |

Figure 10.3 Characteristics of concrete operational thought.

stage—such as preoperational thought— can be trained to reason at a higher cognitive stage—such as concrete operational thought. This poses a problem for Piaget, who argued that such training works only on a superficial level and is ineffective unless the child is at a transitional point from one stage to the next. Fourth, some cognitive abilities emerge earlier than Piaget believed and their subsequent development may be more prolonged than he thought. Conservation of number has been demonstrated in children as young as 3 years of age, although Piaget did not believe that it came about until 7 years of age; some aspects of formal operational thought that involve abstract reasoning do not consistently appear as early in adolescence as Piaget believed.

Information Processing

Among the highlights of changes in information processing during middle and late childhood are improvements in memory, schemata, and scripts. Remember also, from chapter 8, that the attention of most children improves dramatically during middle and late childhood, and that at this time children attend more to the task-relevant features of a problem than to the salient features.

Memory

In chapter 8, we concluded that tasks involving short-term memory—the memory span task, for example—reveal a considerable increase in short-term memory during early childhood, but after the age of 7 do not show as much increase. Is the same pattern found for **long-term memory,** *a relatively permanent and unlimited type of memory?* Long-term memory increases with age during middle and late childhood. Two aspects of memory related to improvement in long-term memory are control processes and learner characteristics.

If we know anything at all about long-term memory, it is that long-term memory depends on the learning activities individuals engage in when learning and remembering information. **Control processes** *are cognitive processes that*

Our life is what our thoughts make it.

~ *Marcus Aurelius,* Meditations, *2d Century* B.C.

Physical and Cognitive Development in Middle and Late Childhood

do not occur automatically but require work and effort. They are under the learner's conscious control and they can be used to improve memory. They are also appropriately called strategies (McGilly & Siegler, 1989; Pressley & Harris, 1990). Three important control processes involved in children's memory are rehearsal, organization, and imagery.

Rehearsal is a control process that improves memory. It is the repetition of information after it has been presented. An example of rehearsal occurs when children hear a phone number, then repeat the number several times to improve their memory of it. Researchers have found that children's spontaneous use of rehearsal increases between 5 and 10 years of age (Flavell, Beach, & Chinsky, 1966). The use of organization also improves memory. As with rehearsal, children in middle and late childhood are more likely to spontaneously organize information to be remembered than are children in early childhood (Moely & others, 1969).

Another control process that develops as children move through middle and late childhood is imagery. A powerful imagery strategy is the *keyword method,* which has been used to practical advantage by teaching elementary schoolchildren how to quickly master new information such as foreign vocabulary words, the states and capitals of the United States, and the names of U.S. presidents. For example, in remembering that Annapolis is the capital of Maryland, children were taught the keywords for the states, such that when a state was given (*Maryland*), they could supply the keyword (*marry*) (Levin, 1980). Then, children were given the reverse type of keyword practice with the capitals. That is, they had to respond with the capital (*Annapolis*) when given a keyword (*apple*). Finally, an illustration was provided (figure 10.4). The keyword strategy's use of vivid mental imagery, such as the image in figure 10.4, was effective in increasing children's memory of state capitals. Developmentalists today encourage the use of imagery in our nation's schools, believing that it helps to increase the child's memory (McDaniel & Pressley, 1987).

In addition to these control processes, characteristics of the child influence memory. Apart from the obvious variable of age, many characteristics of the child determine the effectiveness of memory. These characteristics include attitude, motivation, and health. However, the characteristic that has been examined the most thoroughly is the child's previously acquired knowledge. What the child knows has a tremendous effect on what the child remembers. In one investigation, 10-year-old children who were chess experts remembered chessboard positions much better than adults who did not play much chess (Chi, 1978). However, the children did not do as well as the adults when both groups were asked to remember a group of random numbers; the children's expertise in chess gave them superior memories, but only in chess.

Metacognitive Knowledge

Metacognitive knowledge *is the segment of the acquired world knowledge that involves cognitive matters. It is the knowledge children have accumulated through experience and stored in long-term memory that concerns the human mind and its workings,* not politics or football or electronics, or sewing or some other domain. Many developmentalists believe that metacognitive knowledge is beneficial in school learning, and if students, especially younger ones, are deficient in metacognitive knowledge, this knowledge can possibly be taught to them (Flavell, 1985). Several researchers have developed school programs to impart metacognitive knowledge to children in the areas of reading comprehension, writing, and mathematics. In the following discussion you will read about cognitive monitoring, including information about the role of cognitive monitoring in reading comprehension, which is an excellent example of how metacognitive knowledge can be taught to children.

Figure 10.4 Use of the keyword method to improve children's memory. To help children remember the state capitals, the keyword method was used. A special component of the keyword method is the use of mental imagery, which was stimulated by the presentation to the children of a vivid visual image, such as the one shown here of two apples being married. The strategy is to help the children associate apple *with Annapolis and* marry *with Maryland (Levin, 1980).*

Middle and Late Childhood

Cognitive Monitoring

Cognitive monitoring *is the process of taking stock of what you are currently doing, what you will do next, and how effectively the mental activity is unfolding.* When children engage in an activity like reading, writing, or solving a math problem, they are repeatedly called on to take stock of what they are doing and what they plan to do next (Baker & Brown, 1984; Brown & Palincsar, 1989). For example, when children begin to solve a math problem—especially one that might take awhile to finish—they must figure out what kind of problem they are working on and what would be a good approach in solving it. Once they undertake a problem solution, it is helpful to check whether the solution seems to be working or whether some other approach would be better.

The source of much of young children's cognitive monitoring is other people—especially parents and teachers. Adults provide a lot of guidance and direction for children's activities and they tell children what specific strategies to use to complete different cognitive tasks (Wertsch, 1985; Yussen, 1985). They suggest when children should start an activity, they intervene at points when they think children might encounter difficulty (to explain difficult words, how to get started writing on a topic, a strategy for looking at math problems, a good study strategy), and they check children's progress and understanding (giving oral spelling quizzes, asking for explanations, holding discussions). An important aspect of children's progress in cognitive monitoring as they mature, then, is their abilities to take independent control of their own cognitive activities and to develop their knowledge base to permit significant, strategic performances.

Instructional programs in reading comprehension (Brown & Palincsar, 1984, 1989), writing (Scardamalia, Bereiter, & Steinbach, 1984), and mathematics (Schoenfeld, 1985) have been designed to foster the development of cognitive monitoring (Collins, Brown, & Newman, 1989; Glaser, 1989). Ann Brown and Annemarie Palincsar's program for reading comprehension is an excellent example of a cognitive monitoring instructional program. Students in the program acquire specific knowledge and also learn strategies for monitoring their understanding. **Reciprocal teaching** *is an instructional procedure used by Brown and Palincsar to develop cognitive monitoring; it requires that students take turns in leading the group in the use of strategies for comprehending and remembering text content that the teacher models for the class.* The instruction involves a small group of students, often working with an adult leader, actively discussing a short text, with the goal of *summarizing* it, asking *questions* to promote understanding, offering *clarifying* statements for difficult or confusing words and ideas, and *predicting* what will come next. The procedure involves children in an active way, it teaches them some techniques to reflect about their own understanding, and the group interaction is highly motivating and engaging.

Schema and Scripts

In chapter 9, we described gender schema theory and defined a *schema* as a cognitive structure, a network of associations that organizes and guides an individual's perceptions. Schema is an important cognitive concept in memory and information processing. Schemas come from prior encounters with the environment and influence the way children encode, make inferences about, and retrieve information. Children have schema for stories, scenes, spatial layouts (a bathroom or a park, for example), and common events (such as going to a restaurant, playing with toys, or practicing soccer).

Children frequently hear and tell stories. And as they develop the ability to read, they are exposed to many kinds of stories in print. Simple stories have a structure to them and after hearing enough stories, children develop a strong

Figure 10.5 "Albert, the fish," a
representative story.

Setting	1 Once there was a big gray fish named Albert.
	2 He lived in a pond near the edge of a forest.
Initiating event	3 One day Albert was swimming around the pond.
	4 Then he spotted a big juicy worm on top of the water.
Internal response	5 Albert knew how delicious worms tasted.
	6 He wanted to eat that one for his dinner.
Attempt	7 So he swam very close to the worm.
	8 Then he bit into him.
Consequence	9 Suddenly, Albert was pulled through the water into a boat.
	10 He had been caught by a fisherman.
Reaction	11 Albert felt sad.
	12 He wished he had been more careful.

expectation about what kind of information will be contained in a story. This expectation is a *story schema*. For example, a story tells about what happens in a particular place and circumstance. This content is called the setting. A story will also have at least one main character, the protagonist, who attempts to achieve some purposeful goal for some clear reason. The protagonist's actions are usually captured in one or more episodes of a story, which can be further broken down, depicting a fairly simple, one-episode story (figure 10.5).

A decade of research has shown that children at a very young age are able to use structures like these to fill in missing information, remember better, and tell relatively coherent stories (Ackerman, 1988; Buss & others, 1983; Rahman & Bisanz, 1986; Stein & Glenn, 1979; Yussen & others, 1988). Changes occur throughout the childhood years, however, in children's abilities to identify salient events in stories, to unscramble mixed-up stories, and to keep multiple plot lines straight in their minds when facing more complex stories involving several episodes and more than one major character.

A **script** *is a schema for an event* (Schank & Abelson, 1977). Children's first scripts appear very early in development, perhaps as early as the first year of life. Children clearly have scripts by the time they enter school (Firush & Cobb, 1989; Flannagan & Tate, 1989; Furman & Walden, 1989, 1990; Krackow, 1991). As they develop, their scripts become less crude and more sophisticated. For example, a 4-year-old's script for a restaurant might include information only about sitting down and eating food. By middle and late childhood, the child adds information to the restaurant script about the types of people who serve food, paying the cashier, and so on.

So far, we have learned a great deal about the way children process information about their world. Through a number of chapters, we have studied how children attend to information, perceive it, retain it over time, and draw inferences about it. As we discussed earlier, computers have played an important role in the development of the information processing approach. Next, we examine the role of computers in children's lives.

Children and Computers

At the middle of the twentieth century, commercial television had barely made its debut and IBM had yet to bring its first computer to market. Now as we move toward the close of the twentieth century, both television *and* computers are important influences in children's lives. For some, the computer is a pos-

Middle and Late Childhood

itive tool with the power to transform our schools and revolutionize children's learning. For others, the computer is a menacing force, more likely to undermine than to improve children's education and learning. Let's examine some of the possible positive and negative influences of computers in children's lives.

The influence of computer use on children's learning, motivation, and social behavior continues to be a source of debate and controversy.

Positive Influences of Computers on Children

Among the potential positive influences of computers on children's development are those involving the computer as a personal tutor, as a multipurpose tool, and the motivational and social effects of computers (Lepper & Gurtner, 1989), each of which we consider in turn.

Computer-assisted instruction *uses the computer as a tutor to individualize instruction. The concept behind computer-assisted instruction is to use the computer to present information, give students practice, assess their level of understanding, and provide additional instruction if needed.* Computer-assisted instruction requires the active participation of the student, and in giving immediate feedback to students is patient and nonjudgmental. Over the past two decades, more than 200 research studies involving computer-assisted instruction have been conducted. In general, the effects of computer-assisted instruction are positive. More precisely, the effects are more positive with programs involving tutorials rather than drill and practice, with younger rather than older students, and with lower ability rather than average or unselected populations (Lepper & Gurtner, 1989).

A second important influence of the computer in children's lives is its role in experiential learning. Some experts view the computer as an excellent medium for open-ended, exploratory, and experiential learning (Nelson & Watson, 1991). The most widely studied activity has been the use of the Logo computing language, especially its simplified "turtle graphics" programming environment, as a way to improve children's planning and problem-solving abilities (Papert, 1980). The turtle graphics involve moving a small triangular cursor, called a "turtle," on the screen. However, the research on the effects of Logo are mixed. Although the early studies of Logo essentially found no benefits for children's learning, more recent studies have been supportive of Logo. In the successful recent studies, more favorable adult-child ratios are present, prepared support materials and explicit task requirements are included, younger children are studied, and a wider array of dependent variable measures are used (such as creativity, cognitive monitoring, and solution checking).

A third important influence of the computer in children's lives is its function as a multipurpose tool in helping children achieve academic goals and become more creative. The computer is especially helpful in improving children's writing and communication skills (Collins, 1986). Word-processing programs diminish the drudgery of writing, increasing the probability that children will edit and revise their work. Programs that assist students in outlining a paper may help students organize their thoughts before they write.

Several other themes appear in the discussion of the computer's positive influence on children's development. For one, computer adherents argue that the computer makes learning more intrinsically motivating (Lepper, 1985). Computer enthusiasts also argue that the computer can make learning more fun. And, lessons can often be embedded in instructional "games" or puzzles that encourage children's curiosity and sense of challenge. Some computer adherents also argue that expanded computer use in schools will increase cooperation and collaboration on the part of students, as well as increase intellectual discussion among students. And if the computer does increase students' interest, it may free teachers to spend more time working individually with students. Finally, computer adherents hope that the computer can increase the equality of educational opportunity (Becker & Sterling, 1987). Since the computer allows students to work at their own pace, it may help students who do not normally succeed in schools. Because the computer is fair and impartial, it should minimize the adverse influences of teacher prejudice and stereotyping.

The Negative Influences of Computers on Children

Among the potential negative influences of computers on children's development are those involving regimentation and dehumanization of the classroom, unwarranted "shaping" of the curriculum, and generalization and limitations of computer-based teaching (Lepper & Gurtner, 1989), each of which we discuss in turn.

Skeptics worry that rather than increased individualization of instruction, computers will bring a much greater regimentation and homogenization of classroom learning experiences. While some students may prefer to work autonomously and may learn most effectively when they are allowed to progress on their own, other students may rely on social interaction with guidance by the teacher for effective learning. And, some computer skeptics worry that the computer will ultimately increase inequality, rather than equality, in educational outcomes. School funding in middle-class neighborhoods is usually better than in low-income areas, and homes of children in middle-class neighborhoods are more likely to have computers than those in low-income neighborhoods. Thus, an increasing emphasis on computer literacy may be inequitable for children from low-income backgrounds because they have likely had less opportunities to use computers. Some critics also worry about the dehumanization of the classroom. They argue that school is a social world as well as a cognitive, learning world. From this perspective, children plugged into a computer all day long have little opportunity to engage in social interaction.

A further concern is that computers may inadvertently and inappropriately shape the curriculum. Some subjects, such as mathematics and science, seem to be more easily and successfully adapted to computers than subjects such as art and literature. Consequently, there is concern that the computer may eventually shape the curriculum in the direction of science and math because these areas are more easily computerized.

Yet another concern is the transfer of learning and motivation outside the computer domain. If the instructional effectiveness and motivational appeal of computer-based education depends on the use of impressive technical devices such as color, animation, and sound effects, how effectively will student learning or motivation transfer to other contexts without these technical supports? Will children provided with the editorial assistance of the computer still learn the basic skills needed to progress to more complex forms of creative writing later in their careers? Will children using computers in math gain the proficiency to deal with more complicated math in the future or will their ability to solve complex conceptual problems in the absence of the computer have atrophied? Presently, we do not know the answers to these important questions, but they do raise some important concerns about the computer's role in children's development.

At this point we have discussed a number of ideas about Piaget's theory and concrete operational thought, and about information processing in middle and late childhood. A summary of these ideas is presented in concept table 10.2. Now we turn our attention to the nature of children's intelligence.

Concept Table 10.2: Piaget's Theory and Concrete Operational Thought, and Information Processing

Concept	Processes/Related Ideas	Characteristics/Description
Piaget's Theory and Concrete Operational Thought	Concrete Operational Thought	Concrete operational thought is made up of operations, mental actions that allow the child to do mentally what was done before physically. Concrete operations are also mental actions that are reversible. The concrete operational child shows conservation and classification skills. The concrete operational child needs clearly available perceptual supports to reason; later in development, thought becomes more abstract.
	Piaget and Education	Piaget's ideas have been applied extensively to children's education. Emphasis is on communication and the belief that the child has many ideas about the world, that the child is always learning and unlearning, and that the child is by nature a knowing creature.
	Contributions and Criticisms	Piaget was a genius at observing children and he developed fascinating insights about children's cognition; he showed us some important things to look for in development and mapped out some general cognitive changes in development. Criticisms of Piaget's ideas focus on the belief that the stages are not as unitary as he thought, that small changes in procedures affect the child's cognition, that children can sometimes be trained to think at higher stages, and that some cognitive skills appear earlier than Piaget thought, while others are more protracted than he thought.
Information Processing	Memory	Children's long-term memory improves during middle and late childhood. Control processes or strategies such as rehearsal, organization, and imagery are among the important influences that are responsible for improved long-term memory. Children's knowledge also influences their memory.
	Metacognitive Knowledge	This is the segment of acquired knowledge that involves cognitive matters, especially the way the human mind works. Many developmentalists believe metacognitive knowledge is beneficial in school learning.
	Cognitive Monitoring	This is the process of taking stock of what one is currently doing, what will be done next, and how effectively the mental activity is unfolding. The source of much cognitive monitoring in children is other people. Instructional programs in reading comprehension, writing, and math have been designed to foster children's cognitive monitoring of these activities. Reciprocal teaching is an instructional procedure used to develop children's cognitive monitoring.
	Schema and Scripts	A schema is a cognitive structure, a network of associations that organizes and guides an individual's perceptions. Schemas influence the way children process information. A script is a schema for an event.
	Computers and Children	Among the potential positive effects of computers on children's development are those involving the computer as a personal tutor (computer-assisted instruction), as a multipurpose tool, and the motivational and social aspects of computers. Among the potential negative effects of computers are those involving regimentations and dehumanization of the classroom, unwarranted "shaping" of the curriculum, and generalization and limitations of computer-based teaching.

Intelligence

Intelligence is an abstract concept that is difficult to define (Thorndike, 1990). While many psychologists and laypeople equate intelligence with verbal ability and problem-solving skills, others prefer to define it as the individual's ability to learn from and adapt to the experiences of everyday life. If we were to settle on a definition of intelligence based on these criteria, it would be that **intelligence** *is verbal ability, problem-solving skills, and the ability to learn from and adapt to the experiences of everyday life.*

The components of intelligence are very close to the information-processing and language skills we have discussed at various points in children's development. The difference between how we discussed information-processing skills and language and how we will discuss intelligence lies in the concepts of individual differences and assessment. Individual differences are simply the consistent, stable ways we differ from each other. The history of the study of intelligence has focused extensively on individual differences and their assessment. For example, an intelligence test will inform us whether a child can reason more logically than most other children who have taken the test. Our coverage of intelligence focuses on the components of intelligence, cultural bias, the use and misuse of intelligence tests, and the extremes of intelligence. As you think about intelligence, keep in mind our discussion of intelligence in chapter 3, in which we concluded that intelligence is influenced by the interaction of heredity and environment, rather than either factor alone.

One Face or Many?

Is it more appropriate to think of intelligence as an individual's general ability or as a number of specific abilities? As we explore different approaches to what intelligence is and how it should be measured, you will discover that intelligence is probably *both*.

In 1904, the French Ministry of Education asked psychologist Alfred Binet to devise a method that would determine which students did not profit from typical school instruction. School officials wanted to reduce overcrowding by placing those who did not benefit from regular classroom teaching in special schools. To meet this request, Binet and his student Theophile Simon developed an intelligence test. The test, referred to as the 1905 Scale, consisted of thirty different items ranging from the ability to touch one's nose or ear when asked to the ability to draw designs from memory and define abstract concepts.

Binet developed the concept of **mental age (MA)**—*an individual's level of mental development relative to others.* Binet reasoned that mentally retarded children would perform like normal children of a younger age. He developed norms for intelligence by testing fifty nonretarded children from 3 to 11 years of age. Children suspected of mental retardation were tested, and their performance was compared with children of the same chronological age in the normal sample. Average mental-age scores (MA) correspond to chronological age (CA), which is age since birth. A bright child has an MA above CA, a dull child has an MA below CA.

The term **intelligence quotient (IQ)** *was devised by William Stern. IQ is the child's mental age divided by chronological age multiplied by 100:*

$$IQ = \frac{MA}{CA} \times 100$$

If mental age is the same as chronological age, then the child's IQ is 100; if mental age is above chronological age, the IQ is more than 100; if mental age is below chronological age, the IQ is less than 100.

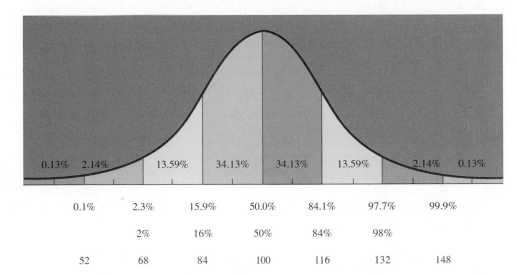

Percent of cases under portions of the normal curve	0.13%	2.14%		13.59%	34.13%	34.13%	13.59%	2.14%	0.13%
Cumulative percentages		0.1%	2.3%	15.9%	50.0%	84.1%	97.7%	99.9%	
			2%	16%	50%	84%	98%		
Stanford-Binet IQs		52	68	84	100	116	132	148	

Figure 10.6 *The normal curve and Stanford-Binet IQ scores. The distribution of IQ scores approximates a normal curve. Most of the population falls in the middle range of scores. Notice that extremely high and extremely low scores are very rare. Slightly more than two-thirds of the scores fall between 84 and 116. Only about 1 in 50 individuals has an IQ of more than 132 and only about 1 in 50 individuals has an IQ of less than 68.*

Over the years extensive effort has been expended to standardize the Binet test, which has been given to thousands of children and adults of different ages, selected at random from different parts of the United States. By administering the test to large numbers of individuals and recording the results, it has been found that intelligence measured by the Binet approximates a normal distribution (see figure 10.6). A **normal distribution** *is symmetrical with a majority of cases falling in the middle of the possible range of scores and few scores appearing toward the extremes of the range.*

The current Stanford-Binet (named after Stanford University, where revisions of the test were constructed) is given to persons from the age of 2 through adulthood. It includes a wide variety of items, some requiring verbal responses, others nonverbal responses. For example, items that characterize a 6-year-old's performance on the test include the verbal ability to define at least six words such as *orange* and *envelope,* and the nonverbal ability to trace a path through a maze. Items that reflect the average adult's intelligence include defining words such as *disproportionate* and *regard,* explaining a proverb, and comparing idleness and laziness.

The fourth edition of the Stanford-Binet was published in 1985 (Thorndike, Hagan, & Sattler, 1985). One important addition to this version is the analysis of responses in four content areas: verbal reasoning, quantitative reasoning, abstract/visual reasoning, and short-term memory (Keith & others, 1988). A general composite score is also obtained to reflect overall intelligence. The Stanford-Binet continues to be one of the most widely used individual tests of children's intelligence.

Besides the Stanford-Binet, the other most widely used individual intelligence tests are the *Wechsler scales,* developed by David Wechsler. They include the Wechsler Adult Intelligence Scale—Revised (WAIS-R); the Wechsler Intelligence Scale for Children—Third Edition (WISC-III), for use with children between the ages of 6 and 16; and the Wechsler Preschool and Primary Scale of Intelligence—Revised (WPPSI-R), for use with children from the ages of 4 to 6½ (Wechsler, 1949, 1955, 1967, 1974, 1981, 1989, 1991).

The Wechsler scales not only provide an overall IQ, but the items are grouped according to twelve subscales, six verbal and six nonverbal. This allows the examiner to obtain separate verbal and nonverbal IQ scores and to see quickly in which areas of mental performance the child is below average, average, or above average. The inclusion of a number of nonverbal subscales

Verbal subtests

Information
The individual is asked a number of general information questions about experiences that are considered normal for individuals in our society.
For example, "How many hours apart are eastern standard time and pacific standard time?"

Similarities
The individual must think logically and abstractly to answer a number of questions about how things are similar.
For example, "In what way are boats and trains the same?"

Arithmetic
Problems measure the individual's ability to do arithmetic mentally and include addition, subtraction, multiplication, and division.
For example, "If oranges are $1.20 per dozen, how much does one orange cost?"

Vocabulary
To evaluate word knowledge, the individual is asked to define a number of words. This subtest measures a number of cognitive functions, including concept formation, memory, and language.
For example, "What does the word *disparate* mean?"

Comprehension
This subtest is designed to measure the individual's judgement and common sense.
For example, "Why do individuals buy automobile insurance?"

Digit span
This subtest primarily measures attention and short-term memory. The individual is required to repeat numbers forward and backward.
For example, "I am going to say some numbers and I want you to repeat them backward: 4 7 5 2 8."

Performance subtests

Picture completion
A number of drawings are shown, each with a significant part missing. Within a period of several seconds, the individual must differentiate essential from nonessential parts of the picture and identify which part is missing. This subtest evaluates visual alertness and the ability to organize information visually.
For example, "I am going to show you a picture with an important part missing. Tell me what is missing."

Picture arrangement
A series of pictures out of sequence are shown to the individual, who is asked to place them in their proper order to tell an appropriate story. This subtest evaluates how individuals integrate information to make it logical amd meaningful.
For example, "The pictures below need to be placed in an appropriate order to tell a meaningful story."

Object assembly
The individual is asked to assemble pieces into something. This subtest measures visual motor coordination and perceptual organization.
For example, "When these pieces are put together correctly, they make something. Put them together as quickly as you can."

Block design
The individual must assemble a set of multi-colored blocks to match designs that the examiner shows. Visual-motor coordination, perceptual organization, and the ability to visualize spatially are measured.
For example, "Use the four blocks on the left to make the pattern on the right."

Coding
This subtest evaluates how quickly and accurately an individual can link code symbols and digits. The subtest assesses visual-motor coordination and speed of thought.
For example, "As quickly as you can, transfer the appropriate code symbols to the blank spaces."

Code

1	2	3	4	5
●	□	★	△	╱

Test

3	5	2	4	1	2	4	3	5	2	1	4	3	5

Figure 10.7   Sample subtests of the Wechsler Intelligence Scale for Children—Third Edition.

makes the Wechsler test more representative of verbal *and* nonverbal intelligence; the Binet test includes some nonverbal items but not as many as the Wechsler scales. The subscales on the Wechsler Intelligence Scale for Children—Third Edition are shown in figure 10.7 along with examples of each subscale.

(a)

(b)

(c)

The contemporary theory of Robert J. Sternberg (1986, 1989) states that intelligence has three factors. **Triarchic theory** *is Sternberg's theory that intelligence consists of componential intelligence, experiential intelligence, and contextual intelligence.* Consider Ann, who scores high on traditional intelligence tests like the Stanford-Binet and is a star analytical thinker; Todd, who does not have the best test scores but has an insightful and creative mind; and Art, a street-smart person who has learned to deal in practical ways with his world, although his scores on traditional IQ tests are low.

Sternberg calls Ann's analytical thinking and abstract reasoning *componential intelligence;* it is the closest to what we call intelligence in this chapter and what is commonly measured by intelligence tests. Sternberg calls Todd's insightful and creative thinking *experiential intelligence*, and he calls Art's street smarts and practical know-how *contextual intelligence* (see figure 10.8).

In Sternberg's view of componential intelligence, the basic unit in intelligence is a *component,* simply defined as a basic unit of information processing. Sternberg believes such components include the ability to acquire or store information; to retain or retrieve information; to transfer information; to plan, make decisions, and solve problems; and to translate our thoughts into performance. Notice the similarity of these components to our description of information processing earlier in this chapter.

The second part of Sternberg's model focuses on experience. According to Sternberg, intellectual individuals have the ability to solve new problems quickly, but they also learn how to solve familiar problems in an automatic, rote way so their minds are free to handle other problems that require insight and creativity.

The third part of the model involves practical intelligence—such as how to get out of trouble, how to replace a fuse, and how to get along with people. Sternberg describes this practical or contextual intelligence as all of the important information about getting along in the real world that you are not taught in school. He believes contextual intelligence is sometimes more important than the "book knowledge" that is often taught in school.

Yet another developmental psychologist, Howard Gardner (1983), believes there are seven types of intelligence: verbal, mathematical, ability to spatially analyze the world, movement skills, insightful skills for analyzing

Figure 10.8   Sternberg's triarchic model of intelligence.
(a) Componential intelligence is the closest to what is commonly measured on intelligence tests and is reflected in the ability to process information as we learn how to use a computer. (b) Experiential intelligence involves creativity and insight. (c) Contextual intelligence refers to practical knowledge, such as knowing how to get along well with other people.

"You're wise, but you lack tree smarts."

ourselves, insightful skills for analyzing others, and musical skills. Gardner believes that each of the seven types of intelligence can be destroyed by brain damage, that each involves unique cognitive skills, and that each shows up in exaggerated fashion in both the gifted and idiot savants (individuals who are mentally retarded but who have unbelievable skill in a particular domain, such as drawing, music, or computing). I remember vividly an individual from my childhood who was mentally retarded but could instantaneously respond with the correct day of the week (say Tuesday or Saturday) when given any date in history (say June 4, 1926, or December 15, 1746).

Gardner is especially interested in musical intelligence, particularly when it is exhibited at an early age. He points out that musically inclined preschool children not only have the remarkable ability to learn musical patterns easily, but that they rarely forget them. He recounts a story about Stravinsky, who as an adult could still remember the musical patterns of the tuba, drums, and piccolos of the fife-and-drum band that marched outside his home when he was a young child.

To measure musical intelligence in young children, Gardner might ask a child to listen to a melody and then ask the child to recreate the tune on some bells he provides. He believes such evaluations can be used to develop a profile of a child's intelligence. He also believes that it is during this early time in life that parents can make an important difference in how a child's intelligence develops.

Critics of Gardner's approach point out that we have geniuses in many domains other than music. There are outstanding chess players, prize fighters, writers, politicians, physicians, lawyers, preachers, and poets, for example; yet we do not refer to chess intelligence, prize-fighter intelligence, and so on.

Are Intelligence Tests Culturally Biased?

Many of the early intelligence tests were culturally biased, favoring urban children over rural children, middle-class children over lower-class children, and White children over minority children (Miller-Jones, 1989). The norms for the early tests were based almost entirely on White, middle-class children. And some of the items themselves were culturally biased. For example, one item on an early test asked what you should do if you find a 3-year-old child

1. A "gas head" is a person who has a:
   (a) fast-moving car
   (b) stable of "lace"
   (c) "process"
   (d) habit of stealing cars
   (e) long jail record for arson

2. "Bo Diddley" is a:
   (a) game for children
   (b) down-home cheap wine
   (c) down-home singer
   (d) new dance
   (e) Moejoe call

3. If a pimp is uptight with a woman who gets state aid, what does he mean when he talks about "Mother's day"?
   (a) second Sunday in May
   (b) third Sunday in June
   (c) first of every month
   (d) none of these
   (e) first and fifteenth of every month

4. A "handkerchief head" is:
   (a) a cool cat
   (b) a porter
   (c) an Uncle Tom
   (d) a hoddi
   (e) a preacher

5. If a man is called a "blood," then he is a:
   (a) fighter
   (b) Mexican-American
   (c) Negro
   (d) hungry hemophile
   (e) red man, or Indian

6. Cheap chitlings (not the kind you purchase at a frozen-food counter) will taste rubbery unless they are cooked long enough. How soon can you quit cooking them to eat and enjoy them?
   (a) forty-five minutes
   (b) two hours
   (c) twenty-four hours
   (d) one week (on a low flame)
   (e) one hour

Answers: 1. c 2. c 3. e 4. c 5. c 6. c

Figure 10.9 *Sample items from the Chitling Intelligence Test.*
Source: Adrian Dove, 1968.

in the street; the correct answer was "Call the police." Children from impoverished inner-city families might not choose this answer if they have had bad experiences with the police; rural children might not choose it, because they may not have police nearby. Such items do not measure the knowledge necessary to adapt to one's environment or to be "intelligent" in an inner-city minority neighborhood or in rural America (Scarr, 1984). The contemporary versions of intelligence tests attempt to reduce cultural bias (Angoff, 1989).

Even if the content of test items is appropriate, another problem may exist with intelligence tests. Since many questions are verbal in nature, minority groups may encounter problems in understanding the language of the questions (Gibbs & Huang, 1989). Minority groups often speak a language that is very different from standard English. Consequently, they may be at a disadvantage when they take intelligence tests oriented toward middle-class Whites. Such cultural bias is dramatically underscored by tests like the one in figure 10.9. The items in this test were developed to reduce the cultural disadvantage Black children might experience on traditional intelligence tests.

Culture-fair tests *are tests that are designed to reduce cultural bias.* Two types of culture-fair tests have been developed. The first includes items that are familiar to individuals from all socioeconomic and ethnic backgrounds, or items that are at least familiar to the people taking the test. A child might be asked how a bird and a dog are different, on the assumption that all children have been exposed to birds and dogs. The second type of culture-fair test has all the verbal items removed. Figure 10.10 shows a sample item from the Raven Progressive Matrices Test, which exemplifies this approach. Even though tests like the Raven Test are designed to be culture fair, people with more education score higher on them than those with less education (Anastasi, 1988).

Culture-fair tests remind us that traditional intelligence tests are probably culturally biased, yet culture-fair tests do not provide a satisfactory alternative. Constructing a test that is truly culture fair—one that rules out the role of experience emanating from socioeconomic and ethnic background—has been difficult and may be impossible. Consider, for example, that the intelligence of the Iatmul people of Papua, New Guinea, involves the ability to remember the names of some 10,000 to 20,000 clans; by contrast, the intelligence of islanders in the widely dispersed Caroline Islands involves the talent of navigating by the stars.

Physical and Cognitive Development in Middle and Late Childhood

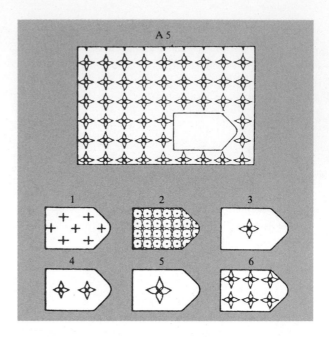

Figure 10.10 Sample item from the Raven Progressive Matrices Test. The individual is presented with a matrix arrangement of symbols, such as the one at the top, and must then complete the matrix by selecting the appropriate missing symbol from a group of symbols.

The Use and Misuse of Intelligence Tests

Psychological tests are tools. Like all tools, their effectiveness depends on the knowledge, skill, and integrity of the user. A hammer can be used to build a beautiful kitchen cabinet or it can be used as a weapon of assault. Like a hammer, intelligence tests can be used for positive purposes or they can be abusive. It is important for both the test constructor and the test examiner to be familiar with the current state of scientific knowledge about intelligence and intelligence tests (Anastasi, 1988).

Even though they have limitations, intelligence tests are among psychology's most widely used tools. To be effective, though, intelligence tests must be viewed realistically. They should not be thought of as a fixed, unchanging indicator of a person's intelligence. They should also be used in conjunction with other information about a person and should not be relied upon as the sole indicator of intelligence. For example, an intelligence test should not be used as the sole indicator of whether a child should be placed in a special-education or gifted class. The child's developmental history, medical background, performance in school, social competencies, and family experiences should be taken into account, too.

The single number provided by many IQ tests can easily lead to stereotypes and expectations about a person. Many people do not know how to interpret the results of an intelligence test, and sweeping generalizations about a person are too often made on the basis of an IQ score. Imagine, for example, that you are a teacher sitting in the teacher's lounge the day after school has started in the fall. You mention a student—Johnny Jones—and a fellow teacher remarks that she had Johnny in class last year, and goes on to say that he was a real dunce, pointing out that his IQ is 78. You cannot help but remember this information, and it may lead you to think that Johnny Jones is not very bright so it is useless to spend much time teaching him. In this way, IQ scores are misused and stereotypes are formed (Rosenthal, 1987; Rosenthal & Jacobsen, 1968).

We have a tendency in our culture to consider intelligence or a high IQ as the ultimate human value. It is important to keep in mind that our value as people includes other matters: consideration of others, positive close relationships, and competence in social situations, for example. The verbal and problem-solving skills measured on traditional intelligence tests are only one part of human competence.

Despite their limitations, when used judiciously by a competent examiner, intelligence tests provide valuable information about people. There are not many alternatives to intelligence tests. Subjective judgments about individuals simply reintroduce the biases the tests were designed to eliminate.

The Extremes of Intelligence

Intelligence tests have been used to discover indications of mental retardation or intellectual giftedness, the extremes of intelligence. At times intelligence tests have been misused for this purpose. Keeping in mind the theme that an intelligence test should not be used as the sole indicator of mental retardation or giftedness, we explore the nature of these intellectual extremes.

Mental Retardation

The most distinctive feature of mental retardation is inadequate intellectual functioning. Long before formal tests were developed to assess intelligence, the mentally retarded were identified by a lack of age-appropriate skills in learning and caring for oneself. With the development of intelligence tests, more emphasis was placed on IQ as an indicator of mental retardation. But it is not unusual to find two retarded individuals with the same low IQ, one of whom is married, employed, and involved in the community and the other requiring constant supervision in an institution. These differences in social competence led psychologists to include deficits in adaptive behavior in their definition of mental retardation. **Mental retardation** *is a condition of limited mental ability in which the individual has a low IQ, usually below 70 on a traditional test of intelligence, and has difficulty adapting to everyday life.* About 5 million Americans fit this definition of mental retardation.

There are different classifications of mental retardation. About 80 percent of the mentally retarded fall into the mild category, with IQs of 50 to 70. About 12 percent are classified as moderately retarded, with IQs of 35 to 49; these individuals can attain a second-grade level of skills and may be able to support themselves as adults through some type of labor. About 7 percent of the mentally retarded are in the severe category, with IQs of 20 to 34; these individuals learn to talk and engage in very simple tasks, but they require extensive supervision. Only 1 percent of the mentally retarded fall into the profound classification with IQs below 20; they are in constant need of supervision.

What causes mental retardation? The causes are divided into two categories: organic and cultural-familial. **Organic retardation** *is mental retardation caused by a genetic disorder or brain damage; organic refers to the tissues or organs of the body, so there is some physical damage in organic retardation.* Down syndrome, a form of mental retardation (see figure 10.11), occurs when an extra chromosome is present in the individual's genetic makeup, for example. It is not known why the extra chromosome is present, but it may involve the health or age of the female ovum or male sperm. Although those who suffer organic retardation are found across the spectrum of IQ distribution, most have IQs between 0 and 50.

Cultural-familial retardation *is mental retardation in which there is no evidence of organic brain damage; individuals' IQs range from 50 to 70. Psychologists seek to find the cause of this type of retardation in impoverished environments.*

Figure 10.11 A Down syndrome child. What causes a child to develop Down syndrome? In which major classification of mental retardation does the condition fall?

Even with organic retardation, though, it is wise to think about the contributions of genetic-environment interaction. Parents with low IQs may not only be more likely to transmit genes for low intelligence to their offspring but they may also tend to provide them with a less enriched environment (Landesman & Ramey, 1989).

Giftedness

Conventional wisdom has identified some individuals in all cultures and historical periods as special or exceptional because they have talents not evident in the majority of people. Individuals who are **gifted** *have above-average intelligence (an IQ of 120 or higher) and/or a superior talent for something.* Most school systems emphasize intellectual superiority and academic aptitude when selecting children for gifted programs, rarely considering competence and potential in the visual and performing arts (arts, drama, dance), psychomotor abilities (tennis, golf, basketball), or other special aptitudes.

A classic study of the gifted was begun by Lewis Terman (1925) more than sixty years ago. Terman studied approximately 1,500 children whose Stanford-Binet IQs averaged 150. His goal was to follow these children through their adult lives—the study will not be complete until the year 2010.

The accomplishments of the 1,500 children in Terman's study are remarkable. Of the 800 males, 78 have obtained PhDs (they include two past presidents of the American Psychological Association), 48 have earned MDs, and 85 have been granted law degrees. Nearly all of these figures are ten to thirty times greater than found among 800 men of the same age chosen randomly from the overall population. These findings challenge the commonly held belief that the intellectually gifted are disturbed emotionally or maladjusted socially, which is based on striking instances of mental disturbances among the gifted. Sir Frances Galton suffered from an anxiety disorder and had two nervous breakdowns, for example. Sir Isaac Newton, Vincent Van Gogh, Leonardo da Vinci, Socrates, and Edgar Allan Poe all had emotional

Never to be cast away are the gifts of the gods, magnificent.

~ *Homer,*
The Iliad, *9th Century* B.C.

problems. But these are the exception rather than the rule; no relation between giftedness and mental disturbance has been found. A number of studies support Terman's conclusion that, if anything, the gifted tend to be more mature and have fewer emotional problems than others (Janos & Robinson, 1985).

In one investigation, people with exceptional talents as adults were interviewed about what they believe contributed to their giftedness (Bloom, 1983). The 120 people had excelled in one of six fields: concert pianists and sculptors (arts), Olympic swimmers and tennis champions (psychomotor), and research mathematicians and research neurologists (cognitive). They said that the development of their exceptional accomplishments required special environmental support, excellent teaching, and encouragement. Each experienced years of special attention under the tutelage and supervision of a remarkable set of teachers and coaches. They also were given extensive support and encouragement from parents. All of these stars devoted exceptional time to practice and training, easily outdistancing the amount of time spent in all other activities combined. Of course, not every parent wants to raise a star, but too many parents develop unrealistic expectations for their offspring, putting unbearable pressure on them and wanting them to achieve things that far exceed their talents. For every Chris Evert, there are thousands of girls with only mediocre tennis talent whose parents have wanted them to become "another" Chris Evert. Such unreal expectations always meet with failure and place children under considerable stress. And all too often parents try to push children and adolescents into activities that bore rather than excite them (Feldman, 1989; Hennessey & Amabile, 1988). The importance of family processes in the development of the gifted was recently underscored by the finding that the personal adjustment of gifted individuals at midlife was strongly related to the harmony that existed in their family of origin as they were growing up in childhood (Tomlinson-Keasey & Little, 1990).

Each of us would like to be talented. And if we have children, we would like to be able to develop their talents. Some children become extraordinarily gifted, reaching the status of "star." Becoming a "star" takes years of special tutelage with remarkable coaches, extensive support by parents, and day after day, week after week, month after month, and year after year of practice.

Creativity

Most of us would like to be both gifted and creative. Why was Thomas Edison able to invent so many things? Was he simply more intelligent than most individuals? Did he spend long hours toiling away in private? Surprisingly, when Edison was a young boy his teacher told him he was too dumb to learn anything! Other examples of famous individuals whose creative genius went unnoticed when they were young include Walt Disney, who was fired from a newspaper job because he did not have any good ideas; Enrico Caruso, whose music teacher told him that his voice was terrible; and Winston Churchill, who failed one year of secondary school.

Edison, Disney, Caruso, and Churchill were intelligent individuals, but experts on creativity believe intelligence and creativity are not the same thing (Winner, 1989). One common distinction is between **convergent thinking,** *which produces one correct answer and is characteristic of the kind of thinking on standardized intelligence tests,* and **divergent thinking,** *which produces many different answers to the same question and is more characteristic of creativity* (Guilford, 1967). For example, the following intellectual problem-solving task characteristic of intelligence test items has one correct answer and thus requires convergent thinking: "How many quarters will you get in return for 60 dimes?" But the following question, an example of an item used to assess creative thinking, has many possible answers: What images does "sitting alone in a dark room" make you think of? (Baron, 1989). Answering "the sound of a violin with no strings" and "patience" are considered creative answers, while answering "a person in a crowd" or "insomnia" are considered common, and thus not very creative, responses.

Creativity *is the ability to think about something in a novel and unusual way and to come up with unique solutions to problems.* When individuals in the arts and sciences who fit the description of "creative" are asked what enables them to produce their creative works, they say they generate large amounts of associative content when solving problems and they have the time and independence to entertain a wide range of possible solutions in an enjoyable setting. How strongly is creativity related to intelligence? A certain level of intelligence is required to be creative in most fields, but many highly intelligent individuals (as measured by IQ tests) are not very creative (Runco, 1991; Wakefield, 1991).

Some experts remain skeptical that we will ever fully understand the creative process. Other experts believe that a psychology of creativity is in reach. Most experts do agree that the concept of creativity as spontaneously bubbling up from a magical well is a myth. Momentary flashes of insight, accompanied by images, make up only a small part of the creative process. At the heart of the creative process are ability and experience that shape an individual's intentional and sustained effort, often over the course of a lifetime.

Language Development

As children develop during middle and late childhood, changes in their vocabulary and grammar take place. Reading assumes a prominent role in their language world. An increasingly important consideration is bilingualism. We will consider each of these aspects of children's language development in turn.

Vocabulary and Grammar

During middle and late childhood, a change occurs in the way children think about words. They become less tied to the actions and perceptual dimensions associated with words, and they become more analytical in their approach to words. For example, when asked to say the first thing that comes to mind when they hear a word such as *dog,* preschool children often respond with a word related to the immediate context of a dog. A child might associate *dog* with a word that indicates its appearance (*black, big*) or to an action associated with it (*bark, sit*). Older children more frequently respond to *dog* by associating it with an appropriate category (*animal*) or to information that intelligently expands the context (*cat, veterinarian*) (Holzman, 1983). The increasing ability elementary children have in analyzing words helps them to understand words that have no direct relationship to their own personal experiences. This allows children to add more abstract words to their vocabulary. For example, *precious stones* may be understood by understanding the common characteristics of *diamonds* and *emeralds.* Also, children's increasing analytic abilities allow them to distinguish between similar words such as *cousin* and *nephew,* or *city, village,* and *suburb.*

Children make similar advances in grammar. The elementary schoolchild's improvement in logical reasoning and analytical skills helps in the understanding of such constructions as the appropriate use of comparatives (*shorter, deeper*) and subjectives ("If you were president. . . ."). By the end of the elementary school years, children can usually apply many of the appropriate rules of grammar when asked to (de Villiers & de Villiers, 1978).

Reading

Reading becomes a special skill during the elementary school years. Not being a competent reader places a child at a substantial disadvantage in relation to his or her peers.

In the history of learning-to-read techniques, three approaches have dominated: ABC method, whole-word method, and phonics method. The **ABC method** *is a learning-to-read technique that emphasizes memorizing the names*

and letters of the alphabet. The **whole-word method** *is a learning-to-read technique that emphasizes learning direct associations between whole words and their meanings.* The **phonics method** *is a learning-to-read technique that emphasizes the sounds that letters make when in words (such sounds can differ from the names of these letters, as when the sound of the letter c is not found in cat).* The ABC method is in ill repute today. Because of the imperfect relationship between the names of letters and their sounds in words, the technique is regarded as ineffective, if not harmful, in teaching children to read. Despite its poor reputation, the ABC method was the technique by which many children in past generations learned to read successfully.

Disputes in recent years have centered on the merits of the whole-word and phonics methods (Goswani & Bryant, 1990). Although some research has been done comparing these two techniques, the findings have not been conclusive (Carbo, 1987). However, there is evidence that drill practice with the sounds made by letters in words (part of some phonics methods) improves reading ability (Williams, 1979). Many current techniques of reading instruction incorporate components of both whole-word and phonics (Karlin & Karlin, 1987).

Reading is more than the sum of whole-word and phonics methods. Information-processing skills are also involved in successful reading (Hall, 1989; Rieben & Perfetti, 1991). When children read, they process information and interpret it. So reading serves as a practical example to illustrate the approach of information processing we have talked about at various other times in this book. Remember that information processing is concerned with how children analyze the many different sources of information available to them in the environment and how they make sense of those experiences. When children read, for example, they have available to their senses a rich and complex set of visual symbols. The symbols are associated with sounds, the sounds are combined to form words, and the words and large units that contain them (phrases, sentences, paragraphs) have conventional meanings. To read effectively, children have to perceive and attend to words and sentences. Another process in reading is holding the information in memory while new information is processed. A number of information processing skills, then, are involved in children's ability to read effectively.

A difficult task faced by the more than 6 million children who come from homes in which the primary language is not English is to master both their native tongue, spoken at home, and English, to make their way in the larger society.

Bilingualism

Octavio's Mexican parents moved to the United States one year before Octavio was born. They do not speak English fluently and have always spoken to Octavio in Spanish. At 6 years of age, Octavio has just entered the first grade at an elementary school in San Antonio, Texas, and he speaks no English. What is the best way to teach Octavio? How much easier would elementary school be for Octavio if his parents had been able to speak to him in Spanish and English when he was an infant?

Well over 6 million children in the United States come from homes in which English is not the primary language. Often, like Octavio, they live in a community where the same non-English language is the main means of communication. These children face a more difficult task than most of us: They must master the native tongue of their family to communicate effectively at home, and they must also master English to make their way in the larger society. The number of bilingual children is expanding at such a rapid rate in our country (some experts predict a tripling of their number early in the twenty-first century) that they constitute an important subgroup of language learners to be dealt with by society. Although the education of such children in the public schools has a long history, only recently has a national policy evolved to guarantee a quality language experience for them.

Bilingual education *refers to programs for students with limited proficiency in English that instruct students in their own language part of the time while English is being learned.* The rationale for bilingual education was provided by the U.S. Civil Rights Commission (1975): Lack of English proficiency is the main reason language minority students do poorly in school; bilingual education should keep students from falling so far behind in a subject while they are learning English. Bilingual programs vary extensively in content and quality. At a minimum, they include English instruction as a second language for students with limited English proficiency. Bilingual programs often include some instruction in Spanish as well. The largest number of bilingual programs in the United States are in Spanish, so our examples refer to Spanish, although the principles apply to bilingual programs in other languages. Bilingual programs differ in the extent the Hispanic culture is taught to all students. And some bilingual programs teach Spanish to all students, regardless of whether their primary language is Spanish.

Most bilingual education programs are simply transitional programs developed to support students in Spanish until they can understand English well enough to function in the regular classroom that is taught in English. A typical bilingual program begins teaching students in their primary language in kindergarten and then changes to English-only classes by the end of the first or second grade (Slavin, 1988).

Research evaluation of bilingualism has led to the conclusion that bilingualism does not interfere with performance in either language (Hakuta & Garcia, 1989). There is no evidence that the native language should be eliminated as early as possible because it might interfere with learning a second language. Indeed, higher degrees of bilingualism are associated with cognitive flexibility and improved concept formation (Diaz, 1983). These findings are based primarily on research in additive bilingual settings, that is, in settings where the second language is added as an enrichment to the native language and not at the expense of the native language. Causal relations between bilingualism and cognitive or language competence are difficult to establish, but in general, positive outcomes are often noted in communities where bilingualism is not socially stigmatized.

Increasingly, researchers are recognizing the complexity of the effects of bilingualism (Beals & De Temple, 1991; Dickinson & Moreton, 1991). For example, as we indicated earlier, the nature of bilingual programs varies enormously; some are of excellent quality, others are of poor quality. Some teachers in bilingual education programs are completely bilingual, others are not. Some programs begin in kindergarten, and others begin in elementary school. Some programs end in the first or second grade, and others continue through the fifth or sixth grade. Some include instruction in the Hispanic culture, others focus only on language instruction itself. Some researchers select outcome measures that include only proficiency in English; some focus on cognitive variables, such as cognitive flexibility and concept formation; and others include more social variables, such as integration into the school, self-esteem, and attitude toward school. In sum, there is more to understanding the effects of bilingual education than simply proficiency in language (Hakuta & Garcia, 1989).

One final point about bilingualism deserves attention. The United States in one of the few countries in the world where most students graduate from high school knowing only their own language. For example, in the Soviet Union, schools have ten grades, called forms, which correspond roughly to the twelve grades in American schools. Children begin school at age 7. In the third form, Russian students begin learning English. Because of the emphasis on teaching English in their schools, today most Soviet citizens under the age of 35 speak at least some English (Cameron, 1988).

Achievement

Yet another important dimension of cognitive development in middle and late childhood is children's achievement. We are a species motivated to do well at what we attempt, to gain mastery over the world in which we live, to explore with enthusiasm and curiosity unknown environments, and to achieve the heights of success. We live in an achievement-oriented world with standards

that tell children that success is important. The standards suggest that success requires a competitive spirit, a desire to win, a motivation to do well, and the wherewithal to cope with adversity and persist until an objective is reached. Some developmentalists, though, believe that we are becoming a nation of hurried, "wired" people who are raising our children to become the same way—uptight about success and failure and far too worried about what we accomplish in comparison to others (Elkind, 1981). It was in the 1950s that an interest in achievement began to flourish. The interest initially focused on the need for achievement.

Need for Achievement

Think about yourself and your friends for a moment. Are you more achievement oriented than they are, or are you less so? If we asked you and your friends to tell stories about achievement-related themes, could we accurately determine which of you is the most achievement oriented?

Some individuals are highly motivated to succeed and they expend a lot of effort striving to excel. Other individuals are not as motivated to succeed and don't work as hard to achieve. These two types of individuals vary in their **achievement motivation (or need for achievement),** *the desire to accomplish something, to reach a standard of excellence, to expend effort to excel.* Borrowing from Henry Murray's (1938) theory and measurement of personality, psychologist David McClelland (1955) assessed achievement by showing individuals ambiguous pictures that were likely to stimulate achievement-related responses. The individuals were asked to tell a story about the picture, and their comments were scored according to how strongly they reflected achievement.

A host of studies have correlated achievement-related responses with different aspects of the individual's experiences and behavior. The findings are diverse, but they do suggest that achievement-oriented individuals have a stronger hope for success than a fear of failure, are moderate rather than high or low risk-takers, and persist for appropriate lengths of time in solving difficult problems (Atkinson & Raynor, 1974). Early research indicated that independence training by parents promoted children's achievement, but more recent research reveals that parents, to increase achievement, need to set high standards for achievement, model achievement-oriented behavior, and reward their children for their achievements (Huston-Stein & Higgens-Trenk, 1978).

Middle and Late Childhood

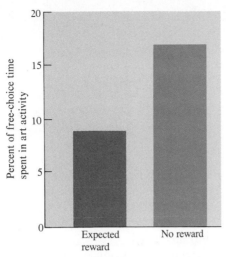

Figure 10.12 Intrinsic motivation and drawing activity. Students with an initial high interest in art spent more time in art activity when no reward was mentioned than when they expected a reward for the participation.

Intrinsic and Extrinsic Motivation

Our achievement motivation—whether in school, at work, or in sports—can be divided into two main types: **intrinsic motivation,** *the internal desire to be competent and to do something for its own sake;* and **extrinsic motivation,** *which is influenced by external rewards and punishments.* If you work hard in college because a personal standard of excellence is important to you, intrinsic motivation is involved. But if you work hard in college because you know it will bring you a higher paying job when you graduate, extrinsic motivation is at work.

An important consideration when motivating a child to do something is whether or not to offer an incentive (Ames & Ames, 1989; Gottfried, Gottfried, & Ames, 1988; Rotter, 1989). If a child is not doing competent work, is bored, or has a negative attitude, it may be worthwhile to consider incentives to improve motivation. However, there are times when external rewards can get in the way of motivation. In one investigation, children with a strong interest in art spent more time in a drawing activity when they expected no reward than their counterparts who knew that they would be rewarded (figure 10.12) (Lepper, Greene, & Nisbett, 1973).

Intrinsic motivation implies that internal motivation should be promoted and external factors deemphasized. In this way, children learn to attribute to themselves the cause of their success and failure, and especially how much effort they expend. But in reality, achievement is motivated by both internal and external factors; children are never divorced from their external environment. Some of the most achievement-oriented children are those who have a high personal standard for achievement and are also highly competitive. In one investigation, low-achieving boys and girls who engaged in individual goal setting (intrinsic motivation) and were given comparative information about peers (extrinsic motivation) worked more math problems and got more of them correct than their counterparts who experienced either condition alone (Schunk, 1983). Other research suggests that social comparison by itself is not a wise strategy (Nicholls, 1984). The argument is that social comparison puts the child in an ego-involved, threatening, self-focused state rather than in a task-involved, effortful, strategy-focused state.

Another important consideration is the role of the child's home environment in promoting internal motivation (Gottfried, 1990; Gottfried & Gottfried, 1991). In a recent investigation, Adele and Allen Gottfried (1989) found that greater variety of home experiences, parental encouragement of com-

The reward of a thing well done is to have done it.

~ *Ralph Waldo Emerson,*
Essays: Second Series, *1844.*

petence and curiosity, and home emphasis on academically related behaviors were related to children's internal motivation for achievement.

An extremely important aspect of internal causes of achievement is *effort*. Unlike many causes of success, effort is under the child's control and amenable to change (Carr, Borkowski, & Maxwell, 1991; Jagacinski & Nicholls, 1990; Schunk, 1990). The importance of effort in achievement is recognized by most children. In one recent study, third to sixth grade students felt that effort was the most effective strategy for good school performance (Skinner, Wellborn, & Connell, 1990).

Mastery Orientation versus Helpless Orientation

Closely related to an emphasis on intrinsic motivation, attributions of internal causes of behavior, and the importance of effort in achievement is a mastery orientation (Le Gall, 1990). Developmental psychologists Valanne Henderson and Carol Dweck (1990) have found that children and adolescents show two distinct responses to difficult or challenging circumstances: The **helpless orientation** *describes children who seem trapped by the experience of difficulty. They attribute their difficulty to a lack of ability.* They frequently say things like, "I'm not very good at this," even though they may have demonstrated earlier their ability through numerous successes. And once they view their behavior as failure, they often feel anxious about the situation and their performance worsens even further. The **mastery orientation** *describes children who are task oriented. Instead of focusing on their ability, they become concerned about their learning strategies.* Mastery-oriented children often instruct themselves to pay attention, to think carefully, and to remember strategies that have worked for them in previous situations. They frequently report feeling challenged and excited by difficult tasks rather than being threatened by them.

What psychological factors have been found to undergird the mastery and helpless achievement orientations? In one recent investigation, students were followed over the first few months of the seventh grade, their first year of junior high school (Henderson & Dweck, 1989). Students who believed that their intelligence is malleable and who had confidence in their abilities earned significantly higher grades than their counterparts who believed their intelligence is fixed and who did not have much confidence in their abilities. Students who believed that their intelligence is fixed also had higher levels of anxiety than students who believed it is changeable. Apparently, then, the way students think about their intelligence and their confidence in their abilities may affect their ability and desire to master academic material. Believing that learning new material increases one's intelligence may actually promote academic mastery (Henderson, 1991).

In summary, we have seen that a number of psychological and motivational factors influence children's achievement. Especially important in the child's ability to adapt to new academic and social pressures are achievement motivation, internal attributions of effort, intrinsic motivation, and a mastery achievement orientation. Next, we examine the role of ethnicity in children's achievement.

Achievement in Minority-Group Children

Too often, research on minority groups has been interpreted as "deficits" by middle-class White standards. Rather than characterizing individuals as *culturally different,* many conclusions unfortunately characterize the cultural distinctiveness of Blacks, Hispanics, and other minority groups as deficient in some way (Jones, 1990; Ramirez, 1990; Sue & Okazaki, 1990).

Much of the research on minority-group children is plagued by a failure to consider socioeconomic status (determined by some combination of education, occupation, and income). In many instances, when ethnicity *and* socioeconomic status (also called social class) are investigated in the same study, social class is a far better predictor of achievement orientation than ethnicity. Middle-class individuals fare better than their lower-class counterparts in a variety of achievement-oriented circumstances—expectations for success, achievement aspirations, and recognition of the importance of effort, for example (McAdoo & McAdoo, 1985).

Educational psychologist Sandra Graham has conducted a number of investigations that reveal not only stronger social class than ethnic-group differences, but also the importance of studying minority-group motivation in the context of general motivational theory (Graham, 1986, 1987, 1990). Her inquiries focus on the causes Blacks give for their achievement orientation—why they succeed or fail, for example. She is struck by how consistently middle-class Black children do not fit our stereotypes of either deviant or special populations. They, like their middle-class White counterparts, have high expectations and understand that failure is often due to lack of effort rather than to luck.

It is always important to keep in mind the diversity that exists within an ethnic group (Phinney, 1991; Slaughter-DeFoe & others, 1990; Spencer, 1991). Consider Asian American children. Many Asian American children fit the "whiz kid, super-achiever" image, but there are still many Asian American children who are struggling just to learn English. The "whiz kid" image fits many of the children of Asian immigrant families who arrived in the United States in the late 1960s and early 1970s. Many of these immigrants came from Hong Kong, South Korea, India, and the Philippines. The image also fits many of the more than 100,000 Indochinese (primarily Vietnamese) immigrants who arrived in the United States after the end of the Vietnam War in 1975. Both groups included mostly middle- to upper-income professional people who were reasonably well educated and who passed along a strong interest in education and a strong work ethic to their children. For thousands of other Asian Americans, including a high percentage of the 600,000 Indochinese refugees who fled Vietnam, Laos, and Cambodia in the late 1970s, the problems are legion. Many in this wave of refugees lived in poor surroundings in their homelands. They came to the United States with few skills and little education. They speak little English and have a difficult time finding a decent job. They often share housing with relatives. Adjusting to school is difficult for their children; some drop out and some are attracted to gangs and drugs. Better school systems use a variety of techniques to help these Asian Americans, including English as a second language class, as well as a range of social services.

American children are more achievement oriented than children in many countries. However, there has recently been concern about the achievement most American children display in comparison with children in other countries with strong educational orientations—Japan, China, and Russia, for example. To learn more about the achievement orientation of American children compared to Japanese and Chinese children, turn to Cultural Worlds of Development 10.1.

At this point we have discussed a number of ideas about children's intelligence, language, and achievement. A summary of these ideas is presented in concept table 10.3. This concludes our discussion of physical and cognitive development in middle and late childhood. In the next chapter, we will study about the nature of social development in middle and late childhood.

COMPARISONS OF CHILDREN'S MATH ACHIEVEMENT IN JAPAN, CHINA, AND THE UNITED STATES

*H*arold Stevenson and his colleagues (Chen & Stevenson, 1989; Stevenson, Stigler, & Lee, 1986; Stevenson & others, 1990, 1991) have conducted extensive investigations of children's math achievement in the first and fifth grades in Japan, China, and the United States. The stimulation for this research comes from the poor performance of American students on tests of mathematics and science in comparison to students in other countries. For example, in a cross-national study of math achievement, American eighth- and twelfth-grade students were below the international average in problem solving, geometry, algebra, calculus, and other areas of math (Garden, 1987; McKnight and others, 1987). In contrast, Japanese eighth graders had the highest average scores of children from twenty countries, and in the twelfth grade, Japanese students were second only to Chinese students in Hong Kong. Why are Chinese and Japanese students consistently among the top achievers in international comparisons and American students among the lowest achievers?

The amount of time spent in school and math classes is probably an important factor. The Japanese school year consists of 240 days of instruction, and each school week is 5½ days long. The American school year consists of 178 days of instruction and each school week is 5 days long. In the fifth grade, Japanese children were in school an average of 37.3 hours per week, American children only 30.4 hours. Observations in the children's classrooms revealed that Japanese teachers spent far more time teaching math than did American teachers; approximately one-fourth of total classroom time in

Japanese children's math achievement is considerably higher than American children's. What reasons have developmentalists given for this difference?

the first grade was spent in math instruction in Japan, only approximately one-tenth in the United States. Observations also indicated that Japanese children attended more efficiently to what the teacher was saying than American children did. And Japanese children spent far more time doing homework than American children—on weekends, 66 minutes versus 18 minutes, respectively.

And in another recent investigation, Chinese children were assigned more homework and spent more time on homework than Japanese children, who in turn were assigned more homework and spent more time on homework than American children (Chen & Stevenson, 1989). Chinese children had more positive attitudes about homework than Japanese children, who in turn had more positive attitudes

about homework than American children.

In the most recent investigation by Stevenson and his colleagues (1990), special attention was given to the family's role in comparisons of children's math achievement in Japan, China, and the United States. Background information about children's everyday lives indicated much greater attention to academic activities among Chinese and Japanese than among American children. Children's academic achievement did not appear to be a central concern to American mothers, while Japanese and Chinese mothers viewed this as their child's most important pursuit. When the children entered elementary school, Chinese and Japanese parents provided much greater assistance to their children's academic activities than did American parents. Chinese and Japanese mothers had higher standards for their children's achievement than American mothers. American mothers, though, were more likely than Chinese and Japanese mothers to overestimate their children's abilities and express greater satisfaction with their accomplishments. Chinese and Japanese mothers stressed the importance of hard work as a basis for children's achievement, while American mothers gave more emphasis to innate ability than did Chinese and Japanese mothers. In sum, the poor performance of American children in math achievement was due to a number of factors related to cultural dimensions of achievement orientation. Stevenson and his colleagues (1991) believe that good teaching, interested parents, and hard work could go a long way in enhancing American children's math achievement.

Concept Table 10.3: Intelligence, Language, and Achievement

Concept	Processes/Related Ideas	Characteristics/Description
Intelligence	What Is Intelligence?	An abstract concept that is measured indirectly. Psychologists rely on intelligence tests to estimate intelligence. Verbal ability, problem-solving skills, and the ability to learn from and adapt to everyday life are involved in intelligence.
	One Face or Many?	The Binet and Wechsler scales are the most widely used individual tests of intelligence. Both evaluate intelligence as a general ability while the Wechsler also evaluates a number of components of intelligence. Psychologists debate whether intelligence is a general ability or a number of specific abilities.
	Cultural Bias	Early intelligence tests favored White, middle-class, urban individuals. Current tests try to reduce this bias. Culture-fair tests are alternatives to traditional tests, but most psychologists believe they cannot replace traditional tests.
	The Use and Misuse of Intelligence Tests	Despite limitations, when used by a judicious examiner, tests can be valuable tools for determining individual differences in intelligence. The tests should be used with other information about the individual. IQ scores can produce unfortunate stereotypes and expectations. Intelligence or a high IQ is not necessarily the ultimate human value.
	The Extremes of Intelligence	These involve mental retardation, giftedness, and creativity. A mentally retarded person has a low IQ and has difficulty adapting to everyday life. A gifted person is one who has well-above-average intelligence, a superior talent, or both. Creativity is the ability to think in a novel or unusual way and to come up with unique solutions to problems.
Language	Vocabulary and Grammar	In middle and late childhood, children become more analytical and logical in their approach to words and grammar.
	Reading	In the history of learning to read, three techniques dominate: ABC, whole-word, and phonics. Current strategies often focus on some combination of the whole-word and phonics methods. But reading is much more than the sum of these approaches. Understanding how reading works requires consideration of information processing.
	Bilingualism	This has become a major issue in our nation's schools, with debate raging over the best way to conduct bilingual education. No negative effects of bilingualism have been found, and bilingual education is often associated with positive outcomes, although causal relations are difficult to establish. Increasingly, researchers recognize the complexity of bilingual education.
Achievement	Its Nature	Early interest, stimulated by McClelland's ideas, focused on the need for achievement. Contemporary ideas include the distinction between intrinsic and extrinsic motivation, a mastery orientation versus a helpless orientation, as well as a concern for achievement motivation in children from ethnic minority groups.

Summary

I. Body Changes

During the elementary school years, children grow an average of 2 to 3 inches a year. Muscle mass and strength gradually increase. Legs become longer and trunks slimmer as "baby fat" decreases. Growth is slow and consistent. During the middle and late childhood years, children's motor development becomes much smoother and more coordinated. Children gain greater control over their bodies and can sit and attend for longer periods of time. However, their lives should be activity focused and very active. Increased myelinization of the central nervous system is reflected in improved fine motor skills. Improved fine motor development is reflected in children's writing skills over the course of middle and late childhood. Boys are usually better at gross motor skills, girls at fine motor skills.

II. Exercise

Every indication suggests that our nation's children are not getting enough exercise. Television viewing, parents being poor role models for exercise, and the lack of adequate physical education classes in schools may be the culprits.

III. Handicapped Children

An estimated 10 to 15 percent of children in the United States are handicapped in some way. Public Law 94–142 ordered a free, appropriate education for every handicapped child. The law emphasizes an individually tailored program for every child and provision of a least restrictive environment, which has led to extensive mainstreaming of handicapped children into the regular classroom. Mainstreaming has been a controversial topic. Another issue is the labeling of handicapped children and its benefits and drawbacks. Children with learning disabilities have normal or above-normal intelligence, have difficulties in some areas but not in others, and do not suffer from some other disorder that could explain their learning problems. Learning disabilities are complex and multifaceted and require precise analysis. Attention-deficit hyperactivity disorder is the technical term for what is commonly called hyperactivity. This disorder is characterized by a short attention span, distractibility, and high levels of physical activity. Possible causes include heredity, prenatal damage, diet, family dynamics, and physical environment. Amphetamines have been used with some success in treatment, but they do not work with all hyperactive children.

IV. Piaget's Theory and Concrete Operational Thought

Concrete operational thought is made up of operations, mental actions that allow the child to do mentally what was done physically before. Concrete operations are also mental actions that are reversible. The concrete operational child shows conservation and classification skills. The concrete operational child needs clearly available perceptual supports to reason; later in development, thought becomes more abstract. Piaget's ideas have been applied extensively to education. Piaget was a genius at observing children; he showed us some important things to look for and mapped out some general cognitive changes. Criticisms of his theory focus on such matters as stages, which are not as unitary as he believed and do not always follow the timetable he envisioned.

V. Information Processing and Computers

Children's long-term memory improves during middle and late childhood. Control processes or strategies such as rehearsal, organization, and imagery are among the important influences responsible for improved long-term memory. Children's knowledge also influences their memory. Metacognitive knowledge is the segment of acquired knowledge that involves cognitive matters, especially the way the human mind works. Many developmentalists believe metacognitive knowledge is beneficial in school learning. Cognitive monitoring is the process of taking stock of what one is doing, what will be done next, and how effectively the mental activity is unfolding. The source of much cognitive monitoring in children is other people. Instructional programs in reading comprehension, writing, and math have been designed to foster children's cognitive monitoring of those activities. Reciprocal teaching is an instructional procedure that is used to develop cognitive monitoring. A schema is a cognitive structure, a network of associations that organizes and guides an individual's perceptions. Schema influences the way children process information. A script is a schema for an event. Among the potential positive effects of computers on children's development are those involving the computer as a personal tutor (computer-assisted instruction), as a multipurpose tool, and the motivational and social aspects of computers. Among the potential negative effects of computers are regimentation and dehumanization of the classroom, unwarranted "shaping" of the curriculum, and limitations of computer-based teaching.

VI. Intelligence

Intelligence is an abstract ability that is measured indirectly. Psychologists use intelligence tests to estimate intelligence. Verbal ability, problem-solving skills, and the ability to learn from and adapt to everyday life are involved in intelligence. The Binet and Wechsler scales are the most widely used individual tests of intelligence. Both evaluate intelligence as a general ability, while the Wechsler evaluates a number of other components of intelligence. Psychologists debate whether intelligence is a general ability or a number of specific abilities. Prominent issues in intelligence are the cultural bias of intelligence tests and the use and misuse of intelligence tests.

VII. The Extremes of Intelligence

These involve mental retardation, giftedness, and creativity. A mentally retarded person has a low IQ and has difficulty adapting to everyday life. A gifted person is one who has well-above-average intelligence, a superior talent, or both. Creativity is the ability to think in a novel or unusual way and to come up with unique solutions to problems.

VIII. Language

In the middle and late childhood years, children become more analytical and logical in their approach to words and grammar. In the history of learning to read, ABC, whole-word, and phonics methods have dominated. Current strategies often focus on some combination of the whole-word and phonics methods. But reading is much more than the sum of these approaches. Understanding how reading works requires consideration of information processing. Bilingualism has become a major issue in our nation's schools, with debate raging over the best way to conduct bilingual education.

IX. Achievement

Early interest, stimulated by McClelland's ideas, focused on the need for achievement. Contemporary ideas include the distinction between intrinsic and extrinsic motivation, a mastery orientation versus a helpless orientation, as well as a concern for achievement motivation in minority-group children.

Key Terms

Suggested Readings

Anastasi, A. (1988). *Psychological testing* (6th ed.). New York: Macmillan.
This widely used text on psychological testing provides extensive information about intelligence tests for children.

Batshaw, M. L., & Perret, Y. M. (1986). *Children with handicaps.* Baltimore: Paul H. Brooks.
A comprehensive treatment of handicapped children. Includes chapters on dental care, vision, hearing, attention-deficit hyperactivity disorder, and cerebral palsy.

Brown, A. L., & Palincsar, A. M. (1989). Guided, cooperative learning and individual knowledge acquisition. In L. B. Resnick (Ed.), *Knowing and learning: Essays in honor of Robert Glaser.* Hillsdale, NJ: Erlbaum.
A detailed presentation of Brown and Palincsar's provocative ideas about teaching cognitive monitoring skills to children.

Horowitz, F. D., & O'Brien, M. (Eds.). (1985). *The gifted and the talented.* Washington, DC: The American Psychological Association.
This volume pulls together what we currently know about the gifted and the talented. Experts contributed chapters on the diverse nature of the gifted and the talented.

Journal of School Health
This journal includes a number of articles about children's nutrition, health, illness, and exercise. Leaf through the issues of the last several years to get a feel for the type of interventions being used in school settings to improve children's health.

Lepper, M. R., & Gurtner, J. (1989). Children and computers: Approaching the twenty-first century. *American Psychologist, 44,* 170–178.
This article provides an excellent, well-balanced treatment of the computer's role in children's development.

McAdoo, H. P., & McAdoo, J. L. (1985). *Black children: Social, educational, and parental environments.* Beverly Hills, CA: Sage.
This book provides a contemporary look at the nature of achievement orientation in Black children.

CHAPTER 11

Social Development in Middle and Late Childhood

*C*an children in middle and late childhood understand concepts like discrimination, economic inequality, affirmative action, and comparable worth? Probably not, if we used these terms. But might we be able to construct circumstances illustrating these concepts that they might be able to understand? Phyllis Katz (1987) asked a group of children to pretend that they had taken a long ride on a spaceship to a make-believe planet called Pax and to give opinions about different situations in which they found themselves. The situations involved conflict, socioeconomic inequality, and civil-political rights. Conflict items included asking what a teacher should do when two students were tied for a prize or when they had been fighting. The economic equality dilemmas included a proposed field trip that not all students could afford, a comparable worth situation in which janitors were paid more than teachers, and an employment situation that discriminated against those with dots on their noses instead of stripes. The rights items dealt with minority rights and freedom of the press.

The elementary schoolchildren did indeed recognize injustice and often came up with interesting solutions to problems. For example, all but two children believed that teachers should earn as much as janitors. The holdouts said that teachers should make less because they stay in one room or because cleaning toilets is disgusting and therefore deserves higher wages. Children were especially responsive to the economic inequality items. All but one thought that not giving a job to a qualified applicant who had different physical characteristics (a striped nose rather than a dotted nose) was unfair. The majority recommended an affirmative action solution—giving the job to the one from the discriminated minority. None of the children verbalized the concept of freedom of the press or seemed to understand that a newspaper could have the right to criticize a mayor in print without being punished. Some of the courses of action suggested by the students were intriguing. Several argued that the reporters should be jailed. One child said that if she were mayor, she would worry, make speeches, and say, "I didn't do anything wrong," not unlike what American presidents have done in recent years. Another child said that the mayor should not put newspaper people out of work because that might make them print more bad things. "Make them write comics instead," he suggested.

Children believed that poverty exists on earth, but mainly in Africa, big cities, or Vietnam. War was mentioned as the biggest problem on earth, although children were not certain where that is currently happening. Other problems mentioned were crime, hatred, school, smog, and meanness. Overall, the types of rules the children believed a society should abide by were quite sensible; almost all included the need for equitable sharing of resources and work, and prohibition against aggression.

Later in this chapter, we will further discuss children's thoughts about rules and regulations, as we continue our description of moral development. Additional aspects of the self and gender roles are also presented. To begin the chapter, we examine the social worlds of children's families, peers, and schools in middle and late childhood.

Families

As children move into the middle and late childhood years, parents spend considerably less time with them. In one investigation, parents spent less than half as much time with their children aged 5 to 12 in caregiving, instruction, reading, talking, and playing as when the children were younger (Hill & Stafford, 1980). This drop in parent-child interaction may be even more extensive in families

> *C*hildren know nothing about childhood and have little to say about it. They are too busy becoming something they have not quite grasped yet, something which keeps changing . . . Nor will they realize what is happening to them until they are too far beyond it to remember how it felt.
>
> *Alistair Reed*

An important dimension of parenting is adapting to developmental changes in children.

with little parental education. While parents spend less time with their children in middle and late childhood than in early childhood, parents continue to be extremely important socializing agents in their children's lives. What are some of the most important parent-child issues in middle and late childhood?

Parent-Child Issues

Parent-child interactions during early childhood focus on such matters as modesty, bedtime regularities, control of temper, fighting with siblings and peers, eating behavior and manners, autonomy in dressing, and attention seeking. While some of these issues—fighting and reaction to discipline, for example—are carried forward into the elementary school years, many new issues appear by the age of 7 (Maccoby, 1984). These include whether children should be made to perform chores, and if so, whether they should be paid for them; how to help children learn to entertain themselves rather than relying on parents for everything; and how to monitor children's lives outside the family in school and peer settings.

School-related matters are especially important for families during middle and late childhood. Later in this chapter, we will see that school-related difficulties are the number one reason that children in this age group are referred for clinical help. Children must learn to relate to adults outside the family on a regular basis—adults who interact with the child much differently than parents. During middle and late childhood, interactions with adults outside the family involve more formal control and achievement orientation.

Discipline during middle and late childhood is often easier for parents than it was during early childhood; it may also be easier than during adolescence. In middle and late childhood, children's cognitive development has matured to the point where it is possible for parents to reason with them about resisting deviation and controlling their behavior. By adolescence, children's reasoning has become more sophisticated and they may be less likely to accept parental discipline. Adolescents also push more strongly for independence, which contributes to parenting difficulties. Parents of elementary schoolchildren use less physical discipline than do parents of preschool children. By contrast, parents of elementary schoolchildren are more likely to use deprivation of privileges, appeals directed at the child's self-esteem, comments designed to increase the child's sense of guilt, and statements indicating to the child that she is responsible for her actions.

Of all the animals, the boy is the most unmanageable, inasmuch as he has the fountain of reason in him not yet regulated; He is the most insidious, sharp-witted, and insubordinate of animals. Wherefore he must be bound with many bridles.

~ *Plato, 350 B.C.*

During middle and late childhood, some control is transferred from parent to child, although the process is gradual and involves *coregulation* rather than control by either the child or the parent alone (Maccoby, 1984). The major shift to autonomy does not occur until about the age of 12 or later. During middle and late childhood, parents continue to exercise general supervision and exert control while children are allowed to engage in moment-to-moment self-regulation. This coregulation process is a transition period between the strong parental control of early childhood and the increased relinquishment of general supervision of adolescence.

During this coregulation, parents should

- monitor, guide, and support children at a distance;
- effectively use the times when they have direct contact with the child;
- strengthen in their children the ability to monitor their own behavior, to adopt appropriate standards of conduct, to avoid hazardous risks, and to sense when parental support and contact are appropriate.

In middle and late childhood, parents and children increasingly label each other and make attributions about each others' motives. Parents and children do not react to each other only on the basis of each others' past behavior; rather, their reactions to each other are based on how they interpret behavior and their expectations for behavior. Parents and children label each other broadly. Parents label their children smart or dumb, introverted or extraverted, mannerly or unruly, and lazy or hard-working. Children label their parents as cold or warm, understanding or not understanding, and so on. Even though there are probably specific circumstances when children and parents do not conform to these labels, the labels represent a distillation of many hours, days, months, and years of learning what each other is like as a person.

Life changes in parents also influence the nature of parent-child interaction in middle and late childhood; parents become more experienced in childrearing. As childrearing demands are reduced in middle and late childhood, mothers are more likely to consider returning to a career or beginning a new career. Marital relationships change as less time is spent in childrearing and more time is spent in career development, especially for mothers.

Societal Changes in Families

As we discussed in chapter 9, increasing numbers of children are growing up in divorced and working-mother families. But there are several other major shifts in the composition of family life that especially affect children in middle and late childhood. Parents are divorcing in greater numbers than ever before, but many of them remarry. It takes time for parents to marry, have children, get divorced, and then remarry. Consequently, there are far more elementary and secondary schoolchildren than infant or preschool children living in stepfamilies. In addition, an increasing number of elementary and secondary schoolchildren are latchkey children.

Stepfamilies

The number of remarriages involving children has steadily grown in recent years, although both the rate of increase in divorce and stepfamilies slowed in the 1980s. Stepfather families, in which a woman has custody of children from a previous marriage, make up 70 percent of stepfamilies. Stepmother families make up almost 20 percent of stepfamilies, and a small minority are blended with both partners bringing children from a previous marriage. A substantial percentage of stepfamilies produce children of their own.

Research on stepfamilies has lagged behind research on divorced families, but recently a number of investigators have turned their attention to this increasingly common family structure (Bray, 1988; Bray & others, 1991; Furstenburg, 1988; Hetherington, 1991; Pasley & Ihinger-Tallman, 1987; Santrock & Sitterle, 1987; Santrock, Sitterle, & Warshak, 1988). Following remarriage of their parents, children of all ages show a resurgence of behavior problems. Younger children seem to eventually form an attachment to a stepparent and accept the stepparenting role. However, the developmental tasks facing adolescents make them especially vulnerable to the entrance of a stepparent. At the time they are searching for an identity and exploring sexual and other close relationships outside the family, a nonbiological parent may increase the stress associated with these important tasks.

Following the remarriage of the custodial parent, an emotional upheaval usually occurs in girls, and problems in boys often intensify. Over time, preadolescent boys seem to improve more than girls in stepfather families. Sons who frequently are involved in conflicted or coercive relations with their custodial mothers probably have much to gain from living with a warm, supportive stepfather. In contrast, daughters who have a close relationship with their custodial mothers and considerable independence frequently find a stepfather both disruptive and constraining.

Children's relationships with their biological parents are more positive than with their stepparents, regardless of whether a stepmother or a stepfather family is involved. However, stepfathers are often distant and disengaged from their stepchildren. As a rule, the more complex the stepfamily, the more difficult the child's adjustment. Families in which both parents bring children from a previous marriage have the highest level of behavioral problems.

In sum, as with divorce, entrance into a stepfamily involves a disequilibrium in children's lives. Most children initially find their parents' remarriage as stressful. Remarriage, though, can remove children from stressful single-parent circumstances and provide additional resources for children, such as increased involvement with parents and improved economic circumstances. Many children emerge from their remarried family as competent individuals. As with divorced families, it is important to consider the complexity of stepfamilies, the diversity of possible outcomes for the child, and the factors that facilitate children's adjustment in stepfamilies (Hetherington, 1991; Santrock, Sitterle, & Warshak, 1988).

Latchkey Children

We concluded in chapter 9 that the mother's working outside the home does not necessarily have negative outcomes for her children. However, a certain set of children from working-mother families deserve further scrutiny: latchkey children. These children typically do not see their parents from the time they leave for school in the morning until about 6:00 or 7:00 P.M. They are called latchkey children because they are given the key to their home, take the key to school, and then use it to let themselves into the home while their parents are still at work. Latchkey children are largely unsupervised for two to four hours a day during each school week. During the summer months, they may be unsupervised for entire days, five days a week.

Thomas and Lynette Long (1983) interviewed more than 1,500 latchkey children. They concluded that a slight majority of these children had had negative latchkey experiences. Some latchkey children may grow up too fast, hurried by the responsibilities placed on them (Elkind, 1981). How do latchkey children handle the lack of limits and structure during the latchkey hours? Without limits and parental supervision, latchkey children find their way into trouble more easily, possibly stealing, vandalizing, or abusing a sibling. The

• *Critical Thinking* •

What might parents do to improve the adjustment of children in stepfamilies?

Middle and Late Childhood

Longs point out that 90 percent of the juvenile delinquents in Montgomery County, Maryland, are latchkey children. Joan Lipsitz (1983), in testifying before the Select Committee on Children, Youth, and Families, called the lack of adult supervision of children in the after-school hours one of today's major problems. Lipsitz calls it the "three-to-six o'clock problem" because it is during this time that the Center for Early Adolescence in North Carolina, of which Lipsitz is director, experiences a peak of referrals for clinical help. And in a 1987 national poll, teachers rated the latchkey children phenomenon the number one reason that children have problems in schools (Harris, 1987).

But while latchkey children may be vulnerable to problems, the experiences of latchkey children vary enormously, just as do the experiences of all children with working mothers. Parents need to give special attention to the ways in which their latchkey children's lives can be effectively monitored. Variations in latchkey experiences suggest that parental monitoring and authoritative parenting help the child cope more effectively with latchkey experiences, especially resisting peer pressure (Galambos & Maggs, 1989; Belle & others, 1991; Steinberg, 1986). The degree of developmental risk to latchkey children remains undetermined. One positive sign is that researchers are beginning to conduct more fine-grained analysis of children's latchkey experiences to determine which aspects of latchkey circumstances are the most detrimental (Rodman, Pratto, & Nelson, 1988; Steinberg, 1988).

Peer Relations

During middle and late childhood, children spend an increasing amount of time in peer interaction. In one investigation, children interacted with peers 10 percent of their day at the age of 2, 20 percent at age 4, and more than 40 percent between the ages of 7 and 11. Episodes with peers totaled 299 times per typical school day (Barker & Wright, 1951).

What do children do when they are with their peers? In one study, sixth graders were asked what they do when they are with their friends (Medrich & others, 1982). Team sports accounted for 45 percent of boys' nominations but only 26 percent of girls'. General play, going places, and socializing were common listings for both sexes. Most peer interactions occur outside the home (although close to home), occur more often in private than in public places, and occur more between children of the same sex than between children of different sexes.

> The little ones leaped, and shouted, and Laugh'd and all the hills echoed.
>
> ~ *William Blake*

Peer Popularity, Rejection, and Neglect

Children often think, "What can I do to get all of the kids at school to like me?" or "What's wrong with me? Something must be wrong with me or I would be more popular." What makes a child popular with peers? Children who give out the most reinforcements are often popular. So are children who listen carefully to other children and maintain open lines of communication with peers. Being themselves, being happy, showing enthusiasm and concern for others, and being self-confident but not conceited are characteristics that serve children well in their quest for popularity among peers (Hartup, 1983).

Recently, developmentalists have distinguished between two types of children who are not popular with their peers: those who are neglected and those who are rejected (Asher & Parker, in press; Coie & Koeppl, 1990; Parker & Asher, 1987; Parkhurst & others, 1991). **Neglected children** *receive little attention from their peers but they are not necessarily disliked by their peers.* **Rejected children** *are disliked by their peers. They are more likely to be disruptive and aggressive than neglected children.* Rejected children often have more serious adjustment problems later in life than do neglected children

(Dodge & others, 1986). For example, in one recent study, 112 fifth-grade boys were evaluated over a period of seven years until the end of high school (Kupersmidt & Coie, 1990). The key factor in predicting whether rejected children would engage in delinquent behavior or drop out of school later during adolescence was aggression toward peers in elementary school.

How can neglected children be trained to interact more effectively with their peers? The goal of training programs with neglected children is often to help them attract attention from their peers in positive ways and to hold their attention by asking questions, listening in a warm and friendly way, and by saying things about themselves that relate to the peers' interests. They are also taught to enter groups more assertively (Duck, 1988).

The goal of training programs with rejected children is often to help them listen to peers and "hear what they say" instead of trying to dominate peer interactions. Rejected children are trained to join peers without trying to change what is taking place in the peer group.

Children may need to be persuaded or motivated that these strategies work effectively and are satisfying. In some programs children are shown videotapes of appropriate peer interaction; then they are asked to comment on them and to draw lessons from what they have seen. In other training programs, popular children are taught to be more accepting of neglected or rejected peers.

One issue that has recently been raised in improving the peer relations of rejected children is whether the focus should be on improving their prosocial skills (better empathy, careful listening, improved communication skills, and so on) or directed more specifically at reducing their aggressive, disruptive behavior and improving their self-control (Coie & Koeppl, 1990). On the one hand, children who acquire the skills to relate to their peers more effectively will likely find themselves resorting less often to aggressive solutions in peer interaction. On the other hand, acquiring positive status with peers may take time to achieve, so it may be hard for peers to change their opinion if the child frequently engages in aggressive behavior. Further, aggression often leads to reinforcement. In these latter instances, then, the argument is that it may be necessary to eliminate or significantly reduce the child's aggressive actions before prosocial strategies can be effectively taught. Next we turn our attention to the role of social cognition in understanding peer relations. As part of this discussion, we will further consider ideas about reducing the aggression of children in their peer encounters.

Social Cognition

Earlier we found that the mutual cognitions of children and parents become increasingly important in family relationships during middle and late childhood. Children's social cognitions about their peers also become increasingly important for understanding peer relationships in middle and late childhood. Of special interest are how children process information about peer relations and their social knowledge.

A boy accidentally trips and knocks a peer's soft drink out of his hand. The peer misinterprets the encounter as hostile, which leads him to retaliate aggressively against the boy. Through repeated encounters of this kind, other peers come to perceive the aggressive boy as habitually acting in inappropriate ways. Kenneth Dodge (1983) argues that children go through five steps in processing information about their social world: decoding social cues, interpreting, searching for a response, selecting an optimal response, and enacting. Dodge has found that aggressive boys are more likely to perceive another child's actions as hostile when the child's intention is ambiguous. And when aggressive boys search for cues to determine a peer's intention, they respond more rapidly, less efficiently, and less reflectively than nonaggressive children. These are among the social cognitive factors believed to be involved in the nature of children's conflicts (Shantz, 1988).

Social knowledge is also involved in children's ability to get along with peers. An important part of children's social life involves what goals to pursue in poorly defined or ambiguous situations. Social relationship goals are also important, such as how to initiate and maintain a social bond. Children need to know what scripts to follow to get children to be their friends. For example, as part of the script for getting friends, it helps to know that saying nice things, regardless of what the peer does or says, will make the peer like the child more.

From a social cognitive perspective, children who are maladjusted do not have adequate social cognitive skills to effectively interact with others. (Kelly & deArmas, 1989; Weisberg, Caplan, & Sivo, 1989). One investigation explored the possibility that children who are maladjusted do not have the social cognitive skills necessary for positive social interaction (Asarnow & Callan, 1985). Boys with and without peer adjustment difficulties were identified, and their social cognitive skills were assessed. Boys without peer adjustment problems generated more alternative solutions to problems, proposed more assertive and mature solutions, gave less intense aggressive solutions, showed more adaptive planning, and evaluated physically aggressive responses less positively than boys with peer adjustment problems.

The world of peers is one of varying acquaintances; children interact with some children they barely know and with others for hours every day. It is to the latter type—friends—that we now turn.

Friends

"My best friend is nice. She is honest and I can trust her. I can tell her my innermost secrets and know that nobody else will find out about them. I have other friends, but she is my best friend. We consider each other's feelings and don't want to hurt each other. We help each other out when we have problems. We make up funny names for people and laugh ourselves silly. We make lists of which boys we think are the ugliest, which are the biggest jerks, and so on. Some of these things we share with other friends, some we don't." This is a description of a friendship by a 10-year-old girl. It reflects the belief that children are interested in specific peers—in Barbara and Tommy—not just any peers. They want to share concerns, interests, information, and secrets with them.

Why are children's friendships important? They serve six functions: companionship, stimulation, physical support, ego support, social comparison, and intimacy/affection (Gottman & Parker, 1987; Parker & Gottman, 1989). Concerning companionship, friendship provides children with a familiar partner and playmate, someone who is willing to spend time with them and join in collaborative activities. Concerning stimulation, friendship provides children with interesting information, excitement, and amusement. Concerning physical support, friendship provides time, resources, and assistance. Concerning ego support, friendship provides the expectation of support, encouragement, and feedback that helps children maintain an impression of themselves as competent, attractive, and worthwhile individuals. Concerning social comparison, friendship provides information about where the child stands vis-à-vis others and whether the child is doing OK. Concerning intimacy and affection, friendship provides children with a warm, close, trusting relationship with another individual in which self-disclosure takes place (figure 11.1).

A man's growth is seen in the successive choirs of his friends.
~ *Ralph Waldo Emerson, 1841*

Figure 11.1 Children's friendships serve many different functions.

Functions of children's friendships

- Companionship
- Stimulation
- Physical support
- Ego support
- Social comparison
- Intimacy/affection

While friendships exist in early childhood, they become more predominant during middle and late childhood. Robert Selman (1980) proposed a developmental model that highlights the changing faces of friendship. Friendship begins at 3 to 7 years of age with momentary friendships; friends are valued because they are nearby and have nice toys. At 4 to 9 years, friendship involves one-way assistance; friends are friends because they do what you want them to do. At 6 to 12 years of age, friendship consists of two-way fair-weather cooperation, followed at 9 to 15 years of age by intimate, mutually shared relationships. Finally, at 12 years of age and older, children gain enough perspective for autonomous, interdependent friendships to become possible.

Two of friendship's most common characteristics are intimacy and similarity. **Intimacy in friendships** *is defined as self-disclosure and the sharing of private thoughts.* Research reveals that intimate friendships may not appear until early adolescence (Berndt, 1982; Berndt & Perry, 1990; Buhrmester, 1989). Also, throughout childhood, friends are more similar than dissimilar in terms of age, sex, race, and many other factors. Friends often have similar attitudes toward school, similar educational aspirations, and closely aligned achievement orientations. Friends like the same music, the same kind of clothes, and the same kind of leisure activities.

Schools

It is justifiable to be concerned about the impact of schools on children: By the time students graduate from high school, they have spent 10,000 hours in the classroom. Children spend many years in schools as members of a small society in which there are tasks to be accomplished, people to be socialized and socialized by, and rules that define and limit behavior, feelings, and attitudes.

The Transition to School

For most children, entering the first grade signals a change from being a "homechild" to being a "schoolchild" in which new roles and obligations are experienced. Children take up a new role (being a student), interact and develop relationships with new significant others, adopt new reference groups, and develop new standards by which to judge themselves. School provides children with a rich source of new ideas to shape their sense of self.

• *Critical Thinking* •

Why does early elementary school involve so much negative feedback? What aspects of our culture and the nature of education are responsible?

Middle and Late Childhood

A special concern about children's early school experiences is emerging. Evidence is mounting that early schooling proceeds mainly on the basis of negative feedback. For example, children's self-esteem in the latter part of elementary school is lower than it is in the earlier part, and older children rate themselves as less smart, less good, and less hard-working than do younger ones (Blumenfeld & others, 1981). In one investigation, the first year of school was identified as a period of considerable importance in shaping achievement, especially for ethnic-minority children (Alexander & Entwisle, 1988). Black and White children began school with similar achievement test scores, but by the end of the first year, Black children's performance lagged noticeably behind that of White children, and the gap widened over the second year of schooling. The grades teachers gave to Black children in the first two grades of school were also lower than those they gave to White children.

In school, as well as out of school, children's learning, like children's development, is *integrated* (NAEYC, 1988). One of the main pressures on elementary teachers has been the need to "cover the curriculum." Frequently, teachers have tried to do so by tightly scheduling discrete time segments for each subject. This approach ignores the fact that children often do not need to distinguish learning by subject area. For example, they advance their knowledge of reading and writing when they work on social studies projects; they learn mathematical concepts through music and physical education (Katz & Chard, 1989; Van Deusen-Henkel & Argondizza, 1987). A curriculum can be facilitated by providing learning areas in which children plan and select their activities. For example, the classroom may include a fully equipped publishing center, complete with materials for writing, illustrating, typing, and binding student-made books; a science area with animals and plants for observation and books to study; and other similar areas (Van Deusen-Henkel & Argondizza, 1987). In this type of classroom, children learn reading as they discover information about science; they learn writing as they work together on interesting projects. Such classrooms also provide opportunities for spontaneous play, recognizing that elementary schoolchildren continue to learn in all areas through unstructured play, either alone or with other children.

Education experts Lilian Katz and Sylvia Chard (1989) described two elementary school classrooms they recently visited. In one, children spent the entire morning making identical pictures of traffic lights. There was no attempt by the teacher to get the children to relate the pictures to anything else the class was doing. In the other class, children were investigating a school bus. They wrote to the district and asked if they could have a bus parked at their school for a few days. They studied the bus, discovered the functions of its different parts, and discussed traffic rules. Then, in the classroom, they built their own bus out of cardboard. The children had fun, but they also practiced writing, problem solving, and even some arithmetic. When the class had their parents' night, the teacher was ready with reports on how each child was doing. However, all the parents wanted to see was the bus because their children had been coming home and talking about it for weeks. Many contemporary education experts believe that this is the kind of education all children deserve. That is, they believe children should be taught through concrete, hands-on experience.

Teachers

Teachers have a prominent influence in middle and late childhood. Teachers symbolize authority and establish the classroom's climate, conditions of interaction among students, and the nature of group functioning.

Children in the early elementary school years learn best through concrete, hands-on experience. For example, 6-year-olds can easily understand addition and subtraction if they have actual objects to count instead of a series of numbers written on the chalkboard. For the child shown here, the numbers don't seem so abstract and forbidding when he counts colored balls.

Almost everyone's life is affected in one way or another by teachers. You were influenced by teachers as you grew up; you may become a teacher yourself or work with teachers through counseling or psychological services; and you may one day have children whose education will be guided by many different teachers through the years. You can probably remember several of your teachers vividly: Perhaps one never smiled, another required you to memorize everything in sight, and yet another always appeared happy and vibrant and encouraged verbal interaction. Psychologists and educators have tried to create a profile of a good teacher's personality traits, but the complexity of personality, education, learning, and individual differences make the task difficult. Nonetheless, some teacher traits are associated with positive student outcomes more than others; enthusiasm, ability to plan, poise, adaptability, warmth, flexibility, and awareness of individual differences are a few (Gage, 1965).

Erik Erikson (1968) believes that good teachers should be able to produce a sense of industry, rather than inferiority, in their students. Good teachers are trusted and respected by the community and know how to alternate work and play, study and games, says Erikson. They know how to recognize special efforts and to encourage special abilities. They also know how to create a setting in which children feel good about themselves and how to handle those children to whom school is not important. In Erikson's (1968) own words, children should be "mildly but firmly coerced into the adventure of finding out that one can learn to accomplish things which one would never have thought of by oneself" (p. 127).

Teacher characteristics and styles are important, but they need to be considered in concert with what children bring to the school situation (Linney & Seidman, 1989). Some children may benefit more from structure than others, and some teachers may be able to handle a flexible curriculum better than others. **Aptitude-treatment interaction (ATI)** *stresses the importance of children's aptitudes or characteristics and the treatments or experiences they are given in classrooms.* Aptitude refers to such characteristics as academic potential and personality characteristics on which students differ; treatment refers to educational techniques, such as structured versus flexible classrooms (Cronbach & Snow, 1977). Researchers have found that children's achievement level (aptitude) interacts with classroom structure (treatment) to produce the best learning (Peterson, 1977). For example, students who are highly achievement oriented usually do well in a flexible classroom and enjoy it; low-achievement-oriented students usually fare worse and dislike the flexibility. The reverse often appears in structured classrooms.

Social Class and Ethnicity

Sometimes it seems as though the main function of schools is to train children to contribute to a middle-class society. Politicians who vote on school funding are usually middle-class, school board members are usually middle-class, and principals and teachers are usually middle-class. Critics argue that schools have not done a good job of educating lower-class children to overcome the barriers blocking the enhancement of their position (Alexander & Entwisle, 1988; McAdoo, 1988).

Teachers have lower expectations for children from low-income families than for children from middle-income families. A teacher who knows that a child comes from a lower-class background may spend less time trying to help the child solve a problem and may anticipate that the child will get into trouble. The teacher may believe that the parents in low-income families are not interested in helping the child, so she may make fewer efforts to communicate with them. There is evidence that teachers with lower-class origins may have

Some critics argue that one of the main functions for schools has been to train children to contribute to a middle-class, white society. These critics argue that schools have not done a competent job of educating low-income, ethnic-minority children.

different attitudes toward lower-class students than teachers from middle-class origins (Gottlieb, 1966). Perhaps because they have experienced many inequities themselves, teachers with lower-class origins may be more empathetic to problems that lower-class children encounter. When asked to rate the most outstanding characteristics of their lower-class students, middle-class teachers checked lazy, rebellious, and fun-loving; lower-class teachers checked happy, cooperative, energetic, and ambitious. The teachers with lower-class backgrounds perceived the lower-class children's behaviors as adaptive; the middle-class teachers viewed the same behaviors as falling short of middle-class standards.

In his famous speech, "I Have a Dream," Martin Luther King said, "I have a dream that my four little children will one day live in a nation where they will not be judged by the color of their skin but by the content of their character." Children from lower-class backgrounds are not the only students who had difficulties in school; so have children from different ethnic backgrounds (Tharp, 1989). In most American schools, Blacks, Mexican Americans, Puerto Ricans, Native Americans, Japanese, and Asian Indians are minorities. Many teachers have been ignorant of the different cultural meanings non-Anglo children have learned in their community (Huang & Gibbs, 1989). The social and academic development of children from minority groups depends on teacher expectations, the teacher's experience in working with children from different backgrounds, the curriculum, the presence of role models in the schools for minority students, the quality of relations between school personnel and parents from different ethnic, economic, and educational backgrounds, and the relations between the school and the community (Minuchin & Shapiro, 1983).

My country is the world;
My countrymen are mankind.
~ *William Lloyd Garrison, 1803*

THE JIGSAW CLASSROOM

Aronson stressed that the reward structure of the elementary school classrooms needed to be changed from a setting of unequal competition to one of cooperation among equals, without making any curriculum changes. To accomplish this, he put together the *jigsaw classroom.* How might this work? Consider a class of thirty students, some White, some Black, some Hispanic. The lesson to be learned in the class focuses on the life of Joseph Pulitzer. The class might be broken up into five groups of six students each, with the groups being as equal as possible in terms of ethnic composition and academic achievement level. The lesson about Pulitzer's life could be divided into six parts, with one part given to each member of the six-person group. The parts might be paragraphs from Pulitzer's biography, such as how the Pulitzer family came to the United States, Pulitzer's childhood, his early work, and so on. The components are like parts of a jigsaw puzzle. They have

to be put together to form the complete puzzle.

Each student in the group is given an allotted time to study his part. Then the group meets and each member tries to teach a part to the group. After an hour or so, each member is tested on the entire life of Pulitzer, with each member receiving an individual rather than a group score. Each student, therefore, must learn the entire lesson; learning depends on the cooperation and effort of the other members. Aronson (1986) believes that this type of learning increases the students' interdependence through cooperatively reaching the same goal.

The strategy of emphasizing cooperation rather than competition and the jigsaw classroom have been widely used in classrooms in the United States. A number of research studies reveal that this type of cooperative learning is associated with increased self-esteem, better academic performance, friendships among classmates, and improved

interethnic perceptions (Aronson, 1986; Slavin, 1987, 1989).

While the cooperative classroom strategy has many merits, it may have a built-in difficulty that restricts its effectiveness. Academic achievement is as much an individual as a team "sport" (Brown, 1986). It is individuals, not groups, who enter college, take jobs, and follow careers. A parent with an advantaged child in the jigsaw classroom might react with increased ethnic hostility when the child brings home a lower grade than she had been used to getting before the jigsaw classroom was introduced. The child tells the father, "The teacher is getting us to teach each other. In my group, we have a kid named Carlos who can barely speak English." While the jigsaw classroom can be an important strategy for reducing interracial hostility, caution needs to be exercised in its use because of the unequal status of the participants and the individual nature of achievement.

Our most basic common link is that we all inhabit this planet. We all breathe the same air. We all cherish our children's future.

~ *John F. Kennedy, address. The American University, 1963*

When the schools of Austin, Texas, were desegregated through extensive busing, the outcome was increased racial tension among Blacks, Mexican Americans, and Whites, producing violence in the schools. The superintendent consulted with Eliot Aronson, a prominent social psychologist, who was at the University of Texas at Austin at the time. Aronson thought it was more important to prevent racial hostility than to control it. This led him to observe a number of elementary school classrooms in Austin. What he saw was fierce competition between persons of unequal status. To learn how Aronson proposed to reduce the tension and fierce competition, turn to Cultural Worlds of Development 11.1.

American anthropologist John Ogbu (1974, 1986, 1989) proposed a controversial view that ethnic-minority children are placed in a position of subordination and exploitation in the American educational system. He believes that ethnic-minority children, especially Black and Hispanic Americans, have inferior educational opportunities, are exposed to teachers and administrators who have low academic expectations for them, and encounter negative stereotypes about ethnic-minority groups. Ogbu states that ethnic-minority opposition to the middle-class White educational system stems from a lack of

trust because of years of discrimination and oppression. Says Ogbu, it makes little sense to do well academically if occupational opportunities are often closed to ethnic-minority youth.

Completing high school, or even college, does not always bring the same job opportunities for many ethnic minority youth as for White youth (Entwisle, 1990). In terms of earnings and employment rates, Black American high school graduates do not do as well as their White counterparts. Giving up in school because of a perceived lack of reward involving inadequate job opportunities characterizes many Hispanic American youth as well.

According to American educational psychologist Margaret Beale Spencer and sociologist Sanford Dornbusch (1990), a form of institutional racism prevails in many American schools. That is, well-meaning teachers, acting out of misguided liberalism, often fail to challenge ethnic-minority students. Knowing the handicaps these children face, some teachers accept a low level of performance from them, substituting warmth and affection for academic challenge and high standards of performance. Ethnic-minority students, like their White counterparts, learn best when teachers combine warmth with challenging standards.

One person who is trying to do something about the poor quality of education for inner city children is Black American psychiatrist James Comer (1988). He has devised an intervention model that is based on a simple principle: Everyone with a stake in a school should have a say in how it's run. Comer's model calls for forming a school-governance team, made up of the principal, psychologists, and even cafeteria workers. The team develops a comprehensive plan for operating the school, including a calendar of academic and social events that encourage parents to come to school as often as possible. Comer is convinced that a strong family orientation is a key to educational success, so he tries to create a familylike environment in schools and also make parents feel comfortable in coming to their children's school. Among the reasons for Comer's concern about the lack of parental involvement in Black

Concept Table 11.1: Families, Peers, and Schools

Concept	Processes/Related Ideas	Characteristics/Description
Families	Parent-Child Interaction and Issues	Parents spend less time with children during middle and late childhood, including less time in caregiving, instruction, reading, talking, and playing. Nonetheless, parents still are powerful and important socializing agents during this period. New parent-child issues emerge, and discipline changes. Control is more coregulatory, children and parents label each other more, and parents mature just as children do.
	Societal Changes in Families	During middle and late childhood, two major changes in many children's lives are movement into a stepfamily and becoming a latchkey child. Just as divorce produces disequilibrium and stress for children, so does the entrance of a stepparent. Over time, preadolescent boys seem to improve more than girls in stepfather families. Adolescence appears to be an especially difficult time for adjustment to the entrance of a stepparent. Latchkey children may become vulnerable when they are not monitored by adults in the after-school hours.
Peers	Peer Interaction	Children spend considerably more time with peers in middle and late childhood.
	Popularity, Rejection, and Neglect	Listening skills and effective communication, being yourself, being happy, showing enthusiasm and concern for others, and having self-confidence, but not being conceited, are predictors of peer popularity. The risk status of neglected children is unclear. Rejected children are at risk for the development of problems. A special interest focuses on improving the peer relations of neglected and rejected children. One issue involving rejected children is whether to initially train their prosocial skills or reduce their aggressive behavior and improve their self-control. It is important to remember that rejected children reflect a heterogeneous grouping.
	Social Cognition	Social information-processing skills and social knowledge are two important dimensions of social cognition in peer relations.
	Friends	Children's friendships serve six functions: companionship, stimulation, physical support, ego support, social comparison, and intimacy/affection. Intimacy and similarity are common characteristics of friendships.
Schools	Transition to School	Children spend more than 10,000 hours in the classroom as members of a small society in which there are tasks to be accomplished, people to be socialized and socialized by, and rules that define and limit behavior. A special concern is that early schooling proceeds mainly on the basis of negative feedback to children. The curriculum in elementary schools should be integrated.
	Teachers	Teachers have prominent influences in middle and late childhood. Aptitude-treatment interaction is an important consideration.
	Social Class and Ethnicity	Schools have a stronger middle-class than lower-class orientation. Many lower-class children have problems in schools, as do children from ethnic-minorities. Efforts are being made to reduce this bias, among them the jigsaw classroom. Ogbu proposed a controversial view that ethnic-minority children are placed in a position of subordination and exploitation in the American educational system. Some experts believe a form of institutional racism exists in some schools because teachers fail to academically challenge ethnic-minority students.

American and Hispanic American children's education is the high rate of single parent families in these ethnic-minority groups. A special concern is that 70 percent of the Black American and Hispanic American single parent families headed by mothers are in poverty (McLoyd, in press). Poor school performance among many ethnic-minority children is related to this pattern of single-parenting and poverty (Dornbusch & others, 1985; Spencer & Dornbusch, 1990).

Thus far, we have discussed many ideas about families, peers, and schools in middle and late childhood. These ideas are summarized in concept table 11.1. We turn next to the continuing development of the self in middle and late childhood.

The Self

What is the nature of the child's self-understanding in the elementary school years? What is the role of perspective taking in self-understanding? What is the nature of children's self-esteem? What issue does Erikson believe children face in middle and late childhood? We consider each of these questions in turn.

The Development of Self-Understanding

In middle and late childhood, self-understanding increasingly shifts from defining oneself through external characteristics to defining oneself through internal characteristics. Elementary school-aged children are also more likely to define themselves in terms of social characteristics and social comparison.

In middle and late childhood, children not only recognize differences between inner and outer states, but are also more likely to include subjective inner states in their definition of self. For example, in one investigation, second-grade children were much more likely than younger children to name psychological characteristics (such as preferences or personality traits) in their self-definition and less likely to name physical characteristics (such as eye color or possessions) (Aboud & Skerry, 1983). For example, 8-year-old Todd includes in his self-description, "I am smart and I am popular." Ten-year-old Tina says about herself, "I am pretty good about not worrying most of the time. I used to lose my temper but I'm better about that now. I also feel proud when I do well in school."

In addition to the increase of psychological characteristics in self-definition during the elementary school years, the *social aspects* of the self also increase at this point in development. In one investigation, elementary school children often included references to social groups in their self-descriptions (Livesly & Bromsley, 1973). For example, some children referred to themselves as Girl Scouts, as Catholics, or as someone who has two close friends.

Children's self-understanding in the elementary school years also includes increasing reference to *social comparison*. At this point in development, children are more likely to distinguish themselves from others in comparative rather than in absolute terms. That is, elementary-school-aged children are no longer as likely to think about what *I* do or do not do, but are more likely to think about what I can do in *comparison with others*. This developmental shift provides an increased tendency of establishing one's differences as an individual from others. In a series of studies, Diane Ruble and her colleagues (1989) investigated children's use of social comparison in their self-evaluations. Children were given a difficult task and then offered feedback on

Table 11.1: Selman's Stages of Perspective Taking

Perspective Taking Stage	Age	Description
Egocentric Viewpoint	3 to 6	Child has a sense of differentiation of self and other but fails to distinguish between the social perspective (thoughts, feelings) of other and self. Child can label other's overt feelings but does not see the cause-and-effect relation of reasons to social actions.
Social-Informational Perspective Taking	6 to 8	Child is aware that other has a social perspective based on other's own reasoning, which may or may not be similar to child's. However, child tends to focus on one perspective rather than coordinating viewpoints.
Self-Reflective Perspective Taking	8 to 10	Child is conscious that each individual is aware of the other's perspective and that this awareness influences self and other's view of each other. Putting self in other's place is a way of judging other's intentions, purposes, and actions. Child can form a coordinated chain of perspectives, but cannot yet abstract from this process to the level of simultaneous mutuality.
Mutual Perspective Taking	10 to 12	Child realizes that both self and other can view each other mutually and simultaneously as subjects. Child can step outside the two-person dyad and view the interaction from a third-person perspective.
Social and Conventional System Perspective Taking	12 to 15	Person realizes mutual perspective taking does not always lead to complete understanding. Social conventions are seen as necessary because they are understood by all members of the group (the generalized other), regardless of their position, role, or experience.

From R. L. Selman, "The Development of Social-Cognitive Understanding: A Guide to Educational and Clinical Practice" in *Moral Development and Behavior: Theory, Research and Social Issues,* edited by Thomas Lickona. Copyright © 1986 Holt, Rinehart & Winston, Inc., Orlando, FL. Reprinted by permission of Thomas Lickona.

their own performance as well as information about the performances of other children their age. The children were then asked for self-evaluations. Children younger than 7 made virtually no reference to the information about other children's performances. However, children older than 7 often included socially comparative information in their self-descriptions.

The Role of Perspective Taking in Self-Understanding

Many child developmentalists believe that perspective taking plays an important role in self-understanding. **Perspective taking** *is the ability to assume another person's perspective and understand his or her thoughts and feelings.* Robert Selman (1980) has proposed a developmental theory of perspective taking that has been given considerable attention. He believes perspective taking involves a series of five stages, ranging from 3 years of age through adolescence (see table 11.1). These stages begin with the egocentric viewpoint in early childhood and end with in-depth perspective taking in adolescence.

Middle and Late Childhood

To study children's perspective taking, Selman individually interviews the child, asking the child to comment on such dilemmas as the following:

> Holly is an 8-year-old girl who likes to climb trees. She is the best tree climber in the neighborhood. One day while climbing down from a tall tree, she falls . . . but does not hurt herself. Her father sees her fall. He is upset and asks her to promise not to climb trees any more. Holly promises.
>
> Later that day, Holly and her friends meet Shawn. Shawn's kitten is caught in a tree and can't get down. Something has to be done right away or the kitten may fall. Holly is the only one who climbs trees well enough to reach the kitten and get it down but she remembers her promise to her father (Selman, 1976, p. 302).

Subsequently, Selman asks the child a series of questions about the dilemma, such as:

- Does Holly know how Shawn feels about the kitten?
- How will Holly's father feel if he finds out she climbed the tree?
- What does Holly think her father will do if he finds out she climbed the tree?
- What would you do in this situation?

After analyzing children's responses to these dilemmas, Selman (1980) concluded that children's perspective taking follows the developmental sequence described in table 11.1.

Children's perspective taking not only can increase their self-understanding, but it can also improve their peer group status and the quality of their friendships. For example, in one investigation, the most popular children in the third and eighth grades had competent perspective-taking skills (Kurdek & Krile, 1982). Children who are competent at perspective taking are better at understanding the needs of their companions, so they are likely to communicate more effectively with them (Hudson, Forman, & Brion-Meisels, 1982).

Self-Esteem

In chapter 2, we described Carl Rogers' humanistic theory, which stresses the importance of the self in understanding development. We described Rogers' ideas about self-concept, the overall perception of oneself. In recent years, developmentalists have given special attention to two aspects of the self, or self-conception: self-understanding and self-esteem. We have already studied self-understanding—the cognitive representation of self. What is self-esteem? **Self-esteem** *is the evaluative and affective dimension of self-concept. Self-esteem is also referred to as self-worth or self-image.* That is, a child may perceive that she is not merely a student, but a *good* student. Another child may perceive that he is not merely a basketball player, but a *good* basketball player. These self-evaluations often stimulate an emotional reaction. The good student feels proud that she just received an A on an exam; the good basketball player feels elated that he scored the winning basket in last night's game. Of course, not all self-evaluations are positive. A child may feel sad that she is not a good student. Another child may feel ashamed that he is a poor reader. These are all evaluative judgments regarding the child's self-esteem.

Until recently, theorists and researchers conceptualized self-esteem as a general, global judgment about the self. However, children make evaluative judgments about many different aspects of their life. For example, they perceive that they are good or bad in physical skills, good or bad in cognitive skills, and good or bad in social skills. As we see next, interest in the domain-specific aspects of self-esteem has led to the development of new measures of self-esteem.

Figure 11.2   Harter's Perceived Competence Scale for Children.

General self-worth

Cognitive skills

Social skills

Physical skills

Measuring Self-Esteem

While it is recognized that all children evaluate their self-worth, psychologists have had a difficult time trying to measure self-worth or self-esteem (Wylie, 1979). One method that has frequently been used is the Piers-Harris Scale (Piers & Harris, 1964), which consists of eighty items designed to measure the child's overall self-esteem. School psychologists often use this scale with children who have been referred to them for evaluation. By responding yes or no to such items as "I have good ideas," children reveal whether they have high or low self-esteem.

However, as we just indicated, a child's self-esteem may vary according to different skill domains and areas of competence. A well-received addition to the assessment of self-esteem or self-worth was Susan Harter's **Perceived Competence Scale for Children** (Harter, 1982), *a measure consisting of four components. One set of questions measures general self-worth ("I am sure of myself," "I am happy the way I am"), while three other sets of questions measure self-esteem in three domains of competence—physical ("I do well at sports," "I'm usually the one chosen for games"), cognitive ("I am good at homework," "I remember things easily"), and social ("I have a lot of friends," "Most kids like me").* (A summary of the four categories on the Perceived Competence Scale for Children is presented in figure 11.2.) Harter's scale does an excellent job of separating children's feelings of self-worth in different skill areas. And when general self-worth is assessed, questions that focus on overall perceptions of self-esteem are used rather than questions directed at specific skill domains. The Perceived Competence Scale for Children was standardized for use with children in the third through sixth grades. Harter also has developed separate scales for young children (Harter & Pike, 1984) and for adolescents (Harter, 1989).

Parent-Child Relationships and Self-Esteem

In the most extensive investigation of parent-child relationships and self-esteem, a measure of self-esteem was given to elementary school boys, and the boys and their mothers were interviewed about their family relationships (Coopersmith, 1967). Based on these assessments, the following parenting attributes were associated with boys' high self-esteem:

- expression of affection
- concern about the child's problems
- harmony in the home
- participation in joint family activities
- availability to give competent, organized help to the boys when they need it
- setting clear and fair rules
- abiding by these rules
- allowing the children freedom within well-prescribed limits

Remember that these findings are correlational in nature. Because they are correlational, we cannot say that the parenting attributes *cause* children's high self-esteem. Such factors as parental acceptance and allowing children freedom within well-prescribed limits probably are important determinants of children's self-esteem, but based on the available research data, we must still say that they *are related to* rather than cause children's self-esteem.

Ethnicity and Self-Esteem

Many of the early attempts to assess self-esteem in different ethnic groups compared Black and White individuals (Coopersmith, 1967; Deutsch, 1967). The early reports indicated that Black individuals, especially Black children had less self-esteem than White individuals. However, more recent research suggests that Black, Mexican American, and Puerto Rican children and adults report equal if not higher self-esteem than children and adults from other ethnic groups, such as Anglo American children and adults (Allen & Majidi-Ahi, 1989; Powell & Fuller, 1972).

A generation of ethnic awareness and pride appears to have advanced the self-esteem of ethnic-minority groups, especially when comparisons are made between groups that are similar in terms of social class and intelligence (Garbarino, 1985). Ethnic pride based on success within a subgroup has both costs and benefits for individuals. An obvious benefit is that their cultural roles are more clearly defined by the subgroup (such as Black, Mexican American, or Native American) and that they know what they must do to become a competent person in the subculture. In these usually tight-knit neighborhoods, there is a feeling of closeness and support among neighbors. Thus, individuals from the ethnic group can obtain help and learn strategies for coping with problems, which makes developing a positive sense of self somewhat easier. The ethnic-group individual gains a sense of rootedness and acceptance.

However, there is no indication that the distribution of self-acceptance in a group is related to the social prestige of the group in American society at large (Rosenberg, 1965). Thus, there may be a negative reality in the social environment beyond the ethnic-group neighborhood which individuals must eventually come to terms with if they are to succeed in the larger society. The beliefs, values, morals, and behaviors of the ethnic-group neighborhood may not be ones that are accepted by the society as a whole, which can impede the development of social competence in the mainstream of society.

A discussion of ethnicity and self-esteem raises the fundamental question: "What kind of people does the world need?" (Garbarino, 1980, 1985). There is a growing recognition of the need for individuals to develop more harmonious, cooperative relationships if the quality of life on this planet is to be enhanced. Such a society needs persons to define themselves in new ways that deemphasize competition, achievement, and materialism in favor of cooperation, connectedness with others, empathy, and spiritual development. We need to ask whether we are socializing children to develop the kind of self we need people to have in a competent, caring, sustainable society.

Increasing Children's Self-Esteem

Social support in the form of approval and confirmation from others is a powerful influence on children's self-esteem (Harter, 1990a,b). Some children with low self-esteem come from conflicted families or conditions in which they experienced abuse or neglect—situations in which support is unavailable. In some cases, alternative sources of support can be implemented, either informally through the encouragement of a teacher, a coach, or other significant adult, or more formally, through programs such as Big Brothers and Big Sisters. Peer approval becomes increasingly important during late childhood and adolescence, but both adult and peer support are important influences on the child's self-esteem.

According to Susan Harter (1990a,b), identifying the child's sources of self-esteem—that is, competence in domains important to the self—as well as social support, is critical to improving the child's self-esteem. Harter points out that the self-esteem enhancement programs of the 1960s, in which self-esteem itself was the target and children were encouraged to believe that they should feel good about themselves, were ineffective. Rather, Harter believes intervention must take place at the level of the *causes* of self-esteem if a major impact on improving the child's self-esteem is to result.

Industry versus Inferiority

Erikson's fourth stage of the human life cycle, industry versus inferiority, appears during middle and late childhood. The term *industry* expresses a dominant theme of this period: Children become interested in how things are made and how they work. It is the Robinson Crusoe age in that the enthusiasm and minute detail Crusoe uses to describe his activities appeal to the child's budding sense of industry. When children are encouraged in their efforts to make and build and work—whether building a model airplane, constructing a treehouse, fixing a bicycle, solving an addition problem, or cooking—their sense of industry increases. However, parents who see their children's efforts at making things as "mischief" or "making a mess" encourage children's development of a sense of inferiority.

Children's social worlds beyond their families also contribute to a sense of industry. School becomes especially important in this regard. Consider children who are slightly below average in intelligence. They are too bright to be in special classes but not bright enough to be in gifted classes. They fail frequently in their academic efforts, developing a sense of inferiority. By contrast, consider children whose sense of industry is derogated at home. A series of sensitive and committed teachers may revitalize their sense of industry (Elkind, 1970).

Gender

In chapter 9, we discussed the biological, cognitive, and social influences on gender development. Gender is such a pervasive aspect of an individual's identity that we further consider its role in children's development here. Among the gender-related topics we examine are: gender stereotypes, similarities, and differences; gender-role classification; gender and social policy; and gender and ethnicity.

Gender Stereotypes, Similarities, and Differences

How pervasive is gender-role stereotyping? What are the real differences between boys and girls? What is gender's role in achievement? We consider each of these questions in turn.

Gender-Role Stereotyping

Gender-role stereotypes *are broad categories that reflect our impressions and beliefs about females and males.* All stereotypes, whether they are based on gender, ethnicity, or other groupings, refer to an image of what the typical member of a particular social category is like. The world is extremely complex. Every day we are confronted with thousands of different stimuli. The use of stereotypes is one way we simplify this complexity. If we simply assign a label (such as the quality of softness) to someone, we then have much less to consider when we think about the individual. However, once labels are assigned they are remarkably difficult to abandon, even in the face of contradictory evidence.

Many stereotypes are so general they are very ambiguous. Consider the stereotypes for "masculine" and "feminine." Diverse behaviors can be called on to support each stereotype, such as scoring a touchdown or growing facial hair for "masculine" and playing with dolls or wearing lipstick for "feminine." The stereotype may be modified in the face of cultural change. At one point in history, muscular development may be thought of as masculine; at another point, it may be a more lithe, slender physique. The behaviors popularly agreed upon as reflecting a stereotype may also fluctuate according to socioeconomic circumstances. For example, lower socioeconomic groups might be more likely than higher socioeconomic groups to include "rough and tough" as part of a masculine stereotype.

Even though the behaviors that are supposed to fit the stereotype often do not, the label itself can have significant consequences for the individual. Labeling a male "feminine" and a female "masculine" can produce significant social reactions to the individuals in terms of status and acceptance in groups, for example (Mischel, 1970).

How widespread is feminine and masculine stereotyping? According to a far-ranging study of college students in thirty countries, stereotyping of females and males is pervasive (Williams & Best, 1982). Males were widely believed to be dominant, independent, aggressive, achievement oriented, and enduring, while females were widely believed to be nurturant, affiliative, less esteemed, and more helpful in times of distress.

In a more recent investigation, women and men who lived in more highly developed countries perceived themselves more similarly than women and men who lived in less-developed countries (Williams & Best, 1989). In the more highly developed countries, women were more likely to attend college and be gainfully employed. Thus, as sexual equality increases, stereotypes, as well as actual behavioral differences, between women and men may diminish. In this investigation, women were more likely to perceive similarity between the sexes than men were (Williams & Best, 1989). And the sexes were perceived more similarly in Christian than in Muslim societies. Next, we go beyond stereotyping and examine the behavioral similarities and differences between the sexes.

Gender Similarities and Differences

There is a growing consensus in gender research that differences between the sexes have often been exaggerated (Hyde, 1981; Hyde, in press). You might remember our discussion of reducing sexist research in psychology in chapter 1. It is not unusual to find statements such as the following: "While only 32 percent of the females were found to . . . fully 37 percent of the males were. . . ." This difference of 5 percent likely is a very small difference, and may or may not even be statistically significant or capable of being replicated in a separate study (Denmark & Paludi, in press). And when statements are made about female-male comparisons, such as "males outperform females in

Middle and Late Childhood

math," this does not mean all females versus all males. Rather, it usually means the average math achievement scores for males at certain ages is higher than the average math achievement scores for females. The math achievement scores of females and males overlap considerably, so that while an *average* difference may favor males, many females have higher math achievement than many males. Further, there is a tendency to think of differences between females and males as biologically based. Remember that when differences occur they may be socioculturally based.

Let's now examine some of the differences between the sexes, keeping in mind that (a) the differences are averages—not all females versus all males; (b) even when differences are reported, there is considerable overlap between the sexes; and (c) the differences may be due primarily to biological factors, sociocultural factors, or both. First, we examine physical and biological differences, and then we turn to cognitive and social differences.

From conception on, females are less likely than males to die, and females are less likely than males to develop physical or mental disorders. Estrogen strengthens the immune system, making females less resistant to infection, for example. Female hormones also signal the liver to produce more "good" cholesterol, which makes their blood vessels more elastic than males'. Testosterone triggers the production of low-density lipoprotein, which clogs blood vessels. Males have twice the risk of coronary disease as females. Higher levels of stress hormones cause faster clotting in males, but also higher blood pressure than in females. Adult females have about twice the body fat of their male counterparts, most concentrated around breasts and hips. In males, fat is more likely to go to the abdomen. On the average, males grow to be 10 percent taller than females. Male hormones promote the growth of long bones; female hormones stop such growth at puberty. In sum, there are many physical differences between females and males. But are there as many cognitive differences?

According to a classic review of gender differences in 1974, Eleanor Maccoby and Carol Jacklin (1974) concluded that males have better math skills and better visuospatial ability (the kind of skills an architect would need to design a building's angles and dimensions), while females have better verbal abilities. Recently, Maccoby (1987) revised her conclusion about several gender dimensions. She commented that the accumulation of research evidence now indicates that the verbal differences in males and females have virtually disappeared, but that the math and visuospatial differences are still present.

A number of researchers in the gender area point out that there are more cognitive similarities between females and males than differences. They also believe that the differences that do exist, such as the math and visuospatial differences, have been exaggerated. Males do outperform females in math, but only for a certain portion of the population—the gifted (Hyde, in press; Linn & Hyde, 1991). Further, males do not always outperform females on all visuospatial tasks—consistent differences occur only in the ability to rotate objects mentally (Linn & Petersen, 1986). And keep in mind our earlier comment about the considerable overlap that exists between females and males, even when differences are reported. Figure 11.3 shows the small average difference on visuospatial tasks that favors males, but also clearly reveals the substantial overlap in the visuospatial abilities of females and males. Combined with the recent information about convergence in the verbal abilities of males and females (females used to have higher scores on the verbal section of the SAT, but now there are no differences, for example), we can conclude that cognitive differences between females and males do not exist in many areas, are disappearing in other areas, and are small when they do exist.

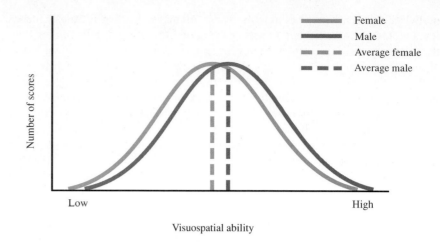

Figure 11.3 The small average difference and substantial overlap between females and males on visuospatial ability. Notice that while the average male's visuospatial ability is higher than the average female's, the overlap between the sexes is substantial. Not all males have better visuospatial ability than all females—the substantial overlap indicates that while the average score of males is higher, many females outperform many males on such tasks (Hyde, 1981).

The most consistent gender differences in social behavior are that males are more active and more aggressive than females (Maccoby, 1987; Maccoby & Jacklin, 1974). The difference in aggression appears in children's development, often present as early as 2 years of age. With regard to emotions, males and females do not experience different emotions, but males and females frequently differ in how they express their emotions and what emotions they feel free to express in public (Doyle & Paludi, 1991). Females grow up to smile more and "read" emotions better than males (Malatesta, 1990). And by elementary school, girls show more helping and caregiving behavior (Zahn-Waxler, 1990). However, in cultures where boys and girls both care for younger siblings, boys and girls show more similar nurturant behavior (Whiting, 1989). Girls also have a wider social network than boys do (Zahn-Waxler, 1990). As we see next, one area of gender that has received considerable attention is achievement.

Achievement For some areas of achievement, gender differences are so large they can best be described as nonoverlapping. For example, no major league baseball players are female, and 96 percent of all registered nurses are female. In contrast, many measures of achievement-related behaviors do not reveal gender differences. For example, girls show just as much persistence at tasks. The question of whether males and females differ in their expectations for success at various achievement tasks is not yet settled (Eccles, 1987).

Because females are often stereotyped as less competent than males, incorporation of gender role stereotypes into a child's self-concept could lead girls to have less confidence than boys in their general intellectual abilities. This could lead girls to have lower expectations for success at difficult academic and vocational activities. It could also lead girls to expect to have to work harder to achieve success at these activities than boys expect to have to work. Evidence supports these predictions (Eccles, Harold-Goldsmith, & Miller, 1989). Either of these beliefs could keep girls from selecting demanding educational or vocational options, especially if these options are not perceived as important or interesting.

Gender roles could also produce different expectations of success depending on the gender stereotyping of the activity. Both educational programs and vocational options are gender stereotyped in our culture. Many high-level professions, especially those that are math-related and scientific/technical, are thought to be male activities. In contrast, teaching below the college level, working in clerical and related support jobs, and excelling in language-related courses are thought to be female activities by both children and adults (Eccles, 1987; Eccles & Hoffman, 1984; Huston, 1983). Incorporating these beliefs

into self-concept could cause girls to have lower expectations for success in male-typed activities and higher expectations for success in female-typed activities. This pattern could lead girls to select female-typed activities over male-typed activities. Some support for this perspective has been found (Eccles, 1987). At times, though, researchers have found no gender differences in achievement expectations.

An intriguing view about gender roles and achievement argues that on the basis of an instrumental-achievement (male) versus an expressive-affiliation (female) dichotomy, we might expect male superiority in achievement patterns. This is not always the case. In an investigation by Lloyd Lueptow (1984), adolescent girls had both higher levels of achievement value orientations and higher levels of academic achievement than did adolescent boys. It may be that achievement is a stronger component of the female gender role than the male gender role. Or, it may be that a distinction is necessary between achievement based on excellence and accomplishment (a stronger focus of females) and achievement based on assertion and aggressive competition (a stronger focus of males). That is, females may be stronger achievers, males stronger competitors. Since researchers have often neglected this distinction, it may be that the achievement orientation of females has been underestimated.

A special concern is that some of the brightest and most gifted girls do not have achievement and career aspirations that match their talents. In one investigation, high-achieving girls had much lower expectations for success than high-achieving boys (Stipek & Hoffman, 1980). In the gifted research program at Johns Hopkins University, many mathematically precocious girls selected scientific and medical careers, although only 46 percent aspired to a full-time career compared to 98 percent of the boys (Fox, Brody, & Tobin, 1979).

To help talented female youth redirect their paths, some high schools are using programs developed by colleges and universities. Project CHOICE (Creating Her Options In Career Education) was designed by Case Western University to detect barriers in reaching one's potential. Gifted eleventh-grade females received individualized counseling that included interviews with female role models, referral to appropriate occupational groups, and information about career workshops. A program at the University of Nebraska (Kerr, 1983) was successful in encouraging talented female high school students to pursue more prestigious careers. This was accomplished by individualized counseling and participation in a "Perfect Future Day," in which girls shared career fantasies and discussed barriers that might impede their fantasies. Internal and external constraints were evaluated, gender-role stereotypes were discouraged, and high aspirations were applauded. While these programs have shown short-term success in redirecting the career paths of high-ability females, in some instances the benefits fade over time—six months or more, for example. It is important to be concerned about improving the awareness of career alternatives for all female youth, however, and not just those of high ability.

Now that we have considered gender stereotyping and the actual similarities and differences between boys and girls, we turn our attention to how gender roles are classified.

Gender-Role Classification: Masculinity, Femininity, and Androgyny

At a point not too long ago, it was accepted that boys should grow up to be masculine and that girls should grow up to be feminine, that boys are made of frogs and snails and puppy dogs' tails and that girls are made of sugar and spice and all that's nice. Today, diversity characterizes gender roles and the feedback individuals receive from their culture. A girl's mother might promote femininity, the girl might be close friends with a tomboy, and the girl's teachers at school might encourage her assertiveness.

In the past, the well-adjusted male was expected to be independent, aggressive, and power oriented. The well-adjusted female was expected to be dependent, nurturant, and uninterested in power. Further, masculine characteristics were considered to be healthy and good by society, female characteristics were considered to be undesirable. A classic study in the early 1970s summarized the traits and behaviors that college students believed were characteristic of males and those they believed were characteristic of females (Broverman & others, 1972). The traits clustered into two groups that were labeled "instrumental" and "expressive." The instrumental traits paralleled the male's purposeful, competent entry into the outside world to gain goods for his family; the expressive traits paralleled the female's responsibility to be warm and emotional in the home. Such stereotypes are more harmful to females than to males because the characteristics assigned to males are more valued than those assigned to females. The beliefs and stereotypes have led to the negative treatment of females because of their sex, or what is called *sexism*. Females receive less attention in schools, are less visible in leading roles on television, are rarely depicted as competent, dominant characters in children's books, are paid less than males even when they have more education, and are underrepresented in decision-making roles throughout our society, from corporate executive suites to Congress.

In the 1970s, as both males and females became dissatisfied with the burdens imposed by their strictly stereotyped roles, alternatives to "masculinity" and "femininity" were explored. Instead of thinking of masculinity and femininity as a continuum, with more of one meaning less of the other, it was proposed that individuals could show both *expressive* and *instrumental* traits. This thinking led to the development of the concept of **androgyny,** *the presence of desirable masculine and feminine characteristics in the same individual* (Bem, 1977; Spence & Helmreich, 1978). The androgynous individual might be a male who is assertive (masculine) and nurturant (feminine), or a female who is dominant (masculine) and sensitive to others' feelings (feminine).

Measures have been developed to assess androgyny. One of the most widely used gender measures, the Bem sex-role inventory, was constructed by a leading early proponent of androgyny, Sandra Bem. To see what the items

(a)

(b)

Androgyny consists of (a) self-assertive characteristics, such as those shown by this young girl's independence, competitiveness, and individualism; and (b) integrative characteristics, such as those shown by these young boys' sympathy, affection, and understanding.

on Bem's measure are like, turn to table 11.2. Based on their responses to the items in the Bem sex-role inventory, individuals are classified as having one of four gender-role orientations: masculine, feminine, androgynous, or undifferentiated (see figure 11.4). The androgynous individual is simply a male or female who has a high degree of both feminine (expressive) and masculine (instrumental) traits. No new characteristics are used to describe the androgynous individual. A masculine individual is high on masculine traits (instrumental) and low on feminine traits (expressive), while a feminine individual shows the reverse of these traits. An undifferentiated individual is not high on masculine or feminine traits. Androgynous individuals are described as more flexible and more mentally healthy than either masculine or feminine individuals. Individuals who are undifferentiated are the least competent. To some degree, though, the context influences which gender role is most adaptive. In close relationships, a feminine or androgynous gender role may be more desirable because of the expressive nature of close relationships. However, a masculine or androgynous gender role may be more desirable in academic and work settings because of the instrumental nature of these settings. And the culture in which individuals live also plays an important role in determining what is adaptive. On the one hand, increasing numbers of children in the United States and other modernized countries such as Sweden are being raised to behave in androgynous ways. On the other hand, traditional gender roles continue to dominate the cultures of many countries around the world. To read about traditional gender role practices in Egypt, as well as the nature of gender roles in China and Russia, turn to Cultural Worlds of Development 11.2.

While androgyny was an improvement over the perspective that femininity and masculinity were opposite ends of gender, it has turned out to be less of a panacea than many of its early proponents envisioned (Doyle & Paludi, 1991). Some theorists, such as Joe Pleck (1981), believe the concept of androgyny should be replaced with the concept of *gender-role transcendence.*

• Critical Thinking •

How extensively are parents rearing their children to become androgynous? Are parents rearing their daughters to be more androgynous than they are their sons? Are middle-class parents more likely to rear their children to be androgynous than parents from low-income backgrounds? Explain.

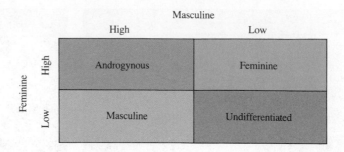

Figure 11.4 Gender role classification.

	Masculine	
	High	Low
Feminine High	Androgynous	Feminine
Feminine Low	Masculine	Undifferentiated

TABLE 11.2: The Bem Sex-Role Inventory: Are You Androgynous?

To find out whether you score as androgynous, first rate yourself on each item, on a scale from 1(never or almost never true) to 7 (always or almost always true).

1. self-reliant	16. strong personality	31. makes decisions easily	46. aggressive
2. yielding	17. loyal	32. compassionate	47. gullible
3. helpful	18. unpredictable	33. sincere	48. inefficient
4. defends own beliefs	19. forceful	34. self-sufficient	49. acts as a leader
5. cheerful	20. feminine	35. eager to soothe hurt	50. childlike
6. moody	21. reliable	feelings	51. adaptable
7. independent	22. analytical	36. conceited	52. individualistic
8. shy	23. sympathetic	37. dominant	53. does not use harsh
9. conscientious	24. jealous	38. soft-spoken	language
10. athletic	25. has leadership abilities	39. likable	54. unsystematic
11. affectionate	26. sensitive to the needs of	40. masculine	55. competitive
12. theatrical	others	41. warm	56. loves children
13. assertive	27. truthful	42. solemn	57. tactful
14. flatterable	28. willing to take risks	43. willing to take a stand	58. ambitious
15. happy	29. understanding	44. tender	59. gentle
	30. secretive	45. friendly	60. conventional

Scoring

(a) Add your ratings for items 1, 4, 7, 10, 13, 16, 19, 22, 25, 28, 31, 34, 37, 40, 43, 46, 49, 52, 55, and 58. Divide the total by 20. That is your masculinity score.

(b) Add your ratings for items 2, 5, 8, 11, 14 17, 20, 23, 26, 29, 32, 35, 38, 41, 44, 47, 50, 53, 56, and 59. Divide the total by 20. That is your femininity score.

(c) If your masculinity score is above 4.9 (the approximate median for the masculinity scale) and your femininity score is above 4.9 (the approximate femininity median), then you would be classified as androgynous on Bem's scale.

Thus, rather than merging their gender roles, Pleck emphasizes that women and men should transcend prescribed gender-role characteristics and stereotypes and more often deal with individuals as persons rather than as females or males. However, the concepts of both androgyny and gender-role transcendence draw attention away from women's unique needs and the power imbalance between women and men in most cultures (Hare-Mustin & Maracek, 1988). The power imbalance between females and males in the United States suggests that attention needs to be given to social policy issues and children's gender.

Gender and Social Policy

Many gender-related research findings have implications for public policy regarding children. Among the areas of gender-related research with important implications for public policy are: Gender-role stereotypes and the media, education, and child care (Jacklin, 1989).

Middle and Late Childhood

GENDER ROLES IN EGYPT, CHINA, AND RUSSIA

*I*n recent decades, roles assumed by males and females in the United States have become increasingly similar—that is, androgynous. In many countries, though, gender roles have remained more gender specific than in the United States. Egypt is one example of such a country. The division of labor between Egyptian males and females is dramatic: Egyptian males are socialized to work in the public sphere, females in the private world of home and childrearing. The Islamic religion dictates that the man's duty is to provide for his family, the woman's duty to care for her family and household (Dickersheid & others, 1988). Any deviations from this traditional gender-role orientation are severely disapproved.

It is not just Egypt that socializes males and females to behave, think, and feel in strongly gender-specific ways. Kenya and Nepal are two other cultures where children are brought up under very strict gender-specific guidelines (Munroe, Himmin, & Munroe, 1984). In the People's Republic of China, the female's status has historically been lower than the male's. The teachings of the fifth century B.C. Chinese philosopher Confucius were used to enforce the female's inferior being. Beginning with the revolution in 1949 women's economic freedom and more equal status in marital relationships were instituted. However, even with the sanctions of a socialist

In Egypt near the Aswan Dam, women are returning from the Nile River where they have filled their water jugs. How might gender role socialization for girls in Egypt compare to that in the United States?

government, the old patriarchal traditions of male supremacy in China have not been completely uprooted. Chinese women still make considerably less money than Chinese men in comparable positions, and in rural China a tradition of male supremacy still governs many women's lives.

The Soviet Union is another country in which a socialist government improved the status of women, but as in China, women still do not have the same status as men. Only 25 percent of the Communist party, the ruling political body, is made up of women, and

just as in the United States, women who work in a career are also primarily responsible for household care and childrearing.

In sum, although females in the United States, Sweden, and other Western countries, as well as China and Russia, have made considerable strides, complete equality has still not been reached. And in many other cultures, such as Egypt and other countries where the Muslim religion predominates, gender-specific behavior is pronounced and females are not given access to high status positions.

Gender Role Stereotypes and the Media

An extensive amount of parents' information about children is brought to them by the media. However, the media can misinform parents. For example, in the early 1980s, a series of articles on gender differences in math were published that caused a stir in the media (Benbow & Stanley, 1980, 1982, 1983). In each of the articles, boys were reported as scoring higher in math than girls. What was especially important about these results is that the authors speculated about the biological causes of their findings. As these speculations became exaggerated in the popular media, they became the overriding message of the studies.

In another investigation, math anxiety, gender-stereotyped beliefs of parents, and the perceived value of math to the student were responsible for the major portion of gender differences in math achievement (Eccles, Adler, & Kaczala, 1982; Eccles & others, 1983). In addition, students' attitudes about math were strongly related to their mothers' beliefs concerning the difficulty of math for their children. Mothers' beliefs were also strongly related to their children's math anxiety.

Might media reports of biologically based gender differences in math ability possibly influence parents' attitudes about boys' and girls' math abilities? In one investigation, parents who were aware of the media-based reports of biological gender differences in math were compared with those who were not aware of them (Eccles & Jacobs, 1986). The uninformed mothers believed the math ability of their sons and daughters was equivalent, while mothers who knew about the biological findings felt that math was much more difficult for their daughters than for their sons. Thus, the media campaign had a direct influence on the attitudes of mothers toward gender-related aspects of math, which was quite clearly harmful for girls. As mothers come to believe that math is much more difficult for girls than for boys, their daughters become less likely to take additional math courses (Jacklin, 1989). These gender expectations for math are not only present in the United States, but in many other cultures as well. For example, in one recent investigation, children and their mothers in the United States, Japan, and Taiwan tended, as early as the first grade, to believe that boys were better at math and girls were better at reading (Lummis & Stevenson, 1990).

Gender and Education

According to psychologist Carol Jacklin (1989), many teachers and parents are not aware of the powerful gender expectations they communicate to children. A specific example, again, involves the area of math abilities. According to Jacklin, most parents and teachers are not aware of how strongly their attitudes influence girls' math orientation. Nationally organized groups, such as the Parent Teacher Association (PTA) could bring findings such as those of Jacqueline Eccles and other colleagues (1983) to parents, but currently do not.

Gender and Child Care

Gender roles and the division of labor play important roles in gender differences. If interacting with infants and children stimulates nurturance in the caregivers, and there is considerable evidence that it does, then, according to Carol Jacklin (1989), we should be rethinking who does the child care in our society. Currently women and girls do most of this care and men and boys may even be discouraged from doing it. Why should nurturance be encouraged in only one sex? According to Jacklin, nurturance may be an antidote for violence.

In sum, changes are needed in the way the media, teachers and parents, and society view gender roles (see figure 11.5). In addition to social policy issues involving children's gender, another important aspect of children's and adult's gender is the way gender roles are prescribed in different ethnic groups.

Gender and Ethnicity

Are gender-related attitudes and behavior similar across different ethnic groups? All ethnic-minority females are females and all ethnic-minority males are males, so there are many similarities in the gender-related attitudes of females across different ethnic-minority groups and of males across different

Middle and Late Childhood

(a)   (b)   (c)

Figure 11.5 Three important social policy issues involving children's gender development. (a) The media can misinform parents about children's gender development, as exemplified in the exaggeration of biological explanations of gender differences in math. (b) Teachers communicate gender expectations to children, and so do parents. Many teachers and parents are not aware of how strongly they communicate gender expectations. (c) Currently girls and women do most of the child care in our society, and boys and men may even be discouraged from it. Might increased child care, especially nurturing infants and young children, reduce male aggression?

ethnic-minority groups. Nevertheless, the different ethnic and cultural experiences of Black American, Hispanic American, Asian American, and Native American females and males need to be considered in understanding their gender-related attitudes and behavior, because in some instances even small differences can be important (Swanson & Cunningham, 1991; Walsh, Katz, & Downey, 1991). For example, the socialization of males and females in other cultures who subsequently migrate to America often reflects a stronger gap between the status of males and females than is experienced in America. Keeping in mind that there are many similarities between females in all ethnic-minority groups and between males in all ethnic-minority groups, we examine, first, information about females from specific ethnic-minority groups, followed by a discussion of males from specific ethnic-minority groups.

Ethnic-Minority Females

Let's now consider the behavior and psychological orientations of females from specific ethnic-minority groups, beginning with Black females, and then in turn, study Asian American females, Hispanic American females, and Native American females.

Researchers in psychology have only begun to focus on the behavior of Black females. For too long, Black females only served as a comparison group for White females on selected psychological dimensions, or they served as the subjects in studies in which the primary research interest related to poverty, unwed motherhood, and so on (Hall, Evans, & Selice, 1989). This narrow research approach could be viewed as attributing no personal characteristics to Black females beyond the labels given to them by society.

The nature and focus of psychological research on Black females has begun to change—to some extent paralleling societal changes (Hall, Evans, & Selice, 1989). In the last decade, more individualized, positive dimensions of Black females are being studied, such as self-esteem, achievement, motivation, and self-control. In the 1980s, psychological studies of Black females began to shift away from studies focused only on the problems of Black females and toward research on the positive aspects of Black females in a pluralistic society.

Black females, as well as other ethnic-minority females, have experienced the double jeopardy of racism and sexism. The ingenuity and perseverance shown by ethnic-minority females as they have survived and grown against the odds is remarkable. For example, 499 Black women earned doctoral degrees in 1986. This represents only 2 percent of the PhD's awarded (compared to the 6.4 percent of the general population represented by Black females). However, the positive side of these figures is that the PhD's earned by Black women in 1986 was almost a 16 percent increase over the number earned in 1977. Despite such gains, our society needs to make a strong commitment to providing Black, and other ethnic-minority, females with the opportunities they deserve.

Asian females are often expected to carry on domestic duties, to marry, to become obedient helpers of their mothers-in-law, and to bear children, especially males (Sue, 1989). In China, the mother's responsibility for the emotional nurturance and well-being of the family, and for raising children, derives from Confucian ethics (Huang & Ying, 1989). However, as China has become modernized, these roles have become less rigid. Similarly, in acculturated Chinese families in the United States, only derivatives of these rigidly defined roles remain. For example, Chinese American females are not entirely relegated to subservient roles.

Traditionally in Mexican families, women assume the expressive role of homemaker and caretaker of children. This continues to be the norm, although less so than in the past (Ramirez, 1989). Historically, the Mexican female's role has been one of self-denial and her needs were considered to be subordinate to those of other family members. Joint decision making and greater equality of males' and females' roles are becoming more characteristic of Mexican American families (Ramirez & Arce, 1981). Of special significance is the increased frequency of Mexican American women's employment outside the home, which in many instances has enhanced a wife's status in the family and in decision making (Baca Zinn, 1980; Marín & Marín, 1991).

For Native Americans, the amount of social and governing control exhibited by women or men depends on the tribe (LaFromboise & Low, 1989). For example, in the traditional matriarchal Navajo family, an older woman might live with her husband, her unmarried children, her married daughter, and the daughter's husband and children (Ryan, 1980). In patriarchal tribes, women function as the central "core" of the family, maintaining primary responsibility for the welfare of children. Grandmothers and aunts often provide child care. As with other ethnic-minority females, Native American females who have moved to urban areas experience the cultural conflict of traditional ethnic values and the values of the American society.

Ethnic-Minority Males

Just as ethnic-minority females have experienced considerable discrimination and have had to develop coping strategies in the face of adversity, so have ethnic-minority males. As with ethnic-minority females, our order of discussion will be Black males, Asian American males, Hispanic American males, and Native American males.

Some statistics provide a portrayal of the difficulties many Black males have faced. Black American males of all ages are three times as likely to live below the poverty line. Black males aged 20 to 44 are twice as likely to die as White males. Black male heads of household earn 70 percent of the income of their White male counterparts. Although they make up only 6.3 percent of the U.S. population, Black males comprise 42 percent of jail inmates and more than 50 percent of men executed for any reason in the last fifty years!

Such statistics do not tell the complete picture (Evans & Whitfield, 1988). The sociocultural aspects of historical discrimination against an ethnic-minority group must be taken into account to understand these statistics. Just as with Black females, researchers are beginning to focus on some of the more positive dimensions of Black males. For example, researchers are finding that Black males are especially efficient at the use of body language in communication, decoding nonverbal cues, multilingual/multicultural expression, and improvised problem solving.

Asian cultural values are reflected in traditional patriarchal Chinese and Japanese families (Sue, 1989). The father's behavior in relation to other family members is generally dignified, authoritative, remote, and aloof. Sons are generally valued over daughters. Firstborn sons have an especially high status.

As with Asian American females, the acculturation experienced by Asian American males has eroded some of the rigid gender roles that characterized Asian families in the past. Fathers still are often the figurative heads of families, especially when dealing with the public, but in private, they have relinquished some of their decision-making power to their wives (Huang & Ying, 1989).

In Mexican families, men traditionally assume the instrumental role of provider and protector of the family (Ramirez, 1989). The concept of machismo—being a macho man—continues to influence the role of the male and the patriarchal orientation of Mexican families, though less so than in the past. Traditionally, this orientation required men to be forceful and strong, and also to withhold affectionate emotions. Ideally, it involved a strong sense of personal honor, family, loyalty, and care for children. However, it also has involved exaggerated masculinity and aggression (Trankina, 1983). The concepts of machismo and absolute patriarchy are currently diminishing in influence. Adolescent males are still given much more freedom than adolescent females in Mexican American families.

Some Native American tribes are also patriarchal, with the male being the head of the family and primary decision maker. In some tribes, though, child care is shared by men. For example, Mescalero Apache men take responsibility for children when not working away from the family (Ryan, 1980). Autonomy is highly valued among the male children in many Native American tribes, with the males operating semi-independently at an early age (LaFromboise & Low, 1989). As with Native American females, increased movement to urban areas has led to modifications in the values and traditions of some Native American males.

At this point we have discussed a number of ideas about gender. Another important topic in children's development that requires further discussion is moral development.

Moral Development

Remember from chapter 9 our description of Piaget's view of moral development. Piaget believed that younger children are characterized by heteronomous morality, but that by 10 years of age they have moved into a higher stage called autonomous morality. According to Piaget, older children consider the intentions of the individual, believe that rules are subject to change, and are aware that punishment does not always follow a wrongdoing. A second major cognitive perspective on moral development was proposed by Lawrence Kohlberg.

Kohlberg's Theory of Moral Development

Kohlberg stressed that moral development is based primarily on moral reasoning and unfolds in stages (Kohlberg, 1958, 1976, 1986). Kohlberg arrived at his view after some twenty years of using a unique interview with children. In the interview, children are presented with a series of stories in which characters face moral dilemmas. The following is the most popular Kohlberg dilemma:

> In Europe a woman was near death from a special kind of cancer. There was one drug that the doctors thought might save her. It was a form of radium that a druggist in the same town had recently discovered. The drug was expensive to make, but the druggist was charging ten times what the drug cost him to make. He paid $200 for the radium and charged $2,000 for a small dose of the drug. The sick woman's husband, Heinz, went to everyone he knew to borrow the money, but he could only get

together $1,000 which is half of what it cost. He told the druggist that his wife was dying and asked him to sell it cheaper or let him pay later. But the druggist said, "No, I discovered the drug, and I am going to make money from it." So Heinz got desperate and broke into the man's store to steal the drug for his wife. (Kohlberg, 1969, p. 379)

This story is one of eleven devised by Kohlberg to investigate the nature of moral thought. After reading the story, the interviewee answers a series of questions about the moral dilemma. Should Heinz have stolen the drug? Was stealing it right or wrong? Why? Is it a husband's duty to steal the drug for his wife if he can get it no other way? Would a good husband steal? Did the druggist have the right to charge that much when there was no law setting a limit on the price? Why or why not?

Based on the reasons interviewees gave for this and other moral dilemmas, Kohlberg believed three levels of moral development exist, each of which is characterized by two stages. A key concept in understanding moral development, especially Kohlberg's theory, is **internalization,** *the developmental change from behavior that is externally controlled to behavior that is internally controlled.*

Level One: Preconventional Reasoning
Preconventional reasoning *is the lowest level in Kohlberg's theory of moral development. At this level, the child shows no internalization of moral values—moral reasoning is controlled by external rewards and punishments.*

> *Stage 1.* **Punishment and obedience orientation** *is the first stage in Kohlberg's theory of moral development. At this stage, moral thinking is based on punishment.* Children obey because adults tell them to obey.
>
> *Stage 2.* **Individualism and purpose** *is the second stage in Kohlberg's theory of moral development. At this stage, moral thinking is based on rewards and self-interest.* Children obey when they want to obey and when it is in their best interest to obey. What is right is what feels good and what is rewarding.

Level Two: Conventional Reasoning
Conventional reasoning *is the second or intermediate level in Kohlberg's theory of moral development. At this level, the individual's internalization is intermediate. The person abides by certain standards (internal), but they are the standards of others (external), such as parents or the laws of society.*

> *Stage 3.* **Interpersonal norms** *is the third stage in Kohlberg's theory of moral development. At this stage, the person values trust, caring, and loyalty to others as the basis of moral judgments.* Children often adopt their parents' moral standards at this stage, seeking to be thought of by their parents as a "good girl" or a "good boy."
>
> *Stage 4.* **Social system morality** *is the fourth stage in Kohlberg's theory of moral development. At this stage, moral judgments are based on understanding the social order, law, justice, and duty.*

Level Three: Postconventional Reasoning
Postconventional reasoning *is the highest level in Kohlberg's theory of moral development. At this level, morality is completely internalized and not based on others' standards.* The person recognizes alternative moral courses, explores the options, and then decides on a personal moral code.

Stage description	Examples of moral reasoning that support Heinz's theft of the drug	Examples of moral reasoning that indicate Heinz should not steal the drug
Preconventional morality		
Stage 1: Avoid punishment	Heinz should not let his wife die; if he does, he will be in big trouble.	Heinz might get caught and sent to jail.
Stage 2: Seek rewards	If Heinz gets caught, he could give the drug back and maybe they would not give him a long jail sentence.	The druggist is a businessman and needs to make money.
Conventional morality		
Stage 3: Gain approval/ avoid disapproval especially with family	Heinz was only doing something that a good husband would do; it shows how much he loves his wife.	If his wife dies, he can't be blamed for it; it is the druggist's fault. He is the selfish one.
Stage 4: Conformity to society's rules	If you did nothing, you would be letting your wife die; it is your responsibility if she dies. You have to steal it with the idea of paying the druggist later.	It is always wrong to steal; Heinz will always feel guilty if he steals the drug.
Postconventional morality		
Stage 5: Principles accepted by the community	The law was not set up for these circumstances; taking the drug is not really right, but Heinz is justified in doing it.	You can't really blame someone for stealing, but extreme circumstances don't really justify taking the law in your own hands. You might lose respect for yourself if you let your emotions take over; you have to think about the long-term.
Stage 6: Individualized conscience	By stealing the drug, you would have lived up to society's rules, but you would have let down your conscience.	Heinz is faced with the decision of whether to consider other people who need the drug as badly as his wife. He needs to act by considering the value of all the lives involved.

Figure 11.6   Examples of moral reasoning at Kohlberg's six stages in response to the Heinz and the druggist story.

Stage 5. **Community rights versus individual rights** *is the fifth stage in Kohlberg's theory of moral development. At this stage, the person understands that values and laws are relative and that standards may vary from one person to another.* The person recognizes that laws are important for society but knows that laws can be changed. The person believes that some values, such as liberty, are more important than the law.

Stage 6. **Universal ethical principles** *is the sixth and highest stage in Kohlberg's theory of moral development. At this stage, persons have developed a moral standard based on universal human rights.* When faced with a conflict between law and conscience, the person will follow conscience, even though the decision might involve personal risk.

Some specific responses to the dilemma of Heinz and the druggist are given in figure 11.6, which should provide you with a better sense of reasoning at the six stages in Kohlberg's theory. Notice that whether Heinz steals the drug is not the important issue in Kohlberg's cognitive developmental theory. What is crucial is how the person reasons about the moral dilemma.

Kohlberg believed that these levels and stages occur in a sequence and are age related: Before age 9, most children reason about moral dilemmas in a preconventional way; by early adolescence, they reason in more conventional ways; and by early adulthood, a small number of people reason in postconventional ways. In a 20-year longitudinal investigation, the uses of stages 1 and 2 decreased (Colby & others, 1983). Stage 4, which did not appear at all in the moral reasoning of the 10-year-olds, was reflected in 62 percent of the moral thinking of the 36-year-olds. Stage 5 did not appear until the age of 20 to 22 and never characterized more than 10 percent of the individuals. Thus, the moral stages appeared somewhat later than Kohlberg initially envisioned, and the higher stages, especially stage 6, was extremely elusive. Recently, stage 6 was removed from the Kohlberg scoring manual, but it is still considered to be theoretically important in the Kohlberg scheme of moral development.

Kohlberg's Critics

Kohlberg's provocative view continues to generate considerable research on moral development, but critics challenge his theory. One criticism of Kohlberg's view is that moral reasons are often a shelter for immoral behavior. When bank embezzlers and presidents are asked about their moral *reasoning,* it may be advanced, even at Kohlberg's post-conventional level, but when their own *behavior* is examined it may be filled with cheating, lying, and stealing. The cheaters, liars, and thieves may *know* what is right and what is wrong, but still *do* what is wrong.

A second major criticism of Kohlberg's view is that it does not adequately reflect relationships and concern for others. The **justice perspective** *is a moral perspective that focuses on the rights of the individual; individuals stand alone and independently make moral decisions. Kohlberg's theory is a justice perspective.* By contrast, the **care perspective** *is a moral perspective developed by Carol Gilligan (1982) that sees people in terms of their connectedness with others and focuses on interpersonal communication, relationships with others, and concern for others.* According to Gilligan, Kohlberg greatly underplayed the care perspective in moral development. She believes this may have happened because he was a male, most of his research was with males rather than females, and he used male responses as a model for his theory.

Recently, Gilligan conducted extensive interviews with girls from 6 to 18 years of age (Brown & Gilligan, 1990; Gilligan, 1990; Gilligan, Brown, & Rogers, 1990). She and her colleagues found that girls consistently revealed reported detailed knowledge about human relationships, based on listening and watching what happens between people. According to Gilligan, girls have the ability to sensitively pick up different rhythms in relationships and are often able to follow the pathways of feelings.

Gilligan also believes that girls reach a critical juncture in their development when they reach adolescence. Gilligan says that at the edge of adolescence, at about 11 to 12 years of age, girls become aware that their intense interest in intimacy is not prized by the male-dominated culture, even though society values females as caring and altruistic. The dilemma, says Gilligan, is that girls are presented with a choice that makes them appear either selfish (if they become independent and self-sufficient) or selfless (if they remain responsive to others). Gilligan states that as young adolescent girls experience this dilemma, they increasingly "silence" their distinctive voice. They become less confident and more tentative in offering their opinions, which often persists into adulthood. Some researchers believe this self-doubt and ambivalence too often translates into depression and eating disorders among adolescent girls.

Some critics argue that Gilligan and her colleagues overemphasize differences in gender. One of those critics is developmentalist Eleanor Maccoby, who says that Gilligan exaggerates the differences in intimacy and connectedness between males and females. Other critics fault Gilligan's research strategy, which rarely includes a comparison group of boys, and rarely includes statistical analysis. Instead, Gilligan conducts extensive interviews with girls and then provides excerpts from the girls' narratives to buttress her ideas. Other critics fear that Gilligan's findings reinforce stereotypes—females as nurturing and sacrificing, for example—that might undermine females'

Carol Gilligan with some of the students she has interviewed about the importance of relationships in a female's development. According to Gilligan, the sense of relationships and connectedness is at the heart of a female's development.

struggle for equality. These critics say that Gilligan's different voice should perhaps be called "the voice of the victim."

In reply, revisionists such as Gilligan say that their work provides a way to liberate females and transform a society that has far too long discriminated against females. They also say that if females' approach to life is acknowledged as authentic, they will no longer have to act like males. The revisionists state that females' sensitivity in relationships is a special gift in our culture. Influenced by Gilligan's and other feminists' thinking, some schools are beginning to incorporate the feminine voice into their curriculum. For example, at the Emma Willard School in Troy, New York, the entire curriculum has been revamped to emphasize cooperation rather than competition, and to encourage girls to analyze and express ideas from their own perspective rather than responding in stereotyped or conformist ways (Gilligan, 1990; Gilligan, Lyons, & Hanmer, 1990; Gilligan, Rogers, & Brown, 1990; Gilligan, Ward, & Taylor, 1988).

Gilligan argues that moral development has three basic levels. She calls Level I preconventional morality, which reflects a concern for self and survival. Level II, conventional morality, shows a concern for being responsible and caring for others. Level III, postconventional morality, shows a concern for

AMY SAYS THEY SHOULD JUST TALK IT OUT AND FIND SOME OTHER WAY TO MAKE MONEY

◆

*T*he main character in Kohlberg's most widely used dilemma is a male, Heinz. Females may have a difficult time identifying with him. Some of Kohlberg's dilemmas are gender neutral, but one concerns the captain of a company of marines, which is highly masculine. The subjects in Kohlberg's original research were all males. Going beyond her critique of Kohlberg's failure to consider females, Gilligan (1982) argues that an important voice is not present in his view. Following are two excerpts from children's responses to the story of Heinz and the druggist, one from 11-year-old Jake, the other from 11-year-old Amy. Jake's comments:

For one thing, human life is worth more than money, and if the druggist only makes $1,000, he is still going to live, but if Heinz doesn't steal the drug, his wife is going to die. (Why is life worth more than money?) Because the druggist can get $1,000 later from rich people with cancer, but Heinz can't get his wife again. (Gilligan, 1982, p. 26)

Carol Gilligan believes that Kohlberg's theory does not place enough emphasis on the importance of relationships and caring in development. According to Gilligan, the American culture has promoted the care perspective in the socialization of females, but not in males.

Amy's comments:

I think there might be other ways besides stealing it, like if he could borrow the money or make a loan or something, but he really shouldn't steal the drug—but his

wife shouldn't die either. (Why shouldn't he steal the drug?) If he stole the drug, he might save his wife then, but if he did, he might have to go to jail, and then his wife might get sicker again, and he couldn't get more of the drug, and it might not be good. So, they should really just talk it out and find some other way to make the money. (Gilligan, 1982, p. 28)

Jake's comments are a mixture of Kohlberg's stages 3 and 4, but they also include some of the components of a mature level 3 moral thinker. Amy, by contrast, does not fit into Kohlberg's scoring system so well. Jake sees the problem as one of rules and balancing the rights of people. However, Amy views the problem as involving relationships: The druggist's failure to live up to his relationship to the needy woman, the need to maintain the relationship between Heinz and his wife, and the hope that a bad relationship between Heinz and the druggist can be avoided. Amy concludes that the characters should talk it out and try to repair their relationships.

self and others as interdependent. Gilligan believes Kohlberg underemphasized the care perspective in the moral development of *both* males and females and that the highest level of morality for both sexes involves a search for moral equality between one's self and others. To read further about Gilligan's ideas on moral development, turn to Perspective on Life-Span Development 11.1.

A third major criticism of Kohlberg's view is that it is culturally biased (Bronstein & Paludi, 1988). In a review of research on moral development in 27 countries, it was concluded that moral reasoning is more culture specific than Kohlberg envisioned and that Kohlberg's scoring system does not recognize higher level moral reasoning in certain cultural groups (Snarey, 1987). Examples of higher level moral reasoning that would not be recognized as such by Kohlberg's system are values related to communal equity and collective happiness in Israel, the unity and sacredness of all life forms in India, or the relation of the individual to the community in New Guinea. These examples of moral reasoning would not be scored at the highest level in Kohlberg's system because they emphasize the individual's rights and abstract principles of justice.

Altruism

Altruism *is an unselfish interest in helping someone.* Human acts of altruism are plentiful—the hardworking laborer who places five dollars in a Salvation Army kettle, rock concerts to feed the hungry, help farmers, and fund AIDS research, and a child who takes in a wounded cat and cares for it. How do developmentalists account for such frequent acts of altruism?

According to William Damon (1988), children's altruism follows a developmental sequence. He especially believes that sharing is an important dimension of altruism. Most sharing during the first three years of life is done for nonempathic reasons, such as the fun of the social play ritual or out of mere imitation. Then at about 4 years of age, the combination of empathic awareness and adult encouragement produces a sense of obligation on the part of the child to share with others. This obligation forces the child to share even though the child may not perceive this as the best way to have fun. However, most 4-year-olds are not selfless saints. Children now believe they have an obligation to share, but they do not necessarily think they should be as generous to others as to themselves. Nor do their actions always support their beliefs, especially when the object is a coveted one. What is important developmentally is that the child now has an internal belief that sharing is an obligatory part of a social relationship, and that this involves a question of right and wrong. However, the preschool child's sense of reciprocity does not constitute a moral duty but rather a pragmatic means of getting one's way. Despite their shortcomings, these early ideas about justice set the stage for giant strides that will be made in the next several years.

By the start of the elementary school years, children begin to genuinely express more objective ideas about fairness. These notions about fairness have been used throughout history to distribute goods and to resolve conflicts. They involve principles of equality, merit, and benevolence. *Equality* means that everyone is treated the same. *Merit* means giving extra rewards for hard work, a talented performance, or some other laudatory behavior. *Benevolence* means giving special consideration for individuals in a disadvantaged condition. Equality is the first of these principles used regularly by elementary school children. It is common to hear 6-year-old children use the word *fair* as synonymous with *equal* or *same*. By mid- to late-elementary school years, children also believe equity means special treatment for those who deserve it—the principles of merit and benevolence. A summary of Damon's developmental sequence of sharing is presented in figure 11.7.

Missing from the concerns that have been identified as guiding children's sharing is one that many adults might expect to be the most influential of all: the motivation to obey adult authority figures. Surprisingly, a number of studies have shown that adult authority has only a small influence on children's sharing. For example, when child developmentalist Nancy Eisenberg (1982) asked children to explain their own real life altruistic acts, they mainly gave empathic and pragmatic reasons for their spontaneous acts of sharing. Not one of the children referred to the demands of adult authority. Parental advice and prodding certainly foster standards of sharing, but the give-and-take of peer requests and arguments provide the most immediate stimulation of sharing. Parents may set examples that children carry into peer interaction and communication, but parents are not present during all of their children's peer exchanges. The day-to-day construction of fairness standards is done by children in collaboration and negotiation with each other. Over the course of many years and thousands of encounters, children's understanding of altruism deepens. With this conceptual elaboration, which involves such notions as equality, merit, benevolence, and compromise, comes a greater consistency and generosity in children's sharing behavior (Damon, 1988).

Age period	Nature of sharing
0 to 3 years	Sharing is done but for nonempathic reasons, such as for the fun of the social play ritual or out of mere imitation.
4 years of age	Combination of empathic awareness and adult encouragement produces a sense of obligation on the part of the child to share with others. Children now believe they have an obligation to share, but that they don't have to be as generous to others as to themselves. Nor do their actions always support their beliefs. Sharing is usually not a moral duty but a pragmatic means of getting one's way.
Early elementary school years	Children begin to genuinely show more objective ideas about fairness. At this point, sharing often involves the principle of equality — that everyone should be treated the same.
Middle-late elementary school years	In addition to the principle of equality, children now add the principles of merit, giving extra rewards for hard work or laudatory performance, and benevolence, giving special consideration for individuals in disadvantaged conditions.

Figure 11.7 Damon's description of children's development of sharing.

At this point we have discussed a number of ideas about the self, gender, and moral development in children's lives. A summary of these ideas is presented in concept table 11.2. In the book's next section, we turn our attention to adolescent development, beginning with a description of adolescents' physical and cognitive development in chapter 12.

Summary

I. Families

Parents spend less time with children during middle and late childhood, including less time in caregiving, instruction, reading, talking, and playing. Nonetheless, parents are still powerful and important socializing agents during this period. New parent-child issues emerge and discipline changes. Control is more coregulatory, children and parents label each other more, and parents mature just as children do. During middle and late childhood, two major changes in many children's lives are movement into a stepfamily and becoming a latchkey child. Just as divorce produces disequilibrium and stress for children, so does the entrance of a stepparent. Over time, preadolescent boys seem to improve more than do girls in stepfather families. Adolescence appears to be an especially difficult time for adjustment to the entrance of a stepparent. Latchkey children may become vulnerable when they are not monitored in the after-school hours.

II. Peer Relations

Children spend considerably more time with peers in middle and late childhood. Listening skills, effective communication, being yourself, being happy, showing enthusiasm and concern for others, and having self-confidence, but not being conceited, are predictors of peer popularity. The risk status of neglected children is unclear. Rejected children are at risk for the development of problems. A special interest focuses on improving the peer relations of neglected and rejected children. One issue involving rejected children is whether to initially train their prosocial skills or reduce their aggression and improve their self-control. It is important to remember that rejected children reflect a heterogeneous grouping. Social information-processing skills and social knowledge are two important dimensions of social cognition in peer relations. Children's friendships serve six functions: companionship, stimulation, physical support, ego support, social comparison, and intimacy/affection. Intimacy and similarity are two common characteristics of friendships.

III. Schools

Children spend more than 10,000 hours in the classroom as members of a small society in which there are tasks to be accomplished, people to be socialized and socialized by, and rules that define and limit behavior, feelings, and attitudes. A special concern is that early schooling proceeds mainly on the basis of negative feedback to children. The curriculum in elementary schools should be integrated. Teachers play

Middle and Late Childhood

Concept Table 11.2: The Self, Gender, and Moral Development in Middle and Late Childhood

Concept	Processes/Related Ideas	Characteristics/Description
The Self	Self-Understanding	The internal self, the social self, and the socially comparative self become more prominent in self-understanding during middle and late childhood. Elementary school-aged children increasingly describe themselves with internal, psychological characteristics. They are also more likely to define themselves in terms of social characteristics and social comparison.
	Perspective Taking	This is the ability to assume another person's perspective and understand his or her thoughts and feelings. Selman proposed a developmental theory of perspective taking with five stages, ranging from 3 years of age through adolescence, beginning with the egocentric viewpoint in early childhood and ending with the in-depth perspective taking of adolescence.
	Self-Esteem	This is the evaluative and affective dimension of self-concept. Self-esteem is also referred to as self-worth or self-image. Until recently, self-esteem was described in global terms. Today, domain-specific aspects of self-esteem are also considered. Measuring self-esteem is a difficult task. Harter's Perceived Competence Scale for Children is a promising measure of self-esteem because it recognizes the importance of assessing children's general self-worth and their perceived competencies in different skill domains—physical, cognitive, and social. In Coopersmith's study, children's self-esteem was associated with such parenting attributes as parental acceptance and allowing children freedom within well-prescribed limits. It is important to remember that these associations are correlational in nature. A special interest has developed in the self-esteem of ethnic-minority children, which has increased in recent years. Social support in the form of approval and confirmation from others is a powerful influence on children's self-esteem. Both adult and peer support are important in increasing children's self-esteem. Identifying the sources of self-esteem is critical to improving the child's self-esteem.
Gender	Gender Stereotypes, Similarities, and Differences	Gender-role stereotypes are broad categories that reflect our impressions and beliefs about males and females. These stereotypes are widespread around the world, especially emphasizing the male's power and the female's nurturance. However, in more highly developed countries, females and males are more likely to be perceived as more similar. Many gender researchers believe a number of differences between females and males have been exaggerated. In considering differences, it is important to recognize that the differences are averages, there is considerable overlap between the sexes, and the differences may be due primarily to biological factors, sociocultural factors, or both. There are a number of physical differences between the sexes, but cognitive differences are either small or nonexistent. At the level of the gifted, the average male does outperform the average female in math achievement. In terms of social behavior, males are more aggressive and active than females, but females are usually more adept at "reading" emotions, show more helping behavior, and have a wider social network than males. Overall, though, there are more similarities than differences between females and males.
	Gender-Role Classification	In the past, the well-adjusted male was supposed to show instrumental traits, the well-adjusted female expressive traits. Masculine traits were more valued by society. Sexism was widespread. In the 1970s, alternatives to traditional masculinity and femininity were explored. It was proposed

[continued]

Concept	Processes/Related Ideas	Characteristics/Description
		that individuals could show both expressive and instrumental traits. This thinking led to the development of the concept of androgyny, the presence of desirable masculine and feminine traits in the same individual. Gender-role measures often categorize individuals as masculine, feminine, androgynous, or undifferentiated. Androgynous individuals are often flexible and mentally healthy, although the particular context and the individual's culture also determine the adaptiveness of a gender-role orientation. One alternative to androgyny is gender-role transcendence, but like androgyny, it diverts attention away from the imbalance of power between females and males.
	Gender and Social Policy	Many gender-related findings have implications for social policy regarding children. Three areas are gender-role stereotypes and the media, education, and child care. Changes are needed in the way the media, teachers and parents, and society view gender roles.
	Gender and Ethnicity	There are many similarities between females in different ethnic-minority groups and between males in different ethnic-minority groups, but even small differences can sometimes be important. Researchers in psychology have only begun to focus on female behavior in specific ethnic groups in a positive way. Many ethnic-minority females have experienced the double jeopardy of racism and sexism. In many instances, Asian American, Hispanic American, and Native American females have lived in patriarchal, male-dominated families, although gender roles have become less rigid in these ethnic groups in recent years. Just as ethnic-minority females have experienced considerable discrimination and have had to develop coping strategies in the face of adversity, so have ethnic-minority males. Just as with Black females, researchers are beginning to focus more on the positive dimensions of Black males. A patriarchal, male-dominant orientation has characterized many ethnic-minority groups, such as Asian American, Hispanic American, and Native American, although females are gaining greater decision making in these cultures, especially those who develop careers and work outside of the home.
Moral Development	Kohlberg's Theory	Kohlberg proposed three levels (each with two stages) that vary in the degree moral development is internalized: preconventional, conventional, and postconventional.
	Kohlberg's Critics	Moral reasons can always be a shelter for immoral behavior. Gilligan believes that Kohlberg vastly underplayed the care perspective in moral development and that girls reach a critical juncture in their development at about 11 to 12 years of age. There is greater cultural variation in moral development than Kohlberg envisioned.
	Altruism	Altruism is an unselfish interest in helping someone. Damon described a developmental sequence of altruism, especially sharing. Up to 3 years of age, sharing is done for nonempathic reasons; at about 4 years, the combination of empathic awareness and adult encouragement produces a sense of obligation to share; in the early elementary years, children begin to genuinely show more objective ideas about fairness, at which time the principle of equality is understood; in the middle to late elementary years, the principles of merit and benevolence are understood.

prominent roles in the school's influence on children. A profile of a good teacher's personality traits has been difficult to establish, although some traits are clearly superior to others. Aptitude-treatment interaction is an important consideration. Schools have a stronger middle-class than lower-class orientation. Not only do many lower-class children have problems in school, so do children from ethnic minorities. Efforts are being made to reduce this bias, among them the jigsaw classroom. Ogbu proposed a controversial view that ethnic-minority children are placed in a position of subordination and exploitation in the American educational system. Some experts believe a form of institutional racism exists in some schools because teachers fail to academically challenge ethnic-minority children.

IV. **Self-Understanding and Perspective Taking**

The internal self, the social self, and the socially comparative self become more prominent in self-understanding during middle and late childhood. Elementary school-aged children increasingly describe themselves with internal, psychological characteristics. They are also more likely to define themselves in terms of social characteristics and social comparison. Perspective taking is the ability to assume another person's perspective and understand his or her thoughts and feelings. Selman proposed a developmental theory of perspective taking with five stages, ranging from 3 years of age (egocentric viewpoint) to adolescence (in-depth perspective taking).

V. **Self-Esteem**

Self-esteem is the evaluative and affective dimension of self-concept. Self-esteem is also referred to as self-worth or self-image. Until recently, self-esteem was described in global terms. Today, domain-specific aspects of self-esteem are also considered. Measuring self-esteem is a difficult task. Harter's Perceived Competence Scale for Children is a promising measure of self-esteem because it recognizes the importance of assessing children's general self-worth and their perceived competencies in different skill domains—physical, cognitive, and social. In Coopersmith's study, children's self-esteem was associated with such parenting attributes as parental acceptance and allowing children freedom within well-prescribed limits. It is important to remember that these associations are correlational in nature. A special interest has developed in the self-esteem of ethnic-minority children, which has increased in recent years. Social support in the form of approval and confirmation from others is a powerful influence on the child's self-esteem. Both adult and peer support are important in increasing the child's self-esteem. Identifying the sources of self-esteem is critical to improving the child's self-esteem.

VI. **Gender Stereotypes, Similarities, and Differences**

Gender-role stereotypes are broad categories that reflect our impressions and beliefs about males and females. These stereotypes are widespread around the world, especially emphasizing the male's power and the female's nurturance. However, in more highly developed countries, females and males are more likely to be perceived as similar. Many gender researchers believe that a number of differences between females and males have been exaggerated. In considering differences, it is important to recognize that the differences are averages, there is considerable overlap between the sexes, and the differences may be due primarily to biological factors, sociocultural factors, or both. There are a number of physical differences between females and males, but cognitive differences are either small or nonexistent. At the level of the gifted, the average male does outperform the average female in math achievement. In terms of social behavior, males are more aggressive and active than females; but females are usually more adept at "reading" emotions, show more helping behavior, and have a wider social network than males. Overall, though, there are more similarities than differences between females and males.

VII. **How Can Gender Roles Be Classified?**

In the past, the well-adjusted male was supposed to show instrumental traits, the well-adjusted female expressive traits. Masculine traits were more valued by society. Sexism was widespread. In the 1970s, alternatives to traditional masculinity and femininity were explored. It was proposed that individuals could show both expressive and instrumental traits. This thinking led to the development of the concept of androgyny, the presence of desirable masculine and feminine traits in the same individual. Gender-role measures often categorize individuals as masculine, feminine, androgynous, or undifferentiated. Androgynous individuals are often flexible and mentally healthy, although the particular context and the individual's culture also determine the adaptiveness of a gender-role orientation. One alternative to androgyny is gender-role transcendence, but like androgyny, it draws attention from the imbalance of power between females and males.

VIII. **Gender and Social Policy with Children**

Many gender-related findings have important implications for social policy regarding children. Three areas are gender role stereotypes and the media, education, and child care. Changes are needed in the way the media, teachers and parents, and society view gender roles.

IX. Gender and Ethnicity

There are many similarities between females in different ethnic-minority groups and between males in different ethnic-minority groups, but even small differences are sometimes significant. Researchers in psychology have only begun to focus on female behavior in specific ethnic groups in a positive way. Many ethnic-minority females have experienced the double jeopardy of racism and sexism. In many instances, Asian American, Hispanic American, and Native American females have lived in patriarchal, male-dominated families, although gender roles have become less rigid in these ethnic groups in recent years. Just as ethnic-minority females have experienced considerable discrimination and have had to develop coping strategies in the face of adversity, so have ethnic-minority males. Just as with Black females, researchers are beginning to focus more on the positive dimensions of Black males. A patriarchal, male-dominant orientation has characterized many ethnic-minority groups, such as Asian American, Hispanic American, and Native American, although females are gaining greater decision making in these cultures, especially those who develop careers and work outside of the home.

X. Kohlberg's Theory and Kohlberg's Critics

Kohlberg proposed three levels (each with two stages) that vary in the degree moral development is internalized: preconventional, conventional, and postconventional. Criticisms of Kohlberg's view include: Moral reasons can always be a shelter for immoral behavior; Gilligan believes Kohlberg vastly underplayed the care perspective in moral development and that girls reach a critical juncture in their development at about 11 to 12 years of age; there is greater cultural variation in moral development than Kohlberg envisioned.

XI. Altruism

Altruism is an unselfish interest in helping someone. Damon described a developmental sequence of altruism, especially sharing: Up to 3 years of age, sharing is done for nonempathic reasons; at about 4 years, the combination of empathic awareness and adult encouragement produces a sense of obligation to share; in the early elementary years, children begin to genuinely show more objective ideas about fairness, at which time the principle of equality is understood; in the middle to late elementary years, the principles of merit and benevolence are understood.

Key Terms

neglected children   345
rejected children   345
intimacy in friendships   348
aptitude-treatment interaction (ATI)
350
perspective taking   356
self-esteem   357
Perceived Competence Scale for
Children   359
gender-role stereotypes   362

androgyny   366
internalization   374
preconventional reasoning   374
punishment and obedience orientation
374
individualism and purpose   374
conventional reasoning   374
interpersonal norms   374

social system morality   374
postconventional reasoning   374
community rights versus individual
rights   375
universal ethical principles   375
justice perspective   376
care perspective   376
altruism   379

Suggested Readings

Asher, S. R., & Coie, J. D. (Eds.), *Peer rejection in childhood*. New York: Cambridge University Press.
This book includes a number of recent ideas about the nature of peer rejection and ways to intervene in the lives of peer-rejected children.

Damon, W., & Hart, D. (1988). *Self-understanding in childhood and adolescence*. New York: Cambridge University Press.
An extensive description of the development of self-understanding is provided, including Damon and Hart's integrative, developmental model of self-understanding.

Development during middle childhood (1984). Washington, DC: National Academy Press.
An excellent collection of essays about what is currently known about the elementary school years. Includes chapters on families, peers, self, and problems and disturbances.

Doyle, J. A., & Paludi, M. A. (1991). *Male and female* (2nd ed.). Dubuque, IA: Wm. C. Brown Publishers.
An excellent overview of gender, with special attention given to the female role.

Gilligan, C., Lyons, N., & Hanmer, T. J. (Eds.). (1990). *Making connections*. Cambridge, MA: Harvard University Press.
Gilligan's ideas about the importance of relationships and connectedness are presented, along with many excerpts from 10- to 18-year-old girls at the Emma Willard School in Troy, New York.

Gottman, J. M., & Parker, J. G. (Eds.). (1987). *Conversations of friends*. New York: Cambridge University Press.
An excellent volume on how children become friends; explores the rich conversations of children.

Minuchin, P. P., & Shapiro, E. K. (1983). The school as a context for social development. In P. H. Mussen (Ed.), *Handbook of child psychology* (4th ed., Vol. 4). New York: Wiley.
An authoritative review of the school's role in children's development.

S·E·C·T·I·O·N

VI

ADOLESCENCE

> *I*n no order of things is adolescence
> the time of simple life.
>
> Janet Erskine Stewart

CHAPTER 12

Physical and Cognitive Development in Adolescence

A s in the development of children, genetic, biological, environmental, and social factors interact in adolescent development. Also, continuity and discontinuity characterize adolescent development. The genes inherited from parents still influence thought and behavior during adolescence, but inheritance now interacts with the social conditions of the adolescent's world—with family, peers, friendships, dating, and school experiences. An adolescent has experienced thousands of hours of interaction with parents, peers, and teachers in the past ten to thirteen years of development. Still new experiences and developmental tasks appear during adolescence. Relationships with parents take a different form, moments with peers become more intimate, dating occurs for the first time as does sexual exploration and possibly intercourse. The adolescent's thoughts are more abstract and idealistic. Biological changes trigger a heightened interest in body image. Adolescence, then, has both continuity and discontinuity with childhood.

Imagine a toddler displaying all the features of puberty. Think about a 3-year-old girl with fully developed breasts or a boy just slightly older with a deep male voice. That is what we would see by the year 2250 if the age at which puberty arrives kept getting younger at its present pace (Petersen, 1979).

In Norway, **menarche**—*the girl's first menstruation*—occurs at just over 13 years of age, as opposed to 17 years of age in the 1840s. In the United States—where children mature up to a year earlier than children in European countries—the average age of menarche has declined from 14.2 in 1900 to about 12.45 today. The age of menarche has been declining at an average of about four months per decade for the past century (see figure 12.1).

Fortunately, however, we are unlikely to see pubescent toddlers, since what has happened in the past century is special. The best guess is that the something special is a higher level of nutrition and health (Brooks-Gunn, 1991; Eveleth & Tanner, 1990). The available information suggests that menarche began to occur earlier at about the time of the Industrial Revolution, a period associated with increased standards of living and advances in medical science.

In this chapter, we consider further puberty's fascinating changes and other dimensions of the adolescent's physical development. The equally fascinating changes of cognitive development in adolescence are charted. The important contexts of school and work in adolescence are also evaluated. To conclude the chapter, we examine the current status of adolescents and at-risk youth.

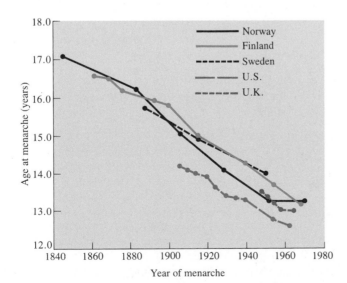

Figure 12.1 Age at menarche in selected northern European countries and the United States from 1845 to 1969.

Physical and Cognitive Development in Adolescence

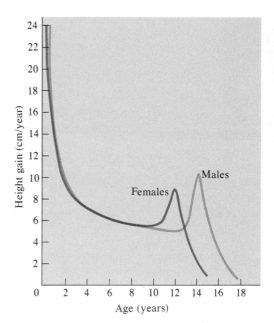

Figure 12.2   The pubertal growth spurt. On the average, the growth spurt that characterizes pubertal change occurs two years earlier for girls (10½ years) than for boys (12½ years).

Physical Development

Menarche is one event that characterizes puberty, but there are others as well. What are puberty's markers? What are the psychological accompaniments of physical changes in adolescence? We consider each of these questions in turn.

Pubertal Change

Puberty *is a period of rapid skeletal and sexual maturation that occurs mainly in early adolescence.* However, puberty is not a single sudden event. It is part of a gradual process. We know when a young person is going through puberty, but pinpointing its beginning and its end is difficult. Except for menarche, which occurs rather late in puberty, no single marker heralds puberty. For boys, the first whisker or first wet dream are events that could mark its appearance but both may go unnoticed.

Behind the first whisker in boys and widening of hips in girls is a flood of hormones, powerful chemical substances secreted by the endocrine glands

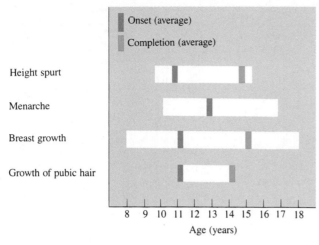

Figure 12.3 *Normal range and average age of the development of sexual characteristics in females.*
From "Growing Up," by J. M. Tanner. Copyright © 1973 Scientific American, Inc. All rights reserved.

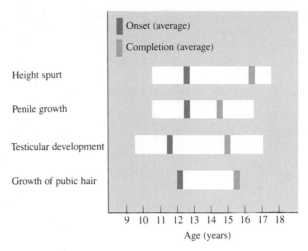

Figure 12.4 *Normal range and average age of the development of sexual characteristics in males.*
From "Growing Up," by J. M. Tanner. Copyright © 1973 Scientific American, Inc. All rights reserved.

and carried through the body by the bloodstream. The concentrations of certain hormones increase dramatically during adolescence (Rabin & Chrousos, 1991; Susman & Dorn, 1991). **Testosterone** *is a hormone associated with the development of genitals, an increase in height, and a change in voice in boys.* **Estradiol** *is a hormone associated with breast, uterine, and skeletal development in girls.* In one investigation, testosterone levels increased eighteenfold in boys but only two-fold in girls during puberty; estradiol increased eightfold in girls but only two-fold in boys (Nottelmann & others, 1987).

These hormonal and body changes occur on the average about two years earlier in females (10½ years of age) than in males (12½ years of age) (see figure 12.2). Four of the most noticeable areas of body change in females are height spurt, menarche, breast growth, and pubic hair; four of the most noticeable areas of body change in males are height spurt, penile growth, testes growth, and pubic hair (Malina, 1991; Tanner, 1973, 1991). The normal and average range of these characteristics is shown in figures 12.3 and 12.4. Among the most remarkable normal variations is that two boys (or two girls) may be the same chronological age, and yet one may complete the pubertal sequence before the other has even begun it. For most girls, the first menstrual period may occur as early as 10 years of age or as late as 15½ years and still be considered normal, for example (Brooks-Gunn, 1988).

Psychological Accompaniments of Physical Changes

A host of psychological changes accompany an adolescent's physical development. Imagine yourself as you were beginning puberty. Not only did you probably think about yourself differently, but your parents and peers probably began acting differently toward you. Maybe you were proud of your changing body, even though you were perplexed about what was happening. Perhaps your parents no longer perceived you as someone they could sit in bed and watch television with or as someone who should be kissed goodnight.

One thing is certain about the psychological aspects of physical change in adolescence: Adolescents are preoccupied with their bodies and develop individual images of what their bodies are like. Perhaps you looked in the mirror daily or even hourly to see if you could detect anything different about your changing body. Preoccupation with one's body image is strong throughout adolescence, but it is especially acute during puberty, a time when adolescents are more dissatisfied with their bodies than in late adolescence (Wright, 1989).

Puberty: the time of life when the two sexes begin to first become acquainted.

~ *Samuel Johnson*

If we listen to boys and girls at the very moment they seem most pimply, awkward and disagreeable, we can partly penetrate a mystery most of us once felt heavily within us, and have now forgotten. This mystery is the very process of creation of man and woman.

~ *Colin Macinnes,*
The World of Children

Physical and Cognitive Development in Adolescence

From *Penguin Dreams and Stranger Things* by Berke Breathed. Copyright © 1985 by The Washington Post Company.

Being physically attractive and having a positive body image are associated with an overall positive conception of one's self. In one investigation, girls who were judged as being physically attractive and who generally had a positive body image had higher opinions of themselves in general (Lerner & Karabenick, 1974). In another investigation, breast growth in girls 9 to 11 years old was associated with a positive body image, positive peer relationships, and superior adjustment (Brooks-Gunn & Warren, 1988).

Some of you entered puberty early, others late, and yet others on time. When adolescents mature earlier or later than their peers, might they perceive themselves differently? Some years ago, in the California Longitudinal Study, early-maturing boys perceived themselves more positively and had more successful peer relations than did their late-maturing counterparts (Jones, 1965). The findings for early-maturing girls were similar but not as strong as for boys. When the late-maturing boys were in their thirties, however, they had developed a stronger sense of identity than the early-maturing boys (Peskin, 1967). Possibly this occurred because the late-maturing boys had more time to explore life's options or because the early-maturing boys continued to focus on their advantageous physical status instead of on career development and achievement.

More recent research confirms, though, that at least during adolescence, it is advantageous to be an early-maturing rather than late-maturing boy (Blyth, Bulcroft, & Simmons, 1981; Simmons & Blyth, 1987). The more recent findings for girls suggest that early maturation is a mixed blessing: These girls experience more problems in school but also more independence and popularity with boys. The time that maturation is assessed is also a factor. In the sixth grade, early-maturing girls showed greater satisfaction with their figures than late-maturing girls, but by the tenth grade, late-maturing girls were more satisfied (figure 12.5). The reason for this is that by late adolescence, early-maturing girls are shorter and stockier, while late-maturing girls are taller and thinner. The late-maturing girls in late adolescence have bodies that more closely approximate the current American ideal of feminine beauty—tall and thin.

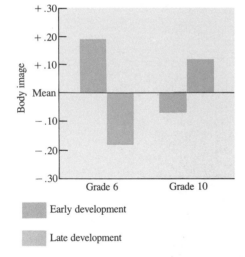

Early development

Late development

Figure 12.5 Early and late maturing adolescent girls' perceptions of body image in early and late adolescence.

Are Puberty's Effects Exaggerated?

Some researchers have begun to question whether puberty's effects are as strong as once believed (Brooks-Gunn & Warren, 1989; Lerner, Petersen, & Brooks-Gunn, 1991; Montemayor, Adams, & Gulotta, 1990). Have the effects of puberty been exaggerated? Puberty affects some adolescents more strongly than others, and some behaviors more strongly than others. Body image, dating interest, and sexual behavior are quite clearly affected by pubertal change. The recent questioning of puberty's effects suggests that if we look at overall development and adjustment in life's human cycle, puberty and its variations have less dramatic effects for most individuals than is commonly thought. For some young adolescents the transition through puberty is stormy, but for most it is not. Each period of life's human cycle has its stresses. Puberty is no different. It imposes new challenges resulting from emerging developmental changes, but the vast majority of adolescents weather these stresses nicely. In thinking about puberty's effects, also keep in mind that the world of adolescents involves not only biological influences on development, but also cognitive and social or environmental influences. As with all periods of human development, these processes work in concert to produce who we are in adolescence. Singling out biological changes as the dominating change in adolescence may not be a wise strategy.

While extreme early or late maturation may be risk factors in development, we have seen that the overall effects of early or late maturation are often not great. Not all early maturers will date, smoke, and drink, and not all late maturers will have difficulty in peer relations. In some instances, the effects of grade in school are stronger than maturational timing effects (Petersen & Crockett, 1985). Because the adolescent's social world is organized by grade rather than pubertal development, this finding is not surprising. However, this does not mean maturation has no influence on development. Rather, we need to evaluate puberty's effects within the larger framework of interacting biological, cognitive, and social contexts (Brooks-Gunn, 1988; Paikoff & Brooks-Gunn, 1990).

Cognitive Developmental Changes

Adolescents' developing power of thought opens up new cognitive and social horizons. Their thought becomes more abstract, logical, and idealistic; more capable of examining one's own thoughts, others' thoughts, and what others are thinking about oneself; and more likely to interpret and monitor the social world. First, we evaluate ideas about Piaget's view of adolescent thought, second, about social cognition in adolescence, and third, about decision making and critical thinking.

Formal Operational Thought

Piaget believed that formal operational thought comes into play between the ages of 11 and 15. Formal operational thought is more *abstract* than a child's thinking. Adolescents are no longer limited to actual concrete experience as the anchor of thought. Instead, they may conjure up make-believe situations, hypothetical possibilities, or purely abstract propositions and reason about them. The adolescent increasingly thinks about thought itself. One adolescent pondered, "I began thinking about why I was thinking what I was. Then I began thinking about why I was thinking about why I was thinking about what I was." If this sounds abstract, it is, and it characterizes the adolescent's increased interest on thought itself and the abstractness of thought.

Accompanying the abstract nature of adolescent thought is the quality of idealism. Adolescents begin to think about ideal characteristics for themselves and others and to compare themselves and others to these ideal standards. In contrast, children think more in terms of what is real and what is limited. During adolescence, thoughts often take fantasy flights into the future. It is not unusual for the adolescent to become impatient with these newfound ideal standards and to be perplexed over which of many ideal standards to adopt.

The error of youth is to believe that intelligence is a substitute for experience, while the error of age is to believe that experience is a substitute for intelligence.

~ *Slyman Bryson*

Figure 12.6   *Formal operational thought.*

Abstract	Idealistic	Logical
Adolescents think more abstractly than children. Formal operational thinkers can solve abstract algebraic equations, for example.	Adolescents often think about what is possible. They think about ideal characteristics of themselves, others, and the world.	Adolescents begin to think more like scientists, devising plans to solve problems and systematically testing solutions. Piaget called this type of logical thinking hypothetical-deductive reasoning.

At the same time adolescents think more abstractly and idealistically, they also think more logically (Kuhn, 1991; Linn, M.C.). Adolescents begin to think more like a scientist, devising plans to solve problems and systematically testing solutions. This type of problem solving has an imposing name. **Hypothetical-deductive reasoning** *is Piaget's formal operational concept that adolescents have the cognitive ability to develop hypotheses, or best guesses, about ways to solve problems, such as an algebraic equation. They then systematically deduce, or conclude, which is the best path to follow in solving the equation.* By contrast, children are more likely to solve problems in a trial-and-error fashion. Figure 12.6 summarizes the main features of formal operational thought.

Some of Piaget's ideas on formal operational thought are currently being challenged (Byrnes, 1988; Danner, 1989; Keating, in press; Lapsley, 1989; Overton & Byrnes, 1991; Overton & Montangero, 1991). There is much more individual variation in formal operational thought than Piaget envisioned. Only about one in three young adolescents is a formal operational thinker. Many American adults never become formal operational thinkers, and neither do many adults in other cultures. Consider the following conversation between a researcher and an illiterate Kpelle farmer in the West African country of Liberia (Scribner, 1977):

> *Researcher:* All Kpelle men are rice farmers. Mr. Smith is not a rice farmer. Is he a Kpelle man?
>
> *Kpelle farmer:* I don't know the man. I have not laid eyes on the man myself.

Members of the Kpelle culture who had gone through formal schooling answered the researcher in a logical way. As with our discussion of concrete operational thought in chapter 10, we find that cultural experiences influence whether individuals reach a Piagetian stage of thought. Education in the logic of science and mathematics is an important cultural experience that promotes the development of formal operational thinking.

Also, for adolescents who become formal operational thinkers, assimilation (incorporating new information into existing knowledge) dominates the initial development of formal operational thought and the world is perceived too subjectively and idealistically. Later in adolescence, as intellectual balance is restored, these individuals accommodate (adjust to new information) to the cognitive upheaval that has occurred.

Social Cognition

Impressive changes in social cognition characterize adolescent development. Adolescents develop a special type of egocentrism, begin to think about personality not unlike the way personality theorists do, and monitor their social world in sophisticated ways.

Adolescent thought is egocentric. David Elkind (1976) believes that **adolescent egocentrism** *has two parts: an imaginary audience and a personal fable.* The **imaginary audience** *is the adolescent's belief that others are as preoccupied with her as she herself* is. Attention-getting behavior, so common in adolescence, reflects egocentrism and the desire to be on stage, noticed, and visible. Imagine the eighth-grade boy who thinks he is an actor and all the others are the audience as he stares at the small spot on his trousers. Imagine the seventh-grade girl who thinks that all eyes are riveted on her complexion because of the tiny blemish she has.

Jennifer talks with her best friend, Anne, about something she has just heard. "Anne, did you hear about Barbara. You know she fools around a lot. Well, the word is she is pregnant. Can you believe it? That would never happen to me." Later in the conversation, Anne tells Jennifer, "I really like Bob, but sometimes he is a jerk. He just can't understand me. He has no clue about what my personal feelings are." The **personal fable** *is the part of the adolescent egocentrism involving an adolescent's sense of uniqueness.* Adolescents' sense of personal uniqueness makes them feel that no one can understand how they really feel. For example, an adolescent girl thinks that in no way can her mother sense the hurt that she feels because her boyfriend broke up with her. As part of their effort to retain a sense of personal uniqueness, adolescents may craft a story about the self that is filled with fantasy, immersing themselves in a world that is far removed from reality. Personal fables frequently show up in adolescent diaries.

Developmentalists have increasingly studied adolescent egocentrism in recent years. The research interest focuses on what the components of egocentrism really are, the nature of self-other relationships, why egocentric thought emerges in adolescence, and the role of egocentrism in adolescent problems. For example, David Elkind (1985) believes that adolescent egocentrism is brought about by formal operational thought. Others, however, argue that adolescent egocentrism is not entirely a cognitive phenomenon. Rather, they think the imaginary audience is due both to the ability to think hypothetically (formal operational thought) and the ability to step outside oneself and anticipate the reactions of others in imaginative circumstances (perspective taking) (Lapsley, 1985, 1990, 1991; Lapsley & others, 1986; Lapsley & Murphy, 1985; Lapsley & Rice, 1988; O'Connor & Nikolio, 1990).

Some developmentalists believe that egocentrism may account for some of the seemingly reckless behavior of adolescents, including drug use, suicidal thoughts, and failure to use contraceptives during intercourse (Elkind, 1978;

The colorful attire of this skateboarder reflects adolescent egocentrism. Attention-getting behavior reflects the desire to be on stage and noticed. The risk-taking behavior of skateboarding, as well as racing cars, taking drugs, and many other behaviors, reflects adolescents' sense of indestructibility. Joseph Conrad once commented, "I remember my youth and the feeling that never came back anymore—the feeling that I could last forever, outlast the sea, the earth, and all men."

I remember my youth and that feeling that never came back to me anymore—the feeling that I could last forever, outlast the sea, the earth, and all men.

~ *Joseph Conrad*

Dolcini & others, 1989). The reckless behavior may stem from the egocentric characteristics of uniqueness and invulnerability. In one recent investigation, eleventh and twelfth grade females who were high in adolescent egocentrism estimated they were less likely to get pregnant if they engaged in sex without contraception than those who were low in adolescent egocentrism (Arnett, 1990).

Adolescents also begin to interpret personality not unlike the way personality theorists do (Barenboim, 1981, 1985). First, when adolescents are given information about another person, they consider previously acquired information and current information and do not rely solely on the concrete information at hand, as children do. Second, adolescents are more likely to detect the contextual or situational variability in the behavior of themselves and others, rather than thinking that they and others always behave consistently. Third, rather than merely accepting surface traits as a valid description of another person or themselves, adolescents begin to look for deeper, more complex—even hidden—causes of personality.

As part of their increased awareness of others—including what others are doing and thinking—adolescents engage in social monitoring. For example, Bob, a 16-year-old, feels he does not know as much as he wants or needs to know about Sally, another 16-year-old. He also wants to know more about Sally's relationship with Brian, a 17-year-old. Bob decides that he wants to know more about the groups Sally belongs to—her student council friends, the clique she is in, and so on. Adolescents use a number of social monitoring methods on a daily basis. For example, an adolescent may check incoming information about an organization (school, club, or group of friends) to determine if it is consistent with the adolescent's impression of the group. Still another adolescent may question someone or paraphrase what that person has just said about her feelings to ensure that he has understood them correctly. Yet another adolescent may meet someone new and quickly think, "It's going to be hard to really get to know him" (Flavell, 1979).

Decision Making and Critical Thinking

Adolescence is a time of increased decision making and also an important juncture in the development of critical thinking. Adolescence is a time when individuals make decisions about the future, which friends to choose, whether to go to college, which person to date, whether to have sex, whether to take drugs, whether to buy a car, and so on. How competent are adolescents at making decisions? Older adolescents are more competent than younger adolescents, who in turn are more competent than children (Keating, 1990). Young adolescents are more likely than children to generate options, to examine a situation from a variety of perspectives, to anticipate the consequences of decisions, and to consider the credibility of sources (Mann, Harmoni, & Power, in press). However, young adolescents are less competent at these decision-making skills than are older adolescents.

Transitions in decision making appear at approximately 11 to 12 years of age and at 15 to 16 years of age. For example, in one study, eighth-, tenth-, and twelfth-grade students were presented with dilemmas involving the choice of a medical procedure (Lewis, 1981). The oldest students were most likely to spontaneously mention a variety of risks, to recommend consultation with an outside specialist, and to anticipate future consequences. For example, when asked a question about whether to have cosmetic surgery, a twelfth grader said that different aspects of the situation need to be examined along with its effects on the individual's future, especially relationships with other people. By contrast, an eighth grader provided a more limited view, commenting on the surgery's effects on getting turned down for a date, the money involved, and being teased at school by peers.

However, the decision-making skills of older adolescents and adults is often far from perfect. And the ability to make decisions does not guarantee that such decisions will be made in everyday life, where breadth of experience often comes into play (Jacobs & Potenza, 1990; Keating, 1990). For example, driver training courses improve the adolescent's cognitive and motor skills to levels equal to, or sometimes superior to, those of adults. However, driver training has not been effective in reducing adolescents' high rate of traffic accidents (Potvin, Champagne, & Laberge-Nadeau, 1988). Thus, an important research agenda is to study the ways adolescents make decisions in practical situations.

Adolescents need more opportunities to practice and discuss realistic decision making. Many real-world decisions occur in an atmosphere of stress, involving such factors as time constraints and emotional involvement. One strategy to improve adolescent decision making about real-world choices involving such matters as sex, drugs, and daredevil driving is for schools to develop more opportunities for adolescents to engage in role playing and group problem solving related to such circumstances (Mann, Harmoni, & Power, in press).

In some instances, adolescents' decision making may be blamed when in reality the problem involves society's orientation toward adolescents and the failure to provide adolescents adequate choices (Keating, 1990). For example, a mathematically precocious ninth-grade girl may abandon mathematics not because of poor decision-making skills but because of a stronger motivation to maintain positive peer relations that would be threatened if she stayed in the math tract. The decision of an adolescent in a low-income inner city area to engage in drug trafficking even at considerable risk may not be a consequence of the adolescent's failure to consider all of the relevant information, but may be the outcome of quite sophisticated thinking about risk-benefit ratios in oppressive circumstances offering limited or nonexistent options. As cognitive developmentalist Daniel Keating observes, if we dislike adolescents' choices, perhaps we need to provide them with better options from which to choose.

Closely related to making competent decisions is engaging in critical thinking, a current buzzword in education and psychology (Ennis, 1991; Jones, Idol, & Brandt, 1991). Although today's definitions of **critical thinking** *vary, they have in common the notions of grasping the deeper meaning of problems, of keeping an open mind about different approaches and perspectives, and of deciding for oneself what to believe or do.* Another, often implicit assumption is that critical thinking is a very important aspect of everyday reasoning (Galotti, 1989). Adolescents should be encouraged to engage in critical thinking, not just inside the classroom but outside it as well.

Adolescence is an important transitional period in the development of critical thinking (Keating, 1990, 1991). Among the important cognitive changes that allow improved critical thinking in adolescence are:

- increased speed, automaticity, and capacity of information processing, which free cognitive resources for other purposes
- more breadth of content knowledge in a variety of domains
- increased ability to construct new combinations of knowledge
- a greater range and more spontaneous use of strategies or procedures for applying or obtaining knowledge, such as planning, considering alternatives, and cognitive monitoring

While adolescence is an important period in the development of critical thinking skills, without the development of a solid basis of fundamental skills (such as literacy and math skills) in childhood, such critical thinking skills are

Concept Table 12.1: Physical and Cognitive Development in Adolescence

Concept	Processes/Related Ideas	Characteristics/Description
Physical Development	Pubertal Change	Puberty is a period of rapid skeletal and sexual maturation that occurs mainly in early adolescence. Testosterone plays an important role in male pubertal development, estradiol in female pubertal development. The growth spurt for boys occurs about two years later than for girls, with 12½ being the average age of onset for boys, 10½ for girls. Individual maturation in pubertal change is extensive.
	Psychological Accompaniments of Pubertal Changes	Adolescents show a heightened interest in their body image. Early maturation favors boys, at least during adolescence. As adults, though, late maturing boys achieve more successful identities. The results are more mixed for girls.
	Are Puberty's Effects Exaggerated?	Recently, some scholars have expressed doubt that puberty's effects on development are as strong as once believed. It is important to keep in mind that adolescent development is influenced by an interaction of biological, cognitive, and social factors, rather than being dominated by biology. While extreme early or late maturation may place an adolescent at risk, the overall effects of early and late maturation are not great. This is not the same as saying puberty and early or late maturation have no effect on development. They do, but puberty's changes always need to be considered in terms of the larger framework of interacting biological, cognitive, and social factors.
Cognitive Development	Formal Operational Thought	Piaget believed that formal operational thought comes into play between 11 and 15 years of age. Formal operational thought is more abstract, idealistic, and logical than concrete operational thought. Piaget believed that adolescents become capable of using hypothetical deductive reasoning. Some of Piaget's ideas on formal operational thought are currently being challenged.
	Social Cognition	Impressive changes in social cognition characterize adolescent development. Adolescents develop a special type of egocentrism that involves an imaginary audience and a personal fable about being unique. They begin to think about personality not unlike the way personality theorists do, and they monitor their social world in more sophisticated ways.
	Decision Making and Critical Thinking	Adolescence is a time of increased decision making. Older adolescents are more competent at decision making than younger adolescents, who in turn are more competent than children. The ability to make decisions does not guarantee they will be made in practice, because in real life breadth of experience comes into play. Adolescents need more opportunities to practice and discuss realistic decision making. In some instances, adolescents' faulty decision making may be blamed when in reality the problem is society's orientation toward adolescents and failure to provide them with adequate choices. Adolescence is an important transitional period in critical thinking because of such cognitive changes as increased speed, automaticity, and capacity of information processing, more breadth of content knowledge, increased ability to construct new combinations of knowledge, and a greater range and more spontaneous use of strategies. Nonetheless, for critical thinking to develop effectively in adolescence a solid foundation in basic skills and knowledge in childhood is required.

unlikely to mature in adolescence. For the subset of adolescents who lack such fundamental skills, potential gains in adolescent thinking are not likely to occur.

At this point we have discussed a number of ideas about adolescents' physical and cognitive development. A summary of these ideas is presented in concept table 12.1. Now we turn our attention to schools and their effects on adolescent development.

Schools

The impressive changes in adolescents' cognition lead us to examine the nature of schools for adolescents. In chapter 11, we discussed different ideas about the effects of schools on children's development. Here we focus more exclusively on the nature of secondary schools. Among the questions we try to answer are the following: What should be the function of secondary schools? What is the nature of the transition from elementary to middle or junior high school? What is the nature of high school dropouts, and how can we reduce the number of dropouts? Does working part-time affect students' schooling and grades?

> In youth we learn, in age we understand.
>
> ~ *Marie Ebner von Eschenbach,*
> Aphorism, *1904*

The Controversy Surrounding Secondary Schools

During the twentieth century, schools have assumed a more prominent role in the lives of adolescents. From 1890 to 1920, virtually every state developed laws that excluded youth from work and required them to attend school. In this time frame, the number of high school graduates increased 600 percent (Tyack, 1976). By making secondary education compulsory, the adult power structure placed adolescents in a submissive position and made their move into the adult world of work more manageable. In the nineteenth century, high schools were mainly for the elite, with the main educational emphasis on classical liberal arts courses. By the 1920s, educators perceived that the secondary school curriculum needed to be changed. Schools for the masses, it was thought, should not just involve intellectual training, but should also involve training for work and citizenship. The curriculum of secondary schools became more comprehensive and grew to include general education, college preparatory, and vocational education courses. As the twentieth century unfolded, secondary schools continued to expand their orientation, adding courses in music, art, health, physical education, and other topics. By the middle of the twentieth century, schools had moved further toward preparing students for comprehensive roles in life (Conant, 1959). Today, secondary schools have retained their comprehensive orientation, designed to train adolescents intellectually; but they now also train students in many other ways as well, such as vocationally and socially.

While there has been a consistent trend of increased school attendance for more than 150 years, the distress over alienated and rebellious youth led some social scientists to question whether secondary schools actually benefit adolescents. During the early 1970s, three independent panels agreed that high schools contribute to adolescent alienation and actually restrict the transition to adulthood (Brown, 1973; Coleman & others, 1974; Martin, 1976). These prestigious panels argued that adolescents should be given educational alternatives to the comprehensive high school, such as on-the-job community work, to increase their exposure to adult roles and to decrease their sense of isolation from adults. To some degree in response to these reports, a number of states lowered the age at which adolescents could leave school from 16 to 14.

As we enter the last decade of the twentieth century, the back-to-basics movement has gained momentum, with proponents arguing that the main function of schools should be rigorous training of intellectual skills through subjects like English, math, and science (Kearns, 1988). Advocates of the back-to-basics movement point to the excessive fluff in secondary school curricula,

Schools play a prominent role in adolescents' development. Controversy has surrounded just what the nature of this role should be.

with students being allowed to select from many alternatives that will not give them a basic education in intellectual subjects. Some critics also point to the extensive time students spend in extra-curricular activities. They argue that schools should be in the business of imparting knowledge to adolescents and not be so concerned about their social and emotional lives. Related to the proverbial dilemma of schools' functions is whether schools should include a vocational curriculum in addition to training in basic subjects such as English, math, and science. Some critics of the fluff in secondary schools argue that the school day should be longer and that the school year should be extended into the summer months. Such arguments are made by critics who believe that the main function of schools should be the training of intellectual skills. Little concern for adolescents' social and emotional development appear in these arguments (Duke & Canady, 1991; Perkinson, 1991).

Should the main—and perhaps only—major goal of schooling for adolescents be the development of an intellectually mature individual? Or should schools also focus on the adolescent's maturity in social and emotional development? Should schools be comprehensive, providing a multifaceted curriculum that includes many electives and alternative subjects to basic core courses? These are provocative questions that continue to be heatedly debated in educational and community circles (Bloome, 1989; Goodlad, 1983; Sizer, 1984; Tharp & Gallimore, 1989).

Tension may always characterize debate about the function of schools. Should intellectual development be emphasized more than it is even today? Or, should intellectual development be only one of the school's functions? Should preparation of the individual for work, a thirst for lifelong learning in many areas of life, and social and emotional development also be part of the schooling equation? Patricia Cross (1984) argues that tension produces shifts of emphases much like a swinging pendulum, moving toward basic skills at one point in time, and toward options, frills, or comprehensive training for life at another, and so on back and forth. What we should strive for is not a swinging pendulum, but rather something like a spiral staircase. That is, we might continually be developing more sophisticated ways of fulfilling the varied and changing functions of schools.

The transition from elementary to middle or junior high school occurs at the same time a number of other changes are taking place in development. Biological, cognitive, and social changes converge with this schooling transition to make it a time of considerable adaptation.

Transition to Middle or Junior High School

The emergence of junior high schools in the 1920s and 1930s was justified on the basis of physical, cognitive, and social changes that characterize early adolescence, as well as the need for more schools for the growing student population. Old high schools became junior high schools and new regional high schools were built. In most systems, the ninth grade remained a part of the high school in content, although physically separated from it in a 6-3-3 system. Gradually, the ninth grade has been restored to the high school as many school systems have developed middle schools that include the seventh and eighth grades, or sixth, seventh, and eighth grades. The creation of middle schools has been influenced by the earlier onset of puberty in recent decades.

One worry of educators and psychologists is that junior high and middle schools have simply become watered-down versions of high schools, mimicking their curricular and extracurricular schedules (Hill, 1980). The critics argue that unique curricular and extracurricular activities reflecting a wide range of individual differences in biological and psychological development in early adolescence should be incorporated into our junior high and middle schools. The critics also stress that many high schools foster passivity rather than autonomy, and that schools should create a variety of pathways for students to achieve an identity.

The transition to middle school or junior high school from elementary school interests developmentalists because, even though it is a normative experience for virtually all children, the transition can be stressful. Why? Because the transition takes place at a time when many changes—in the individual, in the family, and in school—are taking place simultaneously (Eccles & Midgely, 1990; Hawkins & Berndt, 1985; Hirsch, 1989; Simmons & Blyth, 1987). These changes include puberty and related concerns about body image;

the emergence of at least some aspects of formal operational thought, including accompanying changes in social cognition; increased responsibility and independence in association with decreased dependency on parents; change from a small, contained classroom structure to a larger, more impersonal school structure; change from one teacher to many teachers and a small, homogeneous set of peers to a larger, more heterogeneous set of peers; and increased focus on achievement and performance, and their assessment. This list includes a number of negative, stressful features, but there can be positive aspects to the transition. Students are more likely to feel grown up, have more subjects from which to select, have more opportunities to spend time with peers and to locate compatible friends, enjoy increased independence from direct parental monitoring, and may be more challenged intellectually by academic work.

When students make the transition from elementary school to middle or junior high school, they experience the **top-dog phenomenon,** *the circumstance of moving from the top position (in elementary school, the oldest, biggest, and most powerful students in the school) to the lowest position (in middle or junior high school, the youngest, smallest, and least powerful students in the school).* Researchers who have charted the transition from elementary to middle or junior high school find that the first year of middle or junior high school can be difficult for many students (Eccles & Midgely, 1990; Hawkins & Berndt, 1985; Simmons & Blyth, 1987). For example, in one investigation of the transition from sixth grade in an elementary school to the seventh grade in a junior high school, adolescents' perceptions of the quality of their school life plunged in the seventh grade (Hirsch & Rapkin, 1987). In the seventh grade, the students were less satisfied with school, were less committed to school, and liked their teachers less. The drop in school satisfaction occurred regardless of how academically successful the students were.

What kind of experiences might ease the transition from elementary school to middle or junior high school? Schools that provide more support, less anonymity, more stability, and less complexity improve student adjustment during the transition from elementary school to middle or junior high school (Fenzel, Blyth, & Simmons, 1991). For example, in one investigation, 101 students were studied at three points in time: spring of the sixth grade (pretransition), fall of the seventh grade (early transition), and spring of the seventh grade (late transition) (Hawkins & Berndt, 1985). Two different schools were sampled—one a traditional junior high school, the other a junior high in which the students were grouped into small teams (100 students, four teachers). The students' adjustment was assessed through self-reports, peer ratings, and teacher ratings. Adjustment dropped during the post-transition. For example, the self-esteem of students was lower in the seventh grade than in the sixth grade. More teacher support was reported by students in the team-oriented junior high school, and the nature of friendship was also related to the students' adjustment. Students with greater friendship contact and a higher quality of friendship had a more positive perception of themselves and of their junior high school. These data indicate that a supportive, more intimate school environment and friendship can ease students' stressful school transitions.

What makes a successful middle school? Joan Lipsitz (1984) and her colleagues searched the nation for the best middle schools. Extensive contacts and observations were made. Based on the recommendations of education experts and observations in schools in different parts of the United States, four middle schools were chosen for their outstanding ability to educate young adolescents. What were these middle schools like? The most striking feature was

Much of the educational reform implemented in the last decade has emphasized "back to basics" and removing the "fluff" from secondary schools. However, many experts on middle schools believe that the best schools for young adolescents emphasize social development as well as cognitive development, and adapt their practices to individual differences in students.

their willingness and ability to adapt all school practices to the individual differences in physical, cognitive, and social development of their students. The schools took seriously the knowledge we have developed about young adolescents. This seriousness was reflected in the decisions about different aspects of school life. For example, one middle school fought to keep its schedule of minicourses on Friday so that every student could be with friends and pursue personal interests. Two other middle schools expended considerable energy on a complex school organization so that small groups of students worked with small groups of teachers who could vary the tone and pace of the school day, depending on the students' needs. Another middle school developed an advisory scheme so that each student had daily contact with an adult who was willing to listen, explain, comfort, and prod the adolescent. Such school policies reflect thoughtfulness and personal concern about individuals who have compelling developmental needs.

Another aspect of the effective middle schools was that, early in their existence—the first year in three of the schools and the second year in the fourth school—they emphasized the importance of creating an environment that was positive for the adolescent's social and emotional development. This goal was established not only because such environments contribute to academic excellence, but also because social and emotional development are intrinsically valued as important in themselves in adolescents' schooling.

Recognizing that the vast majority of middle schools do not approach the excellent schools described by Joan Lipsitz (1984), in 1989 the Carnegie Corporation issued an extremely negative evaluation of our nation's middle schools. In the report, "Turning Points: Preparing American Youth for the 21st Century," the conclusion was reached that most young adolescents attend massive, impersonal schools, learn from seemingly irrelevant curricula, trust few adults in school, and lack access to health care and counseling. The Carnegie report recommends the following:

- Develop smaller "communities" or "houses" to lessen the impersonal nature of large middle schools.
- Lower student-to-counselor ratios from several hundred-to-1 to 10-to-1.
- Involve parents and community leaders in schools.

• *Critical Thinking* •

Analyze your own middle school or junior high school. How did it measure up to Lipsitz's criteria for effective schools for young adolescents?

- Develop curriculum that produces students who are literate, understand the sciences, and have a sense of health, ethics, and citizenship.
- Have teachers team teach in more flexibly designed curriculum blocks that integrate several disciplines instead of presenting students with disconnected, rigidly separated 50-minute segments.
- Boost students' health and fitness with more in-school programs and help students who need public health care to get it.

Many of these same recommendations were echoed in a report from the National Governor's Association (America in Transition, 1989), which stated that the very structure of middle school education in America neglects the basic developmental needs of young adolescents. Many educators and psychologists strongly support these recommendations (Entwistle, 1990). The Edna McConnell Clark Foundation's Program for Disadvantaged Youth is an example of a multiyear, multisite effort designed to implement many of the proposals for middle school improvement. The Foundation has engaged the Center for Early Adolescence at the University of North Carolina to guide five urban school districts in their middle school reform (Scales, 1990). In sum, middle schools throughout the nation need a major redesign if they are to be effective in educating adolescents for becoming competent adults in the twenty-first century.

High School Dropouts

For many decades, dropping out of high school has been viewed as a serious educational and societal problem. By leaving high school before graduating, many dropouts take with them educational deficiencies that severely curtail their economic and social well-being throughout their adult lives (Rumberger, 1987). We will study the scope of the problem, the causes of dropping out, and ways to reduce dropout rates. While dropping out of high school often has negative consequences for youth, the picture is not entirely bleak (William T. Grant Foundation Commission on Work, Family, and Citizenship, 1988). Over the last forty years, the proportion of adolescents who have not finished high school has decreased considerably. In 1940, more than 60 percent of all individuals 25 to 29 years of age had not completed high school. By 1986, this proportion had dropped to less than 14 percent. From 1973 to 1983, the annual dropout rate nationwide fell by almost 20 percent, from 6.3 to 5.2 percent.

Despite the decline in overall high school dropout rates, a major concern is the higher dropout rate of minority group and low-income students, especially in large cities (Carrasquillo, 1991; Eccles, 1991; McCall, 1991). While the dropout rates of most minority group students have been declining, they remain substantially above those of White students. Hispanic youth made up a disproportionate percentage of high school dropouts in 1986. More than one-third of Hispanic youth, about 17 percent of Black youth, and 13.5 percent of White youth had dropped out (William T. Grant Foundation, 1989). Dropout rates are also high for Native Americans (fewer than 10 percent graduate from high school) (LaFromboise & Low, 1989). In some inner city areas the dropout rate for ethnic-minority students is especially high, reaching more than 50 percent in Chicago, for example (Hahn, 1987).

Students drop out of schools for many reasons (Bachman, 1991; Goertz, Ekstrom, & Rock, 1991). In one investigation, almost 50 percent of the dropouts cited school-related reasons for leaving school, such as not liking school or being expelled or suspended (Rumberger, 1983). Twenty percent of the dropouts (but 40 percent of the Hispanic students) cited economic reasons for leaving school. One-third of the female students dropped out for personal reasons, such as pregnancy or marriage.

To help reduce the dropout rate, community institutions, especially schools, need to break down the barriers between work and school. Many youth step off the education ladder long before reaching the level of a professional career, often with nowhere to step next, left to their own devices to search for work. These youth need more assistance than they are now receiving. Among the approaches worth considering are (William T. Grant Foundation on Work, Family, and Citizenship, 1988):

- monitored work experiences, such as through cooperative education, apprenticeships, internships, preemployment training, and youth-operated enterprises.
- community and neighborhood services, including voluntary and youth-guided services.
- redirected vocational education, the principal thrust of which should not be preparation for specific jobs but acquisition of basic skills needed for a wide range of jobs.
- guarantees of continuing education, employment, or training, especially in conjunction with mentor programs.
- career information and counseling to expose youth to job opportunities and career options as well as to successful role models.
- school volunteer programs, not only for tutoring but also for providing access to adult friends and mentors.

For more information about improving our nation's education of minority-group students, turn to Cultural Worlds of Development 12.1.

Part-Time Work and School

In 1940, only 1 of 25 tenth-grade males attended school while working part-time. In the 1970s, the number had increased to more than 1 of every 4. And, in the 1980s, as just indicated, 3 of 4 combined school and part-time work. Adolescents are also working longer hours now than in the past. For example, the number of 14- and 15-year-olds who work more than 14 hours per week has increased substantially since 1960. A similar picture emerges for 16-year-olds. In 1960, 44 percent of 16-year-old males who attended school worked more than 14 hours a week, but by the 1980s, the figure had increased to more than 60 percent.

What kinds of jobs are adolescents working at today? About 17 percent who work do so in restaurants, such as McDonald's, Burger King, and the like, waiting on customers, cleaning up, and so on. Other adolescents work in retail stores as cashiers or salespeople (about 20%), in offices as clerical assistants (about 10%), or as unskilled laborers (about 10%) (Cole, 1981).

Do male and female adolescents take the same type of jobs and are they paid equally? Some jobs are held almost exclusively by male adolescents— busboys, gardeners, manual laborers, and newspaper carriers—while other jobs are held almost exclusively by female adolescents—babysitters and maids. Male adolescents work longer hours and are paid more per hour than female adolescents (Helson, Elliott, & Leigh, 1989).

Does the increase in work have benefits for adolescents? In some cases, yes; in others, no. Ellen Greenberger and Laurence Steinberg (1981) examined the work experiences of students in four California high schools. Their

HELPING HISPANIC YOUTH STAY IN SCHOOL AND GO TO COLLEGE

*T*he Hispanic population in the United States is increasing more rapidly than any other ethnic minority. Educators are increasingly interested in helping Hispanic adolescents stay in school and succeed in the courses needed for educational and occupational success. As colleges compete to recruit seniors from the small pool of college-eligible and college-ready Hispanics, it is apparent that the pool itself needs to be greatly expanded. Gloria De Necochea (1988) described seven strategies to help keep Hispanic adolescents in school and get them ready to go to college:

1. Identify students early for a college preparatory curriculum. As early as the sixth grade, both students and parents need to know about the college preparatory curriculum and the long-term consequences of choices.
2. Give more attention to math and science. Mathematics and science are critical for both college admissions and a range of career options, but these subjects pose big barriers for Hispanic students. Success can be increased by teaching the complex academic language necessary to tackle these subjects effectively. This is especially important in grades 7 through 9, where the gatekeeping course—algebra—for future scientific and technical courses is taught.
3. Increase school participation. Counselors and teachers can make college-related information more visible throughout the school. Precollege clubs can be developed. Administrators can invite college representatives,

These Hispanic youth leaders, participating in a mock legislation session, are positive examples of the increased concern for helping Hispanic youth stay in school and go to college.

alumni, and individuals in different careers to address students. Critical-thinking skills can be stressed. And teachers can occasionally tailor the structure of exams to be more like the SAT and the ACT.
4. Expose students to the world of college. College recruiters, faculty, and financial-aid officers are important role models and sources of current information. Visits to colleges enable youth to gain firsthand knowledge about campus life (Justiz & Rendon, 1989).
5. Increase workshops. Study skills, assertiveness training, and survival tips can be taught. College-related topics such as

"How to choose a college" and "What to say to college admissions officers" should be offered during the senior year.
6. Involve parents. Invitations to all activities should be bilingual and mailed home well in advance of the event. To increase attendance, students can provide child care. Parents should be encouraged to come to workshops and to participate in planning activities.
7. Organize outside support. Better coordination between community organizations and schools could provide a central source for descriptions of available programs at the school and in the community.

findings disproved some common myths. For example, generally it is assumed that adolescents get extensive on-the-job training when they are hired for work; the reality is that they get little training at all. Also, it is assumed that youths, through work experiences, learn to get along better with adults. However, adolescents reported that they rarely felt close to the adults with whom they worked. The work experiences of the adolescents did help them to understand how the business world works, how to get and keep a job, and how to manage money. Working also helped adolescents learn to budget their time, to take pride in their accomplishments, and to evaluate their goals. But working adolescents often have to give up sports, social affairs with peers, and sometimes sleep. And they have to balance the demands of work, school, family, and peers.

Greenberger and Steinberg asked students about their grade-point averages, school attendance, satisfaction from school, and the number of hours spent studying and participating in extracurricular activities since they began working. They found that working adolescents have lower grade-point averages than nonworking adolescents. More than one of four students reported that their grades dropped when they began working; only one of nine said that their grades improved. But it was not just working that affected adolescents' grades; more importantly, it was *how long* they worked. Tenth-graders who worked more than 14 hours a week suffered a drop in grades. Eleventh-graders worked up to 20 hours a week before their grades dropped. When adolescents work more than 20 hours per week, they have little time to study for tests and to complete homework assignments.

Problems and Disturbances

What are some of the major problems and disturbances that adolescents may encounter? They include drug and alcohol abuse, delinquency, adolescent pregnancy, suicide, and eating disorders, each of which we consider in turn.

Drugs and Alcohol

The 1960s and 1970s were a time of marked increases in the use of illicit drugs. During the social and political unrest of those years, many youth turned to marijuana, stimulants, and hallucinogens. Increases in alcohol consumption by adolescents also were noted (Robinson & Greene, 1988). More precise data about drug use by adolescents have been collected in recent years. Each year since 1975, Lloyd Johnston, Patrick O'Malley, and Gerald Bachman (1988, 1989, 1990, 1991), working at the Institute of Social Research at the University of Michigan, have carefully monitored drug use by America's high school seniors in a wide range of public and private high schools. From time to time, they also sample the drug use of younger adolescents and adults as well.

An encouraging finding from the most recent survey (conducted in 1990) of 15,676 high school seniors is the continued gradual decrease in the use of illicit drugs (Johnston, O'Malley, & Bachman, 1991). Nonetheless, the United States still has the highest rate of drug use among the world's industrialized nations. In 1990, 48 percent of the nation's high school seniors had tried an illicit drug other than marijuana. A special concern is the use of alcohol and cocaine by adolescents, each of which we consider in turn.

Alcohol

Some mornings, 15-year-old Annie was too drunk to go to school. Other days, she'd stop for a couple of beers or a screwdriver on the way to school. She was tall, blonde, and good looking, and no one who sold her liquor, even at 8:00 in

What is the pattern of alcohol consumption among adolescents?

the morning, questioned her age. Where did she get her money? From baby-sitting and from what her mother gave her to buy lunch. Annie used to be a cheerleader, but no longer; she was kicked off the squad for missing practice so often. Soon, she and several of her peers were drinking almost every morning. Sometimes, they skipped school and went to the woods to drink. Annie's whole life began to revolve around her drinking.

This routine went on for two years, and during the last summer, any time anyone saw her, she was drunk. After a while, Annie's parents discovered her problem. But even though they punished her, it did not stop her drinking. Finally, this year, Annie started dating a boy she really liked and who would not put up with her drinking. She agreed to go to Alcoholics Anonymous and has just successfully completed treatment. She has stopped drinking for four consecutive months now, and she hopes that her abstinence will continue.

Alcohol is the drug most widely used by adolescents in our society. For them, it has produced many enjoyable moments and many sad ones as well. Alcoholism is the third-leading killer in the United States, with more than 13 million people classified as alcoholics, many of whom established their drinking habits during adolescence. Each year, approximately 25,000 people are killed and 1.5 million injured by drunk drivers. In 65 percent of the aggressive male acts against females, the offender has been under the influence of alcohol (Goodman & others, 1986). In numerous instances of drunk driving and assaults on females, the offenders have been adolescents.

How extensive is alcohol use by adolescents? Although the use of marijuana and other drugs among adolescents has declined recently, adolescents do not seem to be drinking more to offset their reduced intake of other drugs. Alcohol use by high school seniors has gradually declined. Monthly use declined from 72 percent in 1980 to 60 percent in 1989. The prevalence of drinking five or more drinks in a row during the prior two-week interval fell from 41 percent in 1983 to 32 percent in 1990. There remains a substantial sex difference in heavy adolescent drinking: 28 percent of females versus 46 percent for males in 1986, although this difference diminished gradually during the 1980s. However, data from college students show only a slight drop in alcohol use and heavy drinking. For example, 75 percent of the college students surveyed in 1990 said they had consumed alcohol in the prior month, down from a high of 83 percent in 1982, and 41 percent reported at least one occasion of heavy drinking in the prior two weeks, down from a high of 45 percent in 1986. Heavy drinking at parties among college males continues to be common (Johnston, O'Malley, & Bachman, 1991).

Cocaine

Did you know that cocaine was once an ingredient in Coca-Cola? Of course, it has long since been removed from the soft drink. *Cocaine* comes from the coca plant, native to Bolivia and Peru. For many years Bolivians and Peruvians chewed the plant to increase their stamina. Today cocaine is usually snorted, smoked, or injected in the form of crystals or powder. The effect is a rush of euphoric feelings, which eventually wear off, followed by depressive feelings, lethargy, insomnia, and irritability.

Cocaine is a highly controversial drug. Users claim it is exciting, makes them feel good, and increases their confidence. Yet it is clear that cocaine has potent cardiovascular effects and is potentially addictive. The deaths of sports stars, such as University of Maryland basketball player Len Bias, demonstrate how lethal cocaine can be. When the drug's effects are extreme, it can cause a heart attack, a stroke, or a brain seizure. The increase in cocaine-related deaths is often traced to very pure or tainted forms of the drug (Gold, Gallanter, & Stimmel, 1987).

Adolescence

Cocaine use, which remained at peak levels throughout much of the 1980s, began an important decline in 1987 that continued through 1990 in high school and college students (Johnston, O'Malley, & Bachman, 1991). Among high school seniors the proportion who are current users of cocaine fell dramatically from 1986 to 1990, from 6.2 percent to 1.9 percent. An even larger proportional drop in current use was observed among American college students over the same time interval—from 7 percent to 1.2 percent. A growing proportion of high school seniors and college students are reaching the conclusion that cocaine use holds considerable, unpredictable risk for the user.

The Role of Parents, Peers, and Schools in Adolescent Drug Use
Most adolescents become drug users at some point in their development, whether their use is limited to alcohol, caffeine, and cigarettes or extended to marijuana, cocaine, and hard drugs. A special concern occurs when adolescents use drugs as a way of coping with stress, a practice that can interfere with the development of competent coping skills and responsible decision making. Researchers have found that when drug use occurs initially in childhood or early adolescence, it has more detrimental long-term effects on the development of responsible, competent behavior than when drug use occurs initially in late adolescence (Newcomb & Bentler, 1988). By using drugs to cope with stress, young adolescents often enter adult roles of marriage and work prematurely without adequate socioemotional growth, and they experience greater failure in adult roles (Gabrielli, 1990; Moos, Finney, & Cronkite, 1990).

A special concern in the use of drugs by adolescents is the role parents, peers, and schools play in preventing and reducing drug use. Families play an important role in adolescent drug use (Dielman, Shope, & Butchart, 1990; Brook & Brook, in press; Brook & others, 1990; Cohen, Brook, & Kandel, 1991; Kandel, 1991). In one recent longitudinal investigation, boys' poor self-control at age 4 was related to their drug use in adolescence, and permissive parenting in the families of girls at age 4 was related to their drug use in adolescence (Block & Block, 1988). In another investigation, social support during adolescence substantially reduced drug use (Newcomb & Bentler, 1988). In this study, social support included good relationships with parents, other adults, siblings, and peers. Another researcher found that the greatest use of drugs by adolescents takes place when both the adolescents' parents take drugs (such as tranquilizers, amphetamines, alcohol, or nicotine) and the adolescents' peers take drugs (Kandel, 1974).

Schools are involved in drug use because they frequently are the place where peers initiate and maintain drug use (Dryfoos, 1990). Schools can play an important role in preventing or reducing drug use; there are few other settings where the adolescent population congregates on such a frequent basis. Although most schools have established policies on drug use, some have gone further and developed drug prevention or intervention programs (Bailey, 1989; Minuchin & Shapiro, 1983). The most promising school programs have been those involving comprehensive long-term approaches, not only providing specific information and services, but dealing with the social organization of the school as a whole as well. Programs that have emphasized detection, discipline, and scare tactics have been the least effective in preventing or reducing drug use by adolescents.

Juvenile Delinquency
Arnie is 13 years old. His history includes a string of thefts and physical assaults. The first theft occurred when Arnie was 8; he stole a SONY walkman from an electronics store. The first physical assault took place a year later

when he shoved his 7-year-old brother up against the wall, bloodied his face, and then threatened to kill him with a butcher knife. Recently, the thefts and physical assaults have increased. In the last week, he stole a television set and struck his mother repeatedly and threatened to kill her. He also broke some neighborhood street lights and threatened some youths with a wrench and a hammer. Arnie's father left home when Arnie was 3 years old. Until the father left, his parents argued extensively and his father often beat up his mother. Arnie's mother indicates that when Arnie was younger, she was able to control his behavior; but in the last several years she has not been able to enforce any sanctions on his antisocial behavior. Because of Arnie's volatility and dangerous behavior, it was recommended that he be placed in a group home with other juvenile delinquents.

The label **juvenile delinquent** *is applied to an adolescent who breaks the law or engages in behavior that is considered illegal.* Like other categories of disturbance, juvenile delinquency is a broad concept; legal infractions range from littering to murder. Because the adolescent technically only becomes a juvenile delinquent after being judged guilty of a crime by a court of law, official records do not accurately reflect the number of illegal acts juvenile delinquents commit. Estimates regarding the number of juvenile delinquents in the United States are sketchy, but FBI statistics indicate that at least 2 percent of all youths are involved in juvenile court cases. The number of girls found guilty of juvenile delinquency has increased substantially in recent years. Delinquency rates among Blacks, other minority groups, and the lower class are especially high in proportion to the overall population of these groups. However, such groups have less influence over the judicial decision-making process in the United States and therefore may be judged delinquent more readily than their White, middle-class counterparts (Gold, 1987; Polier, 1989).

What causes delinquency? Many causes have been proposed, including heredity, identity problems, community influences, and family experiences (Kennedy, 1991). Erik Erikson (1968), for example, believes that adolescents whose development has restricted them from acceptable social roles or made them feel that they cannot measure up to the demands placed on them may choose a negative identity. The adolescent with a negative identity may find support for his delinquent image among peers, reinforcing the negative identity. For Erikson, delinquency is an attempt to establish an identity, although it is a negative identity.

Although delinquency is less exclusively a lower-class phenomena than it was in the past, some characteristics of the lower-class culture may promote delinquency (Simons & Gray, 1989). The norms of many lower-class peer groups and gangs are antisocial, or counterproductive, to the goals and norms of society at large. Getting into and staying out of trouble became prominent features of life for some adolescents in low-income neighborhoods. Adolescents from low-income backgrounds may sense that they can gain attention and status by performing antisocial actions. Being "tough" and "masculine" are high-status traits for lower-class boys, and these traits are often measured by the adolescent's success in performing and getting away with delinquent acts. A community with a high crime rate also lets the adolescent observe many models who engage in criminal activities. These communities may be characterized by poverty, unemployment, and feelings of alienation toward the middle class. Quality schooling, educational funding, and organized neighborhood activities may be lacking in these communities (Chesney-Lind, 1989).

Family support systems are also associated with delinquency. Parents of delinquents are less skilled in discouraging antisocial behavior and in encouraging skilled behavior than are parents of nondelinquents. Parental monitoring of adolescents is especially important in determining whether an adolescent becomes a delinquent (Patterson, DeBarsyhe, & Ramsey, 1989;

Patterson & Grimaldi, 1991). "Its 10 P. M.; do you know where your children are?" seems to be an important question for parents to answer affirmatively. Family discord and inconsistent and inappropriate discipline are also associated with delinquency.

A special concern in delinquency has surfaced recently: escalating gang violence, which is being waged on a level more lethal than ever before. Knives and clubs have been replaced by grenades and automatic weapons, frequently purchased with money made from selling drugs. The lure of gang membership is powerful, especially for children and adolescents who are disconnected from family, school, work, and the community. Children as young as 9 years of age cling to the fringes of neighborhood gangs, eager to prove themselves worthy of membership by the age of 12. Once children are members of a gang, it is difficult to get them to leave. Recommendations for prevention of gang violence involve identification of disconnected children in elementary schools and initiation of counseling with the children and their families (Calhoun, 1988).

A large book could be filled just with brief descriptions of the varied attempts to reduce delinquency. These attempts include forms of individual and group psychotherapy, family therapy, behavior modification, recreation, vocational training, alternative schools, survival camping and wilderness canoeing, incarceration and probation, "Big Brothers" and "Big Sisters," community organizations, and Bible reading (Gold & Petronio, 1980). However, we actually know surprisingly little about what actually helps reduce delinquency, and in many instances, prevention and intervention have not been successful (Leitenberg, 1986; Lundman, 1984; Rabkin, 1987).

While few successful models of delinquency prevention and intervention have been identified, there are a number of points that many experts on delinquency agree should be examined more closely because they are likely candidates for better prevention and intervention (Dryfoos, 1990):

1. Programs should be broader than just focusing on delinquency (O'Donnell, Manos, & Chesney-Lind, 1987). For example, it is virtually impossible to improve delinquency prevention without considering the quality of education available to high-risk youth.

2. Programs should have multiple components because no one component has been found to be the "magic bullet" that decreases delinquency.

3. Programs should begin early in the child's development to prevent learning and conduct problems (Berrueta-Clement & others, 1986).

4. Schools play an important role. Schools with strong governance, fair discipline policies, student participation in decision making, and high investment in school outcomes by both students and staff are important candidates for improving the school's role in curbing delinquency (Hawkins & Lam, 1986; Hawkins & Lishner 1987).

5. Efforts should often be directed at institutional rather than individual change. Especially important is upgrading the quality of education for disadvantaged children.

6. While point 5 is accurate, researchers have found that intensive individual attention and personalized planning are important factors in working with children at high risk for becoming delinquent.

7. Program benefits often "wash out" after the program stops. Thus, maintenance programs and continued effort are usually necessary.

In her recent review of delinquency prevention, Joy Dryfoos (1990) also outlined what has not worked in preventing delinquency. What doesn't work in preventing or reducing delinquency includes preventive casework, group counseling, pharmacological interventions (except for extremely violent behavior), work experience, vocational education, "scaring straight" efforts, and the juvenile justice system. Current school practices that are ineffective in reducing delinquency include suspension, detention, expulsion, security guards, and corporal punishment.

Adolescent Pregnancy

Angela is 15 years old and pregnant. She reflects, "I'm three months pregnant. This could ruin my whole life. I've made all of these plans for the future and now they are down the drain. I don't have anybody to talk to about my problem. I can't talk to my parents. There is no way they can understand." Pregnant adolescents were once practically invisible and unmentionable. But yesterday's secret has become today's national dilemma (Rosenbaum & Kandel, 1990; Scott-Jones & White, 1990).

They are of different ethnic groups and from different places, but their circumstances have a distressing sameness. Each year more than 1 million American teenagers will become pregnant, four out of five of them are unmarried. They represent a flaw in our nation's social fabric. Like Angela, many become pregnant in their early or middle adolescent years, 30,000 of them under the age of 15. In all, this means that one of every ten adolescent females in the United States becomes pregnant each year, with eight of the ten pregnancies unintended (National Research Council, 1987). As one 17-year-old Los Angeles mother of a 1-year-old boy said, "We are children having children." The only bright spot in the adolescent pregnancy statistics is that the adolescent pregnancy rate, after increasing during the 1970s, has leveled off and may even be beginning to decline (Hofferth, 1990; National Research Council, 1987).

The adolescent pregnancy rate in the United States is the highest of any in the Western world. It is more than twice the rates in England, France, or Canada, almost three times the rate in Sweden, and seven times the rate in the Netherlands (Alan Guttmacher Institute, 1981; Forrest, 1990; Jones & others, 1985) (see figure 12.7). Although American adolescents are no more sexually active than their counterparts in these other nations, they are many more times likely to become pregnant.

Adolescent pregnancy is a complex American problem, one that strikes many nerves. The subject of adolescent pregnancy touches on many explosive social issues: the battle over abortion rights, contraceptives and the delicate question of whether adolescents should have easy access to them, and the perennially touchy subject of sex education in the public schools (Hofferth, 1990).

Dramatic changes involving sexual attitudes and social morals have swept through the American culture in the last three decades. Adolescents actually gave birth at a higher rate in 1957 than they do today, but that was a time of early marriage, with almost 25 percent of 18- and 19-year-olds married. The overwhelming majority of births to adolescent mothers in the 1950s occurred within a marriage and mainly involved females 17 years of age and older. Two or three decades ago, if an unwed adolescent girl became pregnant, in most instances her parents had her swiftly married off in a shotgun wedding. If marriage was impractical, the girl would discreetly disappear, the child would be put up for adoption, and the predicament would never be discussed again. Abortion was not a real option for most adolescent females until 1973, when the Supreme Court ruled it could not be outlawed.

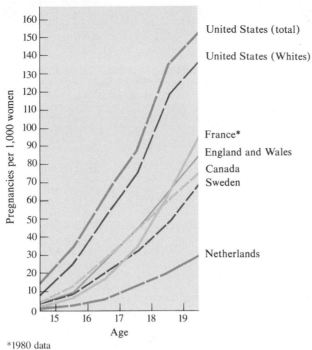

*1980 data

Note: pregnancies are defined here as births plus abortions; age is the age at outcome.

Figure 12.7 **Pregnancy rates per 1,000 women, by age, 1981 (Jones & others, 1985).**

In today's world of adolescent pregnancies, a different scenario unfolds. If the girl does not choose to have an abortion (some 45 percent of pregnant adolescent girls do), she usually keeps the baby and raises it without the traditional involvement of marriage. With the stigma of illegitimacy largely absent, girls are less likely to give up their babies for adoption. Fewer than 5 percent do, compared with about 35 percent in the early 1960s. But while the stigma of illegitimacy has waned, the lives of most pregnant teenagers are anything but rosy.

The consequences of our nation's high adolescent pregnancy rate are of great concern. Adolescent pregnancy increases the health risks of both the child and the mother. Infants born to adolescent mothers are more likely to have low birth weights (a prominent cause of infant mortality), as well as neurological problems and childhood illnesses (Dryfoos, 1990; Furstenberg, Brooks-Gunn, & Chase-Lansdale, 1989). Adolescent mothers often drop out of school, fail to gain employment, and become dependent on welfare. Although many adolescent mothers resume their education later in life, they generally do not catch up with women who postpone childbearing. In the National Longitudinal Survey of Work Experience of Youth, it was found that only half of the women 20 to 26 years old who first gave birth at age 17 had completed high school by their twenties. The percentage was even lower for those who gave birth at a younger age (table 12.1) (Mott & Marsiglio, 1985). By contrast, among young females who waited until age 20 to have a baby, more than 90 percent had obtained a high school education. Among the younger adolescent mothers, almost half had obtained a General Equivalency Diploma (GED), which does not often open up good employment opportunities.

These educational deficits have negative consequences for the young women themselves and for their children (Kenney, 1987). Adolescent parents are more likely than those who delay childbearing to have low-paying, low-status jobs or to be unemployed. The mean family income of White females

Table 12.1: Percentage Distribution of Women, age 20 to 26 in 1983, by Type of High School Completion, According to Age at First Birth

Age at First Birth	High School Completion by 1983		
	Total (%)	Diploma (%)	GED (%)
15	45	24	21
16	49	28	21
17	53	38	15
18	62	52	10
19	77	68	9
Under 20	90	86	4

Source: Frank L. Mott and William Marsiglio, "Early Childbearing and Completion of High School" in *Family Planning Perspectives*, September/October 1985. Copyright © 1985 Alan Guttmacher Institute, New York, NY.

who give birth before age 17 is approximately half that of families in which the mother delays birth until her mid- or late twenties.

Serious, extensive efforts need to be developed to help pregnant adolescents and young mothers enhance their educational and occupational opportunities. Adolescent mothers also need extensive help in obtaining competent day care and in planning for the future (Furstenberg, 1991; Furstenberg, Brooks-Gunn, & Morgan, 1987). Experts recommend that to reduce the high rate of teen pregnancy, adolescents need improved sex-education and family-planning information, greater access to contraception, and broad community involvement and support (Conger, 1988; Treboux & Busch-Rossnagel, 1991; Wallace & Vienonen, 1989). And another very important consideration, especially for young adolescents, is abstention, which is increasingly being included as a theme in sex education classes.

As indicated earlier, adolescent pregnancy is not a major problem in many European countries, especially the Scandinavian countries and Holland. To learn more about adolescent sexual orientation in Holland and Sweden, turn to Perspective on Life-Span Development 12.1.

Suicide

Suicide is a common problem in our society. Its rate has tripled during the last thirty years in the United States; each year about 25,000 people take their own lives. Beginning at about the age of 15, the rate of suicide begins to rise rapidly. Suicide accounts for about 12 percent of the mortality in the adolescent and young adult age group (Brent, 1989). Males are about three times as likely to commit suicide as females; this may be because of their more active methods for attempting suicide—shooting, for example. By contrast, females are more likely to use passive methods such as sleeping pills, which are less likely to produce death. While males commit suicide more frequently, females attempt it more frequently (Maltsberger, 1988).

Estimates indicate that for every suicide in the general population, six to ten suicide attempts are made. For adolescents the figure is as high as fifty attempts for every life taken. As many as two in every three college students has thought about suicide on at least one occasion; their methods range from drugs to crashing into the White House in an airplane.

Why do adolescents attempt suicide? There is no simple answer to this important question. It is helpful to think of suicide in terms of proximal and

• *Critical Thinking* •

You have been assigned to design a community program to reduce the rate of adolescent pregnancy in your community. What would the program be like?

Adolescence

ADOLESCENT SEXUAL ORIENTATION IN HOLLAND AND SWEDEN

◆

*I*n Holland, as well as in other European countries, such as Sweden, sex does not carry the mystery and conflict it does in American society. Holland does not have a mandated sex-education program, but adolescents can obtain contraceptive counseling at government-sponsored clinics for a small fee. The Dutch media also have played an important role in educating the public about sex through frequent broadcasts focused on birth control, abortion, and related matters. Most Dutch adolescents do not consider having sex without birth control.

Swedish adolescents are sexually active at an earlier age than are American adolescents, and they are exposed to even more explicit sex on television. However, the Swedish National Board of Education has developed a curriculum that ensures that every child in the country, beginning at age 7, will experience a thorough grounding in reproductive biology, and by the ages of 10 or 12 will have been introduced to information about various forms of contraceptives. Swedish teachers are expected to handle the subject of sex whenever it becomes relevant, regardless of the subject they are teaching. The idea is to dedramatize and demystify sex so that familiarity will make the individual less vulnerable to unwanted pregnancy and sexually transmitted diseases (Wallis, 1985). American society is not nearly so open about sex education.

distal factors. Proximal, or immediate, factors can trigger a suicide attempt. Highly stressful circumstances such as the loss of a boyfriend or a girlfriend, failing a class at school, or an unwanted pregnancy can produce a suicide attempt. Drugs also have been involved more often in recent suicide attempts than in attempts in the past (Rich, Young, & Fowler, 1986).

But distal, or earlier, experiences are often involved in suicide attempts as well. A longstanding history of family instability and unhappiness may be present (Shapiro & Freedman, 1989). Just as a lack of affection and emotional support, high control, and pressure for achievement by parents during childhood are related to adolescent depression, so are such combinations of family experiences likely to show up as distal factors in suicide attempts. Lack of supportive friendships may also be present (Rubenstein & others, 1989). In an investigation of suicide among gifted women, previous suicide attempts, anxiety, conspicuous instability in work and in relationships, depression, or alcoholism were also present in the women's lives (Tomlinson-Keasey, Warren, & Elliott, 1986). These factors are similar to those found to predict suicide among gifted men (Shneidman, 1971).

Just as genetic factors are associated with depression, so are they associated with suicide. The closer the genetic relationship a person has to someone who has committed suicide, the more likely that person is to commit suicide (Wender & others, 1986). The advice offered in table 12.2 provides valuable information about what to do and what not to do when you suspect an adolescent is contemplating suicide.

Eating Disorders

Fifteen-year-old Jane gradually eliminated foods from her diet to the point where she subsisted by eating *only* applesauce and eggnog. She spent hours observing her own body, wrapping her fingers around her waist to see if it was getting any thinner. She fantasized about becoming a beautiful fashion model who would wear designer bathing suits. But even when she reached 85 pounds, Jane still felt fat. She continued to lose weight, eventually emaciating herself. She was hospitalized and treated for **anorexia nervosa,** *an eating disorder that*

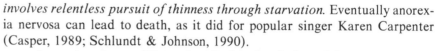

TABLE 12.2: What to Do and What Not to Do When You Suspect Someone Might Commit Suicide

What to Do

1. Calmly ask direct, straightforward questions: "Are you thinking about hurting yourself?"
2. Assess the seriousness of the suicidal intent by asking questions about feelings, important relationships, whom else the person has talked with, and the amount of thought given to the means to be used. If a gun, pills, rope, or other means has been obtained and a precise plan developed, the situation is dangerous. Stay with the person until help arrives.
3. Be a good listener and be very supportive without being falsely reassuring.
4. Try to persuade the person to obtain professional help and assist him or her in getting it.

What Not to Do

1. Do not ignore the warning signs.
2. Do not refuse to talk about suicide if a person approaches you about the topic.
3. Do not react with horror, disapproval, or repulsion.
4. Do not give false reassurances by saying such things as "Everything is going to be OK." Also do not give simple answers or platitudes such as "You have everything to be thankful for."
5. Do not abandon the person after the crisis has passed or after professional help has commenced.

From *Living With 10- to 15-Year-Olds: A Parent Education Curriculum* by Gayle Dorman, et al. Copyright 1982 by the Center for Early Adolescence, University of North Carolina at Chapel Hill, Carrboro, NC. Reprinted by permission.

Anorexia nervosa has become an increasingly frequent problem among adolescent females.

involves relentless pursuit of thinness through starvation. Eventually anorexia nervosa can lead to death, as it did for popular singer Karen Carpenter (Casper, 1989; Schlundt & Johnson, 1990).

Anorexia nervosa afflicts primarily females during adolescence and early adulthood (only about 5 percent of anorexics are male). Most individuals with this disorder are White and from well-educated middle- and upper-income families. Although anorexics avoid eating, they have an intense interest in food, they cook for others, they talk about food, and they insist on watching others eat. Anorexics have a distorted body image, perceiving themselves as beautiful even when they have become skeletal in appearance. As self-starvation continues and the fat content of the body drops to a bare minimum, menstruation usually stops. Behavior is often hyperactive (Polivy & Thomsen, 1987).

Numerous causes of anorexia nervosa have been proposed. They include societal, psychological, and physiological factors (Attie & Brooks-Gunn, 1989; Brumberg, 1988; Fisher & Brone, 1991; Litt, 1991; Stern & others, 1989). The societal factor most often held responsible is the current fashion of thinness. Psychological factors include motivation for attention, desire for individuality, denial of sexuality, and a way of coping with overcontrolling parents. Anorexics sometimes have families that place high demands for achievement on them. Unable to meet their parents' high standards, anorexics feel unable to control their own lives. By limiting their food intake, anorexics gain some sense of self-control. Physiological causes focus on the hypothalamus, which becomes abnormal in a number of ways when the individual is anorexic (Brumberg, 1988). At this time, however, we are not exactly certain what causes anorexia nervosa.

Bulimia *is an eating disorder that involves a binge-and-purge sequence on a regular basis.* The bulimic binges on large amounts of food and then purges by self-induced vomiting or use of a laxative. The binges sometimes alternate with fasting; at other times they alternate with normal eating behavior. Like anorexia nervosa, bulimia is primarily a female disorder. Bulimia has become prevalent among college women. Some estimates suggest that one in two college women binge and purge at least some of the time. However, recent estimates suggest that true bulimics—those who binge and purge on a regular basis—make up less than 2 percent of the college female population (Stunkard, 1987). While anorexics can control their eating, bulimics cannot. Depression is a common characteristic of bulimics (Levy, Dixon, & Stern, 1989). Many of the same causes proposed for anorexia nervosa are offered for bulimia.

So far we have discussed a number of specific problems and disturbances in adolescence. As we see next, many adolescents do not experience a single problem, but rather their problems are often interrelated.

The Current Status of Today's Adolescents and At-Risk Youth

What is the current status of adolescents in the United States? Do adults have idealized images of adolescents and does society communicate ambivalent messages to adolescents? Which youth are at risk? We consider each of these questions in turn.

The Current Status of Adolescents

Today's adolescents face demands and expectations, as well as risks and temptations, that appear to be more numerous and complex than did adolescents only a generation ago (Feldman & Elliott, 1990). Nonetheless, contrary to the popular stereotype of adolescents as highly stressed and incompetent, the vast majority of adolescents successfully negotiate the path from childhood to adulthood (Offer & Church, 1991). By some criteria, today's adolescents are doing better than their counterparts from a decade or two earlier. Today, more adolescents complete high school, especially Black American adolescents. In the last few years, accidents and homicides have declined somewhat, as have drug use, juvenile delinquency, and adolescent pregnancy rates. The majority of adolescents today have positive self-conceptions and have positive relationships with others. Such contemporary findings do not reveal a portrayal of adolescence as a highly disturbed, overly stressful time period in the life cycle. Rather, the majority of adolescents find the transition from childhood to adulthood to be a time of physical, cognitive, and social development that provides considerable challenge, opportunities, and growth (Santrock, in press).

While the majority of adolescents experience the transition from childhood to adulthood more positively than is portrayed by many adults and the media, too many adolescents today are not provided with adequate opportunities and support to become competent adults. In many ways, today's adolescents are presented with a less stable environment than adolescents of a decade or two ago. High divorce rates, high adolescent pregnancy rates, and increased geographic mobility of families contribute to this lack of stability in adolescents' lives. Today's adolescents are exposed to a complex menu of life-style options through the media. And while the adolescent drug rate is beginning to show signs of decline, the rate of adolescent drug use in the United States is the highest of any country in the industrialized Western world. Many of today's adolescents face these temptations, as well as sexual activity, at increasingly young ages.

The above discussion underscores an important point about adolescents: They are not a homogeneous group of individuals. The majority of adolescents negotiate the lengthy path to adult maturity successfully, but too large a minority do not. Ethnic, cultural, gender, socioeconomic, age, and life-style differences influence the actual life trajectory of each adolescent.

Different portrayals of adolescence often emerge, depending on the particular group of adolescents being described. As we see next, some of the problems faced by today's adolescents involve adults' idealized images of what adolescence should be and society's ambivalent messages to adolescents.

Idealized Images of Adolescence and Society's Ambivalent Messages to Adolescents

Adolescent developmental researchers Shirley Feldman and Glenn Elliott (1990) recently described how our society seems to be uncertain about what adolescence should be or should not be. The following examples illustrate how adults' idealized images of adolescence and society's ambivalent messages to adolescents may contribute to adolescent problems:

- Many adults treasure the independence of youth, yet insist that adolescents do not have the maturity to make autonomous, competent decisions about their lives. Some of the ambiguity in messages about adult status and maturity that society communicates to adolescents appears in the form of laws dictating that they cannot drive until they are 16, vote until they are 18, or drink until age 21, yet in some states, 14-year-olds now have the legal right to choose the parent with whom they want to live after a parental divorce and to override parental wishes about such medical matters as abortion and psychiatric care.
- Society's sexual messages to adolescents are especially ambiguous. Adolescents are somehow supposed to be sexually naive but become sexually knowledgeable. The message to many adolescents is: You can experiment with sex and "sow your wild oats," but be sure to maintain high standards of maturity and safety. Adolescents must negotiate this formidable task in a society that cannot agree on how much and what kind of explicit sex education adolescents should be given. This same society sanctions alluring messages about the power and attractiveness of sexuality in the media.
- Laws prohibit adolescents from using alcohol, tobacco, or other drugs, and adults decry the high level of drug use by adolescents. Yet many of the very same adults who stereotype and criticize adolescents for their drug use are themselves drug abusers and heavy cigarette smokers.
- Society promotes education and the development of knowledge as essential to success as an adult. Yet, adolescents frequently observe the rewards society doles out to individuals who develop their athletic skills and business acumen. As adolescents interact with adults who do not value the process of learning, adolescents may attach more importance to simply attaining a diploma than to the process of getting one.

At-Risk Youth

While adolescence is best viewed as a time of decision making and commitment rather than a time of crisis and pathology, a large subset of adolescents are at risk because their likelihood of becoming productive adults is limited.

Adolescence

Four areas of special concern that make up a large portion of at-risk youth are: delinquency, substance abuse, adolescent pregnancy, and school failure or dropout (Dryfoos, 1990). Earlier in the chapter, we considered each of these problems separately. However, there is a growing awareness that these high-risk behaviors often overlap with many adolescents showing problems in more than one area (Scales, 1990). No actual data exist to quantify at-risk status of youth, but experts on adolescence estimate that *very high-risk youth*—those with multiple-problem behaviors—make up about 5 to 10 percent of the adolescent population (Dryfoos, 1990). This group includes adolescents who have been arrested or have committed serious offenses, have dropped out of school or are behind their grade level, are users of "heavy" drugs, drink frequently, regularly use cigarettes and marijuana, and are sexually active but do not use contraception. Many but not all very high-risk youth "do it all."

High-risk youth include another 10 to 15 percent of the youth population. They participate in these same behaviors with a lower frequency and less deleterious consequences. They commit less serious delinquent offenses; however they are heavy users of alcohol, cigarettes, and marijuana; they engage in unprotected sexual intercourse; and they are behind in school. This group often engages in two or three problem behaviors. Overall, 2 to 3 million adolescents are at very high risk, while 3 to 4 million are at high risk (Dryfoos, 1990). Very high-risk and high-risk adolescents are more often males than females, live in cities rather than suburban or rural areas, and often come from families that are poor and have low education levels.

In a recent analysis of successful programs focused on at-risk youth, conducted for the Carnegie Foundation, Joy Dryfoos (1990) found that two approaches had the widest application: providing individual attention to at-risk children and adolescents, and developing broad community-wide interventions. In successful programs, at-risk youth are attached to a responsible adult who pays attention to the adolescent's specific needs. For example, in substance abuse programs, a student assistance counselor might be available full-time for individual counseling. In delinquency prevention, a family worker might give "intensive" support to a predelinquent and the family so they will make the necessary changes to avoid repeated delinquent acts. In pregnancy prevention, a full-time social worker might be placed in the school system for individual counseling. In school remediation, a prevention specialist might work with at-risk adolescents and their families to improve school attendance.

The basic concept of community-wide programs is that to improve the lives of at-risk youth a number of programs and services need to be in place. For example, a substance abuse program might involve a community-wide health promotion that uses local media and community education in conjunction with a substance abuse prevention curricula in the schools. A delinquency program might consist of a neighborhood development program that includes local residents in neighborhood councils who work with schools, police, courts, gang leaders, and the media. A pregnancy prevention program might concentrate on community education through media and a speaker's bureau; training of parents, clergy, and other community leaders; and developing and implementing a comprehensive sex and family life education program in the schools. The problem of dropping out of school might be addressed by an all-out community effort involving schools and local businesses, local government agencies, and universities in planning, teacher training, and student training and job placement.

As the twenty-first century approaches, the well-being of adolescents should be one of America's foremost concerns. We all cherish the future of our youth, because they are the future of any society. Adolescents who do not

Concept Table 12.2: Schools, Problems, and Disturbances; and the Current Status of Today's Adolescents and At-Risk Youth

Concept	Processes/Related Ideas	Characteristics/Description
Schools	Function of Schools	In the nineteenth century, secondary schools were for the elite. By the 1920s, they had changed, becoming more comprehensive and training adolescents for work and citizenship, as well as improving their intellect. The comprehensive high school remains today, but the function of secondary schools continues to be debated. Some maintain that the function should be intellectual development; others argue for more comprehensive functions.
	Transition to Middle or Junior High School	The emergence of junior high schools in the 1920s and 1930s was justified on the basis of physical, cognitive, and social changes in early adolescence and the need for more schools in response to a growing student population. Middle schools have become more popular in recent years, coinciding with puberty's earlier arrival. The transition to middle or junior high school coincides with many social, familial, and individual changes in the adolescent's life. The transition involves moving from the top-dog to the bottom-dog position. Successful schools for young adolescents take individual differences in development seriously, show a deep concern for what is known about early adolescence, and emphasize social and emotional development as much as intellectual development.
	High School Dropouts	Dropping out has been a serious problem for decades. Many dropouts have educational deficiencies that curtail their economic and social well-being for much of their adult lives. Some progress has been made; dropout rates for most ethnic-minority groups have declined in recent decades, although dropout rates for inner-city, low-income minorities are still precariously high. Students drop out of school for school-related, economic, and personal reasons. To reduce the dropout rate, community institutions, especially schools, need to break down the barriers between work and school.
	Part-Time Work and School	There has been a tremendous increase in the number of adolescents who work part-time and go to school, which has both advantages and disadvantages.

reach their full potential, who are destined to make fewer contributions to society than it needs, and who do not take their place as productive adults diminish the power of that society's future (Horowitz & O'Brien, 1989).

At this point we have discussed a number of ideas about schools, problems and disturbances, and the current status of adolescents and at-risk youth. A summary of these ideas is presented in concept table 12.2. In the next chapter, we turn our attention to the social worlds of adolescence.

Concept	Processes/Related Ideas	Characteristics/Description
Problems and Disturbances	Drugs and Alcohol	The United States has the highest adolescent drug use rate of any industrialized nation. The 1960s and 1970s were a time of marked increase in adolescent drug use. Since the mid-1980s there has been a slight overall downturn in drug use among adolescents. Alcohol is the drug most widely used by adolescents; alcohol abuse by adolescents is a major problem. Heavy drinking is common. Cocaine is a highly controversial drug. Its use by high school seniors dropped off for the first time in eight years in 1987, a trend that has continued. Parents, peers, and schools play important roles in adolescent drug use.
	Juvenile Delinquency	A juvenile delinquent is an adolescent who breaks the law or engages in conduct that is considered illegal. Heredity, identity problems, community influences, and family experiences have been proposed as causes of delinquency. Parents' failure to discourage antisocial behavior and encourage skilled behavior, as well as parents' lack of monitoring of the adolescent's whereabouts, are related to delinquency. Successful programs do not focus on delinquency alone (rather they include other components, such as education), have multiple components but no one component is a "magic bullet," begin early in the child's development, often involve schools, focus on institutions, also emphasize giving individual attention to delinquents, and include maintenance.
	Adolescent Pregnancy	More than 1 million American adolescents become pregnant each year. Eight of 10 adolescent pregnancies are unintended. Our nation's adolescent pregnancy rate is the highest in the Western world. Dramatic changes have swept through the American culture in the last three decades regarding adolescent sexuality and pregnancy. The consequences of adolescent pregnancy include health risks for the mother and the offspring. Adolescent mothers often drop out of school, fail to gain employment, and become dependent on welfare. Experts are calling for increased sex education and family planning, access to contraceptive methods, and broad community involvement and support. Abstinence should also be considered in adolescence.

(continued on next page)

Summary

I. Pubertal Change

Puberty is a period of rapid skeletal and sexual maturation that occurs mainly during early adolescence. Testosterone plays an important role in male pubertal development, es-tradiol in female pubertal development. The growth spurt for boys occurs about two years later than for girls with 12½ being the average age of onset for boys, 10½ for girls. Individual maturation in pubertal change is extensive.

II. Psychological Accompaniments of Pubertal Change and Evaluation of Pubertal Effects

Adolescents show a heightened interest in their body image. Early maturation favors boys, at least during adolescence. As adults,

Concept	Processes/Related Ideas	Characteristics/Description
	Suicide	The rate of suicide has increased. Beginning at about the age of 15, the rate of suicide increases dramatically. Both proximal and distal factors are involved in suicide's causes.
	Eating Disorders	Anorexia nervosa and bulimia have increasingly become problems for adolescent females. Societal, psychological, and physiological causes of these disorders have been proposed.
The Current Status of Adolescents and At-Risk Youth	The Current Status of Adolescents	The majority of adolescents today successfully negotiate the path from childhood to adulthood. By some criteria, today's adolescents are also doing better than their counterparts from a decade or two earlier. However, too many of today's adolescents are not provided with adequate opportunities and support to become competent adults. In many ways, today's adolescents are presented with a less stable environment than a decade or two ago. It is important to view adolescents as a heterogeneous group because a different portrayal emerges depending on the particular set of adolescents being described.
	Idealized Images of Adolescence and Society's Ambivalent Messages to Adolescents	Our society seems to be uncertain about what adolescence should be or should not be. There are many areas, such as independence, sexuality, laws and values, and education, in which adults entertain idealized images of adolescents but communicate ambivalent messages to adolescents that may contribute to adolescents' problems.
	At-Risk Youth	There is a growing awareness that high-risk behaviors in adolescence often overlap with four areas of special concern: delinquency, substance abuse, adolescent pregnancy, and school failure or dropout. From 15 to 25 percent of adolescents are at risk because their likelihood of becoming productive adults is limited. Two approaches have the widest application to improving the lives of at-risk youth: providing individual attention to at-risk children and adolescents and developing broad community-wide interventions.

though, late-maturing boys achieve more successful identities. The results are more mixed for girls. Recently some scholars have expressed doubt that puberty's effects are as strong as once believed. It is important to keep in mind that adolescent development is influenced by an interaction of biological, cognitive, and social factors, rather than being dominated by biology. While extreme early or late maturation can place an adolescent at risk, the overall effects of early and late maturation are not great. This is not the same thing as saying puberty and early or late maturation have no effect on development. They do, but puberty's changes always need to be considered in terms of the larger framework of interacting biological, cognitive, and social factors.

III. Formal Operational Thought
Piaget believed that formal operational thought comes into play between 11 and 15 years of age. Formal operational thought is more abstract, idealistic, and logical than concrete operational thought.

Piaget believed that adolescents become capable of using hypothetical deductive reasoning. Some of Piaget's ideas on formal operational thought are currently being challenged.

IV. Social Cognition, Decision Making, and Critical Thinking

Impressive changes in social cognition characterize adolescent development. Adolescents develop a special type of egocentrism that involves an imaginary audience and a personal fable about being unique. They begin to think not unlike the way personality theorists do, and they monitor their social world in more sophisticated ways. Adolescence is a time of increased decision making. Older adolescents are more competent at decision making than younger adolescents, who in turn are more competent than children. The ability to make decisions does not guarantee they will be made in practice, because in real life breadth of experience comes into play. Adolescents need more opportunities to practice and discuss realistic decision making. In some instances, adolescents' faulty decision making may be blamed when in reality the problem is society's orientation toward adolescents and failure to provide them with adequate choices. Adolescence is also an important transitional period in critical thinking because of such cognitive changes as increased speed, automaticity, and capacity for information processing, more breadth of content knowledge, increased ability to construct new combinations of knowledge, and a greater range and more spontaneous use of strategies. Nonetheless, for critical thinking to develop effectively in adolescence, a solid foundation in basic skills and knowledge in childhood is required.

V. Function of Schools

In the nineteenth century, secondary schools were for the elite. By the 1920s, they had changed, becoming more comprehensive and training adolescents for work and citizenship, as well as intellect. The comprehensive high school remains today, but the function of secondary schools continues to be debated. Some maintain that the function of secondary schools should be intellectual development; others argue for more comprehensive functions.

VI. Transition to Middle or Junior High School

The emergence of junior high schools in the 1920s and 1930s was justified on the basis of physical, cognitive, and social changes in early adolescence and the need for more schools in response to a growing student population. Middle schools have become more popular in recent years, coinciding with the earlier arrival of puberty. The transition to middle or junior high school coincides with many social, familial, and individual changes in the adolescent's life. The transition involves moving from the top-dog to the bottom-dog position. Successful schools for young adolescents take individual differences in development seriously, show a deep concern for what is known about early adolescence, and emphasize social and emotional development as much as intellectual development.

VII. High School Dropouts and Part-Time Work and Schools

Dropping out of school has been a serious problem for decades. Many dropouts have educational deficiencies that curtail their economic and social well-being for much of their adult lives. Some progress has been made, however; dropout rates for most ethnic-minority groups have declined in recent decades, although the dropout rates for inner-city, low-income minorities are still precariously high. Students drop out of school for school-related, economic, and personal reasons. To reduce the drop-out rate, community institutions, especially schools, need to break down the barriers between work and school. There has been a tremendous increase in the number of adolescents who work part-time and go to school, which has both advantages and disadvantages.

VIII. Drugs and Alcohol

The United States has the highest adolescent drug use rate of any industrialized nation. The 1960s and 1970s were a time of marked increase in adolescent drug use. Since the mid-1980s, there has been a slight downturn in drug use among adolescents. Alcohol is the drug most widely used by adolescents; alcohol abuse by adolescents is a major problem. Heavy drinking is common. Cocaine is a highly controversial drug. Its use by high school seniors dropped off for the first time in eight years in 1987, a trend that has continued. Parents, peers, and schools play important roles in adolescent drug use.

IX. Adolescent Pregnancy

More than 1 million American adolescents become pregnant each year. Eight of ten adolescent pregnancies are unintended. Our nation's adolescent pregnancy rate is the highest in the Western world. Dramatic changes have swept through the American culture in the last three decades regarding adolescent sexuality and pregnancy. The consequences of adolescent pregnancy include health risks for the mother and the offspring. Adolescent mothers often drop out of school, fail to gain employment, and become dependent on welfare. Experts are calling for increased sex education and family planning, access to contraceptive methods, and broad community involvement and support. Abstinence should also be considered in adolescence.

X. Juvenile Delinquency

A juvenile delinquent is an adolescent who breaks the law or engages in illegal conduct. Heredity, identity problems, community influences, and family experiences have been proposed as delinquency's causes. Parents' failure to discourage antisocial behavior and encourage skilled behavior, as well as parents' lack of monitoring of the adolescent's whereabouts, are related to delinquency. Successful programs do not focus on delinquency alone (rather they include other components such as education), have multiple components but no one component is a "magic bullet," begin early in the child's development, often involve schools, focus on institutions, also emphasize giving individual attention to delinquents, and include maintenance.

XI. **Suicide and Eating Disorders**
The rate of suicide has increased; suicide increases dramatically at about the age of 15. Both proximal and distal factors are involved in suicide's causes. Anorexia nervosa and bulimia have become increasing problems for adolescents. Societal, psychological, and physiological causes of these disorders have been proposed.

XII. **The Current Status of Today's Adolescents, Idealized Images of Adolescence, and Society's Ambivalent Messages to Adolescents**
The majority of adolescents today successfully negotiate the path from childhood to adulthood. By some criteria, today's adolescents are doing better than their counterparts from a decade or two earlier. However, too many of today's adolescents are not provided adequate opportunities and support to become competent adults. In many ways, today's adolescents are presented with a less stable environment than a decade or two ago. It is important to view adolescents as a heterogeneous group because a different portrayal of adolescence emerges depending on the set of adolescents being described. Our society seems uncertain about what adolescents should be or should not be. There are many areas, such as independence, sexuality, laws and values, and education, in which adults entertain idealized images of adolescence but communicate ambivalent messages to adolescents that may contribute to their problems.

XIII. **At-Risk Youth**
There is a growing awareness that high-risk behaviors in adolescence often overlap with four areas of special concern: delinquency, substance abuse, adolescent pregnancy, and school failure or dropout. From 15 to 25 percent of adolescents are at risk because their likelihood of becoming productive adults is limited. Two approaches have the widest application to improving the lives of at-risk youth: providing individual attention to at-risk children and adolescents, and developing broad community-wide interventions.

Key Terms

Suggested Readings

Dryfoos, J. G. (1990). *Adolescents at risk: Prevalence and prevention.* New York: Oxford University Press.
This excellent book provides a broad overview of at-risk youth and programs to improve their lives.

Keating, D. P. (1990). Adolescent thinking. In S. S. Feldman & G. R. Elliott (Eds.), *At the threshold: The developing adolescent.* Cambridge, MA: Harvard University Press.
This is an authoritative, up-to-date overview of a wide-ranging set of ideas about adolescent cognition. Especially valuable are the author's discussions of decision making and critical thinking in adolescence.

Lipsitz, J. (1984). *Successful schools for young adolescents.* New Brunswick, NJ: Transaction Books.
Important reading for anyone interested in better schools for young adolescents. Filled with rich examples of adolescents in schools.

Paikoff, R. L., & Brooks-Gunn, J. (1990). Physiological processes: What role do they play during the transition to adolescence? In R. Montemayor, G. R. Adams, & T. P. Gulotta (Eds.), *From childhood to adolescence: A transitional period.* Newbury Park, CA: Sage.
Different models for interpreting puberty's effects on adolescent development are presented and evaluated, along with a very up-to-date research overview of what is known about pubertal changes and psychological development.

Phi Delta Kappan. A leading educational journal. Leaf through the issues of the 1980s to get a feel for controversial, widely debated ideas in secondary education.

The William T. Grant Foundation Commission on Work, Family and Citizenship. (1980). *The forgotten half: Non-college youth in America.* New York.
This excellent report on the status of non-college youth in America calls attention to ways our society can help these individuals more effectively make the transition to work.

CHAPTER 13

Social Development in Adolescence

Y ou have lived through adolescence. I, too, was an adolescent. No one else experienced adolescence in quite the same way you or I did— your thoughts, feelings, and actions during your adolescent years, like mine, were unique. But we also encountered and handled some experiences in the same ways during adolescence. In high school, we learned many of the same skills that other students learned and grew to care about the same things others cared about. Peers were important to us. And, at one time or another, we probably felt that our parents had no idea what we were all about.

Not only did we feel that our parents misunderstood us, but our parents felt that we misunderstood them. Parents want to know why adolescents have mercurial moods—happy one moment, sad the next. They want to know why their teenagers talk back to them and challenge their rules and values. They want to know what parenting strategies will help them rear a psychologically healthy, competent adolescent who will become a mature adult. What should they do when their adolescents increasingly rely on peers to influence their decisions—in some cases, peers whose backgrounds the parents detest? Parents worry that their adolescent will have a drinking problem, a smoking problem, a drug problem, a sex problem, a school problem, and so on. They want to know if the situations they are experiencing with their adolescents are unique, or if other parents are experiencing the same difficulties and frustrations with their youth.

The social worlds of adolescents are many and fascinating. Through experiences with parents, siblings, peers, friends, clique members, teachers, and other adults, adolescents make the transition from being a child to being an adult. There are many hills and valleys in this transition, and there are times when parent-child relationships become strained. But a large majority of adolescents make the transition from childhood to adulthood competently, continuing to be attached to their parents and exploring an ever-widening social world as they move toward more autonomous behavior and decision making. As they make the transition from child to adult, a major concern of adolescents is the development of an identity: Who am I, What am I all about, and Where am I headed in life? In this chapter, we explore the social worlds of adolescents and the adolescent's concern with identity.

Families

In chapter 11 we discussed how parents spend less time with their children during middle and late childhood than in early childhood, how discipline involves an increased use of reasoning and deprivation of privileges, how there is a gradual transfer of control from parents to children but still within the boundary of coregulation, and how parents and children increasingly respond to each other on the basis of labels. What are some of the most important issues and questions that need to be raised about family relationships in adolescence? They include: What is the nature of autonomy and attachment in adolescence? How extensive is parent-adolescent conflict and how does it influence the adolescent's development? Do maturation of the adolescent and maturation of parents contribute to understanding parent-adolescent relationships?

Autonomy and Attachment

The adolescent's push for autonomy and a sense of responsibility puzzles and angers many parents. Parents see their teenager slipping from their grasp. They may have an urge to take stronger control as the adolescent seeks autonomy and responsibility. Heated emotional exchanges may ensue, with either side calling names, making threats, and doing whatever seems necessary to gain control. Parents may seem frustrated because they *expect* their teenager to heed their advice, to want to spend time with the family, and to grow up to do what is right. Most parents anticipate that their teenager will have some difficulty adjusting to the changes that adolescence brings, but few parents can imagine and predict just how strong an adolescent's desires will be to spend time with peers and how adolescents want to show that it is they—not their parents—who are responsible for their successes and failures.

Expectations for adolescents' autonomy sometimes vary from one culture to another. For example, Western adolescents expect to achieve autonomy earlier than Eastern adolescents. In one recent study of 200 tenth- and eleventh-grade students, Hong Kong youth expected to achieve autonomy earlier than their American-born Caucasian counterparts in the United States (Feldman & Rosenthal, 1990a). And, Chinese youth who reside in the United States and Australia have later expectations for autonomy than their Western counterparts (Feldman & Rosenthal, 1990b). With such cultural variations in mind, let's examine more closely what autonomy is.

The ability to attain autonomy and gain control over one's behavior in adolescence is acquired through appropriate adult reactions to the adolescent's desire for control. At the onset of adolescence, the average individual does not have the knowledge to make appropriate or mature decisions in all areas of life. As the adolescent pushes for autonomy, the wise adult relinquishes control in those areas where the adolescent can make reasonable decisions but continues to guide the adolescent to make reasonable decisions in areas where the adolescent's knowledge is more limited. Gradually, adolescents acquire the ability to make mature decisions on their own.

But adolescents do not simply move away from parental influence into a decision-making process all their own. There is continued connectedness to parents as adolescents move toward and gain autonomy. In the last decade, developmentalists have begun to explore the role of secure attachment, and related concepts such as connectedness to parents, in adolescent development (Fisher & Jenkins, 1991). They believe that attachment to parents in adolescence may facilitate the adolescent's social competence and well-being, as reflected in such characteristics as self-esteem, emotional adjustment, and physical health (Armsden & Greenberg, 1987; Bell & others, 1985; Kobak & Sceery, 1988; Papini, Micka, & Barnett, 1989; Papini, Roggman, & Anderson, 1990). For example, adolescents who have secure relationships with their parents have higher self-esteem and more emotional well-being (Armsden & Greenberg, 1987). In contrast, emotional detachment from parents is associated with greater feelings of parental rejection and a lower sense of one's own social and romantic attractiveness (Ryan & Lynch, 1989). Thus, attachment to parents during adolescence may serve the adaptive function of providing a secure base from which adolescents can explore and master new environments and a widening social world in a psychologically healthy manner. Secure attachment to parents may buffer adolescents from the anxiety and potential feelings of depression or emotional distress associated with the transition from childhood to adulthood. In one recent study, when young adolescents had a secure attachment to their parents, they perceived their family as cohesive and reported little social anxiety or feelings of depression (Papini, Roggman, & Anderson, 1990).

Secure attachment or connectedness to parents promotes competent peer relations and positive close relationships outside of the family. In one investigation, attachment to parents and peers was assessed (Armsden & Greenberg, 1984). Adolescents who were securely attached to parents were also securely attached to peers; those who were insecurely attached to parents were also more likely to be insecurely attached to peers. In another investigation,

We cannot build the future for our youth, but we can build our youth for the future.

~ *Franklin D. Roosevelt, 1940*

Adolescence

college students who were securely attached to their parents as young children were more likely to have securely attached relationships with friends, dates, and spouses than their insecurely attached counterparts (Hazen & Shaver, 1987). And in yet another investigation, older adolescents who had an ambivalent attachment history with their parents reported greater jealousy, conflict, and dependency along with less satisfaction in their relationship with their best friend than their securely attached counterparts (Fisher, 1990). There are times when adolescents reject closeness, connection, and attachment to their parents as they assert their ability to make decisions and to develop an identity. But for the most part, the worlds of parents and peers are coordinated and connected, not uncoordinated and disconnected.

Parent-Adolescent Conflict

While attachment and connectedness to parents remains strong during adolescence, the attachment and connectedness is not always smooth. Early adolescence is a time when conflict with parents escalates beyond childhood levels (Montemayor & Flannery, 1991; Montemayor & Hanson, 1985; Steinberg, 1987, 1990, 1991). This increase may be due to a number of factors: the biological changes of puberty, cognitive changes involving increased idealism and logical reasoning, social changes focused on independence and identity, maturational changes in parents, and violated expectations on the part of parents and adolescents. The adolescent compares her parents to an ideal standard and then criticizes the flaws. A 13-year-old girl tells her mother, "That is the tackiest-looking dress I have ever seen. Nobody would be caught dead wearing that." The adolescent demands logical explanations for comments and discipline. A 14-year-old boy tells his mother, "What do you mean I have to be home at 10 P.M. because it's the way we do things around here? Why do we do things around here that way? It doesn't make sense to me."

Many parents see their adolescent changing from a compliant child to someone who is noncompliant, oppositional, and resistant to parental standards. When this happens, parents tend to clamp down and put more pressure on the adolescent to conform to parental standards (Collins, 1989, 1990). Parents often expect their adolescents to become mature adults overnight instead of understanding that the journey takes ten to fifteen years. Parents who recognize that this transition takes time handle their youth more competently and calmly than those who demand immediate conformity to adult standards. The opposite tactic—letting adolescents do as they please without supervision—is also unwise.

While conflict with parents does increase in early adolescence, it does not reach the tumultuous proportions G. Stanley Hall envisioned at the beginning of the twentieth century. Rather, much of the conflict involves the everyday events of family life such as keeping a bedroom clean, dressing neatly, getting home by a certain time, not talking forever on the phone, and so on. The conflicts rarely involve major dilemmas like drugs and delinquency.

It is not unusual to talk to parents of young adolescents and hear them ask, "Is it ever going to get better?" Things usually do get better as adolescents move from early to late adolescence. Conflict between parents usually escalates during early adolescence, remains somewhat stable during the high school years, and then lessens as the adolescent reaches 17 to 20 years of age. Parent-adolescent relationships become more positive if adolescents go away to college than if they stay at home and go to college (Sullivan & Sullivan, 1980).

The everyday conflicts that characterize parent-adolescent relationships may serve a positive developmental function (Blos, 1989; Hill, 1983). These minor disputes and negotiations facilitate the adolescent's transition from being

> When I was a boy of 14, my father was so ignorant I could hardly stand to have the man around. But when I got to be 21, I was astonished at how much he had learnt in 7 years.
>
> ~ *Mark Twain*

Old model		New model	
Autonomy, detachment from parents; parent and peer worlds are isolated	Intense, stressful conflict throughout adolescence; parent-adolescent relationships are filled with storm and stress on virtually a daily basis	Attachment and autonomy; parents are important support systems and attachment figures; adolescent-parent and adolescent-peer worlds have some important connections	Moderate parent-adolescent conflict common and can serve a positive developmental function; conflict greater in early adolescence, especially during the apex of puberty

Figure 13.1   The old and new models of parent-adolescent relationships.

It is not enough for parents to understand children. They must accord children the privilege of understanding them.

~ *Milton Sapirstein,*
Paradoxes of Everyday Life, *1955*

dependent on parents to becoming an autonomous individual. For example, in one investigation, adolescents who expressed disagreement with parents explored identity development more actively than adolescents who did not express disagreement with their parents (Cooper & others, 1982).

As suggested earlier, one way for parents to cope with the adolescent's push for independence and identity is to recognize that adolescence is a ten-to fifteen-year transitional period in the journey to adulthood rather than an overnight accomplishment. Recognizing that conflict and negotiation can serve a positive developmental function can tone down parental hostility, too. Understanding parent-adolescent conflict, though, is not simple.

In sum, the old model of parent-adolescent relationships suggested that as adolescents mature they detach themselves from parents and move into a world of autonomy apart from parents. The old model also suggested that parent-adolescent conflict is intense and stressful throughout adolescence. The new model emphasizes that parents serve as important attachment figures and support systems as adolescents explore a wider, more complex social world. The new model also emphasizes that in the majority of families, parent-adolescent conflict is moderate rather than severe, and that the everyday negotiations and minor disputes are normal and can serve the positive developmental function of helping the adolescent make the transition from childhood dependency to adult independence (see figure 13.1).

Still, a high degree of conflict characterizes some parent-adolescent relationships. One estimate of the percentage of parents and adolescents who engage in prolonged, intense, repeated, unhealthy conflict is about one in five families (Montemayor, 1982). While this figure represents a minority of adolescents, it indicates that 4 to 5 million American families encounter serious, highly stressful parent-adolescent conflict. And, this prolonged, intense conflict is associated with a number of adolescent problems—moving away from home, juvenile delinquency, school dropout rates, pregnancy and early marriage, joining religious cults, and drug abuse (Brook & others, 1990; Kandel, Dessler, & Margulies, 1978; Ullman, 1982).

The Maturation of Adolescents and Parents

Physical, cognitive, and social changes in the adolescent's development influence the nature of parent-adolescent relationships. Parental changes also influence the nature of these relationships. Among the changes in the adolescent are puberty, expanded logical reasoning and increased idealistic and egocentric thought, violated expectations, changes in schooling, peers, friendship, and dating, and movement toward independence. Several recent investigations have shown that conflict between parents and adolescents is the most stressful during the apex of pubertal growth (Hill & others, 1985; Silverberg & Steinberg, 1990; Steinberg, 1981, 1988).

Parental changes include those involving marital dissatisfaction, economic burdens, career reevaluation and time perspective, and health and body concerns. Marital dissatisfaction is greater when the offspring is an adolescent rather than a child or an adult. A greater economic burden is placed on parents during the rearing of their adolescents. Parents may reevaluate their occupational achievement, deciding whether they have met their youthful aspirations for success. Parents may look to the future and think about how much time they have remaining to accomplish what they want. Adolescents, however, look to the future with unbounded optimism, sensing that they have an unlimited amount of time to accomplish what they desire. Health concerns and an interest in body integrity and sexual attractiveness become prominent themes of adolescents' parents. Even when their body and sexual attractiveness are not deteriorating, many parents of adolescents perceive that they are. By contrast, adolescents are beginning to reach the peak of their physical attractiveness, strength, and health. While both adolescents and their parents show a heightened preoccupation with their bodies, the adolescent's outcome is probably more positive.

• Critical Thinking •

As the parents of adolescents will be increasingly older in the future because of delays in marriage and childbearing, how do you think this will influence the nature of parent-adolescent relationships?

Peers

In chapter 11, we discussed how children spend more time with their peers in middle and late childhood than in early childhood. We also found that friendships become more important in middle and late childhood, and that popularity with peers is a strong motivation for most children. Advances in cognitive development during middle and late childhood also allow children to take the perspective of their peers and friends more readily, and their social knowledge of how to make and keep friends increases.

Imagine you are back in junior or senior high school, especially during one of your good times. Peers, friends, cliques, dates, parties, and clubs probably come to mind. Adolescents spend huge chunks of time with peers, more than in middle and late childhood. Among the important issues and questions to be asked about peer relations in adolescence are: What is the nature of peer pressure and conformity? How important are cliques in adolescence? How do children and adolescent groups differ? What is the nature of dating in adolescence?

Peer Pressure and Conformity

Consider the following statement made by an adolescent girl:

> Peer pressure is extremely influential in my life. I have never had very many friends, and I spend quite a bit of time alone. The friends I have are older. . . . The closest friend I have had is a lot like me in that we are both sad and depressed a lot. I began to act even more depressed than before when I was with her. I would call her up and try to act even more depressed than I was because that is what I thought she liked. In that relationship, I felt pressure to be like her. . . .

During adolescence, especially early adolescence, we conformed more to peer standards than we did in childhood. Investigators have found that around the eighth and ninth grades, conformity to peers—especially to their antisocial standards—peaks (Berndt, 1979; Berndt & Perry, 1990). At this point adolescents are most likely to go along with a peer to steal hubcaps off a car, draw grafitti on a wall, or steal cosmetics from a store counter.

Each of you, individually, walkest with the tread of a fox, but collectively ye are geese.

~ Solon, Ancient Greece

(a)

(b)

Most adolescents conform to the mainstream standards of their peers. However, the rebellious or anticonformist adolescent reacts counter to the mainstream peer group's expectations, deliberately moving away from the actions or beliefs they advocate. Two contemporary versions of anticonformist teenagers are the (a) "skinheads" and (b) punks.

Cliques and Crowds

Most peer group relationships in adolescence can be categorized in one of three ways: the crowd, the clique, or individual friendships. The **crowd** *is the largest and least personal of adolescent groups.* Members of the crowd meet because of their mutual interest in activities, not because they are mutually attracted to each other. **Cliques** *are smaller, involve greater intimacy among members, and have more group cohesion than crowds.*

Allegiance to cliques, clubs, organizations, and teams exerts powerful control over the lives of many adolescents. Group identity often overrides personal identity. The leader of a group may place a member in a position of considerable moral conflict by asking, in effect, "What's more important, our code or your parents'?" or "Are you looking out for yourself, or the members of the group?" Labels like "brother" and "sister" are sometimes adopted and used in the members' conversations with each other. These labels symbolize the bond between the members and suggest the high status of group membership.

One of the most widely cited studies of adolescent cliques and crowds is that of James Coleman (1961). Students from ten different high schools were asked to identify the leading crowds in their schools. They were also asked to identify the students who were the most outstanding in athletics, popularity, and different school activities. Regardless of the school sampled, the leading crowds were composed of athletes and popular girls. Much less power in the leading crowd was attributed to the bright student. Coleman's finding that being an athlete contributes to popularity for adolescent boys was reconfirmed in another investigation (Eitzen, 1975).

Think about your high school years. What were the cliques, and which one were you in? While the names of the cliques change, we could go to almost any high school in the United States and find three to six well-defined cliques or crowds. In one recent investigation, six peer group structures emerged: populars, unpopulars, jocks, brains, druggies, and average students (Brown & Mounts, 1989). The proportion of students in these cliques was much lower in multiethnic schools because of the additional existence of ethnically based crowds.

One investigation revealed that clique membership is associated with the adolescent's self-esteem (Brown & Lohr, 1987). Cliques included jocks (athletically oriented), populars (well-known students who lead social activities), normals (middle-of-the-road students who make up the masses), druggies or toughs (known for illicit drug use or other delinquent activities), and nobodies (low in social skills or intellectual abilities). The self-esteem of the jocks and the populars was highest while that of the nobodies was the lowest. But one group of adolescents not in a clique had self-esteem equivalent to that of the jocks and the populars; this group was the independents, who indicated that clique membership was not important to them. Keep in mind that these data are correlational; self-esteem could increase an adolescent's probability of becoming a clique member just as clique membership could increase the adolescent's self-esteem.

Children and Adolescent Groups

Children groups differ from adolescent groups in several important ways. The members of children groups are often friends or neighborhood acquaintances. Their groups are usually not as formalized as many adolescent groups. During the adolescent years, groups tend to include a broader array of members. In other words, adolescents other than friends or neighborhood acquaintances are often members of adolescent groups. Try to recall the student council, honor society, or football team at your junior high school. If you were a member of any of these organizations, you probably remember that they were made up of many adolescents you had not met before and that they were a more heterogeneous group than your childhood peer groups. For example, peer groups in adolescence are more likely to have a mixture of individuals from different ethnic groups than peer groups in childhood. To read further about ethnic-minority adolescents' peer groups, turn to Cultural Worlds of Development 13.1. Also, in adolescent peer groups, rules and regulations are usually defined more precisely than in children's peer groups. For example, captains or leaders are often formally elected or appointed in adolescent peer groups.

A well-known observational study by Dexter Dunphy (1963) supports the notion that opposite-sex participation in groups increases during adolescence. In late childhood, boys and girls participate in small, same-sex cliques. As they move into the early adolescent years, the same-sex cliques begin to interact with each other. Gradually, the leaders and high-status members form further cliques based on heterosexual relationships. Eventually, the newly created heterosexual cliques replace the same-sex cliques. The heterosexual cliques interact with each other in large crowd activities, too—at dances and

ETHNIC-MINORITY ADOLESCENTS' PEER RELATIONS

*F*or many ethnic-minority youth, especially immigrants, peers from their own ethnic group provide a crucial sense of brotherhood or sisterhood within the majority culture. Peer groups may form to oppose those of the majority group and to provide adaptive support that reduces feelings of isolation (Spencer & Dornbusch, 1990).

As ethnic-minority children move into adolescence and enter schools with more heterogeneous school populations, they become more aware of their ethnic-minority status. Ethnic-minority adolescents may have difficulty joining peer groups and clubs in predominantly White schools. However, schools are only one setting in which peer relations take place.

Adolescent peer relations take place in diverse settings—at school, in the neighborhood, and in the community. Ethnic-minority adolescents often have two sets of peer relationships—one at school, and another in the community. Community peers are more likely to be from their own ethnic group in their immediate neighborhood. Sometimes they go to the same church and participate in activities together, such as Black History Week, Chinese New Year's, or Cinco de Mayo Festival. Because ethnic-group adolescents usually have two sets of peers and friends, researchers asking about their peers and friends should focus on relationships both at school and in the neighborhood and community. Ethnic-minority group adolescents who are social isolates at school may be sociometric stars in their segregated neighborhood. Also, because adoles-

As boys and girls move into adolescence, they become more aware of their ethnic backgrounds. While ethnic-minority adolescents may have trouble joining peer groups in predominantly White schools, it is important to keep in mind that peer relations take place in many settings other than the school, such as in the neighborhood and in the community.

cents are more mobile than children, inquiries should be made about the scope of their social networks (Gibbs & Huang, 1989).

In one recent investigation, the school and neighborhood friendship patterns of 292 Black and White adolescents who attended an integrated junior high school were studied (Dubois and Hirsch, 1990). Most students reported having another ethnic friend, but only 28 percent saw such a friend frequently outside of school. Black adolescents were more likely than White adolescents to have extensive neighborhood friendship networks, but Black adolescents said they talked with fewer friends during the school day.

A special interest is the degree of peer support for an ethnic-minority adolescent's achievement orientation. Some researchers argue that peers often dissuade Black adolescents from doing well in school (Fordham & Ogbu, 1986; Fuller, 1984). However, in one recent investigation, peer support was relatively high among Asian American adolescents, moderate among Black American and Hispanic adolescents, and relatively low among Anglo American adolescents (Brown & others, 1990). Possibly the low peer support of achievement among Anglo American adolescents is due to their strong individual, competitive, and social comparison orientation.

athletic events, for example. In late adolescence, the crowd begins to dissolve as couples develop more serious relationships and make long-range plans that may include engagement and marriage.

Dating

Dating takes on added importance during adolescence. As comedian Dick Cavett (1974) remembers, the thought of an upcoming dance or sock hop was absolute agony: "I knew I'd never get a date. There seemed to be only this limited set of girls I could and should be seen with, and they were all taken by the jocks." Adolescents spend considerable time either dating or thinking about dating, which has gone far beyond its original courtship function to a form of recreation, a source of status and achievement, and a setting for learning about close relationships.

Most girls in the United States begin dating at the age of 14, while most boys begin sometime between the ages of 14 and 15 (Douvan & Adelson, 1966; Sorenson, 1973). The majority of adolescents have their first date between the ages of 12 and 16. Fewer than 10 percent have a first date before the age of 10, and by the age of 16, more than 90 percent have had at least one date. More than 50 percent of high school students average one or more dates per week (Dickinson, 1975). About 15 percent date less than once per month, and about three of every four students have gone steady at least once by the end of high school.

Female adolescents bring a stronger desire for intimacy and personality exploration to dating than do male adolescents (Duck, 1975). Adolescent dating is a context in which gender-related role expectations intensify. Males feel pressured to perform in "masculine" ways and females feel pressured to perform in "feminine" ways. Especially in early adolescence when pubertal changes are occurring, the adolescent male wants to show that he is the very best male possible, and the adolescent female wants to show that she is the very best female possible.

The sociocultural context exerts a powerful influence on adolescent dating patterns (Xiaohe & Whyte, 1990). Values and religious beliefs of people in various cultures often dictate the age at which dating begins, how much freedom in dating is allowed, whether dates must be chaperoned by adults or

• Critical Thinking •

How do you think variations in adolescents' observations of their parents' marital lives and in their own relationships with their parents influence dating relationships in adolescence?

Concept Table 13.1: Families and Peers

Concept	Processes/Related Ideas	Characteristics/Description
Families	Autonomy and Attachment	Many parents have a difficult time handling the adolescent's push for autonomy, even though this push is one of the hallmarks of adolescent development. Adolescents do not simply move into a world isolated from parents; attachment to parents increases the probability that the adolescent will be socially competent and explore a widening social world in healthy ways.
	Parent-Adolescent Conflict	Conflict with parents often increases in early adolescence. Such conflict is usually moderate. The increase in conflict probably serves the positive developmental function of promoting autonomy and identity. A small subset of adolescents experience high parent-adolescent conflict that is related to various negative outcomes for adolescents.
	The Maturation of the Adolescent and Parents	Physical, cognitive, and social changes in the adolescent's development influence parent-adolescent relationships. Parental changes—marital dissatisfaction, economic burdens, career reevaluation and time perspective, and health and body concerns—also influence parent-adolescent relationships.
Peers	Peer Pressure and Conformity	The pressure to conform to peers is strong during adolescence, especially during the eighth and ninth grades.
	Cliques and Crowds	There are usually three to six well-defined cliques in every secondary school. Membership in certain cliques—especially jocks and populars—is associated with increased self-esteem. Independents also show high self-esteem.
	Children and Adolescent Groups	Children groups are less formal, less heterogeneous, and less heterosexual than adolescent groups. Dunphy found that the development of adolescent groups moves through five stages.
	Dating	Dating can be a form of mate selection, recreation, a source of status and achievement, and a setting for learning about close relationships. Most adolescents are involved in dating. Adolescent females appear to be more interested in intimacy and personality exploration than adolescent males are. Dating varies cross-culturally.

parents, and the roles of males and females in dating. For example, Hispanic American and Asian American cultures have more conservative standards regarding adolescent dating than the Anglo American culture. Dating may be a source of cultural conflict for many immigrants and their families who have come from cultures in which dating begins at a late age, little freedom in dating is allowed, dates are chaperoned, and adolescent girls' dating is especially restricted.

Thus far, we have discussed a number of ideas about families and peers during adolescence. These ideas are summarized in concept table 13.1. We turn next to a discussion of values, religion, and cults in adolescence.

Values, Religion, and Cults

What are adolescents' values like today? How powerful is religion in adolescents' lives? Why do some adolescents run away to join cults? We consider each of these questions in turn.

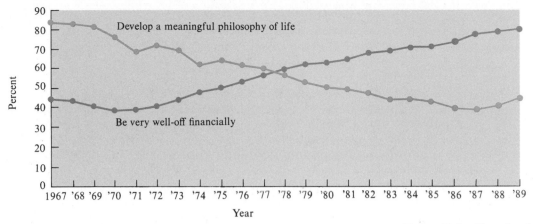

Figure 13.2 Changing freshman life goals, 1967–1989.

Values

Adolescents carry with them a set of values that influences their thoughts, feelings, and actions. What were your values like when you were an adolescent? Are the values of today's adolescents changing?

Over the past two decades, adolescents have shown an increased concern for personal well-being and a decreased concern for the well-being of others, especially for the disadvantaged (Astin, Green, & Korn, 1987; Astin, Korn, & Berz, 1989). As shown in figure 13.2, today's college freshmen are more strongly motivated to be well-off financially and less motivated to develop a meaningful philosophy of life than were their counterparts twenty or even ten years ago. Among high school seniors, increasing numbers are motivated by the opportunity to make a considerable amount of money (Bachman, Johnston, & O'Malley, 1987).

However, two aspects of values that increased during the 1960s continue to characterize today's youth: self-fulfillment and self-expression (Conger, 1981, 1988). As part of their motivation for self-fulfillment, many adolescents show great interest in their physical health and well-being. Greater self-fulfillment and self-expression can be laudable goals, but if they become the only goals, self-destruction, loneliness, or alienation may result. Young people also need to develop a corresponding sense of commitment to others' welfare. Encouraging adolescents to have a strong commitment to others, in concert with an interest in self-fulfillment, is a major task for our nation at the close of the twentieth century.

There are some signs that today's adolescents are shifting toward a stronger interest in the welfare of our society. For example, between 1986 and 1989, there was a small increase in the percentage of college freshmen who said they were strongly interested in participating in community action programs (23 percent in 1989 compared to 18 percent in 1986) and helping promote racial understanding (35 percent in 1989 compared to 27 percent in 1986) (Astin, Korn, & Berz, 1989). More adolescents are showing an active interest in the problems of homelessness, child abuse, hunger, and poverty (Conger, 1988). The percentage of adolescents who believe it is desirable to work for a social service organization rose from 11 percent in 1980 to 17 percent in 1989 (Bachman, Johnston, & O'Malley, 1987; Johnston, Bachman, & O'Malley, 1990). Whether these small increments in concern for the community and society will continue to increase in the remainder of the 1990s is difficult to predict.

Religious Beliefs and the Church

Adolescents are more interested in religion and spiritual beliefs than are children. Their increasing abstract thoughts and their search for an identity make religion and spiritual matters attractive concerns.

The Development of Religious Concepts

In a series of studies, David Elkind (1978) interviewed several hundred Jewish, Catholic, and Protestant boys and girls from 5 to 14 years of age. He asked questions such as "Are you a Catholic?" "Is your family Jewish?" "Are all boys and girls in the world Christians?" He also asked questions like, "What is a Jew?" "How do you become a Catholic?" and "Can you be an American and a Protestant (or Jew, or Catholic) at the same time?" The formal operational thinkers—those who were in early adolescence—had a different way of thinking about religious concepts than the concrete operational thinkers—those in childhood. The formal operational thinkers were more reflective than their younger counterparts. They no longer looked for manifestations of religious identity in an individual's outward behavior but rather in the evidence of innermost beliefs and convictions. For example, one concrete operational thinker said that the way you can tell an individual is a Catholic is by whether the person goes to church or not. By contrast, one formal operational thinker said that you can tell an individual is a Protestant because the person is free to repent and to pray to God.

Another perspective on the development of religious concepts was proposed by James Fowler (1976). **Individuating-reflexive faith** *is Fowler's stage in late adolescence, which is an important time in the development of a religious identity. For the first time in their lives, individuals take full responsibility for their religious beliefs.* Earlier they relied heavily on their parents' beliefs. During late adolescence, individuals come face to face with personal decisions, evaluating such questions as, "Do I consider myself first, or should I consider the welfare of others first?" "Are the doctrines that have been taught to me absolute, or are they more relative than I had been led to believe?" Fowler believes there is a close relation between the adolescent's development of moral values and religious values. He also acknowledges that the stage of individuating-reflexive faith has much in common with Kohlberg's highest level of moral reasoning, postconventional morality.

Spiritual Interest and Church Influences

The sociocultural conditions in which adolescents grow up combine with their developing cognitive capacities to influence their religious identity. The formal operational characteristics of abstract thought and idealism contribute to the adolescent's spiritual interest. Adolescents do show a strong interest in spiritual matters. For example, in one national survey, almost 9 of 10 adolescents said they pray (Gallup & Poling, 1980). Compared to children's prayers, adolescents' prayers are more likely to be characterized by responsibility, subjectivity, and intimacy (Scarlett & Perriello, 1990). In the national survey just mentioned, more than 9 of 10 adolescents said they believed in God or a universal spirit. Only 1 in 1,000 had no religious preference or affiliation. At the same time, though, many adolescents say that organized religion has little meaning for them and that the church's doctrines are outmoded. In the national poll just mentioned, only 25 percent said they have a high degree of confidence in organized religion. About 40 percent said that the honesty and personal ethics of the clergy are average to very low.

One area of religion's influence on adolescent development involves sexual activity. Although variability and change in church teachings make it difficult

Shown here are adolescents at San Fernando parish in San Antonio, Texas. Adolescents show a strong interest in spiritual matters. In one national survey, almost nine of ten adolescents said they pray, for example.

to characterize religious doctrines simply, most churches discourage premarital sex. Since most religious groups discourage premarital sex, the degree of adolescents' participation in religious organizations may be more important than religious affiliation as a determinant of premarital sexual attitudes and behavior. Adolescents who attend religious services may frequently hear messages about abstaining from sex. Involvement of adolescents in religious organizations also enhances the probability that they will become friends with adolescents who have restrictive attitudes toward premarital sex. In one recent study, adolescents who attended church frequently and valued religion in their lives were less experienced sexually and had less permissive attitudes toward premarital sex than their counterparts who attended church infrequently and said that religion did not play a strong role in their lives (Thorton & Cambrun, 1989). However, while religious involvement is associated with a lower incidence of sexual activity among adolescents, adolescents who are religiously involved and sexually active are less likely to use medical methods of contraception (especially the pill) than their sexually active counterparts with low religious involvement (Studer & Thorton, 1987, 1989).

Cults

Barb is 17 years old. She grew up in an affluent family and was given all of the material things she wanted. When she was 15, her parents paid her way to Europe, and for the last three years she has been attending a private boarding school. Her parents attended a Protestant church on a regular basis, and when Barb was home they took her with them. Six months ago, Barb shocked her parents by joining the "Moonies."

There are six unorthodox religious movements that have attracted attention from America's youth: Transcendental Meditation (TM), yoga, the charismatic movement, mysticism, faith healing, and various Eastern religions (Gallup & Poling, 1980). More than 27 million Americans have been touched by these religions, either superficially or deeply. In all, there are more than 2,500 cults in the United States. Two to three million youth and young adults are cult members (Levine, 1984; Swope, 1980). Among the more specific religious cults that have attracted the attention of youth are the Unification Church of Sun Myung Moon (the Moonies), the Divine Light Mission of Maharaj Ji, the Institute of Krishna Consciousness, the Children of God, and the Church of Scientology. Some experts on cults believe that such cults appeal to youth because of weaknesses in organized religion and in families.

The most recent concerns about cults focus on satanism, or devil worship. The nightmarish tale of human sacrifice that unfolded in the spring of 1989 in Matamoros, Mexico, brought national attention to the increasing prevalence of devil worship. Some of the bodies in the mass grave had been decapitated. Investigation of the Satanic cult revealed its ties to drugs. The cult's ringleader, Adolpho de Jesus Constanzo, controlled members' lives, getting them to believe that the devil has supernatural powers.

Critics of the cults argue that the cult leaders are hypocritical, exploit members to gain wealth, brainwash youth, and cast a hypnotic spell over their lives. In some cases, cults have been accused of kidnapping youth and placing them in deprived circumstances to gain control over their minds. Most cults have elaborate training programs in which the cult's teachings are memorized. Cult members are usually required to turn over their wealth to the cult leaders. And cult members are often told that they can associate with or marry only other members of the cult (Galanter, 1989).

Culture and Rites of Passage

Ideas about the nature of adolescents and orientation toward adolescents may vary from culture to culture and within the same culture over different time periods (Whiting, 1989). For example, some cultures have more permissive attitudes toward adolescent sexuality than the American culture (the Mangaian culture in the South Sea islands, for example), and some cultures have more conservative attitudes toward adolescent sexuality than the American culture (the Ines Beag culture off the coast of Ireland, for example). Over the course of the twentieth century, attitudes toward sexuality—especially for females—have become more permissive in the American culture.

Some societies have elaborate ceremonies that signal the adolescent's move to maturity and achievement of adult status. A **rite of passage** *is a ceremony or a ritual that marks an individual's transition from one status to another. The most interest in rites of passage focuses on the transition to adult status.* In many primitive cultures, rites of passage are the avenue through which adolescents gain access to sacred adult practices, to knowledge, and to sexuality (MacDonald, 1991; Sommer, 1978). These rites often involve dramatic practices intended to facilitate the adolescent's separation from the immediate family, especially the mother. The transformation is usually characterized by some form of ritual death and rebirth, or by means of contact

Adolescence

Nigeria girl, painted for festival dance of "OBITUN" (coming of age).

with the spiritual world. Bonds are forged between the adolescent and the adult instructors through shared rituals, hazards, and secrets to allow the adolescent to enter the adult world. This kind of ritual provides a forceful and discontinuous entry into the adult world at a time when the adolescent is perceived to be ready for the change.

Africa has been the location of many rites of passage for adolescents, especially Sub-Saharan Africa. Under the influence of Western culture, many of the rites are disappearing today, although some vestiges remain. In locations where formal education is not readily available, rites of passage are still prevalent.

Do we have such rites of passage for American adolescents? We certainly do not have universal formal ceremonies that mark the passage from adolescence to adulthood. Certain religious and social groups do go through initiation ceremonies that indicate an advance in maturity has been reached—the Jewish bar mitzvah, the Catholic confirmation, and social debuts, for example. School graduation ceremonies come the closest to being culture-wide rites of passage in the United States. The high school graduation ceremony has become nearly universal for middle-class adolescents and increasing numbers of adolescents from low-income backgrounds (Fasick, 1988). Nonetheless, high school graduation does not result in universal changes; many high school graduates continue to live with their parents, continue to be economically dependent on them, and continue to be undecided about career and lifestyle matters. Another rite of passage that has characterized increasing numbers of American adolescents is sexual intercourse (Allen & Santrock, in press). By the end of adolescence, more than 70 percent of American adolescents have had sexual intercourse.

This young Jewish boy is shown at his bar mitzvah, a Jewish initiation ceremony that takes place when the boy reaches the age of 13. The bar mitzvah gives the boy adult status in the Jewish religion.

Graduating from high school is one of the few rites of passage in the United States.

The absence of clear-cut rites of passage make the attainment of adult status ambiguous. Many individuals are unsure whether or not they have reached adult status. In Texas, the age for beginning employment is 15, but many younger adolescents and even children are employed, especially Mexican immigrants. The age for driving is 16, but when emergency need is demonstrated, a driver's license can be obtained at 15. Even at age 16, some parents may not allow their son or daughter to obtain a driver's license, believing they are too young for this responsibility. The age for voting is 18; the age for drinking has recently been raised to 21. Exactly when adolescents become adults in America has not been clearly delineated as it has been in some primitive cultures, where rites of passage are universal in the culture.

Identity

By far the most comprehensive and provocative story of identity development has been told by Erik Erikson. As you may remember from chapter 2, identity versus identity confusion (diffusion) is the fifth stage in Erikson's eight stages of the life cycle, occurring at about the same time as adolescence. It is a time of interest in finding out who one is, what one is all about, and where one is headed in life.

During adolescence, world views become important to the individual, who enters what Erikson (1968) calls a "psychological moratorium," a gap between the security of childhood and the autonomy of adulthood. Adolescents experiment with numerous roles and identities they draw from the surrounding culture. The youth who successfully copes with these conflicting identities during adolescence emerges with a new sense of self that is both refreshing and acceptable. The adolescent who does not successfully resolve this identity crisis is confused, suffering what Erikson calls identity confusion. This confusion takes one of two courses: The individual withdraws, isolating himself from peers and family; or he may lose his identity in the crowd.

Some Contemporary Thoughts about Identity

Contemporary views of identity development suggest several important considerations. First, identity development is a lengthy process; in many instances it is a more gradual, less cataclysmic transition than Erikson's term *crisis* implies. Second, identity development is extraordinarily complex (Marcia, 1980, 1987). Identity formation neither begins nor ends with adolescence. It begins with the appearance of attachment, the development of a sense of self, and the emergence of independence in infancy, and reaches its final phase with a life review and integration in old age. What is important about identity in adolescence, especially late adolescence, is that for the first time physical development, cognitive development, and social development advance to the point at which the individual can sort through and synthesize childhood identities and identifications to construct a viable pathway toward adult maturity. Resolution of the identity issue at adolescence does not mean identity will be stable through the remainder of one's life. A person who develops a healthy identity is flexible, adaptive, and open to changes in society, in relationships, and in careers. This openness assures numerous reorganizations of identity features throughout the life of the person who has achieved identity.

Identity formation does not happen neatly, and it usually does not happen cataclysmically. At the bare minimum, it involves commitment to a vocational direction, an ideological stance, and a sexual orientation. Synthesizing the identity components can be a long, drawn-out process with many negations and affirmations of various roles and faces. Identities are developed in bits and pieces. Decisions are not made once and for all, but have to be made again

Drawing by Koren; © 1988 The New Yorker Magazine, Inc.

"Do you have any idea who I am?"

and again. And the decisions may seem trivial at the time: whom to date, whether or not to break up, whether or not to have intercourse, whether or not to take drugs, whether to go to college after high school or get a job, which major to choose, whether to study or whether to play, whether or not to be politically active, and so on. Over the years of adolescence, the decisions begin to form a core of what the individual is all about as a person—what is called identity (Archer, 1989; Baumeister, 1991; Papini, Micka, & Barnett, 1989).

The Four Statuses of Identity

Canadian psychologist James Marcia (1966, 1980, 1991) analyzed Erikson's theory of identity development and concluded that four identity statuses, or modes of resolution, appear in the theory: identity diffusion, identity foreclosure, identity moratorium, and identity achievement. The extent of an adolescent's commitment and crisis is used to classify the individual according to one of the four identity statuses. **Crisis** *is defined as a period of identity development during which the adolescent is choosing among meaningful alternatives.* Most researchers now use the term *exploration* rather than *crisis,* although in the spirit of Marcia's original formulation, we will use the term *crisis.* **Commitment** *is defined as the part of identity development in which adolescents show a personal investment in what they are going to do.*

Identity diffusion *is the term Marcia uses to describe adolescents who have not yet experienced a crisis (that is, they have not yet explored meaningful alternatives) or made any commitments.* Not only are they undecided about occupational and ideological choices, they are also likely to show little interest in such matters. **Identity foreclosure** *is the term Marcia uses to describe adolescents who have made a commitment but have not experienced a crisis.* This occurs most often when parents hand down commitments to their adolescents, more often than not in an authoritarian manner. In these circumstances, adolescents have not had adequate opportunities to explore different approaches, ideologies, and vocations on their own. **Identity moratorium** *is the term Marcia uses to describe adolescents who are in the midst of a crisis, but*

Table 13.1: The Four Statuses of Identity

	Identity Status			
Position on Occupation and Ideology	Identity Moratorium	Identity Foreclosure	Identity Diffusion	Identity Achievement
Crisis	Present	Absent	Absent	Present
Commitment	Absent	Present	Absent	Present

their commitments are either absent or only vaguely defined. **Identity achievement** *is Marcia's term for adolescents who have undergone a crisis and have made a commitment.* Marcia's four statuses of identity are summarized in table 13.1.

Developmental Changes

Early adolescents are primarily in Marcia's identity diffusion or moratorium statuses. At least three aspects of the young adolescent's development are important in identity formation (Marcia, 1987). Young adolescents must establish confidence in parental support, develop a sense of industry, and gain a self-reflective perspective on their future.

Some researchers believe the most important identity changes take place in youth rather than earlier in adolescence. For example, Alan Waterman (1985, 1989) has found that from the years preceding high school through the last few years of college, an increase in the number of individuals who are identity achieved occurs, along with a decrease in those who are identity diffused. College upperclassmen are more likely to be identity achieved than college freshmen or high school students. Many young adolescents are identity diffused. These developmental changes are especially true for vocational choice. For religious beliefs and political ideology, fewer college students have reached the identity achieved status, with a substantial number characterized by foreclosure and diffusion. Thus, the timing of identity may depend on the particular role involved, and many college students are still wrestling with ideological commitments (Arehart & Smith, 1990; Harter, 1990a,b).

Many identity status researchers believe that a common pattern of individuals who develop positive identities is to follow what are called "MAMA" cycles of *moratorium-achiever-moratorium-achiever* (Archer, 1989). These cyles may be repeated throughout life (Francis, Fraser, & Marcia, 1989; Marcia, 1991). Personal, family, and societal changes are inevitable, and as they occur, the flexibility and skill required to explore new alternatives and develop new commitments are likely to facilitate an individual's coping skills.

Family Influences on Identity

Parents are important figures in the adolescent's development of identity. In studies that relate identity development to parenting styles, democratic parents, who encourage adolescents to participate in family decision making, foster identity achievement. Autocratic parents, who control the adolescent's behavior without giving the adolescent an opportunity to express opinions, encourage identity foreclosure. Permissive parents, who provide little guidance to adolescents and allow them to make their own decisions, promote identity diffusion (Bernard, 1981; Enright & others, 1980; Marcia, 1980).

In addition to studies on parenting styles, researchers have also examined the role of individuality and connectedness in the development of identity. Developmentalist Catherine Cooper and her colleagues (Carlson, Cooper, & Hsu, 1990; Cooper & Carlson, 1991; Cooper & Grotevant, 1989; Grotevant & Cooper, 1985) believe that the presence of a family atmosphere that promotes both individuality and connectedness are important in the adolescent's identity development. **Individuation** *consists of two dimensions: self-assertion, the ability to have and communicate a point of view, and separateness, the use of communication patterns to express how one is different from others.* **Connectedness** *also consists of two dimensions: mutuality, sensitivity to and respect for others' views, and permeability, openness to others' views.* In general, Cooper's research findings reveal identity formation is enhanced by family relationships that are both individuated, which encourages adolescents to develop their own point of view, and connected, which provides a secure base from which to explore the widening social worlds of adolescence.

Stuart Hauser and his colleagues (Hauser, 1991; Hauser & Bowlds, 1990; Hauser & others, 1984; Powers, Hauser, & Kilner, 1989) have also illuminated family processes that promote the adolescent's identity development. They have found that parents who use *enabling* behaviors (such as explaining, accepting, and giving empathy) facilitate the adolescent's identity development more than parents who use *constraining* behaviors (such as judging and devaluing). In sum, family interaction styles that give the adolescent the right to question and to be different, within a context of support and mutuality, foster healthy patterns of identity development (Harter, 1990b).

Cultural and Ethnic Aspects of Identity

Erikson is especially sensitive to the role of culture in identity development. He points out that, throughout the world, ethnic-minority groups have struggled to maintain their cultural identities while blending into the dominant culture (Erikson, 1968). Erikson says that this struggle for an inclusive identity, or identity within the larger culture, has been the driving force in the founding of churches, empires, and revolutions throughout history.

For ethnic-minority individuals, adolescence is often a special juncture in their development (Spencer, 1991; Spencer, 1987; Spencer & Dornbusch, 1990; Spencer & Markstrom-Adams, 1990). Although children are aware of some ethnic and cultural differences, most ethnic-minority individuals consciously confront their ethnicity for the first time in adolescence. In contrast to children, adolescents have the ability to interpret ethnic and cultural information, to reflect on the past, and to speculate about the future (Harter, 1990a,b). As they cognitively mature, ethnic-minority adolescents become acutely aware of the evaluations of their ethnic group by the majority White culture (Comer, 1988; Ogbu, 1989). As one researcher commented, the young Black American child may learn that Black is beautiful, but conclude as an adolescent that White is powerful (Semaj, 1985).

Ethnic-minority youths' awareness of negative appraisals, conflicting values, and restricted occupational opportunities can influence life choices and plans for the future (Spencer & Dornbusch, 1990). As one ethnic-minority youth stated, "The future seems shut off, closed. Why dream? You can't reach your dreams. Why set goals? At least if you don't set any goals, you don't fail."

For many ethnic-minority youth, a lack of successful ethnic-minority role models with whom to identify is a special concern. The problem is especially acute for inner-city ethnic-minority youth. Because of the lack of adult ethnic-minority role models, some ethnic-minority youth may conform to middle-class White values and identify with successful White role models.

However, for many adolescents, their ethnicity and skin color constrain their acceptance by the White culture. Thus, many ethnic-minority adolescents have a difficult task: negotiating two value systems—that of their own ethnic group and that of the White society. Some adolescents reject the mainstream, foregoing the rewards controlled by White Americans; others adopt the values and standards of the majority White culture; and yet others take the difficult path of biculturality.

In one recent investigation, ethnic identity exploration was higher among ethnic-minority than among White American college students (Phinney & Alipuria, 1990). In this same investigation, ethnic-minority college students who had thought about and resolved issues involving their ethnicity had higher self-esteem than their ethnic-minority counterparts who had not. In another investigation, the ethnic-identity development of Asian American, Black American, Hispanic American, and White American tenth-grade students in Los Angeles was studied (Phinney, 1989). Adolescents from each of the three ethnic-minority groups faced a similar need to deal with their ethnic-group identification in a predominately White American culture. In some instances, the adolescents from the three ethnic-minority groups perceived different issues to be important in their resolution of ethnic identity. For Asian American adolescents, pressures to achieve academically and concerns about quotas that make it difficult to get into good colleges were salient issues. Many Black American adolescent females discussed their realization that White American standards of beauty (especially hair and skin color) did not apply to them; Black American adolescent males were concerned with possible job discrimination and the need to distinguish themselves from a negative societal image of Black male adolescents. For Hispanic American adolescents, prejudice was a recurrent theme, as was conflicting values between their Hispanic cultural heritage and the majority culture. To read further about identity development in ethnic-minority youth, turn to Perspective on Life-Span Development 13.1.

Gender

In Erikson's (1968) classic presentation of identity development, the division of labor between the sexes was reflected in his assertion that males' aspirations were mainly oriented toward career and ideological commitments, while females' were centered around marriage and childrearing. In the 1960s and 1970s researchers found support for Erikson's assertion about gender differences in identity. For example, vocational concerns were more central to the identity of males, and affiliative concerns were more important in the identity of females (LaVoie, 1976). However, in the last decade, as females have developed stronger vocational interests, sex differences are turning into sex similarities (Waterman, 1985).

Some investigators believe the order of stages proposed by Erikson are different for females and males. One view is that for males, identity formation precedes the stage of intimacy, while for females, intimacy precedes identity (Douvan & Adelson, 1966). These ideas are consistent with the belief that relationships and emotional bonds are more important concerns of females, while autonomy and achievement are more important concerns of males (Gilligan, 1990). In one study, the development of a clear sense of self by adolescent girls was related to their concerns about care and response in relationships (Rogers, 1987). In another investigation, a strong sense of self in college women was associated with their ability to solve problems of care in relationships while staying connected with both self and others (Skoe & Marcia, 1988).

The task of identity exploration may be more complex for females than males in that females may try to establish identities in more domains than

THE DEVELOPMENT OF IDENTITY IN NATIVE AMERICAN ADOLESCENTS

Substandard living conditions, poverty, and chronic unemployment place many Native American youth at risk for school failure and poor health, which can contribute to problems in developing a positive identity (LaFromboise & Low, 1989; Spencer & Markstrom-Adams, 1990). A special concern is the negative image of Native Americans that has been perpetuated for centuries in the majority White American culture. To consider further the development of identity in Native American youth, let's examine the experiences of a 12-year-old Hopi Indian boy.

The Hopi Indians are a quiet, thoughtful people, who go to great lengths not to offend anyone. In a pueblo north of Albuquerque, a 12-year-old boy speaks: "I've been living in Albuquerque for a year. The Anglos I've met, they're different. I don't know why. In school, I drew a picture of my father's horse. One of the other kids wouldn't believe that it was ours. He said, 'You don't really own that horse.' I said, 'It's a horse my father rides, and I feed it every morning.' He said, 'How come?' I said, 'My uncle and my father are good riders, and I'm pretty good.' He said, 'I can ride a horse better than you, and I'd rather be a pilot.' I told him I never thought of being a pilot."

The 12-year-old Indian boy continues, "Anglo kids, they won't let you get away with anything. Tell them something, and fast as lightning and loud as thunder, they'll say, 'I'm better than you, so there!' My father says it's always been like that."

Native American adolescents are not really angry or envious of White adolescents. Maybe they are in awe of their future power; maybe they fear it. White adolescents can't keep from wondering if, in some way, they have missed out on something, and may end up "losing" (Coles, 1986).

Like children and adolescents from other ethnic minority groups, Native

The American Indian adolescent's quest for identity involves a cultural meshing of tribal customs and the technological, educational demands of modern society.

American youths often are confronted with conflicting values and expectations—those of the larger society and those of their ethnic group—from which they must choose an identity (Spencer & Markstrom-Adams, 1990). Tribal spirituality continues to be an important aspect of Native American culture. Native American children and adolescents are expected to participate in ceremonies related to these spiritual practices, which may violate attendance policies of Anglo-operated schools (LaFromboise & Low, 1989). The Native American youths' task of sorting through the values and expectations of the larger society and the Native American culture and then arriving at a coherent identity is a formidable one. If Native American youths develop an identity that in-

cludes many ingredients of the larger culture, they risk being rejected by their tribal members. Many Native American adolescents oscillate between an identity with the larger Anglo society and an identity with a tribe.

The following words of an American Indian vividly capture some important aspects of Native American youth's search for an identity:

> Rivers flow.
> The sea sings.
> Oceans roar.
> Tides rise.
> Who am I?
>
> A small pebble
> On a giant shore;
> Who am I
> To ask who I am?
> Isn't it enough to be?

Concept Table 13.2: Values, Religion, and Cults; Culture; and Identity

Concept	Processes/Related Ideas	Characteristics/Description
Values, Religion, and Cults	Values	Over the last two decades, adolescents have shown an increased concern for personal well-being and a decreased concern for the welfare of others. Recently, adolescents have shown a slight increase in concern for community and societal issues.
	Religious Beliefs and the Church	Both Elkind's and Fowler's views illustrate the increased abstractness in adolescents' thinking that improves their understanding of the nature of religion. Adolescents show a strong interest in spiritual matters but believe that organized religion does not provide them with the spiritual understanding they are seeking. Adolescents who attend church and value religion in their lives are less experienced sexually and have less permissive attitudes toward sexual activity than their counterparts who have low religious involvement.
	Cults	Cult membership in the United States is extensive among youth. Cults may appeal to adolescents because of weaknesses in organized religion and families.
Culture and Rites of Passage	Its Nature	As in other periods of development, culture influences adolescents' development. Ceremonies mark an individual's transition from one status to another, especially into adulthood. In primitive cultures, rites of passage are often well defined. In contemporary America, rites of passage to adulthood are ill-defined.
Identity	Erikson's Theory	This is the most comprehensive and provocative view of identity development. Identity versus identity confusion is the fifth stage in Erikson's life-cycle theory. During adolescence, world views become important and the adolescent enters a psychological moratorium, a gap between childhood security and adult autonomy.
	Some Contemporary Thoughts about Identity	Identity development is extraordinarily complex. It is done in bits and pieces. For the first time in development, during adolescence, individuals are physically, cognitively, and socially mature enough to synthesize their lives and pursue a viable path toward adult maturity.

males. In today's world, the options for females have increased, and thus may at times be confusing and conflicting, especially for females who hope to successfully integrate family and career roles (Archer, 1989, 1991; Gilligan, 1990).

At this point we have studied a number of different ideas about values, religion, and cults; about culture; and about identity. A summary of these ideas is presented in concept table 13.2. This concludes our discussion of adolescence. In the next section of the book we turn our attention to development in early adulthood.

Summary

I. Autonomy and Attachment
Many parents have a difficult time handling the adolescent's push for autonomy, even though this push is one of the hallmarks of adolescent development. Adolescents do not simply move into a peer world isolated from parents. Attachment to parents increases the likelihood the adolescent will be socially competent and explore a widening social world in healthy ways.

II. Parent-Adolescent Conflict and the Maturation of the Adolescent and Parents
Conflict with parents usually increases in early adolescence. This conflict often is of the moderate variety. The increase in conflict probably serves a positive developmental function of promoting autonomy and identity. A small subset of adolescents experience high parent-adolescent conflict that is related to various negative outcomes for adolescents. Physical, cognitive, and

Concept	Processes/Related Ideas	Characteristics/Description
	The Four Statuses of Identity	Marcia proposed that four statuses of identity exist, based on a combination of conflict and commitment: identity diffusion, identity foreclosure, identity moratorium, and identity achievement.
	Developmental Changes	Some experts believe the main identity changes take place in late adolescence or youth rather than in early adolescence. College upperclassmen are more likely to be identity achieved than freshmen or high school students, although many college students are still wrestling with ideological commitments. Individuals often follow "moratorium-achievement-moratorium-achievement" cycles.
	Family Influences	Parents are important figures in adolescents' identity development. Democratic parenting facilitates identity development in adolescence; autocratic and permissive parenting do not. Cooper and her colleagues have shown that both individuation and connectedness in family relations make important contributions to adolescent identity development. Hauser has shown that enabling behaviors promote identity development more than constraining behaviors.
	Cultural and Ethnic Influences	Erikson is especially sensitive to the role of culture in identity development, underscoring how throughout the world ethnic-minority groups have struggled to maintain their cultural identities while blending into the majority culture. Adolescence is often a special juncture in the identity development of ethnic-minority individuals because, for the first time, they consciously confront their ethnic identity.
	Gender	While Erikson's classical theory argued for sex differences in identity development, more recent studies have shown that as females have developed stronger vocational interests, sex differences in identity are turning into similarities. However, others argue that relationships and emotional bonds are more central to the identity development of females than males, and that female identity development today is more complex than male identity development.

social changes in the adolescent's development influence parent-adolescent relationships. Parental changes—marital dissatisfaction, economic burdens, career reevaluation and time perspective, and health and body concerns—also influence parent-adolescent relationships.

III. **Peer Pressure and Conformity, Cliques and Crowds**

The pressure to conform to peers is strong in adolescence, especially during the eighth and ninth grades. There are usually three to six well-defined cliques in every secondary school. Membership in certain cliques—especially jocks and populars—is associated with increased self-esteem. Independents also show high self-esteem.

IV. **Children and Adolescent Groups, and Dating**

Children groups are less formal, less heterogeneous, and less heterosexual than adolescent groups. Dunphy found that the development of adolescent groups moves through five stages. Dating can be a form of mate selection, recreation, a source of status and achievement, and a setting for learning about close relationships. Most adolescents are involved in dating. It appears that adolescent females are more interested in intimacy and personality exploration than adolescent males are. Dating varies cross-culturally.

V. **Values, Religion, and Cults**

Over the last two decades adolescents have shown an increased concern for personal well-being and a decreased concern for the welfare of others. Recently, adolescents have shown a slight increase in concern for community and societal issues. Both Elkind's and Fowler's views illustrate the increased abstractness in adolescents' thinking that improves their understanding of the nature of religion. Adolescents show a strong interest in spiritual matters but believe that organized religion does not provide them with the spiritual understanding they are seeking. Adolescents who attend church and value religion in their lives are less experienced sexually and have less permissive attitudes toward sexual activity than their counterparts who have low religious involvement. Cult membership in the United States is extensive. It may appeal to adolescents because of weaknesses in organized religion and families.

VI. Rites of Passage

Rites of passage are ceremonies that mark an individual's transition from one status to another, especially into adulthood. In primitive cultures, rites of passage are often well defined. In contemporary America, rites of passage to adulthood are ill-defined.

VII. Erikson's Theory and Some Contemporary Thoughts on Identity

Erikson's theory is the most comprehensive and provocative view of identity development. Identity versus identity confusion is the fifth stage in Erikson's life-cycle theory. During adolescence, world views become important, and the adolescent enters a psychological moratorium, a gap between childhood security and adult autonomy. Identity development is extraordinarily complex. It is done in bits and pieces. For the first time in development, during adolescence, individuals are physically, cognitively, and socially mature enough to synthesize their lives and pursue a viable path toward adult maturity.

VIII. The Four Statuses of Identity and Developmental Changes

Marcia proposed four identity statuses—identity diffusion, identity foreclosure, identity moratorium, and identity achievement—that are based on crisis (exploration) and commitment. Some experts believe the identity status approach oversimplifies Erikson's ideas. Some experts believe the main identity changes take place in youth rather than earlier in adolescence. College upperclassmen are more likely to be identity achieved than freshmen or high school students, although many college students are still wrestling with ideological commitments. Individuals often follow "moratorium-achievement-moratorium-achievement" cycles throughout life.

IX. Family Influences on Identity

Parents are important figures in adolescents' identity development. Democratic parenting facilitates identity development in adolescence; autocratic and permissive parenting do not. Cooper and her colleagues have shown that both individuation and connectedness in family relations are important contributers to adolescent identity development. Hauser has shown that enabling behaviors promote identity development more than contraining behaviors.

X. Cultural and Ethnic Factors in Identity

Erikson is especially sensitive to the role of culture in identity development, underscoring how throughout the world ethnic-minority groups have struggled to maintain their cultural identities while blending into the dominant culture. Adolescence is often a special juncture in the identity development of ethnic-minority individuals because for the first time they consciously confront their ethnic identity.

XI. Gender and Identity

Erikson's classical theory argued for sex differences in identity development. More recent studies have shown that as females have developed stronger vocational interests, sex differences in identity are often turning into similarities. However, others argue that relationships and emotional bonds are more central to the identity development of females than males, and that female identity development today is more complex than male identity development.

Key Terms

crowd   432
cliques   432
individuating-reflexive faith   438
rite of passage   440

crisis   443
commitment   443
identity diffusion   443
identity foreclosure   443

identity moratorium   443
identity achievement   444
individuation   445
connectedness   445

Suggested Readings

Berndt, T. J., & Ladd, G. W. (1989). *Peer relationships in child development.* New York: Wiley. *These writers give very up-to-date, authoritative information about the nature of peer relations in childhood and adolescence.*

Collins, W. A. (1990). Parent-child relationships in the transition to adolescence: Continuity and change in interaction, affect, and cognition. In R. Montemayor, G. R. Adams, & T. P. Gulotta (Eds.), *From childhood to adolescence: A transitional period?* Newbury Park, CA: Sage. *This chapter provides a thorough summary of the key ideas involved in early adolescent-parent relationships.*

Erikson, E. H. (1969). *Gandhi's truth.* New York: W. W. Norton. *In this Pulitzer prize-winning novel, Erikson weaves an insightful picture of Gandhi's identity development.*

Feldman, S. S., & Elliott, G. R. (1990). Progress and promise of research on adolescence. In S. S. Feldman & G. R. Elliott (Eds.), *At the threshold: The developing adolescent.* Cambridge, MA: Harvard University Press. *This excellent overview of the contemporary status of research on adolescence examines many of the issues we have discussed in this chapter.*

Levine, S. V. (1984, August). Radical departures. *Psychology Today,* 18–27. *This article gives an in-depth discussion of cults and includes a discussion of how families should deal with cults and strategies for helping adolescents who have joined cults.*

Marcia, J. (1987). The identity status approach to the study of ego identity development. In T. Honess & K. Yardley (Eds.), *Self and identity: Perspectives across the life-span.* London: Routledge & Kegan Paul. *Marcia presents his concept of the four statuses of identity development and describes the complexity of the identity process.*

Spencer, M. B., & Dornbusch, S. M. (1990). Challenges in studying minority youth. In S. S. Feldman & G. R. Elliott (Eds.), *At the threshold: The developing adolescent.* Cambridge, MA: Harvard University Press. *A superb review of the issues involved in ethnic minority identity development is presented.*

S·E·C·T·I·O·N
VII

EARLY ADULTHOOD

> *H*ow many roads must a man walk down
> before you call him a man?
>
> *Bob Dylan*

CHAPTER 14

Physical and Cognitive Development in Early Adulthood

Robert is in his senior year of college and just had his twenty-first birthday last week. Looking to his future and pondering what life might be like over the next few years, he came up with the following tongue-in-cheek reasons not to take a job:

1. You have to work.
2. It's habit forming. Once you get a job, you'll want another, and then another. . . . It's better not to start at all. Why do you think they call it work?
3. Once you stop being a student, you can never go back. Remember those pathetic people who came back to hang around your high school? You'll look even sillier showing up at mixers, pep rallies, and Sadie Hawkins dances after you have taken a position with some respectable accounting firm.
4. It's unbearably tedious. Not only that, but employees and their families are not eligible to win.
5. Taking a job means taking on new responsibilities. Before you know it, you will be married to an overweight hypochondriac with four sickly brats with crooked teeth and a house in the 'burbs. You will have to take out insurance policies on everything from health care to rodent invasions. Soon you will seriously be considering purchasing a condominium in Fort Lauderdale or Rio Rancho Retirement Village. All this can be avoided by the simple decision not to take a job.
6. People will start calling you "mister" and "sir." Hippies will resent you and call you a "capitalist roader." People with better jobs will shake their heads and say, "What a waste of human talent."
7. Fully employed people can never have sex.
8. You will have to say nice things about the boss's new "flame-thrower red" polyester golf pants, laugh at the boss's jokes about people who mismanage their finances, and carry on endless conversations with your boss about "pennant rallies," "the primaries," and "resort areas." You will have to nod your head with conviction when he refers to his employees as a "team" that works together to "bring home the bacon."
9. If you take a job, you will be an adult (*The Harvard Lampoon Big Book of College Life*).

In this chapter, we explore what it is like to take a job as the nature of careers and work in early adulthood is described. You will also read about changes in our cognitive development in early adulthood and the importance of sexuality in our lives as young adults. Information about physical changes in early adulthood is presented, too, but first we think about the transition from adolescence to adulthood.

The Transition from Adolescence to Adulthood

As Bob Dylan asked at the opening of section VII, "How many roads must a man walk down before you call him a man?" when does an adolescent become an adult? In chapter 12, we saw that it is not easy to tell when a boy or girl enters adolescence. Many developmentalists, though, believe the task of determining adolescence's beginning is easier than determining its end and adulthood's beginning. Although no consensus exists as to when adolescence is left behind and adulthood is entered, some criteria have been proposed.

> *We are born twice over; the first time for existence, the second for life; once as human beings and later as men or as women.*
>
> *Jean-Jacques Rousseau*

Youth and the Criteria for Becoming an Adult

Faced with a complex world of work, with highly specialized tasks, many post-teenagers spend an extended period of time in technical institutes, colleges, and postgraduate centers to acquire specialized skills, educational experiences, and professional training. Earning levels are low and sporadic, and established residences may change frequently. Marriage and a family may be shunned. This period often lasts from two to eight years, although it is not unusual for it to last a decade or longer.

Youth *is sociologist Kenneth Kenniston's (1970) term for the transitional period between adolescence and adulthood that is a time of extended economic and personal temporariness.* Kenniston argues that youth have not settled the questions whose answers once defined adulthood—questions about one's relation to the existing society, about vocation, and about social roles and life-styles. Youth differs from adolescence because of youth's struggle between developing an autonomous self and becoming socially involved in contrast to adolescence's struggle for self-definition.

Two criteria that have been proposed as signaling the end of youth and the beginning of early adulthood are economic independence and independent decision making. Probably the most widely recognized marker of adulthood's entrance is the occasion when the individual takes a more-or-less permanent full-time job. This usually occurs when the individual finishes school—high school for some, college for others, and graduate school for still others. For those who finish high school, move away from home, and assume a career, the transition to adulthood seems to have taken place. But one out of every four individuals does not complete high school, and many individuals who finish college cannot find a job. Further, only a small percentage of graduates settle into jobs that remain permanent throughout their adult lives. Also, attaining economic independence from parents is usually a gradual, rather than an abrupt, process. It is not unusual to find college graduates getting a job and continuing to live, or returning to live, with their parents, especially in today's economic climate.

The ability to make decisions is another characteristic that does not seem to be fully developed in youth. We refer broadly here to decision making about a career, about values, about family and relationships, and about life-style. As a youth, the individual may still be trying out many different roles, exploring alternative careers, thinking about a variety of life-styles, and considering the variety of relationships that are available. The individual who enters adulthood usually has made some of these decisions, especially in the areas of life-style and career.

While change characterizes the transition from adolescence to adulthood, keep in mind that considerable continuity still glues these periods together. Consider the data collected in a longitudinal study of more than 2,000 males from the time they were in the tenth grade until five years after high school (Bachman, O'Malley, & Johnston, 1978). Some of the males dropped out, others graduated from high school; some took jobs after graduating from high school, others went to college; some were employed, others were unemployed. The dominant picture of the males as they went through this eight-year period was stability rather than change. For example, the tenth graders who had the highest self-esteem were virtually the same individuals who had the highest self-esteem five years after high school. A similar patterning was found for achievement orientation—those who were the most achievement oriented in the tenth grade remained the most achievement oriented eight years later. Some environmental changes produced differences in this transition period. For example, marriage reduced drug use, unemployment increased it.

The process of entering into adulthood is more lengthy and complex than has usually been imagined. It begins around 17 and continues until 33. . . . A young man needs about 15 years to emerge from adolescence, find his place in adult society and commit himself to a more stable life.

~ *Daniel J. Levinson,*
Seasons of a Man's Life *1978*

Early Adulthood

Success in college and career increased achievement orientation; less education and poor occupational performance diminished achievement orientation.

Transition from High School to College

Just as the transition from elementary school to middle or junior high school involves change and possible stress, so does the transition from high school to college. In many instances, there are parallel changes in the two transitions. Going from a senior in high school to a freshman in college replays the top-dog phenomenon of going from the oldest and most powerful group of students to the youngest and least powerful group of students that occurred earlier as adolescence began. For many of you, the transition from high school to college was not very long ago. You may vividly remember the feeling of your first days, weeks, and months on campus. You were called a freshman. Dictionary definitions of *freshmen* describe students as being in the first year of high school or college, and as novices and beginners. *Senior* designates them as being in the final year of high school or college, and as above others in decision-making power. The transition from high school to college involves movement to a larger, more impersonal school structure; interaction with peers from more diverse geographical and sometimes more diverse ethnic backgrounds; and increased focus on achievement and its assessment (Belle & Paul, 1989; Upcraft & Gardner, 1989).

But as with the transition from elementary to middle or junior high school, the transition from high school to college can involve positive features. Students are more likely to feel grown up, have more subjects from which to select, have more time to spend with peers, have more opportunities to explore different life-styles and values, enjoy greater independence from parental monitoring, and are more likely to be challenged intellectually by academic work.

However, today's college freshmen appear to be experiencing more stress and depression than in the past, according to a survey of more than 300,000 freshmen at more than 500 colleges and universities (Astin, Green, & Korn, 1989). In 1987, 8.7 percent of freshmen reported feeling depressed often; in 1988, the figure rose to 10.5 percent. Fear of failing in a success-oriented world is frequently given as a reason for stress and depression among college students. The pressure to succeed in college, get an outstanding job, and make lots of money is pervasive, according to many of the students.

Some college students report that they feel "burned out." **Burnout** *is a hopeless, helpless feeling brought on by relentless, work-related stress.* Burnout leaves its sufferers in a state of physical and emotional exhaustion that

Weight lifting has helped some athletes gain their peak performance at an older age than in the past. In the 1988 Olympics, Florence Griffith Joyner broke world records in the 100 and 200 meters at the age of 28. In previous Olympics, dating back to 1896, the average age of Olympic champion female sprinters was 22 years of age.

includes chronic fatigue and low energy. Burnout usually does not occur because of one or two traumatic events but because of a gradual accumulation of heavy, work-related stress (Garden, 1989; Pines & Aronson, 1988).

On a number of campuses, college burnout is the most frequent reason students leave school before earning their degrees, reaching a rate of 25 percent at some schools. Dropping out of college for a semester or two used to be considered a sign of weakness. Now sometimes called "stopping out" because the student fully intends to return, it may be encouraged for some students who feel overwhelmed with stress. Before recommending "stopping out" though, most counselors suggest first examining ways the overload could be reduced and possible coping strategies that would allow the student to remain in school. The simple strategy of taking a reduced or better balanced class load sometimes works, for example. Most college counseling services have professionals who can effectively work with students to alleviate the sense of being overloaded and overwhelmed by life (Leafgren, 1989; Rayman & Garis, 1989).

Physical Development

Physical status not only reaches its peak in early adulthood, it also begins to decline during this period. An interest in health has increased among young adults, with special concerns about diet, weight, and exercise.

The Peak and Slowdown in Physical Performance

For most of us, our peak physical performance is reached under the age of 30, often between the ages of 19 and 26. This peak of physical performance not only occurs for the average young adult, but for outstanding athletes as well. Even though athletes keep getting better—running faster, jumping higher, and lifting more weight—the age at which they reach their peak performance has remained virtually the same. Richard Schultz and Christine Curnow (1988) analyzed records from track and field, swimming, baseball, tennis, and golf to learn at which age athletes turned in their best performances. For example, in track and field they studied Olympic results from 1896 through 1980. Overall, the mean age of the winners from 1896 to 1936 was about the same as from 1948 to 1980. In the 1,500 meter race, the earlier winners averaged 25 years of age, the more recent winners averaged 24.6 years of age. For marathoners, the average age of Olympic champions was 27. The average age for swimming champions was 20 years for males, 18 for females. This gender difference also held for track and field, although the difference was only one year. For professional baseball players, the mean age of peak performance was consistently 27 to 28 years, based on wins, strikeouts, and earned run averages for pitchers, and batting averages, home runs, and runs batted in for nonpitchers. For tennis and golf, world professional rankings were examined. In tennis, the champions' mean ages were 25.4 for males, 24.5 for females. In golf, stars' peak performances were 31 years for males, 30 years for females.

In sum, the strength and speed events peak relatively early, compared to those requiring more diverse motor and cognitive skills. In recent years, though, the "biological window" of peak performance has widened in some individual cases. Weight training, once unthinkable for female athletes, has become standard procedure for such athletic stars as Florence Griffith Joyner. Her ability to lift 320 pounds helped build the strength behind the explosive start and leg drive that produced world records at the age of 28, of 10.49 seconds in the 100 meters and 21.34 seconds in the 200 meters, in the 1988 Olympics. Figure 14.1 summarizes the age of peak performances in professional baseball, the Olympics, tennis, and golf.

Peak performances in baseball	
Pitchers	**Mean age**
Wins	27.3
Strikeouts	27.3
Earned run average	27.7
Nonpitchers	
Batting average	26.5
Home runs	27.3
Runs batted in	28.0

Peak performance age, by event		
	Men	**Women**
18		Swimming
19		
20	Swimming	
21		
22		Running short distance
23	Running short distance	
24	Jumping	Running medium distance
	Running medium distance Tennis	Tennis
25		
26		
27	Running long distance	Running long distance
28	Baseball	
29		
30		Golf
31	Golf	
32		

Figure 14.1 Age at peak performance by professional baseball players, Olympic champions, tennis players, and golfers.
Source: PSYCHOLOGY TODAY MAGAZINE, December 1988. Copyright © 1988 (PT Partners, L. P.).

We not only reach our peak physical performance during early adulthood, but during this time we are also the healthiest. Few young adults have chronic health problems, and they have fewer colds and respiratory problems than when they were children. Most college students know what it takes to prevent illness and promote health. In one study, college students' ranking of health-protective activities—nutrition, sleep, exercise, watching one's weight, and so on—virtually matched that of licensed nurses (Turk, Rudy, & Salovey, 1984).

While most college students know what it takes to prevent illness and promote health, they don't fare very well when it comes to applying this information to themselves. In one investigation, college students reported that they probably would never have a heart attack or drinking problem, but that other college students would (Weinstein, 1984). The college students also said no relation exists between their risk of heart attack and how much they exercise, smoke, or eat meat or high cholesterol food such as eggs, even though they correctly recognized that factors such as family history influence risk. Many college students, it seems, have unrealistic, overly optimistic beliefs about their future health risks.

As individuals move from adolescence to early adulthood, they often increase their use of drugs. For example, in one longitudinal investigation, as individuals moved from the tenth grade to five years after high school, they increased their cigarette smoking, drinking, marijuana smoking, and use of amphetamines, barbiturates, and hallucinogens (Bachman, O'Malley, & Johnston, 1978). Other data confirm that the period from late adolescence to the late twenties is a time of peak levels for many drugs (Johnston, O'Malley, & Bachman, 1987; 1991). Special concerns are the increase in party drinking by college students and the increased use of cocaine by young adults. Heavy party drinking by college males is common and becoming more common (Johnston, O'Malley, & Bachman, 1991). Fortunately, cocaine use by college students declined from 17.1 percent annual prevalence in 1986 to 8.6 percent in 1990. Still, the number of college students who use cocaine is precariously high, and is likely higher among non-college youth.

In early adulthood, few individuals stop to think about how their personal life-styles will affect their health later in their adult lives. As young adults, many of us develop a pattern of not eating breakfast, not eating regular meals, and relying on snacks as our main food source during the day, eating excessively to the point we exceed the normal weight for our age, smoking moderately or excessively, drinking moderately or excessively, failing to exercise, and getting by with only a few hours of sleep at night. These poor personal life-styles were associated with poor health in one investigation of 7,000 individuals from the ages of 20 to 70 (Belloc & Breslow, 1972). In the California Longitudinal Study—in which individuals were evaluated over a period of forty years—physical health at age 30 predicted life satisfaction at age 70, more so for men than women (Mussen, Honzik, & Eichorn, 1982).

There are some hidden dangers in the peaks of performance and health in early adulthood. While young adults can draw on physical resources for a great deal of pleasure, often bouncing back easily from physical stress and abuse, this may lead them to push their bodies too far. The negative effects of abusing one's body may not show up in the first part of early adulthood, but they probably will surface later in early adulthood or in middle adulthood.

Not only do we reach our peak in physical performance during early adulthood, but it is during this age period that we also begin to decline in physical performance. Muscle tone and strength usually begin to show signs of decline around the age of 30. Sagging chins and protruding abdomens may also begin to appear for the first time. The lessening of physical abilities is a common complaint among the just-turned-thirties. Says one 30-year-old, "I played tennis last night. My knees are sore and my lower back aches. Last month, it was my elbow that hurt. Several years ago it wasn't that way. I could play all day and not be sore the next morning." Sensory systems show little change in early adulthood, but the lens of the eye loses some of its elasticity and becomes less able to change shape and focus on near objects. Hearing peaks in adolescence, remains constant in the first part of early adulthood, and then begins to decline in the last part of early adulthood. And in the mid to late twenties, the body's fatty tissue increases.

The health profile of our nation's young adults can be improved by reducing the incidence of certain health-impairing life-styles, such as over-eating, and by engaging in health-improving life-styles that include good nutrition and exercise.

Nutrition and Eating Behavior

A tall, slender female goes into the locker room of the fitness center, hurls her towel across the bench, looks squarely in the mirror and says, "You fat pig. You are nothing but a fat pig." The alarm goes off and 33-year-old Robert jumps out of bed, throws on his jogging shorts, and begins his daily predawn three-mile-run. Returning to shower and dress, he too observes his body in the mirror, tugging at the flabby overhang and commenting, "Why did you eat that bowl of ice cream last night?" The Chicago Bears' William "the Refrigerator" Perry ballooned to 350 pounds and Bears' coach Mike Ditka suspended him, requiring him to enroll in a 28-day eating-disorder program.

> The tissue of life to be
> We weave with colors all our own
> And in the field of destiny
> We reap as we have sown.
> ~ *John Greenleaf Whittier*
> Raphael, *1842*

> Life is not living, but living in health.
> ~ *Martial,*
> Epigrams, A.D. *86*

Early Adulthood

We are a nation obsessed with food, spending an extraordinary amount of time thinking about, eating, and avoiding food. What causes us to be overweight? Which weight-loss program is the most effective?

What Causes People To Be Overweight?

Understanding why we get to be overweight is complex, involving genetic inheritance, physiological mechanisms, cognitive factors, and environmental influences (Carroll & Miller, 1991; Logue, 1986; Simmons, 1991; Stunkard, 1989). Some individuals may have inherited a tendency to be overweight. Only 10 percent of children who do not have obese parents become obese themselves, whereas about 40 percent of children who have one obese parent become obese, and about 70 percent of children who have two obese parents become obese. The extent this is due to genes or experiences with parents cannot be determined in research with humans, but animals can be bred to have a propensity for fatness (Blundell, 1984).

The amount of stored fat in your body is an important factor in your body weight's **set point,** *the weight maintained when no effort is made to gain or lose weight.* Fat is stored in adipose cells. When these cells are filled, you do not get hungry. When we gain weight the number of fat cells increases, and we may not be able to get rid of them. A normal weight individual has 30 to 40 billion fat cells. An obese individual has 80 to 120 billion fat cells. Interestingly, adults who were not obese as children but who become overweight as adults have larger fat cells than their normal weight counterparts, but they do not have more fat cells (VanItallie, 1984).

How much fat should we eat on a daily basis? What is the latest word on what we should eat to be healthy? In 1989, the National Research Council published a 1300 page document, *Diet and Health: Implications for reducing chronic disease risk,* the most comprehensive and detailed set of dietary guidelines ever. By following its recommendations, Americans could cut the risk of developing coronary heart disease by at least 20 percent, and could substantially lower the risk for a host of other ailments, including cancer, stroke, high blood pressure, obesity, osteoporosis, and liver disease. The document was prepared by a 19-member panel of health scientists after reviewing more than 5,000 research studies. Their recommendations include:

- Limit fats to 30 percent of daily calories (currently we average 40 percent), with saturated fats making up less than 10 percent of the intake. Keep cholesterol consumption below 300 milligrams daily. Diets should emphasize fish, skinless poultry, lean meats and low- or non-fat dairy products, and cut back on fried and other fatty foods, such as pastries, spreads, and dressings. To reduce cholesterol, limit consumption of egg yolks and high-cholesterol meats.
- Make carbohydrates account for at least 55 percent of your daily calories, rather than the present average of 45 percent. Eat five or more servings of vegetables daily, preferably the green and yellow kind, and fruits, especially citrus. Also eat complex carbohydrates such as pasta, whole-wheat breads, and cereals, which are usually low in fat and rich in vitamins, minerals, and fiber.
- Eat only moderate amounts of protein. A 120 pound woman fulfills her entire daily protein requirement with a 5.6-ounce hamburger; a 180 pound man meets it with an 8.4-ounce patty. Diets rich in animal protein have no known health benefits and

"Let's just go in and see what happens."

Drawing by Booth; © 1986 The New Yorker Magazine, Inc.

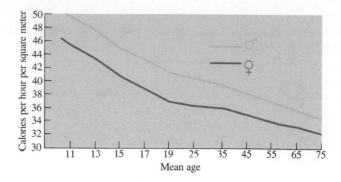

may increase the risk of colon or breast cancer. It is not known whether protein is the villain because meats are typically loaded with fat.

The panel of health experts vehemently condemned the use of dietary supplements. Some 40 to 60 percent of Americans routinely swallow vitamins, mineral tablets, protein powders, and the like. Most individuals do not need more than the recommended daily allowances for vitamins and minerals, which can easily be achieved through a varied diet. Megadoses of vitamins and minerals have no known benefits, and can actually be toxic. There is also no evidence that calcium supplements help to prevent osteoporosis, a crippling bone disease prevalent in older women. The recommended daily allowance of calcium is 800 milligrams. Women now consume about three-fourths of that amount. They could make up the shortfall by drinking one 5-ounce glass of low-fat milk each day. Fish oil capsules also got a thumbs down. Eating marine fish one or more times a week is believed to lower cholesterol, but proof that concentrated fish oil has the same result has not surfaced. Nor are fiber supplements warranted as a hedge against cancer of the stomach, large intestine, or lungs. The panel of experts endorses eating more high-fiber foods, but it is not known if the beneficial effects result from the fiber itself.

Health experts also point out that metabolic rate is important in understanding weight. **Basal metabolism rate (BMR)** *is the minimum amount of energy an individual uses in a resting state.* As shown in figure 14.2, BMR varies with age and sex. Rates decline precipitously during adolescence and then more gradually during adulthood, and they are slightly higher for males than females. Many individuals gradually increase their weight over a period of many years. Figure 14.2 suggests that to some degree the weight gain is due to a declining basal metabolism rate. The declining BMR underscores that to maintain weight in adulthood we have to reduce our food intake.

An Increasingly Heavy Population and Weight-Loss Programs
Our gustatory system and taste preferences developed at a time when food was scarce. Few calories were easily accessible in the environment first encountered by *Homo sapiens*. A concentrated source of sugar (and thus calories) was ripe fruit. Early in the history of our species a preference for sweet food and drinks probably developed because ripe fruit was so accessible. Today food and drinks with high concentrations of sugar are readily available to most of us. But unlike the ripe fruit of our ancestors, which contained sugar *plus* vitamins and minerals, Gummie Bears and Cocoa Crispies fill us with empty calories.

Estimates indicate that about one-half of the middle-aged population in the United States weighs over the upper limit of their normal weight range (Andres, 1989). As many as 25 percent of today's adolescents are estimated to be overweight. Further, the proportion of American children who are overweight increased more than 50 percent over the two decades from the 1960s to the 1980s (Dietz, 1986). Medical personnel and psychologists have become increasingly concerned about poor eating habits established in childhood and adolescence. Eating patterns in childhood and adolescence are strongly associated with obesity in adulthood—80 percent of obese adolescents become obese adults, for example (Brone & Fisher, 1988).

As individuals' weights have increased, interest in losing weight has become a national obsession. Throughout history there have been dieters. Even ancient Roman women were known to starve themselves. But never before has there been a time when so many people spent so much time, energy, and money on their weight. Since its inception in 1963, Weight Watchers alone has enrolled more than 15 million members. Although men *and* women have gained weight and both sexes show concern about losing weight, the obsession with dieting seems to be more intense among women.

A myriad of ways to lose weight exist: bypass surgery, exercise, diets, and different forms of psychotherapy. Which ones work? Does one work better than the rest? Do any of them work at all?

The most dramatic form of losing weight involves bypass surgery, which is an intestinal or gastric bypass operation. This procedure is recommended only for individuals who are 100 pounds or more overweight, in which case the obesity may be life threatening. Bypass surgery has been successful in reducing overeating. In one investigation of more than 700 patients followed for one year or longer, 55 percent of the overweight pounds were lost (Halmi, 1980). In some instances, though, bypass operations have serious side effects, among them liver disease. For extremely obese individuals, the benefits may be greater than the adverse side effects; for example, a more positive mood and increased physical exercise sometimes accompany reduced calorie intake in these individuals.

Drugs are also used to help individuals lose weight. Amphetamines are widely used to decrease food consumption, although they often have adverse side effects such as increased blood pressure and possible addiction. Weight loss with amphetamines is usually short-lived. The ineffective drugs include over-the-counter drugs such as Dexatrim. No drug is currently available that has been proven successful in long-term weight reduction (Logue, 1986).

Exercise is a much more attractive alternative than weight-loss drugs such as amphetamines. Exercise not only burns up calories, but it continues to raise the metabolic rate for several hours *after* the exercise. Exercise actually lowers your body's set point for weight, making it much easier to maintain a lower weight (Bennett & Gurin, 1982). Nonetheless, it is difficult to convince obese individuals to exercise. One problem is that moderate exercise does not reduce calorie consumption and in many cases individuals who exercise take in more calories than their sedentary counterparts (Stern, 1984). Still, exercise combined with conscious self-control of eating habits can produce a viable weight-loss program (Ogden & Wardle, 1991; Polivy & Herman, 1991). When exercise is a component of weight-loss programs, individuals keep weight off longer than when calorie reduction alone is followed.

A special concern has developed about very low calorie diets, especially powdered protein mixes (Wadden, 1990). Risks include cardiovascular problems and excessive muscle loss. The low calorie diets can be used effectively

This exhausted runner at the end of a grueling marathon endorses the "no pain, no gain" philosophy of the role of exercise in health. An alternative philosophy for most individuals is that moderate exercise is more pleasurable and easier to participate in over the long term. For some, intense exercise may be best, for others moderate exercise is best, but a sedentary life with little exercise should be avoided.

if supervised by a doctor, dietician, or behavioral psychologist. No diet or treatment program, though, is the panacea hoped for by millions of individuals who earnestly want to lose weight (Stunkard, 1989). If one program worked for everyone, the turnover rate in diet programs would not be so high.

Exercise

In 1961, President John F. Kennedy offered the following message: "We are underexercised as a nation. We look instead of play. We ride instead of walk. Our existence deprives us of the minimum of physical activity essential for healthy living." Without question, people are jogging, cycling, and aerobically exercising more today than in 1961, but far too many of us are still couch potatoes. **Aerobic exercise** *refers to sustained exercise—jogging, swimming, or cycling, for example—that stimulates heart and lung activity* (Cooper, 1970).

Effects of Exercise on Physical and Mental Health

The greatest effort to study the effects of exercise on health involves the role of exercise in preventing heart disease. Most health experts recommend that you should try to raise your heart rate to 60 percent of your maximum heart rate. Your maximum heart rate is calculated as 220 minus your age, so if you are 20, you should aim for an exercise heart rate of 120 (220 − 20 = 200 × .60 = 120). Some occupations require more vigorous exercise than others. For example, longshoremen have about half the risk of fatal heart attacks as co-workers, such as crane drivers and clerks, who have physically less demanding jobs. Further, in one elaborate investigation of 17,000 male alumni of Harvard University, those who played strenuous sports regularly had a lower risk of heart disease and were more likely to be alive (Paffenbarger & others, 1986). Based on such findings, some health experts conclude that regardless of other risk factors (smoking, high blood pressure, overweight, heredity), if you exercise enough to burn more than 2,000 calories per week, you can cut your risk of heart attack by an impressive two-thirds (Sherwood, Light, & Blumenthal, 1989). Burning up 2,000 calories a week through exercise requires a lot of effort, far more than most of us are willing to expend. To burn 300 calories a day, through exercise, you would have to do one of the following: swim or run for about 25 minutes, walk for 45 minutes at about 4 miles an hour, or participate in aerobic dancing for 30 minutes.

The risk of heart attack can also be cut by as much as one-third over a seven-year period with moderate exercise such as rapid walking and gardening. The catch is that you have to spend an hour a day in these activities to get them to pay off healthwise. Health experts uniformly recommend that if you are unaccustomed to exercise, always start any exercise program slowly.

Robert Ornstein and David Sobel (1989) believe that exercise should be pleasurable, not painful, which is contrary to the "no pain, no gain" philosophy. They point out that 20 percent of joggers running 10 miles a week suffer significant injuries, such as torn knee cartilage and pulled hamstring muscles. Ornstein and Sobel argue that most individuals can stay healthy by participating in exercise that burns up only 500 calories a week. They believe it is overkill to run 8-minute miles, 3 miles at a time, five days a week, for example. Not only are fast walking and gardening on their recommended list of exercises, so are 20 minutes of sex (110 calories), 20 minutes of playing with children (106 calories), and 45 minutes of dancing (324 calories).

Researchers have not only found exercise benefits for physical health, but also for mental health. Positive benefits of exercise on self-concept, anxiety, and depression have been demonstrated (Brown, 1991; Doyne & others, 1987; Lobstein, Ismail, & Rasmussen, 1989; Ossip-Klein & others, 1989; Plante & Rodin, 1990). In one recent investigation, 109 nonexercising vol-

In one recent experiment, the self-concept of depressed women was improved by either weight lifting or running (Ossip-Klein & others, 1989).

unteers were randomly assigned to one of four conditions: high-intensity aerobic training, moderate-intensity aerobic training, low-intensity nonaerobic training, and waiting list (Moses & others, 1989). In the high-intensity aerobic group, participants engaged in a continuous walk-jog program that elevated their heart rate 70 to 75 percent of maximum. In the moderate-intensity aerobic group, participants engaged in walking or jogging that elevated their heart rate 60 percent of maximum. In the low-intensity nonaerobic group, participants engaged in strength, mobility, and flexibility exercises in a slow, discontinuous manner for approximately 30 minutes. Each of these programs was held three to five times a week. In the wait list group, no exercise training or participation took place. The programs lasted for ten weeks. As expected, the high-intensity aerobic condition produced the most improved aerobic fitness when tested in a 12-minute walk-run. The moderate and low exercise conditions were also superior to the wait list condition in improving the fitness of the participants. However, psychological benefits were found only in the moderate intensity aerobic training condition. These benefits appeared immediately in the form of reduced tension and anxiety, and after three months in the form of improved ability to cope with stress.

Why were the psychological benefits superior in the moderate intensity aerobic condition? Possibly the participants in the high-intensity condition found the training too demanding, which would not be surprising because these individuals were nonexercisers prior to the study. The superiority of the moderate aerobic training condition over the nonaerobic low-exercise condition suggests that a minimum level of aerobic conditioning may be required to obtain important psychological benefits.

The accumulating evidence on the benefits of exercise suggests that both moderate and intense activities produce important physical and psychological gains. Some individuals enjoy rigorous, intense exercise. Others enjoy more moderate exercise routines. The enjoyment and pleasure we derive from exercise cooperate with its aerobic benefits to make exercise one of life's most important activities.

Sexuality

The importance of sex in our adult lives was vividly captured by Woody Allen's observation, "Sex without love is an empty experience. Yes, but as empty experiences go, it is one of the best." Allen's comments suggest not only a

"Don't encourage him Sylvia."

Reprinted by permission of Chronicle Features, San Francisco, CA.

• *Critical Thinking* •

Why have we historically had a double standard in sexual relations?

motivation for sex, but also interpretation of its role in our lives. What are our sexual attitudes and behavior as young adults like?

Sexual Attitudes and Behavior

Four percent of the male elephant seals off the coast of California were responsible for 85 percent of the copulations in one recent breeding season. Television soap operas might lead us to conclude that humans are not very different from the elephant seal, mating and moving from partner to partner. However, humans do show more allegiance to one partner than most species. Our advanced brains enable us to ponder about the best strategy for us.

Gathering information about sexual attitudes and behavior has not always been a straightforward affair. Consider how you would respond if someone asked you, How often do you have intercourse? or How many different sexual partners have you had? When sexual surveys are conducted, the people most likely to respond are those with liberal sexual attitudes who engage in liberal sexual behaviors. Thus, what we know is limited by the reluctance of individuals to candidly answer questions about extremely personal matters, and by our inability to get any answer, candid or otherwise, from individuals who believe that talking about sex with strangers should not be done (Allen & Santrock, in press). With these cautions in mind, we now examine a number of surveys of sexual attitudes and behavior at different points in the twentieth century, considering, first, heterosexual attitudes and behavior, and second, homosexual attitudes and behavior.

Heterosexual Attitudes and Behavior

If you had been a college student in 1940, you probably would have had a very different attitude toward many aspects of sexuality than you do today, especially if you are a female. A review of college students' sexual practices and attitudes from 1900 to 1980 reveals two important trends (Darling, Kallen, & VanDusen, 1984). First, the percentage of young people reporting intercourse has dramatically increased, and second, the proportion of females reporting sexual intercourse has increased more rapidly than in the case of males, although the initial base for males was greater. Prior to 1970, about twice as many college males as females reported they had engaged in sexual intercourse, but since 1970, the proportion of males and females is about equal. These changes suggest that major shifts in the standards governing sexual behavior have taken place. That is, there has been a movement away from the double standard in which it was more appropriate for males than females to have intercourse (Robinson & others, 1991).

Two surveys that include wider age ranges of adults verify these trends. Morton Hunt's survey of more than 2,000 adults in the 1970s revealed more permissiveness toward sexuality than Alfred Kinsey's inquiries in the 1940s (Hunt, 1974; Kinsey, Pomeroy, & Martin, 1948). Hunt's survey, though, may have overestimated sexual permissiveness because it was based on a sample of *Playboy* magazine readers. Kinsey found that foreplay consisted of a kiss or two, but by the 1970s Hunt discovered that foreplay had lengthened, now averaging fifteen minutes. Hunt also found that individuals in the 1970s were using more varied sexual techniques in their lovemaking. Oral-genital sex, virtually taboo at the time of Kinsey's survey, was more accepted by the 1970s.

Two more things about heterosexual attitudes and behavior are important to consider: the double standard we mentioned earlier and the nature of extramarital sex. While it has become more appropriate for females to engage in premarital sex, some vestiges of the double standard still exist (Bancroft, 1990; Erickson & Rapkin, 1991). Matters are often left up to the female to set the limits on the male's overtures. And although it is often thought that

Early Adulthood

the female should not plan ahead to have sexual intercourse (by taking contraceptive precautions), it is permissible for her to be swept up in the passion of the moment.

The double standard is at work in extramarital relations, too, although not as extensively as in earlier years. In Kinsey's research, about half of the husbands and one-fourth of the wives had engaged in sexual intercourse with someone other than their spouse during their marriage. In Hunt's survey in the 1970s, the figure was still about the same for males, but had increased for females, especially younger females. The majority of us still disapprove of extramarital sex; but while we disapprove of it, we still engage in it, a clear instance of a gap between sexual attitudes and behavior.

Homosexual Attitudes and Behavior

Both the early (Kinsey) and more recent (Hunt) surveys indicate that about 4 percent of males and 3 percent of females are exclusively homosexual. While the incidence of homosexual behavior does not seem to have increased, attitudes toward homosexuality were becoming more permissive, at least until recently. In 1986, the Gallup poll began to detect a shift in attitudes brought about by public awareness of AIDS. For example, in 1985, slightly more than 40 percent of Americans believed that "homosexual relations between consenting adults should be legal"; by 1986, the figure had dropped to just above 30 percent (Gallup Report, 1987). Individuals who have negative attitudes toward homosexuals are also likely to favor severe controls for AIDS, such as excluding AIDS carriers from the workplace and school (Fish & Rye, 1991; Pryor & others, 1988).

Why are some individuals homosexual whereas others are heterosexual? Speculation about this question has been extensive, but no firm answers are available. Homosexual and heterosexual males and females have similar physiological responses during sexual arousal and seem to be aroused by the same types of tactile stimulation. Investigators find that in terms of a wide range of attitudes, behaviors, and adjustments, no differences between homosexuals and heterosexuals are present (Bell, Weinberg, & Mammersmith, 1981). Recognizing that homosexuality is not a form of mental illness, the American Psychiatric Association discontinued its classification of homosexuality as a disorder, except in those cases where the individuals themselves consider the sexual orientation to be abnormal.

An individual's sexual orientation—heterosexual or homosexual—is most likely determined by a combination of genetic, hormonal, and environmental factors (McWhirter, Reinisch, & Sanders, 1989; Money, 1987; Remafedi, 1991). Most experts on homosexuality believe that no one factor alone causes homosexuality and that the relative weight of each factor may vary from one individual to the next. In truth, no one knows *exactly* what causes an individual to become a homosexual. Scientists have a clearer picture of what does not cause homosexuality than what does cause it. For example, children raised by gay or lesbian parents or couples are no more likely to be homosexual than are children raised by heterosexual parents. There is also no evidence that male homosexuality is caused by a dominant mother or a weak father, or that female homosexuality is caused by girls choosing male role models. Among the biological factors believed to be involved in homosexuality are prenatal hormone conditions (Ellis & Ames, 1987). In the second to fifth months after conception, exposure to hormone levels characteristic of females is speculated to cause the individual (male or female) to become attracted to males. If the prenatal critical period hypothesis turns out to be correct, it would explain why researchers and clinicians have found a homosexual orientation difficult to modify.

How have sexual attitudes and behavior changed during the twentieth century? You probably can think of your own conversations and experiences with others to document these changes. Earlier generations had a more conservative orientation toward sexuality, especially females. However, the epidemics of AIDS and Herpes have produced a more conservative sexual orientation in the last several years.

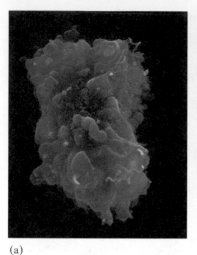
(a)

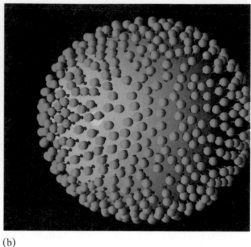
(b)

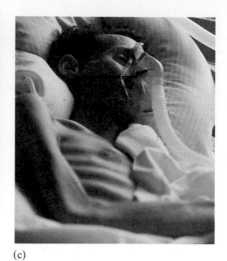
(c)

Figure 14.3   The AIDS virus. (a) The AIDS virus can remain dormant for months or years. Once activated though, it reproduces and bursts through the cell. Then, the AIDS virus (in blue above) attacks healthy cells (in tan above). (b) Shown above is a computer-generated model of the AIDS virus. (c) The virus destroys the body's immune system, as reflected in the weakened state of this AIDS patient.

AIDS

Sexual diseases have plagued human beings throughout history. Hippocrates wrote about syphilis in 460 B.C. The first major recorded epidemic of syphilis appeared in Naples, Italy, two years after Columbus's first return. It is believed that millions of people died of the disease, which is sexually transmitted through intercourse, kissing, or intimate body contact. The cause of syphilis is a tiny bacterium that requires warm, moist surfaces to penetrate the body. It was not until 400 years after the Italian outbreak that penicillin, a successful treatment for syphilis was discovered. Today we harbor the same fear of sexually transmitted disease as in Columbus's time, but instead of syphilis, the fear is of AIDS, a major sexually related problem that has generated considerable fear in today's world. **AIDS (Acquired Immune Deficiency Syndrome)** *is a virus that destroys the body's immune system* (see figure 14.3). *Consequently, many germs that usually do not harm someone with a normal immune system produce devastating results and eventually death.*

In 1981, when AIDS was first recognized in the United States, there were fewer than 60 reported cases. Beginning in 1990, according to Dr. Frank Press, President of the National Academy of Sciences, we began losing as many Americans each year to AIDS as we lost in the Vietnam War. Almost 60,000 Americans died in that war. According to federal health officials, 1 to 1.5 million Americans are now asymptomatic carriers of AIDS—those who are infected with the virus and presumably capable of infecting others but who show no clinical symptoms of AIDS. In 1989, the first attempt to assess AIDS among college students was made. Testing of 16,861 students found 30 students infected with the virus (American College Health Association, 1989). If the 12.5 million students attending college were infected at the same rate, 25,000 students would have the AIDS virus.

Experts say that AIDS can be transmitted only by sexual contact, sharing needles, or blood transfusion. While 90 percent of AIDS cases continue to occur among homosexual males or intravenous drug users, a disproportionate increase among females who are heterosexual partners of bisexual males or of intravenous drug users has been recently noted (Cantor & others, 1991; Smith, 1991). This increase suggests the risk of AIDS may be increasing among heterosexual individuals who have multiple sexual partners (Boyer & Hein, 1991; Corless & Pittman-Lindeman, 1989). Table 14.1 describes what's risky and what's not regarding AIDS.

Evidence that the AIDS epidemic has begun to reduce promiscuous behavior in both homosexual and heterosexual individuals is appearing

Table 14.1: Understanding AIDS—What's Risky, What's Not

The AIDS virus is not transmitted like colds or the flu, but by an exchange of infected blood, semen, or vaginal fluids. This usually occurs during sexual intercourse, in the sharing of drug needles, or to babies infected before or during birth.

You won't get AIDS from:
— Everyday contact with individuals around you in school or the workplace, at parties, in child-care centers, or in stores
— Swimming in a pool, even if someone in the pool has the AIDS virus
— A mosquito bite or from bedbugs, lice, flies, or other insects
— Saliva, sweat, tears, urine, or a bowel movement
— A kiss
— Clothes, telephones, or toilet seats
— Using a glass or eating utensils that someone else has used
— Being on a bus, train, or crowded elevator with an individual who is infected with the virus or who has AIDS

Blood donations and transfusions:
— You will not come into contact with the AIDS virus by donating blood at a blood bank
— The risk of getting AIDS from a blood transfusion has been greatly reduced. Donors are screened for risk factors, and donated blood is tested.

Risky behavior includes:
— Having a number of sexual partners
— Sharing drug needles and syringes
— Engaging in anal sex with or without a condom
— Performing vaginal or oral sex with someone who shoots drugs or engages in anal sex
— Engaging in sex with someone you don't know well or with someone who has several sexual partners
— Engaging in unprotected sex (without a condom) with an infected individual

Safe behavior includes:
— Not having sex
— Having sex with one mutually faithful, uninfected partner
— Having sex with proper protection
— Not shooting drugs

Source: United States government educational pamphlet: *America Responds to AIDS,* 1988.

(Kalichman, Kelly, & St. Lawrence, in press). In one investigation, single heterosexual males decreased their number of sexual partners from 2.8 to 1.8 from 1984 to 1986 (Winkelstein & others, 1987). In another investigation of 5,000 homosexual males, the percentage who said they were either celibate or monogamous increased from 14 to 39 percent between 1984 and 1986 (Fineberg, 1988). While these figures are encouraging in the latter study, virtually all of the homosexual males knew that condoms reduce the risk of contracting AIDS, yet 60 percent did not use them.

Given the high number of sexually transmitted diseases, a special concern is the knowledge individuals have about these diseases as well as other aspects of sexuality (Siegel & Krauss, 1991). How sexually literate are Americans?

Sexual Knowledge

According to June Reinisch (1990), director of the Kinsey Institute for Sex, Gender, and Reproduction, the United States is a nation whose citizens know more about how their automobiles function than how their bodies function sexually. Reinisch directed a recent national assessment of basic sexual knowledge, given to 1,974 adults. Among the results of the assessment:

- 65 percent did not know that most erection difficulties begin with physical problems
- 75 percent did not know that approximately 40 percent of American men have had an extramarital affair (some experts believe the rate of male infidelity is 60 percent or more)
- 50 percent did not know that oil-based lubricants should not be used with condoms or diaphragms; some cause holes in less than 60 seconds.

And American adolescents also have woefully inadequate sexual knowledge. In one investigation, a majority of adolescents believed that pregnancy risk is greatest during menstruation (Zelnik & Kantner, 1977).

Of course, it's not that American adolescents and adults are sheltered from sexual messages. According to Reinisch, we are inundated with sexual messages, but not sexual facts. Sexual information is abundant, but much of it is misinformation (Mueller & Powers, 1990). In some cases, even sex education teachers display sexual ignorance. One high school sex education teacher referred to erogenous zones as "erroneous zones," possibly causing the students to wonder if their sexually sensitive zones were characterized by error!

The Menstrual Cycle and Hormones

From early adolescence until some point in middle adulthood, a woman's body undergoes marked changes in hormone levels that are associated with the menstrual cycle. The latter part of the menstrual cycle, from about day 22 on, is associated with a greater incidence of depression, anxiety, and irritability than is the middle of the menstrual cycle, when ovulation is occurring. Women show higher levels of self-esteem and confidence during ovulation in comparison to other phases of the menstrual cycle (Bardwick, 1971). The weight of the evidence shows that mood swings are definitely associated with the middle of the menstrual cycle and the later premenstrual phase. However, it is not entirely clear whether the mood changes are due to positive upswing of mood during the middle phase, a downward swing during the premenstrual phase, or a combination of both. Moreover, as many as 25 percent of all women report no mood shifts at all during these two phases (Hyde, 1985).

What causes the changes in mood that affect 75 percent of all women? Hormonal changes are clearly one factor. Female hormones reach their peak at about day 22 to day 24 of the menstrual cycle, just at the time when depression and irritability peak. By contrast, mood changes could affect hormone levels. If so, intense feelings of irritability and depression may feed back to the endocrine system and produce more estrogen.

So far we have discussed a number of important issues involving sexuality that include sexual attitudes and behavior, AIDS, and the menstrual cycle. But it is important to also consider another topic involving sexuality, the forcible sexual behavior of rape.

Rape

Rape *is forcible sexual intercourse with a person who does not give consent.* Legal definitions of rape may differ from state to state. For example, in some states husbands are not prohibited from forcing their wives to have intercourse, although this law has been challenged in several states (Byer & Shainberg, 1991). Because of difficulties involved in reporting cases of rape, the actual incidence of rape is difficult to determine. Rape does occur most often in large cities, where it has been reported that 8 of every 10,000 women 12 years and older are raped each year. Reported rapes are close to the 200,000 per year mark.

Why is rape so pervasive in the American culture? Feminist writers believe males are socialized to be sexually aggressive, to regard women as inferior beings, and to view their own pleasure as the most important objective. Researchers have found the following characteristics common among rapists: aggression enhances the offender's sense of power or masculinity; anger toward women is present and the rapist wants to hurt the victim (Knight, Rosenberg, & Schneider, 1985).

An increasing concern is **date or acquaintance rape,** *which is coercive sexual activity directed at someone with whom the individual is at least casually acquainted.* Date rape is an increasing problem (Lloyd, 1991). In one investigation, almost two-thirds of college men admitted that they fondled women against their will, and one half admitted to forced sexual activity (Burkhart, 1983).

Rape is a traumatic experience for the victim and those close to her. The rape victim initially feels shock and numbness, and is often acutely disorganized. Some women show their distress through words and tears, others show more internalized suffering. The victims then strive to get their lives back to normal, although depression, fear, and anxiety may stay with them for many months and years. Sexual dysfunctions such as reduced sexual desire and the absence of orgasms occur in 50 percent of rape victims (Sprei & Courtois, 1988). Many rape victims make changes in their life-style, such as moving to a new apartment or refusing to go out at night. A woman's recovery depends on her coping resources as well as how well adjusted she was before the assault. Social support from parents, boyfriend/girlfriend or husband, and others close to her are important factors in her recovery, as is the availability of professional counseling, which is sometimes obtained through a rape crisis center.

At this point we have discussed a number of ideas about the transition from adolescence to adulthood, physical development, and sexuality. A summary of these ideas is presented in concept table 14.1. Now we examine the possibility that cognitive changes take place in early adulthood.

Cognitive Development

Do people continue to develop cognitively in adulthood or are they as smart as they ever will be by the end of adolescence? Do people continue to develop their creative skills in adulthood or are they as creative as they ever will be in childhood and adolescence?

Cognitive Stages

Piaget believed that an adolescent and an adult think in the same way. But some developmentalists believe it is not until adulthood that individuals consolidate their formal operational thinking. That is, they may begin to plan and hypothesize about problems as adolescents, but they become more systematic in approaching problems as adults. While some adults are more proficient at developing hypotheses and deducing solutions to problems than adolescents, many adults do not think in formal operational ways at all (Keating, 1980, 1990).

Other developmentalists believe that the absolute nature of adolescent logic and youth's buoyant optimism diminish in early adulthood. According to Gisela Labouvie-Vief (1982, 1986), a new integration of thought takes place in early adulthood. She thinks the adult years produce pragmatic constraints

Concept Table 14.1: The Transition from Adolescence to Adulthood, Physical Development, and Sexuality		
Concept	**Processes/Related Ideas**	**Characteristics/Description**
Transition from Adolescence to Adulthood	Youth	This transition was proposed by Kenniston; it is a period of economic and personal temporariness, and struggle between interest in self-autonomy and becoming socially involved. The period of youth averages two to eight years but can be longer.
	Criteria for Adulthood	Two criteria are economic independence and independent decision making. However, clear-cut criteria are yet to be established.
	Continuity and Change	There is both change and continuity in the transition from adolescence to adulthood.
Physical Development	The Peak and Slowdown in Physical Performance	Peak physical status is reached between 18 and 30, especially between 19 and 26. Individuals' health also peaks during these years. There is a hidden hazard in these peaks of physical performance and health; bad health habits may be formed. Toward the latter part of early adulthood, a detectable slowdown and decline in physical status is apparent.
	Nutrition and Eating Behavior	The causes for being overweight are complex and involve genetic factors, physiological mechanisms, cognitive factors, and environmental influences. Individuals have too much fat in their diet, cholesterol needs to be reduced, carbohydrates should be increased, and protein intake should be moderated. The population is increasingly heavy, and weight-loss programs abound. Cognitive strategies, especially self-control techniques, and exercise are helpful in weight reduction.
	Exercise	Both moderate and intense physical exercise produce important physical and psychological gains, such as lowered risk of heart disease and reduced anxiety. Experts increasingly recommend that your level of exercise should be pleasurable.

that require an adaptive strategy of less reliance on logical analysis in solving problems. Commitment, specialization, and channeling energy into finding one's niche in complex social and work systems replace the youth's fascination with idealized logic. If we assume that logical thought and buoyant optimism represent the criteria for cognitive maturity, we would have to admit that the cognitive activity of adults is too concrete and pragmatic. But from Labouvie-Vief's view, the adult's understanding of reality's constraints reflects cognitive maturity, not immaturity.

Our cognitive abilities are very strong during early adulthood, and they do show adaptation to the pragmatic aspects of our lives. Less clear is whether our logical skills actually decline. Competence as a young adult probably requires doses of both logical thinking skills and pragmatic adaptation to reality. For example, as architects design a building, they logically analyze and plan the structure but understand the cost constraints, environmental concerns, and time it will take to get the job done effectively.

William Perry (1970) has also charted some important changes in the way young adults think differently than adolescents. He believes adolescents often view the world in a basic dualistic fashion of polarities—right/wrong, we/they, or good/bad, for example. As youth mature and move into the adulthood years, they gradually become aware of the diversity of opinion and the multiple perspectives that others hold, which shakes their dualistic percep-

• *Critical Thinking* •

Other than an increase in pragmatic thinking, can you think of other ways that our cognitive development advances in early adulthood?

Concept	Processes/Related Ideas	Characteristics/Description
Sexuality	Heterosexual Attitudes and Behavior	Increased liberalization has occurred. Some dimensions of the double standard, however, still exist.
	Homosexual Attitudes and Behavior	Rates of homosexuality have remained constant in the twentieth century. Homosexuality is no longer classified as a disorder. Until recently acceptance of homosexuality was increasing, but in concert with the AIDS epidemic, acceptance of homosexuality has recently decreased. No definitive conclusions about the cause of homosexuality have been reached.
	AIDS	AIDS (Acquired Immune Deficiency Syndrome) is caused by a virus that destroys the body's immune system. AIDS can only be transmitted through sexual contact, sharing needles, or blood transfusion, or to babies before or during birth.
	Sexual Knowledge	According to a recent national survey, Americans are not very knowledgeable about sex. Many American adolescents and adults have misconceptions about sex.
	The Menstrual Cycle and Hormones	The relation between the menstrual cycle and personality fluctuations in females have been studied, and there is a relation between mood swings and the middle and later premenstrual phases of the cycle.
	Rape	This is forcible sexual intercourse with a person who does not give consent. Feminist writers believe rape is pervasive because males are socialized to be sexually aggressive, to regard women as inferior, and to view their own pleasure as the most important objective. An increasing concern is date or acquaintance rape. Rape is a traumatic experience for the victim. The support systems of family, boyfriend/girlfriend, and friends, as well as professional counseling, can help rape victims cope more effectively.

tions. Their *dualistic thinking* gives way to *multiple thinking,* as individuals come to understand that authorities may not have all of the answers. They begin to carve out their own territory of individualistic thinking, often believing that others are entitled to their own opinions and that one's personal opinion is as good as anyone else's. As these personal opinions become challenged by others, multiple thinking yields to *relative subordinate thinking,* in which an analytical, evaluative approach to knowledge is consciously and actively pursued. Only in the shift to *full relativism* does the adult completely comprehend that truth is relative, that the meaning of an event is related to the context in which the event occurs, and is confined to the framework that the knower uses to understand that event. In full relativism, the adult recognizes that relativism pervades all aspects of life, not just the academic world, and the adult also understands that knowledge is constructed, not given; it is contextual, not absolute. Perry's ideas have been widely used by educators and counselors in working with young adults in academic settings. Perry's ideas are oriented toward well-educated, bright individuals.

Another perspective on adult cognitive changes is offered by K. Warner Schaie (1977). He believes that Piaget's cognitive changes describe increasing efficiency in the *acquisition* of new information. It is doubtful that adults go beyond the powerful methods of scientific thinking characteristic of formal operational thought in their quest for knowledge. However, according to Schaie,

What can be known? The unknown. My true self runs toward a hill. More! O more! Visible.

~ *Theodore Roethke*

adults do progress beyond adolescents in their *use* of intellect. For example, in early adulthood, we typically switch from acquiring knowledge to applying knowledge, using what we know to pursue careers and families. The **achieving stage** *is Schaie's early adulthood stage that involves the application of intelligence to situations that have profound consequences for achieving long-term goals, such as those involving careers and knowledge.* These solutions must be integrated into a life plan that extends far into the future.

Schaie believes that young adults who master the cognitive skills needed to monitor their own behavior, and have therefore acquired considerable independence, move on to the next stage that involves social responsibility. The **responsibility stage** *is Schaie's stage that occurs when a family is established and attention is given to the needs of a spouse and offspring.* Similar extensions of cognitive skills are needed as the individual's career develops and responsibility for others arises on the job and in the community. The responsibility stage often begins in early adulthood and extends into middle adulthood.

The **executive stage** *is Schaie's middle adulthood stage in which people are responsible for societal systems and organizations (government or business, for example). In the executive stage the individual develops an understanding of how societal organizations work and the complex relationships that are involved.* In middle age, individuals may become presidents of business firms, deans of academic institutions, officials of churches, or take other positions that require a knowledge of how an organization works and the complex relationships that are involved. Executives need to know who answers to whom, and for what purpose. They must monitor organizational activities over time (past, present, and future) and up and down the organizational hierarchy. Attainment of the executive stage, of course, depends on exposure to opportunities that permit the development and practice of relevant skills.

The **reintegrative stage,** *which occurs in late adulthood, is Schaie's final stage that involves older adults choosing to focus their energy on the tasks and activities that have meaning for them.* In late adulthood, the need to acquire knowledge declines further. The need to monitor decisions also declines, because the future appears short and inconsequential. Executive monitoring also declines because most individuals have retired from the position that required this type of intellectual application. What, then, is the nature of the older adult's cognitive stage? In Schaie's view, it is reintegrative, which closely corresponds to Erikson's final stage in the life cycle, integrity versus despair. Elderly people's acquisition and application of knowledge is—to a greater extent than earlier in life—related to their interests, attitudes, and values. The elderly are less likely to waste time on tasks that have little or no meaning for them. They are less likely to expend effort to solve a problem unless that problem is one they face in their lives. For example, they tend to show little interest in abstract questions, such as "Which is better, communism or capitalism?" unless the questions relate to their motivation to make sense out of their lives as a whole, such as, "What is the purpose of life?" or "What comes after death?" A summary of Schaie's adult cognitive stages, along with those proposed by Piaget, Labouvie-Vief, and Perry is presented in table 14.2.

Creativity

At the age of 30, Thomas Edison invented the phonograph, Hans Christian Anderson wrote his first volume of fairy tales, and Mozart composed *The Marriage of Figaro.* It hardly seems that these represent a decline in creativity during early adulthood. In several investigations, the quality of productivity of recognized adults was the highest during their thirties; approximately 80 percent of the most important creative contributions were completed by the age of 50 (Dennis, 1966; Lehman, 1960) (see figure 14.4). In another approach, the total productivity, not just the superior works, of creative individ-

The artist finds a greater pleasure in painting than in having completed the picture.

~ *Seneca,*
Letter to Lucilius, *1st Century*

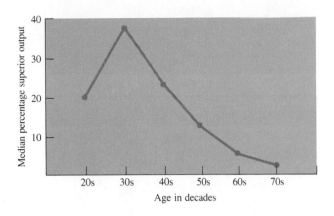

Figure 14.4 *Percentage of superior output as a function of age. In several investigations the quality of creative works was highest in the age period of the thirties.*

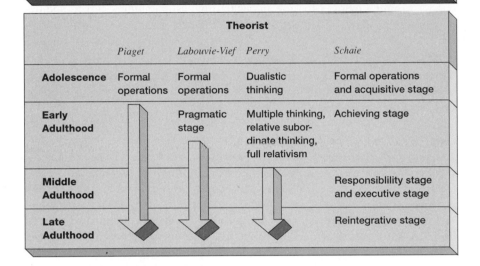

Table 14.2: The Cognitive Stages of Adulthood—Piaget, Labouvie-Vief, Perry, and Schaie

	Theorist			
	Piaget	*Labouvie-Vief*	*Perry*	*Schaie*
Adolescence	Formal operations	Formal operations	Dualistic thinking	Formal operations and acquisitive stage
Early Adulthood		Pragmatic stage	Multiple thinking, relative subordinate thinking, full relativism	Achieving stage
Middle Adulthood				Responsiblility stage and executive stage
Late Adulthood				Reintegrative stage

uals in the arts, sciences, and humanities who had lived long lives was investigated (Dennis, 1966). As shown in figure 14.5, the point in adult development at which creative production peaked varied from one discipline to another. In the humanities, the seventies was just as creative a decade as the forties. Artists and scientists, though, began to show a decline in creative productivity in their fifties. In all instances, the twenties was the least productive decade in terms of creativity. There are exceptions, of course. In the sciences, Benjamin Duggar discovered the antibiotic aureomycin when he was 72. The first major paper of Nobel laureates in science was published at the average age of 25. All laureates who were past 70, however, continued to publish scholarly papers in scientific journals. These data support the belief that individuals who are bright and productive during their early adult years maintain their creativity in their later years. It is inappropriate to conclude that there is a linear decrease in creativity during the adult years (Simonton, 1989).

Careers and Work

At age 21, Thomas Smith graduated from college and accepted a job as a science teacher at a high school in Boston. At age 26, Sally Caruthers graduated from medical school and took a job as an intern at a hospital in Los Angeles. At age 20, Barbara Breck finished her training at a vocational school

Whatever you can do, or dream you can, begin it. Boldness has genius, power and magic in it.

~ *Johann Wolfgang von Goethe*

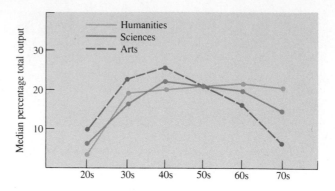

Figure 14.5 Percentage of total output as a function of age. The point in adult development at which creative production peaked varied from one discipline to another. In the humanities, the seventies were just as creative as the forties. Artists and scientists, though, began to show a decline in creative productivity in their fifties.

and went to work as a computer programmer for an engineering firm in Chicago. Earning a living, choosing an occupation, establishing a career, and developing in a career—these are important themes of early adulthood.

Theories of Career Development

Three dominant theories describe the manner in which individuals make choices about careers—Ginzberg's developmental theory, Super's self-concept theory, and Holland's personality type theory.

Ginzberg's Developmental Theory

The **developmental theory of career choice** *is Eli Ginzberg's view that individuals go through three career choice stages—fantasy, tentative, and realistic* (Ginzberg & others, 1951). When asked what they want to be when they grow up, young children may answer "a doctor," "a superhero," "a teacher," "a movie star," "a sports star," or any number of other occupations. In childhood, the future seems to hold almost unlimited opportunities. Ginzberg argues that until about the age of 11, children are in the *fantasy stage* of career choice. From the ages of 11 to 17, adolescents are in the *tentative stage* of career development, a transition from the fantasy stage of childhood to the realistic decision making of young adulthood. He believes that adolescents progress from evaluating their interests (11 to 12 years of age) to evaluating their capacities (13 to 14 years of age) to evaluating their values (15 to 16 years of age). Thinking shifts from less subjective to more realistic career choices at around 17 to 18 years of age. The period from 17 to 18 years of age through the early twenties is called the *realistic stage* of career choice by Ginzberg. At this time, the individual extensively explores available careers, then focuses on a particular career, and finally selects a specific job within the career (such as family practitioner or orthopedic surgeon within the career of doctor).

Critics have attacked Ginzberg's theory on a number of grounds. For one, the initial data were collected from middle-class youth, who probably had more career options open to them. And, as with other developmental theories (such as Piaget's), the time frames are too rigid. Moreover, Ginzberg's theory does not take into account individual differences—some persons make mature decisions about careers (and stick with them) at much earlier ages than specified by Ginzberg. Not all children engage in career fantasies either. In a revision of his theory, Ginzberg (1972) conceded that lower-class individuals do not have as many options available to them as middle-class individuals do. Ginzberg's general point—that at some time during late adolescence or early adulthood more realistic career choices are made—is probably correct.

Early Adulthood

Super's Self-Concept Theory

The **career self-concept theory** *is Donald Super's view that the individual's self-concept plays a central role in career choice. Super believes a number of developmental changes in vocational self-concept take place during the adolescent and young adulthood years* (Super, 1967, 1976). First, at about 14 to 18 years of age, adolescents develop ideas about work that mesh with their already existing global self-concept—this phase is called *crystallization*. Between 18 and 22 years of age, they narrow their career choices and initiate behavior that enables them to enter some type of career—this phase is called *specification*. Between 21 and 24 years of age, young adults complete their education or training and enter the world of work—this phase is called *implementation*. The decision on a specific, appropriate career is made between 25 and 35 years of age—this phase is called *stabilization*. Finally, after the age of 35, individuals seek to advance their careers and reach higher-status positions—this phase is called *consolidation*. The age ranges should be thought of as approximate rather than rigid. Super believes that career exploration in adolescence is a key ingredient of the adolescent's career self-concept. He constructed the Career Development Inventory to assist counselors in promoting adolescents' career exploration.

Holland's Personality-Type Theory

Personality-type theory *is John Holland's view that it is important to match the individual's personality with a particular career. Holland proposed six basic personality types that he believes match up with certain careers* (Holland, 1973, 1987). In Holland's view, once individuals find a career that fits their personality, they are more likely to enjoy the career and stay in a job for a longer period of time than individuals who work at jobs that are not suited to their personality (Gati, 1991; Gottfreedson & Holland, 1990). Following are Holland's six personality types and their career matchups:

Realistic. These individuals show characteristically "masculine" traits. They are physically strong, deal in practical ways with problems, and have very little social know-how. They are best oriented toward practical careers such as labor, farming, truck driving, and construction.

Intellectual. These individuals are conceptually and theoretically oriented. They are thinkers rather than doers. Often they avoid interpersonal relations, and are best suited to careers in math and science.

Social. These individuals often show characteristically "feminine" traits, especially those associated with verbal skills and interpersonal relations. They are likely to be best equipped to enter "people" professions such as teaching, social work, counseling, and the like.

Conventional. These individuals show a distaste for unstructured activities. They are best suited for jobs as subordinates, such as bank tellers, secretaries, and file clerks.

Enterprising. These individuals energize their verbal abilities toward leading others, dominating individuals, and selling people on issues or products. They are best counseled to enter careers such as sales, politics, and management.

Artistic. These individuals prefer to interact with their world through artistic expression, avoiding conventional and interpersonal situations in many instances. They should be oriented toward careers such as art and writing.

If all individuals fell conveniently into Holland's personality types, career counselors would have an easy job. But individuals are more varied and complex than Holland's theory suggests. Even Holland (1987) now admits that most individuals are not pure types. Still, the basic idea of matching the abilities and attitudes of individuals to particular careers is an important contribution to the career field (Hackett, Lent, & Greenhaus, 1991; Kahn & Alvi, 1991). Holland's personality types are incorporated into the Strong-Campbell Vocational Interest Inventory, a widely used measure in career guidance (Randahl, 1991).

Exploration, Planning, and Decision Making

At some point toward the end of adolescence or the beginning of early adulthood, most individuals enter some type of occupation. Exploration of a number of career options is widely recommended by career counselors. Individuals often approach career exploration and decision making with ambiguity, uncertainty, and stress (Lock, 1988). In one investigation of individuals after they left high school, over half the position changes (such as student to student, student to job, job to job) made between leaving school and the age of 25 involved floundering and unplanned changes. The young adults were neither systematic nor intentional in their career exploration and planning (Super, Kowalski, & Gotkin, 1967).

Predicting career choices and guiding individuals toward rewarding occupations is a complex undertaking (Vondracek, 1991). In the first several years of college, most students cannot accurately chart their career path through the adult years. Many students change majors while in college, discover that their employment after college is not directly related to their college major, and change careers during the course of adulthood (Rothstein, 1980). To some career counselors, the unpredictability of career pursuit by college students means that many students should not follow a path of narrow vocational training but rather a course of broad liberal education. Other career counselors believe that to increase the probability of getting a good job, an intense, focused course of study in a particular discipline is a wise strategy.

The Life Contour of Work in Adulthood

The occupational cycle has four main stages: selection and entry, adjustment, maintenance, and retirement (see figure 14.6). These stages are readily identifiable in careers that move in an orderly progression; they become more obscure in disorderly work patterns or work changes that require some form of readjustment. In chapter 16, we will discuss the stage of maintenance and career change in middle adulthood, and in chapter 18, we will address the stage of retirement and the work world of older adults. Here we focus on the two initial stages that take place primarily in early adulthood—selection and entry, and adjustment.

Entering an occupation signals the beginning of new roles and responsibilities for the individual. The career role is different from the role the individual might have had as a temporary or part-time worker during adolescence. Career role expectations for competence are high and the demands are real for the young adult. When individuals enter a job for the first time, they may be confronted by unanticipated problems and conditions. Transitions are required as the individual tries to adjust to the new role. Meeting the expectations of a career and adjusting to a new role are crucial for the individual at this time in adult development (Heise, 1991; Smither, 1988).

Adjustment is the key label in the second stage of life's work contour. This is the period Daniel Levinson (1978) calls "Age 30 Transition" in men.

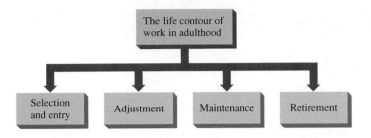

Figure 14.6 *The life contour of work in adulthood. The occupational cycle has four main stages: selection and entry, adjustment, maintenance, and retirement.*

According to Levinson, once an individual enters an occupation, he must develop a distinct occupational identity and establish himself in the occupational world. Along the way, he may fail, drop out, or begin a new path. He may stay narrowly on a single track or try several new directions before settling firmly on one. This adjustment phase lasts several years. A professional may spend several years in academic study while an executive may spend his early years in lower- or middle-management jobs. Hourly workers usually need several years to explore the work world, become familiar with the industry and the labor union, and move beyond the apprentice status to a permanent occupational role.

The level of attainment reached by individuals in their early thirties varies (Landy, 1989). A professional may just be getting started or may have already become well established and widely known. One executive may be on the bottom rung of the corporate ladder; another may be already near the top. An hourly worker may be an unskilled laborer without job security or a highly skilled craftsman earning more than some executives or professionals. As suggested in Cultural Worlds of Development 14.1, however, some individuals face unemployment, a circumstance that produces stress whether the job loss is temporary, cyclical, or permanent.

We have seen how the early years of adulthood mark the development and integration of cognitive capacities that enable individuals to attain purposeful, organized mastery of their personal lives and work. We have also seen the importance of work's role in our lives as young adults. Next, we consider one of the major changes in the work role.

Women's Changing Work Roles

Mary is a 26-year-old policewoman. Nancy is a 30-year-old electrical engineer. Barbara is a 32-year-old brick layer. The occupations of these women underscore the dramatic changes of women's changing work roles.

Culture and History

Gender roles vary across cultures and over time (Moen, 1991). In agricultural societies, women usually stay close to home, working in the fields and rearing their children, while men have considerably more freedom. In nomadic societies, the gender roles are less distinct (Van Leeuwen, 1978). In industrialized societies, the work roles of men and women may vary from one culture to another. For example, in the United States, most physicians and dentists are men; in Russia, most physicians are females; and in Denmark, most dentists are females.

In an intriguing analysis of gender roles over historical time, Marcia Guttentag and Paul Secord (1983) analyzed cultures ranging from classical Greece to modern America and found that gender roles vary in predictable ways over many centuries. In eras when marriageable women are in short supply, women are given protection and marital commitment is strong. When historical events such as migration or war generate a relative oversupply of

UNEMPLOYMENT

*I*t is well documented that professional, semiskilled, and unskilled workers experience stress from losing their jobs (Jahoda, 1988; Liem & Liem, 1988). However, the psychological effects of unemployment may depend on a number of factors, including the individual's personality, social status, and resources (Davy, Kinick, & Scheck, 1991; McReynolds & Gilbert, 1991; Winefield & others, 1991). For example, a 50-year-old married worker with two adolescents, a limited education, no transferable job skills, and no pension will not react in the same way to the loss of a job as a 21-year-old apprentice electrician.

In one investigation of job loss, researchers studied how the shutdown of a steel plant in Youngstown, Ohio, affected workers (Buss & Redburn, 1983). The managers were less affected than the steelworkers after the plant closed. The steelworkers felt more helpless, victimized, and distrustful, tended to avoid social interaction, and were more aggressive. They were also more depressed and showed a greater

The unemployed worker shown here is applying for welfare. Many individuals who lose their jobs experience a great deal of stress.

degree of perceived immobility. Over time, the steelworkers were less trustful and continued to feel immobile, helpless, and stressed. They also reported

more health problems and increased their alcohol consumption. In contrast, managers coped better than the steelworkers. Except for a lack of trust, their psychological profile either continued to improve or remained the same. However, in a second wave of interviews, the managers reported more family problems and an increased tendency to take over-the-counter drugs, but they were still less severely affected than the steelworkers. In sum, unemployment had stressful effects on both managers and steelworkers, but managers coped more effectively with the stress.

Being unemployed in the 1990s may be as bad as, or in some cases worse than, in the 1930s. The unemployed in the 1930s had a strong feeling their jobs would return. However, because many of today's workers are being replaced by technology, expectations that their jobs will return are less realistic, although the possibilities for retraining are more numerous.

younger women, men show more sexual promiscuity and women become more independent. In these circumstances, women are more likely to work outside the home and to organize social protests to improve their status.

Guttentag and Secord (1983) comment, however, that these sex ratio imbalances will likely not have the same effects in the future, at least in the United States and in other countries with similar cultures. Conditions that contrived in past times to keep women in the home have changed. Without effective means of contraception, many wives were pregnant most of the time, bearing one child after another. Before the advent of bottle-feeding, mothers also had to breast-feed their young. And in preindustrial societies, the home was the center of domestic production. Women made clothes and other items needed for daily living, and food production began with the raw product, often involving many steps before reaching the table. Women were so fully occupied that there was little or no time for thinking about how their young daughters could leave home and get a better education or earn an income by working outside the home on a full-time basis.

The situation for women has changed dramatically. Modern contraceptive methods have made it possible for women to limit the number of children they have, and oftentimes to plan births to minimally disrupt their career. With modern medical care, women have fewer complications during pregnancy and birth. Childrearing has changed, too. Domestic burdens are relatively light in modern society and various types of child care facilities have become available.

The effect of these various changes has been to create a society that makes task demands on men and women that are vastly different from those of the past. Men no longer gain appreciable advantages from superior physical strength, women are no longer confined solely to bearing and rearing children, and performing domestic tasks. Women who are economically independent do not have an economic need to marry, so they feel less pressure to marry. They may marry for other reasons, but marriage is not their only option. And those who choose not to be mothers, though married, may relate to men in markedly different ways from women who do.

Women in the Workforce

The changing role of women is evident in the increasing rate of women's employment (London & Greller, 1991). In 1960, only one-third of women with children were employed; but in 1988, 55 percent of married women with infants and 61 percent of women with preschool children worked outside the home. Women's occupations are also changing. Four in ten college women today intend to pursue careers in law, business, medicine, or engineering, while in 1970 only two in ten said they intended to pursue these male-dominated careers (Astin, Green, & Korn, 1987). In one recent investigation, gender-role orientation was related to females' stress in male-dominated occupations (Long, 1989). High-masculine (self-assertive) women reported less anxiety and strain in their jobs than did low-masculine women.

Today, women fill nearly one-third of management positions, an improvement from the 19 percent level in 1972, but most are in jobs with little authority and low pay (Doyle & Paludi, 1991). Only 2 percent of senior executives are women, and only 1.7 percent of corporate officers of Fortune 500 companies are women. A special concern about the career development of females, as well as ethnic-minority individuals, is the experience of a "glass ceiling" in management. The glass ceiling concept was popularized in the 1980s to describe a subtle barrier that is virtually transparent, yet is so strong it prevents females from moving up in the management hierarchy. This discrimination still often portrays the "good manager" as "masculine" rather than "androgynous," or simply competent, in many organizations (Morrison & Von Glinow, 1990).

Dual-Career Marriage

As growing numbers of females pursue careers, they are faced with questions involving career and family (Anderson & Leslie, 1991; Gustafson & Magnusson, 1991; Spade & Reese, 1991; Steil & Weltman, 1991). Should they delay marriage and childbearing and establish their career first? Or should they combine their career, marriage, and childbearing in their twenties? Some females continue to embrace the domestic patterns of an earlier historical period. They have married, borne children, and committed themselves to full-time mothering. These "traditional" females have worked outside the home only intermittently, if at all, and have subordinated the work role to the family role. Many other females, though, have veered from this time-honored path. They have postponed motherhood, or in some cases chosen not to have children. They have developed committed, permanent ties to the workplace that

One can live magnificently in this world, if one knows how to work and how to love.

~ *Count Leo Tolstoy, 1856*

THE LIFE AND CAREER PATHS OF JOANNE AND JOAN

---◆---

*T*he life paths of Joanne and Joan were very different (Gerson, 1986). Joanne grew up in a typical American family. While her father earned only a modest wage as a repairman, her mother stayed home to rear four children because both parents believed that full-time mothering for the children was more important than additional income. However, they hoped that Joanne would educate herself for a better life. But Joanne was more interested in dating than in schoolwork or in her part-time job at a fast-food restaurant. When she became pregnant at 17, she was happy to marry her boyfriend and assume the role of a full-time mother. Two children, several brief and disenchanting sales jobs and ten years later, Joanne still finds satisfaction in full-time mothering. At times she feels financial pressure to give up homemaking for paid work and resents being snubbed when she says her family is her career. But every time she searches the want ads, she vividly remembers how much she disliked her temporary jobs. Since her husband earns enough money to make ends meet, the urge to go to work quickly passes. Instead, Joanne is seriously thinking about having another child.

Joanne's life history reflects the traditional model of female development. An adult woman chooses a domestic life for which she was prepared emotionally and practically since childhood. Approximately 20 percent of women from a variety of social class and family backgrounds are believed to follow this life course (Gerson, 1986). These women are insulated from events that might steer them away from their expected paths. They are

neither pushed out of the home by economic necessity or marital instability nor pulled into the workplace by enticing opportunities. Instead, they remain committed to the domestic role that they assume is the woman's proper and natural place in society.

In contrast, consider Joan's path. Like Joanne, Joan believed as a child that when she grew up she would marry, have children, and live happily ever after as a housewife. She harbored a vague wish to go to college, but her father thought women should not go to college, and as a low-paid laborer he could not afford to send her to college, anyway. Joan worked after high school as a filing clerk and married Frank, a salesman, two years later. Within six months of the ceremony, she was pregnant and planning to stay home with her young child. But things changed soon after her daughter was born. Unlike Joanne, she became bored and unhappy as a full-time mother. Taking care of the baby was not the ultimate fulfillment for Joan. Motherhood was a mixture of feelings for her—alternately rewarding and frustrating, joyful and depressive. Despite her reluctance to admit these feelings to anyone but herself, a growing sense of emptiness and the need for additional income spurred Joan to look for paid work. She took a job as a bank teller, perceiving it to be a temporary way to boost family income. But the right time to quit never came. Frank's income consistently fell short of their needs, and as his work frustrations mounted, their marriage began to falter. When Frank pressured Joan to have another child, she began to think more seriously about whether she

wanted to remain married to Frank. Just when the marriage seemed unbearable, Joan's boss gave her a chance to advance. She accepted the advance and decided to divorce Frank. Today, more than a decade later, Joan is dedicated to her career, aspires to upper-level management, and does not plan to remarry or expand her family beyond one child. Joan's life represents an increasingly common pattern among women—one of rising work aspirations and ambivalence toward motherhood. Like their traditional counterparts, these women grew up wanting and preparing for a domestic role, only to find that events stimulated them to move in a different direction. About one-third of women today seem to follow this life pattern (Gerson, 1986). These women are more likely to experience unstable relationships with men, unanticipated opportunities for job advancement, economic squeezes at home, and disappointments with mothering and full-time homemaking. As a consequence, heightened work ambitions replace their earlier home-centered orientation. Although Joanne and Joan experienced similar childhood backgrounds and aspirations, their lives diverged increasingly as they were confronted with the opportunities and restrictions of early adulthood.

There are a number of other life trajectories that the career and family paths of women in early adulthood can take. More about the increasing dilemma of career and family roles in early adulthood appears in the next chapter as we discuss the nature of marriage, family, and adult life-styles.

resemble the pattern once reserved only for men. When they have had children, they have strived to combine a career and motherhood. While there have always been "career" females, their numbers are growing at an unprecedented rate. More about work and family developmental paths is presented in Perspective on Life-Span Development 14.1.

What issues do women face as they combine a career and family?

Dual-career marriages can have advantages and disadvantages for individuals (Thompson & Walker, 1989; Zedeck & Mosier, 1990). Of course, one of the main advantages is financial. One of every three wives earns 30 to 50 percent of the family's total income, which helps to explain why most first-time home buyers are dual-career couples. Other than financial benefits, dual-career marriages can contribute to a more equal relationship between husband and wife and enhanced feelings of self-esteem for women. Among the possible disadvantages or stresses of dual-career marriages are added time and energy demands, conflict between work and family roles, competitive rivalry between husband and wife, and if the family includes children, concerns of whether the children's needs are being adequately met.

Many men, especially those with low earnings, have a difficult time accepting their wives' employment. For example, in one investigation, married men who opposed their wives' employment were more depressed when their own earnings were low rather than high (Ulbrich, 1988). These men apparently experience a double insult to themselves as providers. Many husbands whose wives work report that they would like to have a wife who is a full-time homemaker. For example, in one study, although husbands appreciated their wives' earnings, they felt they had lost the services of a full-time home-maker—someone who is there when they get home, someone who cooks all their meals, and someone who irons all their clothes (Ratcliff & Bogdan, 1988). Some husbands, of course, encourage their wives' employment, or support their decision to pursue a career. In one investigation of high-achieving women, many of their husbands took pride in their wives' accomplishments and did not feel competitive with them (Epstein, 1987).

At this point we have discussed a number of ideas about cognitive development and careers and work in early adulthood. A summary of these ideas is presented in concept table 14.2. In the next chapter, we continue our discussion of early adulthood, focusing on social development.

• *Critical Thinking* •

As women's work roles have changed, what adaptations has this forced men to make?

Summary

I. Transition from Adolescence to Adulthood

Kenniston proposed that the transition from adolescence to adulthood be called youth, a period of economic and personal temporariness, and struggle between interest in self-autonomy and becoming socially involved. This period averages from two to eight years but can be longer. Two criteria for adulthood are economic independence and independent decision making. However, clear-cut criteria are yet to be established. Both change and continuity occur in the transition from adolescence to adulthood.

Concept Table 14.2: Cognitive Development and Careers and Work

Concept	Processes/Related Ideas	Characteristics/Description
Cognitive Development	Cognitive Stages	It is not until adulthood that many individuals consolidate their formal operational thinking, and many other adults do not think in formal operational ways at all. Labouvie-Vief argues that young adults enter a pragmatic stage of thought. Perry theorized that as individuals move into adulthood, their thinking becomes more relativistic. Schaie proposed a sequence of cognitive stages: acquisitive, achieving, responsibility, executive, and reintegrative.
	Creativity	The highest productivity of superior works seems to be in the thirties, although when total productivity is considered, it depends on the discipline.
Careers and Work	Theories of Career Development	Three major theories have been proposed—Ginzberg's developmental theory of career choice, Super's career self-concept theory, and Holland's personality-type theory.
	Exploration, Planning, and Decision Making	Everything we know about career development suggests that young people should explore a variety of career options. Planning and decision making about careers is often disorganized and vaguely pursued. Predicting career choices and guiding individuals toward rewarding occupations is a complex undertaking.
	The Life Contour of Work in Adulthood	The contour follows this course: selection and entry, adjustment, maintenance, and retirement.
	Women's Changing Work Roles	Gender roles vary across cultures and over time. Over many centuries sex-ratio imbalances have been related to gender roles, but the dramatic changes in gender roles today suggest these imbalances will not have the same effects in the future. There has been a tremendous influx of women into the labor force in recent years. Women have increased their presence in occupations previously dominated by men, although women, as well as ethnic minorities, still experience a "glass ceiling" in management. As greater numbers of women pursue careers, they face issues involving career and family. Dual-career marriages can involve advantages as well as stresses.

II. Physical Development: The Peak and Slowdown

Peak physical status is reached between 18 and 30, especially between 19 and 26. Individuals' health also peaks in these years. There is a hidden hazard in these peaks of physical performance and health; bad health habits can be formed. Toward the latter part of early adulthood, a detectable slowdown and decline in physical status is apparent.

III. Nutrition and Eating Behavior

The causes for being overweight are complex and involve genetic factors, physiological mechanisms, cognitive factors, and environmental influences. Individuals consume too much fat, cholesterol needs to be lowered, carbohydrates need to be increased, and protein intake should be moderated. The population is increasingly heavy and weight-loss programs abound. Cognitive strategies, especially self-control techniques, and exercise are helpful in weight reduction.

IV. Exercise

Both moderate and intense physical exercise produce important physical and psychological gains, such as lowered risk of heart disease and reduced anxiety. Experts increasingly recommend that the level of exercise you participate in should be pleasurable.

V. Sexuality

Increased liberalization of heterosexual attitudes and behavior has occurred. Some dimensions of the double standard, however, still exist. Rates of homosexuality have remained constant in the twentieth century. Homosexuality is no longer classified as a disorder. Until recently acceptance of homosexuality was increasing, but in concert with the AIDS epidemic, acceptance of homosexuality has decreased. No definitive conclusions about the cause of homosexuality have been reached. AIDS (Acquired Immune Deficiency Syndrome) is caused by a virus that destroys the body's immune system. AIDS can only be transmitted through sexual contact, sharing needles, or blood transfusion, or to babies infected before or during birth. According to a recent national survey, Americans are not very knowledgeable about sex. Many American adolescents and adults have misconceptions about sex. The relation between the menstrual cycle and personality fluctuations in females have been studied and there is a relation between mood swings and the middle and later premenstrual phases of the cycle. Rape is forcible sexual behavior with a person who does not give consent. Feminist writers believe rape is pervasive because males are socialized to be sexually aggressive, to regard women as inferior, and to view their own pleasure as the most important objective. An increasing concern is date or acquaintance rape. Rape is a traumatic experience for the victim. The support systems of family, boyfriend/girlfriend, and friends, as well as professional counseling, can help rape victims cope more effectively.

VI. Cognitive Stages
It is not until adulthood that many individuals consolidate their formal operational thinking, and many other adults do not think in formal operational ways at all. Labouvie-Vief argues that young adults enter a pragmatic stage of thought. Perry theorized that as individuals move into adulthood their thinking becomes more relativistic. Schaie proposed a sequence of cognitive stages: acquisitive, achieving, responsibility, executive, and reintegrative.

VII. Creativity
The highest productivity of superior works seems to be in the thirties, although when total productivity is considered, it depends on the discipline.

VIII. Careers and Work
Three major theories of career development have been proposed—Ginzberg's developmental theory of career choice, Super's career self-concept theory, and Holland's personality-type theory. Everything we know about career development suggests that young people should explore a variety of career options. Planning and decision making about careers is often disorganized and vaguely pursued. Predicting career choices and guiding individuals toward rewarding occupations is a complex undertaking. The contour of work in adulthood follows this sequence: selection and entry, adjustment, maintenance, and retirement.

IX. Women's Changing Work Roles
Gender roles vary across cultures and over time. Over many centuries sex ratio imbalances have been related to gender roles, but the dramatic changes in gender roles today suggest these imbalances will not have the same effects in the future. There has been a tremendous influx of women into the labor force in recent years. Women have increased their presence in occupations previously dominated by men, although women, as well as ethnic minorities, still experience a "glass ceiling" in management. As greater numbers of women pursue careers, they are facing issues involving career and family. Dual-career marriages can involve advantages as well as stresses.

Key Terms

youth 456
burnout 457
set point 461
basal metabolism rate (BMR) 462
aerobic exercise 464

AIDS (Acquired Immune Deficiency Syndrome) 468
rape 470
date or acquaintance rape 471
achieving stage 474
responsibility stage 474
executive stage 474

reintegrative stage 474
developmental theory of career choice 476
career self-concept theory 477
personality-type theory 477

Suggested Readings

Byer, C. O., & Shainberg, L. W. (1991). Dimensions of human sexuality (3rd ed.). Dubuque, IA: Wm. C. Brown.
This book covers a diversity of topics related to sexuality, ranging from the physiological bases of sexuality to developmental aspects of sexuality to sexual orientation to sexually transmitted diseases.

Gerson, K. (1986). Hard choices: How women decide about work, career, and motherhood. Berkeley: University of California Press.
This book addresses the increasing conflict between career and family faced by women. Includes many case studies of the life and career paths of women.

Logue, A. W. (1986). *The psychology of eating and drinking.* New York: W. H. Freeman.
A well-written and authoritative coverage of what we know about eating behavior, obesity, and weight-loss programs.

Ornstein, R., & Sobel, D. (1989). *Healthy pleasures.* Reading, MA: Addison-Wesley.
A fascinating look at the role of pleasure in health. Ornstein and Sobel argue that we should engage in healthy practices we enjoy doing.

Smelser, N. J., & Erikson, E. H. (1980). *Themes of work and love in adulthood.* Cambridge, MA: Harvard University Press.
A volume of essays focused on the themes of work and love in adulthood, written by experts such as Erik Erikson, Roger Gould, and Daniel Levinson.

CHAPTER 15

Social Development in Early Adulthood

Phil is a lovesick man. On two consecutive days he put expensive ads in New York City newspapers, urging, begging, pleading a woman named Edith to forgive him and continue their relationship. The first ad read as follows:

> **Edith**
> I was torn two ways.
> Too full of child
> to relinquish the lesser.
> Older now,
> a balance struck,
> that a child forever behind me.
> Please forgive me,
> reconsider.
> Help make a new us;
> better now than before.
> **Phil**

This ad was placed in the *New York Post* at a cost of $3,600. Another full-page ad appeared in the *New York Times* at a cost of $3,408. Phil's ads stirred up quite a bit of interest. Forty-two Ediths responded; Phil said he thought the whole process would be more private. As Phil would attest, relationships are very important to us. Some of us will go to almost any length and spend large sums of money to restore lost relationships (Worschel & Cooper, 1979).

Sherry is not searching for a particular man. She is at the point where she is, well, looking for Mr. Anybody. Sherry is actually more particular than she says, although she is frustrated by what she calls the great man shortage in this country. According to the 1980 United States Census, for every 100 men over 15 years of age who have never been married or are widowed or divorced, there are 123 women; for blacks the ratio is 100 men for every 133 women.

William Novak (1983), author of the *Great Man Shortage,* believes it is the quality of the gap that bothers most women. He says the quality problem stems from the fact that in the last two decades, the combination of the feminist movement and women's tendency to seek therapy when their personal relationships do not work out has made women outgrow men emotionally. He points out that many women are saying to men, "You don't have to earn all the money anymore, and I don't want to have to do all the emotional work." Novak observes that the whole issue depresses many women because society has conditioned them to assume that their lack of a marriage partner is their fault. One 37-year-old woman told Novak, "I'm no longer waiting for a man on a white horse. Now I'd settle for the horse."

Our close relationships bring us warm and cherished moments. They can also bring us moments we would rather forget, moments that are highly stressful. Among the questions we ask and examine in this chapter are: What attracts us to others and what are love's faces? What is the nature of marriage and the family in early adulthood? What are the life-styles of single adults and divorced adults like? How do we juggle our motivation for both intimacy and independence? What is the nature of women's development and gender issues? How much continuity and discontinuity is there between the adult and childhood years?

Attraction, Love, and Close Relationships

What attracts us to others and motivates us to spend more time with them? And another question needs to be asked, one that has intrigued philosophers,

And then, from across the room, their eyes met.

THE FAR SIDE cartoon by Gary Larson is reprinted by permission of Chronicle Features, San Francisco, CA.

Ask a toad what is beauty . . . he will answer that it is a female with two great round eyes coming out of her little head, a large flat mouth, a yellow belly and a brown back.

~ *Voltaire,*
Philosophical Dictionary, *1764*

• *Critical Thinking* •

Think about your life and the lives of other people you know. What are the common faces of love that appear in each of your lives?

poets, and songwriters for centuries: What is love? Is it lustful and passionate? Or should we be more cautious in our pursuit of love, as a Czech proverb advises, "Do not choose your wife at a dance, but in the fields among the harvesters."

Of equal importance is why relationships dissolve. Many of us know all too well that an individual we thought was a marvelous human being who we wanted to spend the rest of our life with may not turn out to be so marvelous after all. But often it is said that it is better to have loved and lost than never to have loved at all. Loneliness is a dark cloud over many individuals' lives, something few human beings want to feel. These are the themes of our exploration of close relationships: how they get started in the first place, the faces of love, and loneliness.

What Attracts Us to Others in the First Place?

Does just being around someone increase the likelihood of a relationship developing? Do birds of a feather flock together; that is, are we likely to associate with those who are similar to us? How important is the attractiveness of the other person?

Physical proximity does not guarantee that we will develop a positive relationship with an individual. Familiarity can breed contempt, but familiarity is a condition that is necessary for a close relationship to develop. For the most part, friends and lovers have been around each other for a long time; they may have grown up together, gone to high school or college together, worked together, or gone to the same social events. Once we have been exposed to someone for a period of time, what is it that makes the relationship breed friendship and even love?

Birds of a feather do indeed flock together. One of the most powerful lessons generated by the study of close relationships is that we like to associate with people who are similar to us. Our friends, as well as our lovers, are much more like us than unlike us. We have similar attitudes, behavior, and characteristics, as well as clothes, intelligence, personality, other friends, values, life-style, physical attractiveness, and so on. In some limited cases and on some isolated characteristics, opposites may attract. An introvert may wish to be with an extravert, or someone with little money may wish to associate with someone who has a lot of money, for example. But overall we are attracted to individuals with similar rather than opposite characteristics (Berndt & Perry, 1990). In one recent study, for example, the old adage "misery loves company" was supported as depressed college students preferred to meet unhappy others while nondepressed college students preferred to meet happy others (Wenzlaff & Prohaska, 1989).

Consensual validation *provides an explanation of why individuals are attracted to people who are similar to them. Our own attitudes and behavior are supported when someone else's attitudes and behavior are similar to ours; their attitudes and behavior* validate *ours.* Also, because dissimilar others are unlike us and therefore more unknown, we may be able to gain more control over similar others, whose attitudes and behavior we can predict. And similarity implies that we will enjoy interacting with the other person in mutually satisfying activities, many of which require a partner with similarly disposed behavior and attitudes.

The Faces of Love

Love refers to a vast and complex territory of human behavior. How can we classify and study such a vast and complex phenomenon as love? A common classification is to describe four forms of love: altruism, friendship, romantic or passionate love, and affectionate or companionate love (Berscheid, 1988).

Table 15.1: Sample Items from Rubin's Loving and Liking Scales

Love Scale
1. I feel that I can confide in _____ about virtually everything.
2. If I could never be with_____ , I would feel miserable.
3. One of my primary concerns is_____'s welfare.

Liking Scale
1. I would highly recommend _____ for a responsible job.
2. Most people would react favorably to _____ after a brief acquaintance.
3. _____ is the sort of person whom I myself would like to be.

Note: Subjects are asked to fill out the questionnaire in terms of their feelings for their boyfriend or girlfriend and in terms of their feelings for a platonic friend of the opposite sex.

From Zick Rubin, "Measurement of Romantic Love" in *Journal of Personality and Social Psychology,* 16:267. Copyright © 1970 by the American Psychological Association. Reprinted by permission of the author.

We discussed altruism in chapter 11. Let's now examine friendship, romantic or passionate love, and affectionate or companionate love.

Friendship

For many of us, finding a true friend is not an easy task. In the words of American historian Henry Adams, "One friend in life is much, two are many, and three hardly possible." **Friendship** *is a form of close relationship that involves enjoyment (we like to spend time with our friends), acceptance (we accept our friends without trying to change them), trust (we assume our friends will act in our best interest), respect (we think our friends make good judgments), mutual assistance (we help and support our friends and they us), confiding (we share experiences and confidential matters with a friend), understanding (we feel that a friend knows us well and understands what we like), and spontaneity (we feel free to be ourselves around a friend)* (Davis, 1985). In an inquiry of more than 40,000 individuals, many of these characteristics were given when people were asked what a best friend should be like (Parlee, 1979).

How is friendship different from love? The difference can be seen by looking at the scales of liking and loving developed by social psychologist Zick Rubin (1970) (see table 15.1). Rubin says that liking involves our sense that someone else is similar to us; it includes a positive evaluation of the individual. Loving, he believes, involves being close to someone; it includes dependency, a more selfless orientation toward the individual, and qualities of absorption and exclusiveness.

But friends and lovers are similar in some ways. Keith Davis (1985) revealed that friends and romantic partners share the characteristics of acceptance, trust, respect, confiding, understanding, spontaneity, mutual assistance, and happiness. However, he found that relationships with our spouses or lovers are more likely to also involve fascination and exclusiveness. Relationships with friends were perceived as more stable, especially more than those among unmarried lovers.

Romantic or Passionate Love

Romantic love *is also called passionate love or Eros; it has strong sexual and infatuation components, and it often predominates in the early part of a love*

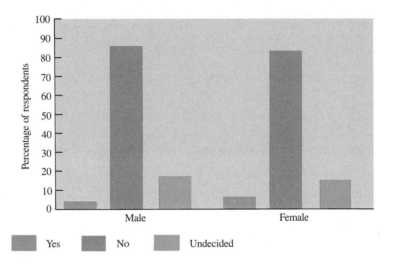

Figure 15.2 Percentage of respondents who would marry someone that they are not in love with in 1984.

I flee who chases me, and chase who flees me.

~ *Ovid,*
The Loves, A.D.*8*

relationship. The fires of passion burn hot in romantic love. It is the type of love Juliet had in mind when she cried "O Romeo, Romeo, wherefore art thou Romeo?" It is the type of love portrayed in a new song that hits the charts virtually every week. It sells millions of books for writers like Danielle Steele. Well-known love researcher Ellen Berscheid (1988) says that it is romantic love we mean when we say that we are "in love" with someone. It is romantic love she believes we need to understand if we are to learn what love is all about.

Romantic love is the main reason we get married. In 1967, a research study showed that men maintained that they would not get married if they were not "in love," women either were undecided or said that they would get married even if they did not love their prospective husband (see figure 15.1) (Kephart, 1967). In the 1980s, women and men agree that they would not get married unless they were "in love" (see figure 15.2). And more than half of today's men and women say that not being "in love" is sufficient reason to dissolve a marriage (Simpson, Campbell, & Berscheid, 1986).

Romantic love is especially important among college students. In one investigation, unattached college males and females were asked to identify their closest relationship (Berscheid, Snyder, & Omoto, 1989). More than half named a romantic partner rather than a parent, sibling, or friend. It is about a romantic partner that an individual says, "I am *in love,*" not just "I *love.*"

Early Adulthood

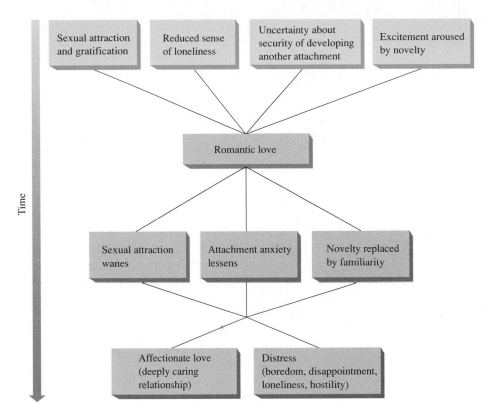

Time

Sexual attraction and gratification	Reduced sense of loneliness	Uncertainty about security of developing another attachment	Excitement aroused by novelty

Romantic love

Sexual attraction wanes	Attachment anxiety lessens	Novelty replaced by familiarity

Affectionate love (deeply caring relationship)	Distress (boredom, disappointment, loneliness, hostility)

Figure 15.3 Phillip Shaver's developmental model of love.

The importance of romantic love appeared in a biography of actress Ingrid Bergman (Leamer, 1986). She once told a man she cared about him deeply, valued his friendship and affection, but simply was not in love with him. Upon hearing this, the man committed suicide. Romantic love has an awesome power—its fires are based on more than liking.

Romantic love includes a complex intermingling of different emotions—fear, anger, sexual desire, joy, and jealousy, for example. Note that not all of these emotions are positive. In one investigation, romantic lovers were more likely to be the cause of depression than friends (Berscheid & Fei, 1977).

Berscheid (1988; Berscheid, Snyder, & Omoto, 1989) believes sexual desire is vastly neglected in the study of romantic love. When pinned down to say what romantic love truly is, she concluded, "It's about 90 percent sexual desire." Berscheid said that this is still an inadequate answer but "to discuss romantic love without also prominently mentioning the role sexual arousal and desire plays in it is very much like printing a recipe for tiger soup that leaves out the main ingredient."

Affectionate or Companionate Love
Love is more than just passion. **Affectionate love,** *also called companionate love, is the type of love that occurs when individuals desire to have the other person near and have a deep, caring affection for the person.*

There is a growing belief that the early stages of love have more romantic ingredients, but as love lasts, passion tends to give way to affection. Phillip Shaver (1986) described this developmental course (see figure 15.3). The initial phase of romantic love is fueled by a mixture of sexual attraction and gratification, a reduced sense of loneliness, uncertainty about the security of developing another attachment, and excitement from exploring the novelty of another human being. With time, sexual attraction wanes, attachment anxieties either lessen or produce conflict and withdrawal, novelty is replaced with

Love is a canvas furnished by nature and embroidered by imagination.

~ *Voltaire*

familiarity, and lovers either find themselves securely attached in a deeply caring relationship or distressed—feeling bored, disappointed, lonely, or hostile, for example. In the latter case, one or both partners may eventually seek another close relationship.

When two lovers go beyond their preoccupation with novelty, unpredictability, and the urgency of sexual attraction, they are more likely to detect deficiencies in each other's caring (Vannoy-Hiller & Philliber, 1989). This may be the point in a relationship when women, who often are better caregivers than men, sense that the relationship has problems. Wives are almost twice as likely as husbands to initiate a divorce (National Center for Health Statistics, 1989).

Friends, dates, lovers, and marital partners bring to their relationships a long history of relationships (Duck & Pond, 1989; Hartup, 1989; Hendrick, 1989). Each partner has internalized a relationship with parents, one that may have been (or continues to be) warm and affectionate or cold and aloof. One partner may have extensive experience in romantic relationships, the other little or none. These experiences are carried forward and influence our relationships with others. For example, adults who were securely attached to their parents as young children are more likely to have securely attached emotional relationships than adults who were insecurely attached (Hazan & Shaver, 1987).

So far we have described two forms of love: romantic or passionate and affectionate or companionate. Robert J. Sternberg (1988) believes affectionate love actually consists of two types of love: intimacy and commitment. The **triangular theory of love** *is Sternberg's theory that love has three main forms: passion, intimacy, and commitment.* Passion, as we described earlier, is the physical and sexual attraction to a lover. Intimacy is the emotional feelings of warmth, closeness, and sharing in a relationship. Commitment is our cognitive appraisal of the relationship and our intent to maintain the relationship even in the face of problems. If only passion is present (with intimacy and commitment low or absent), *infatuation* is present. This might occur in an affair or a fling in which there is little intimacy and even less commitment. If the relationship has intimacy and commitment, but passion is low or absent, *companionate* or *affectionate love* is present, a pattern often found in happy couples who have been married for many years. If passion and commitment are present but intimacy is not, Sternberg calls the relationship *fatuous love*, as when one person worships another from a distance. Only when all three of love's parts are present—passion, intimacy, and commitment—is the strongest, fullest type of love experienced, what Sternberg labels *consummate love* (see figure 15.4). Based on his observations of love, Sternberg (1988) described a number of rules for a successful loving relationship. To read about these rules, turn to Perspective on Life-Span Development 15.1.

Loneliness

Some of us are lonely individuals. We may feel that no one knows us very well. We may feel isolated and sense that we do not have anyone we can turn to in times of need or stress. Our society's contemporary emphasis on self-fulfillment and achievement, the importance we attach to commitment in relationships, and the decline in stable close relationships are among the reasons feelings of loneliness are common today (de Jong-Gierveld, 1987).

Loneliness is associated with an individual's gender, attachment history, self-esteem, and social skills. A lack of time spent with females, on the part of both males and females, is associated with loneliness. Individuals who are lonely often have a history of poor relationships with their partners. Early

Early Adulthood

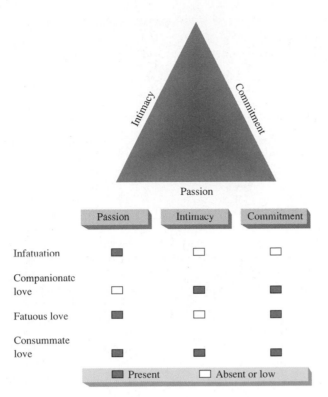

Figure 15.4 Sternberg's triangle of love.

	Passion	Intimacy	Commitment
Infatuation	■	☐	☐
Companionate love	☐	■	■
Fatuous love	■	☐	■
Consummate love	■	■	■

■ Present	☐ Absent or low

It is important to distinguish being alone from being lonely. Most of us cherish the moments we can be left alone for awhile. Aloneness can heal, but loneliness can hurt.

experiences of rejection and loss (as when a parent dies) can cause a lasting effect of feeling alone. Lonely individuals often have low self-esteem and tend to blame themselves more than they deserve for their inadequacies (Frankel & Prentice-Dunn, 1990). And lonely individuals are deficient in social skills (Riggio, Throckmorton, & DePaola, 1990; Jones, Hobbs, & Hockenbury, 1982). For example, they show inappropriate self-disclosure, self-attention at the expense of attention to a partner, or an inability to develop comfortable intimacy.

TEN RULES FOR LOVE

◆

Sternberg (1988) spells out ten rules that males and females who seek a satisfying love relationship should find helpful:

1. *Successful partners do not take their relationship for granted.* The seeds of a relationship's destruction are planted when one or both partners take the other member for granted. When we are dating, we often make a special effort to impress each other by paying attention to the way we look, act, and set priorities. In dating, we are usually aware of the possibility of losing each other, so we put forth an extra effort to keep the relationship stimulating. Dating is like an agreement written in paper and pencil, marriage is like an agreement etched in stone, says Sternberg, but stone is not indestructible, and under certain conditions, it will crumble.

2. *Successful partners make their relationship an important priority.* In dating, we often put the relationship first because we want something—the love and possibly marital commitment of the other individual. As time passes, the press of careers, family, and other matters tempt us to give less attention to the relationship. The relationship can share first place with other priorities, but once it drops below them, its life is jeopardized.

3. *Successful partners actively seek to meet each other's needs.* Active, self-initiated meeting of your partner's needs shows you care and understand your partner. Don't wait for your partner to request something, anticipate your partner's wants and desires. Do whatever it is that satisfies your partner's needs before you are asked and the value of what you do will be much greater.

4. *Successful partners know when, and when not, to change in response to the other.* Successful partners in a love relationship are flexible and adaptive, willing to change to satisfy a partner's needs. Only by being flexible can partners meet the challenge to grow that each change in the nature of the relationship demands. Successful partners not only know when to give in, but also when not to give in. They are aware of what they can be and what they cannot be, not striving to meet requests they know are impossible and compromise being true to themselves.

5. *Successful partners value themselves.* Abraham Maslow distinguished between deficiency love and being love. In deficiency love, you seek out another individual to attain something you lack in yourself; in being love, you seek out another individual to enhance an already competent self. Most loves are probably a combination of deficiency and being loves, a blend that varies over time. If you seek self-worth in another individual that you cannot find in yourself, you probably will be disappointed.

6. *Successful partners love each other, not their idealization of each other.* It is much easier to fall in love with an ideal person than a real person. An ideal person is without flaws, does not

The social transition to college is a time when loneliness may develop as individuals leave behind the familiar world of their hometown and family. Many college freshmen feel anxious about meeting new people and developing a new social life. As one student commented:

My first year here at the university has been pretty lonely. I wasn't lonely at all in high school. I lived in a fairly small town—I knew everyone and everyone knew me. I was a member of several clubs and played on the basketball team. It's not that way at the university. It is a big place and I've felt like a stranger on so many occasions. I'm starting to get used to my life here, and the last few months I've been making myself meet people and get to know them, but it hasn't been easy.

As reflected in the comments of this freshman, individuals usually can't bring their popularity and social standing from high school into the college environment. There may even be a dozen high school basketball stars, National Merit scholars, and former student council presidents in a single dor-

make unreasonable demands, has all the characteristics we want in a true love, and does not talk back. The problem with an ideal love is that such a person only exists in one's mind. You can be in love with an idealized person rather than a real person, and the relationship can go on for some time. You tend to see only what you want to see and ignore or make excuses about your lover's flaws. Sooner or later, though, the bubble bursts as you eventually get to really know your partner. You become disappointed because your partner is not the ideal love you initially thought. In a successful relationship, partners love each other for who they are, not what they want each other to be.

7. *Successful partners tolerate what they cannot change.* We can change some things in our partner, other things we cannot. A key ingredient of a successful love relationship is to develop the wisdom to recognize which is which. If your partner is short and you want someone tall, you are not going to be able to change that characteristic of your partner. You either have to accept your partner's short stature or give up the relationship. If your partner is moody and has been that way for a long time, the partner will probably continue to be moody. If you want to make the relationship work, you may have to cope with your partner's moody tendencies.

8. *Successful partners are open with each other.* We all have our faults, but most of us are not too good at admitting them. Sometimes the easy way out is to lie or hold back the truth instead of divulging errors and shortcomings. The problem is that omissions, distortions, and flat out lies can be damaging to a relationship. Once they start, they tend to spread and can ultimately destroy the relationship. Once you see you can get by with a small lie, you may try to get by with a bigger one next time. Eventually, the relationship becomes like a shell. When the partners talk, they say empty things because the relationship has lost its depth and trust.

9. *Successful partners make good times together and grow through the bad ones.* They participate in joint activities that are enjoyable and provide companionship. Instead of waiting for good times to happen, they create them. At the same time, they recognize life is not always perfect. Successful partners, though, use the bad times as opportunities to grow. You can be truly honest with each other and still not prevent problems from developing in a relationship. However, by using problems as an opportunity to cope and mutually grow, you can come out stronger.

10. *Successful partners do unto each other as they would have the other do unto them.* It is easy to want to give less than we get. If you really want the relationship to work, see things from your partner's viewpoint, and treat your partner the way you want to be treated. This helps you to develop empathy and understanding that are important in a successful love relationship.

mitory wing. Especially if students attend college away from home, they face the task of forming completely new social relationships.

In one investigation conducted two weeks after the school year began, 75 percent of 354 college freshmen said they felt lonely at least part of the time since arriving on campus (Cutrona, 1982). More than 40 percent said their loneliness was moderate to severe in intensity. Students who were the most optimistic and had the highest self-esteem were more likely to overcome their loneliness by the end of their freshmen year. Loneliness is not reserved only for college freshmen, though. It is not uncommon to find a number of upperclassmen who are also lonely.

How do you determine if you are lonely? The types of questions on scales of loneliness ask you to respond to questions such as,

"I don't feel in tune with the people around me."
"I can't find companionship when I want it."

If you consistently respond that you never or rarely feel in tune with people around you and rarely or never can find companionship when you want it, you are likely to fall into the category of individuals described as moderately or intensely lonely.

How can individuals who are lonely reduce their loneliness? Two recommendations are: (1) change your actual social relations or (2) change your social needs and desires (Peplau & Perlman, 1982). Probably the most direct and satisfying way to become less lonely is to improve your social relations (Rokach, 1990). This can be accomplished by forming new relationships, by using your existing social network more competently, or by creating "surrogate" relationships with pets, television personalities, and the like. A second way to reduce loneliness is to reduce your desire for social contact. Over the short run, this might be accomplished by selecting activities you can enjoy alone rather than selecting activities that require someone's company. Over the long run, though, effort should be made to form new relationships. A third coping strategy some individuals unfortunately adopt is to distract themselves from their painful feelings by drinking to "drown their sorrows" or by becoming a workaholic. Some of the negative health consequences of loneliness may be the product of such maladaptive coping strategies (McWhirter, 1990). If you perceive yourself as being a lonely individual, you might consider contacting the counseling center at your college for advice on ways to reduce your loneliness and improve your social relations skills.

Marriage and the Family

Should I get married? If I wait any longer, will it be too late? Will I get left out? Should I stay single or is it too lonely a life? If I get married, do I want to have children? How will it affect my marriage? These are questions that many young adults pose to themselves as they consider their life-style options.

Trends in Marriage

Until about 1930, the goal of a stable marriage was widely accepted as a legitimate endpoint of adult development. In the last sixty years, however, we have seen the emergence of personal fulfillment both inside and outside a marriage that competes with marriage's stability as an adult developmental goal. The changing norm of male-female equality in marriage has produced marital relationships that are more fragile and intense than they were earlier in the twentieth century. More adults are remaining single longer in the 1990s and the average duration of a marriage in the United States is currently just over nine years. The divorce rate, which increased astronomically in the 1970s, has finally begun to slow down, although it still remains alarmingly high. Even with adults remaining single for longer and divorce a frequent occurrence, Americans still show a strong predilection for marriage—the proportion of women who never marry has remained at about 7 percent throughout the twentieth century, for example.

The sociocultural context is a powerful influence on the nature of marriage. The age at which individuals marry, expectations about what the marriage will be like, and the developmental course of the marriage, may vary not only across historical time within a given culture, but also across cultures. For example, you might remember from chapter 2 that a new marriage law took effect in China in 1981. The law sets a minimum age for marriage—22 years for males, 20 years for females. Late marriage and late childbirth are critical efforts in China's attempt to control population growth. More information about the nature of marriage in different cultures appears in Cultural Worlds of Development 15.1.

When two people are under the influence of the most violent, most insane, most delusive, and most transient of passions, they are required to swear that they will remain in that excited, abnormal, and exhausting condition continuously until death do them part.

~ *George Bernard Shaw*

Early Adulthood

MATE SELECTION AROUND THE WORLD

*W*hat characteristic in marital selection do you think varies the most in cultures around the world? In one recent large-scale research investigation of 9,474 individuals from 37 different cultures on six continents and five islands, chastity was the marital preference characteristic that varied the most (Buss & others, 1990). Chastity—desiring a marital partner with no previous experience in sexual intercourse—was the most important factor in marital selection in China, India, Indonesia, Iran, Taiwan, and the Palestinian Arab culture. Individuals in Ireland and Japan placed moderate importance on chastity. But in contrast, individuals in Finland, Norway, the Netherlands, and West Germany generally said that chastity was not important in selecting a marital partner.

In this study, two traditionally domestic characteristics also varied considerably across cultures. Individuals from the Zulu culture in South Africa, Estonia (a Soviet republic), and Colombia placed a high value on housekeeping skills in their marital preference. By contrast, individuals in the United States, Canada, and all Western European countries except Spain said that housekeeping was not an important factor in marital selection.

Religion plays an important role in marital preferences in many cultures. For example, in the Arabic world in the Middle East, the Islam religion stresses the honor of the male and the purity of the female. An emphasis is placed on the female's role in childbearing, childrearing, educating children, and instilling the Islamic faith in their children.

International comparisons of marriage also reveal that individuals in Scandinavian countries marry late, while their counterparts in Eastern Europe marry early (Bianchi & Spani,

1986). For example, in the 1980s, almost 80 percent of the women and 90 percent of the men in Denmark aged 20 to 24 had never been married. By contrast, in the 1980s less than 40 percent of the women and 70 percent of the men in Hungary aged 20 to 24 had never been married. In Scandinavian countries, cohabitation is popular among young adults. Most Scandinavians eventually marry—in the 1980s, only 5 percent of the women and 11 percent of the men had never been married by their early forties. Many Soviet influenced countries, such as Hungary, encourage early marriage and childbearing to offset current and future population losses. Like Scandinavian countries, Japan has a high proportion of unmarried young people, but rather than cohabitate as the Scandinavian young adults do, unmarried Japanese young adults live at home longer with their parents before marrying.

In Scandinavian countries, cohabitation is popular; only a small percentage of 20- to 24-year-olds are married.

Many Soviet-influenced countries encourage early marriage and childbearing to offset current and future population issues.

A Muslim wedding ceremony. The Islam religion stresses the honor of the male and the purity of the female.

"You have no idea how nice it is to have someone to talk to."

Marital Expectations and Myths

Among the explanations of our nation's high divorce rate and high degree of dissatisfaction in many marriages is that we have such strong expectations of marriage. We expect our spouse to simultaneously be a lover, a friend, a confidant, a counselor, a career person, and a parent, for example. In one research investigation, unhappily married couples expressed unrealistic expectations about marriage (Epstein & Eidelson, 1981). Underlying unrealistic expectations about marriage are numerous myths about marriage. A myth is a widely held belief unsupported by facts.

To study college students' beliefs in the myths of marriage, Jeffry Larson (1988) constructed a marriage quiz to measure college students information about marriage and compared their responses with what is known about marriage in the research literature. The college students responded incorrectly to almost half of the items. Female students missed fewer items than male students, and students with a less romantic perception of marriage missed fewer items than more romantically inclined students. See figure 15.5 to take the marriage quiz.

Marital Satisfaction and Conflict

Beyond our unrealistic expectations, what else makes us satisfied with our marriage or so dissatisfied that we consider a divorce? Two views of marital satisfaction and conflict are: behavioral exchange and developmental construction. **Behavior exchange theory** *emphasizes the hedonism and competence involved in marital relationships.* Hedonism is reflected in the belief that each partner's reinforcement value for the other determines the degree of marital satisfaction; competency is reflected in the belief that the mastery of specific relationship skills determines the degree of marital satisfaction. In one investigation, the reward-punishment ratio of social exchanges was a good predictor of marital satisfaction; that is, the more rewards marital partners gave each other, the more satisfied they were with their marriage (Barnett & Nietzel, 1979). In another investigation, couples who were planning to marry were followed for two and a half years; the partner's rating of their positive communication was highly predictive of their marital satisfaction two and a half years later (Markman, 1979).

When two people marry, each individual brings to the marriage a long history of relationships with many people. The **developmental construction view** *of marital satisfaction emphasizes the history of relationships and the manner in which they are carried forward.* Each of the partners has internalized a

Early Adulthood

Figure 15.5 The marriage quiz.

Take out a sheet of paper and number from 1 to 15. Answer each of the following items true or false. After completing the quiz, turn to the end of the chapter for the correct answers.

Marriage Quiz Items

1. A husband's marital satisfaction is usually lower if his wife is employed full time than if she is a full-time homemaker.
2. Today most young, single, never-married people will eventually get married.
3. In most marriages having a child improves marital satisfaction for both spouses.
4. The best single predictor of overall marital satisfaction is the quality of a couple's sex life.
5. The divorce rate in America increased from 1960 to 1980.
6. A greater percentage of wives are in the work force today than in 1970.
7. Marital satisfaction for a wife is usually lower if she is employed full time than if she is a full-time homemaker.
8. If my spouse loves me, he/she should instinctively know what I want and need to be happy.
9. In a marriage in which the wife is employed full time, the husband usually assumes an equal share of the housekeeping.
10. For most couples, marital satisfaction gradually increases from the first year of marriage through the childbearing years, the teen years, the empty nest period, and retirement.
11. No matter how I behave, my spouse should love me simply because he/she *is* my spouse.
12. One of the most frequent marital problems is poor communication.
13. Husbands usually make more life-style adjustments in marriage than wives.
14. Couples who cohabitated before marriage usually report greater marital satisfaction than couples who did not.
15. I can change my spouse by pointing out his/her inadequacies, errors, etc.

relationship with parents. The partners come from families that were divorced, widowed, or intact. Each of the partners may have had romantic relationships with individuals other than the spouse. Psychoanalytic theory has recognized the importance of carrying forward relationships but too often this has been tied to the first five years of life and to psychosexual development. The contemporary developmental construction view considers not only the early childhood years, but the continuing experiences of individuals later in childhood, adolescence, and adulthood. In addition, it is important to evaluate the nature of cohort effects. The immense change in the woman's career role and her increased assertiveness in male-female relationships undoubtedly has had a strong impact on how marital relationships are constructed.

Howard Markman, director of the Center for Marital and Family Studies at the University of Denver, believes that one of the best predictors of marital success is a couple's ability to handle conflict constructively. To strengthen marriages, Markman recommends that couples develop ground rules for discussing marital problems. Markman's suggestions for marital negotiation include:

Make a date for discussion and negotiation. Tell your partner you want to talk about such-and-such and ask if this is a good time. Your partner can refuse to discuss it then, but must respond within 24 hours.

Social Development in Early Adulthood

Focus on the problem. Talk face to face with no distractions. Discuss the problem itself, not the solution at this point. Markman believes that about 70 percent of relationship problems do not need to be solved, but rather people just want their opinions recognized as valid.

Reserve the right to take a break. Either partner can call for a time out, agreeing to resume the discussion within 24 hours, so that both may leave without resentment if the discussion becomes too heated.

Deal with obstacles. If your partner won't talk, have your partner talk about the reasons why. Often the partner is afraid that a fight will break out. Assure your partner that will not happen, and don't let it happen.

Go on to problem solving if needed. Brainstorm solutions, writing them down. Then focus on some form of compromise.

Try out the solution. Renegotiate if necessary.

Try holding a weekly half-hour meeting. Establish a set time to talk about relationship issues, a time for bringing up subjects that may cause conflict.

Markman says that if your partner absolutely refuses to talk and the relationship seems very troubled, you probably need to seek counseling to improve the relationship.

Gender, Intimacy, and Family Work in Marriage

The experiences and implications of marriage may differ for the wife and for the husband (Thompson & Walker, 1989). This is especially true in the expression of intimacy and in family work. In one investigation, only one-third of married, Black women said they would go to their husbands first for support if they had a serious problem, such as being depressed or anxious (Brown & Gary, 1985). And only one-third of these women named their husbands as one of the three people closest to them. More men than women view their spouses as best friends (Rubin, 1984).

Wives consistently disclose more to their partners than husbands do (Peplau & Gordon, 1985). And women tend to express more tenderness, fear, and sadness than their partners. For many men, controlled anger is a common emotional orientation (Cancian & Gordon, 1988). A common complaint expressed by women in a marriage is that their husbands do not care about their emotional lives and do not express their own feelings and thoughts (Rubin, 1984). Women often point out that they have to literally pull things out of their husbands and push them to open up. Men frequently respond either that they are open or that they do not understand what their wives want from them. It is not unusual for men to protest that no matter how much they talk it is not enough for their wives. Women also say they want more warmth as well as openness from their husbands. For example, women are more likely than men to give their partners a spontaneous kiss or hug when something positive happens (Blumstein & Schwartz, 1983). Overall, women are more expressive and affectionate than men in marriage, and this difference bothers many women.

Not only are there gender differences in intimacy in marriages, but there are also strong gender differences in family work (Burley, 1991; Duxbury & Higgins, 1991; Suitor, 1991; Thompson & Walker, 1989). Wives typically do much more family work than husbands (Warner, 1986). Most women and men agree that women should be responsible for family work and that men should "help out" (Szinovacz, 1984). Most wives report they are satisfied with the small amount of family work their husbands do (Peplau & Gordon, 1985). Most wives do two to three times more family work than their husbands (Kamo, 1988). In one study, only 10 percent of husbands did as much family work as their wives (Berk, 1985). These "exceptional" men usually were in circumstances with many, usually young, children and a wife who worked full time.

The nature of women's involvement in family work is often different than men's. Besides doing more, what women do and how they experience family work are different than men's experiences. The family work most women do is unrelenting, repetitive, and routine, often involving cleaning, cooking, child care, shopping, laundry, and straightening up. The family work most men do is infrequent, irregular, and nonroutine, often involving household repairs, taking out the garbage, mowing the lawn, yard work, and gardening. Women often report having to do several tasks at once, which may explain why they find domestic work less relaxing and more stressful than men do (Shaw, 1988).

Because family work is intertwined with love and embedded in family relations, it has complex and contradictory meanings (DeVault, 1987). Most women experience family tasks as mindless but essential work done for the people they love. Most women usually enjoy tending to the needs of their loved ones and keeping the family going, even if they do not find the activities enjoyable and fulfilling. Women experience both positive and negative family work conditions. They are unsupervised and rarely criticized, they plan and control their own work, and they have only their own standards to meet. However, women's family work is often worrisome, tiresome, menial, repetitive, isolating, unfinished, inescapable, and often unappreciated. Thus, it is not surprising that many women have mixed feelings about family work.

Families are undergoing significant changes. The number of one-child families is increasing. And men are apt to increase the amount of time they spend in fathering.

The Parental Role

For many adults, the parental role is well planned and coordinated with other roles in life and is developed with the individual's economic situation in mind. For others, the discovery that they are about to become parents is a startling surprise. In either event, the prospective parents may have mixed emotions and romantic illusions about having a child. Parenting consists of a number of interpersonal skills and emotional demands, yet there is little in the way of formal education for this task. Most parents learn parenting practices from their own parents—some they accept, some they discard. Husbands and wives may bring different viewpoints of parenting practices to the marriage. Unfortunately, when methods of parents are passed on from one generation to the next, both desirable and undesirable practices are perpetuated.

The needs and expectations of parents have stimulated many myths about parenting (Okun & Rappaport, 1980):

- The birth of a child will save a failing marriage
- As a possession or extension of the parent, the child will think, feel, and behave like the parents did in their childhood
- Children will take care of parents in old age
- Parents can expect respect and get obedience from their children
- Having a child means that the parents will always have someone who loves them and is their best friend
- Having a child gives the parents a "second chance" to achieve what they should have achieved
- If parents learn the right techniques, they can mold their children into what they want
- It's the parents fault when children fail
- Mothers are naturally better parents than fathers
- Parenting is an instinct and requires no training

In earlier times, women considered being a mother a full-time occupation. Currently, there is a tendency to have fewer children, and as birth control has become common practice, many individuals choose when they will have children and how many children they will raise. The number of one-child families is increasing, for example. Giving birth to fewer children and reduced demands of child care free a significant portion of a woman's life span for other endeavors. Three accompanying changes are: (1) as a result of the increase in working women, there is less maternal investment in the child's development; (2) men are apt to invest a greater amount of time in fathering; and (3) parental care in the home is often supplemented by institutional care (day care, for example).

As more women show an increased interest in developing a career, they are not only marrying later, but also having children later. What are some of the advantages of having children early or late? Some of the advantages of having children early are: Parents are likely to have more physical energy (for example, they can cope better with such matters as getting up in the middle of the night with infants, and waiting up until adolescents come home at night); the mother is likely to have fewer medical problems with pregnancy and child-birth; and the parents may be less likely to build up expectations for their children, as do many couples who have waited many years to have children. By contrast, there are also advantages to having children late: Parents will have had more time to consider their goals in life, such as what they want from their family and career roles; parents will be more mature and will be able to benefit from their life experiences to engage in more competent parenting; and parents will be better established in their careers and have more income for childrearing expenses (Olds, 1986).

At this point, we have discussed a number of ideas about attraction and close relationships, and about marriage and the family in early childhood. A summary of these ideas is presented in concept table 15.1. Next, we consider the diversity of life-styles in adulthood.

The Diversity of Adult Life-Styles

Today's adult life-styles are diverse. We have single-career families, dual-career families, single-parent families, including mother custody, father custody, and joint custody, the remarried or stepfamily, the kin family (made up of bilateral or intergenerationally linked members), or even the experimental family (individuals in multiadult households—communes—or cohabiting adults). And, of course, there are many single adults.

Single Adults

There is no rehearsal. One day you don't live alone, the next day you do. College ends. Your wife walks out. Your husband dies. Suddenly, you live in this increasingly modern condition, living alone. Maybe you like it, maybe you don't. Maybe you thrive on the solitude, maybe you ache as if in exile. Either way, chances are you are only half-prepared, if at all, to be sole proprietor of your bed, your toaster, and your time. Most of us were raised in the din and clutter of family life, jockeying for a place in the bathroom in the morning, fighting over the last piece of cake, and obliged to compromise on the simplest of choices—the volume of the stereo, the channel on the TV, for example. Few of us grew up thinking that home would be a way station in our life course (Schmich, 1987).

The number of individuals who live alone began to grow in the 1950s but it was in the 1970s that the pace skyrocketed. In the decade of the sev-

Early Adulthood

Concept Table 15.1: Attraction, Love, and Close Relationships; and Marriage and the Family

Concept	Processes/Related Ideas	Characteristics/Description
Attraction, Love, and Close Relationships	What Attracts Us to Others in the First Place?	Familiarity precedes a close relationship. We like to associate with individuals who are similar to us.
	The Faces of Love	Berscheid believes love has four forms: altruism, friendship, romantic or passionate love, and affectionate or companionate love. Friends and lovers have similar and dissimilar characteristics. Romantic love is involved when we say we are "in love"; it includes passion, sexuality, and a mixture of emotions, some of which may be negative. Affectionate love is more important as relationships age. In Sternberg's triangular theory of love, love has three forms: passion, intimacy, and commitment. The high or low presence of these ingredients can produce infatuation, companionate love, fatuous love, or consummate love.
	Loneliness	An individual's gender, attachment history, self-esteem, and social skills are associated with loneliness. The transition to college is a time when loneliness often surfaces.
Marriage and the Family	Trends in Marriage	Even though adults are remaining single longer and the divorce rate is high, we still show a strong predilection for marriage. The age at which individuals marry, expectations about what the marriage will be like, and the developmental course of marriage may not only vary across historical time within a culture, but also across cultures.
	Marital Expectations and Myths	Unrealistic expectations and myths about marriage contribute to marital dissatisfaction and divorce.
	Marital Satisfaction and Conflict	Two views are behavior exchange theory and the developmental construction view.
	Gender, Intimacy, and Family Work in Marriage	Overall, women are more expressive and affectionate in marriage, and this difference bothers many women. Women do much more family work than men, and they experience family work differently than men do.
	The Parental Role	For some, the parental role is well planned and coordinated. For others, there is surprise and sometimes chaos. There are many myths about parenting, among them the myth that the birth of a child will save a failing marriage. Families are becoming smaller and many women are delaying childbirth until they have become well established in a career. There are some advantages to having children earlier in adulthood, and some advantages to having them later.

enties, the number of men living by themselves increased 97 percent, the number of women, 55 percent. In the eighties, the growth slowed considerably, but it continues and is expected to do so at least through the end of the century. In 1985, 20.6 million individuals lived alone in the United States, accounting for 11 percent of adults and 24 percent of all households. In some respects, the number of individuals living alone is a symptom of other changes: low birthrates, high divorce rates, long lives, and late marriages. But the group that grew the fastest in the 1970s was young adults, the majority of them young men. In that decade, the number of never-married people under 30 living by themselves more than tripled. For them, marriage was no longer the only way out of the house or the only route to sexual fulfillment. In figure 15.6, the percentages of never-married individuals in 1970 and 1988 are compared.

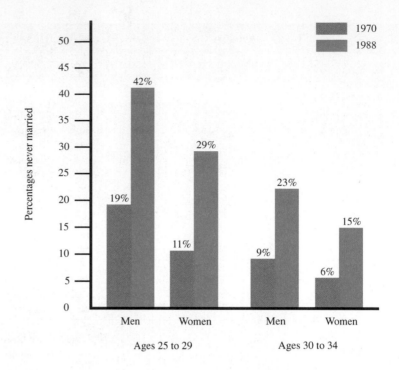

Figure 15.6 Percentages of never-married individuals in 1970 and 1988. Notice the dramatic increase from 1970 to 1988 of never-married individuals, both men and women, during the early adulthood years.

A history of myths and stereotypes are associated with being single, ranging from "the swinging single" to "desperately lonely, suicidal single." Most singles, of course, are somewhere between these extremes. Single adults are often challenged by others to get married so they will no longer be termed selfish, irresponsible, impotent, frigid, and immature. Clearly, though, being a single adult has some advantages—time to make decisions about one's life course, time to develop personal resources to meet goals, freedom to make autonomous decisions and pursue one's own schedule and interests, opportunity to explore new places and try out new things, and availability of privacy.

Common problems of single adults focus on intimate relationships with other adults, confronting loneliness, and finding a niche in a society that is marriage oriented. Many single adults cite personal freedom as one of the major advantages of being a single adult. One woman who never married commented, "I enjoy knowing that I can satisfy my own whims without someone else's interferences. If I want to wash my hair at two o'clock in the morning, no one complains. I can eat when I'm hungry and watch my favorite television shows without contradictions from anyone. I enjoy these freedoms. I would feel very confined if I had to adjust to another person's schedule."

Some adults never marry. Initially, they are perceived as living glamorous, exciting lives. But once we reach the age of 30, there is increasing pressure on us to settle down and get married. If a woman wants to bear children, she may feel a sense of urgency when she reaches 30. This is when many single adults make a conscious decision to marry or to remain single. As one 30-year-old male recently commented, "It's real. You are supposed to get married by 30—that is a standard. It is part of getting on with your life that you are supposed to do. You have career and who-am-I concerns in your 20s. In your 30s, you have to get on with it, keep on track, make headway, financially and familywise." But, to another 30-year-old, getting married is less important than buying a house and some property. A training manager for a computer company, Jane says, "I'm competent in making relationships and being committed, so I don't feel a big rush to get married. When it happens, it happens."

Early Adulthood

Divorced Adults

Divorce has become epidemic in our culture. Until recently, it was increasing annually by 10 percent, although its rate of increase is now slowing. While divorce has increased for all socioeconomic groups, those in disadvantaged groups have a higher incidence of divorce. Youthful marriage, low educational level, and low income are associated with increases in divorce. So too is premarital pregnancy. One investigation revealed that half of the women who were pregnant before marriage failed to live with the husband for more than five years (Sauber & Corrigan, 1970).

For those who do divorce, separation and divorce are complex and emotionally charged (Bursik, 1991). In one investigation, 6 of the 48 divorced couples continued to have sexual intercourse during the first two years after separation (Hetherington, Cox, & Cox, 1978). Prior social scripts and patterns of interaction are difficult to break. Although divorce is a marker event in the relationship between spouses, it often does not signal the end of the relationship. Attachment to each other endures regardless of whether the former couple respects, likes, or is satisfied with the present relationship. Former spouses often alternate between feelings of seductiveness and hostility. They may also have thoughts of reconciliation. And while at times they may express love toward their former mate, the majority of feelings are negative and involve anger and hate.

The stress of separation and divorce place both men and women at risk for psychological and physical difficulties (Chase-Lansdale & Hetherington, in press; Coombs, 1991). Separated and divorced men and women have higher rates of psychiatric disturbance, admission to psychiatric hospitals, clinical depression, alcoholism, and psychosomatic problems, such as sleep disturbances, than do married adults. There is increasing evidence that stressful events of many types—including marital separation—reduce the immune system's capabilities, rendering separated and divorced individuals vulnerable to disease and infection. In one investigation, the most recently separated women (one year or less) were more likely to show impaired immunological functioning than women whose separations had occurred several years earlier (one to six years) (Kiecolt-Glaser & Glaser, 1988). Also in this investigation, unhappily married individuals had immune systems that were not functioning as effectively as those of happily married individuals.

Special problems surface for the divorced woman who is a displaced homemaker. She assumed that her work would probably always be in the home. Although her expertise in managing the home may be considerable, future employers do not recognize this experience as work experience. Donna is typical of a divorced displaced homemaker. She married young, and at age 18 had her first child. Her work experience consisted of a part-time job as a waitress in high school. Now 32 with three children—aged 14, 12, and 6—her husband recently divorced her and married someone else. The child support payments are barely enough for rent, clothing, and other necessities. Without any marketable skills, Donna is working as a salesclerk in a local department store. She cannot afford a housekeeper and worries about the children being unsupervised while she works. Creating a positive single identity is essential for divorced adults such as Donna, so they can come to grips with their loneliness, lack of autonomy, and financial hardship (Ahrons & Rodgers, 1987; McLanahan & Booth, 1989). Men, however, do not go through a divorce unscathed. They usually have fewer rights to their children, experience a decline in income (though not nearly as great as their ex-wives), and receive less emotional support. Divorce can also have a negative impact on a man's career.

Separation and divorce are highly charged emotional affairs. No one gets married to get divorced. Attachment in some form often continues after the separation and divorce. Prior social scripts and interactions are difficult patterns to break. Former spouses may vacillate between hostility and seduction.

Intimacy, Independence, and Women's Development

As we go through our early adult years, most of us are motivated not only by intimacy but also by independence. What is the nature of intimacy's development? How do we juggle the motivation for intimacy and the motivation for independence?

Intimacy

Erik Erikson (1968) believes that intimacy should come after individuals are well on their way to establishing a stable and successful individual identity. Intimacy is another life crisis in Erikson's scheme—if intimacy is not developed in early adulthood, the individual may be left with what Erikson calls isolation. Intimacy versus isolation is the sixth stage in Erikson's eight-stage life-cycle perspective, corresponding roughly to the early adulthood years. Erikson refers to intimacy in both sexual relationships and friendships:

> As the young individual seeks at least tentative forms of playful intimacy in friendship and competition, in sex play and love, in argument and gossip, he is apt to experience a peculiar strain, as if such tentative engagement might turn into an interpersonal fusion amounting to a loss of identity and requiring, therefore, a tense inner reservation, a caution in commitment. Where a youth does not resolve such a commitment, he may isolate himself and enter, at best, only stereotyped and formalized interpersonal relations; or he may, in repeated hectic attempts and dismal failures, seek intimacy with the most improbable of partners. For where an assured sense of identity is missing, even friendships and affairs become desperate attempts at delineating the fuzzy outlines of identity by mutual narcissistic mirroring; to fall in love means to fall in love with one's mirror image, hurting oneself and damaging the mirror. (p. 167)

An inability to develop meaningful relationships with others in early adulthood can be harmful to an individual's personality. It may lead individuals to repudiate, ignore, or attack those who frustrate them. Such circumstances account for the shallow, almost pathetic attempts of youth to merge themselves with a leader. Many youths want to be apprentices or disciples of leaders and adults who will shelter them from the harm of an "outgroup" world. If this fails, and Erikson believes that it must, sooner or later the individuals will recoil into a self-search to discover where they went wrong. This introspection sometimes leads to painful depression and isolation, and may contribute to mistrust of others and restrict the willingness to act on one's own initiative.

There are different styles of intimate interaction. One classification suggests five styles: intimate, preintimate, stereotyped, pseudointimate, and isolated (Orlofsky, Marcia, & Lesser, 1973). The **intimate style** *is a form of social interaction in which the individual maintains one or more deep and long-lasting love relationships.* The **preintimate style** *is a form in which the individual has mixed emotions about commitment. This ambivalence is reflected in a strategy of offering love without obligations or long-lasting bonds.* The **stereotyped style** *is a form in which the individual engages in superficial relationships that tend to be dominated by same-sex friendships rather than opposite-sex relationships.* The **pseudointimate style** *is a form in which the individual maintains a long-lasting heterosexual attachment with little or no depth or closeness.* And, the **isolated style** *is a form in which the individual withdraws from social encounters and has little or no intimate attachment to same- or opposite-sex individuals.* Occasionally, the isolate shows signs of developing interpersonal relationships, but usually the interactions are stressful. In one investigation, intimate and preintimate individuals were more sensitive

Early Adulthood

to their partner's needs and were more open in their friendships than individuals who were categorized according to the other three intimacy statuses (Orlofsky, 1976).

A desirable goal is to develop a mature identity and have positive close relationships with others (Whitbourne, 1991; Whitbourne & Ebmeyer, 1990). Kathleen White and her colleagues (Paul & White, 1990; White & others, 1986; White & others, 1987) developed a model of relationship maturity that includes this goal at its highest level. Individuals are described as moving through three levels of relationship maturity: self-focused, role-focused, and individuated-connected.

The **self-focused level** *is the first level of relationship maturity, at which one's perspective of another or a relationship is concerned only with how it affects the self.* The individual's own wishes and plans overshadow those of others, and the individual shows little concern for others. Intimate communication skills are in the early developing, experimental stages. In terms of sexuality, there is little understanding of mutuality or consideration of another's sexual needs.

The **role-focused level** *is the second or intermediate level of relationship maturity, at which perceiving others as individuals in their own right begins to develop. However, at this level, the perspective is stereotypical and emphasizes social acceptability.* Individuals at this level know that acknowledging and respecting another is part of being a good friend or a romantic partner. Yet commitment to an individual, rather than the romantic partner role itself, is not articulated. Generalizations about the importance of communication in relationships abound, but underlying this talk is a shallow understanding of commitment.

The **individuated-connected level** *is the highest level of relationship maturity, at which there is evidence of an understanding of one self, as well as consideration of others' motivation and anticipation of their needs. Concern and caring involve emotional support and individualized expression of interest.* Commitment is made to specific individuals with whom they share a relationship. At this level, individuals understand the personal time and investment needed to make a relationship work. In White's view, it is not until adulthood that the individuated-connected level is likely to be reached. She believes most individuals making the transition from adolescence to adulthood are either self-focused or role-focused in their relationship maturity. Next, we further examine the nature of intimacy and independence.

Intimacy and Independence

The early adult years are a time when individuals usually develop an intimate relationship with another individual. An important aspect of this relationship is the commitment of the individuals to each other. At the same time, individuals show a strong interest in independence and freedom. Development in early adulthood often involves an intricate balance of intimacy and commitment on the one hand, and independence and freedom on the other (McAdams, 1988).

Recall that intimacy is the aspect of development that follows identity in Erikson's eight stages of development. A related aspect of developing an identity in adolescence and early adulthood is independence. At the same time individuals are trying to establish an identity, they face the difficulty of having to cope with increasing their independence from their parents, developing an intimate relationship with another individual, and increasing their friendship commitments, while also being able to think for themselves and do things without always relying on what others say or do.

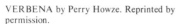

VERBENA by Perry Howze. Reprinted by permission.

The extent to which the young adult has begun to develop autonomy has important implications for early adulthood maturity. The young adult who has not sufficiently moved away from parental ties may have difficulty in both interpersonal relationships and a career. Consider the mother who overprotects her daughter, continues to support her financially, and does not want to let go of her. In early adulthood, the daughter may have difficulty developing mature intimate relationships and she may have career difficulties. When a promotion comes up that involves more responsibility and possibly more stress, she may turn it down. When things do not go well in her relationship with a young man, she may go crying to her mother.

The balance between intimacy and commitment on the one hand, and independence and freedom on the other, is delicate. Keep in mind that these important dimensions of adult development are not necessarily opposite ends of a continuum—some individuals are able to experience a healthy independence and freedom along with an intimate relationship. These dimensions may also fluctuate with social and historical change. Keep in mind that intimacy and commitment, and independence and freedom, are not just concerns of early adulthood; they are important themes of development that are worked and reworked throughout the adult years. And as we have seen, changing gender roles have increased the motivation of many women to gain more independence and self-determination. Next, we examine the nature of women's development, their competence in connectedness and relationships, and the feminist perspective on development.

Women's Development and Gender Issues

Many feminist scholars believe that much of psychology's history portrays human behavior and development with a "male dominant theme" (DeFour & Paludi, in press; Denmark & Paludi, in press). Feminist scholars are developing new perspectives that focus on women's life experiences and development. These perspectives include an emphasis on girls and women as authorities about their own experiences, or as Harvard psychologist Carol Gilligan (1990) advocates, listening to women's voices; on women's ways of knowing (Belenky & others, 1986); on abuse of women and rape (Koss, 1990; Russo, 1990); on women's career and family roles (Baruch, Biener, & Barnett, 1987; Russo, 1990); and on women's experiences of connectedness and self-determination (Brown & Gilligan, 1990; Chodorow, 1989; Gilligan, Brown, & Rogers, 1990; Josselson, 1987; Lerner, 1989; Miller, 1986).

In the last decade it has become clearer that if women are trying to define and create a full personhood, we are engaged in a huge undertaking. We see that this attempt means building a new way of living which encompasses all realms of life, from global economic, social, and political levels to the most intimate personal relationships.

~ *Jean Baker Miller,*
Toward a New Psychology
of Women, *1986*

Jean Baker Miller (1976, 1986) has been an important voice in stimulating examination of psychological issues from a female perspective. She believes the study of women's psychological development opens up paths to a better understanding of all psychological development. She also concludes that when researchers examine what women have been doing in life, a large part of it is active participation in the development of others. In Miller's view, women often try to interact with others in ways that will foster the other person's development along many dimensions—emotionally, intellectually, and socially. Many women are very competent at building other people's strengths, resources, and well-being.

Many feminist thinkers believe it is important for women to not only maintain their competency in relationships, but to balance this other-oriented competence with an increased motivation for self-determination. Many women came from a position in which their lives were extensively determined by others as they grew up in a male-dominated culture that dictated what women should be like. Miller believes that through increased self-determination, coupled with already developed relationship skills, many women will discover the route to a deserved status of greater power in the American culture. And as feminist scholar Harriet Lerner (1989) concludes in her book, *The Dance of Intimacy*, it is important for women to bring to their relationships nothing less than a strong, assertive, independent, and authentic self. She believes competent relationships are those in which the separate "I-ness" of both persons can be appreciated and enhanced while still staying emotionally connected to the significant other.

In discussing social and personality development in adulthood, we have talked almost exclusively about adults' current experiences and personality. But just as children do not enter adolescence with a blank slate, neither do youths enter adulthood with a blank slate.

Continuity and Discontinuity from Childhood to Adulthood

It is a common finding that the closer in time we measure personality characteristics the more similar an individual will look. Thus, if we measure an individual's self-concept at the age of 20 and then again at the age of 30 we will probably find more stability than if we measured the individual's self-concept at the age of 10 and then again at the age of 30. We no longer believe in the infant determinism of Freud's psychosexual theory, which argued that our personality as adults is virtually cast in stone by the time we are 5 years of age. But the first twenty years of life are not meaningless in predicting an adult's personality. And there is every reason to believe that later experiences in the early adult years are important in determining what the individual is like as a young adult. In trying to understand the young adult's personality, it would be misleading to look only at the adult's life in present tense, ignoring the developmental unfolding of personality. So, too, would it be far off target to only search through a 30-year-old's first five to ten years of life in trying to predict why he is having difficulty in a close relationship. The truth about adult personality development, then, lies somewhere between the infant determinism of Freud and a contextual approach that ignores the antecedents of the adult years altogether.

At this point we have discussed a number of ideas about the diversity of adult life-styles, intimacy and independence, and continuity and discontinuity. A summary of these ideas is presented in concept table 15.2.

Jean Baker Miller, a leading feminist scholar, believes it is important for women to not only maintain their competency in relationships, but to balance this other-oriented competence with an increased motivation for self-determination.

• *Critical Thinking* •

What gender issues do you believe women will face in the year 2000? Will they be the same issues women face today?

Concept Table 15.2: The Diversity of Adult Life-Styles, Intimacy and Independence, and Continuity and Discontinuity

Concept	Processes/Related Ideas	Characteristics/Description
The Diversity of Adult Life-Styles	Single Adults	Being single has become an increasingly prominent life-style. Myths and stereotypes about singles abound, ranging from "swinging single" to "desperately lonely, suicidal single." There are advantages and disadvantages to being single, autonomy being one of the advantages. Intimacy, loneliness, and a marriage-oriented society are concerns of single adults.
	Divorced Adults	Divorce has increased dramatically, although its rate of increase has begun to slow. Divorce is complex and emotional. In the first year following divorce, a disequilibrium in the divorced adult's behavior occurs, but by several years after the divorce, more stability has been achieved. The divorced displaced homemaker may encounter excessive stress. Men do not go through a divorce unscathed either.
Intimacy and Independence	Intimacy	Erikson argues that intimacy versus isolation, the sixth stage in his eight-stage theory of the life cycle, coincides with early adulthood. Five styles of intimate interaction are: intimate style, preintimate style, stereotyped style, pseudointimate style, and isolated style. White proposed a model of relationship maturity in which individuals move through three levels: self-focused, role-focused, and individuated-connected.
	Intimacy and Independence	There is a delicate balance between intimacy and commitment on the one hand, and independence and freedom on the other. These themes are germane to understanding early adulthood, but they are usually worked and reworked throughout the adult years.
	Women's Development and Gender Issues	Feminist scholars are developing new perspectives that focus on women's experiences and development. Women's strengths have been especially important in relationships and connections with others. A special emphasis is that while staying emotionally connected to significant others, women can enhance their well-being by developing stronger self-determination.
Continuity and Discontinuity	Its Nature	The closer in time we measure personality, the more continuity we find. The first twenty years are important in predicting an adult's personality, but so, too, are continuing experiences in the adult years. The first five years are not as powerful as Freud believed in determining an adult's personality.

Summary

I. Attraction, Love, and Close Relationships

Familiarity precedes a close relationship. We like to associate with individuals who are similar to us. Berscheid believes love has four forms: altruism, friendship, romantic or passionate love, and affectionate or companionate love. Friends and lovers have similar and dissimilar characteristics. Romantic love is involved when we say we are "in love"; it includes passion, sexuality, and a mixture of emotions, some of which may be negative. Affectionate love is more important as relationships age. In Sternberg's triangular theory of love, love has three forms: passion, intimacy, and commitment. The high or low presence of these ingredients can produce infatuation, companionate love, fatuous love, or consummate love. Loneliness is associated with gender, attachment history, self-esteem, and social skills. The transition to college is a time when loneliness often surfaces.

II. Trends in Marriage

Even though adults are remaining single longer and the divorce rate is high, we still show a strong predilection for marriage. The age at which individuals marry, expectations about marriage, and the developmental course of marriage, not only vary across historical time within a culture, but also across cultures.

III. The Nature of Marriage

Unrealistic expectations and myths about marriage contribute to marital dissatisfaction and divorce. Two views about the nature of marital satisfaction are behavioral exchange theory and the developmental construction view. Overall, women are more expressive and affectionate in marriage, and this difference bothers many women. Women do much more family work than men, and they experience family work differently than men do.

IV. The Parental Role

For some, the parental role is well planned and coordinated. For others, there is surprise and sometimes chaos. There are many myths about parenting, among them the myth that the birth of a child will save a failing marriage. Families are becoming smaller and many women are delaying childbirth until they have become well established in a career. There are some advantages to having children earlier in adulthood, and some advantages to having them later.

V. Single Adults

Being single has become an increasingly prominent life-style. Myths and stereotypes about singles abound, ranging from "swinging single" to "desperately lonely, suicidal single." There are advantages and disadvantages to being single, one of the advantages being autonomy. Intimacy, loneliness, and a marriage-oriented society are concerns of single adults.

VI. Divorced Adults

Divorce has increased dramatically, but its rate has begun to slow. Divorce is complex and emotional. In the first year following divorce, a disequilibrium in the divorced adult's behavior occurs, but by several years after the divorce, more stability has been achieved. The divorced displaced homemaker may encounter excessive stress. Men do not go through a divorce unscathed.

VII. Intimacy

Erikson argues that intimacy versus isolation, the sixth stage in his eight-stage theory of the life cycle, coincides with early adulthood. Five styles of intimate interaction are: intimate style, preintimate style, stereotyped style, pseudointimate style, and isolated style. White proposed a model of relationship maturity in which individuals move through three levels: self-focused, role-focused, and individuated-connected.

VIII. Intimacy and Independence

There is a delicate balance between intimacy and commitment on the one hand, and independence and freedom on the other. These themes are germane to understanding early adulthood, but they usually are worked and reworked throughout the adulthood years.

IX. Women's Development and Gender Issues

Feminist scholars are developing new perspectives that focus on women's experiences and development. Women's strengths have been especially important in relationships and connections with others. A special emphasis is that while staying emotionally connected to significant others, women can enhance their well-being by developing stronger self-determination.

X. Continuity and Discontinuity

The closer in time we measure personality the more continuity we find. The first twenty years are important in predicting an adult's personality development, but so, too, are continuing experiences in the adult years. The first five years are not as powerful as Freud believed in determining an adult's personality.

Key Terms

consensual validation 488
friendship 489
romantic love 489
affectionate love 491
triangular theory of love 492

behavior exchange theory 498
developmental construction view 498
intimate style 506
preintimate style 506
stereotyped style 506

pseudointimate style 506
isolated style 506
self-focused level 507
role-focused level 507
individuated-connected level 507

Suggested Readings

Ahrons, C. R., & Rodgers, R. H. (1987). *Divorced families*. New York: W. W. Norton.
A contemporary look at the nature of divorce and its effects on adult development and life-styles.

Hatfield, E., & Sprecher, S. (1986). *Mirror, mirror. . . . The importance of looks in everyday life*. Albany: State University of New York Press.
Elaine Hatfield (formerly Elaine Walster) is a pioneer in the field of physical attractiveness and close relationships. This entertaining, insightful book details how looks affect sex, marriage, self-image, personality, and social skills.

Harayda, J. (1986). *The joy of being single*. New York: Doubleday.
This popular book describes many of the myths about single life and chronicles how being single is more adaptive today than it used to be.

Hendrick, C. (Ed.). (1989). *Close relationships*. Newbury Park, CA: Sage.
This book includes a number of insightful chapters about the nature of close relationships, including the topics of envy and jealousy in relationships, emotional communication, marital satisfaction, and trust.

Journal of Marriage and the Family
This journal includes a wide-ranging set of articles about marital and family relationships. Leaf through the issues of the last several years to discover the topics that interest researchers in this area.

Rubin, L. B. (1984). *Intimate strangers: Men and women together*. New York: Harper & Row.
This extremely popular best-selling book describes in insightful and interesting ways the role that gender plays in our intimate relationships.

Sternberg, R. J. (1988). *The triangle of love*. New York: Basic Books.
Sternberg outlines his theory of love based on passion, intimacy, and commitment. Includes valuable information about what makes a successful love relationship as well as what causes problems in love.

Answers to the Marriage Quiz (Figure 15.5)

1. False
2. True
3. False
4. False
5. True

6. True
7. False
8. False
9. False
10. False

11. False
12. True
13. False
14. False
15. False

S·E·C·T·I·O·N

VIII

MIDDLE ADULTHOOD

*G*enerations will depend on the ability
of every procreating individual to face
his children.

Erik Erikson

CHAPTER 16

Physical and Cognitive Development in Middle Adulthood

*O*ur perception of time depends on where we are in the life cycle. We are more concerned about time at some points in life than others. Jim Croce's *Time in a Bottle* reflects a time perspective that develops in the adult years.

> If I could save time in a bottle
> the first thing that I'd like to do
> is save every day till eternity passes away
> just to spend them with you. . . .
>
> But there never seems to be enough time to do
> the things you want to do once you find them.
> Looked around enough to know that you're the one
> I want to go through time with
>
> Jim Croce, *Time in a Bottle*

As young adults, love and intimacy assume prominent roles in our lives. We begin to look back at where we have been. As middle-aged adults, we reflect even more on what we have done with the time we have had. We look toward the future more in terms of how much time remains to accomplish what we wish to do with our lives.

When we think about what happens to us when we become middle-aged, physical changes leap to the forefront of our thoughts—the lessening of physical powers, the arrival of sags, spreads, and lines, the appearance of menopause. Middle age also brings forth thoughts about whether our mind slows down at this point in the life cycle. We wonder, "Will my memory be worse when I become middle-aged?" for example. And we imagine where we will be in our careers in middle age. We think, "Will I be able to reach and maintain satisfaction in my career?" "Will I possibly change careers in mid-life?" "Will I be able to find enough time for leisure and lead a balanced, happy life?" These are the themes of this chapter—physical, cognitive, and career development in middle adulthood.

Physical Development

I am 46 years of age at the time of this writing. When I was an adolescent and my father was 46 years old, I thought he was old. I could not conceive of myself ever being that old! But it happened, and now I've got a few gray hairs, I'm wearing reading glasses while I'm typing this sentence, and I can't run as fast as I could, although I still run about 15 miles every week to keep my body from falling apart. At some point in our forties we become middle-aged. What physical changes accompany this change to middle adulthood? What is the health status of middle-aged adults? What kind of sexual changes occur?

Physical Changes

A host of physical changes characterize middle adulthood—some began to appear earlier in the individual's thirties, but at some point in the forties, decline in physical development indicates that middle adulthood has arrived.

Seeing and hearing are two of the most troublesome and noticeable changes in middle adulthood. Accommodation of the eye—the ability to focus and maintain an image on the retina—experiences its sharpest decline between 40 and 59 years of age. In particular, middle-aged individuals begin to have difficulty viewing close objects (Kline & Schieber, 1985). The eye's blood supply also diminishes, although usually not until the fifties or sixties. The reduced blood supply may decrease the visual field's size and account for an increase in the eye's blind spot. And there is some evidence that the retina

I wear them. They help me. But I don't care for them . . .
My gaze feels aimed. It is as if two manufactured beams had been lodged in my sockets— hollow stiff and gray.
Like mailing tubes—and when I pivot, vases topple down from tabletops, and women frown.

~ *John Updike*

A host of physical changes accompany middle age, among them accommodation of the eye.

For most of us, some aspect of our health deteriorates in middle adulthood. Being overweight has become epidemic in our culture. For overweight middle-aged individuals, the probability of dying increases by about 40 percent. Think about the middle-aged individuals you know. What percentage of them are overweight?

Middle age is when your age starts to show around your middle.

~ Bob Hope

becomes less sensitive to low levels of illumination. In one investigation, the effects of illumination level on the work productivity of individuals in early and middle adulthood were studied (Hughes, 1978). The workers were asked to look for 10 target numbers printed on sheets that had a total of 420 numbers printed on them. Each of the workers performed the task under three different levels of illumination. While increased levels of illumination increased performance for both age groups, the performance of middle-aged workers improved the most.

Hearing may also start to decline by the age of 40. Sensitivity to high pitches usually declines first; the ability to hear low pitched sounds does not seem to decline much in middle adulthood, though. And men usually lose their sensitivity to high pitched sounds sooner than women do. However, this sex difference might be due to the greater exposure to noise by men in occupations such as mining, automobile work, and so on (Olsho, Harkins, & Lenhardt, 1985).

As individuals go through their adult years, they get shorter—our bodies cannot hold off gravity forever! As muscles weaken, an adult's back weakens. As the disks between the bones of the spine deteriorate, the bones move closer to one another. For example, a man who is 5 feet 10 inches tall at age 30 will probably be 5 feet 9 ⅞ inches by age 50, and only 5 feet 9 ¼ inches by age 60.

Health Status

Health status becomes a major concern in middle adulthood. More time is spent worrying about health now than in early adulthood. Because middle adulthood is characterized by a general decline in physical fitness, some deterioration in health is to be expected. The main health nemeses of middle-aged adults are cardiovascular disease, cancer, and weight. Cardiovascular disease is the number one killer in the United States, followed by cancer. Smoking-related cancer often surfaces for the first time in middle adulthood. And the Harvard Medical School Health Letter indicates that about 20 million Americans are on a serious diet at any particular moment. Being overweight is a critical health problem in middle adulthood. For individuals who are 30 percent or more overweight, the probability of dying in middle adulthood increases by about 40 percent. Obesity increases the probability that an individual will suffer a number of other ailments, among them hypertension and digestive disorders.

Since a youthful appearance is stressed in our culture, many individuals whose hair is graying, whose skin is wrinkling, whose body is sagging, and whose teeth are yellowing strive to make themselves look younger. Undergoing cosmetic surgery, dying hair, purchasing a wig, enrolling in a weight reduction program, participating in an exercise regimen, and taking heavy doses of vitamins are frequent occurrences in middle age. One investigation found that middle-aged women focus more attention on facial attractiveness than do older or younger women (Nowak, 1977). In this same investigation, middle-aged women were more likely to perceive the signs of aging as having a negative effect on their physical appearance. In our culture, some aspects of aging in middle adulthood are taken as signs of attractiveness in men; similar signs may be perceived as unattractive in women. Facial wrinkles and gray hair symbolize strength and maturity in men but may be perceived as unattractive in women.

How individuals deal with physical change and decline varies greatly from one individual to the next. One individual may be able to function well with severe physical problems or deteriorating health; another with the same

Middle Adulthood

problems may be hospitalized and bedridden. Some individuals call a doctor at the slightest hint of something being physically amiss; others ignore serious physical signs that might indicate the presence of a heart condition or cancer.

Life-Style, Personality, and Health
Emotional stability and personality are related to health in middle adulthood. In the California Longitudinal Study, as individuals aged from 34 to 50, those who were the most healthy were also the most calm, the most self-controlled, and the most responsible (Livson & Peskin, 1981). Two clusters of personality characteristics that have been extensively investigated as factors in stress and health are Type-A behavior pattern and hardiness. And considerable interest has developed in the role of stress and diet in cancer.

Cardiovascular Disease and the Type A Behavior Pattern
The heart and coronary arteries change in middle adulthood. The heart of a 40-year-old pumps only 23 liters of blood per minute; the heart of a 20-year-old pumps 40 liters under comparable conditions. Just as the coronary arteries that supply blood to the heart narrow during middle adulthood, the level of cholesterol in the blood increases with age—at age 20, it is 180 milligrams; at 40, 220 mg; at age 60, 230 mg—and begins to accumulate on the artery walls, which are also thickening. The net result: Arteries are more likely to become clogged, increasing the pressure on the arterial walls, which in turn pushes the heart to work harder to pump blood, thus making a stroke or heart attack more likely. Blood pressure, too, usually rises in the forties and fifties. At menopause, a woman's blood pressure rises sharply and usually remains above that of a man through life's later years.

Might an individual's personality characteristics contribute to the likelihood of having cardiovascular disease? In the late 1950s, a secretary for two California cardiologists, Meyer Friedman and Ray Rosenman, observed that the chairs in their waiting room were tattered and worn, but only on the front edge. The cardiologist had noticed the impatience of their cardiac patients, often arriving exactly on time for an appointment and in a great hurry to leave. Subsequently they conducted a study of 3,000 healthy men between the ages of 35 and 59 over an eight-year period (Friedman & Rosenman, 1974). During the eight years, one group of men had twice as many heart attacks or other forms of heart disease as anyone else. And autopsies of the men who died revealed that this same group had coronary arteries that were more obstructed than other men. Friedman and Rosenman described the coronary-disease group as characterized by **Type A behavior pattern,** *a cluster of characteristics— excessively competitive, hard-driven, impatient and hostile—thought to be related to the incidence of heart disease.*

Since the original research of Friedman and Rosenman, an extensive effort examining the link between Type A behavior and coronary disease has cast some doubt on the strength of the association (Edwards & Baglion, 1991; Siegman & Dembrowski, 1989; Williams, 1989b). Studies with large samples of Type-A subjects (on the order of 1,000 or more) and carefully designed interviewing techniques still reveal an association between Type A behavior and coronary risk, but the association is not as strong as was believed. Researchers have examined the different components of Type A behavior, such as hostility, to determine a more precise link with coronary risk. People who are hostile or consistently turn anger inward are more likely to develop heart disease (Siegman, 1989; Williams, 1989 a, b). Hostile, angry individuals have been labeled "hot reactors," meaning they have intense physiological reactions to stress—their hearts race, their breathing hurries, and muscles tense up—

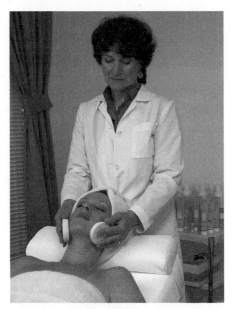

How do individuals deal with physical changes in middle age? A youthful appearance is stressed in our culture. Many individuals go to great lengths to make themselves look younger. Face lifts and tummy tucks are more common today than in prior decades, especially in women. Why might women in our culture be more motivated than men to change their physical appearance in middle age?

When more time stretches before one, some assessments, however reluctantly and incompletely, begin to be made.

~ *James Baldwin*

All men should strive to learn before they die
What they are running from, and to, and why.

~ *James Thurber,*
The Shore and the Sea, *1956*

Table 16.1: Illness of High-Stress Business Executives—The Effects of Personal Hardiness, Exercise, and Support Systems

Resistance Sources	Number of Illnesses
All three high	357
Two high	2,049
One high	3,336
None high	6,474

Note: The measure of illnesses is based on the seriousness of illness survey, a self-report checklist of 126 commonly recognized illnesses—severity weights were given to illnesses based on ratings by large numbers of physicians and lay persons.

Reprinted with permission from *Journal of Psychosomatic Research,* 29:525–533, S. C. Kobasa, et al., "Relative Effectiveness of Hardiness, Exercise, and Social Support as Resources Against Illness," Copyright 1985, Pergamon Press plc.

which could lead to heart disease. Redford Williams, a behavioral medicine specialist and a leading researcher in charting the behavioral and psychological dimensions of heart disease, believes each of us has the ability to control our anger and develop more trust in others, which he believes will reduce the risk for heart disease.

The dust has not completely settled in the debate about whether Type A behavior in general should be abandoned in favor of its more precise components. Meyer Friedman still believes the cluster of anger, impatience, competiveness, and irritation is related to heart disease, for example. And his clinical staff reports success with counseling and behavior modification programs designed to reduce the intensity of the cluster in coronary risk patients. As one 64-year-old heart attack victim who went through counseling commented, "I realized that there is more than one way of getting from point A to point B. . . . If I had a problem before, I'd just drive forward and solve it at any cost. Now I know what I don't complete I'll finish tomorrow." (Fischman, 1987, p. 50). Thus, while empirical research studies have chipped away at the Type A behavior pattern, trying to find which of its components are most strongly associated with coronary disease, the Type A behavior pattern continues to play an important role in clinical analysis and treatment.

Hardiness

Hardiness *is a personality style characterized by a sense of commitment (rather than alienation), control (rather than powerlessness), and a perception of problems as challenges (rather than threats)* (Maddi, 1986). In the Chicago Stress Project, business managers 32 to 65 years of age were studied over a five-year period. During the five years, most of the managers experienced stressful events, such as divorce, job transfers, the death of a close friend, inferior performance evaluations at work, and working at a job with an unpleasant boss. In one investigation, managers who developed an illness (ranging from the flu to a heart attack) were compared with those who did not (Kobasa, Maddi, & Kahn, 1982). The latter group was more likely to have a hardy personality. In another study of business executives, hardiness along with exercise and social support were evaluated to determine whether they buffered stress and reduced illness. As shown in table 16.1, when all three were present in the executive's life, the level of illness dropped dramatically. Thus, a combination of factors, rather than a single factor, often helps to buffer stress (Allred & Smith, 1989; Wiebe, 1991).

• *Critical Thinking* •

A sense of commitment, control, and a perception of problems predicted resistance to illness in middle-aged men. Can you think of other factors that might prevent illness in middle age?

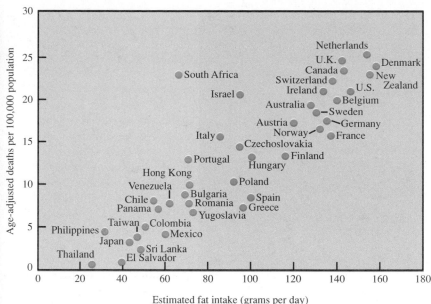

In countries where individuals have a low daily intake of fat, the rate of breast cancer is low (in Thailand, for example). In countries where individuals have a high daily intake of fat, the rate of breast cancer is high (in the Netherlands, for example).

Stress, Diet, and Cancer

If we lead less stressful lives and improve our diet, are we less likely to develop cancer? Findings that associate stress with cancer are controversial. In one investigation, the Minnesota Multiphasic Personal Inventory (MMPI) personality test was given to 2,018 middle-aged men in 1958 (Persky, Kepthorne-Rawson, & Skekelle, 1987). In the next twenty years, the middle-aged men who were the least depressed were less likely to die of cancer, a finding that was not due to their age, smoking, drinking, or other physical characteristics. And researchers have found that cancer patients who hold their negative emotions inside and do not psychologically fight the disease have less effective immune systems and less chance of survival (Jensen, 1987; Levy, 1985).

The relation of emotions to cancer should not be overstated. There is no evidence that stress causes cancer (Levenson & Bemis, 1991). Rather, stress likely influences how rapidly the cancer spreads by weakening the body's immune system, rendering it less effective in its fight against malignant cells.

Not only is stress related to cancer (although it does not cause it), but so is diet. In a recent cross-cultural comparison of diet and cancer, a strong positive correlation between fat consumption and death rates from breast cancer in different nations was found (see figure 16.1) (Cohen, 1987). And laboratory experiments with mice reveal that mice on a high-fat diet are more likely to develop breast cancer than other mice. One of the most informative comparisons of death rates due to cancer is between the United States and Japan. Both countries have similar levels of industrialization and education, and high medical standards. While the overall cancer rates of the two countries are similar, cancers of the breast, colon, and prostate are common in the United States but rare in Japan. By contrast, cancer of the stomach is common in Japan but rare in the United States. Within two generations, Japanese immigrants to Hawaii and California begin to have breast cancer rates that approach those of Americans and are significantly higher than those of Japanese. Many researchers believe the high fat intake of Americans and the low fat intake of Japanese are implicated in the different cancer rates of the two countries.

Figure 16.1 Cross-cultural comparisons of diet and cancer.
Graph from "Diet and Cancer," by L.A. Cohen. Copyright © 1987 by Scientific American, Inc. All rights reserved.

Physical and Cognitive Development in Middle Adulthood

521

Toward Healthier Lives

We have seen that staying healthy involves far more than simply going to the doctor when you get sick and being treated for disease. We are becoming increasingly aware that our behavior determines whether we will develop a serious illness and when we will die (Erben, 1991; Minkler, 1989; Siegler, 1989; Stanhope & Lancaster, 1991). Seven of the ten leading causes of death in the United States are associated with the *absence* of health behaviors. Diseases such as influenza, polio, and rubella are no longer major causes of death. More deaths are caused by heart disease, cancer, and stroke. As we have seen in this chapter, personal habits and life-style play key roles in such diseases. This has led health psychologists to predict that the next major step in improving the general health of the American population will be primarily behavioral, not medical.

What should be our nation's health goals? A number of recommendations are being made for the year 2000. Among them are objectives of the federal government and the Society for Public Health Education (Lorion, 1991; McGinnis, 1991; Schwartz & Eriksen, 1989):

- the need to develop preventive services targeting diseases such as cancer, heart disease, stroke, unintended pregnancy (especially among adolescents), and AIDS.
- the need for health promotion, including behavior modification and health education. Stronger programs are urged for dealing with smoking, alcohol and drug abuse, nutrition, physical fitness, and mental health.
- the need for cleaner air and water, and the need to improve workplace safety, including reducing exposure to toxic chemicals.
- meeting the health needs of special populations, such as a better understanding of health prevention in Black and Hispanic populations. Ethnic-minority groups suffer disproportionately from cancer, heart disease, diabetes, and other major diseases. More information about the health of individuals from ethnic-minority backgrounds appears in Cultural Worlds of Development 16.1.

America's health costs have soared and are moving toward the $1 trillion mark annually. Health experts hope a dent can be made in these costs by encouraging people to live healthier lives. Many corporations have begun to recognize that health promotion for their employees is cost effective. Businesses are increasingly examining their employees' health behavior and the workplace environment as they recognize the role health plays in productive work. Smoke-free work environments, on-site exercise programs, bonuses to quit smoking and lose weight, and company-sponsored athletic events are increasingly found in American businesses.

Sexuality

What kind of sexual changes take place during middle adulthood? What are the biological factors involved? What are our sexual attitudes and behavior like as we go through middle adulthood?

Biological Changes

Most of us know something about menopause. But is what we know accurate? Stop for a moment and think about your knowledge of menopause. What is menopause? When does it occur? Can it be treated? Most of us share some

THE HEALTH STATUS OF BLACK AMERICANS, HISPANIC AMERICANS, AND ASIAN AMERICANS

*I*n considering the health of ethnic-minority groups, it is important to recognize that there are large within-group differences in living conditions and life-styles and that these differences are influenced by social class, status as an immigrant, social skills, language skills, occupational opportunities, and social resources such as the availability of meaningful social support networks. Felipe Castro and Delia Magaña (1988) developed a course in health promotion in ethnic minority populations, which they teach at UCLA. A summary of some of the issues they discuss in the course follows.

For Black Americans, historical issues of prejudice and racial segregation are important considerations. The chronic stress of discrimination and poverty continue to negatively affect the health of many Black Americans. Personal and support systems are viable ways to improve the health of Black Americans. Their extended family network may be especially helpful in coping with stress (Boyd-Franklin, 1989; McAdoo, 1988).

For many Hispanic Americans, some of the same stressors mentioned for Black Americans are associated with migration to the United States by Puerto Ricans, Mexicans, and Latin Americans. Language is likely a barrier for unacculturated Hispanics in doctor-patient communications. In addition, there is increasing evidence that diabetes occurs at an above average rate in Hispanics (Gardner & others, 1984), making this disease a major health problem that parallels the above average rate of high blood pressure among Blacks.

For Asian Americans, it is important to consider their broad diversity in national backgrounds and life-styles. They range from highly acculturated Japanese Americans who may be better educated than many Anglo Americans and have excellent access to health care to the many Indo-Chinese refugees who have few economic resources and a poor health status.

Cultural barriers to adequate health care include the above-mentioned financial resources and language skills. In addition, members of ethnic-minority groups are often unfamiliar with how the medical system operates, confused about the need to see numerous people, and uncertain about why they have to wait so long for service (Snowden & Cheung, 1990).

Other barriers may be specific to certain cultures, reflecting differing ideas about what causes disease and how disease should be treated. For example, Chinese Americans have access to folk healers in every Chinatown in the United States. Depending on their degree of acculturation to Western society, a Chinese American may go to a folk healer first, or to a Western doctor first, but invariably consults a folk healer for follow-up care. Chinese medicines are usually used for home care. These include ginseng tea, boiled centipede soup for cancer, and eucalyptus oil for dizziness resulting from hypertension.

Native Americans view Western medicine as a source of crisis intervention, quick fixes for broken legs, or other symptom cures. They do not view Western medicine as a source for treatment of the causes of disease, or for prevention. For example, they are unlikely to attend a seminar on the prevention of alcohol abuse. They are also reluctant to become involved in care that requires long hospitalization or that necessitates surgery.

Both Navajo Indians and Mexican Americans rely on family members to make decisions about treatment choices. Doctors who expect such patients to decide on the spot whether or not to undergo treatment will likely embarrass the patient or force the patient to give an answer that may lead to cancelled appointments if the family members veto the decision.

Mexican Americans also believe that some illnesses are due to natural causes, while others are due to supernatural causes. Depending on their level of acculturation, they may be disappointed and confused by doctors who do not show an awareness of how to treat diseases with supposed supernatural origins.

Health-care professionals can increase their effectiveness with culturally diverse populations by improving their knowledge of what patients bring to the health-care setting in the way of attitudes, beliefs, and folk-health practices. Such information should be integrated into the Western-prescribed treatment rather than ignored at the risk of alienating the patient.

assumptions about menopause—we may think that it is a deficiency disease, that it involves numerous complaints, that women who are undergoing menopause deeply regret losing their reproductive capacity, their sexuality, and their femininity, and that they become deeply depressed. Are these assumptions accurate?

Menopause *is the time in middle age, usually in the late forties or early fifties, when a woman's menstrual periods and childbearing capability cease completely.* There is a dramatic decline in the production of estrogen by the ovaries. Estrogen decline produces some uncomfortable symptoms in some menopausal women—"hot flashes," nausea, fatigue, and rapid heart beat, for example. Some menopausal women report depression and irritability, but in some instances, these feelings are related to other circumstances in the women's life, such as becoming divorced, losing a job, caring for a sick parent, and so on (Dickson, 1990; Strickland, 1987).

The comments of the following two women reveal the extensive variation menopause may bring. One woman commented, "I had hot flashes several times a week for almost six months. I didn't get as embarrassed as some of my friends who also had hot flashes, but I found the 'heat wave' sensation uncomfortable." Another woman commented, "I am constantly amazed and delighted to discover new things about my body, something menstruation did not allow me to do. I have new responses, desires, sensations, freed and apart from the distraction of menses (periods)."

Recent research investigations reveal that menopause does not produce psychological problems or physical problems for the majority of women. For example, in a large survey of more than 8,000 randomly selected women, the majority judged menopause to be a positive experience—feeling relief that they no longer had to worry about becoming pregnant or having periods—or a neutral experience—with no particular feelings at all about it (McKinlay & McKinlay, 1984). Only 3 percent said they regretted reaching menopause. Except for some temporary bothersome symptoms, such as hot flashes, sweating, and menstrual irregularity, most women simply said that menopause was not nearly the big deal that a lot of people make it out to be.

Why, then, do so many individuals have the idea that menopause is such a big deal? Why do we have so many erroneous assumptions—that menopausal women will lose their sexuality and femininity, that they will become deeply depressed, and that they will experience extensive physical pain? Much of the research on menopause is based on small, selective samples of women who go to physicians or therapists because they are having problems associated with menopause. These women are unrepresentative of the large population of women in the United States.

For the minority of menopausal women whose experiences are physically painful and psychologically difficult, estrogen replacement therapy may be beneficial. The painful symptoms are usually related either to low estrogen levels or to hormonal imbalance. Estrogen replacement therapy has been successful in relieving low-estrogen menopausal symptoms like hot flashes and sweating. Medical experts increasingly recommend that, prior to menopause, women have their level of estrogen monitored. In this way, once menopause occurs and estrogen level declines, the physician knows how much estrogen to replace to maintain a woman's normal level.

Our portrayal of menopause has been much more positive than was usually painted in the past. While menopause overall is not the negative experience for most women it was once thought to be, the loss of fertility is an important marker for women—it means that they have to make final decisions about having children. Women in their thirties who have never had children sometimes speak about being up against the biological clock, because they cannot postpone questions about having children much longer (Blechman & Brownell, 1987).

Do men go through anything like the menopause that women experience? That is, is there a male menopause? During middle adulthood, most men do not lose their capacity to father children, although there usually is a modest decline in their sexual potency at this time. Men do experience hormonal changes in their fifties and sixties, but nothing like the dramatic drop in estrogen that women experience. Testosterone production begins to decline about 1 percent a year during middle adulthood, and sperm count usually shows a slow decline, but men do not lose their fertility in middle age. What has been referred to as male menopause, then, probably has less to do with hormonal change than with the psychological adjustment men must make when they are faced with declining physical energy and family and work pressures. Testosterone therapy has not been found to relieve such symptoms, suggesting that they are not induced by hormonal change.

Sexual Attitudes and Behavior

Although the ability of a man or woman to function sexually shows little biological decline in middle adulthood, sexual activity usually occurs on a less frequent basis than in early adulthood. Career interests, family matters, energy level, and routine may contribute to this decline. But a large percentage of individuals in middle adulthood continue to engage in sexual activity on a reasonably frequent basis. For example, in one national survey of 502 men and women between 46 and 71 years of age, approximately 68 percent of the 51- to 55-year-old respondents said that they had a moderate or strong interest in sex, and approximately 52 percent said that they had sexual intercourse once a week or more (Pfeiffer, Verwoerdt, & Davis, 1974).

At this point we have discussed a number of ideas about physical development in middle adulthood. A summary of these ideas is presented in concept table 16.1. Next, we study the possibility of cognitive change in middle adulthood.

• *Critical Thinking* •

What will sex probably be like in the next generation of middle-aged women and men?

Concept Table 16.1: Physical Development in Middle Adulthood

Concept	Processes/Related Ideas	Characteristics/Description
Physical Changes	Their Nature	A host of physical changes occur—at some point in the forties, decline in physical development usually indicates that middle adulthood has arrived. Seeing and hearing decline, and individuals actually become shorter.
	Health Status	Health status becomes a major concern in middle adulthood. Some deterioration is to be expected. The main health nemeses of middle adulthood are cardiovascular disease, cancer, and weight. How individuals deal with physical decline varies greatly from one individual to the next.
Life-Style, Personality, and Health	Cardiovascular Disease and the Type A Behavior Pattern	The heart and coronary arteries become less efficient in middle age, and cardiovascular disease is the number one cause of death. Type A behavior pattern refers to a cluster of characteristics—excessively competitive, hard-driven, impatient, and hostile—thought to be related to heart disease. The Type A pattern is controversial, with some researchers arguing that only specific components of the cluster, such as hostility, are associated with heart disease.
	Hardiness	Hardiness is a personality style characterized by a sense of commitment, control, and a perception of problems as challenges rather than threats. Hardiness is a buffer of stress and is related to reduced illness.
	Stress, Diet, and Cancer	The link between cancer and stress is controversial. Stress does not cause cancer, but some researchers believe stress is related to how rapidly cancer grows. A high fat diet is associated with breast cancer.
	Toward Healthier Lives	Seven of the ten leading causes of death—heart disease, cancer, and stroke, for example—are associated with the absence of health behaviors. The next major improvement in general health may be behavioral, not medical. A number of health goals for the year 2000 have been proposed and businesses are increasingly interested in improving their employees' health.
Sexuality	Biological Changes	Menopause is a marker that signals the cessation of childbearing capability, arriving usually in the late forties and early fifties. The vast majority of women do not have substantial problems with menopause, although the public perception of menopause has often been negative. Estrogen replacement therapy is effective in reducing the physical pain of menopause. Men do not experience an inability to father children, although their testosterone level gradually drops off; clearly, a male menopause, like the dramatic decline in estrogen in women, does not occur.
	Sexual Attitudes and Behavior	Sexual behavior usually occurs on a less frequent basis in middle adulthood than in early adulthood. Nonetheless, a majority of middle-aged adults show a moderate or strong interest in sex.

Cognitive Development

We have seen that the decline in some physical characteristics during middle adulthood is not just imagined. Middle-aged adults may not see as well, run as fast, or be as healthy as in their twenties and thirties. But what about cognitive characteristics? In chapter 14, we saw that our cognitive abilities are very strong during early adulthood. Do they decline as we enter and move through middle adulthood?

The aspect of cognition that has been investigated more than any other in this regard is memory. Putting the pieces of this research together, we find that memory decline in middle adulthood is more likely to occur when long-term rather than short-term memory is involved (Craik, 1977). For example, a middle-aged man can remember a phone number he heard twenty seconds ago, but he probably won't remember it as efficiently the next day. Memory is also more likely to decline when organization and imagery are not used (Hultsch, 1971; Smith, 1977). By using memory strategies, such as organizing lists of phone numbers into different categories or imagining that the phone numbers represent different objects around the house, memory in middle adulthood can be improved. Memory also tends to decline when the information to be recalled is recently acquired information or when the information is not used often (Riege & Inman, 1981). For example, a middle-aged adult may easily remember chess moves, baseball rules, or television schedules if she has used this information extensively in the past. And finally, memory tends to decline if recall rather than recognition is required (Mandler, 1980). If the middle-aged man is shown a list of phone numbers and asked to select the numbers he heard yesterday (recognition), this can be done more efficiently than recalling the number without the list. To see how the recall-recognition distinction works with remembering the names and faces of high school classmates, turn to Perspective on Life-Span Development 16.1. Memory in middle adulthood will also decline if health is poor and attitudes are negative (Poon, 1985; Salthouse, 1989). More about the nature of cognitive changes in adulthood appears in chapter 18, where we discuss general changes in intelligence, problem-solving skills, and further ideas about memory.

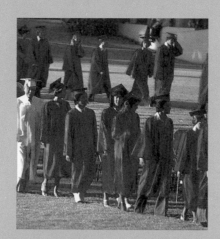
One of the saddest things is that the only thing a man can do for eight hours a day, day after day, is work. You can't eat eight hours a day nor drink for eight hours a day nor make love for eight hours.

~ *William Faulkner*, Writers at Work, *1958*

• *Critical Thinking* •

What might be the most important ingredients of job satisfaction in middle adulthood? That is, what is it about jobs in middle age that cause people to enjoy them?

Careers, Work, and Leisure

Are middle-aged workers as satisfied with their jobs as young adult workers? What is the career ladder in middle adulthood like? How extensive is mid-life career change? What are some different pathways for men and women in the workplace? What is leisure at mid-life like? These are among the most important questions to answer about careers, work, and leisure in middle adulthood—we consider each of them in turn.

Job Satisfaction

Work satisfaction increases steadily throughout the work life—from age 20 to at least age 60, for both college-educated and noncollege-educated adults (Rhodes, 1983; Tamir, 1982) (see figure 16.2). This same pattern has been found for both women and men. Satisfaction probably increases because as we get older we get paid more, we are in higher positions, and we have more job security. There is also a greater commitment to the job as we get older—we take our jobs more seriously, have lower rates of avoidable absenteeism, and are more involved with our work in middle adulthood than in early adulthood. Younger adults are still experimenting with their work, still searching for the right occupation, so they may be inclined to seek out what is wrong with their current job rather than focusing on what is right about it (Rhodes, 1983).

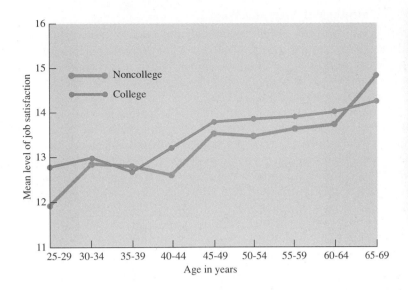

Figure 16.2 Age and job
satisfaction. Job satisfaction
increases with age, for both college
and noncollege educated adults.
Among the reasons for increased
satisfaction are more income, higher
status jobs, greater job security, and
stronger job commitment.

Career Ladders

Many of us think of our adult work life as a series of discrete steps, much like
the rungs on a ladder. In a factory, an individual might move from laborer, to
foreman, to superintendent, to production manager, and so on up the ladder.
In a business, an individual might move from salesperson, to sales manager,
to regional sales manager, to national sales manager, to vice-president of the
company, and then even possibly to president of the company, for example.
Not all occupations have such clearly defined steps, but most jobs involve a
hierarchy in which low-level workers and high-level workers are clearly distinguished. How can an individual move up the career ladder?

Having a college education helps a great deal; a college degree is associated with earlier career advancement and greater career advancement (Bray
& Howard, 1983; Golan, 1986). And individuals who are promoted early go
further up the career ladder than those who are promoted late. Most career
advancement occurs early in our adult lives. By the ages of 40 to 45, most of
us have gone as far as we will up the career ladder. In one investigation of a
large corporation, this occurred regardless of whether the positions were non-
management, lower management, or foreman (Rosenbaum, 1984).

Mid-Life Career Change

Only about 10 percent of Americans change jobs in mid-life; as we saw earlier,
job satisfaction usually increases in mid-life. But for those 10 percent who do
change jobs in mid-life, what are some of the psychological reasons behind
this dramatic life change? Of course, some of these individuals get fired but
others may change course because of their own motivation. The mid-life career
experience has been described as a turning point in adulthood by Daniel Levinson (1978). One aspect of the mid-life period involves adjusting idealistic
hope to realistic possibilities in light of how much time is left in an occupation.
Middle-aged adults may focus on how much time they have left before retirement and the speed with which they are reaching their occupational goals
(Pines & Aronson, 1988). If individuals perceive that they are behind schedule,
or if their goals are now perceived as unrealistic, reassessment and readjustment may take place. Levinson (1978) believes this may result in a sadness
over unfulfilled dreams. He found that many middle-aged men feel con-
strained by their bosses, their wives, and their children. Such feelings, he says,
may produce rebellion, which can assume several forms—extramarital affairs,
divorce, alcoholism, suicide, or career change.

A number of career patterns may be followed by the professional or career woman during her adulthood years.

Work Pathways of Men and Women

Most men begin work in early adulthood and work more or less continuously until they retire, unless they return to school or become unemployed. Unstable patterns of work are much more common among low-income workers than among middle-income workers, although a continuous pattern of work is still the norm among low-income workers.

The most common path for the middle-class woman is to work for awhile after finishing high school or even college; to marry and have children; then, when the children are a little older, to go back to part-time work to supplement the husband's income. As the children begin to leave home, the woman goes back to school for some updating of earlier skills or for a retraining program so she can assume a full-time paid job in her forties and fifties, when she is relatively free of responsibilities.

For the professional or career woman, the picture is somewhat different, since she has more invested in keeping up her professional skills. Four career patterns among professional women have been identified (Golan, 1986): (1) *regular,* the woman who pursued her professional training immediately after graduation, who began to work and continued to do so without interruption or with minimal interruption throughout the years; (2) *interrupted career,* the woman who began as in the regular pattern but interrupted her career for several years—usually for childrearing—and then went back to work full-time; (3) *second career,* the woman who started her professional training near or after the time the children left home or after a divorce; and (4) *modified second career,* the woman who started her professional training while the children were still at home but old enough not to need full-time mothering, then started to work, possibly part-time, until the last child left home or became independent at which time she shifted to a full-time career.

Why do women go back to work during middle adulthood? What stands out is that reasons are rarely as simple as earning money, although in those families where the husband has become ill or disabled, or, for other reasons, has not been able to keep up his breadwinner role, income is undoubtedly the main motive. Many middle-aged women enter the labor force when they are confronted with the need to support themselves and their family, but boredom, loneliness, and the desire for new interests are probably involved, too. Today's 50-year-old women are taking courses in computer programming, enrolling in schools of social work and studying for a real estate salesperson's license in far greater numbers than their mothers or grandmothers did in similar circumstances. The trend toward dual career couples, so prevalent in their children's generation, is also now penetrating middle adulthood. Both positive and negative reasons may be behind a middle-aged woman entering the labor force as exemplified in the situation discussed in Perspective on Life-Span Development 16.2.

Researchers who study women at mid-life have found that employment plays an important role in many women's psychological well-being (Baruch, & Barnett, 1987). In one recent investigation, higher earnings were related to life satisfaction, and being overworked was related to unhappiness, in middle-aged women (Crohan, Antonucci, Adelmann, & Coleman, 1989).

Leisure

As adults, we must not only learn how to work well, but we also need to learn how to relax and enjoy leisure. Henry Ford was known as a man who emphasized that our salvation rests in our work. Few people were aware of Ford's frequent trips to his mansion in Dearborn, Michigan, where he relaxed and participated extensively in leisure activities. Similarly, President George Bush

There is only one cure for birth and death, save to enjoy the interval.

~ *George Santayana*

Middle Adulthood

MARTHA, THE PATHS OF HER WORK

◆

*M*artha, dressed in a tailored gray suit, had signed up for an adult education course, "Real Estate Sales." At the coffee break, another student in the course asked Martha why she was taking the course. Martha said that she had worked since she was an adolescent. Back in Omaha, where she was raised, her father was an alcoholic. He used to beat up her mother and sometimes he took out his frustrations on Martha and her eight brothers and sisters. She decided to get out as soon as she could. While still in high school, she worked part-time as a cashier. She went back to the restaurant to work full-time when she graduated. There she met her first husband, Bobby, a jazz drummer. Once they moved to Chicago, she immediately found a new job, this time as a waitress. She held on to it through the birth of her two sons because Bobby traveled most of the time and stopped over only when the band was in town.

Then one day she found a note saying that the band was moving east and he would not be back. She packed the kids in the car and moved to Los Angeles, where she found a job as a telephone operator, working nights. Once the boys were in school for the full day, she took a secretarial course and eventually started to work in the typing pool of an aircraft company. She moved up the secretarial ranks until she became a private secretary for a sales executive. Eventually she married her boss. They bought a nice house in Pasadena and settled down. She had to give up her job because it was against company policy for executives' wives to work for the company.

For the next thirteen years, Martha was a company wife, entertaining the right people, showing up with her husband at the right places, organizing and running the household. She worked hard to keep the kids in line and eventually they made it through college. Once the kids were gone, she and Roy socialized a lot and sometimes she would travel with him when he was on company business. Then suddenly, three years ago, the roof fell in. The aircraft industry was experiencing a recession and her husband's company was being taken over by another company. Without warning, Roy, her husband, was fired. Martha tried to help him as much as she could. She worked up his job resume and sent out dozens of letters to other companies for him. Unfortunately, employment opportunities for a man of Roy's status and age were drying up. Besides, Roy took his firing hard and began to drink heavily. Martha would come home from shopping and find him sitting in the den with a drink in his hand instead of pursuing employment leads.

By now, Martha felt that she was a survivor, that she could take care of herself. After two more years of pampering Roy, she realized that he seemed to have lost his motivation and probably would never get a decent job again. She decided it was up to her, so she compiled a quick inventory of what she had to offer and decided that she probably would do best by going into sales herself. That was when she noticed the ad for this course and decided to enroll. What are Martha's plans? She already passed her realtor's exam and has started to sell property. She is thinking of moving away from Los Angeles, possibly up the coast to Santa Barbara. She does not have much to tie her down since she and Roy are on the verge of obtaining a divorce (Golan, 1986).

seems to have found a better balance between work and leisure than many of us. With the kind of work ethic on which our country is based, it is not surprising to find that many adults view leisure as boring and unnecessary. But even Aristotle recognized leisure's importance in life, stressing that we should not only work well but use leisure well. He even described leisure as better because it was the end of work. How can we define leisure? **Leisure** *refers to the pleasant times after work when individuals are free to pursue activities and interests of their own choosing—hobbies, sports, or reading, for example.*

Ninety years ago, the average work week was 72 hours. Only in the last three to four decades has it averaged 40 hours. What do most of us do now that we have more free time than cohorts at the beginning of this century? One of the basic themes of research on leisure is the increasing reliance on television over other forms of mass media as a form of entertainment. Sports are also an integral part of the nation's leisure activities, either through direct

participation or as a spectator. The diversity of sports allows many individuals to escape the rigors and pressures of everyday life, even if only for a few hours a week.

What is leisure in middle adulthood like? When Mark became 40 years old, he decided that he needed to develop some leisure activities and interests. He bought a personal computer and joined a computer club. Now Mark looks forward to coming home from work and "playing with his toy." At the age of 43, Barbara sent her last child off to college and told her husband that she was going to spend the next several years reading the many books she had bought but had never found time to read. Mark and Barbara chose different leisure activities, but their actions suggest that middle adulthood is a time when leisure activities assume added importance. For example, some developmentalists believe that middle adulthood is a time of questioning how time should be spent and of reassessing priorities (Gould, 1978).

Leisure may be an especially important aspect of middle adulthood because of the changes many individuals experience at this point in the adult life cycle. The changes include physical changes, relationship changes with spouse and children, and career changes. By middle adulthood, more money is available to many individuals, and there may be more free time and paid vacations. These mid-life changes may produce expanded opportunities for leisure. For many individuals, middle adulthood is the first time in their lives when they have the opportunity to diversify their interests.

Adults at mid-life need to begin preparing both financially and psychologically for retirement. Constructive and fulfilling leisure activities in middle adulthood are an important part of this preparation. If an adult develops leisure activities that can be continued into retirement, the transition from work to retirement may be less stressful.

We have discussed a number of ideas about cognitive development and about careers, work, and leisure. A summary of these ideas is presented in concept table 16.2.

Concept Table 16.2: Cognitive Development and Careers, Work, and Leisure

Concept	Processes/Related Ideas	Characteristics/Description
Cognitive Development	Its Nature	Some decline in memory occurs during middle adulthood, although strategies can be used to reduce the decline. Deficits are greater in long-term than in short-term memory. Processes such as organization and imagery can be used to reduce deficits in memory. Deficits are greater when the information is recently acquired or not used often, and when recall rather than recognition is assessed. Poor health and negative attitudes are related to memory decline.
Careers, Work, and Leisure	Job Satisfaction	Work satisfaction increases steadily throughout life—from age 20 to at least age 60, for both college-educated and noncollege-educated adults.
	Career Ladders	Many of us think of our adult work life as a series of discrete steps, much like the rungs of a ladder. Having a college education helps us move up the ladder. Most career advancement occurs early in our adult lives, at least by 40 to 45, and individuals who are promoted early go further.
	Mid-Life Career Change	Only about 10 percent of Americans change jobs in mid-life, some because they are fired, others because of their own motivation. In mid-life, we often evaluate our possibilities in terms of how much time we have left in an occupation.
	Work Pathways of Men and Women	A continuous pattern of work is more common among men than among women, although low-income men have more unstable work patterns than middle-income men. It is not unusual for women to go back to work for reasons other than money.
	Leisure	We not only need to learn to work well but we also need to learn to enjoy leisure. Mid-life may be an especially important time for leisure because of the physical changes that occur and because of preparation for an active retirement.

Summary

I. Physical Changes and Health Status in Middle Adulthood

A host of physical changes occur. At some point in the forties, decline in physical development usually indicates that middle adulthood has arrived. Seeing and hearing decline, and individuals actually become shorter. Health status becomes a major concern in middle adulthood. Some deterioration is to be expected. The main health nemeses of middle adulthood are cardiovascular disease, cancer, and weight. How individuals deal with physical decline varies greatly from one individual to the next.

II. Cardiovascular Disease and the Type A Behavior Pattern

The heart and coronary arteries become less efficient in middle age, and cardiovascular disease is the number one cause of death. Type A behavior pattern refers to a cluster of characteristics—excessively competitive, hard-driven, impatient, and hostile—thought to be related to heart disease. The Type A behavior pattern is controversial, with some researchers arguing that only specific components of the cluster, such as hostility, are associated with the disease.

III. Hardiness and Stress, Diet, and Cancer

Hardiness is a personality style characterized by a sense of commitment, control, and a perception of problems as challenges rather than threats. Hardiness is a buffer of stress and is related to reduced illness. The link between cancer and stress is controversial. Stress does not cause cancer, but some researchers believe stress is related to how rapidly cancer spreads. A high fat diet is associated with breast cancer.

IV. Toward Healthier Lives

Seven of the ten leading causes of death—heart disease, cancer, and stroke, for example—are associated with the absence of health behaviors. The next major improvement in general health may be behavioral, not medical. A number of health goals for the year 2000 have been proposed and businesses are increasingly interested in improving their employees' health.

V. Biological Changes in Sexuality

Menopause is a marker that signals the cessation of childbearing capability, usually arriving in the late forties and early fifties. The vast majority of women do not have substantial problems with menopause, although the public perception of menopause has often been negative. Estrogen replacement therapy is effective in reducing the physical pain of menopause. Men do not experience an inability to father children, although their testosterone level gradually drops off; clearly, a male menopause, like the dramatic decline in women's estrogen, does not occur.

VI. Sexual Attitudes and Behavior

Sexual behavior usually occurs on a less frequent basis in middle adulthood than in early adulthood. Nonetheless, a majority of middle-aged adults show a moderate or strong interest in sex.

VII. Cognitive Development

Some decline in memory occurs during middle adulthood, although strategies such as organization and imagery can be used to reduce the decline. Deficits are greater in long-term than in short-term memory, when information is recently acquired or not used often, when recall rather than recognition is assessed, and when health is poor and attitudes are negative.

VIII. Job Satisfaction and Career Ladders

Work satisfaction increases steadily throughout life—from age 20 to at least age 60, for both college-educated and noncollege-educated adults. Many of us think of our adult work life as a series of discrete steps, much like the rungs of a ladder. Having a college education helps us move up the ladder. Most career advancement occurs early in our adult lives, at least by 40 to 45, and individuals who are promoted early go further.

IX. Mid-Life Career Change and Work Pathways of Men and Women

Only about 10 percent of Americans change jobs in mid-life, some because they are fired, others because of self-motivation. In mid-life, we often evaluate our possibilities in terms of how much time we have left in an occupation. A continuous pattern of work is more common among men than among women, although low-income men have more unstable work patterns than middle-income men. It is not unusual for women to go back to work for reasons other than money.

X. Leisure

We not only need to learn how to work well but we also need to learn how to enjoy leisure. Mid-life may be an especially important time for leisure because of the physical changes that occur and because of preparation for an active retirement.

Key Terms

Type A behavior pattern 519
hardiness 520

menopause 524
leisure 531

Suggested Readings

Baruch, G., & Brooks-Gunn, J. (Eds.). (1985). *Women in midlife.* New York: Plenum.
This authoritative overview of many aspects of women's development in middle adulthood includes chapters on sexuality, health care, and reproductive issues, including menopause.

Carroll, C., & Miller, D. (1991). *Health: The science of human adaptation.* Dubuque, IA: William C. Brown.
This book includes extensive information about mid-life health issues.

Golan, N. (1986). *The perilous bridge.* New York: Free Press.
This is an easy-to-read book on helping individuals through mid-life transitions. It includes a number of case studies.

Okun, B. F. (1984). *Working with adults: Individual, family, and career development.* Monterey, CA: Brooks/Cole.
Valuable information on counseling individuals about career decisions at mid-life is given.

Tamir, L. M. (1982). *Men in their forties.* New York: Springer.
This excellent research report on the mid-life concerns of men includes valuable information about their work orientation.

CHAPTER 17

Social Development in Middle Adulthood

*F*orty-five-year-old Sarah feels tired, depressed, and angry. She became pregnant when she was 17 and married Ben. They stayed together for three years and then he left her for another woman. Sarah went to work as a sales clerk to help make ends meet. She remarried eight years later to Alan who had two children of his own from a previous marriage. Sarah stopped working for several years, but then Alan started going out on her. She found out about it from a friend. Sarah stayed with Alan for another year, but finally he was gone so much that she could not take it anymore and she decided to divorce him. Sarah went back to work again as a sales clerk; she has been in the same position for sixteen years now. During those sixteen years, she has dated a number of men but the relationships never seem to work out. Her son never finished high school and has drug problems. Her father just died last year and Sarah is trying to help her mother financially, although she can barely pay her own bills. Sarah looks in the mirror and does not like what she sees— she sees her past as a shambles and the future does not look rosy, either.

Forty-five-year-old Wanda feels energetic, happy, and satisfied. She graduated from college and worked for three years as a high school math teacher. She married Andy, who had just finished law school. One year later, they had their first child, Josh. Wanda stayed home with Josh for two years, then returned to her job as a math teacher. Even during her pregnancy, Wanda stayed active and exercised regularly, playing tennis almost every day. After her pregnancy, she kept up her exercise habits. Wanda and Andy had another child, Wendy, and now as they move into their middle-aged years, Josh and Wendy are both off to college, and Wanda and Andy are enjoying spending more time with each other. Last weekend they visited Josh at his college and the weekend before they visited Wendy at her college. Wanda continued working as a high school math teacher until six years ago. She had developed considerable computer skills as part of her job and taken some computer courses at a nearby college, doubling up during the summer months. She resigned her math teaching job and took a job with a computer company, where she has already worked her way into management. Wanda looks in the mirror and likes what she sees—she sees her past as enjoyable, although not without hills and valleys, and she looks to the future with zest and enthusiasm.

The life paths of Sarah and Wanda have been very different. They represent the individual variation, the divergence of what mid-life is like. For some, mid-life is the worst time period of life; for others, it is the best. In this chapter we explore some of the common themes of mid-life—the nature of relationships, the chances that we will experience a mid-life crisis or not, the personality characteristics that take on greater meaning in mid-life, and the degree we change or stay the same as we go through the years of middle adulthood.

Close Relationships

Attachment and love are important to our well-being throughout our lives. What are marital relationships like in middle adulthood? Do our friendships change? What is the nature of sibling relationships in middle adulthood? How do intergenerational relationships contribute to our development? These are among the important questions about relationships in middle adulthood that we address.

Love and Marriage at Mid-Life

Remember from chapter 15 that two major forms of love are romantic love and affectionate love. The fires of romantic love are strong in early adulthood. Affectionate or companionate love increases during middle adulthood. That

Figure 17.1 *The development of relationships. One view of how close relationships develop states that we begin a relationship with someone at a zero point of contact (top) and then gradually move from a surface relationship into more intense, mutual interaction, sharing ourselves more and more with the other person as the relationship develops. At the final stage, a major intersection, we are probably experiencing affectionate or companionate love (bottom).*

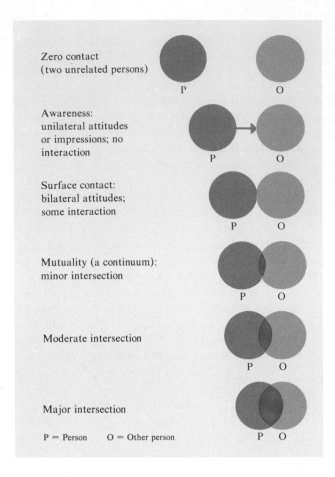

is, physical attraction, romance, and passion are more important in new relationships, especially in early adulthood, whereas security, loyalty, and mutual emotional interest become more important as relationships mature, especially in middle adulthood. Some developmentalists believe mutuality plays a key role in the maturity of relationships, occurring when partners share knowledge with each other, assume responsibility for each other's satisfaction, and share private information that governs their relationship (Berscheid, 1985; Levinger, 1974; Rusbult & others, 1991). For example, as indicated in figure 17.1, we begin a relationship with someone at a zero point of contact and then gradually move from a surface relationship into more intense, mutual interaction, sharing ourselves more and more with the other individual as the relationship deepens. At the final stage, a major intersection, we are probably experiencing affectionate or companionate love.

To explore the nature of age and sex differences in satisfying love relationships, in one investigation 102 happily married couples in early adulthood (average age 28), middle adulthood (average age 45), and late adulthood (average age 65) were interviewed (Reedy, Birren, & Schaie, 1981). As indicated in figure 17.2, passion and sexual intimacy were more important in early adulthood, and tender feelings of affection and loyalty were more important in later-life love relationships. Young adult lovers also rated communication as more characteristic of their love than their older counterparts. Aside from the age differences, however, there were some striking similarities in the nature of satisfying love relationships. At all ages, emotional security was ranked as the most important factor in love, followed by respect, communication, help and play behaviors, sexual intimacy, and loyalty. Clearly,

Middle Adulthood

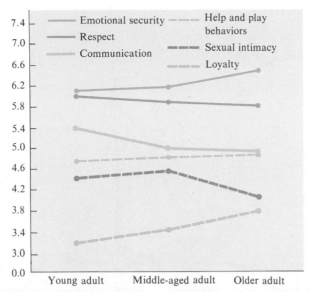

Figure 17.2 *Changes in satisfying love relationships across the adult years. In the investigation by Reedy, Birren, and Schaie (1981), emotional security was the most important factor in love at all ages. Sexual intimacy was more important in early adulthood, while affection and loyalty were more important in the love relationships of older adults. Young adult lovers also rated communication as more important in love than their older counterparts.*

there is more to satisfying relationships than sex. The findings in this research also suggested that women believe emotional security is more important in love than men do.

Even some marriages that were difficult and rocky during early adulthood turn out to be better adjusted during middle adulthood (Rollins, 1989). Although the partners may have lived through a great deal of turmoil, they eventually discover a deep and solid foundation on which to anchor their relationship. In middle adulthood, the partners may have fewer financial worries, less housework and chores, and more time with each other. Partners who engage in mutual activities usually view their marriage as more positive at this time.

As marital partners grow older, many of their earlier incompatibilities brought about by differences in religion, ethnicity, social class, levels of education, family backgrounds, and personality patterns have either been worked out and adjusted to or have contributed to the breakup of the marriage (Golan, 1986). Divorce in middle adulthood may be more positive in some ways, more

"Thus ends another evening of dancing on the edge of the volcano."

negative in others, than divorce in early adulthood. For mature individuals, the perils of divorce may be fewer and less intense than for younger individuals. They have more resources, and they can use this time as an opportunity to simplify their lives by disposing of possessions, such as a large home, which they no longer need. Their children are adults and may be able to cope with their parents' divorce more effectively. The partners may have attained a better understanding of themselves and may be searching for changes that could include the end to a poor marriage.

In contrast, the emotional and time commitment to marriage that has existed for so many years may not be lightly given up. Many mid-life individuals perceive this as failing in the best years of their lives. The divorcer may see the situation as an escape from an untenable relationship; the divorced partner, however, usually sees it as betrayal, the ending of a relationship that had been built up over many years and that involved a great deal of commitment and trust.

The Empty Nest and Its Refilling

An important event in a family is the launching of a child into adult life, to a career or family independent of the family of origin. Parents face new adjustments as disequilibrium is created by a child's absence (Bassoff, 1988). The **empty nest syndrome** *states that marital satisfaction will decrease because parents derive considerable satisfaction from their children, and therefore, the children's departure will leave parents with empty feelings. While the empty nest syndrome may hold true for some parents who live vicariously through their children, the empty nest usually does not lower marital satisfaction. Rather, just the opposite happens; marital satisfaction increases in the post-childrearing years* (Sherman, 1987). Now with children gone, marital partners have more time to pursue career interests and more time for each other.

In today's uncertain economic climate, the refilling of the empty nest is becoming a common occurrence as adult children return to live at home after an unsuccessful career or a divorce. And some individuals don't leave home at all until their middle to late twenties because they cannot financially support themselves. The middle generation has always provided support for the younger generation, even after the nest is bare (Stevens-Long, 1988). Through loans and monetary gifts for education, and through emotional support, the middle generation has helped the younger generation. Adult children appreciate the financial and emotional support their parents provide them at a time when they often feel considerable stress about their career, work, and lifestyle. And parents feel good that they can provide this support.

However, as with most family living arrangements, there are both pluses and minuses when adult children return to live at home. Many parents have developed expectations that their adult children would be capable of supporting themselves. And adult children had expectations that they would be on their own as young adults. In one investigation, 42 percent of middle-aged parents said they had serious conflicts with their resident adult children (Clemens & Axelson, 1985). One of the most common complaints voiced by both adult children and their parents is a loss of privacy. The adult children complain that their parents restrict their independence, cramp their sex lives, reduce their rock music listening, and treat them as children rather than adults. Parents often complain that their quiet home has become noisy, that they stay up late worrying when their adult children will come home, that meals are difficult to plan because of conflicting schedules, that their relationship as a married couple has been invaded, and that they have to shoulder too much responsibility for their adult children. In sum, when adult children return home to live, a disequilibrium in family life is created, which requires considerable adaptation on the part of parents and their adult children. This living arrangement usually works best when there is adequate space, when parents treat their adult children more like adults than children, and when there is an atmosphere of trust and communication.

Sibling Relationships and Friendships

Sibling relationships also persist over the entire life cycle for most adults. Eighty-five percent of today's adults have at least one living sibling. Sibling relationships in adulthood may be extremely close, apathetic, or highly rivalrous. The majority of sibling relationships in adulthood have been found to be close in several investigations (Cicirelli, 1982, 1991; Gold, Woodbury, & George, 1990; Scott, 1983). Those siblings who are psychologically close to each other in adulthood tended to be that way in childhood; it is rare for sibling closeness to develop for the first time in adulthood (Dunn, 1984).

Friendships continue to be important in middle adulthood just as they were in early adulthood (Antonnuci, 1989; Rook, 1987). It takes time to develop intimate friendships, so friendships that have endured over the adult years are often deeper than those that have just been formed in middle adulthood.

Intergenerational Relationships

In Samuel Butler's (1902) novel, *The Way of All Flesh,* Theobold Pontifex had been raised by a harsh father but believed that he would be more lenient toward his own son than his father had been toward him. But he also believed, as had his father, that he must be on guard against being too indulgent. Theobold thrashed his son, Ernest, for mispronouncing a word. With each new generation, personality characteristics, attitudes, and values are replicated or changed. As older family members die, their emotional, intellectual, personal, and genetic legacies are carried on in the next generation. Their children become the oldest generation and their grandchildren the second generation (Datan, Greene, & Reese, 1986).

I vividly remember the day four years ago when we returned to our house after taking our youngest daughter to college. The silence was deafening. The house was quieter after our first daughter had left for college four years earlier, but this time the quiet was even more noticeable. Even two decades ago it was believed that marital satisfaction decreased when children left home to attend college or pursue an occupation. In today's world, the evidence indicates the opposite—an upswing in marital satisfaction as the nest empties. Why do you think this cohort effect has taken place?

In the investigation by Alice Rossi (1989), mothers and their daughters had much closer relationships during their adult years than mothers and sons, fathers and daughters, and fathers and sons. Married men were more involved with their wives' kin than their own. And maternal grandmothers and maternal aunts were cited twice as often as their counterparts on the paternal side of the family as the most important or loved relative.

• *Critical Thinking* •

Are we likely to see more or less contact across generations in future decades? Explain your answer.

In case you're worried about what's going to become of the younger generation, it's going to grow up and start worrying about the younger generation.

~ *Roger Allen*

For the most part, family members maintain considerable contact across generations (Sprei, 1991). As we continue to maintain contact with our parents and our children as we age, both similarity and dissimilarity across generations are found. For example, parent-child similarity is most noticeable in religious and political areas, least in gender roles, life-style, and work orientation. An example of how relationships are transmitted across generations appeared in the California Longitudinal Study (Elder, Caspi, & Downey, 1986). Children whose parents had a high degree of marital conflict and who were unaffectionate subsequently had tension in their own marriages and were ineffective in disciplining their own children (now the third generation).

Gender differences also characterize intergenerational relationships (Nydegger & Mitteness, 1991; Troll, 1989; Troll & Bengston, 1982). In one recent investigation, mothers and their daughters had much closer relationships during their adult years than mothers and sons, fathers and daughters, and fathers and sons (Rossi, 1989). Also, in this same investigation, married men were more involved with their wives' kin than their own. And maternal grandmothers and maternal aunts were cited twice as often as their counterparts on the paternal side of the family as the most important or loved relative. These findings underscore the significance of a woman's role as mother in monitoring access to and feelings toward kin (Barnett & others, 1991; Fischer, 1991).

Middle-aged adults play an important role in intergenerational relationships (Brody, 1990; Crosby & Ayers, 1991; Richards, Bengston, & Miller, 1989). They have been described as the "sandwich" generation. Their situation has been labeled the "generation squeeze" or "generational overload." The demands they face, as both children of elderly parents and parents of adolescents or young adults, have implications for individual life-course development and for the family systems to which they belong. While middle-aged adults are guiding and financially supporting their adolescents, they may have to support elderly parents who no longer have a secure base in times of emotional difficulties or financial problems. Instead, the older parents may need affection and financial support from their middle-aged children. These simultaneous pressures from adolescents or young adult children and aging parents may contribute to stress in middle adulthood. When adults immigrate to another country, intergenerational stress may also be increased (Curtis, 1990). To read about the role of immigration and acculturation in intergenerational relationships among Mexican Americans, turn to Cultural Worlds 17.1.

INTERGENERATIONAL RELATIONSHIPS IN MEXICAN AMERICAN FAMILIES— THE EFFECTS OF IMMIGRATION AND ACCULTURATION

*I*n the last several decades, increasing numbers of Mexicans have immigrated to the United States, and their numbers are expected to increase. The pattern of immigration usually involves separation from the extended family. It may also involve separation of immediate family members, with the husband coming first and then later bringing his wife and children. Initially isolated, especially the wife, they experience considerable stress due to relocation and the absence of family and friends. Within several years, a social network is usually established in the ethnic neighborhood.

As soon as some stability in their lives is achieved, Mexican families may sponsor the immigration of extended family members, such as a maternal or paternal sister or mother who provides child care and enables the mother to go to work. In some cases the older generation remains behind and joins their grown children in old age. The accessibility of Mexico facilitates visits to and from the native village for vacations or at a time of crisis, such as when an adolescent runs away from home.

Three levels of acculturation often exist within the Mexican American family (Falicov & Karrer, 1980). The mother and the grandparents may be at the beginning level, the father at an intermediate level, and the children at an advanced level. The discrepancies between acculturation levels can give rise to conflicting expectations within the family. The immigrant parents' model of childrearing may be out of phase with the dominant culture's

How might the acculturation experiences of Mexican American families influence the nature of intergenerational relations?

model, which may cause reverberations through the family's generations. For example, the mother and grandparents may be especially resistant to the demands for autonomy and dating made by adolescent daughters, and so may the father. And in recent years an increasing number of female youth are leaving their Mexican American homes to further their education, an event that is often stressful for families with strong ties to Mexican values.

As children leave home, parents begin to face their future as a middle-aged couple. This may be difficult for many Mexican American middle-aged couples because their value orientations have prepared them better for parenting than for relating as a married couple. Family therapists who

work with Mexican Americans frequently report that a common pattern is psychological distance between the spouses and a type of emotional separation in mid-life, with the marital partners continuing to live together and carrying on their family duties but relating to each other only at a surface level. The younger generation of Mexican Americans may find it difficult to accept their parents' life-style, may question their marital arrangement, and may rebel against their value orientations. Despite the intergenerational stress that may be brought about by immigration and acculturation, the majority of Mexican American families maintain considerable contact across generations and continue to have a strong family orientation.

Concept Table 17.1: Close Relationships in Middle Adulthood

Concept	Processes/Related Ideas	Characteristics/Description
Love and Marriage at Mid-Life	Their Nature	Affectionate or companionate love increases in middle adulthood, especially in marriages that have endured many years. Divorce in middle adulthood may be more positive or more negative than divorce in early adulthood.
The Empty Nest and Its Refilling	The Empty Nest Syndrome	This states that marital satisfaction will decrease when children leave home after adolescence because parents derive considerable pleasure from their children. However, rather than decreasing marital satisfaction, the empty nest usually increases it.
	When Adult Children Return Home to Live	Increasing numbers of young adult children continue to live with their parents or refill the empty nest by returning home after a failed marriage, economic difficulties, college or loss of a job. The refilling of the empty nest requires considerable adaptation on the part of parents and their adult children.
Sibling Relationships and Friendships	Sibling Relationships	They continue thoughout life. Many sibling relationships in adulthood are close, especially if they were close in childhood, although some are apathetic or highly conflicted.
	Friendships	Friendships continue to be important in middle adulthood. Longstanding friendships are often deeper and more intimate.
Intergenerational Relationships	Contact	There is generally continuing contact across generations in families. Greater continuity occurs in political and religious attitudes, lesser continuity occurs in gender roles, life-styles, and work orientation.
	Gender	Mothers and daughters have the closest relationship in adulthood. Women play an important role in the monitoring of access to and feelings toward kin.
	Middle Age	The middle-aged generation has been called the "sandwich" generation because financial and caregiving obligations to youth and to aging parents may create stress for middle-aged adults. The middle-aged generation plays an important role in linking generations.

At this point we have discussed a number of ideas about close relationships in middle adulthood. A summary of these ideas is presented in concept table 17.1. Now we turn our attention to theories of adult personality development, especially the way they conceptualize the middle adulthood years.

Personality Theories and Development in Middle Age

How should we conceptualize personality in middle age? Is mid-life a stage that is beset with crisis? How important are life events, like divorce and death, in understanding personality at mid-life? To what extent do social and historical circumstances modify how personality develops in middle adulthood? How much individual variation characterizes middle adulthood?

The Adult Stage Theories

Adult stage theories have been plentiful and they have contributed to the view that mid-life is a crisis in development. Three prominent adult stage theories

> Perhaps middle-age is, or should be, a period of shedding shells; the shell of ambition, the shell of material accumulations and possessions, the shell of ego.
>
> ~ *Ann Morrow Lindbergh,*
> Gift from the Sea, *1955*

Biological generativity	Parental generativity
Adults conceive and give birth to infants.	Adults provide nurturance and guidance to children.

Work generativity	Cultural generativity
Adults develop skills that are passed down to others.	Adults create, renovate, or conserve some aspect of the culture that survives.

Figure 17.3 Four paths to developing generativity.

are Erik Erikson's life-cycle view, Roger Gould's transformations, and Daniel Levinson's seasons of a man's life. George Valliant's view represents an important expansion of Erikson's theory. We consider each of these perspectives in turn.

Erikson's Stage of Generativity Versus Stagnation

Erikson (1968) believes that middle-aged adults face a significant issue in life—generativity versus stagnation, which is the name Erikson gave to the seventh stage in his life-span theory. Generativity encompasses adults' plans for what they hope to do to leave a legacy of themselves to the next generation. Through generativity, the adult achieves a kind of immortality by leaving one's legacy to the next generation (McAdams, 1990). By contrast, stagnation (sometimes called self-absorption) develops when individuals sense that they have done nothing for the next generation.

Middle-aged adults can develop generativity in a number of different ways (Kotre, 1984). Through biological generativity, adults conceive and give birth to an infant. Through parental generativity, adults provide nurturance and guidance to children. Through work generativity, adults develop skills that are passed down to others. The generative individual in this instance is the apprentice who learns the skill. And through cultural generativity, adults create, renovate, or conserve some aspect of culture that ultimately survives. In this instance, the generative object is the culture itself. (Figure 17.3 shows these four different ways middle-aged adults can develop generativity.)

Through generativity, adults promote and guide the next generation through such important aspects of life as parenting, teaching, leading, and doing things that benefit the community (McAdams, 1990). Generative adults commit themselves to the continuation and improvement of society as a whole through their connection to the next generation. Generative adults develop a positive legacy of the self and then offer it as a gift to the next generation.

In one research investigation, Carol Ryff (1984) compared the views of women and men from different age groups. She found that generativity was a major concern of the middle-aged adults in her study. They saw themselves as leaders and decision makers who were interested in helping and guiding younger people.

Table 17.1: Gould's Transformations in Adult Development

Stage	Approximate Age	Development(s)
1	16 to 18	Desire to escape parental control.
2	18 to 22	Leaving the family; peer group orientation.
3	22 to 28	Developing independence; commitment to a career and to children.
4	29 to 34	Questioning self; role confusion; marriage and career vulnerable to dissatisfaction.
5	35 to 43	Period of urgency to attain life's goals; awareness of time limitation; realignment of life's goals.
6	43 to 53	Settling down; acceptance of one's life.
7	53 to 60	More tolerance; acceptance of past; less negativism; general mellowing.

From Roger L. Gould, M.D., *Transformations.* Copyright © 1978 by Roger Gould, M.D. Reprinted by permission of Simon & Schuster, Inc.

> Whoever, in middle age, attempts to realize the wishes and hopes of his early youth, invariably deceives himself.
>
> ~ *Goethe,*
> Elective Affinities, *1809*

Gould's Transformations

Psychiatrist Roger Gould (1975, 1978, 1980) links stage and crisis in his view of developmental transformations. He emphasizes that mid-life is every bit as turbulent as adolescence, with the exception that during middle adulthood striving to handle crisis will probably produce a happier, healthier life. Gould studied 524 men and women, whom he described as going through seven stages of adult life (see table 17.1). He believes that in our twenties we assume new roles; in our thirties we begin to feel stuck with our responsibilities; and in our forties we begin to feel a sense of urgency that our lives are speeding by. Handling the mid-life crisis and realizing that a sense of urgency is a natural reaction to this stage helps to keep us on the path of adult maturity, Gould says. His study has been criticized—it contains middle-class bias, no reliability of clinical judgments was conducted, and no statistical analysis was performed.

Levinson's Seasons of a Man's Life

In *Seasons of a Man's Life,* clinical psychologist Daniel Levinson (1978, 1980) and his colleagues at Yale University reported the results of their extensive interviews with forty middle-aged men. His interviews were conducted with hourly workers, business executives, academic biologists, and novelists. He bolstered his conclusions with information from the biographies of famous men and the development of memorable characters in literature. Although Levinson's major interest focused on mid-life change, he described a number of stages and transitions in the life cycle, ranging from 17 to 65 years of age, which are shown in figure 17.4.

Like Robert Havighurst (1972), Levinson emphasizes that developmental tasks must be mastered at each of these stages. In early adulthood, the two major tasks to be mastered are exploring the possibilities for adult living and developing a stable life structure. Levinson sees the twenties as a *novice phase* of adult development. At the end of one's teens, a transition from dependence to independence should occur. This transition is marked by the

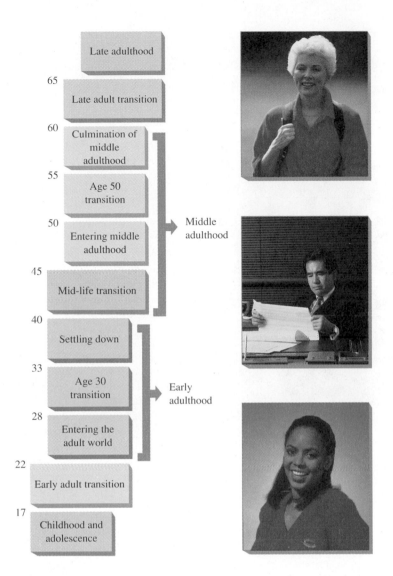

Figure 17.4   Daniel Levinson's periods of adult development.

Late adulthood

65

Late adult transition

60

Culmination of middle adulthood

55

Age 50 transition

50

Entering middle adulthood

Middle adulthood

45

Mid-life transition

40

Settling down

33

Age 30 transition

Early adulthood

28

Entering the adult world

22

Early adult transition

17

Childhood and adolescence

formation of a dream—an image of the kind of life the youth wants to have, especially in terms of a career and marriage. The novice phase is a time of reasonably free experimentation and of testing the dream in the real world.

From about the ages of 28 to 33, the individual goes through a transition period in which he must face the more serious question of determining his goals. During the thirties, the individual usually focuses on family and career development. In the later years of this period, the individual enters a phase of Becoming One's Own Man (or BOOM, as Levinson calls it). By age 40, the individual has reached a stable location in his career, has outgrown his earlier, more tenuous attempts at learning to become an adult, and now must look forward to the kind of life he will lead as a middle-aged adult.

According to Levinson, the change to middle adulthood lasts about five years and requires the adult to come to grips with four major conflicts that have existed in his life since adolescence: (1) being young versus being old (more about this polarity in mid-life is presented in Perspective on Life-Span Development 17.1); (2) being destructive versus being constructive; (3) being masculine versus being feminine; and (4) being attached to others versus being separated from them. Seventy to eighty percent of the men Levinson interviewed found the mid-life transition (ages 40 to 45) tumultuous and psychologically painful, as many aspects of their lives came into question. According

> Middle age is such a foggy place.
> ~ *Roger Rosenblatt, 1987*

THE SENSE OF MORTALITY AND THE WISH FOR IMMORTALITY

*F*or Daniel Levinson (1978), in the mid-life transition, the young versus the old polarity is experienced with a special force. As early adulthood comes to a close, the individual is faced with new fears of the loss of youth. He feels that the young—represented by the child, the adolescent, and the young adult—is dying. The image of old age hangs over him like a pall.

The individual's physical decline is normally very moderate and allows for competent functioning. But the physical decline may be experienced catastrophically. He fears that he will soon lose all the youthful qualities that made life worthwhile. Reminders of mortality occur in more frequent illness, death, and loss of others. In the late thirties and early forties the probability of such losses go up considerably. There are more heart attacks, more depressions, alcoholism, job failures, troubles with children or parents, stress of all kinds, says Levinson.

Why should the recognition of mortality be so painful? Levinson believes the answer lies in our wish for immortality. At mid-life, the growing recognition of mortality collides with the powerful wish for immortality. Beyond the concern with personal survival, there is a concern with meaning. It is not unusual for the 40-year-old to feel that his life has been wasted, that it just has not had any meaning. Levinson describes billionaire Howard

Daniel J. Levinson, Yale psychologist, believes that the mid-life transition involves a confrontation with feeling young versus feeling old. New fears of losing one's youth spring forth. The young—represented by the child, the adolescent, and the young adult—is dying. The image of old age occupies the middle-aged adult's mind. Is the middle-age adult's preoccupation with the young-old polarity as pervasive as Levinson argues? Is there more individual variation than his view suggests?

Hughes as a dramatic example of decline in mid-life. He converted a small fortune into a fantastic empire. But in the end, with all his power, he died of starvation, disease, and emotional iso-lation. He could invest his money for great profit, but he could not invest his self in successful interpersonal relations or obtain any psychological benefits from it. He finally suffocated within the cocoon he had built around himself.

During and after the mid-life transition, the individual tries to transform the young-old polarity and create a middle-aged self, wiser and more mature than before, yet still connected to the youthful sources of energy, imagination, and daring. He comes to grasp more clearly the flow of generations and the continuity of the human species. His personal immortality, whatever its form, lies within the larger human continuity. He feels more responsible for the generations that will follow his own. Acquiring a greater individuality, a firmer sense of who he is and what matters most to him, he also understands more deeply that he is merely a speck of sand in the vast history of humankind.

In a poem written when he was about 50, the American poet Theodore Roethke portrays his own experience of mortality:

> . . . he dares to live
> Who stops being a bird, yet
> beats his wings
> Against the immense
> immeasurable
> emptiness of things.

• *Critical Thinking* •

Levinson argues that his adult stages are basically the same for women as for men. Can you think of some types of women for whom the stages might not be as accurate?

to Levinson, the success of the mid-life transition rests on how effectively the individual reduces the polarities and accepts each of them as an integral part of his being.

Because Levinson interviewed middle-aged males, we can consider the data about middle adulthood more valid than the data about early adulthood. When individuals are asked to remember information about earlier parts of their lives, they may distort and forget things. The original Levinson data included no females, although Levinson (1987) reported that his stages, transitions, and the crisis of middle age hold for females as well as males. Like

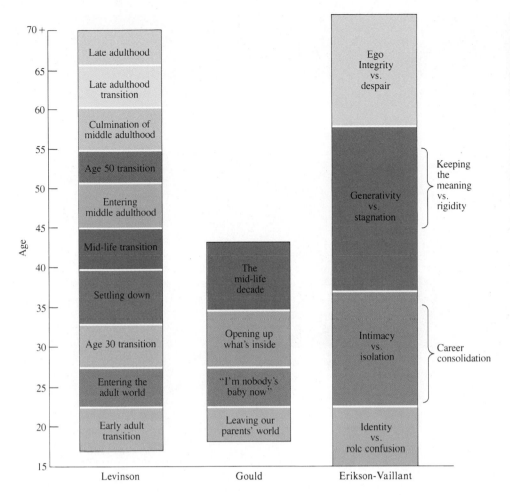

Figure 17.5 Comparison of the adult developmental stages proposed by Levinson, Gould, and Vaillant. When Vaillant's stages are added to Erikson's stages, some agreement between the adult stage theories of Levinson, Gould, and Vaillant is apparent. All would concur with a general outline of adult development that begins with a change from identity to intimacy, then from career consolidation to generativity, and finally from searching for meaning to some final integration.

Gould's report, Levinson's work included no statistical analysis. However, the quality and quantity of the Levinson biographies are outstanding in the clinical tradition.

Vaillant's Expansion of Erikson's Stages

Adult developmentalist George Vaillant (1977) believes two additional stages should be added to Erikson's adult stages. **Career consolidation** *is Vaillant's stage that occurs from approximately 23 to 35 years of age. Career consolidation is a period in which an individual's career becomes more stable and coherent.* **Keeping the meaning versus rigidity** *is Vaillant's stage that occurs from approximately 45 to 55 years of age. At this time a more relaxed feeling characterizes adults if they have met their goals, or if they have not, accept the fact. At this time adults become concerned about extracting some meaning from their lives and fight against falling into a rigid orientation.*

Conclusions about the Adult Stage Theories

When Vaillant's stages are added to Erikson's stages, there is at least reasonable agreement among Gould, Levinson, and Vaillant about adult stages. All would concur with a general outline of adult development that begins with the change from identity to intimacy, then from career consolidation to generativity, and finally from searching for meaning to some final integration. Thus, although the labels are different, the underlying themes of these adult developmental stage theories are remarkably similar (see figure 17.5).

You come to a place in your life when what you've been is going to form what you will be. If you've wasted what you have in you, it's too late to do much about it. If you've invested yourself in life, you're pretty certain to get a return. If you are inwardly a serious person, in the middle years it will pay off.

~ Lillian Hellman

WHY GAIL SHEEHY'S *PASSAGES* IS NOT ACCEPTED BY SCIENTISTS

*I*n 1976, Gail Sheehy's book, *Passages,* was so popular that it topped the *New York Times* best-seller list for 27 weeks. Sheehy's goal in *Passages* was to describe adult development. She cited discussions about Daniel Levinson and Roger Gould and information from interviews with 115 men and women as her main sources.

Sheehy argues that we all go through developmental stages roughly bound by chronological age. Each stage contains problems we must solve before we can progress to the next stage. The periods between the stages are called *passages.* Sheehy uses catchy phrases to describe each stage: the "trying twenties," "catch-thirty," the "deadline decade" (between thirty-five and forty-five), and the "age forty crucible." Sheehy's advice never wavers: adults in transition may feel miserable, but those who face up to agonizing self-evaluation, who appraise their weaknesses as well as their strengths, who set goals for the future, and who try to

Gail Sheehy's book, Passages, was a dramatic success. Why did developmentalists show much less appreciation of Sheehy's book than the public?

be as independent as possible will be happier than those who do not fully experience these trials.

Sheehy believes these passages earn us an *authentic identity.* This identity

is not based on the authority of one's parents or on cultural prescriptions. Instead, it is constructed through one's own strenuous efforts. Sheehy says that adults who allow themselves to fully experience life's issues and examine their lives are the individuals who find their identity and thrive.

Unfortunately, Sheehy does not disclose such elementary information as the sex and ethnic composition of her sample of 115 adults, how the sample was selected, what questions were asked in the interviews and by whom, and the length of the interviews. The data may be biased toward individuals experiencing a great deal of stress because a disproportionate number of divorced adults were in the sample. The author described the cases only to buttress a point about adult development; no mention was made of how representative the cases were. In addition, Sheehy conducted no statistical analyses.

• Critical Thinking •

How culture bound do you think the stage perspectives of Erikson, Gould, Levinson, and Vaillant are? Are there some primitive island cultures and possibly some non-Western societies to which the stages would not apply?

The adult developmental perspectives of Erikson, Gould, Levinson, and Vaillant emphasize the importance of developmental stages in the life cycle. Though information about stages can be helpful in pinpointing dominant themes that characterize many individuals at particular points in development, there are several important ideas to keep in mind when considering these perspectives as viable models of adult development. First, the research on which they are based has not been very scientific. Second, there has been a tendency to focus on the stages as crises in development, especially the mid-life crisis. Third, there is an alternative perspective that emphasizes the importance of life events rather than stages in development. Fourth, there often is considerable individual variation in the way people experience the stages. In Perspective on Life-Span Development 17.2, further critical evaluation of the popular stage-crisis theories suggests why some scientists are skeptical about their claims.

Crisis and Cohort

Daniel Levinson (1978, 1987) views mid-life as a crisis, believing that the middle-aged adult is suspended between the past and the future, trying to cope with this gap that threatens life's continuity. George Vaillant (1977) concludes that just as adolescence is a time for detecting parental flaws and discovering

Drawing by Leo Cullum; © 1984 The New Yorker Magazine, Inc.

"Goodbye, Alice. I've got to get this California thing out of my system."

the truth about childhood, the forties is a decade of reassessing and recording the truth about the adolescent and adulthood years. However, while Levinson sees mid-life as a crisis, Vaillant believes that only a minority of adults experience a mid-life crisis:

> Just as pop psychologists have reveled in the not-so-common high drama of adolescent turmoil, just so the popular press, sensing good copy, had made all too much of the mid-life crisis. The term mid-life crisis brings to mind some variation of the renegade minister who leaves behind four children and the congregation that loved him in order to drive off in a magenta Porsche with a 25-year-old striptease artiste. . . . As with adolescent turmoil, mid-life crises are much rarer in community samples (pp. 222–23).

Vaillant's study—called the Grant Study—involved a follow-up of Harvard University men in their early thirties and in their late forties, who initially had been interviewed as undergraduates. In Vaillant's words, "The high drama in Gail Sheehy's best-selling *Passages* was rarely observed in the lives of the Grant Study men," p. 223.

Some developmentalists believe that changing times and different social expectations influence how different cohorts—remember that these are groups of individuals born in the same year or time period—move through the life cycle. Bernice Neugarten (1964) has been emphasizing the power of age-group or cohort since the 1960s. Our values, attitudes, expectations, and behaviors are influenced by the period in which we live. For example, individuals born during the difficult times of the Depression may have a different outlook on life than those born during the optimistic 1950s, says Neugarten.

Neugarten (1986) believes that the social environment of a particular age group can alter its **social clock**—*the timetable according to which individuals are expected to accomplish life's tasks, such as getting married, having children, or establishing themselves in a career.* Social clocks provide guides for our lives; individuals whose lives are not synchronized with these social clocks find life to be more stressful than those who are on schedule, says Neugarten.

The popular conception of adolescence has been one of storm and stress. So it also has become with mid-life. The popular press has promoted a conception of middle age as a turbulent time filled with upheaval and stress. Recently, the sexual indiscretions of such well-known evangelists as Jim Bakker and Jimmy Swaggart have only fueled this popular conception. But few amongst us middle-aged adults drive off into the sunset in a 911 Porsche with a 25-year-old striptease dancer draped over our body. As with adolescent turmoil, mid-life crises are much rarer than the popular press's stories would lead us to believe.

Table 17.2: Individuals' Conceptions of the Right Age for Major Life Events and Achievements (late 1950s and late 1970s)

Activity/Event	Appropriate Age Range	Late '50s Study % Who Agree		Late '70s Study % Who Agree	
		Men	*Women*	*Men*	*Women*
Best age for a man to marry	20 to 25	80%	90%	42%	42%
Best age for a woman to marry	19 to 24	85	90	44	36
When most people should become grandparents	45 to 50	84	79	64	57
Best age for most people to finish school and go to work	20 to 22	86	82	36	38
When most men should be settled on a career	24 to 26	74	64	24	26
When most men hold their top jobs	45 to 50	71	58	38	31
When most people should be ready to retire	60 to 65	83	86	66	41
When a man has the most responsibilities	35 to 50	79	75	49	50
When a man accomplishes most	40 to 50	82	71	46	41
The prime of life for a man	35 to 50	86	80	59	66
When a woman has the most responsibilities	25 to 40	93	91	59	53
When a woman accomplishes most	30 to 45	94	92	57	48

Note: There has been a dramatic decline in middle-aged adults' conceptions of the right age for major life events and achievements.

Source: P. M. Passuth, D. R. Maines, and B. L. Neugarten, 1984. "Age Norms and Age Constraints Twenty Years Later," paper presented at the annual meeting of the Midwest Sociological Society, Chicago.

Neugarten first began examining adults' social clocks for significant life events in the late 1950s. In the late 1970s, she examined their social clocks once again. As shown in table 17.2, there has been a dramatic decline in middle-class, middle-aged individuals' conceptions about the right age for major life events and achievements.

Trying to tease out universal truths and patterns about adult development from one birth cohort is complicated because the findings may not apply to another birth cohort. Most of the individuals studied by Levinson, Gould, and Vaillant, for example, were born before and during the Depression. What was true for these individuals may not be true for today's forty-year-olds, born in the optimistic aftermath of World War II, or the post baby-boom generation as they approach the mid-life transition. The profile of mid-life men in Levinson's, Gould's, and Vaillant's studies may have been burned out at a premature age rather than reflecting a normal developmental pattern that all men go through so early in life (Rossi, 1988).

Gender, Culture, and Middle Age

Do women experience middle age differently than men do? How do women in other cultures, especially nonindustrialized cultures, experience middle age? Do most cultures around the world show as much interest in mid-life crises as North Americans do?

Gender

Critics say that the stage theories of adult development have a male bias (Deutsch, 1991; Grambs, 1989; Mercer, Nichols, & Doyle, 1989). For example, the central focus of stage theories is on career choice and work achievement, which historically have dominated men's life choices and life chances more than women's. The stage theories do not adequately address women's concerns about relationships, interdependence, and caring (Gilligan, 1982). The adult stage theories have also placed little importance on childbearing and childrearing. Women's family roles are complex and often have a higher salience in their lives than in men's lives. The role demands that women experience in balancing career and family are usually not experienced as intensely by men.

One of the problems in making stage theory comparisons of males and females is the assumption of a normative sequence of development by the stage theories. That is, the stage theories assume that most people will encounter a given developmental stage at more or less the same time: graduation from high school and college, getting married, starting a family, becoming grandparents, and retiring, for example. However, our contemporary life challenges many of these "normative" experiences. Many women are returning to college to obtain an education and further their career after a number of years of starting a family. Many other women are delaying marriage and childbearing until after they have successfully established a career. Yet other women continue in the tradition of women earlier in this century by getting married, having children, and not pursuing a career outside the home. As the roles of women have become more complex and varied, defining a normative sequence of development for them has become difficult, if not impossible (Germain, 1990).

Middle-aged Women in Nonindustrialized Societies

What is middle age like for women in other cultures? The nature of middle age for women in other cultures depends on the modernity of the culture and the culture's view of gender roles. Anthropologist Judith Brown (1985) believes that middle age in many nonindustrialized societies has more advantages than in industrialized nations like the United States. She argues that as women reach middle age in many nonindustrialized societies three changes take place that improve their status. First, they are often freed from cumbersome restrictions that were placed on them when they were younger. For example, in middle age they enjoy greater geographical mobility. Child care has ceased or can be delegated, and domestic chores are reduced. Commercial opportunities, visitation of relatives living at a distance, and religious opportunities provide an opportunity to venture forth from the village. A second major change brought on by middle age is a woman's right to exercise authority over specified younger kin. Middle-aged women can extract labor from younger family members. The work of the middle-aged woman tends to be administrative, delegating tasks and making assignments to younger women. The middle-aged woman also makes important decisions for certain members

Critics say the stage theories of adult development have a male bias by emphasizing career choice and achievement. The stage theories do not adequately address women's concerns about relationships, interdependence, and caring. The stage theories assume a normative sequence of development, but as women's roles have become more varied and complex, determining what is normative is difficult.

Gusii dancers perform on habitat day, Nairobi, Kenya. Movement from one status to the other in the Gusii culture is due primarily to life events, not age. The Gusii do not have a clearly labeled mid-life transition.

of the younger generation: what a grandchild is to be named, who is ready to be initiated, and who is eligible to marry whom. A third major change brought on by middle age in nonindustrialized societies is the eligibility of the woman for special statuses and the possibility that these provide recognition beyond the household. These statuses include the vocation of midwife, curer, holy woman, and matchmaker.

Cultural Conceptions of Middle Age

We have already seen that mid-life crises are less pervasive in the United States than is commonly believed (Chiriboga, 1989; Haan, 1989). How common are mid-life crises in other cultures? There has been little cross-cultural research on middle adulthood, and adult stage theories, such as Levinson's seasons of a man's life, have not been tested in other cultures. In many cultures, though, especially nonindustrialized cultures, the concept of middle age is not very clear, or in some cases is absent. It is common in nonindustrialized societies to describe individuals as young or old, but not as middle-aged (Foner, 1984; Grambs, 1989). And some cultures have no words for "adolescent," "young adult," or "middle-aged adult."

Consider the Gusii culture, located south of the equator in the African country of Kenya. The Gusii divide the life course differently for females and males (LeVine, 1979):

Females	**Males**
1. Infant	1. Infant
2. Uncircumcised girl	2. Uncircumcised boy
3. Circumcised girl	3. Circumcised boy warrior
4. Married woman	4. Male elder
5. Female elder	

Thus, movement from one status to the next is due primarily to life events, not age, in the Gusii culture. While the Gusii do not have a clearly labeled mid-life transition, some of the Gusii adults do reassess their lives around the age of 40. At this time, these Gusii adults examine their current status and the limited time they have remaining in their lives. Their physical strength is decreasing and they know they cannot farm their land forever, so they seek spiritual powers by becoming ritual practitioners or healers. As in the American culture, however, a mid-life crisis in the Gusii culture is the exception rather than the rule.

At this point we have discussed a number of ideas about adult stage theories, crisis and cohort, and gender and culture. A summary of these ideas is presented in concept table 17.2.

Concept Table 17.2: Adult Stage Theories, Crisis and Cohort, Gender and Culture

Concept	Processes/Related Ideas	Characteristics/Description
Adult Stage Theories	Generativity versus Stagnation	In middle adulthood, individuals need to assist the next generation in developing and leading useful lives.
	Gould's Transformations	Mid-life is as turbulent as adolescence except that during mid-life striving to handle a crisis produces a healthy, happier life. In our forties we begin to feel a sense of urgency as we see our lives speeding by.
	Levinson's Seasons of a Man's Life	Developmental tasks should be mastered at different points in development. Changes in middle adulthood focus on four conflicts: being young vs. being old; being destructive vs. being constructive; being masculine vs. being feminine; being attached to others vs. being separated from them.
	Vaillant's Expansion of Erikson's Stages	Career consolidation occurs from 23 to 35 years of age; keeping the meaning vs. rigidity occurs from 45 to 55 years of age.
	Conclusions	Adult development begins with a change from identity to intimacy, then from career consolidation to generativity, and finally from searching for meaning to some final integration. Criticisms of the stage theories have been made.
Crisis and Cohort	Crisis	A majority of individuals in the United States do not experience a mid-life crisis.
	Cohort	Neugarten believes the social environment of a particular cohort can alter its social clock—the timetable according to which individuals are expected to accomplish life's tasks—such as getting married, having children, or establishing a career.
Gender, Culture, and Middle Age	Gender	Critics say the adult stage theories have a male bias by emphasizing career choice and achievement. The stage theories do not adequately address women's concerns about relationships, interdependence, and caring. The stage theories assume a normative sequence of development, but as women's roles have become more varied and complex, determining what is normative is difficult.
	Culture	In many nonindustrialized societies, a woman's status often improves in middle age. In many cultures, the concept of middle age is not clear. Some cultures do not have words for "adolescent," "young adult," or "middle-aged adult." However, most cultures distinguish between the young and the old.

The Life-Events Approach

An alternative to the stage approach to adult development is the life-events approach. In the early version of the life-events approach, life events were viewed as taxing circumstances for individuals, forcing them to change their personality (Holmes & Rahe, 1967). Such events as the death of a spouse, divorce, marriage, and so on were believed to involve varying degrees of stress, and therefore, likely to influence the individual's development.

Today's life-events approach is more sophisticated (Brim & Ryff, 1980; Hansell, 1991; Hultsch & Plemons, 1979). The **contemporary life-events approach** *emphasizes that how life events influence the individual's development depends not only on the life event, but also on mediating factors (physical*

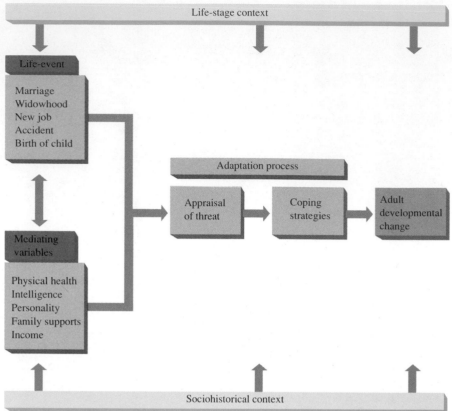

Figure 17.6 A contemporary life-events framework for interpreting adult developmental change.

The flow chart in the figure contains the following labeled boxes:

Life-stage context

Life-event
Marriage
Widowhood
New job
Accident
Birth of child

Mediating variables
Physical health
Intelligence
Personality
Family supports
Income

Adaptation process
Appraisal of threat → Coping strategies → Adult developmental change

Sociohistorical context

It's not the large things that send a man to the madhouse . . . no, it's the continuing series of small tragedies that send a man to the madhouse . . . not the death of his love but a shoelace that snaps with no time left.

~ *Charles Bukowski*

health, family supports, for example), the individual's adaptation to the life event (appraisal of the threat, coping strategies, for example), the life-stage context, and the sociohistorical context (see figure 17.6). If individuals are in poor health and have little family support, life events are likely to be more stressful. One individual may perceive a life event as highly stressful, another individual may perceive the same event as a challenge. And, a divorce may be more stressful after many years of marriage when adults are in their fifties than when they have only been married several years and are in their twenties (Chiriboga, 1982). Adults may be able to cope more effectively with divorce in the 1990s than in the 1950s because divorce has become more commonplace and accepted in today's society.

Though the life-events approach is a valuable addition to understanding adult development, like other approaches to adult development, it has its drawbacks (Dohrenwend & Dohrenwend, 1978). One of the most significant drawbacks is that the life-events approach places too much emphasis on change, not adequately recognizing the stability that, at least to some degree, characterizes adult development. Another drawback is that it may not be life's major events that are the primary sources of stress, but our daily experiences. Enduring a boring but tense job or marriage and living in poverty do not show up on scales of major life events. Yet the everyday pounding we take from these living conditions can add up to a highly stressful life and eventually illness. Some psychologists believe we can gain greater insight into the source of life's stresses by focusing more on daily hassles and daily uplifts (Chamberlin & Zika, 1990; Kanner & Feldman, 1991; Lazarus & Folkman, 1984).

In one investigation of 210 Florida police officers, the day-to-day friction associated with an inefficient justice system and distorted press accounts of police work were more stressful than responding to a felony in progress or making an arrest (Spielberger & Grier, 1983). In another investigation, the

Table 17.3: Ten Most Frequent Daily Hassles and Uplifts of Middle-Aged Adults over a Nine-Month Period

Daily Hassles	% of Times Checked*	Daily Uplifts	% of Times Checked
1. Concerns about weight	52.4	1. Relating well with your spouse or lover	76.3
2. Health of a family member	48.1	2. Relating well with friends	74.4
3. Rising prices of common goods	43.7	3. Completing a task	73.3
4. Home maintenance	42.8	4. Feeling healthy	72.7
5. Too many things to do	38.6	5. Getting enough sleep	69.7
6. Misplacing or losing things	38.1	6. Eating out	68.4
7. Yard work or outside home maintenance	38.1	7. Meeting your responsibilities	68.1
8. Property, investment, or taxes	37.6	8. Visiting, phoning, or writing someone	67.7
9. Crime	37.1	9. Spending time with family	66.7
10. Physical appearance	35.9	10. Home (inside) pleasing to you	65.5

* The "% of times checked" figures represent the mean percentage of people checking the item each month averaged over the nine monthly administrations.

most frequent daily hassles of college students were wasting time, concerns about meeting high standards, and being lonely (Kanner & others, 1981). Among the most frequent uplifts of the college students were entertainment, getting along well with friends, and completing a task. In this same investigation, the most frequent daily hassles of middle-aged adults were concerns about weight and the health of a family member, while their most frequent daily uplifts involved relating well with a spouse or lover, or a friend (see table 17.3). And the middle-aged adults were more likely than the college students to report that their daily hassles involved economic concerns (rising prices and taxes, for example). Critics of the daily hassles approach argue that some of the same problems involved with life-events scales occur when daily hassles are assessed (Dohrenwend & Shrout, 1985). For example, knowing about an adult's daily hassles tells us nothing about physical changes, how the individual copes with hassles, and how the individual perceives hassles.

Individual Variation

One way to look at personality development is to focus on similarities; another way is to focus on differences (Meyer 1991; Schooler, 1991). The stage theories of Erikson, Gould, Levinson, and Vaillant all attempt to describe the universals—not the individual variation—in adult development. In an extensive investigation of a random sample of 500 men at mid-life, Michael Farrell and Stanley Rosenberg (1981) concluded that extensive individual variation characterized the men. They emphasize the individual as an active agent who interprets, shapes, alters, and gives meaning to his life.

The ability to set aside unproductive worries and preoccupations is believed to be an important factor in functioning under stress. In Vaillant's (1977) Grant Study, pervasive personal preoccupations were maladaptive in both the work and marriage of college students over a thirty-year period after leaving college. Some individuals in the Grant Study had personal preoccupations, while others did not. While collectively we are geese, each of us, individually, walks with the tread of a fox. In the words of Simon Weil, "Every person cries out to be read differently."

If a man does not keep pace with his companions, perhaps it is because he hears a different drummer. Let him step to the music he hears, however measured or far away.

~ *Henry David Thoreau, 1854*

Longitudinal Studies of Personality Development in Adulthood

A number of longitudinal studies have assessed the personality development of adults. These studies are especially helpful in charting the most important dimensions of personality at different points in adult development and in evaluating the degree personality changes or stays the same.

One of the earliest longitudinal studies of adult personality development was conducted by Bernice Neugarten (1964). Known as the Kansas City Study, it involved the investigation of individuals 40 to 80 years of age over a ten-year period. The adults were given personality tests, they filled out questionnaires, and they were interviewed. Neugarten concluded that both continuity and age-changes in personality were present. Adaptive characteristics showed the most stability—these included styles of coping, attaining life satisfaction, and strength of goal-directed behavior. Some consistent age differences occurred in the individual's inner versus outer orientation and active versus passive mastery. For example, 40-year-olds felt that they had control over their environment and risk taking did not bother them much. However, 60-year-olds were more likely to perceive the environment as threatening and sometimes dangerous and they had a more passive view of the self. This personality change in adulthood was described by Neugarten as going from active to passive mastery. As shown in figure 17.7, this change occurred for both males and females.

Another major longitudinal study of adult personality development has been conducted by Paul Costa and R. R. McRae at the Veterans Administration Outpatient Clinic in Boston. It involves approximately 2,000 men in their twenties through their eighties. Measures include assessments of personality, attitudes, and values (Costa & McRae, 1980, 1989; Costa & others, 1987). Costa and McRae believe that personality can be best understood in terms of three dimensions: neuroticism, extraversion, and openness to experience. Neuroticism includes how anxious, stable, depressed, self-conscious, impulsive, and vulnerable the individual is; extraversion includes the individual's attachment, gregariousness, assertiveness, activity, excitement seeking, and positive emotions; and openness to experience includes the individual's openness to fantasy, feelings, ideas, and values. Costa and McRae conclude that considerable stability in these three dimensions of personality—neuroticism, extraversion, and openness to experience—characterizes adult development.

By far the longest longitudinal study is the California Longitudinal Study. Initially, more than 500 children and their parents were studied in the late 1920s and early 1930s. In *Present and Past in Middle Life* (Eichorn & others, 1981), the profile of these individuals' lives was described as they became middle aged. The results from early adolescence to mid-life did not support either extreme in the debate over whether personality is characterized by stability or change. Some characteristics were more stable than others, however. Dimensions more directly concerned with self (cognitively invested, self-confident, and open or closed self) were more consistent than dimensions more directly concerned with interpersonal relationships (nurturant or hostile and undercontrolled or overcontrolled).

Another recent longitudinal investigation of adult personality development was conducted by Ravenna Helson and her colleagues (Helson, Mitchell, & Moane, 1984; Helson & Moane, 1987; Helson & Wink, 1987). They initially studied 132 women who were seniors at Mills College in California in the late 1950s; in 1981, when the women were 42 to 45 years old, they were studied again. Helson, and her colleagues distinguished three main groups among the Mills women: family-oriented, career-oriented (whether or not they

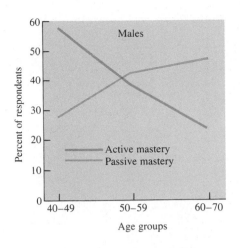

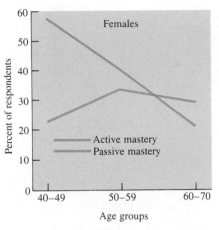

Figure 17.7 *Active and passive mastery through the adult years. In Neugarten's Kansas City study, as individuals went through middle age their active mastery decreased and their passive mastery increased.*

also wanted families); and those who followed neither path (women with no children who pursued only low-level work). Despite their different college profiles and their diverging life paths, the women in all three groups experienced some similar psychological changes over their adult years, although the women in the third group changed less than those committed to career or family. Between the ages of 27 and the early forties, there was a shift toward less traditionally feminine attitudes, including greater dominance, greater interest in events outside the family, and more emotional stability. This may have been due to societal changes from the 1950s to the 1980s rather than to age changes.

During their early forties, many of the women shared the concerns that stage theorists such as Levinson and Gould found in men: concern for young and old, introspectiveness, interest in roots, and awareness of limitation and death. However, the researchers in the Mills College study concluded that rather than being a mid-life crisis, what was being experienced was *mid-life consciousness*. They also indicated that commitment to the tasks of early adulthood—whether to a career or family (or both)—helped women learn to control their impulses, develop interpersonal skills, become independent, and work hard to achieve goals. Women who did not commit themselves to one of these life-style patterns faced fewer challenges and did not develop as fully as the other women (Rosenfeld & Stark, 1987).

What can we conclude from the series of longitudinal studies about constancy and change in personality during the adult years? Richard Alpert was an achievement-oriented, hardworking college professor in the 1960s. In the 1970s, Richard Alpert became Ram Dass, a free-spirited guru in search of an expanded state of consciousness. Most individuals would look at Alpert and Ram Dass and see two very different people. But Harvard psychologist David McClelland, who has known Alpert and Ram Dass well, says that Dass is the same old Richard, still charming, still concerned with inner experience, and still power hungry.

Jerry Rubin views his own transformation from yippie to Wall Street businessman in a way that underscores continuity in personality. Rubin says that discovering his identity was accomplished in a typical Jerry Rubin fashion—trying out anything and everything, jumping around wild-eyed and crazy. Whether yippie or Wall Street businessman, Rubin approached life with enthusiasm and curiosity (Rubin, 1981).

William James (1890/1950) said that our basic personality is set like plaster by the time we are 30 and never softens again. Like Jerry Rubin and David McClelland, James believed that our bodies and attitudes may change through the adult years, but not the basic core of our personality. Paul Costa's (1986, 1987) research clearly supports this stability. He believes that whether

(a)

(b)

How much does our personality change and how much does it stay the same through adulthood? In the early 1970s, Jerry Rubin was a Yippie demonstrator (a), but in the 1980s, Rubin became a Wall Street businessman (b). Rubin says that his transformation underscores continuity in personality: Whether Yippie or Wall Street Yuppie, he approached life with curiosity and enthusiasm.

We are adaptive human beings, resilient throughout our adult lives, but we do not become entirely new personalities. In a way we change but remain the same—amidst change is an underlying coherence and stability. Think about adults you know or have known. How well does their adult development fit our description of both stability and change in their lives?

October answers to that period in the life of man when he is no longer dependent on his transient moods, when all his experiences ripen into wisdom, but every root, branch, leaf of him glows with maturity. What he has been and done in his spring and summer appears. He bears fruit.

~ *Ralph Waldo Emerson*

we are extraverted or introverted, how adjusted we are, and how open we are to new experience do not change much during our adult lives. Look at an individual at age 25 who is shy and quiet and then observe the individual again at age 50, says Costa, and you will find the same shy and quiet individual.

Yet many adult developmentalists are enthusiastic about our capacity for change as adults, arguing that too much importance has been attached to personality change in childhood and not enough importance has been placed on change in adulthood. A more moderate view on the stability-change view comes from the California Longitudinal Study (Eichorn & others, 1981; Mussen, Honzik, & Eichorn, 1982). They believe some stability exists over

Concept Table 17.3: The Life-Events Approach, Individual Variation, and Longitudinal Studies

Concept	Processes/Related Ideas	Characteristics/Description
The Life-Events Approach	Early Version	Life events produce taxing circumstances that produce stress in individuals' lives.
	Contemporary Version	This emphasizes that how life events influence the individual's development depends not only on the life event but also on mediating factors, the individual's adaptation to the life event, the life-stage context, and the sociohistorical context.
Individual Variation	Its Nature	One approach to adult personality development emphasizes similarities, another emphasizes differences. The adult stage approach emphasizes similarities. However, there is substantial individual variation in adult development.
Longitudinal Studies of Personality Development in Adulthood	Neugarten's Study	The most consistent characteristics were adaptive characteristics—styles of coping, attaining life satisfaction, and strength of goal-directed behavior. Two significant changes in middle age were increases in both passive mastery and interiority.
	Costa and McRae's View	They report extensive stability in adult personality development, especially in neuroticism, extraversion, and openness to experience.
	California Longitudinal Study	The extremes in the stability-change argument were not supported. Characteristics associated with the self were more stable than those associated with interpersonal relationships.
	Mills College Study	In this study of adult women, there was a shift toward less traditionally feminine characteristics from age 27 to the early forties, but this may have been due to societal changes. In their early forties, women experienced many of the concerns stage theorists such as Levinson and Gould found in men. However, rather than a mid-life crisis, this change was described as mid-life consciousness.
	Conclusions	The longitudinal studies portray adults as becoming different but still remaining the same—amidst change there is still some underlying coherence and stability.

the long course of adult development, but that adults are more capable of change than Costa thinks. For example, shy, introverted individuals at age 25 may not be completely extraverted at age 50, but they may be less introverted than they were when they were 25. Perhaps they married someone who encouraged them to be more outgoing and supported their social ventures; perhaps they changed jobs at age 30 and became a salesperson, placing them in a circumstance that required them to develop their social skills.

Humans are adaptive beings; we are resilient throughout our adult lives. But we do not become entirely new personalities either. In a sense we become different but we are still the same—amidst change is some underlying coherence and stability.

At this point we have discussed a number of ideas about personality theories and development in middle age. A summary of these ideas is presented in concept table 17.3. This chapter concludes our examination of the middle adulthood years. In the book's next section we turn our attention to the final period in life's human cycle—the late adulthood years.

Summary

I. Love and Marriage at Mid-Life and the Empty Nest

Affectionate or companionate love increases in middle adulthood, especially in marriages that have endured many years. Divorce in middle adulthood may be more positive or more negative than divorce in early adulthood. The empty nest syndrome states that marital satisfaction will decrease when children leave home after adolescence because parents derive considerable pleasure from their children. However, rather than decreasing marital satisfaction, the empty nest usually increases it. Increasing numbers of adult children continue to live with their parents or refill the empty nest by returning home after a failed marriage, economic difficulties, loss of a job, or college. The refilling of the empty nest requires considerable adaptation on the part of parents and their adult children.

II. Sibling Relationships and Friendships

Sibling relationships continue throughout life. Many adult sibling relationships are close, especially if they were close in childhood, although some are apathetic or highly conflicted. Friendships continue to be important in the middle adulthood years. Longstanding friendships are often deeper and more intimate.

III. Intergenerational Relationships

There generally is continuing contact across generations in families. Greater continuity occurs in political and religious attitudes, lesser continuity occurs in gender roles, life-styles, and work orientation. Mothers and daughters have the closest relationship in adulthood.

Women play an important role in the monitoring of access to and feelings toward kin. The middle-aged generation has been called the "sandwich" generation because financial obligations to youth and to aging parents may create stress for middle-aged adults. The middle-aged generation plays an important role in linking generations.

IV. Adult Stage Theories

In Erikson's life-cycle theory, generativity versus stagnation is the seventh stage, corresponding roughly with middle adulthood; it is a time when adults need to assist the next generation in developing and leading useful lives. In Gould's transformations, mid-life is as turbulent as adolescence except that during mid-life striving to handle a crisis produces a healthy, happier life. For Gould, our forties represent a time when we begin to feel a sense of urgency as we see our lives speeding by. In Levinson's seasons of a man's life, developmental tasks should be mastered at different points in development. Changes in middle adulthood focus on four conflicts: being young vs. being old, being destructive vs. being constructive, being masculine vs. being feminine, and being attached to others vs. being separated from them. In Vaillant's expansion of Erikson's stages, career consolidation occurs from 23 to 35 years of age; keeping the meaning vs. rigidity occurs from 45 to 55 years of age. In conclusion, the adult stage theories suggest that adult development begins with a change from identity to intimacy, then from career consolidation to generativity, and finally from searching for meaning to some final integration. Criticisms of the stage theories have been made.

V. Crisis and Cohort

A majority of individuals in the United States do not experience a mid-life crisis. Neugarten believes the social environment of a particular cohort can alter its social clock—the timetable according to which individuals are expected to accomplish life's tasks, such as getting married, having children, or establishing a career.

VI. Gender and Culture

Critics say the adult stage theories have a male bias by emphasizing career choice and achievement. The stage theories do not adequately address women's concerns about relationships, interdependence, and caring. The stage theories assume a normative sequence of development, but as women's roles have become more varied and complex, determining what is normative is difficult. In many nonindustrialized societies, a woman's status improves in middle age. In many cultures, the concept of middle age is not clear. Some cultures do not have words for "adolescent," "young adult," or "middle-aged adult." However, most cultures distinguish between the young and the old.

VII. The Life-Events Approach

In the early version, life events were perceived as taxing circumstances and were studied for their stressful impact. In today's more sophisticated version, sociohistorical circumstances, factors that mediate life events, appraisal of the life events, and how the individual copes with the events are considered. Too much emphasis on change and inadequate attention to life's daily hassles and uplifts are criticisms of the life-events approach.

VIII. Individual Variation

One approach to adult personality development emphasizes similarities, another emphasizes differences. The adult stage theories emphasize similarity; however, there is substantial individual variation in adult development.

IX. Longitudinal Studies of Personality Development in Adulthood

In Neugarten's study, the most consistent characteristics were adaptive characteristics—styles of coping, attaining life satisfaction, and strength of goal-directed behavior. Two significant changes as individuals went through middle age were an increase in passive mastery and interiority. Costa and McRae report extensive stability in adult personality development, especially in neuroticism, extraversion, and openness to experience. In the California Longitudinal Study, the extremes in the stability-change argument were not supported. Characteristics associated with the self were more stable than those associated with interpersonal relationships. In the Mills College Study of adult women, there was a shift toward less traditionally feminine characteristics from age 27 to the early forties, but this may have been due to societal changes. In their early forties, these women experienced many of the concerns stage theorists such as Gould and Levinson found in men. However, it was concluded that rather than a mid-life crisis, this represented mid-life consciousness. In summary, the longitudinal studies portray individuals as becoming different but still remaining the same—amidst change there is some underlying coherence and stability.

Key Terms

empty nest syndrome   540
career consolidation   549

keeping the meaning versus rigidity   549

social clock   551
contemporary life-events approach   555

Suggested Readings

Eichorn, D. H., Clausen, J. A., Haan, N., Honzik, M. P., & Mussen, P. H. (1981). *Present and past in middle life.* New York: Academic Press. *Includes details about the California Longitudinal Study, that spans from childhood through middle age.*

Grambs, J. D. (1989). *Women over forty* (rev. ed.). New York: Springer. *Includes up-to-date information about women in mid-life and old age. Among the chapters are "Is there life after menopause?" "Older and female: myths and realities," and "The older woman in historical and cross-cultural perspective."*

Hunter, S., & Sundel, M. (1989). (Eds.), *Mid-life Myths.* Newbury Park, CA: Sage. *This book includes discussion of many issues involving development in middle adulthood. Among the chapters are "Marital quality at mid-life," "Dual-career families at mid-life," "Myths of intergenerational relationships," and "Modern myths about men at mid-life."*

Levinson, D. (1978). *Seasons of a man's life.* New York: Ballantine Books. *Levinson's well-known book provides extensive biographical material about forty men and their adult development as well as commentary about the adult development of famous individuals.*

Scholossberg, N. K. (1984). *Counseling adults in transition.* New York: Springer. *A helping skills model is developed for counseling individuals in middle adulthood.*

Sherman, E. (1987). *Meaning in mid-life transitions.* Albany: State University of New York Press. *Extensive case studies of individuals as they make the transition through mid-life. Separate chapters on generativity and mortality.*

S·E·C·T·I·O·N

IX

LATE ADULTHOOD

To be seventy years young is sometimes far more cheerful and hopeful than to be forty years old.

Oliver Wendell Holmes

CHAPTER 18

Physical Development in Late Adulthood

J onathan Swift said, "No wise man ever wished to be younger." Without doubt, a 70-year-old body does not work as well as it once did. It is also true that an individual's fear of aging is often greater than it needs to be. As more individuals live to a ripe *and* active old age, our image of aging and how we react to aging is changing. While on the average, a 75-year-old's joints should be stiffening, individuals can practice not to be average. For example, a 70-year-old man may *choose* to train for and run a marathon; an 80-year-old woman whose capacity for work is undiminished may *choose* to continue making and selling children's toys.

We ask some exciting and provocative questions in this chapter. How long can we live? What are your chances for living to be 100? Why do we age? What is the nature of physical changes in late adulthood? Do older adults have sex? What kind of health treatment do older adults receive? Can more exercise and better nutrition make us healthier in old age, and possibly even extend the life span?

Longevity

Linus Pauling, now in his eighties, believes that vitamin C diminishes the aging process. Aging researcher Roy Walford fasts two days a week because he believes undernutrition (not malnutrition) also diminishes the aging process. In animals, underfeeding has been shown to not only delay death but to forestall the decay of the immune system. In humans, though, we do not have evidence that underfeeding or vitamin C prolongs life. What do we know about longevity?

Life Expectancy and Life Span

We are no longer a youthful society. Remember from chapter 1 that, as more individuals live to older ages, the proportion of individuals at different ages has become increasingly similar. Indeed, the concept of a period called late adulthood is a recent one—until the twentieth century most individuals died before they were 65. In the 1980 census, the number of persons 65 and older climbed by 28 percent over figures for 1970. In the United States today, there are more than 25 million people in the 65 and over category.

However, while a much greater percentage of persons live to an older age, the life span has remained virtually unchanged since the beginning of recorded history. **Life span** *is the upper boundary of life, the maximum number of years an individual can live. The maximum life span of human beings is approximately 115 to 120 years of age.* **Life expectancy** *is the number of individuals expected to reach a particular age in life.* Improvements in medicine, nutrition, exercise, and life-style have increased our life expectancy an average of 22 additional years since 1900. However, few of us will live to be 100 (32,000 Americans lived to be 100 in 1980), although the number is increasing.

Supposedly, one American, Charlie Smith (ca1842–1979), lived to be 137 years old. Charlie was very, very old, but documentation of his age is sketchy. In 1956, the Social Security Administration began to collect information about American centenarians (those who live to be 100 or older) who were receiving benefits. Charlie Smith was visited in 1961. He gave his birthdate as July 4, 1842, and his place of birth as Liberia. By the end of the nineteenth century, Charlie had settled in Florida. He worked in turpentine camps, and at one point owned a turpentine farm in Homeland, Florida. Smith's records at the Social Security Administration do not provide evidence of his birthdate, but they do mention he began to earn benefits based on Social Security credits by picking oranges at the age of 113 (Freeman, 1982).

AGING IN RUSSIA, ECUADOR, AND KASHMIR

*I*magine that you are 120 years old. Would you still be able to write your name? Could you think clearly? What would your body look like? Would you be able to walk? To run? Could you still have sex? Would you have an interest in sex? Would your eyes and ears still function? Could you work?

Has anyone ever lived to be 120 years old? Supposedly. In three areas of the world, not just a single person but many people have reportedly lived more than 130 years. These areas are the Republic of Georgia in Russia, the Vilcabamba valley in Ecuador, and the province of Hunza in Kashmir (in Northern India). Three people over 100 years old (centenarians) per 100,000 people is considered normal. But in the Russian region where the Abkhasian people live, approximately 400 centenarians per 100,000 people have been reported. Some of the Abkhasians are said to be 120 to 170 years old (Benet, 1976).

However, there is reason to believe that some of these claims are false

Selakh Butka, who says he is 113 years old, is shown with his wife, who says she is 101. The Butkas live in the Georgian Republic of the Soviet Union, where reports of unusual longevity have surfaced. Why are scientists skeptical about their age?

Eighty-seven year-old José Maria Roa is from the Vilcabamba region of Ecuador, which also is renowned for the longevity of its inhabitants.

(Medvedev, 1974). Indeed, we really do not have sound documentation of anyone living more than approximately 115 to 120 years. In the case of the Abkhasians, birth registrations and other documents, such as marriage certificates and military registrations, are not available. In most instances, the ages of the Abkhasians have been based on the individuals' recall of important historical events and interviews with other members of the village (Benet, 1976). In the Russian villages where

people have been reported to live a long life, the elderly experience unparalleled esteem and honor. Centenarians are often given special positions in the community, such as the leader of social celebrations. Thus there is a strong motivation to give one's age as older than one really is. One individual who claimed to be 130 years of age was found to have used his father's birth certificate during World War I to escape army duty. Later it was discovered that he only was 78 years old (Hayflick, 1975).

Charlie Smith lived to be very old—exactly how old we will never know. He lived an active life, even after the age of 100. Many other Americans have lived to be 100. In the book, *Living to be 100: 1200 who did and how they did it* (Segerberg, 1982), Social Security Administration interviews with 1,127 individuals who lived to be 100 were described. Especially interesting are some of the bizarre reasons several of the centenarians gave as to why they were able to live so long were: "because I slept with my head facing the north," "because of eating a lot of fatty pork and salt," and "because I don't believe in germs." More accurate reasons given by these individuals as to why they had lived to be 100 were their organized, purposeful behavior, discipline and hard work, freedom and independence, balanced diet, positive family relations, and the support of friends. In some areas of the world large numbers of individuals reportedly live to be very old. To learn more about these areas, turn to Cultural Worlds of Development 18.1.

What about you? What chance do you have of living to be 100? By taking the test in table 18.1, you can obtain a rough estimate of your chance

Table 18.1: Can You Live to Be 100?

The following test gives you a rough guide for predicting your longevity. The basic life expectancy for males is age 71, and for females 78. Write down your basic life expectancy. If you are in your fifties or sixties, you should add ten years to the basic figure because you have already proved yourself to be a durable individual. If you are over age sixty and active, you can even add another two years.

Basic Life Expectancy _____

Decide how each item below applies to you and add or subtract the appropriate number of years from your basic life expectancy.

1. Family history
   Add five years if two or more of your grandparents lived to 80 or beyond. _____
   Subtract four years if any parent, grandparent, sister, or brother died of heart attack or stroke before 50. _____
   Subtract two years if anyone died from these diseases before 60. _____
   Subtract three years for each case of diabetes, thyroid disorder, breast cancer, cancer of the digestive system, asthma, or chronic bronchitis among parents or grandparents. _____

2. Marital status
   If you are married, add four years. _____
   If you are over twenty-five and not married, subtract one year for every unwedded decade. _____

3. Economic status
   Add two years if your family income is over $40,000 per year. _____
   Subtract three years if you have been poor for the greater part of your life. _____

4. Physique
   Subtract one year for every ten pounds you are overweight. _____
   For each inch your girth measurement exceeds your chest measurement deduct two years. _____
   Add three years if you are over forty and not overweight. _____

5. Exercise
   Add three years if you exercise regularly and moderately (jogging three times a week). _____
   Add five years if you exercise regularly and vigorously (long-distance running three times a week). _____
   Subtract three years if your job is sedentary. _____
   Add three years if your job is active. _____

6. Alcohol
   Add two years if you are a light drinker (one to three drinks a day). _____
   Subtract five to ten years if you are a heavy drinker (more than four drinks per day). _____
   Subtract one year if you are a teetotaler. _____

7. Smoking
   Subtract eight years if you smoke two or more packs of cigarettes per day. _____
   Subtract two years if you smoke one to two packs per day. _____
   Subtract two years if you smoke less than one pack. _____
   Subtract two years if you regularly smoke a pipe or cigars. _____

8. Disposition
   Add two years if you are a reasoned, practical person. _____
   Subtract two years if you are aggressive, intense, and competitive. _____
   Add one to five years if you are basically happy and content with life. _____
   Subtract one to five years if you are often unhappy, worried, and often feel guilty. _____

9. Education
   Subtract two years if you have less than a high school education. _____
   Add one year if you attended four years of school beyond high school. _____
   Add three years if you attended five or more years beyond high school. _____

10. Environment
   Add four years if you have lived most of your life in a rural environment. _____
   Subtract two years if you have lived most of your life in an urban environment. _____

11. Sleep
   Subtract five years if you sleep more than nine hours a day. _____

12. Temperature
   Add two years if your home's thermostat is set at no more than 68° F. _____

13. Health care
   Add three years if you have regular medical checkups and regular dental care. _____
   Subtract two years if you are frequently ill. _____

Your Life Expectancy Total _____

Table 18.2: Differences in the Life Expectancies of Females and Males

Sex	Year		
	1950	*1985*	*2020* *(projected)*
Female	71.0	78.2	82.0
Male	65.5	71.2	74.2

Source: Data from the *Duke Longitudinal Study.*

'Tis very certain that the desire for life prolongs it.

~ *Byron,*
Don Juan, *1819*

• *Critical Thinking* •

What factors do you believe will be the most important in increasing longevity fifty years from now, in approximately the year 2040? Will they be any different than those that are the most critical today? Will some factors assume more importance, less importance?

and discover some of the most important contributors to longevity. According to the questionnaire, heredity and family health (weight, diet, smoking, and exercise), education, personality, and life-style are factors in longevity.

Just as actuaries predict longevity for the purpose of insurance risks on the basis of age, sex, and ethnicity, developmentalists have also evaluated the factors that predict longevity. In the most comprehensive investigation of longevity, known as the Duke Longitudinal Study (Palmore, 1982), older adults were assessed over a 25-year period. A total of 270 volunteers were examined for the first time in 1959 with a series of physical, mental, social, and laboratory tasks. At that time, the adults ranged in age from 60 to 94 with a mean age of 70. What were the factors that predicted their longevity 25 years later? Not surprisingly, health was the best predictor. Nonsmoking, intelligence, education, work satisfaction, usefulness, and happiness in 1959 also predicted whether these individuals would still be alive in 1981. Also, finances predicted longevity for men; activity level predicted longevity for women.

Beginning at the age of 25, females outnumber males, a gap that widens during the remainder of the adult years (see table 18.2). By the time adults are 75 years of age, more than 61 percent of the population is female; for those 85 and over, the figure is almost 70 percent female. Why might this be so? Social factors such as health attitudes, habits, life-styles, and occupation are probably important. For example, among such leading causes of death in the United States as cancer of the respiratory system, motor vehicle accidents, suicide, cirrhosis of the liver, emphysema, and coronary heart disease, men are more likely to die from such factors than are women. These causes of death are associated with life-style. For example, the sex difference in deaths due to lung cancer and emphysema is probably associated with men being heavier smokers than women.

However, if life expectancy is influenced extensively by the stress of work, the sex difference in longevity should be narrowing, since so many more women have entered the labor force. Yet in the last forty years, just the opposite has occurred. Apparently, self-esteem and work satisfaction outweigh the stress of work when the longevity of women is at issue.

The sex difference in longevity is also influenced by biological factors. In virtually all species, females outlive males. Women have more resistance to infections and degenerative diseases. For example, the female's estrogen production helps to protect her from arteriosclerosis (hardening of the arteries). And the X chromosome women carry may be associated with the production of more antibodies to fight off disease.

Late Adulthood

Heredity is an important component of how long we will live. For example, in table 18.1, you were able to add five years to your life expectancy if two or more of your grandparents lived to eighty or beyond. And if you were born a female you get to start out with a basic life expectancy that is seven years older than if you were born a male. The three sisters shown above are all in their eighties.

Biological Theories of Aging

Even if we keep a remarkably healthy profile through our adult lives, we begin to age at some point. What are the biological explanations of aging? **Microbiological theories of aging** *look within the body's cells to explain aging. The label micro is used because a cell is a very small unit of analysis.* **Macrobiological theories of aging** *examine life at a more global level of analysis than the cell. Macro refers to a larger, more global level of analysis.* Some microbiological and macrobiological theories attribute aging to wear and tear on the body, others to a biological clock within the body.

Microbiological Theories

As cells age, they have more difficulty disposing of their wastes. Eventually this "garbage" takes up as much as 20 percent of a cell's space. Imagine the cell's working molecules as waiters in a nightclub trying to move across a dance floor that becomes increasingly crowded. Service becomes slower and slower until eventually it might come to a complete standstill. Most scientists view this phenomenon as a result, rather than a cause, of aging, though.

As cells age, their molecules can become linked or attached to each other in ways that stop vital biochemical cycles and create other forms of havoc as they disrupt cell functioning (Bruce, 1991; Pacifici & Davies, 1991). The cross-linkage view, like the garbage-accumulation view, is now thought to be a consequence rather than a cause of aging.

Might there also be a biological clock within our cells that causes us to age? Leonard Hayflick (1977, 1987) thinks so. He has demonstrated that the body's cells can only divide a limited number of times. Cells from human embryonic tissue can divide only about fifty times, for example. Cells extracted from older individuals still have dividing capability, however, so we rarely live to the end of our life-span potential. Based on the way human cells divide, scientists place the upper limit of the human life span at 115 to 120 years.

Macrobiological Theories

Aging also may be influenced by the immune system, the brain, and homeostasis. Regarding the immune system, in early adulthood, the thymus (a gland in the upper chest whose hormones stimulate the white blood cells needed to fight infection and cancer) has already begun to shrink. As life continues, the immune system loses some of its ability to recognize and attack bacteria and other invaders, as well as cancer cells. The immune cells may also start to attack the body's own healthy cells, possibly producing autoimmune diseases such as rheumatoid arthritis and some kidney ailments (Walford, 1969).

Other scientists argue that the aging timer is located in the brain, more specifically the hypothalamus and pituitary gland, which are involved in the release of hormones. In this view, beginning at puberty, the pituitary gland releases a hormone, or a family of hormones, that causes the body to decline at a programmed rate. This "aging" hormone—which has not yet been isolated or proven to exist—hinders the cell's ability to take in thyroxine, the hormone secreted by the thyroid gland. Thyroxine controls the metabolic rate in the body's key cardiovascular and immune systems, whose failure often is involved in many diseases that kill older individuals.

Aging might also be related to the decline in the body's organ reserve. At the level of the organism, life may be defined as internal homeostasis (balance). The body's internal world is balanced and regulated within strict limits. Neural and endocrine systems monitor heart, lungs, liver, kidneys, and other organs to maintain this balance. In young adulthood, biologists estimate that we have an organ reserve that is ten times that required to sustain life. This organ reserve allows a stressed individual to restore homeostasis, or balance, when the body is damaged by something external. But beginning at about 30 years of age, our organ reserve begins a gradual drop that continues through the remainder of our life. Eventually our organ reserve capacity reaches zero, and we die even if a disease is not present. After the age of 30, an individual's mortality rate doubles every eight years because of this decline in organ reserve (Upton, 1977).

While no one knows for sure why we age, scientists today believe we have a biological clock that ultimately will be identified. Some scientists argue that the clock resides in the cells of the body, others argue that it lies in the brain or certain glands, and yet others argue that it lies in the homeostatic balance of the body and organ reserve in general. A summary of the theories of aging we have described is shown in figure 18.1.

The Course of Physical Decline in Late Adulthood

What are some of the common ravages that hit us sooner or later in old age? At 30 we are not bad specimens—a little slower, a little plumper probably, but already our body had passed its peak. At 50, we probably are not the specimens we were when we were 30. We become shorter, our reflexes diminish, we gain even more weight, we do not have as much stamina, and our cardiovascular system is less efficient. By 70, the human specimen shows further decline.

The Brain and Nervous System

The brain is of considerable interest to scientists who study the course of physical decline in late adulthood. As we age we lose a number of neurons, the basic cellular unit of the nervous system. Some researchers estimate that the loss may be as high as 50 percent over the adult years, although others believe the loss is substantially less and that an accurate assessment of neuron loss has not been made in human brains (Bondareff, 1985). Perhaps a more reasonable estimate is that 5 to 10 percent of our neurons atrophy until we reach the seventies. After that, neuron loss may accelerate.

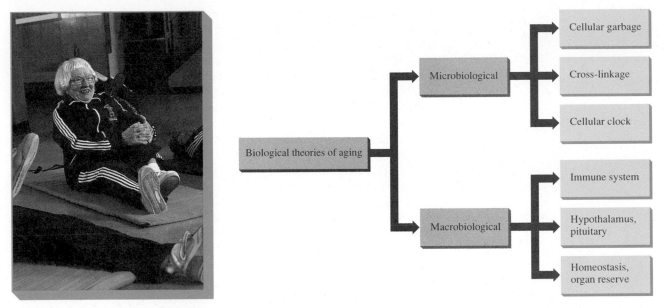

Figure 18.1   *Biological theories of aging.*

A significant aspect of the aging process may be that neurons do not replace themselves (Moushegian, 1991). Nonetheless, generally it is believed that the brain has remarkable recovery and repair capability, losing only a small portion of its ability to function in the late adulthood years (Labouvie-Vief, 1985). The adaptive nature of the brain was demonstrated in one investigation (Coleman, 1986). From the forties through the seventies, the growth of dendrites increased. Dendrites are the receiving part of the neuron or nerve cell. They are thought to be especially important because they make up approximately 95 percent of the neuron's surface. But in very old people, those in their nineties, dendritic growth was no longer taking place. Through the seventies, then, dendritic growth may compensate for neuron loss, but not when individuals reach their nineties.

Sensory Development

Sensory physical changes in late adulthood involve vision, hearing, taste, smell, and pain. In late adulthood, the decline in vision that, for most of us, began in early or middle adulthood becomes more pronounced (Kosnick & others, 1989). Night driving becomes especially difficult, to some extent because tolerance for glare diminishes. Dark adaptation is slower, meaning that older individuals take longer to recover their vision when going from well-lighted rooms to semidarkness. The area of the visual field becomes smaller, suggesting that a stimulus's intensity in the peripheral area of the visual field needs to be increased if the stimulus is to be seen. Events taking place away from the center of the visual field may not be detected (Kline & Schieber, 1985).

This visual decline can usually be traced to reduction in the quality or intensity of light reaching the retina. In extreme old age, these changes may be accompanied by degenerative changes in the retina, causing severe difficulty in seeing. Large print books and magnifiers may be needed in such cases. Legal blindness is defined as corrected distance vision of 20/200 in the better eye or a visual field restricted to 20 degrees as large as the diameter. Legal blindness occurs in less than 100 out of every 100,000 individuals under the age of 21; it increases to 1400 out of every 100,000 individuals at the age of 69, still indicating that the vast majority of older adults can see quite well with glasses.

Although hearing impairment may begin in middle adulthood, it usually does not become much of an impediment until late adulthood. Even then, some but not all hearing problems may be corrected by hearing aids. Only 19 percent of individuals from 45 to 54 experience some type of hearing problem, but from 75 to 79 the figure has reached 75 percent (Harris, 1975). It has been estimated that 15 percent of the population over the age of 65 is legally deaf, usually due to the degeneration of the cochlea, the primary neural receptor for hearing in the inner ear (Olsho, Harkins, & Lenhardt, 1985). Wearing two hearing aids that are balanced to correct each ear separately can sometimes help hearing-impaired adults.

Not only do we experience declines in vision and hearing as we age, but we may also become less sensitive to taste and smell. Sensitivity to bitter and sour tastes persists longer than sensitivity to sweet and salty tastes. However, in healthy older adults, there is less decline in sensitivity to taste and smell than in those who are not healthy (Engen, 1977). One loss of sensory sensitivity as we age may be advantageous, though. Older adults are less sensitive to pain and suffer from it less than younger adults. Of course, although decreased sensitivity to pain may help the elderly cope with disease and injury, it can be harmful if it masks injury and illness that need to be treated.

The Circulatory System

The diminished efficiency of the circulatory system is a special concern (Miller & Gottlieb, 1991). There is less *elastin,* the molecules that dictate the heart's elasticity, and there is more *collagen,* the stiff protein that makes up about one third of the body's protein. An individual's heart rate does not rise as predictably in response to stress as was the case during middle adulthood. The heart muscle cannot contract and relax as fast. The arteries are more resistant to blood flow. Heart output—about 5 quarts a minute at age 50—subsequently drops about one percent a year. With the heart muscle less efficient and the vessels more resistant, heart rate and blood pressure both rise—and both are related to heart disease. Even for the healthy older individual, blood pressure that was 100/75 at age 25 probably will be 160/90 at age 70. The blood also carries less oxygen to the brain and lungs. If elderly individuals rise too quickly from a chair, they may get dizzy; if they climb a set of stairs too speedily, they may get out of breath.

Sexuality

Aging does induce some changes in human sexual performance, more so in the male than in the female. Orgasm becomes less frequent in males, occurring in every second to third act of intercourse rather than every time. More direct stimulation usually is needed to produce an erection. In the absence of two circumstances—actual disease and the belief that old people are or should be asexual—sexuality can be lifelong. Even when actual intercourse is impaired by infirmity, other relationship needs persist, among them closeness, sensuality, and being valued as a man or a woman.

Such a view, of course, is contrary to folklore, to the beliefs of many individuals in society, and even to many physicians and health-care personnel. Fortunately, many elderly individuals went on having sex without talking about it, unabashed by the accepted and destructive social image of the dirty old

Late Adulthood

Concept Table 18.1: Longevity and the Course of Physical Decline in Late Adulthood

Concept	Processes/Related Ideas	Characteristics/Description
Longevity	Life Expectancy and Life Span	Life expectancy is increasing but the life span is not. Among the most important factors in longevity are heredity and family, health, personality characteristics, and life-style. Beginning at age 25, females outnumber males, a gap that widens as individuals age; this sex difference is probably due to social and biological factors.
	Biological Theories of Aging	Microbiological theories of aging look within the body's cells for the clues to aging. The most popular microbiological theories are cellular garbage, cross-linkage, and cellular clock. Macrobiological theories look for more global causes of aging than the cellular, microbiological theories. Three popular macrobiological theories involve the immune system, the hypothalamus and pituitary gland, and organ reserve and homeostasis.
The Course of Physical Decline	The Brain and Nervous System	Although we lose some neurons as we age, the extent to which neuron loss is incapacitating is debated. It is generally believed that the brain has remarkable repair capacity. Dendritic growth may take place until adults become very old.
	Sensory Development	The visual system declines in late adulthood, but the vast majority of older adults can have their vision corrected so they can continue to work or function in their world. Hearing decline often begins in middle adulthood, but it usually does not become much of an impediment until late adulthood. Hearing aids can diminish the problem of hearing for many older adults. Decline in taste and smell may occur, although the decline is barely noticeable in healthy older adults. Sensitivity to pain decreases in late adulthood.
	The Circulatory System	The diminished efficiency of the circulatory system is a special concern in late adulthood. Heart rate and blood pressure both rise and the blood carries less oxygen to the brain.
	Sexuality	Aging in late adulthood does include some changes in sexual performance, more so for males than for females. Nonetheless, there are no known age limits to sexual activity.

man and the asexual, undesirable older woman. Bear in mind that many individuals who are now in their eighties were reared when there was a Victorian attitude toward sex. In early surveys of sexual attitudes, older individuals were not asked about their sexuality, possibly because everyone thought they did not have sex or because the investigators believed it would be embarrassing to ask them about sex (Pfeiffer & Davis, 1974).

Various therapies for elderly individuals who report sexual difficulties have been effective. In one investigation, sex education—which consisted largely of simply giving sexual information—led to increased sexual interest, knowledge, and activity in the elderly (White & Catania, 1981).

At this point we have discussed a number of ideas about the nature of longevity and the course of physical decline in late adulthood. A summary of these ideas is presented in concept table 18.1. Now we turn our attention to the nature of health in older adults.

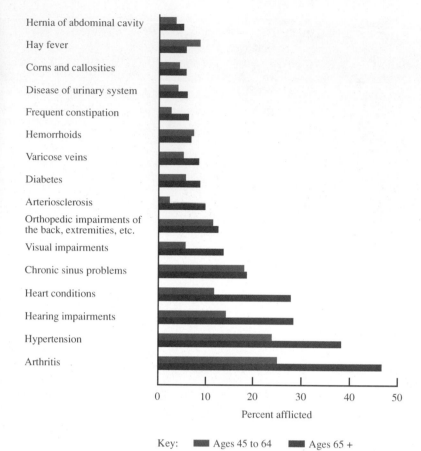

Figure 18.2 *Most prevalent chronic conditions in middle and late adulthood.*

Hernia of abdominal cavity
Hay fever
Corns and callosities
Disease of urinary system
Frequent constipation
Hemorrhoids
Varicose veins
Diabetes
Arteriosclerosis
Orthopedic impairments of the back, extremities, etc.
Visual impairments
Chronic sinus problems
Heart conditions
Hearing impairments
Hypertension
Arthritis

0   10   20   30   40   50
Percent afflicted

Key: ■ Ages 45 to 64   ■ Ages 65 +

> How many of us older persons have really been prepared for the second half of life, for old age, and eternity?
>
> ~ *Carl Jung,*
> Modern Man in Search of a Soul,
> *1933*

Health

What are the major health problems in old age? What are the main causes of death in older adults?

Health Problems

As we age, the probability we will have some disease or illness increases. For example, the majority of adults who are still alive at the age of 80 are likely to have some impairment.

Chronic disorders *are characterized by a slow onset and a long duration. Chronic disorders rarely develop in early adulthood, increase during middle adulthood, and become common in late adulthood.* As shown in figure 18.2, arthritis is the most common chronic disorder in late adulthood, followed by hypertension. Elderly women have higher incidences of arthritis and hypertension, are more likely to have visual problems, but are less likely to have hearing problems than elderly men do.

Although adults over the age of 65 often have a physical impairment, many of them can still carry on their everyday activities or work. Chronic conditions associated with the greatest limitation on work are heart condition (52 percent), diabetes (34 percent), asthma (27 percent), and arthritis (27 percent) (Harris, 1978). Low income is also strongly related to health problems in late adulthood. Approximately three times as many poor as nonpoor older adults report that their activities are limited by chronic disorders.

Table 18.3: The Six Leading Causes of Death in Americans 65 Years and Older

Rank	Cause of Death	Rate per 100,000 Population in the 65 and Over Age Group
1	Heart disease	2,173
2	Cancer	1,047
3	Cerebrovascular disease (stroke)	464
4	Lung Diseases	213
5	Pneumonia and influenza	206
6	Diabetes	96

Source: National Center for Health Statistics, 1987.

Causes of Death in Older Adults

Nearly three-fourths of all older adults die of heart disease, cancer, or cerebrovascular disease (stroke). Chronic lung diseases, pneumonia and influenza, and diabetes round out the six leading causes of death among older adults (see table 18.3). If cancer, the second leading cause of death in older adults, were completely eliminated, the average life expectancy would rise by only one to two years. However, if all cardiovascular and kidney diseases were eradicated, the average life expectancy of older adults would increase by approximately ten years (Butler, 1975). This increase in longevity is already underway as the number of strokes among older adults has declined considerably in the last several decades. The decline in strokes is due to improved treatment of high blood pressure, a decrease in smoking, better diet, and an increase in exercise.

Arthritis

Arthritis *is an inflammation of the joints accompanied by pain, stiffness, and movement problems. Arthritis is especially common in older adults.* This disorder can affect hips, knees, ankles, fingers, and vertebrae. Individuals with arthritis often experience pain and stiffness, as well as problems in moving about and performing routine daily activities. There is no known cure for arthritis. However, the symptoms of arthritis can be reduced by drugs, such as aspirins, range-of-motion exercises for the afflicted joints, weight reduction, and, in extreme cases, replacement of the crippled joint with a prothesis (Aiken, 1989).

Osteoporosis

Normal aging involves some loss of bone tissue from the skeleton (Kiebzak, 1991). However, in some instances loss of bone tissue can become severe. **Osteoporosis** *is an aging disorder involving an extensive loss of bone tissue. Osteoporosis is the main reason many older adults walk with a marked stoop. Women are especially vulnerable to osteoporosis, the leading cause of broken bones in women.* Almost two-thirds of all women over the age of 60 are affected by osteoporosis. Osteoporosis is more common in White, thin, and small-framed women. This aging disorder is related to deficiencies in calcium, Vitamin D, estrogen depletion, and lack of exercise (Dawson-Hughes, 1990). To prevent osteoporosis, young and middle-aged women should eat foods richer in calcium, get more exercise, and avoid smoking. Calcium-rich foods include dairy products (low-fat milk and low-fat yogurt, for example) and certain vegetables (broccoli, turnip greens, and kale, for example). Estrogen replacement therapy may also be recommended for middle-aged women at especially high risk for developing osteoporosis.

Accidents

Accidents are the seventh leading cause of death among older adults. Injuries resulting from a fall at home or during a traffic accident in which an older adult is a driver or an older pedestrian is hit by a vehicle are common. Each year, approximately 200,000 adults over the age of 65 (most of them women) fracture a hip in a fall. Half of these older adults die within 12 months, frequently from pneumonia. Because healing and recuperation are slower in older adults, an accident that is only a temporary setback for a younger person may result in long-term hospital or home care for an older adult.

Health Treatment

What are the health costs of the elderly and how are they handled? What is the quality of nursing homes and other extended care facilities for older adults? What is the nature of the relationship between older adults and health-care providers? We consider each of these questions in turn.

Health Costs

Compared to individuals under the age of 65, the elderly spend more days in bed, visit doctors more often, have longer and more frequent stays in hospitals, and consume more medications (Aiken, 1989). The expenses associated with these health problems would be impossible for most elderly adults and their families to meet without turning to the federal and state government agencies for assistance. Expenditures for health-care costs are heading toward an average of $5,000 per person per year for individuals 65 years and older. Medicare and Medicaid, the federal government's health-care programs for the elderly, account for approximately two-thirds of the elderly's health-care costs. Escalating medical costs are stimulating considerable discussion about better ways to meet the health-care needs of older adults (DeFriese & Womert, 1991). One consideration is for the government to pay for long-term, home-based care, which is much less costly than nursing home residency. Another consideration is some form of national health insurance. Continued reevaluation of the government's role in health care for the elderly is needed because, despite billions of dollars appropriated each year by the federal government for Medicare and Medicaid, medical bills often deplete the savings and income of many older adults.

Nursing Homes

Only about 5 percent of adults 65 years of age and over reside in a nursing home at any point in time in our society. However, as older adults age their probability of being in a nursing home or other extended care facility increases (Baines, 1991). Twenty-three percent of adults 85 years of age and older live in nursing homes or other extended care facilities.

Three kinds of services or levels of nursing care are provided by various types of nursing homes. In a *skilled* nursing facility, the most extensive nursing care is found. This type of nursing home is carefully reviewed and monitored by federal and state governments. In an *intermediate or ordinary* nursing facility, nursing care is less extensive than in a skilled nursing facility. In a *residential* nursing facility, qualification standards are the least restrictive.

Late Adulthood

Residential nursing care is mainly routine "maintenance" and personal assistance in meeting day-to-day needs. Residential care may include provision for some rehabilitation. The costs for residential care are lower than for the other two types of nursing homes.

The quality of nursing homes and other extended care facilities for elderly adults varies enormously and is a source of continuing national concern (Cherry, 1991; Kanda & Mezey, 1991). Investigations of nursing homes reveal that more than one-third are seriously deficient in one or more areas (Maddox, 1987). Even many of the skilled nursing homes are unaccredited (they fail to pass federally mandated inspections) because they do not meet the minimum standards for physicians, pharmacists, and various rehabilitation specialists (occupational and physical therapists). Further concerns focus on the patient's right to privacy, access to medical information, safety, and life-style freedom within the individual's range of mental and physical capabilities.

The decision to place an elderly parent or relative in a nursing home or other extended care facility is often preceded by a number of years of attempting to cope with the increasing physical and emotional demands of care-taking (Rybash, Roodin, & Santrock, 1991). The decision to place an elderly person in a nursing home is often a stressful one. Anticipation of a move to a nursing home raises the following concerns among the elderly: How well will I adjust to living in a nursing home? How much independence will I lose and how dependent will I become on the staff? What is the quality and availability of medical care? Will they give me tender loving care? Do they have sufficient space?

Nursing home costs continue to escalate each year. A recent survey of adults conducted by the American Association of Retired Persons (1990) indicated they believe that protection against the high cost of nursing homes is the most important coverage in a long-term health-care program. The average cost of staying in a nursing home for one year ranges from $25,000 to $34,000. Medicare only pays for 100 days a year and patients must share the cost after 20 days. Most older adults need supplemental nursing home insurance, yet few obtain this coverage. They incorrectly believe Medicare or other government programs will cover all of their hospital and nursing home expenses, or they find nursing home insurance premiums to be too expensive. In the recent AARP survey, 88 percent of the adults said they would support a government-sponsored program to cover the costs of nursing home care.

Because of the inadequate quality of many nursing homes and the escalating costs of nursing home care, many gerontologists and geriatric specialists (*geriatrics* is the branch of medicine dealing with the health problems of the aged) believe alternatives to nursing homes need to be considered. These alternatives include home health care, day-care centers, and preventive medicine clinics (Aiken, 1989; Miller, 1991). The alternatives are potentially less expensive than hospitals and nursing homes, and are also less likely to engender feelings of depersonalization and dependency that occur so often among residents of institutions.

Giving Options for Control and Teaching Coping Skills

An important factor related to health, and even survival, in a nursing home is the patient's feelings of control and self-determination (Baltes & Wahl, 1991; Schmidt, 1990). In one investigation, a group of elderly nursing home residents were encouraged to make more day-to-day choices and thus feel they had more responsibility for and control over their lives (Rodin & Langer, 1977). They began to decide such matters as what they ate, when their visitors could come, what movies they saw, and who could come to their rooms. A similar group in the same nursing home was told by the administrator how caring the nursing home was and how much the staff wanted to help, but these elderly

Giving nursing home residents options for control and teaching them coping skills are important factors in their health and psychological well-being.

nursing home residents were given no opportunities to take more control over their lives. Eighteen months later, the residents given responsibility and control were more alert and active, and said they were happier, than the residents who were only encouraged to feel that the staff would try to satisfy their needs. And the "responsible" or "self-control" group had significantly better improvement in their health than did the "dependent" group. Even more important was the finding that after 18 months only half as many nursing home residents in the "responsibility" group had died as in the "dependent" group. Perceived control over one's environment, then, may literally be a matter of life or death.

In another investigation, Richard Schulz (1976) gave nursing home residents different amounts of control over visits they received from local college students. Having control over the visits, or at least advance information about them, made the nursing home residents more active, happier, and healthier, probably because control makes life less stressful by making it more predictable. When the experiment ended, so did the visits by the college students. In a follow-up two years later, the researchers found that the nursing home residents who had been given control over scheduling of visits, and then had the visits, and the control, taken away, were doing worse psychologically than the others (Schulz & Hanusa, 1978). Loss of control may even be worse than lack of control in some cases.

How can a psychological factor, such as the feeling of control, have such dramatic effects on health? American psychologist Judith Rodin (1986, 1990; Rodin & Timko, 1991) says that individuals who believe they have a high degree of control are more likely to feel their actions can make a difference in their lives, so they are more likely to take better care of themselves by eating healthier foods and exercising. In contrast, those who have reduced feelings of control are likely to feel that what they do will not make a difference, and thus do not even bother to try to make a difference. Rodin also believes the perception of control can have a direct effect on the body. For example, being in control reduces stress and its stress-related hormones. When stress-related hormones remain elevated, there is more wear and tear on the body; high blood pressure, heart disease, arthritis, and certain types of ulcers have all been linked with excessive stress.

Following up on this line of thinking, Rodin (1983) measured stress-related hormones in several groups of nursing home residents and then taught the residents coping skills to help them deal better with day-to-day problems.

Late Adulthood

She taught the residents how to say no when they did not want something, without worrying whether they would offend someone. She gave them assertiveness training, and she also taught them time management skills. After the training, the nursing home residents had greatly reduced levels of cortisol, a hormone closely related to stress that has been implicated in a number of diseases. The cortisol levels of the "assertive training" residents remained lower, even after 18 months. Further, these nursing home residents were healthier and had a reduced need for medication, compared to residents who had not been taught the coping skills. In sum, Rodin's research has shown that simply giving nursing home residents options for control and teaching them coping skills can change their behavior and improve their health (Trotter, 1990).

The Older Adult and Health-Care Providers

The attitudes of both the health-care provider and the older adult are important aspects of the older adult's health care (Morse & Johnson, 1991). Unfortunately, health-care providers too often share society's stereotypes and negative attitudes toward the elderly. In a heath-care setting, these attitudes can take the form of avoidance, dislike, and begrudged tolerance rather than positive, hopeful treatment. Health-care personnel are more likely to be interested in treating younger persons who more often have acute problems with a higher prognosis for successful recovery than older persons who are more likely to have chronic problems with a lower prognosis for successful recovery (Butler, 1975).

Health-care personnel also report that they have a more difficult time communicating with older persons than younger persons. In one investigation, the communication between a group of middle-aged physicians and their patients of different ages was examined (Greene & others, 1987). The physicians raised fewer psychosocial issues (asking patients questions about their general anxieties and worries, feelings of depression, economic problems, leisure activities, family relationships, and so on) with older patients than younger patients. And when the older patients raised psychosocial concerns, the physicians were less responsive to them than when their younger patients raised such issues. Such findings are important because older adults are more satisfied with their physicians and show better improvement in their health when physicians raise various psychosocial issues or respond positively when older patients want to talk about psychosocial issues.

• Critical Thinking •

Other than giving options for control and teaching coping skills, can you think of other psychological interventions that could benefit nursing home residents?

Physical Development in Late Adulthood

Active older people are more satisfied with their lives than inactive older people. Older people should be encouraged to take trips, exercise, attend meetings, and get out in the world rather than merely sit at home.

All we know about older adults indicates that they are healthier and happier the more active they are. Several decades ago, it was believed that older adults should be more passive and inactive to be well adjusted and satisfied with life. In today's world, we believe that, while older adults may be in the evening of life's human cycle, they were not meant to passively live out their remaining years.

Not only are physicians less responsive to older patients, but older patients often take a less active role in medical encounters with health-care personnel than do younger patients (Woodward & Wallston, 1987). Older adults should be encouraged to take a more active role in their own health care.

Exercise, Nutrition, and Weight

An important aspect of preventing health problems in older adults and improving their health is to encourage individuals to exercise more and to develop better nutritional habits.

Exercise

While we may be in the evening of our lives in late adulthood, we are not meant to passively live out our remaining years. Everything we know about older adults suggests they are healthier and happier the more active they are. The possibility that regular exercise can lead to a healthier late adulthood, and possibly extend life, has been raised (O'Brien & Vertinsky, 1991; Schilke, 1991).

In one recent study, the cardiovascular fitness of 101 older men and women (average age = 67 years) was examined (Blumenthal & others, 1989). The older adults were randomly assigned to an aerobic exercise group, a yoga and flexibility control group, and a waiting list control group. The programs lasted 4 months. Prior to and following the 4-month program, the older adults underwent comprehensive physiological examinations. In the aerobic group, the older adults participated in three supervised exercise sessions per week for 16 weeks. Each session consisted of a 10-minute warm-up, 30 minutes of continuous exercise on a stationary bicycle, 15 minutes of brisk walking/jogging, and a 5-minute cool down. In the yoga and flexibility control group, the older adults participated in 60 minutes of supervised yoga exercises at least twice a week for 16 weeks. Over the 4-month period, the cardiovascular fitness—such as peak oxygen consumption, cholesterol level, and blood pressure—of the aerobic exercise group significantly improved. In contrast, the cardiovascular fitness of the yoga and the waiting list groups did not improve.

In another recent investigation, exercise literally meant a difference in life or death for middle-aged and older adults (Blair, 1990; Blair & Kohl, 1988). More than 17,000 men and women were studied at the Aerobic Institute in Dallas, Texas. Sedentary participants were more than twice as likely to die during the 8 year time span of the study than those who were moderately fit. Examples of exercise programs included running two miles in 20 minutes twice a week or walking three miles in 45 minutes twice a week.

Exercise is an excellent way to maintain health. Being fit means being able to do the things you want to do, whether you are young or old. While there is usually a need for a decrease in exercise intensity as the older adult ages, individuals vary extensively in the degree to which such reduction is necessary. The body's capacity for exercise in late adulthood is influenced by the extent the body has been kept in shape at earlier points in the life cycle. It is not uncommon to discover individuals in late adulthood who participate in the Senior Olympics—athletic competition for senior citizens—to have a greater capacity for exercise than some young adults (Wiswell, 1980). More about exercise's role in maintaining a healthier and happier life as an older adult is discussed in Perspective on Life-Span Development 18.1.

Nutrition and Weight

English philosopher and essayist Francis Bacon (1561–1626) was the first author to recommend scientific evaluation of diet and longevity. He advocated

582

Late Adulthood

A 72-YEAR-OLD COMPETITIVE RUNNER AND JOGGING HOGS

*I*magine you are 72 years old. You have just awakened from 10 hours of restful sleep. You fix yourself a yogurt shake for breakfast and then put on your Nike running shoes and shorts. You drive to the location where the race is to begin. The New York Marathon will start in 30 minutes. You see some friendly competitors, most of whom are much younger than you, but you also see some others who look to be about your age. You chat with them for a few minutes about the race conditions. John Pianfetti, age 72, and Madge Sharples, age 65, recently completed the New York Marathon. Older adults do not have to run marathons to be healthy and happy, but even moderate exercise can benefit their health. By getting men and women aged 50 to 87 to do calisthenics, walk, run, stretch, and swim for 42 weeks, researchers found dramatic changes in the oxygen transport systems of the participants' bodies (Adams & deVries, 1973; deVries, 1970). The improvements occurred regardless of age or prior exercise history.

Jogging hogs have shown the dramatic effects of exercise on health. In

The Experimental setup in Bloor and White's study of exercise and health. Hogs, such as the one shown here, were trained to run approximately 100 miles per week. Then the experimenters narrowed the arteries that supplied blood to the hogs' hearts. The jogging hogs' hearts developed alternative pathways for blood supply, while a group of nonjogging hogs was less likely to recover.

one investigation, a group of hogs were trained to run approximately 100 miles per week (Bloor & White, 1983). Then, the researchers narrowed the arteries that supplied blood to the hogs' hearts. The hearts of the jogging hogs developed extensive alternate pathways for blood supply and 42 percent of the threatened heart tissue was salvaged compared to only 17 percent in a control group of nonjogging hogs.

Many older adults simply feel that they do not need to exercise, yet most aging experts emphasize that the single most effective way to accelerate the aging process is to do nothing. In some instances, the news media have promoted barriers to exercise in older adults by dramatizing the occasional cardiac problem that occurs during exercise. In practical terms, though, we can expect an exercise class of fifty individuals meeting three times a week to have only one cardiac fatality in every 6.5 years. Deciding to exercise is a crucial step for the older adult. Current health should be carefully reviewed and realistic goals for improvement should be set.

---

a frugal diet. Does a restricted intake of food increase longevity or could it possibly even extend the human life span? Before we tackle these intriguing possibilities, we need to examine the nutritional requirements of older adults.

Nutritional Requirements of Older Adults

A common belief is that older adults have poorer dietary habits than middle-aged adults, and therefore, they should use vitamin and mineral supplements. However, this belief appears to be unfounded for most older adults, at least until they become very old (Cavanaugh, 1990). Some older adults do have nutritional problems, especially the institutionalized elderly and the elderly with little income.

What are the dietary requirements for older adults? Only recently have nutritionists turned their attention to guidelines for older adults. For the majority of nutrients, recommended intakes are the same for younger and older adults, although adjustments are usually made for energy requirements (Schlenker, 1988). Energy needs decrease in late adulthood as a result of a

> • Critical Thinking •
>
> What can we do as a society to get older people to exercise more? Should the government be involved? If so, how?

Table 18.4: Recommended Calorie Intake for Older Adults

	51 to 75 Years	76+ Years
Females Calories	1800 (range 1400–2200)	1600 (range 1200–2000)
Males Calories	2400 (range 2000–2800)	2050 (range 1650–2450)

Source: Data modified from Food and Nutrition Board, National Research Council, *Recommended Dietary Allowances,* 9th ed. National Academy of Sciences, Washington, DC.

decline in both basal metabolism rate and physical activity. Table 18.4 presents some general guidelines for energy intake by older adults. Nutrition experts conclude that the protein needs of healthy older adults do not differ from those of younger adults. However, the protein needs of aged persons with serious chronic diseases are usually increased. Vitamin needs usually do not increase in healthy older adults, and megavitamin fads should be avoided (Herbert, 1988).

Food Restriction and Weight

Scientists have accumulated considerable evidence that food restriction in laboratory animals (in most cases rats) can increase the animals' life span (Adelman, 1988; Dax & others, 1989). Animals fed diets restricted in calories, although adequate in protein, vitamins, and minerals, live as much as 40 percent longer than animals given unlimited access to food. And, chronic problems such as kidney disease appear at a later age. Diet restriction also delays biochemical alterations such as the age-related rise in cholesterol observed in both humans and animals. Whether similar very low-calorie diets (in some instances the animals eat 40 percent less than normal) can stretch the human life span is not known. Most nutritional experts do not recommend very low-calorie diets for older adults, but rather a well-balanced, low-fat diet that includes the nutritional factors needed to maintain good health.

Human studies of weight and mortality reveal that despite the association between obesity, chronic disease, and mortality in younger age groups, reasonable numbers of persons who are both old and overweight have been identified (Schlenker, 1988). Overweight persons, recognizing their increased risk, may seek medical check-ups regularly and make a greater effort toward preventive health. Smoking is also a factor. Underweight persons are more likely to be smokers than overweight persons and smokers have an increased mortality rate (Simopoulos & Van Itallie, 1984). Being extremely overweight, though, increases risk in older adults. In one recent study of 8,428 adults, obesity was associated with mortality only when the individuals were 100 percent or more overweight (Potter, Schafer, & Bohi, 1988).

At this point we have discussed a number of important ideas about health and health treatment, and about exercise, nutrition, and weight, in older adults. A summary of these ideas is presented in concept table 18.2. In the next chapter we turn our attention to the cognitive changes that characterize older adults.

Concept Table 18.2: Health, Health Treatment, and Exercise, Nutrition, and Weight

Concept	Processes/Related Ideas	Characteristics/Description
Health	Health Problems	As we age, the probability we will have some disease or illness increases. Chronic disorders rarely develop in early adulthood, increase in middle adulthood, and become common in late adulthood. The most common chronic problem is arthritis, followed by hypertension.
	Causes of Death in Older Adults	Nearly three-fourths of older adults die of heart disease, cancer, or cerebrovascular disease (stroke).
	Arthritis	Arthritis is an inflammation of the joints accompanied by pain, stiffness, and movement problems. Arthritis is especially common among older adults.
	Osteoporosis	Osteoporosis is an aging disorder involving an extensive loss of bone tissue. Osteoporosis is the main reason many older adults walk with a stoop. Women are especially vulnerable to osteoporosis.
	Accidents	Accidents are the seventh leading cause of death among older adults. Accidents are usually more debilitating to older adults than to younger adults.
Health Treatment	Health Costs	Compared to individuals under the age of 65, the elderly spend more days in bed, visit doctors more often, have longer and more frequent stays in the hospital, and consume more medications. Health-care costs for the elderly are escalating. Government programs, such as Medicare and Medicaid, cover approximately two-thirds of the older adult's health-care costs.
	Nursing Homes	Although only 5 percent of adults 65 and over reside in nursing homes, 23 percent of adults 85 and over do. Three types of nursing homes are skilled, intermediate or ordinary, and residential. The quality of nursing homes varies enormously. The decision to place an elderly person in a nursing home is often a stressful one. Nursing home costs are escalating and alternatives to nursing homes are being proposed.
	Giving Options for Control, and Teaching Coping Skills	Simply giving nursing home residents options for control and teaching coping skills can change their behavior and improve their health.
	The Older Adult and Health-Care Providers	The attitudes of both the health-care provider and the older adult patient are important aspects of the older adult's health care. Too often health-care personnel share society's negative view of older adults. Discussion of psychosocial issues with the older patient and encouragement of the older adult patient's active role in medical care are recommended strategies.
Exercise, Nutrition, and Weight	Exercise	Although there may be some need for reduction in exercise in late adulthood, the physical benefits of exercise have been demonstrated. Recently, researchers documented a relation between exercise and longevity, but no evidence exists that exercise can extend the human life span.
	Nutrition and Weight	A common belief is that most older adults have poor nutritional habits and need dietary supplements. Some older adults do have nutritional problems, but the dietary requirements of healthy older adults are similar to middle-aged adults, although adjustments are usually made for energy requirements. Food restriction in animals can increase the animals' life span, but whether this works with humans is not known. In humans, only being extremely overweight is associated with an increased mortality rate. Most nutritional experts recommend a well-balanced, low-fat diet for older adults, but do not recommend an extremely low-calorie diet.

Summary

I. Life Expectancy and Life Span
Life expectancy is increasing but the life span is not. Among the most important factors in longevity are heredity and family, health, personality characteristics, and lifestyle. Beginning at age 25, females outnumber males, a gap that widens as individuals age. This sex difference is probably due to social and biological factors.

II. Biological Theories of Aging
Microbiological theories of aging look within the body's cells for the clues to aging. The most popular microbiological theories are cellular garbage, cross-linkage, and cellular clock. Macrobiological theories look for more global causes of aging than the cellular, microbiological theories. Three popular macrobiological theories involve the immune system, the hypothalamus and pituitary gland, and organ reserve and homeostasis.

III. The Course of Physical Decline
While we lose some neurons as we age, the extent to which neuron loss is incapacitating is debated. It is generally believed that the brain has remarkable repair capacity. Dendritic growth may take place until adults become very old. The visual system declines in late adulthood, but the vast majority of older adults can have their vision corrected so they can continue to work or function in their world. Hearing decline often begins in middle adulthood, but it is usually not much of an impediment until late adulthood. Hearing aids can diminish the problem of hearing for many older adults. Decline in taste and smell may occur, although the decline is barely noticeable in healthy older adults. Sensitivity to pain decreases in late adulthood. The diminished efficiency of the circulatory system is a special concern in late adulthood. Both heart rate and blood pressure rise, and the blood carries less oxygen to the brain.

IV. Sexuality
Aging in late adulthood does include some changes in sexual performance, more so for males than for females. Nonetheless, there are no known age limits to sexual activity.

V. Health Problems and Causes of Death in Older Adults
As we age the probability we will have some disease or illness increases. Chronic disorders rarely develop in early adulthood, increase in middle adulthood, and become common in late adulthood. The most common chronic problem is arthritis, followed by hypertension. Nearly three-fourths of older adults die of heart disease, cancer, or cerebrovascular disease (stroke).

VI. Arthritis, Osteoporosis, and Accidents
Arthritis is an inflammation of the joints accompanied by pain, stiffness, and movement problems. This disorder is especially common in late adulthood. Osteoporosis is an aging disorder involving an extensive loss of bone tissue. Osteoporosis is the main reason many older adults walk with a stoop. Women are especially vulnerable to osteoporosis. Accidents are the seventh leading cause of death among older adults. Accidents are usually more debilitating to older adults than to younger adults.

VII. Health Costs and Nursing Homes
Compared to individuals under the age of 65, the elderly spend more days in bed, visit doctors more often, have longer and more frequent stays in the hospital, and consume more medication. Health-care costs for the elderly are escalating. Government programs, such as Medicare and Medicaid, cover approximately two-thirds of the older adult's health-care costs. Although only 5 percent of adults 65 and over reside in nursing homes, 23 percent of adults 85 and over do. Three types of nursing homes are skilled, intermediate or ordinary, and residential. The quality of nursing homes varies enormously. The decision to place an elderly person in a nursing home is often a stressful one. Nursing home costs are escalating and alternatives to nursing homes are being proposed. Simply giving nursing home residents options for control and teaching coping skills can change their behavior and improve their health.

VIII. The Older Adult and Health-Care Providers
The attitudes of both the health-care provider and the older adult patient are important aspects of the older adult's health care. Too often health-care personnel share society's negative view of older adults. Discussion of psychosocial issues with the older patient and encouragement of the older adult's active role in medical care are recommended strategies.

IX. Exercise
While there may be some need for reduction in exercise in late adulthood, the physical benefits of exercise have been demonstrated. Recently, researchers documented a relation between exercise and longevity, but no evidence exists that exercise can extend the human life span.

X. Nutrition and Weight
A common belief is that most older adults have poor nutritional habits and need dietary supplements. Some older adults do have nutritional problems, but the dietary requirements of healthy older adults are similar to middle-aged adults, although adjustments are usually made for energy requirements. Food restriction in animals can increase the animals' life span, but whether this works with humans is not known. In humans, only being extremely overweight is associated with an increased mortality rate. Most nutritional experts recommend a well-balanced, low-fat diet for older adults, but do not recommend an extremely low-calorie diet.

Key Terms

life span 567
life expectancy 567
microbiological theories of aging 571
macrobiological theories of aging 571
chronic disorders 576
arthritis 577
osteoporosis 577

Suggested Readings

Cart, C. S., Metress, E. K., & Metress, S. P. (1988). *Aging, health, and society* (2nd ed.). Boston: Jones & Bartlett.
This is an excellent source of age-related changes in the body.

Kent, B., & Butler, R. (Eds.). (1988). *Human aging research: Concepts and techniques.* New York: Raven.
This book includes a far ranging set of articles on the nature of human aging. A chapter by Meier on skeletal aging provides especially good information about osteoporosis.

Office of Disease Prevention and Health Promotion, United States Public Health Service. (1988). *Disease prevention/health promotion: The facts.* Palo Alto, CA: Bull Publishing.
This is an excellent source of information about the statistical incidence of illness and impairment. Includes information about the health problems of older adults.

Ostrow, A. C. (1984). *Physical activity and the older adult: Psychological Perspectives.* Princeton, NJ: Princeton Book Co.

Ostrow covers a wide range of changes in physical development brought about by aging, and discusses the effects of exercise on these changes.

Woodruff, D. E. (1977). *Can you live to be 100?* New York: Chatham Square Press.
Woodruff describes factors that influence longevity and gives considerable information that allows you to estimate your chances of living to be 100.

CHAPTER 19

Cognitive Development in Late Adulthood

*I*magine that you are a healthy 60-year-old faced with the possibility of early retirement from a position with a large corporation. Your career has been successful and you have received steady increases in pay. However, you have not been given a major promotion in the last ten years. You sense that the company has put you on the shelf and is simply waiting for you to retire so that a younger employee on the way up can fill your position. Further, the company is offering attractive early-retirement options that are beginning to look tempting to you. Indeed, the company recently paid your way (and that of other employees in their late fifties and early sixties) to a retirement seminar at a golf resort. You attended several sessions led by psychologists that focused on the benefits of early retirement. One psychologist commented, "Early retirement will allow you to travel and pursue your own interests while you are young enough to still have your health." The sessions were thought-provoking. What should you do?

On the one hand, you enjoy your work. You know that you are competent at your job and do many good things for the company (although you don't think they are always appreciated). You believe that you are every bit as sharp as the younger employees in your department. Your greater experience has been invaluable on countless occasions when critical decisions had to be made. And, aside from a little arthritis, your health is excellent and you have not missed a day of work in fifteen years. So, why should you retire?

Later in the chapter we discuss the changing worlds of work and retirement in late adulthood. The nature of older adults' mental health problems and treatment is also described. Before we examine these areas of older adults' lives, though, we evaluate the issues in the debate about whether older adults are less intelligent than younger adults.

> *It is always in season for the old to learn.*
>
> *Aeschylus, 524–456* B.C.

Cognitive Functioning in Older Adults

At the age of 70, Dr. John Rock introduced the birth-control pill. At age 89, Arthur Rubinstein gave one of his best performances at New York's Carnegie Hall. From 85 to 90 years of age, Pablo Picasso completed three sets of drawings. And at age 76, Anna Mary Robertson Moses took up painting; as Grandma Moses, she became internationally famous and staged fifteen one-woman shows throughout Europe. Figure 19.1 shows her painting of a New York winter when she was 84 years old. Are these feats rare exceptions?

> Age only matters when one is aging. Now that I have arrived at a great age. I might just as well be twenty.
>
> ~ *Picasso*

(a)

(b)

Figure 19.1 (a) Grandma Moses continued to produce artistic masterpieces in her late adulthood years. (b) At age 84, in 1944, she painted this picture of Hoosick Falls, New York.

(a) "Grandma Moses at her Painting Table," 1948. Photo by Otto Kallir. Copyright © 1982 Grandma Moses Properties Co., New York. (b) Grandma Moses (1860–1961): *Hoosick Falls in the Winter.* Copyright © 1987, Grandma Moses Properties Co., New York, and The Phillips Collection, Washington, DC.

Figure 19.2 *Fluid and crystallized intellectual development across the life span. According to Horn, crystallized intelligence (based on cumulative learning experiences) increases throughout the life span, but fluid intelligence (the ability to perceive and manipulate information) steadily declines from middle adulthood.*

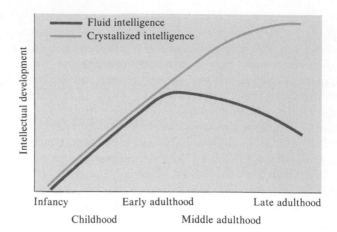

"I was grinding out barnyards and farmhouses and cows in the meadow. And then, suddenly, I figured to hell with it."

Drawing by Stevenson; © 1971 The New Yorker Magazine, Inc.

The Debate about Intellectual Decline in Late Adulthood

The issue of intellectual decline through the adult years is a provocative one. David Wechsler (1972), who developed the Wechsler scales of intelligence, concluded that adulthood is characterized by intellectual decline due to the aging process everyone experiences. But the issue is more complex. For example, John Horn thinks some abilities decline while others do not (Horn & Donaldson, 1980). Horn argues that **crystallized intelligence,** *an individual's accumulated information and verbal skills, increases with age,* while **fluid intelligence,** *one's ability to reason abstractly, steadily declines from middle adulthood* (see figure 19.2).

Paul Baltes and K. Warner Schaie seriously question Horn's claims (Baltes, 1987; Schaie, 1984). They believe many of the data on intelligence and aging, such as Horn's, are flawed because they were collected in a cross-sectional manner. Recall from chapter 1 that in a cross-sectional study, indi-

Late Adulthood

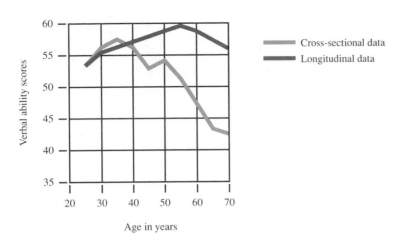

Figure 19.3 Intellectual development in adulthood: A comparison of cross-sectional and longitudinal data. In one investigation involving a test of verbal intelligence, when the cross-sectional strategy was used, test scores decreased in the middle and late adulthood years (Schaie & Strother, 1968). However, when the longitudinal strategy was followed (adults tested over a number of years), intelligence test scores increased until late adulthood, at which point they only slightly decreased.

viduals of different ages are tested at the same time. For example, a cross-sectional study might assess the intelligence of different groups of 40- and 70-year-old individuals in a single evaluation, say in 1986. The average 40-year-old individual and the average 70-year-old individual tested in 1986 were born and reared in different eras, which produced different socioeconomic and educational opportunities. For instance, as the 70-year-old individuals grew up, they had fewer educational opportunities, which probably influenced their scores on intelligence tests; so, if we find differences in intelligence levels of 40- and 70-year-old individuals when we assess them in a cross-sectional manner, the differences may be due to educational opportunities instead of age.

By contrast, a longitudinal study might evaluate the intelligence of the same individuals at age 40 and then again at age 70. Remember from chapter 1 that in a longitudinal study, the same individuals are retested after a period of years. The longitudinal data collected by Schaie (1984) and others do not reveal an intellectual decline in adulthood (see figure 19.3).

In thinking about how to study intelligence in late adulthood, we need to consider what components should be investigated and how they should be measured (Salthouse, 1989, 1991; Sternberg, 1990). Horn, Baltes, and Schaie, for the most part, have studied general intelligence and several of its subfactors, such as fluid and crystallized intelligence, through psychometric testing (standardized intelligence tests). Are we likely to find a decline in intelligence if we focus on important intellectual processes such as speed of processing, memory, and problem solving and observe them in different contexts?

Life-span developmentalist K. Warner Schaie believes there is considerable plasticity in the intelligence of older adults. Schaie and his colleagues have conducted important studies that reveal the role of cohort effects in intelligence.

Speed of Processing, Memory, and Problem Solving

While our speed of processing information seems to slow down in late adulthood, there is considerable individual variation in this ability. And when the slowdown occurs, it is not clear that this affects our lives in any substantial way. For example, in one experiment, the reaction time and typing skills of typists of all ages were studied (Salthouse, 1984). While the reactions of the older typists were usually slower, they actually typed just as fast as the younger typists. Possibly the older typists were faster when they were younger and had slowed down, but the results in another condition lead the researchers to think that something else was involved. When they limited the number of characters that the typists could look ahead, the older typists slowed substantially; the younger typists were affected much less by this restriction. The researchers believe the older typists had learned to look farther ahead, allowing them to type as fast as their younger counterparts.

Shown here is 77-year-old Etta Kallman, who recently returned to New York University to further her education. She is a straight A student.

A substitution of experience for speed may explain how older individuals maintain their skills in many cognitive domains, among them memory and problem solving (Poon, 1985, 1990). Because of this, many researchers now realize that measuring performance in the laboratory may only give a rough estimate of an individual's ability in the real world. If we observed memory and problem solving in the real world, we might discover less decline in late adulthood. Nancy Denney (1986) pointed out that most tests of memory and problem-solving abilities measure how older adults perform abstract or trivial activities, not unlike those found on school exams.

In her research, Denney assessed cognition among older adults by observing how they handled a landlord who would not fix their stove and what they would do if a Social Security check did not arrive on time. Denney revealed that the ability to solve such practical problems actually increased through the forties and fifties as individuals got practical experience. She also found that individuals in their seventies were no worse at this type of practical problem solving than their counterparts in their twenties, who were quite good at solving practical problems.

We have already seen that understanding the nature of cognitive functioning in late adulthood is not so simple as examining general, overall decline in intelligence on a traditional test of intelligence. We found that some aspects of cognitive functioning are more likely to decline (such as speed of processing information) than others (such as problem solving in natural contexts). Other aspects of understanding cognitive functioning in older adults include education, health, work, terminal drop, cognitive skills training, and wisdom, each of which we consider in turn.

Education, Work, and Health

Education, work, and health are three important influences on the cognitive functioning of older adults. They are also three of the most important factors involved in understanding why cohort effects need to be taken into account in studying the cognitive functioning of older adults (Baltes, 1987).

Education

Successive generations in America's twentieth century have been better educated. Not only were today's older adults more likely to go to college when they were young adults than their parents or grandparents, but more older adults are returning to college today to further their education than in past generations. Educational experiences are positively correlated with scores on intelligence tests.

Older adults may seek more education for a number of reasons (Willis, 1985). They may want to better understand the nature of their aging. They may want to learn more about the social and technological changes that have produced dramatic changes in their lives. They may want to discover relevant knowledge and to learn relevant skills to cope with societal and job demands in later life. They may recognize that they need further education to remain competitive and stay in the work force. Earlier in this century, individuals made career choices in adolescence and young adulthood and never wavered from those choices throughout their adult years. Today, that pattern does not always occur. Technological changes have meant that some of the occupations of fifteen years ago no longer exist. And some of today's occupations could not even be identified fifteen years ago. Finally, older adults may seek more education to enhance their self-discovery and the nature of leisure activities that will enable them to make the adjustment to retirement more smoothly.

Successive generations of Americans have been healthier in the twentieth century. Healthy older adults who exercise regularly function better cognitively than their counterparts who are in poor health and do not exercise. Shown here is a 72-year-old former engineer who recognizes the importance of exercise in maintaining physical and cognitive functioning in late adulthood.

Work

Successive generations have also had work experiences that include a stronger emphasis on cognitively oriented labor. Our great-grandfathers and grand-fathers were more likely to be manual laborers than our fathers, who are more likely to be involved in cognitively oriented occupations. As the industrial society continues to be replaced by the information society, younger generations will have more experience in jobs that require considerable cognitive investment. The increased emphasis on information processing in jobs likely enhances an individual's intellectual abilities.

Health

Successive generations have also been healthier in late adulthood as better treatments for a variety of illnesses (such as hypertension) have been developed. Many of these illnesses have a negative impact on intellectual performance. In one investigation, hypertension was related to decreased performance on the WAIS (Wechsler Adult Intelligence Scale) by individuals over the age of 60 (Wilkie & Eisdorfer, 1971). The older the population, the greater the number of persons with health problems will be (Siegler & Costa, 1985). Thus, some of the decline in intellectual performance found for older adults is likely due to health-related factors rather than age per se.

In chapter 18 we found that exercise is related to longevity. Might exercise also help older adults to think more efficiently while they are living longer? In one recent investigation, the relation between vigorous physical exercise and cognitive ability in men and women 55 to 91 years of age was examined (Clarkson-Smith & Hartley, 1989). *Vigorous exercisers* were older adults who engaged in at least 1¼ hours of strenuous exercise per week. *Low exercisers* were older adults who spent less than 10 minutes per week exercising. The older adults who exercised vigorously performed better on tests of reasoning, memory, and reaction time than the older adults who exercised little, if at all. These results occurred regardless of the age, educational level, and health status of the older adults. Other researchers have also begun to confirm that exercise is a very important factor in improving the cognitive functioning of older adults (Stones & Komza, 1989). Of course, prior to beginning an exercise program, older adults should have a thorough physical examination and begin with a level of exercise that is tailored to their physical status.

While the memory of older adults may show some decline, memory activities can be used to improve their memory. The older adults shown here can use the technique of chunking, for example, to improve their memory of such items as telephone numbers, social security numbers, and license plate numbers.

Terminal Drop

Related to the idea that health status is an important factor in the cognitive functioning of older adults is the **terminal drop hypothesis,** *which states that death is preceded by a decrease in cognitive functioning over approximately a five-year-period prior to death.* Thus, distance from death in a subsequently deceased population should be correlated with performance on tests of cognitive functioning if they were administered during the critical five-year-period (Riegel & Riegel, 1972). In investigations that compare older and younger adults, many more of the older adults are likely to be within five years of their death than the younger adults. The chronic diseases these older adults may have are likely to decrease their motivation, alertness, and energy to perform competently when they are given tests of cognitive functioning. Thus, the negative findings for older adults found in some investigations that compare older adults with younger adults may be due in part to age from death rather than simply age from birth. One issue in considering terminal drop is in keeping with our emphasis on assessing a number of aspects of cognitive functioning rather than general intelligence alone. In one recent investigation, the terminal drop hypothesis was supported for tests of vocabulary, but not for numerical facility and perceptual speed (White & Cunningham, 1989).

Training Cognitive Skills

If cognitive skills are atrophying in late adulthood, can they be retrained? An increasing number of developmentalists believe they can be (Denney, 1982; Meyer, Young, & Bartlett, 1989; Perlmutter, 1990; Willis, 1989, 1990; Willis & Schaie, 1990; Yesavage, Lapp, & Sheikh, 1989). For example, in the investigation conducted by life-span developmentalists K. Warner Schaie and Sherry Willis (1986), more than 4,000 adults, most of whom were older adults, were studied. Using individualized training, the researchers improved the spatial orientation and reasoning skills for two-thirds of the adults. Nearly 40 percent of those whose abilities had declined returned to a level they reached fourteen years earlier.

Mnemonics can also be used to improve older adults' cognitive skills. **Mnemonics** *is a term that describes the techniques designed to make memory more efficient.* In the fifth century B.C., the Greek poet Simonides attended a banquet. After he left, the building collapsed, crushing the guests and maiming their bodies beyond recognition. Simonides was able to identify the bodies using a memory technique. He generated vivid images of each individual and pictured where they had sat at the banquet table. The *method of loci,* Simonides' technique, was used in one study to improve the memory of older adults (Kliegl & Baltes, 1987). The method of loci training involved practice with a map of 40 Berlin landmarks. The older adults were also trained to use *chunking*—organizing items into meaningful or manageable units—to improve their memory of Berlin landmarks. Telephone numbers, social security numbers, and license plate numbers are common examples of how chunking can help us and elderly adults remember large amounts of information in our everyday lives. Using the method of loci and chunking, the elderly adults could recall more than 32 of the 40 Berlin landmarks. Later they were able to apply what they had learned in their method of loci and chunking training to recall long lists of digits. One 69-year-old woman correctly recalled 120 digits presented in intervals of eights. Such results suggest substantial memory capacity in healthy, mentally fit older adults. In another recent study, the method of loci was again effective in improving the memory of older adults (Kliegl, Smith, & Baltes, 1990).

In a seven-year-longitudinal study, Sherry Willis and Carolyn Nesselroade (1990) examined the effectiveness of cognitive training on the maintenance of fluid intelligence with advancing age. The older adults were taught strategies for identifying the rule or pattern required in problem solutions. Adults in their seventies and eighties performed at a higher level than they had in their late sixties following the cognitive training, which consisted of the trainer modeling the use of correct strategies in solving tasks, individual practice on training items, feedback about correct solutions of practice problems, and group discussion.

According to Sherry Willis (1990), cognitive training research contributes in three ways to understanding the cognitive mechanisms of old age. First, this research underscores the plasticity in older adults' cognitive performance (Lerner, 1990). Second, findings from cognitive training research contribute to an understanding of the cognitive processes associated with developmental change in old age, especially those involved in age-related decline (Campbell & Charness, 1990). Third, cognitive training research has the potential of contributing relevant information to the development of programs and services for older adults that will improve their ability to live independently and productively.

Wisdom

Wisdom, like good wine, may get better with age. What is this thing we call wisdom? **Wisdom** *is expert knowledge about the practical aspects of life* (Baltes & Smith, in press; Kliegl, Smith, & Baltes, 1989; Baltes & others, in press). This practical knowledge involves exceptional insight into human development and life matters, good judgment, and an understanding of how to cope with difficult life problems. Thus, wisdom, more than standard conceptions of intelligence, focuses on life's pragmatic concerns and human conditions. This practical knowledge system takes many years to acquire, accumulating through intentional, planned experiences and through incidental experiences. Of course, not all older adults solve practical problems in wise ways. In one recent investigation, only 5 percent of adults' responses to life-planning problems were considered wise, and these wise responses were equally distributed across the early, middle, and late adulthood years (Smith & Baltes, in press).

With the ancient is wisdom; and in the lengths of days understanding.

~ Job *12:12*

Older adults may not be as quick with their thoughts as younger adults, but when it comes to wisdom, that may be an entirely different matter. This elderly woman shares the wisdom of her experiences with a classroom of children.

Concept Table 19.1: Cognitive Functioning in Older Adults

Concept	Processes/Related Ideas	Characteristics/Description
The Debate about Intellectual Decline in Late Adulthood	Horn's Position	John Horn thinks that some abilities decline but others do not. He argues that fluid intelligence (one's ability to reason abstractly) declines but that crystallized intelligence (an individual's accumulated information and verbal skills) increases.
	Schaie and Baltes' Position	They argue that longitudinal data reveal little or no decline in intelligence while cross-sectional data do because of cohort effects.
Speed of Processing, Memory, and Problem Solving	Speed of Processing	Speed of processing declines in late adulthood, but strategies can be used to reduce the impact of this decline.
	Memory and Problem Solving	Recent naturalistic research on memory and problem solving suggests that the decline in these cognitive processes may have been exaggerated.
Education, Work, and Health	Education	Successive generations of Americans have been better educated. Education is positively correlated with scores on intelligence tests. Older adults may return to education for a number of reasons.
	Work	Successive generations have had work experiences that include a stronger emphasis on cognitively oriented labor. The increased emphasis on information processing in jobs likely enhances an individual's intellectual abilities.
	Health	Successive generations have been healthier. Poor health is related to decreased performance on intelligence tests in late adulthood. Exercise is related to improved cognitive functioning among older adults.
Terminal Drop	Its Nature	The terminal drop hypothesis states that death is preceded by a decrease in cognitive functioning over approximately a five-year-period prior to death. Probably because of their poor health preceding death, older adults' cognitive functioning has been shown to decline in this period prior to death.
Training Cognitive Skills	Its Nature	We have increasing evidence that the elderly's cognitive skills can be trained through techniques such as mnemonics.
Wisdom	Its Nature	Wisdom, more so than standard conceptions of intelligence, focuses on life's pragmatic concerns and human conditions. Many developmentalists believe that wisdom increases in late adulthood.

• *Critical Thinking* •

Do you agree with the components of wisdom we have outlined? What would you add or subtract from the list?

What does the possibility that older adults are as wise or wiser than younger adults mean in terms of the basic issue of intellectual decline in adulthood? Remember that intelligence comes in different forms. In many instances, older adults are not as intelligent as younger adults when speed of processing is involved, and this probably harms their performance on many traditional school-related tasks and standardized intelligence tests. But when we consider general knowledge and something we call wisdom, that may be an entirely different matter.

At this point we have discussed a number of ideas about cognitive functioning in late adulthood. A summary of these ideas is presented in concept table 19.1. Now we turn our attention to the nature of work and retirement in older adults.

McDonald's created McMasters, a four-week job training program for people over fifty. Katherine Galik (shown here) went through the training and was hired to work part-time at McDonalds. The percentage of older adults who work part-time has increased dramatically in the twentieth century.

Table 19.1: The Increase in Part-Time Work among Older Adults

	1960	1972	1986
Males 65+	30%	38%	48%
Females 65+	43%	49%	61%

Source: U.S. Bureau of Labor Statistics, 1986.

Work and Retirement

What percentage of older adults continue to work? How productive are they? Do older adults go through phases of retirement? Who adjusts best to retirement? What is the changing pattern of retirement in the United States and around the world? These are some of the questions we now examine.

Work

In the 1980s the percentage of men over the age of 65 who continued to work full-time was less than at the beginning of the twentieth century. The decline from 1900 through the 1980s was as much as 70 percent (Douvan, 1983). One important change in older adults' work patterns is the increase in part-time work. For example, of the more than 3 million adults over the age of 65 who worked in 1986, more than half were part-time workers. As indicated in table 19.1, the percentage of older adults who work part-time has steadily increased since 1960.

Some individuals maintain their productivity throughout their lives. These older adults may follow a work agenda that exhausts younger workers, and some older workers demonstrate highly creative skills, at times outperforming their younger counterparts (Landy, 1989). In business and industry, a positive relation between age and productivity favors the older worker. For example, older workers have a 20 percent better attendance record than

At some point in our lives, we face the issue of how to handle retirement in a work-oriented world. Some individuals, such as those shown here, may have looked forward most of their lives to retirement and greatly enjoy its more relaxed freedom. Others may not know what to do with themselves when they retire—their life satisfaction might be improved if they were to continue working.

The night hath not yet come: We are not quite cut off from labor by the failing light; some work remains for us to do and dare.

~ *Henry Wadsworth Longfellow,* Morituri Salutamous, *1875*

Work is what you do so that some time you won't have to do it anymore.

~ *Alfred Polgar*

• *Critical Thinking* •

Issues of work and retirement will affect each of us in the coming decades. Where do you stand on the issue of forced retirement at a specific age, such as 65 or 70? Explain why.

younger workers. Somewhat surprisingly, they also have fewer disabling injuries and their frequency of accidents is lower than for young adults. Recent changes in the federal law that allow individuals over the age of 65 to continue working sounds like a wise and humane decision.

One national survey focused on the characteristics of older workers in the United States (Flanagan, 1981). The individuals ranged in age from 68 to 73. Each of the 500 men and 500 women participated in an extensive four- to five-hour interview about their education, family, employment, and quality of life. Only 4 percent of the men were working full-time, while an additional 12 percent were working part-time. The same percentage of women were working full-time but only 8 percent were working part-time. Most of the men were in jobs that did not require professional training. About 41 percent were in general labor and service-type jobs requiring no special skills. Nearly 14 percent more were in mechanical, technical, or construction trades, while 33 percent were in sales or clerical positions. Only about 12 percent were in jobs requiring college training. However, more women (29 percent) were in occupations requiring college training, with teachers accounting for the bulk of these jobs. Unskilled labor jobs accounted for about 31 percent of the women who worked, while sales and clerical jobs represented 39 percent of women who worked either full- or part-time. The older adults expressed a great deal of pride and life satisfaction in their ability to continue their work into late adulthood.

Retirement in the United States and Other Countries

A retirement option for older workers is a late twentieth century phenomenon in America. Recall from our earlier discussion that a much higher percentage of older Americans worked full-time in the early 1900s than today. The Social Security system, which establishes benefits for older workers when they retire, was implemented in 1935. On the average, today's workers will spend 10 to 15 percent of their lives in retirement.

In 1967, the Age Discrimination Act made it a federal policy to prohibit the firing of employees because of their age before they reach the mandatory retirement age. In 1978, Congress extended the mandatory retirement age from 65 to 70 in business, industry, and the federal government. In 1986, Congress voted to ban mandatory retirement for all but a few occupations, such as police officers, firefighters, and airline pilots, where safety is an issue. Federal law now prohibits employers from firing older workers, who have seniority and higher salaries, just to save money. As mandatory retirement continues to lessen, older workers will face the decision of when to retire rather than be forced into retirement.

Late Adulthood

WORK AND RETIREMENT IN JAPAN, THE UNITED STATES, ENGLAND, AND FRANCE

*A*re a larger percentage of older adults in Japan in the labor force than in the United States and other industrialized countries? What are the attitudes of older Japanese adults toward work and retirement compared to their counterparts in other industrialized countries? To answer these questions, the Japanese Prime Minister's Office (1982) conducted national surveys of adults 60 years and older in four industrialized nations—Japan, the United States, England, and France. A much larger percentage of the men over 60 in Japan were in the labor force (57%) than in the United States (33%), England (13%), and France (8%).

When asked, "What do you think is the best age to retire?" a majority of the older men in England and France said 60 years of age. In sharp contrast, only 14 percent of the older men in Japan and 16 percent of the older men in the United States chose such an early age to retire (see table 19.A). Another question the older men in the four countries were asked was, "Where should an older person's income come from?" In Japan and the United States, the proportion of older men who favored saving while working was at least twice that advising reliance on social security. In contrast, older adult men in France and England favored reliance on social security (see table 19.B).

Sociologists Alex Inkeles and Chikako Usui (1989) believe these cross-cultural data suggest that the marked differences in the rate of employment among those over 60 in Japan and the United States, compared to England and France, are mainly due to attitudes and values about work, and about reliance on oneself (and on relatives in the case of Japan) rather than on the government and its social security system.

Table 19.A   *Preferred Age of Retirement by Men 60 Years and Older in Japan, the United States, England, and France*

	Japan	U.S.	England	France
55 years	1	6	5	20
60 years	14	16	55	54
65 years	34	31	23	15
70+ years	39	22	2	3
Other	8	25	13	4

Source: Data from Japan Prime Minister's Office, 1982.
Note: Numbers represent percentages

Table 19.B   *Attitudes about Where Older People's Income Should Come from in Japan, the United States, England, and France*

	Japan	U.S.	England	France
Save while Working	60	64	42	29
Social Security	24	25	50	67
Family	12	1	0	1
Other	3	10	8	3

Source: Data from Japan Prime Minister's Office, 1982.
Note: Numbers represent percentages

While the United States has extended the retirement age upward, early retirement continues to be followed in large numbers (Stanford & others, 1991). In many European countries—both capitalist and Communist-bloc—officials have experimented with various financial inducements designed to reduce or control unemployment by encouraging the retirement of older workers. West Germany, Sweden, Great Britain, Italy, France, Czechoslovakia, Hungary, and the Soviet Union are among the nations that are moving toward earlier retirement. More information about cultural variations in retirement appears in Cultural Worlds of Development 19.1.

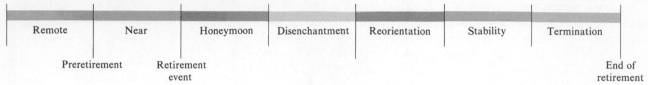

| Remote | Near | Honeymoon | Disenchantment | Reorientation | Stability | Termination |

Preretirement   Retirement   End of
                        event   retirement

Figure 19.4 Seven phases of retirement. Gerontologist Robert Atchley believes individuals experience seven phases of retirement. However, because individuals retire at different ages for different reasons, there is considerable variation in the timing and sequencing of various aspects of retirement.

Phases of Retirement

Gerontologist Robert Atchley (1976) described seven phases of retirement he believes adults go through—remote, near, honeymoon, disenchantment, re-orientation, stability, and termination (see figure 19.4).

Most of us go to work with the vague belief that we will not die on the job but will enjoy the fruits of our labor at some point in the distant future. In the **remote phase,** *most individuals do little in the way of preparing for retirement.* As they age toward possible retirement, they may deny that retirement will ever happen. In the **near phase,** *the worker begins to participate in a preretirement program.* These programs usually help adults decide when and how they should retire by familiarizing them with the benefits and pensions they can expect to receive, or involve discussion of more comprehensive issues, such as physical and mental health. As adults have become more aware of the importance of financial planning, a surge of participation in preretirement planning has occurred in the last decade.

Five phases occur after retirement. In the **honeymoon phase,** *the earliest phase of retirement, many individuals feel euphoric.* They may be able to do all of the things they never had time to do before and they may enjoy leisure activities more. However, adults who are forced to retire, or who retire because they are angry about their job, or because of ill health, are less likely to experience the positive aspects of the honeymoon stage. In the **disenchantment stage,** *older adults recognize that their preretirement fantasies about retirement were unrealistic.* After the honeymoon stage, older adults often fall into a routine. If the routine is satisfying, adjustment to retirement is usually successful. Adults whose life-styles did not entirely revolve around their jobs before retirement are more likely to make the retirement adjustment and develop a satisfying routine than those who did not develop leisure activities during their working years. Even adults who initially experience retirement as a honeymoon often later feel some type of letdown, or in some cases, depression.

In the **reorientation phase,** *retirees take stock, pull themselves together, and develop more realistic life alternatives.* They explore and evaluate the type of life-style that is likely to bring them life satisfaction. In the **stability phase,** *adults have decided upon a set of criteria for evaluating choices in retirement and how they will perform once they have made these choices.* For some adults, this phase follows the honeymoon phase, but for others the transition is slower and more difficult. In the **termination phase,** *the retirement role is replaced by the sick or dependent role because the older adult can no longer function autonomously and be self-sufficient.*

For some adults, the retirement role may lose its significance and relevance. They may go to work again, often accepting a job that is totally unrelated to what they had done prior to retirement. Full-time leisure may become boring to them or they may need money to support themselves.

Because individuals retire at different ages and for different reasons, there is no particular timing or sequencing of the seven stages. Nonetheless, the seven stages help us to think about the different ways we can experience retirement and the adjustments that are involved.

Even for those who do not move, retirement is a moving experience.

~ *Richard Armour*

Those Who Adjust Best to Retirement

Who adjusts best to retirement? Older adults who adjust best to retirement are healthy, have adequate income, are active, are better educated, have an extended social network including both friends and family, and usually were satisfied with their lives before they retired (Palmore & others, 1985). Older adults with inadequate income, poor health, and who must adjust to other stress that occurs at the same time as retirement, such as the death of a spouse, have the most difficult time adjusting to retirement (Stull & Hatch, 1984).

In the last chapter we discussed the importance of options for control and self-determination in the health, and even the longevity, of nursing-home residents. Choice and self-determination are also important factors in successful work and retirement (Herzog, House, & Morgan, 1991). The less choices older adults have regarding their retirement, the less satisfied they are with their lives. Options for control and self-determination are important aspects of the mental health of older adults (Fry, Slivinske, & Fitch, 1989).

The Mental Health of Older Adults

What is the nature of mental health among older adults? What are the most common mental health problems? What are the most effective mental health treatments for older adults?

The Nature of Mental Health in Older Adults

While a substantial portion of the population can now look forward to a longer life, the life may unfortunately be hampered by a mental disability in old age. This prospect is both troubling to the individual and costly to society. Mental disturbance makes an individual increasingly dependent on the help and care of others; the cost of mental health disturbance in older adults is estimated at more than $40 billion per year in the United States. More important than the loss in dollars, though, is the loss of human potential and the suffering (Gatz, 1989; Siegler, 1989; Wetle, 1991).

Mental health not only embraces the absence of mental illness, difficulties, and frustrations but also reflects one's ability to deal with life's issues in effective and satisfying ways. Because older adults are more likely to have some type of physical illness, the interweaving of physical and mental problems is more common in later adulthood than in early adulthood (Birren & Sloane, 1985).

How common is mental disturbance in older adults? At least 10 percent of individuals over 65 have mental health problems severe enough to warrant professional attention (La Rue, Dessonville, & Jarvik, 1985). Two disorders that are especially prevalent among older adults are depression and Alzheimer's disease.

Depression

Major depression *is a mood disorder in which the individual is deeply unhappy, demoralized, self-derogatory, and bored. The individual with major depression does not feel well, loses stamina easily, has a poor appetite, and is listless and unmotivated. Major depression is so widespread it has been called the "common cold" of mental disorders.* Estimates of depression's frequency among older adults vary (Lewinsohn & others, 1991). As many as 80 percent of older adults who show depressive symptoms receive no treatment at all. Major depression may not only envelop the individual in sadness, but may also evoke suicidal tendencies. Nearly 25 percent of individuals who

Retirement comes in many forms. Regardless of its form, individuals can adapt more efficiently to retirement if they familiarize themselves with the benefits and pensions they can expect to receive long before retirement begins. In the last decade, Americans have increased their participation in financial planning for retirement.

HEMINGWAY

◆

*S*uicide was a recurrent theme in Ernest Hemingway's (1899–1961) life. Even before his father's suicide, Hemingway seemed obsessed by the theme of self-destruction. As a young boy, he enjoyed reading Stevenson's "The Suicide Club." At one point in his adult life, Hemingway said he would rather go out in a blaze of light than have his body worn out and old and his illusions shattered.

Hemingway's suicidal thoughts sometimes coincided with his marital crisis. Just before marrying Hadley, Hemingway became apprehensive about his new responsibilities and alarmed her by the mention of suicide. Five years later, during a crisis with Pauline, he calmly told her he would have committed suicide if their love affair had not been resolved happily. Hemingway was strangely comforted by the morbid thoughts of death. When feeling low, he would think about death and ways of dying; the best way he thought, unless he could arrange to die in his sleep, would be to go off an ocean liner at night.

Hemingway committed suicide in his sixties. His suicide raised the question of why a man with good looks, sporting skills, friends, women, wealth, fame, genius, and a Nobel Prize would kill himself. Hemingway developed a combination of physical and mental disturbances. He had neglected his

Hemingway as a healthy, productive adult.

A depressed Hemingway shortly before his suicide.

health for many years, suffering from weight loss, skin disease, alcoholism, diabetes, hypertension, and impotence. His body was in a shambles. He dreaded becoming an invalid and the slow death this would bring. At this point, the severely depressed Hemingway was losing his memory and no

longer could write. One month before his suicide, Hemingway said, "Staying healthy. Working good. Eating and drinking with his friends. Enjoying himself in bed. I haven't any of them." (Meyers, 1985, p. 559)

commit suicide in the United States are older than 65 years of age (Church, Siegel, & Foster, 1988). The four greatest risk factors related to suicide in older adults are living alone, being male, losing a spouse, and experiencing failing health. To read about one famous individual, American author Ernest Hemingway, who experienced major depression and committed suicide, turn to Perspective on Life-Span Development 19.1.

Alzheimer's Disease

Mary's family thought she was having vision problems when at age 65 she could not remember how to do the crossword puzzles she loved so much. Soon her family detected other symptoms pointing to a more serious condition. Mary no longer recognized her husband and even ran away from him in terror several times. She thought he was a stranger who was going to attack her, although he was an extremely kind and gentle man. Mary's family finally took her to a hospital, where she was diagnosed as having **Alzheimer's disease,** *a progressive, irreversible brain disorder characterized by gradual deterioration of memory, reasoning, language, and eventually, physical function.*

Alzheimer's disease was discovered in 1906, and researchers have still not found the causes or cure for it. Approximately 2.5 million individuals over the age of 65 in the United States have Alzheimer's disease. As increasing numbers of individuals live to older ages, it has been predicted that Alzheimer's disease could triple in the next fifty years. Because of the increasing prevalence of Alzheimer's disease, researchers have stepped up their efforts to understand the causes of the disease and to discover more effective ways to treat it (Davidson & Stern, 1991; Jarvik's & Winograd, 1988; Morris & Rubin, 1991).

For roughly one in ten Alzheimer's victims, the disease is clearly inherited. On the average, Alzheimer's will strike 50 percent of the offspring of someone with this hereditary form of the disease. Families with an incidence of Alzheimer's disease are three times as likely to have a case of Down's syndrome, a severe form of mental retardation, in their family as well. Scientists have yet to isolate the gene or genetic combination responsible, but they are getting closer—it is on chromosome twenty-one (Barnes, 1987). The brains of Alzheimer's patients are filled with plaque, formed from pieces of nerve cells and a protein called amyloid. The plaque accumulates at sites of nerve cell connections and chokes off communication between nerve cells (Kosik, 1989). But it is not known whether the plaque causes Alzheimer's or is a secondary effect caused by other factors. Researchers are currently investigating the genes that control amyloid production for possible clues about the cause of Alzheimer's disease (Blass, Ko, & Wishiewski, 1991).

Something also goes wrong with the neurotransmitter acetylcholine in Alzheimer's patients; this chemical is especially important in memory and the motor control of muscles (McDonald & Nemeroff, 1991). It may be that the problems in acetylcholine production are due to a defective gene. One strategy for treating Alzheimer's patients involves the use of drugs to block the pathway that leads to acetylcholine breakdown. In one investigation, a drug by the name of THA improved the memory and coping skills of 16 of 17 Alzheimer's patients by increasing acetylcholine production (Summers, 1986). But most scientists believe that increasing acetylcholine production does not attack the cause of Alzheimer's disease. Eventually, the acetylcholine-producing cells in Alzheimer's patients die and THA only works as long as there is at least some acetylcholine around.

With more knowledge about the genetic basis of Alzheimer's disease, though, scientists are optimistic that the cause of Alzheimer's disease will be discovered and the expression of the disorder curtailed. Even if the gene defect is discovered, it is clear that more than just a gene defect is involved. Some trigger must set off the disease. What that trigger (or triggers) might be is still not known, although Alzheimer's disease is associated with diet, smoking, stress, head injury, and thyroid problems.

Written reminders help this Alzheimer's victim lead a relatively normal life. In the early phases of Alzheimer's disease, older adults can often remember how to do something if they are reminded to do it. In the later phases of the disease, they may lose the ability to perform even simple tasks.

Whether or not special living conditions can improve the motor skills of Alzheimer's patients is being studied, too. Color codes and bright lights may help the daily functioning of the Alzheimer's patient. Dance and exercise may improve motor abilities. The family's role as a support system for Alzheimer's patients is also being evaluated. Psychologists believe the family can help improve the mental outlook of the Alzheimer's patient (Biegel, Sales, & Schulz, 1991; Kinney & Ogrocki, 1991).

Fear of Victimization and Crime

Some of the physical decline and limitations that characterize development in late adulthood contribute to a sense of vulnerability and fear among older adults. The fear of crime may become a deterrent to travel, attendance at social events, and the pursuit of an active life-style among some elderly adults. Almost one-fourth of older adults say they have a basic fear of being the victim of a crime. However, in reality, possibly because of the precautions they take, older adults are less likely than younger adults to be the victim of a crime. However, the crimes committed against the elderly are likely to be serious offenses, such as armed robbery. The elderly are also victims of nonviolent crimes such as fraud, vandalism, purse snatching, and harassment. Estimates of the incidence of crimes against the elderly may be low because older adults fear retribution from criminals or believe the criminal justice system cannot help them (Church, Siegel, & Foster, 1988; Fevitz & Gurnack, 1991).

Meeting the Mental Health Needs of Older Adults

Older adults receive disproportionately few mental health services. One estimate is that only 2.7 percent of all clinical services provided by psychologists go to older adults, although individuals aged 65 and over make up more than 11 percent of the population. The proportion of community mental health services rendered to older adults has remained relatively stable—at or about 4 percent in the 1970s and 1980s (Lebowitz, 1987; VandenBos, Stapp, & Kilburg, 1981).

Psychotherapy can be expensive. Although reduced fees and sometimes no fee can be arranged in public hospitals for older adults from low income backgrounds, many older adults who need psychotherapy do not get it. It has been said that psychotherapists like to work with young, attractive, verbal, intelligent, and successful clients (called YAVISes) rather than those who are quiet, ugly, old, institutionalized, and different (called QUOIDs). While mental health professionals have become increasingly sensitive to such problems, surveys indicate that 70 percent of psychotherapists report never seeing older clients (VandenBos, Stapp, & Kilburg, 1981). Psychotherapists have been accused of failing to see older adults because they perceive that older adults have a poor prognosis for therapy success, they do not feel they have adequate training to treat older adults, who may have special problems requiring special treatment, and they may have stereotypes that label older adults as low status and unworthy recipients of treatment.

There are many different types of mental health treatment available to older adults. Some common mechanisms of change that improve the mental health of older adults are (Gatz, 1989; Gatz & others, 1985; Tobin, 1991; Waters & Goodman, 1990): (1) fostering a sense of control, self-efficacy, and hope; (2) establishing a relationship with a helper; (3) providing or elucidating a sense of meaning; and (4) promoting educative activities and the development of skills.

How can we better meet the mental health needs of the elderly? First, psychologists must be encouraged to include more older adults in their client lists, and the elderly must be convinced that they can benefit from therapy.

Late Adulthood

Concept Table 19.2: Work and Retirement, and the Mental Health of Older Adults

Concept	Processes/Related Ideas	Characteristics/Description
Work and Retirement	Work	In the 1980s the percentage of men over the age of 65 who continued to work full-time was less than at the beginning of the twentieth century. One important change in older adults' work patterns is the increase in part-time work. Some individuals continue a life of strong productivity throughout late adulthood.
	Retirement in the United States and Other Countries	A retirement option for older workers is a late twentieth century phenomenon in America. The United States has extended the mandatory retirement age upward, and efforts have been made to reduce age discrimination in work-related circumstances. While the United States has moved toward increasing the age for retirement, many European companies have lowered it.
	Phases of Retirement	One theory of retirement emphasizes seven phases: remote, near, honeymoon, disenchantment, reorientation, stability, and termination. Many individuals do not experience the phases in this order, although the phases can help us to think about the different ways we can experience retirement.
	Those Who Adjust Best to Retirement	Individuals who are healthy, have adequate income, are active, are better educated, have an extended social network of friends and family, and usually were satisfied with their lives before they retired adjust best to retirement.
The Mental Health of Older Adults	Its Nature	At least 10 percent of older adults have mental health problems sufficient to need professional help.
	Depression	Depression has been called the "common cold" of mental disorders. However, a majority of older adults with depressive symptoms never receive mental health treatment.
	Alzheimer's Disease	Approximately 2.5 million older adults have this progressive, irreversible brain disorder characterized by gradual deterioration of memory, reasoning, language, and, eventually, physical function. Special attention is being given to Alzheimer's cellular and genetic basis.
	Fear of Victimization and Crime	Some of the physical decline and limitations that characterize development in late adulthood contribute to a sense of vulnerability and fear among older adults. Almost one-fourth of older adults say they have a basic fear of being the victim of a crime.
	Meeting the Mental Health Needs of the Elderly	A number of barriers to mental health treatment in older adults exist; older adults receive disproportionately less mental health treatment. There are many different ways to treat the mental health problems of the elderly.

Second, we must make mental health care affordable: Medicare currently pays lower percentages for mental health care than for physical health care, for example (Roybal, 1988).

At this point we have discussed a number of ideas about the nature of work and retirement, and about the mental health of older adults. A summary of these ideas is presented in concept table 19.2. In the next chapter we continue our discussion of late adulthood as we describe the social development of older adults.

Summary

I. The Debate about Intellectual Decline in Late Adulthood

Horn thinks that some abilities decline but others do not. He argues that fluid intelligence (one's ability to reason abstractly) declines but that crystallized intelligence (an individual's accumulated information and verbal skills) increases. Schaie and Baltes argue that longitudinal data reveal little or no decline in intelligence while cross-sectional data do because of cohort effects.

II. Speed of Information Processing, Memory, and Problem Solving

Speed of processing declines in late adulthood but strategies can be used to reduce the impact of this decline. Recent naturalistic research on memory and problem solving suggests the decline in these cognitive processes may have been exaggerated.

III. Education, Work, and Health

Successive generations of Americans have been better educated. Education is positively correlated with scores on intelligence tests. Older adults return to education for a number of reasons. Successive generations have had work experiences that include a stronger emphasis on cognitively oriented labor. The increased emphasis on information processing in jobs likely enhances an individual's cognitive functioning. Successive generations have also been healthier. Poor health is related to decreased performance on intelligence tests in late adulthood. Exercise is associated with improved cognitive functioning by older adults.

IV. Terminal Drop

The terminal drop hypothesis states that death is preceded by a decrease in cognitive functioning over approximately a five-year-period prior to death. Probably because of their poor health preceding death, older adults' cognitive functioning has been shown to decline in this period prior to death.

V. Training Cognitive Skills and Wisdom

We have increasing evidence that the elderly's cognitive skills can be trained through techniques such as mnemonics. Wisdom, more so than standard conceptions of intelligence, focuses on life's pragmatic concerns and human conditions. Many developmentalists believe wisdom increases in late adulthood.

VI. Work in Late Adulthood

In the 1980s the percentage of men over the age of 65 who continued to work full-time was less than at the beginning of the twentieth century. One important change in older adults' work patterns is the increase in part-time work. Some individuals continue a life of strong productivity throughout late adulthood.

VII. Retirement in the United States and Other Countries

A retirement option for older workers is a late twentieth century phenomenon in America. The United States has extended the mandatory retirement age upward, and efforts have been made to reduce age discrimination in work-related circumstances. While the United States has moved toward increasing the age for retirement, many European countries have lowered it.

VIII. Phases of Retirement and Those Who Adjust Best to Retirement

One theory of retirement emphasizes seven phases: remote, near, honeymoon, disenchantment, reorientation, stability, and termination. Many adults do not experience the phases in this order, although the phases can help us to think about the different ways we can experience retirement. Adults who adjust best to retirement are individuals who are healthy, have adequate income, are active, are better educated, have an extended social network of friends and family, and usually were satisfied with their lives before they retired.

IX. The Nature of Older Adults' Mental Health

At least 10 percent of older adults have mental health problems that need professional help. Depression is called the "common cold" of mental disorders. A majority of depressed older adults do not receive mental health treatment. Approximately 2.5 million older adults have Alzheimer's disease, a progressive, irreversible brain disorder characterized by gradual deterioration of memory, reasoning, language, and, eventually, physical function. Special attention is given to Alzheimer's cellular and genetic basis.

X. Fear of Victimization and Crime, and Meeting the Mental Health Needs of the Elderly

Some of the physical decline and limitations that characterize development in late adulthood contribute to a sense of vulnerability and fear among older adults. Almost one-fourth of older adults say they have a basic fear of being the victim of a crime. A number of barriers to mental health treatment in older adults exist. Older adults receive disproportionately less mental health treatment. There are many different ways to treat the mental health problems of the elderly.

Key Terms

Suggested Readings

Gatz, M. (1989). Clinical psychology and aging. In M. Storandt & G. R. VandenBos (Eds.), *The adult years: Continuity and change.* Washington, DC: American Psychological Association.
A leading researcher in mental health and aging, Gatz spells out how to clinically work with older adults and provides several case studies to illustrate her ideas.

Palmore, E. B., Burchett, B. M., Fillenbaum, G. G., George, L. K., &

Wallman, L. M. (1985). *Retirement: Causes and Consequences.* New York: Springer.
Why we retire and what happens to us after we retire are described.

Poon, L. W., Rubin, D. C., & Wilson, B. C. (Eds.). (1989). *Everyday cognition in adulthood and later life.* New York: Cambridge University Press.
An up-to-date, authoritative treatment of cognitive processes in aging is presented with special

attention to the nature of cognition in the everyday lives of older adults.

Rybash, J. W., Roodin, P. A., & Santrock, J. W. (1991). *Adult development and aging* (2nd ed.). Dubuque, IA: Wm. C. Brown.
This text includes considerable detail about the cognitive changes of older adulthood. Chapters also focus on the nature of work and retirement, and on the mental health of older adults.

CHAPTER 20

Social Development in Late Adulthood

Edna is a 75-year-old woman who has spent more time reflecting on what her life has been like since she entered late adulthood. Recently, she thought to herself:

I think about my life a lot—it is in the back of my mind on many occasions. Thoughts of the past come into my mind when I look at my children and their children. When I walk down the street I think back to when I was a young girl . . . to the enjoyable moments with my friends and my parents. I think about my husband, our wedding . . . the times we struggled but made ends meet. He is gone now, but I have so many good memories of him.

On another occasion, Edna passed by a mirror and looked at herself:

I see all these wrinkles and this little old lady whose body is slumping. I said to myself how old I looked. It made me think of death. It made me think of my past—what I had done wrong, what I had done right.

Several years ago after her husband had died, Edna was hospitalized for two months. She thought to herself:

I feel so unhappy, so depressed. My husband is gone forever. I'm mad. I hate all of this. Why does it have to be this way? I'm mad at myself. When I look myself over, I think, "You could have done things a lot better. Maybe if you had done things differently you wouldn't feel like this."

On yet another occasion, some six months after she left the hospital, Edna's reflections revealed some of the adaptive and constructive outcomes a life review can provide:

I am a lot more optimistic about my life now than I was six months ago. I have six marvelous grandchildren and two great daughters. I decided to get a tape recorder and talk about my positive feelings I had been having lately about my life. I wanted to tell my life story so my grandchildren could listen to it when they grow up. I acted like I was telling the story directly to them. I hope they will listen to it after I am gone.

Late adulthood is a time when we review our lives—later in the chapter we will explore this pervasive characteristic of older adults more fully and describe other aspects of older adults' personality development. Among the other topics we evaluate are the social worlds of older adults; the roles of ethnicity, gender, and culture in aging; and marital, family, and social relationships.

The Social Worlds of Older Adults

Could social experiences partly explain why we age? Do we stereotype old people in the United States? What social policy issues does an aging society raise? How devastating is poverty to the elderly? What are the living arrangements of older adults?

Social Theories of Aging

For too many years, it was believed that the best way to age was to be disengaged. **Disengagement theory** *argues that as older adults slow down they gradually withdraw from society* (Cumming & Henry, 1961). Disengagement is a mutual activity in which the older adult not only disengages from society, but society disengages from the older adult. According to the theory, the older adult develops an increasing self-preoccupation, lessens emotional ties with others, and shows a decreasing interest in society's affairs. Reduction of social interaction and increased self-preoccupation was thought to increase life satisfaction among older adults.

As individuals survey their life history in late adulthood, one common theme for grandparents is the satisfaction derived from their grandchildren. Imagine yourself as an older adult. Expand your imaginative powers and speculate about what your life review might be like if you were engaging in a life review as an older adult. If you already are an older adult, you probably will have engaged in this practice on a number of occasions.

Figure 20.1   Social breakdown syndrome.

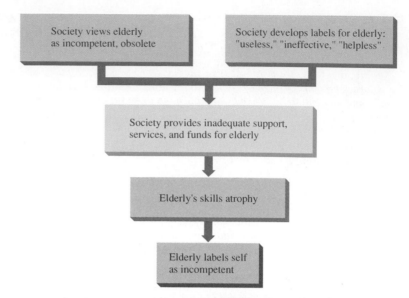

```
┌──────────────────────────┐      ┌──────────────────────────────┐
│  Society views elderly    │      │ Society develops labels for     │
│  as incompetent, obsolete │      │ elderly: "useless,"             │
│                           │      │ "ineffective," "helpless"       │
└──────────────────────────┘      └──────────────────────────────┘
              │                                  │
              └─────────────┬────────────────────┘
                            ▼
              ┌────────────────────────────────┐
              │  Society provides inadequate support,  │
              │  services, and funds for elderly        │
              └────────────────────────────────┘
                            │
                            ▼
              ┌────────────────────────────────┐
              │     Elderly's skills atrophy      │
              └────────────────────────────────┘
                            │
                            ▼
              ┌────────────────────────────────┐
              │      Elderly labels self          │
              │      as incompetent               │
              └────────────────────────────────┘
```

Disengagement theory predicted that low morale would accompany high activity, that disengagement is inevitable, and that disengagement is sought out by the elderly. Disengagement theory was in error. A series of investigations failed to support these contentions (Maddox, 1968; Neugarten, Havighurst, & Tobin, 1968; Reichard, Levson, & Peterson, 1962). When individuals continue to live active, energetic, and productive lives as older adults, their life satisfaction does not go down; sometimes it even goes up.

According to **activity theory,** *the more active and involved older adults are, the less likely they will age and the more likely they will be satisfied with their lives.* Activity theory suggests that individuals should continue their middle adulthood roles through late adulthood; if these roles are taken away from them (such as forced retirement, for example), it is important for them to find substitute roles that keep them active and involved in society's activities.

A third social theory of aging is **social breakdown-reconstruction theory** (Kuypers & Bengston, 1973). *This theory argues that aging is promoted through negative psychological functioning brought about by negative societal views of older adults and inadequate provision of services for them. Social reconstruction can occur by changing society's view of older adults*

Late Adulthood

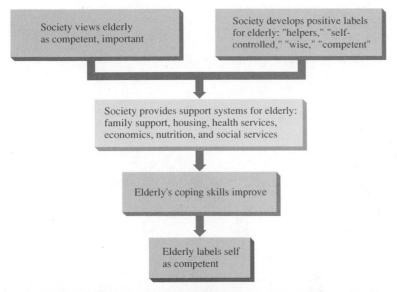

Figure 20.2   Social reconstruction syndrome.

```
┌─────────────────────────┐   ┌─────────────────────────┐
│  Society views elderly  │   │ Society develops positive│
│  as competent, important│   │ labels for elderly:      │
│                         │   │ "helpers," "self-        │
│                         │   │ controlled," "wise,"     │
│                         │   │ "competent"              │
└─────────────────────────┘   └─────────────────────────┘

        ┌───────────────────────────────────────┐
        │ Society provides support systems for   │
        │ elderly: family support, housing,      │
        │ health services, economics, nutrition, │
        │ and social services                    │
        └───────────────────────────────────────┘

              ┌───────────────────────────┐
              │ Elderly's coping skills    │
              │ improve                    │
              └───────────────────────────┘

                    ┌───────────────────┐
                    │ Elderly labels self│
                    │ as competent       │
                    └───────────────────┘
```

and by providing adequate support systems for them. As suggested in figure 20.1, social breakdown begins with negative social views and ends with identifying and labeling oneself as incompetent. Figure 20.2 shows how social reconstruction could reverse social breakdown. Both activity theory and social breakdown-reconstruction theory argue that older adults' capabilities and competence are far greater than society has acknowledged in the past. Encouragement of older adults' active participation in society should increase their life satisfaction and positive feelings about themselves. Perspective on Life-Span Development 20.1 describes a program that provides meaningful activity for older adults.

Stereotyping Older Adults

Ageism *is prejudice against older adults.* Like sexism, it is one of society's uglier words. Many older adults face painful discrimination and may be too polite and too timid to attack it. Older adults may not be hired for new jobs or may be eased out of old ones because they are perceived as too rigid or feebleminded, or because it is cost effective. They may be shunned socially, possibly because they are perceived as senile or boring. At other times, they may be perceived as children and described with adjectives such as "cute"

THREE GENERATIONS OF LOVE

*T*he Foster Grandparent Program in Wayne County, Michigan, serves the needs of two increasing populations—elderly adults who need some meaningful activity and teenage parents who need understanding and guidance in raising their children (Walls, 1987). The Teenage Parent Alternative School Program includes a Child Care Center where, each weekday morning, the blue Foster Grandparent Program van pulls up in front of the school and nine older women step out in their bright red smocks, ready to begin their four-hour day. They play with the infants, feed them, take them for walks, and give them a great deal of warmth and attention.

When the teenage parents are in the room, the foster grandparents talk with them, listen to their problems, and give them support. One foster grandparent commented that several of the teenage girls enjoyed talking about their boyfriends or problems they might be having. She said that this was part of her responsibility—to listen to their problems and hope that she can help them. Most of the teenage girls do not have extended families; the foster grandparent program allows them to see another generation's view of life—a generation with which they would otherwise have little association. In some cases, foster grandmothers take the place of the grandmother the adolescent girl does not have or rarely sees. The grandmothers take great

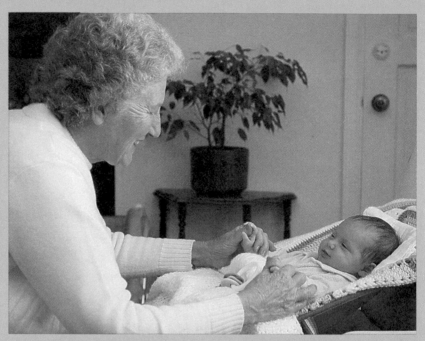

This foster grandmother has gained tremendous satisfaction by volunteering her services. Working with foster grandchildren has given her life renewed energy and reduced her loneliness.

pride in their "grandchildren," giving glowing reports to what "their" grandchild learned to do that day.

The work is important to the older women. Not only are they keeping themselves busy and useful by volunteering, but they also form new friendships and sometimes create new "families." For some of the grandparents, working at the school is their main social outlet. They have little contact

with their families, so the program fills a void in their lives. One foster grandmother said, "I'm reborn! It takes me out of my apartment for four hours. I was a very lonely, lonely person before I joined" (Walls, 1987, p. 4). She recalls with pleasure her return to the school after several days vacation. When she came into the room, three of the children ran to her excitedly and exclaimed, "Grandma's back!"

• Critical Thinking •

Can you think of programs in addition to the foster grandparent program described in Perspective on Life-Span Development 20.1 that improve the active participation of the elderly in society? Describe one or more of these programs.

and "adorable." The elderly may be edged out of their family life by children who see them as sick, ugly, and parasitic. In sum, the elderly may be perceived as incapable of thinking clearly, learning new things, enjoying sex, contributing to the community, and holding responsible jobs—inhumane perceptions to be sure, but often painfully real (Butler, 1987; Chinn, 1991; Gatz, 1989).

The increased number of adults living to an older age has led to active efforts at improving society's image of the elderly, obtaining better living conditions for the elderly, and gaining political clout. The American Association of Retired Persons (AARP), with almost 30 million members, is bigger than

(a)

(b)

most countries. The Gray Panthers, with 80,000 members, pressures Congress on everything from health insurance to housing costs. These groups have developed a formidable gray lobbying effort in state and national politics.

Policy Issues in an Aging Society

The aging society and older persons' status in this society raise policy issues about the well-being of older adults, among them the status of the economy and the viability of the Social Security System, the provision of health care, supports for families who care for elderly adults, and generational inequity, each of which we consider in turn (Neugarten, 1988; Neugarten & Neugarten, 1989).

An important issue involving the economy and aging is the concern that our economy cannot bear the burden of so many older persons, who by reason of their age alone are usually consumers rather than producers. However, not all persons 65 and over are nonworkers and not all persons 18 to 64 are workers. And considerably more individuals in the 55 to 64 age group are in the work force—three out of five men—than a decade ago. Thus, it is incorrect to simply describe older adults as consumers and younger adults as producers. Another concern about the economy and aging is the viability of the Social Security system. Scares in the mid- to late-1980s about the Social Security system going bankrupt have now eased, and the Social Security system is no longer in jeopardy.

An aging society also brings with it various problems involving health care. Escalating health-care costs are currently causing considerable concern. One factor that contributes to the surge in health costs is the increasing number of older adults. Older adults have more illnesses than younger adults, despite the fact that many older adults report their health as good. Older adults see doctors more often, are hospitalized more often, and have longer hospital stays. Approximately one-third of the total health bill of the United States is for the care of adults 65 and over, who comprise only 12 percent of the population. The health-care needs of the elderly are reflected in Medicare, the program that provides health care insurance to adults over 65 under the Social Security system. Of interest is the fact that the United States is the only industrialized nation that provides health insurance specifically for older adults rather than to the population at large, and the only industrialized nation currently without

(a) The Gray Panthers is actively involved in pressuring Congress on everything from health insurance to housing costs. Along with the American Association for Retired Persons, they have developed a formidable gray lobbying effort in state and national politics. (b) Maggie Kuhn, founder of the Gray Panthers.

"I used to be old, too, but it wasn't my cup of tea."

Drawing by Weber; © 1977 The New Yorker Magazine, Inc.

a national health-care system. Older adults themselves still pay about one-third of their total health-care costs. Thus, older adults as well as younger adults, are adversely affected by rising medical costs.

A special concern is that while many of the health problems of the elderly are chronic rather than acute, the medical system is still based on a "cure" rather than a "care" model. Chronic illness is long-term, often life-long, and requires long-term, if not life-term, management. Chronic illness often follows a pattern of an acute period that may require hospitalization, followed by a longer period of remission, and then repetitions of this pattern. The patient's home, rather than the hospital, often becomes the center of managing the patient's chronic illness. In a home-based system, a new type of cooperative relationship between doctors, nurses, patients, family members, and other service providers needs to be developed. Health-care personnel need to be trained and be available to provide home services, sharing authority with the patient and perhaps yielding to it over the long term (Corbin & Strauss, 1988; Quality Health Care, 1988).

Eldercare *is the physical and emotional caretaking of older members of the family, whether that care is day-to-day physical assistance or responsibility for arranging and overseeing such care.* An important issue involving eldercare is how it can best be provided (Barusch, 1991; Cantor, 1991; Hoyert, 1991; Montgomery & Hirshorn, 1991). With so many women in the labor market, who will replace them as caregivers? An added problem is that many caregivers are in their sixties, some of whom are ill themselves. They may find it especially stressful to be responsible for the care of relatives who are in their eighties or nineties.

Some gerontologists advocate that the government should provide financial support to families to help with home services or substitute for the loss of income if a worker reduces outside employment to care for an aging relative (England & others, 1991). Some large corporations are helping workers with parent-caring by providing flexible work schedules and creating more part-time or at-home jobs. Government supports have been slow to develop. One reason for their slow development is that some persons believe such government interventions will weaken the family's responsibility and thus have a negative effect on the well-being of older, as well as younger, adults.

Yet another policy issue involving aging is **generational inequity,** *which states that an aging society is being unfair to its younger members because older adults pile up advantages by receiving an inequitably large allocation of resources* (Bengston, Marti, & Roberts, 1991). Some authors have argued that generational inequity produces intergenerational conflict and divisiveness in the society at large (Longman, 1987). The generational equity issue raises questions about whether the young should be required to pay for the old. One claim is that today's baby boomers, now in their thirties and forties, will receive lower Social Security payments than are presently being payed out, or none at all, when they reach retirement age. However, our earlier comments indicated that this is highly unlikely. The generational equity issue sometimes also takes the form of whether the "advantaged" old population is using up resources that should go to disadvantaged children (Hirshorn, 1991; Sapp, 1991; Welch, 1991). The argument is that older adults are advantaged because they have publicly provided pensions, health care, food stamps, housing subsidies, tax breaks, and other benefits that younger age groups do not have. While the trend of greater services for the elderly has been occurring, the percentage of children living in poverty has been increasing. Distinguished developmentalist Bernice Neugarten (1988) says it is undeniable that the large numbers of poor children is a disgrace to an affluent society like the United States. She stresses that the problem should not be viewed as one of generational equity, but rather as a major shortcoming of our broader economic and social policies. In conclusion, Neugarten envisions that we would do better to

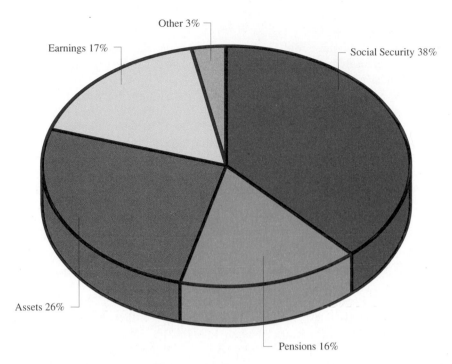

Earnings 17%

Other 3%

Social Security 38%

Assets 26%

Pensions 16%

Figure 20.3   Income sources of Americans aged 65 and older. Social Security is the largest contributor to the income of older Americans, followed by assets, earnings, and pensions. Most of the "other" category consists of a small amount of money received from children or other relatives. Data are for 1986.

think about what a positive spirit of aging would mean to America and to what extent this positive spirit could improve the range of options for people of all ages.

Income

The elderly poor are a special concern (Krause, Jay, & Liang, 1991). In 1988, 3,482,000 individuals aged 65 and over in the United States were classified as poor by the federal government (U.S. Bureau of the Census, 1990). Poverty level is determined by the minimum income required to sustain families of various sizes. For example, in 1988 the federal poverty level for an elderly person living alone was $5,674 and for an elderly couple it was $7,158. The percentage of elderly poor would be greater if the "hidden poor," those who have been taken in by relatives who are not poor, were included. A special concern is the elderly who are widowed and the elderly who are single, showing poverty rates of 40 percent or higher in various parts of the United States (Hurd & Wise, 1989).

Many older adults are understandably concerned about their income. The average income of retired Americans is only about half of what they earned when they were fully employed. While retired individuals need less income for job-related and social activities, adults 65 and over spend a greater proportion of their income for food, utilities, and health care. They spend a smaller proportion for transportation, clothing, pension and life insurance, and entertainment than do adults under the age of 65. As indicated in figure 20.3, Social Security is the largest contributor to the income of older Americans (38%), followed by assets, earnings, and pensions.

The majority of older adults face a life of reduced income. Far too few middle-aged adults adequately plan for this life of reduced income. For instance, middle-aged Americans who will retire in 20 to 25 years will need an income equal to 75 percent of their current annual expenditures (adjusted for inflation) to maintain their current, middle-aged life-style (Taylor, 1988).

Despite the sizable number of elderly adults who still fall below the poverty level, the reduction of poverty among older Americans is one of the few success stories of the federal government's war on poverty. During the 1970s and 1980s, poverty rates declined for both elderly and nonelderly adults (Aiken, 1989).

Social Development in Late Adulthood

Living Arrangements

One stereotype of older adults is that they are often residents in institutions—hospitals, mental hospitals, nursing homes, and so on. However, nearly 95 percent of older adults live in the community. Almost two-thirds of older adults live with family members—spouse, a child, a sibling, for example—while almost one-third live alone (Church, Siegel, & Foster, 1988). The older people become, the greater are their odds for living alone. The majority of older adults living alone are widowed. As with younger adults, living alone as an older adult does not mean being lonely (Kasper, 1988). Elderly adults who can sustain themselves while living alone often have good health and few disabilities, and they may have regular social exchanges with relatives, friends, and neighbors.

For many years researchers who studied the living arrangements of older adults focused on special situations such as nursing homes, public housing, mobile home parks, welfare hotels, or retirement communities. However, less than 10 percent of older adults live in these types of housing arrangements. Nonetheless, the quality of housing for the elderly is far from perfect (Baker & Prince, 1991; Pastalan, 1991). The vast majority of older adults prefer to live independently—either alone or with a spouse—rather than with a child, a relative, or in an institution (Beland, 1987).

While only 5 percent of adults 65 years of age and older live in institutions, the older adults become, the more likely they are to live in an institution. For example, 23 percent of adults 85 years and over live in institutions. The majority of the elderly adults in institutions are widows, many of whom cannot physically navigate their environment, are mentally impaired, or are incontinent (cannot control their excretory functions). Because the population is aging and because wives' life expectations are increasing more rapidly than husbands', we are likely to witness even greater numbers of widows in institutions in the future.

Ethnicity, Gender, and Culture

What are the roles of ethnicity and gender in aging? What are the social aspects of aging in different cultures?

Ethnicity and Gender

Of special concern are the ethnic-minority elderly, especially Black Americans and Hispanic Americans, who are overrepresented in the elderly poor (Atchley, 1989; Hernandez, 1991; Stanford, 1990; Watson, 1990). Consider Harry, a 72-year-old Black American who lives in a rundown hotel in Los Angeles. He suffers from arthritis and uses a walker. He has not been able to work for years and government payments are rarely enough to meet his needs. Nearly one-third of elderly Black Americans live on less than $5,300 per year. Among Black American women living alone the figure is 55 percent. Almost one-fourth of elderly Hispanic Americans are below the poverty line. Only 10 percent of elderly White Americans fall below the poverty line (Bahr, 1989).

Comparative information about Black Americans, Hispanic Americans, and White Americans indicates a possible double jeopardy for elderly ethnic-minority individuals, who face problems related to *both* ageism and racism (Dowd & Bengston, 1978; Kart, 1990; Milligan, 1990; Tran, Wright, & Chatters, 1991). Both the wealth and the health of ethnic-minority elderly decrease more rapidly than for elderly White Americans. Ethnic-minority elderly are more likely to become ill but less likely to receive treatment. They are also more likely to have a history of less education, unemployment, worse housing

• *Critical Thinking* •

Do you have any ideas about how we can intervene to make the lives of low income and ethnic-minority older adults healthier and happier? Describe at least one strategy that could be implemented.

conditions, and shorter life expectancies than their elderly White American counterparts. And many ethnic-minority workers never enjoy the Social Security and Medicare benefits to which their earnings contribute, because they die before reaching the age of eligibility for benefits (Gelfand, 1982; Skinner, 1990; Williams, 1990).

A possible double jeopardy also faces many women—the burden of *both* ageism and sexism (Datan, 1989; Gerlach, 1991; Harrison, 1991; Kite, Deaux, & Miele, 1991; Macdonald, 1989). The poverty rate for elderly females is almost double that of elderly males. According to Congresswoman Mary Rose Oakar, the number one priority for mid-life and older women should be economic security. She predicts that 25 percent of all women working today can expect to be poor in old age (Porcino, 1983). Yet only recently has scientific and political interest in the aging woman developed. For many years, the aging woman was virtually invisible in aging research and in protests involving rights for the elderly. An important research and political agenda for the 1990s is increased interest in the aging and rights of elderly women.

Not only is it important to be concerned about the double jeopardy of ageism and sexism involving older women, but special attention also needs to be devoted to the elderly who are female ethnic-minority individuals. They face what could be described as triple jeopardy—ageism, sexism, and racism (Edmonds, 1990). Income is a special problem for these women. For example, more than one-third of older Black American women have income below the poverty level (compared to less than one-fourth of older Black American men and approximately 13 percent of older White American women). One-fourth of older Hispanic American women have income below the poverty level (compared to 19% of Hispanic American men) (United States Bureau of the Census, 1990). More information about being female, ethnic, and old appears in Cultural Worlds of Development 20.1.

Despite the stress and discrimination elderly ethnic-minority individuals face, many of these older adults have developed coping mechanisms that allow them to survive in the dominant White American world (Markides & Mindel, 1987). Extension of family networks helps elderly minority-group individuals cope with the bare essentials of living, and gives them a sense of being loved. The Black church, as well as the Catholic church in Hispanic communities, provides avenues for meaningful social participation, feelings of power, and

Social Development in Late Adulthood

BEING FEMALE, ETHNIC, AND OLD

*P*art of the unfortunate history of ethnic-minority groups in the United States has been the negative stereotypes against members of their groups (Grambs, 1989). Many have also been hampered by their immigrant origins in that they are not fluent or literate in English, may not be aware of the values and norms involved in American social interaction, and may have life-styles that differ from mainstream America. Often included in these cultural differences is the role of women in the family and in society. Many but not all immigrant ethnic groups traditionally have relegated the woman's role to family maintenance. Many important decisions may be made by a woman's husband or parents, and she is often not expected to seek an independent career or enter the work force except in the case of dire financial need.

Some ethnic-minority groups may define the older woman's role as unimportant, especially if she is unable to contribute financially. However, in some ethnic-minority groups, the older woman's social status improves. For example, older Black American women can express their own needs, and can be given status and power in the community. Despite their positive status in

A special concern is stress faced by Black elderly women, many of whom view religion as a source of strength.

the Black family and the Black culture, Black women over the age of 70 are the poorest population group in the United States. Three of five elderly Black women live alone; most of them are widowed. The low income of elderly Black women translates into less than adequate access to health care.

Substantially lower income for Black American elderly women is related to the kinds of jobs they held, which either were not covered by Social Security, or in the case of domestic service, were not reported even when legally required.

A portrayal of the older Black woman in the city reveals some of her survival strategies. She highly values the family as a system of mutual support and aid, adheres to the American work ethic, and views religion as a source of strength. The use of religion as a way of coping with stress has a long history in the Black culture, with roots in the slave experience. The Black church came to fulfill needs and functions once met by religious-based tribal and community organizations that Blacks brought from Africa (McAdoo, 1979). In one investigation, elderly Black women valued church organizations more than their male counterparts, especially valuing the church's group activities and organizations (Taylor, 1982).

In sum, Black elderly women have faced considerable stress in their lives (Edmonds, 1990). In the face of this stress, they have shown remarkable adaptiveness, resilience, responsibility, and coping skills.

a sense of internal satisfaction. And residential concentrations of ethnic-minority groups give their elderly members a sense of belonging. Nonetheless, the income and health of elderly ethnic-minority individuals are important concerns in our aging society.

Culture

For many generations, the elderly in China and Japan experienced higher status than the elderly in the United States (Ikels, 1989; Palmore, 1975). In Japan, the elderly are more integrated into their families than the elderly in most industrialized countries. More than 75 percent live with their children; few single older adults live alone. Respect for the elderly surfaces in many circumstances: the best seats may be reserved for the elderly, cooking caters to the tastes of the elderly, and individuals bow to the elderly.

An older adult fabric weaver in Kyoto, Japan. As Japan has become more urbanized and Westernized, fewer elderly adults live with their children and more elderly adults return to work. Today, respect for the elderly in Japan is greater than in the United States, but not as strong as the idealized images we sometimes have.

However, the image of elderly Japanese who are spared the heartbreak associated with aging in the United States by the respect and devotion they receive from children, grandchildren, and society is probably idealized and overexaggerated (Tobin, 1987). Americans' images of the elderly in other cultures may be idealized, too—we imagine elderly Eskimos adrift on blocks of ice and 120-year-old Russian yogurt eaters, in addition to the honored elders of Japan. For example, as Japan has become more urbanized and Westernized, fewer elderly live with their children and more elderly adults return to work, usually in a lower-status job, with lower pay, a loss of fringe benefits, and a loss of union membership. The Japanese culture has acted as a powerful brake in slowing the decline in the respect for the elderly—today respect for the elderly is greater in Japan than in the United States, but not as strong as the idealized images we sometimes have (Usui, 1989).

What factors are associated with whether the elderly are accorded a position of high status in a culture? Seven factors are most likely to predict high status for the elderly in a culture (Cogwill, 1974; Sangree, 1989; Sokolovsky, 1983):

1. Older persons have valuable knowledge.
2. Older persons control key family/community resources.
3. Older persons are permitted to engage in useful and valued functions as long as possible.
4. There is role continuity throughout the life span.
5. Age-related role changes involve greater responsibility, authority, and advisory capacity.
6. The extended family is a common family arrangement in the culture, and the older person is integrated into the extended family.
7. The culture is more collectivistic than individualistic.

At this point we have discussed a number of ideas about the social worlds of older adults, and about the roles of ethnicity, gender, and culture in aging. A summary of these ideas is presented in concept table 20.1. Now we turn our attention to the nature of families and social relationships in late adulthood.

Concept Table 20.1: The Social Worlds of Older Adults; and Ethnicity, Gender, and Culture

Concept	Processes/Related Ideas	Characteristics/Description
The Social and Cultural Worlds of Older Adults	Social Theories of Aging	Three prominent theories are disengagement theory, activity theory, and social breakdown-reconstruction theory. No support has been found for disengagement theory. Both activity theory and social breakdown-reconstruction theory argue that older adults' capabilities are far greater than was acknowledged in the past.
	Stereotyping of Older Adults	Ageism is prejudice against older adults. Too many negative stereotypes of older adults still exist.
	Policy Issues in an Aging Society	According to Neugarten, some of the important policy issues in an aging society of the United States are the status of the economy and the viability of the Social Security system, the provision of health care, eldercare, and generational inequity.
	Income	A special concern is the elderly poor. Older adults who are widowed or single have especially high poverty rates, although overall, there are fewer older adults living in poverty today than in earlier decades. Nonetheless, the majority of older adults face a life of reduced income.
	Living Arrangements	A stereotype of older adults is that they often live in institutions, but almost 95 percent live in the community. The majority of older adults living alone are widowed. The older adults become, the more likely they are to live in an institution (23 percent of adults 85 and over, for example). Almost two-thirds of older adults live with family members.
Ethnicity, Gender, and Culture	Ethnicity and Gender	The ethnic-minority elderly face special burdens, having to cope with the possible double jeopardy of ageism and racism. Many older women also face a possible double jeopardy—ageism and racism. Only recently have scientific and political interests focused on the aging woman. Older ethnic-minority women face a possible triple jeopardy—the burdens of ageism, racism, and sexism. Nonetheless, despite the stress and discrimination elderly ethnic-minority persons face, many of these older adults have developed coping mechanisms that allow them to survive in the dominant White American culture.
	Culture	For many generations the elderly in China and Japan have experienced higher status than the elderly in the United States. Today, respect for the elderly in Japan has diminished somewhat, but still remains above that accorded the elderly in the United States. The factors that predict high status for the elderly across cultures include their valuable knowledge, their control of family/community resources, allowing older persons to engage in useful functions, role continuity, age-related role changes that involve greater responsibility, integration in an extended family, and a collectivistic rather than an individualistic cultural orientation.

Families and Social Relationships

What is the nature of marital relationships in older adults? Do older adults date? What is the nature of their friendships and social networks? What is the grandparent's role? These are some of the important questions to ask about the families and social relationships of older adults.

The Aging Couple, Life-Styles, Dating, and Friendship

The time from retirement until death is sometimes referred to as the final stage in the marriage process. Retirement alters a couple's life-style, requiring adaptation (Mann, 1991; Vinick & Ekerdt, 1991). The greatest changes occur in the traditional family, in which the husband works and the wife is a home-maker. The husband may not know what to do with his time, and the wife may feel uneasy having him around the house all of the time. In traditional families, both partners may need to move toward more expressive roles. The husband must adjust from being the good provider to being a helper around the house; the wife must change from being only a good homemaker to being even more loving and understanding. Marital happiness as an older adult is also affected by each partner's ability to deal with personal conflicts, including aging, illness, and eventual death (Condi, 1989; Duvall & Miller, 1985).

Individuals who are married in late adulthood are usually happier than those who are single (Lee, 1978). Marital satisfaction is greater for women than for men, possibly because women place more emphasis on attaining satisfaction through marriage than men do. However, as more women develop careers, this sex difference may not continue.

Not all older adults are married. At least 8 percent of all individuals who reach the age of 65 have never been married. Contrary to the popular stereotype, older adults who have never been married seem to have the least difficulty coping with loneliness in old age. Many of them discovered long ago how to live autonomously and how to become self-reliant (Gubrium, 1975).

Few of us imagine older couples taking an interest in the opposite sex other than for companionship—perhaps being interested in a game of bridge or conversation on the porch, but not much else. In fact, there are a number of older adults who date. The increased health and longevity of older adults has resulted in a much larger pool of active older adults. And the increased divorce rate has added many more older adults to this pool. More about the dating world of older adults is presented in Perspective on Life-Span Development 20.2.

Regardless of their age, individuals also seem to place a high value on time spent with friends, at times higher than time spent with relatives. Life events may influence our friendships. In divorce or death, friendship usually provides an important support system; these events may intensify our friendships. Friendships among the elderly may become especially important in the years to come. Because individuals are having fewer children, families are

So closely interwoven have been our lives, our purposes, and experiences that, separated, we have a feeling of incompleteness—united, such strengths of self-assertion that no ordinary obstacles, differences, or dangers ever appear to us insurmountable.

~ *Elizabeth Cady Stanton,*
Eighty Years and More

The richest love is that which submits to the arbitration of time.

~ *Lawrence Durrell,*
Clea, *1960*

I could be handy, mending a fuse when your lights are gone.
You can knit a sweater by the fireside, Sunday morning go for a ride.
Doing the garden, digging the weeds, who could ask for more?
Will you still need me, will you still feed me, when I'm sixty-four?

~ *John Lennon and Paul McCartney*

OLDER ADULTS' DATING

◆

Kris Bulcroft and Margaret O'Conner-Roden (1986) observed singles' dances for older adults at a senior center. They noticed a sense of anticipation, festive dress, and flirtatious behavior that were not dissimilar from what we perceive in young adults. They subsequently interviewed 45 older adults between the ages of 60 and 92 (average age = 68) who were widowed or divorced and who had been actively dating during the last year. Most of the older adults were from middle-class backgrounds and they were asked questions about how they met, what they did on a date, how important sexuality is in their relationship, and the nature of family and friends' reactions to their dating.

Most of the elderly daters did not approach dating with a casual attitude of "playing the field." They saw dating as distinct from friendship, although companionship was a key ingredient of over-60 dating. One of the main findings was the similarity between how older and younger daters feel when they fall in love—perspiring hands, a feeling of awkwardness, an inability to concentrate, anxiety when away from the loved one, and heart palpitations.

Older adults were just as likely as younger adults to desire romantic displays like candlelight dinners, long walks in the park, and gifts of candy or flowers. In addition to traditional dates of going out for pizza and to dances, older couples also went

Sexuality is an important consideration in the dating relationship of older adults. Sexuality includes intercourse, but stronger emphasis is placed on hugging, kissing, and touching.

camping, enjoyed the opera, and flew to Hawaii for the weekend. The pace of dating seemed to be accelerated in later life. Older adults said they simply did not have time to play the field, favoring a more direct, no-game-playing approach to building a relationship with the opposite sex. Sexuality was an important aspect of the dating relationship for most of the older adults. Sexuality included intercourse, but the stronger emphasis was on hugging, kissing, and touching. This physical closeness helped to fulfill the intimacy needs of the older adults. Recall from our discussion in chapter 15 that passionate love is especially intense among

young adults. For older daters, it is different. They have learned from experience that passionate love cannot be maintained with the same early level of intensity. But since most of them have been in marriages that lasted for decades, most of them know companionate love's value.

Older couples also felt the need to hide the intimate aspects of their dating because they feared social disapproval. As one 63-year-old retiree commented, "Yeah, my girlfriend (age 64) lives just down the hall from me . . when she spends the night she usually brings her cordless phone . . . just in case her daughter calls." Another 61-year-old woman said that her 68-year-old boyfriend had been spending three or four nights a week at her house for the past year, but she has not been able to tell her family, and she hides his shoes when her grandchildren visit. However, most family and friends supported the dating of the older adults, including them in family and social gatherings.

What is the age of love? The star-crossed lovers Romeo and Juliet were adolescents; Anthony and Cleopatra's intense love affair took place in the prime of their health and beauty; Lady Di was barely 20 when she married Prince Charles. But as we have seen, old is never too old for blushing cheeks, sparkling eyes, and affectionate touches (Bulcroft & Bulcroft, 1991).

becoming smaller. As individuals age, they will have fewer individuals to depend on for emotional and financial support. The mobility of our society also increases the distance between older and younger adults. Friendships with unrelated adults may help to replace the warmth, companionship, and nurturance traditionally supplied by families. In sum, friends play an important role in the support systems of older adults (Adams, 1989; Crohan & Antonucci, 1989).

Grandparenting

Think for a moment about your images of grandparents. We generally think of grandparents as old people, but there are many middle-aged grandparents

At some point in our middle or late adulthood years, the majority of us will become grandparents. What are the different meanings attached to the grandparent role? What do you think you will be like as a grandparent? Would you treat your grandchildren any differently than your grandparents treated you?

too. About three of every four adults over the age of 65 has at least one living grandchild, and most grandparents have some regular contact with their grandchildren (Bahr, 1989). About 80 percent of grandparents say they are happy in their relationships with their grandchildren, and a majority of grandparents say that grandparenting is easier than parenthood and enjoy it more than parenthood (Brubaker, 1985). In one investigation, grandfathers were less satisfied with grandparenthood than grandmothers, and middle-aged grandparents (aged 45–60) were more willing to give advice and to assume responsibility for watching and disciplining grandchildren than older grandparents (aged 60 and older) (Thomas, 1986). Also, maternal grandparents often interact more with their grandchildren than paternal grandparents (Bahr, 1989).

What is the meaning of the grandparent role? Three prominent meanings are attached to being a grandparent (Neugarten & Weinstein, 1964). For some older adults, being a grandparent is a source of biological reward and continuity. In such cases, feelings of renewal (youth) or extensions of the self and family into the future emerge. For others, being a grandparent is a source of emotional self-fulfillment, generating feelings of companionship and satisfaction that may have been missing in earlier adult-child relationships. And for yet others, being a grandparent is not as important as it is for some individuals, experienced as a remote role.

The grandparent role may have different functions in different families, in different ethnic groups and cultures, and in different situations. For example, in one investigation of White, Black, and Mexican American grandparents and grandchildren, the Mexican American grandparents saw their grandchildren more frequently, provided more support for the grandchildren and their parents, and had more satisfying relationships with their grandchildren (Bengston, 1985). And, in an investigation of three generations of families in Chicago, grandmothers had closer relationships with their children and grandchildren and gave more personal advice than grandfathers did (Hagestad, 1985).

The diversity of grandparenting was also apparent in an early investigation of how grandparents interacted with their grandchildren (Neugarten & Weinstein, 1964). Three styles were dominant—formal, funseeking, and distant figure. In the formal style, the grandparent performed what was considered to be a proper and prescribed role. These grandparents showed a strong

I am the family face;
Flesh perishes, I live on,
Projecting trait and trace
Through time to times anon,
And leaping from place to place
Over oblivion.

~ Thomas Hardy, 1917

• Critical Thinking •

How do you think the grandparent's role will change in the future? Consider such factors as the increased mobility of our society, the increased number of people growing up in divorced and stepparent families, the increased longevity of our population, and changing gender roles.

interest in their grandchildren, but left parenting to the parents and were careful not to give childrearing advice. In the funseeking style, the grandparent was informal and playful. Grandchildren were a source of leisure activity; mutual satisfaction was emphasized. A substantial portion of grandparents were distant figures. In the distant figure style, the grandparent was benevolent but interaction occurred on an infrequent basis. Grandparents who were over the age of 65 were more likely to display a formal style of interaction; those under 65 were more likely to display a funseeking style.

As more individuals live to an old age and as more families live in varied family structures, we can expect the nature of the grandparent's role and social interaction with grandchildren to change (Cherlin & Furstenberg, 1988; Peterson, 1989). Because of the aging of our society, an increasing number of grandparents are also great-grandparents. At the turn of the century, the three-generation family was common, but now the four-generation family is common. As divorce and remarriage have become more common, a special concern of grandparents is visitation privileges with their grandchildren. In the last ten to fifteen years, most states have passed laws giving grandparents the right to petition a court to legally obtain visitation privileges with their grandchildren. Now, even if a parent objects, grandparents may be permitted to spend time with their grandchildren. Whether such forced visitation rights for grandparents are in the child's best interests is still being debated.

Personality Development in Late Adulthood

Does our personality change when we become old? Do we enter a new stage of personality development? What contributes to our life satisfaction as an older adult? Do our gender roles change when we become old? We consider each of these questions in turn.

The Nature of Personality Development

Psychoanalytic theorists Sigmund Freud and Carl Jung saw old age as similar to childhood. For example, Freud believed that in old age we return to the narcissistic interests of early childhood. Jung said that in old age thought is deeply submerged in the unconscious mind; little contact with reality in old age was possible, he thought. More recently, developmentalists have crafted a view of old age that is more constructive and adaptive (Erikson, Erikson, & Kivnick, 1986).

Erikson's Final Stage: Integrity versus Despair
Erik Erikson (1968) believes that late adulthood is characterized by the last of the eight life cycle stages, *integrity versus despair.* In Erikson's view, the later years of life are a time for looking back at what we have done with our lives. Through many different routes, the older adult may have developed a positive outlook in each of the preceding periods. If so, retrospective glances and reminiscence will reveal a picture of a life well spent, and the older adult will be satisfied (integrity). But if the older adult resolved one or more of the earlier stages in a negative way (being isolated in early adulthood or stagnated in middle adulthood, for example), retrospective glances may reveal doubt, gloom, and despair over the total worth of one's life. Erikson's own words capture the richness of his thought about the crisis of integrity versus despair in older adults:

> *A meaningful old age, then . . . serves the need for that integrated heritage which gives indispensable perspective to the life cycle. Strength here takes the form of that detached yet active concern with life bounded by death, which we call* wisdom *in its many connotations from ripened "wits" to accumulated knowledge, mature judgment, and inclusive understanding. Not that each man can evolve wisdom for himself. For most, a* living tradition *provides the essence of it. But the end of the life cycle also evokes "ultimate concerns" for what change may have to transcend the limitations of his identity. . . .*
>
> *To whatever abyss ultimate concerns may lead individual men, man as a psychosocial creature will face, toward the end of his life, a new edition of the identity crisis which we may state in the words, "I am what survives of me." (1968, pp. 140–41.)*

Robert Peck's Reworking of Erikson's Final Stage
Robert Peck (1968) reworked Erikson's final stage of development, integrity versus despair, by describing three developmental tasks, or issues, that men and women face when they become old. **Differentiation versus role preoccupation** *is Peck's developmental task in which older adults must redefine their worth in terms of something other than work roles.* Peck believes older adults need to pursue a set of valued activities so that time previously spent in an occupation and with children can be filled. **Body transcendence versus body preoccupation** *is Peck's developmental task in which older adults must cope with declining physical well-being.* As older adults age, they may experience a chronic illness and considerable deterioration in their physical capabilities. For men and women whose identity has revolved around their physical well-being, the decrease in health and deterioration of physical capabilities may present a severe threat to their identity and feelings of life satisfaction. However, while most older adults experience illnesses, many enjoy life through human relationships that allow them to go beyond a preoccupation with their aging body. **Ego transcendence versus ego preoccupation** *is Peck's development task in which older adults must recognize that while death is inevitable and probably not too far away, they feel at ease with themselves by realizing that they have contributed to the future through the competent rearing of their children or through their vocation and ideas.*

Life Review
Life review *is a common theme in theories of personality development in late adulthood. Life review involves looking back at one's life experiences, evaluating them, interpreting them, and often reinterpreting them.* Distinguished aging researcher Robert Butler (1975) believes the life review is set in motion by looking forward to death. Sometimes the life review proceeds quietly, at other times it is intense, requiring considerable work to achieve some sense of

In Erikson's final stage, the older adult faces the developmental task of integrity versus despair. In this late adulthood period, the older adult engages in a life review, and the retrospective analysis yields a picture of a life well spent and life satisfaction (integrity) or a picture of doubt, gloom, and unhappiness (despair).

Virtually every older adult engages in a life review process. As the past marches in review, the older adult surveys it, observes it, and reflects on it. You might want to talk with several older adults and ask them to tell you about their lives to get a sense for how older adults review their life histories.

personality integration. The life review may be observed initially in stray and insignificant thoughts about oneself and one's life history. These thoughts may continue to emerge in brief intermittent spurts or become essentially continuous. One 76-year-old man commented, "My life is in the back of my mind. It can't be any other way. Thoughts of the past play on me. Sometimes I play with them, encouraging and savoring them; at other times I dismiss them."

As the past marches in review, the older adult surveys it, observes it, and reflects on it. Reconsideration of previous experiences and their meaning occurs, often with revision or expanded understanding taking place (Haight, 1991). This reorganization of the past may provide a more valid picture for the individual, providing new and significant meaning to one's life. It may also help prepare the individual for death, in the process reducing fear. Remember our description of the 75-year-old woman at the beginning of the chapter, who decided to get a tape recorder and describe her life so her grandchildren would have something to remember her by when she is gone.

As the life review proceeds, the older adult may reveal to a spouse, children, or other close associates, unknown characteristics and experiences that previously had been undisclosed. In return, they may reveal previously unknown or undisclosed truths. Hidden themes of great meaning to the individual may emerge, changing the nature of the older adult's sense of self. Successful aging, though, doesn't mean spending all of one's time thinking about the past. In one study, older adults who were obsessed about the past were less well adjusted than older adults who integrated their past and present (Wong & Watt, 1991).

Life Satisfaction

Life satisfaction *is psychological well-being in general or satisfaction with life as a whole. Life satisfaction is a widely used index of psychological well-being in older adults* (Lawton, 1989). Income, health, an active life-style, and a network of friends and family are associated with older adults' life satisfaction in predictable ways. Older adults with adequate income and good health are more likely to be satisfied with their lives than their counterparts who have little income and poor health (Markides & Martin, 1979). An active life-style is associated with psychological well-being in older adults—older adults who go to church, go to meetings, go on trips, play golf, go to dances, and exercise regularly are more satisfied with their lives than older adults who stay at home and wrap themselves in a cocoon. Older adults who have an extended social network of friends and family are also more satisfied with their lives than older adults who are more socially isolated (Chappell & Badger, 1989; Palmore & others, 1985). Some researchers, though, believe a close attachment to one or more individuals is more important than support networks as a whole (Levitt, 1989; Levitt & others, in press).

Gender Roles

Do our gender roles change when we become older adults? Some developmentalists believe there is decreasing femininity in women and decreasing masculinity in men when they reach the late adulthood years (Gutmann, 1975). The evidence suggests that older men do become more feminine—nurturant, sensitive, and so on—but it appears that older women do not necessarily become more masculine—assertive, dominant, and so on (Turner, 1982). Keep in mind that cohort effects are especially important to consider in areas like gender roles. As sociohistorical changes take place and are assessed more frequently in life-span investigations, what were once perceived to be age effects may turn out to be cohort effects (Szinovacz, 1989).

Concept Table 20.2: Families and Social Relationships, and Personality Development in Late Adulthood

Concept	Processes/Related Ideas	Characteristics/Description
Families and Social Relationships	The Aging Couple, Life-Styles, Dating, and Friendship	The time from retirement until death is sometimes referred to as the final stage in the marriage process. Retirement alters a couple's life-style, requiring adaptation. Married adults in old age are usually happier than single adults, although single adults may adjust easier to loneliness. Dating has become increasingly common in older adults. In some cases it is similar to dating in younger adults, and in other cases it is dissimilar. Regardless of age, friendships are an important dimension of social relationships; they may become more intense in times of loss.
	Grandparenting	About 80 percent of grandparents say they are happy in their relationships with grandchildren. Maternal grandparents interact with grandchildren more than paternal grandparents. The grandparent role has at least three meanings—biological, emotional, and remote; and it has at least three styles of interaction—formal, funseeking, and distant. Grandparents' roles may vary across cultures and ethnic groups, and because of our aging society, an increasing number of grandparents are also great-grandparents. As divorce and remarriage have become more common, a special concern is the visitation rights of grandparents.
Personality Development	Its Nature	Erikson proposed that late adulthood is characterized by the stage of integrity versus despair, a time when older adults look back and evaluate what they have done with their lives. Peck reworked Erikson's final stage. He proposed three developmental tasks older adults face: differentiation versus role preoccupation, body transcendence versus body preoccupation, and ego transcendence versus ego preoccupation. Life review is a common theme in personality theories of late adulthood.
	Life Satisfaction	This refers to psychological well-being in general. Income, health, an active life-style, and a network of family and friends are associated with older adults' life satisfaction in predictable ways.
	Gender Roles	There is stronger evidence that men become more "feminine" (nurturant, sensitive) as older adults than there is that women become more "masculine" (assertive, dominant) as older adults.

At this point, we have discussed a number of ideas about families and social relationships, and about personality development, in late adulthood. A summary of these ideas is presented in concept table 20.2. In the next chapter we turn our attention to another pervasive theme of late adulthood and aging— the nature of death and the dying process.

Summary

I. Social Theories of Aging

Three prominent theories are disengagement theory, activity theory, and social breakdown-reconstruction theory. No support has been found for disengagement theory. Both activity theory and social breakdown-reconstruction theory argue that older adults' capabilities are far greater than was acknowledged in the past.

II. Stereotyping of Older Adults and Policy Issues in an Aging Society

Ageism is prejudice against older adults. Too many negative stereotypes of older adults still exist. Among the important policy issues in the aging society of the United States are the status of the economy and the viability of the Social Security system, the provision of health care, eldercare, and generational inequity.

III. Income and Living Arrangements

A special concern is the elderly poor. Older adults who are widowed or single have especially high poverty rates, although overall there are fewer older adults living in poverty today than in earlier decades. Nonetheless, the majority of older adults face a life of reduced income. A stereotype of older adults is that they often live in institutions, yet almost 95 percent live in the community. The majority of older adults who live alone are widowed. The older adults become, the more likely they are to live in an institution (23% of adults 85 and over, for example). Almost two thirds of older adults live with family members.

IV. Ethnicity and Gender

The ethnic-minority elderly face special burdens, having to cope with the possible double jeopardy of ageism and racism. Many older women also face a possible double jeopardy—ageism and sexism. Only recently have scientific and political interests focused on the aging woman. Older ethnic-minority women face a possible triple jeopardy—the burdens of ageism, racism, and sexism. Nonetheless, despite the stress and discrimination elderly ethnic-minority individuals face, many of these older adults have developed coping mechanisms that allow them to survive in the dominant White American culture.

V. Culture

For many generations the elderly in China and Japan have experienced a higher status than the elderly in the United States. Today, respect for the elderly in Japan has diminished somewhat, but still remains above that accorded older persons in the United States. The factors that predict high status for the elderly across cultures include their valuable knowledge, their control of family/community resources, allowing older persons to engage in useful functions, role continuity, age-related role changes that involve greater responsibility, integration in an extended family, and a collectivistic rather than an individualistic cultural orientation.

VI. The Aging Couple, Life-Styles, Dating, and Friendship

The time from retirement until death is sometimes referred to as the final stage of the marital process. Retirement alters a couple's lifestyle, requiring adaptation. Married couples in old age are usually happier than single adults, although single adults may adjust more easily to loneliness. Dating has become increasingly common in older adults. In some cases it is similar to dating in younger adults, and in other cases it is dissimilar. Regardless of age, friendships are an important dimension of social relationships; they may intensify in times of loss.

VII. Grandparenting

About 80 percent of grandparents say they are happy in their relationships with their grandchildren. Maternal grandparents interact more with grandchildren than do paternal grandparents. The grandparent role has at least three meanings (biological, emotional, and remote) and at least three styles of interaction (formal, funseeking, and distant). Grandparents' roles may vary across cultures and ethnic groups, and because of our aging society, an increasing number of grandparents are also great-grandparents. As divorce and remarriage have become more common, a special concern is the visitation rights of grandparents.

VIII. The Nature of Personality Development in Late Adulthood

Erikson proposed that late adulthood is characterized by the stage of integrity versus despair, a time when older adults look back and evaluate what they have done with their lives. Peck reworked Erikson's final stage. He proposed three developmental tasks older adults face: differentiation versus role preoccupation, body transcendence versus body preoccupation, and ego transcendence versus ego preoccupation. Life review is a common theme in personality theories of late adulthood.

IX. Life Satisfaction and Gender Roles

Life satisfaction is psychological well-being in general. Income, health, an active life-style, and a network of family and friends are associated with older adults' life satisfaction. There is stronger evidence that men become more "feminine" (nurturant, sensitive) as older adults than there is that women become more "masculine" (assertive, dominant) as older adults.

Key Terms

disengagement theory 609
activity theory 610
social breakdown-reconstruction
theory 610
ageism 611

eldercare 614
generational inequity 614
differentiation versus role
preoccupation 625
body transcendence versus body
preoccupation 625

ego transcendence versus ego
preoccupation 625
life review 625
life satisfaction 626

Suggested Readings

Aiken, L. R. (1989). *Later life* (3rd edition). Hillsdale, NJ: Erlbaum.
This book by gerontologist Lewis Aiken includes extensive discussion of social status and roles, living conditions, and victimization of the elderly. An appendix listing agencies, organizations, and programs for the elderly is provided by the author.

Bahr, S. J., & Peterson, E. T. (Eds.). (1989). *Aging and the family.* Lexington, MA: Lexington Books.
This book includes a variety of chapters focused on the aging family, including the topics of older married couples, grandparenting, extended family ties, and the economic well-being of families.

Kertzer, D. I., & Schaie, K. W. (Eds.). (1989). *Age structuring in comparative perspective.* Hillsdale, NJ: Erlbaum.
A number of cross-cultural comparisons of social and psychological aspects of aging are presented. Comparisons include many European countries, China, Japan, and Africa.

The Gerontologist
This journal includes many articles on the social aspects of aging. Find a library that has this journal and leaf through the issues of the last several years to discover researchers' interests in the social aspects of aging.

Whitbourne, S. (1987). Personality development in adulthood and old age. In K. W. Schaie (Ed.), *Annual review of gerontology and geriatrics* (Vol. 7). New York: Springer.
Coverage of personality change in old age is included; the roles of coping, adaptation, and context are emphasized.

S·E·C·T·I·O·N X

DEATH AND DYING

*Y*ears following years steal something
every day:
At last they steal us from ourselves away.

Alexander Pope

CHAPTER 21

Death and Dying

O n December 2, 1982, Barney Clark became the first human to be given a permanent artificial heart. The retired Seattle dentist seemed ideally suited for the new technique. He was dying of a heart disease that did not respond to other treatments, and, at age 65, Barney was considered too old for a conventional transplant. Otherwise he was in good physical condition. Psychologically, Barney also seemed to be a good candidate: He had a strong will to live, an intelligent, thorough understanding of his disease and his options, and a loving, supportive family.

Barney Clark's options—no doubt preferable to death—were not without their drawbacks. Unlike a transplant, the artificial heart would not let him be completely mobile. For the remainder of his life, Barney would be connected to a bulky compressor by two 6-foot hoses. Everyone involved was uncertain what the quality of Barney's life would be like with the artificial heart. Barney chose to have the implantation and the event received an enormous amount of publicity, virtually all of it ecstatic over the new technology. One small item, though, was often overlooked in the publicity surrounding the artificial heart operation. Barney Clark had been given a key that he could use to turn off the compressor if at any time he wanted to cease living. Barney Clark never used the key, however. Fifteen weeks after the history-making operation, he died. Although he never used the key, the fact that he was given such an option raises some important ethical issues about voluntary death (Rachels, 1986).

Giving Barney Clark the key acknowledged that, in his case, suicide was permissible. This is unusual because in our society we rarely have acknowledged the permission to commit suicide. Giving him the key symbolized social acceptance of the act. Would it have been acceptable for Barney Clark to solicit the help of others to end his life? Should he also have been given the right to have his wife or his best friend turn the key for him? These are difficult questions and we explore them further in this chapter. Among other intriguing questions we evaluate are the following: How do we define death? How is death viewed in different cultures? How is death viewed at different points in the life cycle? How do we face our own death? How should we communicate with a dying person? How do we cope with the death of someone else? What are the contexts in which people die? What is the nature of death education?

Defining Death

Is there one point in the process of dying that is *the* point at which death takes place, or is death a more gradual process? Should we painlessly put to death people who are suffering extensively?

Issues in Determining Death

Twenty-five years ago, determining if someone was dead was more simple than it is today (Veatch, 1988). The end of certain biological functions, such as breathing and blood pressure, and the rigidity of the body (rigor mortis) were considered to be clear signs of death. In the past several decades, defining death has become more complex. Consider the circumstance of Philadelphia Flyers hockey star Pelle Lindbergh, who slammed his Porsche into a cement wall on November 10, 1985. The newspaper headline the next day read "Flyers' Goalie Is Declared Brain Dead." In spite of the claim that he was "brain dead," the story reported that Lindbergh was listed in "critical condition" in the intensive care unit of a hospital.

Brain death *is a neurological definition of death, which states that a person is "brain dead" when all electrical activity of the brain has ceased for a specified period of time. A flat EEG (electroencephalogram) recording for a specified period of time is one criterion of brain death.* The higher portions

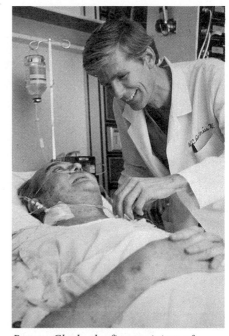

Barney Clark, the first recipient of an artificial heart, is shown with his doctor. What ethical issues were raised by giving Barney Clark a key that he could use to turn off the compressor if at any time he wanted to stop living?

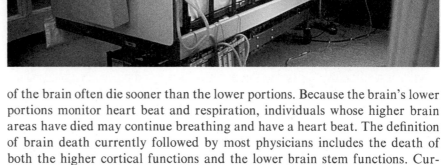

• Critical Thinking •

Considering our discussion of the factors involved in defining death, how would *you* define death?

of the brain often die sooner than the lower portions. Because the brain's lower portions monitor heart beat and respiration, individuals whose higher brain areas have died may continue breathing and have a heart beat. The definition of brain death currently followed by most physicians includes the death of both the higher cortical functions and the lower brain stem functions. Currently 36 states and the District of Columbia have adopted a statute endorsing the cessation of brain function as a standard for determining death.

One of the most famous cases of brain death is that of Karen Ann Quinlin, whose higher cortical functioning stopped because she had taken a potent mixture of alcohol and barbiturates. However, because the lower portion of her brain still functioned, she continued to survive on her own. Because of such cases as Karen Ann Quinlin and hockey star Pelle Lindbergh, some medical experts are debating the possibility that the criteria for death should include only higher cortical functioning. If the cortical death definition were adopted, then physicians could claim a person is dead who has no cortical functioning even though the lower brain stem is functioning. Supporters of the cortical death policy argue that the functions we associate with being human, such as intelligence and personality, are located in the higher cortical part of the brain. They believe that when these functions are lost, the "human being" is no longer alive. To date, the cortical definition of death is not a legal definition of death anywhere in America (Cavanaugh, 1990).

Euthanasia

Euthanasia *is the act of painlessly putting to death persons who are suffering from an incurable disease or severe disability. Sometimes euthanasia is called "mercy killing."* Distinctions are made between two types of euthanasia— active and passive. **Active euthanasia** *occurs when death is induced by a deliberate attempt to end a person's life, such as the injection of a lethal dose of a drug.* **Passive euthanasia** *occurs when a person is allowed to die by withholding an available treatment, such as withdrawing a life-sustaining therapeutic device* (turning off a respirator or a heart-lung machine, for example). Some medical ethicists argue that passive euthanasia is not a form of euthanasia at all, but simply letting nature take its course. Today, active euthanasia is illegal in all countries of the world, except in several specific circumstances in the Netherlands (Levinson, 1987).

Technological advances in life-support devices raise the issue of quality of life. Should individuals be kept alive in undignified and hopeless states? The trend is toward acceptance of passive euthanasia in the case of terminally ill patients. The inflammatory argument that once equated this practice with

Perspective on Life-Span Development 21.1
BABY JANE DOE

◆

On October 11, 1983, an infant known to the public only as "Baby Jane Doe" was born in New York. She suffered from multiple defects including spina bifida (a broken and protruding spine), hydrocephaly (excess fluid on the brain), and microencephaly (an abnormally small brain). A CAT scan indicated that part of her cerebral cortex was missing completely. The parents were told that, without surgery, the infant would die in two years; with surgery, she would have a 50–50 chance of surviving into her twenties, but even then she would be severely mentally retarded, paralyzed, epileptic, and unable to leave her bed, and there would be a continuous risk of such diseases as meningitis. In the face of all these devastating problems, the parents chose not to authorize the surgery.

A lawyer representing a conservative right-to-life group petitioned the New York State Supreme Court to order that the surgery be performed on Baby Jane Doe. However, higher courts in New York quickly overturned the order, calling it "offensive." He then asked the Supreme Court to order the surgery; the Court declined to hear the case.

Then the executive branch of the federal government entered the case. The Department of Justice filed suit, demanding to see hospital records for Baby Jane Doe; the Department argued that she was being discriminated against. However, the suit was dismissed in federal court, with the judge concluding that:

The papers submitted to the court demonstrate conclusively that the decision of the parents to refuse consent to the surgical procedures was a reasonable one based on due consideration of the medical op-

tions available and on a genuine concern for the best interests of the child.

In May, 1984, though, Congress passed *new* "Baby Jane Doe" legislation, requiring states receiving federal child-abuse prevention grants to adopt rules covering "medical neglect." The American Medical Association promised to fight the legislation in court.

The debate over the Baby Jane Doe case focuses primarily on the question of parental autonomy—whether parents have the right to decide if life-saving surgery should be performed on a child who will have an extremely subnormal life—and the question of the value of an infant's life. Again, the point is made that these are questions with no easy answers and questions that involve issues about which each of us may have deeply held convictions (Rachels, 1986).

suicide rarely is heard today. However, experts do not yet entirely agree on the precise boundaries or the exact mechanisms by which treatment decisions should be implemented. Can a comatose patient's life-support systems be disconnected when the patient has left no written instructions to that effect? Does the family of a comatose patient have the right to overrule the attending physician's decision to continue life-support systems? These are searching questions with no simple or universally agreed upon answers. A provocative case involving an infant named "Baby Jane Doe" is presented in Perspective on Life-Span Development 21.1, where issues are raised pertaining to parents' rights and the value of a human life.

Death and Sociohistorical, Cultural Contexts

When, where, and how people die have changed historically in the United States, and attitudes toward death vary across cultures.

Changing Historical Circumstances

We have already described one of the historical changes involving death—the increasing complexity of determining when someone is truly dead. Another historical change in death is in the age group it strikes most often. Two hundred years ago, almost one of every two children died before the age of 10, and one parent died before children grew up. Today, death occurs most often among the elderly. Life expectancy has increased from 47 years for a person born in

(a)

(b)

(c)

Figure 21.1 Rituals associated with death in different cultures. (a) A Chinese burial service in Singapore; (b) family memorial day at the National Cemetery in Seoul, Korea; and (c) the deceased person's belongings are left on a mountainside in Tibet.

1900 to 75 years for someone born today. As our population has aged and become more mobile, more older adults die apart from their families. In the United States today, more than 80 percent of all deaths occur in institutions or hospitals. The care of a dying older person has shifted away from the family and minimized our exposure to death and its painful surroundings.

Death in Different Cultures

The ancient Greeks faced death as they faced life—openly and directly. To live a full life and die with glory was the prevailing goal of the Greeks. Individuals are more conscious of death in times of war, famine, and plague. Whereas Americans are conditioned from early in life to live as though they were immortal, in much of the world this fiction cannot be maintained. Death crowds the streets of Calcutta in daily overdisplay, as it does the scrubby villages of Africa's Sahel. Children live with the ultimate toll of malnutrition and disease, mothers lose as many babies as survive into adulthood, and it is rare that a family remains intact for many years. Even in peasant areas where life is better, and health and maturity may be reasonable expectations, the presence of dying people in the house, the large attendance at funerals, and the daily contact with aging adults prepare the young for death and provide them with guidelines of how to die. By contrast, in the United States, it is not uncommon to reach adulthood without having seen someone die.

Most societies throughout history have had philosophical or religious beliefs about death, and most societies have a ritual that deals with death (see figure 21.1). For example, elderly Eskimos in Greenland who can no longer contribute to their society may walk off alone never to be seen again, or they may be given a departure ceremony at which they are honored, then ritually killed. In some tribes, an old man wants his oldest son or favorite daughter to put a string around his neck and hoist him to his death. This may be performed at the height of a party where there is good food, gaiety, and dancing (Freuchen, 1961).

In most societies, death is not viewed as the end of existence—though the biological body has died, the spiritual body is believed to live on. This religious perspective is favored by Americans as well. However, cultures may differ in their perceptions of death and their reactions to it. In the Gond culture of India, death is believed to be caused by magic and demons. The members of the Gond culture react angrily to death. In the Tanala culture of Madagascar, death is believed to be caused by natural forces. The members of the Tanala culture show a much more peaceful reaction to death than their counterparts in the Gond culture (see figure 21.2). Other cultural variations in attitudes toward death include beliefs about reincarnation, which is an important aspect of the Hindu and Buddhist religions (see figure 21.3).

Perceptions of death vary and reflect diverse values and philosophies. Death may be seen as a punishment for one's sins, an act of atonement, or a judgment of a just God. For some, death means loneliness; for others, death is a quest for happiness. For still others, death represents redemption, a relief from the trials and tribulations of the earthly world. Some embrace death and welcome it; others abhor and fear it. For those who welcome it, death may be seen as the fitting end to a fulfilled life. From this perspective, how we depart from earth is influenced by how we have lived. In the words of Leonardo da Vinci, death should come to an individual after a full life, just as sleep comes after a hard day's work.

In many ways, we are death avoiders and death deniers in the United States. This denial can take many forms:

- The tendency of the funeral industry to gloss over death and fashion lifelike qualities in the dead
- The adoption of euphemistic language for death—for example, exiting, passing on, never say die, and good for life, which implies forever
- The persistent search for a fountain of youth
- The rejection and isolation of the aged, who may remind us of death
- The adoption of the concept of a pleasant and rewarding afterlife, suggesting that we are immortal
- The medical community's emphasis on the prolongation of biological life rather than an emphasis on diminishing human suffering

Even though we are death avoiders and death deniers, ultimately we face death—others' and our own.

Figure 21.2 A death ritual in the Tanala culture of Madagascar, where death is dealt with in a peaceful manner.

• *Critical Thinking* •

How many different rituals for death can you think of that take place in the United States? Describe them, and explain their role in death and life.

(a)

(b)

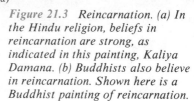

Figure 21.3 Reincarnation. (a) In the Hindu religion, beliefs in reincarnation are strong, as indicated in this painting, Kaliya Damana. (b) Buddhists also believe in reincarnation. Shown here is a Buddhist painting of reincarnation.

A Developmental Perspective on Death

Do the causes of death vary across the human life cycle? Do we have different expectations about death as we develop through the life span? What are our attitudes toward death at different points in our development?

Causes of Death and Expectations About Death

Although we often think of death as occurring in old age, death can occur at any point in the human life cycle. Death can occur during prenatal development through miscarriages or stillborn births. Death can also occur during the birth process or in the first few days after birth, which usually happens because of a birth defect or because infants have not developed adequately to sustain life outside the uterus. An especially tragic form of death in infants is **sudden infant death syndrome (SIDS),** *which is the sudden death of an apparently healthy infant. SIDS occurs most often between 2 and 4 months of age. The immediate cause of SIDS is that the infant stops breathing, but the underlying cause is not yet known.* An infant's death from SIDS is difficult for parents to cope with because the infant appears to have been very healthy until death suddenly arrived. Thus, the death of some persons seems more tragic than that of others. The death of a 90-year-old woman is considered to be natural, since she has lived a long, full life, whereas the death of an infant is considered to be tragic because a life has ended before it has barely begun.

In childhood, death occurs most often because of accidents or illness. Accidental death in childhood can be the consequence of automobile accidents, drowning, poisoning, death in a fire, or a fall from a high place. Major illnesses that cause death in children are heart disease, cancer, and birth defects, and it is not unusual for terminally ill children to distance themselves from their parents as they approach the final phase of their illness (Wass & Stillion, 1988). The distancing may be due to the depression that many dying patients experience or it may be a child's way of protecting parents from the overwhelming grief they will experience at the death. Most dying children know they have a terminal illness. Their developmental level, social support, and coping skills influence how well they cope with knowing they will die.

Compared to childhood, death in adolescence is more likely to occur because of suicide, motor vehicle accidents, and homicide. Many motor vehicle accidents that cause death in adolescence are alcohol-related.

Older adults are more likely to die from chronic diseases, such as heart disease and cancer, whereas younger adults are more likely to die from accidents. Older adults' diseases often incapacitate before they kill, which produces a course of dying that slowly leads to death. Of course, many young and middle-aged adults die of diseases, such as heart disease and cancer too. Younger adults who are dying often feel cheated more than do older adults who are dying (Kalish, 1987). Younger adults are more likely to feel they have not had the opportunity to do what they want to with their lives. Younger adults perceive they are losing what they might achieve; older adults perceive they are losing what they have (Cavanaugh, 1990).

Attitudes Toward Death at Different Points in the Life Span

The ages of children and adults influence the way they experience and think about death. A mature, adultlike conception of death includes an understanding that death is final and irreversible, that death represents the end of life, and that all living things die (Speece & Brent, 1984). Most researchers have found that, as children grow, they develop a more mature approach to death (Wass & Stillion, 1988).

Childhood

Most researchers believe that infants do not have even a rudimentary concept of death. However, as infants develop an attachment to a caregiver, they can experience loss or separation and an accompanying anxiety. However, young children do not perceive time the way adults do. Even brief separations may be experienced as total losses. For most infants, the reappearance of the caregiver provides a continuity of existence and a reduction of anxiety. We know very little about the infant's actual experiences with bereavement, although the loss of a parent, especially if the caregiving is not replaced, can negatively affect the infant's health.

Even children 3 to 5 years of age have little or no idea of what death really means. They may confuse death with sleep or ask in a puzzled way, "Why doesn't it move?" Preschool-aged children rarely get upset by the sight of a dead animal or by being told that a person has died. They believe that the dead can be brought back to life spontaneously by magic or by giving them food or medical treatment (Lonetto, 1980). Young children often believe that only people who want to die, or who are bad or careless, actually die. They also may blame themselves for the death of someone they know well, illogically reasoning that the event may have happened because they disobeyed the person who died.

Sometime in the middle and late childhood years these illogical ways of conceptualizing death give way to more realistic perceptions of death. In one early investigation of children's perception of death, children 3 to 5 years of age denied that death exists, children 6 to 9 years of age believed that death exists but only happens to some people, and children 9 years of age and older recognized death's finality and universality (Nagy, 1948).

Most psychologists believe that honesty is the best strategy in discussing death with children. Treating the concept as unmentionable is thought to be an inappropriate strategy, yet most of us have grown up in a society in which death is rarely discussed. In one investigation, the attitudes of 30,000 young adults toward death were evaluated (Shneidman, 1973). More than 30 percent said they could not recall any discussion of death during their childhood; an equal number said that, although death was discussed, the discussion took place in an uncomfortable atmosphere. Almost one of every two respondents said that the death of a grandparent was their first personal encounter with death.

Adolescence

In adolescence, the prospect of death, like the prospect of aging, is regarded as a notion that is so remote that it does not have much relevance. The subject of death may be avoided, glossed over, kidded about, neutralized, and controlled by a cool, spectatorlike orientation. This perspective is typical of the adolescent's self-conscious thought; however, some adolescents do show a concern for death, both in trying to fathom its meaning and in confronting the prospect of their own demise.

Adolescents develop more abstract conceptions of death than children do. For example, adolescents describe death in terms of darkness, light, transition, or nothingness (Wenestam & Wass, 1987). They also develop religious and philosophical views about the nature of death and whether there is life after death.

Adulthood

There is no evidence that a special orientation toward death develops in early adulthood. An increase in consciousness about death accompanies individuals' awareness that they are aging, which usually intensifies in middle adulthood. In our discussion of middle adulthood, we indicated that mid-life is a time when adults begin to think more about how much time is left in their lives. Researchers have found that middle-aged adults actually fear death more than young adults or older adults (Kalish & Reynolds, 1976). Older adults, though, think about death more and talk about it more in conversations with others than do middle-aged and young adults. They also have more direct experience with death as their friends and relatives become ill and die. Older adults are forced to examine the meanings of life and death more frequently than are younger adults.

In old age, one's own death may take on an appropriateness it lacked in earlier years. Some of the increased thinking and conversing about death, and an increased sense of integrity developed through a positive life review, may help older adults accept death. Older adults are less likely to have unfinished business than are younger adults. They usually do not have children who need to be guided to maturity, their spouses are more likely to be dead, and they are less likely to have work-related projects that require completion. Lacking such anticipations, death may be less emotionally painful to them. Even among older adults, however, attitudes toward death are sometimes as individualized as the people holding them. One 82-year-old woman declared that she had lived her life and was now ready to see it come to an end. Another 82-year-old woman declared that death would be a regrettable interruption of her participation in activities and relationships.

At this point, we have discussed a number of ideas about defining death; death and sociohistorical, cultural contexts; and a developmental perspective on death. A summary of these ideas is presented in concept table 21.1.

Facing One's Own Death

This chapter opened with a quote from Erich Fromm (1955) about people being the only animals who know they must die. Knowledge of death's inevitability permits us to establish priorities and structure our time accordingly.

As we age, these priorities and structurings change in recognition of diminishing future time. Values concerning the most important uses of time also change. For example, when asked how they would spend six remaining months of life, younger adults described such activities as traveling and accomplishing things they previously had not done; older adults described more inner-focused activities—contemplation and meditation, for example (Kalish & Reynolds, 1976).

Most dying individuals want an opportunity to make some decisions regarding their own life and death. Some individuals want to complete unfinished business; they want time to resolve problems and conflicts and to put their affairs in order. Might there be a sequence of stages we go through as we face death?

Kübler-Ross's Stages of Dying

Elisabeth Kübler-Ross (1969) divided the behavior and thinking of dying persons into five stages: denial and isolation, anger, bargaining, depression, and acceptance. **Denial and isolation** *is Kübler-Ross's first stage of dying, in which the person denies that death is really going to take place.* The person may say, "No, it can't be me. It's not possible." This is a common reaction to terminal illness. However, denial is usually only a temporary defense and is eventually replaced with increased acceptance when the person is confronted with such matters as financial considerations, unfinished business, and worry about surviving family members.

Anger *is Kübler-Ross's second stage of dying, in which the dying person recognizes that denial can no longer be maintained. Denial often gives way to anger, resentment, rage, and envy.* The dying person's question is, "Why me?" At this point, the person becomes increasingly difficult to care for as anger may become displaced and projected onto physicians, nurses, family members, and even God. The realization of loss is great, and those who symbolize life, energy, and competent functioning are especially salient targets of the dying person's resentment and jealousy.

Bargaining *is Kübler-Ross's third stage of dying, in which the person develops the hope that death can somehow be postponed or delayed.* Some persons enter into a bargaining or negotiation—often with God—as they try to delay their death. Psychologically, the person is saying, "Yes, me, but . . ." In exchange for a few more days, weeks, or months of life, the person promises to lead a reformed life dedicated to God or to the service of others.

Depression *is Kübler-Ross's fourth stage of dying, in which the dying person comes to accept the certainty of death. At this point, a period of depression or preparatory grief may appear.* The dying person may become silent, refuse visitors, and spend much of the time crying or grieving. This behavior should be perceived as normal in this circumstance and is actually an effort to disconnect the self from all love objects. Attempts to cheer up the dying person at this stage should be discouraged, says Kübler-Ross, because the dying person has a need to contemplate impending death.

Acceptance *is Kübler-Ross's fifth stage of dying, in which the person develops a sense of peace; an acceptance of one's fate; and, in many cases, a desire to be left alone.* This stage may be virtually absent of feelings and physical pain. Kübler-Ross describes this fifth stage as the end of the dying struggle, the final resting stage before death. A summary of Kübler-Ross's dying stages is presented in figure 21.4.

No one has been able to confirm that people go through the stages in the order described by Kübler-Ross. Kübler-Ross herself feels that she has been misread, saying that she never intended the stages to be an invariant sequence

Death and Dying

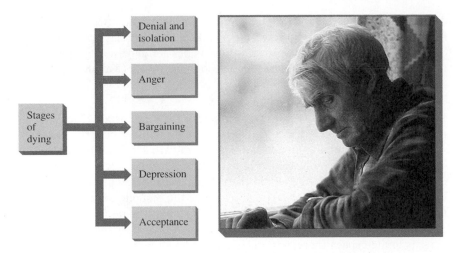

Figure 21.4   Kubler-Ross's stages of dying.

According to Elisabeth Kübler-Ross, we go through five stages of dying: denial and isolation, anger, bargaining, depression, and acceptance. Today's interpretation of Kübler-Ross's stages suggests that adaptation does not require us to go through the stages in the order described by Kübler-Ross.

of steps toward death. Even though Kübler-Ross (1974) recognizes the importance of individual variation in how we face death, she still believes that the optimal way to face death is in the sequence she has proposed.

Some individuals, though, struggle until the end, desperately trying to hang onto their lives. Acceptance of death never comes for them. Some psychologists believe that the harder individuals fight to avoid the inevitable death they face and the more they deny it, the more difficulty they will have in dying peacefully and in a dignified way; other psychologists argue that not confronting death until the end may be adaptive for some individuals (Kalish, 1988; Lifton, 1977; Shneidman, 1973). At any one moment, a number of emotions may wax and wane. Hope, disbelief, bewilderment, anger, and acceptance may come and go as individuals try to make sense of what is happening to them.

Perceived Control and Denial

Perceived control and denial may work together as an adaptive strategy for some older adults who face death. When individuals are led to believe they can influence and control events—such as prolonging their lives—they may become more alert and cheerful. Remember from our discussion in chapter 18 that giving nursing home residents options for control improved their attitudes and increased their longevity (Rodin & Langer, 1977).

Denial also may be a fruitful way for some individuals to approach death. It is not unusual for dying individuals to deny death right up until the time they die. Life without hope represents learned helplessness in its most extreme form. Denial can protect us from the tortuous feeling that we are going to die. Denial may come in different forms (Weisman, 1972). First, we can deny the facts. For example, a woman who has been told by her physician that a scheduled operation is for cancer may believe that the operation is for a benign tumor. Second, we can deny the implications of a disease or life-threatening situation. For example, a man may accept the fact that he has a disease but may deny that it leads to death. Third, we can deny that we will be extinguished even if we die biologically; we can have faith in our spiritual immortality.

Denial can be adaptive or maladaptive. Denial can be used to avoid the destructive impact of shock by delaying the necessity of dealing with one's

Do not go gentle into that good night
Old age should burn and rave at close of day;
Rage, rage against the dying of the light.

~ *Dylan Thomas*

death. Denial can insulate the individual from having to cope with intense feelings of anger and hurt; however, if denial keeps us from having a life-saving operation, it clearly is maladaptive. Denial is neither good nor bad; its adaptive qualities need to be evaluated on an individual basis (Kalish, 1981).

The Contexts in Which People Die

For dying individuals, the context in which they die is important. Most deaths in the United States occur in a hospital; a smaller number occur in other institutions such as nursing homes and board-and-care centers. Hospitals offer several important advantages to the dying individual—professional staff members are readily available and the medical technology present may prolong life, for example, yet a hospital may not be the best place for many people to die. Most individuals say they would rather die at home (Kalish & Reynolds, 1976). Many feel, however, that they will be a burden at home, that there is limited space there, and that dying at home may alter prior relationships such as being cared for by one's children. Individuals who are facing death also worry about the competency and availability of emergency medical treatment if they remain at home.

In addition to hospital and home, a third context for dying that has received increased attention in recent years is the **hospice,** *a humanized institution committed to making the end of life as free from pain, anxiety, and depression as possible. The hospice's goals contrast with those of a hospital, which are to cure illness and prolong life*. The hospice movement began toward the end of the 1960s in London, when a new kind of medical institution, St. Christopher's Hospice, opened. Little effort is made to prolong life at St. Christopher's—there are no heart-lung machines and there is no intensive care unit, for example. A primary goal is to bring pain under control and to help dying patients face death in a psychologically healthy way. The hospice also makes every effort to include the dying individual's family; it is believed that this strategy not only benefits the dying individual but family members as well, probably diminishing their guilt after the death.

The hospice movement has grown rapidly in the United States. In 1987, there were close to 200 hospices (Kitch, 1987). The hospice advocates continue to underscore that it is possible to control pain for almost any dying individual and that it is possible to create an environment for the patient that is superior to that found in most hospitals.

Coping with the Death of Someone Else

Loss can come in many forms in our lives—divorce, a pet's death, loss of a job—but no loss is greater than that which comes through the death of someone we love and care for—a parent, sibling, spouse, relative, or friend. In the ratings of life's stresses that require the most adjustment, death of a spouse is given the highest number. How should we communicate with a dying individual? How do we cope with the death of someone we love?

Communicating with a Dying Person

Most psychologists believe that it is best for dying individuals to know that they are dying and that significant others know they are dying so they can interact and communicate with each other on the basis of this mutual knowledge. What are some of the advantages of this open awareness context for the dying individual? Four such advantages are: dying individuals can close their life in accord with their own ideas about proper dying; dying individuals may be able to complete some plans and projects, can make arrangements for sur-

One must have looked into the greyness of the night that every man passes through and not flinch in order to hold the hands of those who are making the great transition. All of the defenses and denials we ascribe to others may in reality be projections of our own extinction. When one has achieved some composure about his own death, he may finally be able to listen creatively with responses and silences that help others have an appropriate death.

~ *James Peterson, 1980*

vivors, and can participate in decisions about a funeral and burial; dying individuals have the opportunity to reminisce, to converse with others who have been important individuals in their life, and to end life conscious of what life has been like; and dying individuals have more understanding of what is happening within their body and what the medical staff is doing to them (Kalish, 1981).

It may be easier to die when people we love and like can converse freely with us about what is happening to us, even if it involves considerable sadness. Perspective on Life-Span Development 21.2 describes an open communication with a dying 81-year-old woman.

In addition to an open communication system, what are some other suggestions for conversing with a dying individual? Some experts believe that conversation should not focus on mental pathology or preparation for death but should focus on strengths of the individual and preparation for the remainder of life. Since external accomplishments are not possible, communication should be directed more at internal growth. Keep in mind also that caring does not have to come from a mental health professional only; a concerned nurse, an attentive physician, a sensitive spouse, or an intimate friend can provide an important support system for a dying individual.

Stages and Dimensions of Grief

Grief *is the emotional numbness, disbelief, separation anxiety, despair, sadness, and loneliness that accompany the loss of someone we love.* One view indicates that we go through three stages of grief after we lose someone we

• *Critical Thinking* •

Consider your close relationships with the people in your life. How would you communicate with them if they were dying? Would their developmental status affect how you talked to them? If so, how?

Grief is the emotional numbness, disbelief, separation anxiety, despair, sadness, and loneliness that accompany the loss of someone we love. While the sense of separation anxiety and loss may continue to the end of one's life, most of us emerge from grief's tears, turning our attention once again to productive tasks and gaining a more positive view of life.

It is sweet to mingle tears with tears; griefs; where they wound in solitude, wound more deeply.

~ *Senaca*

love: shock, despair, and recovery (Averill, 1968). Another perspective indicates that we go through four stages: numbness, pining, depression, and recovery (Parkes, 1972).

In the first view of grief, at stage one the survivor feels shock, disbelief, and numbness, often weeping or becoming easily agitated. This stage occurs just after death and usually lasts for 1 to 3 days. It is like the denial and anger stages Kübler-Ross proposed for the dying individual. At stage two, there is painful longing for the dead, memories and visual images of the deceased, sadness, insomnia, irritability, and restlessness. Beginning not long after the death, this stage often peaks in the second to fourth weeks following the death and may subside after several months, although it can persist for one to two years. Elements of bargaining for the return of the deceased person may appear, again corresponding to one of Kübler-Ross's stages. Stage three usually appears within a year after the death. Analogous to Kübler-Ross's acceptance stage, this grief resolution stage is marked by a resumption of ordinary activities, a greater probability of recalling pleasant memories about the deceased, and the establishment of new relationships with others.

However, just as we found that Kübler-Ross's stages of dying are not invariant and that individuals do not have to go through them in the order she suggested to adapt effectively, the same can be said for grief's stages (Campbell, Swank, & Vincent, 1991; Klass, 1988). Rather than talking about grief's stages, perhaps it is more accurate to talk about grief's dimensions. One description emphasized that grief is not a simple, decrescendoing emotional state but, rather, a complex, evolving process with multiple dimensions (Jacobs & others, 1987). In this view, pining for the lost person is one important dimension. Pining or yearning reflects an intermittent, recurrent wish or need to recover the lost person. Another important dimension of grief is separation anxiety, which includes not only pining and preoccupation with thoughts of the deceased person but also focuses on places and things associated with the deceased, as well as crying or sighing as a type of suppressed cry. Another dimension of grief is the typical immediate reaction to a loss discussed earlier—emotional blunting, numbness, disbelief, and outbursts of panic or extreme tearfulness. Yet another dimension of grief involves despair and sadness, which include a sense of hopelessness and defeat, depressive symptoms, apathy, loss of meaning for activities that used to involve the person who is gone, and growing desolation. This dimension does not represent a clear-cut stage but, rather, occurs repeatedly in one context or another shortly after a loss. Nonetheless, as time passes, pining and protest over the loss tend to diminish, although episodes of depression and apathy may remain or increase. Although the sense of separation anxiety and loss may continue to the end of one's life, most of us emerge from grief's tears, turning our attention once again to productive tasks and regaining a more positive view of life (Rando, 1988).

Making Sense of the World

One beneficial aspect of grieving is that it stimulates many individuals to try to make sense of their world. A common occurrence is to go over again and again all of the events that led up to the death. In the days and weeks after the death, the closest family members share experiences with each other, sometimes reminiscing over family experiences (Kalish, 1981).

Each individual may offer a piece of death's puzzle. "When I saw him last Saturday, he looked as though he were rallying," says one family member. "Do you think it might have had something to do with his sister's illness?" remarks another. "I doubt it, but I heard from an aide that he fell going to the bathroom that morning," comments yet another. "That explains the bruise on his elbow," says the first individual. "No wonder he told me that he was angry because he could not seem to do anything right," chimes in a fourth family member. So it goes in the attempt to understand why someone who was rallying on Saturday was dead on Wednesday.

When a death is caused by an accident or a disaster, the effort to make sense of it is pursued more vigorously. As added pieces of news come trickling in, they are integrated into the puzzle. The bereaved want to put the death into a perspective that they can understand—divine intervention, a curse from a neighboring tribe, a logical sequence of cause and effect, or whatever it may be.

In some instances, when famous individuals die, solving the puzzle of the death may become a national obsession and can drag on for years. Such was the case in the assassination of President John F. Kennedy. Some individuals are still trying to make sense of the event. That the death was the act of one unstable man working alone strikes many individuals as improbable. "How can such an absurd set of circumstances destroy such a powerful man?" ask some individuals.

Eventually, each of us finds an adequate "story" of the dying and death— of John F. Kennedy, of our father, or of our friend. Versions of the death may differ—whether their doctors did all they could to save the patient, whether Aunt Bertha showed up frequently at the hospital or not, whether the operation succeeded or not, whether the individual was ready to die or not. Each individual develops a satisfactory version, and, with slight modifications, it becomes the official version for the teller.

Widowhood

Usually the most difficult loss is the death of a spouse. There are more than 12 million widowed people in the United States; widows outnumber widowers above five-fold. The death of a spouse is usually unpreventable, may involve the shattering of a long-term bond, may require the pursuit of new roles and statuses, may lead to financial hardship, and may leave the survivor without a major support system. Thus, it is not surprising that a spouse's death is associated with depression, increases in physician consultations, hospitalization, increase in health-compromising behaviors such as smoking and drinking, and mortality rates above the expected norm (Zisook, Schuchter, & Lyons, 1987).

Widowhood may be experienced differently depending on sociohistorical circumstances. Modernization of societies has resulted in many widows living independently, free from the control of the patriarchal family and able to maintain themselves economically through paid employment or the Social Security System, in the United States. Although there are isolated widows— unable to reengage in social relations and social roles after a past tie is broken through death—many widows have support systems and eventually reimmerse themselves in their families, their neighborhood, friendship networks, or occupations and organizations. Social support for caregivers of dying individuals helps them adjust to the death (Bass, Bowman, & Noelker, 1991; LaGrand, 1991; Sankar, 1991; Worden, 1991).

Keep in mind that widowhood may be experienced in many different ways (Lopata, 1987; O'Bryant, 1991). Some widows are passive, accepting changes produced by the death of a husband. Others acquire personal abilities and may even bloom in widowhood. Some stay in pockets of high tradition, surrounded by, but almost oblivious to, changes around them. Others eagerly seek new resources and social roles. Sometimes the initiative to cope with widowhood comes from within; at other times it comes from support systems.

(a)   (b)

Figure 21.5 Cultural comparisons
of the rituals surrounding death. (a)
A New Orleans street funeral, a
ritual that includes a march through
the streets with music and dancing.
(b) The cremation of this 98-year-
old woman in Bali, Indonesia, is a
festive occasion. Strangers and
townspeople alike are invited to
share a feast with music and
dancing.

Forms of Mourning and the Funeral

Suttee *is the now-outlawed Hindu practice of burning to death a dead man's widow to increase his family's prestige and firmly establish an image of her in his memory.* In some cultures, a ceremonial meal is held. In others, a black armband is worn for one year following a death (see figure 21.5). From these examples, it is obvious that cultures vary in how they practice mourning.

The funeral is an important aspect of mourning in many cultures. One consideration involves what to do with the body. In the United States, most bodies are placed in caskets under the earth or in mausoleums. About 9 percent are cremated. Most individuals who are cremated have their ashes spread in the crematorium's garden; others wish their ashes to be taken to specific locations. A viewing of the body occurs after about 75 percent of the deaths in the United States.

The funeral industry has been the source of controversy in recent years (Fulton, 1988). Funeral directors and their supporters argue that the funeral provides a form of closure to the relationship with the deceased, especially when there is an open casket. Their dissenters, however, stress that funeral directors are just trying to make money; they further argue that the art of embalming is grotesque.

One way to avoid the exploitation that may occur because bereavement may make us vulnerable to more expensive funeral arrangements is to purchase them in advance. However, most of us do not follow this procedure. In one survey, only 24 percent of individuals 60 and over had made any funeral arrangements (Kalish & Reynolds, 1976).

Some cultures have elaborate mourning systems. To learn about two cultures with extensive mourning systems, turn to Cultural Worlds of Development 21.1.

Death Education

The art of living well and the art
of dying well are one.

~ *Epicurus, 3rd Century* B.C.

Thanatologists, *persons who study death and dying,* believe that death education provides a positive preparation for both dying and living. Many of them stress that confronting one's own mortality and that of others is important for developing the mature perspective necessary for making decisions about crucial life and death events (Durlak & Riesenberg, 1991; Wass, Berardo, & Neimeyer, 1988). Some thanatologists also argue that, although our society has developed greater permissiveness toward the open discussion of formerly taboo topics, we may have merely developed a more sophisticated level of denial (Morgan, 1988). The avoidance of discussing death and dying that characterized the American culture two decades ago still appears in too many instances today.

Death and Dying

THE FAMILY AND THE COMMUNITY IN MOURNING—
THE AMISH AND TRADITIONAL JUDAISM

*T*he family and the community have important roles in mourning in some cultures. Two of those cultures are the Amish and traditional Judaism (Worthington, 1989).

The Amish are a conservative group with approximately 80,000 members in the United States, Ontario, and several small settlements in South and Central America. The Amish live in a family-oriented society in which family and community support are essential for survival. Today, they live at the same unhurried pace as that of their ancestors, using horses instead of cars and facing death with the same steadfast faith as their forebears. At the time of death, close neighbors assume the responsibility of notifying others of the death. The Amish community handles virtually all aspects of the funeral. Family members dress the body in white garments—the wearing of white clothes signifies the high ceremonial emphasis on death as the final rite of passage to a new and better life (Bryer, 1979). The funeral service is held in a barn on warmer months and in a house during colder months. Calm acceptance of death, influenced by a deep religious faith, is an integral part of the Amish culture. Following the funeral, a high level of support is given to the bereaved family for at least a year. Visits to the family, special scrapbooks

An Amish funeral procession in Pennsylvania. The funeral service is held in the barn in the warmer months and in the house during the colder months. Following the funeral, a high level of support is given to the bereaved family for at least a year.

and handmade items for the family, new work projects started for the widow, and quilting days that combine fellowship and productivity are among the supports given to the bereaved family.

The family and community also have specific and important roles in mourning in traditional Judaism. The program of mourning is divided into graduated time periods, each with its appropriate practices (Gerson, 1977). The observance of these practices is required of the spouse and the immediate blood relatives of the deceased.

The first period is *aninut,* the period between death and burial. The next two periods make up *avelut,* or mourning proper. The first of these is *shivah,* a period of seven days, which commences with the burial. This is followed by *sheloshim,* the thirty-day period following the burial, including shivah. At the end of sheloshim, the mourning process is considered over for all but one's parents. In this case, mourning continues for eleven months, although observances are minimal. The seven-day period of the shivah is especially important in mourning in traditional Judaism. The Jewish community provides considerable support during the mourning process (Kidorf, 1966). The mourners, sitting together as a group through an extended period, have an opportunity to project their feelings to the group as a whole. Visits from others during shivah may help the mourner deal with feelings of guilt. After shivah, the mourner is encouraged to resume normal social interaction. In fact, it is customary for the mourners to walk together a short distance as a symbol of their return to society. In its entirety, the elaborate mourning system of traditional Judaism is designed to promote personal growth and to reintegrate the individual into the community.

Consider the findings of a research investigation indicating diminished mourning by adult children and a decrease in ceremonial grief expressions throughout our American culture (Fulton, 1988). Children are often kept from attending funerals, so they may not even learn the *forms* of our rituals for death. Television also gives minimal attention to such rituals. In an investigation of more than 1,500 commercial television programs aired at prime time and on weekday afternoons, there were approximately 300 incidents of one

Concept Table 21.2: Facing One's Own Death, Coping with the Death of Someone Else, and Death Education

Concept	Processes/Related Ideas	Characteristics/Description
Facing One's Own Death	Kübler-Ross's Stages of Dying	She proposed five stages: denial and isolation, anger, bargaining, depression, and acceptance. Not all individuals go through the same sequence. Some individuals may struggle to the end.
	Perceived Control and Denial	Perceived control and denial may work together as an adaptive orientation for the dying individual. Denial can be adaptive or maladaptive, depending on the circumstance.
	The Contexts in Which People Die	Most deaths in the United States occur in hospitals; this has advantages and disadvantages. Most individuals say they would rather die at home, but they worry that they will be a burden and they worry about the lack of medical care. The hospice is a humanized environment with a commitment to making the end of life as free from pain and depression as possible; the hospice movement has grown rapidly.
Coping with the Death of Someone Else	Communicating with a Dying Person	Most psychologists recommend an open communication system; this system should not dwell on pathology or preparation for death but should emphasize the dying person's strengths.
	Stages and Dimensions of Grief	Grief is the emotional numbness, disbelief, separation, anxiety, despair, sadness, and loneliness that accompany the loss of someone we love. One view suggests we go through three stages of grief: shock, despair, and recovery. Another indicates that we go through four stages: numbness, pining, depression, and recovery. We do not necessarily go through the stages in order; many developmentalists believe we should describe grief's dimensions rather than grief's stages. In some cases, grieving may last for years.
	Making Sense of the World	The grieving process may stimulate individuals to strive to make sense out of their world; each individual may contribute a piece to death's puzzle.
	Widowhood	Usually the most difficult loss is the death of a spouse. A spouse's death is associated with depression, health-compromising behavior, and increased mortality rates. Widowhood is experienced differently depending on sociohistorical circumstances.
	Forms of Mourning and the Funeral	They vary from culture to culture. The most important aspect of mourning in most cultures is the funeral. In recent years, the funeral industry has been the focus of controversy.
Death Education	Its Nature	Thanatologists, persons who study death and dying, believe death education provides a positive preparation for both dying and living. In many ways, we still are a death-avoiding society. Death education is rarely incorporated in a systematic way in elementary schools, although high school and college students are more likely to experience some death education.

death or multiple deaths, 80 percent of them caused by violence. However, grief reactions were shown in fewer than 30 of the deaths, and only 9 funerals were shown (Wass, 1985).

Despite the efforts of thanatologists to educate children more extensively about death, death education has not received widespread acceptance in elementary schools (Wass, Berardo, & Neimeyer, 1988). How death-related crises are handled in schools is related more to teachers' qualities, including their rapport with children, their comfort with the topic, and their degree of empathy, than to any special preparation or curriculum.

High school students are more likely to be exposed to some death education, although sometimes it is only a brief presentation as part of a health class. In one survey, 14 percent of the health educators in high schools in the state of New York taught a unit on death and another 64 percent discussed death as part of another unit (Cappiello & Troyer, 1979). Many colleges and universities now have one or more courses in death or dying. These courses are taught in a variety of disciplines such as psychology, sociology, religion, anthropology, the humanities, and philosophy. Death educators hope that such courses provide students with important information about the nature of death and dying, help them clarify their values, and improve their coping skills (Knott, 1979).

At this point, we have discussed a number of ideas about facing one's own death, coping with the death of someone else, and death education. A summary of these ideas is presented in concept table 21.2. We have come to the end of life's journey. The hope is that you now have a better understanding of the journey and that the wisdom this understanding might bring can help you in your own journey through life's remaining years.

> • *Critical Thinking* •
>
> Imagine that you have been hired as a consultant to an elementary school system as an expert on death education. Design a curriculum of death education for elementary school children.

Summary

I. Defining Death
Twenty-five years ago, determining if someone was dead was simpler than today. Brain death is a neurological definition of death, which states that a person is "brain dead" when all electrical activity of the brain has ceased for a specified period of time. Medical experts debate whether this should mean the higher and lower brain functions or just the higher cortical functions. Currently, most states have a statute endorsing the cessation of brain function (both higher and lower) as a standard for determining death. Euthanasia is the act of painlessly putting to death a person who is suffering from an incurable disease or disability. Distinctions are made between active and passive euthanasia.

II. The Changing Historical Circumstances of Death
When, where, and why people die have changed historically. Today, death occurs most often among the elderly. More than 80 percent of all deaths in the United States now occur in a hospital or an institution. Our exposure to death in the family has been minimized.

III. Death in Different Cultures
Most societies throughout history have had philosophical or religious beliefs about death, and most societies have rituals that deal with death. Most cultures do not view death as the end of existence—spiritual life is thought to continue. The United States has been described as a death-denying and death-avoiding culture.

IV. Causes of Death and Expectations about Death
Although death is more likely to occur in late adulthood, death can come at any point in development. The death of some persons, especially children and younger adults, is often perceived to be more tragic than that of others, such as very old adults, who have had an opportunity to live a long life. Death in children and younger adults is more likely to occur because of accidents but is more likely to occur in older adults because of chronic diseases.

V. Attitudes Toward Death at Different Points in the Life Span
Infants do not have a concept of death. Preschool children have little concept of death, showing no upset at the sight of a dead animal or

person. Preschool children sometimes blame themselves for a person's death. In the elementary school years, children develop a more realistic orientation toward death. Most psychologists believe honesty is the best strategy for helping children cope with death. Death may be glossed over in adolescence. Adolescents have more abstract, philosophical views of death than children do. There is no evidence that a special orientation toward death emerges in early adulthood. Middle adulthood is a time when adults show a heightened consciousness about death and death anxiety. Older adults often show less death anxiety than middle-aged adults, but older adults experience and converse about death more. Attitudes about death may vary considerably among adults of any age.

VI. Kübler-Ross's Stages of Dying
She proposed five stages: denial and isolation, anger, bargaining, depression, and acceptance. Not all individuals go through the same sequence. Some individuals may struggle to the end.

VII. Perceived Control and Denial
Perceived control and denial may work together as an adaptive orientation for a dying individual.

Denial can be adaptive or maladaptive, depending on the circumstance.

VIII. The Contexts in Which People Die
Most deaths in the United States occur in hospitals; this has advantages and disadvantages. Most individuals say they would rather die at home, but they worry that they will be a burden and worry about the lack of medical care. A hospice is a humanized environment with a commitment to making the end of life as free of pain and depression as possible; the hospice movement has grown rapidly.

IX. Communicating with a Dying Person
Most psychologists recommend an open communication system; this system should not dwell on pathology or preparation for death but emphasize the dying person's strengths.

X. Stages and Dimensions of Grief
Grief is the emotional numbness, disbelief, separation anxiety, despair, sadness, and loneliness that accompany the loss of someone we love. One view suggests that we go through three stages of grief—shock, despair, and recovery; another view suggests four stages—numbness, pining, depression, and recovery. We do not necessarily go through the stages in order; many

developmentalists believe we should describe grief's dimensions rather than grief's stages. In some cases, grieving may last for years. The grieving process may stimulate individuals to strive to make sense of their world; each individual may contribute a piece of death's puzzle. Usually the most difficult loss is a spouse's death, which is associated with depression, health-compromising behavior, and increased mortality rates. Widowhood is experienced differently, depending on sociohistorical circumstances.

XI. Forms of Mourning and the Funeral
Mourning varies from culture to culture. The most important aspect of mourning in most cultures is the funeral. In recent years, the funeral industry has been enveloped in controversy.

XII. Death Education
Thanatologists, persons who study death and dying, believe death education provides a positive preparation for both dying and living. In many ways, we still are a death-avoiding society. Death education is rarely incorporated in a systematic way in elementary schools, although high school and college students are more likely to experience some death education.

Key Terms

Suggested Readings

Campbell, S., & Silverman, P. R. (1987). *Widower*. New York: Prentice-Hall Press.
This book is about what happens to men when their wives die, and includes many detailed case studies of widowers.

Kalish, R. A. (1981). *Death, grief, and caring relationships*. Monterey, CA: Brooks/Cole.
Kalish gives an excellent overview of death's many faces and includes considerable information about communicating with the dying individual.

Kastenbaum, R. (1985). Dying and death: A life-span approach. In J. E. Birren & K. W. Schaie (Eds.), *Handbook of the psychology of aging* (2nd ed.). New York: Van Nostrand Reinhold.
Kastenbaum focuses on the experience of death and attitudes toward death at different points in the human life cycle.

Lopata, H. Z. (Ed.). (1987). *Widows*. Durham, NC: Duke University Press.
Information is provided about widows in different cultures, with special attention given to the Middle East, Asia, and the Pacific; emphasis is placed on support systems for widows.

Wass, H., Berardo, F. M., & Neimeyer, R. A. (Eds.). (1988). *Dying: Facing the facts* (2nd ed.). Washington, DC: Hemisphere.
This edited volume includes a number of articles by thanatologists that focus on a wide-ranging set of topics related to death and dying. Chapter topics include the definition of death; problems for public policy; death anxiety; hospice care for the dying; death in the lives of children and adolescents; the funeral in contemporary society; the right to die; ethical and medical issues; and bereavement and mourning.

GLOSSARY

A

ABC method This learning-to-read technique emphasizes memorizing the names of the letters of the alphabet. *328*

acceptance In Kübler-Ross's fifth stage of dying, the person develops a sense of peace, acceptance of his fate, and in many cases, a desire to be left alone. *642*

accommodation This is the process, according to Piaget, that occurs when individuals adjust to new information. *54*

achievement motivation (need for achievement) This is a desire to accomplish something, to reach a standard of excellence, to expend effort to excel. *332*

achieving stage Schaie's early adulthood stage, the achieving stage, involves the application of intelligence to situations that have profound consequences for achieving long-term goals, such as those involving careers and knowledge. *474*

active euthanasia Death is induced by a deliberate attempt to end a person's life, such as the injection of a lethal dose of a drug. *634*

activity level In this style of temperament, the child's tempo and vigor of movement are involved. *97*

activity theory This theory argues that the more active and involved older adults are, the less likely they will age and the more likely they will be satisfied with their lives. *610*

adolescence This developmental period, entered at approximately 10 to 12 years and ending at 18 to 22 years, is the period of transition from childhood to early adulthood. *15*

adolescent egocentrism David Elkind believes that adolescent egocentric thought has two parts: an imaginary audience and a personal fable. *395*

adoption study In this type of study, investigators seek to discover whether behavior and psychological characteristics of adopted children are more like their adoptive parents, who contributed a home environment, or their biological parents, who contributed their heredity. *94*

aerobic exercise Jogging, swimming, and cycling are examples of the sustained aerobic exercise that stimulates heart and lung activity. *464*

affectionate love Also called companionate love, this type of love occurs when an individual desires to have the other person near and have a deep, caring affection for the person. *491*

afterbirth The third stage of birth, the afterbirth, consists of detaching and expelling the placenta, umbilical cord, and other membranes. *117*

ageism This is the concept of prejudice against older adults, based on the stereotypes about aging. *611*

AIDS (Acquired Immune Deficiency Syndrome) A virus destroys the body's immune system, allowing germs that usually do not harm a person with a normal immune system, to produce devastating illnesses and death. *468*

altruism This is an unselfish interest in helping someone. *379*

Alzheimer's disease This progressive, irreversible brain disorder is characterized by gradual deterioration of memory, reasoning, language, and physical function. *603*

amniocentesis In this prenatal medical procedure, a sample of amniotic fluid is withdrawn by syringe and tested to discover if the fetus is suffering from any chromosomal or metabolic disorders. It is performed between the 12th and 16th weeks of pregnancy. *91*

amnion The bag or envelope containing clear fluid in which the developing embryo floats provides an environment that is shockproof, and temperature and humidity controlled. *104*

anal stage The second Freudian stage of development, in which the child's greatest pleasure involves the anus or the eliminative functions associated with it; occurs between 1½ and 3 years of age. *45*

androgyny Desirable masculine and feminine characteristics are present in the same individual. *366*

anger During Kübler-Ross's second stage of dying, the dying person recognizes that denial cannot be maintained, and often gives way to anger, resentment, rage, and envy. *642*

animism A feature of preoperational thought, animism is the belief that inanimate objects have lifelike qualities and are capable of action. *227*

anorexia nervosa This eating disorder involves the relentless pursuit of thinness through starvation. *415*

anoxia Insufficient oxygen is available to the infant, which may result in brain damage. *117*

Apgar scale This widely used method assesses the health of newborns 1 and 5 minutes after birth; the scale evaluates heart rate, respiratory effort, muscle tone, body color, and reflex irritability. *123*

aptitude-treatment interaction This concept stresses the importance of children's aptitudes or characteristics and the treatments or experiences they are given in classrooms. *350*

arthritis Especially common in older adults, arthritis is an inflammation of the joints accompanied by pain, stiffness, and movement problems. *577*

assimilation This process, described by Piaget, is the incorporation of new knowledge into an individual's existing knowledge. *54*

associative play Play involves social interaction with little or no organization; one of Mildred Parten's categories of play. *270*

attachment This is a close emotional bond between the infant and the caregiver. *190*

attention-deficit hyperactivity disorder This disorder, commonly called hyperactivity, is characterized by a short attention span, distractibility, and high levels of physical activity. *307*

authoritarian parenting This restrictive, punitive style of parenting exhorts the child to follow the parent's directions and to respect work and effort. Authoritarian parenting places firm limits and controls on the child, allows little verbal exchange, and is associated with social incompetence. *256*

authoritative parenting This parenting style encourages children to be independent but still places limits and controls on their actions. Authoritative parenting is associated with extensive verbal exchange, warm and nurturant parenting, and social competence in children. *256*

autonomous morality Piaget's second stage of moral development is displayed by children about 10 years of age and older. The child becomes aware that rules and laws are created by people and that in judging an action, one should consider intentions as well as consequences. *289*

autonomy versus shame and doubt Erikson's second stage of development is experienced during later infancy and toddlerhood (1 to 3 years). After gaining trust in one's caregivers, infants begin to discover that their behavior is their own. *50*

B

bargaining In Kübler-Ross's third stage of dying, the person develops the hope that death can somehow be postponed or delayed. *642*

basal metabolism rate (BMR) This is the minimum amount of energy a person uses in the resting state. *223, 462*

Bayley Scales of Infant Development This infant development assessment, developed by Nancy Bayley, has three components: a mental scale, a motor scale, and an infant behavior profile. *172*

behavior exchange theory This theory emphasizes the hedonism and competence involved in marital relationships. *498*

behavior genetics This branch of genetics is concerned with the degree and nature of behavior's hereditary basis. *93*

behaviorism This approach, primarily associated with the work of B. F. Skinner, emphasizes the scientific study of observable behavioral responses and their environmental determinants. *60*

bilingual education These programs for students with limited proficiency in English instructs students in their own language part of the time, while English is being learned. *330*

biological processes These are changes that involve the individual's physical nature. *14*

blastocyst This inner layer of cells develops during the germinal period, and later develops into the embryo. *103*

body transcendence versus body preoccupation One of three developmental tasks of aging described by Peck, older adults must cope with declining physical well-being. *625*

bonding Close contact, especially close physical contact, between parents and child in the period shortly after birth, is thought by some physicians to be a critical time for the formation of an important emotional attachment that will provide a foundation for optimal development in the future. *125*

brain death The neurological definition of death states that a person is "brain dead" when all electrical activity of the brain has ceased for a specified period of time. A flat EEG recording is one criterion of brain death. *633*

Brazelton Neonatal Behavioral Assessment The newborn's neurological development, reflexes, and reactions to people are assessed several days after birth with this method. *124*

Brazelton training The Brazelton Scale is used to show parents how their newborn responds to people. A sluggish response can be improved through proper stimulation. *125*

breech position The baby's position in the uterus is such that the buttocks, rather than the head, emerge through the vagina first. *117*

bulimia This eating disorder involves regularly occurring binging and purging sequences. *416*

burnout This hopeless, helpless feeling is brought on by relentless, work-related stress. *457*

C

canalization This term describes the narrow path or developmental course that certain characteristics take. Apparently, preservative forces help to protect or buffer a person from environmental extremes. *92*

care perspective Carol Gilligan described this moral perspective as viewing people in terms of their connectedness to others, and focuses on interpersonal communication, relationships with others and concern for others. *376*

career consolidation One of Vaillant's adult stages of development that occurs from about 23 to 35 years of age, in which an individual's career becomes more stable and coherent. *549*

career self-concept theory Donald Super holds the view that the individual's self-concept plays a central role in career choice. He believes a number of developmental changes in vocational self-concept take place during the adolescent and young adulthood years. *477*

case study This is an in-depth look at one individual, used mainly by clinical psychologists when the unique aspects of an individual's life cannot be duplicated, either for practical or ethical reasons. *26*

centration A characteristic of preoperational thought, centration involves focusing attention on one characteristic, to the exclusion of all others. *231*

cephalocaudal pattern This rule states that the greatest growth always occurs at the head (the top) with physical growth in size, weight, and feature differentiation gradually working down from top to bottom. *140*

cesarean section This is the surgical removal of the baby from the uterus through the abdomen. *117*

child-centered kindergarten In this type of kindergarten, education involves the whole child and includes concern for the child's physical, cognitive, and social development. Instruction is organized around the child's needs, interests, and learning styles. *241*

chorionic villus test In this prenatal medical procedure, done between the 8th and 11th weeks of pregnancy, a small sample of the placenta is removed for examination. *91*

chromosomes Threadlike structures that come in 23 pairs; one member of each pair of chromosomes comes from each parent. The chromosomes contain DNA. *85*

chronic disorders These disorders are characterized by a slow onset and long duration: they rarely develop in early adulthood, increase during middle adulthood, and become chronic in late adulthood. *576*

chronosystem In Bronfenbrenner's ecological theory, the chronosystem involves the patterning of environmental events and transitions over the life course. *72*

cliques A small group, cliques involve greater intimacy among members than crowds, and have greater group cohesion. *432*

cognitive developmental theory of gender Children's gender typing occurs after they have developed a concept of gender. Once they consistently conceive of themselves as male or female, children often organize their world on the basis of gender. *286*

cognitive monitoring This is the process of taking stock of what you are currently doing, what you will do next, and how effectively the mental activity is unfolding. *313*

cognitive processes These changes involve the individual's thought, intelligence, and language. *14*

cohort effects These effects are due to a subject's time of birth or generation, but not to actual age. *32*

commitment James Marcia defines commitment as the part of identity development in which adolescents show a personal investment in what they are going to do. *443*

community rights versus individual rights In this fifth stage of Kohlberg's theory of moral development, the person understands that values and laws are relative and that standards may vary from one person to another. *375*

computer-assisted instruction The computer is used as a tutor to individualize instruction. The concept behind computer-assisted instruction is to use the computer to present information, give students practice, and provide additional instruction if needed. *315*

concrete operational stage Piaget's third stage lasts from approximately 7 to 11 years of age. Children can perform operations. Logical reasoning replaces intuitive thought as long as the principles can be applied to specific, concrete examples. *55*

conditional positive regard This is Carl Rogers' concept that love and praise are often not given unless an individual conforms to parental or social standards, resulting in lowered self-esteem. *63*

connectedness The two dimensions of connectedness are (1) mutuality—sensitivity and respect for other's views; and (2) permeability—openness to other's views. *445*

consensual validation This concept explains why individuals are attracted to people who are similar to them. Our own attitudes and behavior are supported, or validated, when someone else's attitudes and behavior are similar to ours. *488*

conservation This Piagetian concept is demonstrated in the idea that the amount stays the same, regardless of how the containers change. *231*

constructive play The child combines sensorimotor/practice repetitive activity with symbolic ideas; children engage in self-regulated creation or construction of a product or problem solution. *272*

constructivist view The view, advocated by Piaget, that the main perceptual abilities are completely uncoordinated at birth and that young infants do not have intermodal perception. Infant perception involves a representation of the world that builds up as the infant constructs an image of experiences. *155*

contemporary life events approach This approach emphasizes that how life events influence the individual's development depends not only on the life event, but also on mediating factors, the individual's adaptation to the event, the life-stage context, and the sociohistorical context. *555*

continuity of development This view states that development involves gradual, cumulative change from conception to death. *18*

control processes Also called strategies, these are cognitive processes that do not occur automatically, but require work and effort. They are under the learner's conscious control and can be used to improve memory. *311*

conventional reasoning In this second, intermediate level of Kohlberg's theory of moral development, the individual's internalization is incomplete. The person abides by certain standards (internal), but they are the standards of others, such as parents or the laws of society. *374*

convergent thinking The kind of thinking that is characteristically used on standardized tests, convergent thinking produces one correct answer. *327*

cooperative play Play involves social interaction in a group, with a sense of group identity and organized activity; one of Mildred Parten's categories of play. *270*

coordination of secondary circular reactions In Piaget's fourth sensorimotor substage, which develops between 8 and 12 months of age, significant changes take place involving the coordination of schemes and intentionality. *162*

correlational strategy The goal of this strategy is to describe the strength of the relation between two or more events or characteristics. The more strongly events are correlated, the more we can predict one from the other. *28*

creativity This ability to think about something in a novel and unusual way produces unique solutions to problems. *328*

crisis James Marcia defines crisis as a period of identity development during which an adolescent is exploring meaningful alternatives. *443*

critical period According to ethologists, there is a fixed time period, very early in development, during which certain behaviors optimally emerge. *69*

critical thinking Although definitions vary, they commonly describe the notions of grasping the deeper meanings of problems, of keeping an open mind about different approaches and perspectives, and of deciding for oneself what to believe or do. *397*

cross-sectional approach This is a research strategy in which individuals of different ages are compared at one time. *31*

crowd A large group, the crowd is the least personal of adolescent groups. *432*

crystallized intelligence This is one's accumulated information and verbal skills, which increase with age. *590*

cultural-familial retardation There is no evidence of organic brain damage in this form of mental retardation. The IQ ranges from 50 to 70. Psychologists seek to find the cause of this type of retardation in impoverished environments. *325*

culture This refers to the behavior patterns, beliefs, and all other products of a particular group of people that are passed on from generation to generation. *71*

culture-fair tests These tests are designed to reduce cultural bias. *323*

D

date or acquaintance rape Coercive sexual activity is directed at someone with whom the individual is at least casually acquainted. *471*

deep structure This is the syntactic relation of the words in a sentence. *176*

defense mechanisms This is a psychoanalytic term for unconscious methods, by which the ego distorts reality, thereby protecting it from anxiety. *43*

deferred imitation This type of imitation occurs after a time delay of hours or days. *170*

deficiency needs According to Maslow, if physiological and psychological needs are not fulfilled, an individual will try to make up for them in some way. *65*

denial and isolation Kübler-Ross's first stage of dying consists of denial that death is really going to take place. *642*

Denver Developmental Screening Test This widely used test measures young children's motor development. It is especially helpful in assessing developmental delay in motor skills and can be used with children from birth through 6 years of age. *221*

dependent variable This is the factor that is measured in the experiment; it may change because of the manipulation of the independent variable. It is labeled "dependent" because this variable depends on what happens to the subjects in the experiment. *29*

depression In Kübler-Ross's fourth stage of dying, the person comes to accept the certainty of death, and may enter a period of depression or preparatory grief. *642*

development The pattern of movement or change that begins at conception continues through the life cycle.

developmental construction view This view of marital satisfaction emphasizes the history of relationships and the manner in which they are carried forward. *498*

developmental quotient (DQ) This overall developmental quotient combines subscores in motor, language, adaptive, and personal-social domains in the Gesell Assessment of Infants. *172*

developmental theory of career choice Eli Ginzberg holds the view that individuals go through three career choice stages: fantasy, tentative, and realistic. *476*

developmentally appropriate practice This type of schooling is based upon knowledge of the typical development of children within an age span as well as the uniqueness of the child. Developmentally appropriate practice contrasts with developmentally inappropriate practice, which ignores the concrete, hands-on approach to learning, and teaches largely through abstract activities presented to large groups of young children. *243*

dialectical model Riegel states that each individual continually changes because of various forces that push and pull development forward. Each person is viewed as acting on and reacting to social and historical developments. *20*

differentiation versus role preoccupation One of three developmental tasks of aging described by Peck, older adults must redefine their worth in terms of something other than work roles. *625*

difficult child In this style of temperament, the child tends to react negatively and cry frequently, engages in irregular daily routines, and is slow to accept new experiences. *96*

direct perception view This viewpoint states that infants are born with intermodal perception abilities that enable them to display intermodal perception early in infancy. Infants only have to attend to the appropriate information; they do not have to build up an internal representation of the information through experience. *154*

discontinuity of development This view states that development involves distinct stages in the life span. *20*

disenchantment phase In the fourth of Robert Atchley's phases of retirement, older adults recognize that their preretirement fantasies about retirement were unrealistic. *600*

disengagement theory This theory proposes that as older adults slow down they gradually withdraw from society. *609*

dishabituation An infant shows renewed interest in a stimulus. *167*

displacement A psychoanalytic defense mechanism, displacement occurs when the individual shifts unacceptable feelings from one object to another, more acceptable object. *44*

divergent thinking Characteristic of creative thinking, divergent thinking produces many answers to the same problem. *327*

DNA Deoxyribonucleic acid is a complex molecule, contained in chromosomes, that contains genetic information. *85*

dominant-recessive genes principle If one gene of a pair is dominant and one is recessive (goes back, recedes), the dominant gene exerts its effect, overriding the potential influence of the other, recessive gene. A recessive gene exerts its influence only if both genes of a pair are recessive. *89*

Down syndrome Caused by the presence of an extra (47th) chromosome, Down syndrome is the most common genetically transmitted form of mental retardation. *89*

E

early adulthood This developmental period begins in the late teens or early twenties and continues through the thirties. *15*

early childhood This developmental period, also called the preschool years, extends from the end of infancy to about 5 or 6 years. *14*

easy child In this style of temperament, the child is generally in a positive mood, quickly establishes regular routines in infancy, and adapts easily to new experiences. *96*

echoing The child's words are repeated, especially if it is an incomplete phrase or sentence in this language teaching strategy. *181*

echolalia This is a speech disorder, associated with autism, in which children echo what they hear. *212*

ecological theory Bronfenbrenner's sociocultural view of development consists of five developmental systems, ranging from the fine-grained inputs of direct interactions with social agents to the broad-based inputs of culture. The five systems of the ecological theory are: microsystem, mesosystem, exosystem, macrosystem, and chronosystem. *70*

ectoderm This outermost layer of embryonic cells will become the nervous system, sensory receptors, and skin parts. *104*

ego In Freudian personality theory, the ego is a structure of personality that deals with the demands of reality. It is called the executive branch of personality because it makes rational decisions. *42*

ego transcendence versus ego preoccupation One of three developmental tasks of aging described by Peck, older adults must recognize that while death is inevitable, they feel at ease with themselves by realizing that they have contributed to the future through the competent rearing of children or through their vocation or ideas. *625*

egocentrism This salient feature of preoperational thought is the inability to distinguish between one's own perspective and the perspective of another. *227*

eldercare Whether day-to-day physical assistance or the responsibility for arranging such care, eldercare is the physical and emotional caretaking of older members of the family. *614*

embryonic period During the embryonic period, which occurs from 2 until 8 weeks after conception, the rate of cell differentiation intensifies, support systems for the cells form, and organs appear. *103*

emotionality In this style of temperament, the child has a tendency to be distressed. *97*

empathy Another's feelings may engender an emotional response that is similar to the other's responses. *291*

empty nest syndrome It is expected that marital satisfaction will decrease when children leave home, because parents derive considerable satisfaction from their children. The empty nest syndrome may hold true for some parents who live vicariously through their children, but marital satisfaction usually increases in post-childbearing years. *540*

endoderm This inner layer of cells of the embryo will develop into the digestive and respiratory systems. *104*

epigenetic principle This is Erikson's term for the process that guides development through the life cycle. This principle states that anything that grows has a blueprint. Each part has a time of ascendancy, until all of the parts have arisen to make a functioning whole. *50*

erogenous zones At each stage of development, according to Freud, one part of the body has especially strong pleasure-giving qualities. *45*

estradiol This hormone is associated with breast, uterine, and skeletal development in girls. *391*

ethnicity An important dimension of culture, ethnicity is based on cultural heritage, nationality characteristics, religion, and language. The word *ethnic* comes from the Greek word for "nation." *72*

ethology Behavior is strongly influenced by biology, is tied to evolution, and is characterized by sensitive or critical periods, according to Konrad Lorenz, the most famous ethologist. *68*

euthanasia Sometimes called "mercy killing," euthanasia is the act of painlessly putting to death a person who is suffering from an incurable disease or a severe disability. *634*

executive stage In Schaie's middle adult stage, people become responsible for societal systems and organizations. The individual develops an understanding of how societal organizations work and the complex relationships that are involved. *474*

exosystem In Bronfenbrenner's ecological theory, the exosystem is involved when experiences in another social setting, in which the individual does not have an active role, influence what the individual experiences in an immediate context. *70*

expanding The child's words are repeated in a linguistically more sophisticated way in this language teaching strategy. *181*

experimental strategy The causes of behavior may be precisely determined using this strategy. The researcher performs an experiment, in a carefully regulated setting in which one or more of the factors believed to influence the behavior being studied are manipulated and all others are held constant. *28*

extrinsic motivation This is motivation influenced by external rewards and punishments. *333*

F

fetal alcohol syndrome FAS is a cluster of abnormalities that appear in the offspring of mothers who drink heavily during pregnancy. The abnormalities include physical deformities, below average intelligence, including mental retardation. *111*

fetal period This refers to the prenatal period of development that begins two months after conception and lasts for about seven months. *105*

fine motor skills These activities involve finely tuned movements, such as finger dexterity. *140*

first habits and primary circular reactions In Piaget's second sensorimotor substage, which develops between 1 and 4 months of age, the infant learns to coordinate sensation and types of schemes or structures—that is, habits and primary circular reactions. *161*

fixation A psychoanalytic defense mechanism, fixation occurs when the individual remains locked into an earlier developmental stage because needs are over- or under-gratified. *45*

fluid intelligence The ability to reason abstractly, it is argued that this may steadily decline from middle adulthood on. *590*

formal operational stage Piaget's fourth and final stage appears between the ages of 11 and 15. Individuals move beyond the world of concrete experience and think in abstract and more logical terms. *55*

fraternal twins Dizygotic (fraternal) twins develop from separate eggs, making them genetically less similar than identical twins. *93*

friendship This close relationship involves enjoyment, acceptance, trust, respect, mutual assistance, confiding, understanding, and spontaneity. *489*

G

games These are activities engaged in for pleasure; they often include rules and competition with other individuals. *272*

gametes These are the cells of human reproduction, created in the testes of males and the ovaries of females. *86*

gender This refers to the social dimensions of being male or female. *281*

gender identity The sense of being male or female; most children acquire their gender identity by the time they are 3 years old. *281*

gender role This set of expectations prescribes how females and males should think, act, and feel. *281*

gender schema This schema organizes the world in terms of male and female. *287*

gender schema theory The theory argues that children's attention and behavior are guided by an internal motivation to conform to gender-based, sociocultural standards and stereotypes. *287*

gender-role stereotypes These are broad categories that reflect our impressions and beliefs about males and females. *362*

generational inequity This viewpoint states that an aging society is unfair to its younger members because older adults have the advantage of receiving an inequitably large allocation of resources. *614*

generativity versus stagnation Erikson's seventh developmental stage is experienced during middle adulthood. A chief concern is to assist the younger generation in developing and leading useful lives. *51*

genes Hereditary information is carried on these short segments of the DNA double-helix "staircase." Genes act as a blueprint for cells to reproduce themselves and manufacture the proteins that maintain life. *85*

genital stage The fifth and final stage of Freudian development, the genital stage occurs from puberty on. This is a time of sexual reawakening, and the source of sexual pleasure becomes someone outside of the family. *48*

genotype This is the person's genetic heritage, the actual genetic material. *91*

germinal period The period of prenatal development, which takes place in the first two weeks after conception, includes creation of the zygote, continuation of cell division, and attachment of the zygote to the uterine wall. *103*

giftedness The gifted show above average intelligence, with an IQ of above 120, and/or a superior talent for something. *326*

grammar This is the formal description of syntactical rules. *176*

grasping reflex When something touches the infant's palm, he or she responds by grasping tightly. *134*

grief Accompanying the loss of someone we love are the emotions of grief: numbness, disbelief, separation anxiety, despair, sadness, and loneliness. *645*

gross motor skills These activities involve large muscles, such as moving the arms, and walking. *140*

H

habituation In this process, repeated presentation of the same stimulus causes reduced attention to the stimulus. *167*

hardiness This personality style is characterized by a sense of commitment rather than alienation, control rather than powerlessness, and a perception of problems as challenges rather than threats. *520*

helpless orientation This describes children who seem trapped by the experience of difficulty; they attribute their difficulty to a lack of ability. *334*

hermaphrodites These are individuals whose genital development is intermediate between male and female because of a hormonal imbalance. *281*

heteronomous morality Piaget's first stage of moral development occurs from about 4 to 7 years of age. Justice and rules are conceived of as unchangeable properties of the world, removed from the control of people. *289*

hierarchy of needs Certain basic needs, according to Maslow, must be met before we can satisfy the highest need for self-actualization. The basic needs include physiological needs, safety, love and belongingness, and self-esteem. *65*

holophrase hypothesis This concept states that a single word is used to imply a complete sentence. *181*

honeymoon phase In the third of Robert Atchley's phases of retirement, and the earliest phase after retirement, many individuals feel euphoric. *600*

hospice A humanized institution committed to making the end of life as free from pain, anxiety, and depression as possible. The goals of the hospice are different from those of hospitals, which are to cure illness and prolong life. *644*

humanistic approach This is the most widely known phenomenological approach to personality. It stresses the person's capacity for personal growth, freedom to choose one's own destiny, and positive qualities. Carl Rogers and Abraham Maslow are the principle architects of the humanistic approach. *62*

hypotheses These are the assumptions underlying a theory that can be tested to determine their accuracy. *23*

hypothetical-deductive reasoning According to Piaget's formal operational concept, adolescents have the cognitive ability to develop hypotheses about ways to solve problems such as an algebraic equation. They then systematically deduce, or conclude which is the best path for solving the equation. *394*

I

id In Freudian theory, the id is a structure of personality consisting of instincts, which are the individual's reservoir of psychic energy. The id is unconscious, lacking contact with reality. *42*

identical twins Monozygotic (identical) twins develop from a single fertilized egg that splits into two genetically identical replicas, each of which becomes a person. *93*

identification theory Freud held that children acquire masculine and feminine attitudes from their parents because the preschool child develops a sexual attraction to the same-sex parent, then renounces this attraction by 6 or 7 years of age because of anxious feelings, and subsequently identifies with the same-sex parent, adopting that parent's characteristics. *282*

identity achievement Marcia uses this term to describe adolescents who have undergone a crisis and have made a commitment. *444*

identity diffusion James Marcia uses this term to describe adolescents who have not yet experienced a crisis, that is, they have not explored alternatives, or made any commitments. *443*

identity foreclosure Marcia uses this term to describe adolescents who have made a commitment but have not experienced a crisis. *443*

identity moratorium Marcia uses this term to describe adolescents who are in the midst of a crisis, but their commitments are either absent or only vaguely defined. *443*

identity versus identity confusion Erikson's fifth stage of development is experienced during adolescence. Individuals are faced with finding out who they are, what they are about, and where they are going in life. *50*

imaginary audience According to Elkind, adolescents believe that others are as preoccupied with them as they are with themselves. *395*

immanent justice The heteronomous thinker, according to Piaget, believes that if a rule is broken, justice will be meted out immediately. *290*

implantation The attachment of the zygote to the uterine wall takes place about 10 days after conception. *103*

imprinting This ethological concept states that rapid, innate learning occurs within a critical period of time, and involves attachment to the first moving object seen. *68*

in vitro fertilization Conception outside the body takes place as a result of medical procedures. *86*

independent variable This is the manipulated, influential, and experimental factor in the experiment. It is called 'independent' because it can be changed independently of other factors. *29*

individualism and purpose In the second stage of Kohlberg's theory of moral development, moral thinking is based on rewards and self-interest. *374*

individuated-connected level In this highest level of relationship maturity, there is evidence of an understanding of oneself, as well as consideration of the other's motivation and anticipation of his or her needs. Concern and caring involve emotional support and individualized expression of interest. *507*

individuating-reflexive faith Fowler's stage in late adolescence defines an important time in the development of a religious identity. For the first time in their lives, individuals take full responsibility for their religious beliefs. *438*

individuation The two dimensions of individuality are self-assertion, the ability to have and communicate a point of view, and separateness, the use of communication patterns to express how one is different from others. *445*

industry versus inferiority Erikson's fourth stage of development occurs approximately during the elementary school years. Children's initiative brings them in contact with a wealth of new experiences. Moving toward middle and late childhood, they direct their energy toward mastering knowledge and intellectual skills. *50*

infancy This is the developmental period extending from birth to 18 or 24 months. *14*

infantile amnesia As children and adults, humans have little or no memory for events experienced before 3 years of age. *169*

infantile autism This severe developmental disturbance has its onset in infancy, and includes deficiencies in social relationships, abnormalities in communication, and restricted, repetitive, and stereotyped patterns of behavior. *211*

infinite generativity Individuals have the ability to generate an infinite number of meaningful sentences using a finite set of words and rules, which makes language a highly creative enterprise. *175*

information processing approach This approach is concerned with how individuals process information about their world—how information enters the mind, how it is stored, and how it is retrieved to perform such complex activities as problem solving and reasoning. *55*

initiative versus guilt Erikson's third stage of development occurs during the preschool years. As children encounter a widening social world, they are challenged more than they were as infants. Active, purposeful behavior is needed to cope with these challenges. *50*

innate goodness Jean Jacques Rousseau presented the view that children are inherently good. *8*

integrity versus despair Erikson's eighth and final stage of development is experienced during late adulthood. Through many different routes, the older person may have achieved a positive outlook in most of the previous stages of development. If so, the retrospective overview will reveal a life well spent, resulting in satisfaction; integrity will be achieved. *51*

intelligence This is a complex concept that includes verbal ability, problem-solving skills, and the ability to learn from and adapt to the experiences of everyday life. *318*

intelligence quotient (IQ) William Stern devised the term, which is the child's mental age divided by chronological age, multiplied by 100. *318*

intermodal perception This ability allows an individual to relate and integrate information about two or more sensory modalities, such as vision and hearing. *154*

internalization This is the developmental change from behavior that is externally controlled to behavior that is internally controlled. *374*

internalization of schemes In Piaget's sixth and final sensorimotor substage, which develops between 18 and 24 months, the infant's mentality shifts from a purely sensorimotor plane to a symbolic plane, and the infant develops the ability to use primitive symbols. *162*

interpersonal norms In the third stage of Kohlberg's theory of moral development, the person values trust, caring, and loyalty to others as the basis of moral judgment. *374*

intimacy in friendships In friendships, intimacy is defined as self-disclosure and the sharing of private thoughts. *348*

intimacy versus isolation Erikson's sixth developmental stage is experienced during early adulthood. Individuals face the task of forming intimate relationships with others. *51*

intimate style In this form of social interaction, an individual maintains one or more deep and long-lasting love relationships. *506*

intrinsic motivation This is an internal desire to be competent and to do something for its own sake. *333*

intuitive thought substage According to Piaget, this is the second substage of preoperational thought, occurring between 4 and 7 years of age. Children begin to use primitive reasoning and want to know the answers to all sorts of questions; they seem to be sure about their knowledge, but unaware of how they know what they know. *229*

isolated style In this form of social interaction, the individual withdraws from social encounters and has little or no intimate attachment to same- or opposite-sex individuals. *506*

J

justice perspective Kohlberg described a moral perspective that focuses on the rights of the individual; individuals stand alone and independently make moral decisions. *376*

juvenile delinquent This label is applied to an adolescent who breaks the law or engages in behavior that is considered illegal. *411*

K

keeping the meaning versus rigidity Vaillant's stage of adult development that occurs from 45 to 55 years of age, in which a more relaxed feeling characterizes adults if they have met their goals, or, if not, they have accepted the fact. At this time, adults become concerned about extracting some meaning from their lives and resist falling into a rigid orientation. *549*

Klinefelter syndrome This is a genetic disorder in which males have an extra X chromosome, making them XXY instead of XY, and resulting in abnormal secondary sex characteristics. *89*

L

labeling The names of objects are identified in this language teaching strategy. *181*

laboratory Research is conducted in the laboratory, a controlled setting from which many of the complex factors of the "real world" are removed. *24*

Lamaze method Developed by French obstetrician Fernand Lamaze, this form of prepared or natural childbirth involves helping the pregnant mother to cope with childbirth in an active way. *116*

language A system of symbols is used to communicate with others. In humans, language is characterized by infinite generativity and rule systems. *175*

language acquisition device (LAD) Noam Chomsky believes that children are biologically prewired to enable the detection of certain language categories, such as phonology, syntax, and semantics. *176*

late adulthood This developmental period begins in the sixties or seventies and lasts until death. *15*

latency stage The fourth Freudian stage of development, in which the child represses interest in sexuality and develops intellectual and social skills; occurs between 6 years of age and puberty. *48*

learning disabilities The criteria for being diagnosed as having learning disabilities include (1) having normal intelligence or above, (2) having difficulties in some academic areas, but not in others, and (3) not suffering from other conditions or disorders that could explain the learning problem. *306*

Leboyer method Developed by French obstetrician Frederick Leboyer, this procedure is intended to make the birth process less stressful for infants. It is referred to as "birth without violence." *115*

leisure This refers to the pleasant times after work when individuals are free to pursue activities and interests of their own choosing. *531*

life expectancy The number of individuals who are expected to reach a particular age in life. *567*

life review A common theme in personality development theories, life review involves looking back at one's life experiences, evaluating them, interpreting them, and often reinterpreting them. *625*

life satisfaction A widely used index of psychological well-being in older adults, life satisfaction is psychological well-being in general, or satisfaction with life as a whole. *626*

life span The upper boundary of life, life span is the maximum number of years an individual can live. *567*

life-span perspective Baltes includes seven basic characteristics of this perspective: development is life-long, multidimensional, multidirectional, plastic, historically embedded, multidisciplinary, and contextual. *11*

longitudinal approach This is a research strategy in which the same individuals are studied over a period of time, usually several years or more. *31*

long-term memory This type of memory is relatively permanent and unlimited. *311*

low-birthweight infants Babies who are full-term (38–42 weeks) but who weigh less than 5½ pounds are considered to be low birthweight and at higher risk. *118*

M

macrobiological theories of aging These theories examine life at a more global level of analysis than the cell. *571*

macrosystem In Bronfenbrenner's ecological theory, the macrosystem involves the culture in which the individual lives. *71*

mainstreaming Handicapped children enter the mainstream of education in the school by attending classes with non-handicapped children, rather than being separated from them. *304*

major depression An individual suffering this mood disorder is deeply unhappy, demoralized, self-derogatory, and bored. The person does not feel well, has little stamina, has a poor appetite, and is listless and unmotivated. Major depression is so widespread it has been called the "common cold" of mental disorders. *601*

marasmus This severe protein-calorie deficiency causes a wasting away of body tissues, usually in the first year of life. *145*

mastery orientation This describes children who are task oriented; they focus on their learning strategies rather than their ability. *334*

maturation An orderly sequence of changes is dictated by the genetic blueprint we each have. *17*

Maximally Discriminative Facial Movement Coding System (MAX) Carroll Izard developed this system of coding infant's facial expressions related to emotion. *201*

mean length of utterance (MLU) Roger Brown proposed this index of language development based on the number of words per sentence a child produces in a sample of 50–100 sentences. *182*

meiosis In the process of cell division, each pair of chromosomes in the cell separates, with one member of each pair going into each gamete, or daughter cell. *86*

memory This is the retention of information over time. *168*

menarche This refers to the occurrence of a girl's first menstruation. *389*

menopause A woman's menstrual periods and childbearing capability cease completely during menopause, which usually occurs in the late 40s or early 50s. *524*

mental age (MA) Binet developed the concept that an individual's level of mental development is relative to others. *318*

mental retardation This is a condition of limited mental ability; the individual has a low IQ, and has difficulty adapting to everyday life. *325*

mesoderm This middle layer of embryonic cells will become the circulatory system, bones, muscle, excretory system, and reproductive system. *104*

mesosystem In Bronfenbrenner's ecological theory, the mesosystem involves relations between microsystems or contexts; for example, the relations between family and school experiences. *70*

metacognitive knowledge This is the segment of acquired world knowledge that involves cognitive matters. It is the knowledge that children have accumulated through experience and stored in long-term memory that concerns the domain of the human mind and its workings. *312*

metaneeds These growth needs refer to Maslow's concept of higher, self-actualization needs, and include truth, goodness, beauty, wholeness, aliveness, uniqueness, perfection, justice, richness, and playfulness. *65*

microbiological theories of aging These theories look within the body's cells to explain aging. *571*

microsystem In Bronfenbrenner's ecological theory, the microsystem is the setting in which the individual lives. These contexts include the person's family, peers, school, and neighborhood. Most direct interactions with social agents—teachers, peers, and parents—take place in the microsystem. *70*

middle adulthood This developmental period begins at approximately 35 to 45 years and extends to the sixties. *15*

middle and late childhood This developmental period, also called the elementary school years, extends from 6 to about 11 years. *15*

mnemonics These are techniques designed to make memory more efficient. *594*

moral development This is an area that concerns rules and conventions about what people should do in their interactions with other people. *289*

Moro reflex This infantile startle response is common to neonates, but disappears by about 3 months of age. When startled, the neonate arches its back, throws back its head, and flings out its arms and legs. Then the arms and legs are rapidly brought back to the center of the body. *134*

morphology This is the system of rules for combining morphemes, the smallest string of sounds that gives meaning to what we see and hear. *175*

motherese This type of language, often used by adults when they talk to babies, uses higher than normal frequency, greater than normal pitch, and simple words and sentences. *180*

N

natural selection This is the evolutionary process that favors individuals of a species that are best adapted to survive and reproduce. *84*

naturalistic observation The scientist observes behavior in real-world settings and makes no effort to manipulate or control the situation. *25*

nature-nurture controversy Nature refers to an organism's biological inheritance, and nurture refers to environmental experiences. The "nature" proponents claim that biological influences on development are the most important; the "nurture" proponents claim that environmental influences are the most important. *18*

near phase In the second of Robert Atchley's phases of retirement, the worker begins to participate in a preretirement program. *600*

neglected children These children receive little attention from their peers, but are not necessarily disliked by their peers. *345*

neo-ethological theory Robert Hinde applies ethological theory to human development, but emphasizes sensitive, rather than critical periods of development, social development, and relationships. *69*

non-normative life events There are unusual occurrences that have a major effect on an individual's life. The occurrence, patterning, and sequence of these events are not applicable to many individuals. *13*

nonnutritive sucking This sucking behavior is unrelated to the infant's feeding but is a frequently used measure in neonatal research. *134*

normal distribution This is a symmetrical distribution, with a majority of cases falling in the middle of the possible range of scores and few scores appearing toward the extremes of the range. *319*

normative age-graded influences Individuals in a particular age group have biological and environmental influences that are similar. *13*

normative history-graded influences People of a particular generation have common biological and environmental influences that are associated with history. *13*

O

object permanence Piaget named this important infant accomplishment: understanding that objects and events continue even when they cannot directly be seen, heard, or touched. *162*

Oedipus complex A Freudian concept, this describes the young child's intense desire to replace the parent of the same sex and enjoy the affections of the opposite-sexed parent. *45*

onlooker play The child watches others play, but does not enter in; one of Mildred Parten's categories of play. *270*

operant conditioning This is a form of learning in which the consequences of behavior lead to changes in the probability of that behavior's occurrence. *60*

operations According to Piaget, these internalized sets of actions allow the child to do mentally what before was done physically. *226*

oral rehydration therapy (ORT) This treatment is designed to prevent dehydration during episodes of diarrhea by giving the child a large volume of fluids. *224*

oral stage The first Freudian stage of development, in which the infant's pleasure centers around the mouth; occurs during the first 18 months of life. *45*

organic retardation Organic refers to the tissues or organs of the body; there is some physical damage in organic mental retardation, and it is usually caused by a genetic disorder or brain damage. *325*

organogenesis The process of organ formation takes place during the first two months of prenatal development. *105*

original sin Children were perceived, especially during the Middle Ages, as being born as basically bad, evil beings. *8*

osteoporosis This disorder of aging involves an extensive loss of bone tissue. Women are especially vulnerable; it is the main reason many older adults walk with a marked stoop. *577*

oxytocin This hormone stimulates and regulates uterine contractions and has been widely used as a drug to speed up delivery; its use is controversial *118*

P

parallel play The child plays separately from the others, but with similar toys, or in a manner that mimics their play; one of Mildred Parten's categories of play. *270*

passive euthanasia A person is allowed to die by withholding an available treatment, such as withdrawing life-sustaining therapeutic devices. *634*

peers These are individuals who are at about the same age or maturity level. *267*

Perceived Competence Scale for Children Susan Harter's scale measures four components: general self-worth and perceived competence in three skill domains: physical, cognitive, and social. *359*

perception The interpretation of what is sensed is perception. *149*

permissive-indifferent parenting This is a parenting style in which the parent is very uninvolved with the child's life; it is associated with social incompetence in children, especially a lack of self-control. *257*

permissive-indulgent parenting This is a parenting style in which parents are highly involved with their children but place few demands or controls on them. It is associated with children's social incompetence, especially a lack of self-control. *257*

personal fable According to Elkind, the adolescent's egocentrism involves a sense of uniqueness so that others cannot truly understand how he or she feels. *395*

personality-type theory John Holland holds the view that it is important to match the individual's personality with a particular career. Holland proposed six basic personality types that he believes match up with certain careers. *477*

perspective taking One is able to assume another person's perspective and understand his or her thoughts and feelings. *356*

phallic stage The third Freudian stage of development, in which pleasure focuses on the genitals, occurs between the ages of 3 and 6 years. The name comes from the Latin word "phallus," which means penis. *45*

phenomenological approach This approach stresses the importance of our perceptions of ourselves and our world in understanding personality: for each individual, reality is what is perceived. *62*

phenotype This is the way an individual's genotype is expressed in observed and measurable characteristics. *92*

phenylketonuria PKU is a genetic disorder in which the individual cannot properly metabolize protein. If not treated, it can result in mental retardation and hyperactivity. *88*

phonics method This learning to read technique emphasizes the sounds that letters make when used in words. *329*

phonology This is the study of a language's system of sounds.

placenta The life-support system of the embryo consists of a disk-shaped group of tissues in which small blood vessels from the mother and the offspring intertwine but do not mix. *104*

play This is a pleasurable activity which is engaged in for its own sake. *268*

play therapy This form of therapy allows the child to work off frustrations and is a medium through which the therapist can analyze the child's conflicts and ways of coping with them. Children may feel less threatened and be more likely to express their true feelings in the context of play. *268*

pleasure principle The id, according to this Freudian concept, always seeks pleasure and avoids pain. *42*

polygenic inheritance This genetic principle describes the interaction of many genes to produce a particular characteristic. *91*

postconventional reasoning In this highest level of Kohlberg's theory of moral development, morality is completely internalized and not based on other's standards. *374*

practice play The child repeats behavior when new skills are being learned, or when physical or mental mastery and coordination of skills is required for games or sports; practice play is engaged in throughout life. *271*

pragmatics These rules of language involve the ability to engage in context-appropriate conversation. *176*

precipitate In this too rapid delivery, the baby takes less than 10 minutes to be squeezed through the birth canal, resulting in abnormal stress on the infant. *117*

preconventional reasoning In this lowest level in Kohlberg's theory of moral development, the child shows no internalization of moral values; moral reasoning is controlled by external rewards and punishments. *374*

preintimate style In this form of social interaction, an individual has mixed emotions about commitment. The ambivalence is reflected in a strategy of offering love without obligations or long-lasting bonds. *506*

prenatal period This includes the time period from conception to birth. *14*

preoperational stage Piaget's second stage lasts from approximately 2 to 7 years of age. Children begin to represent the world with words, images, and drawings. *55*

pretense/symbolic play The child transforms the physical environment into a symbol. *271*

preterm infants A preterm, or premature, infant is one who is born prior to 38 weeks after conception. *118*

primary circular reaction This is a scheme based on the infant's attempt to reproduce an interesting or pleasurable event that initially occurred by chance. *161*

Project Follow Through This adjunct to Project Head Start, implemented in 1967, devised various programs to maintain the enrichment programs throughout the first years of elementary school. *248*

Project Head Start This compensatory education program is designed to provide children from low income families the opportunity to acquire the skills and experiences important for success in school. *248*

projection A psychoanalytic defense mechanism, projection occurs when we attribute our own shortcomings, problems, and faults to others. *44*

proximodistal pattern This rule of development states that growth starts at the center of the body and moves toward the extremities. *140*

pseudointimate style In this form of social interaction, an individual maintains a long-lasting heterosexual attachment with little or no depth or closeness. *506*

puberty This is a period of rapid sexual and skeletal maturation that occurs mainly in early adolescence. *390*

Public Law 94–142 This 1975 law, also called the Education for All Handicapped Children Act, is the federal government's mandate to all states to provide a free, appropriate education for all children. A key provision of the bill was the development of an individualized education program for each identified handicapped child. *304*

punishment In contrast to reinforcement, the probability that a behavior will occur is decreased when the consequence of that behavior is negative (punishment). *60*

punishment and obedience orientation In this first stage of Kohlberg's theory of moral development, moral reasoning is based on punishment. *374*

Q

questionnaire Respondents read questions and mark their answers on paper rather than respond verbally as they would in an interview. *26*

R

random assignment Researchers assign subjects by chance to experimental and control conditions, thus reducing the likelihood that the results of the experiment will be due to some preexisting differences in the two groups. *29*

rape Forcible sexual intercourse with a person who does not give consent constitutes rape. *470*

rationalization A psychoanalytic defense mechanism, rationalization occurs when the real motive for an individual's behavior is not accepted by the ego and is replaced by a cover motive. *43*

reaction formation A psychoanalytic defense mechanism, reaction formation occurs when we express an unacceptable impulse by transforming it into its opposite. *44*

reaction range This term is used to describe the range of phenotypes for each genotype, suggesting the importance of an environment's restrictiveness or enrichment. *92*

reality principle According to Freud, the ego tries to abide by this principle, bringing the individual pleasure, within the boundaries of reality. *42*

recasting A sentence is phrased in a different way, while retaining the same meaning in this language teaching strategy. *181*

reciprocal socialization This is the view that socialization is bidirectional; children socialize parents just as parents socialize children. *188*

reciprocal teaching This is an instructional procedure used by Brown and Palinscar to develop cognitive monitoring; it requires that students take turns in leading the group in the use of strategies for comprehending and remembering text content that the teacher models for the class. *313*

reflexive smile This type of smile is not associated with external stimuli; it occurs during the first month of life, during irregular patterns of sleep. It does not occur when the infant is in an alert state. *137*

regression A psychoanalytic defense mechanism, regression occurs when we behave in a way that characterizes a previous developmental level. *44*

reinforcement The probability that a behavior will occur is increased when that behavior is reinforced (rewarded). *60*

reintegrative stage Schaie's final stage occurs in late adulthood, when older adults choose to focus their energy on the tasks and activities that have meaning for them. *474*

rejected children These children are disliked by their peers, and are more likely to be disruptive and aggressive than neglected children. *345*

REM (rapid eye movement) sleep Vivid dreams commonly occur among both adults and children during this recurring sleep stage. *139*

remote phase In the first of Robert Atchley's seven phases of retirement, most individuals do little to prepare for retirement. *600*

reorientation phase In the fifth stage of Robert Atchley's phases of retirement, retirees take stock, pull themselves together, and develop more realistic life alternatives. *600*

repression According to Freud, this is the most powerful and pervasive defense mechanism. It works to push unacceptable id impulses out of awareness and back into the unconscious mind. *43*

reproduction When a female gamete (ovum) is fertilized by a male gamete (sperm), the reproductive process begins. *86*

responsibility stage Schaie's adult stage occurs when a family is established and attention is given to the needs of a spouse and offspring. *474*

rite of passage Rituals and ceremonies mark the individual's transition from one status to another. Most rites of passage focus on the transition to adult status. *440*

role-focused level In this second, or intermediate level of relationship maturity, one begins to perceive others as individuals in their own right. *507*

romantic love Also called passionate love or Eros, romantic love has strong sexual and infatuation components, and often predominates in the early part of a love relationship. *489*

rooting reflex When an infant's cheek is stroked, or the side of the mouth is touched, the infant turns its head to the side that was touched in an apparent effort to find something to suck. *133*

S

scaffolding This term describes an important caregiving role in early parent-child interaction. Through their attention and choice of behaviors, caregivers provide a framework around which they interact with their infants. One function scaffolding serves is to introduce infants to social rules, especially turn taking. *189*

schema This cognitive structure is a network of associations that organizes and guides an individual's perceptions. *287*

scheme Piaget's term describes the basic unit for an organized pattern of sensorimotor functioning—also called a schema. *160*

scientific method This approach, which can be used to discover accurate information about behavior and development, includes the following steps: identify and analyze the problem, collect data, draw conclusions, and revise theories. *23*

script This is a schema for an event. *314*

secondary circular reactions In Piaget's third sensorimotor substage, which develops between 4 and 8 months of age, the infant becomes more object-oriented, or focused on the world, moving beyond the preoccupation with the self in sensorimotor interactions. *161*

secure attachment Infants use the caregiver as a secure base from which to explore the environment; believed to provide an important foundation for psychological development later in life.

self-actualization This is Maslow's term for the highest human need, defined as the motivation to develop one's full potential as a human being. *65*

self-concept A central theme in Rogers' and other humanists' views, self-concept refers to individuals' overall perception of their abilities, behavior, and personality. *63*

self-esteem Also referred to as self-worth or self-image, self-esteem is the evaluative and affective dimension of self-concept. *357*

self-focused level In this first level of relationship maturity, one's perspective of another or a relationship is concerned only with how it affects the self. *507*

self-understanding This is the substance and content of the child's self-conception, the cognitive representation of self. *280*

semantics This refers to the meanings of words and sentences. *176*

sensation When information contacts sensory receptors—the eyes, ears, tongue, nostril, and skin—sensation occurs. *149*

sensitive period This ethological concept describes a more flexible band of time for behavior to emerge than does the concept of a critical period. *69*

sensorimotor play Infants engage in this play behavior to derive pleasure from exercising their sensorimotor schemas. *271*

sensorimotor stage Piaget's first stage lasts from birth to about 2 years of age. Infants construct an understanding of the world by coordinating sensory experiences such as seeing and hearing, with physical, motoric actions—hence the term, sensorimotor. *54*

sequential approach This approach combines cross-sectional and longitudinal designs. Usually, this approach starts with a cross-sectional study that includes individuals of different ages. Some time after the initial assessment, the same individuals are tested again. This is the longitudinal aspect of the design. At this later time, a new group of subjects is assessed at each age level. *32*

set point This is the weight that is maintained when no effort is made to gain or lose weight. *461*

short-term memory Individuals retain information for up to 15 to 30 seconds, assuming there is no rehearsal. *235*

sickle-cell anemia This is a genetic disorder that affects the red blood cells, and occurs most often in Blacks. *89*

simple reflexes In Piaget's first sensorimotor substage, corresponding to the first month after birth, the basic means of coordinating sensation and action is through reflexive behaviors, such as rooting and sucking, which are present at birth. *161*

slow-to-warm-up child In this style of temperament, the child has a low activity level, is somewhat negative, shows low adaptability, and displays a low intensity of mood. *96*

sociability In this style of temperament, the child has a tendency to prefer the company of others to being alone. *97*

social breakdown-reconstruction theory This theory argues that aging is promoted through negative psychological functioning brought about by negative societal views of older adults and inadequate provision of services for them. Social reconstruction can occur by changing society's view of older adults and by providing adequate support systems for them. *610*

social clock Neugarten proposed a timetable according to which individuals are expected to accomplish life's tasks, such as getting married, having children, or establishing a career. *551*

social learning theory, The key factors in learning, according to this theory, are behavior, environment, and cognition; this approach is associated primarily with the work of Bandura and Mischel. *60*

social learning theory of gender This theory holds that children's gender development occurs through observation and imitation of gender behavior, and through the rewards and punishments they receive for gender appropriate and inappropriate behavior. *283*

social play The child plays in a way that involves social interaction with peers. *272*

social processes These processes involve changes in the individual's relationships with other people, in emotions, and in personality. *14*

social smile This type of smile occurs in response to an external stimulus, such as a face. *137*

social system morality In this fourth stage of Kohlberg's theory of moral development, moral judgments are based on understanding the social order, law, justice, and duty. *374*

solitary play The child plays alone and independently of others; one of Mildred Parten's categories of play. *270*

stability phase In the sixth stage of Robert Atchley's phases of retirement, adults have decided upon a set of criteria or evaluation choices in retirement and how they will perform once they have made these choices. *600*

stability-change issue Addressing whether development is best described by stability or change, this issue involves the degree to which we become older renditions of our earlier experience or whether we develop into someone different than we were at an earlier stage of development. *20*

standardized tests People answer a series of written or oral questions. The tests have two distinct features: First, psychologists usually total an individual's score, to yield a single score, or set of scores that reflects something about the individual. Second, the individual's scores are compared to the scores of a large group of similar people to determine how the individual responded relative to others. *26*

stereotyped style In this form of social interaction the individual engages in superficial relationships that tend to be dominated by same-sex friendships rather than opposite sex relationships. *506*

storm and stress view Adolescence, according to G. Stanley Hall, is a turbulent time charged with conflict and mood swings. *8*

sublimation A psychoanalytic defense mechanism, sublimation occurs when a useful course of action replaces a distasteful one; it is a form of displacement. *44*

sucking reflex Newborns automatically suck an object placed in their mouth; this enables newborns to get nourishment before they have associated a nipple with food. *133*

sudden infant death syndrome SIDS is the sudden death of an apparently healthy infant, and occurs most often between 2 and 4 months of age. The immediate cause of death is that the infant stops breathing, but the underlying cause is unknown. *638*

superego In Freudian personality theory, the superego is a structure of personality that is the moral branch of personality, taking into account whether something is right or wrong. *43*

surface structure This is the actual order of words in a sentence. *176*

suttee A now-outlawed Hindu practice, suttee is the burning to death of a dead man's widow to increase his family's prestige and firmly establish an image of her in his memory. *648*

symbolic function substage In Piaget's first substage of preoperational thought, occurring roughly between 2 and 4 years, the child gains the ability to mentally represent an object that is not present. *226*

syntax These are the rules that involve the way words are combined to form acceptable phrases and sentences. *175*

T

telegraphic speech This is the use of short and precise words to communicate. It is characteristic of young children's two-word utterances. *182*

temperament This concept refers to an individual's behavioral style and characteristic way of responding. *96*

teratogen Derived from the Greek word *tera,* meaning "monster," a teratogen is any agent that causes a birth defect. Teratology is the field of study that investigates the causes of birth defects. *107*

terminal drop hypothesis This hypothesis states that death is preceded by a decrease in cognitive functioning over approximately a five-year period prior to death. *594*

termination phase In the seventh of Robert Atchley's phases of retirement, the retirement role is replaced by the sick or dependent role because older adults can no longer function autonomously and be self-sufficient. *600*

tertiary circular reactions, novelty, and curiosity In Piaget's fifth sensorimotor substage, which develops between 12 and 18 months of age, infants become intrigued by the variety of properties that objects possess and by the multiplicity of things they can cause to happen to objects. *162*

testosterone This hormone is associated with the development of genitals, an increase in height, and a change in voice in boys. *391*

thanatologists These are people who study death and dying. *648*

theory A theory is a coherent set of ideas that helps to explain data and to make predictions. *23*

top-dog phenomenon This describes the circumstances of moving from the top position in elementary school to the lowest position in middle school or junior high. *402*

triangular theory of love Sternberg's theory says that love has three main forms: passion, intimacy, and commitment. *492*

triarchic theory Sternberg's theory holds that intelligence consists of componential intelligence, experiential intelligence, and contextual intelligence. *321*

trophoblast The outer layer of cells that develops during the germinal period later provides nutrition and support for the embryo. *103*

trust versus mistrust Erikson's first psychosocial stage is experienced in the first year. A sense of trust requires a feeling of physical comfort and a minimal amount of fear and apprehension about the future. *50*

Turner syndrome This is a genetic disorder in which females are missing an X chromosome, making them XO instead of XX. *89*

twin study Behaviors of identical and fraternal twins are compared in this type of study. *93*

type A babies These babies exhibit insecurity by avoiding the mother, by ignoring her, averting her gaze, failing to seek proximity. *192*

Type A behavior pattern This cluster of characteristics—excessively competitive, hard-driving, impatient, and hostile—is thought to be related to the incidence of heart disease. *519*

type B babies These babies use the caregiver as a secure base from which to explore the environment. *192*

type C babies These babies exhibit insecurity by resisting the mother; for example, clinging to her but, at the same time, fighting against the closeness. *192*

U

ultrasound sonography In this prenatal medical procedure, high-frequency sound waves are directed into the pregnant woman's abdomen to detect malformations. *91*

umbilical cord This part of the life support system of the embryo contains two arteries and one vein, and connects the baby to the placenta. *104*

unconditional positive regard A concept, proposed by Carl Rogers, in which one is accepting, valuing, and positive toward another person regardless of that person's behavior. *64*

universal ethical principles In this sixth and highest stage of Kohlberg's theory of moral development, persons have developed a moral standard based on universal human rights. *375*

unoccupied play A child, not engaged in play as it is commonly understood, may stand in one spot, look around the room, or perform random movements that do not seem to have a goal; one of Mildred Parten's categories of play. *269*

W

whole word method This learning to read technique emphasizes learning direct associations between whole words and their meanings. *329*

wisdom According to Baltes, wisdom is the expert knowledge about the practical aspects of life. *595*

X

XYY syndrome This is a genetic disorder in which the male has an extra Y chromosome; it was thought that aggression and violence would be more likely in these men. *89*

Y

youth Kenneth Kenniston described this transitional period between adolescence and adulthood as a time of extended economic and personal temporariness. *456*

Z

zone of proximal development (ZPD) This is Vygotsky's term for tasks too difficult to master alone, but that can be mastered with the guidance of adults or more skilled children. *238*

zygote A zygote is a single cell, which is formed through fertilization and combines the two sets of unpaired chromosomes from the parents. *86*

REFERENCES

A

Aboud, F. E., & Skeery, S. A (1983). Self and ethnic concepts in relation to ethnic constancy. *Canadian Journal of Behavioral Science, 15,* 14–26.

Abramovitch, R., Corter, C., Pepler, D. J., & Stanhope, L. (1986). Sibling and peer interaction: A final follow-up and comparison. *Child Development, 47,* 217–229.

Achenbach, T. M., Phares, V., Howell, V. A., & Nurcombe, B. (1990). Seven-year outcome of the Vermont Intervention Program for Low-Birthweight Infants. *Child Development, 61,* 1672–1681.

Ackerman, B. P. (1988). Thematic influences on children's judgments about story accuracy. *Child Development, 59,* 918–938.

Acredolo, L. P., & Hake, J. L. (1982). Infant perception. In B. B. Wolman (Ed.), *Handbook of developmental psychology.* Englewood Cliffs, NJ: Prentice-Hall.

Adams, G. M., & deVries, H. A. (1973). Physiological effects of an exercise training regimen among women aged 52 to 79. *Journal of Gerontology, 28,* 50–55.

Adams, R. G. (1989). Conceptual and methodological issues in studying friendships of older adults. In R. G. Adams & R. Blieszner (Eds.), *Older adult friendship.* Newbury Park, CA: Sage.

Adelman, R. C. (1988). The importance of basic biological science to gerontology. *Journal of Gerontology: Biological Sciences, 43,* B1–2.

Adler, T. (1991, January). Seeing double? Controversial twins study is widely reported, debated. *APA Monitor, 22,* 1,8.

Ahrons, C. R., & Rodgers, R. H. (1987). *Divorced families.* New York: W. W. Norton.

Aiken, L. R. (1989). *Later life* (3rd ed.). Hillsdale, NJ: Erlbaum.

Ainsworth, M. D. S. (1979). Infant-mother attachment. *American Psychologist, 34,* 932–937.

Alan Guttmacher Institute. (1981). *Teenage pregnancy: The problem that has not gone away.* New York.

Alexander, K. L., & Entwisle, D. R. (1988). Achievement in the first two years of school: Patterns and processes. *Monographs of the Society for Research in Child Development, 53,* (2, Serial No. 218).

Allen, L., & Majidi-Ahi, S. (1989). *Black American children.* In J. T. Gibbs & L. N. Huang (Eds.), Children of color. San Francisco: Jossey-Bass.

Allen, L., & Santrock, J. W. (in press). *Psychology: The contexts of behavior.* Dubuque, IA: Wm. C. Brown.

Allred, K. D., & Smith, T. W. (1989). The hardy personality: Cognitive and physiological responses to evaluative threat. *Journal of Personality and Social Psychology, 56,* 257–266.

America in Transition (1989). Washington, DC: National Governors' Association Task Force on Children.

American Association for Protecting Children (1986). *Highlights of Official Child Neglect and Abuse Reporting: 1984,* American Humane Association, Denver, CO.

American Association of Retired Persons. (1990, January). *Survey of the most important coverages in long-term health care.* Washington, DC: AARP.

American College Health Association (1989, May). *Survey of AIDS on American college and university campuses.* Washington, DC: American College Health Association.

American Psychological Association (1989, January). *APA research review finds no evidence of "post abortion syndrome," but research studies on psychological effects of abortion inconclusive.* Washington, DC: American Psychological Association.

Ames, C., & Ames, R. (Eds.). (1989). *Research on motivation in education.* (Vol. 3) *Goals and cognitions.* San Diego: Academic Press.

Ammerman, R. T., & Hersen, M. (Eds.). (1990). *Children at risk.* New York: Plenum.

Amsterdam, B. K. (1968). *Mirror behavior in children under two years of age.* Unpublished doctoral dissertation, University of North Carolina, Chapel Hill.

Anastasi, A. (1988). *Psychological testing* (6th ed.). New York: Macmillan.

Anderson, D. R., Lorch, E. P., Field, D. E., Collins, P. A., & Nathan, J. G. (1985, April). *Television viewing at home: Age trends in visual attention and time with TV.* Paper presented at the biennial meeting of the Society for Research in Child Development, Toronto.

Anderson, E. A., & Leslie, L. A. (1991). Coping with employment and family stress: Employment arrangement and gender differences. *Sex Roles, 24,* 223–237.

Anderson, L. W. (1989, April). *The impact of sex and age on the resolutions of preschool children's conversational disagreements.* Paper presented at the biennial meeting of the Society for Research in Child Development, Kansas City, MO.

Anderson, N. B. (1989). Health status of aged minorities: Directions for clinical research. *Journal of Gerontology, 44,* M1–M2.

Andres, R. (1989). Does the "best" body weight change with age? In A. J. Stunkard & A. Baum, (Eds.), *Perspectives on behavioral medicine.* Hillsdale, NJ: Erlbaum.

Angoff, W. (1989, August). *Perspectives on bias in mental testing.* Paper presented at the meeting of the American Psychological Association, New Orleans.

Antonucci, T. C. (1989). Understanding adult social relationships. In K. Kreppner & R. M. Lerner (Eds.), *Family systems and life-span development.* Hillsdale, NJ: Erlbaum.

Archer, S. L. (1989). The status of identity: Reflections on the need for intervention. *Journal of Adolescence, 12,* 345–359.

Archer, S. L. (1991). Identity development, gender differences in. In R. M. Lerner, A. C. Petersen, & J. Brooks-Gunn (Eds.), *Encyclopedia of adolescence* (Vol. 1). New York: Garland.

Arehart, D. M., & Smith, P. H. (1990). Identity in adolescence: Influences on dysfunction and psychosocial task issues. *Journal of Youth and Adolescence, 19,* 63–72.

Aries, P. (1962). *Centuries of childhood* (R. Baldrick, Trans.). New York: Knopf.

Arman-Nolley, S. (1989, April). *Vygotsky's perspective on development of creativity and imagination.* Paper presented at the biennial meeting of the Society for Research on Child Development, Kansas City, MO.

Armsden, G. C., & Greenberg, M. T. (1987). The inventory of parent and peer attachment: Individual differences and their relationship to psychological well-being in adolescence. *Journal of Youth and Adolescence, 16,* 427–454.

Arnett, J. (1990). Contraceptive use, sensation seeking, and adolescent egocentrism. *Journal of Youth and Adolescence, 19,* 171–180.

Aronson, E. (1986, August). *Teaching students things they think they already know about: The case of prejudice and desegregation.* Paper presented at the meeting of the American Psychological Association, Washington, DC.

Asarnow, J. R., & Callan, J. W. (1985). Boys with peer adjustment problems: Social cognitive processes. *Journal of Consulting and Clinical Psychology, 53,* 80–87.

Asher, J., & Garcia, R. (1969). The optimal age to learn a foreign language. *Modern Language Journal, 53,* 334–341.

Asher, S. R., & Parker, J. G. (in press). The significance of peer relationship problems in childhood. In B. H. Schneider, G. Attili, J. Nadel, & R. P. Weisberg (Eds.), *Social competence in developmental perspective.* Amsterdam: Kluwer Academic Publishing.

Ashmead, D. H., & Perlmutter, M. (1979, August). *Infant memory in everyday life.* Paper presented at the meeting of the American Psychological Association, New York City.

Astin, A. W., Green, K. C., & Korn, W. S. (1987). *The American freshman: Twenty year trends.* Los Angeles: UCLA Higher Education Research Institute.

Astin, A. W., Green, K. C., & Korn, W. S. (1989). *The American freshman, 1988.* Unpublished manuscript, Higher Education Institute, University of California, Los Angeles.

Astin, A. W., Korn, W. S., & Berz, E. R. (1989). *The American freshman: National norms for fall 1989.* Los Angeles: Higher Education Research Institute, University of California, Los Angeles.

Atchley, R. C. (1976). *The sociology of retirement.* Cambridge, MA: Schenkman.

Atchley, R. C. (1989). Demographic factors and adult psychological development. In K. W. Schaie & C. Schooler (Eds.), *Social structure and aging.* Hillsdale, NJ: Erlbaum.

Atkinson, J. W., & Raynor, I. O. (1974). *Motivation and achievement.* New York: Wiley.

Attie, I., & Brooks-Gunn, J. (1989). The development of eating problems in adolescent girls: A longitudinal study. *Developmental Psychology, 25,* 70–79.

Averill, J. R. (1968). Grief: Its nature and significance. *Psychological Bulletin, 6,* 721–748.

Baca Zinn, M. (1980). Employment and education of Mexican-American women: The interplay of modernity and ethnicity in eight families. *Harvard Educational Review, 50,* 47–62.

Bachman, J., O'Malley, P., & Johnston, L. (1978). *Youth in transition: Vol. VI. Adolescence to adulthood—change and stability of the lives of young men.* Ann Arbor: Institute of Social Research, University of Michigan.

Bachman, J. G. (1991). Dropouts, school. In R. M. Lerner, A. C. Petersen, & J. Brooks-Gunn (Eds.), *Encyclopedia of adolescence* (Vol. 1). New York: Garland.

Bachman, J. G., Johnston, L. P., & O'Malley, P. M. (1987). *Monitoring the future.* Ann Arbor: University of Michigan Institute of Social Research.

Bahr, S. J. (1989). Prologue: A developmental overview of the aging family. In S. J. Bahr & E. T. Peterson (Eds.), *Aging and the family.* Lexington, MA: Lexington Books.

Bahrick, H. P., Bahrick, P. O., & Wittlinger, R. P. (1975). Fifty years of memory for names and faces: A cross-sectional approach. *Journal of Experimental Psychology: General, 104,* 54–75.

Bahrick, L. E. (1988). Intermodal learning in infancy: Learning on the basis of two kinds of invariant relations in audible and visible events. *Child Development, 59,* 197–209.

Bailey, G. W. (1989). Current perspectives on substance abuse in youth. *Journal of the American Academy of Child and Adolescent Psychiatry, 28,* 151–162.

Baines, E. M. (1991). Perspectives on gerontological nursing. Newbury Park, CA: Sage.

Bakeman, R., & Brown, J. V. (1980). Early interaction: Consequences for social and mental development at three years. *Child Development, 51,* 437–447.

Baker, L., & Brown, A. L. (1984). Metacognitive skills and reading. In P. D. Pearson (Ed.), *Handbook of reading research, Part 2.* New York: Longman.

Baker, P. M., & Prince, M. J. (1991). Supportive housing preferences among the elderly. *Journal of Housing for the Elderly, 7,* 5–24.

Ballenger, M. (1983). Reading in the kindergarten: Comment. *Childhood Education, 59,* 187.

Baltes, M. M., & Wahl, H. W. (1991). The behavior system of dependency in long-term care institutions. In M. G. Ory, R. P. Abeles, & P. D. Lipman (Eds.), *Aging, health, and behavior.* Newbury Park, CA: Sage.

Baltes, P. B. (1987). Theoretical propositions of life-span developmental psychology: On the dynamics between growth and decline. *Developmental Psychology, 23,* 611–626.

Baltes, P. B. (1989). The dynamics between growth and decline. *Contemporary Psychology, 34,* 983–984.

Baltes, P. B., Featherman, D. L., & Lerner, R. M. (1990). *Life-span development and behavior.* (Vol. 10). Hillsdale, NJ: Erlbaum.

Baltes, P. B., & Smith, J. (in press). Toward a psychology of wisdom and its ontogenesis. In R. J. Sternberg (Ed.), *Wisdom: Its nature, origins, and development.* New York: Cambridge University Press.

Baltes, P. B., Smith, J., Staudinger, U. M., & Sowarka, D. (in press). Wisdom: One facet of successful aging? In M. Perlmutter (Ed.), *Late-life potential.* Washington, DC: Gerontological Association of America.

Bancroft, J. (1990). The impact of sociocultural influences on adolescent development: Further considerations. In J. Bancroft & J. Reinisch (Eds.), *Adolescence and Puberty.* New York: Plenum.

Bancroft, J., & Reinisch, J. M. (1990). *Adolescence and puberty.* New York: Oxford University Press.

Bandura, A. (1965). Influence of models' reinforcement contingencies on the acquisition of imitative responses. *Journal of Personality and Social Psychology, 1,* 589–595.

Bandura, A. (1977). *Social learning theory.* Englewood Cliffs, NJ: Prentice-Hall.

Bandura, A. (1986). *Social foundations of thought and action: A social cognitive theory.* Englewood Cliffs, NJ: Prentice-Hall.

Bandura, A. (1989). Social cognitive theory. In R. Vasta (Ed.), *Six theories of child development.* Greenwich, CT: JAI Press.

Bandura, A. (1991). Self-efficacy: Impact of self-beliefs on adolescent life paths. In R. M. Lerner, A. C. Petersen, & J. Brooks-Gunn (Eds.), *Encyclopedia of adolescence* (Vol. 2). New York: Garland.

Banks, M. S., & Salapatek, P. (1983). Infant visual perception. In P. H. Mussen (Ed.), *Handbook of child psychology* (4th ed., Vol. 2). New York: Wiley.

Bardwick, J. (1971). *The psychology of women: A study of biocultural conflicts.* New York: Harper & Row.

Barenboim, C. (1981). The development of person perception in childhood and adolescence: From behavioral comparisons to psychological constructs to psychological comparisons. *Child Development, 52,* 129–144.

Barenboim, C. (1985, April). *Person perception and interpersonal behavior.* Paper presented at the biennial meeting of the Society for Research in Child Development, Toronto.

Barkeley, R. (1989). Attention deficit disorders: History, definition, diagnosis. In M. Lewis & S. Miller (Eds.), *Handbook of developmental psychopathology.* New York: Plenum.

Barnes, D. M. (1987). Defect in Alzheimer's is on Chromosome 21. *Science, 235,* 846–847.

Barnes, K. E. (1971). Preschool play norms: A Replication. *Developmental Psychology, 4,* 99–103.

Barnett, L. R., & Netzel, M. T. (1979). Relationship of instrumental and affection behaviors and self-esteem to marital satisfaction in distressed and nondistressed couples. *Journal of Consulting and Clinical Psychology, 47,* 946–954.

Barnett, R. C., Kibria, N., Baruch, G. K., & Pleck, J. H. (1991). Adult daughter-parent relationships and their associations with daughters' subjective well-being and psychological distress. *Journal of Marriage and the Family, 53,* 29–42.

Baron, F. (1989, April). The birth of a notion: Exercises to tap your creative potential. *Omni, 11,* pp. 112–119.

Barr, R. G., Desilets, J., & Rotman, A. (1991, April). *Parsing the normal crying curve: Is it really the evening fussing curve?* Paper presented at the biennial meeting of the Society for Research in Child Development, Seattle.

Barrett, K. C., & Campos, J. J. (1987). A functionalist approach to emotions. In J. D. Osofsky (Ed.), *Handbook of infant development.* New York: Wiley.

Baruch, C. (1991, April). *The influence of the mother-child relationship on the emergence of symbolic play.* Paper presented at the biennial meeting of the Society for Research in Child Development, Seattle.

Baruch, G. K., & Barnett, R. C. (1987). Role quality and psychological well-being. In F. J. Crosby (Ed.), Spouse, parent, worker: On gender and multiple roles. New Haven, CT: Yale University Press.

Baruch, G. K., Biener, L., & Barnett, R. C. (1987). Women and gender in research on work and family. *American Psychologist, 42,* 130–136.

Barusch, A. S. (Ed.). (1991). *Elder care.* Newbury Park, CA: Sage.

Baskett, L. M., & Johnston, S. M. (1982). The young child's interaction with parents versus siblings. *Child Development, 53,* 643–650.

Bass, D. M., Bowman, K., & Noelker, L. S. (1991). The influence of caregiving and bereavement support on adjusting to an older relative's death. *The Gerontologist, 31,* 31, 32–41.

Bassoff, E. (1988). *Mothers and daughters: Loving and letting go.* New York: New American Library.

Bateson, G. (1956). The message, "This is play." In B. Schaffner (Ed.), *Group processes.* New York: Josiah Macy Foundation.

Batshaw, M. L., & Perret, Y. M. (1986). *Children with handicaps.* Baltimore: Paul H. Brooks.

Baumeister, R. F. (1991). Identify crisis. In R. M. Lerner, A. C. Petersen, & J. Brooks-Gunn (Eds.), *Encyclopedia of adolescence* (Vol. 1). New York: Garland.

Baumrind, D. (1971). Current patterns of parental authority. *Developmental Psychology Monographs, 4* (1, Pt. 2).

Baumrind, D. (1989, April). *Sex-differentiated socialization effects in childhood and adolescence.* Paper presented at the biennial meeting of the Society for Research in Child Development, Kansas City, MO.

Baumrind, D. (1991). Effective parenting during the early adolescent transition. In P. A. Cowan & E. M. Hetherington (Eds.), *Advances in family research* (Vol. 2). Hillsdale, NJ: Erlbaum.

Bayley, N. (1969). *Manual for the Bayley Scales of infant development.* New York: The Psychological Corporation.

Beals, D. E., & De Temple, J. (1991, April). *Reading, reporting, and repast: Three R's for co-constructing language and literacy skills.* Paper presented at the biennial meeting of the Society for Research in Child Development, Seattle.

Becker, H. J., & Sterling, C. W. (1987). Equity in school computer use: National data and neglected considerations. *Journal of Educational Computing Research 3,* 289–311.

Becker, J. A. (1991). Processes in the acquisition of pragmatic competence. In G. Conti-Ramsden & C. E. Snow (Eds.), *Children's language* (Vol. 7). Hillsdale, NJ: Erlbaum.

Becker, R. O. (1990). *Cross currents: The perils of electropollution.* Los Angeles: Tarcher.

Beckwith, L., & Howard, J. (1991, April). *Development of toddlers exposed prenatally to PCP and cocaine.* Paper presented at the biennial meeting of the Society for Research in Child Development, Seattle.

Behnke, M., & Eyler, F. D. (1991, April). *Issues in perinatal cocaine abuse research: The interface between medicine and child development.* Paper presented at the biennial meeting of the Society for Research in Child Development, Seattle.

Beilin, H. (1989). Piagetian theory. In R. Vasta (Ed.), *Six theories of child development: Revised formulations and current issues.* Greenwich, CT: JAI Press.

Beland, F. (1987). Living arrangement preferences among elderly people. *The Gerontologist, 27,* 797–803.

Belenky, M. F., Clinchy, B. M., Goldberger, N. R., & Tarule, J. M. (1986). *Women's ways of knowing: The development of self, voice, and mind.* New York: Basic Books.

Bell, A. P., Weinberg, M. S., & Mammersmith, S. K. (1981). *Sexual preference: Its development in men and women.* New York: Simon & Schuster.

Bell, N. J., Avery, A. W., Jenkins, D., Feld, J., & Schoenrock, C. J. (1985). Family relationships and social competence during late adolescence. *Journal of Youth and Adolescence, 14,* 109–119.

Bell, S. M., & Ainsworth, M. D. S. (1972). Infant crying and maternal responsiveness. *Child Development, 43,* 1171–1190.

Belle, D. (1990). Poverty and women's mental health. *American Psychologist, 45,* 385–389.

Belle, D., Burr, R., Shadmon, O., Woodbury, A., Heffernan, M., & Ozer, D. (1991, April). *Unsupervised after-school time, social support, and children's well-being.* Paper presented at the biennial meeting of the Society for Research in Child Development, Seattle.

Belle, D., & Paul, E. (1989, April). *Structural and functional changes accompanying the transition to college.* Paper presented at the biennial meeting of the Society for Research in Child Development, Kansas City, MO.

Bellinger, D., Leviton, A., Waternaux, C., Needleman, H., & Rabinowitz, M. (1987). Longitudinal analysis of prenatal and postnatal lead exposure and early cognitive development. *New England Journal of Medicine, 316,* 1037–1043.

Belloc, N. B., & Breslow, L. (1972). Relationships of physical health status and health practices. *Preventive Medicine, 1,* 409–421.

Bell-Scott, P., & Taylor, R. L. (1989). Introduction: The multiple ecologies of black adolescent development. *Journal of Adolescent Research, 4,* 117–118.

Belmont, J. M. (1989). Cognitive strategies and strategic learning: The socio-instructional approach. *American Psychologist, 44,* 142–148.

Belsky, J. (1981). Early human experience: A family perspective. *Developmental Psychology, 17,* 3–23.

Belsky, J. (1989). Infant-parent attachment and day care: In defense of the stranger situation. In J. S. Lande, S. Scarr, & N. Gunzenhauser (Eds.), *Caring for Children: Challenge to America.* Hillsdale, NJ: Erlbaum.

Belsky, J., Rovine, M., & Fish, M. (1989). The developing family system. In M. R. Gunnar & E. Thelen (Eds.), *Systems and development: The Minnesota Symposia on Child Psychology Series* (Vol. 22). Hillsdale, NJ: Erlbaum.

Belson, W. (1978). *Television violence and the adolescent boy.* London: Saxon House.

Bem, S. L. (1977). On the utility of alternative procedures for assessing psychological androgyny. *Journal of Consulting and Clinical Psychology, 45,* 196–205.

Bem, S. L. (1981). Gender schema theory: A cognitive account of sex-typing. *Psychological Review, 88,* 354–364.

Benbow, C. P., & Stanley, J. C. (1980). Sex differences in mathematics ability: Fact or artifact? *Science, 210,* 1262–1264.

Benbow, C. P., & Stanley, J. C. (1982). Consequences in high school and college of sex differences in mathematical reasoning ability: A longitudinal perspective. *American Educational Research Journal, 19,* 598–622.

Benbow, C. P., & Stanley, J. C. (1983). Sex differences in mathematical reasoning ability: More facts. *Science, 222,* 1029–1031.

Benet, S. (1976). *How to live to be 100.* New York: The Dial Press.

Bengston, V. L. (1985). Diversity and symbolism in grandparental roles. In V. L. Bengston & J. Robertson (Eds.), *Grandparenthood.* Newbury Park, CA: Sage.

Bengston, V. L., Marti, G., & Roberts, R. E. L. (1991). Age group relationships: Generational equity and inequity. In K. Pillemer & K. McCartney (Eds.), *Parent-child relations throughout life.* Hillsdale, NJ: Erlbaum.

Bennett, W. I., & Gurin, J. (1982). *The dieter's dilemma: Eating less and weighing more.* New York: Basic Books.

Berensen, G. (1989, February). *The Bogalusa heart study.* Paper presented at the science forum, American Heart Association, Monterey, CA.

Berg, W. K., & Berg, K. M. (1987). Psychophysiological development in infancy: State, startle, & attention. In J. D. Osofsky (Ed.), *Handbook of infant development* (2nd ed.). New York: Wiley.

Bergin, D. (1988). Stages of play development. In D. Bergin (Ed.), *Play as a medium for learning and development.* Portsmouth, NH: Heinemann.

Berk, S. F. (1985). *The gender factory: The apportionment of work in American households.* New York: Plenum.

Berko, J. (1958). The child's learning of English morphology. *Word, 14,* 150–177.

Berlyne, D. E. (1960). *Conflict, arousal, and curiosity.* New York: McGraw-Hill.

Bernard, H. S. (1981). Identity formation in late adolescence: A review of some empirical findings. *Adolescence, 16,* 349–358.

Berndt, T. J. (1979). Developmental changes in conformity to peers and parents. *Developmental Psychology, 15,* 608–616.

Berndt, T. J. (1982). The features and effects of friendships in early adolescence. *Child Development, 53,* 1447–1460.

Berndt, T. J., & Perry, T. B. (1990). Distinctive features and effects of early adolescent friendships. In R. Montemayor (Ed.), *Advances in adolescent research.* Greenwich, CT: JAI Press.

Berrueta-Clement, J., Schweinhart, L., Barnett, W., & Weikart, D. (1986). The effects of early educational intervention on crime and delinquency in adolescence and early adulthood. In J. Burchard & S. Burchard (Eds.), *Prevention of delinquent behavior.* Newbury Park, CA: Sage.

Berscheid, E. (1985). Interpersonal attraction. In G. Lindzey & E. Aronson (Eds.), *Handbook of social psychology* (3rd ed., Vol. 2). New York: Random House.

Berscheid, E. (1988). Some comments on love's anatomy: Or, whatever happened to old-fashioned lust? In R. J. Sternberg & M. L. Barnes (Eds.), *Anatomy of love.* New Haven: Yale University Press.

Berscheid, E., & Fei, J. (1977). Sexual jealousy and romantic love. In G. Clinton & G. Smith (Eds.), *Sexual jealousy.* Englewood Cliffs, NJ: Prentice-Hall.

Berscheid, E., Snyder, M., & Omoto, A. M. (1989). *Issues in studying close relationships: Conceptualizing and measuring closeness.* Newbury Park, CA: Sage.

Bianchi, S. M., & Spani, D. (1986). *American women in transition.* New York: Russell Sage Foundation.

Biegel, D. E., Sales, E., & Schulz, R. (1991). *Family caregiving in chronic illness.* Newbury Park, CA: Sage.

Birren, J. E., & Sloane, R. B. (Eds.). (1985). *Handbook of mental health and aging.* Englewood Cliffs, NJ: Prentice-Hall.

Bjorklund, D. F. (1989). *Children's thinking.* Belmont, CA: Brooks/Cole.

Blair, S. N. (1990, January). *Personal communication.* Aerobics Institute, Dallas, TX.

Blair, S. N., & Kohl, H. W. (1988). Physical activity: Which is more important for health? *Medicine and Science and Sports and Exercise, 20* (2), Supplement, pp. 5–7.

Blass, J. P., Ko, L., & Wisniewski, H. (1991). Pathology of Alzheimer's disease. *Psychiatric Clinics of North America, 14,* 397–420.

Blechman, E. A., & Brownell, K. D. (Eds.). (1987). *Handbook of behavioral medicine for women.* Elmsford, NY: Pergamon.

Block, J., & Block, J. H. (1988). Longitudinally foretelling drug usage in adolescence: Early childhood personality and environmental precursors. *Child Development, 59,* 336–355.

Block, J. H., Block, J., & Gjerde, P. F. (1986). The personality of children prior to divorce. *Child Development, 57,* 827–840.

Bloom, B. S. (1983, April). *The development of exceptional talent.* Paper presented at the biennial meeting of the Society for Research in Child Development, Detroit.

Bloome, D. (1989). *Classrooms and literacy.* Norwood, NJ: Ablex.

Bloor, C., & White, F. (1983). Unpublished manuscript. University of California at San Diego, LaJolla, CA.

Blos, P. (1989). The inner world of the adolescent. In A. H. Esman (Ed.), *International Annals of Adolescent Psychiatry.* Chicago: University of Chicago Press.

Blum, R. W., & Goldhagen, J. (1981). Teenage pregnancy in perspective. *Clinical Pediatrics, 20,* 335–340.

Blumenfeld, P. C., Pintrich, P. R., Wessles, K., & Meece, J. (1981, April). *Age and sex differences in the impact of classroom experiences on self-perceptions.* Paper presented at the biennial meeting of the Society for Research in Child Development, Boston.

Blumenthal, J. A., Emery, C. F., Madden, D. J., George, L. K., Coleman, R. E., Riddle, M. W., McKee, D. C., Reasoner, J., & Williams, R. S. (1989). Cardiovascular and behavioral effects of aerobic exercise training in healthy older men and women. *Journal of Gerontology: Medical Sciences, 44,* M147–157.

Blumstein, P., & Schwartz, P. (1983). *American couples: Money, work, sex.* New York: Morrow.

Blundell, J. E. (1984). Systems and interactions: An approach to the pharmacology of feeding. In A. J. Stunkard & E. Stellar (Eds.), *Eating and its disorders.* New York: Raven Press.

Blyth, D. A., Bulcroft, R., & Simmons, R. G. (1981, August). *The impact of puberty on adolescents: A longitudinal study.* Paper presented at the meeting of the American Psychological Association, Los Angeles.

Bohannon, J. N., III, & Stanowicz, L. (1988). The issue of negative evidence: Adult responses to children's language errors. *Developmental Psychology, 24,* 684–689.

Bondareff, W. (1985). The neural basis of aging. In J. E. Birren & K. W. Schaie (Eds.), *Handbook of the psychology of aging* (2nd ed.). New York: Van Nostrand Reinhold.

Bornstein, M. H. (Ed.) (1987). *Sensitive periods in development.* Hillsdale, NJ: Erlbaum.

Bornstein, M. H. (1988). Perceptual development across the life cycle. In M. H. Bornstein & M. E. Lamb (Eds.), *Developmental Psychology* (2nd ed.). Hillsdale, NJ: Erlbaum.

Bornstein, M. H. (1989). Stability in early mental development. In M. H. Bornstein & N. A. Krasnegor (Eds.), *Stability and continuity in mental development.* Hillsdale, NJ: Erlbaum.

Bornstein, M. H., & Krasnegor, N. A. (1989). *Stability and continuity in mental development.* Hillsdale, NJ: Erlbaum.

Bornstein, M. H., & Sigman, M. D. (1986). Continuity in mental development from infancy. *Child Development, 57,* 251–274.

Borovsky, D., Hill, W., & Rovee-Collier, C. (1987, April). *Developmental changes in infant long-term memory.* Paper presented at the biennial meeting of the Society for Research in Child Development, Baltimore.

Borstelmann, L. J. (1983). Children before psychology: Ideas about children from antiquity to the late 1800s. In P. H. Mussen (Ed.), *Handbook of Child Psychology* (4th ed., Vol. 1). New York: Wiley.

Bouchard, T. J., Heston, L., Eckert, E., Keyes, M., & Resnick, S. (1981). The Minnesota study of twins reared apart: Project description and sample results in the developmental domain. *Twin Research, 3,* 227–233.

Bouchard, T. J., Lykken, D. T., McGue, M., Segal, N. L., & Tellegen, A. (1990). Source of human psychological differences: The Minnesota Study of Twins Reared Apart. *Science, 250,* 223–228.

Bower, B. (1985). The left hand of math and verbal talent. *Science News, 127,* 263.

Bower, T. G. R. (1989). *The rational infant.* San Francisco: W. H. Freeman.

Bower, T. G. R. (1991, February). Personal communication. Program in psychology and human development, University of Texas at Dallas, Richardson, TX.

Bower, T. G. R. (1991, May). [Personal communication.] Program in Psychology, University of Texas at Dallas, Richardson.

Bowlby, J. (1969). *Attachment and loss* (Vol. 1). London: Hogarth.

Bowlby, J. (1989). *Secure attachment.* New York: Basic Books.

Bowman, P. J., & Howard, C. (1985). Race-related socialization, motivation, and academic achievement: A study of Black youths in three-generation families. *Journal of the American Academy of Child Psychiatry, 24,* 134–141.

Boyd-Franklin, N. (1989). *Black families in therapy: A multisystems approach.* New York: Guilford.

Boyer, C. B., & Hein, K. (1991). AIDS and HIV infection in adolescents: The role of education and antibody testing. In R. M. Lerner, A. C. Petersen, & J. Brooks-Gunn (Eds.), *Encyclopedia of adolescence* (Vol. 1). New York: Garland.

Brackbill, Y. (1979). Obstetric medication and infant behavior. In J. D. Osofsky (Ed.), *Handbook of infant development.* New York: Wiley.

Bracken, M. B., Eskenazi, B., Sachse, K., McSharry, J., Hellenbrand, K., & Leo-Summers, L. (1990). Association of cocaine use with sperm concentration, motility, and morphology. *Fertility and Sterility, 53,* 315–322.

Brady, M. P., Swank, P. R., Taylor, R. D., & Freiberg, H. J. (1988). Teacher-student interactions in middle school mainstreamed classes: Differences with special and regular students. *Journal of Educational Research, 81,* 332–340.

Bray, D. W., & Howard, A. (1983). The AT&T longitudinal studies of managers. In K. W. Schaie (Ed.), *Longitudinal studies of adult psychological development.* New York: Guilford Press.

Bray, J. H. (1988). The effects of early remarriage on children's development: Preliminary analyses of the developmental issues in stepfamily research project. In E. M. Hetherington & J. D. Arasteh (Eds.), *Impact of divorce, single-parenting, and stepparenting on children.* Hillsdale, NJ: Erlbaum.

Bray, J. H., Berger, S., Pacey, K., & Boethel, C. (1991, April). Longitudinal predictors of children's adjustments to divorce and remarriage. Paper presented at the biennial meeting of the Society for Research in Child Development, Seattle.

Brazelton, T. B. (1956). Sucking in infancy, *Pediatrics, 17,* 400–404.

Brazelton, T. B. (1973). *Neonatal Behavioral Assessment Scale.* London: Heinemann Medical Books.

Brazelton, T. B. (1984). *Neonatal Behavioral Assessment Scale* (2nd ed.). Philadelphia: Lippincott.

Brazelton, T. B. (1987, August). *Opportunities for intervention with infants at risk.* Paper presented at the meeting of the American Psychological Association, New York City.

Brazelton, T. B. (1989). Observations of the neonate. In C. Rovee-Collier & L. P. Lipsitt (Eds.), *Advances in infancy* (Vol. 6). Norwood, NJ: Ablex.

Brazelton, T. B. (1990). Saving the bathwater. *Child Development, 61,* 1661–1671.

Brazelton, T. B., Nugent, J. K., & Lester, B. M. (1987). Neonatal Behavioral Assessment Scale. In J. D. Osofsky (Ed.), *Handbook of infant development* (2nd ed.). New York: Wiley.

Bredakamp, S. (1987). *Developmentally appropriate practice in early childhood programs serving children from birth through age 8.* Washington, DC: National Association for the Education of Young Children.

Bredekamp, S., & Shepard, L. (1989). How to best protect children from inappropriate school expectations, practices, and policies. *Young Children, 44,* 14–24.

Brent, D. A. (1989). Suicide and suicidal behavior in children and adolescents. *Pediatrics in Review, 10,* 269–275.

Bretherton, I., Fritz, J., Zahn-Waxler, C., & Ridgeway, D. (1986). Learning to talk about emotions. *Child Development, 57,* 529–548.

Brim, O. G., & Ryff, C. D. (1980). On the properties of life events. In P. B. Baltes & O. G. Brim (Eds.), *Life-span development and behavior.* New York: Academic Press.

Brislin, R. W. (1990). Applied cross-cultural psychology: An introduction. In R. W. Brislin (Ed.), *Applied cross-cultural psychology.* Newbury Park, CA: Sage.

Brody, E. M. (1990). *Women in the middle: Their parent-care years.* New York: Springer.

Brodzinsky, D. M., Schechter, D. E., Braff, A. M., & Singer, L. M. (1984). Psychological and academic adjustment in adopted children. *Journal of Consulting and Clinical Psychology, 52,* 582–590.

Brone, R. J., & Fisher, C. B. (1988). Determinants of adolescent obesity: A comparison with anorexia nervosa. *Adolescence, 23,* 155–169.

Bronfenbrenner, U. (1970). *Two worlds of childhood: U.S. and U.S.S.R.* Newbury Park, CA: Sage.

Bronfenbrenner, U. (1979). Contexts of child rearing: Problems and prospects. *American Psychologist, 34,* 844–850.

Bronfenbrenner, U. (1986). Ecology of the family as a context for human development: Research perspectives. *Developmental Psychology, 22,* 723–742.

Bronfenbrenner, U. (1989, April). *Ecology of the family as a context for human development.* Paper presented at the biennial meeting of the Society for Research in Child Development, Kansas City, MO.

Bronfenbrenner, U. (1989, April). *The developing ecology of human development.* Paper presented at the biennial meeting of the Society for Research in Child Development, Kansas City, MO.

Bronstein, P. (1988). Marital and parenting roles in transition. In P. Bronstein & C. P. Cowen (Eds.), *Contemporary fatherhood.* New York: Wiley.

Bronstein, P., & Paludi, M. (1988). The introductory course from a broader human perspective. In P. A. Bronstein & K. Quina (Eds.), *Teaching a psychology of people.* Washington, DC: American Psychological Association.

Bronstein, P. A., & Quina, K. (1988). Perspectives on gender balance and cultural diversity in the teaching of psychology. In P. A. Bronstein & K. Quina (Eds.), *Teaching a psychology of people: Resources for gender and sociocultural awareness.* Washington, DC: American Psychological Association.

Brook, D. W., & Brook, J. S. (in press). Family processes associated with alcohol and drug use and abuse. In E. Kaufman & P. Kaufman (Eds.), *Family therapy of drug and alcohol abuse: Ten years later.* New York: Gardner Press.

Brook, J. S., Brook, D. W., Gordon, A. S., Whiteman, M., & Cohen, P. (1990). The psychological etiology of adolescent drug use: A family interactional approach. *Genetic, Social, and General Psychology Monographs, 116,* 110–267.

Brooks-Gunn, J. (1988). Antecedents and consequences of variations in girls' maturational training. In M. D. Levine & E. R. McAnarney (Eds.), *Early adolescent transitions.* Lexington, MA: Lexington Books.

Brooks-Gunn, J., & Warren, M. P. (1988). The psychological significance of secondary sexual characteristics in 9- to 11-year-old girls. *Child Development, 59,* 161–169.

Brooks-Gunn, J. & Warren, M. P. (1989, April). *How important are pubertal and social events for different problem behaviors and contexts.* Paper presented at the biennial meeting of the Society for Research in Child Development, Kansas City, MO.

Broughton, J. M. (1978). Development of concepts of self, mind, reality, and knowledge. In W. Damon (Ed.), *Social cognition.* San Francisco: Jossey-Bass.

Broverman, I., Vogel, S., Boverman, D., Clarkson, F., & Rosenkranz, P. (1972). Sex-role stereotypes: A current appraisal. *Journal of Social Issues, 28,* 59–78.

Brown, A. L., Bransford, J. D., Ferrara, R. A., & Campione, J. C. (1983). Learning, remembering, and understanding. In P. H. Mussen (Ed.), *Handbook of child psychology* (4th ed., Vol. 3). New York: Wiley.

Brown, A. L., & Palincsar, A. M. (1984). Reciprocal teaching of comprehension-fostering and monitoring activities. *Cognition and Instruction, 1,* 175–177.

Brown, A. L., & Palincsar, A. M. (1989). Guided, cooperative learning and individual knowledge acquisition. In L. B. Resnick (Ed.), *Knowing and learning: Essays in honor of Robert Glaser.* Hillsdale, NJ: Erlbaum.

Brown, B. B., & Lohr, M. J. (1987). Peer group affiliation and adolescent self-esteem: An integration of ego identity and symbolic interaction theories. *Journal of Personality and Social Psychology, 52,* 47–55.

Brown, B. B., & Mounts, N. (1989, April). *Peer group structures in single versus multiethnic high schools.* Paper presented at the biennial meeting of the Society for Research in Child Development, Kansas City, MO.

Brown, B. B., Steinberg, L., Mounts, N., & Phillipp, M. (1990, March). *The comparative influence of peers and parents on high school achievement: Ethnic differences.* Paper presented at the meeting of the Society for Research in Adolescence, Atlanta, GA.

Brown, D. R., & Gary, L. E. (1985). Social support network differentials among married and nonmarried Black females. *Psychology of Women Quarterly, 9,* 229–241.

Brown, F. (1973). *The reform of secondary education: Report of the national commission on the reform of secondary education.* New York: McGraw-Hill.

Brown, J. D. (1991). Staying fit and staying well: Physical fitness as a moderator of life stress. *Journal of Personality and Social Psychology, 60,* 555–561.

Brown, J. K. (1985). Introduction. In J. K. Brown & V. Kerns (Eds.), *In her prime: A new view of middle-aged women.* South Hadley, MA: Bergin & Garvey.

Brown, J. L. (1964). States in newborn infants. *Merrill-Palmer Quarterly, 10,* 313–327.

Brown, J. L., & Pizer, H. F. (1987). *Living hungry in America.* New York: Macmillan.

Brown, L. M. & Gilligan, C. (1990, March). *The psychology of women and the development of girls.* Paper presented at the meeting of the Society for Research on Adolescence, Atlanta, GA.

Brown, R. (1973). *A first language: The early stages.* Cambridge, MA: Harvard University Press.

Brown, R. (1986). *Social psychology* (2nd ed.). New York: Free Press.

Brubaker, T. H. (1985). *Later life families.* Newbury Park, CA: Sage.

Bruce, S. A. (1991). Ultrastructure of dermal fibroblasts during development and aging: Relationship to in vitro senescence of dermal fibroblasts. *Experimental Gerontology, 26,* 3–16.

Brumberg, J. J. (1988). *Fasting girls.* Cambridge, MA: Harvard University Press.

Bruner, J. S. (1989, April). *The state of developmental psychology.* Paper presented at the biennial meeting of the Society for Research in Child Development, Kansas City, MO.

Bruner, J. S. (1991, April). *Social-cultural determinants of concept of mind.* Paper presented at the biennial meeting of the Society for Research in Child Development, Seattle.

Bryer, K. B. (1979). The Amish way of death: A study of family support systems. *American Psychologist, 34,* 255–261.

Buhrmester, D. (1989). *Changes in friendship, interpersonal competence, and social adaptation during early adolescence.* Unpublished manuscript, Department of Psychology, UCLA, Los Angeles.

Buhrmester, D., & MacDonald, V. (1991, April). *The effects of hyperactivity and stimulant medication on prosocial behavior.* Paper presented at the biennial meeting of the Society for Research in Child Development, Seattle.

Bulcroft, K. A., & Bulcroft, R. A. (1991). The nature and functions of dating in later life. *Research on Aging, 13,* 244–256.

Bulcroft, K. A., & O'Connor-Roden, M. (1986, June). Never too late. *Psychology Today,* pp. 66–69.

Burkhart, B. (1983). Acquaintance rape on college campuses. Paper presented at the Rape Prevention on College Campuses Conference in Louisville, KY.

Burley, K. A. (1991). Family-work spillover in dual-career couples: A comparison of two time perspectives. *Psychological Reports, 68,* 471–480.

Bursik, K. (1991). Adaptation to divorce and ego development in adult women. *Journal of Personality and Social Psychology, 60,* 300–306.

Burts, D. C., Charlesworth, R., & Fleege, P. O. (1991, April). *Achievement in kindergarten children in developmentally appropriate and developmentally inappropriate classrooms.* Paper presented at the biennial meeting of the Society for Research in Child Development, Seattle.

Burts, D. C., Hart, C. H., Charlesworth, R., Fleege, P. O., Mosley, J., & Thomasson, R. (in press). Observed activities and stress behaviors of children in developmentally appropriate and inappropriate kindergarten classrooms. *Early Childhood Research Quarterly.*

Burts, D. C., Hart, C. H., Charlesworth, R., Hernandez, S., Kirk, L., & Mosley, J. (1989, March). *A comparison of the frequencies of stress behaviors observed in kindergarten children in classrooms with developmentally appropriate vs. developmentally inappropriate instructional practices.* Paper presented at the annual meeting of the American Educational Research Association, San Francisco, CA.

Buss, A. H., & Plomin, R. (1984). *A temperament theory of personality development.* New York: Wiley-Interscience.

Buss, A. H., & Plomin, R. (1987). Commentary. In H. H. Goldsmith, A. H. Buss, R. Plomin, M. K. Rothbart, A. Thomas, A. Chess, R. R. Hinde, & R. B. McCall. Roundtable: What is temperament? Four approaches. *Child Development, 58,* 505–529.

Buss, D. & others. (1990). International preferences in selecting mates. *Journal of Cross-Cultural Psychology, 21,* (1), 5–47.

Buss, R. R., Yussen, S. R., Mathews, S. R., Miller, G. E., & Rembold, K. L. (1983). Development of children's use of a story schema to retrieve information. *Developmental Psychology, 19,* 22–28.

Buss, T., & Redburn, F. S. (1983). Unpublished manuscript, Center for Urban Studies, Youngstown State University, Youngstown, OH.

Butler, R. N. (1975). *Why survive? Being old in America.* New York: Harper & Row.

Butler, R. N. (1987). Ageism. In G. L. Maddox (Ed.), *The encyclopedia of aging.* New York: Springer.

Butler, S. (1902). The way of all flesh. In Shrewsbury (Ed.), *The works of Samuel Butler* (Vol. 17). New York: AMS Press.

Byer, C. O. & Shainberg, L. W. (1991). *Dimensions of human sexuality* (3rd ed.). Dubuque, IA: Wm. C. Brown.

Byrnes, J. P. (1988). Formal operations: A systematic reformulation. *Developmental Review, 8,* 66–87.

C

Cairns, R. B. (1991). Multiple metaphors for a singular idea. *Developmental Psychology, 27,* 23–236.

Cairns, R. B., & Cairns, B. D. (1989, April). *Risks and lifelines in adolescence.* Paper presented at the biennial meeting of the Society for Research in Child Development, Kansas City, MO.

Caldwell, B. (1964). The effects of infant care. In M. Hoffman & L. Hoffman (Eds.), *Review of child development research* (Vol. 1). New York: Russell Sage.

Caldwell, B. (1991, October). *Impact on the child.* Paper presented at the symposium on day care for children, Arlington, VA.

Calhoun, J. A. (1988, March). *Gang violence.* Testimony to the House Select Committee on Children, Youth, and Families, Washington, DC.

Camara, K. A., & Resnick, G. (1988). Interparental conflict and cooperation: Factors moderating children's post-divorce adjustment. In E. M. Hetherington & J. D. Arasteh (Eds.), *Impact of divorce, single-parenting, and stepparenting on children.* Hillsdale, NJ: Erlbaum.

Cameron, D. (1988 February). Soviet schools. *NEA Today,* p. 15.

Campbell, J., Swank, P., & Vincett, K. (1991). The role of hardiness in the resolution of grief. *Omega, 23,* 53–65.

Campbell, J. I. D., & Charness, N. (1990). Age-related declines in working-memory skills: Evidence from a complex calculation task. *Developmental Psychology, 26,* 879–888.

Campos, J. J., Langer, A., & Krowitz, A. (1970). Cardiac responses on the visual cliff in prelocomotor human infants. *Science, 170,* 196–197.

Cancian, F. M., & Gordon, S. L. (1988). Changing emotion norms in marriage: Love and anger in U.S. women's magazines since 1900. *Gender and Society, 2,* 308–342.

Cantor, K. P., Weiss, S. H., Goedert, J. J., & Battjes, R. J. (1991). HTLV–I/II seroprevalence and HIV/HTLV coinfection among U.S. intravenous drug users. *Journal of Acquired Immune Deficiency Syndromes, 4,* 460–467.

Cantor, M. H. (1991). Family and community: Changing roles in an aging society. *The Gerontologist, 31,* 337–346.

Cappiello, L. A., & Troyer, R. E. (1979). A study of the role of health educators in teaching about death and dying. *Journal of School Health, 49,* 397–399.

Carbo, M. (1987). Reading styles research: "What works" isn't always phonics. *Phi Delta Kappan, 68,* 431–435.

Carey, S. (1977). The child as word learner. In M. Halle, J. Bresman, & G. A. Miller (Eds.), *Linguistic theory and psychological reality.* Cambridge: Massachusetts Institute of Technology Press.

Carlson, C., Cooper, C., & Hsu, J. (1990, March). *Predicting school achievement in early adolescence: The role of family process.* Paper presented at the meeting of the Society for Research in Adolescence, Atlanta, GA.

Carnegie Corporation (1989). *Turning points: Preparing youth for the 21st century.* New York: Carnegie Corporation.

Carper, L. (1978, April). Sex roles in the nursery. *Harper's.*

Carr, M., Borkowski, J. G., & Maxwell, S. E. (1991). Motivational components of underachievement. *Developmental Psychology, 27,* 108–118.

Carrasquillo, A. L. (1991). Hispanic children and youth in the United States. New York: Garland.

Carroll, C., & Miller, D. (1991). *Health* (5th ed.). Dubuque, IA: Wm. C. Brown.

Carskadon, M. A., & Dement, W. C. (1989). Normal human sleep: An overview. In M. H. Kryger, T. Roth, & W. C. Dement (Eds.), *Principles and practices of sleep medicine.* San Diego: Harcourt Brace Jovanovich.

Carter, D. B., & Levy, G. D. (1988). Cognitive aspects of children's early sex-role development: The influence of gender schemas on preschoolers' memories and preferences for sex-typed toys and activities. *Child Development, 59,* 782–793.

Carter, D. B., & Taylor, R. D. (in press). The development of children's awareness and understanding of flexibility in sex-role stereotypes: Implications for preferences, attitude, and behavior. *Sex Roles.*

Carter-Saltzman, L. (1980). Biological and sociocultural effects on handedness: Comparison between biological and adoptive families. *Science, 209,* 1263–1265.

Case, R. (1991). Advantages and disadvantages of the Neo-Piagetian position. In R. Case (Ed.), *The mind's staircase.* Hillsdale, NJ: Erlbaum.

Case, R., Kurland, D. M., & Goldberg, J. (1982). Operational efficiency and the growth of short-term memory span. *Journal of Experimental Child Psychology, 33,* 386–404.

Casper, R. C. (1989). Psychodynamic psychotherapy in acute anorexia nervosa and acute bulimia nervosa. In A. H. Esman (Ed.), *International annals of adolescent psychiatry.* Chicago: University of Chicago Press.

Castro, F. G., & Magaña, D. (1988). A course in health promotion in ethnic minority populations. In P. A. Bronstein & K. Quina (Eds.), *Teaching a psychology of people.* Washington, D.C. American Psychological Association.

Cavanaugh, J. C. (1990). *Adult development and aging.* Belmont, CA: Wadsworth.

Cavett, D. (1974). *Cavett*. San Diego: Harcourt Brace Jovanovich.

Cazden, C. B. (1988). *Classroom discourse*. Portsmouth, NH: Heinemann.

Ceci, S. J. (1991, April). *Intellectual development in context*. Paper presented at the biennial meeting of the Society for Research in Child Development, Seattle.

Chalfant, J. C. (1989). Learning disabilities: Policy issues and promising approaches. *American Psychologist, 44,* 392–398.

Chappell, N. L., & Badger, M. (1989). Social isolation and well-being. *Journal of Gerontology, 14,* S169–S176.

Charlesworth, R. (1989). "Behind" before they start? *Young Children, 44,* 5–13.

Charlesworth, R., Hart, C. H., Burts, D. C., & Hernandez, S. (in press). Kindergarten teachers' beliefs and practices. *Early Child Development and Care*.

Chase-Lansdale, P. L., & Hetherington, E. M. (in press). The impact of divorce on life-span development: Short- and long-term effects. In P. B. Baltes, D. L. Featherman, & R. M. Lerner (Eds.), *Life-span development and behavior*. Hillsdale, NJ: Erlbaum.

Chasnoff, I. J. (1991, April). *Cocaine versus tobacco: Impact on infant and child outcome*. Paper presented at the biennial meeting of the Society for Research in Child Development, Seattle.

Chasnoff, I. J., Griffith, D. R., MacGregor, S., Dirkes, K., & Burns, K. A. (1989). Temporal patterns of cocaine use in pregnancy. *Journal of the American Medical Association, 261,* 1741–1744.

Chen, C., & Stevenson, H. W. (1989). Homework: A cross-cultural examination. *Child Development, 60,* 551–561.

Cherlin, A. J., & Furstenberg, F. F. (1988). *The new American grandparent*. New York: Basic Books.

Cherry, R. L. (1991). Agents of nursing home quality of care: Ombudsmen and staff ratios revisited. *The Gerontologist, 31,* 302–308.

Chesney-Lind, M. (1989). Girls' crime and woman's place: Toward a feminist model of female delinquency. *Crime and Delinquency, 35,* 5–30.

Chess, S., & Thomas, A. (1977). Temperamental individuality from childhood to adolescence. *Journal of Child Psychiatry, 16,* 218–226.

Chi, M. T. (1978). Knowledge structures and memory development. In R. S. Siegler (Ed.), *Children's thinking: What develops?* Hillsdale, NJ: Erlbaum.

Chinn, P. L. (1991). Aging and ageism. *Advances in Nursing Science, 13,* vii.

Chiriboga, D. A. (1982). Adaptation to marital separation in later and earlier life. *Journal of Gerontology, 37,* 109–114.

Chodorow, N. J. (1978). *The reproduction of mothering*. Berkeley: University of California Press.

Chodorow, N. J. (1989). *Feminism and psychoanalytic theory*. New Haven, CT: Yale University Press.

Chomsky, N. (1957). *Syntactic structures*. The Hague: Mouton.

Church, D. K., Siegel, M. A., & Foster, C. D. (1988). *Growing old in America*. Wylie, TX: Information Aids.

Cicchetti, D., Beeghly, M., Carlson, V., Coster, W., Gersten, M., Rieder, C., & Kegan, R. (1991). Development and psychopathology: Lessons from the study of maltreated children. In D. P. Keating & H. G. Rosen (Eds.), *Constructivist perspectives on atypical development*. Hillsdale, NJ: Erlbaum.

Cicirelli, V. G. (1977). Family structure and interaction: Sibling effects on socialization. In M. McMillan & M. Sergio (Eds.), *Child psychiatry: Treatment and research*. New York: Brunner/Mazel.

Cicirelli, V. G. (1982). Sibling influence throughout the life span. In M. E. Lamb & B. Sutton-Smith (Eds.), *Sibling relationships*. Hillsdale, NJ: Erlbaum.

Cicirelli, V. G. (1991). Sibling relationships in adulthood. *Marriage and Family Review, 16,* 291–310.

Clark, E. V. (1983). Meanings and concepts. In P. H. Mussen (Ed.), *Handbook of child psychology* (4th ed., Vol. 4). New York: Wiley.

Clark, H. H., & Clark, E. V. (1977). *Psychology and language*. New York: Harcourt Brace Jovanovich.

Clarke-Stewart, K. A. (1989). Infant day care: Maligned or malignant? *American Psychologist, 44,* 266–273.

Clarke-Stewart, K. A., & Fein, G. G. (1983). Early childhood programs. In P. H. Mussen (Ed.), *Handbook of child psychology* (4th ed., Vol. 2). New York: Wiley.

Clarkson-Smith, L., & Hartley, A. A. (1989). Relationships between physical exercise and cognitive abilities in older adults. *Psychology and Aging, 4,* 183–189.

Clemens, A. W., & Axelson, L. J. (1985). The not-so-empty nest: The return of the fledgling adult. *Family Relations, 34,* 259–264.

Cogwill, D. O. (1974). Aging and modernization: A revision of theory. In J. Gubrium (Ed.), *Late Life*. Springfield, IL: Charles C Thomas.

Cohen, C. P., & Naimark, H. (1991). United Nations convention on the rights of the child: Individual rights concepts and their significance for social scientists. *American Psychologist, 46,* 60–65.

Cohen, L. A. (1987, November). Diet and cancer. *Scientific American*, pp. 128–137.

Cohen, P., Brook, J. S., & Kandel, D. B. (1991). Drug use, predictors, and correlates of. In R. M. Lerner, A. C. Petersen, & J. Brooks-Gunn (Eds.), *Encyclopedia of adolescence* (Vol. 1). New York: Garland.

Cohen, P., Velez, C. N., Brook, J., & Smith, J. (1989). Mechanisms of the relation between perinatal problems, early childhood illness, and psychopathology in late childhood and adolescence. *Child Development, 60,* 701–709.

Cohn, J. F., & Tronick, E. Z. (1988). Mother-infant face-to-face interaction. Influence is bidirectional and unrelated to periodic cycles in either partner's behavior. *Developmental Psychology, 24,* 396–397.

Coie, J. D., & Koeppl, G. K. (1990). Adapting intervention to the problems of aggressive and disruptive rejected children. In S. R. Asher & J. D. Coie (Eds.), *Peer rejection in childhood*. New York: Cambridge University Press.

Colby, A., Kohlberg, L., Gibbs, J., & Lieberman, M. (1983). A longitudinal study of moral judgment. *Monographs of the Society for Research in Child Development* (Serial No. 201).

Cole, S. (1981). *Working kids on working*. New York: Lothrop, Lee, & Shephard.

Coleman, J. S. (1961). *The adolescent society*. New York: Free Press.

Coleman, J. S., et al. (1974). *Youth: Transition to adulthood*. Report of the Panel on Youth of the President's Science Advisory Committee. Chicago: University of Chicago Press.

Coleman, P. D. (1986, August). *Regulation of dendritic extent: Human aging brain and Alzheimer's disease*. Paper presented at the meeting of the American Psychological Association, Washington, DC.

Coles, C. D., Platzman, K. A., & Smith, I. E. (1991, April). *Substance abuse and neonates: Alcohol and cocaine effects*. Paper presented at the biennial meeting of the Society for Research in Child Development, Seattle.

Coles, R. (1986). *The political life of children*. Boston: Little, Brown.

Collins, A. (1986). Teaching reading and writing with personal computers. In J. Oransanu (Ed.), *A decade of reading research: Implications for practice*. Hillsdale, NJ: Erlbaum.

Collins, A., Brown, J. S., & Newman, S. E. (1989). Cognitive apprenticeship: Teaching the craft of reading, writing, and mathematics. In L. B. Resnick (Ed.), *Knowing and learning: Essays in honor of Robert Glaser*. Hillsdale, NJ: Erlbaum.

Collins, W. A. (1989, April). *Parents' relational cognitions and developmental changes in relationships during adolescence*. Paper presented at the biennial meeting of the Society for Research in Child Development, Kansas City, MO.

Collins, W. A. (1990). Parent-child relationships in the transition to adolescence: Continuity and change in interaction, affect, and cognition. In R. Montemayor, G. R. Adams, & T. P. Gulotta (Eds.), *From childhood to adolescence: A transitional period?* Newbury Park, CA: Sage.

Colombo, J., Moss, M., & Horowitz, F. D. (1989). Neonatal state profiles: Reliability and short-term prediction of neurobehavioral status. *Child Development, 60,* 1102–1110.

Columbo, J., & Fagen, J. W. (1991). (Eds.). *Individual differences in infancy*. Hillsdale, NJ: Erlbaum.

Comer, J. P. (1988). Educating poor minority children. *Scientific American, 259,* 42–48.

Committee for Economic Development (1987). *Children in need: Investment strategies for the educationally disadvantaged*. Washington, DC: Committee for Economic Development.

Conant, J. B. (1959). *The American high school today*. New York: McGraw-Hill.

Condi, S. J. (1989). Older married couples. In S. J. Bahr & E. T. Peterson (Eds.), *The aging family*. Lexington, MA: Lexington Books.

Condry, J. C. (1989). *The psychology of television*. Hillsdale, NJ: Erlbaum.

Conger, J. J. (1981). Freedom and commitment: Families, Youth, and Social Change. *American Psychologist, 36,* 1475–1484.

Conger, J. J. (1988). Hostages to the future: Youth, values, and public interest. *American Psychologist, 43,* 291–300.

Conti-Ramsden, G., & Snow, C. E. (1991). (Eds.). Children's language: How it develops and how it is used. In G. Conti-Ramsden & C. E. Snow (Eds.), *Children's language* (Vol. 7). Hillsdale, NJ: Erlbaum.

Coombs, R. H. (1991). Marital status and personal well-being: A literature review. *Family Relations, 40,* 97–102.

Coons, S., & Guilleminault, C. (1984). Development of consolidated sleep and wakeful periods in relation to the day/night cycle of infancy. *Developmental Medicine and Child Neurology, 26,* 169–176.

Cooper, C. R., & Carlson, C. (1991, April). Continuity and change in adolescents' family communication: Developmental, gender, and ethnic perspectives. Paper presented at the biennial meeting of the Society for Research in Child Development, Seattle.

Cooper, C. R., & Grotevant, H. D. (1989, April). *Individuality and connectedness in the family and adolescents' self and relational competence*. Paper presented at the biennial meeting of the Society for Research in Child Development, Kansas City, MO.

Cooper, C. R., Grotevant, H. D., Moore, M. S., & Condon, S. M. (1982, August). *Family support and conflict: Both foster adolescent identity and role taking*. Paper presented at the meeting of the American Psychological Association, Washington, D.C.

Cooper, K. (1970). *The new aerobics*. New York: Bantam.

Coopersmith, S. (1967). *The antecedents of self-esteem*. San Francisco: W. H. Freeman.

Corbin, J., & Strauss, A. (1988). *Unending work and care: Managing chronic illness at home.* San Francisco: Jossey-Bass.

Corless, I. B., & Pittman-Lindeman, M. (1989). *AIDS: Principles, practices, and politics.* New York: Hemisphere.

Corrigan, R. (1981). The effects of task and practice on search for invisibly displaced objects. *Developmental Review, 11,* 1–17.

Corser, J., Stevenson, H. W., & Lee, S. (1989, April). *Education for excellence: The Asian experience.* Paper presented at the biennial meeting of the Society for Research in Child Development, Kansas City, MO.

Corwin, V. (1989, March). *Sesame Street* abroad. *Sesame Street Magazine Parent's Guide,* pp. 24, 26.

Costa, P. T. (1986, August). *The scope of individuality.* Paper presented at the meeting of the American Psychological Association, Washington, DC.

Costa, P. T., & McRae, R. R. (1980). Still stable after all these years: Personality as a key to some issues in aging. In P. B. Baltes & O. G. Brim (Eds.), *Life-span development and behavior.* New York: Academic Press.

Costa, P. T., & McRae, R. R. (1989). Personality continuity and the changes of adult life. In M. Storandt & G. R. VandenBos (Eds.), *The adult years: Continuity and change.* Washington, DC: American Psychological Association.

Costa, P. T., Zonderman, A. B., McCrae, R. R., Cornon-Huntely, J., Locke, B. Z., & Barbano, H. E. (1987). Longitudinal analyses of psychological well-being in a national sample: Stability and mean levels. *Journal of Gerontology, 42,* 50–55.

Cowan, C. P., Cowan, P. A., Heming, G., & Miller, N. (1991). Becoming a family: Marriage, parenting, and child development. In P. A. Cowan & E. M. Hetherington (Eds.), *Family transitions.* Hillsdale, NJ: Erlbaum.

Cowan, P. A. (1988). Becoming a father: A time of change, an opportunity for development. In P. Bronstein & C. P. Cowan (Eds.), *Fatherhood today.* New York: Wiley.

Cowan, P. A. (1991). Individual and family life transitions: A proposal for a new definition. In P. A. Cowan & E. M. Hetherington (Eds.), *Family transitions.* Hillsdale, NJ: Erlbaum.

Cowan, P. A., & Cowan, C. P. (1989, April). *From parent adaptation pregnancy to child adaptation in kindergarten.* Paper presented at the biennial meeting of the Society for Research in Child Development, Kansas City, MO.

Cowley, G. (1988, May 23). The wisdom of animals. *Newsweek,* pp. 52–58.

Craik, F. I. M. (1977). Age differences in human memory. In J. E. Birren & K. W. Schaie (Eds.), *Handbook of the psychology of aging.* New York: Van Nostrand Reinhold.

Crisafi, M. A., & Driscoll, J. M. (1991, April). *Developmental outcome in very low birth-weight infants at three years of age.* Paper presented at the biennial meeting of the Society for Research in Child Development, Seattle.

Crittenden, P. (1988). Family and dyadic patterns of functioning in maltreating families. In K. Browne, C. Davies, & P. Stratton (Eds.), *Early prediction and prevention of child abuse.* New York: Wiley.

Crittenden, P., & Partridge, M. (1991, April). *Maltreating couples' representations of attachment.* Paper presented at the biennial meeting of the Society for Research in Child Development, Seattle.

Crohan, S. E., & Antonucci, T. C. (1989). Friends as a source of social support in old age. In R. G. Adams & R. Blieszner (Eds.), *Older adult friendships.* Newbury Park, CA: Sage.

Crohan, S. E., Antonucci, T. C., Adelmann, P. K., & Coleman, L. M. (1989). Job characteristics and well-being at mid-life: Ethnic and gender comparisons. *Psychology of Women Quarterly, 13,* 223–235.

Cronbach, L. J., & Snow, R. E. (1977). *Aptitudes and instructional methods.* New York: Irvington Books.

Crosby, F., & Ayers, L. (1991). In the middle. *Contemporary Psychology, 36,* 565–566.

Cross, K. P. (1984, November). The rising tide of school reform reports. *Phi Delta Kappan,* pp. 167–172.

Cumming, E., & Henry, W. (1961). *Growing old.* New York: Basic Books.

Cummings, E. M., Greene, A. L., & Karraker, K. H. (1991). *Life-span developmental psychology: Perspectives on stress and coping.* Hillsdale, NJ: Erlbaum.

Curtiss, S. (1977). *Genie.* New York: Academic Press.

Cutrona, C. E. (1982). Transition to college: Loneliness and the process of social adjustment. In L. A. Peplau & D. Perlman (Eds.), *Loneliness: A sourcebook of current theory, research and therapy.* New York: Wiley.

D

Damon, W. (1988). *The moral child.* New York: Free Press.

Damon, W., & Hart, D. (1988). *Self-understanding in childhood and adolescence.* New York: Cambridge University Press.

Danner, F. (1989). Cognitive development in adolescence. In J. Worrell & F. Danner (Eds.), *The adolescent as decision maker.* New York: Academic Press.

Darling, C. A., Kalles, D. J., & VanDusen, J. E. (1984). Sex in transition, 1900–1984. *Journal of Youth and Adolescence, 13,* 385–399.

Darlington, R. B. (1991). The long-term effects of model preschool programs. In L. Okagaki & R. J. Sternberg (Eds.), *Directors of development: Influences on the development of children's thinking.* Hillsdale, NJ: Erlbaum.

Daro, D. (1988). *Confronting child abuse.* New York: Free Press.

Darwin, C. (1859). *On the origin of species.* London: John Murray.

Datan, N. (1989). Aging women: The silent majority. *Women's Studies Quarterly,* 12–19.

Datan, N., Greene, A. L., & Reese, H. W. (1986). *Life-span developmental psychology.* Hillsdale, NJ: Erlbaum.

Davidson, M., & Stern, R. G. (1991). The treatment of cognitive impairment in Alzheimer's disease: Beyond the cholinergic approach. *Psychiatric Clinics of North America, 14,* 461–482.

Davis, K. E. (1985, February). Near and dear: Friendship and love compared. *Psychology Today,* pp. 22–29.

Davy, J. A., Kinicki, A. J., & Scheck, C. L. (1991). Developing and testing a model of survivor responses to layoffs. *Journal of Vocational Behavior, 38,* 302–317.

Dawson, G. (Ed.). (1989). *Autism: Nature, diagnosis, and treatment.* New York: Guilford.

Dawson-Hughes, B., Dallal, G. E., Krall, E. A., Sadowski, L., Sahyoun, N., & Tannebaum, S. (1990). A controlled trial of the effect of calcium supplementation on bone density in postmenopausal women. *New England Journal of Medicine, 323,* 878–883.

Dax, E. M., Ingram, D. K., Partilla, J. S., & Gregerman, R. I. (1989). Food restriction prevents an age-associated increase in rat liver beta-adrenergic receptors. *Journal of Gerontology: Biological Sciences, 44,* B72–76.

Day, N. (1991, April). *Effects of alcohol and marijuana on growth and development.* Paper presented at the biennial meeting of the Society for Research in Child Development, Seattle.

De Casper, A. J. & Spence, M. J. (1986). Prenatal Maternal Speech Influences Newborns' Perception of Speech Sounds. *Infant Behavior and Development, 9,* 133–150.

DeAngelis, T. (1990, June). House child-care bill ignores quality issue. *APA Monitor,* p. 21.

Dedrick, C., Dedrick, R., Plunkett, J., Berlin, M., & Meisels, S. (1991, April). Persistence of effects of prematurity in the second year of life: Maternal behavior and infant security. Paper presented at the biennial meeting of the Society for Research in Child Development, Seattle.

DeFour, D. C., & Paludi, M. A. (in press). Integrating scholarship on ethnicity into the psychology of women course. *Teaching of Psychology.*

DeFriese, G. H., & Womert, A. (1991). Informal and formal health care systems serving older people. In M. G. Ory, R. P. Abeles, & P. D. Lipman (Eds.), *Aging, health, and behavior.* Newbury Park, CA: Sage.

DeHart, G., & Smith, B. (1991, April). *The role of age and gender composition in sibling pretend play.* Paper presented at the biennial meeting of the Society for Research in Child Development, Seattle.

de Jong-Gierveld, J. (1987). Developing and testing a model of loneliness. *Journal of Personality and Social Psychology, 53,* 119–128.

DeLoache, J. S., Cassidy, D. J., & Carpenter, C. J. (1987). The Three Bears are all boys: Mothers' gender labeling of neutral picture book characters. *Sex Roles, 17,* 163–178.

Dempster, F. N. (1981). Memory span: Sources of individual and developmental differences. *Psychological Bulletin, 80,* 63–100.

De Necochea, G. (1988, May). Expanding the Hispanic college pool. *Change,* pp. 61–62.

Denmark, F. L. & Paludi, M. A. (Eds.). (in press). *Handbook on the psychology of women.* Westport, CT: Greenwood Press.

Denmark, F. L., Russo, N. F., Frieze, I. H., Sechzur, J. (1988). Guidelines for avoiding sexism in psychological research: A report of the Ad Hoc Committee on nonsexist research. *American Psychologist, 43,* 582–585.

Denney, N. (1982). Aging and cognitive changes. In B. B. Wolman (Ed.), *Handbook of developmental psychology.* Englewood Cliffs, NJ: Prentice-Hall.

Denney, N. (1986, August). *Practical problem solving.* Paper presented at the meeting of the American Psychological Association, Washington, DC.

Dennis, W. (1966). Creative productivity between the ages of 20 and 80 years. *Journal of Gerontology, 21,* 1–18.

Deutsch, F. M. (1991). Women's lives: The story not told by theories of development. *Contemporary Psychology, 36,* 237–238.

Deutsch, M. (Ed.). (1967). *The disadvantaged child.* New York: Basic Books.

DeVault, M. L. (1987). *Doing housework: Feeding and family life.* In N. Gerstel & H. E. Gross (Eds.), *Families and work.* Philadelphia: Temple University Press.

de Villiers, J. G., & de Villiers, P. A. (1978). *Language acquisition.* Cambridge, MA: Harvard University Press.

deVries, H. A. (1970). Physiological effects of an exercise training regimen upon men aged 52 to 88. *Journal of Gerontology, 25,* 325–336.

Diamond, A. (1989, April). *Behavioral and anatomical approaches to the study of frontal and hippocampal functions in infants and toddlers.* Paper presented at the biennial meeting of the Society for Research in Child Development, Kansas City, MO.

Diaz, R. M. (1983). Thought and two languages: The impact of bilingualism on cognitive development. *Review of Research in Education, 10,* 23–54.

Dickerscheid, J. D., Schwarz, P. M., Noir, S., & El-Taliawy, T. (1988). Gender concept development of preschool-aged children in the United States and Egypt. *Sex Roles, 18,* 669–677.

Dickinson, D. K., & Moreton, J. (1991, April). *Predicting specific kindergarten literacy skills from three-year-olds' preschool experiences.* Paper presented at the biennial meeting of the Society for Research in Child Development, Seattle.

Dickinson, G. E. (1975). Dating behavior of black and white adolescents before and after desegregation. *Journal of Marriage and the Family, 37,* 602–608.

Dickson, G. L. (1990). A feminist post-structuralist analysis of the knowledge of menopause. *Advances in Nursing Science, 12,* 15–31.

Dielman, T. E., Shope, J. T., & Butchart, A. T. (1990, March). *Peer, family, and intrapersonal predictors of adolescent alcohol use and misuse.* Paper presented at the meeting of the Society for Research in Adolescence, Atlanta, GA.

Dietz, W. (1986, March). *Comments at the workshop on childhood obesity.* Washington, DC: National Institute of Health.

Dixon, S. D. (1991, April). *Infants exposed perinatally to cocaine or methamphetamine demonstrate behavioral and neurophysiologic changes.* Paper presented at the biennial meeting of the Society for Research in Child Development, Seattle.

Dodge, K. A. (1983). Behavioral antecedents of peer social status. *Child Development, 54,* 1386–1399.

Dodge, K. A., Petit, G. S., McClaskey, C. L., & Brown, M. M. (1986). Social competence in children. *Monographs of the Society for Research in Child Development, 55,* 1646–1650.

Dohrenwend, B. S., & Dohrenwend, B. P. (1978). Some issues in research on stressful life events. *Journal of Nervous and Mental Disease, 166,* 7–15.

Dohrenwend, B. S., & Shrout, P. E. (1985). "Hassles" in the conceptualization and measurement of life stress variables. *American Psychologist, 40,* 780–785.

Dolcini, M. M., Coh, L. D., Adler, N. E., Millstein, S. G., Irwin, C. E., Kegeles, S. M., & Stone, G. C. (1989). Adolescent egocentrism and feelings of invulnerability: Are they related? *Journal of Early Adolescence, 9,* 409–418.

Dolgin, K. G., & Behrend, D. A. (1984). Children's knowledge about animates and inanimates. *Child Development, 55,* 1646–1650.

Doll, G. (1988, Spring). Day care. *Vanderbilt Magazine,* p. 29.

Dornbusch, S. M., Carlsmith, J. M., Bushwall, S. J., Ritter, P. I., Leidman, P. H., Hastorf, A. H., & Gross, R. T. (1985). Single parents, extended households, and the control of adolescents. *Child Development, 56,* 326–341.

Douvan, D. (1983). Listening to a different drummer. *Contemporary Psychology, 28,* 261–262.

Douvan, E., & Adelson, J. (1966). *The adolescent experience.* New York: John Wiley.

Dowd, J. J., & Bengston, V. L. (1978). Aging in minority populations: An examination of the double jeopardy hypothesis. *Journal of Gerontology, 30,* 584–593.

Downey, A. M., Frank, G. C., Webber, L. S., Harsha, D. W., Virgilio, S. J., Franklin, F. A., & Berenson, G. S. (1987). Implementation of "Heart Smart": A cardiovascular school health promotion program. *Journal of School Health, 57,* 98–104.

Doyle, J. A., & Paludi, M. A. (1991). *Sex and gender: The human experience* (2nd ed.). Dubuque, IA: Wm. C. Brown.

Doyne, E. J., Ossip-Klein, D. J., Bowman, E. D., Osborne, K. M., McDougall-Wilson, I. B., & Neimeyer, R. A. (1987). Running versus weight lifting in the treatment of depression. *Journal of Consulting and Clinical Psychology, 55,* 748–754.

Dryfoos, J. G. (1990). *Adolescents at risk: Prevalence and prevention.* New York: Oxford University Press.

Dubois, D. L., & Hirsch, B. J. (1990). School and neighborhood friendship patterns of Blacks and Whites in early adolescence. *Child Development, 61,* 524–536.

Duck, S., & Pond, K. (1989). Friends, Romans, countrymen, lend me your retrospections: Rhetoric and reality in personal relationships. In C. Hendrick (Ed.), *Close Relationships.* Newbury Park, CA: Sage.

Duck, S. W. (1975). Personality similarity and friendship choices by adolescents. *European Journal of Social Psychology, 5,* 351–365.

Duck, S. W. (1988). Child and adolescent friendships. In P. Marsh (Ed.), *Eye to Eye: How people interact.* Topsfield, MA: Salem House.

Duke, D. L., & Canady, R. L. (1991). School policy. New York: McGraw-Hill.

Duncan, R. M. (1991, April). *An examination of Vygotsky's theory of children's private speech.* Paper presented at the biennial meeting of the Society for Research in Child Development, Seattle.

Dunn, J. (1984). Sibling studies and the developmental impact of critical incidents. In P. B. Baltes & O. G. Brim (Eds.), *Life-span development and behavior* (Vol. 6). Orlando, FL: Academic Press.

Dunn, J., & Kendrick, C. (1982). *Siblings.* Cambridge, MA: Harvard University Press.

Dunphy, D. C. (1963). The social structure of urban adolescent peer groups. *Society, 26,* 230–246.

Durkin, K. (1985). Television and sex-role acquisition: 1. Content. *British Journal of Social Psychology, 24,* 101–113.

Durlak, J. A., & Riesenberg, L. A. (1991). The impact of death education. *Death Studies, 15,* 39–58.

Duvall, E. M., & Miller, B. C. (1985). *Marriage and family development* (6th ed.). New York: Harper & Row.

Duxbury, L. E., & Higgins, C. A. (1991). Gender differences in work-family conflict. *Journal of Applied Psychology, 76,* 60–74.

E

Eccles (Parsons), J. S., Alder, T. F., Futterman, R., Goff, S. B., Kaczala, C. M., Meece, J. L., & Midgley, C. (1983). Expectations, values, and academic behaviors. In J. T. Spence (Ed.), *Achievement and achievement motivation.* San Francisco: Jossey-Bass.

Eccles, J. S. (1987). Gender roles and achievement patterns: An expectancy value perspective. In J. M. Reinisch, L. A. Rosenblum, & S. A. Sanders (Eds.), *Masculinity/Femininity.* New York: Oxford University Press.

Eccles, J. S. (1991). Academic achievement. In R. M. Lerner, A. C. Petersen, & J. Brooks-Gunn (Eds.), *Encyclopedia of adolescence* (Vol. 1). New York: Garland.

Eccles, J. S., Adler, T. F., & Kaczala, C. M. (1982). Socialization of achievement attitudes and beliefs: Parental influences. *Child Development, 53,* 310–321.

Eccles, J. S., Harold-Goldsmith, R., & Miller, C. R. (1989, April). *Parents' stereotyping beliefs about gender differences in adolescence.* Paper presented at the biennial meeting of the Society for Research in Child Development, Kansas City, MO.

Eccles, J. S., & Hoffman, L. W. (1984). Sex roles, socialization, and occupational behavior. In H. W. Stevenson & A. E. Siegel (Eds.), *Research in Child Development and Public Policy* (Vol. 1). Chicago: University of Chicago Press.

Eccles, J. S., & Jacobs, J. E. (1986). Social forces shape math attitudes and performance. *Signs, 11,* 367–389.

Eccles, J. S., MacIver, D., & Lange, L. (1986). *Classroom practices and motivation to study math.* Paper presented at the annual meeting of the American Educational Research Association, San Francisco.

Eccles, J. S., & Midgley, C. (1990). Changes in academic motivation and self-perception during early adolescence. In R. Montemayor, G. R. Adams, & T. P. Gullotta (Eds.), *From childhood to adolescence: A transitional period?* Newbury Park, CA: Sage.

Edelman, M. W. (1987). *Families in peril: An agenda for social change.* New York: Alan Guttmacher Institute.

Edmonds, M. Mc. (1990). The health of the black aged female. In Z. Harel, E. A. McKinney, & M. Williams (Eds.), *Black aged.* Newbury Park, CA: Sage.

Edwards, J. R., & Baglioni, A. J. (1991). Relation between Type A behavior pattern and mental and physical symptoms: A comparison of global and component measures. *Journal of Applied Psychology, 76,* 276–290.

Egeland, B. (1989, January). *Secure attachment in infancy and competence in the third grade.* Paper presented at the meeting of the American Association for the Advancement of Science, San Francisco.

Ehrhardt, A. A. (1987). A transactional perspective on the development of gender differences. In J. M. Reinisch, L. A. Rosenblum, & S. A. Sanders (Eds.), *Masculinity/femininity: Basic perspectives.* New York: Oxford University Press.

Eichorn, D. H., Clausen, J. A., Haan, N., Honzik, M. P., & Mussen, P. H. (Eds.). (1981). *Present and past in middle life.* New York: Academic Press.

Eiferman, R. R. (1971). Social play in childhood. In R. E. Herron & B. Sutton-Smith (Eds.), *Child's play.* New York: Wiley.

Eisenberg, N. (Ed.). (1982). *The development of prosocial behavior.* New York: Wiley.

Eitzen, D. S. (1975). Athletics in the status system of male adolescents. A replication of Coleman's *The Adolescent Society. Adolescence, 10,* 267–276.

Elder, G. H., & Caspi, A. (in press). Studying lives in a changing society. In A. I. Rabin, R. A. Zucker, S. Franck, & R. Emmons (Eds.), *Study in persons and lives.* New York: Springer.

Elder, G. H., Caspi, A., & Burton, L. M. (1988). Adolescent transition in developmental perspective: Sociological and historical insights. In M. R. Gunnar & W. A. Collins (Eds.), *Development during the transition to adolescence.* Hillsdale, NJ: Erlbaum.

Elder, G. H., Caspi, A., & Downey, G. (1986). Problem behavior and family relationships: A multigenerational analysis. In A. Sorensen, F. Weinert, & L. Sherrod (Eds.), *Human development and the life course.* Hillsdale, NJ: Erlbaum.

Elkind, D. (1970, April 5). Erik Erikson's eight ages of man. *New York Times Magazine.*

Elkind, D. (1976). *Child development and education: A Piagetian perspective.* New York: Oxford University Press.

Elkind, D. (1978). Understanding the young adolescent. *Adolescence, 13,* 127–134.

Elkind, D. (1981). *The hurried child.* Reading, MA: Addison-Wesley.

References

Elkind, D. (1985). Reply to D. Lapsley and M. Murphy's *Developmental Review* paper. *Developmental Review, 5,* 218–226.

Elkind, D. (1987). *Miseducation: Preschoolers at risk.* New York: Knopf.

Elkind, D. (1988, January). Educating the very young: A call for clear thinking. *NEA Today,* pp. 22–27.

Ellis, L., & Ames, M. A. (1987). Neurohormonal functioning and sexual orientation: A theory of homosexuality-heterosexuality. *Psychological Bulletin, 101,* 233–258.

Emde, R. N., Gaensbauer, T. G., & Harmon, R. J. (1976). Emotional expression in infancy: A biobehavioral study. *Psychological Issues, Monograph Series, 10* (No. 37).

Emery, R. E. (1989). Family violence. *American Psychologist, 44,* 321–328.

Emmerich, W., Goldman, K. S., Kirsch, B., & Sharabany, R. (1977). Evidence for a transitional phase in the development of gender constancy. *Child Development, 48,* 930–936.

Engen, T. (1977). Taste and smell. In J. E. Birren & K. W. Schaie (Eds.), *Handbook of the psychology of aging.* New York: Van Nostrand.

England, S. E., Linsk, N. L., Simon-Rusinowitz, L., & Keigher, S. M. (1991). Paying kin for care: Agency barriers to formalizing informal care. *Journal of Aging and Social Policy, 2,* 63–86.

Engle, P. L. (1991, April). *The effects of nutritional supplementation on cognitive functioning of preschoolers in Guatemala.* Paper presented at the biennial meeting of the Society for Research in Child Development, Seattle.

Enkin, M. W. (1989). Cesarian section: Why do the rates differ? *Birth, 16,* 207–208.

Ennis, R. H. (1991). Critical thinking: Literature review and needed research. In L. Idol & B. F. Jones (Eds.), *Educational values and cognitive instruction.* Hillsdale, NJ: Erlbaum.

Enright, R. D., Lapsley, D. K., Dricas, A. S., & Fehr, L. A. (1980). Parental influence on the development of adolescent autonomy and identity. *Journal of Youth and Adolescence, 9,* 529–546.

Entwistle, D. R. (1990). Schools and the adolescent. In S. S. Feldman & G. R. Elliott (Eds.), *At the threshold: The developing adolescent.* Cambridge, MA: Harvard University Press.

Epstein, C. F. (1987). Multiple demands and multiple roles: The conditions of successful management. In F. J. Crosby (Ed.), *Spouse, Parent, Worker: On gender and multiple roles.* New Haven, CT: Yale University Press.

Epstein, N., & Eidelson, R. J. (1981). Unrealistic beliefs of clinical couples: Their relationship to expectations, goals, and satisfaction. *American Journal of Family Therapy, 9,* 13–21.

Erben, R. (1991). Health challenges for the year 2000: Health promotion and AIDS. *Health Education Quarterly, 18,* 29–37.

Erikson, E. H., Erikson, J. M., & Kivnick, H. Q. (1986). *Vital involvement in old age.* New York: W. W. Norton.

Erickson, P. I., & Rapkin, A. J. (1991). Unwanted sexual experiences among middle and high school youth. *Journal of Adolescent Health, 12,* 319–325.

Erikson, E. H. (1950). *Childhood and society.* New York: W. W. Norton.

Erikson, E. H. (1968). *Identity: Youth and crisis.* New York: W. W. Norton.

Esty, E. T., & Fisch, S. M. (1991, April). *SQUARE ONE TV: Using television to enhance children's problem solving.* Paper presented at the biennial meeting of the Society for Research in Child Development, Seattle.

Evans, B. J., & Whitfield, J. R. (Eds.). (1988). *Black males in the United States: An annotated bibliography from 1967 to 1987.* Washington, DC: American Psychological Association.

Eveleth, P. B., & Tanner, J. M. (1990). *Worldwide variation in human growth* (2nd ed.). Cambridge, England: Cambridge University Press.

Eyler, F. D., Behnke, M. L., & Stewart, N. J. (1990). *Issues in identification and follow-up of cocaine-exposed neonates.* Unpublished manuscript, University of Florida, Gainesville, FL.

F

Fagan, J. F., & Knevel, C. R. (1989, April). *The prediction of above average intelligence from infancy.* Paper presented at the biennial meeting of the Society for Research in Child Development, Kansas City, MO.

Falbo, T., & Polit, D. F. (1986). A quantitative review of the only-child literature. Research evidence and theory development. *Psychological Bulletin, 100,* 176–189.

Falicov, C. J., & Karrer, B. M. (1980). Cultural variations in the family life cycle: The Mexican-American family. In E. A. Carter & M. McGoldrick (Eds.), The family life cycle: A framework for family therapy. New York: Gardner Press.

Fantz, R. L. (1963). Pattern vision in newborn infants. *Science, 140,* 296–297.

Farley, J. E. (1990). *Sociology.* Englewood Cliffs, NJ: Prentice-Hall.

Farrell, M. P., & Rosenberg, S. D. (1981). *Men at mid-life.* Boston: Auburn House.

Fasick, F. A. (1988). Patterns of formal education in high school as rites of passage. *Adolescence, 23,* 457–468.

Featherman, D. L. (1989). "What develops in adulthood?" In K. W. Schaie & C. Schooler (Eds.), *Social structure and aging: Psychological Processes.* Hillsdale, NJ: Erlbaum.

Fein, G. G. (1986). Pretend play. In D. Görlitz & J. F. Wohlwill (Eds.), *Curiosity, imagination, and play.* Hillsdale, NJ: Erlbaum.

Feingold, A. (1988). Cognitive gender differences are disappearing. *American Psychologist, 43,* 95–103.

Feldman, D. H. (1989). Creativity: Proof that development occurs. In W. Damon (Ed.), *Child development today and tomorrow.* San Francisco: Jossey-Bass.

Feldman, S. S., & Elliott, G. R. (Eds.). (1990). *At the threshold: The developing adolescent.* Cambridge, MA: Harvard University Press.

Feldman, S. S., & Rosenthal, D. A. (1990a). *The influence of family variables and adolescents' values on age expectations of behavioral autonomy: A cross cultural study of Hong Kong, Australian, and American youth.* Unpublished manuscript, Stanford Center for the Study of Families.

Feldman, S. S., & Rosenthal, D. A. (1990b). The acculturation of autonomy expectations in Chinese high schoolers residing in two Western nations. *International Journal of Psychology, 25,* 259–281.

Fenzel, L. M., Blyth, D. A., & Simmons, R. G. (1991). School transition, secondary. In *Encyclopedia of adolescence* (Vol. 2). New York: Garland.

Ferber, R. (1989). Sleeplessness in the child. In M. H. Kryger, T. Roth, & W. C. Dement (Eds.), *Principles and practices of sleep medicine.* San Diego: Harcourt Brace Jovanovich.

Ferguson, D. M., Harwood, L. J., & Shannon, F. T. (1987). Breastfeeding and subsequent social adjustment in 6- to 8-year-old children. *Journal of Child Psychology and Psychiatry, 28,* 378–386.

Field, T. M. (1979). Visual and cardiac responses to animate and inanimate faces by young term and preterm infants. *Child Development, 50,* 188–194.

Field, T. M. (1987, January). Interview. *Psychology Today,* p. 31.

Field, T. M. (1990). Alleviating stress in newborn infants in the intensive care unit. In B. M. Lester & E. Z. Tronick (Eds.), *Stimulation and the preterm infant: The limits of plasticity.* Philadelphia: W. B. Saunders.

Field, T. M. (1991). Reducing stress in child and psychiatric patients by massage and relaxation therapy. In T. M. Field, P. M. McCabe, & Schneiderman (Eds.), *Stress and coping in infancy and childhood* (Vol. 4). Hillsdale, NJ: Erlbaum.

Field, T. M., Scafidi, F., & Schanberg, S. (1987). Massage of preterm newborns to improve growth and development. *Pediatric Nursing, 13,* 385–387.

Field, T. M., Woodson, R., Greenberg, R., & Cohen, D. (1982). Discrimination and imitation of facial expressions by neonates. *Science, 218,* 179–181.

Fincher, J. (1982). Before their time. *Science '82.*

Fineberg, H. V. (1988). Education to prevent AIDS: Prospects and obstacles. *Science, 239,* 592–596.

Firush, R., & Cobb, P. A. (1989, April). *Developing scripts.* Paper presented at the biennial meeting of the Society for Research in Child Development, Kansas City, MO.

Fischer, L. R. (1991). Between mothers and daughters. *Marriage and Family Review, 16,* 237–248.

Fischman, J. (1987, February). Type A on trial. *Psychology Today,* pp. 42–50.

Fish, M. (1989, April). *Temperament and attachment of separation intolerance at three years.* Paper presented at the biennial meeting of the Society for Research in Child Development, Kansas City, MO.

Fish, T. A., & Rye, B. J. (1991). Attitudes toward a homosexual or heterosexual person with AIDS. *Journal of Applied Psychology, 21,* 651–667.

Fisher, C. B., & Brone, R. J. (1991). Eating disorders in adolescence. In R. M. Lerner, A. C. Petersen, & J. Brooks-Gunn (Eds.), *Encyclopedia of adolescence* (Vol. 1). New York: Garland.

Fisher, D. A. (1990, March). *Effects of attachment on adolescents' friendships.* Paper presented at the meeting of the Society for Research in Adolescence, Atlanta, GA.

Fisher, D. A., & Jenkins, V. Y. (1991, April). *Attachment in adolescence: Relationship quality and conflict resolution.* Paper presented at the biennial meeting of the Society for Research in Child Development, Seattle.

Flanagan, J. (1981, August). *Some characteristics of 70-year-old workers.* Paper presented at the meeting of the American Psychological Association, Los Angeles.

Flannagan, D. A., & Tate, C. S. (1989, April). *The effects of children's script knowledge on their communication and recall of scenes.* Paper presented at the biennial meeting of the Society for Research in Child Development, Kansas City, MO.

Flavell, J. H. (1979). Metacognition and cognitive monitoring: A new area of psychological inquiry. *American Psychologist, 34,* 906–911.

Flavell, J. H. (1985). *Cognitive development* (2nd ed.). Englewood Cliffs, NJ: Prentice-Hall.

Flavell, J. H., Beach, D. R., & Chinsky, J. M. (1966). Spontaneous verbal rehearsal in a memory task as a function of age. *Child Development, 37,* 283–299.

Flavell, J. H., Friedrichs, A. G., & Hoyt, J. D. (1970). Developmental changes in memorization processes. *Cognitive Psychology, 1,* 324–340.

Fleming, A. S., Ruble, D. N., Flett, G. L., & Shaul, D. L. (1988). Postpartum adjustment in first-time mothers: Relations between mood, maternal attitudes, and mother-infant interactions. *Developmental Psychology, 24,* 71–81.

Fogel, A., Toda, S., & Kawai, M. (1988). Mother-infant face-to-face interaction in Japan and the United States: A laboratory comparison using 3-month-old infants. *Developmental Psychology, 24,* 398–406.

Foner, N. (1984). Ages in conflict. New York: Columbia University Press.

Fordham, S., & Ogbu, J. U. (1986). Black students' school success: Coping with the burden of "acting white." *Urban Review, 18,* 176–206.

Forrest, J. D. (1990). Cultural influences on adolescents' reproductive behavior. In J. Bancroft & J. M. Reinisch (Eds.), Adolescence and puberty. New York: Oxford University Press.

Forsyth, B. W. C., Leventhal, J. M., & McCarthy, P. L. (1985). Mothers' perceptions of feeding and crying behaviors. *American Journal of Diseases of Children, 139,* 269–272.

Fowler, J. W. (1976). Stages in faith: The structural developmental approach. In T. Hennessy (Ed.), *Values and moral development*. New York: Paulist Press.

Fox, L. H., Brody, L., & Tobin, D. (1979). *Women and mathematics*. Baltimore, MD: Intellectually Gifted Study Group, Johns Hopkins University.

Fox, N. A., Kagan, J., & Weiskopf, F. (1979). The growth of memory during infancy. *Genetic Psychology Monographs, 99,* 91–130.

Fox, N. A., Sutton, B., Aaron, N., & Luebering, A. (1989, April). *Infant temperament and attachment: A new look at an old issue*. Paper presented at the biennial meeting of the Society for Research in Child Development, Kansas City, MO.

Francis, J., Fraser, G., & Marcia, J. E. (1989). *Cognitive and experimental factors in Moratorium-Achievement (MAMA) cycles*. Unpublished manuscript, Department of Psychology, Simon Fraser University, Burnaby, British Columbia.

Frankel, A., & Prentice-Dunn, S. (1990). Loneliness and the processing of self-relevant information. *Journal of Social and Clinical Psychology, 9,* 303–315.

Freedman, D. G. (1971). Genetic influences on development of behavior. In G. B. A. Stoelinga & J. J. Van Der Werff Ten Bosch (Eds.), *Normal and abnormal development of behavior*. Leiden: Leiden University Press.

Freedman, D. G., & Freedman, N. (1969). Behavioral differences between Chinese-American and European-American newborns. *Nature, 224,* 1127.

Freedman, J. L. (1984). Effects of television violence on aggressiveness. *Psychological Bulletin, 96,* 227–246.

Freeman, J. (1982). The old, old, very old Charlie Smith. *The Gerontologist, 22,* 532.

Freuchen, P. (1961). *Book of the Eskimos*. Cleveland: World Press.

Freud, A., & Dann, S. (1951). Instinctual anxiety during puberty. In A. Freud (Ed.), *The ego and its mechanisms of defense*. New York: International Universities Press.

Freud, S. (1917). *A general introduction to psychoanalysis*. New York: Washington Square Press.

Fried, P., & O'Connell, C. (1991, April). *Marijuana and tobacco as prenatal correlates of child behavior: Follow-up to school age*. Paper presented at the biennial meeting of the Society for Research in Child Development, Seattle.

Fried, P. A., & Watkinson, B. (1990). 36- and 48-month neurobehavioral follow-up of children prenatally exposed to marijuana, cigarettes, and alcohol. *Developmental and Behavioral Pediatrics, 11,* 49–58.

Fried, P. A., Watkinson, B., & Dillon, R. F. (1987). Neonatal neurological status in a low-risk population after prenatal exposure to cigarettes, marijuana, and alcohol. *Journal of Developmental and Behavioral Pediatrics, 8,* 318–326.

Friedman, H., & Caron, B. (1991, April). *Trends in outcome of very low birthweight (VLBW) children*. Paper presented at the biennial meeting of the Society for Research in Child Development, Seattle.

Friedman, M., & Rosenman, R. (1974). *Type A behavior and your heart*. New York: Knopf.

Friedrich, L. K., & Stein, A. H. (1973). Aggressive and prosocial TV programs and the natural behavior of preschool children. *Monographs of the Society for Research in Child Development, 38* (4, Serial No. 151).

Fromm, E. (1955). *The sane society*. New York: Fawcett.

Fry, P. S., Slivinske, L. R., & Fitch, V. L. (1989). Power, control, and well-being of the elderly: A critical reconstruction. In P. S. Fry (Ed.), *Psychological perspectives of helplessness and control in the elderly*. Amsterdam: North Holland.

Fuller, M. (1984). Black girls in a London comprehensive school. In M. Hammersley & P. Woods (Eds.), *Life in school: The sociology of pop culture*. New York: Open University Press.

Fulton, R. (1988). The funeral in contemporary society. In H. Wass, F. M. Berardo, & R. A. Neimeyer (Eds.), *Dying: Facing the facts* (2nd ed.). Washington, DC: Hemisphere.

Furman, L. N., & Walden, T. A. (1989, April). *The effect of script knowledge on children's communicative interactions*. Paper presented at the biennial meeting of the Society for Research in Child Development, Kansas City, MO.

Furman, L. N., & Walden, T. A. (1990). Effects of script knowledge on preschool children's communicative interactions. *Developmental Psychology, 26,* 227–233.

Furrow, D., & Moore, C. (1991, April). *Mothers' feedback to children's utterances: The role of context*. Paper presented at the biennial meeting of the Society for Research in Child Development, Seattle.

Furstenberg, F. F. (1988). Child care after divorce and remarriage. In E. M. Hetherington & J. Arasteh (Eds.), *Impact of divorce, single-parenting, and stepparenting on children*. Hillsdale, NJ: Erlbaum.

Furstenberg, F. F. (1991). Pregnancy and childbearing: Effects on teen mothers. In R. M. Lerner, A. C. Petersen, & J. Brooks-Gunn (Eds.), *Encyclopedia of adolescence* (Vol. 2). New York: Garland.

Furstenberg, J. J., Brooks-Gunn, J., & Morgan, S. P. (1987). *Adolescent mothers in later life*. New York: Cambridge University Press.

Furth, H. G., & Wachs, H. (1975). *Thinking goes to school*. New York: Oxford University Press.

Fustenberg, F. F., Brooks-Gunn, J., & Chase-Lansdale, L. (1989). Teenaged pregnancy and childbearing. *American Psychologist, 44,* 313–320.

G

Gabrielli, W. (1990, June). *Alcoholism from a biological perspective*. Paper presented at the meeting of the American Psychological Society, Dallas, TX.

Gage, N. L. (1965). Desirable behaviors of teachers. *Urban Education, 1,* 85–96.

Galambos, N. L., & Maggs, J. L. (1989, April). *The after-school ecology of young adolescents and self-reported behavior*. Paper presented at the biennial meeting of the Society for Research in Child Development, Kansas City, MO.

Galanter, M. (1989). *Cults: Faith, healing, and coercion*. New York: Oxford University Press.

Gallagher, J. J., Trohanis, P. L., & Clifford, R. M. (1989). *Policy implementation and PL 99–457*. Baltimore: Paul H. Brooks.

Gallup, A. M., & Clark, D. L. (1987). The 19th annual Gallup poll of the public's attitude toward the public schools. *Phi Delta Kappan, 69,* 17–30.

Gallup, G., & Poling, D. (1980). *The search for America's faith*. New York: Abington.

Galotti, K. M. (1989). Approaches to studying formal and everyday reasoning. *Psychological Bulletin, 105,* 331–351.

Garbarino, J. (1976). The ecological correlates of child abuse: The impact of socioeconomic stress on mothers. *Child Development, 47,* 178–185.

Garbarino, J. (1980). The issue of human quality: In praise of children. *Children and Youth Services Review, 1,* 353–377.

Garbarino, J. (1985). *Adolescent development: An ecological perspective*. Columbus, OH: Merrill.

Garbarino, J. (1989). *The psychologically battered child*. San Francisco: Jossey-Bass.

Garden, A. (1989). Burnout: The effect of psychological type on research findings. *Journal of Occupational Psychology, 62,* 223–234.

Garden, R. A. (1987). The second IEA mathematics study. *Comparative Education Review, 31,* 47–68.

Gardner, B. T., & Gardner, R. A. (1971). Two-way communication with an infant chimpanzee. In A. Schrier & F. Stollnitz (Eds.), *Behavior of nonhuman primates* (Vol. 4). New York: Academic Press.

Gardner, H. (1983). *Frames of mind*. New York: Basic Books.

Gardner, L. I., Stern, M. P., Haffner, S. M., Gaskill, S. P., Hazuda, H. P., Relethford, J. H., & Eifter, C. W. (1984). Prevalence of diabetes in Mexican Americans: Relationships to percent of gene pool derived from Native American sources. *Diabetes, 33,* 86–92.

Gardner, R. A., Gardner, B. T., & Van Cantfort, T. E. (Eds.). (1989). *Teaching Sign Language to Chimpanzees*. Albany, N.Y.: State University of New York Press.

Garrison, W. T., & McQuiston, S. (1989). *Chronic illness during childhood and adolescence*. Newbury Park, CA: Sage.

Garvey, C. (1977). *Play*. Cambridge, MA: Harvard University Press.

Gati, I. (1991). The structure of vocational interests. *Psychological Bulletin, 109,* 309–324.

Gatz, M. (1989). Clinical psychology and aging. In M. Storandt & G. R. VandenBos (Eds.), *The adult years: Continuity and change*. Washington, DC: American Psychological Association.

Gatz, M., Popkin, S. J., Pino, C. D., & VandenBos, G. R. (1985). Psychological interventions with older adults. In J. E. Birren & K. W. Schaie (Eds.), *Handbook of the psychology of aging* (2nd ed.). New York: Van Nostrand Reinhold.

Gelfand, D. E. (1982). *Aging: The ethnic factor*. Boston: Little Brown.

Gelman, R. (1969). Conservation acquisition: A problem of learning to attend to relevant attributes. *Journal of Experimental Child Psychology, 7,* 67–87.

Gelman, R. (1972). Logical capacity of very young children: Number invariance rules. *Child Development, 43,* 75–90.

Gelman, R. (1991). Epigenetic foundations of knowledge structures: Initial and transcendent constructions. In S. Carey and R. Gelman (Eds.), *The epigenesis of mind: Essays on biology and cognition*. Hillsdale, NJ: Erlbaum.

Gelman, R., & Baillargeon, R. (1983). A review of some Piagetian concepts. In P. H. Mussen (Ed.), *Handbook of child psychology* (4th ed., Vol. 3). New York: Wiley.

Gerlach, J. (1991). Introduction: Women, education, and aging. *Educational Gerontology, 17,* iii.

Gerson, G. S. (1977). The psychology of grief and mourning in Judaism. *Journal of Religion and Health, 16,* 260–274.

Gerson, K. (1986). *Hard choices: How women decide about work, career, and motherhood.* Berkeley, CA: University of California Press.

Gesell, A. (1934). *An atlas of infant behavior.* New Haven, CT: Yale University Press.

Gewirtz, J. (1977). Maternal responding and the conditioning of infant crying: Directions of influence within the attachment-acquisition process. In B. C. Etzel, J. M. LeBlanc, & D. M. Baer (Eds.), *New developments in behavioral research.* Hillsdale, NJ: Erlbaum.

Gibbs, J. T. (1989). Black American adolescents. In J. T. Gibbs & L. N. Huang (Eds.), *Children of color.* San Francisco: Jossey-Bass.

Gibbs, J. T., & Huang, L. N. (1989). A conceptual framework for assessing and treating minority youth. In J. T. Gibbs & L. N. Huang (Eds.), *Children of color.* San Francisco, CA: Jossey-Bass.

Gibson, E. J. (1969). *The principles of perceptual learning and development.* New York: Appleton-Century-Crofts.

Gibson, E. J., & Spelke, E. S. (1983). The development of perception. In P. H. Mussen (Ed.), *Handbook of child psychology* (4th ed., Vol. 3). New York: Wiley.

Gibson, E. J., & Walk, R. D. (1960). The "visual cliff." *Scientific American, 202,* 64–71.

Gilligan, C. (1982). *In a different voice.* Cambridge, MA: Harvard University Press.

Gilligan, C. (1990). Teaching Shakespeare's sister. In C. Gilligan, N. Lyons, and T. Hanmer (Eds.), *Making connections: The relational worlds of adolescent girls at Emma Willard School.* Cambridge: Harvard University Press.

Gilligan, C. (1991, April). Discussant, *Psychology and the good: How should "we" talk about development?* Symposium at the biennial meeting of the Society for Research in Child Development, Seattle.

Gilligan, C., Brown, L. M., & Rogers, A. G. (1990). Psyche embedded: A place for body, relationships, and culture in personality theory. In A. I. Rabin, R. A. Zucker, R. A. Emmons, & S. Frank (Eds,. *Studying persons and lives.* New York: Springer.

Gilligan, C., Lyons, N. P., & Hanmer, T. J. (1990). *Making connections.* Cambridge, MA: Harvard University Press.

Gilligan, C., Rogers, A., & Brown, L. M. (1990). Soundings into development. In C. Gilligan, N. P. Lyons, & T. J. Hanmer (Eds.), *Making connections.* Cambridge, MA: Harvard University Press.

Gilligan, C., Ward, J., & Taylor, J. (Eds.). (1988). *Mapping the moral domain: A contribution to women's thinking to psychology and education.* Cambridge, MA: Harvard University Graduate School of Education.

Ginsburg, H., & Opper, S. (1988). *Piaget's theory of intellectual development.* Englewood Cliffs, NJ: Prentice-Hall.

Ginzberg, E. (1972). Toward a theory of occupational choice: A restatement. *Vocational Guidance Quarterly, 20,* 169–176.

Ginzberg, E., Ginzberg, S. W., Axelrad, S., & Herman, J. L. (1951). *Occupational choice.* New York: Columbia University.

Glaser, R. (1989). The reemergence of learning theory within instructional research. *American Psychologist, 45,* 29–39.

Gleason, J. B. (1988). Language and socialization. In F. Kessel (Ed.), *The development of language and language researchers.* Hillsdale, NJ: Erlbaum.

Glick, J. (1991, April). *The uses and abuses of Vygotsky.* Paper presented at the biennial meeting of the Society for Research in Child Development, Seattle.

Goertz, M. E., Ekstrom, R. B., & Rock, D. (1991). Dropouts, high school: issues of race and sex. In R. M. Lerner, A. C. Petersen, & J. Brooks-Gunn (Eds.), *Encyclopedia of adolescence* (Vol. 1). New York: Garland.

Golan, N. (1986). *The perilous bridge.* New York: Free Press.

Gold, M. (1987). Social ecology. In H. C. Quay (Ed.), *Handbook of juvenile delinquency.* New York: Wiley.

Gold, M., & Petronio, R. J. (1980). Delinquent behavior in adolescence. In J. Adelson (Ed.), *Handbook of adolescent psychology.* New York: Wiley.

Gold, M. S., Gallanter, M., & Stimmel, B. (1987). *Cocaine.* New York: Haworth Press.

Goldman-Rakic, P. S., Isseroff, A., Schwartz, M. L., & Bugbee, N. M. (1983). The neurobiology of cognitive development. In P. H. Mussen (Ed.), *Handbook of child psychology* (4th ed., Vol. 2). New York: Wiley.

Goldsmith, H. H. (1988, August). *Does early temperament predict late development?* Paper presented at the meeting of the American Psychological Association, Atlanta, GA.

Goldsmith, H. H., & Gottesman, I. I. (1981). Origins of variation in behavioral style: A longitudinal study of temperament in young twins. *Child Development, 52,* 91–103.

Goldsmith, H. H., Rothbart, M. K., Crowley, J. M., Harmon-Losova, S. G., & Bowden, L. M. (1991, April). *Behavioral assessment of early temperament in the laboratory.* Paper presented at the biennial meeting of the Society for Research in Child Development, Seattle.

Goodchilds, J. D., & Zellman, G. L. (1984). Sexual signaling and sexual aggression in adolescent relationships. In N. M. Malamuth & E. D. Donnerstein (Eds.), *Pornography and sexual aggression.* New York: Academic Press.

Goodlad, J. (1983). *A place called school.* New York: McGraw-Hill.

Goodman, R. A., Mercy, J. A., Loya, F., Rosenberg, M. L., Smith, J. C., Allen, N. H., Vargas, L., & Kolts, R. (1986). Alcohol use and interpersonal violence: Alcohol detected in homicide victims. *American Journal of Public Health, 76,* 144–149.

Goodman, S. (1979). *You and your child: From birth to adolescence.* Skokie, IL: Rand McNally.

Gordon, D. (1991, April). *Supportive policies for children of color: Strategies for the year 2000 and beyond.* Keynote address at the SRCD pre-conference on ethnicity and diversity, Seattle.

Gorman, K., & Pollitt, E. (1991, April). *The effects of early supplementary feeding on cognitive outcomes in adolescence in rural Guatemala.* Paper presented at the biennial meeting of the Society for Research in Child Development, Seattle.

Goswami, U., & Bryant, P. (1990). *Phonological skills and learning to read.* Hillsdale, NJ: Erlbaum.

Gotowiec, A., & Ames, E. W. (1989, April). *Crying and behavioral state organization in 6- to 8-week-old infants.* Paper presented at the biennial meeting of the Society for Research in Child Development, Kansas City, MO.

Gottfredson, G. D., & Holland, J. L. (1990). A longitudinal test of the influence of congruence: Job satisfaction, competency utilization, and counterproductive behavior. *Journal of counseling psychology, 37,* 389–398.

Gottfried, A. E., & Gottfried, A. W. (1989, April). *Home environment and children's academic intrinsic motivation: A longitudinal study.* Paper presented at the biennial meeting of the Society for Child Development, Kansas City, MO.

Gottfried, A. E., & Gottfried, A. W. (1991, April). *Parents' reward strategies and children's academic intrinsic motivation and school performance.* Paper presented at the biennial meeting of the Society for Research in Child Development, Seattle.

Gottfried, A. E., Gottfried, A. W., & Bathurst, K. (1988). Maternal employment, family environment, and children's development: Infancy through the school years. In A. E. Gottfried & A. W. Gottfried (Eds.), *Maternal employment and children's development: Longitudinal Research.* New York: Plenum.

Gottlieb, D. (1966). Teaching and students: The views of Negro and white teachers. *Sociology of Education, 37,* 345–353.

Gottlieb, G. (1991a). Epigenetic systems view of human development. *Developmental Psychology, 27,* 33–34.

Gottlieb, G. (1991b). Experiential canalization of behavioral development theory. *Developmental Psychology, 27,* 4–13.

Gottman, J. M., & Parker, J. G. (Eds.). (1987). *Conversations of friends.* New York: Cambridge University Press.

Gould, R. L. (1975). Adult life stages: Growth toward self-tolerance. *Psychology Today, 8,* 74–78.

Gould, R. L. (1978). *Transformations: Growth and change in adult life.* New York: Simon & Schuster.

Gould, R. L. (1980). Transformations during early and middle adult years. In N. J. Smelser & E. H. Erikson (Eds.), *Themes of work and love in adulthood.* Cambridge, MA: Harvard University Press.

Graham, D. (1981). The obstetric and neonatal consequences of adolescent pregnancy. In E. R. McAnarney & G. Stickle (Eds.), *Pregnancy and childbearing during adolescence: Research priorities for the 1980s.* New York: Alan R. Liss.

Graham, S. (1986, August). *Can attribution theory tell us something about motivation in Blacks?* Paper presented at the meeting of the American Psychological Association, Washington, DC.

Graham, S. (1987, August). *Developing relations between attributions affect and intended social behavior.* Paper presented at the meeting of the American Psychological Association, New York.

Graham, S. (1990). Motivation in Afro-Americans. In G. L. Berry & J. K. Asamen (Eds.), *Black students: Psychosocial issues and academic achievement.* Newbury Park, CA: Sage.

Grambs, J. D. (1989). *Women over forty* (rev. ed.). New York: Springer.

Granrud, C. E. (1989, April). *Visual size and shape constancy in 4-month-old infants.* Paper presented at the biennial meeting of the Society for Research in Child Development, Kansas City, MO.

Grant, J. P. (1986). *State of the World's Children.* New York: UNICEF and Oxford University Press.

Grant, J. P. (1991). *The state of the world's children.* New York: UNICEF and Oxford University Press.

Green, J. (1991). Analyzing individual differences in development. In J. Columbo & J. W. Fagen (Eds.), *Individual differences in infancy.* Hillsdale, NJ: Erlbaum.

Greenberg, J. S., Bruess, C. E., Mullen, K. D., & Sand, D. W. (1989). *Sexuality* (2nd ed.). Dubuque, IA: Wm. C. Brown.

Greenberger, E., & Steinberg, L. (1981). *Project for the study of adolescent work: Final report.* Report prepared for the National Institute of Education, U.S. Department of Education, Washington, DC.

Greene, M. G., Hoffman, S., Charon, R., & Adelman, R. (1987). Psychosocial concerns in the medical encounter: A comparison of the interaction of doctors with their old and young patients. *The Gerontologist, 27,* 164–168.

Grossman, F. K., Pollack, W. S., & Golding, E. (1988). Fathers and children: Predicting the quality and quantity of fathering. *Developmental Psychology, 24,* 82–91.

Grotevant, H. D., & Cooper, C. R. (1985). Patterns of interaction in family relationships and the development of identity exploration in adolescence. *Child Development, 56,* 415–428.

Gubrium, J. F. (1975). *Living and dying at Murray Manor.* New York: St. Martin's Press.

Guilford, J. P. (1967). *The structure of intellect.* New York: McGraw-Hill.

Gunnar, M. R., Malone, S., & Fisch, R. O. (1987). The psychobiology of stress and coping in the human neonate: Studies of the adrenocortical activity in response to stress in the first week of life. In T. Field, P. McCabe, & N. Scheiderman (Eds.), *Stress and coping.* Hillsdale, NJ: Erlbaum.

Gustafson, G. E. (1989, April). *On some common assumptions about cry perception and infant development.* Paper presented at the biennial meeting of the Society for Research in Child Development, Kansas City, MO.

Gustafson, G. E., & Green, J. A. (1989). On the importance of fundamental frequency and other acoustic features in cry perception and infant development. *Child Development, 60,* 772–780.

Gustafson, G. E., & Green, J. A. (1991, April). Infant crying as a moving target. Paper presented at the biennial meeting of the Society for Research in Child Development, Seattle.

Gustafson, S. B., & Magnusson, D. (1991). *Female life careers: A pattern approach.* Hillsdale, NJ: Erlbaum.

Gutmann, D. L. (1975). Parenthood: A key to the comparative study of the life cycle. In N. Datan & L. Ginsberg (Eds.), *Life-span developmental psychology: Normative life crises.* New York: Academic Press.

Guttentag, M., & Secord, P. F. (1983). *Too many women? The sex-ratio question.* Newbury Park, CA: Sage.

H

Hackett, G., Lent, R. W., & Greenhaus, J. H. (1991). Advances in vocational theory and research: A 20-year retrospective. *Journal of Vocational Behavior, 38,* 3–38.

Hagestad, G. O. (1985). Continuity and connectedness. In V. L. Bengston (Ed.), *Grandparenthood.* Beverly Hills, CA: Sage.

Hahn, A. (1987, December). Reaching out to America's dropouts: What to do? *Phi Delta Kappan,* pp. 256–263.

Haight, B. K. (1991). Reminiscing: The state of the art as a basis for practice. *International Journal of Aging and Human Development, 33,* 1–32.

Haith, M. H. (1991, April). *Setting a path for the '90s: Some goals and challenges in infant sensory and perceptual development.* Paper presented at the biennial meeting of the Society for Research in Child Development, Seattle.

Hakuta, K., & Garcia, E. E. (1989). Bilingualism and education. *American Psychologist, 44,* 374–379.

Hall, C. C. I., Evans, B. J., & Selice, S. (Eds.). (1989). *Black females in the United States.* Washington, DC: American Psychological Association.

Hall, G. S. (1904). *Adolescence* (Vols. I and II). Englewood Cliffs, NJ: Prentice-Hall.

Hall, W. S. (1989). Reading comprehension. *American Psychologist, 44,* 157–161.

Hallahan, D. P., Kauffman, J. M., Lloyd, J. W., & McKinney, J. D. (1988). Questions about the regular education initiative. *Journal of Learning Disabilities, 21,* 3–5.

Halmi, D. (1980). Gastric bypass for massive obesity. In A. J. Stunkard (Ed.), *Obesity.* Philadelphia: Saunders.

Hanks, R. S. (1991). An intergenerational perspective on family ethical dilemmas. *Marriage and Family Review, 16,* 161–174.

Hans, S. (1989, April). *Infant behavioral effects of prenatal exposure to methadone.* Paper presented at the biennial meeting of the Society for Research in Child Development, Kansas City, MO.

Hansell, S. (1991). The meaning of stress. *Contemporary Psychology, 36,* 112–114.

Hardyck, C., & Petrinovich, L. F. (1977). Left-handedness. *Psychological Bulletin, 84,* 385–404.

Hare-Muston, R., & Marecek, J. (1988). The meaning of difference: Gender theory, postmodernism, and psychology. *American Psychologist, 43,* 455–464.

Harlow, H. F., & Zimmerman, R. R. (1959). Affectional responses in the infant monkey. *Science, 130,* 421–432.

Harris, C. S. (1978). *Fact book on aging: A profile of America's older population.* Washington, DC: National Council on Aging.

Harris, L. (1975). *The myth and reality of aging in America.* Washington, DC: National Council on Aging.

Harris, L. (1987, September 3). The latchkey child phenomena. *Dallas Morning News,* pp. 1A, 10A.

Harrison, C. A. (1991). Older women in our society: America's silent, invisible majority. *Educational Gerontology, 17,* 111–122.

Hart, S. N. (1991). From property to person status: Historical perspectives on children's rights. *American Psychologist, 46,* 53–59.

Harter, S. (1982). The Perceived Competence Scale for Children. *Child Development, 53,* 87–97.

Harter, S. (1988). Developmental processes in the construction of self. In T. D. Yawkey & J. E. Johnson (Eds.), *Integrative processes and socialization: Early to middle childhood.* Hillsdale, NJ: Erlbaum.

Harter, S. (1989). Self-perception profile for adolescents. Denver, CO: University of Denver.

Harter, S. (1990a). Processes underlying adolescent self-concept formation. In R. Montemayor, G. R. Adams, & T. P. Gulotta (Eds.), *From childhood to adolescence: A transitional period?* Newbury Park, CA: Sage.

Harter, S. (1990b). Self and identity development. In S. S. Feldman & G. R. Elliott (Eds.), *At the threshold: The developing adolescent.* Cambridge, MA: Harvard University Press.

Harter, S., Alexander, P. C., & Neimeyer, R. A. (1988). Long-term effects of incestuous child abuse in college women: Social adjustment, social cognition, and family characteristics. *Journal of Consulting and Clinical Psychology, 56,* 5–8.

Harter, S., & Pike, R. (1984). The Pictorial Scale of Perceived Competence and Social Acceptance for Young Children. *Child Development, 55,* 1969–1982.

Hartshorne, H., & May, M. S. (1928–1930). *Moral studies in the nature of character: Studies in the nature of character.* New York: Macmillan.

Hartup, W. W. (1983). Peer relations. In P. H. Mussen (Ed.), *Handbook of child psychology* (4th ed., Vol. 4). New York: Wiley.

Hartup, W. W. (1989). Social relationships and their developmental significance. *American Psychologist, 44,* 120–126.

Haskins, R. (1989). Beyond metaphor: The efficacy of early childhood education. *American Psychologist, 44,* 274–282.

Haugard, J. J., & Emery, R. E. (in press). Methodological issues in child sex abuse research. *Child Abuse and Neglect.*

Hauser, S. T. (1991, April). *Antecedents of young adult ego development: The contributions of adolescent and parent ego development.* Paper presented at the biennial meeting of the Society for Research in Child Development, Seattle.

Hauser, S. T., & Bowlds, M. K. (1990). Stress, coping, and adaptation. In S. S. Feldman & G. R. Elliott (Eds.), *At the threshold: The developing adolescent.* Cambridge, MA: Harvard University Press.

Hauser, S. T., Powers, S. I., Noam, G. G., Jacobson, A. M., Weisse, B., & Follansbee, D. J. (1984). Familial contexts of adolescent ego development. *Child Development, 55,* 195–213.

Havighurst, R. J. (1972). *Developmental tasks and education* (3rd ed.). New York: McKay.

Havighurst, R. J. (1973). History of developmental psychology: Socialization and personality development through the life span. In P. B. Baltes & K. W. Schaie (Eds.), *Life-span developmental psychology.* New York: Academic Press.

Havighurst, R. J. (1987). Adolescent culture and subculture. In V. B. Van Hasselt & M. Hersen (Eds.), *Handbook of adolescent psychology.* New York: Pergamon.

Hawkins, D., & Lam, T. (1986). Teacher practices, social development, and delinquency. In J. Buchard & S. Buchard (Eds.), *Prevention of delinquent behavior.* Newbury Park, CA: Sage.

Hawkins, D., & Lishner, D. (1987). School and delinquency. In E. Johnson (Ed.), *Handbook on crime and delinquency prevention.* Westport, CA: Greenwood Press.

Hawkins, J., Pea, R. D., Glick, J., & Scribner, S. (1984). "Merds that laugh don't like mushrooms": Evidence for deductive reasoning by preschoolers. *Developmental Psychology, 20,* 584–594.

Hawkins, J. A., & Berndt, T. J. (1985, April). *Adjustment following the transition to junior high school.* Paper presented at the biennial meeting of the Society for Research in Child Development, Toronto.

Hayden-Thomson, L., Rubin, K. M., & Hymel, S. (1987). Sex preferences in sociometric choices. *Developmental Psychology, 23,* 558–562.

Hayflick, L. (1975, September). Why grow old? *Stanford Magazine,* 36–43.

Hayflick, L. (1977). The cellular basis for biological aging. In C. E. Finch & L. Hayflick (Eds.), *Handbook of the biology of aging.* New York: Van Nostrand.

Hayflick, L. (1987). The cell biology and theoretical basis of aging. In L. Carstensen & B. A. Edelstein (Eds.), *Handbook of clinical gerontology.* New York: Pergamon.

Hazan, C., & Shaver, P. (1987). Romantic love conceptualized as an attachment process. *Journal of Personality and Social Psychology, 51,* 511–524.

Heath, S. B. (1983). *Ways with words: Language, life, and work in communities and classrooms.* Cambridge, MA: Cambridge University Press.

Heath, S. B. (1989). Oral and literate traditions among Black Americans living in poverty. *American Psychologist, 44,* 367–373.

Heath, S. B. (in press). The children of Trackton's children: Spoken and written language in social change. In J. Stigler, G. Herdt, & R. A. Shweder (Eds.), *Cultural psychology: The Chicago symposia.* New York: Cambridge University Press.

Heise, D. R. (1991). Careers, career trajectories and the self. In J. Rodin, C. Schooler, & K. W. Schaie (Eds.), *Self-directedness and efficacy.* Hillsdale, NJ: Erlbaum.

Helson, R., Elliot, T., & Leigh, J. (1989). Adolescent antecedents of women's work patterns. In D. Stern & D. Eichorn (Eds.), *Adolescence and work.* Hillsdale, NJ: Erlbaum.

Helson, R., Mitchell, V., & Moane, G. (1984). Personality change in women from college to midlife. *Journal of Personality and Social Psychology, 53,* 176–186.

Helson, R., & Moane, G. (1987). Personality change in women from college to midlife. *Journal of Personality and Social Psychology, 53,* 176–186.

Helson, R., & Wink, P. (1987). Two conceptions of maturity examined in the findings of a longitudinal study. *Journal of Personality and Social Psychology, 53,* 531–541.

Henderson, V. L. (1991, April). *Self-conceptions of intelligence and developmental transitions.* Paper presented at the biennial meeting of the Society for Research in Child Development, Seattle.

Henderson, V. L., & Dweck, C. S. (1989, April). *Predicting individual differences in school anxiety in early adolescence.* Paper presented at the meeting of the Society for Research in Child Development, Kansas City, MO.

Henderson, V. L., & Dweck, C. S. (1990). Motivation and achievement. In S. S. Feldman & G. R. Elliott (Eds.), *At the threshold: The developing adolescent.* Cambridge, MA: Harvard University Press.

Hendrick, C. (Ed.). (1989). *Close Relationships.* Newbury Park, CA: Sage.

Hendry, J. (1986). *Becoming Japanese: The world of the preschool child.* Honolulu: University of Hawaii Press.

Henker, B., & Whalen, C. K. (1989). Hyperactivity and attention deficits. *American Psychologist, 44,* 216–223.

Hennessey, B. A., & Amabile, T. M. (1988). The conditions of creativity. In R. J. Sternberg (Ed.), *The nature of creativity.* New York: Cambridge University Press.

Herbert, V. (1988). Megavitamins, food fads, and quack nutrition in health promotion: Myths and risks. In R. Chernoff & D. A. Lipschitz (Eds.), *Health promotion and disease prevention in the elderly.* New York: Raven Press.

Hernandez, G. G. (1991). Not so benign neglect: Researchers ignore ethnicity in defining family caregiver burden and recommending services. *The Gerontologist, 31,* p. 271.

Hertzig, M., & Shapiro, T. (in press). Autism and pervasive developmental disorders. In M. E. Lewis & S. M. Miller (Eds.), *Handbook of developmental psychopathology.* New York: Plenum.

Herzog, A. R., House, J. S., & Morgan, J. N. (1991). Relation of work and retirement to health and well-being in older age. *Psychology and Aging, 6,* 202–211.

Hetherington, E. M. (1989). Coping with family transitions: Winners, losers, and survivors. *Child Development, 60,* 1–14.

Hetherington, E. M. (1991). The role of individual differences and family relationships in coping with divorce and remarriage. In P. A. Cowan & E. M. Hetherington (Eds.), *Family transitions.* Hillsdale, NJ: Erlbaum.

Hetherington, E. M., & Baltes, P. B. (1989). Child psychology and life-span development. In E. M. Hetherington, R. M. Lerner, & M. Perlmutter (Eds.), *Child development in a life-span perspective.* Hillsdale, NJ: Erlbaum.

Hetherington, E. M., Cox, M., & Cox, R. (1978). The aftermath of divorce. In J. H. Stevens & M. Mathews (Eds.), *Mother-child/father-child relations.* Washington, DC: NAEYC.

Hetherington, E. M., Cox, M., & Cox, R. (1979). Play and social interaction in children following divorce. *Journal of Social Issues, 35,* 26–49.

Hetherington, E. M., Cox, M., & Cox, R. (1982). Effects of divorce on children and parents. In M. E. Lamb (Ed.), *Nontraditional families.* Hillsdale, NJ: Erlbaum.

Hetherington, E. M., Hagan, M. S., & Anderson, E. R. (1989). Family transitions: A child's perspective. *American Psychologist, 44,* 303–312.

Hightower, E. (1990). Adolescent interpersonal and familial precursors of positive mental health at midlife. *Journal of Youth and Adolescence, 19,* 257–275.

Hill, C. R., & Stafford, F. P. (1980). Parental care of children: Time diary estimate of quantity, predictability, and variety. *Journal of Human Resources, 15,* 219–239.

Hill, J. P. (1980). The early adolescent and the family. In M. Johnson (Ed.), *The 79th Yearbook of the National Society for the Study of Education.* Chicago: University of Chicago Press.

Hill, J. P. (1983, April). *Early adolescence: A research agenda.* Paper presented at the biennial meeting of the Society for Research in Child Development, Detroit.

Hill, J. P., Holmbeck, G. N., Marlow, L., Green, T. M., & Lynch, M. E. (1985). Pubertal status and parent-child relations in families of seventh-grade boys. *Journal of Early Adolescence, 5,* 31–44.

Hinde, R. A. (1983). Ethology and child development. In P. H. Mussen (Ed.), *Handbook of child psychology* (4th ed., Vol. 2). New York: Wiley.

Hinde, R. A. (1989). Ethological and relationship approaches. In R. Vasta (Ed.), *Six theories of child development: Revised formulations and current issues.* Greenwich, CT: JAI Press.

Hinde, R. A. (1989, April). *Differential treatment of particular characteristics in boys and girls.* Paper presented at the biennial meeting of the Society for Research in Child Development, Kansas City, MO.

Hinde, R. A., & Gorebel, J. (1989). The problem of aggression. In J. Gorebel & R. A. Hinde (Eds.), *Aggression and war: Their biological bases.* New York: Cambridge University Press.

Hines, M. (1982). Prenatal gonadal hormones and sex differences in human behavior. *Psychological Bulletin, 92,* 56–80.

Hirsch, B. J. (1989, April). *School transitions and psychological well-being in adolescence: Comparative longitudinal analyses.* Paper presented at the biennial meeting of the Society for Research in Child Development, Kansas City, MO.

Hirsch, B. J., & Rapkin, B. D. (1987). The transition to junior high school: A longitudinal study of self-esteem, psychological symptomatology, school life, and social support. *Child Development, 58,* 1235–1243.

Hirsh-Pasek, K., Hyson, M., Rescorla, L., & Cone, J. (1989, April). *Hurrying children: How does it affect their academic, social, creative, and emotional development?* Paper presented at the biennial meeting of the Society for Research in Child Development, Kansas City, MO.

Hirshorn, B. (1991). Sharing or competition: Multiple views of the intergenerational flow of society's resources. *Marriage and Family Review, 16,* 175–192.

Ho, D. Y. F. (1987). Fatherhood in Chinese culture. In M. E. Lamb (Ed.), *The father's role: Cross-cultural perspectives.* Hillsdale, NJ: Erlbaum.

Hobbs, N. (Ed.). (1975). *Issues in the classification of children* (Vol. 1). San Francisco: Jossey-Bass.

Hoff-Ginsberg, E. (1991, April). *Why and how some mothers talk more to their children than other mothers.* Paper presented at the biennial meeting of the Society for Research in Child Development, Seattle.

Hofferth, S. L. (1990). Trends in adolescent sexual activity, contraception, and pregnancy in the United States. In J. Bancroft & J. M. Reinisch (Eds.), *Adolescence and puberty.* New York: Oxford University Press.

Hoffman, L. W. (1979). Maternal employment: 1979. *American Psychologist, 34,* 859–865.

Hoffman, L. W. (1989). Effects of maternal employment in two-parent families. *American Psychologist, 44,* 283–293.

Hofstede, G. (1980). *Culture's consequences.* Newbury Park, CA: Sage.

Holland, J. L. (1973). *Making vocational choices: A theory of careers.* Englewood Cliffs, NJ: Prentice-Hall.

Holland, J. L. (1987). Current status of Holland's theory of careers: Another perspective. *Career Development Quarterly, 36,* 24–30.

Holmes, D. L., Reich, J. N., Y Gyurke, J. S. (1989). The development of high-risk infants in low-risk families. In F. J. Morrison, C. Lord, & D. P. Keating (Eds.), *Psychological development in infancy.* San Diego: Academic Press.

Holtzmann, W. H. (1982). Cross-cultural comparisons of personality development in Mexico and the United States. In D. A. Wagner & H. W. Stevenson (Eds.), *Cultural perspectives on child development.* New York: W. H. Freeman.

Horn, J. L., & Donaldson, G. (1980). Cognitive development II: Adulthood development of human abilities. In O. G. Brim & J. Kagan (Eds.) *Constancy and change in human development.* Cambridge, MA: Harvard University Press.

Horne, M. D. (1988). Handicapped, disabled, or exceptional: Terminological issues. *Psychology in the Schools, 25,* 419–421.

Horney, K. (1967). *Feminine psychology.* New York: W. W. Norton.

Horowitz, F. (1991). Developmental models of early individual differences. In J. Columbo & J. W. Fagen (Eds.), *Individual differences in infancy.* Hillsdale, NJ: Erlbaum.

Horowitz, F. D., & O'Brien, M. (1989). In the interest of a nation: A reflective essay on the state of knowledge and the challenges before us. *American Psychologist, 44,* 441–445.

House, J. S. (1989). Social structure and interpersonal relations. In K. W. Schaie & C. Schooler (Eds.), *Social structure and aging: Psychological Processes.* Hillsdale, NJ: Erlbaum.

Howard, J. (1982). Counseling: A developmental approach. In E. E. Bleck & D. A. Nagel (Ed.), *Physically handicapped children.* New York: Grune & Stratton.

Howes, C. (1988, April). *Can the age of entry and the quality of infant child care predict behaviors in kindergarten?* Paper presented at the International Conference on Infant Studies, Washington, D.C.

Howes, C., Unger, O., & Seidner, L. B. (1989). Social pretend play in toddlers: Parallels with social play and solitary pretend. *Child Development, 60,* 77–84.

Hoyert, D. L. (1991). Financial and household exchanges between generations. *Research on Aging, 13,* 205–226.

Huang, L. N., & Gibbs, J. T. (1989). Future directions: Implications for research, training, and practice. In J. T. Gibbs & L. N. Huang (Eds.), *Children of color.* San Francisco: Jossey-Bass.

Huang, L. N., & Ying, Y. (1989). Japanese children and adolescents. In J. T. Gibbs & L. N. Huang (Eds.), *Children of color*. San Francisco: Jossey-Bass.

Hudson, L. M., Forman, E. R., & Brion-Meisels, S. (1982). Role-taking as a predictor of prosocial behavior in cross-age tutors. *Child Development, 53,* 222–234.

Huesmann, L. R. (1986). Psychological processes promoting the relation between exposure to media violence and aggressive behavior by the viewer. *Journal of Social Issues, 42,* 125–139.

Huesmann, L. R., Eron, L. D., Klein, R., Brice, P., & Fischer, P. (1983). Mitigating the imitation of aggressive behaviors by changing children's attitudes about media violence. *Journal of Personality and Social Psychology, 44,* 899–910.

Hughes, P. C. Reported in Fozard, J. L., & Popkin, S. J. (1978). Optimizing adult development. *American Psychologist, 33,* 975–989.

Hui, C. H., & Villareal, M. J. (1989). Individualism-collectivism and psychological needs. *Journal of Cross-Cultural Psychology, 20,* 310–323.

Hultsch, D. F. (1971). Adult age differences in free classification and free recall. *Developmental Psychology, 4,* 338–342.

Hultsch, D. F., & Plemons, J. K. (1979). Life events and life-span development. In P. B. Baltes & O. G. Brim (Eds.), *Life-span development and behavior*. New York: Academic Press.

Hunt, J. V., & Cooper, B. A. (1989). Determining the risk for high-risk preterm infants. In M. Bornstein & N. A. Krasnegor (Eds.), *Stability and continuity in mental development*. Hillsdale, NJ: Erlbaum.

Hunt, M. (1974). *Sexual behavior in the 1970s*. Chicago: Playboy Press.

Hurd, M. D., & Wise, D. A. (1989). The wealth and poverty of widows: Assets before and after the husband's death. In D. A Wise (Ed.), *The economics of aging*. Chicago: University of Chicago Press.

Huston, A. C. (1983). Sex-typing. In P. H. Mussen (Ed.), *Handbook of child psychology* (Vol. 4, 4th ed.). New York: Wiley.

Huston, A. C., Seigle, J., & Bremer, M. (1983, April). *Family environment and television use by preschool children*. Paper presented at the biennial meeting of the Society for Research in Child Development, Detroit.

Huston, A. C., Watkins, B. A., & Kunkel, D. (1989). Public policy and children's television. *American Psychologist, 44,* 424–433.

Huston-Stein, A., & Higgens-Trenk, A. (1978). Development of females from childhood through adulthood: Career and feminine role orientations. In P. Baltes (Ed.), *Life-span development and behavior* (Vol. 1). New York: Academic Press.

Hutchings, D. E., & Fifer, W. P. (1986). Neurobehavioral effects in human and animal offspring following prenatal exposure to methadone. In E. P. Riley & C. V. Vorhees (Eds.), *Handbook of behavioral teratology*. New York: Plenum.

Hyde, J. S. (1981). How large are cognitive gender differences? A meta-analysis using w^2 and *d*. *American Psychologist, 36,* 892–901.

Hyde, J. S. (1985). *Half the human experience*. (3rd ed.). Lexington, MA: D. C. Heath.

Hyde, J. S. (in press). Meta-analysis and the psychology of women. In F. L. Denmark & M. A. Paludi (Eds.), *Handbook on the psychology of women*. Dubuque, IA: Wm. C. Brown.

Hynd, G. W., & Obrzut, J. E. (1986). Exceptionality: Historical antecedents and present positions. In R. T. Brown & C. R. Reynolds (Eds.), *Psychological perspectives on childhood exceptionality: A handbook*. New York: Wiley.

I

Ikels, C. (1989). Becoming a human being in theory and practice: Chinese views of human development. In D. I. Kertzer & K. W. Schaie (Eds.), *Age structuring in comparative perspective*. Hillsdale, NJ: Erlbaum.

Ingelhart, R., & Rabier, J. (1986). Aspirations adapt to situations—but why are the Belgians so much happier than the French? A cross-cultural analysis of the subjective quality of life. In F. M. Andrews (Ed.), *Research on the quality of life*. Ann Arbor, MI: Institute of Social Research, University of Michigan.

Inkeles, A., & Usui, C. (1989). Retirement patterns in cross-national perspective. In D. I. Kertzer & K. W. Schaie (Eds.), *Age structuring in comparative perspective*. Hillsdale, NJ: Erlbaum.

Irvine, M. J., Johnston, D. W., Jenner, D. A., & Marie, G. V. (1986). Relaxation and stress management in the treatment of essential hypertension. *Journal of Psychosomatic Research, 30,* 437–450.

Izard, C. E. (1982). *Measuring emotions in infants and young children*. New York: Cambridge University Press.

Izard, C. E. (1991). Studies of the development of emotion-cognition relations. In C. E. Izard (Ed.), *The development of emotion-cognition relations*. Hillsdale, NJ: Erlbaum.

Izard, C. E., & Malatesta, C. Z. (1987). Differential emotions theory of early emotional development. In J. D. Osofsky (Ed.), *Handbook of infant development*. New York: Wiley.

J

Jacklin, C. N. (1989). Female and male: Issues of gender. *American Psychologist, 44,* 127–133.

Jackson, J. S. (1989). Race, ethnicity, and psychological theory and research. *Journal of Gerontology, 44,* P1–P2.

Jacobs, J. E., & Potenza, M. (1990, March). *The use of decision making strategies in late adolescence*. Paper presented at the meeting of the Society for Research in Adolescence, Atlanta, GA.

Jacobs, S. C., Dosten, T. R., Kasl, S. V., Ostfield, A. M., Berkman, L., & Charpentier, M. P. H. (1987). Attachment theory and multiple dimensions of grief. *Omega, 18,* 41–52.

Jacobson, J. L., Jacobson, S. W., Fein, G. G., Schwartz, P. M., & Dowler, J. K. (1984). Prenatal exposure to an environmental toxin: A test of the multiple-effects model. *Developmental Psychology, 20,* 523–532.

Jagacinski, C. M., & Nicholls, J. G. (1990). Reducing effort to protect perceived ability: "They'd do it but I wouldn't." *Journal of Educational Psychology, 82,* 15–21.

Jahoda, M. (1988). Economic recession and mental health: Some conceptual issues. *Journal of Social Issues, 44,* 13–24.

James, W. (1890/1950). *The principles of psychology*. New York: Dover.

Janos, P. M., & Robinson, N. M. (1985). Psychosocial development in intellectually gifted children. In F. D. Horowitz & M. O'Brien (Eds.), *The gifted and the talented*. Washington, DC: American Psychological Association.

Japanese Prime Minister's Office. (1982). *International comparative survey of life and perception of the old*. Tokyo, Japan: Office of the Aged, Prime Minister's Office.

Jarvik, L. F., & Winograd, C. H. (1988). *Treatments for the Alzheimer's patient*. New York: Springer.

Javernik, E. (1988, January). Johnny's not jumping: Can we help obese children? *Young Children*, pp. 18–23.

Jeans, P. C., Smith, M. B., & Stearns, G. (1955). Incidence of prematurity in relation to maternal nutrition. *Journal of the American Dietary Association, 31,* 576–581.

Jensen, A. R. (1969). How much can we boost IQ and scholastic achievement? *Harvard Educational Review, 39,* 1–123.

Jensen, M. R. (1987). Psychobiological factors predicting the course of breast cancer. *Journal of Personality, 55,* 317–342.

John-Steiner, V. (1985). Notebooks of the mind: Explorations of thinking. Albuquerque, NM: University of New Mexico Press.

Johnston, L., Bachman, J. G., & O'Malley, P. M. (1990). *Monitoring the future*. Ann Arbor, MI: Institute of Social Research, University of Michigan.

Johnston, L. D., O'Malley, P. M., & Bachman, J. G. (1987). *National trends in drug use and related factors among American high school students and young adults, 1975–1986*. Institute of Social Research, University of Michigan, Ann Arbor.

Johnston, L. D., O'Malley, P. M., & Bachman, J. G. (1988). *Illicit drug use, smoking, and drinking by America's high school students, college students, and young adults, 1975–1987*. Washington, DC: National Institute of Drug Abuse.

Johnston, L. D., O'Malley, P. M., & Bachman, J. G. (1989, February 24). *Teen drug use continues decline*. New Release, Institute for Social Research, University of Michigan, Ann Arbor.

Johnston, L. D., O'Malley, P. M., & Bachman, J. G. (1990, February 13). *Drug Use continues to decline*. News Release, Institute for Social Research, University of Michigan, Ann Arbor.

Johnston, L. D., O'Malley, P. M., & Bachman, J. G. (1991, January 23). *News release on national drug use by young Americans*. Ann Arbor, MI: Institute for Social Research.

Jones, B. F., Idol, L., & Brandt, R. S. (1991). Dimensional thinking. In B. F. Jones & L. Idol (Eds.), Dimensions of thinking and cognitive instruction. Hillsdale, NJ: Erlbaum.

Jones, E. (1953). *The life and work of Sigmund Freud* (Vol. 1). New York: Basic Books.

Jones, E. R., Forrest, J. D., Goldman, N., Henshaw, S. K., Lincoln, R., Rosoff, J. I., Westoff, C. G., & Wulf, D. (1985). Teenage pregnancy in developed countries: Determinants and policy implications. *Family Planning Perspectives, 17,* 53–63.

Jones, J. M. (1990, August). *Psychological approaches to race: What have they been and what should they be?* Paper presented at the meeting of the American Psychological Association, Boston, MA.

Jones, M. C. (1965). Psychological correlates of somatic development. *Child Development, 36,* 899–911.

Jones, W. H., Hobbs, S. A., & Hockenbury, D. (1982). Loneliness and social skills deficits. *Journal of Personality and Social Psychology, 42,* 682–689.

Josselson, R. (1987). *Finding herself*. San Francisco: Jossey-Bass.

Justiz, M. J. & Rendon, L. I. (1989). Hispanic students. In M. L. Upcraft & J. N. Gardner (Eds.), *The freshman experience*. San Francisco: Jossey-Bass.

K

Kagan, J. (1984). *The nature of the child*. New York: Basic Books.

Kagan, J. (1987). Perspectives on infancy. In J. D. Osofsky (Ed.), *Handbook on infant development*. (2nd ed.). New York: Wiley.

Kagan, J. (1989). *Unstable ideas: Temperament, cognition, and self*. Cambridge, MA: Harvard University Press.

Kagan, J., Kearsley, R. B., & Zelazo, P. R. (1978). *Infancy.* Cambridge, MA: Harvard University Press.

Kagan, S. L. (1988, January). Current reforms in early childhood education: Are we addressing the issues? *Young Children, 43,* 27–38.

Kagitcibasi, C. (1988). Diversity of socialization and social change. In P. R. Dasen, J. W. Berry, & N. Sartorious (Eds.), *Health and cross-cultural Psychology: Toward applications.* Newbury Park, CA: Sage.

Kagitcibasi, C., & Berry, J. W. (1989). Cross-cultural psychology: Current research and trends. *Annual Review of Psychology, 40.* Palo Alto, CA: Annual Reviews.

Kalichman, S. C., Kelly, J. A., & St. Lawrence, J. S. (in press). Factors influencing reduction of sexual risk behaviors for HIV infection. *Annals of Sex Research.*

Kalish, R. A. (1981). *Death, grief, and caring relationships.* Monterey, CA: Brooks/Cole.

Kalish, R. A. (1987). Death. In G. L. Maddox (Ed.), *Encyclopedia of aging.* New York: Springer.

Kalish, R. A. (1988). The study of death: A psychosocial perspective. In H. Wass, F. M. Berardo, & R. A. Niemeyer (Eds.), *Dying: Facing the facts* (2nd ed.). Washington, DC: Hemisphere.

Kalish, R. A., & Reynolds, D. K. (1976). *An overview of death and ethnicity.* Farmingdale, NY: Baywood.

Kamerman, S. B. (1989). Child care, women, work, and the family: An international overview of child-care services and related policies. In J. S. Lande, S. Scarr, & N. Gunzenhauser (Eds.), *Caring for children: Challenge to America.* Hillsdale, NJ: Erlbaum.

Kamerman, S. B., & Kahn, A. J. (1988). Social policy and children in the United States and Europe. In J. L. Palmer, T. Smeeding, & B. B. Torrey (Eds.), *The vulnerable America's young and old in the industrialized world.* Washington, DC: The Urban Institute.

Kamo, Y. (1988). Determinants of the household division of labor: Resources, power, and ideology. *Journal of Family Issues, 9,* 177–200.

Kanda, K., & Mezey, M. (1991). Registered nursing staffing in Pennsylvania nursing homes: Comparison before and after implementation of Medicare's prospective payment system. *The Gerontologist, 31,* 318–324.

Kandel, D. B. (1974). The role of parents and peers in marijuana use. *Journal of Social Issues, 30,* 107–135.

Kandel, D. B. (1991). Drug use, epidemiology and developmental stages of involvement In R. M. Lerner, A. C. Petersen, & J. Brooks-Gunn (Eds.), *Encyclopedia of adolescence* (Vol. 1). New York: Garland.

Kandel, D. B., Dessler, R. C., & Margulies, R. Z. (1978). Antecedents of adolescent initiation into stages of drug use: A developmental analysis. In D. B. Kandel (Ed.), *Longitudinal research on drug use.* New York: Wiley.

Kanner, A. D., Coyne, J. C., Schaefer, C., & Lazarus, R. S. (1981). Comparison of two modes of stress measurement: Daily hassles and uplifts versus major life events. *Journal of Behavioral Medicine, 4,* 1–39.

Kanner, A. D., & Feldman, S. S. (1991). Control over uplifts and hassles and its relationship to adaptational outcomes. *Journal of Behavioral Medicine, 14,* 187–196.

Kantrowitz, B. & Wingert, P. (1989, April 17). How kids learn. *Newsweek,* pp. 4–10.

Kaplan, P., Fox, K., & Huckeby, B. (1991, April). *Do faces sensitize young infants?* Paper presented at the biennial meeting of the Society for Research in Child Development, Seattle.

Karlin, R., & Karlin, A. R. (1987). *Teaching elementary reading.* San Diego: Harcourt Brace Jovanovich.

Kart, C. S. (1990). *Diversity among aged black males.* In Z. Harel, E. A. McKinney, & M. Williams (Eds.), *Black aged.* Newbury Park, CA: Sage.

Kasper, J. D. (1988). *Aging alone: Profiles and projections.* Report of the Commonwealth Fund Commission: Elderly People Living Alone. Baltimore, MD: Commonwealth Fund Commission.

Katz, L., & Chard, S. (1989). *Engaging the minds of young children: The project approach.* Norwood, NJ: Ablex.

Katz, P. A. (1987, August). *Children and social issues.* Paper presented at the meeting of the American Psychological Association, New York.

Kearns, D. T. (1988, April). An education recovery plan for America. *Phi Delta Kappan,* pp. 565–570.

Keating, D. (1980). Thinking processes in adolescence. In J. Adelson (Ed.), *Handbook of adolescent psychology.* New York: Wiley.

Keating, D. P. (1990). Adolescent thinking. In S. S. Feldman & G. R. Elliott (Eds.), *At the threshold: The developing adolescent.* Cambridge, MA: Harvard University Press.

Keating, D. P. (1991). Cognition, adolescent. In R. M. Lerner, A. C. Petersen, & J. Brooks-Gunn (Eds.), *Encyclopedia of adolescence* (Vol. 1). New York: Garland.

Keating, D. P. (in press). Structuralism, deconstruction, reconstruction: The limits of reasoning. In W. F. Overton (Ed.), *Reasoning, necessity, and logic: Developmental perspectives.* Hillsdale, NJ: Erlbaum.

Keefe, S. E., & Padilla, A. M. (1987). *Chicano ethnicity.* Albuquerque, NM: University of New Mexico Press.

Keith, T. Z., Cool, V. A., Novak, C. G., White, L. J., & Pottebaum, S. M. (1988). Confirmatory factor analysis of the Stanford-Binet Fourth Edition: Testing the theory-test match. *Journal of School Psychology, 26,* 253–274.

Keller, A., Ford, L., & Meacham J. (1978). Dimensions of self-concept in preschool children. *Developmental Psychology, 14,* 483–489.

Kelly, J. A., & de Armas, A. (1989). Social relationships in adolescence: Skill development and training. In J. Worell & F. Danner (Eds.), *The adolescent as decision-maker.* San Diego: Academic Press.

Kelly, J. B. (1987, August). *Children of divorce: Long-term effects and clinical implications.* Paper presented at the meeting of the American Psychological Association, New York City.

Kennedy, R. E. (1991). Delinquency. In R. M. Lerner, A. C. Petersen, & J. Brooks-Gunn (Eds.), *Encyclopedia of adolescence* (Vol. 1). New York: Garland.

Kenney, A. M. (1987, June). Teen pregnancy: An issue for schools. *Phi Delta Kappan,* pp. 728–736.

Kenniston, K. (1970). Youth: A "new" stage of life. *The American Scholar, 39,* 631–654.

Kephart, W. M. (1967). Some correlates of romantic love. *Journal of Marriage and the Family, 29,* 470–474.

Kerr, B. A. (1983). Raising the career aspirations of gifted girls. *Vocational Guidance Quarterly, 32,* 37–43.

Kessen, W., Haith, M. M., & Salapatek, P. (1970). Human infancy. In P. H. Mussen (Ed.), *Manual of child psychology* (3rd ed., Vol. 1). New York: Wiley.

Khan, S. B., & Alvi, S. A. (1991). The structure of Hooland's typology: A study in a non-western culture. *Journal of Cross-Cultural Psychology, 22,* 283–292.

Kidorf, I. W. (1966). The shiva: A form of group psychotherapy. *Journal of Religion and Health, 5,* 43–46.

Kiebzak, G. M. (1991). Age-related bone changes. *Experimental Gerontology, 26,* 171–188.

Kiecolt-Glaser, J. K., & Glaser, R. (1988). Behavioral influences on immune function. In T. Field, P. McCabe, & N. Schneiderman (Eds.), *Stress and coping across development.* Hillsdale, NJ: Erlbaum.

King, H. E. (1961). Psychological effects of excitation of the limbic system. In D. E. Sheer (Ed.), *Electrical stimulation of the brain.* Austin, TX: University of Texas Press.

King, N. (1982). School uses of materials traditionally associated with children's play. *Theory and research in social education, 10,* 17–27.

Kinney, J. M., & Ogrocki, P. K. (1991). Stressors and well-being among caregivers to older adults with Dementia: The in-home versus nursing home experience. *The Gerontologist, 31,* 217–223.

Kinsey, A. C., Pomeroy, W. B., & Martin, E. E. (1948). *Sexual behavior in the human male.* Philadelphia: W. B. Saunders.

Kitch, D. L. (1987). Hospice. In R. J. Corsini (Ed.), *Concise encyclopedia of psychology.* New York: Wiley.

Kite, M. E., Deaux, K., & Miele, M. (1991). Stereotypes of young and old: Does age outweigh gender? *Psychology and aging, 6,* 19–27.

Klahr, D. (1989). Information-processing approaches. In R. Vasta (Ed.), *Six theories of child development: Revised formulations and current issues.* Greenwich, CT: JAI Press.

Klass, D. (1988). *Parental grief.* New York: Springer.

Klaus, M., & Kennell, H. H. (1976). *Maternal-infant bonding.* St. Louis: Mosby.

Klein, S. S. (1988). Using sex equity research to improve education policies. *Theory into Practice, 27,* 152–160.

Kliegl, R., & Baltes, P. B. (1987). Theory-guided analysis of mechanisms of development and aging through testing-the-limits and research on expertise. In C. Schooler & K. W. Schaie (Eds.), *Cognitive functioning and social structure over the life course.* Norwood, NJ: Ablex.

Kliegl, R., Smith, J., & Baltes, P. B. (1989). Testing-the-limits and the study of age differences in cognitive plasticity of a mnemonic skill. *Developmental Psychology, 25,* 247–256.

Kliegl, R., Smith, J., & Baltes, P. B. (1990). On the locus and process of magnification of age differences during mnemonic training. *Developmental Psychology, 26,* 894–904.

Kline, D. W., & Schieber, F. (1985). Vision and aging. In J. E. Birren & K. W. Schaie (Eds.), *Handbook of the psychology of aging* (2nd ed.). New York: Van Nostrand Reinhold.

Knight, R. A., Rosenberg, R., & Schneider, B. (1985). Classification of sexual offenders: Perspectives, methods, and validation. In A. W. Burgess (Ed.), *Rape and sexual assault.* New York: Garland.

Knott, J. E. (1979). Death education for all. In H. Wass (Ed.), *Dying: Facing the facts.* Washington, DC: Hemisphere.

Kobak, R. R., & Sceery, A. (1988). Attachment in late adolescence: Working models, affect regulation, and representations of self and others. *Child Development, 59,* 135–146.

Kobasa, S. C., Maddi, S., & Kahn, S. (1982). Hardiness and health: A prospective study. *Journal of Personality and Social Psychology, 42,* 168–177.

Kohlberg, L. (1958). *The development of modes of moral thinking and choice in the years 10 to 16.* Unpublished doctoral dissertation, University of Chicago, Chicago, IL.

Kohlberg, L. (1966). A cognitive-developmental analysis of children's sex-role concepts and attitudes. In E. E. Maccoby (Ed.), *The development of sex differences.* Palo Alto, CA: Stanford University Press.

Kohlberg, L. (1969). Stage and sequence: The cognitive-developmental approach to socialization. In D. A. Goslin (Ed.), *Handbook of socialization theory and research.* Chicago: Rand McNally.

Kohlberg, L. (1976). Moral stages and moralization: The cognitive-development approach. In T. Lickona (Ed.), *Moral development and behavior.* New York: Holt, Rinehart, & Winston.

Kohlberg, L. (1986). A correct statement on some theoretical issues. In S. Modgil & C. Modgil (Eds.), *Lawrence Kohlberg.* Philadelphia: Falmer Press.

Kohn, M. L. (1977). Class and conformity: A study in values (2nd ed.). Chicago: University of Chicago Press.

Kopp, C. B. (1983). Risk factors in development. In P. H. Mussen (Ed.), *Handbook of child psychology* (4th ed., Vol. 2). New York: Wiley.

Kopp, C. B. (1987). Developmental risk: Historical reflections. In J. D. Osofsky (Ed.), *Handbook of infant development* (2nd ed.). New York: Wiley.

Kopp, C. B., & Kaler, S. R. (1989). Risk in infancy: Origins and implications. *American Psychologist, 44,* 224–230.

Korner, A. F. (1990). Infant stimulation: Issues of theory and research. In B. M. Lester & E. Z. Tronick (Eds.), *Stimulation and the preterm infant: The limits of plasticity.* Philadelphia: W. B. Saunders.

Kosik, K. S. (1989). The molecular and cellular pathology of Alzheimer neurofibrillary lesions. *Journal of Gerontology: Biological Sciences, 44,* B55–58.

Kosnik, W., Winslow, L., Kline, D., Rasinski, K., & Sekuler, R. (1989). Visual changes in daily life through adulthood. *Journal of Gerontology: Psychological Sciences, 43,* P63–P70.

Koss, M. P. (1990). The women's mental health research agenda: Violence against women. *American Psychologist, 45,* 374–381.

Kotre, J. (1984). Outliving the self: Generativity and the interpretation of lives. Baltimore: MD: Johns Hopkins University Press.

Krackow, E. (1991, April). *Preschool children's memory for repeated changes in the lunch routine.* Paper presented at the biennial meeting of the Society for Research in Child Development, Seattle.

Krause, N., Jay, G., & Liang, J. (1991). Financial strain and psychological well-being among the American and Japanese elderly. *Psychology and Aging, 6,* 17–181.

Kübler-Ross, E. (1969). *On death and dying.* New York: Macmillan.

Kübler-Ross, E. (1974). *Questions and answers on death and dying.* New York: Macmillan.

Kuhn, D. (1991a). Education for thinking: What can psychology contribute? In M. Schwebel, C. A. Maher, & N. S. Fagley (Eds.), *Promoting cognitive growth over the life span.* Hillsdale, NJ: Erlbaum.

Kuhn, D. (1991b). Reasoning, higher-order in adolescence. In R. M. Lerner, A. C. Petersen, & J. Brooks-Gunn (Eds.), *Encyclopedia of adolescence* (Vol. 2). New York: Garland.

Kupersmidt J. B. & Coie, J. D. (1990). Preadolescent peer status, aggression, and school adjustment as predictors of externalizing problems in adolescence. *Child Development, 61,* 1350–1363.

Kurdek, L. A., & Krile, D. (1982). A developmental analysis of the relation between peer acceptance and both interpersonal understanding and perceived social self-competence. *Child Development, 53,* 1485–1491.

Kusche, C. A. (1991, April). *Improving classroom behavior and emotional understanding in special needs children: The effects of the PATHS curriculum.* Paper presented at the biennial meeting of the Society for Research in Child Development, Seattle.

Kuypers, J. A., & Bengston, V. L. (1973). Social breakdown and competence. A model of normal aging. *Human Development, 16,* 181–201.

L

Labouvie-Vief, G. (1982). Dynamic development and mature autonomy: A theoretical prologue. *Human Development, 25,* 161–191.

Labouvie-Vief, G. (1985). Intelligence and cognition. In J. E. Birren & K. W. Schaie (Eds.), *Handbook on the psychology of aging* (2nd ed.). New York: Van Nostrand Reinhold.

Labouvie-Vief, G. (1986, August). *Modes of knowing and life-span cognition.* Paper presented at the meeting of the American Psychological Association, Washington, DC.

LaFromboise, T. D., & Low, K. G. (1989). American Indian children and adolescents. In J. T. Gibbs & L. N. Huang (Eds.), *Children of color.* San Francisco: Jossey-Bass.

Lagerspetz, K. (1979). Modification of aggressiveness in mice. In S. Feshbach & A. Fraczek (Eds.), *Aggression and behavior change: Biological and social processes.* New York: Praeger.

LaGrand, L. E. (1991). United we cope: Support groups for the dying and bereaved. *Death Studies, 15,* 207–230.

Lamb, M. E. (1977). The development of mother-infant and father-infant attachments in the second year of life. *Developmental Psychology, 13,* 637–648.

Lamb, M. E. (Ed.). (1986). *The father's role: Applied perspectives.* New York: Wiley.

Lamb, M. E., Frodi, A. M., Hwang, C. P., Frodi, M., & Steinberg, J. (1982). Mother- and father-infant interaction involving play and holding in traditional and nontraditional Swedish families. *Developmental Psychology, 18,* 215–221.

Lamb, M. E., Thompson, R. A., Gardner, W. R., Charnov, E. L., & Estes, D. P. (1984). Security of infantile attachment as assessed in the "strange situation": Its study and biological interpretation. *The Behavioral and Brain Sciences, 7,* 121–171.

Lambert, N. M., & Hartsough, C. S. (1984). Contribution of predispositional factors to the diagnosis of hyperactivity. *American Journal of Orthopsychiatry, 54,* 97–109.

Landesman, S., & Ramey, C. (1989). Developmental psychology and mental retardation: Integrating scientific principles with treatment practices. *American Psychologist, 44,* 409–415.

Landesman-Dwyer, S., & Sackett, G. P. (1983, April). *Prenatal nicotine exposure and sleep-wake patterns in infancy.* Paper presented at the biennial meeting of the Society for Research in Child Development, Detroit.

Landy, F. J. (1989). *Psychology of work behavior* (4th ed.). Chicago: Dorsey Press.

Lane, H. (1976). *The wild boy of Aveyron.* Cambridge, MA: Harvard University Press.

Langer, J. (1969). *Theories of development.* New York: Holt, Rinehart & Winston.

Lapsley, D. G. (1989). Continuity and discontinuity in adolescent social cognitive development. In R. Montemayor, G. Adams, & T. Gullota (Eds.), *Advances in adolescence research* (Vol. 2), Orlando, FL: Academic Press.

Lapsley, D. K. (1990). The adolescent egocentrism theory and the "new look" at the imaginary audience and personal fable. In R. M. Lerner, A. C. Petersen, & J. Brooks-Gunn (Eds.), *The Encyclopedia of adolescence.* New York: Garland.

Lapsley, D. K. (1991). Egocentrism theory and the "new look" at the imaginary audience and personal fable in adolescence. In R. M. Lerner, A. C. Petersen, & J. Brooks-Gunn (Eds.), *Encyclopedia of adolescence.* New York: Garland.

Lapsley, D. K., Enright, R. D., & Serlin, R. C. (1985). Toward a theoretical perspective on the legislation of adolescence. *Journal of Early Adolescence, 5,* 441–466.

Lapsley, D. K., Milstead, M., Qunitana, S. M., Flannery, D., & Buss, R. R. (1986). Adolescent egocentrism and formal operations: Tests of a theoretical assumption. *Developmental Psychology, 22,* 800–807.

Lapsley, D. K., & Murphy, M. N. (1985). Another look at the theoretical assumptions of adolescent egocentrism. *Developmental Review, 5,* 201–217.

Lapsley, D. K., & Rice, K. G. (1988). The "new look" at the imaginary audience and personal fable: Toward an integrative model of adolescent ego development. In D. K. Lapsley & F. C. Power (Eds.), *Self, ego, and identity: Integrative approaches.* New York: Springer-Verlag.

Larson, J. H. (1988). The Marriage Quiz: College students' beliefs in selected myths about marriage. *Family Relations, 37,* 3–11.

LaRue, A., Dessonville, C., & Jarvik, L. F. (1985). Aging and mental disorders. In J. E. Birren & K. W. Schaie (Eds.), *Handbook of the psychology of aging* (2nd ed.). New York: Van Nostrand Reinhold.

LaVoie, J. (1976). Ego identity formation in middle adolescence. *Journal of Youth and Adolescence, 5,* 371–385.

Lawton, M. P. (1989). Behavior-relevant ecological factors. In K. W. Schaie & C. Schooler (Eds.), *Social structure and aging.* Hillsdale, NJ: Erlbaum.

Lazar, I., Darlington, R., & Collaborators. (1982). Lasting effects of early education: A report from the consortium for longitudinal studies. *Monographs of the Society for Research in Child Development, 47.*

Lazarus, R. S., & Folkman, S. (1984). *Stress, appraisal, and coping.* New York: Springer.

Leafgren, A. (1989). Health and wellness programs. In M. L. Upcraft & J. N. Gardner (Eds.), *The freshman year experience.* San Francisco: Jossey-Bass.

Leamer, I. (1986). *As time goes by.* New York: Harper & Row.

Lebowitz, B. D. (1987). Mental health services. In G. L. Maddox (Ed.), *The encyclopedia of aging.* New York: Springer.

Leboyer, F. (1975). *Birth without violence.* New York: Knopf.

Lee, G. R. (1978). Marriage and morale in late life. *Journal of Marriage and the Family, 40,* 131–139.

Lee, V. E., Brooks-Gunn, J., & Schnur, E. (1988). Does Head Start Work? A 1-year follow-up comparison of disadvantaged children attending Head Start, no preschool, and other preschool programs. *Developmental Psychology, 24,* 210–222.

LeGall, S. (1990). Academic achievement orientation and help-seeking behavior in early adolescent girls. *Journal of Early Adolescence, 10,* 176–190.

Lehman, H. C. (1960). The age decrement in outstanding scientific creativity. *American Psychologist, 15,* 128–134.

Leifer, A. D. (1973). *Television and the development of social behavior.* Paper presented at the meeting of the International Society for the Study of Behavioral Development, Ann Arbor, MI.

Leifer, A. D., Gordon, N. J., & Graves, S. B. (1974). Children's television: More than entertainment. *Harvard Educational Review, 44,* 213–245.

Leitenberg, H. (1986). Primary prevention in delinquency. In J. Burchard & S. Burchard (Eds.), *Prevention of delinquent behavior.* Newbury Park, CA: Sage.

Lenneberg, E. H., Rebelsky, F. G., & Nichols, I. A. (1965). The vocalization of infants born to deaf and hearing parents. *Human Development, 8,* 23–37.

Lepper, M., Greene, D., & Nisbett, R. R. (1973). Undermining children's intrinsic interest with extrinsic rewards. *Journal of Personality and Social Psychology, 28,* 129–137.

Lepper, M. R. (1985). Microcomputers and education: Motivational and social issues. *American Psychologist, 40,* 1–18.

Lepper, M. R., & Gurtner, J. (1989). Children and computers: Approaching the twenty-first century. *American Psychologist, 44,* 170–178.

Lerner, H. G. (1989). *The dance of intimacy.* New York: Harper & Row.

Lerner, J. W. (1988). *Learning disabilities.* Boston, MA: Houghton Mifflin.

Lerner, J. W. (1989). Educational interventions in learning disabilities. *Journal of the American Academy of Child and Adolescent Psychiatry, 28,* 326 331.

Lerner, J. V., Hertzog, C., Hooker, K. A., Hassibi, M., & Thomas, A. (1988). A longitudinal study of negative emotional states and adjustment from early childhood through adolescence. *Child Development, 59,* 129–137.

Lerner, J. V., & Hess, L. E. (1991). Maternal employment influences on adolescent development. In R. M. Lerner, A. C. Petersen, & J. Brooks-Gunn (Eds.), *Encyclopedia of adolescence* (Vol. 2). New York: Garland.

Lerner, M. (1976). When, why, and where people die. In E. S. Shneidman (Ed.), *Death: Current perspectives.* Palo Alto, CA: Mayfield.

Lerner, R. M. (1990). Plasticity, person-context relations, and cognitive training in the aged years: A developmental contextual perspective. *Developmental Psychology, 26,* 911–915.

Lerner, R. M. (1991). Changing organism-context relations as the basic process of development: A developmental-contextual perspective. *Developmental Psychology, 27,* 27–32.

Lerner, R. M., & Karabenick, S. A. (1974). Physical attractiveness, body attitudes, and self-concept in late adolescence. *Journal of Youth and Adolescence, 3,* 307–316.

Lerner, R. M., Petersen, A. C., & Brooks-Gunn, J. (Eds.) (1991). *Encyclopedia of Adolescence.* New York: Garland.

Lester, B. M. (1991, April). *Neurobehavioral syndromes in cocaine-exposed newborn infants.* Paper presented at the biennial meeting of the Society for Research in Child Development, Seattle.

Lester, B. M., & Boukydis, C. F. Z. (1991, April). *Infant cry characteristics and maternal cry perception: Is a 'good fit' for good development?* Paper presented at the biennial meeting of the Society for Research in Child Development, Seattle.

Lester, B. M., Boukydis, C. F., McGarth, M., Censullo, M., Zahr, L., & Brazelton, T. B. (1990). Behavioral and psychophysiologic assessment of the newborn. In B. M. Lester & E. Z. Tronick (Eds.), *Stimulation and the preterm infant: The limits of plasticity.* Philadelphia: W. B. Saunders.

Lester, B. M., & Tronick, E. Z. (1990a). Preface. In B. M. Lester & E. Z. Tronick (Eds.), *Stimulation and the preterm infant: The limits of plasticity.* Philadelphia: W. B. Saunders.

Lester, B. M., & Tronick, E. Z. (1990b). Introduction. In B. M. Lester & E. Z. Tronick

(Eds.), *Stimulation and the preterm infant: The limits of plasticity.* Philadelphia: W. B. Saunders.

Levenson, J. L., & Bemis, C. (1991). The role of psychological factors in cancer onset and progression. *Psychosomatics, 32,* 124–132.

Levin, J. R. (1980). *The mnemonic '80s: Keywords in the classroom.* Theoretical paper No. 86, Wisconsin Research and Development Center for Individualizing Schooling, Madison, WI.

LeVine, S. (1979). *Mothers and wives: Gusii women of East Africa.* Chicago: The University of Chicago Press.

Levine, S. V. (1984, August). Radical departures. *Psychology Today,* 18–27.

Levinger, G. (1974). A three-level approach to attraction: Toward an understanding of pair relatedness. In T. Huston (Ed.), *Foundations of interpersonal attraction.* New York: Academic Press.

Levinson, D. J. (1978). *The seasons of a man's life.* New York: Knopf.

Levinson, D. J. (1980). Toward a conception of the adult life course. In N. J. Smelser & E. H. Erikson (Eds.), *Themes of work and love in adulthood.* Cambridge, MA: Harvard University Press.

Levinson, D. J. (1987, August). *The seasons of a woman's life.* Paper presented at the meeting of the American Psychological Association, New York City.

Levinson, R. J. (1987). Euthanasia. In G. L. Maddox (Ed.), *The encyclopedia of aging.* New York: Springer.

Levitt, M. J. (1989). Attachment and close relationships: A life-span perspective. In J. L. Gewirtz & W. F. Kurtines (Eds.), *Intersections with attachment.* Hillsdale, NJ: Erlbaum.

Levitt, M. J., Clark, M. C., Rotton, J., & Finley, G. E. (in press). Social support, perceived control, and well-being: A study of an environmentally distressed population. *International Journal of Aging and Human Development.*

Levy, A. B., Dixon, K. N., & Stern, S. L. (1989). How are depression and bulimia related? *American Journal of Psychiatry, 146,* 162–169.

Levy, G. D. (1991, April). *Effects of gender constancy, figure's sex and size on preschoolers' gender constancy: Sometimes big girls do cry.* Paper presented at the biennial meeting of the Society for Research in Child Development, Seattle.

Levy, G. D., & Carter, D. B. (1989). Gender schema, gender constancy, and gender-role knowledge: The roles of cognitive factors in preschoolers' gender-role stereotype attributions. *Developmental Psychology, 25,* 444–449.

Levy, S. (1985). *Behavior and cancer.* San Francisco: Jossey-Bass.

Lewinsohn, P. M., Antonuccio, D. O., Steinmetz, J., & Teri, L. (1984). *The coping with depression course: A psychoeducational intervention for unipolar depression.* Eugene, OR: Castalia.

Lewinsohn, P. M., Rohde, P., Seeley, J. R., & Fischer, S. A. (1991). Age and depression: Unique and shared effects. *Psychology and Aging, 6,* 246–260.

Lewis, C. G. (1981). How adolescents approach decisions: Changes over grades seven to twelve and policy implications. *Child Development, 52,* 538–554.

Lewis, M. (1987). Early sex-role behavior and school age adjustment. In J. M. Reinisch, L. A. Rosenblum, & S. A. Sanders (Eds.), *Masculinity/femininity: Basic perspectives.* New York: Oxford University Press.

Lewis, M. (1989). What do we mean when we say emotional development? In L. Cirillo, B.

Kaplan, & S. Wapner (Eds.), *Emotions in ideal human development.* Hillsdale, NJ: Erlbaum.

Lewis, M., & Brooks-Gunn, J. (1979). *Social cognition and the acquisition of the self.* New York: Plenum.

Lewis, M., & Feinman, S. (1991). (Eds.), *Social influences and socialization in infancy.* New York: Plenum.

Lewis, M., Sullivan, M. W., Sanger, C., & Weiss, M. (1989). Self development and self-conscious emotions. *Child Development, 60,* 146–156.

Lewkowicz, D. J. (1988). Sensory dominance in infants: 1. Six-month-old infants' response to auditory-visual compounds. *Developmental Psychology, 24,* 155–171.

Liben, L. S., & Signorella, M. L. (Eds.). (1987). *Children's gender schemata: New directions in child development.* San Francisco: Jossey-Bass.

Liebert, R. M., & Sprafkin, J. N. (1988). *The early window: Effects of television on children and youth* (3rd ed.). Elmsford, NY: Pergamon.

Liem, R., & Liem, J. H. (1988). Psychological effects of unemployment on workers and their families. *Journal of Social Issues, 44,* 87–106.

Lifshitz, F., Pugliese, M. T., Moses, N., & Weyman-Daum, M. (1987). Parental health beliefs as a cause of non-organic failure to thrive. *Pediatrics, 80,* 175–182.

Lifton, R. J. (1977). The sense of immortality: On death and the continuity of life. In H. Feifel (Ed.), *New meanings of death.* New York: McGraw-Hill.

Linn, M. C. (1991). Scientific reasoning, adolescent. In R. M. Lerner, A. C. Petersen, & J. Brooks-Gunn (Eds.), *Encyclopedia of adolescence* (Vol. 2). New York: Garland.

Linn, M. C., & Hyde, J. S. (1991). Cognitive and psychosocial gender differences, trends in. In R. M. Lerner, A. C. Petersen, & J. Brooks-Gunn (Eds.), *Encyclopedia of adolescence.* (Vol. 1). New York: Garland.

Linn, M. C., & Peterson, A. C. (1986). A meta-analysis of gender differences in spatial ability: Implications for mathematics and science achievement. In J. S. Hyde & M. C. Linn (Eds.), *The psychology of gender: Advances through meta-analysis.* Baltimore, MD: Johns Hopkins University Press.

Linney, J. A., & Seidman, E. (1989). The future of schooling. *American Psychologist, 44,* 336–340.

Lipsitt, L. P., Reilly, B. M., Butcher, M. J., & Greenwood, M. M. (1976) The stability and interrelationships of newborn sucking and heart rate. *Developmental Psychology, 9,* 305–310.

Lipsitz, J. (1983, October). *Making it the hard way: Adolescents in the 1980s.* Testimony prepared for the Crisis Intervention Task Force, House Select Committee on Children, Youth, and Families, Washington, D.C.

Lipsitz, J. (1984). *Successful schools for young adolescents.* New Brunswick, NJ: Transaction Books.

Litt, I. F. (1991). Eating disorders, medical complications of. In R. M. Lerner, A. C. Petersen, & J. Brooks-Gunn (Eds.), *Encyclopedia of adolescence* (Vol. 1). New York: Garland.

Little, B. B., Snell, L. M., Klein, V. R., & Gilstrap, L. C. (1989). Cocaine abuse during pregnancy: Maternal and fetal implications. *Obstetrics and Gynecology, 73,* 157–160.

Livesley, W. J., & Bromley, D. B. (1973). *Person perception in childhood and adolescence.* New York: Wiley.

Livson, N., & Peskin, H. (1981). Psychological health at age 40. Prediction from adolescent personality. In D. M. Eichorn, J. Clausen, N. Haan, M. Honzik, & P. Mussen (Eds.), *Present and past in middle life.* New York: Academic Press.

Lloyd, S. A. (1991). The darkside of courtship: Violence and sexual exploitation. *Family Relations, 40,* 14–20.

Lobstein, D. D., Ismail, A. H., & Rasmussen, C. L. (1989). Beta-endorphin and components of emotionality discriminate between physically active and sedentary men. *Biological Psychiatry, 26,* 3–14.

Lock, A. (1991). The role of social interaction in early language development. In N. A. Krasnegor, D. M. Rumbaugh, M. Studdert-Kennedy, & R. L. Schiefelbusch (Eds.), Biological and behavioral determinants of language development. Hillsdale, NJ: Erlbaum.

Lock, R. D. (1988). *Job search and taking care of your career direction.* Pacific Grove, CA: Brooks/Cole.

Locke, J. L., Bekken, K. E., Wein, D., & Ruzecki, V. (1991, April). *Neuropsychology of babbling: Laterality effects in the production of rhythmic manual activity.* Paper presented at the biennial meeting of the Society for Research in Child Development, Seattle.

Loge, D. V., & Schatz, J. (1991, April). *Social interactions of children with Attention Deficit Disorder: The role of emotions and self-control.* Paper presented at the biennial meeting of the Society for Research in Child Development, Seattle.

Logue, A. W. (1986). *Eating and drinking.* New York: W. H. Freeman.

Lombardi, J. (1991, October). *Type and availability of day care for children in America.* Paper presented at the symposium on day care for children, Arlington, VA.

London, M., & Greller, M. M. (1991). Demographic trends and vocational behavior: A twenty year retrospective and agenda for the 1990s. *Journal of Vocational Behavior, 38,* 125–164.

Lonetto, R. (1980). *Children's conception of death.* New York: Springer.

Long, B. C. (1989). Sex-role orientation, coping strategies, and self-efficacy of women in traditional and nontraditional occupations. *Psychology of Women Quarterly, 13,* 307–324.

Long, T., & Long, L. (1983). *Latchkey children.* New York: Penguin.

Longman, P. (1987). *Born to pay: The new politics of aging in America.* Boston: Houghton Mifflin.

Lonner, W. J. (1988). *The introductory psychology text and cross-cultural psychology: A survey of cross-cultural psychologists.* Bellingham, WA: Center for Cross-Cultural Research, Western Washington University.

Lonner, W. J. (1990). An overview of cross-cultural testing and assessment. In R. W. Brislin (Ed.), *Applied cross-cultural psychology.* Newbury Park, CA: Sage.

Lopata, H. Z. (Ed.). (1987). Widowhood. In G. L. Maddox (Ed.), *The encyclopedia of aging.* New York: Springer.

Lorenz, K. Z. (1965). *Evolution and the modification of behavior.* Chicago: University of Chicago Press.

Lorion, R. P. (1991). Prevention and public health: Psychology's response to the nation's health care crisis. *American Psychologist, 46,* 516–519.

Lozoff, B. (1989). Nutrition and Behavior. *American Psychologist, 44,* 231–236.

Ludtke, M. (1988, August 8). John David. *Time,* pp. 44–48.

Lueptow, L. (1984). Adolescent sex roles and social change. New York: Columbia University Press.

Lummis, M., & Stevenson, H. W. (1990). Gender differences in beliefs and achievement. A cross-cultural study. *Developmental Psychology, 26,* 254–263.

Lundman, R. (1984). *Prevention and control of juvenile delinquency.* New York: Oxford University Press.

Luria, A., & Herzog, E. (1985, April). *Gender segregation across and within settings.* Paper presented at the biennial meeting of the Society for Research in Child Development, Toronto.

Lyle, J., & Hoffman, H. R. (1972). Children's use of television and other media. In E. A. Rubenstein, G. A. Comstock, & J. P. Murray (Eds.), *Television and social behavior,* (Vol. 4). Washington, DC: U.S. Government Printing Office.

Lynch, M. A., & Roberts, J. (1982). *The consequences of child abuse.* New York: Academic Press.

Lyons, J. M. (1991, April). *The influence of parental scaffolding on the development of coping skills in clinically distressed and nondistressed children.* Paper presented at the biennial meeting of the Society for Research in Child Development, Seattle.

M

Maccoby, E. E. (1980). *Social development.* San Diego: Harcourt Brace Jovanovich.

Maccoby, E. E. (1984). Middle childhood in the context of the family. In *Development during middle childhood.* Washington, DC: National Academy Press.

Maccoby, E. E. (1987). The varied meanings of "masculine" and "feminine." In J. M. Reinisch, L. A. Rosenblum, & S. A. Sanders (Eds.), *Masculinity/femininity: Basic perspectives.* New York: Oxford University Press.

Maccoby, E. E. (1987, November). Interview with Elizabeth Hall: All in the family. *Psychology Today,* pp. 54–60.

Maccoby, E. E. (1989, August). *Gender and relationships: A developmental account.* Paper presented at the meeting of the American Psychological Association, New Orleans.

Maccoby, E. E., & Jacklin, C. N. (1974). *The psychology of sex differences.* Palo Alto, CA: Stanford University Press.

Maccoby, E. E., & Jacklin, C. N. (in press). Gender segregation in childhood. In H. Reese (Ed.), *Advances in child development and behavior* (Vol. 20). New York: Academic Press.

Maccoby, E. E., & Martin, J. A. (1983). Socialization in the context of the family: Parent-child interaction. In P. H. Mussen (Ed.), *Handbook of child psychology* (4th ed., Vol. 4). New York: Wiley.

Macdonald, B. (1989). Outside the sisterhood: Ageism in women's studies. *Women's Studies Quarterly,* 6–11.

MacDonald, K. (1991). Rites of passage. In R. M. Lerner, A. C. Petersen, & J. Brooks-Gunn (Eds.), *Encyclopedia of adolescence* (Vol. 2). New York: Garland.

MacDonald, K. B., Cluff, C., Kosmos, J., & Jones, C. (1991, April). *The effects of hyperactivity and stimulant medication on prosocial behavior.* Paper presented at the biennial meeting of the Society for Research in Child Development, Seattle.

MacFarlane, J. A. (1975). Olfaction in the development of social preferences in the human neonate. In *Parent-infant interaction,* Ciba Foundation Symposium, 33. Amsterdam: Elsevier.

Maddi, S. (1986, August). *The great stress-illness controversy.* Paper presented at the meeting of the American Psychological Association. Washington, DC.

Maddox, G. L. (1968). Disengagement theory: A critical evaluation. *The Gerontologist, 4,* 80–83.

Mahler, M. (1979). *Separation-individuation* (Vol. 2). London: Jason Aronson.

Main, M. (1990). Cross-cultural studies of attachment organization: Recent studies, changing methodologies, and the concept of conditional strategies. *Human Development, 33,* 48–61.

Malatesta, C. (1990, May 28). Commentary. *Newsweek,* p. 61.

Malina, R. M. (1991). Growth spurt, adolescent. II. In R. M. Lerner, A. C. Petersen, & J. Brooks-Gunn (Eds.), *Encyclopedia of adolescence* (Vol. 1). New York: Garland.

Malinowski, B. (1927). *Sex and repression in savage society.* New York: Humanities Press.

Maltsberger, J. T. (1988). *Suicide risk.* New York: Human Sciences Press.

Mandler, G. (1980). Recognizing the judgment of previous occurrence. *Psychology Review, 87,* 252–271.

Mandler, G. (1991, April). *The foundation of symbolic thought in infancy.* Paper presented at the biennial meeting of the Society for Research in Child Development, Seattle.

Mandler, J. M. (1983). Representation. In P. H. Mussen (Ed.), *Handbook of child psychology* (4th ed., Vol. 3). New York: Wiley.

Mandler, J. M. (1990). A new perspective on cognitive development. *American Scientist, 78,* 236–243.

Mann, J. (1991). Discussion—Retirement: What happens to husband-wife relationships? *Journal of Geriatric Psychiatry, 24,* 41–46.

Mann, L., Harmoni, R., & Power, C. N. (in press). Adolescent decision making: The development of competence. *Journal of Adolescence.*

Marín, G., & Marín, B. V. (1991). *Research with Hispanic populations.* Newbury Park, CA: Sage.

Maratsos, M. P. (1983). Some current issues in the study of the acquisition of grammar. In P. H. Mussen (Ed.), *Handbook of child psychology* (4th ed., Vol. 3). New York: Wiley.

Maratsos, M. P. (1991). How the acquisition of nouns may be different from that of verbs. In N. A. Krasnegor, D. M. Rumbaugh, M. Studdert-Kennedy, & R. L. Schiefelbusch (Eds.), *Biological and behavioral determinants of language development.* Hillsdale, NJ: Erlbaum.

Marcia, J. E. (1966). Identity six years after: A follow-up study. *Journal of Youth and Adolescence, 5,* 145–160.

Marcia, J. E. (1980). Ego identity development. In J. Adelson (Ed.), *Handbook of adolescent psychology.* New York: Wiley.

Marcia, J. E. (1987). The identity status approach to the study of ego identity development. In T. Honess & K. Yardley (Eds.), *Self and identity: Perspectives across the lifespan.* London: Routledge & Kegan Paul.

Marcia, J. E. (1991). Identity and self-development. In R. M. Lerner, A. C. Petersen, & J. Brooks-Gunn (Eds.), *Encyclopedia of adolescence* (Vol. 1). New York: Garland.

Marieskind, H. I. (1989). Cesarean section in the United States: Has it changed since 1979? *Birth, 16,* 196–202.

Markides, K., & Martin, H. (1979). A causal model of life satisfaction among the elderly. *Journal of Gerontology, 34,* 86–93.

Markides, K. S., & Mindel, C. H. (1987). *Aging and ethnicity.* Newbury Park, CA: Sage.

Markman, H. J. (1979). Application of a behavioral model of marriage in predicting relationship satisfaction of couples planning marriage. *Journal of Consulting and Clinical Psychology, 47,* 743–749.

Marquis, K. S., & Detweiler, R. A. (1985). Does adopted mean different? An attributional analysis. *Journal of Personality and Social Psychology, 48,* 1054–1066.

References

Martin, C. L. (1989, April). *Beyond knowledge-based conceptions of gender schematic processing.* Paper presented at the biennial meeting of the Society for Research in Child Development, Kansas City, MO.

Martin, C. L., & Halverson, C. F. (1981). A schematic processing model of sex-typing and stereotyping in children. *Child Development, 52,* 1119–1132.

Martin, C. L., & Halverson, C. F. (1987). The role of cognition in sex-role acquisition. In D. B. Carter (Ed.), *Current conceptions of sex roles and sex-typing: Theory and research.* New York: Praeger.

Martin, C. L., & Rose, H. A. (1991, April). *Children's gender-based distinctive theories.* Paper presented at the biennial meeting of the Society for Research in Child Development, Seattle.

Martin, J. (1976). *The education of adolescents.* Washington, DC: U.S. Office of Education.

Maslow, A. H. (1954). *Motivation and personality.* New York: Harper & Row.

Maslow, A. H. (1971). *The farther reaches of human nature.* New York: Viking.

Matas, L., Arend, R. A., & Sroufe, L. A. (1978). Continuity in adaptation: Quality of attachment and later competence. *Child Development, 49,* 547–556.

Matheny, A. P., Dolan, R. S., & Wilson, R. S. (1976). Relation between twin's similarity: Testing an assumption. *Behavior Genetics, 6,* 343–351.

McAdams, D. P. (1988). *Power, intimacy, and the life story.* New York: Guilford.

McAdams, D. P. (1990). Unity and purpose in human lives: The emergence of identity as a life story. In A. I. Rabin, R. A. Zucker, R. A. Emmons, & S. Frank (Eds.), *Studying persons and lives.* New York: Springer.

McAdoo, H. P. (Ed.). (1988). *Black families* (2nd ed.). Newbury Park, CA: Sage.

McAdoo, H. P., & McAdoo, J. L. (Eds.). (1985). *Black children: Social, educational, and parental environments.* Beverly Hills, CA: Sage.

McAdoo, J. L. (1979). Well-being and fear of crime among the Black elderly. In D. E. Gelfand & A. J. Kuztik (Eds.), *Ethnicity and aging.* New York: Springer.

McBride, A. B. (1990). Mental health effects of women's multiple roles. *American Psychologist, 45,* 381–384.

McBride, B. A. (1991, April). *Variations in father involvement with preschool-aged children.* Paper presented at the biennial meeting of the Society for Research in Child Development, Seattle.

McCall, R. B. (1991). Underachievers and dropouts. In R. M. Lerner, A. C. Petersen, & J. Brooks-Gunn (Eds.), *Encyclopedia of adolescence* (Vol. 2). New York: Garland.

McCarley, R. W. (1989). The biology of dreaming sleep. In M. H. Kryger, T. Roth, & W. C. Dement (Eds.), *Principles and practices of sleep medicine.* San Diego: Harcourt Brace Jovanovich.

McCartney, K., Robeson, W. W., Jordon, E., & Mouradian, V. (1991, April). *Mothers' language with first- and second-born children: A within-family study.* Paper presented at the biennial meeting of the Society for Research in Child Development, Seattle.

McClelland, D. C. (1955). Some social consequences of achievement motivation. In M. R. Jones (Ed.), *The Nebraska Symposium on Motivation.* Lincoln: University of Nebraska Press.

McCue, M., & Bouchard, T. J. (1989). Genetic and environmental determinants of information processing and special mental abilities. In R. J. Sternberg (Ed.), *Advances in the psychology of human intelligence.* Hillsdale, NJ: Erlbaum.

McDaniel, M. A., & Pressley, M. (1987). *Imagery and related mnemonic processes.* New York: Springer-Verlag.

McDonald, W. M., & Nemeroff, C. B. (1991). Neurotransmitters and neuropeptides in Alzheimer's disease. *Psychiatric Clinics of North America, 14,* 421–442.

McGhee, P. E. (1984). Play, incongruity, and humor. In T. Yawkey & A. D. Pellegrin (Eds.), *Child's play: Developmental and applied.* Hillsdale, NJ: Erlbaum.

McGilly, K., & Siegler, R. S. (1989). How children choose among serial recall strategies. *Child Development, 60,* 172–182.

McGinnis, J. M. (1991). Health objectives for the nation. *American Psychologist, 46,* 520–524.

McHugh, M., Koeske, R., & Frieze, I. H. (1986). Issues to consider in conducting nonsexist psychological research: A guide for researchers. *American Psychologist, 41,* 879–890.

McKinlay, S. M., & McKinlay, J. B. (1984). *Health status and health care utilization by menopausal women.* Unpublished manuscript, Cambridge Research Center, American Institutes for Research, Cambridge, MA.

McKnight, C. C., Crosswhite, F. J., Dossey, J. A., Kifer, E., Swafford, J. O., Travers, K. J., & Cooney, T. J. (1987). *The underachieving curriculum: Assessing U.S. school mathematics from an international perspective.* Champaign, IL: Stipes.

McLanahan, S., & Booth, K. (1989). Mother-only families: Problems, prospects, and politics. *Journal of Marriage and the Family, 51,* 557–580.

McLoyd, V. (in press). The declining fortunes of Black children: Psychological distress, parenting, and socioemotional development in the context of economic hardship. *Child Development.*

McLoyd, V. C., & Wilson, L. (1990). Maternal behavior, social support, and economic conditions as predictors of distress in children. In V. C. McLoyd & C. A. Flanagan (Eds.), *Economic stress: Effects on family life and child development.* San Francisco: Jossey-Bass.

McWhirter, B. T. (1990). Loneliness: A review of current literature, with implications for counseling and research. *Journal of counseling and development, 68,* 417–422.

McWhirter, D. P., Reinisch, J. M., & Sanders, S. A. (1989). *Homosexuality/heterosexuality.* New York: Oxford University Press.

Medrich, E. A., Rossen, J., Rubin, V., & Buckley, S. (1982). *The serious business of growing up.* Berkeley, CA: University of California Press.

Medvedev, Z. A. (1974). The nucleic acids in the development of aging. In B. L. Strehler (Ed.), *Advances in gerontological research* (Vol. 1). New York: Academic Press.

Melton, G. B. (1991). Socialization in the global community: Respect for the dignity of children. *American Psychologist, 46,* 66–71.

Meltzoff, A. N. (1988). Infant imitation and memory: Nine-month-old infants in immediate and deferred tests. *Child Development, 59,* 217–225.

Meltzoff, A. N. (1990, June). *Infant Imitation.* Invited address at the University of Texas at Dallas, School of Human Development and Communication Sciences, Richardson, TX.

Meltzoff, A. N., & Kuhl, P. (1989). Infants' perceptions of faces and speech sounds: Challenges to developmental theory. In P. R. Zelazo & R. Barr (Eds.), *Challenges to developmental paradigms.* Hillsdale, NJ: Erlbaum.

Mercer, R., Nichols, E. G., & Doyle, G. C. (1989). Transitions in a woman's life: Major life events in developmental context. New York: Springer.

Meredith, H. V. (1978). Research between 1960 and 1970 on the standing height of young children in different parts of the world. In H. W. Reece & L. P. Lipsitt (Eds.), *Advances in child development and behavior* (Vol. 12). New York: Academic Press.

Meyer, B. J. F., Young, C. J., & Bartlett, B. J. (1989). *Memory improved: Reading and memory enhancement across the life span through strategic text structures.* Hillsdale, NJ: Erlbaum.

Meyer, J. W. (1991). Individualisms: Social experience and cultural formulation. In J. Rodin, C. Schooler, & K. W. Schaie (Eds.), *Self-directedness and efficacy.* Hillsdale, NJ: Erlbaum.

Meyerhoff, M. K., & White, B. L. (1986). Making the grades as parents. *Psychology Today.* September, 38–45.

Meyers, J. (1985). *Hemingway.* New York: Harper & Row.

Michel, G. L. (1981). Right-handedness: A consequence of infant supine head-orientation preference? *Science, 212,* 685–687.

Milham, J., Widmayer, S., Bauer, C. R., & Peterson, L. (1983, April). *Predictory cognitive deficits for preterm, low birthweight infants.* Paper presented at the biennial meeting of the Society for Research in Child Development, Detroit.

Miller, C. A. (1987). A review of maternity care programs in Western Europe. *Family Planning Perspectives, 19,* 207–211.

Miller, G. (1981). *Language and speech.* New York: W. H. Freeman.

Miller, G. (1989). Foreward. In J. T. Gibbs & L. N. Huang (Eds.), *Children of color.* San Francisco: Jossey-Bass.

Miller, J. A. (1991). *Community-based long-term care.* Newbury Park, CA: Sage.

Miller, J. B. (1976). *Toward a new psychology of women.* Boston: Beacon Press.

Miller, M., & Gottlieb, S. O. (1991). Preventive maintenance of the aging heart. *Geriatrics, 46,* 22–30.

Miller-Jones, D. (1989). Culture and testing. *American Psychologist, 44,* 360–366.

Milligan, S. E. (1990). Understanding diversity of the urban black aged: Historical perspectives. In Z. Harel, E. A. McKinney, & M. Williams (Eds.), *Black aged.* Newbury Park, CA: Sage.

Minkler, M. (1989). Health education, health promotion and the open society: A historical perspective. *Health Education Quarterly, 16,* 17–30.

Minnett, A. M., Vandell, D. L., & Santrock, J. W. (1983). The effects of sibling status on sibling interaction: Influence of birth order, age spacing, sex of the child, and sex of the sibling. *Child Development, 54,* 1064–1072.

Minuchin, P. P., & Shapiro, E. K. (1983). The school as a context for social development. In P. H. Mussen (Ed.), *Handbook of child psychology* (4th ed., Vol. 4). New York: Wiley.

Mischel, W. (1970). Sex-typing and socialization. In P. H. Mussen (Ed.), *Manual of child psychology* (Vol. 2, 3rd ed.). New York: Wiley.

Mischel, W. (1973). Toward a cognitive social learning reconceptualization of personality. *Psychological Review, 80,* 252–283.

Mischel, W. (1984). Convergences and challenges in the search for consistency. *American Psychologist, 39,* 351–364.

Mischel, W., & Patterson, C. J. (1976). Substantive and structural elements of effective plans for self-control. *Journal of Personality and Social Psychology, 34,* 942–950.

Moely, B. E., Olson, F. A., Halwes, T. G., & Flavell, J. H. (1969). Production deficiency in young children's clustered recall. *Developmental Psychology, 1,* 26–34.

Moen, P. (1991). Transitions in mid-life: Women's work and family roles in the 1970s. *Journal of Marriage and the Family, 53,* 135–150.

Moll, I. (1991, April). *The material and the social in Vygotsky's theory of cognitive development.* Paper presented at the biennial meeting of the Society for Research in Child Development, Seattle.

Money, J. (1987). Sin, sickness, or status? Homosexual gender identity and psychoneuroendrocrinology. *American Psychologist, 42,* 384–399.

Montemayor, R. (1982). The relationship between parent-adolescent conflict and the amount of time adolescents spend with parents, peers, and alone. *Child Development, 53,* 1512–1519.

Montemayor, R., Adams, G. R., & Gulotta, T. P. (Eds.). (1990). *From childhood to adolescence: A transitional period?* Newbury Park, CA: Sage.

Montemayor, R., & Flannery, D. J. (1991). Parent-adolescent relations in middle and late adolescence. In R. M. Lerner, A. C. Petersen, & J. Brooks-Gunn (Eds.), *Encyclopedia of adolescence* (Vol. 2). New York: Garland.

Montemayor, R., & Hanson, E. (1985). A naturalistic view of conflict between adolescents and their parents and siblings. *Journal of Early Adolescence, 5,* 23–30.

Montgomery, R. J., & Hirshorn, B. A. (1991). Current and future family help with long-term care needs of the elderly. *Research on Aging, 13,* 171–204.

Moos, R. H., Finney, J. W., & Cronkite, R. C. (1990). Alcoholism treatment: Contexts, process, and outcome. New York: Oxford University Press.

Morgan, J. D. (1988). Living our dying: Social and cultural considerations. In H. Wass, F. N. Berardo, & R. A. Neimeyer (Eds.), *Dying: Facing the facts* (2nd ed.). Washington, DC: Hemisphere.

Morris, J. C., & Rubin, E. H. (1991). Clinical diagnosis and course of Alzheimer's disease. *The Psychiatric Clinics of North America, 14,* 223–236.

Morrison, A. M., & Von Glinow, M. A. (1990). Women and minorities in management. *American Psychologist, 45,* 200–208.

Morrongiello, B. A., Fenwick, K. D., & Chance, G. (1990). Sound localization acuity in very young infants: An observer-based testing procedure. *Developmental Psychology, 26,* 75–84.

Morse, J. M., & Johnson, J. L. (1991) (Eds.). *The illness experience.* Newbury Park, CA: Sage.

Moses, J., Steptoe, A., Mathews, A., & Edwards, S. (1989). The effects of exercise training on mental well-being in the normal population: A controlled trial. *Journal of Psychosomatic Research, 33,* 47–61.

Mott, F. L., & Marsiglio, W. (1985, September/October). Early childbearing and completion of high school. *Family Planning Perspectives,* p. 234.

Moushegian, G. (1991, January). Personal Communication. Program in Psychology and Human Development, University of Texas at Dallas, Richardson, TX.

Moyer, J., Egertson, H., & Isenberg, J. (1987). The child-centered kindergarten. *Childhood Education, 63,* 235–242.

Mueller, K. E., & Powers, W. G. (1990). Parent-child sexual discussion: Perceived communicator style and subsequent behavior. *Adolescence, 25,* 469–482.

Munroe, R. H., Himmin, H. S., & Munroe, R. L. (1984). Gender understanding and sex role preference in four cultures. *Developmental Psychology, 20,* 673–682.

Munroe, R. L., & Munroe, R. H. (1975). *Cross-cultural human development.* Monterey, CA: Brooks/Cole.

Murphy, K. C., Talley, J. A., & Huston, A. C. (1991, April). *Family ecology and young children's viewing of television designed for children.* Paper presented at the biennial meeting of the Society for Research in Child Development, Seattle.

Murphy, M. P., & Carter, D. B. (1991, April). *Familial characteristics and the development of gender schemas.* Paper presented at the biennial meeting of the Society for Research in Child Development, Seattle.

Murray, H. A. (1938). *Explorations in personality.* New York: Oxford University Press.

Mussen, P. H., Honzik, M., & Eichorn, D. (1982). Early adult antecedents of life satisfaction at age 70. *Journal of Gerontology, 37,* 316–322.

Musun-Miller, L. (1991, April). *Children's birth order as a mediator in responses by mothers and siblings.* Paper presented at the biennial meeting of the Society for Research in Child Development, Seattle.

Myers, D. G. (1989). Psychology (2nd ed.). New York: Worth.

N

Nagy, M. (1948). The child's theories concerning death. *Journal of Genetic Psychology, 73,* 3–27.

National Association for the Education of Young Children. (1986a). *How to choose a good early childhood program.* Washington, DC: NAEYC.

National Association for the Education of Young Children. (1986b). Position statement on developmentally appropriate practice in programs for 4- and 5-year-olds. *Young Children, 41,* 20–29.

National Association for the Education of Young Children. (1988). NAEYC position statement on developmentally appropriate practices in the primary grades, serving 5- through 8-year-olds. *Young Children, 43,* 64–83.

National Association for the Education of Young Children. (1990). NAEYC position statement on school readiness. *Young Children, 46,* 21–28.

National Center for Health Statistics. (1987, August 28). Advance report of the final mortality statistics, 1985. *Monthly Vital Statistics Report, 36* (5). Hyattsville, MD: Public Health Service.

National Center for Health Statistics. (1989, June). *Statistics on marriage and divorce.* Washington, DC: U.S. Government Printing Office.

National Research Council. (1987). *Risking the future: Adolescent sexuality, pregnancy, and childbearing.* Washington, DC: National Academy Press.

National Research Council. (1989). *Diet and Health: Implications for reducing chronic disease risk.* Washington, DC: National Research Council.

Nelson, C. S., & Watson, J. A. (1991, April). *Computer-based interactive media as an educational tool: Evaluation of a first grade multimedia/videodisc science lesson.* Paper presented at the biennial meeting of the Society for Research in Child Development, Seattle.

Nelson, K. (1991). *Representational change and the emergence of autobiographical memory.* Paper presented at the biennial meeting of the Society for Research in Child Development, Seattle.

Neugarten, B. L. (1964). *Personality in middle and late life.* New York: Atherton Press.

Neugarten, B. L. (1980). Must everything be a mid-life crisis? Annual editions, *Human Development 80/81.* Guilford, CT: Dushkin.

Neugarten, B. L. (1986). The aging society. In A. Pifer & L. Bronte (Eds.), *Our aging society: Paradox and promise.* New York: W. W. Norton.

Neugarten, B. L. (1988, August). *Policy issues for an aging society.* Paper presented at the meeting of the American Psychological Association, Atlanta.

Neugarten, B. L., Havighurst, R. J., & Tobin, S. S. (1968). Personality and patterns of aging. In B. L. Neugarten (Ed.), *Middle age and aging.* Chicago: University of Chicago Press.

Neugarten, B. L., & Neugarten, D. A. (1989). Policy issues in an aging society. In M. Storandt & G. R. VandenBos (Eds.), *The adult years: Continuity and change.* Washington, DC: American Psychological Association.

Neugarten, B. L., & Weinstein, K. K. (1964). The changing American grandparent. *Journal of Marriage and the Family, 26,* 199–204.

Newcomb, M. D., & Bentler, P. M. (1988). Substance use and abuse among children and teenagers. *American Psychologist, 44,* 242–248.

Nicholls, J. G. (1984). Conceptions of ability and achievement motivation. In R. E. Ames & C. Ames (Eds.), *Motivation in education.* New York: Academic Press.

Nitz, V., & Lerner, J V. (1991). Temperament during adolescence. In R. M. Lerner, A. C. Petersen, & J. Brooks-Gunn (Eds.), *Encyclopedia of adolescence* (Vol. 2). New York: Garland.

Nottelman, E. D., Inoff-Germain, G., Susman, E. J., & Chrousos, G. P. (1990). Hormones and behavior at puberty. In J. Bancroft & M. Reinisch (Eds.), *Adolescence and puberty.* New York: Oxford University Press.

Nottelmann, E. D., Susman, E. J., Blue, J. H., Inoff-Germain, G., Dorn, L. D., Loriaux, D. L., Cutler, G. B., & Chrousos, G. P. (1987). Gonadal and adrenal hormone correlates of adjustment in early adolescence. In R. M. Lerner & T. T. Foch (Eds.), *Biological-psychological interactions in early adolescence.* Hillsdale, NJ: Erlbaum.

Novak, W. (1983). *The great American man shortage.* New York: Basic Books.

Novick, B. (1989). Pediatric AIDS: A medical overview. In J. M. Seibert & R. A. Olson (Eds.), *Children, adolescents, and AIDS.* Lincoln: University of Nebraska Press.

Nowak, C. A. (1977). Does youthfulness equal attractiveness? In L. E. Troll, J. Israel, & K. Israel (Eds.), *Looking ahead: A woman's guide to the problems and joys of growing older.* Englewood Cliffs, NJ: Prentice-Hall.

Nydegger, C. N., & Mitteness, L. S. (1991). Fathers and their adult sons and daughters. *Marriage and Family Review, 16,* 249–266.

O

O'Brien, S. J., & Vertinsky, P. A. (1991). Unfit survivors: Exercise as a resource for aging women. *The Gerontologist, 31,* 347–357.

O'Bryant, S. L. (1991). Older widows and independent life-styles. *International Journal of Aging and Human Development, 32,* 41–52.

O'Conner, B. P., & Nikolic, J. (1990). Identity development and formal operations as sources of adolescent egocentrism. *Journal of Youth and Adolescence, 19,* 149–158.

O'Donnel, B. (1989, April). *Altering children's gender stereotypes about adult occupations with nonsexist books.* Paper presented at the biennial meeting of the Society for Research in Child Development, Kansas City, MO.

O'Donnell, C., Manos, M., & Chesney-Lind, M. (1987). Diversion and neighborhood delinquency programs in open settings. In E. Morris & C. Braukmann (Eds.), *Behavioral approaches to crime and delinquency*. New York: Plenum.

Offer, D., & Church, R. B. (1991). Turmoil, adolescent. In R. M. Lerner, A. C. Petersen, & J. Brooks-Gunn (Eds.), *Encyclopedia of adolescence* (Vol. 2). New York: Garland.

Offer, D., Ostrov, E., Howard, K. I., & Atkinson, R. (1988). *The teenage world: Adolescents' self-image in ten countries*. New York: Plenum.

Ogbu, J. U. (1974). *The next generation: An ethnography of education in an urban neighborhood*. New York: Academic Press.

Ogbu, J. U. (1986). The consequences of the American caste system. In U. Neisser (Ed.), *The school achievement of minority children: New perspectives*. Hillsdale, NJ: Erlbaum.

Ogbu, J. U. (1989, April). *Academic socialization of Black children: An innoculation against future failure?* Paper presented at the meeting of the Society for Research in Child Development, Kansas City, MO.

Ogden, J., & Wardle, J. (1991). Cognitive and emotional responses to food. *International Journal of Eating Disorders, 10*, 297–311.

Okun, B. F., & Rappaport, L. J. (1980). *Working with families: An introduction to family therapy*. North Scituate, MA: Duxbury Press.

Olds, S. W. (1986). *Working parents' survival guide*. New York: Bantam.

Olsho, L. W., Harkins, S. W., & Lenhardt, M. L. (1985). Aging and the auditory system. In J. E. Birren & K. W. Schaie (Eds.), *Handbook of the psychology of aging* (2nd ed.). New York: Van Nostrand Reinhold.

Olweus, D. (1980). Bullying among schoolboys. In R. Barnen (Ed.), *Children and violence*. Stockholm: Adaemic Litteratur.

Olweus, D. (1989, April). *Peer relationships problems: Conceptual issues and a successful intervention program against bully/victim problems*. Paper presented at the biennial meeting of the Society for Research in Child Development, Kansas City, MO.

Orlofsky, J. (1976). Intimacy status: Relationship to interpersonal perception. *Journal of Youth and Adolescence, 5*, 73–88.

Orlofsky, J., Marcia, J., & Lesser, I. (1973). Ego identity status and the intimacy vs. isolation crisis of young adulthood. *Journal of Personality and Social Psychology, 27*, 211–219.

Ornstein, R., & Sobel, D. (1989). *Healthy pleasures*. Reading, MA: Addison-Wesley.

Osofsky, J. D. (1989, April). *Affective relationships in adolescent mothers and their infants*. Paper presented at the biennial meeting of the Society for Research in Child Development, Kansas City, MO.

Osofsky, J. D. (1990, Winter). Risk and protective factors for teenage mothers and their infants. SRCD Newsletter, pp. 1–2.

Ossip-Klein, D. J., Doyne, E. J., Bowman, E. D., Osborn, K. M., McDougall-Wilson, I. B., & Neimeyer, R. A. (1989). Effects of running or weight lifting on self-concept in clinically depressed women. *Journal of Consulting and Clinical Psychology, 57*, 158–161.

Ottinger, D. R., & Simmons, J. E. (1964). Behavior of human neonates and prenatal maternal anxiety. *Psychological Reports, 14*, 391–394.

Overton, W. F., & Byrnes, J. P. (1991). Cognitive Development. In R. M. Lerner, A. C. Petersen, & J. Brooks-Gunn (Eds.), *Encyclopedia of adolescence* (Vol. 1). New York: Garland.

Overton, W. F., & Montangero, J. (1991). Piaget, Jean. In R. M. Lerner, A. C. Petersen, & J. Brooks-Gunn (Eds.), *Encyclopedia of adolescence* (Vol. 2). New York: Garland.

P

Pacheco, S., & Valdes, L. F. (1989, August). *The present state and future directions of Hispanic psychology*. Paper presented at the meeting of the American Psychological Association, New Orleans.

Pacifici, R. E., & Davies, K. J. A. (1991). Protein, lipid and DNA repair systems in oxidative stress: The free-radical theory of aging revisited. *Gerontology, 37*, 166–182.

Paffenbarger, R. S., Hyde, R. T., Wing, A. L., & Hsieh, C. (1986). Physical activity, all-cause mortality, and longevity of college alumni. *New England Journal of Medicine, 314*, 605–612.

Paikoff, R. L., & Brooks-Gunn, J. (1990). Physiological processes: What role do they play during the transition to adolescence? In R. Montemayor, G. R. Adams, & T. P. Gulotta (Eds.), *From childhood to adolescence: A transitional period?* Newbury Park, CA: Sage.

Palmore, E. B. (1975). *The honorable elders: A cross-cultural analysis of aging in Japan*. Durham, NC: Duke University Press.

Palmore, E. B. (1982). Predictors of the longevity difference: A 25-year follow-up. *The Gerontologist, 22*, 513–518.

Palmore, E. B., Burchett, B. M., Fillenbaum, C. G., George, L. K., & Wallman, L. M. (1985). *Retirement: Causes and consequences*. New York: Springer.

Pan, B. A., Rollins, P. R., & Snow, C. E. (1991, April). *Pragmatic development and its relationship to morphosyntactic indices*. Paper presented at the biennial meeting of the Society for Research in Child Development, Seattle.

Papert, S. (1980). *Mindstorms: Children, computers, and powerful ideas*. New York: Basic Books.

Papini, D. R., Micka, J., & Barnett, J. (1989). Perceptions of intrapsychic and extrapsychic functioning as bases of adolescent ego identity statuses. *Journal of Adolescent Research, 4*, 460–480.

Papini, D. R., Roggman, L. A., & Anderson, J. (1990, March). *Early adolescent perceptions of attachment to mother and father: A test of the emotional distancing hypothesis*. Paper presented at the meeting of the Society for Research in Adolescence, Atlanta, GA.

Parcel, G. S., Simons-Morton, G. G., O'Hara, N. M., Baranowski, T., Kolbe, L. J., & Bee, D. E. (1987). School promotion of healthful diet and exercise behavior: An integration of organizational change and social learning theory interventions. *Journal of School Health, 57*, 150–156.

Paris, S. C., & Lindauer, B. K. (1982). The development of cognitive skills during childhood. In B. B. Wolman (Ed.), *Handbook of developmental psychology*. Englewood Cliffs, NJ: Prentice-Hall.

Parish, T. S. (1988). Evaluations of family as a function of one's family structure and sex. *Perceptual and Motor Skills, 66*, 25–26.

Parish, T. S., & Osterberg, J. (1985). Evaluations of self, parents, and family: Variations caused by family structure and personal stress. *Journal of Psychology, 119*, 231–233.

Parke, R. D., & Sawin, D. B. (1980). The family in early infancy. In F. Pedersen (Ed.), *The father-infant relationship: Observational studies in family context*. New York: Praeger.

Parke, R. D., & Suomi, S. (1981). Adult male-infant relationships: Human and non-human primate evidence. In K. Immelmann, G. W. Barlow, L. Petrinovitch, & M. Main (Eds.), *Behavioral development: The Bielefeld Interdisciplinary Project*. New York: Cambridge University Press.

Parker, J. G., & Asher, S. R. (1987). Peer relations and later personal adjustment: Are low accepted children at risk? *Psychological Bulletin, 102*, 357–389.

Parker, J. G., and Gottman, J. M. (1989). Social and emotional development in a relational context: Friendship interaction from early childhood to adolescence. In T. J. Berndt & G. W. Ladd (Eds.), *Peer relations in child development*. New York: Wiley.

Parkes, C. M. (1972). *Bereavement: Studies of grief in adult life*. New York: International University Press.

Parkhurst, J. T., Roedel, T. D., Bendixen, L. D., & Potenza, M. T. (1991, April). *Subgroups of rejected middle school students: Their behavioral characteristics, friendships, social concerns*. Paper presented at the biennial meeting of the Society for Research in Child Development, Seattle.

Parlee, M. B. (1979, April). The friendship bond: PT's survey report on friendship in America. *Psychology Today*, pp. 43–54, 113.

Parmalee, A. H. (1986). Children's illnesses: Their beneficial effects on behavioral development. *Child Development, 57*, 1–10.

Parmalee, A. H., Wenner, W., & Schulz, H. (1964). Infant sleep patterns from birth to 16 weeks of age. *Journal of Pediatrics, 65*, 572–576.

Parten, M. (1932). Social play among preschool children. *Journal of Abnormal and Social Psychology, 27*, 243–269.

Pascual-Leone, J., & Johnson, J. (1991). The psychological unit and its role in task analysis: A reinterpretation of object permanence. In M. Chandler & M. Chapman (Eds.), *Criteria for competence*. Hillsdale, NJ: Erlbaum.

Pasley, K., & Ihinger-Tallman, M. (Eds.). (1987). *Remarriage and stepparenting*. New York: Guilford.

Pastalan, P. M. (1991). Introduction: Optimizing housing for the elderly. *Journal of Housing for the Elderly, 7*, 1–4.

Patterson, G. R., Capaldi, D., & Bank, L. (1991). An early starter model for predicting delinquency. In D. Pepler & K. Rubin (Eds.), *The development and treatment of aggression in childhood*. Hillsdale, NJ: Erlbaum.

Patterson, G. R., DeBarsyshe, B. D., & Ramsey, E. (1989). A developmental perspective on antisocial behavior. *American Psychologist, 44*, 329–335.

Patterson, G. R., & Grimaldi, D. M. (1991). Antisocial parents: Unskilled and vulnerable during family transitions. In P. A. Cowan & E. M. Hetherington (Eds.), *Family transitions*. Hillsdale, NJ: Erlbaum.

Paul, E. L., & White, K. M. (1990). The development of intimate relationships in late adolescence, *Adolescence, 25*, 375–400.

Peck, R. C. (1968). Psychological developments in the second half of life. In B. L. Neugarten (Ed.), *Middle age and aging*. Chicago: University of Chicago Press.

Pederson, D. R., Moran, G., Sitko, C., Campbell, K., Ghesquire, K., & Acton, H. (1989, April). *Maternal sensitivity and the security of infant-mother attachment*. Paper presented at the biennial meeting of the Society for Research in Child Development, Kansas City, MO.

Penner, S. G. (1987). Parental responses to grammatical and ungrammatical child utterances. *Child Development, 58*, 376–384.

Peplau, L. A., & Gordon, S. L. (1985). Women and men in love: Gender differences in close heterosexual relationships. In V. E. O'Leary, R. K. Unger, & B. S. Wallston (Eds.), *Women, gender, and social psychology*. Hillsdale, NJ: Erlbaum.

Peplau, L. A., & Perlman, D. (Eds.). (1982). *Loneliness: A sourcebook of current theory, research and therapy.* New York: Wiley.

Perkinson, H. J. (1991). *The imperfect panacea: American faith in education, 1865–1990* (3rd ed.). New York: McGraw-Hill.

Perlmutter, M. (1990, April). *Practical intelligence across adulthood.* Paper presented at the 12th West Virginia conference on life-span developmental psychology, Morgantown, WV.

Perry, W. G. (1970). *Forms of intellectual and ethical development in the college years.* New York: Holt, Rinehart & Winston.

Persky, V. W., Kepthorne-Rawson, J., & Skekelle, R. B. (1987). Personality and risk of cancer: 20-year follow-up of the Western Electric study. *Psychosomatic Medicine, 49,* 435–449.

Peskin, H. (1967). Pubertal onset and ego functioning. *Journal of Abnormal Psychology, 72,* 1–15.

Petersen, A. C. (1979, January). Can puberty come any faster? *Psychology Today,* pp. 45–56.

Petersen, A. C. (1987, September). Those gangly years. *Psychology Today,* pp. 28–34.

Petersen, A. C., & Crockett, L. (1985). Pubertal timing and grade effects on adjustment. *Journal of Youth and Adolescence, 14,* 191–206.

Peterson, E. T. (1989). Grandparenting. In S. J. Bahr & E. T. Peterson (Eds.), *Aging and the family.* Lexington, MA: Lexington Books.

Peterson, L. M., Widmayer, S. M., Bacon, K. L., Burns, W. J., & Calderon, A. E. (1991, April). *Developmental outcome of HIV positive infants.* Paper presented at the biennial meeting of the Society for Research in Child Development, Seattle.

Peterson, P. L. (1977). Interactive effects of student anxiety, achievement orientation, and teacher behavior on student achievement and attitude. *Journal of Educational Psychology, 69,* 779–792.

Pettit, G. S., Dodge, K. A., & Brown, M. M. (1988). Early family experience, social problem-solving patterns, and children's social competence. *Child Development, 59,* 107–120.

Pfeiffer, E., & Davis, G. (1974). Determinants of sexual behavior in middle and old age. In E. Palmore (Ed.). *Normal aging II.* Durham, NC: Duke University Press.

Pfeiffer, E., Verwoerdt, A., & Davis, G. C. (1974). Sexual behavior in middle life. In E. Palmore (Ed.), *Normal aging II: Reports from the Duke longitudinal studies, 1970–1973.* Durham, NC: Duke University Press.

Phillips, D. (1989). Future directions and needs for child care in the United States. In J. Lande, S. Scarr, & N. Gunzenhauser (Eds.), *Caring for children: Challenge to America.* Hillsdale, NJ: Erlbaum.

Phinney, J. S. (1989). Stages of ethnic identity development in minority group adolescents. *Journal of Early Adolescence, 9,* 34–49.

Phinney, J. S. (1991, April). *Research with ethnic minority adolescents: Problems of data collection and interpretation.* Paper presented at the biennial meeting of the Society for Research in Child Development, Seattle.

Phinney, J. S., & Alipura, L. L. (1990). Ethnic identity in college students from four ethnic groups. *Journal of Adolescence, 13,* 171–183.

Piaget, J. (1932). *The moral judgment of the child.* New York: Harcourt Brace Jovanovich.

Piaget, J. (1936). *The origins of intelligence in children.* New York: W. W. Norton.

Piaget, J. (1952). *The origins of intelligence in children.* New York: International Universities Press.

Piaget, J. (1954). *The construction of reality in the child.* New York: Basic Books.

Piaget, J. (1962). *Play, dreams, and imitation in childhood.* New York: W. W. Norton.

Piaget, J. (1967). The child's conception of the world. Totowa, NJ: Littlefield, Adams, & Co.

Piaget, J., & Inhelder, B. (1969). *The child's conception of space* (F. J. Langdon & J. L. Lunzer, Trans.). New York: W. W. Norton.

Pierce, E. W. (1991, April). *Impulsivity as a component of behavior problems in preschool boys.* Paper presented at the biennial meeting of the Society for Research in Child Development, Seattle.

Piers, E. V., & Harris, D. V. (1964). Age and other correlates of self-concept in children. *Journal of Educational Psychology, 55,* 91–95.

Pines, A., & Aronson, E. (1988). *Career burnout: Causes and cures.* New York: Free Press.

Pipes, P. (1988). Nutrition in childhood. In S. R. Williams & B. S. Worthington-Roberts (Eds.), *Nutrition throughout the life cycle.* St. Louis: Times Mirror/Mosby.

Plante, T. G., & Rodin, J. (1990). Physical fitness and enhanced psychological health. *Current psychology research and reviews, 9,* 3–24.

Pleck, J. (1981). *Three conceptual issues in research on male roles.* Working paper no. 98, Wellesley College Center for Research on Women, Wellesley, MA.

Pleck, J. H. (1984). *Working wives and family well-being.* Beverly Hills, CA: Sage.

Plomin, R. (1989). Environment and genes: Determinants of behavior. *American Psychologist, 44,* 105–111.

Plomin, R. (1991, April). *The nature of nurture: Genetic influence on "environmental" measures.* Paper presented at the biennial meeting of the Society for Research in Child Development, Seattle.

Plomin, R., DeFries, J. C., & McClearn, G. E. (1990). *Behavioral genetics: A primer.* New York: W. H. Freeman.

Plomin, R., & Thompson, L. (1987). Life-span developmental behavior genetics. In P. B. Baltes, D. L. Featherman, & R. M. Lerner (Eds.), *Life-span development and behavior* (Vol. 7). Hillsdale, NJ: Erlbaum.

Poest C. A., Williams, J. R., Witt, D. D., & Atwood, M. E. (1990). Challenge me to move: Large muscle development in young children. *Young Children, 45,* 4–10.

Polier, J. W. (1989). *Juvenile justice in double jeopardy.* Hillsdale, NJ: Erlbaum.

Polivy, J., & Herman, C. P. (1991). Good and bad dieters: Self-perception and reaction to a dietary challenge. *International Journal of Eating Disorders, 10,* 91–99.

Polivy, J., & Thomsen, L. (1987). Eating, dieting, and body image. In E. A. Blechman & K. D. Brownell (Eds.), *Handbook of behavioral medicine for women.* Elmsford, NY: Pergamon.

Pomerleau, A. (1989). Commentary. *Human Development, 32,* 167–191.

Poon, L. W. (1985). Differences in human memory with aging: Nature causes, and clinical implications. In J. E. Birren & K. W. Schaie (Eds.), *Handbook of the psychology of aging* (2nd ed.). New York: Van Nostrand Reinhold.

Poon, L. W. (1990, April). *What is everyday cognition? Some validity and generalization considerations.* Paper presented at the 12th West Virginia conference on life-span developmental psychology, Morgantown, WV.

Porcino, J. (1983). *Growing older, getting better: A handbook for women in the second half of life.* Reading, MA: Addison-Wesley.

Porter, F. L., Porges, S. W., & Marshall, R. E. (1988). Newborn pain cries and vagal tone: Parallel changes in response to circumcision. *Child Development, 59,* 495–515.

Potter, J. F., Schafer, D. F., & Bohi, R. L. (1988). In-hospital mortality as a function of body mass index: An age-dependent variable. *Journal of Gerontology: Medical Sciences, 43,* M59–632.

Potvin, L., Champagne, F., & Laberge-Nadeau, C. (1988). Mandatory driver training and road safety: The Quebec experience. *American Journal of Public Health, 78,* 1206–1212.

Powell, G. J., & Fuller, M. (1972). The variables for positive self-concept among Southern Black adolescents. *Journal of the National Medical Association, 42,* 72–79.

Powers, S. I., Hauser, S. T., & Kilner, L. A. (1989). Adolescent mental health. *American Psychologist, 44,* 200–208.

Pressley, M., & Harris, K. R. (1990). What we really know about strategy instruction. *Educational Leadership, 48,* 31–34.

Price, J., & Feshbach, S. (1982, August). *Emotional adjustment correlates of television viewing in children.* Paper presented at the meeting of the American Psychological Association, Washington, DC.

Puffer, J. C. (1987, September). *Risky sports for young children.* Paper presented at the annual meeting of the American Academy of Family Physicians, San Francisco.

Q

Quality health care: Critical issues before the nation (1988, March). Washington, DC: Health Care Quality Alliance.

Quina, K. (1986). *Teaching research methods: A multidimensional feminist curricular transformation plan.* Wellesley College Center for Research on Women. Working Paper No. 164.

R

Rabin, D. S., & Chrousos, G. P. (1991). Androgens, Gonadal. In R. M. Lerner, A. C. Petersen, & J. Brooks-Gunn (Eds.), *Encyclopedia of adolescence* (Vol. 1). New York: Garland.

Rabkin, J. (1987). *Epidemiology of adolescent violence: Risk factors, career patterns, and intervention programs.* Paper presented at the conference on adolescent violence, Stanford University, Stanford, CA.

Rachels, J. (1986). *The end of life.* New York: Oxford University Press.

Rahman, T., & Bisanz, G. L. (1986). Reading ability and use of a story schema in recalling and reconstructing information. *Journal of Educational Psychology, 5,* 323–333.

Ramirez, M. (1990). *Psychotherapy and counseling with minorities.* Riverside, NJ: Pergamon.

Ramirez, O. (1989). Mexican American children and adolescents. In J. T. Gibbs & L. N. Huang (Eds.), *Children of Color.* San Francisco: Jossey-Bass.

Ramirez, O., & Arce, C. Y. (1981). The contemporary Chicago family: An empirically based review. In A. Baron (Ed.), *Explorations in Chicano psychology.* New York: Praeger.

Ramsay, D. S. (1980). Onset of unimanual handedness in infants. *Infant Behavior and Development, 3,* 377–385.

Randahl, G. J. (1991). A typological analysis of the relations between measured vocational interests and abilities. *Journal of Vocational Behavior, 38,* 333–350.

Rando, T. A. (1988). *Grieving: How to go on living when someone you love dies.* Lexington, MA: Lexington Books.

Ratcliff, K. S., & Bogdan, J. (1988). Unemployed women: When 'social support' is not supportive. *Social Problems, 35,* 54–63.

Rayman, J, R., & Garis, J. W. (1989). Counseling. In M. L. Upcraft & J. N. Gardner (Eds.), *The freshman year experience.* San Francisco: Jossey-Bass.

Reedy, M. N., Birren, J. E., & Schaie, K. W. (1981). Age and sex differences in satisfying relationships across the adult life span. *Human Development, 24,* 52–66.

Reichard, S., Levson, F., & Peterson, P. (1962). *Aging and personality: A study of 87 older men.* New York: Wiley.

Reid, D. K. (1988). *Teaching the learning disabled.* Boston, MA: Allyn & Bacon.

Reilly, R. (1988, August 15). Here no one is spared. *Sports Illustrated, 69* (7), 70–77.

Reinisch, J. M. (1990). *The Kinsey Institute New Report on Sex: What You Must Know to be Sexually Literate.* New York: St. Martin's Press.

Remafedi, G. (1991). Homosexuality, adolescent. In R. M. Lerner, A. C. Petersen, & J. Brooks-Gunn (Eds.), *Encyclopedia of adolescence* (Vol. 1). New York: Garland.

Revitch, E., & Schlesinger, L. B. (1978). Murder: Evaluation, classification, and prediction. In I. L. Kutash, S. B. Kutash, & L. B. Schlesinger (Eds.), *Violence.* San Francisco: Jossey-Bass.

Reynolds, S., & Gilbert, P. (1991). Psychological impact of unemployment: Interactive effects of vulnerability and protective factors on depression. *Journal of Counseling Psychology, 38,* 76–84.

Rhodes, S. R. (1983). Age-related differences in work attitudes and behavior: A review and conceptual analysis. *Psychological Bulletin, 93,* 329–367.

Rice, F. P. (1989). *Human sexuality.* Dubuque, IA: Wm. C. Brown.

Rice, M. B. (1991). Preschoolers' QUIL: Quick incidental learning of words. In G. Conti-Ramsden & C. E. Snow (Eds.), *Children's language* (Vol. 7). Hillsdale, NJ: Erlbaum.

Rice, M. L. (1989). Children's language acquisition. *American Psychologist, 44,* 149–156.

Rich, C. L., Young, D., & Fowler, R. C. (1986). San Diego suicide study. *Archives of General Psychiatry, 43,* 577–582.

Richards, L. N., Bengston, V. L., & Miller, R. B. (1989). The "generation in the middle": Perceptions of changes in adults' intergenerational relationships. In K. Kreppner & R. M. Lerner (Eds.), *Family systems and life-span development.* Hillsdale, NJ: Erlbaum.

Rieben, L., & Perfetti, C. A. (1991). *Learning to read: Basic research and its implications.* Hillsdale, NJ: Erlbaum.

Riege, W. H., & Inman, V. (1981). Age differences in nonverbal memory tasks. *Journal of Gerontology, 36,* 51–58.

Riegel, K. F. (1975). Toward a dialectical theory of development. *Human Development, 18,* 50–64.

Riegel, K. F. (1977). The dialectics of time. In N. Datan & H. W. Reese (Eds.), *Life-span developmental psychology: Dialectical perspective on experimental research.* New York: Academic Press.

Riegel, K. F., & Riegel, R. M. (1972). Development, drop, and death. *Developmental Psychology, 6,* 306–319.

Riggio, R. E., Throckmorton, B., & DePaola, S. (1990). *Social skills and self-esteem: Personality and individual differences, 11,* 799–804.

Riley, M. W. (1989). Foreward: Why this book? In K. W. Schaie & C. Schooler (Eds.), *Social structure and aging: Psychological Processes.* Hillsdale, NJ: Erlbaum.

Riley, M. W., & Foner, A. (1968). *Aging and society* (Vol. 1). New York: Russell Sage.

Risser, W. L. (1989). Exercise for children. *Pediatrics in Review, 10,* 131–140.

Robinson, D. P., & Greene, J. W. (1988). The adolescent alcohol and drug problem: A practical approach. *Pediatric Nursing, 14,* 305–310.

Robinson, I., Ziss, K., Ganza, B., Katz, S., & Robinson, E. (1991). Twenty years of the sexual revolution, 1965–1985: An update. *Journal of Marriage and the Family, 53,* 216–220.

Rode, S. S., Chang, P., Fisch, R. O., & Sroufe, L. A. (1981). Attachment patterns of infants separated at birth. *Developmental Psychology, 17,* 188–191.

Rodin, J. (1983). Behavioral medicine: Beneficial effects of self-control training in aging. *International Review of Applied Psychology, 32,* 153–181.

Rodin, J. (1986). Health, control, and aging. In M. M. Baltes & P. B. Baltes (Eds.), *The psychology of control and aging.* Hillsdale, NJ: Erlbaum.

Rodin, J. (1990, January). Conversation with Robert Trotter. *Longevity,* pp. 60–67.

Rodin, J., & Langer, E. J. (1977). Long-term effects of a control-relevant intervention with the institutionalized aged. *Journal of Personality and Social Psychology, 35,* 397–402.

Rodin, J., & Timko, C. (1991). Sense of control, aging, and health. In M. G. Ory, R. P. Abeles, & P. D. Lipman (Eds.), *Aging, health, and behavior.* Newbury Park, CA: Sage.

Rodman, H., Pratto, D. J., & Nelson, R. S. (1988). Toward a definition of self-care children: A commentary on Steinberg (1986). *Developmental Psychology, 24,* 292–294.

Rodriguez-Haynes, M., & Crittenden, P. M. (1988). *Ethnic differences among abusing, neglecting, and non-maltreating families.* Paper presented at the Southeastern Conference on Human Development, Charleston, SC.

Roff, M., Sells, S. B., & Golden, M. W. (1972). *Social adjustment and personality development in children.* Minneapolis, MN: University of Minnesota Press.

Rogers, A. (1987). *Questions of gender differences: Ego development and moral voice in adolescence.* Unpublished manuscript, Department of Education, Harvard University.

Rogers, C. R. (1961). *On becoming a person.* Boston: Houghton Mifflin.

Rogers, C. R. (1963). The actualizing tendency in relation to "motives" and consciousness. In M. R. Jones (Ed.), *Nebraska Symposium on Motivation.* Lincoln: University of Nebraska Press.

Rogers, C. R. (1967). Carl R. Rogers. In E. G. Boring & G. Lindzey (Eds.), *A history of psychology in autobiography.* New York: Macmillan.

Rogers, C. R. (1974). In retrospect: Forty-six years. *American Psychologist, 29,* 115–123.

Rogers, C. R. (1980). *A way of being.* Boston: Houghton-Mifflin.

Rogers, C. S., & Sawyers, J. K. (1988). *Play in the lives of children.* Washington, DC: NAEYC.

Rogler, L. H., Cortes, D. E., & Malgady, R. G. (1991). Acculturation and mental health status among Hispanics: Convergence and new directions for research. *American Psychologist, 46,* 585–597.

Rogoff, B. (1990). *Apprenticeship in thinking: Cognitive development in social context.* New York: Oxford University Press.

Rogoff, B. (in press). Peer influences on cognitive development: Piagetian versus Vygotskian perspectives. In M. H. Bornstein & J. S. Bruner (Eds.), *Interaction in human development.* Hillsdale, NJ: Erlbaum.

Rogoff, B., & Morelli, G. (1989). Perspectives on children's development from cultural psychology. *American Psychologist, 44,* 343–348.

Rohner, R. P., & Rohner, E. C. (1981). Parental acceptance-rejection and parental control: Cross-cultural codes. *Ethnology, 20,* 245–260.

Rokach, A. (1990). Surviving and coping with loneliness. *Journal of psychology, 124,* 39–54.

Rollins, B. C. (1989). Marital quality at mid-life. In S. Hunter & M. Sundel (Eds.), *Midlife myths.* Newbury Park, CA: Sage.

Rook, K. (1987). Reciprocity of social exchange and social satisfaction among older women. *Journal of Personality and Social Psychology, 52,* 145–154.

Rose, R. J., Koskenvuo, M., Kaprio, J., Sarna, S., & Langinvainio, H. (1988). Shared genes, shared experiences, and similarity of personality: Data from 14,228 adult Finnish co-twins. *Journal of Personality and Social Psychology, 54,* 161–171.

Rose, S. A. (1989). Measuring infant intelligence: New perspectives. In M. H. Bornstein & N. A. Krasnegor (Eds.), *Stability and continuity in mental development.* Hillsdale, NJ: Erlbaum.

Rose, S. A., Feldman, J. F., McCarton, C. M., & Wolfson, J. (1988). Information processing in seven-month-old infants as a function of risk status. *Child Development, 59,* 489–603.

Rose, S. A., & Ruff, H. A. (1987). Cross-modal abilities in human infants. In J. D. Osofsky (Ed.), *Handbook of infant development* (2nd ed.). New York: Wiley.

Rosenbaum, E., & Kandel, D. B. (1990). Early onset of adolescent sexual behavior and drug involvement. *Journal of Marriage and the Family, 52,* 783–798.

Rosenbaum, J. E. (1984). *Career mobility in a corporate hierarchy.* New York: Academic Press.

Rosenberg, N. (1965). Society and the adolescent self-image. Princeton, NJ: Princeton University Press.

Rosenblith, J. F., & Sims-Knight, J. E. (1985). *In the beginning: Development in the first two years.* Monterey, CA: Brooks/Cole.

Rosenfeld, A., & Stark, E. (1987, May). The prime of our lives. *Psychology Today,* pp. 62–72.

Rosenthal, R. (1987). Pygmalion effects: Existence, magnitude, and social importance. *Educational Researcher, 16,* 37–41.

Rosenthal, R., & Jacobsen, L. (1968). *Pygmalian in the classroom.* New York: Holt, Rinehart & Winston.

Rossi, A. S. (1989). A life-course approach to gender, aging, and intergenerational relations. In K. W. Schaie & C. Schooler (Eds.), *Social structure and aging.* Hillsdale, NJ: Erlbaum.

Rothbart, M. K. (1971). Birth order and mother-child interaction. *Dissertation Abstracts, 27,* 45–57.

Rothbart, M. K. (1988). Temperament and the development of inhibited approach. *Child Development, 59,* 1241–1250.

Rothstein, W. G. (1980). The significance of occupations in work careers: An empirical and theoretical review. *Journal of Vocational Behavior, 17,* 343–378.

Rotter, J. B. (1989, August). *Internal versus external locus of control of reinforcement: A case history of a variable.* Paper presented at the meeting of the American Psychological Association, New Orleans.

Rovee-Collier, C. (1987). Learning and memory in children. In J. D. Osofsky (Ed.), *Handbook of infant development* (2nd ed.). New York: Wiley.

Rowe, D. C., & Rodgers, J. E. (1989). Behavioral genetics, adolescent deviance, and "d" contributions and issues. In G. R. Adams, R. Montemayor, & T. P. Gulotta (Eds.), *Biology of adolescent behavior and development.* Newburg, CA: Sage.

Roybal, E. R. (1988). Mental health and aging: The need for an expanded federal response. *American Psychologist, 43,* 189–194.

Rubin, K. H., Maioni, T. L., & Hornung, M. (1976). Free play behaviors in middle and lower social class preschoolers: Parten and Piaget revisited. *Child Development, 47,* 414–419.

Rubin, K. N., Fein, G. G., & Vandenberg, B. (1983). Play. In P. H. Mussen (Ed.), *Handbook of child psychology* (4th ed., Vol. 4). New York: Wiley.

Rubin, L. B. (1984). *Intimate strangers: Men and women working together.* New York: Harper & Row.

Rubin, Z. (1970). Measurement and romantic love. *Journal of Personality and Social Psychology, 16,* 265–273.

Rubin, Z. (1981, May). Does personality really change after 20? *Psychology Today.*

Rubin, Z., & Mitchell, C. (1976). Couples research as couples counseling. *American Psychologist, 31,* 17–25.

Ruble, D. N., Boggiano, A. K., Feldman, N. S., & Loebl, J. H. (1989). Developmental analysis of the role of social comparison in self-evaluation. *Developmental Psychology, 16,* 105–115.

Ruebenstein, J., Heeren, T., Housman, D., Rubin, C., & Stechler, G. (1989). Suicidal behavior in "normal" adolescents: Risk and protective factors. *American Journal of Orthopsychiatry, 59,* 59–71.

Rumbaugh, D. M., Hopkins, W. D., Washburn, D. A., & Savage-Rumbaugh, E. S. (1991). Comparative perspectives of brain, cognition, and language. In N. A. Krasnegor, D. M. Rumbaugh, M. Studdert-Kennedy, & R. L. Schiefelbusch (Eds.), *Biological and behavioral determinants of language development.* Hillsdale, NJ: Erlbaum.

Rumberger, R. W. (1983). Dropping out of high school: The influence of race, sex, and family background. *American Educational Research Journal, 20,* 199–220.

Rumberger, R. W. (1987). High school dropouts: A review of the issues and evidence. *Review of Educational Research, 57,* 101–121.

Runco, M. A. (1991). *Divergent thinking.* Norwood, NJ: Ablex.

Russo, N. F. (1990). Overview: Forging research priorities for women's mental health. *American Psychologist, 45,* 368–374.

Rutter, M. (1983, April). *Influences from family and school.* Paper presented at the meeting of the Society for Research in Child Development, Detroit.

Rutter, M., & Schopler, E. (1987). Autism and pervasive developmental disorders: Concepts and diagnostic issues. *Journal of Autism and Developmental Disorders, 17,* 159–186.

Ryan, R. A. (1980). Strengths of the American Indian family: State of the art. In F. Hoffman (Ed.), The American Indian family: Strengths and stresses. Isleta, NM: American Indian Social Research and Development Association.

Ryan, R. M., & Lynch, J. H. (1989). Emotional autonomy versus detachment: Revisiting the vicissitudes of adolescence and young adulthood. *Child Development, 60,* 340–356.

Rybash, J. W., Roodin, P. A., & Santrock, J. W. (1991). *Adult Development and Aging* (2nd ed.). Dubuque, IA: Wm. C. Brown.

Ryff, C. D. (1984). Personality development from the inside: The subjective experience of change in adulthood and aging. In P. B. Baltes & O. G. Brim (Eds.), *Life-span development and behavior.* New York: Academic Press.

S

Sadker, M., & Sadker, D. (1986, March). Sexism in the classroom: From grade school to graduate school. *Phi Delta Kappan,* pp. 512–515.

Sadker, M., Sadker, D., & Klein, S. S. (1986). Abolishing misperceptions about sex equity in education. *Theory into Practice, 25,* 219–226.

Sagan, C. (1977). *Dragons of Eden.* New York: Random House.

St. James-Roberts, Bowyer, J., & Hurry, J. (1991, April). *Delineating "problem" infant crying: Findings in community and referred infants, using tape recordings, diaries, and direct questionnaires.* Paper presented at the biennial meeting of the Society for Research in Child Development, Seattle.

Salthouse, T. A. (1984). Effects of age and skill in typing. *Journal of Experimental Psychology: General, 113,* 345–371.

Salthouse, T. A. (1989). Age-related changes in basic cognitive processes. In M. Storandt & G. R. VandenBos (Eds.), *The adult years: Continuity and change.* Washington, DC: American Psychological Association.

Salthouse, T. A. (1991). Theoretical perspectives on cognitive aging. Hillsdale, NJ: Erlbaum.

Sangree, W. H. (1989). Age and power: Life-course trajectories and age structuring of power relations in East and West Africa. In D. I. Kertzer & K. W. Schaie (Eds.), *Age structuring in comparative perspective.* Hillsdale, NJ: Erlbaum.

Sankar, A. (1991). Ritual and dying: A cultural analysis of social support for caregivers. *The Gerontologist, 31,* 43–50.

Santrock, J. W. (1990a). Children of divorce: A concise eclectic review. *Contemporary Psychology, 35,* 559–560.

Santrock, J. W. (1990b). The changing tapestry of children's family worlds. *Contemporary Psychology, 35,* 692–693.

Santrock, J. W. (in press). *Adolescence* (5th ed.). Dubuque, IA: Wm. C. Brown.

Santrock, J. W., & Bartlett, J. C. (1986). *Developmental psychology.* Dubuque, IA: Wm. C. Brown.

Santrock, J. W., & Sitterle, K. A. (1987). Parent-child relationships in stepmother families. In K. Pasley & M. Ihinger-Tallman (Eds.), *Remarriage and stepparenting.* New York: Guilford.

Santrock, J. W., Sitterle, K. A., & Warshak, R. A. (1988). Parent-child relationships in stepfather families. In P. Bronstein & C. Cowan (Eds.), *The father's role today: Men's changing roles in the family.* New York: Wiley.

Santrock, J. W., & Warshak, R. A. (1979). Father custody and social development in boys and girls. *Journal of Social Issues, 35,* 112–125.

Santrock, J. W., & Warshak, R. A. (1986). Development, relationships, and legal/clinical considerations in father custody families. In M. E. Lamb (Ed.), *The father's role: Applied perspectives.* New York: Wiley.

Sapp, S. (1991). Ethical issues in intergenerational equity. *Journal of Religious Gerontology, 7,* 1–16.

Sauber, M., & Corrigan, E. M. (1970). *The six year experience of unwed mothers as parents.* New York: Community Council of Greater New York.

Savage-Rumbaugh, E. S. (1991). Language learning in the Bonobo: How and why they learn. In N. A. Krasnegor, D. M. Rumbaugh, M. Studdert-Kennedy, & R. L. Schiefelbusch (Eds.), *Biological and behavioral determinants of language development.* Hillsdale, NJ: Erlbaum.

Saxe, G. B., Guberman, S. R., & Gearhart, M. (1987). Social processes in early number development. *Monographs of the Society for Research in Child Development, 52* (2, Serial No. 216).

Scales, P. (1990). Developing capable young people: An alternative strategy for prevention programs. *Journal of Early Adolescence, 10,* 420–438.

Scardamalia, M., Bereiter, C., & Steinbach, R. (1984). Teachability of reflective processes in written composition. *Cognitive Science, 8,* 173–190.

Scarlett, W. G., & Perriello, L. (1990, March). *The development of prayer in adolescence.* Paper presented at the meeting of the Society for Research in Adolescence, Atlanta, GA.

Scarr, S. (1984). *Mother care/Other care.* New York: Basic Books.

Scarr, S. (1984, May). Interview. *Psychology Today,* pp. 59–63.

Scarr, S. (1989, April). *Transracial adoption.* Discussion at the biennial meeting of the Society for Research in Child Development, Kansas City, MO.

Scarr, S. (1991, April). *Developmental theories for the 1990s.* Presidential address, biennial meeting of the Society for Research in Child Development, Seattle.

Scarr, S. (1991, October). *A study of the quality of day care in three states.* Paper presented at the symposium on day care for children, Arlington, VA.

Scarr, S., & Kidd, K. K. (1983). Developmental behavior genetics. In P. H. Mussen (Ed.), *Handbook of child psychology* (4th ed., Vol. 2). New York: Wiley.

Scarr, S., Lande, J., & McCartney, K. (1989). Child care and the family: Complements and interactions. In J. Lande, S. Scarr, & N. Gunzenhauser, (Eds.), *Caring for children: Challenge to America.* Hillsdale, NJ: Erlbaum.

Scarr, S., & Weinberg, R. A. (1980). Calling all camps! The war is over. *American Sociological Review, 45,* 859–865.

Scarr, S., & Weinberg, R. A. (1983). The Minnesota adoption studies: Genetic differences and malleability. *Child Development, 54,* 253–259.

Schaie, K. W. (1973). Methodological problems in descriptive developmental research on adulthood and aging. In J. R. Nesselroade & H. W. Reese (Eds.), *Life-span developmental psychology: Methodological issues.* New York: Academic Press.

Schaie, K. W. (1977). Toward a stage theory of adult cognitive development. *Aging and Human Development, 8,* 129–138.

Schaie, K. W. (1984). The Seattle Longitudinal Study: A 21-year exploration of psychometric intelligence in adulthood. In K. W. Schaie (Ed.), *Longitudinal studies of adult psychological development.* New York: Guilford Press.

Schaie, K. W. (1989). Introduction. In K. W. Schaie & C. Schooler (Eds.), *Social structure and aging: Psychological Processes.* Hillsdale, NJ: Erlbaum.

Schaie, K. W. (1991). Developmental designs revisited. In S. H. Cohen & H. W. Reese (Eds.), *Life-span developmental psychology: Methodological innovation.* Hillsdale, NJ: Erlbaum.

Schaie, K. W., & Strother, C. R. (1968). A cross-sequential study of age changes in cognitive behavior. *Psychological Bulletin, 70,* 671–680.

Schaie, K. W., & Willis, S. L. (1986). Can adult intellectual decline be reversed? *Developmental Psychology, 22,* 223–232.

Schank, R., & Abelson, R. (1977). *Scripts, plans, goals, and understanding.* Hillsdale, NJ: Erlbaum.

Schegloff, E. A. (1989). Reflections on language, development, and the interactional character of talk-in-interaction. In M. H. Bornstein & J. S. Bruner (Eds.), *Interaction in human development*. Hillsdale, NJ: Erlbaum.

Schilke, J. M. (1991). Slowing the aging process with physical activity. *Gerontological Nursing, 17*, 4–8.

Schlenker, E. D. (1988). Nutrition for aging and the aged. In S. R. Williams & B. S. Worthington-Roberts (Eds.), Nutrition throughout the life cycle. St. Louis: Times Mirror/Mosby.

Schlundt, D. G., & Johnson, W. G. (1990). *Assessment and treatment of anorexia nervosa and bulimia nervosa.* Needham Heights, MA: Allyn & Bacon.

Schmich, M. T. (1987, July 29). *Living alone.* Dallas Morning News, Section C, pp. 1, 4.

Schmidt, M. G. (1990). *Negotiating a good old age.* San Francisco: Jossey-Bass.

Schneider-Rosen, K., & Cicchetti, D. (1991). Self-knowledge and emotional development: Visual self-recognition and affective reactions to mirror self-images in maltreated and non-maltreated toddlers. *Developmental Psychology, 27*, 471–478.

Schoenfeld, A. H. (1985). *Mathematical problem solving.* Orlando, FL: Academic Press.

Schooler, C. (1991). Individualism and the historical and social structural determinants of people's concern over self-directedness and efficacy. In J. Rodin, C. Schooler, & K. W. Schaie (Eds.), *Self-directedness and efficacy.* Hillsdale, NJ: Erlbaum.

Schrag, S. G., & Dixon, R. L. (1985). Occupational exposure associated with male reproductive dysfunction. *Annual Review of Pharmacology and Toxicology, 25*, 467–592.

Schulz, R. (1976). Effects of control and predictability on the physical and psychological well-being of the institutionalized aged. *Journal of Personality and Social Psychology, 33*, 563–573.

Schultz, R., & Curnow, C. (1988). Peak performance and age among superathletes: Track and field, swimming, baseball, tennis, and golf. *Journal of Gerontology, 43*, P113–120.

Schulz, R., & Hanusa, B. H. (1978). Long-term effects of control and predictability-enhancing interventions: Findings and ethical issues. *Journal of Personality and Social Psychology, 11*, 1194–1201.

Schunk, D. H. (1983). Developing children's self-efficacy and skills: The roles of social comparative information and goal-setting. *Contemporary Educational Psychology, 8*, 76–86.

Schunk, D. H. (1990). Introduction to the special section on motivation and efficacy. *Journal of Educational Psychology, 82*, 3–6.

Schwartz, B. (1990). The creation and destruction of value. *American Psychologist, 45*, 7–15.

Schwartz, D., & Mayaux, M. J. (1982). Female fecundity as a function of age: Results of artificial insemination in nullparous women with azoospermic husbands. *New England Journal of Medicine, 306*, 304–406.

Schwartz, R., & Eriksen, M. (1989). Statement of the Society for Public Health Education on the national health promotion disease prevention objectives for the year 2000. *Health Education Quarterly, 16*, 3–7.

Scott, J. P. (1983). Siblings and other kin. In T. Brubaker (Ed.), *Family relationships in later life.* Beverly Hills, CA: Sage.

Scott-Jones, D., & White, A. B. (1990). Correlates of sexual activity in early adolescence. *Journal of Early Adolescence, 10*, 221–238.

Scribner, S. (1977). Modes of thinking and ways of speaking: Culture and logic reconsidered. In F. N. Johnson-Laird & P. C. Wason (Eds.), *Thinking: Readings in Cognitive Science.* New York: Cambridge University Press.

Sears, R. R., & Feldman, S. S. (Eds.). (1973). *The seven ages of man.* Los Altos, CA: William Kaufmann.

Segerberg, O. (1982). *Living to be 100: 1200 who did and how they did it.* New York: Charles Scribner's Sons.

Seibert, J. M. & Olson, R. A. (Eds.). (1989). *Children, adolescents, and AIDS.* Lincoln: University of Nebraska Press.

Selman, R. L. (1976). Social-cognitive understanding: A guide to educational and clinical practice. In T. Lickona (Ed.), *Moral development and behavior: Theory, research, and social issues.* New York: Holt, Rinehart, & Winston.

Selman, R. L. (1980). *The growth of interpersonal understanding.* New York: Academic Press.

Semaj, L. T. (1985). Afrikanity, cognition, and extended self-identity. In M. B. Spencer, G. K. Brookins, & W. R. Allen (Eds.), *Beginnings: The social and affective development of Black children.* Hillsdale, NJ: Erlbaum.

Serbin, L. A., & Sprafkin, C. (1986). The salience of gender and the process of sex-typing in three- to seven-year-old children. *Child Development, 57*, 1188–1209.

Sexton, M., & Hebel, J. R. (1984). A clinical trial of change in maternal smoking and its effects on birth weight. *Journal of the American Medical Association, 251*, 911–915.

Shakeshaft, C. (1986, March). A gender at risk. *Phi Delta Kappan*, pp. 499–503.

Shantz, C. O. (1988). Conflicts between children. *Child Development, 58*, 283–305.

Shantz, C. U. (1983). Social cognition. In P. H. Mussen (Ed.), *Handbook of child psychology* (4th ed., Vol. 3). New York: Wiley.

Shapiro, E. R., & Freedman, J. (1989). Family dynamics of adolescent suicide. In A. H. Esman (Ed.), *International Annals of Adolescent Psychiatry.* Chicago: University of Chicago Press.

Shaver, P. (1986, August). *Being lonely, falling in love: Perspectives from attachment theory.* Paper presented at the meeting of the American Psychological Association, Washington, DC.

Shaw, S. M. (1988). Gender differences in the definition and perception of household labor. *Family Relations, 37*, 333–337.

Sheehy, G. (1976). *Passages.* New York: Dutton.

Sheingold, K., & Tenney, Y. J. (1982). Memory for a salient childhood event. In U. Neisser (Ed.), *Memory observed.* New York: W. H. Freeman.

Sherman, E. (1987). *Meaning in mid-life transitions.* Albany: State University of New York Press.

Sherwood, A., Light, K. C., & Blumenthal, J. A. (1989). Effects of aerobic exercise training on hemodynamic responses during psychosocial stress in normotensive and borderline hypertensive Type A men: A preliminary report. *Psychosomatic Medicine, 51*, 123–136.

Shneidman, E. S. (1971). Suicide among the gifted. *Suicide and Life-threatening Behavior, 1*, 23–45.

Shneidman, E. S. (1973). *Deaths of man.* New York: Quadrangle/New York Times.

Siegel, K., & Krauss, B. J. (1991). Living with HIV infection: Adaptive tasks of seropositive gay men. *Journal of Health and Social Behavior, 32*, 17–32.

Siegel, L. S. (1989, April). *Perceptual-motor, cognitive, and language skills as predictors of cognitive abilities at school age.* Paper presented at the biennial meeting of the Society for Research in Children, Kansas City, MO.

Siegel, L. S., & Ryan, E. B. (1989). The development of working memory in normally achieving and subtypes of learning disabled children. *Child Development, 69*, 973–980.

Siegler, I. C. (1989). Developmental health psychology. In M. Storandt & G. R. VandenBos (Eds.), *Developmental health psychology.* Washington, DC: American Psychological Association.

Siegler, I. C. (1989). Developmental health psychology. In M. Storandt & G. R. VandenBos (Eds.), *The adult years: Continuity and change.* Washington, DC: American Psychological Association.

Siegler, I. C., & Costa, P. T. (1985). Health behavior relationships. In J. E. Birren & K. W. Schaie (Eds.), *Handbook of the psychology of aging* (2nd ed.). New York: Van Nostrand Reinhold.

Siegman, A. W. (1989). The role of hostility, neuroticism, and speech style in coronary-artery disease. In A. W. Siegman & T. Dembrowski (Eds.), *In search of coronary-prone behavior: Beyond Type A.* Hillsdale, NJ: Erlbaum.

Siegman, A. W., & Dembrowski, T. (Eds.). (1989). *In search of coronary-prone behavior: Beyond Type A.* Hillsdale, NJ: Erlbaum.

Sigman, M., Asarnow, R., Cohen, S., & Parmalee, A. H. (1989, April). *Infant attention as a measure of information processing.* Paper presented at the biennial meeting of the Society for Research in Child Development, Kansas City, MO.

Silver, L. B. (1987). *Attention deficit disorders.* Summit, NJ: CIBA.

Silver, L. B. (1989). Learning disabilities. *Journal of the American Academy of Child and Adolescent Psychiatry, 28*, 309.

Silverberg, S. B., & Steinberg, L. (1990). Psychological well-being of parents with early adolescent children. *Developmental Psychology, 26*, 658–666.

Simmons, D. D. (1991). Dietary restraint as values-related motivation: A psychometric clarification. *The Journal of Psychology, 245*, 189–194.

Simmons, R. G., & Blyth, D. A. (1987). *Moving into adolescence.* Hawthorne, NY: Aldine.

Simons, R. L., & Gray, P. A. (1989). Perceived blocked opportunity as an explanation of delinquency among lower-class Black males: A research note. *Journal of Research in Crime and Delinquency, 26*, 90–101.

Simons, R. L., Whitbeck, L. B., Conger, R. B., & Chyi-In, W. (1991). Intergenerational transmission of harsh parenting. *Developmental Psychology, 27*, 159–171.

Simonton, D. K. (1989). Age and creative productivity: Nonlinear estimation of an information-processing model. *International Journal of Aging and Human Development, 29*, 23–27.

Simopoulos, A. P., & Van Itallie, T. B. (1984). Body weight, health, and longevity. *Annual of Internal Medicine, 100*, 285.

Simpson, J. A., Campbell, B., & Berscheid, E. (1986). The association between love and marriage: Kephart (1967) twice revisited. *Personality and Social Psychology Bulletin, 12*, 363–372.

Singer, D. G., & Singer, J. L. (1987). Practical suggestions for controlling television. *Journal of Early Adolescence, 7*, 365–369.

Singer, J. L. (1984). *The human personality.* San Diego: Harcourt Brace Jovanovich.

Singer, J. L., & Singer, D. G. (1988). Imaginative play and human development: Schemas, scripts, and possibilities. In D. Bergin (Ed.), *Play as a medium for learning and development.* Portsmouth, NH: Heinemann.

Singer, M. (1991). *Psychology of language: An introduction to sentence and discourse processes.* Hillsdale, NJ: Erlbaum.

Sizer, T. R. (1984). *Horace's compromise: The dilemma of the American high school today.* Boston: Houghton Mifflin.

Skinner, B. F. (1938). *The behavior of organisms: An experimental analysis.* New York: Appleton-Century-Crofts.

Skinner, B. F. (1948). *Walden two.* New York: Macmillan.

Skinner, B. F. (1957). *Verbal behavior.* New York: Appleton-Century-Crofts.

Skinner, E. A., Wellborn, J. G., & Connell, J. P. (1990). What it takes to do well in school and whether I've got it: A process model of perceived control and children's engagement and achievement in school. *Journal of Educational Psychology, 82,* 22–32.

Skinner, J. H. (1990). Targeting benefits for the black elderly: The Older Americans Act. In Z. Harel, E. A. McKinney, & M. Williams (Eds.), *Black aged.* Newbury Park, CA: Sage.

Skoe, E. E., & Marcia, J. E. (1988). Ego identity and care-based moral reasoning in college women. Unpublished manuscript, Acadia University.

Slater, A., Cooper, R., Rose, D., & Morrison, V. (1989). Prediction of cognitive performance from infancy to early childhood. *Human Development, 32,* 137–147.

Slaughter-Defoe, D. T., Nakagawa, K., Takanishi, R., & Johnson, D. J. (1990). Toward cultural/ecological perspectives on schooling and achievement in Africa- and Asian-American children. *Child Development, 61,* 363–383.

Slavin, R. E. (1987). Developmental and motivational perspectives on cooperative learning: A reconciliation. *Child Development, 58,* 1161–1167.

Slavin, R. E. (1989). Cooperative learning and student achievement. In R. E. Slavin (Ed.), *School and classroom organization.* Hillsdale, NJ: Erlbaum.

Slobin, D. (1972, July). Children and language: They learn the same way all around the world. *Psychology Today,* pp. 71–76.

Small, M. (1990). *Cognitive development.* San Diego: Harcourt Brace Jovanovich.

Smith, A. D. (1977). Adult age differences in cued recall. *Developmental Psychology, 13,* 326–331.

Smith, B. A., Fillion, T. J., & Blass, E. M. (1990). Orally mediated sources of calming in 1- to 3-day-old human infants. *Developmental Psychology, 26,* 731–737.

Smith, J., & Baltes, P. B. (1991). A life-span perspective on thinking and problem solving. In M. Schwebel, C. A. Maher, & N. S. Fagley (Eds.), *Promoting cognitive growth over the life span.* Hillsdale, NJ: Erlbaum.

Smith, J., & Baltes, P. B. (in press). A study of wisdom-related knowledge: Age-cohort differences in responses to life-planning problems. *Developmental Psychology.*

Smith, J. E. (1985). A familistic religion in modern society. In K. Davis (Ed.), *Contemporary marriage.* New York: Russell Sage Foundation.

Smith, T. W. (1991). Adult sexual behavior in 1989: Number of partners, frequence of intercourse, and risk of AIDS. *Family Planning Perspectives, 23,* 102–107.

Smither, R. D. (1988). *The psychology of work and human performance.* New York: Harper & Row.

Smolucha, F. (1989, April). *Vygotsky's theory of creative imagination and its relevance for research on play.* Paper presented at the biennial meeting of the Society for Research on Child Development, Kansas City, MO.

Snarey, J. (1987, June). A question of morality. *Psychology Today,* pp. 6–8.

Snow, C. E. (1989a). Understanding social interaction in language interaction: Sentences are not enough. In M. H. Bornstein & J. S. Bruner (Eds.), *Interaction in human development.* Hillsdale, NJ: Erlbaum.

Snow, C. E. (1989b, April). *Imitation as one path to language acquisition.* Paper presented at the biennial meeting of the Society for Research in Child Development, Kansas City, MO.

Snowden, L. R., & Cheung, F. K. (1990). Use of inpatient mental health services by members of ethnic minority groups. *American Psychologist, 45,* 347–355.

Sokolovsky, J. (1983). *Growing old in different societies: Cross-cultural perspectives.* Belmont, CA: Wadsworth.

Sommer, B. B. (1978). *Puberty and adolescence.* New York: Oxford University Press.

Sorensen, R. C. (1973). *Adolescent sexuality in contemporary America.* New York: World.

Spade, J. Z., & Reese, C. A. (1991). We've come a long way, maybe: College students' plans for work and family. *Sex Roles, 24,* 309–322.

Speece, M., & Brent, S. (1984). Children's understanding of death: A review of three components of a death concept. *Child Development, 55,* 1671–1686.

Spelke, E. S. (1991). Physical knowledge in infancy: Reflections on Piaget's theory. In S. Carey & R. Gelman (Eds.), *The epigenesis of mind: Essays on biology and cognition.* Hillsdale, NJ: Erlbaum.

Spence, J. T., & Helmreich, R. (1978). *Masculinity and femininity: Their psychological dimensions.* Austin, TX: University of Texas Press.

Spencer, M. B. (1987). Black children's ethnic identity formation: Risk and resilience of castelike minorities. In J. S. Phinney & M. J. Rotheram (Eds.), *Children's ethnic socialization: Pluralism and development.* Newbury Park, CA: Sage.

Spencer, M. B. (1991, April). *Research methods: Prospects, perils, and "pearls of opportunity."* Paper presented at the biennial meeting of the Society for Research in Child Development, Seattle.

Spencer, M. B. (1991). Identity, minority development of. In R. M. Lerner, A. C. Petersen, & J. Brooks-Gunn (Eds.), *Encyclopedia of adolescence* (Vol. 1). New York: Garland.

Spencer, M. B., & Dornbusch, S. M. (1990). Challenges in studying minority youth. In S. S. Feldman & G. R. Elliott (Eds.), *At the threshold: The developing adolescent.* Cambridge, MA: Cambridge University Press.

Spencer, M. B., & Markstrom-Adams, C. (1990). Identity processes among racial and ethnic minority children in America. *Child Development, 61,* 290–310.

Spencer, M. L. (1986). Sex equity in bilingual education, English as a second language, and foreign language instruction. *Theory into Practice, 25,* 257–266.

Spielberger, C. D., & Grier, K. (1983). Unpublished manuscript. University of South Florida, Tampa.

Sprei, J. E., & Courtois, C. A. (1988). The treatment of women's sexual dysfunctions arising from sexual assault. In R. A. Brown & J. R. Field (Eds.), *Treatment of sexual problems in individual and couples therapy.* Great Neck, NY: PMA.

Sprey, J. (1991). Generational and intergenerational connections within the family and the community. *Marriage and Family Review, 16,* 221–236.

Sroufe, L. A. (1985). Attachment classification from the perspective of infant-caregiver relationships and infant temperament. *Child Development, 56,* 1–14.

Sroufe, L. A. (1987). *The role of infant-caregiver attachment in development.* Unpublished manuscript, Institute of Child Development, University of Minnesota.

Sroufe, L. A. (in press). Pathways to adaptation and maladaptation: Psychopathology as developmental deviation. In D. Cicchetti (Ed.), *Developmental psychopathology: Past, present, and future.* Hillsdale, NJ: Erlbaum.

Sroufe, L. A., & Waters, E. (1976). The ontogenesis of smiling and laughter: A perspective on the organization of development in infancy. *Psychological Review, 83,* 173–189.

Stage, E. K., Kreinberg, N., Eccles, J., & Becker, J. R. (1985). Increasing the participation and achievement of girls and women in mathematics, science, and engineering. In S. S. Klein (Ed.), *Handbook for achieving sex equity through education.* Baltimore, MD: Johns Hopkins University Press.

Stallings, J. (1975). Implementation and child effects of teaching practices in Follow Through classrooms. *Monographs of the Society for Research in Child Development, 40* (Serial No. 163).

Stanford, E. P. (1990). Diverse Black aged. In Z. Harel, E. A. McKinney, & M. Williams, (Eds.), *Black aged.* Newbury Park, CA: Sage.

Stanford, E. P., Happersett, C. J., Morton, D. J., Molgaard, C. A., & Peddecord, K. M. (1991). Early retirement and functional impairment from a multi-ethnic perspective. *Research on Aging, 13,* 5–38.

Stanhope, M., & Lancaster, J. (1991). Toward a healthy tomorrow. *Family and Community Health, 14,* 1–7.

Steil, J. M., & Weltman, K. (1991). Marital inequality: The importance of resources, personal attributes, and social norms on career valuing and the allocation of domestic responsibilities. *Sex Roles, 24,* 161–180.

Stein, N. L., & Glenn, C. G. (1979). An analysis of story comprehension in elementary school children. In R. O. Freedle (Ed.), *Discourse processing: Multidisciplinary perspectives* (pp. 53–120). Norwood, NJ: Ablex.

Steinberg, L. D. (1981). Transformations in family relations at puberty. *Developmental Psychology, 17,* 833–840.

Steinberg, L. D. (1986). Latchkey children and susceptibility to peer pressure: An ecological analysis. *Developmental Psychology, 22,* 433–439.

Steinberg, L. D. (1987). Impact of puberty on family relations: Effects of pubertal status and pubertal timing. *Developmental Psychology, 23,* 451–460.

Steinberg, L. D. (1988a.). Reciprocal relation between parent-child distance and pubertal maturation. *Developmental Psychology, 24,* 122–128.

Steinberg, L. D. (1988b.). Simple solutions to a complex problem: A response to Rodman, Pratto, and Nelson (1988). *Developmental Psychology, 24,* 295–296.

Steinberg, L. D. (1990). Autonomy, conflict, and harmony in the family relationship. In S. S. Feldman & G. R. Elliott (Eds.), *At the threshold: The developing adolescent.* Cambridge, MA: Harvard University Press.

Steinberg, L. D. (1991). Parent-adolescent relations. In R. M. Lerner, A. C. Petersen, & J. Brooks-Gunn (Eds.), *Encyclopedia of adolescence.* New York: Garland.

Steiner, J. E. (1979). Human facial expressions in response to taste and smell stimulation. In H. Reese & L. Lipsitt (Eds.), *Advances in child development and behavior* (Vol. 13). New York: Academic Press.

Stern, D. N., Beebe, B., Jaffe, J., & Bennett, S. L. (1977). The infant's stimulus world during social interaction: A study of caregiver behaviors with particular reference to repetition and timing. In H. R. Schaffer (Ed.), *Studies in mother-infant interaction.* London: Academic Press.

Stern, J. S. (1984). Is obesity a disease of inactivity? In A. J. Stunkard & E. Stellar (Eds.), *Eating and its disorders.* New York: Raven Press.

Stern, S. L., Dixon, K. N., Jones, D., Lake, M., Nemzer, E., & Sansone, R. (1989). Family environment in anorexia nervosa and bulimia. *International Journal of Eating Disorders, 8,* 25–31.

Sternberg, R. J. (1986). *Intelligence Applied.* San Diego: Harcourt Brace Jovanovich.

Sternberg, R. J. (1988). *The triangle of love.* New York: Basic Books.

Sternberg, R. J. (1989). Introduction. In R. J. Sternberg (Ed.), *Advances in the psychology of human intelligence.* (Vol. 5). Hillsdale, NJ: Erlbaum.

Sternberg, R. J. (1990, April). *Academic and practical cognition as different aspects of intelligence.* Paper presented at the 12th West Virginia conference on life-span developmental psychology, Morgantown, WV.

Sternberg, R. J., & Okagaki, L. (1989). Continuity and discontinuity in intellectual development are not a matter of 'either-or.' *Human Development, 32,* 158–166.

Sternglanz, S. H., & Serbin, L. A. (1974). Sex-role stereotyping in children's television programming. *Developmental Psychology, 10,* 710–715.

Steur, F. B., Applefield, J. M., & Smith, R. (1971). Televised aggression and interpersonal aggression of preschool children. *Journal of Experimental Child Psychology, 11,* 442–447.

Stevens, J. H. (1984). Black grandmothers' and Black adolescents mothers' knowledge about parenting. *Developmental Psychology, 20,* 1017–1025.

Stevens-Long, J. (1988). *Adult life* (3rd ed.). Mountain View, CA: Mayfield.

Stevenson, H. W., Chen, C., Lee, S., & Fulgni, A. J. (1991). Schooling, culture, and cognitive development. In L. Okagaki & R. J. Sternberg (Eds.), *Directors of development: Influences on the development of children's thinking.* Hillsdale, NJ: Erlbaum.

Stevenson, H. W., Lee, S., Chen, C., Stigler, J., Hsu, C., & Kitamura, G. (1990). *Contexts of achievement.* Monograph of the Society for Research in Child Development (Serial No. 221, Vol. 55, Nos. 1–2).

Stevenson, H. W., Stigler, J. W., & Lee, S. (1986). Achievement in mathematics. In H. W. Stevenson, H. Azuma, & K. Hakuta (Eds.), *Child development and education in Japan.* San Francisco: W. H. Freeman.

Stewart, N. (1990, January 27). *The effects of cocaine use by pregnant mothers on the development of their offspring.* Invited presentation, School of Human Development, University of Texas at Dallas, Richardson, TX.

Stine, E. L., & Bohannon, J. N., III. (1984). Imitations, interactions, and language acquisition. *Journal of Child Language, 10,* 589–603.

Stipek, D. J., & Hoffman, J. M. (1980). Children's achievement-related expectancies as a function of academic performance histories and sex. *Journal of Educational Psychology, 72,* 861–865.

Stock, W. A., Okun, M. A., Haring, M. J., & Witter, R. A. (1983). Age and subjective well-being: A meta-analysis. In R. J. Light (Ed.), *Evaluation studies: Review annual* (Vol. 8). Newbury Park, CA: Sage.

Stocker, C., & Dunn, J. (1991). Sibling relationships in adolescence. In R. M. Lerner, A. C. Petersen, & J. Brooks-Gunn (Eds.), *Encyclopedia of adolescence.* (Vol. 2). New York: Garland.

Stones, M. J., & Kozman, A. (1989). Age, exercise, and coding performance. *Psychology and Aging, 4,* 190–194.

Streissguth, A. P., Carmichael-Olson, H., Sampston, P. D., & Barr, H. M. (1991, April). *Alcohol vs. tobacco as prenatal correlates of child behavior.* Paper presented at the biennial meeting of the Society for Research in Child Development, Seattle.

Streissguth, A. P., Martin, D. C., Barr, H. M., Sandman, B. M., Kirshner, G. L., & Darby, B. L. (1984). Intrauterine alcohol and nicotine exposure: Attention and reaction time in 4-year-old children. *Developmental Psychology, 20,* 533–541.

Strickland, B. R. (1987). Menopause. In E. A. Blechaman & K. D. Brownell (Eds.), *Handbook of behavioral medicine for women.* Elmsford, NY: Pergamon.

Studdert-Kennedy, M. (1991). Language development from an evolutionary perspective. In N. A. Krasnegor, D. M. Rumbaugh, M. Studdert-Kennedy, & R. L. Schiefelbusch (Eds.), *Biological and behavioral determinants of language development.* Hillsdale, NJ: Erlbaum.

Studer, M., & Thorton, A. (1987). Adolescent religiosity and contraceptive usage. *Journal of Marriage and the Family, 49,* 117–128.

Studer, M., & Thorton, A. (1989). The multifaceted impact of religiosity on adolescent sexual experience and contraceptive usage: A reply to Shornack and Ahmed. *Journal of Marriage and the Family, 51,* 1085–1089.

Stull, D. E., & Hatch, L. R. (1984). Unravelling the effects of multiple life changes. *Research on Aging, 6,* 560–571.

Stunkard, A. J. (1987). The regulation of body weight and the treatment of obesity. In H. Weiner & A. Baum (Eds.), *Eating regulation and discontrol.* Hillsdale, NJ: Erlbaum.

Stunkard, A. J. (1989). Perspectives on human obesity. In A. J. Stunkard & A. Baum (Eds.), *Perspectives on behavioral medicine: Eating, sleeping, and sex.* Hillsdale, NJ: Erlbaum.

Sue, D. W. (1989). Ethnic identity: The impact of two cultures on the psychological development of Asians in America. In D. R. Atkinson, G. Morten, & D. W. Sue (Eds.), *Counseling American minorities* (3rd ed.). Dubuque, IA: Wm. C. Brown.

Sue, S. (1990, August). *Ethnicity and culture in psychological research and practice.* Paper presented at the meeting of the American Psychological Association, Boston, MA.

Sue, S. & Okazaki, S. (1990). Asian-American educational achievements. *American Psychologist, 45,* 913–920.

Sugarman, S. (1990). *Cognitive development.* New York: Cambridge University Press.

Suitor, J. J. (1991). Marital quality and satisfaction with the division of household labor across the family life cycle. *Journal of Marriage and the Family, 53,* 221–230.

Sullivan, K., & Sullivan, A. (1980). Adolescent-parent separation. *Developmental Psychology, 16,* 93–99.

Summers, W. K. (1986). About a drug THA that improves memory of Alzheimer's victims. *The New England Journal of Medicine.*

Suomi, S. J., Harlow, H. F., & Domek, C. J. (1970). Effect of repetitive infant-infant separations of young monkeys. *Journal of Abnormal Psychology, 76,* 161–172.

Super, C. M., Herrera, M. G., & Mora, J. O. (1990). Long-term effects of food supplementation and psychosocial intervention on the physical growth of Columbian infants at risk of malnutrition. *Child Development, 61,* 29–49.

Super, C. M., Herrera, M. G., & Mora, J. O. (1991, April). *Cognitive outcomes of early nutritional intervention in the Bogota study.* Paper presented at the biennial meeting of the Society for Research in Child Development, Seattle.

Super, D. E. (1967). *The psychology of careers.* New York: Harper & Row.

Super, D. E. (1976). *Career education and the meanings of work.* Washington, DC: U.S. Office of Education.

Super, D. E., Kowalski, R., & Gotkin, E. (1967). *Floundering and trial after high school.* Unpublished manuscript, Columbia University.

Susman, E. J., & Dorn, L. D. (1991). Hormones and behavior in adolescence. In R. M. Lerner, A. C. Petersen, & J. Brooks-Gunn (Eds.), *Encyclopedia of adolescence.* New York: Garland.

Swanson, D. P., & Cunningham, M. (1991, April) *Issues in gender and racial socialization of African American children.* Paper presented at the biennial meeting of the Society for Research in Child Development, Seattle.

Swope, G. (1980). Kids and cults: Who joins and why? *Media and Methods, 16,* 18–21.

Szinovacz, M. E. (1989). Retirement, couples, and household work. In S. J. Bahr & E. T. Peterson (Eds.), *Aging and the family.* Lexington, MA: Lexington Books.

Szinovacz, M. E. (1984). Changing family roles and interactions. In B. B. Hess & M. B. Sussman (Eds.), *Women and the family: Two decades of change.* New York: Hayworth Press.

T

Tager-Flusberg, H. (in press). A psycholinguistic perspective on language development in autistic children. In G. Dawson (Ed.), *Autism: New directions on diagnosis, nature, and treatment.* New York: Guilford.

Takahashi, K. (1990). Are the key assumptions of the 'strange situation' procedure universal? A view from Japanese research. *Human Development, 33,* 23–30.

Tamir, L. M. (1982). *Men in their forties.* New York: Springer.

Tamis-LeMonda, C. S., & Bornstein, M. H. (1989). Habituation and maternal encouragement of attention in infancy as predictors of toddler language, play, and representational competence. *Child Development, 60,* 738–751.

Tangney, J. P. (1988). Aspects of the family and children's television viewing content preferences. *Child Development, 59,* 1070–1079.

Tanner, J. M. (1991). Growth spurt, adolescent. I. In R. M. Lerner, A. C. Petersen, & J. Brooks-Gunn (Eds.), *Encyclopedia of adolescence.* (Vol. 1). New York: Garland.

Task Force on Pediatric AIDS (1989). Pediatric AIDS and human immunodeficiency virus infection. *American Psychologist, 44,* 248–264.

Tavris, C., & Wade, C. (1984). *The longest war: Sex differences in perspective* (2nd ed.). San Diego: Harcourt Brace Jovanovich.

Taylor, S. P. (1982). Mental health and successful coping among aged Black women. In R. C. Manuel (Ed.), *Minority aging.* Westport, CT: Greenwood Press.

Taylor, W. (1988). Real problems, real answers. *Boston Magazine, 80,* 176–228.

Terman, L. (1925). *Genetic studies of genius: Vol. 1. Mental and physical traits of a thousand gifted children.* Stanford, CA: Stanford University Press.

Teti, D. M., Corns, K., Das-Eiden, R., Kucera, E., & Sakin, J. (1991, April). *Transition to siblinghood among preschool-aged children: Changes in security of attachment following the birth of a baby.* Paper presented at the biennial meeting of the Society for Research in Child Development, Seattle.

Tharp, R. G. (1989). Psychocultural variables and constants: Effects on teaching and learning in schools. *American Psychologist, 44,* 349–359.

Tharp, R. G., & Gallimore, R. G. (1989). *Rousing minds to life.* New York: Cambridge University Press.

Thomas, A., & Chess, S. (1987). Commentary. In H. H. Goldsmith, A. H. Buss, R. Plomin, M. K. Rothbart, A. Thomas, A. Chess, R. R. Hinde, & R. B. McCall. Roundtable: What is temperament? Four approaches. *Child Development, 58,* 505–529.

Thomas, A., & Chess, S. (1991). Temperament in adolescence and its functional significance. In R. M. Lerner, A. C. Petersen, & J. Brooks-Gunn (Eds.), *Encyclopedia of adolescence* (Vol. 2). New York: Garland.

Thomas, J. L. (1986). Age and sex differences in perceptions of grandparenting. *Journal of Gerontology, 41,* 417–23.

Thompson, L., & Walker, A. J. (1989). Gender in families: Women and men in marriage, work, and parenthood. *Journal of Marriage and the Family, 51,* 845–871.

Thompson, R. A. (1991). Construction and reconstruction of early attachments: Taking perspective on attachment theory and research. In D. P. Keating & H. G. Rosen (Eds.), Constructivist perspectives on atypical development. Hillsdale, NJ: Erlbaum.

Thompson, R. J., & Oehler, J. M. (1991, April). *Very low birthweight (VLBW) infants: Maternal stress, coping, and psychological adjustment.* Paper presented at the biennial meeting of the Society for Research in Child Development, Seattle.

Thorndike, R. L. (1990). Is there any future for intelligence? In R. E. Snow & D. E. Wiley (Eds.), *Improving inquiry in social science.* Hillsdale, NJ: Erlbaum.

Thorndike, R. L., Hagen, E. P., & Sattler, J. M. (1985). *Stanford-Binet* (4th ed.). Chicago: Riverside Publishing.

Thorpy, M. J., & Glovinsky, P. B. (1989). Headbanging (*Jactatio capitis nocturna*). In M. H. Kryger, T. Roth, & W. C. Dement (Eds.), *Principles and practices of sleep medicine.* San Diego: Harcourt Brace Jovanovich.

Thorton, A., & Cambrun, D. (1989). Religious participation and sexual behavior and attitudes. *Journal of Marriage and the Family, 51,* 641–653.

Timberlake, B., Fox, R. A., Baisch, M. J., & Goldberg, B. D. (1987). Prenatal education for pregnant adolescents. *Journal of School Health, 57,* 105–108.

Tobin, J. J. (1987). The American idealization of old age in Japan. *The Gerontologist, 27,* 53–58.

Tobin, J. J., Wu, D. Y. H., & Davidson, D. H. (1989). Preschool in three cultures. New Haven, CT: Yale University Press.

Tobin, S. S. (1991). *Personhood in advanced old age.* New York: Springer.

Tomlinson-Keasey, C., & Little, T. D. (1990). Predicting educational attainment, occupational achievement, intellectual skill, and personal adjustment among gifted men and women. *Journal of Educational Psychology, 82,* 442–455.

Tomlinson-Keasey, C., Warren, L. W., & Elliott, J. E. (1986). Suicide among gifted women: A prospective study. *Journal of Abnormal Psychology, 95,* 123–130.

Toth, A. (1991). *The fertility solution.* New York: Atlantic Monthly Press.

Tran, T. V., Wright, R., & Chatters, L. (1991). Health, stress, psychological resources, and subjective well-being among older Blacks. *Psychology and Aging, 6,* 100–108.

Trankina, F. (1983). Clinical issues and techniques in working with Hispanic children and their families. In G. J. Powell, J. Yamamoto, A. Romero, & A. Morales (Eds.). *The psychosocial development of minority group children.* New York: Brunner/Mazel.

Treboux, D. A., & Busch-Rossnagel, N. A. (1991). Sexual behavior, sexual attitudes, and contraceptive use, age differences in adolescent. In R. M. Lerner, A. C. Petersen, & J. Brooks-Gunn (Eds.), *Encyclopedia of adolescence* (Vol. 2). New York: Garland.

Trehub, S. E., Schneider, B. A., Thorpe, L. A., & Judge, P. (1991). Observational measures of auditory sensitivity in early infancy. *Developmental Psychology, 27,* 40–49.

Triandis, H. (1985). Collectivism vs. individualism: A reconceptualization of a basic concept in cross-cultural social psychology. In C. Bagley & G. K. Verman (Eds.), *Personality, cognition, and values.* London: Macmillan.

Trickett, P. K., Aber, J. L., Carlson, V., & Cicchetti, D. (1991). Relationship of socioeconomic status to the etiology and developmental sequalae of physical child abuse. *Developmental Psychology, 27,* 148–158.

Trimble, J. E. (1989). *The enculturation of contemporary psychology.* Paper presented at the meeting of the American Psychological Association, New Orleans.

Trimble, J. E. (in press). Ethnic specification, validation prospects and the future of drug use research. *International Journal of Addiction.*

Troll, L. E. (1989). Myths of mid-life intergenerational relationships. In S. Hunter & M. Sundel (Eds.), *Mid-life myths.* Newbury Park, CA: Sage.

Troll, L. E., & Bengston, V. L. (1982). Intergenerational relations through the life span. In B. B. Wolman (Ed.), *Developmental psychology.* Englewood Cliffs, NJ: Prentice-Hall.

Trotter, R. J. (1987, December). Project Day-Care. *Psychology Today,* pp. 32–38.

Trotter, R. J. (1990, January). Regaining control. Longevity, pp. 60–67.

Tucker, L. A. (1987). Television, teenagers, and health. *Journal of Youth and Adolescence, 16,* 415–425.

Tuckman, B. W., & Hinkle, J. S. (1988). An experimental study of the physical and psychological effects of aerobic exercise on school children. In B. G. Melamed, K. A. Matthews, D. K. Routh, B. Stabler, & N. Schneiderman (Eds.), *Child health psychology.* Hillsdale, NJ: Erlbaum.

Turk, D. C., Rudy, T. E., & Salovey, P. (1984). Health protection: Attitudes and behaviors of LPN's, teachers, and college students. *Health Psychology, 3,* 189–210.

Turner, B. F. (1982). Sex-related differences in aging. In B. B. Wolman (Ed.), *Handbook of developmental psychology.* Englewood Cliffs, NJ: Prentice-Hall.

Tyack, D. (1976). Ways of seeing: An essay on the history of compulsory schooling. *Harvard Educational Review, 46,* 355–389.

U

U.S. Bureau of the Census. (1990). *Statistical Abstracts of the United States, 1990.* Washington, DC: U.S. Dept. of Commerce.

Ulbrich, P. M. (1988). The determinants of depression in two-income marriages. *Journal of Marriage and the Family, 50,* 121–131.

Ullman, C. (1982). Cognitive and emotional antecedents of religious conversion. *Journal of Personality and Social Psychology, 43,* 183–192.

Unger, R. (1990, August). *Source of variability: A feminist analysis.* Paper presented at the meeting of the American Psychological Association, Boston, MA.

United States Bureau of the Census. (1987). Current Population Reports: Consumer Income, Series P-60, No. 157. *Income and poverty status of families and persons in the United States, 1986.* Washington, DC: U.S. Government Printing Office.

United States Commission on Civil Rights (1975). *A better chance to learn: Bilingual bicultural education.* Washington, DC: U.S. Government Printing Office.

United States Senate Special Committee on Aging. (1983). *Aging America.* Washington, DC: United States Government Printing Office.

Upcraft, M. L., & Gardner, J. N. (1989). *The freshman year experience.* San Francisco: Jossey-Bass.

Upton, A. C. (1977). Pathology: In L. E. Finch & L. Hayflick. (Eds.). *Handbook of the biology of aging.* New York: Van Nostrand.

Usui, C. (1989). Can Japanese society promote individualism? In D. I. Kertzer & K. W. Schaie (Eds.), *Age structuring in comparative perspective.* Hillsdale, NJ: Erlbaum.

V

Vaillant, G. E. (1977). *Adaptation to life.* Boston: Little, Brown.

Vandell, D. L. (1987). Baby sister/Baby brother: Reactions to the birth of a sibling and patterns of early sibling relations. In F. F. Schachter & R. K. Stone (Eds.), *Practical concerns about siblings.* New York: The Haworth Press.

Vandell, D. L., & Corasaniti, M. A. (1988). Variations in early child care: Do they predict subsequent social, emotional, and cognitive differences? *Child Development, 59,* 176–186.

Vandell, D. L., & Wilson, K. S. (1988). Infants' interactions with mother, sibling, and peer: Contrasts and relations between interaction systems. *Child Development, 48,* 176–186.

VandenBos, G. R., Stapp, J., & Kilburg, R. R. (1981). Health service providers in psychology: Results of the 1978 APA Human Resources Survey. *American Psychologist, 36,* 1395–1418.

Van Deusen-Henkel, J., & Argondizza, M. (1987). Early elementary education: Curriculum planning for the primary grades. In *A framework for curriculum design.* Augusta, ME: Division of Curriculum, Maine Department of Educational and Cultural Services.

Van Itallie, T. B. (1984).The enduring storage capacity for fat: Implications for treatment of obesity. In A. J. Stunkard & F. Stellar (Eds.), *Eating and its disorders.* New York: Raven Press.

Van Leeuwen, M. S. (1978). A cross-cultural examination of psychological differentiation in males and females. *International Journal of Psychology, 13,* 87–122.

Vannoy-Hiller, D., & Philliber, W. W. (1989). *Equal partners: Successful women in marriage.* Newbury Park, CA: Sage.

Veatch, R. M. (1988). The definition of death: Problems for public policy. In H. Wass, F. M. Berardo, & R. A. Neimeyer (Eds.), *Dying: Facing the facts* (2nd ed.). Washington, DC: Hemisphere.

Vinick, B. H., & Ekerdt, D. J. (1991). Retirement: What happens to husband-wife relationships. *Journal of Geriatric Psychiatry, 24,* 23–40.

Vondracek, F. W. (1991). Vocational development and choice in adolescence. In R. M. Lerner, A. C. Petersen, & J. Brooks-Gunn (Eds.), *Encyclopedia of adolescence* (Vol. 2). New York: Garland.

von Tetzchner, S., & Siegel, L. S. (1989). *The social and cognitive aspects of normal and atypical language development.* New York: Springer-Verlag.

Vorhees, C. V., & Mollnow, E. (1987). Behavioral teratogenesis: Long-term influences in behavior from early exposure to environmental agents. In J. D. Osofsky (Ed.), *Handbook of infant development.* New York: Wiley.

Vygotsky, L. S. (1962). *Thought and language.* Cambridge: Massachusetts Institute of Technology Press.

W

Wadden, T. A., Van Italie, T. B., & Blackburn, G. L. (1990). Responsible and Irresponsible use of very-low-calorie diets in the treatment of obesity. *Journal of the American Medical Association, 263,* 83–85.

Waddington, C. H. (1957). *The strategy of the genes.* London: Allen & Son.

Wahlsten, D. (1991, April). *Molecular biology requires a reformulation of the nature-nurture question in developmental psychology.* Paper presented at the biennial meeting of the Society for Research in Child Development, Seattle.

Wakefield, J. F. (1991). *Creative thinking: Problem solving skills and the arts orientation.* Norwood, NJ: Ablex.

Walford, R. L. (1969). *The immunologic theory of aging.* Baltimore: Williams & Wilkins.

Wallace, H. M., & Vienonen, M. (1989). Teenage pregnancy in Sweden and Finland: Implications for the United States. *Journal of Adolescent Health Care, 10,* 231–236.

Wallerstein, J., Corbin, S. B., & Lewis, J. M. (1988). Children of divorce: A ten-year study. In E. M. Hetherington & J. Arasteh (Eds.), *Impact of divorce, single-parenting, and stepparenting on children.* Hillsdale, NJ: Erlbaum.

Wallerstein, J. S., & Kelly, J. B. (1980). *Surviving the breakup: How children actually cope with divorce.* New York: Basic Books.

Wallis, C. (1985, December 9). Children having children. *Time,* pp. 78–88.

Walls, N. (1987, Spring). Three generations of love. *Aging International,* pp. 2–5.

Walsh, P. V., & Katz, P. A., & Downey, E. P. (1991, April). *A longitudinal perspective on race and gender socialization in infants and toddlers.* Paper presented at the biennial meeting of the Society for Research in Child Development, Seattle.

Walton, M. D., & Vallelunga, L. R. (1989, April). *The role of breastfeeding in establishing early mother-infant interactions.* Paper presented at the biennial meeting of the Society for Research in Child Development, Kansas City, MO.

Warner, R. L. (1986). Alternative strategies for measuring household division of labor: A comparison. *Journal of Family Issues, 7,* 179–185.

Warshak, R. A. (1991, January 15). Personal Communication, Department of Psychology, University of Texas at Dallas, Richardson, TX.

Wass, H. (1985). Depiction of death, grief, and funerals on national television. *Research Record, 2,* 81–82.

Wass, H., Berardo, F. N., & Neimeyer, R. A. (1988). Dying: Integrating the facts. In H. Wass, F. N. Berardo, & R. A. Neimeyer (Eds.), *Dying: Facing the facts* (2nd ed.). Washington, DC: Hemisphere.

Wass, H., & Stillion, J. M. (1988). Death in the lives of children and adolescents. In H. Wass, F. M. Berardo, & R. A. Neimeyer (Eds.), *Dying: Facing the facts* (2nd ed.). Washington, DC: Hemisphere.

Waterman, A. S. (1985). Identity in the context of adolescent psychology. In A. S. Waterman (Ed.), *Identity in adolescence: Processes and contents.* San Francisco: Jossey-Bass.

Waterman, A. S. (1989). Curricula interventions for identity change: Substantive and ethical considerations. *Journal of Adolescence, 12,* 389–400.

Waters, E. (1991). Individual differences in infant-mother attachment. In J. Columbo & J. W. Fagen (Eds.), *Individual differences in infancy.* Hillsdale, NJ: Erlbaum.

Waters, E. B., & Goodman, J. G. (1990). *Empowering older adults: Practical strategies for counselors.* San Francisco: Jossey-Bass.

Watson, J. B. (1928). *Psychological care of infant and child.* New York: W. W. Norton.

Watson, W. H. (1990). Family care, economics, and health. In Z. Harel, E. A. McKinney, & M. Williams (Eds.), *Black aged.* Newbury Park, CA: Sage.

Wechsler, D. (1949). *Wechsler Intelligence Scale for Children.* New York: The Psychological Corporation.

Wechsler, D. (1955). *Wechsler Adult Intelligence Scale.* New York: The Psychological Corporation.

Wechsler, D. (1967). *Wechsler Preschool and Primary Scale for Intelligence.* New York: The Psychological Corporation.

Wechsler, D. (1972). "Hold" and "Don't Hold" test. In S. M. Chown (Ed.). *Human aging.* New York: Penguin.

Wechsler, D. (1974). *Wechsler Intelligence Scale for Children-Revised.* New York: The Psychological Corporation.

Wechsler, D. (1981). *Wechsler Adult Intelligence Scale-Revised.* New York: The Psychological Corporation.

Wechsler, D. (1989). *Wechsler Preschool and Primary Scale of Intelligence—Revised.* San Antonio, TX: The Psychological Corporation.

Wechsler, D. (1991). *Wechsler Intelligence Scale for Children—Third Edition.* San Antonio, TX: The Psychological Corporation.

Wegman, W. E. (1986). Annual summary of vital statistics—1985. *Pediatrics, 78,* 983–984.

Weinberg, R. A. (1989). Intelligence and IQ: Landmark issues and great debates. *American Psychologist, 44,* 98–104.

Weinstein, N. D. (1984). Reducing unrealistic optimism about illness susceptibility. *Health Psychology, 3,* 431–457.

Weisberg, R. P., Caplan, M. Z., & Sivo, P. J. (1989). A new conceptual framework for establishing school-based social competence promotion programs. In L. A. Bond, B. E. Compas, & C. Swift (Eds.), *Prevention in the schools.* Menlo Park, CA: Sage.

Weisman, A. T. (1972). On dying and denying: A psychiatric study of terminality. In M. Lowenthal, M. Turnher, & D. Chiriboga (Eds.), *Four stages of life.* San Francisco: Jossey-Bass.

Weiss, G., & Hechtman, L. T. (1986). *Hyperactive children grown up.* New York: Guilford Press.

Welch, H. G. (1991). Comparing apples and oranges: Does cost-effectiveness analysis deal fairly with the old and young? *The Gerontologist, 31,* 332–336.

Wender, P. H., Kety, S. S., Rosenthal, D., Schulsinger, F., Ortmann, J., & Lunde, I. (1986). Psychiatric disorders in the biological and adoptive families of adopted individuals with affective disorders. *Archives of General Psychiatry, 43,* 923–929.

Wenestam, C. G., & Wass, H. (1987). Swedish and U.S. children's thinking about death: A qualitative study and cross-cultural comparison. *Death Studies, 11,* 99–121.

Wenzlaff, R. M., & Prohaska, M. L. (1989). When misery loves company: Depression, attributions, and responses to others' moods. *Journal of Experimental Social Psychology, 25,* 220–223.

Werner, E. E. (1979). *Cross-cultural child development: A view from planet earth.* Monterey, CA: Brooks/Cole.

Werner, E. E., & Smith, R. S. (1982). *Vulnerable but invincible: A longitudinal study of resilient children and youth.* New York: McGraw-Hill.

Wertsch, J. V. (1985). Adult-child interaction as a source of self-regulation in children. In S. R. Yussen (Ed.), *The growth of reflection in children.* New York: Academic Press.

Whaley, L. F., & Wong, D. L. (1989). *Essentials of pediatric nursing.* St. Louis, MO: Mosby.

Whitbourne, S. K. (1991). Intimacy. In R. M. Lerner, A. C. Petersen, & J. Brooks-Gunn (Eds.), *Encyclopedia of adolescence* (Vol. 1). New York: Garland.

Whitbourne, S. K., & Ebmeyer, J. B. (1990). *Identity and intimacy in marriage: A study of couples.* New York: Springer-Verlag.

White, B. L. (1988). *Educating the infant and toddler.* Lexington, MA: Lexington Books.

White, B. L. (1990). *The first three years.* New York: Prentice-Hall.

White, C. B., & Catania, J. (1981). Psychoeducational intervention for sexuality with the aged, family members of the aged, and people who work with the aged. *International Journal of Aging and Human Development.*

White, K. M., Speisman, J. C., Costos, D., & Smith, A. (1987). Relationship maturity: A conceptual and empirical approach. In J. Meacham (Ed.), *Interpersonal relations: Family, peers, friends.* Basel, Switzerland: Karger.

White, K. M., Speisman, J. C., Jackson, D., Bartis, S., & Costos, D. (1986). Intimacy maturity and its correlates in young married couples. *Journal of Personality and Social Psychology, 50*(1), 152–162.

White, N., & Cunningham, W. R. (1989). Is terminal drop pervasive or specific? *Journal of Gerontology: Psychological Sciences, 43,* P141–144.

Whitehurst, G. J., & Valdez-Menchaca, M. C. (1988). What is the role of reinforcement in early language acquisition? *Child Development, 59,* 430–440.

Whiting, B. B. (1989, April). *Culture and interpersonal behavior.* Paper presented at the biennial meeting of the Society for Research in Child Development, Kansas City, MO.

Whiting, B. B., & Edwards, C. P. (1988). *Children of different worlds.* Cambridge, MA: Harvard University Press.

Widmayer, S., & Field, T. (1980). Effects of Brazelton demonstrations on early patterns of preterm infants and their teenage mothers. *Infant Behavior and Development, 3,* 79–89.

Wiebe, D. J. (1991). Hardiness and stress moderation: A test of proposed mechanisms. *Journal of Personality and Social Psychology, 60,* 89–99.

Wilkie, F. & Eisdorfer, C. (1971). Intelligence and blood pressure in the aged. *Science, 172,* 959–962.

Willer, B., & Bredekamp, S. (1990). Redefining readiness: An essential requisite for educational reform. *Young Children, 45,* 22–26.

William T. Grant Foundation Commission on Work, Family, and Citizenship. (1988, February). *The forgotten half: Non-college-bound youth in America.* Washington, DC: William T. Grant Foundation.

William T. Grant Foundation (1989). *American Youth: A statistical snapshot.* Washington, DC: William T. Grant Foundation.

Williams, J. (1979). Reading instruction today. *American Psychologist, 34,* 917–922.

Williams, J. E., & Best, D. L. (1982). *Measuring sex stereotypes: A thirty nation study.* Newbury Park, CA: Sage.

Williams, J. E., & Best, D. L. (1989). *Sex and psyche: Self-concept viewed cross-culturally.* Newbury Park, CA: Sage.

Williams, M. (1990). African American elderly experiences with Title II: Program assumptions and economic well-being. In Z. Harel, E. A. McKinney, & M. Williams (Eds.), *Black aged.* Newbury Park, CA: Sage.

Williams, M. F., & Condry, J. (1989, April). *Living color: Minority portrayals and cross-racial interactions on television.* Paper presented at the biennial meeting of the Society for Research in Child Development, Kansas City, MO.

Williams, R. B. (1989a) Biological mechanisms mediating the relationship between behavior and coronary prone behavior. In A. W. Siegman & T. Dembrowski (Eds.), *In search of coronary-prone behavior: Beyond Type A.* Hillsdale, NJ: Erlbaum.

Williams, R. B. (1989b). *The trusting heart: Great news about Type A behavior.* New York: Random House.

Willis, S. L. (1985). Towards an educational psychology of the adult learner. In J. E. Birren & K. W. Schaie (Eds.), *Handbook of the psychology of aging* (2nd ed.). New York: Van Nostrand Reinhold.

Willis, S. L. (1989). Cohort differences in cognitive aging: A sample case. In K. W. Schaie & C. Schooler (Eds.), *Social structure and aging: Psychological processes.* Hillsdale, NJ: Erlbaum.

Willis, S. L. (1990). Introduction to the special section on cognitive training in later adulthood. *Developmental Psychology, 26,* 875–879.

Willis, S. L., & Nesselroade, C. S. (1990). Long-term effects of fluid ability training in old age. *Developmental Psychology, 26,* 905–910.

Willis, S. L., & Schaie, K. W. (1986). Training the elderly on the ability factors of spatial orientation and inductive reasoning. *Psychology and Aging, 1,* 239–247.

Willis, S. L., & Schaie, K. W. (1990, April). *Methodological and taxonomic considerations in research on everyday cognition.* Paper presented at the 12th West Virginia conference on life-span developmental psychology, Morgantown, WV.

Wilson, L. C. (1990). *Infants and toddlers: Curriculum and teaching.* Albany, NY: Delmar.

Wilson, M., Kohn, L., Hinton, I., Underwood, A., & Do, L. (1991, April). *The context of socialization in diverse Black families.* Paper presented at the biennial meeting of the Society for Research in Child Development, Seattle.

Wilson, M. N. (1989). Child development in the context of the extended family. *American Psychologist, 44,* 380–385.

Windle, W. F. (1940). *Physiology of the human fetus.* Philadelphia: Saunders.

Winefield, A. H., Winefield, H. R., Tiggemann, M., & Goldney, R. D. (1991). A longitudinal study of the psychological effects of unemployment and unsatisfactory employment on young adults. *Journal of Applied Psychology, 76,* 424–431.

Winkelstein, W., Samuel, M., Padian, N. S., & Wiley, J. A. (1987). Selected sexual practices of San Francisco heterosexual men and risk of infection by human immunodeficiency virus. *Journal of the American Medical Association, 257,* 1470.

Winner, E. (1986, August). Where pelicans kiss seals. *Psychology Today,* pp. 24–35.

Winner, E. (1989). Development in the visual arts. In W. Damon (Ed.), *Child development today and tomorrow.* San Francisco: W. H. Freeman.

Winner, E., & Gardner, H. (1988). Creating a world with words. In F. Kessel (Ed.), *The development of language and language researchers.* Hillsdale, NJ: Erlbaum.

Wiswell, R. A. (1980). Relaxation, exercise, and aging. In J. E. Birren & R. B. Sloane (Eds.), *Handbook of mental health and aging.* Englewood Cliffs, NJ: Prentice-Hall.

Witkin, H. A., Mednick, S. A., Schulsinger, R., Bakkestrom, E., Christiansen, K. O., Goodenbough, D. R., Hirchhorn, K., Lunsteen, C., Owen, D. R., Philip, J., Ruben, D. B., & Stocking, M. (1976). Criminality in XYY and XXY men. *Science, 193.* 547–555.

Wong, P. T. P., & Watt, L. M. (1991). What types of reminiscence are associated with successful aging? *Psychology and Aging, 6,* 272–279.

Wood, F. H. (1988). Learners at risk. *Teaching Exceptional Children, 20,* 4–9.

Woodward, N. J., & Wasslston, B. S. (1987). Age and health-care beliefs: Self-efficacy as a mediator of low desire for control. *Psychology and Aging, 2,* 3–8.

Worden, J. W. (1991). Grief counseling and grief therapy (2nd ed.). New York: Springer.

Worobey, J. & Belsky, J. (1982). Employing the Brazelton Scale to influence mothering: An experimental comparison of three strategies. *Developmental Psychology, 18,* 736–743.

Worschel, S., & Cooper, J. (1979). *Understanding social psychology.* Homewood, IL: Dorsey.

Worthington, E. L. (1989). Religious faith across the life span: Implications for counseling and research. *The Counseling Psychologist, 17,* 555–612.

Worthington-Roberts, B. S. (1988). Lactation and human milk. In S. R. Williams & B. S. Worthington-Roberts (Eds.), *Nutrition throughout the life cycle.* St. Louis: Times Mirror/Mosby.

Wright, M. R. (1989). Body image satisfaction in adolescent girls and boys. *Journal of Youth and Adolescence, 18,* 71–84.

Wroblewski, R., & Huston, A. C. (1987). Televised occupational stereotypes and their effects on early adolescents: Are they changing? *Journal of Early Adolescence 7,* 283–297.

Wylie, R. C. (1979). *The self-concept* (Vol. 2). Lincoln, NE: University of Nebraska Press.

X

Xiaohe, X., & Whyte, M. K. (1990). Love matches and arranged marriages. *Journal of Marriage and the Family, 52,* 709–722.

Y

Yekel, C. A., Bigler, R. S., & Liben, L. S. (1991, April). *Children's gender schemata: Occupation, activity, and trait.* Paper presented at the biennial meeting of the Society for Research in Child Development, Seattle.

Young, K. T. (1990). American conceptions of infant development from 1955 to 1984: What the experts are telling parents. *Child Development, 61,* 17–28.

Yussen, S. R. (1985). The role of metacognition in contemporary theories of cognitive development. In D. Forrest-Pressley and G. Waller (Eds.), *Contemporary research in cognition and metacognition.* Orlando, FL: Academic Press.

Yussen, S. R., Mathews, S., Huang, S., & Evans, R. (1988). The robustness and temporal course of the story schema's influence on recall. *Journal of Experimental Psychology: Learning, Memory, and Cognition 14,* 173–179.

Z

Zahn-Waxler, C. (1990, May 28). Commentary. *Newsweek,* p. 61.

Zedeck, S., & Mosier, K. L. (1990). Work in the family and employing organization. *American Psychologist, 45,* 240–251.

Zeiss, A. M., & Lewinsohn, P. M. (1986, Fall). Adapting behavioral treatment of depression to meet the needs of the elderly. *Clinical Psychologist,* 98–100.

Zelnik, M., & Kantner, J. F. (1977). Sexual and contraceptive experiences of young unmarried women in the United States, 1976 and 1971. *Family Planning Perspectives, 9,* 55–71.

Zeskind, P. S., & Marshall, T. R. (1988). The relation between variations in pitch and maternal perception of infant crying. *Child Development, 59,* 193–196.

Zevitz, R. G., & Gurnack, A. M. (1991). Factors related to elderly crime victims' satisfaction with police service: The impact of Milwaukee's "Gray Squad." *The Gerontologist, 31,* 92–101.

Zigler, E. (1987, April). *Child care for parents who work outside the home: Problems and solutions.* Paper presented at the biennial meeting of the Society for Research in Child Development, Baltimore.

Zigler, E. (1991, October). *Day care in America: What is needed.* Paper presented at the symposium on day care for children, Arlington, VA.

Zisook, S., Schuchter, S. R., & Lyons, L. E. (1987). Predictors of psychological reactions during the early stages of widowhood. *Psychiatric Clinics of North America, 10,* 355–368.

Zukow, P. G. (Ed.). (1989). *Sibling interaction across cultures.* New York: Springer-Verlag.

References

CREDITS

Chapter 3

Poem, page 86: From *Verses From 1929 On* by Odgen Nash. Copyright 1940 by Ogden Nash. By permission of Little, Brown and Company; reprinted by permission of Curtis Brown, Ltd, copyright © 1945 Curtis Brown; and reprinted by permission of Andre Deutsch Ltd.

Figure 3.7: From I. Gottesman, "Genetic Aspects of Intellectual Behavior" in *Handbook of Mental Deficiency,* Norman R. Ellis, Ed. Copyright © McGraw-Hill, Inc. Reprinted by permission.

Chapter 4

Figure 4.4: From Keith L. Moore, *The Developing Human: Clinically Oriented,* 3d ed. Copyright © 1982 W. B. Saunders Company, Philadelphia, PA. Reprinted by permission.

Chapter 5

Poem, page 137: From *W. H. AUDEN: COLLECTED POEMS* by W. H. Auden, ed. by Edward Mendelson. Copyright 1942 by W. H. Auden. Copyright © 1976 by Edward Mendelson, William Meredith and Monroe K. Spears, Executors of the Estate of W. H. Auden. Reprinted by permission of Random House, Inc.

Figure 5.1 (top): From Howard P. Roffwarg, et al., "Ontogenetic Development of the Human Sleep-Dream Cycle" in *Science,* 152:608. Copyright 1966 by the AAAS. Reprinted by permission of the publisher and the author.

Figure 5.2: From Patten, *Human Embryology.* Copyright © 1933 McGraw-Hill, Inc. Reprinted by permission.

Figure 5.4: J. L. Conel (1939–1963), *Postnatal Development of the Human Cerebral Cortex,* Vols. I–VI. Copyright © Harvard University Press, Cambridge, MA. Reprinted by permission.

Chapter 6

Poem, page 159: Source: Walt Whitman, *Leaves of Grass,* 1945. Random House Modern Library, New York, NY.

Figure 6.5: From *Memory Observed: Remembering in Natural Contexts.* By Ulric Neisser. Copyright © 1982 by W. H. Freeman and Company. Reprinted with permission.

Figure 6.6 (left): From Tiffany M. Field, et al., "Discrimination and Imitation of Facial Expressions by Neonates" in *Science,* Vol. 218, No. 4568: 179–181, 8 October 1982. Copyright 1982 by the AAAS. Reprinted by permission.

Figure 6.9: From R. Brown, C. Cazden, and U. Bella-Klima, "The Child's Grammar from 1–3" in *Minnesota Symposium on Child Psychology,* Vol. 2, J. P. Hill, editor, University of Minnesota Press. Copyright © 1969 University of Minnesota.

Chapter 7

Figure 7.3: From Jay Belsky, "Early Human Experience: A Family Perspective" in *Developmental Psychology,* 17:3–23. Copyright 1981 by the American Psychological Association. Reprinted by permission.

Figure 7.6 (left): From M. Lewis and J. Brooks-Gunn, *Social Cognition and the Acquisition of the Self.* Copyright © 1979 Plenum Publishing Corporation, New York, NY. Reprinted by permission.

Chapter 8

Figure 8.1 (left): From George H. Lowrey, *Growth and Development of Children,* 7th ed. Copyright © 1978 Year Book Medical Publishers.

Figure 8.A: D. Wolf/J. Nove.

Figure 8.B: Reprinted by permission of Ellen Winner.

Figure 8.C: Reprinted by permission of Ellen Winner.

Figure 8.7: From Daniel R. Anderson, et al., "Television Viewing at Home: Age Trends in Visual Attention and Time with TV," paper presented at the meeting of the Society for Research in Child Development. Reprinted by permission of the author.

Figure 8.8: From Frank N. Dempster, "Memory Span: Sources of Individual and Developmental Differences" in *Psychological Bulletin,* 89:63–100. Copyright © 1981 by the American Psychological Association. Reprinted by permission of the author.

Figure 8.10: From J. Berko, "The Child's Learning of English Morphology" in *Word,* 14:361, 1958. Copyright © 1958 International Linguistic Association, NY.

Chapter 9

Figure 9.2: Source: Data from U.S. Government Printing Office, Washington, DC.

Chapter 10

Figure 10.4: From Joel Levin, et al., "The Keyword Method in the Classroom" in *Elementary School Journal,* 80(4). Copyright © 1980 The University of Chicago Press, Chicago, IL. Reprinted by permission.

Figure 10.5: From S. Yussen, et al., "The Robustness and Temporal Cause of the Story Schemics Influence on Recall" in *Journal of Experimental Psychology Learning, Memory, and Cognition,* 14:173–179. Copyright 1988 by the American Psychological Association. Reprinted by permission.

Figure 10.6: From Jerome M. Sattler, *Assessment of Children's Intelligence and Special Abilities,* Second Edition. Copyright © 1982 by Allyn and Bacon, Inc. Reprinted with permission.

Figure 10.10: Figure A5 from the Raven *Standard Progressive Matrices* reproduced by J. C. Raven Limited.

Figure 10.12: From Mark R. Lepper, et al., "Undermining Children's Intrinsic Interest with Extrinsic Rewards" in *Journal of Personality and Social Psychology,* 28:129–137. Copyright 1973 by the American Psychological Association. Reprinted by permission.

Chapter 11

Figure 11.3: From J. S. Hyde, "How Large Are Cognitive Gender Differences? A Meta-Analysis Using w^2 and d" in *American Psychologist,* 36:899. Copyright 1981 by the American Psychological Association. Reprinted by permission.

Chapter 12

Figure 12.1: From A. F. Roche, "Secular Trends in Stature, Weight, and Maturation" in *Monographs of The Society for Research in Child Development,* Ser. No. 179, Vol. 44. Copyright © 1977 The Society for Research in Child Development.

Figure 12.2 (graph): From J. M. Tanner, R. H. Whitehouse, and M. Takaishi, "Standards from Birth to Maturity for Height, Weight, Height Velocity, and Weight Velocity: British Children 1965" in *Archives of Diseases in Childhood,* 41, 1966. Reprinted by permission of the British Medical Society and the author.

Figure 12.5: From D. A. Blythe, et al., "The Impact of Puberty on Adolescence: A Longitudinal Study" in *Girls at Puberty* by Jeanne Brooks-Gunn. Copyright © 1981 Plenum Publishing Co., Inc., New York, NY. Reprinted by permission.

Figure 12.7: Reprinted with permission from *Family Planning Perspectives,* vol. 17, no. 2, March/April 1985. The Alan Guttmacher Institute, 1985.

Chapter 13

Figure 13.2: Source: Data from The Higher Education Research Institute, Graduate School of Education, University of California, Los Angeles, 1987.

Section VII

Excerpt, page 453: Copyright © 1962 WARNER BROS. MUSIC; copyright renewed 1990, BOB DYLAN. This arrangement copyright 1992, Special Rider Music. All rights reserved. International copyright secured. Used by permission.

Chapter 14

Excerpt, page 455: Source: S. Christ and G. Meyer, "10 Reasons Not to Get a Job" in *The Harvard Lampoon Big Book of College Life.* Copyright © Harvard Lampoon, Inc., Cambridge, MA.

Figure 14.2: From L. L. Langley, *Physiology of Man.* Copyright © 1971 Van Nostrand Reinhold Company. Reprinted by permission of the publisher and the author.

Poem, page 473: "Once More, The Round," copyright © 1962 by Beatrice Roethke, Administratrix of the Estate of Theodore Roethke, from *The Collected Poems of Theodore Roethke* by Theodore Roethke. Used by permission of Doubleday, a division of Bantam Doubleday Dell Publishing Group, Inc.; reprinted by permission of Faber and Faber Ltd from *Collected Poems by Roethke.*

Figure 14.4: From Jack Botwinick, *Cognitive Processes in Maturity and Old Age.* Copyright © 1967 Springer Publishing Co., Inc., New York, NY. Reprinted by permission.

Figure 14.5: From Jack Botwinick, *Cognitive Processes in Maturity and Old Age.* Copyright © 1967 Springer Publishing Co., Inc., New York, NY. Reprinted by permission.

Chapter 15

Figure 15.1: From W. M. Kephart, "Some Correlates of Romantic Love" in *Journal of Marriage and the Family,* 29. Copyright 1967 by the National Council on Family Relations, 3989 Central Avenue, N.E., Suite #550, Minneapolis, MN 55421. Reprinted by permission.

Figure 15.2: Reprinted with permission from T. Chess and A. Thomas, "Temperamental Individuality from Childhood to Adolescence" in *Journal of Child Psychiatry,* 16. Copyright 1977, Pergamon Press PLC.

Figure 15.4: Source: Data from R. J. Sternberg, *The Triangle of Love.* Copyright © 1988 Basic Books, New York, NY.

Figure 15.5: From J. Larson, "The Marriage Quiz: College Students' Beliefs in Selected Myths about Marriage" in *Family Relations,* 37:4. Copyright 1988 by the National Council on Family Relations, 3989 Central Avenue, N.E., Suite #550, Minneapolis, MN 55421. Reprinted by permission.

Figure 15.6: Source: U.S. Bureau of the Census, *Population Statistics,* 1989.

Chapter 16

Excerpt, page 517: "TIME IN A BOTTLE" by Jim Croce. © 1972 BLENDINGWELL MUSIC INC., 1985 SAJA MUSIC. ℗ 1985 DENJAC MUSIC CO.

Figure 16.2 (graph): From Lois M. Tamir, *Men In Their Forties: The Transition to Middle Age* (Book No. 363). Copyright © 1982 Springer Publishing Co., Inc., New York, NY. Reprinted by permission.

Chapter 17

Figure 17.1: From George Levinger and Diedrick Snoek, *Attraction in Relationship: A New Look at Interpersonal Attraction*. General Learning Press, 1972. Reprinted by permission of the author.

Figure 17.2 (top): From M. N. Reedy, J. E. Birren, and K. W. Schaie, "Age and Sex Differences in the Life Span" in *Human Development,* 24:52–66. Copyright © 1981 S. Karger, A. G., Basel, Switzerland. Reprinted by permission.

Figure 17.4 (left): From D. J. Levinson, "Toward a Conception of the Adult Life Course" in N. J. Smelzer and E. H. Erickson (eds.), *Themes of Work and Love in Adulthood.* Copyright © 1980 Harvard University Press, Cambridge, MA. Reprinted by permission.

Poem, page 548: From "They Sing, They Sing" in *The Collected Poems of Theodore Roethke.* Copyright © 1966 Doubleday, a division of Bantam Doubleday Dell Publishing Group, Inc. Reprinted by permission, reprinted by permission of Faber and Faber Ltd, London, England.

Excerpt, page 554: From S. LeVine, *Mothers and Wives: Gusii Women of East Africa.* Copyright © 1979 University of Chicago Press, Chicago, IL. Reprinted by permission.

Figure 17.6 (right): From D. F. Hultsch and J. K. Plemons, "Life Events and Life Span Development" in *Life Span Development and Behavior,* Vol. 2 by P. B. Baltes and O. G. Brim. Copyright © 1979 Academic Press, Inc. Reprinted by permission of the publisher and the author.

Figure 17.7: From D. Hultsch and F. Deutsch, *Adult Development and Aging.* Copyright © 1980 McGraw-Hill, Inc. Reprinted by permission.

Chapter 18

Figure 18.2 (right): Source: Data from Advocate for the U.S. Senate, Special Committee on Aging, 1983, p. 50, "Aging in America." Washington, DC: U.S. Government Printing Office.

Chapter 19

Figure 19.3: From K. W. Schaie and C. R. Strother, "A Cross-Sequential Study of Age Changes in Cognitive Behavior" in *Psychological Bulletin,* 70:671–680. Copyright 1968 by the American Psychological Association. Reprinted by permission.

Figure 19.4: From *The Social Forces in Later Life* by Robert C. Atchley. © 1977 by Wadsworth Publishing Company. Reprinted by permission.

Chapter 20

Figure 20.3: Source: S. Grad, "Income of the Population 55 or Over," publication number 13–111871. Washington, DC: U.S. Social Security Administration.

Excerpt, page 621: "WHEN I'M SIXTY-FOUR" Words and Music by JOHN LENNON and PAUL McCARTNEY. © Copyright 1967 NORTHERN SONGS. All rights controlled and administered by MCA MUSIC PUBLISHING, a Division of MCA INC., under license from NORTHERN SONGS. ALL RIGHTS RESERVED. INTERNATIONAL COPYRIGHT SECURED. USED BY PERMISSION.

Poem, page 623: Reprinted with permission of Macmillan Publishing Company from *The Complete Poems of Thomas Hardy* (New York: Macmillan, 1978).

Chapter 21

Poem, page 643: Dylan Thomas: *Poems of Dylan Thomas.* Copyright 1952 by Dylan Thomas. Reprinted by permission of New Directions Publishing Corporation.

NAME INDEX

Brice, P., 277
Brim, O. G., 555
Brion-Meisels, S., 357
Brislin, R. W., 18
Brody, E. M., 542
Brody, L., 365
Bromsley, D. B., 355
Brone, R. J., 416, 463
Bronfenbrenner, U., 25, 70, 73
Bronstein, P. A., 7, 378
Brook, D. W., 409, 430
Brook, J. S., 120, 409, 430
Brooks-Gunn, J., 203, 249, 389, 391–393, 413–414, 416
Broughton, J. M., 280
Broverman, I., 366
Brown, A. L., 313
Brown, B. B., 432–434
Brown, D. R., 500
Brown, F., 399
Brown, J. D., 464
Brown, J. K., 553
Brown, J. L., 137, 147
Brown, J. S., 313
Brown, J. V., 126
Brown, L. M., 7, 376–377, 508
Brown, M. M., 268, 345
Brown, R., 179
Brownell, K. D., 525
Brownn, R., 181–182
Brubaker, T. H., 623
Bruce, S. A., 571
Brumberg, J. J., 416
Bruner, J. S., 18, 189
Bryant, P., 329
Bryer, K. B., 649
Buckley, S., 345
Bugbee, N. M., 143
Buhrmester, D., 307, 348
Bukowski, C., 556
Bulcroft, K. A., 622
Bulcroft, R., 392
Bulcroft, R. A., 622
Burchett, B. M., 601
Burkhart, B., 471
Burley, K. A., 500
Burns, K. A., 113
Burns, W. J., 109
Bursik, K., 505
Burton, L. M., 9
Burts, D. C., 246
Busch-Rossnagel, N. A., 414
Bushwall, S. J., 355
Buss, D., 497
Buss, R. R., 314, 395
Buss, T., 480
Butchart, A. T., 409
Butcher, M. J., 153
Butler, R. N., 577, 581, 612, 625
Butler, S., 226, 541
Byer, C. O., 109, 470
Byrnes, J. P., 394
Byron, 570

C

Cairns, B. D., 267
Cairns, R. B., 93, 267
Calderon, A. E., 109
Caldwell, B., 144, 198
Calhoun, J. A., 411
Callan, J. W., 347
Camara, K. A., 265
Cambrun, D., 439
Cameron, D., 331
Campbell, B., 490
Campbell, J., 646
Campbell, J. I. D., 595
Campbell, K., 192
Campos, J. J., 150, 200
Canady, R. L., 400
Cancian, F. M., 500
Cantor, K. P., 468
Cantor, M. H., 614

Capaldi, D., 25
Caplan, M. Z., 347
Cappiello, L. A., 651
Carbo, M., 329
Carey, S., 238
Carlsmith, J. M., 355
Carlson, C., 445
Carlson, V., 209–211
Carpenter, C. J., 288
Carper, L., 255
Carr, M., 334
Carrasquillo, A. L., 404
Carroll, C., 461
Carskadon, M. A., 139
Carter, D. B., 287
Carter-Saltzman, L., 222
Case, R., 235, 310
Casper, R. C., 416
Caspi, A., 9, 72, 542
Cassidy, D. J., 288
Castro, F. G., 523
Catania, J., 575
Cavanaugh, J. C., 583, 634, 639
Cavett, D., 435
Cazden, C. D., 242
Ceci, S. J., 18
Censullo, M., 123
Chalfant, J. C., 306
Champagne, F., 397
Chance, G., 152
Chang, P., 126
Chappell, N. L., 626
Chard, S., 301, 349
Charlesworth, R., 241, 246
Charness, N., 595
Charnov, E. L., 193
Charon, R., 581
Charpentier, M. P. H., 646
Chase-Landsdale, P. L., 264, 413, 505
Chasnoff, I. J., 111, 113
Chatters, L., 616
Chen, C., 336
Cherlin, A. J., 624
Cherry, R. L., 579
Chesney-Lind, M., 410, 411
Chesquire, K., 192
Chess, S., 96–97
Cheung, F. K., 523
Chi, M. T., 312
Chinn, P. L., 612
Chinsky, J. M., 312
Chiriboga, D. A., 554, 556
Chodorow, N. J., 47, 508
Chomsky, N., 176
Chrousos, G. P., 27, 391
Church, D. K., 602, 604, 616
Church, R. B., 417
Chyi-In, W., 210
Cicchetti, D., 5, 209–211
Cicirelli, V. G., 262, 541
Clark, D. L., 284
Clark, E. V., 181
Clark, H. H., 181
Clarke, C. C., 626
Clarke-Stewart, K. A., 198, 248
Clarkson, F., 366
Clarkson-Smith, L., 593
Clausen, J. A., 558, 560
Clemens, A. W., 541
Clifford, R. M., 304
Clinchy, B. M., 285, 508
Cluff, C., 307
Cobb, P. A., 314
Cogwill, D. O., 619
Coh, L. D., 395
Cohen, D., 170
Cohen, L. A., 521
Cohen, P., 120, 409, 430
Cohen, S., 172
Coheru, P., 409
Cohn, C.P., 8
Cohn, J. F., 189
Coie, J. D., 267

Colby, A., 375
Cole, J. D., 345–346
Cole, S., 405
Coleman, J. S., 399, 432
Coleman, L. M., 530
Coleman, P. D., 573
Coleman, R. E., 582
Coles, C. D., 111
Coles, R., 447
Collins, A., 313, 315
Collins, P. A., 234
Collins, W. A., 429
Colombo, J., 137, 171
Comer, J. P., 353, 445
Committee for Economic
    Development, 259
Conant, J. B., 399
Condi, S. J., 621
Condon, S. M., 430
Condry, J. C., 275, 277
Cone, J., 247
Conger, J. J., 414, 437
Conger, R. B., 210
Connell, J. P., 334
Conti-Ramsden, G., 183
Cool, V. A., 319
Coombs, R. H., 505
Cooney, T. J., 247, 336
Coons, S., 139
Cooper, B. A., 119
Cooper, C. R., 430, 445
Cooper, J., 487
Cooper, K., 464
Cooper, R., 172
Coopersmith, S., 359–360
Corasaniti, M. A., 198
Corbin, J., 614
Corbin, S. B., 264–265
Corless, I. B., 468
Cornon-Huntley, J., 558
Corns, K., 262
Coron, B., 119
Corrigan, E. M., 505
Corrigan, R., 162
Corser, J., 71
Corter, C., 263
Corwin, V., 276
Costa, P. T., 558–559, 593
Coster, W., 209–210
Costos, D., 507
Courtois, C. A., 471
Cowan, C. P., 188
Cowan, P. A., 188
Cowley, R., 177
Cox, M., 72, 264–265, 272, 505
Cox, R., 72, 264–265, 272, 505
Craik, F. I. M., 527
Cristafi, M. A., 119
Crittenden, P. M., 209–210
Croce, J., 517
Crockett, L., 393
Crohan, S. E., 530, 622
Cronbach, L. J., 350
Cronkite, R. C., 409
Crosby, F., 542
Cross, K. P., 400
Crosswhite, F. J., 247, 336
Crowley, J. M., 96
Cummings, E. M., 9
Cunningham, M., 371
Cunningham, W. R., 594
Curnow, C., 458
Curtiss, S., 178
Cutler, G. B., 391
Cutrona, C. E., 495

D

Damon, W., 280, 291, 379
Dann, S., 267
Danner, F., 394
Darby, B. L., 111, 207
Darling, C. A., 466
Darlington, R. B., 249

Daro, D., 210
Darwin, C., 84
Das-Eiden, R., 262
Datan, N., 541, 617
Davidson, D. H., 247
Davies, K. J. A., 571
Davis, G., 575
Davis, G. C., 525
Davis, K. E., 489
Davison, M., 603
Davy, J. A., 480
Dawson, G., 211
Dawson-Hughes, B., 577
Dax, E. M., 584
DeAngelis, T., 200
deArmas, A., 347
Deaux, K., 617
DeBarsyhe, D. B., 410
DeCasper, A. J., 152
Dedrick, C., 119
Dedrick, R., 119
DeFour, D. C., 7, 508
DeFries, J. C., 96
DeFriese, G. H., 578
DeHart, G., 271
de Jong-Gierveld, J., 492
DeLoache, J. S., 288
Dembrowski, T., 519
Dement, W. C., 139
DeMoss, V., 223
Dempster, F. N., 235
De Necochea, G., 406
Denmark, F. L., 34, 362, 508
Denney, N., 592, 594
Dennis, W., 474–475
DePaola, S., 493
Desilets, J., 136
Dessler, R. C., 430
Dessonville, C., 601
DeTemple, J., 331
Detweiler, R. A., 88
Deusen-Henkel, J. van, 349
Deutsch, F. M., 553
Deutsch, M., 360
DeVault, M. L., 501
de Villiers, J. G., 180, 328
de Villiers, P. A., 180, 328
deVries, H. A., 583
Diamond, A., 169
Diaz, R. M., 331
Dickersheid, J. D., 369
Dickinson, D. K., 331
Dickinson, G. E., 435
Dickson, G. L., 524
Dielman, T. E., 409
Dietz, W., 463
Dillon, R. F., 111
Dirkes, K., 113
Dixon, K. N., 416–417
Dixon, R. L., 112
Dixon, S. D., 113
Do, L., 259
Dodge, K. A., 268, 345–346
Dohrenwend, B. P., 556
Dohrenwend, B. S., 556–557
Dolan, R. S., 98
Dolcini, M. M., 395
Dolgin, K. G., 227
Doll, G., 198
Domek, C. J., 267
Donaldson, G., 590
Dorn, L. D., 27, 391
Dornbusch, S. M., 6, 259, 353, 355, 434, 445
Dossey, J. A., 247, 336
Dosten, T. R., 646
Douvan, D., 597
Douvan, E., 435, 446
Dowd, J. J., 616
Dowler, J. K., 113
Downey, A. M., 302
Downey, E. P., 371
Downey, G., 72, 542
Doyle, G. C., 553

Name Index

Mora, J. O., 146
Moran, G., 192
Morelli, G., 238, 240
Moreton, J., 331
Morgan, J. D., 648
Morgan, J. N., 601
Morgan, S. P., 414
Morris, J. C., 603
Morrison, A. M., 481
Morrison, V., 172
Morrongiello, B. A., 152
Morse, J. M., 581
Morton, D. J., 599
Moses, J., 465
Moses, N., 146
Mosier, K. L., 483
Mosley, J., 241, 246
Moss, M., 137
Mott, F. L., 413
Mounts, N., 432, 434
Mouradian, V., 262
Moushegian, G., 573
Moyer, J., 241
Mueller, K. E., 470
Munroe, R. H., 73, 369
Munroe, R. L., 73, 369
Murphy, K. C., 277
Murphy, M. N., 395
Murphy, M. P., 287
Murray, H. A., 332
Mussen, P. H., 460, 558, 560
Musun-Miller, L., 262

N

Nagy, M., 639
Naimark, H., 8
Nakagawa, K., 335
Nathan, J. G., 234
National Association for the
    Education of Young Children,
    199, 243, 246
National Center for Health Statistics,
    492, 577
National Research Council, 412
Needleman, H., 113
Neimeyer, R. A., 210, 464–465, 648,
    651
Nelson, C. S., 315
Nelson, K., 169
Nelson, R. S., 345
Nemeroff, C. B., 603
Nemzer, E., 416
Nesselroade, C. S., 595
Neugarten, B., 558
Neugarten, B. L., 15, 551, 610,
    613–614, 623
Neugarten, D. A., 15
Newcomb, M. D., 409
Newman, S. E., 313
New Yorker Magazine, The, 116,
    443, 461, 613
Nicholls, J. G., 333–334
Nichols, E. G., 553
Nichols, I. A., 181
Nietzche, F., 435
Nietzel, M. T., 498
Nikolio, J., 395
Nisbett, R. R., 333
Nitz, V., 98
Noam, G. G., 445
Noelker, L. S., 647
Noir, S., 369
Nottleman, E. D., 27, 391
Novak, C. G., 319
Novak, W., 487
Novick, B., 109
Nowak, C. A., 518
Nugent, J. K., 124–125
Nurcomb, B., 119
Nydegger, C. N., 542

O

O'Brien, S.J., 582
O'Brien, M., 420
O'Bryant, S. L., 647
Obrzut, J. E., 306
O'Connell, C., 111
O'Conner-Roden, M., 622
O'Connor, B. P., 395
O'Donnel, B., 288
O'Donnell, C., 411
Oehler, J. M., 119
Offer, D., 9, 417
Ogbu, J. U., 260, 352, 434, 445
Ogden, J., 463
Ogrocki, P. K., 604
O'Hara, N. M., 301
Okagaki, L., 173
Okazaki, S., 334
Okun, B. F., 501
Okun, M. A., 17
Olds, S. W., 502
Olsho, L. W., 518, 574
Olson, F. A., 312
Olson, R. A., 109
Olweus, D., 268
O'Malley, P. M., 407–409, 437,
    459–460
Omoto, A. M., 490–491
Opper, S., 160
Orenek, Don, 498
Orlofsky, J., 506, 507
Ornstein, R., 464
Ortmann, J., 415
Osborn, K. M., 464–465
Osofsky, J. D., 109
Ossip-Klein, D. J., 464–465
Osterberg, J., 264
Ostfield, A. M., 646
Ostrov, E., 9
Ottinger, D. R., 110
Overton, W. F., 394
Ovid, 490
Owen, D. R., 89
Ozer, D., 345

P

Pacey, K., 344
Pacheco, S., 19
Pacific, R. E., 571
Padian, N. S., 469
Padilla, A. M., 259
Paffenbarger, R. S., 464
Paikoff, R. L., 393
Palincsar, A. M., 313
Palmore, E. B., 570, 601, 618, 626
Paludi, M. A., 7, 34, 362, 364, 367,
    378, 481
Pan, B. A., 176
Papert, S., 315
Papini, D. R., 428, 443
Parcel, G. S., 301
Paris, S. C., 235
Parish, T. S., 264
Parke, R. D., 195
Parker, J. G., 347
Parker, S. R., 345
Parkes, C. M., 646
Parkhurst, J. T., 345
Parlee, M. B., 489
Parmalee, A. H., 139, 172
Parten, M., 269–270
Partilla, J. S., 584
Partridge, M., 209
Pascual-Leone, J., 310
Pasley, K., 344
Pastalan, P. M., 615
Patterson, C. J., 291
Patterson, G. R., 25, 410
Paul, E. L., 457, 507
Pauludi, M. A., 508
Pea, R. D., 236
Peck, R. C., 625

Pederson, D. R., 192
Penner, S. C., 180
Peplau, L. A., 496, 500
Pepler, D. J., 263
Percy, W., 442
Perfetti, C. A., 329
Perkinson, H. J., 400
Perlman, S. L., 496
Perlmutter, M., 168, 594
Perret, Y. M., 307
Perriello, L., 438
Perry, T. B., 348, 431, 488
Perry, W., 472
Persky, V. W., 521
Peskin, H., 392, 519
Petersen, A. C., 363, 389, 392–393
Peterson, E. T., 624
Peterson, J., 644
Peterson, L. M., 109
Peterson, P., 610
Peterson, P. L., 350
Petit, G. S., 345
Petrinovich, L. F., 222
Petronio, R. J., 411
Pettit, S. C., 268
Pfeiffer, E., 525, 575
Phares, V., 119
Philip, J., 89
Philliber, W. W., 492
Phillip, M., 434
Phillips, D., 198
Phinney, J. S., 335, 446
Piaget, J., 54, 160–163, 227, 269,
    289, 309
Pierce, E. W., 307
Piers, E. V., 359
Pike, R., 359
Pines, A., 458, 529
Pino, C. D., 604
Pintrich, P. R., 349
Pipes, P., 144, 223
Pittman-Lindeman, M., 468
Pizer, H. F., 147
Plante, T. G., 464
Plato, 342
Platzman, K. A., 111
Pleck, J., 367
Pleck, J. H., 194, 542
Plemons, J. K., 555
Plomin, R., 20, 96, 98–99
Plunkett, J., 119
Poest, C. A., 220
Polgar, A., 598
Polier, J. W., 410
Poling, D., 438–439
Polit, D. F., 263
Polivy, J., 416, 463
Pollack, W. S., 195
Pollitt, E., 146
Pomerleau, A., 173
Pomeroy, A. C., 466
Pond, K., 492
Poon, L. W., 527, 592
Pope, A., 631
Popkin, S. J., 604
Porcino, J., 617
Porges, S. W., 154
Porter, F. L., 154
Potenza, M., 397
Potenza, M. T., 345
Pottbaum, S. M., 319
Potter, J. F., 584
Potvin, L., 397
Powell, G. J., 360
Power, C. N., 396–397
Powers, S. I., 445
Powers, W. G., 470
Pratto, D. J., 345
Prentice-Dunn, S., 493
Pressley, M., 312
Price, J., 278
Prince, M. J., 615
Prohaska, M. L., 488

Pryor, J. B., 467
Psychology Today, 459
Puffer, J. C., 303
Pugliese, M. T., 146

Q

Quality Health Care: Critical Issues
    Before the Nation, 614
Quasimodo, S., 567
Quina, K., 7, 34

R

Rabier, J., 17
Rabin, D. S., 391
Rabinowitz, M., 113
Rabkin, J., 411
Rachels, J., 633, 635
Rahe, R. H., 555
Rahman, T., 314
Ramey, C., 326
Ramirez, M., 334
Ramirez, O., 6, 19, 372
Ramsay, D. S., 222
Ramsey, E., 410
Randahl, G. J., 478
Rando, T. A., 646
Rapkin, A. J., 466
Rapkin, B. D., 402
Rappaport, L. J., 501
Raskinski, K., 573
Ratcliff, K. S., 483
Ray, J., 181
Rayman, J. R., 458
Raynor, I. O., 332
Reasoner, J., 582
Rebelsky, F. G., 181
Redburn, F. S., 480
Reddecord, K. M., 599
Reed, A., 341
Reedy, M. N., 538
Reese, C. A., 481
Reese, H. W., 541
Reich, J. N., 119
Reichard, S., 610
Reid, D. K., 306
Reilly, B. M., 153
Reilly, D., 322
Reilly, R., 300
Reinisch, J. M., 100, 467, 469
Relethford, J. H., 523
Remafed, G., 467
Rembold, K. L., 314
Rescorla, L., 247
Resnick, G., 265
Resnick, S., 83
Revitch, E., 26
Reynolds, D. K., 640, 642, 644, 648
Rhodes, S. R., 528
Rice, K. G., 395
Rice, M. B., 238
Rich, C. L., 415
Richards, L. N., 542
Riddle, M. W., 582
Ridgeway, D., 200
Rieben, L., 329
Rieder, C., 209–210
Riege, W. H., 527
Riegel, K., 9, 20
Riegel, K. M., 594
Riegel, R. M., 594
Riesenberg, L. A., 648
Riggio, R. E., 493
Riley, W. L., 11
Risser, W. L., 303
Ritter, P. I., 355
Roberts, R. E. L., 614
Robeson, W. W., 262
Robinson, D. P., 407
Robinson, E., 466
Robinson, I., 466
Robinson, N. M., 327
Rock, D., 404

Rode, S. S., 126
Rodgers, J. E., 100
Rodgers, R. H., 505
Rodin, J., 464, 579, 580, 643
Rodman, H., 345
Rodriguez-Haynes, M., 210
Roedel, T. D., 345
Roethke, T., 473
Roff, M., 267
Rogers, A., 377, 446
Rogers, A. G., 7, 376, 508
Rogers, C. R., 41, 63–64
Rogers, C. S., 271
Roggman, L. A., 428
Rogoff, B., 18, 238, 240, 242
Rohde, P., 601
Rohner, E. C., 259
Rohner, R. P., 259
Rokach, A., 496
Rollins, B. C., 539
Rollins, P. R., 176
Roodin, P. A., 579
Rook, K., 541
Rose, D., 172
Rose, H. A., 287
Rose, R. J., 94
Rose, S. A., 119, 154, 172
Rosenbaum, F., 412
Rosenbaum, J. E., 529
Rosenberg, M. L., 408
Rosenberg, N., 360
Rosenberg, R., 471
Rosenberg, S. D., 557
Rosenblatt, R., 547
Rosenblith, J. F., 104, 115, 118, 125, 168
Rosenfeld, A., 559
Rosenkranz, P., 366
Rosenman, R., 519
Rosenthal, D., 415
Rosenthal, R., 324
Rosoff, J. L., 412
Rossen, J., 345
Rossi, A., 553
Rossi, A. S., 542
Rothbart, M. K., 96, 98, 262
Rothstein, W. G., 478
Rotman, A., 136
Rotter, J. B., 333
Rousseau, J. J., 160, 217, 455
Rovee-Collier, C., 168
Rovine, M., 190
Rowe, D. C., 100
Roybal, E. R., 605
Ruben, D. B., 89
Rubenstein, J., 415
Rubin, C., 415
Rubin, E. H., 603
Rubin, K. H., 272
Rubin, K. M., 284
Rubin, K. N., 271
Rubin, L. B., 500
Rubin, V., 345
Rubin, Z., 35, 489, 559
Ruble, D. N., 188, 355
Rudy, T. E., 459
Ruff, H. A., 154
Rumbaugh, D. M., 177
Rumberger, R. W., 404
Runco, M. A., 328
Russo, N. F., 34, 508
Rutter, M. M., 211, 213, 264
Rutton, J., 626
Ruzecki, V., 181
Ryan, E. B., 306
Ryan, R. A., 372–373
Ryan, R. M., 428
Rybash, J. W., 579
Rye, B. J., 467
Ryff, C. D., 545, 555

S
Sachse, K., 87
Sackett, G. P., 111
Sadker, D., 285
Sadker, M., 285
Safford, J. O., 247
Sagan, C., 84
Saint-Exupery, 487
St. Lawrence, J. S., 469
Sakin, J., 262
Salapatek, P., 134, 149
Sales, E., 604
Salovey, P., 459
Salthouse, T. A., 527, 591
Sammuel, M., 469
Sanders, S. A., 467
Sandman, B. M., 111, 207, 307
Sanger, C., 203
Sangree, W. H., 619
Sankar, A., 647
Sansone, R., 416
Santayana, G., 530
Santrock, J. W., 6, 57, 263–266, 344, 417, 441, 466, 579
Sapp, S., 614
Sarna, S., 94
Sattler, J. M., 319
Sauber, M., 505
Savage-Rumbaugh, E. S., 177
Sawin, D. B., 195
Sawyers, J. K., 271
Saxe, G. B., 240
Scafidi, F., 122
Scales, P., 404, 419
Scardamalia, M., 313
Scarlett, W. G., 438
Scarr, S., 21, 92, 94, 99, 197, 198, 323
Sceery, A., 428
Schafer, D. F., 584
Schaie, K. W., 32, 34, 473, 538, 590–591, 594
Schalsinger, R., 89
Schanberg, S., 122
Schank, R., 314
Schatz, J., 307
Schechter, D. E., 88
Scheck, C. L., 480
Schegloff, E. A., 179
Schieber, F., 517, 573
Schilke, J. M., 582
Schlenker, E. D., 583, 584
Schlesinger, L. B., 26
Schlundt, D. G., 416
Schmich, M. T., 502
Schmidt, M. G., 579
Schneider, B., 471
Schneider, B. A., 151
Schneider-Rosen, K., 5
Schnur, E., 249
Schoenfeld, A. H., 313
Schoenrock, C. J., 428
Schooler, C., 557
Schopler, E., 211, 213
Schrag, S. G., 112
Schuchter, S. R., 647
Schulsinger, F., 415
Schultz, R., 458, 569, 580
Schulz, C., 263
Schulz, H., 139
Schulz, R., 604
Schunk, D. H., 333–334
Schwartz, B., 73
Schwartz, D., 109
Schwartz, M. L., 143
Schwartz, P., 500
Schwartz, P. M., 113
Schwartz, R., 522
Schweinhart, L., 411
Scott, J. P., 541
Scott-Jones, D., 412
Scribner, S., 236, 394
Sears, R., 10

Sechzur, J., 34
Secord, P. F., 479, 480
Seeley, J. R., 601
Segal, N. L., 83, 96
Segerberg, O., 568
Seibert, J. M., 109
Seidman, E., 350
Seidner, L. B., 271
Seigle, J., 274, 278
Sekuler, R., 573
Selice, S., 371
Sells, S. B., 267
Selman, R. L., 348, 356–357
Semaj, L. T., 445
Serbin, L. A., 286, 287
Serlin, R. C., 9
Sexton, M., 111
Shadmon, O., 345
Shainberg, L. W., 109, 470
Shakeshaft, C., 285
Shakespeare, W., 139
Shannon, F. T., 144
Shantz, C. O., 227, 347
Shapiro, E. K., 351, 409
Shapiro, E. R., 415
Shapiro, T., 211
Sharabany, R., 287
Shaul, D. L., 188
Shaver, P., 429, 491–492
Shaw, G. B., 496
Shaw, S. M., 501
Sheingold, K., 169
Shepard, L., 241
Sherman, E., 540
Sherwood, A., 464
Shneidman, E. S., 415, 639, 643
Shope, J. T., 409
Shrout, P. E., 557
Siegel, J. S., 306
Siegel, K., 469
Siegel, L. S., 172, 183
Siegel, M. A., 602, 604, 616
Siegler, I. C., 522, 593, 601
Siegler, R. S., 312
Siegman, A. W., 519
Sigman, M., 172
Sigman, M. D., 234
Signorella, M. L., 287
Silver, L. B, 306, 307
Silverberg, S. B., 431
Simmons, D. D., 461
Simmons, J. E., 110
Simmons, R. G., 392, 401–402
Simon-Rusinowitz, L., 614
Simons, R. L., 210, 410
Simons-Morton, G. G., 301
Simonton, D. K., 475
Simopoulos, A. P., 584
Simpson, J. A., 490
Sims-Knight, J. E., 104, 115, 118, 125, 168
Singer, D. G., 271, 278
Singer, J. L., 42, 271, 278
Singer, L. M., 88
Singer, M., 237
Sitko, C., 192
Sitterle, K. A., 344
Sivo, P. J., 347
Sizer, T. R., 400
Skekelle, R. B., 521
Skerry, S. A., 355
Skinner, B. F., 58, 60, 179
Skinner, E. A., 334
Skinner, J. H., 617
Skoe, E. E., 446
Slater, A., 172
Slaughter-DeFoe, D. T., 335
Slavin, R. E., 331, 352
Slivinske, L. R., 601
Sloane, R. B., 601
Slobin, D., 182
Small, M., 310
Smith, A., 507
Smith, A. D., 527

Smith, B., 271
Smith, B. A., 153
Smith, I. E., 111
Smith, J., 12, 57, 120, 595
Smith, J. C., 408
Smith, M. B., 110
Smith, P. A., 444
Smith, R., 277
Smith, R. S., 209
Smith, T. W., 468, 520
Smither, R. D., 478
Smolucha, F., 269
Snarey, J., 378
Snell, L. M., 113
Snow, C. E., 176, 179–180, 183
Snow, R. E., 350
Snowden, L. R., 523
Snyder, M., 490–491
Sobel, D., 464
Sokolovsky, J., 619
Solon, 431
Sommer, B. B., 440
Sorenson, R. C., 435
Sowarka, D., 595
Spade, J. Z., 481
Spalding, J. L., 297
Spani, D., 497
Speece, M., 639
Spelke, E. S., 154, 310
Spence, J. T., 366
Spence, M., 152
Spencer, C., 445
Spencer, M. B., 6, 18, 259, 335, 353, 355, 434, 445, 447
Spencer, M. L., 285
Spersman, J. C., 507
Spielberger, J. E., 556
Sprafkin, C., 287
Sprafkin, J. N., 277
Sprei, J., 542
Sprei, J. E., 471
Sroufe, L. A., 126, 137, 192–193
Stafford, F. P., 341
Stage, E. K., 285
Stallings, J., 248
Stanford, E. P., 599, 616
Stanhope, L., 263
Stanhope, M., 522
Stanley, J. C., 369
Stanowicz, L., 180
Stapp, J., 604
Stark, E., 559
Staudinger, U. M., 595
Stearns, G., 110
Stechler, G., 413
Steil, J. M., 481
Stein, A. H., 275
Stein, N. L., 314
Steinbach, R., 313
Steinberg, J., 195
Steinberg, L. D., 345, 405, 429, 431, 434
Steiner, J. E., 152–153
Steinmetz, J., 23
Steptoe, A., 465
Sterling, C. W., 316
Stern, D. N., 189
Stern, J. S., 463
Stern, M. P., 523
Stern, R. G., 603
Stern, S. L., 416–417
Sternberg, R. G., 173
Sternberg, R. J., 321, 492, 494, 591
Sternglanz, S. H., 286
Steur, F. B., 277
Stevens, J. H., 261
Stevens-Long, J., 541
Stevenson, H. W., 71, 336, 370
Stewart, N. J., 113
Stigler, J. W., 336
Stillion, J. M., 638–639
Stimmel, B., 408
Stine, E. L., 180
Stipek, D. J., 365

SUBJECT INDEX